𝔉𝔞𝔰𝔱𝔦 𝔈𝔠𝔠𝔩𝔢𝔰𝔦𝔞𝔢 𝔖𝔠𝔬𝔱𝔦𝔠𝔞𝔫𝔞𝔢

The succession of ministers in the Church of Scotland

from the reformation

(Volume VIII)

Hew Scott

Alpha Editions

This edition published in 2020

ISBN : 9789354033278

Design and Setting By
Alpha Editions
email - alphaedis@gmail.com

As per information held with us this book is in Public Domain.
This book is a reproduction of an important historical work. Alpha Editions uses the best technology to reproduce historical work in the same manner it was first published to preserve its original nature. Any marks or number seen are left intentionally to preserve its true form.

FASTI ECCLESIÆ SCOTICANÆ

COMMITTEE, 1936–49

Sir FRANCIS JAMES GRANT, K.C.V.O., LL.D., W.S., *Convener and General Editor*

*Rev. WILLIAM BURNETT, B.D., Restalrig

Rev. ALFRED BROWN, D.D., Maxwell

Rev. THOMAS CALDWELL, D.D., Aberlady

*Very Rev. ANDREW JAMES CAMPBELL, D.D., Evie

Sir THOMAS CLARK, Bart.

Rev. GEORGE FREDERICK COX, B.D., Harray

*Rev. JAMES TAYLOR COX, D.D., Dyce

Rev. ROBERT MARCUS DICKSON, D.D., Lanark

Rev. WILLIAM MCLAUCHLAN GOLDIE, T.D., Kilmaronock

Rev. JOHN ARNOTT HAMILTON, B.D., Ph.D., Newbattle

Rev. Professor GEORGE DAVID HENDERSON, D.D., D.Litt., Aberdeen

Rev. WALTER ROBERTSON HENDERSON, B.D., Auchencairn

Rev. WILLIAM MCCALLUM, D.D., Makerstoun

*Rev. ARCHIBALD MACDONALD, D.D., Kiltarlity

Rev. DAVID JOHN MCLAREN, M.A., Dundurn

Rev. JOHN SCOTT MACNAUGHTON, D.D., Perth

*Rev. WILLIAM MCMILLAN, D.D., Dunfermline

Rev. ANGUS MCVICAR, M.A., Southend

*Rev. JOHN MUIRHEAD, B.D., Avendale

*Rev. LOUIS CARRICK PHILLIPS, D.D., Fala

*Rev. ALEXANDER MASON SHAND, M.A., Bridge of Weir

Rev. JOHN SINCLAIR, B.D., Glasgow

*Rev. WILLIAM STEPHEN, D.D., Inverkeithing

*Rev. ARTHUR POLLOK SYM, D.D., Lilliesleaf

Rev. JAMES PETER WILSON, B.D., St. Quivox

* Deceased

FASTI ECCLESIÆ SCOTICANÆ

THE SUCCESSION OF MINISTERS IN
THE CHURCH OF SCOTLAND FROM
THE REFORMATION

BY

HEW SCOTT, D.D.

*Revised and continued to the Present Time under the Superintendence of a
Committee appointed by the General Assembly*

VOLUME VIII

MINISTERS OF THE CHURCH FROM DATE OF
PUBLICATION OF VOLUMES I–VII, 1914–28, TO
UNION OF THE CHURCHES, 2nd OCTOBER 1929,
AND ADDENDA AND CORRIGENDA 1560–1949

OLIVER AND BOYD
EDINBURGH: TWEEDDALE COURT
1950

PREFATORY NOTE

DURING the years 1915 to 1928 were published the seven volumes of this work containing the record of the Ministers of the Church of Scotland from 1560 to the date of the issue of the various volumes, viz. I Synods of Lothian and Tweeddale, 1915; II Merse and Teviotdale, Dumfries and Galloway, 1917; III Glasgow and Ayr, 1920; IV Argyll and Perth and Stirling, 1923; V Fife and Angus and Mearns, 1925; VI Aberdeen and Moray, 1926; VII Ross, Sutherland and Caithness; Orkney and Shetland, with Churches Overseas, also University Principals and Professors in the Faculties of Divinity, 1928.

Towards the end of 1936 the General Administration Committee decided that a supplementary volume should be issued to complete the Record of Ministers of the Church of Scotland as it existed before the date of the Union of the Churches on 2nd October 1929 and also to add all the additional information that had been collected since the above-mentioned volumes were published. A sub-committee of the Committee on General Administration was formed to which several others were co-opted to carry out the work —Sir Francis J. Grant, K.C.V.O., LL.D., Convener and General Editor.

Since these seven volumes were printed the present Convener, who had been Joint Editor of the same, has been collecting additional information and keeping the work up to date, and therefore the foundation of the present volume existed and was used as a basis on which to work.

Certain records of the immediate Post-Reformation Period which had not been systematically gone over have now been done so, and many new names and information as to the Clergy, Readers, and Exhorters previous to 1600 have been recovered and many blanks filled in. In regard to these the Committee are indebted to Dr Gordon Donaldson, formerly of the Historical Department of H.M. Register House, and the late Rev. William Stephen, D.D., Inverkeithing. For the continuation of the accounts of the various parishes, presbyteries and synods the Committee have to thank their various members who undertook this work and particularly to the late Rev. William Burnett, B.D., for the Presbytery of Edinburgh; the late Rev. Arthur P. Sym, D.D., for the Synods of Merse, Teviotdale and Dumfries; the Rev. Walter R. Henderson for the Synod of Galloway; the Rev. James P. Wilson, B.D., for the Synod of Ayr; the late Rev. Alexander Mason Shand, M.A., for the Presbytery of Paisley; the late Rev. John Muirhead, B.D., for the Presbytery of Hamilton; the Rev. R. Marcus Dickson, D.D., for the Presbytery of Lanark; the Very Rev. Andrew James Campbell, D.D., for the

Presbytery of Glasgow; the Rev. William McLauchlan Goldie for the Presbytery of Dunbarton; the Rev. Angus J. McVicar, M.A., for the Synod of Argyll; the Rev. John Scott Macnaughton, D.D., for the Presbytery of Perth; the Rev. David J. Maclaren, M.A., for the Presbytery of Auchterarder; the late Rev. William Stephen, D.D., for the Synod of Fife; the late Rev. James Taylor Cox, D.D., for the Synods of Aberdeen and Moray; the late Rev. Archibald Macdonald, D.D., for the Synod of Ross and Sutherland; the Rev. George Frederick Cox, B.D., for the Synod of Orkney, and the Rev. Professor G. D. Henderson for the University of Aberdeen. The Clerks to Presbyteries and the Officials of H.M. Register House and the Ministers' Widows Fund and many others have also contributed much new matter.

The most valuable part of this volume will be the very large additional information regarding the earlier clergy which has been gathered from many sources too numerous to mention and involving much research in records. The volume has further been enriched by a number of Ecclesiological Notes on parishes by the late Dr William Stephen.

The Editor regrets that ten of his valued helpers have passed away since the volume was first undertaken and have not seen the results of their labours and that latterly he has had to complete the same alone.

FRANCIS J. GRANT
Convener and General Editor

April 1950

CONTENTS

	PAGE
ABBREVIATIONS	xii

SYNOD OF LOTHIAN AND TWEEDDALE—
Presbytery of Edinburgh	1
Presbytery of Linlithgow	36
Presbytery of Biggar	51
Presbytery of Peebles	58
Presbytery of Dalkeith	67
Presbytery of Haddington	85
Presbytery of Dunbar	105

SYNOD OF MERSE AND TEVIOTDALE—
Presbytery of Duns	115
Presbytery of Chirnside	122
Presbytery of Kelso	130
Presbytery of Jedburgh	135
Presbytery of Earlston	143
Presbytery of Selkirk	148

SYNOD OF DUMFRIES—
Presbytery of Lochmaben	155
Presbytery of Langholm	162
Presbytery of Annan	165
Presbytery of Dumfries	170
Presbytery of Penpont	182

SYNOD OF GALLOWAY—
Presbytery of Stranraer	187
Presbytery of Wigtown	193
Presbytery of Kirkcudbright	199

SYNOD OF GLASGOW AND AYR—
Presbytery of Ayr	211
Presbytery of Irvine	228
Presbytery of Paisley	237
Presbytery of Greenock	246
Presbytery of Hamilton	251
Presbytery of Lanark	265
Presbytery of Dunbarton	273
Presbytery of Glasgow	285

	PAGE
SYNOD OF ARGYLL—	
Presbytery of Inveraray	312
Presbytery of Dunoon	316
Presbytery of Kintyre	322
Presbytery of Islay and Jura	328
Presbytery of Lorn	331
Presbytery of Mull	337
Presbytery of Abertarff	343
SYNOD OF PERTH AND STIRLING—	
Presbytery of Dunkeld	346
Presbytery of Weem	354
Presbytery of Perth	360
Presbytery of Auchterarder	376
Presbytery of Stirling	386
Presbytery of Dunblane	395
SYNOD OF FIFE—	
Presbytery of Dunfermline	404
Presbytery of Kinross	416
Presbytery of Kirkcaldy	422
Presbytery of Cupar	437
Presbytery of St Andrews	453
SYNOD OF ANGUS AND MEARNS—	
Presbytery of Meigle	471
Presbytery of Forfar	479
Presbytery of Dundee	485
Presbytery of Brechin	497
Presbytery of Arbroath	508
Presbytery of Fordoun	516
SYNOD OF ABERDEEN—	
Presbytery of Aberdeen	526
Presbytery of Kincardine O'Neil	544
Presbytery of Alford	555
Presbytery of Garioch	562
Presbytery of Ellon	572
Presbytery of Deer	578
Presbytery of Turriff	588
Presbytery of Fordyce	596
SYNOD OF MORAY—	
Presbytery of Strathbogie	603
Presbytery of Aberlour	611
Presbytery of Abernethy	615
Presbytery of Elgin	622

	PAGE
SYNOD OF MORAY (*continued*)	
Presbytery of Forres	642
Presbytery of Nairn	647
Presbytery of Inverness	650
SYNOD OF ROSS—	
Presbytery of Chanonry	655
Presbytery of Dingwall	658
Presbytery of Tain	664
SYNOD OF SUTHERLAND AND CAITHNESS—	
Presbytery of Dornoch	671
Presbytery of Tongue	674
Presbytery of Caithness	676
SYNOD OF GLENELG—	
Presbytery of Lochcarron	680
Presbytery of Skye	683
Presbytery of Uist	688
Presbytery of Lewis	692
SYNOD OF ORKNEY—	
Presbytery of Kirkwall	693
Presbytery of Cairston	696
Presbytery of the North Isles	699
SYNOD OF SHETLAND—	
Presbytery of Lerwick	702
Presbytery of Burravoe	704
Presbytery of Olnafirth	706
ARCHBISHOPS	708
BISHOPS	709
UNIVERSITIES OF SCOTLAND	711
MODERATORS OF GENERAL ASSEMBLY	720
ARMY AND NAVY CHAPLAINS	721
CHAPLAINS TO INFIRMARIES AND OTHERS	722
SYNOD OF THE SCOTTISH CHURCH IN ENGLAND—	
I. Presbytery of North of England	723
II. Presbytery of West of England	724
III. Presbytery of London	724
CHARGES IN ENGLAND NOW EXTINCT OR MERGED WITH OTHER CONGREGATIONS	725
IRELAND	725

	PAGE
THE CHURCH OF SCOTLAND OVERSEAS—	
Continent of Europe	
Belgium	727
France	727
Germany	727
Holland	727
Italy	729
Switzerland	729
Continent of Africa	
Egypt	730
Kenya	730
Mauritius	730
Continent of Asia	
Burma	731
Ceylon	731
Indian Chaplains	731
Palestine	732
Australasia	
Australia	734
New Zealand	734
Continent of America	
Dominion of Canada	
Cape Breton	735
Nova Scotia	735
Prince Edward Island	735
Ontario and Quebec	736
Newfoundland	736
United States of America	737
British West Indies	
Grenada	737
Jamaica	737
St Vincent	737
Central America	
British Honduras	737
South America	
British Guiana	737
Argentina	738
Chile	738
FOREIGN MISSIONARIES	739
JEWISH MISSIONARIES	742
PRINCIPAL CLERKS AND DEPUTE CLERKS OF ASSEMBLY	743

	PAGE
PROCURATORS OF THE CHURCH	745
AGENTS FOR THE CHURCH	746
FATHERS OF THE CHURCH	747
INDEX OF PARISHES AND CHAPELS, SCOTLAND AND ENGLAND	749
INDEX OF MINISTERS	767

ABBREVIATIONS

adm.	..	admitted	marr.	.. married
app.	..	appointed	min.	.. minister
bapt.	..	baptized	ord.	.. ordained
coll.	..	collated	pres.	.. presented
cont.	..	contract (marriage)	presb.	.. presbytery
			pro.	.. proclaimed
dem.	..	demitted	res.	.. resigned
dep.	..	deposed	*s.p.*	.. without issue
ind.	..	inducted	trans.	.. translated
inst.	..	instituted	univ.	.. university
licen.	..	licensed	unmarr.	.. unmarried

SYNOD OF LOTHIAN AND TWEEDDALE

PRESBYTERY OF EDINBURGH

ADDIEWELL

1893 WILLIAM PETER McLAREN, his widow, Joan Robertson, died at manse of Trinity Gask 7th Nov. 1924; his son William David, A.M.I.C.E., V.D., died 31st May 1941.

1898 WILLIAM LOW JAMIE, dem. 3rd June 1930; line 6, for "28" read "26"; died at Edinburgh 4th Jan. 1947.

COLINTON

1575 SIR ANDREW BINNING, vicar of "the Kirk at ye brig of Hailes" (Colinton), died Oct. 1575, executor, Walter Binning.—[*Edin. Test.*, iii, 420.]

1686 SAMUEL NIMMO, M.A., in response to his petition stating that on 27th April 1689 his house was invaded by more than 40 armed men with "wicked and bloodie designe" against him, they failed to find him but caused the reader and beadle to tear his gown, sacrilegiously took away the vessels of the sanctuary, and warned him and his family to flit in six days under and professing readiness to pray for William and Mary, Parliament on 3rd May 1689 ordained the communion cups and other things belonging to the church to be recovered and asked the heritors to protect him in the exercise of his ministry and in the possession of his house, resident with his first wife in Lady Yester's Parish, 1st Nov. 1694.—[*Lady Yester's Poll Tax Roll*, 23; *Acts Scott. Parl.*, ix, App. 7.]

1694 THOMAS JOHNSTON, M.A., reader and schoolmaster 1694, had son James.—[*Colinton Poll Tax Roll*, 5.]

1861 WILLIAM LOCKHART. Addl. Publication—*Heaven, its Changed Relationship* (Edin., 1875).

1910 THOMAS MARJORIBANKS, D.D. (Edinburgh 30th June 1932), trans. to Morham 15th Feb. 1932; dem. 31st July 1941; died at St Andrews 30th Jan. 1947; his wife, Mary Ord Logan, died 26th July 1946; his son, James Alexander Milne, in H.M. Consular Service, China; his daugh., Anne Leslie, born 6th May 1915. Addl. publication—*A Ministry Ended: the Rev. James Alexander Milne, M.A., Minister of the Parish of Cramond.*

CORSTORPHINE

In 1128 the church, than a dependent chapel of St Cuthberts, was granted along with 2 bovates and 6 acres of land to Holyrood Abbey by David I; and, probably soon after, Norman, Sheriff of Berwick, made a similar grant to the abbey under the designation "my Chapel of Corstorphine." The chapel was a church before 1158. In the church there was an altar dedicated to the Holy Trinity to which on 18th May 1465 a tenement of land under Edinburgh Castle was granted by Sir John Marschall, chaplain in the collegiate church of Corstorphine, and an annual rent of £5 was granted by Hugh Barr from a tenement in the Cowgate on 16th Dec. 1475. There was also in the church an altar dedicated to St Ann, at which a chaplain was founded in 20th Sept. 1473 by William de Camera, vicar of Kirkurd. In the churchyard and adjoining the church, a chapel dedicated to John the Baptist was founded by Sir Adam Forrester of Corstorphine, who died before 6th Nov. 1405. On 25th Feb. 1425–6 James I gave and confirmed £24 for the endowment of three chaplainries in the chapel, £20 being from the King personally and £4 being an annual rent from Edinburgh, bestowed by the late Sir Adam Forrester; and on 20th May 1429 Dame Margaret Forrester, relict of Sir Adam, and their son, Sir John Forrester, gave an annual rent of £21 13s. 4d. for the support of two additional chaplains and two clerks in the chapel. Probably soon afterwards, and in any case prior to 6th Jan. 1436–7, the said Sir John erected the chapel into a collegiate church for a provost and four prebendaries and two singing boys, and for endowment consigned 120 gold ducats; and on the foregoing date Pope Eugenius IV issued a Bull which, after narrating that Sir John had stated that if the rectory of Ratho Church which was served by a perpetual vicar could be added to the collegiate church, four or five priests could from its fruits be instituted in the said collegiate church, gave mandate to the Abbot of Holyrood, if he found the statement true, to confirm and approve the said foundation and endowment, etc.; and to make appropriation of the said rectory when it became vacant, and after such appropriation that five other priests be instituted. A further Bull of Pope Eugenius, 13th June 1440, suspended *notu proprio* the taking effect of the said appropriation pending a certain contingency; but still another Bull of the same Pope, 15th June 1444, gave mandate to the Abbot of Holyrood to carry out the annexation and appropriation of the rectory and the institution of prebends. Later, however, on a further representation by Sir John Forrester that the priests and two boys could not be maintained and live on the said fruits, the Pope ordered the reduction of the priests from five to four, the establishment thus consisting of a provost, eight prebends, and two boys. On 30th Oct. 1444 the institution was confirmed by James Kennedy, Bishop of St Andrews. Subsequently, on 23rd Jan. 1450–1, papal remit was made to the Abbot of Holyrood to confirm and approve an agreement between the said bishop on the one hand and, on the other, the provost and chaplains of the collegiate church, whereby the latter, in return for the rectory of Ratho being surrendered by the Bishop, should celebrate for ever on the Wednesday after the Feast of St Thomas the Martyr a solemn mass with music during the bishop's life and, after his death, a *requiem* mass. The prebends were Gogar, Hadingston, Haltoun, Dalmahoy, Bonyngtoun, Platt, Nortoun, and Byres. The fruits of the Church of Clerkington were included in Bishop Kennedy's confirmation charter. After the Reformation the Church of Corstorphine was again attached to St Cuthbert's, and was served by a reader. But on 7th March 1587–8 Sir James Forrester and other parishioners presented to the presbytery a claim that Corstorphine was a parish church, and that they should not be "compellit to hant any other paroch kirk nor their awn qlk had been fundit of auld to yt effect." After due enquiry the presbytery on 19th March interponed their authority on the claim, and asked the "Lords Modifiers" to supply a stipend for the minister out of the Thirds of Holyrood. Up to 1633 the collegiate church and the parish church seem to have existed side by side. The collegiate church, however, was dissolved by the provost and first prebend in 1634, an action ratified by Parliament seven years later; and the collegiate building became the parish church in 1646, when, on 6th May of that year, the Kirk Session had estimates for taking down the old parish church and putting up a new aisle, attached to the collegiate fabric, and apparently on the site of the old church.—[*Reg. Great Seal*, ii, 35, 121, 337, 1320, 3564; *Cal. Papal Regs.*, Letters, viii, 265, 595, x, 476–7; *Acts Scott. Parl.*, iv, 677, v, 158, 437; *Excheq. Rolls*, vii, 30, viii, 203, x, 73, etc.; *Charters of St Giles*, 41–2; *Charters of Holyrood*, 3, 4, 6, 7,10.]

THOMAS MARJORIBANKS, son of Thomas M., burgess of Edinburgh, pres. to the prebend of the Collegiate Church of Corstorphine called Halton and Dalmahoy 16th Nov. 1548 on death of Robert Marjoribanks; he was also Vicar of Craigie and Prebendary of Kirkmichael in the cathedral church of Ross, still prebendary in 1567.—[*Comps. Sub Coll. of Thirds, Linlithgow*, etc.; *P. S. Reg.*, iii, 3023, 3026.]
1548

JAMES SCOTT, provost of Corstorphine 18th July 1549, was brother's son and heir of late Sir Alexander Scott, provost of Corstorphine and son and heir of the late Janet Adamson, relict of John Bruce, burgess of Edinburgh; was still provost 15th Oct. 1560, when he had a son William, who was described as grandson and son of the heirs of the late William Adamson, burgess of Edinburgh. He died Sept. 1563 and was succeeded as provost by his nephew William Scott, burgess of Irvine.—[*Acts and Decs.*, iii, 154–5, lx, 20th May 1575; A. Guthrie's *Prot. Book*, i, 174.]
1549

MUNGO WOOD, reader at Gogar, trans. to Corstorphine 1561.—[*Comps. Gen. Coll. of Thirds*, 1561; 97.]
1561

WALTER LANG reader 1568 and 1569.—[*Comps. Sub Coll. of Thirds, Linlithgow*, etc.]
1568

WALTER COUPER, reader 1569 and 1570.—[*Comps. Sub Coll. of Thirds, Linlithgow*, etc.]
1569

ANDREW FORRESTER, as min. here pres. to vicarage vacant by death of last vicar, Adam, Bishop of Orkney.—[*P. S. Reg.*, lxvi, 46.]
1590

ROBERT LINDSAY, had issue—David, bapt. 14th June 1603; Helen, bapt. 14th Nov. 1617; David, bapt. 19th August 1619.
1617

DAVID BALSILLIE, had issue—John.—[*G. R. Sas.*, 2 Ser. v, 354.]
1626

ROBERT HUNTER, afterwards of Bo'ness (*q.v.*).
1655

ROBERT LAW, delete perhaps min. of Kilpatrick.
1689

GEORGE HENRY, M.A., with his wife and children, James, Mary, Edward, Margaret and Janet, resident in Tron Parish 6th Nov. 1684.—[*Tron Poll Tax Roll*, 20.]
1672

ARCHIBALD HAMILTON, marr. 24th March 1694 Sarah, daugh. of William Wynne of Wynne Hall, Ruabon, Denbighshire; she died 14th Aug. 1724. From her daugh., Sarah, was descended the Right Hon. Neville Chamberlain.
1692

GEORGE FORDYCE, had issue—George, Henry, Anna (died 19th May 1791), Sarah, Jean, Martha and Elizabeth.
1709

JOHN CHIESLIE, his son John born 16th Jan. 1760, died 4th Oct. 1761; his daugh. Agnes born 1st March 1765, died 6th Oct. 1766
1768

ROBERT KEITH DICK HORNE, his widow, Helen Macfarlane, died at Eastbourne 11th Nov. 1929, aged 86; his daugh., Caroline, died at Edinburgh 22nd Oct. 1920.
1863

JAMES DODDS, his widow, Elizabeth Leishman, died 5th Nov. 1914; his sons—John Macalister (died 13th Nov. 1921); Sir James Miller (died at London 25th Oct. 1935); his daugh., Mary Janet, O.B.E. (died at Edinburgh 15th Oct. 1947).
1881

JAMES FERGUSSON, clerk of Presbytery 1925–6; died at London 11th Sept. 1926.
1895

OSWALD BELL MILLIGAN, M.C., trans. from Jedburgh 31st March 1927; D.D. (Edinburgh) 30th June 1939; died 2nd April 1940. Addl. issue—Beatrice Moira, born 20th Dec. 1918 (marr. 7th Feb. 1948 Hubert Horace, only son of
1927

Professor Ernest H. Lamb, Cambridge). Publications—*The Story of St Leonard's, Ayr*; *Corstorphine and its Parish Church* (1929); *The Practice of Prayer* (1938).

ST. ANNE'S, CORSTORPHINE

Erected parish quoad sacra 5th Nov. 1915.

JOHN ANDERSON ROBERTSON, dem. 31st Dec. 1932; died 12th Dec. 1941; his sons—Atholl, 2nd Lieut., King's Royal Rifle Corps, born 29th March 1897, killed in action, Civenchy in France, 26th March 1916; Douglas William, D.S.O., M.C., 2nd Lieut., R.F.A., in Administrative Service, Uganda; his daugh. Aileen (marr. 1st Jan. 1926 Field-Marshal William Joseph Slim, M.C., India). His wife, Jean Mathewson, died 1st June 1938. Publication—*The Parish Church of St Anne, History* (1917).
1889

CRAIGLOCKART

ALFRED WILLIAM ANDERSON, died 20th Oct. 1934.
1903

GOGAR

The church of Gogar was dedicated by Bishop de Bernham of St Andrews on 23rd May 1247. The chapel of Ochterogate (Gogar ?) was united by the Ordinary to the Trinity College, Edinburgh, and on the petition of James III, patron of the said chapel, and his mother, Mary of Gueldres, the union was confirmed by Bull of Pope Pius II, 10th July 1462. The hospital of Ochterogate occurs in 1394.—[*Cal. Papal Regs., Letters*, xi, 450, *Petitions* i, 615; *Reg. Great Seal*, vi, 137; Lockhart's *Ch. of Scotland in 13th Century*, 60.]

CRAMOND

On 11th Jan. 1478-9 Alexander Currour, vicar of Dunsyre, founded a chaplainry at the parish altar of St Columba in the "Parish Church of St Columba of Nether Cramond." Another chaplainry in the church was founded by James Howieson in Cramond Regis, with endowment in part from land in the burgh kirk of Cramond. Part of the *reddendo* was 2 sh. annually for the maintenance of the lights of the Blessed Virgin Mary in the church, indicating the existence of an altar dedicated to the Virgin. There was also in the church an altar dedicated to St Thomas. The church was rebuilt in 1654, and enlarged in 1711 and again in 1811; and in recent years it has been twice altered. The tower, which belongs to the 15th century, was finished with the present parapet in 1811. The New Statistical Account records that the bell, which has the inscription "Michael Burgersdyk facit me 1619. Soli Deo Gloria," was "restored from the body of the Civil War by Monk in 1658." In 1569 Patrick Murray was chaplain of the altar in the church founded by John Howieson in Cramond Regis, and in 1571 occurs Matthew Stewart, chaplain of Cramond Regis.—[*Reg. of Abbrev. of Feu Charters of Church Lands*, ii, 69; *Comps. Sub Coll. of Thirds, Roxburgh*, etc.; *Reg. Great Seal*, ii, 1429; iv, 2840; vi, 1146; x, 323; *Reg. Sec. Seal*, xliii, 114; and, 2, *Report Commis. Ancient Monuments, Midlothian*, 27.]

THOMAS SCOTT, M.A., vicar 1568-72. [*Comps. Sub Coll. of Thirds, Linlithgow*, etc.]
1568

WILLIAM CORNWALL, called exhorter 1568.—[*Comps. Sub Coll. of Thirds, Linlithgow*, etc.]
1573

PATRICK SIMSON, as minister pres. to vicarage 24th April 1588 on death of Thomas Scott.—[*P.S. Reg.*, lv, 61.]
1582

MICHAEL CRANSTOUN, pres. to vicarage 11th Feb. 1591-2 on dem. of Patrick Simson.—[*P. S. Reg.*, lxiii, 178.]
1590

WILLIAM DALGLEISH, his son James, merchant, baillie of Queensferry, died 25th Feb. 1719, ancestor of Scotscraig family.
1639

WILLIAM MARTIN, reader; the first entry dated 7th Sept. 1651, in the earliest existing volume of the Kirk Session Records, is—"The Session Book
1651

being lost in the year immediately after Dunbar by Mr William Martin, reader, in whose custody it was, this Book is begun at the minister and the people's return to the parish again. This day was the first Lord's Day after the people were returned from the several places where they were scattered, to the parish again."—[*Memo.* Mr Gordon Stott.]

1666 DAVID FALCONER, marr. Margaret Brydie.—[*Reg. Mag. Sig.*, xi, 1201.]

1675 JOHN SOMERVILLE, line 4 delete "To St Boswells 1662, trans.," line 11 delete from "(1) Esther Scougall to (2)"; died in London 1691.

1694 WILLIAM HAMILTON, tutor in family of Earl of Dundonald, Paisley, in summer.—[*Cramond Poll Tax Roll*, 9th Nov. 1694.]

1737 GILBERT HAMILTON, his daugh., Mary, marr. pro. 5th Nov. 1751.

1816 GEORGE MUIRHEAD, his daugh., Elizabeth, died 1st May 1837.

1843 WALTER LAIDLAW COLVIN, his daughs.—Eliza, died 14th Sept. 1923; Jessie Louisa, died at London 10th Feb. 1938.

1884 JOHN WEBSTER, had issue—James Melville, born 26th Aug. 1858; Robert, born 19th Dec. 1859; John Alexander, born 29th Jan. 1864; Edward, born 30th March 1870, died 18th June 1938.

1907 JAMES ALEXANDER MILNE, his widow, Mary Lee Bowden, died 30th Aug. 1948.

1910 GEORGE GORDON STOTT, D.D. (St Andrews, 1919); his sons, George Gordon, advocate, 1936; Ian Fergusson, Nyasaland Mission; Richard Cossar Gordon, died 23rd Oct. 1947.

ST COLUMBA'S, BLACKHALL (Q.S.)

Erected parish quoad sacra 7th July 1922.

1900 WILLIAM BLACK STEVENSON, D.D., convener of Foreign Mission Committee, died at Aberdeen 5th May 1928. His sons, Robert Dennistoun, killed May 1916; Alexander James, advocate, Carrick Pursuivant 1939–46; Sheriff Substitute, Airdrie, 1946.

1913 CECIL TAYLOR THORNTON, dem. 1916; Lieut. Royal Scots; afterwards min. of St Margaret's, Edinburgh (*q.v.*).

1916 DAVID WILSON BAIRD, adm. from Presbyterian Church of England by General Assembly 1915; app. 1916; adm. to Augustine, Greenock, 15th Dec. 1920.

1921 ANDREW MITCHELL SNADDEN, trans. from Gilmerton 18th May 1921; adm. first min. of parish 31st July 1922; dem. 1931; died at Bishopbriggs 2nd March 1936.

CURRIE

The church was dedicated to St Mungo. —[*P. S. Reg.*, lxvi, 47.]

1571 ALEXANDER BETOUN, archdeacon of Lothian, parson 1571 and parson and vicar 1584. He is to resign the parsonage and vicarage called of old the Archdeaconry of Lothian and its emoluments, to the sustentation of the masters, regents and other residents of the college recently erected by them in the burgh in favour of the provost, bailies, councillors and community 28th March 1584.— [*Comps. Sub Coll. of Thirds, Linlithgow*, etc.; *Cal. of Charters* xii, 2709; *Acts and Dec.*, xxviii, 144.]

1591 MATTHEW LICHTON, pres. to vicarage pensionary Feb. 1593–4 on death of Sir Mark Jamieson.—[*P. S. Reg.*, lxvi, 51.]

1691 HENRY HAMILTON, son of Archibald H., min. of Wigtown.

ROBERT TAYLOR, son of James T., merchant burgess, Edinburgh.
1701

JOHN SPARK, his daugh., Elizabeth, marr. proc. 25th Dec. 1768, William Steedman, Lieut. R.N.
1719

JAMES LANGWILL, his sons—Archibald, died 4th Jan. 1928; Robert Balfour Graham, died Edinburgh 29th July 1932; Hamilton Graham, M.D., died 25th July 1946.
1859

DUDDINGSTON

The church was granted to Kelso Abbey probably in the 12th century and certainly not later than the early part of the 15th, but the exact date of the gift and the identity of the donor do not appear to be on record.

The church is as old as at least the early part of the 12th century, and consisted of a nave and chancel separated by an arch which is the internal feature of the building. By Act of Presbytery of Edinburgh of 18th May 1631 an aisle was appointed to be added to the church for the accommodation of the proprietor of Prestonfield and his tenants, the aisle to be built and supported at his expense. This aisle, on the north side at the east end of the nave, bears the date 1631, and the tower at the west end was added at the same time. The church was described in 1843 as "enlarged, repaired, and painted about 4 years ago."—[*Cart. of Kelso*, i, 196; ii, 347, 348.]

WILLIAM BLACKWOOD, vicar in 1560 and 1566, and 9th June 1574, and chaplain of Our Lady Altar in Dunblane.—[*Laing Charters*, 808; *Acts and Dec.*, lv, 17.]
1560

NINIAN HAMILTON, exhorter 1561, called minister 1568–72, prebendary of Railsteun, brother of John H. in Prestonpans, died before 19th April 1583. Marr. Alison, daugh. of Alexander Heriot in Murehouse.—[*Edin. Com. Dec.* 1587; *Comps. Sub Coll. of Thirds, Linlithgow*, etc.]
1574

CHARLES LUMSDEN, M.A. (1585). Line 7, for 1587 read 1585; as min. here pres. to vicarage 7th Nov. 1588–9 in succession to William Blackwood, last vicar excommunicated.—[*P. S. Reg.*, lix, 17.]
1588

JAMES CRAIG, his son William rector of West Kington.—[*Deeds, Dal.*, 1704, No. 741.]
1694

WILLIAM BENNET, his son Patrick, Ross Herald, 1816–25.
1786

JAMES MACFARLANE, his son William died Peterhead 26th Sept. 1916; his daugh. Eliza died 10th Sept. 1932. Addl. Publication—*The Principles and Duties of the Church of Scotland* (Assembly Address) (Edin., 1865).
1841

JOHN ALLAN HUNTER PATON, his son John Hunter Park died 11th Jan. 1949.
1866

WILLIAM SERLE, died 5th April 1947. He was a keen ornithologist and was one of the official observers for the bird sanctuary of Duddingston Loch.
1903

ST JAMES, PORTOBELLO

JAMES OLIVER, died at Portobello 4th Jan. 1918.
1880

JAMES RAY, trans. from Cellardyke 3rd Oct. 1916; dem. 16th May 1924; died at Harrogate 10th June 1933.
1916

WILLIAM SUTHERLAND BUCHAN, trans. from Liff and Benvie 8th Oct. 1924; trans. to Sanquhar 24th Oct. 1929; trans. to Dunbog 16th Dec. 1949. Addl. Publication—*Young Minds Adventuring* (Edin., 1933).
1924

EDINBURGH, ABBEY

JAMES ROBERTSON SABISTON, died 4th March 1918; his widow, Gretchen Becker, died 24th Jan. 1941.
1889

ARCHIBALD MORRISON, M.A., trans. from Salen (*q.v.*) 23rd Oct. 1918; trans. to Lairg 20th Nov. 1940; trans. to Kilmodan 19th Sept. 1946. Addl. issue—Mary Rose, born 31st Dec. 1924 (marr. 17th Oct. 1944 John Talvethan
1918

Wells, Lieut. North Staffordshire Regiment); Archibald, born 12th March 1925.

BUCCLEUCH

1864 FINLAY MATHIESON, died 26th Nov. 1918.

1882 JOHN CAMPBELL, his son, Ian Wentworth, died at Palmerston, New Zealand, 24th Aug. 1928.

1913 NEIL MACLEOD ROSS, trans. to Laggan 25th Sept. 1923.

1924 JOHN SPENCE EWEN, trans. from Monquhitter 25th Jan. 1924; trans. to Liberton 5th Dec. 1928.

1929 WILLIAM GEMMELL MITCHELL, born 12th Aug. 1893; trans. from Freuchie 16th May 1929. Addl. issue—Robert Gemmell, born 9th Nov. 1925; Jean Gall, born 5th May 1931.

CANONGATE
(HOLYROODHOUSE)

In the Monastery of Holyrood was a parochial aisle with parochial altar, dedicated to the Virgin Mary, founded by Sir John Eastoun, curate. Part of the endowment was "the merck lands called the Crosshouse of the tenements of the Chaplainrie." On 25th May 1487 sasine of 30s. from the Community of the Canongate was given to the image of the Virgin at the said altar, and to Sir George White, chaplain. In the yard of the Palace was a chapel dedicated to St Anne. A short distance north of the Girth Cross was the original boundary of the sanctuary of Holyrood Abbey, there was situated a chapel dedicated to St Thomas the Apostle, with almshouse for seven old men, founded by George Crichton, Bishop of Dunkeld 1527-43, who had previously been Abbot of Holyrood.—[*Acts of Parl.*, vii, 82-3; James Young's *Prot. Book* Nos. 19, 558; *Lord High Treas. Acc.*, ii, 260; iv, 43, Maitland's *Hist. of Edinburgh*, 154.]

1544 JOHN BRAND, his pres. to the chaplaincy of St Ninian, 5th Jan. 1567-8, was on death of Sir William Younger. His son, James, was chaplain of St Thomas situate at the well, that is beside the Abbey.—[*Reg. Pres. Bene.*, i, 1; *Acts and Dec.*, lii, 215.]

1571 ALEXANDER THOMSON, reader 1571-2.—[*Edin. Tests.*, iii, 54].

1635 MATTHEW WEMYSS, his son David bapt. 14th Oct. 1632.

1646 GEORGE LESLIE, M.A., his widow, Elizabeth Charteris, and son, Henry, resident in Tron Parish 3rd Nov. 1694.—[*Tron Poll Tax Roll*, 30.]

1689 THOMAS WILKIE, son of William W., min. of Lilliesleaf, had issue, Christian.—[*Canongate Poll Tax Roll*, 14th Nov. 1694.]

1713 JAMES WALKER, his sons—William, apprenticed to Thomas Gardner, merchant, 1st Aug. 1733; James, bapt. 18th March 1711.—[*Ferryport on Craig Reg.*]

1753 JAMES WATSON, died 1763, not 1673; line 8, for "James Pillans son of a cousin" and line 9 "and Professor of Humanity in the University" read "Alexander Adam".

1769 WILLIAM LOTHIAN, his daugh. Helen died 19th Jan. 1828.

1784 ROBERT WALKER, born at Monkton 3rd May 1755; pres. 29th Dec. 1783; his daugh. Jane (marr. 29th Sept. 1809).

1849 ANDREW REDMAN BONAR, pres. by Queen Victoria 25th Oct. 1849.

1869 JAMES MACNAIR, pres. by Queen Victoria 10th Sept. 1869; his second wife, Harriet Hill, born 24th June 1827.

1889 THOMAS WHITE, died at Bridge of Weir 2nd Dec. 1936; his wife, Janet Barbara Stuart, died 17th March 1936; his son, George Thomas Frood, executive engineer, P.W.D., died at Singapore 15th Oct. 1934; his daugh., Margaret Stewart (marr. 2nd Aug. 1918 Captain James Leggat, R.F.A.).

CANONGATE
SECOND CHARGE

1687 ALEXANDER BURNET, son of Alexander B., alias Buchan, merchant, Aberdeen, Dean of Guild, and grandson of Andrew B., of Kirkhill, resident with his wife and three children in Lady Yester's parish 10th Nov. 1694.—[*Aberdeen Sher. Court Deeds*, 5th Nov. 1692; *Lady Yester's Poll Tax Roll*, 3.]

1709 JOHN WALKER, his son, William min. of Monkton.

1755 JOHN WARDEN, marr. (1) 16th July 1733, Ann Macfarlane, who died 21st Jan. 1748 and had issue—Elizabeth, born 28th March 1734; Helen, born 15th Aug. 1735; Margaret, born 31st March 1737; Lilias, born 24th Dec. 1738; John, born 29th May 1740; William, born 6th Oct. 1745; James, born 25th Jan. 1747.

1765 JOHN WARDEN (MACFARLANE), his daugh., Elizabeth Horne, died 7th April 1794.

1789 WALTER BUCHANAN, marr. Margaret, daugh. of John Stobie, writer, Edinburgh.

DEAN

1865 ROBERT WILLIAM WALKER, his widow, Jane Ogilvie, died 29th March 1919.

1879 JAMES WILLIAMSON, dem. 29th Dec. 1915, died 18th Dec. 1919; his wife, Isabella Agnes Jane Donaldson, died 26th Aug. 1919; his daugh., Mary Gordon, died 7th March 1941; his son, James Gordon, died 22nd Oct. 1934.

1926 JAMES REEKIE, ord. 10th May 1916, trans. to Ashkirk 12th Nov. 1926.

1927 ARTHUR STANLEY MIDDLETON, trans. from Cambuslang West 15th March 1927; dem. 28th Oct. 1945. His wife, Gloriana Margaret Muir, died 14th Jan. 1939; his daugh., Ann Chrystal (marr. 5th April 1941 William Stephen, younger son of William Macdonald, The Knoll, Montgarrie, Aberdeenshire). Addl. issue—James Clyne Wingate, born 24th April 1921, licenciate.

GAELIC CHAPEL OF EASE

1778 JOSEPH MACGREGOR ROBERTSON, marr. Nov. 1771 Janet, daugh. of Thomas Brown, merchant, Aberdeen. His son, Hamilton, died 12th Nov. 1813, aged 21.

GAELIC PARISH (ST ORAN'S)

The Gaelic Church was in Argyll Square, 1815–77.

1840 JAMES NOBLE, marr. Abigail, daugh. of Thomas Ross, LL.D., min. of Lochbroom.

1854 DONALD TOLMIE MASSON, his daugh., Grace Isabella, died 13th March 1915.

1911 JOHN CAMPBELL MACGREGOR, died of wounds in action 4th Nov. 1916; his widow, Robina Ralston McIntyre, died at Connel 25th Oct. 1939; his daughs.—Constance Evelyn Campbell (marr. Dr G. H. Clement, Broadstairs, Kent); Mary Kathleen (marr. 11th Aug. 1934 Allan Lawson Kelly Rankin, M.D., Ph.D., son of Rev. H. M. Rankin, min. of St Andrew's, Galashiels).

1917 JAMES DUFF MACDONALD, trans. from Durness 8th June 1917; died 22nd Oct. 1945.

GREENSIDE

1899 JOHN LAMOND, dem. 3rd Oct. 1923 and became a spiritualist; died at London 19th July 1932; his daugh., Kathleen Ogilvie, died 18th March 1922; his son, John Logan, died at Glasgow 28th Sept. 1940; his widow, Mary Logan, died at Tetbury 9th Nov. 1945.

1924 PETER ALEXANDER DUNN, trans. from Woodside, Aberdeen, 13th May 1924; dem. 7th Oct. 1928 on app. to Central Church, Boston, U.S.A.; trans. to St Paul's, Hamilton, Ontario, 1932; marr. (2) 6th Aug. 1942 Dorothy Burton Dewar.

NEW GREYFRIARS

1929 DUDLEY STUART HOPKIRK, B.D., B.Litt., Ph.D., born Portobello 7th Dec. 1896, son of John Hopkirk; educated at Univ. Edinburgh and Oxford; licen. by Presb. of Edinburgh 1925; assistant Barony, Glasgow, 1925; ord. to Skelmorlie 5th Aug. 1926; trans. and adm. 26th April 1929.

NEW GREYFRIARS

1768 ROBERT HENRY, line 6, for "liii" read "lviii".

1787 WILLIAM MARTIN, marr. Margaret, daugh. of John Cockburn, teacher, Edinburgh.

1814 JOHN THOMSON, his daughs. Nancy Ann, born 28th June 1771, died 7th Feb. 1788; Janet, born 2nd July 1776, died 5th Nov. 1793.

1829 DAVID WILKIE, his son, James of Rathobyres; his daughs.—Christian Stuart (marr. 29th June 1858 Andrew Scott, Glasgow); Caroline (marr. 2nd Jan. 1851 James Malcolm of Olrig, Nova Scotia); Emelia (marr. 15th March 1855 D. J. Dickson).

1839 JOHN JULIUS WOOD, line 3, for "March" read "May"; his daugh., Margaret Hedley, died at Penicuik 3rd March 1929.

1843 WILLIAM ROBERTSON, his son, John Hay, died 1874. Publications—for "Four" read "Six".

1890 ROBERT STEWART, licen. 6th Dec. 1871; his widow, Margaret Brown, died 6th Oct. 1934; his son, John James Erskine Brown, B.A. (Oxon), LL.B. (Edinburgh), 2nd Lieut. Royal Scots, died of wounds 12th June 1917; his daugh., Wilhelmina Jane, died 29th Sept. 1931; his son, William, in Sumatra, died 26th Oct. 1944.

1905 JAMES NICOLL OGILVIE, D.D. (Aberdeen, 1911), dem. 4th June 1919; app. Junior Clerk of Assembly 1st June 1926; died suddenly 9th June 1926; his widow, Elizabeth Johnston Massie, died 6th Jan. 1939. Addl. publication—*Our Empire's Debt to Missions* (London, 1924).

1919 WILLIAM WALLACE DUNLOP GARDINER, D.Litt. (1928), D.D. (Edinburgh, 1st July 1938); trans. from St Madoe's 24th Dec. 1919; trans. to Caddonfoot 4th Sept. 1940; trans. to Onich Ballachulish 28th Oct. 1948; his wife, Ellen Pearl Lindsay Ranken, died at Nethy Bridge 5th Aug. 1936; he marr. (2) 20th Dec. 1938 Margaret Jackson, daugh. of Thomas Miller, 55 Oxgangs Road, Edinburgh.

(*Church united with Old Greyfriars 1st June* 1929.)

ROBERTSON MISSION

1907 WALTER SHAW, trans. to Lairg 23rd Aug. 1916.

1918 JOHN HENDERSON MACKENZIE, ind. 17th Jan. 1918; trans. to Newcastle 22nd Aug. 1918.

1921 THOMAS CONNOLLY, ord. 13th July 1921; afterwards min. of Kelso North and Glasford (*q.v.*).

OLD GREYFRIARS

1689 GILBERT RULE, born 1629, son of George Rule, min. of Mordington and Longformacus, was enrolled at St Andrews Univ. in 1647 (his name does not appear on the lists of Glasgow); Regent at King's College, Aberdeen, 1651–2 and Sub Principal 1652–6; he "came into the College by violence and not minding forms"; he went to Alnwick in 1656 but prior to that he held the degree of M.D., having graduated at Leyden 9th Feb. 1656. On 18th Dec. 1679 he was on the petition of William Hepburn of Beanstoun and remanent heritors allowed to preach in a meeting house at East Linton which had been built for him, but on 17th June 1680 the Sheriff Depute of Haddington was ordered by the Council to demolish it before the end of the month on the ground that it was within a mile of the parish church. He marr., contract 27th Nov. 1655, Elizabeth Birnie and had issue—Elizabeth, bapt. 30th Dec. 1655; Isabel, bapt. 20th Jan. 1657; and (2) before 21st June 1657 Janet, daugh. of John Turnbull, Minto, and had issue—Gilbert, born Berwick 1658-9, M.D. (Leyden, 20th Sept. 1682), F.R.C.P. (Edin. 1695), physician, Heriot's Hospital, 1695.—[*Aberdeen Reg., Old Machar Reg.; Univ. of King's College*, 41, 57, 192-3; *Berwick Sas.*, 1666, 365; *G. R. Sas.*, 33; 309 (1674), 37, 112 (1676), 55, 282 (1687), 58, 345 (1668), 60, 67 (1690); *Edin. Tests*, 82, 23, Feb. 1704; *Index to English Speaking Students at Leyden Univ., Privy Council Reg.*, 3 Ser., vi, 360, 471.]

1702 JAMES HART, marr. (2) Mary, daugh. of James Campbell of Kilpont.

1736 WILLIAM ROBERTSON, his daughs.—Elizabeth, died 27th Feb. 1810 (marr. Archibald Hope, Royal Bank); Jane (marr. William Gifford, farmer); Helenora (marr. 27th Feb. 1757 James Cunningham, baxter); Mary, died 15th Aug. 1837.

1747 JAMES STEVENSON, his daugh., Mary (marr. pro. 2nd June 1771 William Home, upholsterer).

1761 WILLIAM ROBERTSON, his daugh., Mary, died 15th Aug. 1837.

1799 JOHN INGLIS, his daugh., Mary Jane, died 2nd April 1897.

1834 JOHN SYM, his daughs.—Jane Melville, died 21st Dec. 1914; Margaret Scott, died 4th Jan. 1917; Henrietta Wilson, died 25th Sept. 1943; his son, Sir John Munro, died 3rd Oct. 1919.

1877 JOHN GLASSE, died at Edinburgh 8th Feb. 1918; his son, John Morley, M.B., Ch.B., died Haltwhistle 26th Dec. 1943; his widow, Louisa Plymer Gibson, died 12th Aug. 1944.

1910 ALEXANDER BROWN GRANT, trans. to Rosneath 3rd Nov. 1916.

1917 SAMUEL DUNLOP, trans. from Kirkpatrick Irongray 17th May 1917; app. Presb. Clerk 27th Oct. 1926; killed in motor accident 30th Sept. 1928; his widow, Helen Brown Hislop, died 10th June 1930.

OLD GREYFRIARS
SECOND CHARGE

1644 MUNGO LAW, son of William L. in Ballintown, Stirlingshire, and Jean Houston, had a child buried 22nd Aug. 1658; had additional issue—Anna, born 6th May 1647; James, born 28th Aug. 1648; Andrew, born 28th Sept. 1651; David, born 29th Dec. 1652; Marion, born 26th March 1654; Robert, born 19th June 1656; William, born 9th May 1658; his son, John, min. of Symington.—[*G. R. Sas.*, lxi, 32.]

1693 JOHN HAMILTON, line 15, for "Hugh" read "Henry"; his daugh. Jean, marr. Henry, not Hugh, Hawthorn; his son, William, buried 12th Aug. 1685; a child buried 26th March 1698.

1732 JOHN HEPBURN. Addl. issue—Thomas, merchant burgess of Edinburgh, 6th March 1751; Jean (marr. pro. 20th Jan. 1760 John Weir, merchant).

1750 ROBERT HAMILTON, his son, James, died 1845; his daughs.—Catherine, died 1811; Grizel (marr. Aug. 1771).

1754 GEORGE KAY, marr. (2) Ann, daugh. of John Forth, merchant.

The churches of Old and New Greyfriars were united 1st June 1929 and the whole building restored as one church. The church of Lady Yester's was also united 3rd July 1938 and that of New North on 18th June 1941.

ST GILES or THE HIGH KIRK

1560 JOHN KNOX, p. 50, line 15, delete "and again in 1568."

1572 JAMES LAWSON, line 21, for "First" read "Second."

1639 ALEXANDER HENDERSON, line 10 from bottom of p. 57, 2, delete "and was again Moderator in 1639."

1647 GEORGE GILLESPIE. Addl. Publication—*The Testimony of Mr. George Gillespie against association and compliance with malignant enemies of the truth*, 1648 (Paisley, 1791).

ALEXANDER HAMILTON, died 1691, not 1692; p. 60, line 3, for "West Linton" read "Kinglassie." [*G. R. Sas.*, 3 Ser., xxix, 443.]
1689

GEORGE HAMILTON. Addl. issue—Agnes.
1697

JOHN MATHIESON, son of Alexander M., wright burgess of Edinburgh; his daugh., Jean (marr. pro. 6th May 1753 William Currie, merchant, Dumfries); Margaret, died 10th June 1754.
1710

WILLIAM GREENFIELD, his son, James Hunter, died 1st Feb. 1866.
1787

ROBERT GORDON, line 21—delete Professor of Divinity, etc.; min. of Free High Church; line 25, for 1843 read 1847; his daughs., Georgiana White died 11th Jan. 1919; Susan Campbell (marr. Andrew Mackean) died 3rd April 1926.
1836

DAVID ARNOT, his daugh., Anna Fernie (marr. James Gourlay, North British & Mercantile Insurance Co.), died 19th Aug. 1919.
1843

ANDREW WALLACE WILLIAMSON, licen. 13th May 1881; dem. 10th July 1925; created K.C.V.O. 1926; died 10th July 1926; his widow, Elizabeth Mary Phoebe Croall, died 1st March 1946.
1910

CHARLES LAING WARR, educated Glasgow Academy, Univs. of Edinburgh, M.A. (1914), and Glasgow; trans. from St Paul's, Greenock, 11th Feb. 1926; app. Dean of the Thistle and of the Chapel Royal in Scotland, 19th Feb. 1926 and Extra Chaplain in Ordinary to H.M. the King 12th March 1926; Chaplain in Ordinary 1935; Chaplain to Convention of the Royal Burghs of Scotland 1926; Trustee National Library of Scotland 1926; Chaplain to Highland and Agricultural Society 1926; Chaplain to Royal Scottish Academy, 1927; D.D. (Edinburgh, 2nd July 1931); Vice Convener, Home Mission, 1935-6, 1939-41, and Convener 1947; Convener of Committee on Huts and Canteens for Forces 1939-45; Chaplain to King's Body Guard (Royal Company of Archers) 22nd Feb. 1937; Hon. R.S.A. (1927); F.R.S.E.; C.V.O. 10th July 1937; LL.D. (St. Andrews 28th Sept. 1937); Chaplain of the Order of St. John of Jerusalem, 1943, Sub-Prelate 1947, and Prelate of the revived Scottish Priory 1950. Created K.C.V.O. 1950. Marr. 30th April 1918 Christian Lawson Aitken, only daugh. of Robert Rattray Tatlock and Christian, daugh. of Rev. Charles Aitken of Cuparhead, Lanarkshire, Vicar of Carmenellis, Cornwall. Publications—*The Unseen Host* (1916); *Echoes of Flanders* (1916); *Alfred Warr of Rosneath* (1917); *Principal Caird* (1926); *The Call of the Island* (1929); *Scottish Sermons and Addresses* (1930); *The Presbyterian Tradition* (1933); *Bruce* (Walker Trust Lecture) (1936); many contributions to journalism.
1926

ST GILES
SECOND CHARGE

JAMES BALFOUR, line 32, delete "who survived him"; marr. (2) Elizabeth King, buried 10th Sept. 1639.
1598

ALEXANDER THOMSON, line 5, for 1623 read 1619; marr. Margaret, daugh. of Thomas Muirhead, min. of Cambusnethan.
1628

HENRY POLLOCK, trans. from Trinity.
1641

DAVID DICKSON of BUSBY, Moderator in 1639, not 1640; his sons, David and Archibald, matriculated at Glasgow Univ., 1647.
1650

ANDREW CANT, line 10, for "1553" read "1653"; marr. (1) 20th Nov. 1653 Anna Burnett; his son, Andrew, Bishop of Glasgow.—[*Aberdeen Reg.*]
1675

WILLIAM MITCHELL, line 24, marr. (2) "26" not "7."
1721

ROBERT KINLOCH, addl. issue—Robert, bapt. Dundee 9th Aug. 1716.
1728

JAMES BUCHANAN, son of James B., spirit dealer and grain merchant, and Annabella Orr; his daugh., Jean Morrison (marr. 12th Dec. 1862 William Rose Campbell of Ballochyle).
1840

OLD KIRK

ANDREW RAMSAY. (*G. R. Sas.*, xviii, 337; liii, 274).
1641

THOMAS GARVINE, schoolmaster of Irvine; brother of Janet G., who married 1609 James, son of John Spence, portioner of Lathine, Fife; his daugh. Anne (marr. cont, 3rd Jan. 1673 James Caithness, writer, Edinburgh). [*G. R. Sas.*, 2 Ser., xviii, 46; 3 Ser., i, 7; *Edin. Sheriff Court Reg. of Deeds*, 14th June 1707.]
1649

ALEXANDER RAMSAY, his son, Robert, apprenticed to Alexander Callander 17th Aug. 1709; his widow, Jean Orrok, marr. Robert Cheyne, min. of Girthon.
1681

JAMES NISBET, son of James N., M.D.; line 4, for 1625 read 1695; his son, David, merchant, Glasgow.
1718

DANIEL MACQUEEN, marr. Elizabeth, daugh. of Archibald Nisbet of Carfin. Addl. issue—Elizabeth, born 4th April 1745, died 27th March 1746; Ann (marr. 27th July 1769 James Wilkie), died 26th March 1789.
1758

JAMES MACKNIGHT, had issue—William, born 2nd Feb. 1755, died 20th Oct. 1761.
1778

JOHN LEE. Addl. publication—*Evidence before the Committee on Religious Instruction* (Edin., 1837).
1835

OLD KIRK
SECOND CHARGE

JOHN HALL, trans. to Second Charge St Giles after 21st Feb. 1610.
1596

JAMES HAMILTON, son of Gavin H., merchant, Glasgow and Coleraine, and Helen Dunlop; his daughs.—Jane (marr. Archibald Hamilton, min. of Wigtown); a daugh. marr. William Maitland, min. of Beith; Mary (marr. Peter Blair, min. of Jedburgh).—[*Hamilton MS.*, 161.]
1647

GEORGE CAMPBELL of KINNOCHTREE, his daughs.—Rosina (marr. 12th June 1690 Charles Garden, min. of Ashkirk); Marion (marr. George Anderson, min. of Dairsie); Janet, buried 10th June 1676; his son, Alexander, buried 30th Aug. 1699.
1690

JOHN ORR, his daugh., Janet, died 1732 (marr. Andrew Greg, surgeon, Cupar, Fife).
1703

PATRICK CUMING, MS. volume of sermons in Assembly Library.
1732

ROBERT HENRY, marr. Ann, daugh. of Thomas Balderston, surgeon, Berwick.—[*Scots Mag.*, lviii, 293.]
1776

THOMAS MACKNIGHT, line 6, for "Canongate Second Charge" read "South Leith."
1810

(*Second Charge abolished* 1836.)

OLD KIRK PARISH (Q.S.)

JAMES RICHMOND AITKEN, app. Presbytery Clerk 14th Nov. 1928; app. secretary, Church Extension Committee, 1939; D.D. (Edinburgh, 30th June 1932); died 3rd Jan. 1943. His wife, Gertrude Allen, died 9th Dec. 1921. His daugh., Marguerite, marr. Andrew Fraser.
1907

(*Church transported to new site at Crewe Toll*, 7th Jan. 1941.)

LADY GLENORCHY'S (Q.S.)

THOMAS SNELL JONES, marr. (2) pro. 1st Dec. 1783 Mary, daugh. of John Belshes of Invermay, and (3) pro. 30th June 1787 Agnes, daugh. of George Gardiner of Custom House.
1779

GEORGE RAMSAY DAVIDSON, his sons—David William, died Oct. 1886; George Ramsay, died Feb. 1893.
1842

ALEXANDER FYFE BURNS, for "Andrew" read "Alexander."
1877

THOMAS BURNS, D.D., C.B.E., T.D., died 15th Jan. 1938; his wife, Sarah Frances Townsend Murray, died 18th Nov. 1926. He was chairman of the Scottish National Home for Blinded Soldiers (Newington House) and raised large sums of money for this purpose. At the same time the Thomas Burns Home for Blinded Women was founded as a tribute to his work on behalf of the blind. His son, Norman Frederick MacGregor, manager, Banda Kwala Estate, Sumatra; his daugh., Agnes Mary Frances (marr. 30th July 1918 James Thomas Hall, min. of Monymusk).
1882

LADY YESTER'S

THOMAS WILKIE, his son by first marriage, Henry, apprenticed to John Hay, surgeon, 15th Dec. 1695. —[*Lady Yester's Poll Tax Roll*, 35.]
1691

ARCHIBALD GIBSON, probably of Durie family. His mother was Jean Pringle; his daugh., Janet (marr. Jan. 1756 Robert Innes, physician, Edinburgh).
1732

THOMAS FLEMING, his daugh., Ann, born 2nd May 1788, died 25th March 1791.
1806

CHARLES MacGREGOR, died 27th Dec. 1923; his widow, Wilhelmina Blair, died 21st Feb. 1927; his son, Blair, died Oakland, California, 18th April 1937.
1880

JOHN MORRISON McLUCKIE, trans. to Castleton 7th Feb. 1918.
1910

GEORGE SIMPSON MARR, M.A., B.D., D.Litt., M.B., Ch.B. (Edin. 20th Dec. 1923); trans. from Dalzell 2nd Oct. 1918; dem. 2nd July 1938; marr. 5th Feb. 1924 Rhoda Keith Bryden, B.Sc., only daugh. of William Shand, 37 Buckingham Terrace, Edinburgh, whom he divorced for desertion 6th July 1928. Publications—*Periodical Essayists of the Eighteenth Century*: *Happy Youth*: *A Faith for To-day*: *Christianity and the Cure of Disease*.
1918

(*Charge united to Greyfriars 3rd July* 1938.)

MAYFIELD (Q.S.)

ALEXANDER NEIL, dem. 27th Oct. 1920; died at Joppa 13th Oct. 1925; his widow, Cecilia Morrison, died 5th Aug. 1929.
1879

WILLIAM JOHN SYM, trans. from Broughty Ferry 28th April 1921; M.B.E., 1932; Chaplain to Territorial Forces and Senior Chaplain, Aldershot, 1940–3; Convener, Chaplain's Committee, 1938; died 29th Sept. 1946.
1921

MORNINGSIDE (Q.S.)

THOMAS ADDIS, his sons—Rev. William, died 20th Feb. 1917; Thomas Chalmers, died at Colinton 24th Jan. 1918; David Foulis, died 26th Nov. 1924; Sir Charles, K.C.M.G., died 14th Dec. 1945; his daughs.—Henrietta Thorburn (marr. Andrew D. Black) died at Rothesay 14th June 1917; Robina Scott Thorburn, died 16th Aug. 1940; Susan Forbes, died 12th Feb. 1936.
1841

EBENEZER BROWN SPEIRS, his widow, Wilhelmina Amalie Marie Pancke, died 12th Nov. 1935, aged 83; his son, Andrew, died 11th Nov. 1918; his daughs.—Wanda died at Blenay, Switzerland, 26th Jan. 1917; Catherine Vera (marr. 8th May 1920 Frederick K. Watson, B.Sc., New South Wales); Marie, headmistress, Allermuir School, died 23rd Dec. 1943.
1897

ROBERT HOWIE FISHER, trans. to St Cuthbert's 6th May 1914.
1900

ANDREW BROWN, D.D. (St. Andrews 27th June 1930), died 21st March 1943; his sons—David in Ceylon; Douglas, C.A., died from result of an accident, Idwah, Upper Burma, 19th May 1934.
1914

MURRAYFIELD (Q.S.)

ROBERT JOHNSTONE, trans. to Aberdour 18th Nov. 1914.
1901

JAMES ROSSIE BROWN, born 10th July 1886, son of William Rossie B., min. of Ardrossan; educated at High School and Univ. of Glasgow; M.A.
1915

(1907) Berlin and Heidelburg; licen. by Presb. of Irvine 2nd May 1911; app. Chaplain to Duke of Hamilton and ord. by Presb. of Hamilton 29th July 1912; assist. at Glasgow Cathedral, St Cuthbert's Edinburgh, and Peebles; adm. 13th April 1915; served in European War 1914–15 with Royal Scots; Squadron Leader, Auxiliary Air Force; Chaplain, No. 603 City of Edinburgh Squadron, 1929; D.D. St Andrews 30th Nov. 1948.

NEWINGTON (Q.S.)

JOHN ALISON, his widow, Margaret Macgeorge, died at Bournemouth 15th March 1921.
1871

HUGH CAMERON, dem. 15th May 1932, died 21st Aug. 1934; his daughs.—Maud (marr. 26th July 1917 Norman Gottfried Kesting, min. of Kirkhope); Norah (marr. 24th Sept. 1942 Lewis Frederick Armitage).
1898

PRESTONFIELD

DONALD MACMILLAN, dem. 11th Feb. 1926; died 31st July 1944; his wife, Edith Marjorie Eveline Watt, died 26th May 1920; marr. (2) 6th June 1928 Agnes Charteris (died 23rd April 1938), daugh. of James Stirling, 17 Orchardhead Road, Liberton; his daugh., Isabella Catherine, marr. 1st July 1922 John Elder, M.C., M.A., min. of Cults East.
1908

ANDREW ROBERTSON, trans. from Mochrum 6th Oct. 1926; trans. to Oxnam 26th May 1937; his wife, Helen Ferme Lawson, died 22nd Sept. 1939.
1926

RESTALRIG (Q.S.)

JOHN DURIE, exhorter in 1568 and 1569.—[*Comps. Sub Coll. of Thirds, Linlithgow, etc.*]
1568

GEORGE BOYD, his daugh., Elizabeth Mackenzie, died 17th Dec. 1929.
1870

WILLIAM BURNETT, dem. 31st Dec. 1934; died at Leeds 30th May 1946; his daugh., Mary Johnstone, M.A., B.Ed. (marr. 27th July 1932 James Lumsden D.Sc., Ph.D., principal, Technical College, Dundee); his wife, Lena Dawson, died 4th Dec. 1943.
1912

ROBERTSON MEMORIAL (Q.S.)

WILLIAM LYON RIACH, his widow, Agnes Geraldine Potter, died 15th Nov. 1915; his daugh., Agnes Mary (marr. Francis William Gibb, Edinburgh), died 2nd March 1940.
1872

DAVID PAUL, dem. 26th Nov. 1919, died 12th July, 1929; his son, George Morison, died at Malaga 23rd Jan. 1917; his daugh., Alice Mary, died 19th July 1947.
1896

GEORGE VICTOR DUNNETT, trans. from Cockburnspath 4th June 1920; O.B.E. (3rd June 1918); adm. to Flisk 4th Feb. 1937; dem. 21st Dec. 1943. Addl. issue—Alastair Inglis, born 31st March 1920; Stephen Falconer, born 19th Jan. 1923.
1920

ST AIDAN'S

ANDREW BENVIE, dem. 28th Nov. 1926; died 5th Aug. 1930.
1894

NEIL ALEXANDER MACLEAN, born Glasgow 27th June 1895, son of Neil M., Leamington Terrace, Edinburgh; educ. at Univ. of Glasgow; licen. by Presb. of Glasgow 1923; assistant at Paisley Abbey; served in European war as private in H.L.I. and officer in K.R.R.C.; taken prisoner at Cambrai 30th April 1917; ord. to Montrose, Second Charge, 3rd Feb. 1925; trans. and adm. 7th June 1927; dem. 15th May 1936; adm. to St Columba's, Lauriston, Falkirk, 19th Sept. 1939; dem. 15th May 1944. Marr. 17th Sept. 1943 Janet Inglis, daugh. of James Cruickshank, S.S.C.
1927

(*New Church at Saughton dedicated 28th Dec.* 1934.)

ST ANDREW'S

1813 ANDREW GRANT, his son David, born 22nd Sept. 1794, died 13th March 1800.

1837 JOHN BRUCE, his daugh., Isabel Angus, died Edinburgh 21st May 1924.

1843 THOMAS CLARK, his daugh., Janet Gordon, died 19th Sept. 1853.

1857 JOHN STUART, line 7, for "1848" read "1847"; his widow, Jessie Duncan, died 19th March 1922.

1896 PETER HAY HUNTER, his widow, Helen Dawson, died 13th June, 1935.

1908 GEORGE CHRISTIE, D.D. 1927; died 23rd Nov. 1937.

(*St Andrews and Queen Street Churches united 12th Oct.* 1947.)

ST BERNARD'S (Q.S.)

1841 For ANDREW WATSON BROWN read Alexander Watson Brown.

1866 JOHN McMURTRIE, his widow, Beatrix Somerville Brodie, died at Skene Manse 20th April 1920; his daughs.—Beatrix, headmistress, St Columba's School for Girls, Kilmacolm; Agnes Katherine, died 29th Aug. 1936.

1900 ALEXANDER FIDDES, D.D. (Aberdeen, 1929), dem. 12th Nov. 1925; died 29th March 1943; his widow, Mary Ross Allardyie, died 24th Jan. 1948.

1926 ALBERT ALEXANDER DIACK, trans. from Peterhead East 7th July 1926.

ST CUTHBERT'S

In 1128 David I with consent of his son, Henry, granted to Holyrood Abbey the church with the parish and all things pertaining to the church, and with the kirkton, and with the land on which the church is situated, and with the other land which lies beneath the Castle, and two chapels pertaining to the church—the chapel of Corstorphine with two bovates and 6 acres of land, and the chapel of Liberton, with 2 bovates of land, and with all the teinds and rights, both living and dead, of Legbernarde, which Macbeth of Liberton gave to the said church and which the King confirmed. Manifestly the church was founded long prior to the foregoing date; and it may be that it owed its origin to one of the followers of St Cuthbert, or even to that saint himself. There is, however, no certain information with regard to the foundation. The church was dedicated by Bishop de Bernham on 16th March, 1241–2. On 3rd July 1486 William Tours of Inverleith and Alison Home, his wife, granted to a chaplain at the altar of St Anne, mother of the Virgin Mary, situated in St Anne's aisle on the north side of the church, 14 merks annually from a tenement near the place of the Minorite Friars, Edinburgh; and in 1558 George Tours of Inverleith stated that the altar had been founded by his predecessors. On 10th Dec. 1488 Mr Alexander Currour, vicar of Livingstone, granted to a chaplain at an altar in the church dedicated to the Holy Trinity annual rents from tenements on the north and south sides of High Street, in the Canongate, and in *le Forstan's* Wynd on the south side of High Street. There was also in the church an altar dedicated to the Virgin Mary. By Act of Parliament in 1633 St Cuthbert's Church was dissolved from Holyrood; and by Charter of 29th September of that year Charles I annexed it to his newly formed Bishopric of Edinburgh. After the Revolution, when the bishopric was dissolved, the church became independent.

It is presumed that when, in May 1544, under the direction of the Earl of Hertford, the English leader, "the towne (Edinburgh) and also the Abbey of Holyrodehouse" were wholly burned and desolate, St Cuthbert's Church was involved in the conflagration. In any case in 1550 the church is described as "the new parish Church of St Cuthbert's," indicating that at that date a scheme of rebuilding had very recently been carried out. In 1593 the fabric of the church underwent considerable repairs. The Steeple "yat is auld," was taken down in whole or in great part and rebuilt, the walls of the church were heightened, and the roof was covered with slates in place of thatch which had done service. The foregoing description of the steeple clearly indicates that it was of much earlier date than the rest of the church, and therefore had survived the fire of 1544. At the same time a new church was erected at the west end of the church, on the site of the existing tower and the triangular piece of ground adjacent thereto. In Gordon of Rothiemay's map of Edinburgh, 1647, there is a sketch of the church showing it as a plain building consisting of nave and choir, with a south transept at the junction of the nave and choir, and on the south side of the west end a massive square tower. Later illustrations reveal considerable alterations in the external appearance of the building, including the heightening of the nave and an addition in the outside stair to the end of the south transept. These alterations were due to the need of providing lofts for additional accommodation. Mention in 1649 is made of the West Loft called Braid's Loft, at the north end of which provision was made in that year for accommodation for the Town Council, who had become a heritor, entrance to the Council's Loft being secured by a door "broken through the wall." In September 1650, after the battle of Dunbar, in connection with the siege of Edinburgh Castle by Cromwell, the new church was demolished, and of the old church practically nothing but the bare walls remained. In the following year restoration work was begun; and in 1652 sufficient repairs had been carried out in "roof, walls, and windows" to enable the church to be reopened for worship in April of that year. But even in 1655 internal renewal work was still being carried on, for on 13th June of the latter year the Town Council, on the ground that "St Cuthbert's was straitened for fault of lofts and seats therein, that the most part of the congregation goe stragling and wandring up and down to uther kirks and under pretence thereof spend the holie Sabbath ydlie and profanlie," and that their loft if repaired, would provide needed accommodation and thereby make the people "inexcusable for disorderlie living," ordered their said loft to be rebuilt. Probably it was in this connection that the Town Council on 7th Nov. 1655 arranged for a partition wall of "good and sufficient lyme and stane work" being built in the church. In the same period, 1652–5, the walls and roof of the new church were restored, and repairs were carried out on the churchyard dykes which had been built in the early part of 1601. In March–June 1689 the blockade of the Castle, then held by the Duke of Gordon on behalf of James II, led to further severe damage being done to both churches. In course the old church was repaired, while the new church was externally restored. The latter does not appear again to have been used for worship, and in 1753, when it was in a ruinous condition, the roof was removed, and in 1772 the walls were demolished. In 1772 the old church, including the tower, was also demolished, and its place was taken by a building which was opened for worship on 31st July 1775. At the same time the first stage of the tower, which has a sundial with the date 1772 and the motto Vivite Fugio, was built, and in 1789 the tower was completed with funds privately subscribed. The church of 1775 gave place to the present church, which was opened for worship on Wednesday, 11th July 1894. The name, West Church, applied to St Cuthbert's in the 17th century, seems to have originated in the early Covenanting days. But it never really supplanted the old name. Indeed, it had a restricted use, and in course it disappeared. The church lands and glebe, with barn, cornyard, etc., were situated on the east side of the churchyard.

In the parish there were several chapels and religious houses. Near the West Port on the south side of the Castle there was Barras or Barres Chapel, so named from the enclosure for tournaments in the vicinity. Dedicated to the Virgin Mary, it was built by James IV in 1507–8, and appears to have been completed in May of the latter year. On 10th May foresaid King James supplied taffeta red and white "to the courtingis and ruf of the Chapel of the barres" at a cost of £42 5s., and later in the same month, on the 20th and 27th respectively, he made offerings in the chapel then designated "the Chapell of conscience beside the barres." On 25th Feb. 1532-3 James V provided for the chapel, vestments and altar furnishings, and also a bell and an image of the Virgin Mary. The lands of the chapel are described on 31st Oct. 1566 as *lie* Barres and the tail adjoining the same on the west side, and extending to St Margaret's well, lying under the Castle on the south, between Polcatsher's and Orchardfield on the south, the public way leading to St Cuthbert's on the north, the said well on the west, and the lands called *Kingis-Stabillis* on the east. The first chaplain, presented by James IV on 6th June 1508, was Sir James Ellem or Allane, and his successor on 15th Sept. 1545 was Henry Achesoun. At the Burgh Moor, on the ground of St Giles' Grange, there was a chapel founded in honour of St John the Baptist and St John the Evangelist, apparently on 15th Feb. 1512-13, by Sir John Crawford, prebendary of St Giles. Provision was made for (1) a chaplain to celebrate in the chapel, the endowment being 18 acres of the Common Moor, 1¼ acres of land given of charity by the Town Council, and 3½ acres of said moor held by Sir John off the Town Council in feu, and (2) for "a man of advanced age" who "shall reside at the said church, wearing always a white robe and carrying on his breast a sign, viz. the head of John the Baptist, proclaiming his hermitical life, who shall have for his sustenance an acre of land with house and garden adjacent to the same on the south. On 5th Jan. 1516-17 Sir John Crawford conveyed the chapel with the churchyard, houses, yards, lands, to the adjacent Convent of St Catherine of Sienna, and the chapel became the chapel of the convent. Near the foregoing chapel there was a chapel dedicated to St Roc or Rok, founded probably about 1501-2. At that period James IV made various gifts to the chapel, and included in the outlays was a gratuity to the French Friar "that brocht ane bane of Sanct Rouk to the King." Further gifts followed in 1507 and 1512. On 24th Nov. 1532, "for suffrage and prayeris to be done in Sanct Rokis Kirk on the Burowmuir for the souls that lie in the said Kirk and Kirkyard," the Town Council granted to Sir John Young, chaplain in the chapel, and his successors in office 3 acres of the Burgh Moor, with another acre on the south side of the kirkyard of the chapel, to build a yard and house upon—the successive chaplains to "uphold the Kirk in sclates watherticht, glaswyndows, and all uther necessour thingis." Evidently the Town Council was the patron of the chapel, for on 11th Aug. 1537 it granted authority for £10 expenditure "upon heting and mending Sanct Rokis Chapel for the present year," which "is allegit to thame to be reuynous and falling doun." At Newhaven there was a chapel dedicated to the Virgin Mary and St James. In the 16th century up to 1560 it was variously designated the "Chapel of the Blessed Virgin," "Our Lady Kirk of the New Haven," the "Chapel of St Mary at *lie* New Haven or Port of Grace"; but later, and certainly in 1601, it was called the "Chapel of St James, Newhaven." Included in the revenue granted by Crown Charter of 2nd March 1614 to the minister, elders, and deacons of South Leith Church for the Royal Foundation of the Hospital and Poor of Leith, was the place where was the Chapel of St James, Newhaven, formerly called the Chapel of the Blessed Virgin Mary, with the garden of the chapel. Within the lands of Bristo there was a chapel dedicated to St Sebastian, founded on 8th May 1511, by Sir Matthew Doweile, chaplain; and in a charter of 14th April 1439, quoted in a Crown Charter of 2nd Sept. 1458, there appears "the Church of St John the Baptist under the Wall of the Castle." This latter was the chapel attached to the Hospital of the Knight Templars and later the Knights of St John at the Bow Foot in the Grassmarket. In St Ninian's Row in the Low Calton there was a chapel dedicated to St Ninian. Lepers at St Ninian's Chapel are referred to in a charter of 15th Feb. 1541–2, indicating that attached to the chapel there was a house for lepers. The west pier of Regent Bridge is situated on the site of the chapel. The Dominican nunnery of St Catherine of Sienna, the foundation of which was confirmed by Bull of Pope Leo X on 29th March 1517, was situated at the place called the Sciennes. Land for the nunnery was given by John Cant, burgess of Edinburgh, and Sir John Crawford, prebendary of St Giles, and the expense of erection was borne chiefly by Jane Hepburn, wife of George, fourth Lord Seton. Dedicated to the Virgin Mary, the Carmelite convent of St Mary of Placentia was situated a short distance from the south-east corner of the city wall. Alike of the name of the founder and of the date of the foundation nothing is known. The name survives in the pleasance. The hospital, or almshouse, with chapel was situated at the foot of St Leonard's Lane in the old barony of Broughton. It was in existence in the first half of the 12th century, and was granted to Holyrood Abbey by David I, probably at or soon after his foundation of the abbey in 1128. It seems to have had a somewhat chequered career. At any rate, towards the end of the 15th century "time, war, and other inconvenients" had made it "waste and uninhabitable," and on 18th July 1493 it was refounded by Robert Bellenden, Abbot of Holyrood, for six old and frail poor men, and their successors as beneficiaries, with sustenance for them, consisting of two crofts, the Terraris Croft and *le Hermitis* Croft in the said Abbot's territory of St Leonard, and 23s. annual rent from a tenement in the Canongate. Provision was also made for a chaplain for the hospital, who had a manse near the gate of the monastery on the north side of the High Street of the Canongate. Of the two crofts and the annual rent of 20s. sasine was granted by the abbot on 2nd Sept. 1494 to six poor men in the hospital, John Rudry, Thomas Blak, Robert Murray, John Burne, Thomas Rannald, Thomas Huchonson, and their successors.—[*Reg. Great Seal*, i, 805, 1812; ii, 616, 1692, 2192, 3818; iii, 170; iv, 2813; vi, 1181; vii, 1015; viii, 243; *Reg. Sec. Seal*, i, 1689, ii, 2455, iii, 1322; *Acts Scott. Parl.*, v, 54; *Lord High Treas. Accs.*, ii, 68, 146, 346, iii, 293, 1322, iv, 22–3, 38, 41, 181, 183, 191, v, 389, vi, 93, vii, 74, 195, 290; *Exts. from Records of City of Edinburgh*, i, 164; 1528–57, 59, 67; 1557–71, 7; 1589–1603, 285; 1642–55, 275, 391; *Charters of Holyrood*, 3, 4, 6, 234–44; Foular's *Prot. Bk.*, Nos. 110, 253, 713; Young's *Prot. Bk.*, No. 730; Gilbert Grote's *Prot. Bk.*, Nos. 152, 155; *Church of Scotland in 13th Century*, 46; *Scotsman*, 12th July 1894.]

ARCHIBALD HAMILTON, M.A., vicar in 1557 and 7th July 1566.—
1557 [*Col. of Charters*, ix, 1902, 2044; *Reg. Abb. Feu Charters of Church Lands*, i, 183; *Acts and Dec.*, xxxii, 113.]

WILLIAM HARLAW, his pres. to vicarage 6th Feb. 1572 was on death
1560 of William Hamilton.—[*Reg. Pres. Bene.*, i, (4), 4.]

ROBERT PONT, his daugh., Beatrix, was by first marriage; his son, James,
1578 commissary of Dunblane. It does not appear that he actually became min. at St Andrews (*q.v.*).

JAMES REID, line 1, for "John" read
1649 "William."

DAVID WILLIAMSON, his son, George, by 2nd marr., bapt. 15th
1689 Oct. 1668; his son, William, apprenticed to Robert Manderston, merchant, 23rd March 1711. Publications—for "*Two*" read "*Four Single Sermons 1690–1703.*"—[*South Leith Reg.*]

THOMAS PITCAIRN, parentage given is doubtful; his daughs., Jean (marr.
1735 pro. 17th Aug. 1755 David Wardrop, surgeon, Edinburgh); Margaret (marr. pro. 5th Sept. 1756 Alexander Sheriff, merchant, Leith); his son, James, apprenticed to James Hunter, wright, 8th Sept. 1742.

ALEXANDER STUART, marr. (1) Margaret, daugh. of John Heriot,
1762 candlemaker.

SIR HENRY WELWOOD MONCREIFF. 1775 Addl. Publication—*A Brief Account of the Constitution of the Established Church of Scotland* (Edin., 1833).

JOHN PAUL, 1828 his son, Sir James Balfour, died 15th Sept. 1931. Publications—for *"Two"* read *"Four Single Sermons"* (1834-60).

JAMES MacGREGOR, 1873 pres. by Queen Victoria 17th July 1873; his widow, Helen Murray, died 29th May, 1930.

ROBERT HOWIE FISHER, 1914 line 17, "June," not "May"; dem. 12th Nov. 1925; died at Oxford 2nd Nov. 1934.

NORMAN MACLEAN, 1925 trans. to Collegiate Charge from Park, Glasgow, 18th March 1915; became senior minister 12th Nov. 1925; app. Chaplain to the King 24th Aug. 1926; chaplain, St Andrew's, Jerusalem, 1939-40; Moderator of General Assembly, 1927; convener of Life and Work Committee, 1928; preached opening sermon in the Cathedral of Geneva of 10th Assembly of the League of Nations, 1930; dem. 2nd Feb. 1937; his wife, Jane Robertson Macaulay, died 1927. He marr. (2) 3rd April 1929 Hon. Iona Marie Adelaide, only daugh. of Ronald Archibald, Lord Macdonald of Sleat. His daughs.—Margaret Hope (marr. 28th June 1929 Daniel, son of Lachlan Macpherson, Upper Ollach, Portree); Jean (marr. 4th July 1930 Allan Biggar, Bombay); Dileas, M.B., Ch.B. (marr. 1st June 1935 William Douglas Short, B.Sc., Dumbarton). Addl. Publications—*The Message of Bethlehem*; *The Future Life*; *Death Cannot Sever*; *How shall we Escape?*; *In Former Days* (1945); numerous contributions to the *Scotsman* and magazines.

ST CUTHBERT'S
COLLEGIATE CHARGE

WILLIAM KEITH OF AQUHORTIS, 1661 was formerly min. of Udny (*q.v.*). Addl. issue—William, eldest; Robert, called eldest 1694; Jean (marr. cont. 14th March 1720 William Anderson, min. of Daviot.)—[*Aberdeen Inhib.*, 24th July, 1655; *Sher. Court Deeds*, 3rd July 1694.]

NEIL McVICAR, 1707 marr. (2) contract 9th Nov. 1737 Bridget Balfour and had issue—Neil, only son, Jean and Lilias.—[*Reg. of Deeds, Dal.* 161, 12th March 1747.]

JAMES MACKIE, 1758 his Common Place Book and Sermons in Assembly Library.

JOHN GIBSON, 1765 marr. Mary, daugh. of Alexander Tait, merchant, Edinburgh. Addl. issue—Janet, born 30th May 1756.

JAMES VEITCH, 1843 pres. by Queen Victoria 29th Aug. 1842.

JAMES BARCLAY, 1878 died at Keswick 18th March 1928; his widow, Marion Simpson, died 1st April 1942.

WILLIAM LYALL WILSON, 1911 died 1st Aug. 1914; his widow, Margarita MacCulloch, died at Hove, 23rd June 1945; his son, Thomas Leslie Lyall, killed in flying accident Jan. 1945.

NORMAN MACLEAN, 1915 see Senior Charge.

SIR GEORGE FIELDEN MACLEOD, 1926 Bart., born Glasgow 17th June 1895; second son of Sir John Mackintosh Macleod, Bart., C.A., M.P. Glasgow, and Edith Fielden; educ. at Winchester, Oriel College, Oxford, B.A., Edinburgh Univ., Union Theological College, New York; served as Captain, Argyll and Sutherland Highlanders, in European war (Military Cross and Croix de Guerre); licen. by Presb. of Edinburgh 29th June 1921; missioner, British Columbia Lumber Camps 1922; assist. St Giles, Edinburgh; ord. for Social Service with Toc H 17th Dec. 1924; adm. to this charge 24th March 1926; trans. to Govan 8th Oct. 1930; D.D. (Glasgow Univ. 16th June 1937); dem. 31st May 1938 to become leader of the Iona Community; succeeded his nephew as 4th

Baronet, April 1944; marr. 28th Aug. 1948 Lorna Helen Janet, daugh. of Donald Macleod, min. of Inverness. Publications—*Govan Calling, a Book of Broadcast Sermons and Addresses* (1934); contributor to "Way to God" series for the B.B.C.; *Speaking the Truth in Love: a Book on Preaching* (1936).

BONNINGTON

1908 JOHN SUTHERLAND HUNTER, licen. by Presb. of Irvine 8th June 1886; died 15th Jan. 1943; his wife, Lizzie Mathewson, died at Edinburgh 30th April 1924; had issue—May Spedding, born 21st June 1899; Elizabeth Dorothy, born 19th May 1901.

1915 JOHN ANTHONY MACRAE, ord. 8th April 1915; res. 1917; afterwards of St John's, Dundee.

1918 JAMES MILLER, trans. from Dundee.

1920 JOHN W. SPENCE, afterwards of Buckhaven.

(*Charge dissolved* 1924.)

CHARTERIS MEMORIAL ST NINIAN'S

1912 WILLIAM COWAN, died 9th June 1917.

1917 JAMES GILLAN.

1918 ROBERT GEORGE JAMIESON, Indian chaplain locum.

1920 GEORGE CAMPBELL, app. 1920; trans. to Cranshaws 9th April 1925.

1925 THOMAS RAMSAY KEARNEY, formerly of Ichang; adm. 19th April 1925; trans. to Hallside 21st Sept. 1927.

1928 HENRY McKINLEY, born 18th May 1874; son of William M., mining contractor, and Isabella Aitchison; educ. at Tranent Public School, Univ. of Edin. and Congregational Theological Hall; ord. in Congregational Union 10th Aug. 1912; min. at Sullom in Shetland; Old Greyfriars, Edinburgh Jan. 1916 to April 1917; *locum tenens* North Esk 1st May 1917, and assistant Liberton 1st Sept. 1917–25; ord. in Church of Scotland and adm. to Channelkirk 30th April 1925; trans. to Sinclairtown 2nd Nov. 1926; dem. 27th Dec. 1927 on app. to this charge 15th Jan. 1928; trans. to Cambusbarron 13th June 1934; died 24th May 1945. Marr. (1) 1st June 1897 Margaret, daugh. of William Nicolson, Mossbank, Shetland; she died 14th Feb. 1932 and had issue—William, born 28th Aug. 1898; (2) 30th Sept. 1933 Isabel Margaret, youngest daugh. of Norman Macdonald, F.C. Min., Alvie, and Elizabeth Stewart.

ST DAVID'S

1896 WILLIAM RITCHIE BLACK, died 1st Dec. 1944. Line 2, for "6" read "4." He had issue—Marion Galloway (marr. 2nd July 1923 Leonard Langdon Williams, M.S.A., F.R.I.B.A., M.I.P.T., manager, Singapore Improvement Trust); John Murray, M.D., F.R.C.S. (Edin.), Dunfermline; William Galloway, M.A., B.Sc., M.I.C.E.; Robert James, died 15th Sept. 1916; David James Galloway, B.Sc., lecturer in Agriculture, Reading University; Helen Grace, M.A.; Charles Ritchie, M.A., LL.B., W.S., 1937; his wife Euphemia Grace Galloway, died 9th Aug. 1943.

ST GEORGE'S

1814 ANDREW MITCHELL MORRISON, his daugh., Jean (marr. 1st June 1831 Alexander Campbell, writer).

1834 ROBERT SMITH CANDLISH, his daugh., Elizabeth Smith, died 18th July 1915.

1843 ROBERT HORNE STEVENSON, his wife, Frances Cadell, died 27th March 1918; his sons—John Horne, K.C., M.B.E., Marchmont Herald, died 23rd Jan. 1939; Robert Cadell died at Epsom 23rd March 1944; Henry James, W.S., died 8th Aug. 1945; his daugh., Anne Frances, died 25th Dec. 1941.

ARCHIBALD SCOTT, marr. 4th July, *not* June; his sons Archibald, born 10th April 1863, died 31st April 1864; John Robert, born 19th Nov. 1864, died 3rd June 1865; his daugh. Margaret died at Ballater 22nd Sept. 1922; his widow, Marion Elizabeth Rankine, died at Ballater 30th Sept. 1920.
1880

GAVIN LANG PAGAN, enlisted in 15 Royal Scots 1914 and became captain; killed in action 28th April 1917. He marr. 12th Aug. 1915 Jessie Mabel, daugh. of Gordon Douglas, manager of Life Association of Scotland; she marr. (2) 5th Jan. 1927 Cecil Thornton, min. of St Margaret's, Edinburgh.
1909

CHARLES WILLIAM GRAY TAYLOR, trans. from Uddingston 18th Jan. 1918 (*q.v.*), D.D. Edinburgh 30th June 1933; convener of Foreign Mission Committee 1928–36; moderator, General Assembly, 19th May 1942.
1918

ST JAMES (Q.S.)

THOMAS PORTEOUS, dem. 29th Dec. 1931, died 3rd March 1939.
1899

ST JOHN'S

THOMAS GUTHRIE, D.D., his sons—James, died at Brechin 2nd March 1920; Patrick, died at Colinton 30th Nov. 1925; Alexander, died 28th Dec. 1934.
1840

ROBERT WILLIAM FRASER, his daugh. Mary Gertrude (marr. William Cownie) died at Corstorphine 10th July 1922.
1844

JOHN GAVIN DICKSON, born May, *not* Aug.; dem. 18th May 1927; died 31st July 1928; his widow, Agnes McAllum Paul, died 25th Sept. 1930; his son, John Gavin, Lieut. H.L.I., killed in action 8th March 1916; his daughs.—Lilian Paul (marr. 1st Oct. 1925 Peter Dewar, Arnprior), died 16th Jan. 1947; Jean Shearer Paul (marr. 10th Sept. 1930 George Smith Goodall Strachan, W.S.).
1908

SAMUEL JAMES MOORE COMPTON, born Ballymena, Co. Antrim, 6th March 1881, son of James C., timber merchant, Larne, and Margaret Ann Wilson; educ. at Royal Univ. of Ireland, B.A. (1904), and Princeton Theological Seminary, B.D. (1907), Berlin and Halle; licen. by Presb. of Carrickfergus 24th Nov. 1908; assistant, Fitzroy Avenue, Belfast, 1908; ord. 1910, St James, Ballymony, Antrim; trans. to St Andrew's, Kingston, Canada, 1912; served with Canadian Forces in Great War as chaplain; trans. to St Andrew's U.F., Kilmarnock, 1919; St George's Pres. Ch., Southend on Sea, 1925; trans. 21st Dec. 1927; trans. to Skirling 14th April 1943. Marr. 15th July 1913 Ruby, daugh. of Rev. Robert Cameron, Glasgow, and has issue—David Henry Cameron, born 21st June 1914, died 7th Oct. 1914.
1927

ST LEONARD'S (Q.S.)

LEWIS FREDERICK ARMITAGE, his widow, Jane Edmonstone Morham, died 16th Nov. 1918; his daugh. Elizabeth marr. Louis Edmond McVicker, min. of Monigaff.
1879

WILLIAM LIDDLE, his wife, Florence Louisa Nystrom, died 24th Oct. 1929; he died from effects of an accident 12th Sept. 1948.
1913

(*The parish was united with Newington 1st June* 1932.)

ST LUKE'S (Q.S.)

ADAM MOODY STUART, p. 111, line 16, for "a daugh'." read "Adam"; his sons—Alexander, died 22nd Dec. 1915; George, O.B.E., died 30th May 1940; John, died 7th Feb. 1936; his daugh., Eliza, died 30th Jan. 1946.
1835

RANALD MACPHERSON, his daughs.—Jean, died 23rd Feb. 1926; Janet Harvey (Jessie), widow of David Grieve Miller, died 15th June 1946.
1861

DAVID MUNRO MILNE, died 31st March 1927; his wife, Jeannie Mackay, died 12th April 1922; his son, Sir David, K.C.B. (1947), Permanent
1893

Under-Secretary of State for Scotland, 1945; his daughs.—Mary Catherine (marr. 25th March 1924 James Davie, M.C., B.Sc., Kokstadt, South Africa); Agnes (marr. 6th Aug. 1935 Koert Nicholas Pretorius, Livingstone, Northern Rhodesia).

THOMAS DOWNIE MEREDITH, trans. from Inchture 30th Sept. 1927; died 30th Sept. 1944.

1927

ST MARGARET'S (Q.S.)

WILLIAM MORRIS BROWN, line 12, delete "advocate"; formerly a teacher at Constantinople; ord. by Presb. of Aberdeen 14th May 1868, missionary to Jews; his widow, Elizabeth Brodie Powrie, died 2nd Nov. 1927; his son, Alexander Monro, LL.B., died at Regina, Canada, 4th June 1935.

1881

903 JOHN COCHRANE, licen. 1890.

JAMES GILLAN, D.D., dem. 30th Nov. 1910; died 9th May 1932; his widow, Margaret Henderson Wilson, died Aberdeen 25th May 1947, aged 95; his sons—James, Civil Secretary to Sudan Government 1933; Ian Robert Wilson, min. of Fairmilehead, Edinburgh.

1905

WILLIAM VEITCH, dem. 26th Nov. 1920; died at Bridge of Allan 31st Dec. 1937; his daughs.—Helen Flowerdew (marr. 29th July 1921 Prince Demetre Galiczini, Russia); Gladys Muriel (marr. 28th Aug. 1920 Francis William George Urquhart, W.S.).

1911

DAVID BRUCE NICOL, M.C., trans. from Skelmorlie 3rd Aug. 1920; trans. to St Mark's, Dundee, 18th Dec. 1925.

1920

CECIL TAYLOR THORNTON, formerly of Blackhall, adm. 4th March 1926; his wife, Hilda Buchanan Batchelor, died 23rd Jan. 1922; issue—Frances Elizabeth, born 15th Sept. 1915 (marr. 14th July 1940 John, son of Charles Young, Hazledene, Gilmerton); George Hugh Malcolm, born 30th March 1919; marr. (2) 5th Jan. 1927 Mabel, daugh. of

1926

Gordon Douglas, manager of Life Association of Scotland and widow of Gavin Lang Pagan, min. of St George's, and had issue, Gordon Douglas, born 6th Dec. 1927.

ST MARY'S

JAMES GRANT, died Father of the Church; his sons—Archibald Duncan, died 7th May 1915; Andrew, of Pitcorthie, died 23rd Oct. 1924, bequeathed £350,000 to Edinburgh College of Art.

1841

CORNELIUS GIFFEN, his daughs.—Annie, died 15th Dec. 1914; Agnes, died 10th Aug. 1925.

1872

ANDREW TAYLOR LAURENCE, trans. from High Church, Kilmarnock, 4th March 1915.

1915

ST MATTHEW'S (Q.S.)

FRANK HALE MARTIN, convener of Home Mission Committee, died 5th May 1941; marr. 14th Nov. 1923 Helen, youngest daugh. of David Smith Rae, min. of Lethendy; she died 30th May 1939.

1912

ST MICHAEL'S (Q.S.)

GEORGE WILSON, D.D., died at Edinburgh 5th May 1921.

1887

JOHN EDMUND HAMILTON, son of Rev. John Sinclair H.; B.A., M.C.; ord. to Helen's Bay, Co. Down, 1909; trans. A. & S. 20th Dec. 1919; dem. 27th Feb. 1929; re-adm. by General Assembly, May 1930; adm. to St. John's East, Leith, 18th May 1938. Marr. 22nd Sept. 1926 Hon. Lilian, M.B., Ch.B., daugh. of Joseph, 1st Lord Macleay, and has issue—Helen Josephine, born 1927; Martha, born 12th May 1929; Patrick John Sinclair, born 28th July 1934; Colin William, born 12th June, 1937.

1919

JOHN MACDOUGALL, trans. from Wick 30th Sept. 1929; secretary, Church of Scotland Committee on Canteen Work during war 1939–45; O.B.E.

1929

June 1945; trans. to Kincardine and Croick 25th Feb. 1948.

ST OSWALD'S (Q.S.)

1907 HENRY JOHNSTONE WOTHERSPOON, licen. 30th June 1875; dem. 27th June 1923; died unmarried 28th Jan. 1930.

1924 CHARLES GOODALL, trans. from Dailly 15th Jan. 1924; dem. 18th Nov. 1928; app. chaplain to Queensberry House Dec. 1934; died 2nd June 1941. Addl. issue—George Turnbull, born 20th April 1921; his daugh., Patricia, marr. 6th Nov. 1942 Captain J. F. Wilson, R.A.M.C.

1929 CHARLES MONCRIEFF ROBERTSON, trans. from Ferryhill, Aberdeen, 19th April 1929.

ST SERF'S (Q.S.)

1912 DAVID GORDON HAMILTON, line 4, for "Forbes" read "Jones"; marr. Agnes Todd Hunter; trans. to Kelso 21st Sept. 1916.

1917 EDWARD CHARLES HOULISTON, trans. from St Leonard's, Dunfermline, 1st March 1917; served as chaplain, Gallipoli, Egypt, France, 1915-16, Italy Feb. 1918 to Jan 1919; chaplain to Lord High Commissioner 1925 and 1926; died suddenly 2nd Oct. 1926; his widow, Jacobina Scott Mason, died 6th Nov. 1939.

1920 GEORGE TOD WRIGHT, born 21st April 1892, son of Maxwell James W., min. of St Ninian's, Aberdeen; educ. at Annan, Univ. of Aberdeen, M.A. (1913), B.D. (1915); licen. by Presb. of Aberdeen 4th May 1915; chaplain to Forces 26th Dec. 1917-18; assistant St Michael's, Dumfries; ord. to Dryfesdale 6th April 1920; trans. and adm. 5th April 1927; trans. to Carnock, Fife, 20th Feb. 1946. Marr. 20th Nov. 1923 Vera Stewart, daugh. of Samuel Thomas Parish of Todhillmuir, Dumfries-shire, and has issue—Edith Ann, born 26th July 1925 (marr. 16th Feb. 1946 Charles Russell Miller, Dorclyfe House, Rawcliffe, Goole); Maxwell James, born 14th July 1928. Publication—*God and Israel* (Church of Scotland Bible Class Handbook. Edin., 1935).

ST STEPHEN'S

1829 WILLIAM MUIR, his sons—James, engineer to New River Company, London, died Jan. 1889; William, born 5th Sept. 1814, died 4th Nov. 1815.

1867 MAXWELL NICHOLSON, his son, Stuart Oliphant, died 15th Oct. 1923; his daughs.—Anna (Mrs Marshall) died 29th Sept. 1939; Mary (Mrs Ellis) died 12th Dec. 1918; Margaret Marianne (Mrs Rankine) died 1st Jan. 1926; Anne Helen died 3rd April 1917; Frances Maxwell died Buenos Aires 27th April 1947, aged 92.

1891 JOHN FORBES WATSON GRANT, his widow, Diana Shank Cook, died 29th Nov. 1932; his daugh., Mary Elizabeth, died 18th Dec. 1947.

1911 LAUCHLAN McLEAN WATT, trans. to St Mungo's, Glasgow, 26th June 1923.

1923 THOMAS BENTLEY STEWART THOMSON, trans. from Dalzell (*q.v.*) 20th Dec. 1923; assistant Chaplain General, Territorial Army, 1922; Senior Chaplain, Lowland Division, 1928; app. convener of the Committee on Societies for Young Men and Women, 1929; of the Jewish Mission Committee, 1931-4; of the Committee on Desecration of the Sea of Galilee, 1934; app. Senior Chaplain to the Forces (T.A.), Scottish Command, 1934; trans. to Govan Old 27th April 1939; trans. to Dunbarney 16th Feb. 1948. Marr. 4th June 1918 Margaret Rolland Menzies, only daugh. of Robert Mackenzie, M.A., min. of West U.F. Church, Alloa, and has issue—Elizabeth Stewart, born 12th July 1920 (marr. 30th May 1945 Charles Grant, M.B., Ch.B., R.A.M.C.); William Mackenzie Stewart, born 3rd Dec. 1925; Margaret Stewart, born 6th June 1935. Publications—Edited *Alma Mater* (Aberdeen University Magazine) 1912-13; *Crumbs for the Children*, 1923; *Preparing* *for the Lord's Table*, 1925 (fifth impression, 1936); *The Quest of Youth*, 1926; *Studies in the Teaching of Jesus*, 1928; edited *A Book of Prayers for Guild Meetings*, 1928; contributor of sections to *The Expositor's Ministers' Annual*, 1929-30-31; and to *Lovely Britain*, 1935; edited *The Man's Own Paper*, 1928-9; *Historical Notes on the Origin, Progress and Issue of the Great War, with Suggested Form and Order of Service for the use of Educational and other Authorities on the Day of National Remembrance*, 1936; *Bens and Glens—Wayfaring in Scotland*, 1935.

TOLBOOTH PARISH

GEORGE HUTCHESON. (*G. R. Sas.* 2 Ser. x, 134.)
1649

WILLIAM MELDRUM, line 9, for "Colston" read "Colison"; last line, for "1683" read "1681."
1675

WILLIAM GARDYNE, D.D., resident with three children, John, James and Margaret, in Old Kirk parish 9th Nov. 1694.—[*Old Kirk Poll Tax Roll*, 16.]
1686

JOHN TAYLOR, ord. to Tillicoultry 7th July 1714; trans. to Alloa 17th Feb. 1726. Marr. Martha Lindsay and had issue—John, born 1724; Marion (marr. pro. 22nd April 1753).
1735

ALEXANDER WEBSTER, his daugh. Ann marr. pro. 22nd June 1777. Publication — *Observations on Church Affairs* (Edin., 1/34).
1737

WILLIAM KING TWEEDIE, his daugh. Margaret died at Elie 19th July 1927.
1842

GEORGE SMITH, his son Sir Henry died 2nd March 1921.
1844

TOLBOOTH
SECOND CHARGE

JAMES WEBSTER, line 2, p. 124, after "Edin." add "1694." Marr. (1) Margaret, daugh. of Laurence Keir of Forret.—[*Reg. of Deeds Mack*, lxxxv, 1032.]
1693

WILLIAM GUSTHART, his daugh. Elizabeth died 19th Nov. 1792.
1721

DAVID PLENDERLEITH, his daughs.—Alison (marr. pro. 1st March 1779 James Grant, merchant, Edinburgh); Janet (marr. pro. 19th Nov. 1755 Robert Wilson, cabinet-maker, Edinburgh).
1765

JOHN CAMPBELL, had issue—Daniel, born 15th Aug. 1792, died 6th June 1802; Mary, born 12th July, died 15th Sept. 1793; Robert (twin), born 12th July, died 25th Sept. 1793; Elizabeth (marr. 25th June 1839 James Gibson, min. of Kingston, Glasgow), died 9th Aug. 1881; Margaret (marr. 2nd Nov. 1843 Charles James Kerr, C.A.), died 18th Nov. 1891.
1805

TOLBOOTH (Q.S.)

JAMES LUMSDEN, trans. to Ratho, 2nd March 1917.
1900

JOHN CAMPBELL, trans. from Greenock St Paul's 16th Sept. 1917; Librarian, General Assembly Library, 1932; D.D. (Glasgow 17th June 1936); dem. 7th Jan. 1941. His wife, Margaret Swan, died 6th Feb. 1935; his daugh., Effie Jean, marr. 9th March 1940 Daniel Richard Cameron, Bombay, son of David Cameron, Greenock); his sons—John, min. of Dunnottar; Alexander Archibald, ord. *locum* Cromdale, Sept. 1941, ord. to Strathdon 18th Oct. 1943.
1917

(*The charge was united with St John's 2nd Jan.* 1940.)

TRINITY

WALTER BALCANQUHEL, his son Walter D.D. made burgess and guild Brother, Edinburgh, 2nd June 1617.
1598

HEW McKAIL. [*G. R. Sas.*, 2 Ser., xvii, 190.]
1649

ANDREW CANT, M.A., his wife and daughs. resident in Tron Parish 12th Nov. 1694. Marr. (1) Agnes Murray and had issue—Andrew, bapt. 13th June 1672; Alexander, born 25th May 1674; John, born 24th Oct. 1675; Jean, 21st July
1678

1678.—[*Tron Poll Tax Roll*, 56; *S. Leith Reg.*]

1689 HUGH KENNEDY, transfer children to first marriage and add Herbert, regent in Edinburgh University 1684.—[*G. R. Sas.*, 2 Ser., xi, 362.]

1813 WALTER TAIT, his daugh. Aline Elizabeth (marr. John Balleny) died 1892.

1834 WILLIAM CUNNINGHAM, his daugh. Mary Anne died 17th Aug. 1933.

1843 WILLIAM STEVEN, p. 130, line 4, for "1862" read "1826."

1879 ALEXANDER KENNEDY, his sons—Lieut. Colonel MacDougal, D.S.O., C.M.G., died 2nd Nov. 1924; Alexander Burnett died 28th July 1913.

1906 WILLIAM MAIN, trans. to Paisley Abbey 11th Sept. 1925.

1926 ALFRED JAMES MACKENZIE, formerly Professor, Madras Christian College; adm. 3rd March 1926, died 15th March 1930; his son Ian Andrew born 16th Jan. 1924.

TRINITY
SECOND CHARGE

1628 HENRY ROLLOCK, afterwards min. of St Giles 1641.

1635 JAMES ELLIOT, son of James E., min. of Forfar.—[*Reg. of Deeds*, dxli, 383.]

1641 WILLIAM BENNET, had issue—William and Helen (twins), bapt. 13th Aug. 1643; David, bapt. 2nd Jan. 1645; Catherine, bapt. 27th Dec. 1646.

1701 ARCHIBALD RIDDELL, was min. of Kippen for a short time in 1691; marr. (1) "Isobel" not "Helen" Aitkenhead.

1732 GEORGE LOGAN, had issue by first marriage—Alexander, born 1714, W.S. apprentice 1733; John, born 1715; Elizabeth, born 1712; Helen, born 1713; by second marriage—George, min. of Ormiston, born 1723; Jean (marr. pro. 10th March 1754 Archibald Campbell, writer, Edinburgh).

1758 ROBERT DICK, marr. Grizel, daugh. of Robert Ford, Glasgow.

TRON

1663 JOHN PATERSON, one of H.M. Chaplains 6th May 1668 in succession to Dr William Ogstoun.

1687 ALEXANDER MALCOLM, his son William buried 25th June 1688; his daugh. Janet buried 31st Aug. 1697; his son John, schoolmaster of Newbattle; Alexander, writer on mathematics and music, incumbent of St Anne's Parish, Maryland, 26th Sept. 1749, died in Queen Anne's County 15th June 1763.—[*Scot. Notes and Queries*, Dec. 1928, 234.]

1692 GEORGE MELDRUM, M.S. Sermon on Hebrews x, 23, in Assembly Library.

1707 WILLIAM WISHART, his daugh. Cordelia (marr. 6th Jan. 1724 John Moncrieff of Rumgally).

1786 ANDREW HUNTER, born 15th Feb. 1744. Addl. Publication—*The Duties of Subjects, a Sermon* (Edin., 1793).

1874 JOHN BARCLAY, trans. from St George's, Glasgow, not Old Kilpatrick.

1876 WILLIAM CRUICKSHANK EDDIE JAMIESON, his widow, Jessie Archibald, died at Edinburgh 28th June 1924, aged 85.

1885 DAVID MORRISON, his widow, Annie Gray Stirling, died at Dunblane 13th Aug. 1931; his son David Lyall died 16th Dec. 1944.

1908 JOHN WALLACE, trans to Paisley Abbey 2nd Charge, 4th May 1916.

1916 JOHN ARCHIBALD GLOVER THOMSON, trans. from Wallacetown, Ayr, 28th Sept. 1916; trans. to Hawick 19th Nov. 1925.

TRON

JOHN FORD MACLEOD, trans. from Craigrownie 5th May 1926; trans. to Longniddry 4th Sept. 1940. Marr. 21st Sept. 1920 Catherine Maud, younger daugh. of George Cuthbert, Gartlands, Broughty Ferry.
[1926]

TRON
SECOND CHARGE

ROBERT MORTIMER, son of Thomas M., bailie of Aberdeen.
[1665]

JOHN STRACHAN, marr. (1) Janet, daugh. of William Forbes of Finzean, advocate, and (2) Isabel, daugh. of John Irvine of Kincausie; his son Alexander, paymaster of the Forces; his daugh. Isabella bapt. 15th Aug. 1689 (marr. 7th Nov. 1716 Andrew Drummond of Stanmore, banker, Charing Cross) died 13th Feb. 1731. Col. 2, line 1, for "Fingask" read "Finzean."
[1683]

JOHN STEEDMAN, his son Robert apprenticed to Robert Grierson, merchant, Edinburgh, 5th Feb. 1718.
[1710]

WILLIAM WISHART, delete daugh. Cordelia.
[1745]

JOHN JARDINE, born 3rd Jan. 1716, son of Robert J., min. of Lochmaben.
[1754]

JOHN DRYSDALE, born 20th April, 1718; his daugh. Anne marr. Professor Andrew Dalziel.—[*Dict. Net. Biog.*]
[1767]

WILLIAM SIMPSON, his son George, Lieut. R.N., H.M.S. *Fox*, killed in Batavia.
[1789]

TYNECASTLE

JAMES BELL NICOLL, died 22nd Jan. 1924; his daughs.—Janet Maud (marr. 2nd April 1919 Capt. John Frayer Hosken); Elizabeth Bell (marr. 2nd June 1925 Charles Moubray Russell, M.B., Ch.B., Bradford); Jean Mackenzie, died 19th Sept. 1926.
[1891]

JOHN MENZIES BAILLIE DUNCAN, formerly Foreign Missionary (vii, 692), trans. from St Brides 30th April 1924; trans. to Moonzie 19th July 1939; dem. 31st Dec. 1947; his sons—John Henry, missionary, Kikuyu, 18th June 1933; George Baillie, min. of St James Parish Church, Carlisle; his daugh. Clara Cecilia died 6th Sept. 1934.
[1924]

WEST COATES

ROBERT GIBB FORREST, ord. to New Pitsligo 10th Aug. 1865; his son George, C.A., Inverness, died 25th Oct. 1931; his daugh. Elsie died 29th April 1946.
[1872]

WILLIAM ANDREW KNOWLES, trans. to Dalton 21st March 1918.
[1909]

WILLIAM JAMES SOMERVILLE MILLER, trans. from Helensburgh West 26th Sept. 1918; dem. 5th June 1932; his wife, Grace Beveridge Begg, died at Carrick Castle 22nd March 1941.
[1918]

ST BRIDE'S

Erected parish *quoad sacra* 16th March 1923.

WILLIAM GEORGE ANDREWS, died 19th Nov. 1917; marr. 11th April 1917 Elsie Anderson, daugh. of David Williamson Runciman, min. of Leslie, Fife and Auckland, New Zealand.
[1904]

JOHN MENZIES BAILLIE DUNCAN, formerly of Calcutta (vii, 692), adm. 13th Feb. 1918; dem. 1918; app. Joint Secretary for Scotland of Bengal Religious Tract Society 1st June 1920; adm. to Tynecastle 30th April 1924.
[1918]

THOMAS GILLIESON, trans. from Cranshaws 9th Oct. 1919; trans. to Greyfriars, Port of Spain, Trinidad, 30th Sept. 1931; dem.; returned to Scotland and adm. to Bonkle and Preston 3rd Sept. 1935; died 8th June 1946. Issue—Margaret Theodora, born 22nd June 1908; Archibald Hamilton Charteris Phin. B.Sc., Ph.D., born 5th May 1910; John William McIntosh, born 25th April 1911; Marion Catherine, born 1st July 1912; Thomas Lindsay, born 30th Oct. 1915; Flora Patience, born 2nd Dec. 1919; Anne Eddie,
[1919]

born 2nd Aug. 1926; a son born 2nd Dec. 1931. His wife's mother was Margaret Ann Eddie, widow of David Shaw, agent, Bank of Scotland, Bonar Bridge.

WEST ST GILES

1738 ROBERT WALLACE, his daugh. Elizabeth died 6th July 1795.

1843 ROBERT NISBET, his daugh. Jessie Ann died 5th March 1935.

1875 ALEXANDER WILLIAMSON, his widow, Sarah Ann Todd, died Edinburgh 26th Dec. 1924.

1913 JOHN MALCOLM MUNRO, trans. to St Columba's, Glasgow, 18th June 1925.

1925 DAVID BROWN, born 30th Sept. 1890, only son of David B., Newton Stewart; licen. by Presb. of Wigtown,1922; assist. St. Matthew's, Glasgow; ord. to St. Mary's, Dumfries, 30th June 1922; trans. and adm. 24th Sept. 1925; died 14th Jan. 1944. Marr. 12th Sept. 1923 Margaret Cranston, eldest daugh. of Robert Ormiston, Westlea, Alloa; s.p.

WEST ST GILES
COLLEGIAGE CHARGE

1708 ROBERT SANDILANDS, son of Robert S., bailie of Edinburgh.—[Edin. Burgesses, 13th Sept. 1706.]

1732 WILLIAM HAMILTON, marr. Mary, daugh. of John Robertson, merchant, Glasgow; his son Alexander died 1778; his daugh. Janet marr. 1731 James Smith.

1786 THOMAS HARDY, born 22nd April 1748; his daughs.—Agnes, born July, not Nov.; Sophie (marr. (1) 28th Feb. 1811).

1861 DAVID DICKSON, addl. issue—Mary, born 25th Aug. 1785; Alexander, born 7th Jan. 1789.

GILMERTON

1881 JAMES CHRISTIE, his widow, Jane Turner Jack, died 15th Aug. 1939; his daugh. Mary Christina died at Dumfries 15th Sept. 1937; his sons—James Johnston died at St Jovite, Canada, 18th Jan. 1917; Thomas in Calcutta.

1913 JOSEPH MOFFETT, dem. 31st Oct. 1917; adm. to Crown Court, London, 3rd Nov. 1917.

1918 ANDREW MITCHELL SNADDEN, formerly of St George's, Johannesburg (vii, 564); adm. 3rd May 1918; trans. to Blackhall 18th May 1921.

1921 PETER MILNE, formerly chaplain, Duars, India (q.v.); adm. 18th Sept. 1921; trans. to Guthrie 7th Aug. 1929.

GRANTON

1889 THOMAS SMITH GOLDIE, dem 4th Dec. 1927; died at Balerno 30th Nov. 1929; his daughs.—Margaret Somerville (marr. 2nd Aug. 1916 John Crawford, M.A.); Norah Isabella (marr. 14th July 1923 Robert Johnston, Victoria); his widow, Maria Gosling, died 7th Feb. 1936.

1928 THOMAS MALLOCH MACFARLANE, born Dundee 25th Nov. 1897, son of William M.; educated Harris Academy and Univ. of St Andrews, M.A. (1921) and Strasbourg; licen. by Presb. of Dundee 1924; assistant St Mary's, Edinburgh, 1925; ord. 9th May 1928; marr. 24th Sept. 1928 Elizabeth Mary, daugh. of Alexander Low, Dundee.

JUNIPER GREEN

1906 CHARLES MAURICE SHORT, formerly of Congregational Church, Cork, died 3rd Nov. 1925; his widow, Lucy Greig Robertson, died Sept. 1937.

1926 WILLIAM BUCHANAN CULLEN BUCHANAN, born Southend, Argyll, 1899, son of Robert B., Macharioch, Kintyre; educated at Hamilton Academy, Univ. of Edinburgh, M.A., British School of Archaeology, Athens;

served as Flying Officer in Great War in France 1917-19; licen. by Presb. of Edinburgh 1924; assistant St Giles; ord. 18th March 1926; trans. to St Marnoch's, Kilmarnock, 11th Sept. 1930; dem. 8th July 1941 on becoming Chaplain, R.A.F.; adm. to Pollokshields East 30th April 1946; marr. 9th Sept. 1927 Alice Dorothy, younger daugh. of William Sime, N.E.I.S., Dalserf.

KIRKNEWTON

1562 NINIAN BORTHWICK, M.A., min. in 1562, and Prebendary of Corstorphine, called Half Gogar and Aldertoun.—[*Comps. Sub Coll. of Thirds, Linlithgow*, etc.; *Gen. Coll. of Thirds*, 1562, 101.]

1573 JAMES BROWN, sometime parson, rector 2nd April 1556, 16th Feb. 1565-6 and 28th May 1569, formerly rector, was out of office 11th April 1576.—[*Acts and Dec.*, 1, 256; Thomas Johnson's *Prot. Book*, 376, 482, 824, 935.]

1577 SIR JOHN TOD, reader and vicar pensioner 28th March 1574; died before 2nd March 1577.—[*Reg. Pres. Bene.*, i, (2), 66; *Edin. Tests*, iv, 191-2.]

1577 SAMUEL SOMERVILLE, pres. to vicarage pensionary 2nd March 1577 on death of John Tod; designated reader Oct. 1578 and 21st Feb. 1578-9; still vicar 1581.—[*Reg. Pres. Bene.*, i, (2), 66; *Reg. Abbrev. Feu Charters of Church Lands*, ii, 223; *Edin. Tests*, iv, 191-2, vi, 324.]

1699 JOHN THORBURN, his son James, merchant, Keith.—[*Lyon Register*.]

1745 ALEXANDER BRYCE, marr. daugh. of Provost John Gillespie, surgeon, Stirling; his daugh. Janet (2) marr. George Johnston of Hillhouse.

1862 HENRY WALLIS SMITH, p. 153, line 3—for "Auchinleck" read "Auchineck."

1881 GEORGE GARDINER, licen. 16th May 1878; died 21st Jan. 1922; had issue—Euphemia Forgan, born 5th Oct. 1881, died 7th June 1882; Annie Dow, born 10th Oct. 1883; David Forgan Lindsay, born 21st Aug. 1885, died 22nd Sept. 1888; William Wallace Dunlop, min. of Caddonfoot; his widow, Margaret Smith, died 11th March 1936.

1922 CHARLES ORFORD ALLAN, trans. from Logie (Cupar) 20th July 1922. Addl. issue—Kathleen Anderson, born 26th May 1926.

NEWHAVEN

There was at Newhaven a chapel of St James with manse and garden, which took the place of a chapel dedicated to the Virgin Mary.—[*Reg. Mag. Sig.*, vii, 1015.]

1887 THOMAS PEARSON, dem. 17th May 1916, died 20th July 1920; his widow, Eliza Downs, died 2nd June 1930.

1916 MUNRO SOMERVILLE, trans. from Drumelzier (*q.v.*) 12th Oct. 1916; trans. to Ballantrae 5th April 1923.

1923 DAVID SILVER JOHNSTON, trans. from Bervie (*q.v.*) 19th Oct. 1923; trans. to Botriphnie 25th March 1931; died 7th Oct. 1946; his daugh., Elizabeth Marguerite Angela, marr. 24th March 1945 Lieut. Inge Hey, Norwegian Services.

NORTH LEITH

The Act of Parliament, 9th July 1606, which erected the parish, the church then having 1,000 communicants, narrates that the inhabitants of the north and south parts of the Water of Leith being "unable to repair to thair Parish Church of Holyrood, upon thair awin expenss and charges has biggit to themselffis ane kirk upon the north side of the brig of Leith, and has had ministers there 20 years bygone" serving the cure and ministering to them the sacraments. The General Assembly had ratified and approved the erection in 1602. The "kirk" in the narrative has reference to the Chapel of St Ninian which Robert Bannatyne, Abbot of Holyrood, founded in 1493 at the north end of the Bridge of Leith, and to which, for two chaplains to serve at the chapel, he conveyed by charter of 18th July 1493, land or building at the south end of the bridge and various annual rents. In or about 1586 the inhabitants of North Leith acquired the chapel, the chaplain's house, the tithes of certain lands and houses, and also the tithes of fish brought into the harbour. At that time the chapel was rebuilt, or at least enlarged. In 1736 the church was in great measure rebuilt; and of this church only the steeple now remains. The present church is situated farther to the west.—[*Acts Scott. Parl.*, iv, 301–2; *Reg. Great Seal*, i, 2193; *the Stewarton Case*, 114.]

1620 HENRY CHARTERIS, marr. (1) cont. 9th Aug. 1599 Agnes, daugh. of Alexander Barclay, apothecary; (2) 3rd Sept. 1602 Agnes, daugh. of John Mason, merchant; (3) 19th Dec. 1615 Janet, daugh. of John Bell, min. of Cadder and widow of Henry Stirling. Addl. issue—Laurence, min. of Dirleton; James, merchant; Gilbert, died young; Elspeth (marr. George Leslie, min. of Canongate); Thomas, min. of Humbie.

1653 JOHN KNOX, his eldest son, John, garrison surgeon, Edinburgh Castle; his daugh. Margaret bapt. 19th May 1666.—(*Roxburgh Sas.* 22nd Sept. 1683; Burke's *Landed Gentry*, 1937, 2285.]

1672 THOMAS WILKIE, line 5, for "Jan" read "4th June."

1687 JAMES LUNDIE, son of John L., regent, King's College, Aberdeen; had a child buried 5th Feb. 1674; his wife, Agnes Wilkie, buried 20th Jan. 1692; his son James, M.D., Haddington, died 1777.

1708 JOHN WILSON, had issue—Mr Andrew; Rebecca, died before 13th June 1747.

1725 GEORGE LINDSAY, his son Alexander, apprentice to Alexander Kincaid, bookseller, Edinburgh, 12th Oct. 1743; his daugh. Grizel marr. William Porteous, min. of Wynd, Glasgow.

1799 WALTER FOGGO IRELAND, marr. (1) Jane, daugh. of Dr John Alves, Inverness; his daughs.—Thomasina (marr. 13th July 1840 Samuel Miller, min. of Monifeith); Eliza Ann (marr. 18th March 1858 Rev. James Davidson, Saltcoats).

1843 ALEXANDER DAVIDSON, his wife, Margaret Barron, born 4th May 1825.

1884 JOHN HUTTON McCULLOCH, his widow, Anne Louisa Case, died 16th Oct. 1919; his sons—Donald Harry, solicitor, Aberdeen; Alexander Norman, died 7th Oct. 1943.

1913 JAMES ROBERTSON SWEET WILSON, died 11th Feb. 1942; his widow, Helen Cameron Ruthven, died 19th July 1947.

ST JOHN'S (Q.S.)

Was held by the Free Church till 1868.

1880 JAMES PARK, dem. 18th May 1921; died at Blackness 25th Nov. 1931; his wife, Robina Riddell, died 20th Oct. 1918.

1921 DONALD MACASKILL BEGBIE, trans. from Freuchie 23rd Nov. 1921; trans. to Glencorse 5th Dec. 1928.

1929 DONALD MACKILLOP CAMERON, born 15th Nov. 1876; educ. Univ. of Aberdeen and F.C. College; ord. to Ardchattan and Connel F.C. 1907; trans. to Lorne Street U.F., Campbeltown; trans. 14th May 1929; died 26th Oct. 1937. Marr. 7th Oct. 1909 Grace Rae Mary Helen Oridge Peterkin and had issue—Constance Mary, born 27th July 1917; Sheena Marjorie, born 23rd Sept. 1912 (marr. 23rd Nov. 1939 James Sharp Grant, M.D., F.R.C.S.); Grace Rae, born 10th Oct. 1913; Ranald James, born 17th July 1920.

ST PAUL'S (Q.S.)

1883 HUGH MacCULLOCH, adm. from Buncrana, Donegal, April 1883; trans. to Greenlaw 23rd Sept. 1881.

THOMAS MILLAR, his widow, Helen Stuart Watt, marr. (2) 27th Dec. 1911 Dr J. M. Logie, Cuttlehill, Aberdour, and died 15th March 1931; his daughs.—Monica Anderson (marr. 9th Dec. 1920 Alexander John McLaren, Milrig, Kirkliston); Maud, died 4th June 1923.

1893

DUNCAN CAMERON, dem. 30th June 1920 on app. as Director of Religious Instruction in Edinburgh Training College; died 2nd April 1946; his wife, Margaret Shepherd Robertson, died at Auchterarder 21st July 1942; his daugh. Margaret died 28th May 1943. Publication—*A First Hebrew Reader* (Edin., 1919).

1914

GEORGE LINDSAY STEWART, trans. from Annbank (*q.v.*) 9th Dec. 1920; trans. to Houndwood 26th Sept. 1946; his daugh. Louisa Constance (marr. 30th March 1932 Robert Fisher Martin, Dunsley, Dunfermline).

1920

ST THOMAS (Q.S.)

ROBERT GEORGE FRASER, his widow, Margaret Sharp, died 7th March 1933.

1864

JAMES ALEXANDER FLEMING, trans. to Carnoustie 6th Feb. 1919.

1904

ROBERT FORSYTH McGARRITY, trans. from Carfin (*q.v.*) 19th May 1919; adm. to Burray 24th Oct. 1923.

1919

CHARLES KEITH McWILLIAM, trans. from Leadhills 11th April 1923; trans. to Kelso North 17th Feb. 1926.

1923

ALEXANDER MAUCHLINE, trans. from St Mary's, Dalziel, 22nd Sept. 1926; trans. to Rathen 14th Sept. 1928.

1926

JAMES ALEXANDER HAMILTON IRWIN, born 3rd July 1876, son of Samuel Hyndman I., farmer, and Mary Hamilton; educ. at Royal Univ. of Ireland, B.A. (1900), M.A. (1902), B.D. (1907), Ph.D. (1910); Magee College; Univ. of Edinburgh, New College, and Univ. of London; licen. by Presb. of Glendermott May 1903; ord. to Killearn, Co. Antrim, 24th Nov. 1903; dem. 19th Oct. 1926; assistant St Michael's, Edinburgh; adm. by General Assembly on probation 26th May 1927; adm. 19th Dec. 1928; trans. to Lucan and Summerhill, Dublin, 30th May 1935. Marr. (1) 3rd Sept. 1907 Alexandrina Thompson Cheyne (died 11th June 1911), daugh. of Rev. R. J. Morrell, Bangor, and had issue—Samuel Ranald, born 22nd Nov. 1908; Robert John Morrell, born 11th June 1911; (2) 25th April 1916 Amy Marie, daugh. of Francis Hunter and Jane Smith and widow of George Miller, Rothesay.

1928

SOUTH LEITH

DAVID LINDSAY, line 18 from top of column—for "Westruther" read "Westerkirk."

1613

JOHN CRANSTOUN, his son James, writer, Edinburgh.—[*Reg. of Deeds Mack.*, xxv, 210.]

1627

JAMES SHARPE, M.A. (Glasgow 1612); his son John, M.A. (Glasgow 1653).

1639

DAVID ADDINSTOUN, reader, 4th July 1657.—[*Laing Charters*, 2504.]

1657

JAMES WAUGH, marr. Christian Mylne.—[*Edin. Sas.*, xxxiii, 84.]

1682

ROBERT DICKSON, pres. 30th July 1790.

1790

JAMES GRANT, pres. 1824, not 1799.

1824

WILLIAM STEVENSON, pres. by Queen Victoria 14th Feb. 1844.

1844

JAMES MITCHELL, pres. by Queen Victoria 16th June 1862; his widow, Janet Stewart Sceales, died 28th June 1921.

1864

WILLIAM SWAN, died at Greenbank Manse 28th Aug. 1927; his daughs. —Eiladh (marr. James Arthur Coullie, min. of St Columba's, Oban);

1911

Katherine Allison (marr. 22nd April 1924 Rt Hon. William Shepherd Morrison, M.P., K.C., Postmaster-General); Dorothy Mary (marr. 21st April 1931 Dr John Morrison, Hong Kong).

1928 DONALD DAVIDSON, born 26th Nov. 1892, son of Donald D., min. of Invergowrie, educ. Univ. of Edinburgh, M.A. (1914), B.D. (1921), D. Litt. (1923), Ph.D. (Oxon) (1927); licen. by Presb. of Edinburgh 1921; assistant St Mary's, Dundee; ord. to Campbeltown, Lowland Charge, 4th April 1923; trans. to Queen's Park, Glasgow, 20th Jan. 1925; trans. and adm. 28th Feb. 1928; trans. to St Andrews, Bournemouth, 30th Sept. 1937; trans. to St Andrews, Edinburgh, 20th June 1948. Marr. 5th Aug. 1925 Charlotte Brookes, youngest daugh. of Charles Kemp of Auchencrieve, Rothiemay, and has issue—Charles Kemp, born 15th April 1929; Lilian Charlotte, born 6th June 1932. Publications—*Afterthoughts* (Glasgow, 1928); *The Inner Circle* (1928); *The Issues of Life* (1929).

SECOND CHARGE

1570 JOHN DURIE, trans. to St Giles before 6th Aug. 1573.

1659 DAVID ADDINSTOUNE, M.A., reader 13th Dec. 1659 and 12th May 1672.

1681 CHARLES KAY, marr. Janet Turnbull.—[*Reg. of Deeds Mack.*, lxxxiii, 9th Dec. 1698.]

1766 HENRY HUNTER, his son Lieut. Samuel died at Madras 1792.

1804 JAMES ROBERTSON. Addl. issue— James, born 4th July 1790.

1833 DAVID THORBURN, his son John Hay died 22nd Feb. 1931.

1844 HENRY DUFF, his daugh. Mary Anne died 12th Feb. 1927.

ST MUNGO'S (Q.S.)

Erected quoad sacra parish 20th July 1923; now Lockhart Memorial Church.

1901 GEORGE JACK, dem. 1921; became lecturer for International Society of Practical Psychology; his wife, Jeanie Ross, died 9th Oct. 1920; marr. (2) 5th July 1921 Agnes Watson, daugh. of John Hunter, Woodhall, Juniper Green— she died at Buffalo 28th Jan. 1922.

1922 KENNETH DUNBAR, born 18th March 1892; educ. at Univ. of Edin.; became min. of non-subscribing Presb. Church of Ireland; missionary at Kingscavil Oct. 1919; adm. as licentiate by General Assembly May 1920; ind. to this charge 1st Feb. 1922; adm. first min. 21st July 1923; trans. to Broughton 4th Oct. 1934; trans. to Colinton Mains 15th Sept. 1939; dem. 14th Oct. 1945. Marr. 21st Sept. 1933 Barbara Maclean, daugh. of John B. Wallace, Birkenhead, and has issue—Fiona Margaret Wallace, born 27th July 1936; Sheila Rosemary, born 5th April 1938; Henrietta Michael Ian, born 28th Nov. 1939.

LIBERTON

In 1128 the church, at that time a dependent chapel of St Cuthbert's, was granted along with two bovates of land by David I to Holyrood Abbey. Apparently about a century later Liberton was erected into a parish. There was in the church an altar dedicated to St John the Baptist; and lands in the parish called Reinyenielandis and Ninianeslandis indicate that there may also have been in the church an altar dedicated to St Ninian. The church was rebuilt in 1815. On the east side of the Edinburgh-Straiton road, about a quarter-mile north of the Kaimes cross-road, at the place called St Catherine's, there was a chapel dedicated to that saint, termed St Catherine-of-the-Kaimes. Of the chapel it is said on 30th March 1420 that it was "founded of old," and is "devoutly resorted to by Christ's faithful on the Feast of St Catherine," and "for want of means cannot be completely constructed or fittingly ornamented, unless through Papal succour"; and on that date Papal Indulgence was granted to all Christ's faithful giving free caritative subsidies to the construction of the said chapel, or visiting it on the said feast. The spring, called the Balm-Well, which was attached to the chapel, still exists. On the surface of the water there always floats petroleum, issuing, in all probability, from a bed of shale below. To the well curative properties were ascribed. It was visited in 1617 by James VI, who ordered it to be fenced with stones from bottom to top, and a door and staircase to be made for it to facilitate access to the water. In 1650 it was destroyed and filled up by Cromwell's soldiers; but after the Restoration it was again opened up and put in order. It is covered by a small vaulted structure. By charter of 5th June 1502 Archibald Wauchope of Niddrie-Marschall, with consent of Elizabeth Scougal, his wife, granted to Sir William Warrok, chaplain, and his successors in office, for perpetual celebrations at the high altar of the Holy Rood built by him in the town and territory of Niddrie-Marschall, 12 merks annual rent from the lands of Pylmure in the barony of Niddrie-Marschall, in the parish of Currie, land built, planted, and open in the said town and territory of Niddrie-Marschall, and the East Croft, called the Scotis-patis-croft, also in the said town, for glebe and manse, with pasture for two cows in the commonty of the said town. The above description is incomplete; but evidently it implies that the chapel was dedicated to the Holy Rood. Attached to the chapel there was a graveyard which in 1685 was transferred to the south-west side of the garden. At that time or somewhat later there was built the Tomb-house which occupies the site of the chapel. To the latter may have belonged ecclesiastical details which are found in the Tomb-house. After 1511 Sir Simon Preston of Craigmillar, Kt., who died in or before 1520, built and endowed a chapel at the south end of the bridge of Craigmillar. The chapel was dedicated to the Virgin Mary. The *New Statistical Account* tells of a chapel at Bridgend, built by James V, near a place that he used as a hunting lodge, and at the time (1845) that the account was written served as a stable. It may be, however, that the latter chapel was identical with the chapel of Sir Simon Preston, and was erroneously ascribed to James V. There was also at Craigmillar a chapel built and used as a place of worship for the Presbyterians during the Indulgence by James VII. It, too, a century ago was used as an out-house.—[*Reg. Great Seal*, i, 2695, 3616; ix, 138, 1071; John Foular's *Prot. Book*, 315, *Scott. Rec. Soc.*; *Excheq. Rolls*, xiv, 629; *Cal. of Scott. Supplics.*, 186, *S.H.S.*; *Book of Dryburgh*, 3, 4, 6; for traditional story of St Catherine's Chapel see Boece's *Scotorum Historiae*, etc., p. 6, ed. 1574, and Bellenden's *Cronikils of Scotland*, i, xxxviii.]

1561 ALEXANDER CHALMERS, M.A., vicar of Liberton 9th Nov. 1570, designated priest 21st Jan. 1561-2 and earlier was factor and sub-chamberlain and then chamberlain of Holyrood.—[*Reg. of Deeds*, iii, 19, 162, 420; iv, 337; xi, 247, 485.]

1568 JAMES, LORD SOMERVILLE, held parsonage 1568.—[*Reg. Abbrev. Feu Charters of Church Lands Dumfries*, etc.]

1574 JAMES HAMILTON, min. 2nd Nov. 1575.—[*Edin. Tests*, iv, 169.]

1571 NINIAN RAMSAY, vicar 1571.— [*Comps. Sub Coll. of Thirds, Roxburgh.*]

1586 MICHAEL CRANSTOUN, his pres. in 1586 was on death of Alexander Chalmers.—*P. S. Reg.*, lv, 31.]

1586 ALEXANDER CHALMERS, vicar 1586-90.—[*Comps. Sub Coll. of Thirds, Linlithgow*, etc.]

1609 JOHN ADAMSON, line 2, for "Henry" read "James."

1627 ANDREW LEARMONTH, trans. from Saline 1627.

1697 SAMUEL SEMPLE, MS. Sermon preached in 1708 in Assembly Library.

1789 JAMES GRANT, pres. by George III 1st April 1789.

1835 JAMES BEGG, his sons—Ferdinand Faithfull, died at Hove 4th Dec. 1926; Walter Bently (actor), died in Australia Sept. 1927; Charles, M.D., died at Bath 21st April 1931; his daugh. Euphemia died at London 15th Nov. 1926.

1843 JOHN STEWART, pres. by Queen Victoria 14th July 1843.

1896 ROBERT BURNETT, died 22nd May 1928.

1928 JOHN SPENCE EWEN, D.D. (Aberdeen, 1st April 1936), Junior Mathematical Master, Robert Gordon's College, 1898; Headmaster, Lonmay School, 1902; Cullen Secondary School, 1906; Chaplain to 9th Seaforth Highlanders during Great War; was Chaplain to Edinburgh Police, 1926; trans. from Buccleuch 5th Dec. 1928; died 16th Sept. 1941; was a noted Highland athlete in his younger days. His sons—John Clifford Spence, Education Officer, B.B.C., killed mountaineering at Brevart, Switzerland, 21st July 1935; Alastair Hamilton, Assistant Professor, Animal Husbandry, Univ. of Saskatchewan, Canada, 1930.

CRAIGMILLAR

1926 JAMES MATHERS, O.B.E., app. 1926; trans. to Rosewell 3rd Feb. 1927.

EAST CALDER

The church was dedicated by Bishop de Bernham on 30th May 1247.—[Lockhart's *Church of Scotland in 13th Century*.]

1566 JOHN BALFOUR, vicar 14th May 1566, died before 13th July 1582.— [*Reg. Sec. Sig.*, xxxv, 31; *Reg. Pres. Bene.*, ii, 76.]

1582 SAMUEL WARDLAW, M.A., his pres. in 1582 was on death of John Balfour.—[*Reg. Pres. Bene.*, ii, 74.]

1588 WILLIAM GALBRAITH, pres. to vicarage on death of Samuel Wardlaw.—[*P. S. Reg.*, lvii, 139.]

1596 JOHN BROWN, M.A., his pres. in 1596 was on death of John Spottiswood.—[*P. S. Reg.*, lxviii, 37.]

1663 EDWARD KINNEAR, read "Andrew Kinnear."

1694 JOHN KINNAIRD, his widow, Rachel Sandilands (died 30th Dec. 1738), sister of John Sandilands of Bradshaw.—[*Deeds, Durie*, 1704, No. 595.]

MID CALDER

1583 JOHN SPOTTISWOOD, marr. 12th Oct. 1589.

1638 GEORGE DUNBAR, went to Ireland and preached at Carrickfergus 1625, Ballymena 1625 and Inverlarne 1625. His wife, Jean Crawford, died between 13th April 1603 and 15th Oct. 1604. —[*Ayr Sas. Sec. Reg.*, ii, 495.]

1663 JOHN COLVILLE, his son John.— [*G. R. Sas.*, 3 Ser., xxxix, 214, 19th June 1677.]

1907 WILLIAM WEIR CLARK, his sons— William Arthur, C.B.E., Colonial Service, Kenya; Peter George, North Rhodesia, born 23rd Nov. 1915; his wife, Katherine Robertson Dewar, died 19th Dec. 1943; his daugh., Isabel Katherine, born 24th Jan. 1913, marr. 30th Aug. 1945 John Melville Clark, W.S.

WEST CALDER

1645 PATRICK SHIELDS, third son of James S., cooper, Glasgow; his sons —James, apprentice to Henry Brown, surgeon apothecary, 9th Oct. 1667; Walter, apprentice to William Thine, litster, 11th Nov. 1674.—[*Burgess Roll*, 28th Aug. 1658.]

1675 GEORGE ROBERTSON, line 2, delete "Ord. to Queensferry 20th Dec. 1674"; line 4, "trans. to Kirkurd 16th Jan. 1679; dep. 3rd Nov. 1680."

1689 JOHN LAUDER, born 20th Jan. 1631.

ANDREW GLOAG, eldest son of John
1720   G.; marr. pro. 18th Dec. 1721, Christian Ronald, Linlithgow, she was buried 20th July 1729; had issue—John, merchant, Edinburgh; James, apprentice to Robert Straiton, wright, 23rd June 1742; Thomas, apprentice to James Mansfield, merchant, 14th June 1738.

WILLIAM LEARMONTH, his daugh.
1835   Elizabeth Lee died 17th March 1920.

JAMES ALEXANDER ANDERSON,
1874   died 27th June 1927; his wife, Margaret Melville, died at Portrush 22nd Aug. 1921; his son, Gustav Alexander Melville, surgeon, Lieut.-Commander, R.N., died at Plymouth 26th July 1924; his daughs.—Olivia (marr. 24th April 1915 Rowland H. Rawlingson, Lieut., 10 Bat. H.L.I.); Winifred, died at Belfast 22nd Feb. 1936; Eva Melville (marr. Alexander Carstairs, Rio de Janeiro).

JOHN MACDOUGAL, trans. from
1927   Aberfoyle 17th June 1927; trans. to Old Bonhill 8th Feb. 1932; trans. to Daviot, Inverness, 25th Aug. 1937; trans. to Forgan 2nd Sept. 1942.

PORTOBELLO

GEORGE THOMAS JAMIESON, dem.
1866   17th May 1917, died Father of the Church 6th March 1926.

ROBERT DAVIDSON, trans. from
1917   Fisherton (*q.v.*) 15th Nov. 1917; died 24th June 1943.

RATHO

The church was dedicated by Bishop de Bernham on 5th May 1243. By mandate of 15th June 1444 Pope Eugenius IV, at the instance of Sir John Forrester of Corstorphine, Kt., annexed the rectory and vicarage of the church to the Collegiate Church of Corstorphine. About four years later William de Lauder, lord of Haulton (Halton), and all the parishioners of Ratho represented to Pope Nicholas V that on account of said annexation the church and its great and populous parish had been "much weakened and neglected," and that "the cure of the parishioners" could "ill be borne," and accordingly by Bull of 2nd Jan. 1450–1 Pope Nicholas separated from the said collegiate church all the tithes, etc., formerly belonging to the Vicar of Ratho, not exceeding £8 stg. in value, and granted and assigned them for the portion of a vicar to be again instituted in the said Parish Church of Ratho, and moreover erected the said Parish church into another vicarage, and made provision of it, not exceeding £8, to Thomas de Lauder, priest of the Diocese of St Andrews, of a race of barons, by unmarried knight and an unmarried woman.—[Lockhart's *Ch. in Scot. in the 13th Century*, 52; *Collegiate Churches of Midlothian*, 289–303; *Cal. Papal Regs.*, x, 85, 476–7.]

JAMES BISHOP, Vicar pensionary
1577   1577.—[*Comps. Gen. Coll. of Thirds.*]

RICHARD THOMPSON, pres. to
1589   vicarage principal and pensionary 24th Jan. 1588–9 on death of James Bishop.—[*P. S. Reg.*, lviii, 162.]

THOMAS BANNATYNE, M.A., son
1606   of Thomas B. of Newtyle, pres. to vicarage 23rd Oct. 1606 on death of Richard Thompson, but appears to have declined. See Castleton and Douglas.—[*P. S. Reg.*, lxxv, 188.]

JOHN DUNLOP, his son Ludovick,
1607   burgess of Aberdeen 1st Aug. 1636.

JOHN GUTHRIE, his son John apprenticed to Andrew Mowat, merchant,
1703   20th July 1743.

ANDREW DUNCAN. Addl. issue—
1808   James, born 25th Jan. 1789, died 19th Aug. 1799; his daughs.—Hannah died 12th March 1839 (marr. Major H. A. Montgomerie of Arndean, 53 Reg. Indian Army); Margaret (marr. Major David Bruce, Bengal Army), died at Delhi 18th July 1833; Susan (marr. Dr John Wyllie, physician-general H.E.I.C.S.), died at Nagpore, India, 13th Aug. 1828.—[*Tombst. Blairingone Churchyard.*]

1866 ROBERT CHARLES HENRY MACDUFF, his son William Alexander died at London 8th Oct. 1934.

1876 ARCHIBALD BISSET, died 6th Oct. 1916.

1917 JAMES LUMSDEN, trans. from Tolbooth (*q.v.*) 2nd March 1917; D.D. (Aberdeen, 3rd April 1935); his daugh. Margaret Grange (marr. (1) 23rd June 1928 Geronwy Owen, Blue Star Line; (2) 30th April 1945 Alfred Gamble, Liverpool).

EDINBURGH CASTLE

1692 WALTER SMYTH, William, probably his son, apprenticed to Robert Antonious, wright, Edinburgh, 18th Aug. 1725.

1788 JAMES GLASGOW, son of John G., min. of Kilbirnie.—[*Edin. Com. Deeds*, xxxvi, 5th Jan. 1758.]

NEW STREET CHAPEL

1799 DAVID SAVILE, his daugh. Mary marr. 17th Sept. 1833.

ROXBURGH PLACE

1833 JOHN JOHNSTON, line 20, for "1" read "31."

1841 JAMES HAMILTON, his son Robert William died at Newport, Salop, 14th Sept. 1918.

PRESBYTERY OF LINLITHGOW

ABERCORN

1572 SIR JOHN LYTHGOW, vicar in 1572.—[*Reg. Abbrev. Charters of Church Lands*, ii, 190.]

1574 JAMES MOUBRAY, pres. to vicarage 28th Feb. 1574-5 on death of Sir John Lythgow, last vicar.—[*P. S. Reg.*, xlii, 118.]

1583 WILLIAM POWRIE, min. in 1583.—[*Comps. Sub Coll. of Thirds, Linlithgow*, etc.]

1624 JOHN LAING, for "John" read "James."

1642 ROBERT ROW, his widow marr. (2) Luke Greenshiells, min. of Ardrossan.

1662 JOHN ARTHUR, probably brother of Patrick A. of Ballone.

1791 HUGH MEIKLEJOHN, his children—Elizabeth died 1847; James Hope Johnstone died 1856; Hugh Cree died 1847; Andrew died 1844; Alexander died 21st Jan. 1809.

1843 DAVID PLAYFAIR, line 17, for "Nov." read "Feb."; his daugh. Alice Jane Macduff died 10th April 1930.

1908 JOHNSTON OLIPHANT, dem. 10th Jan. 1948.

AIRTH

1900 FREDERIC HENDRY, died 13th July 1937.

ARMADALE

1909 JOHN ALEXANDER CALDWELL DREW, dem. 16th Feb. 1922.

1922 ROBERT MACPHERSON, M.A., ord. 7th June 1922; trans. to Stobhill 23rd Sept. 1927.

1928 ALEXANDER AITKEN MORTON, trans. from Logie, Cupar (*q.v.*), 14th March 1928; trans. to Bourock, Barrhead, 18th March 1931.

BATHGATE

1555 JOHN HAMILTON, reader and vicar 1555, and on a Letter of Collation to him by John, Archbishop of St Andrews, was infeft in the vicarage in the church on 30th March 1567 by sasine in his favour, there being delivered to him the book and church keys; pres. to vicarage 2nd May 1574 on death of John Gray.—[Thomas Johnsoun's *Prot. Book*, 506; *Reg. Pres. Bene.*, i (2), 19; *Reg. Abbrev. of Charters Church Lands*, ii, 1565.]

1567 JOHN GRAY, M.A., had been min. for six years in 1573 in succession to John Layng.—[*Acts and Dec.*, i, 148.]

1574 ROBERT HODGE, also min. at Livingstone and Torphichen.

1579 JOHN LEVERANCE, son of Richard L., messenger-at-arms, Linlithgow; reader at Carmichael; pres. to vicarage 8th June 1579 on death of John Hamilton.—[*P. C. Reg.*, iv, 510, 18th July 1590; *Reg. Sec. Sig.*, xlvi, 8.]

1588 GILBERT TAYLOR, his pres. to parsonage and vicarage ratified as minister.—[*Reg. Sec. Sig.*, lviii, 49.]

1618 JAMES SIMSON, trans. 1618; his daugh. Margaret marr. John Crooks, min. of Ballantrae.—[*G. R. Sas.*, 2 Ser., vi, 75.]

1655 WILLIAM CRICHTON, line 9, for "after 16th Nov. 1660" read "May 1661."

1735 GEORGE BLACKWALL, MS. volume of sermons in Assembly Library.

1665 WALTER RIGG, line 2, for "1655" read "1665."

1825 SAMUEL MARTIN, born 2nd Dec. 1802; his sons—John died 12th Jan. 1854; Samuel died 20th June 1856; Robert died 17th Dec. 1862; David died 1st April 1875; his daugh. Jane died 12th Jan. 1929; his son William Hamilton died 14th Feb. 1854.

1867 JOSEPH MILNE, his widow, Mary L. Burns, died 26th May 1917.

1872 WILLIAM BENNIE, his widow, Catherine E. Craig, died 23rd Oct. 1922.

1898 WILLIAM LAURIE WEBSTER, died Edinburgh 5th Aug. 1941; his daugh. Laura, M.D., Ch.B., marr. 12th July 1928 William Robert Caldwell Campbell, M.B., Ch.B., Newcastle upon Tyne.

BLACKBRAES

1871 IRVING BEATTIE, ord. 1871, died at Edinburgh 24th Nov. 1883.

1890 WILLIAM SMITH, ord. 11th April 1884, died 12th Feb. 1926; his widow, Helen Smith, died 29th Oct. 1937.

1927 JOHN EASTON, born Bathgate 27th Oct. 1887; licen. by Presb. of Linlithgow 1917; M.A.; assistant at Bathgate 1925; South Leith; ord. 9th March 1927.

BORROWSTOUNNESS or KINNEIL

The Church of Kinneil was granted to Holyrood Abbey by Herbert, Chamberlain of Malcolm IV, with consent of his sons, Stephen and William; and this was confirmed by Charter of King Malcolm in 1158-9. Before 1163 there pertained also to the Abbey the teinds of the mill and salt pans of Kinneil. In 1634 the inhabitants of Bo'ness built a church in which the parish minister conducted worship in turn with the parish church at Kinneil. In 1649, Bo'ness being then in a flourishing condition through the increase of trade, the inhabitants petitioned Parliament to the effect that their kirk had been planted with a minister, and that it was expedient that it should be erected into a kirk by itself, "they pledging themselves to provide a stipend of 800 merks for the minister"; and on 9th March of that year Parliament passed an Act dissolving and dividing the church from Kinneil and erecting it into a separate church with an area attached, the stipend as stated to be allocated among the inhabitants. In 1669 William, Duke of Hamilton, and Anna, Duchess of Hamilton, laid a petition before Parliament stating that Kinneil had only 300 communicants, that through the decay of trade and the poverty of the inhabitants of Bo'ness the stipend there could not be yearly collected or recovered without a great deal of trouble and expense, and that the erection of Bo'ness Church into a parish church was for the time illegal as wanting the lawful authority, and done in the absence of the late James, Duke of Hamilton, then a prisoner in England, who had right to the superiority and property of all lands in the barony of Kinneil, and to all the teinds thereof; they craved therefore that the said erection be declared null and void save in relation to the stipend of 800 merks payable by the inhabitants of Bo'ness, and that the Kirk of Bo'ness, situated in the most fit and convenient place within the barony, should be declared the only kirk of the barony and parish, they being willing to provide at Bo'ness for the minister a manse and glebe in lieu of the same at Kinneil. On 23rd Dec. of the same year Parliament passed an Act in terms of the petition, declaring the Kirk of Bo'ness to be the parish church, and annulling the erection of the parish of Bo'ness in 1649 except in regard to the stipend of 800 merks which, with the teind stipend at Kinneil, was to constitute the stipend of the minister. The parish church at Bo'ness was repaired in 1672, when the Duke of Hamilton added a large aisle for himself and his tenants. In 1775 the aisle was removed, and the church was very largely rebuilt to a size of 69 × 48 ft., and in 1820 the south wall and part of the east wall were rebuilt and the galleries reconstructed and made uniform. The present church was built in 1886–8, being opened for worship on 14th Oct. of the latter year. It consists of a nave with aisles, transepts, chancel, and a tower at the north end, and contains a Dutch pulpit said to have been a gift from Dutch sailors, and a ship in the gallery of the west transept, both transferred from the old church. The latter church was for a time the place of worship of the congregation of the Episcopal Church of Scotland, and is now a cinema house. It was burned on Sat., April 7th 1945. Within the policies of Kinneil are the remains of the Church of Kinneil—the west gable with double belfry, and foundations, which show a nave and a chancel with a cross aisle on the south side of the latter. In the vestibule of Bo'ness Church there is a bell which is said to have belonged to Kinneil Church. It is medieval, and has this incomplete inscription on the shoulder in Lombard lettering: EN : KATERINA : VOCOR : UT : PER : ME : VIRGINIS : ALME (Lo, Katherine I am called, that by me . . . of the Blessed Virgin . . .).—[*Charters of Holyrood*, 12, 13–14, 15, 167–171; *Acts Scott. Parl.*, vi (2), 262, vii, 656; *Memo.* Mr. Robert Taylor, Solicitor, Bo'ness.]

1567 JOHN JOHNSTON, exhorter, of Barnecluyth, held the vicarage and apparently was vicar in 1560 and conformed; died after 30th July 1582 and before 24th Jan. 1585–6.—[*Reg. Great Seal*, v, 431, 1040; *Reg. Sec. Seal*, liii, 91.]

1571 PETER HAMILTON, reader; designated Minister in 1574.—[*Sir Thomas Johnsoun's Prot. Bk.*, 906.]

1585 WILLIAM POWRIE, minister 24th Jan. 1585–6, when he was presented to the vicarage vacant by the death of Sir John Johnston; seems identical with William Powrie, minister at Abercorn, holding both charges.—[*Reg. Sec. Seal*, liii, 91; see Abercorn.]

1672 ROBERT HUNTER, his son James died 11th April 1672.

1694 JOHN BRAND, his son John apprentice to Francis Newton, merchant, Edinburgh, 6th May 1726.

1868 HENRY McINTOSH ROBERTSON FULLARTON, his sons—Archibald Louis died 30th Oct. 1918; Henry Argyll died 26th Oct. 1932; Edward Charles died 8th Nov. 1928.

1896 ROBERT GARDNER, died 25th Feb. 1925; his son Roderick James, Lieut. H.M. Submarine H47, which was sunk in collision off West Coast 9th July 1929 but saved; his widow, Jessie Wylie, M.B.E., died at Edinburgh 28th Nov. 1946.

1925 WILLIAM JAMES SMITH, trans. from St Marnoch's, Kilmarnock (*q.v.*), 1st Sept. 1925; trans. to Claremont, Glasgow, 28th Sept. 1933; D.D. (Glasgow, 1948).

BROXBURN

1908 JOHN AITKEN ORR, died 15th Nov. 1919.

1920 WILLIAM McWHIRTER, formerly of British Guiana St Catherine's (*q.v.*), adm. 20th March 1920; trans. to Small Isles 4th July 1930; dem. 30th Aug. 1939; app. to Half Morton by Presb. for three years 5th May 1942; trans. to Hoy and Graemsay 2nd Nov. 1944. Marr. 20th Dec. 1939 Adelaide Geraldine Fitzgerald.

CAMELON

1867 JOHN SCOTT, his son John Michael died 8th Dec. 1942.

1913 ROBERT AGNEW, trans. A. and S. to Clackmannan 19th Jan. 1921.

1921 ROBERT HEADRICK, born 11th April 1893; son of Robert H., bootmaker, Alva, and Helen Macnaughton; educ. Alva Academy and Univ. of St Andrews; M.A. (1914); B.D. (1918); served in Great War as Lieut. in Scottish Rifles; licen. by Presb. of Stirling 1918; assistant St Mungo's, Glasgow; ord. 8th June 1921. Marr. 7th Sept. 1921 Ethel Isabella Lindsay, daugh. of Robert Kirtley.

CARRIDEN

In 1124–42 the church was granted to Holyrood Abbey by Robert, Bishop of St Andrews. It was dedicated by Bishop de Bernham on 7th May 1243. In 1766 the church was removed from the churchyard in the vicinity of Carriden House, a new church being built on a site on the east side of the road a short distance south of Bridgeness. The latter consisted of a nave with a north transept in the middle, and the walls were of rubble. A tower at the east end and a vestry at the west were added considerably later. From the old church to the new there was transferred the pulpit which had the date 1655 and is said to have come from Holland. In 1905 steps were taken to deal with the dilapidated condition of the church, and after protracted negotiations with the heritors it was agreed on 20th March 1907 that that body contribute £1,800 to the building of a new church at a minimum cost of £4,800, the Kirk Session being responsible for the balance of the cost. The church, built to plans by Dr Macgregor Chalmers, Glasgow, was completed prior to 8th Sept. 1909, and ten days later was designated the parish church by the Presbytery. It occupies a site on the North Glebefield, in the vicinity of the old church. The bell and a ship, which presumably had been in the older building in the churchyard prior to 1766, were removed from the old church to the new. The bell is Dutch and bears the inscription PIETER OSTENS GOOT MY TE ROTTERDAM A^s 1674. After the old church was abandoned the heritors agreed to dismantle it, leaving only the tower and vestry intact.—[*Charters of Holyrood*, 10; *Heritors' Records.*]

ALEXANDER HAMILTON, M.A., vicar; presented to the vicarage in 1546 in succession to Sir Archibald Wetherspoon; may have conformed and acted as reader; vicar on 16th April 1560, when, along with William Cornewall, reader, Linlithgow, he certified the publication of the banns of marriage in their respective churches. Evidence that the Reformed Religion was in operation here then. Still in office 11th March 1577–8; died before 17th Sept. 1579; had a natural daughter, Elizabeth, who married (1) John Gardner, (2) Henry Touch in Linlithgow.— [Nicol Brounis *Prot. Bk*. No. 10, 3; *Charters of Holyrood*, 261–2; Sir Thomas Johnsoun's *Prot. Bk.*, 543, 994.]

JOHN LESLIE, exhorter in 1563 and 1569, min. in 1571 and exhorter in 1572.—[*Comps. Sub Coll. of Thirds, Linlithgow*, etc.]

JOHN WESTWATER, pres. to vicar. 17th Sept. 1579 on death of Alexander Hamilton.—*Reg. Pres. Bene.*, ii, 21.]

ROBERT STEEDMAN, eldest son of James S., elder, of Little Sergie.— [*G. R. Sas.*, 2 Ser., xv, 160.]

JOHN TOD, marr. Agnes, daugh. of James Dundas, Southfield, and had issue—James, born 18th Feb. 1705; John, born 21st March 1706; Robert, born 23rd March 1708; Alexander, born 21st July 1710; William, born 1st Feb. 1712; Agnes, born 11th Nov. 1714.—[*Reg. of Deeds, Linlithgow Sher. Court*, 1st April 1709.]

GEORGE ELLIS, his daugh. Mary died at Edinburgh 4th Feb. 1796.

DAVID FLEMING, his daughs.—Janet Carlile (marr. 1st Sept. 1857 Andrew Vannan); Martha Duncanson (marr. 11th Oct. 1854).

WILLIAM DUNDAS, died 9th Nov. 1931; his son William, Captain in Black Watch; his daugh. Harriet Elspeth, B.A., teacher of Greek, Wycombe Abbey School (marr. 12th April 1935 Frederick Sleath, M.A., Scottish author).

DALMENY

There was in the church an altar dedicated to St Bridget; and there was also in the church an altar dedicated to St Adamnan and St Columba. The Church of Auldcathie belonged to the Priory of St Andrews.—[Mackinlay's *Anc. Church Dedications, Non-Scriptural*, 127; *Cal. Papal Regs., Letters*, viii, 376; *Cal. Laing Charters*, 619; *Retours*, xv, 140, xvi, 1.]

1547 JOHN SINCLAIR, provost of Roslin, pres. to vicarage 2nd Jan. 1547–8 on death of Sir Thomas Hulduson, but did not enter.

1547 ALEXANDER FOIRHOUSE, pres. 3rd Jan. 1547–8.—[*P. S. Reg.*, xxii, 3, 63.]

1562 SIR WILLIAM McDOWALL, vicar, also at Dreghorn, Leswalt and Holyroodhouse, and Preceptor of St Paul's Work. at the foot of Leith Wynd, to which he was appointed 1555–6; died in or before 1579.—[*Compts. Gen. Coll. of Thirds; Compts. Sub Coll. of Thirds, Linlithgow*, etc.; *Book of Old Edin. Club*, xvii, 49, 52.]

1569 ROBERT HOGG, exhorter 1569–72.—[*Compts. Sub Coll. of Thirds, Linlithgow*, etc.]

1574 GEORGE LUNDIE, rector of Auldcathie 4th April 1567; pres. on death of Sir William McDowall. Marr. Katherine Loch and had issue—George, his heir.—[*Reg. Mag. Sig.*, iv, 2251; *Reg. Pres. Bene.*, ii, 321; *Pitfirrane Writs*, 335.]

1579 JAMES STEWART, pres. to vicarage 3rd March 1579–80 on death of Sir William McDowall.—[*Reg. Pres. Bene.*, ii, 31.]

1642 JOHN DURIE, 2nd line from foot, for "1660" read "1680."

1656 ALEXANDER HAMILTON, son of John H. of Bangour.—[*Reg. of Deeds*, 14th Aug. 1663.]

1682 ALEXANDER BANKS, had issue—William, bapt. 11th Feb. 1673; Mary, bapt. 3rd March 1675; Katherine, bapt. 7th Jan., died March 1677.—[*Peterhead Reg.*]

1688 GEORGE TURNBULL. On supplication by the parishioners, which stated that George Turnbull "has preached at the meeting-house of the parish some considerable time and exercised the other ministerial functions, and that the kirk was now vacant by the death of Mr Alexander Banks," the Commission of Estates on 15th May 1689 granted warrant allowing Mr Turnbull to preach at the said kirk of Dalmeny and exercise the other parts of the ministerial function without prejudice to the rights of the patron according to law; he was admitted to Alloa 26th Sept. 1690.—[*Acts Scott. Parl.*, ix, App. 26b; see Alloa.]

1711 JAMES NASMYTH, his son Patrick, apprenticed to Ralph Dundas, merchant, Edinburgh, 22nd June 1743.

1776 THOMAS ROBERTSON, his son Charles Hope died 28th Jan. 1806.

1884 ROBERT HUGH MUIR, his widow, Margaret Kerr Black, died 1st Feb. 1921.

1890 PETER DUNN, D.D. (Aberdeen, 1922); dem. 9th Dec. 1925; died 23rd March 1930.

1926 WILLIAM NEIL SUTHERLAND, trans. from Fraserburgh (*q.v.*) 18th June 1926; died 19th June 1946; his wife, Eugenie Florence Natalie Bach, died 15th Feb. 1940. Marr. (2) 31st Oct. 1940 Marion Cunningham, elder daughter of John George Dudgeon, Easter Dalmeny.

ECCLESMACHAN

1561 JOHN MOUBRAY, parson and min., 1561 and 1569–72.—[*Coll. Gen. of Thirds*, 1561*f.* 96; *Acts and Dec.*, xlviii, 67.]

1734 CHARLES WILKIE, marr. Eupham, daugh. of James Flint, merchant and bailie of Edinburgh.

ALEXANDER SHEPHERD, his widow, Jane Douglas Dawson, died Newbury, Berks, 16th July 1926; his daugh. Sophia Hay died at Blair Atholl 26th Aug. 1926.
1869

ARTHUR PENRHYN STANLEY TULLOCH, dem. 6th May 1924 and joined Church of Rome; died 15th Dec. 1945; his son Arthur died 16th April 1937.
1910

ROBERT LANG PINKERTON, trans. from St Leonard's, Lanark (*q.v.*), 17th Sept. 1924; has issue—Jean Haddow Bell, born 11th June 1919; Robert Leonard Cecil Comrie, born 23rd Dec. 1921; Frances Mary Joyce, born 11th April 1926.
1924

FALKIRK

In 1166 Richard, Bishop of St Andrews, for the souls of David I, Malcolm IV, his predecessors, Robert and Arnold, Bishops of St Andrews, Alwin, his uncle, etc., granted to Holyrood Abbey "the Church of Eeiglesbrac" (Falkirk) called Varia Capella, "speckled church." On 12th June 1242 the church was dedicated by Bishop de Bernham of St Andrews. On 24th Feb. 1449 Papal confirmation was given to the erection of the church into a collegiate church by Sir Alexander Livingstone, but the erection was subsequently quashed. There were in the church an altar dedicated to the Virgin Mary, and an altar dedicated to St Michael the Archangel, founded on the north side in 1531 by Sir Robert Batho, chaplain of the said Altar of the Virgin. At Manuel there was a chapel, dedicated to the Virgin Mary, with regard to which there was presented to the Pope by Rankine de Crawford, nobleman, temporal lord of Manuel, and all the inhabitants of Manuel in the parish of Falkirk, a petition to the effect that the church or chapel of the said place of Manuel had from time immemorial a cemetery, baptistry, chrism, vase, burial-place, and a priest who celebrated divine offices there and administered the sacraments to all the inhabitants of the temporal lordship, but that, although other similar neighbouring churches or chapels had their own district and special clerk-minister to the priests and chaplains serving such churches or chapels in divine offices, elected and presented by the inhabitants of such places, the said church or chapel was without such a clerk-minister. The petition craved a clerk-minister, so elected and presented. In response a Papal Mandate was given 4th Apr. 1454 to Robert Lauder, Bishop of Dunblane, to grant power to the place and lordship to elect, with the consent of the chaplain, a clerk-minister to help and minister, according to custom, to the chaplain or priest of the said church or chapel, the emoluments, similar to those in other cases, to be provided by the inhabitants. On 21st Oct. 1300 Edward I made an offering of 7 sh. "at the High Altar of the Priory of Manuel." In the west end of the parish, near St Helen's Loch, which no longer exists, there was a chapel dedicated to St Helen.—[*Cal. Papal Regs., Letters*, x, 691–2; *Cal. Docs. Rel. to Scot.*, iv, 44a; *Church of Scot. in 13th Century*, 48; *Scott. Ch. Hist. Soc.*, vi, 212; *Reg. Great Seal*, ii, 2441; iii, 1333; iv, 815; v, 68.]

SIR ANDREW HOGGE or HEGY, vicar 1560; still in office 1572.— [*Comps. Sub Coll. of Thirds, Dumfries*, etc.]
1560

JAMES ERSKINE, son of James E. of Little Sauchie, pres. to vicarage 14th Nov. 1576 in succession to Sir Andrew Hegy.—[Stephen's, *Inverkeithing and Rosyth*, 528.]
1567

ALEXANDER CUTHBERT, reader 29th Oct. 1574, pres. to vicarage 31st May 1587 on dem. of James Erskine.—[*Reg. Sec. Sig.*, lv, 48.]
1587

JAMES ERSKINE, pres. to vicarage 29th Sept. 1588 on death of Sir James Erskine.—[*Reg. Sec. Sig.*, lviii, 44.]
1588

THOMAS SPITTAL, marr. Elizabeth, daugh. of Adam Spittal of Blairlogy.
1626

1686 ARCHIBALD MUSCHET, marr. (2) proc. 23rd June 1675 Margaret Edward; his son Archibald apprentice to John Hay, surgeon apothecary, Edinburgh, 7th Aug. 1700.

1696 WILLIAM BURNET, his son Alexander, apprentice to Peter Blair, skinner, Edinburgh, 27th Feb. 1723; his daughs.—Catherine (marr. Aug. 1756 Alexander McCulloch, merchant, Edinburgh); Elizabeth (marr. (1) Feb. 1751 Alexander Ross, Edinburgh).

1718 JAMES ANDERSON, his son James, apprentice to Charles Blair, goldsmith, Edinburgh, 12th Sept. 1721.

1744 JOHN ADAMS, line 5, for "1728" read "1727."

1759 JOHN AITCHISON, line 4, for "1759" read "1758."

1787 JOHN MUIR pres. 15th June, 1787.

1840 WILLIAM BEGG, his daugh. Margaret died at Prestwick 6th Aug. 1929.

1888 GEORGE CARRUTHERS, his widow, Mary Russell, died 17th Sept. 1928.

1898 ALEXANDER LOUDON, died 20th March 1940; his son James Alexander, M.B., Ch.B., F.R.C.P.E., lecturer in anatomy, Edinburgh University, died 1st Aug. 1931; his daugh. Helen (marr. 20th Oct. 1931 John A. Balfour, shipbroker, Grangemouth).

LAURIESTON, ST COLUMBA'S

1908 ALEXANDER BARRIE ROBB organised efforts on behalf of Servia during the Great War for which he received the Order of St Sava; died suddenly between services 22nd Jan. 1939.

(*Charges united 25th April* 1945.)

ST MODAN'S

Disjoined from Falkirk 16th March 1923.

1910 JOHN MARSHALL PRYDE, dem. 1916 on appoint. as Chaplain to Forces, Salonica; afterwards of Ruthrieston.

1917 JOHN SPENCE, F.R.A.S. (1897), born Lerwick, 1861; sometime a sailor at Greenland fishing, had command of two sailing vessels, then became a clerk in Edinburgh; ord. to Baptist Church, Arbroath Oct. 1891; went to America 1893; min. of Baptist Church, Chelsea, 1894–1904; of Orange Street Congregational Church, Leicester Square, Hope Park Congregational Church, Edinburgh, 1905 to Feb. 1908; Eccleston Square Congregational Church, Belgravia, 1909 to Nov. 1913; Lerwick Congregational Church 1913 to Jan. 1915; *locum tenens*, Ladhope; adm. as licentiate by General Assembly, assistant Balshagray; ord. 16th Nov. 1917; died 13th Feb. 1921. Marr. Janet Johnston, who died 3rd June 1920, and had issue— James W., min. of Symington, born 19th June 1892, and two daughs. Publications—*The Wonders of the Heavens*; *From Forecastle to Pulpit*; *The Wreck of the World*; *Christ in Astronomy*.

1921 THOMAS MEIKLE WATT, formerly of Congregational Church; ord. 15th June 1921; admitted first min. of parish 17th March 1923; dem. 23rd July 1926 on admission to Scots Church, Geneva (*q.v.*).

1926 WILLIAM ROBERTSON BROWN, trans. from Kerse (*q.v.*) 10th Nov. 1926; trans. to Deskford 6th May 1932; died 20th Jan. 1945.

FAULDHOUSE

1882 GAVIN CRAWFORD, his widow, Jessie Brownlie Craig, died at Alloway Manse 18th March 1932; his son William, min. of Coylton; his daugh. Mary Hamilton (marr. 21st April 1925 John Macfarlane Hamilton, min. of Alloway).

1898 THOMAS WATT McANDREW, trans. to Tollcross, Glasgow, 1st Sept. 1915.

1916 JOHN SINCLAIR, ord. 16th Feb. 1916; trans. to Lundie and Foulis 17th July 1919.

CHARLES WATSON, trans. from Carlisle (*q.v.*) 29th Oct. 1919; dem. 5th July 1932. His wife, Anne Horsburgh Young Williamson, died 5th Nov. 1936. He died at Greenlaw 2nd Oct. 1942.
1919

GRAHAMSTON

ANDREW ROSS TAYLOR, died 11th March 1926.
1881

JAMES FERRIER POLLOCK, trans. from Portmoak (*q.v.*) 1st Oct. 1926; died at Edinburgh 20th Dec. 1948; had issue—Margaret Muriel, born 1st Feb. 1916 (marr. 24th May 1945 Ronald Major, B.Sc. (Agric.)); Freda, born 26th July 1919.
1926

GRANGEMOUTH

GEORGE MILES THOMSON, his son Robert, M.B., Ch.B. (Edin.), died 25th Jan. 1930; his daugh. Jemima, M.A., teacher in Fife.
1884

ALEXANDER MACPHERSON, died at Aberdeen 28th July 1939.
1914

KERSE

WILLIAM ROBERTSON BROWN, trans. to St Modan's, Falkirk, 10th Nov. 1926.
1919

JOHN BARCLAY DAVIE, trans. from Benholm (*q.v.*) 18th May 1927; trans. to St Nicholas, Leith, 26th Feb. 1935; trans. to Coldingham 29th July 1942; had issue—Eleanor Margaret, born 14th Feb. 1926; John Alexander Barclay, born 13th Aug. 1927.
1927

KINNEIL

JOHN JOHNSTON, vicar and reader 1562-7.—[*Comps. Coll. Gen. Thirds and Sub Coll. Thirds, Linlithgow*, etc.]
1562

RICHARD DICKSON, fourth son of William D., burgess of Edinburgh; his daugh. Margaret (marr. Robert Innes, merchant, Edinburgh.—[*Edin. Burgess Roll*, 8th May 1611 and 9th June 1641.]
1625

WILLIAM WISHART, his son, Sir George, died 1725.—[*G. R. Sas.*, 2 Ser., xi, 63.]
1649

KIRKLISTON

The church was dedicated by Bishop de Bernham on 11th Sept. 1244. In response to a petition by James Kennedy, Bishop of St Andrews, the Church of Kirkliston was appropriated by Papal Bull of 26th June 1451 to the episcopal *mensa* of St Andrews. The petition stated that "the said Parish Church is situated within the barony of Kirkliston (which belongs to the episcopal *mensa* of St Andrews, and is not more than six miles distant from the most populous town of the realm, at which town the King of Scotland at times resides) and has a convenient manse for the Bishop's residence." The actual appropriation was to take effect on the resignation or death of the rector, John Gray. By Act of Parliament in 1598 the parsonage and vicarage of the church were dissolved from the Bishopric of St Andrews, and granted to James Law, minister of the parish. In 1383 and later the church was called Liston; and another alternative name was Temple Liston. By Papal Decree of 4th Oct. 1387 the church was annexed to the *mensa* of the Bishop of St Andrews.—[*Cal. Papal Reg., Letters*, x, 220; *Acts Scott. Parl.*, iv, 33; Lockhart's *Ch. in Scot. in 13th Century*, 59; *Cal. Scott. Supplics.*, 53; *Transcripts from Vatican*, i, 283; see Lasswade.]

JOHN MOUBRAY, reader 1568 and 1569.—[*Comps. Sub Coll. of Thirds Linlithgow*, etc.]
1568

GEORGE SPENS, pres. to vicar pensionary in succession to Gilbert McMath.—[*Reg. Pres. Bene.*, i (2), 6.]
1577

JAMES LAW, marr. Marion Dundas.—[*Deeds*, 35, 45, 1588-9.]
1585

GILBERT HALL, had issue—Euphame; Alexander; Janet; Thomas; John.—[*P. Reg. Sas. Edin.*, xxvii, 444.]
1646

1826	ADAM DUNCAN TAIT, marr. Margaret, daugh. of James Hill of Gartloch.
1879	ALEXANDER MASSON, died at Eskbank 18th Feb. 1936; his wife Helen Ogilvie, died 11th May 1929; his daugh. Lennie (marr. 19th Sept. 1933 Dr James Ogilvie, late of Moffat).
1924	ROBERT ALLAN MACLEAN, born 30th Oct. 1891, son of John Allan M., Glasgow, and Barbara White Smith; educ. at Univ. of Glasgow, M.A. (1922); licen. by Presb. of Glasgow 1922; assistant at Bluevale; ord. (assist. and suc.) 8th May 1924; died 22nd July 1940. Marr. 30th April 1924 Edith Miller, M.A., daugh. of Alexander Sinclair Johnston and Margaret Miller, and has issue—Margaret Miller, born 17th July 1925; Robert Allan, born 4th April 1927; Barbara Smith, born 26th Aug. 1928; Edith, born 10th Jan. 1932; Fiona Roberta, born 11th Sept. 1940.

LINLITHGOW

The church was dedicated by Bishop de Bernham of St Andrews on 22nd May 1242. Nearly two years before, on 6th July 1240, Bishop de Bernham confirmed to the Priory of St Andrews the Church and Chapels of Linlithgow, and particularly the Chapel of Binnie, afterwards Church of Binny, and the Chapel of Retrevyn (Torthraven), which had been granted to the priory by his predecessor, William Malvoisine, Bishop 1202–38. The Church of Binny was dedicated to St Giles. In 1120–57 William de Lindsay confirmed to the church ½ caracute of land which had been given by his ancestor, Durand. The patronage of the vicarage of the church belonged to the Priory of Elcho in Rhynd. The Chapel of Torthraven was dedicated to St Leonard the Abbot. To the chapel Sir Richard de Melville, who lived *cir.* 1180–1215, gave ½ caracute of land; and his grandson, George or Gregory, *cir.* 1262–70, 2½ marks annually from the fermes of Lochbersard. On 24th May 1401 Sir James de Douglas of Dalkeith granted to Friar William Cochar, Prior of the Provincial Order of the Carmelites, and to the Chapel of the Virgin (Mary) of Linlithgow and the friars of the Order there, a piece of land of 4 acres at the south side of the chapel, and an acre called "the Hermit's Acre," for building a refectory, dormitory, cloister, etc. This appears to denote the completion of the settlement founded by the burgesses of Linlithgow in 1290. On 26th April 1571, on presentation by James, Lord Ross of Halkhead and Melville, patron, Sir Robert Alisoun was instituted chaplain of the said "Kirk or Chapel" by John Kirkpatrick handing over to him "the Book, the Door Key, and the Desk" of the same. On 2nd Feb. 1502-3 James IV granted to the burgesses of Linlithgow and certain chaplains of Linlithgow Church, the church lands of Magdaleneside, amounting to 6 arable acres, and in exchange received from them 6 arable acres of land beside the hospitium of Sir James Erskill, Chaplain. The latter lands the King gave "for building a Place for the Augustine Friars," no doubt the Hermit Friars of the Order of St Augustine, Observantes. From the King there came to those friars further gifts noted in the Lord High Treasurer's Accounts of 1503: 14th Sept. To the Augustine Freris to thair bigging in Linlithgow, X French Crowns, VII lib.; 29th Oct. To the Augustine Freris at Linlithgow, XIII Sh.; 13th Dec. To the Augustine Freris of Linlithgow to thair bigging, X French Crowns, VII lib. Of the Place nothing further seems to be known. At Linlithgow there was also a leper house dedicated to St Michael. Probably it was to the inmates of this house that James IV made various contributions in 1496 and 1498, under these descriptions: "The pur folk, seke folk, and gangors in Linlithgow"; "The sek folk," "The pur folk", and "The Seik folk at the toun end of Linlithgow." In 1641 Parliament ratified a charter of James VI, 8th May 1591, granting to the town council the endowments of all altarages and chaplainries in the burgh, for the maintenance of a reader at the kirk, and of the poor of the hospital of the burgh.—[*The Church of Scotland in the 13th Century*, 48; *Reg. Priory of St*

Andrews, 169, 180–1, 376–7; Fraser's *The Melvilles*, i, 14–16, iii, 9–10; Sir Thomas Johnsoun's *Prot. Bk.*, 581; *Reg. Great Seal*, ii, 2694; and *MS. Reg.* xiii, 562; *Lord High Treas. Accs.*, i, 286, 288, 307; ii, 254–6; *Acts Scott. Parl.*, v, 460–1; Birch's *Eccles. Seals*, 100; *Reg. Honoris de Morton*, ii, 199, 200.]

PATRICK FRENCH, vicar, still in office 17th June 1588.—[*Cal. of Charters*, xiii, 2973.]
1559

WALTER CORNWALL, reader on 16th April 1560, when he, along with Alexander Hamilton, vicar of Carriden, certified the publication of banns of marriage in their respective churches.—[Nicol Thoun's *Prot. Book*, No. 10, 3.]
1560

PATRICK KINLOQUHY or **KINLOCH**, pres. to vicarage in 1574 on death of Alexander Heriot and on 19th Aug. 1587, on death of Sir Patrick French. He had issue—Pater or Patrick of Kettleston, pedagogue to James, Lord Hamilton, son and heir to John, Marquess of Hamilton; Andrew, fought duel with swords; David; Agnes (marr. Robert Haly, min. of Muiravonside); Elspeth; Marion; Helen (marr. George, son of Nicol Cornwall of Bonhard).—[*Reg. Sec. Sig.*, lvi, 72; *Reg. Pres. Bene.*, i (2), 21; *Linlithgowshire Sas.*, 24th Feb. 1603; *Linlithgow Sher. Court Books*, 24th June 1623; *Part Reg. Inhib.*, 10th Dec. 1612, 26th June 1623.]
1561

WILLIAM SALMONT, M.A., Vicar of Binny 2nd May 1565–72.—[Sir Thomas Johnsoun's *Prot. Book*; *Comps. Sub Coll. of Thirds, Dumfries*; *Reg. of Abbrev. Feu Charters of Church Lands*, i, 283.]
1563

GEORGE HEPBURN, M.A., parson and minister 1568.—[*Comps. Sub Coll. of Thirds, Linlithgow*, etc.]
1568

RICHARD FLEMING, pres. to vicarage of Binny 16th Jan. 1588 on death of William Salmont, was min. of St Laurence Kirk, Slamannan.—[*Reg. Rec. Sig.*, lviii, 105.]
1588

ROBERT CORNWALL, pres. to vicarage on dem. of Patrick Kennaway. —[*P. S. Reg.*, cxv, 228; *G. R. Sas.*, lii, 248.]
1597

EPHRAIM MELVILLE, marr. 24th Feb. 1642 Bessie Yoole.—[*St. Andrews Reg.*]
1650

WILLIAM WEIR, was min. of West Calder in 1672; his widow, Katherine Lunn, buried 24th Feb. 1714; his son James buried 13th Jan. 1728.—[*Reg. of Deeds, Linlithgow Sher. Court*, 22nd Dec. 1716.]
1691

ALEXANDER DALGLEISH, his widow, Susan Campbell, buried 26th July 1743; his daugh. Christian (marr. 16th July 1725 William Dalgleish). —*G. R. Sas.*, xxii, 409; civ, 415.]
1699

ROBERT DALGLEISH, his children— Alexander, buried 16th May 1730; Isobel (Helen), buried 15th Nov. 1734; Mary, buried 12th Sept. 1757; Christian (marr. Dec. 1772 John Short, burgess, Bo'ness).
1727

JAMES DOBIE, marr. (1) Isabella, daugh. of James Stoddart, min. of Kirkintilloch.
1792

JOHN FERGUSON, his widow, Mary Jane Richard, died 4th Feb. 1940.
1878

ROBERT COUPAR, D.D. (St Andrews, 28th June 1929); his wife, Eliza Nicol, died 5th Oct. 1936. He died at Edinburgh 11th Dec. 1945. His son, Sydney Bell Nicol, died in France 1918.
1914

SECOND CHARGE

PATRICK TRENT, his daugh. Christian died before 10th July 1732.
1687

ANDREW BARCLAY, his daugh. Margaret (marr. Sept. 1754 Robert Macfarlane, merchant, Edinburgh); his son Alexander apprenticed to William Mead, surgeon apothecary, Edinburgh, 22nd June 1720.
1700

KINGSCAVIL

1899 THOMAS LUGTON, died 16th Feb. 1917.

LIVINGSTON

The church, with a half-caracute of land and a croft, was given to Holyrood Abbey by Turstan, son of Leuing; and a charter of confirmation, in which the church was designated "the Church of the town of Leuing," was granted by Richard, Bishop of St Andrews, in 1163–5. At Stoneburn in the parish there was a chapel.—[*Charters of Holyrood*, 11, 12, 15–16; *Reg. Great Seal*, v, 69.]

1569 ROBERT BALFOUR, vicar 1569–72 and Provost of Kirk of Field.—[*Comp. Sub Coll. of Thirds, Linlithgow*, etc.]

1573 ROBERT HODGE, M.A., min. here 26th Aug. and 5th Dec. 1575 and 9th Feb. 1578; probably continued in charge here when min. at Bathgate and Torphichen (*q.v.*).—[*Edin. Tests*, vi, 302; *Test. William Moreis*, 26th Aug. 1575, *Inventories MS., Gen. Reg. House.*]

1585 PETER HAMILTON, as min. pres. on dem. of Robert Balfour.—[*P. S. Reg.*, lxxxii, 186.]

1610 PATRICK MONIPENNY, min. at The Hayning; marr. (1) Janet Campbell; (2) Beatrix or Elizabeth Muirhead, who marr. (2) James Flint.—(*Clan Campbell*, vi, 88; *Reg. of Deeds*, cccl, 58.]

1616 JAMES ROSS, his son Walter.

1718 ROBERT HUNTER, son of James H., merchant, burgess, Ayr.

1872 THOMAS AITON, dem. 25th Nov. 1919, died at Edinburgh 24th April 1923; his son William, 2nd Lieut., Rifle Brigade, killed in action 21st March 1917; Agnes Hamilton, his daugh., died at Edinburgh 27th Dec. 1931; his widow, Jane Charteris Scott, died 23rd Jan. 1942; his son, Adam Charteris, died at Glasgow 6th Feb. 1947.

1920 JOHN COPLAND, M.A., Ph.D., trans. from St Andrew's Presbyterian Church, Newcastle upon Tyne, adm. 7th April 1920; trans. to Edzell 23rd Feb. 1928.

1928 JAMES AITKEN, trans. from St James, Forfar (*q.v.*), 14th Sept. 1928, died 13th Feb. 1945.

(*Charges united* 1st Oct. 1945.)

MUIRAVONSIDE

The Cistercian nunnery at Manuel, which was situated on the left bank of the river Avon and was dedicated to the Virgin Mary, was founded by Malcolm IV before 1164, and very probably in 1156. By Charter 1165–71 King William the Lion confirmed to the nuns that land in Manuel which King Malcolm, his brother, gave to them, by its right marches as perambulated . . . with common pasture and easements of wood for building, fencing, and fuel, so far as necessary for their own use. The same Charter also confirmed a tenth of the Mill of Ihetham (Yetholm) given to the nuns by Walter Corbat, and a holding in Rokesburg (Roxburgh), given by Rawenild of Ietham (Yetholm). By Charter of 22nd June 1224 Alexander II granted to them 1½ chalders of salt from the teinds of his saltpans which Ralph Baret then held. The lands of Manuel comprised the lands, town, and manor of Manuel, lands of Walkmilton with the Mill, Myrehead, Williamcraigs, in the barony of Manuel. Other possessions of the nunnery were the grain mill called Mongall, with the mill and mill lands, and the dry multures of Nether and Over Mongall, lying in Mongall, in the barony of West Kers, and at least one half, one and a half fifth-parts and a fifth part of the land of Whitebaukis in the barony of Bellormie. To the nunnery there also pertained an annual rent from the fermes of the Burgh of Linlithgow. On 16th June 1506 Pope Julius II, in response to a petition of James IV, gave commission to the Abbots of Cambuskenneth and Balerimo, and the Provost of Trinity College, Edinburgh, to convert the nunnery into a house of the Hermit Friars of the Order of St Augustine, Observantes. The King stated that no house of the Order existed in Scotland, that he desired the establishment of such a house, and that in the Nunnery of Manuel five nuns were resident. He asked, therefore, that the said nunnery be "suppressed and extinguished," the nuns transferred to another place, and said Order of Friars introduced, a house to be built for their use with church, bell tower, small bell, cloister, refectory, churchyard, etc.; but it is apparent that the change was not carried out. On 10th Jan. 1545-6 the lands of Manuel, as already described, were set in feu by Janet Livingstone, prioress of the nunnery, to Alexander Livingstone, in life rent, and his second son, William, in fee for defence, promised by said Alexander, against those who might do her harm—an illustration of the danger of lawless steps being taken in the interests of a rival to usurp the office of prioress in such houses. Then or soon afterwards the other local possessions of the nunnery were also set in feu by the said Janet. Associated with the office of prioress for a time was a prior. The seal of James Hopper, "Prior of the Monastery of Manuel and the Convent of the Carmelites in Linlithgow," is attached to a charter of 11th Jan. 1559-60.—[*Scotichronicon*, i, 453, *Ed.* 1759; Hailes' *Annals*, i, 130, *Ed.* 1819; *Misc. Scott. Hist. Soc.*, iv, 305, 313; *Transcripts from the Vatican*, i, 148-56, *MS., Reg. Ho.*; *Abbrev. Feu Charters of Church Lands*, i, 167, ii, 103, 202, *MS. Reg. Ho.*; *Reg. Great Seal*, iii, 3308, v, 16, 568, 649, vi, 248, 890; *Excheq. Rolls*, i, 25, iv, 25; Laing's *Cat. Scott. Seals*, ii, 204.]

1642 JOHN BRUCE, his widow, Isobel Ker. —[*G. R. Sas.*, 3 Ser., xxxiv, 271, 20th Nov. 1674.]

1667 ANDREW URIE, resident in Old Kirk Parish, Edinburgh, with three children—Mary, aged 6; Anna (marr. 15th Feb. 1699); Elizabeth, 9th Nov. 1696.—[*Old Kirk Poll Tax Roll*, 23.]

1696 ANDREW BENNET, his daugh. Anna, born 9th Sept. 1713.—[*Bo'ness Court of Regality*, 17th Aug. 1720.]

1834 JAMES MACFARLANE. His issue— Christian (marr. 4th April 1857); Jane (marr. 1872), died 1901; Marianne (marr. 1886), died 1894; Eleanora, died Perth 10th June 1932; Katharine Louise, died 22nd Sept. 1935; Mary Christie (marr. 1910 her brother-in-law Robert Charles Menzies, papermaker, St Michael's, Inveresk). died 9th Dec. 1924.

1897 DAVID BAYNE, dem. 1st July 1940; died at Edinburgh 2nd Sept. 1941.

POLMONT

There was at Polmont, then in the parish of Falkirk, a chapel dedicated to the Virgin Mary, to which on 28th May 1498 Robert Bellenden, Abbot of Holyrood, granted an annual rent of 6 merks from the tenement of the late Alexander Turing in the burgh of Edinburgh, above "the lower arch" of the said burgh on the south side of High Street.—[*Reg. Great Seal*, ii, 244.]

1871 GEORGE KEITH, born 9th March 1844.

1885 OSWALD BELL, his widow, Kate Matilda Keddie, died 3rd June 1934.

1894 JAMES BUCHANAN MACKENZIE, died 4th Feb. 1926; his widow, Mary Bayne Mushet, died 17th July 1935; his son, Archibald, min. of Balfron and Ayr 2nd Charge; his daugh., Janet Buchanan, died 22nd Jan. 1944.

1926 JAMES WALKER MORISON WILLIAMSON, trans. from Pitsligo (*q.v.*) 12th Aug. 1926. His wife, Susan Maxwell Elmslie, died 8th Dec. 1935.

QUEENSFERRY

By Crown Charter 9th July 1635, ratified by Act of Parliament 9th July 1641, the Chapel of St Michael in the Burgh was erected into the parish church.—[*Reg. Mag. Sig.*, 9th July 1635; *Acts of Parl.*, i, 570.]

JOHN PRIMROSE, his widow was resident in Tron Parish, Edinburgh, 8th Nov. 1694.—[*Tron Poll Tax Roll*, 6.]
1652

JOHN PHILIP OF ORMISTON.—*Reg. of Deeds, Mack.* lxxxiii, 10th Nov. 1698.]
1678

JOHN DALGLEISH, marr. Agnes, daugh. of Gideon Wauchope of Pendicle.—[*Reg. of Deeds Dal.*, liii, 576.]
1688

DONALD CAMPBELL, son of John C., min. of Monzieward; his son, John.—[*Reg. of Deeds Mack.*, xc, 22nd Jan. 1702.]
1693

JOHN GRIERSON, his daugh. Janet (marr. William Somerville, min. of Hawick.]
1700

JAMES KID, his son James, apprentice to James Lorimer, merchant, Edinburgh, 20th May 1747.
1710

THOMAS DIMMA, his daugh. Laura (marr. John Gardner, Queensferry, and went to America.)
1820

JOHN WHYTE, his daugh. Mary Ruth (marr. John Stewart, min. of Bridgegate).
1872

DAVID MILLER, his widow, Margaret Fender Hay, died 5th Dec. 1931; his daugh. Elizabeth Constance Winifred (marr. John William Thomson, bank agent, Mid Calder) died 2nd April 1932.
1884

WILLIAM BOWER WILSON, dem. 8th March 1944, died 4th June 1944; his daugh. Molly, M.B., Ch.B. (Edin.), awarded, 18th July 1934, Dorothy Gilfillan Memorial Prize and the Prize of the Scottish Association for Medical Education of Women to most distinguished woman graduate; his daugh. Marion, B.Sc. (marr. 5th July 1939 Dr Charles, lecturer on Applied Mathematics, Liverpool University, son of E. Strachan, 213 Forest Avenue, Aberdeen).
1900

SLAMANNAN

RICHARD FLEMING, reader and vicar pensionary 1565 and in 1569; pres. to vicarage of Binning 16th Jan. 1588.—[*Comps. Sub Coll. of Thirds, Linlithgow and Dumfries*, etc.]
1565

ADAM MURRAY, pres. to parsonage and vicarage 17th May 1566 by John, son and heir of the late John Sandilands of Calder Cleir.—[*Reg. Sec. Sig.*, xxxiv, 81.]
1566

JAMES DALRYMPLE, min. in 1568. —[*Comps. Sub Coll. of Thirds, Linlithgow*, etc.]
1568

GAVIN NASMYTH, Exhorter 1568.— [*Comps. Sub Coll. of Thirds, Linlithgow*, etc.]
1568

THOMAS AMBROSE, eldest son of William A., merchant burgess of Stirling, and Christian Anderson, and brother of Alexander, min. of Newbattle.—[*Edin. Tests*, 3rd Dec. 1606.]
1607

GEORGE PHIN, marr. cont. 25th July 1684, Susannah, daugh. of Alexander Simpson of Stonehouse.—[*G. R. Sas.*, 2 Ser., xiv, 436; *Deeds Durie*, 1706, No. 719.]
1661

JAMES STEVENSON, his son, John, min. of Cathcart.
1691

JOHN STEVENSON, his widow, Isobel Smith, died at Glasgow 16th Jan. 1763.
1709

JAMES MACNAIR, pres. 26th Sept. 1787.
1788

ALEXANDER DAVIDSON, his son Alexander born 24th Oct. 1821, died young; his daugh. Anne (marr. 10th June 1834 Henry James Taylor of Southfield).
1826

ROBERT STEVENSON HORNE, pres. 31st March 1856; his widow, Mary Lochhead, died at Edinburgh 26th Nov. 1925; his sons—Right Hon. Sir Robert Stevenson, P.C., G.B.E., LL.D., M.P. Hillhead, Minister of Labour 1919,
1856

President of the Board of Trade 1920–1, Chancellor of the Exchequer 1921–2, created Viscount 12th May 1937, died 3rd Sept. 1940; Thomas Lochhead, died 2nd Dec. 1916.

1892 ALLAN REID, died 5th Sept. 1922; his widow, Jessie Baird Macdonald, died 30th Sept. 1933.

1923 ARCHIBALD MORTON PATERSON, M.A., ord. 28th Feb. 1923; trans. to Tarbolton 15th Dec. 1927.

1928 NINIAN ELLIOT, born Edinburgh 12th June 1898, son of John E., Surveyor of Taxes, H.M. Customs and Excise, and Margaret Craig Melville, educated at George Watson's College, Edinburgh; Grammar School and Univ. of Aberdeen, M.A. (1920), B.D. (1923); served in Great War as Signaller, R.G.A., in France 1917–18; licen. by Presb. of Aberdeen 1923; assistant Aberdeen West, 1923; ord. to St Leonard's, Lanark, 19th Feb. 1925; trans. and adm. 11th April 1928; trans. to Sorbie 5th April 1945. Marr. 12th Dec. 1939 Margaret, youngest daugh. of Rev. William Skinner, C.I.E., D.D., Principal, Madras College and had issue: Helen, born 14th, died 19th March 1941; Jane Melville, born 23rd March 1943.

(*Charges of Slamannan and Balquhatson united 25th Oct.* 1945.)

TORPHICHEN

There was an altar dedicated to St Ninian and another to the Virgin Mary.—[Nicol Thounis *Prot. Book*, 44ⁿ.]

1567 SIR THOMAS DICKSON, vicar cousin and intimate servitor of John, Archbishop of St Andrews, vicar 1558–71.—[*Cal. of Charters*, x, 2112; *Reg. Abbrev. Feu Charters of Church Lands*, ii, 226; *Compts. Sub Coll. of Thirds, Linlithgow.*]

1572 ROBERT HODGE.—[*G. R. Sas.*, 2 Ser., i, 27.]

1639 THOMAS VASSIE, son of William V., burgess of Lanark.

1682 WILLIAM BAIN, eldest son of John B., wright burgess of Musselburgh; resident with his wife in Tron par., Edinburgh, 9th Nov. 1694; his daugh. Alison (marr. George Boswell, writer, Edinburgh).—[*Tron Poll Tax Roll*, 6; *Abb. Adj.*, 2nd March 1726.]

1879 JOHN McKERLIE JOHNSTONE, licen. 9th May 1871.

1898 GEORGE BEALE, dem. 1931 and charges united 16th May 1931; died 1st Feb. 1945. Publications—Contributions to *West Lothian Courier* on Nature Knowledge, Birds, Folklore, Antiquities, Poetry and General Literature; Brochures on *Torphichen Preceptory, The Knights of St John of Jerusalem*, etc.

UPHALL

1572 ROBERT PITCAIRN, Commendator of Dunfermline, held the parsonage 1572.—[*Compts. Sub Coll. of Thirds, Linlithgow*, etc.]

1572 SIR PATRICK OGSTONE, vicar 1572. —[*Compts. Sub Coll. of Thirds, Linlithgow*, etc.]

1690 GEORGE BARCLAY, min. of meeting house at Gargunnock 1688.

1699 ALEXANDER KEITH, marr. (2) Margaret Hamilton.—[*G. R. Sas.*, 2 Ser., ix, 240, July 1654.]

1763 WILLIAM GIB, marr. Elizabeth, daugh. of Robert Rentoul of Middleton.

1798 JOHN FERGUSON, according to Aberdeen Univ. Records, 346, his father was James F., London.

1868 WILLIAM JOHNSTON, his widow, Elizabeth Arbuckle, died 20th Oct. 1916.

1912 CHARLES DUNN, born Leochel Cushnie, licen. March 1900, died suddenly 13th March 1931.

WHITBURN

1732 ALEXANDER WARDROBE, his son David apprentice to John Wallace, surgeon, Edinburgh, 9th Nov. 1748.

1912 ROBERT BRUCE MACKINNON, his son, Robert Alexander, died 26th Dec. 1922.

WINCHBURGH

1904 HUGH ARMSTRONG, licen. 11th June 1890, died at Edinburgh 9th Feb. 1930. He marr. (2) 22nd Aug. 1916, Amelia Barr, daugh. of J. Miller, Dalry Road, Edinburgh, and had issue—Margaret Sybil Ross (marr. 26th May 1927, Laurence Harrower, Hamilton, Bermuda); Aimes Isabel Josephine, born 4th Jan. 1918; Hugh Ian Oliphant, born 22nd Jan. 1923; Anne Jane, born 24th Nov. 1926.

PRESBYTERY OF BIGGAR

BIGGAR

The church in 1545 was erected on the site of the old building dedicated to St Nicholas. Associated with the church there was a hospital, dedicated to St Leonard, called the House of Biggar. On 10th Aug. 1531 John Tweedie of Drummelziar granted an annual rent of £10 from his lands of Drummelziar to Sir Andrew Brown, Chaplain, and his successors as chaplains, for perpetual celebrations in Biggar Church for the soul of John, Lord Fleming, slain on 1st Nov. 1524 by said John Tweedie's son James and his kinsmen and associates. The grant was in fulfilment of a Decreet Arbitral with reference to the foresaid murder between Malcolm, Lord Fleming, son and successor of the said John, Lord Fleming, and the said John Tweedie. On 10th Jan. 1545–6 Malcolm, Lord Fleming, erected the church into a collegiate church in honour of the Trinity and the Virgin Mary, for a provost, 8 canons and prebendaries, 4 boys having children's voices, and 6 poor men. At his own charge Lord Malcolm built "a stately Church in the village of Biggar, dedicated to our Lady of Assumption." The foundation was confirmed by the Papal Legate on 14th March 1545–6. To the provostry was assigned the Church of Thankerton, with its rents, fruits and emoluments and manse and glebe, the provost being held bound to pay to a curate having the care of the souls of the parishioners of Thankerton £10 Scots besides 2 acres of land of the provostry beside the church for a manse and garden. The First Prebendary was called the Prebendary of the Hospital of St Leonard. He was the preceptor of the Song School; and to him were assigned the lands of Spittal. The Second Prebendary was the Preceptor of Grammar Study; and to him were assigned the lands of Auchinreoch in the barony of Auchtermony in the county of Stirling. The Third Prebendary was the sacrist of the church; and to him were assigned the chaplainry of St Mary at Kirkintilloch, founded upon the lands of Garnegaber and Auchyndavy, 6 merks annual rent in Kirkintilloch and 2 acres for a manse and garden pertaining to the said Chaplainry. The Fourth Prebendary was the preceptor of the praying poor and the administrator and distributer of their victual and other emoluments; and to him were assigned £10 Scots annual rent from the lands of Drummelzier, and £7 6s. 8d. from the fruits, etc., of the parsonage and vicarage of Biggar. To each of the other prebendaries was assigned £7 6s. 8d. from the parsonage and vicarage, and of the church lands of the same. The Eighth Prebendary was the vicar-pensioner of the "Parish Church of Biggar erected into a College"; and he had a seat with the other prebendaries in the choir, and sang and exercised the divine office there except when he was occupied with the cure of the said church and the administration of the Sacraments to the parishioners. In 1555 the Church of Dunrod was collated to the collegiate church. One of the altars in the church was dedicated to the Holy Rood.—[*Reg. Great Seal*, iii, 1093, 1531; Charter Chest of Earl of Wigton, 409, 466, 478, 486–8, 529, 530, 602; *Scott. Rec. Soc.*; *Calendar of Yester Writs*, 117, 157, 160; *Scott. Rec. Soc.*; *Charters of Holyrood*, 294–8; *Mis. of Spalding Club*, v, 296–308; see Thankerton, Dunrod, Kirkintilloch.]

1567 WILLIAM MILLAR, reader, 1567 and 1568.—[*Comps. Sub Coll. of Thirds, Linlithgow.*]

1599 THOMAS CAMPBELL.—[*G. R. Sas.*, 2 Ser., xv, 46.]

1696 ROBERT LIVINGSTON, his son Alexander apprentice to George Lawson, merchant, Edinburgh, 11th Nov. 1705.

1751 WILLIAM HAIG, son of James H. of Orchardfarm.

1754 JOHN JOHNSTON, marr. (1)——; (2) 8th Aug. 1755.

1787 WILLIAM WATSON, his daugh. Janet (marr. 3rd June 1823).

1822 JOHN CHRISTISON, his daugh. Ann Hay (marr. 19th Aug. 1851).

1874 WILLIAM NEWBIGGING, his widow Sarah Wilson died 1st Nov. 1926.

1884 WILLIAM GRANT DUNCAN, died suddenly 22nd Oct. 1933; his wife Ann Williamson Matthew died 5th March 1924; his daughs.—Catherine Matthew (marr. (1) 10th March 1927 John Thomson, Edenside, Strathmiglo; (2) 25th Jan. 1938 Thomas Robinson, Indian Police); Jean Ogilvy (marr. 22nd July 1919, Gerard Hassell Williams, M.C., Birkenhead); Ann Williamson (marr. 10th April 1929 John Myles Caie, M.C., M.B., Ch.B., Biggar).

1928 DAVID SINCLAIR RUTHERFORD, born 25th Nov. 1896, son of Robert William R., min. of Gartsherrie, educ. at Royal High School, Fettes College and Univs. of Edinburgh and Glasgow, M.A. (1920); served in France Aug. 1916 to Dec. 1916, Lieut. 3 Welsh Regiment; Black Bursar; Licen. by Presb. of Hamilton 1921; assist. St Mary's, Edinburgh, 1922; ord. to Ochiltree 3rd May 1923; trans to Biggar (ass. and suc.) 20th June 1928. Marr. 16th April 1924 Catherine Jardine, youngest daughter of Laurence Crawford, J.P., Coatbridge, and has issue—David William, born 28th Nov. 1925; Laurence Crawford, born 9th July 1933.

BROUGHTON

1576 WALTER TWEEDIE, reader and vicar pensioner 1562, designated min. 28th Nov. 1588.—[*Comps. Sub Coll. of Thirds, Roxburgh.*]

1769 THOMAS GRAY, his daugh. Mary (marr. 9th Jan. 1824 James Usher, writer, Edinburgh).

1854 ALEXANDER THOMSON COSENS, his son Peter Hunter, W.S., died 26th Nov. 1931; his daughs.—Alexandra Jeanette died 1st Dec. 1929; Ann Thomson (Mrs Napier) died 14th Feb. 1944; his son Robert Romanes died 5th Sept. 1944.

1892 ANDREW BAIRD, died 7th Jan. 1935.

GLENHOLM

By Bull of 29th July 1272 Pope Gregory X confirmed the grant of the church to the Abbey of Scone by John Fraser of Glenholm.—[*Book of Scone*, 83.]

1568 JOHN PORTEOUS, vicar in 1568 and 1569.—[*Comps. Sub Coll. of Thirds, Dumfries*, etc.]

1569 GEORGE TOD, reader and vicar pensioner 1563 to 18th Dec. 1574.—[*Comps. Sub Coll. of Thirds, Roxburgh*, and *Edin. Tests.*, iii, 441.]

1571 WALTER TWEEDY, appears to have been parson just prior to 1571.—[*Comps. Sub Coll. of Thirds, Roxburgh*, etc.]

1571 JAMES STEWART, son of Sir John S. of Minto and his second wife Margaret, daugh. of James Stewart of Cardonald, and brother of Walter, Prior of Blantyre; pres. to parsonage and vicarage, which is ane chaplaine within the chapel of Stirling, 3rd Aug. 1571, on death of William Hamilton, parson of Cambuslang, last parson and vicar.—[*Scots Peerage*, ii, 80; *P. S. Reg.*, xxxix, 14; *Reg. Pres. Bene.*, i, (2), 18; *Comps. Coll. Gen. of Thirds.*]

1572 JAMES TOD, reader, 20th Feb. 1572-3.—[*Test, Inventories, MS. Reg. Ho.*]

1574 JOHN JAMIESON, vicar pensioner, 13th April 1574.—[*Cal. Laing Charters*, 890.]

1591 JOHN HEPBURN, M.A., pres. to parsonage and vicarage 31st Dec. 1591 on death of James Stewart.—[*P. S. Reg.*, lxiii, 92.]

1636 ROBERT JOHNSTON, marr. Margaret Lawrie; died before 15th Nov. 1642.—[*Reg. of Deeds Dal.*, xxxviii, 212; *Acts and Dec.*, iii, 340.]

1708 SIMON KELLIE, eldest son of John K., tailor burgess of Glasgow. His son John, apprenticed to Robert McKinlay, merchant, Edinburgh, 9th Dec. 1720; his daughs.—Marion (marr. Jan. 1768 James Sommers, writer, Edinburgh); Helen (marr. James Dean, farmer in Chapelgill of Glenholm).

KILBUCHO

There was a hermitage at Kilbucho. Cosmo, hermit of Kylbovkhoe, was witness to a writ regarding the division of Stobo about 1200.—[*Reg. of Glasgow*, i, 89.]

1567 WILLIAM PORTEOUS, reader and vicar pensioner 1559-72; confirmed in office 28th April 1570.—[*Comps. Coll. Gen. of Thirds*; *Edin. Tests.*, iii, 50-1.]

1571 GEORGE AUCHINLECK of BALMANNO, parson 1571-86.—[*Comps. Gen. Coll. of Thirds*; *Comps. Sub Coll. of Thirds*, Roxburgh, etc.]

1574 ANDREW JARDINE, reader, 28th Nov. 1580.—[*Edin. Tests.*, viii, 292.]

1575 WALTER TWEEDIE, min. at Broughton, in charge here.

1700 JOHN TAIT, son of James T., merchant burgess of Edinburgh; his son James, wright, burgess of Edinburgh 15th May 1728; his daugh. Isobel (marr. John Tait, staymaker, Alnwick).

1751 WILLIAM TAIT, marr. Grissel, daugh. of James Dick, min. of Wynd, Glasgow; his son Robert died at sea 17th March 1793.

COULTER

1560 ARCHIBALD LIVINGSTON, rector, 1st Sept. 1563.—[Sir Thos. Johnstoun's *Prot. Book*, 682.]

1563 JAMES FOTHERINGHAM, exhorter, 1563.—[*Comps. Sub Coll. of Thirds, Stirling*, etc.]

1563 JOHN LIVERANCE, exhorter, 1563.—[*Comps. Sub Coll. of Thirds, Stirling*, etc.]

1568 JOHN GOLD, exhorter, 1568.—[*Comps. Sub Coll. of Thirds, Stirling*, etc.]

1576 WILLIAM MILLAR, reader, 5th March 1576.—[*Edin. Tests.*, v, 64.]

1654 ANTHONY MURRAY, had sasine with his wife Grissel Muir, of the lands of Westerhills, Lanarkshire; marr. (2) Jean Murray with issue Jean, both residing in the Canongate 13th Nov. 1694; his widow marr. (2) Alexander Bertram of Nisbet.—[*Canongate Poll Tax Roll*; *G. R. Sas.*, 3 Ser., xxxi, 12th Dec. 1672.]

1700 JAMES FORRESTER, his son Robert, apprenticed to George Andrew, merchant, Edinburgh, 24th Aug. 1720.

1750 JOHN BROWN, his daughs.—Marion (marr. pro. 6th April 1791 John Thomson of Comiston, merchant, Edinburgh); Euphemia, died 5th Dec. 1793.

1862 JOHN ANDERSON, died at Corstorphine 27th March 1922, aged 101.

1891 JOHN COWAN HAMILTON, dem. 30th June 1932; died 1st Aug. 1943; his wife, Jessie Burns Shearer, died 29th Jan. 1938; his son Arnold Angus, M.D., died at Broughton, 9th Sept. 1937; his daugh., Leslie Baillie Shearer (marr. 30th Nov. 1935 Robert Murray Methven, Calcutta).

COVINGTON

1608 HEW LINDSAY, son of John L. of Covington. Marr. Katherine Arthur and had issue—Hew; Patrick.

1621 GEORGE OGSTOUN, marr. Abigail, daugh. of James Baillie, Min. of Lamington.

1691 JOHN BUCHANAN, marr. Catherine Spreull.—[*Abbey Proclam.* 26th June 1692.]

1865 JAMES HOGGAN, his widow, Isabel Gibson, died 30th Sept. 1921.

1890 WILLIAM COVINGTON MACGREGOR, dem. 1st Dec. 1931; died 9th April 1942.

THANKERTON

About 1180 Agnes de Brus granted to Kelso Abbey the church of the town of Thankerton, which is called the Wodekyrch (Woodchurch); and at the same period Simon Lockard made a similar grant, the designation being "the Church which is called the Wudechirche." The confirmation charter of Jocelyn, Bishop of Glasgow, also about the same date, has the description, "the Church of Wudekirche with the whole parish as well of Thankerton as of the town of Symon Lockard." On 1st May 1542 the Archbishop of Glasgow ratified the transference of the patronage of the church by Kelso Abbey on 26th Nov. 1540, with consent of David Hamilton, Rector of Thankerton, to the Collegiate Church of Biggar which Malcolm, Lord Fleming, intended to build. To a vicar-pensioner for Thankerton there was reserved 20 merks Scots with 4 acres of land at Kelso. The consent of the Commendator (Gavin) of Kelso to the transference bears that "all of them in these evil times in the increase of Lutheranism" are "obliged to contribute to so good a work," and that Lord Fleming might not be diverted from so good a work nor receive any prejudice by the abbey having the patronage.—[*Book of Kelso*, i, 227, 318-20; *Reg. Epis. of Glasgow*, ii, 272; *Charter Chest of Earl of Wigton*, 522; *Scott Rec. Soc.*]

1595 THOMAS BAIKIE of St Thomas Chapel, parson and vicar, 1595-7.—[*Comps. Gen. Coll. of Thirds.*]

DOLPHINTON

1569 THOMAS LUNDY, exhorter, 1569.—[*Comps. Sub Coll. of Thirds, Roxburgh*, etc.]

1592 ARCHIBALD DOUGLAS, M.A., pres. to parsonage 28th March 1592 on death of John Cockburn.

1592 JOHN KELLIE, pres. to vicarage 9th April 1592 on death of John Cockburn of Newholm.—[*P. S. Reg.*, lxiii, 229, 248.]

1618 ALEXANDER SOMERVILLE, marr. (2) Margaret Cockburn and had issue—James; John; Agnes; Jean.—[*G. R. Sas.*, xxi, 239, 19th July 1631.]

1665 WILLIAM DUGUID, portioner of Appletree-leaves.—[*G. R. Sas.*, 2 Ser. x, 180.]

1684 JAMES CRUICKSHANKS, marr. Margaret Oswald.—[*Edin. Sas.*, vii, 116.]

1693 JOHN SANDILANDS, his son James apprenticed to Robert Mowbray, wright, Edinburgh, 28th May 1707.

1711 JOHN SANDILANDS, his son John, min. of Sanquhar.

1825 JOHN AITON, his daugh. Ruth died at Musselburgh 24th Nov. 1939.

1899 JAMES RUTH GILRUTH, dep. 1928.

1928 ROBERT BROWN WISEMAN, trans. from St John's, Kirkcaldy, 1st June 1928; dem. 28th May 1938.

(*United to Dunsyre* 28th Dec. 1941.)

DUNSYRE

1577 ROBERT DENHOLME, pres. to vicarage 31st May 1577 on death of Sir Robert Greig.—[*Reg. Pres. Bene.* i, 55.]

ROBERT SOMERVILLE, son of
Patrick S. in Grene, was pres. in
1601 1601 on death of Robert Denholme.
—[*P. S. Reg.*, lxxii, 167.]

THOMAS SOMERVILLE, min. here
pres. to parsonage 22nd Jan. 1603.
1603 —[*P. S. Reg.*, lxxiii, 171.]

ROBERT LOCKHART, marr. (2)
Eleis, daugh. of William Dunlop,
1647 elder of Crage.—[*Reg. of Deeds*, 1st
Dec. 1663.]

ROBERT SKENE, son of James S.,
1678 merchant, Aberdeen; Lyon Depute.

JAMES BRADFUTE, born 22nd July
1681, marr. 4th June 1717; had
1713 issue—Elizabeth, born 13th March
1718; Janet, born 8th May 1720.

JOHN BRADFUTE, born 10th Nov.
1725; his son James min. at Penrith;
1751 his son John, died 16th Jan. 1837.—
[*Ex information* Miss Margaret Tait.]

WILLIAM SMITH, dem. 25th Oct.
1920; died at Carnwath 29th Nov.
1877 1921.

ROBERT WILSON TURNBULL, ord.
11th March 1921; trans. to Kirk-
1921 michael 5th June 1925.

WILLIAM MUIRHEAD, born 16th
March 1864, son of Robert M.,
1925 farmer, and Isabella Wallace; educ.
at Univ. of Glasgow, M.A. (1884); licen.
by Presb. of Dunbarton May 1889; assist.
Langholm 1918-19; *locum* St Margaret's,
Arbroath; assist. St Michael's, Edinburgh;
Temperance Committee Deputy; ord. 11th
Sept. 1925; dem. 24th Feb. 1948.

LIBBERTON

For the souls of himself, Christian, his wife, etc., Sir John Maxwell of Carlaverock, Lord of Maxwell, granted the church to Kilwinning Abbey, the rights of Sir Robert Glene, rector, being reserved. The grant was confirmed by Charter of David II in 1364, and by Bull of Pope Gregory IX, 25th Nov. 1372.—[*Reg. Great Seal*, i, 182; Theiner's *Vet. Mon.*, 347-8.]

GEORGE ALEXANDER, reader, 1569.
1569 —[*Comps. Sub Coll. of Thirds, Linlithgow.*]

ALEXANDER CHALMERS, vicar.—
1574 [*Acts and Dec.*, lvi, 55.]

JAMES HAMILTON.—[*Acts and Dec.*,
1574 cxxx, 258.]

ALEXANDER SPITTAL, was of the
family of Spittal, either of Blairlogie
1590 or Leuchat.—[Stephen's *Inverkeithing and Rosyth*, 482.]

ROBERT LIVINGSTONE, his son
Samuel apprentice to James Tait,
1649 merchant, Edinburgh, 24th July
1672.—[*G. R. Sas.*, 2 Ser., xiv, 171.]

JAMES STUART, marr. a daugh. of
1697 John Ingles of Eastshiel.

JOHN LAWRIE, his widow Isobel
1857 Stark died 14th Nov. 1921.

JOHN PICKEN, died 31st July 1935;
his daugh. Mary (marr. 9th July
1890 1932, Alister John Frazer, B.Sc.,
A.M.I.C.E.).

QUOTHQUAN

JAMES HAMILTON, min. in 1569.—
1569 [*Comps. Sub Coll. of Thirds, Linlithgow,* etc.]

SIR THOMAS SOMERVILLE, parson
and min. in 1576; had a son Thomas.
1592 —[*Reg. Sec. Sig.*, lxiv, 28; *Comps. Sub Coll. of Thirds, Linlithgow,* etc.]

JOHN CHIESLIE, min. 3rd March
1606 1606.—[*Fraser Charters.*]

ROBERT BROWN.—[*G. R. Sas.*, 2 Ser.,
1652 iii, 76, 160, 238.]

SKIRLING

JOHN COCKBURN, of Newholme;
parson 30th April 1558 and 21st
1525 Aug. 1568; also parson of Roberton.
—[*Reg. of Deeds*, ii, 463; vi, 467; viii, 133; xii, 144; *Reg. Sec. Seal*, lxiii, 229, 248.]

1701 JOHN MURRAY, marr. Katherine Douglas (died 6th June 1756).

1888 JOHN BROWN ARMSTRONG, his widow, Rhoda Charlotte Mary Truman, died 3rd April 1948.

1904 THOMAS MUIR, his wife, Joanna Mavor, died 31st May 1933; his son, John, min. of Foulden.

SYMINGTON

At first called the chapel of the town of Symon, the church, under the designation of the Church of Symonstoun, was granted to the Bishopric of Glasgow by Simon Lockard about 1180, with confirmation by William the Lion in 1195-9.—[*Reg. Epis. of Glasgow*, ii, 267, 269, 272.]

1607 ROBERT LINDSAY, M.A.

1665 JOHN LAW, son of Mungo L., min. of Greyfriars, Edinburgh.

1700 PATRICK MITCHELL.—[*Act Book*, 10th March 1712.]

1813 JOHN SMITH, his daughs.—May (marr. 9th Jan. 1828); Grace Henderson, died 28th Dec. 1869.

1840 JOHN FORBES, his daughs.—Elizabeth Isabella (Mrs John Murray Bell) died 7th Sept. 1938; Margaret Matilda died 3rd Nov. 1946.

1851 JOHN ALEXANDER, licen. 15th May 1879; died 29th March 1926. Marr. (2) 20th June 1916 Martha Crouch, who died 27th Oct. 1932.

1891 GEORGE CALDWELL, died 22nd May 1927. His son, James Robert Macdonald, 2 Lieut. R.F.A., killed in action 27th Oct. 1918.

1928 JOHN W. SPENCE, formerly of Buckhaven (*q.v.*), dem. 23rd Nov. 1926; assist. Barony; adm. here 26th Jan. 1928; died 20th Oct. 1945.

(*Charges united 10th Feb.* 1946.)

WALSTON

1560 DAVID DALGLEISH, as Sir David D. held the vicarage at 1560, and, being reader, had conformed; died before 20th May 1567.—[*Reg. Sec. Seal*, xxxvii, 5.]

1567 WALTER TWEEDIE, was pres. to the vicarage 20th May 1567.—[*Reg. Sec. Seal*, xxxvii, 5.]

1580 THOMAS LINDSAY, his daugh. Mary (marr. Robert Nairne, min. of Carmichael).

1621 THOMAS LINDSAY, marr. Mary Livingston.—[*G. R. Sas.*, 2 Ser., vi, 355; *Reg. of Deeds Dal.*, i, 456.]

1689 PATRICK ANDERSON, marr. Margaret, second daugh. of James Threipland, Chamberlain of Biggar.—[*G. R. Sas.*, 3 Ser., iii, 334; xxxvi, 240, 1st Nov. 1675.]

1705 THOMAS LINNING, had a son Thomas.

1788 PATRICK MOLLISON, his daugh. Ann died at London, 6th May 1857.

1904 JAMES EADIE, trans. to Macduff, 16th June 1916.

1916 THOMAS BLANEY, born 2nd Jan. 1885, son of Thomas B., surfaceman, and Agnes Brown Steele; licen. by Presb. of Lanark 6th May 1913; ord. 13th Oct. 1916; marr. 2nd Jan. 1917, Elizabeth, daugh. of William Scott and Jessie Tennant.

WANDEL

1560 NICOL CRAWFORD, M.A., min. parson and vicar of Hartside 1560–69.—[*Comps. of Sub Coll. of Thirds, Dumfries*, etc.]

1664 JOHN HAMILTON, marr. Jean Sharp and had issue—Jane (marr. cont. 22nd and 24th June 1653 Archibald Bannatyne of Lubors); Mary (marr. (1) William Power, merchant, Edinburgh; (2)

Ninian Spence of Wester Kames).—[*House of Hamilton* 549; *G. R. Inhib.*, 200, 1665; *Reg. of Deeds*, dxxxix, 129, 1643; *Argyll Sas.*, i, 87.]

1706 DAVID BLINSHALL, his son Baillie, apprentice to Malcolm Brown, saddler, Edinburgh, 14th June 1749; his daugh. Ann died 8th April 1806.

1821 CHARLES HOPE, his daugh. Janet Sarah died 27th Nov. 1914.

1870 ROBERT RANKIN, marr. Theresa Margaret, daugh. of John George Claus, shipowner, Liverpool; she died 12th June 1937; his sons—Kenneth Phin, died at Plymouth 7th March 1919; Robert Andrew Smith, died 7th Feb. 1943; Right Hon. Sir George Claus, P.C., Chief Justice, Bengal, 1926–34; Member of Judicial Committee of Privy Council, 1935; died 8th April 1946.

1892 CHARLES JOHN RITCHIE, D.D. (St Andrews, 28th June 1932); dem. 31st Jan. 1934; died at Edinburgh 21st March 1937.

LAMINGTON

On 30th March 1448 there occurs Archibald Jardin, rector, of the other or second part, called the Rectory of Hartside, of the parish church of Lamington; the parish church of Hartside is mentioned on 26th Jan. 1451–2; and on 7th July 1460 the Rectory of Hartside is given as constituting the other or second part of the Rectory of Lamington.—[*Cal. Papal Regs.*; *Letters*, x, 184, 550; xi, 575.]

PRESBYTERY OF PEEBLES

DRUMELZIER

On the south side of the stream of Kingledoors there was a chapel dedicated to St Cuthbert. By Sir Simon Fraser, who died a short time prior to 15th Jan. 1291-2, the chapel, along with the lands of South Kingledoors and Hopcarthne, was granted to Melrose Abbey, confirmation being given by Sir Simon's son, Sir Simon Fraser, Kt. Cristin, hermit of Kingledoors, is recorded about 1200. The chapel may have been a hermitage.—[*Munimenta de Melros*, 318-19; *Rotuli Scotiae*, i, 7; *Reg. of Glasgow*, i, 89.]

1563 THOMAS BISSAIT, exhorter, 1563; designated minister 5th Dec. 1575.—[*Test. of Peter Waych*, 11th Jan. 1575-6, *Edin. Commis.*; *Test. Inventories, MS. Reg. Ho.*; *Comps. Sub Coll. of Thirds, Roxburgh*, etc.]

1683 JAMES SIMPSON, eldest son of James S., cordiner, Glasgow.

1787 WILLIAM WELSH, marr. Marion, daugh. of Gavin Waugh, baker, Edinburgh.

1810 JAMES SOMERVILLE, his daugh. Rachel died 2nd Dec. 1875.

1843 JOHN TAYLOR, his daugh. Mary Alison died 12th Jan. 1918.

1877 WILLIAM MILNE, his widow, Alexandrina Hill Lindsay, died Edinburgh 25th Feb. 1932; his daugh. Janette Murray Lindsay (marr. 21st Jan. 1926 John Archibald Hunter, Malay States).

1900 MUNRO SOMERVILLE, trans. to Newhaven 12th Oct. 1916.

1917 NORMAN GOTTFRIED KESTING, M.A., ord. 20th April 1917; trans. to Knoxland 29th Sept. 1927.

1926 GILMOUR NEILL, born 31st Dec. 1880, son of Matthew N., min. of Urney and Sion Mills parish, Tyrone; educ. at Royal School, Raphoe; Royal Univ. of Ireland; Magee College, Londonderry; licen. by Presb. of Strabane, 12th May 1905; assist. First Presbyterian Church, Lisburn; ord. to Hillhall Church 8th May 1907; trans. to St Andrew's Church, Portsmouth, 1913; Chaplain to H.M. Forces, 5th Army; wounded in France 1918; Acting Chaplain to Presbyterian Troops, Portsmouth, Oct. 1920; adm. by General Assembly 26th May 1921, *locum tenens* Moffat, adm. to Moffat 25th Dec. 1921, trans. and adm. 21st May 1926; died 2nd May 1933. Marr. July 1907 Helen Maude Neil (died 26th Nov. 1943) and had issue—Helen Christine, born 8th June 1908.

EDDLESTON

In later medieval times the church was dedicated to the Virgin Mary. About 1140 Eddleston appears on record as Pentjacob or Pentejacob. On 5th April 1170 the designation is Gillemorestun; the "town" of Gille More, St Mary's servant or devotee. Somewhat later, 1176-89, the lands were granted by Richarde de Moreville, constable of Scotland, to Edulf, son of Uchtred, from whom arose the designation Eddleston, Edulfston. The church was rebuilt in 1829. Possibly Harehope in this parish was the site of the "House of St Lazarus of Harop," the Master of which,

Friar William Corbert, in 1296 had letters from Edward I of England to the Sheriff of Edinburgh for restitution of the lands of his house in the shire of Edinburgh. Land in the parish called St Mungo's Row suggests either a chapel or an altar dedicated to that saint.—[*Ancient Church Dedications in Scotland*; *Reg. of Glasgow*, i, 3–5, 23, 39, 140–3; *Lord High Treas. Accs.*, vi, 347; *Rolls of Scot.*, i, 25a; Watson's *Celtic Place-Names*, 135; Mackenzie's *Scott. Place-Names*, 217; *New Stat. Acc.* iii, *Peebles*, 15.]

1560 GEORGE HAY, delete p. 271, line 1, from "and" to line 5 "Assembly." Son of William Hay of Talla. On 19th Jan. 1560–1 he granted to his brother William the lands of Eddleston for a sum of money to repair the church.—[*Reg. Mag. Sig.* iv, 1615.] See Kiltarlity, Ruthven, Renfrew.

1574 ADAM DICKSON, reader. See Peebles.

1589 SIR THOMAS HARGREAVES, vicar pensioner, died before 3rd June 1589.—[*Reg. Mag. Sig.*, v, 1640.]

1665 JAMES SMITH, his sons—Alexander, born 1652, apprentice to Charles Smyth, merchant, Edinburgh, 16th Nov. 1681; died 1689; Charles, apprentice to William Alison, merchant, Edinburgh, 14th Dec. 1670; William, apprentice to Simon Johnston, merchant, Edinburgh, 18th Sept. 1667.—[*Notes and Queries*, 3 Ser., xii, 27.]

1686 JAMES BUCHAN, his son James at Univ. of Aberdeen.

1697 JAMES ROBERTSON, son of James R., tailor, Edinburgh.

1735 ALEXANDER ROBERTSON, his daugh. Christian (marr. 27th April 1776).

1856 ALEXANDER JOHN MURRAY, his son Patrick Maxwell died at Sydney, New South Wales, 27th Nov. 1938.

HOPE KAILZIE

1563 JOHN BULLO, reader in 1563 and 1567.—[*Comps. Sub Coll. of Thirds, Roxburgh*, etc.]

INNERLEITHEN

The church was dedicated to St Mungo. —[*Cal. Papal Regs. Letters*, xii, 277.]

1563 PATRICK SANDERSON, exhorter, in office 1572.—[*Comps. Sub Coll. of Thirds, Roxburgh*, etc.; *Reg. Privy Council*, ii, 306.]

1674 HEW GRAY.—[*G. R. Sas.*, 3 Ser., i, 121.]

1697 THOMAS LAWIS, eldest son of William L. of Plora; marr. cert. 31st March 1658 Janet, daugh. of Francis Scott of Sinton.—[*G. R. Sas.*, 2 Ser., xiv, 406, 407.]

1727 GILBERT HUTCHISON, his son David, apprentice to Patrick Sibbald, locksmith, Edinburgh, 27th Nov. 1754.

1777 ROBERT SCOTT, his daugh., Agnes, died 6th June 1802; his son, Charles James, died at sea 4th June 1807.

1797 JOSEPH JOHNSTON, marr. Christian, daugh. of Hugh Grandison, bailie of Inverkeithing.

1833 PATRICK BOOTH, his children—Patrick, died 19th March 1924; Robina, died Edinburgh 30th Sept. 1924; William, died 17th May 1917; Jane Ann Duff, died London 22nd Nov. 1934.

1878 JAMES BOYD, died 24th Sept. 1919; his daugh. Henrietta (marr. 1st Aug. 1916 Ralph B. Macdonald, Lieut. Seaforth Highlanders).

1917 JOHN YUILL WALKER, trans. (ass. and suc.) from Pathhead (*q.v.*) 9th March 1917; Provost of Innerleithen 1st July 1941; his daugh. Noreen Christian May (marr. 22nd July 1939 Lieut. John Kellwick Wright, R.N.).

KIRKURD

By Bull of Pope Alexander II in 1170 the Church of Ord (Kirkurd) was confirmed to Ingleram, Bishop of Glasgow. In 1186 the church is called the Church of Hurd, and in the early part of the 14th century, Kyrkhurde.—[*Reg. Epis. of Glasgow*, 23, 425, 355; *Reg. Mag. Sig.*, i, 727.]

1561 DAVID GIBSON, M.A., vicar, 4th Aug. 1561.—[*Cal. of Deeds*, iv, 296.]

1563 THOMAS LUMSDEN, exhorter, 1563–71.—[*Comps. Sub Coll. of Thirds, Roxburgh*, etc.]

1574 ARCHIBALD DOUGLAS, had issue—Edward.—[*Stirling Papers* No. 413.]

1576 RICHARD WEIR, still vicar.—[*Stirling Papers* Nos. 418, 427.]

1580 JOHN MEKILL, vicar, 1580.—[*Reg. Mag. Sig.*, v, 86.]

1673 GEORGE ROBERTSON, line 7, delete "He became minister of West Calder 1675."

1681 LAURENCE MERCER, his daughs.—Elizabeth (marr. 14th Sept. 1713); Sarah (marr. John Campbell, second son of Patrick C. of Beath).

1694 ALEXANDER WALKER, his daugh. Isobel (marr. (1) Thomas Baillie of Polkemmet, W.S.; (2) probably John Leirmant of Handaxwood).

1787 DAVID ANDERSON, his daugh. Isabella (marr. 19th Aug. 1835 George I. Moxey, M.D.).

1843 THOMAS GRAY, marr. daugh. of Major-General Burrell, Governor of Hong Kong.

1880 THOMAS DUNCAN MILLAR, dem. 19th Nov. 1919; died 25th July 1936; his son, Archibald William Buchanan, K.O.S.B., killed in action Oct. 1917; his widow, Margaret Julia Grant, died at Perth 25th June 1942.

1920 JOSEPH HARDIE CATTANACH, M.A., B.D., formerly of Scots Church, Paris (*q.v.*); adm. 7th May 1920; trans. to Newton 19th Oct. 1934; died 30th Oct. 1937.

LYNE and MEGGAT

1563 PATRICK GRINTON, reader, 1563–72.—[*Comps. Sub Coll. of Thirds, Roxburgh*, etc.]

1572 JOHN WYHTMAN, vicar, 1572.—[*Comps. Sub Coll. of Thirds, Roxburgh*, etc.]

1575 ARCHIBALD DOUGLAS, M.A., probably identical with A.D. pres. to Kirkurd 1574, dem. before 14th July 1575.—[*Reg. Sec. Sig.*, xliii, 5.]

1575 GILBERT HAY, parson 1584–98; pres. to vicarage 16th July 1575.—[*Reg. Sec. Sig.*, xliii, 15; *Aud. of Exch.* 1584–98, 2.]

1627 HEW KER.—[*G. R. Sas.*, xlvi, 459.]

1660 ROBERT BROWN, tenant in Hallmyre; his daughs., Janet and Margaret.—[*P. C. Reg.*, 2 Ser., ix, 500; x, 308.]

1852 WILLIAM WALKINGSHAW, his daugh., Jane Inglis, died 9th Jan. 1936.

1908 MOSES TAGGART, dem 31st Dec. 1946; died 8th Jan. 1949; his son, Henry Rawson, 2nd Lieut. Argyll and Sutherland Highlanders, killed in action 24th July 1918; his daugh., Christine (marr. 12th Jan. 1927 Hedley Briggs Constable, Kluang, Johore); his wife, Martha Hall Allan, died 6th March 1940.

MANOR

1560 JOHN ALLAN, minister 1560, died in or before 1572.—[*Comps. Sub Coll. of Thirds, Roxburgh*, etc.]

1563 THOMAS PURVES, reader in 1563 and 1565.—[*Comps. Sub Coll. of Thirds, Roxburgh*, etc.]

1574 HECTOR CRANSTON, reader, 16th May 1574 and 8th Jan. 1577–8.—[*Edin. Tests.*, iv, 54; v, 341.]

1663 DAVID THOMSON, his eldest son, Samuel, tailor burgess of Peebles.—[*Reg. of Deeds Mack.*, i, 589; *Reg. Ho. Charters*, 1707.]

1683 ROBERT SMITH, his daugh., Agnes, born 1664.

1743 WILLIAM ANDERSON, his daugh. Margaret (marr. proc. 12th Sept. 1781 John Stewart, student of divinity); a daugh. (marr. –. Somerville) died 14th May 1826.

1788 WILLIAM MARSHALL, his first father-in-law a peruke-maker.

1901 JOHN WILLIAM MURRAY, his wife, Ann Bell, died 11th Oct. 1927. He died 3rd June 1938.

NEWLANDS

In 1317 the patronage of the church was granted to Dunfermline Abbey by John de Grahame; and in 1477 the church became a prebend of the Collegiate Church of Dalkeith.—[*Reg. of Dunfermline*, 236, 403–4.]

1563 THOMAS PATERSON, reader 1563.—[*Comps. Sub Coll. of Thirds, Roxburgh*, etc.]

1566 WILLIAM MURRAY.—[*Acts and Dec.* xxviii, 58.]

1570 ARCHIBALD DOUGLAS, M.A., min. of Kirkurd, held parsonage 1570; min. at West Linton 1576 (*q.v.*); senator of College of Justice.—[*Comps. Sub Coll. of Thirds, Dumfries*, etc.]

1575 SIR JOHN THOMSON, reader, probably vicar before 1560 and conformed, died Oct. 1575. Marr. Margaret Robeson, who survived him and marr. (2) Patrick Thomson in Scotstoun.—[*Edin. Tests.*, viii, 212.]

1592 JOHN COLDEN, coll. and adm. to parsonage by Presb. of Edinburgh and Peebles 20th June 1593.—[*Decr. on Taxation* 22nd Jan. 1593–4.]

1596 JOHN SYDE.—[*G. R. Sas.*, xv. 102.]

1694 ARCHIBALD TORRIE, his son, David.—[*Scroll Reg. P. R. Sas. Fife*, 1716, *War.* 79.]

1709 STEPHEN PATON, his widow, Jane Sibbald, marr. (2) James Lorimer, min. of Yarrow.

1756 DAVID DICKSON, line 22, for "1756" read "1755."

1768 JAMES MOFFAT, marr. Janet, daugh. of Thomas Stoddart of Williamhope.

1834 JAMES CHARTERIS, son of George Charteris of Amisfield.

1870 WILLIAM KELLY, his widow, Catherine Forrester, died at Edinburgh 5th May 1923.

1884 JOHN MILNE, died 26th May, 1918.

1918 HORACE JAMES DICK, trans. from Blythswood (*q.v.*) 25th Oct. 1918; died at Largs 20th Nov. 1944. His daugh. Ella (marr. 10th Dec. 1920 Walter Brotherston, Rangoon); his widow, Elizabeth J. M. Smith, died at Greenock 29th Jan. 1949.

PEEBLES

The earliest patron of Peebles was St Mungo; and St Mungo's Well still survives. About 1116 the church with a caracute of land belonged to the See of Glasgow; and added to it there occurs in 1186 among the possessions of the see the dependent Chapel of Manor. On 29th Oct. 1195 the church was dedicated by Bishop Joceline of Glasgow, and it may be that it was at that date that St Andrew took the place of St Mungo as the patron. Before 1214 Peebles had become a prebend of Glasgow.

In the church there were altars dedicated to—St Mary the Virgin (St Mary of Childbirth); Holy Rood; St Andrew; St Mary of the Geddes Aisle, founded with the aisle or chapel by John Geddes early in the 15th century; St Mary Major; St James, designated also the Altar of St James and St Katharine in a Charter of 17th April 1469, by which William Smaill, priest, granted two annual rents from properties on the north side of High Street, Edinburgh, for masses at the altar; St John the Baptist; St Laurence, founded probably about 1470 by Sir Richard Purdie, Dean of Peebles and Vicar of Pettinain; St. Martin; St Michael the Archangel; St Christopher, founded 29th April 1517 by William Alane, burgess of Peebles; St Peter and St Paul, founded 20th Jan. 1520-1, in virtue of an indenture between the community of the burgh and Sir Patrick Stenhouse, chaplain of the Chapel of St Mary, who gave part of the chapel lands as the endowment. By Crown Charter of 8th June 1543 there was confirmed the erection of the church into a collegiate church by the Bailies, Council, and Community, and John, Lord Hay of Yester, for a provost and 12 prebendaries, and "two young persons having a youthful voice to chant Divine Service." The prebends, identical with the altars, were in the following order: The Virgin Mary of Childbirth, Holy Cross, St Michael the Archangel, St Mary Major, St Peter and St Paul, St John the Baptist, St Mary of Geddes Aisle, St Andrew, St James, St Laurence, St Martin, St Christopher. Each prebendary was to have 24 merkes, a chamber with garden "in the ancient town of Peebles" adjoining the messuage of the Archdeacon of Glasgow, and an acre of the church lands. There was at the Castle of Peebles a chapel founded by David I. To Kelso Abbey King William the Lion (1145-1214) confirmed the chapel, with a caracute of land, and also an annual rent of 10 shillings from the fermes of the burgh of Peebles assigned to the chapel by his grandfather, David I, for perpetual celebrations for the soul of Henry, father of said King William. The abbey was also held bound to make the chapel fitting and beautiful, to equip it with suitable ecclesiastical ornaments, and to provide a chaplain who "shall minister perpetually in it for the soul of Earl Henry." By letters of David II of 8th March 1362-3 the community were enjoined to assign a stance in the common muir to build a Chapel of the Virgin Mary. In the chapel there was an altar dedicated to St Osyth. The Church of the Holy Cross is said by Fordun to have been founded by Alexander III. According to the narrative, the royal action was prompted by the discovery of a stately and venerable cross at Peebles on 9th May 1361. The cross, it was believed, had been hidden by some of the faithful about 296, when the Maximian persecution was raging in Britain. Soon after there was found close to the same spot an urn containing ashes and bones of a man's body torn from limb to limb, as it were. The clue to the identity of the ashes and bones was thought to lie in the inscription on the outside of the stone in which the cross was lying, "Tomb of the Bishop St Nicolas." Miracles were wrought at the place to which people from Scotland and the north of England continued to resort in crowds, bringing offerings to God. And so, with the advice of the Bishop of Glasgow, the King reared a handsome church on the spot in honour of God and the Holy Cross. The church was placed in the custody of Trinitarian or Red Friars; and on 3rd Feb. 1473, in response to a petition by James III and Margaret, his queen, Brother Robert, Head Minister of the Red Friars at the Monastery of Mathuron, Paris, sanctioned the erection of a Trinitarian Monastery at the church, and the annexation thereto of the Trinitarian House at Berwick on Tweed, which had been destroyed by the English. Among the possessions of the house at Berwick on Tweed, so annexed, was the Church of Kettins. James V increased the resources of the monastery by the annexation of the Trinitarian House at Dunbar on 1st July 1529, the monastery being described as the place "quhar ane part of the verray croce that our Salvatour was crucifyit on is honorit and kepit," and by the annexation of the Trinitarian House at Houston in the parish of Prestonkirk, on 2nd Dec. 1531. The high altar of the church was the Black Rood; and there were also altars of the Holy Blood and St Sebastion. After the Reformation the Cross Church became the parish church, and was so used till 1784, when a new church was built on the Castlehill. The latter gave place to the present church in 1887. At Eshiels near Horsburgh Castle there was a hospital with chapel bearing at first the name of St Laurence, and later the name of St Leonard and, maybe, under the invocation of both. Regular payments to the hospital were made from the customs of the burgh, the first occurring in 1327. The site is now called Chapelyards. About 1462 there was founded near the Chapel of the Virgin Mary an almshouse, also dedicated to St Leonard. By Charter of 19th Nov. 1621 James VI granted to the burgh for "the commonne workes of the burgh" the endowments of the following prebends of the former collegiate church, St Mary, Holy Rood, St Michael the Archangel, St Marie major, St John the Baptist, St Mary dallgeddes, St Andrew, St James, St Laurence, St Christopher, "with the chaplanrie callit St Marie"; the lands, tenements, houses, biggins, kirt kirks, with "the hie and Cross Kirk" and kirkyards, chapels, yards, orchards, crofts, rents, teinds, fruits, duties, emoluments, "almous silver, obite silver and anniversaries" pertaining to chaplainries, alterages, prebends founded in any kirk, hospital, chapel, college or hospital in the burgh, or due from any land or tenement in the burgh to any kirk, chaplainry or prebend founded outside the burgh in any part of Scotland. —[*Acts Scott. Parl.*, xii, Supplement 1b; *Excheq. Rolls*, i, 71, ii, 208, 323, etc.; *Reg. of Glasgow*, 5, 55, 95; *Book of Kelso*, 15; *Reg. Sec. Seal*, i, 4110, ii, 203, 1069, 2524, 4207, 4842; *Reg. Great Seal*, ii, 838, iii, 2921; *Chron. of Melrose*, 102; *Charters of Burgh of Peebles*, 8, 9, 10, 14, 43, 50, 54, 61 ff., 64, 73, 76 ff., 81, 91; *Retours*, viii, 275; Fordun's *Scot.*, i, 299, *Scott. Historians*; for details see Dr. C. B. Gunn's *Book of St Andrew's Church*; *Book of the Cross Church* (2 vols.).]

1559 JOHN WALLACE, was probably the first, if unauthorised, preacher of the Reformed Faith in Peebles, for on 3rd March 1559-60 it is narrated that "John Dikesone yr. of Winkieston, and Rollan Scott, bailies, passit to the personale presens of Johne Wallace als appostal, and dischargit him to vse ony new novationes of commoun prayeris or preching becaus the said Johne was nocht electit be the saidis baillies and parochyn, and that the said baillies wald nocht assist to him nor nane of his sect nor opinioun; becaus the saidis baillies wald stand vnder the faith and obedience of thair Prince berand authorite for the tyme, nocht being dischargit be ane ordour and in na contimptioun of the Lordis of the Congregatioun,"—[*Extracts from the Records of the Burgh of Peebles*, 258.]

1560 JOHN DICKSON, min. in 1566.— [*Acts and Dec.*, xxxvi, 374.]

1573 JOHN HOPPRINGLE, chaplain.— [*Acts and Dec.*, liii, 219.]

1575 THOMAS HAY, brother to William, Lord Hay of Yester, provided to the ministry 30th Oct. 1566; res. in favour of his nephew James, 7th Lord Hay of Yester, 15th Jan. 1583-4; died before 11th June 1584.—[*Scots Peerage*, viii, 437; *Acts and Dec.*, lxi, 260, 262.]

1586 ADAM DICKSON, reader at Eddleston, designated minister in Peebles 31st July and 14th Sept. 1577.—[*Edin. Tests.*, v, 242; vii, 219.]

1616 THEODORE HAY.—[*G. R. Sas.*, 25th July 1631, xxxi, 304.]

1696 JAMES THOMSON, his son, William, and his daugh., Susanna, died before 30th March 1737.—[*P. R. Sas. Lanark*, xiv, ii, 354.]

1813 ROBERT BUCHANAN, died Father of the Church.

1911 THOMAS MARTIN, licen. 11th June 1883; Moderator of General Assembly, May 1920; dem. 12th Nov. 1925; died at Davidson's Mains 7th Jan.

1942; his wife, Isabella Robertson, died 14th Aug. 1929; his son, Thomas, M.D., Peebles, died 27th June 1931; his daugh., Christeen Isobell (marr. 4th July 1918 George Thomas Thomson, min. of St Boswells), died 7th Jan. 1937.

1926 BERRY PRESTON, trans. from Riccarton (*q.v.*) 24th March 1926.

STOBO

At Westerhoprew there was a chapel dedicated to St Michael, described in 1503 as founded by the predecessors of John, Lord Hay of Yester, and endowed with certain lands and a manse, the vicar of Stobo being held bound to celebrate service twice weekly in the chapel for the souls of the founders.—[*Yester Writs*, 272, *Scott. Rec. Soc.*]

1560 JOHN COLQUHOUN, M.A., parson 1554, reader 1560; son natural of late James Colquhoun, parson of Luss; held the parsonage of Stobo, of which he was described on 28th April 1566 as now "usufructuar."—[*Reg. of Deeds*, viii, 301*b*; *Comps. Sub Col. of Thirds, Roxburgh*, etc.; *Chiefs of Colquhoun*, i, 100; *Acts and Dec.*, xxiii, 153; xxx, 301; xlvii, 298; xlviii, 216; 1,279; lii, 187; liv, 71, 304, 337; lxi, 389; *Monumenta Univ. Glasgow*, i, 82.]

1562 SIR NINIAN DOUGLAS, vicar 4th Nov. 1562; was in office 19th Dec. 1557; Chaplain of the Altar of the Holy Rood, Dalkeith Coll. Church, 19th Dec. 1551; and on 28th Sept. 1557 was Chaplain of the "Altar in the threshold of said Coll. Church."—[*Laing Charters*, 591, 679, 744; *Reports Hist. MSS. Commis.*, ii, *Duns Castle*, 23.]

1562 SIR THOMAS GODERRALL, vicar 14th July 1562, on which date he received from Sir David Hamilton, vicar-pensioner of Stobo, a letter of tack and assedation of the fruits, rents, teinds, emoluments, and other duties of the vicarage, with glebe, manse, houses, and kirklands, for 5 years.—[Grote's *Prot. Bk.*, 221.]

1566 THOMAS NEILSON, reader, alleged parson; designated exhorter 1569–72.—[*Acts and Dec.*, xxxvii, 157; *Comps. Sub Coll. of Thirds, Roxburgh*, etc.]

1572 JAMES NOBLE, parson 1572.—[*Comps. Sub Coll. of Thirds, Roxburgh*, etc.]

1573 ARCHIBALD COLQUHOUN of Sallochty, parson 2nd Sept. 1566 in succession to his kinsman, John Colquhoun.—[*Reg. of Deeds*, viii, 301; *Acts and Dec.*, l, 279; lii, 187; liv, 71; 302, 337; lxi, 389; lxiii, 377.]

1578 WILLIAM TWEEDIE, reader, 13th Jan. 1578–9.—[*Edin. Tests.*, ix, 239.]

1582 ROBERT DOUGLAS, perpetual vicar 16th July 1565, Provost of Corstorphine 8th Dec. 1575, called vicar 1582.—[*Reg. Abbrev. Feu Charters of Church Lands*, ii, 1580; *Yester Writs*, 731, 812.]

1592 ADAM HEPBURN, pres. to benefice on death of Archibald Colquhoun 30th Sept. 1588 and to parsonage on death of Andrew Murdo.—[*P. S. Reg.*, lx, 65; lxiii, 248.]

1598 ARCHIBALD ROW, pres. to vicarage on depr. of Andrew Cunninghame. —[*P. S. Reg.*, lxx, 51.]

1682 WILLIAM BOLLO, line 2 for "1600" read "1660."

1688 WILLIAM RUSSELL, had issue— Marion, born 18th June 1672; Margaret, born 7th Nov. 1673; John, born 30th Dec. 1675; George, born 6th Feb. 1678; Alexander, born 23rd June 1679; Margaret, born 6th Dec. 1688; William, born 11th Feb. 1691; James, born 28th Sept. 1693; Adam, born 25th Jan. 1697; Daniel; Agnes. Marr. (2) Jean Lindsay.—[*Deeds, Mack.*, 1704, No. 11, 515.]

1701 WILLIAM RUSSELL, his son, William, born 23rd July 1703, apprentice to William Carmichael, merchant, Edinburgh, 28th Feb. 1718.

1787 ALEXANDER KER, his daugh. Isabella [marr. 17th Sept. 1818].

1837 ALEXANDER EDGER, line 6, for "1847" read "1837."

1871 JOHN LIVINGSTON BOOTH, his widow, Julia Ritchie, died 1st Aug. 1928.

1891 JOHN RODGERS CRUICKSHANK, D.D. (Aberdeen, 3rd April 1941), died 6th Oct. 1944.

DAWYCK

1684 GEORGE SMITH, born 1650; marr. 1690 and had issue—Ann.—[*N. and Q.*, 3 Ser., xii, 27.]

TRAQUAIR

1567 ALEXANDER TAIT, vicar pensioner and reader 1567-72; vicar and exhorter 10th April 1575; reader 16th Jan. 1577; afterwards at Bedrule.—[*Comps. Sub Coll. of Thirds, Roxburgh*; *Edin. Tests.*, iii, 189; v, 349; vii, 181.]

1646 WILLIAM THOMSON, his widow, Geilles Millar, and son, Mr Thomas, resident in Tron Par., Edinburgh, 9th Nov. 1694; his daugh. Jean (marr. cont. 30th Nov. 1677 Ewen Campbell in Pelnaneach, Moray).—[*Tron Poll Tax Roll* 10; *Reg. of Deeds Dal.*, 19th Nov. 1720.]

1789 JOHN WALKER, line 3, for "7" read "2."

1859 JARDINE WALLACE, his sons—James Campbell, died 4th Feb. 1935; Jardine, died East Grange, New Jersey, 6th Dec. 1936.

1908 JOHN MAIN, his wife, Elizabeth Kidd Campbell, died at Musselburgh 16th Aug. 1926. Marr. (2) 11th April 1928 Isabella Clark (died 23rd Sept. 1943).

TWEEDSMUIR

Formerly known as the Quarter Kirk.—[*Reg. of Deeds Mack.*, xliii, 201, 1703.]

1698 WILLIAM HIGGINS, M.P., 1689-1700; his son William apprentice to James Chisholm, apothecary, Edinburgh, 26th Jan. 1704.

1793 JAMES GARDNER, his son, George, died 31st July 1842.

1831 GEORGE BURNS, his son, John James, died at Glasgow, 18th Jan. 1917.

1860 JOHN DICK, his daughs.—Mary Gibson, died 23rd March 1915; Eleanora Lidderdale, died 8th Jan. 1933; Jessie Crawford, died 28th Feb. 1933.

1894 WILLIAM SHILLINGLAW CROCKETT, D.D. (Edinburgh, 1929); his wife, Mary Ross, died 5th Jan. 1944. He died 25th June 1945. Addl. Publications—*The Centenary of Waverley* (1915); *Dr Mair of Earlston* (1920); *Berwickshire and Roxburghshire* (Cambridge Series) (1925); *Lays from Leaderside* (1925); *The Berwickshire Scene* (1936); *Tweedsmuir Church and Churchyard* (1936). General Editor of *Fasti Ecclesiae Scoticanae* 1915-28.

WALKERBURN

1908 DONALD MACGREGOR GRANT, dem. 16th May 1918, adm. to Newport 13th Feb. 1920.

1919 ROBERT STEWART, born 22nd Aug. 1864; educ. at Univ. of Glasgow and Original Secession Church Hall; ord. 1888 to Original Session Church, Castletown, Caithness; adm. to Free Church 1895; missionary at Windygates; adm. min. 1899; adm. here 2nd July 1919; dem. 16th May 1924 owing to dispute with congregation; died 3rd Oct. 1927. Marr. 5th July 1888 Isobel Brown, and had issue—William R. B., born 29th April 1889; Anne Isabel B., born 12th Aug. 1890; Grace, born 24th Nov. 1893; Jessie McD., born 15th May 1895; Helene S., born 5th March 1897; Robert A., born 31st Aug. 1899.

1924 FREDERICK ROBERT SIM, born 10th August 1888, youngest son of Robert S., M.D., Affleck House, Monikie, and Isabella Margaret Boosie;

licen. by Presb. of Edinburgh 22nd Dec. 1922; assistant North Esk 1923; ord. 23rd Sept. 1924; trans. to St Columba's, Blackhall, 30th Sept. 1931; died 4th Aug. 1945. Marr. 23rd Dec. 1924 Janet Grant, daugh. of William Smith, Portobello, and has issue—David Robert, born 14th Nov. 1925.

WEST LINTON

There was in the church an aisle of St John the Baptist, no doubt with an altar of that dedication.

In its early designation, Lyntunruderic (Linton Roderick), West Linton is linked up with Roderick (d. 603), Christian King of Strathclyde, Rydderick Hael (Roderick the Liberal), supporter of St Mungo, to whom the church was dedicated. In 1569-72 George Foirhous had the chaplainry of "ye Lady of Linton" to "sustain him at the Schools," indicating the existence of a chapel dedicated to the Virgin.—[*Ancient Ch. Dedications in Soct., Non-Scrip.*, 178-9; *Compts. Sub Coll. of Thirds, Linlithgow*, etc.; *Laing Charters*, 499.

1563 ADAM COLQUHON, exhorter 1563-71 and described as reader 20th Sept. 1574 and 8th June 1575.—[*Edin. Test.*, ii, 47; iii, 267.]

1566 WALTER BALFOUR, afterwards reader at Kinross.

1576 ARCHIBALD DOUGLAS, min. of Kirkurd, had charge here 1574.

1585 ROBERT ALLAN, min. of Newlands, had charge here 1585. (See Newlands.)

1731 THOMAS FINDLATER, born 2nd July 1697.

1836 ALEXANDER McCAUL FORRESTER, died 9th April 1883.

1877 SAMUEL McLINTOCK, died 12th April 1922; his widow, Margaret Bryce Gunn, died 25th Dec. 1938.

1922 JAMES THOMAS HALL, trans. from Tillicoultry (*q.v.*) 6th Oct. 1922; trans. to Holborn 2nd Sept. 1927.

1928 JAMES GRAHAM GOODALL NICOLSON, born Pittenweem 1893, son of Thomas Peter Johnston N., secretary and bailie, Pittenweem, and Margaret Anderson; educ. at Waid Academy and Univ. of St Andrews, M.A. (1916); served in Great War as lieut. in Highland Light Infantry; licen. by Presb. of St Andrews Jan. 1923; Assistant, Dunblane; ord. 13th Dec. 1923 to Saltoun; trans. and adm. 22nd March 1928. Marr. 24th June 1925 Nellie, younger daugh. of James Hebenton, Glasgow, and has issue—Thomas Peter Johnston, born 25th March 1927; Isobel Marion, born and died 12th Jan. 1931; Margaret Helen Rae, born 4th May 1932. Editor *College Echoes* (St Andrews Univ.).

PRESBYTERY OF DALKEITH

BORTHWICK

The Church of Lockerworth was granted to the Abbey of Scone by David I 1124–53, along with a piece of land which the abbey subsequently gave to David de Lyn in exchange for 1 acre of land and a piece of land beside the river under the orchard of the church. The exchange was confirmed by Roger, Bishop of St Andrews, 1188–1202. The teinds, fruits, etc., of the church were granted by William, Lord Crichton, for the institution of prebends of the Collegiate Church of Crichton on its foundation on 26th Dec. 1449. In response to a petition by the Presbytery of Edinburgh which stated that the church had been destitute of the exercise of religion for several years bypast on account of the absence of stipend for a minister, all the teind sheaves and all the teinds of the rectory, great and small, and all the fruits of the parish that pertained to the prebends of Crichton Collegiate Church, and the vicarage of Borthwick, *alias* the vicarage Lochorquhart of Torcrek, with manse and glebe, resigned by Nathaniel Harlaw, Minister of Ormiston, were, by Crown Charter of 4th April 1596, ratified by Parliament in 1606, dissolved from Crichton, and annexed to Borthwick, to be called the Rectory of Borthwick.—[*Book of Scone*, 5–6, 14, 33; *Reg. Great Seal*, vi, 425; *Acts Scott. Parl.*, iv, 327.]

1583 DUNCAN WALKER, min. 27th March 1583.—[*Cal. Laing Charters*, 1060.]

1604 PATRICK TURNER, M.A., pres. in 1604 in succession to John Murray.—[*Reg. Sec. Sig.*, lxxiv, 150.]

1648 ARCHIBALD TURNER, marr. Rebecca, daugh. of Alexander Couper of Failford, W.S.—[*Reg. of Deeds, Dal.*, xix, 587.]

1652 JOHN WEIR, marr. Anne, daugh. of John Hamilton of Gilkerscleuch, parson of Crawfordjohn.

1657 THOMAS PATERSON, had issue (addl.)—Agnes; Helen; Walter.—[*Reg. of Deeds, Mack.*, lxxxvii, 31st Dec. 1700.]

1683 THOMAS PATERSON, M.A., with his wife Ann Murray and three children, the eldest 8 years, and his daughter-in-law Ann White going on 14, was resident in Tron parish, Edinburgh, 16th Nov. 1694. Thomas, probably his son, was apprenticed to David Wemyss, merchant, Edinburgh, 11th Jan. 1703.

1860 WALTER WADDELL, marr. Susan, daugh. of William Morrison, Procurator Fiscal, Fifeshire; she died 13th Sept. 1924; James Cumming Dewar, his son, died at Uddingston 14th Aug. 1932.

1904 THOMAS ALEXANDER BICKERTON, licen. May 1882; dem. 30th Jan. 1922; died at Davidson's Mains 29th Jan. 1923; his wife, Alison Watson Hope Mackenzie, died 4th July 1918.

1922 WILLIAM JOHN MACFARLAND, B.A., trans. from Kelso North 15th Dec. 1922; trans. to Balmerino 6th May 1926.

1926 ANDREW CLARK ORR, born 11th May 1888, son of Robert Clark O., West Kilbride, and Annie Boyd; educ. at Univ. of Edinburgh, M.A. (1915); licen. by Free Church Presb. of Glasgow June 1919; assistant Bluevale; ord. 15th Oct. 1926. Marr. 14th Dec. 1926 Janey Hepburn, M.A., daugh. of Peter Hepburn, Auchterarder.

CARRINGTON

The original parish church was dedicated by Bishop David de Bernham, 2nd May 1243. The church was granted to the Abbey of Scone by David I 1124–53. On 13th Feb. 1356 William, Bishop of St Andrews, on the renunciation of all rights in the church by Scone Abbey, gave in exchange to the said abbey the Church of Blair in Gowrie; the present church was first used 7th Oct. 1911.—[*Bk. of Scone*, 5–6, 14, 130–3; see Blairgowrie.]

1570 GEORGE ALEXANDER, parson of Foulden, pres. to parsonage here on forfeiture of James Hamilton.—[*Reg. Pres. Bene.*, i, (2), 27.]

1574 SIR JAMES HOPKIRK, reader, probably previously vicar in 1549, vicar pensioner, died after 23rd Dec. 1574.—[Wodrow's *Miscel. Prot. Book of Thomas Steven; Edin. Tests.* June 1570, iii, 178; *Reg. Pres. Bene.*, i (2), 32.]

1575 JOHN CHARLES, reader, pres. to vicar; pensionary 15th April 1575 on death of James Hopkirk.—[*Reg. Pres. Bene.*, i (2), 32; *Reg. Mag. Sig.*, iv, 2816, 24th Nov. 1578.]

1585 LUCAS SOUSIE, line 3, for "1586" read "1585–6."

1663 JOHN COLLIER, his wife, Annabella Lindsay, buried 15th March 1693.

1682 ROBERT MONTEITH, bapt. 16th Nov. 1651; marr. Rebecca Higgins; his second son, Patrick.—[*Dumfries Sas.*, iv, 455.]

1688 JAMES KIRKPATRICK, min. at Machars, Co. Down, marr. 1682 (1) and had issue—Anna, Susanna and Christian.—[*Deeds Dal.*, 1706, No. 1029.]

1698 JOHN BISHOP, son of William B., burgess of Edinburgh.

1709 JAMES PATON, his daugh., Rosina (marr. proc. 21st Feb. 1762 George Paton, clerk in Custom House).

1864 WILLIAM GRANVILLE CORE, dem. 19th May 1916; died at Portobello 5th Jan. 1917; his widow, Jessie Braidwood, died 25th Aug. 1920; his daugh. Jessie died at London 16th Dec. 1918.

1916 WILLIAM EDWARD GRIMWOOD, ord. 19th Sept. 1916; trans. to Polwarth 22nd Oct. 1925.

1926 DAVID EDWARD EASSON, born 2nd Aug. 1867, son of David Chapman E. and Isabella Rae Duncan; educ. at Univ. of St Andrews, M.A. (1918), B.D. (1924), Ph.D. (1928); licen. by Presb. of St Andrews 7th May 1924, assistant Inveresk; ord. 8th April 1926; trans. to Mauchline Old Church 5th March 1931; dem. on app. Lecturer on Church History, Univ. of Leeds, 30th Sept. 1947.

COCKPEN

1569 SIR GEORGE RAMSAY, perpetual vicar 24th Dec. 1569; appears to have held office in 1560; died before 1580.—[*Reg. Great Seal*, iv, 3018; *Reg. Pres. of Benefs.*, ii, 44.]

1681 ALEXANDER WOOD, marr. Jean Brown.—[*Reg. of Deeds*, 1700.]

1695 DAVID LINDSAY, his sons—Charles, apprentice to Patrick Gibb, cordiner, Edinburgh, 12th Aug. 1736; David, apprentice to John Sempill, surgeon apothecary, Edinburgh, 8th March 1721.

1903 ROBERT MONTGOMERIE HARDIE, died 13th March 1942; his wife, Mary Smith, died 2nd May 1928; his daugh., Agnes Montgomerie, died 5th Oct. 1937; his sons—Thomas, L.R.C.P. & S.E., died at Hull 24th Nov. 1941; William Towers Hardie, M.D., Ch.B., Glasgow, died 3rd June 1948.

CRANSTOUN

The church was granted to Kelso Abbey by Hugh Riddel, Lord of Cranston, and in 1165–78 the grant was confirmed by William the Lion. On 2nd March 1316–17 the church, with the lands of Preston or Easter Cranston pertaining thereto, was conveyed by the abbey to William Lamberton, Bishop of St Andrews, in exchange for the Church of Nenthorn, with the Chapel of Little Newton. The vicarage of the church became a Prebend of St Salvator's College and Collegiate Church, St Andrews. At least twice at the end of the 16th century the parish was designated Cranston-Riddell. The present church was built in 1825 at the sole expense of Sir John Dalrymple. The old manse, which was situated at Prestonhall, is said to have been a rest-house for pilgrims to Melrose (Kelso ?) Abbey. Over one of the windows was the inscription "*Diversorium infra, Habitaculum supra,*" literally, "Inn below, dwelling above," expressive of the idea of Pilgrimage on earth, Home in heaven. At the village of Cousland there was a chapel dedicated to St Catharine, originally a dependent chapel of Inveresk Church, and as such appearing among the possessions of Dunfermline Abbey confirmed by Robert, Bishop of St Andrews, apparently before 1153, and certainly not later than 1158-9. On 4th June 1509 William Ruthven of Ruthven, Kt., fiar lord of Cousland, and William, Lord of Ruthven, and his wife, Isabel Livingstone, life-renters of Cousland, granted to the chapel 12 merks annually from the lands of Cousland, and a house and garden on the west side of the chapel. The date when Cousland was attached to Cranston parish has not been definitely ascertained; but it is said to have been at or soon after 1560. All traces of the chapel seem to have disappeared some time prior to the close of the 18th century; but local people of that period had recollections of a bell which had been taken away, and of a churchyard.—[*Acts Scott. Parl.*, iv, 28, v, 118; *Reg. Great Seal*, ii, 3358; *Reg. Sec. Seal*, iii, 1716; *Retours*, xliii, 291; *Reg. of Dunfermline*, 55, 57, 59, 63, etc.; *Book of Kelso*, i, 14, 16–18, 197–8, 251–2.]

1563 JAMES MURRAY, vicar 1563, styled min. 20th Nov. 1580; pres. to haill vicarage on dem. of Andrew Blackhall.—*Reg. Sec. Sig.*, lxi, 57; *Comps. Sub Coll. of Thirds, Linlithgow,* etc.]

1597 JAMES WATSON, pres. by David McGill, King's Advocate, before 3rd July 1598.—[*Decreets on the Taxation*, 3rd July 1598.]

1610 JOHN NYMBILL, marr. 21st Feb. 1604 Margaret Danielston.—[*Reg. House Charters.*]

1663 GEORGE KINTORE, had issue, George, bapt. 2nd Nov. 1662.— [*South Leith Reg.*]

1679 JAMES BLAIR, son of Peter B., min. of Jedburgh.

1733 WILLIAM SMITH, his daugh. Margaret (marr. pro. 9th Dec. 1795 Richard Cochrane, late of America.)

1912 SAMUEL STEPHEN WALKER, his wife Anna, daugh. of James Sharp, Aberdeen, died 9th Sept. 1939; marr. (2) 5th July 1944 Helen Alexander, eldest daugh. of John Aikman, 3 Whitehouse Terrace, Edinburgh; his son, James Cadenhead, died prisoner of war, Singapore, 1942.

CRICHTON

On 26th Dec. 1449 William, Lord Crichton, Chancellor of Scotland, "out of thankfulness and gratitude to Almighty God for all the manifold deliverances He has vouchsafed unto him," and "to the praise and Honour of God Omnipotent, and our Lord Jesus Christ, the ever Blessed and Glorious Virgin Mary, St Kentigern, and All Saints and the Elect of God," with consent of his son and heir, Sir James of Frendraucht, founded the Collegiate Church of Crichton in the parish church. Three days later confirmation was given by James Kennedy, Bishop of St Andrews. The foundation was for a provost, eight chaplains or prebendaries, one of whom was to be master or instructor of the school of music, and another master or teacher of the grammar school, two boys, and a sacrist whose duties were to attend to the ringing of the bells, locking the doors, vestments, chalices, and other vessels, and also for the repair of the fabric, furnishing the altar and choir, and other necessaries. The provost was to have the whole fruits of the Rectory of Crichton, along with the rector's manse as residence, subject to a provision of £10 annually with ½ acre of land for manse and garden, to a perpetual vicar who was to have the parochial cure of Crichton, and was also to be the Prebendary of Crichton. To the provostry also pertained the Temple Lands of Crichton. The fruits of the Church of Lockerworth (Borthwick), annexed to the collegiate church, were in the first instance for the provision of a perpetual vicar of Lockerworth, who was to have the church lands or glebe of Lockerworth for his own use, along with the manse and garden formerly pertaining to the rector, and all the teind sheaves and other teinds of Haukerston, and all the teinds of Douglasland and Goldlan. The fruits of the Church of Lockerworth further provided for three prebends—the First Prebend of Middleton and the Second Prebend of Middleton, which had all the teind sheaves and other teinds of the town of Middleton and of Cauldsyde, along with all the teinds of the town of Osperton, and the Prebend of Lockerworth, later called the Prebend of Vogrie, which had all the teind sheaves and other teinds of the lands of Little Lockerworth, with all the teinds of the domicile lands of Lockerworth. For the fabric of the church and the repair of the fabric, and for ornaments, vestments, etc., further teinds of Lockerworth were devoted—the teinds of Arnoldston, Hervistoun, Rathquhillintoun and Catkin, with the teinds of the mills of Catkin and Lockerworth and Vogrie. This appears to be the Prebend of Arnoldston mentioned in a Crown Charter of 4th April 1596. The other three prebends were the prebend called , with endowments of lands and annual rents in *lie Buithraw* in Edinburgh; the Prebend of Hogston, with endowments of an annual rent of 16½ merks from a tenement in Edinburgh, along with the town of Hogston near the Burgh Muir of Edinburgh; and the Prebend of Furde in the barony of Crichton, with endowments of £5 Scots from the east half of the lands of Uggingis between Sleden and Furde, £5 Scots annual rent from the lands of the barony of Crichton, and ½ acre for manse and garden. For the education and sustenance of the two boys there were set apart the teind sheaves and other teinds of Auchinlekhill and Curry, with all the teinds of the lands called *lie Stanis;* and the provision for the sacrist was all the teind sheaves and other teinds of West Caldmure, all portions of the fruits of Lockerworth Church. The Act of Parliament of 1641 which declared the collegiate church to be the parish church for all time, converted and appropriated all the teinds, fruits, rents, emoluments, and other duties whatsoever, "due to the vicares or prebendaries thair," to the said parish kirk and the minister serving or to serve the same.—[*Acts Scott. Parl.*, v. 572; *Reg. Great Seal*, ii, 1784, iv, 2169, vi, 425, vii, 508; *Reg. Sec. Seal*, iii, 2366; *Charters of Coll. Churches of Midlothian*, lxxvii–lxxix, 304–12.]

ADAM JOHNSTON, M.A., min. and provost 1569 and 1572.—[*Comps. Sub Coll. of Thirds, Linlithgow*, etc.]
1569

GIDEON PENMAN, his son, James, apprenticed to James Edmondstoune, merchant, Edinburgh, 13th April 1681.—[*G. R. Sas.*, 2 Ser., ii, 417.]
1639

ANDREW DONN, resident with his wife at Inveresk 1694; his son, Alexander, apprenticed to James Spotswood, barber, 7th March 1701.—[*Inveresk Poll Tax Roll*, 24.]
1682

MATTHEW SELKIRK, marr. Agnes, daugh. of George Cunningham, merchant burgess, Edinburgh; his son, James, apprentice to Robert Geddes, surgeon apothecary, Edinburgh, 2nd Nov. 1709; his daughs.—Janet (marr. John Cleghorn, min. of Wemyss); Agnes (marr. Charles Wright, portioner of Newbigging); Laurence.—[*Edin. Burgess Roll*, 14th June 1695.]
1690

CHARLES PRIMROSE, marr. (1) daugh. of Bailie Duncan McIntosh; (2) Ann, daugh. of Nicolas Moffat, stabler.
1729

1840 JOHN CRAWFORD, his daughs.—Lillian Ann, died 28th Oct. 1918; Georgiana, died 11 May 1923; Agnes, died 11th Jan. 1927.

1884 HENRY DUNCAN, his widow Cecilia Bertram Baillie, died 25th Jan. 1933; his son, Alexander William, died 18th Nov. 1934; his daugh., Mary Henrietta, died at London 26th March 1924.

1902 STEVENSON MACNAB, dem. 5th Dec. 1946, died 14th Oct. 1947.

DALKEITH

In Dec. 1372 Robert II granted licence to Sir James de Douglas, Kt., of Dalkeith, to found a chaplainry or chaplain in the Chapel of St Nicolas, Dalkeith, with an endowment of £6 13s. 4d. stg. annual rent from the lands of Horsbruke in Peebles, and also to Sir Henry de Douglas, Kt., to infeft the foresaid chaplain in 5 merks annual rent from whatever source he pleased. The same king on 25th Oct. 1375 confirmed a charter of Sir James de Douglas, Kt. of Dalkeith, founding in the chapel another chaplainry in honour of the Virgin Mary and St Nicolas, for the souls of Sir John de Douglas, his father, and Lady Agnes, his mother, the endowment being the lands of Suylt and Fethenane in Peebles. On 1st June 1406 Sir James erected the chapel, which he had enlarged and decorated, into a collegiate church for six chaplains, one of whom was provost. To the provost were assigned the lands of Dythment and Holden in the barony of West Calder. The provision for the first chaplain was the tenpound lands of Suylt and Fethenane to the extent of 20 marks annually; for the second, £10 stg., to wit 2 merks of the lands of Louchurde and 40s. annual rent of the lands of Kirkurde in Tweeddale; for the third 10 merks annual rent of the lands of Horsbruke "granted by us," and £3 annually from the lands of Wynkiston, Corstunyngiisfelde and Dillay-islande in the Sheriffdom of Peebles, granted by Sir Henry de Douglas, brother of Sir James, the chaplain to celebrate at the Altar of St Peter in the said chapel (collegiate church); and for the other two chaplains 22 merks and half the lands of Spittalhaulch and Ingalston in Tweeddale, formerly given by "our predecessors to the Culdees and pious uses," in equal portions. Manses were also provided for the provost and chaplains. On 17th May 1477 James, Earl of Morton, erected the collegiate church anew for a provost and six canonries or prebends which were reorganised and augmented, the Churches of Newlands, Kilbocho, and Mordington being appropriated to the collegiate church. The prebends were—Newlands; Romanhouse; Bordland; Kilbocho; Horsbruke; Mordington. Besides the Altar of St Peter, there were at least an Altar of the Virgin Mary, an Altar of the Holy Rood and an Altar of St John the Baptist. On 31st May 1504 James II confirmed a charter, apparently of 21st July 1503, by which Alexander Gifford, Recorder of Newlands, founded two chaplainries in the church, one at the Altar of the Holy Rood, with lands and tenement in Edinburgh, and other buildings, and 14 acres of "my Temple Lands" in Gullane, and the other at the Altar of St John the Baptist in the south aisle, with 5 merks apx. from "my Hospital in the town of Dalkeith on the south side of the highway of the same."

Originally Dalkeith formed part of the parish of Lasswade; but in 1467 the inhabitants of Dalkeith made representations as to the very great inconvenience and danger to which they were exposed during tempestuous weather in having to cross the streams that fell into the Esk, as they resorted to their parish church of Lasswade about 2 miles distant, and also that the vicarage teinds were ample to support two vicars, and craved Patrick Graham, Bishop of St Andrews, to disjoin Dalkeith from Lasswade. On 10th Oct. of the same year the Bishop consented to the proposed disjunction and erected Dalkeith into a separate parish, the inhabitants of the town and Castle of Dalkeith, of the park commonly called Graham's Park, and of Easter and Wester Coldane, etc., to be under the spiritual jurisdiction of a separate vicar who was to perform Divine Service at the Altar of the Virgin Mary in the collegiate church, and was to have the fruits of the said town, etc. The actual disjunction was to take effect upon the death or demission of Mr. James Lewington, vicar of Lasswade. The Altar or Chapel of the Virgin was thus constituted the Parish Church of Dalkeith. The Earl of Morton granted two roods of land for a manse. The rectory of Dalkeith was attached to the deanery of Restalrig; and on the dissolution of the deanery by Act of Parliament in 1592, Dalkeith secured full status as a parish. On 25th Nov. 1531 an indentor was made between James, Earl of Morton, and Sir John Crichtone, vicar of Dalkeith, by which the said vicar, considering the cost and expense incurred of James, Earl of Morton, John, Earl of Morton, and now James, Earl of Morton, "to find and obtene coles of Colden and Dalkeith," and the importance and emoluments the vicar and his successors might have, "if coals were won," for "the utilitie, augmentatioun, and ampler profit of the Kirk and Vicarage of Dalkeith," set and let to the Earl "all and hail the teynd coles of Colden and Dalkeith, with the teind sheaves of the lands of Braidwood," and the Earl, "to the laude glore and Honour of God Omnipotent, the blessit virgine Sanct Marie, His moder, patrones of the paroche kirk of Dalkeith, the bishop Sanct Nicolace, patron of the said nobill and michty Lordis College and Chapel of Dalkeith, and of all the Sancts," to pay to the vicar and his successors 40s. Scots annually.

On 5th Dec. 1384 Sir James de Douglas founded in Dalkeith Castle a chapel dedicated to the Virgin Mary and St John the Baptist, in memory of his wife, Agnes Dunbar, the endowments being the lands of Louchurde and Kirkurd, subsequently annexed to the collegiate church. Provision was made for the services being conducted at Lasswade amid interruptions of war or repairs to the Castle. On 27th June 1396 Sir James de Douglas also founded a "House of God near our Chapel of Dalkeith," for six poor and miserable persons, the endowment being the following annual rents: £6 3s. 4d. stg. from the lands of Esterhopkelyack, £4 stg. from lands of Newby in Peebles, £3 4s. 8d. stg. from lands of Morton in Dalkeith. Described as "two mean old houses called the Beid Houses," the hospital was sold for the benefit of the poor about 1752, when the charity workhouse was built. One house was opposite the old manse, the other a little to the east of the church.—[*Reg. Hon. de Morton*, ii, 98–9, 124–6, 151–4, 197, 211, 226–35, 247, 259–60, 294, 324–8; *Coll. Churches of Midlothian*, lxxxiii, lxxxv, lxxxvi, cxvi–cxix, 323; *Laing Charters*, 28, 160, 230.]

ARCHIBALD BOYD, provost of the collegiate church 10th Feb. 1558-9.
1558 —[*Reg. of Abbrev. Feu Charters of Church Lands*, i, 9.]

ANDREW DAVIDSON, vicar, 25th June 1563.—[*Reg. Mag. Sig.*, v, 1563 1214.]

ARCHIBALD SIMPSON, pres. to Altarage St John in Church 1st
1591 Aug. 1588. For "1586" read "1591."—[*Reg. Sec. Sig.*, lvii, 154.]

HEW CAMPBELL, son of George C., apparent of Shankstoun; marr. (1)
1635 Mary Ross, and had issue—Hugh; John; Elizabeth (marr. 2nd March 1656); Robert.—[*Books of Council and Session* 3rd April 1602; *Ayr Sas.*, iii, 2 Ser., 28th July 1624; *Reg. of Deeds* dcxvi, 19th Dec. 1655; *G. R. Sas.*, liii, 432; *Clan Campbell*, vi, 327.]

WILLIAM CALDERWOOD, his
1659 daugh. Elizabeth.—[*Edin. Sas.*, xxxv, 451.]

ALEXANDER HERIOT, his son
1683 Robert, apprentice to John Wilkie, merchant, Edinburgh, 24th Jan. 1694.

WILLIAM MUIR, marr. cont. recorded.—[*Reg. of Deeds, Dal.*,
1691 xviii, 827.]

JAMES ELPHINSTON, his son, John,
1700 apprentice to George Duncan, surgeon apothecary, 13th Jan. 1721.

DALKEITH—GLENCORSE

ANDREW GRAY, line 23, delete
1876 "Robert John died at school 1877."

DALKEITH WEST

HENRY FARQUHAR, died at London
3rd March 1946; his wife, Annie
1883 Muir Peace, died at Dover 27th
Dec. 1916; his daugh., Jane Lamont, died
at London 8th March 1935.

JOHN SCOTT, trans. to Saughtree 8th
1909 Sept. 1922.

CHARLES MICHAEL HEPBURN,
M.A., B.D., ord. 4th Jan, 1923;
1923 trans. to Moulin 25th Nov. 1926.

DOUGLAS DICKSON ROBERTSON,
trans. from Patna (*q.v.*) 21st April
1927 1927. Had issue—Margaret Selkirk,
born 7th Aug. 1928, died 17th Jan. 1937;
John James (twin), born 7th Aug. 1928,
died 16th Dec. 1943.

FALA

JOHN FERNIE THOMSON, his
widow, Jessie Wood McGowan,
1861 died 27th Nov. 1927.

JAMES HUNTER, died 26th Nov.
1915; his widow, Caroline Helen
1882 Parry, died 8th Sept. 1926; his
sons—David Ainslie, sergeant, Canadians,
killed in action 9th April 1917; Charles
Cook, died at Murtle 21st Nov. 1919.

JAMES ALEXANDER STEPHEN,
trans. from Orphir (*q.v.*) 19th May
1916 1916; min. of United Charge 1937.
Served in Great War as Lieut. R.G.A.
1916-19; died 10th Nov. 1946.

SOUTRA

There was in the church an altar dedicated to the Virgin Mary, the endowment of which was a croft in the burgh of Hawick, and Blacatis-Aiker, East Mains, in the barony of Hawick.—[*Reg. Great Seal*, iv, 1702.]

GLENCORSE

In or about 1230 Sir Henry de Brade granted to Holyrood Abbey the teinds of Baveley (Bavelaw) for the support of the chapel then called the Chapel of St Katherine in Pentland, and later St Katherines (or St Catherines)-in-the Hopes. The grant was confirmed by Charter of King Alexander II in 1236, and Bull of Pope Gregory IX in 1237. In Jan. 1243 David de Bernham, Bishop of St Andrews, confirmed the chapel to the abbey; and a Bull of Pope Innocent IV to the same effect followed in 1247. The foregoing facts hardly support the picturesque story of the founding of the chapel by Sir William St Clair of Rosslyn, which narrates that while hunting in the Pentlands King Robert the Bruce was baulked by a white deer specially fleet of foot, and in his difficulty asked his attendant nobles whether one of their dogs could secure the animal. Without hesitation Sir William St Clair pledged his head against the forest of Pentland Moor that his two dogs would kill the deer before it crossed the march Burn. The king assented; and then came the chase, which went on till it was close on the Burn. In despair of securing the animal, Sir William threw himself from his horse and invoked the aid of St Katherine. At once one of his dogs stopped the deer in the middle of the stream, and the other turned it back to the winning bank and killed it. Sir William's reward was the lands of Logan House, Kirkton, and Earnscraig; and in gratitude for St Katherine's help he built a chapel to her honour on the spot where he had knelt in prayer. While the story can hardly be true, it may be that in some way Sir William was a benefactor of the chapel which was in existence more than a century earlier. Some time prior to 1560 Glencorse became a parish with the chapel as the church; and in the 17th century there occur the designations the Church of St Catherine-in-the-Hopes; and under that designation the church was attached to the Bishopric of Edinburgh on its erection by Charles I in 1633. At an earlier period, apparently in or soon after 1602, the parish had been united to Lasswade. But on 18th June 1612, on the ground that "Glencorse is not able to interteine ane minister for the present as is allegit," and also on account of the distance of Lasswade from Glencorse, the Presbytery consented "to the union of the twa kirks," Glencorse and Penicuik, "ane reasonable augmentation" to be "provyded fra Glencors for the present minister of Penycuik and his successors." The union with Lasswade, however, was not disannulled; and the minister of Lasswade retained his right to the double benefice. In any case the arrangement does not appear to have yielded satisfactory results for Glencorse; and on 26th Oct. 1615 the parishioners complained to the Presbytery "of ye want of the Word and Sacramentis," and desired "most earnestlie ane pastor." The minister of Lasswade agreed, "provyding that in respect of his strict and grit necessities his stipend was not imparit." The lack of stipend prevented Glencorse being made a separate charge; but on 23rd Dec. 1615 the Presbytery resolved that a colleague be appointed to the minister of Lasswade, his particular duty being to overtake the work at Glencorse. In this arrangement the people of Glencorse concurred; and the emoluments of the colleague were provided by the heritors of both parishes. By Act of Parliament on 8th March 1647 Glencorse was disjoined from Lasswade and made into a separate parish. In the same year, on account of the church being situated at the west end of the parish—it was only 20 yards from the March Burn—a new church was erected in a central position on the Erncraig. The work does not appear, however, to have been wholly satisfactory, for on 6th June 1661 there was laid before the Presbytery a reference of the Kirk Session of 1st May narrating the "ruinous state of that part of the kirk from the Eastern door to the Western door, which is holden up for the present by props of timber, notwithstanding whereof the whole side wall in that bounds is most like to fall," and craving speedy repairs. Four years later the church was in large part rebuilt. A new church was in process of building in 1694–5, and in the latter year was burned without being completed. Rebuilding took place in 1699. A scheme of renovation was carried out in 1811, when the tower was added.

The last service took place in the church on 5th Dec. 1885; and thereafter the church, whose ruins still stand on Erncraig, gave place to the present church situated near Milton Bridge. Within the latter church is a baptismal font which was discovered deep down in the middle of the floor of the old church during the renovation work of 1811. Probably it had been removed from the Church of St Catherine in 1647. For the increase of Glencorse stipend Parliament in 1648 mortified a yearly sum of 140 merks which had previously been paid out of the lands of Castlelaw for the maintenance of the organs and singers of the Chapel Royal of Stirling.—[*Charters of Holyrood*, 45–6, 64, 65–6, 179–80; *Acts Scott. Parl.*, vi, (1), 733, vi, (2), 482; Grant's *Call of the Pentlands*, 89–99.]

LANCELOT GIBSON, reader 1573, still in office 1585.—[*Comps. Gen. Coll. of Thirds.*]
1573

THOMAS DOUGLAS, M.A., min. 1576; also in charge at Dalkeith.—[*Comps. Gen. Coll. of Thirds.*]
1576

JAMES PORTEOUS, M.A., min. at Soutra; on 23rd Dec. 1615 the Presbytery, with the concurrence of the parishioners of Glencorse, chose him as colleague to George Ramsay, min. at Lasswade and Glencorse, "to furder (said) Mr George at Leswaid in word and discipline, as also to instruct thaim (parishioners of Glencorse) by preiching and chatechising, yea, administer to thaim also the sacramentis in due and proper season in and at thair awin Kirk at Glencors"; trans. and adm. as colleague 8th Aug. 1616; in 1636 he "related (to the Presbytery) that for sa meikle as ye paroche of Glencors had been annexed to his Kirk (Lasswade) thir many yeirs bygane, and he had been serving yaim according to his abilitie, bot now aige on his pairt, and distance of place and ye charge of his awin Kirk makes him unable to repair thither, and yairfoir hes demitted ye said kirk (Glencorse) to Mr Alexander Robesoun, who hes resaved
1616

presentation yairto be ye Kings Majestie."
—[Grant's *Call of the Pentlands*, 91–3.]

GEORGE PURVES, M.A., on his complaint that notwithstanding that he had given obedience to the proclamation for prayers for the King and Queen, certain persons had come "to his house and discharged him from preaching . . . and took away the keys of the kirk door and the Kirk Byble," Parliament, on 7th May 1689, ordered the keys and the Bible to be restored to him, and the laird of Glencorse to afford him protection.—[*Acts Scott. Parl.*, ix, App. 10a.]
1674

JOHN WILSON, eldest son of Thomas W., merchant burgess of Glasgow, admitted burgess of Glasgow 1748.
1699

ALEXANDER TORRENCE left a bequest of £1,000 in favour of the church, which is said to have been invested in ground annuals in respect of the Municipal Buildings, Portobello.
1818

WILLIAM BAILLIE STRONG, dem. 24th July 1928, died at Edinburgh 17th Dec. 1930; his daughs.—Helen Marjorie (marr. 22nd Nov. 1919 James C. Spence of Debrugarth, Assam); Katherine Baillie (marr. 24th June 1925 John Fleming, C.A.); his son, William, M.A., C.A. assistant controller Transport, Sudan Government.
1878

DONALD MacASKELL BEGBIE, formerly of Freuchie (*q.v.*), trans. from St John's, Leith, 5th Dec. 1928; his son, Donald William David, killed in an accident 20th Feb. 1941.
1928

HERIOT

WILLIAM McGEORGE, son of James McG., schoolmaster, Dumfries, and Marion Gladstanes; marr. Katherine, daugh. of John Coupland, elder and barber of Dumfries, and had issue—Robert, died 17th Dec. 1680. Line 6, delete "son of min. of Caerlaverock."
1689

ADAM STEEL, his daugh. Helen (marr. proc. 21st May 1749 James Robertson, clerk to London Paving Co.).
1734

ALEXANDER HUNTER, marr. (3) Lily, daugh. of Thomas Malcolm, shoemaker, Edinburgh.
1791

DANIEL CAMERON, his daugh., Amelia Nisbet, died 19th April 1931.
1869

JOHN FRANCIS BROWN, dem. 15th Dec. 1927, died at Gorebridge 25th Nov. 1928.
1871

HARRY SMITH, trans. from Old Kilpatrick (*q.v.*) 7th June 1928; dem. 31st March 1936, D.D. (Aberdeen, 1st April 1925); died 8th Aug. 1942; his daughs.—Margaret Miller Frazer (marr. 7th March 1933 Thomas Alexander, elder son of William Mathieson, Shoesbourne, Heriot); Lettice Ruthven, B.Sc. (marr. 18th Dec. 1934 Peter Chalmers Somerville, B.Com., A.I.C.S., Antwerp). Addl. Publications—Editor *Life and Work*, 1925; *Not against Flesh and Blood*, 1923, is included in Modern Scottish Poets: *A Book of Twentieth Century Scottish Verse* and *Oor Mither Tongue*, Scots Anthology.
1928

INVERESK

There was in the church an altar dedicated to St Ninian, and in St Ninian's Aisle there was also an altar dedicated to the Virgin Mary. On 6th March 1475–6 Simon de Preston of Craigmillar, Kt., granted 10 merks of the lands of Cameron for a perpetual chaplain to celebrate in the church. Later this was designated the "Chaplainry of St Ninian called Cameron." In 1804 the old church was taken down and the existing church built. There were at least three chapels in the parish. The chapel dedicated to St Mary Magdalene, called Whitehill, was situated at Hailes on the banks of the Niddry Burn. The chapel dedicated to St James was in existence before 8th Sept. 1491, and may have been the chapel which stood at the head of Market Street where, in the first part of the 19th century, there were the ruins of an almshouse. The beginning of the Chapel of Loretto, dedicated to the Virgin Mary, is narrated in the *Diurnal of*

Occurrents under date 19th April 1533: "In this mene tyme, thair come an heremeit, callit Thomas Douchtie, in Scotland, quha haid been lang capitane (captive ?) befoir the Turk, as was allegit, and brocht ane ymage of our Lady with him, and foundit the cheppill of Laureit beside Musselburgh." There followed on 27th Jan. 1533-4 a charter of the bailies, burgesses and community of Musselburgh, granting in pure alms to Thomas Duchty, hermit of the Order of St Paul, first hermit of Mount Sinai, for his lifetime and for his successors, hermits, for building the Chapel of the Blessed Virgin Mary of Loretto, with small house and garden, as might be pleasing to them, a piece of vacant land of their territory and liberty, containing 5 roods, at the east boundary of the burgh near *le chaypule*, bounded by the common green on the east and west. On 1st Aug. 1534 James V supplied furnishings and vestments for the altar of the chapel, provision being made for embroidering the royal arms on the vestments and "frunlett." The "small house" was a cell, the residence of the hermit, adjoining the chapel; and it may be assumed that Thomas Duchty was "Thomas, Hermeit in Lareit," to whom Alexander, Earl of Glengairn, addressed a satire exposing the hypocrisy of the clergy—"Ane Epistell direct fra the halie Hermeit of Alareit to his Brethern, the Gray Friars." The chapel was destroyed in Hertford's expedition in 1544, but was repaired; and on 10th Dec. 1568 Sir Gavin Walker, hermit of the chapel, with consent of the patrons, the bailies and community of Musselburgh, set in feu to Andrew Sanderson, burgess of the burgh, the chapel with its room and garden. In 1590 the stones of the chapel were utilised for the building of Musselburgh Tolbooth.

The church was dedicated to St Michael and All Angels.—[*Cal. of Scott. Supplications*, 119, S.H.S.; *Reg. Great Seal*, ii, 1228; iii, 1403; iv, 1909; *Lord High Treas. Accs.*, 200-1; *Diurnal of Occurrents*, 17; *Caprington Letter Bk.*, 14; James Young's *Prot. Bk.*, 483, 485; *Ancient Church Dedications in Scotland*, 347.]

JOHN BURNE, min. before Aug. 1567.
1567 —[*Edin. Tests.*, i, 73.]

EDWARD LAYOS or **LYNE**, reader,
1570 pres. to vicarage 26th June 1579 in succession to Thomas Makgill.—[*Reg. Sec. Sig.*, xl, 15.]

ANDREW BLACKHALL, his son,
1574 Andrew, student of grammar, pres. to Prebendary of Restalrig 7th July 1582.—[*Reg. Sec. Sig.*, xlix, 14.]

RICHARD OGILL, son of Henry O.
1590 of Hartramwade, pres. to vicarage 12th May 1590 on death of Michael Baillie.—*Reg. Sec. Sig.*, lx, 128.]

ADAM COLT, pres. to vicarage on
1597 dem. of Edward Lyne, last vicar.—[*Chart. of Dunfermline MS.*, ii, 148a.]

PATRICK HENDERSON, M.A.,
1607 reader, 3rd Jan. 1607 and 4th Aug. 1608.—[*Yester Writs*, 1045, 1062.]

ARTHUR MILLAR, M.A., resident in
1680 Inveresk, with his wife, 1694; had right to half-year's stipend at Whitsunday of that year.—[*Inveresk Poll Tax Book*, 23.]

RICHARD HOWIESON, had five
1694 children; his second son, Richard; Magdalen (marr. Henry Stewart, surgeon, Inverkeithing.—[*Fraser Writs Gen. Reg. House*, 16th Nov. 1707; *Inveresk Poll Tax Roll*, 17.]

JOHN WILLIAMSON, 2 col., line 2,
1702 delete "Agnes marr. Henry Robin, min. of Burntisland."

LESLIE MOODIE, born 29th Dec.
1806 1766.

JOHN GARDINER BEVERIDGE, his
1836 son, William Bryce, died 6th Feb. 1932; his daughs.—Janet Isabella (marr. William Macnab of Keithock); Mary Elizabeth Anne, died 14th Aug. 1933.

JAMES SHARP, licen. 13th May 1885; his daughs.—Muriel Margaret, died 22nd July 1918; Irene, died Edinburgh 28th Sept. 1925; Catherine, died 1st Aug. 1931.

1888

WILLIAM EDIE, D.D. (St Andrews, 5th July 1918), Chaplain to Royal Company of Archers 8th June 1927; M.V.O. 3rd Oct. 1929; died 22nd June 1936; his widow, Jean Irvine Fergusson, died 9th Nov. 1941; his son, Robert Miller, M.A., died 13th Dec. 1919.

1910

LASSWADE

Of the old church, apparently of the 13th century, and therefore in all likelihood the church dedicated by Bishop de Bernham on 6th May 1240, only a portion of the south wall in the old graveyard survives. There is also the ruin of a north transeptal aisle, now a mausoleum of the family of Clerk of Eldin, belonging to the 17th century. The medieval floriated finial cross above the entrance of the Drummond mausoleum in all likelihood belonged to the old church, as also did two sculptured fragments which are in the National Museum of Antiquities of Scotland. The present church was built in 1793. Apparently a short time prior to 1451 the church became a mensal church of the Bishopric of St Andrews. But on 26th June of that year a Papal Decree, in answer to a petition by Bishop Kennedy of St Andrews, revoked and dissolved the appropriation of the church to that purpose, the actual severance to be effected with Kirkliston Church, which was to take the place of Lasswade as a mensal church, became vacant by the death or resignation of the rector thereof. The connection with St Andrews was renewed however, when, during a voidance in the Church of St Andrews and with the consent of the Chapter, Prior David, vicar general, at the instigation of George Abernethy, who had become rector of Lasswade before 5th May 1465, united Lasswade Church in perpetuity to the capitular *mensa* of St Salvator's Church, St Andrews, the said George Abernethy being received as a Canon of St Salvator's. The union did not at once take effect; and on 20th Dec. 1468 the Pope, Paul II, made remit to delegates to enquire into the matter, and if they found that union had been decreed as stated, "to unite in perpetuity the said Church of Lasswade not exceeding 40 merks to the said *mensa*, so that on the resignation or death of said George Abernethy, the Dean and Chapter take possession of the Church and cause its cure of souls to be governed by one of the Canons or Chaplains of St Salvator's." Succeeding stages are marked by Bulls of Pope Sixtus IV, one on 31st May 1473, which united Lasswade (along with other churches) to the episcopal *mensa* of St Andrews, on the death or demission of the rector, and the other on 17th March 1477, which joined to St Salvator's Church a canonry and prebend in the Church of Lasswade, Robert Blackadder, rector of Lasswade, being made canon and prebendary, and 5 merks annually to be paid from the canonry to the common table of St Salvator's. The election of Robert Blackadder to the See of Aberdeen in 1480 rendered the parsonage vacant; and by Bull of Pope Sixtus on 8th Aug. 1482 it was united once more to the *mensa* of St Andrews. Five years later a Papal Bull effected the dissolution of the union with St Andrews, and united Lasswade to the collegiate church, Restalrig, attaching it to the deanery thereof. On 5th June 1592 an Act of Parliament dissolved the Deanery of Restalrig, constituted Lasswade a separate parish, and, excluding Dalkeith which also pertained to the deanery, erected "the haill permanent fruitis of the said deanry of Restalrig and qlk pertenit thairto of auld in ane severall and distinct personage to be callit the personage of Leswaid," and with the vicarage of the church, "quhen it sal happen to vaik," to become the stipend of the minister and his successors "in all tymes cuming." In 1601 the vicarage became part of the stipend; and in 1648 Parliament ratified the mortification by Mr James Fairlie, parson of Lasswade, to Mr John Weir, parson of

Restalrig, of the endowments of the parsonage of Lasswade not lying within that parish, Lasswade thus becoming dependent entirely upon its own parochial endowments. By Bull of 11th March 1478-9 Pope Sixtus IV gave faculty and licence to a hospital, "lately erected" near the church of Lasswade by Robert Blackadder, rector, to God and the Blessed Virgin, and under the invocation of the Blessed Mary of Consolation, "for the poor, for pilgrims, for the infirm, the sick, and other miserable persons wishing to betake themselves to it for a time." By another Bull of the same date the Pope gave executors and keepers of the hospital, and by still another of 4th April previously he had granted indulgences for its erection and maintenance. Beside the "brig of Leswaid" there was a hospital with chapel, dedicated to St Leonard. To it belonged the lands and mill of Powtoun (Polton), which in July 1500 Sir David Ramsay, parson of Foulden and chaplain of the hospital, with consent of his nephew, Sir Alexander Ramsay of Dalhousie, patron of said hospital, granted in feu to William Ramsay of Powtoun (Polton). Evidently one of the Dalhousie family had founded the hospital, the patronage of which continued with that family.—[Lockhart's *Ch. in Scot. in 13th Century*, 46; *Report of Anc. Mon. Commission, Midlothian*, 97; *Cal. Papal Reg., Letters*, x, 220, xii, 635-6, 794; *Acts Scott. Parl.*, iii, 551, vi (2), 84; Theiner's *Vetera Monumenta*, 481, 483, 484; *Reg. Sec. Seal*, i, 551; *Retours*, i, 108, xxxi, 323; *Chart. Coll. Churches of Midlothian*, 237; Walcott's *Anc. Ch. of Scotland*, 389, 409.]

1565 WILLIAM BARBOUR, pres. 1569 on death of Sir Michael Henderson.—[*Reg. Pres. Bene.*, i, 22.]

1581 GEORGE RAMSAY, his pres. to vicarage in 1601 was in consequence of the death of Mr John Manderston and was in terms of the Act of Dissolution of the Deanery of Restalrig, which decreed that he should receive the vicarage when it became vacant.—[*Reg. Pres. Bene.*, iii, 51.]

1592 JOHN MANDERSTON, vicar of Glencorse and Lasswade prior to 1592; died before 1601.—[*Reg. Pres. Bene.*, iii, 51.]

1616 JAMES PORTEOUS, M.A., his pres. to the parsonage and vicarage of Lasswade in 1617 was upon the resignation of George Ramsay, who thus helped to make provision for James Porteous, his colleague in the charge of Lasswade and Glencorse.—[*Reg. Pres. Bene.*, iv, 146.]

1876 JAMES ALEXANDER BURDON, his widow, Marianne Imrie, died 12th Oct. 1927; his son, Harry, died 12th Dec. 1929.

1905 ROBERT HAMILTON PRYDE, app. Presby. Clerk 4th July 1929, died suddenly 6th Jan. 1930; his daugh., Frances (marr. 14th July 1939 Cyril Jones, min. of St Andrews, Lochgelly); his widow, Sarah Eleanor Braithwaite, died 10th March 1943.

LOANHEAD

1884 ALEXANDER STEWART, dem. 13th Oct. 1927, died at Corstorphine 18th Feb. 1929; his widow, Isobel Glover Johnston, died 1st May 1933; his daugh., Jessie Bremner (marr. 4th Jan. 1936 Matthew Campbell Thomson, curator, Carnegie Aquarium, Edinburgh).

1928 THOMAS MAVER PATERSON, born Aberdeenshire 26th May 1901, son of John P., farmer, and Helen Mary Maver; educ. at Univ. of Aberdeen, M.A. (1922); Edin. B.D. (1925); licen. by Presb. of Edinburgh 12th May 1926, assistant, South Leith; ord. 14th March 1928; trans. to Sinclairtown 27th Nov. 1935. Marr. 16th July 1930 Agnes Campbell, M.A., only daugh. of Andrew Bowden, Ryehill Gardens, Leith, and has issue—Agnes Ruth, born 6th May 1931; John Maver, born 6th March 1935; Alistair Andrew, born 25th Dec. 1936, died 22nd June 1937; Helen Campbell, born 14th Aug. 1943.

NEWBATTLE

There was in Newbattle Abbey an altar dedicated to St Katherine.—(*Book of Assumption*, 79, 344.) The patronage of the Church of Masterton (Newbattle) was granted to Newbattle Abbey by Robert I 306-29. The Church of St Mary Newbattle was dedicated by the Bishop of Moray 13th March 1233. At Bryan's Chapel there was a chapel dedicated to St Briox.—[*Reg. Mag. Sig.*, i, app. ii, 525, viii, 1146.]

ROBERT WILSON had parsonage and vicarage in succession to John Hay.
1573 —[*Acts and Dec.*, lv, 12.]

ANDREW MILLAR, pres. to parsonage and vicarage and to be
1583 reader 9th Jan. 1583 and 6th June 1584, on death of Robert Wilson.—[*Reg. Pres. Bene.*, ii (2), 104.]

JOHN HERRIES, pres. on dem. of Andrew Millar, probably son of
1583 Archibald H. of Maidenpap. Marr. Barbara Harlaw and had issue—John, M.A., held Prebend of Kirkbank in the Collegiate Church of St Bothans, which on 22nd March 1608-9 he received for life from James, Lord Hay of Yester, in succession to Daniel Hay. Line 7, delete "probably."—[*Cal. of Yester Writs*, 1058, 1059; *Reg. Sec. Sig.*, lv, 32.]

THOMAS AMBROSE, son of William A., merchant burgess of Stirling.—
1606 [*Edin. Tests.*, 3rd Dec. 1606.]

ANDREW CANT, M.A.; on 19th Dec. 1638, on a supplication by Lord
1639 Lothian from Newbattle, the General Assembly deliberated whether Mr Cant should be transported from Pitsligo to Edinburgh or to Newbattle ("the Commissioners of Edinburgh alledged that they had made an election of him 24 yeares since"), and by a majority decided in favour of Newbattle.—[Peterkin's *Recs. of the Kirk of Scot.*, 187.]

JOHN MOSSMAN, his son, George, apprentice to Alexander Mitchell,
1688 barber, 21st Jan. 1696.

GEORGE SHEPHERD, his son, John,
1784 min. of Muirkirk.

THOMAS GORDON, his daughs.—Amy Mary, died at Crieff 21st Dec.
1843 1938; Janet Elizabeth (Mrs Sym), died 23rd April 1945.

JOHN CHARLES CARRICK, his widow, Annie Jane Russell, died
1885 25th June 1915.

WILLIAM LINDSAY, trans. to Langholm 3rd March 1922.
1913

JOHN ARNOTT HAMILTON, trans. to Kirkfieldbank (*q.v*) 14th July
1922 1922. Addl. Publications—*A Mediaeval City in Greece* (Aberdeen, 1921); *Churches in Palermo* (London, 1929); *Newbattle Parish Church, 1727-1827* (Edinburgh, 1928); *Byzantine Architecture and Decoration* (London, 1933); *The Story of Newbattle Church and Abbey* (1945); *Byzantine Architecture* (London, 1945).

NEWCRAIGHALL

ARCHIBALD PRENTICE, died 16th Nov. 1919; his sons—James Alexan-
1886 der Webster, corporal, 3rd Dragoon Guards, killed in Flanders 6th June 1915; Archibald Hepburn Gardner, died at Mombasa 21st March 1926; his daugh. Maisie (marr. 10th Nov. 1917 Lieut.-Col. William Henry Forsyth, R.A.M.C.); his widow, Jane Ann Russel, died at Tonbridge, Kent, 25th Nov. 1931.

CHARLES HEUGHAN, trans. to Hutchesontown, Glasgow, 29th
1912 March 1917.

ADAM HUNTER, born Sheardale, Dollar, 29th Oct. 1870, son of John
1917 H., colliery manager, Kirkintilloch, and Mary Morris; educ. Dollar Academy, Univ. and Trinity College, Glasgow; licen. by Free Church Presb. of Glasgow, May 1900; Assistant Partick and Springburn, Glasgow; ord. to Shettleston Free Church, 1905; trans. to Glenorchy, 1908; trans. to Rothesay Free Church, 1913; trans. and adm. 4th Sept. 1917. Marr. 16th Dec. 1902 Elizabeth Paul, daugh. of William Gray,

Portobello, and has issue—Elizabeth Paul, born 12th Oct. 1903, M.A. (marr. 6th Sept. 1932 Robert Mitchell, Musselburgh); Mary Morris, L.D.S., R.C.S.E., born 22nd April 1906 (marr. 17th April 1946 Peter Bryce Gunn, min. of Roxburgh); John (Ian), born 9th Nov. 1907; William Gray, born 3rd April 1909.

NEWTON

1561 DAVID BELL, exhorter before 12th March 1561-2 and also 5th Nov. 1569.—[*Edin. Tests.*, i, 332.]

1576 LAURENCE WATSON, reader; for "1576" read "1567"; pres. to vicarage 16th March 1573 on death of Sir John Crawford.—[*Reg. Pres. Bene.*, 1, (2), 17.]

1586 JOHN BARBOUR, reader, Pentland; pres. to vicarage 14th July 1587 on death of Sir Laurence Watson; still reader 1603.—[*Reg. Sec. Sig.*, lv, 99; *Comps. Surplus Thirds of Benefices.*]

1681 ROBERT BANNERMAN, son of Alexander B. of Elsick and his wife, Marion, daughter of Alexander Hamilton of Easter Binning; resident with his wife and son, Alexander, in Tron Parish, Edinburgh, 4th Nov. 1694.—[*Tron Poll Tax Roll*, 2; *Complete Baronetage*, iv, 317.]

1700 THOMAS MOFFAT, his daugh., Mary (marr. proc. 28th March 1762 John Sprott, candlemaker, Edinburgh).

1801 THOMAS SCOTT, his daugh., Margaret Louisa, died 9th July 1836.

1863 MALCOLM MACGREGOR, his widow, Jane Snowdon, died 16th Feb. 1922; his daugh., Margaret Arnot, died 10th July 1945.

1897 JOHN MACBETH, died 5th Oct. 1923.

1924 WILLIAM CARRIC CLARK, ord. 3rd April 1924; trans. to Montrose Second Charge 7th Dec. 1927.

1928 FREDERICK RITCHIE MITCHELL, born 15th May 1899; son of Alexander M., solicitor and provost, Musselburgh, and Annie Rose Ritchie; educ. at Univ. of Edinburgh, M.A. (1922), B.D. (1925); licen. by Presb. of Dalkeith, 1927; assistant St Paul's, Leith; ord. 20th April 1928; trans. to Orwell Park Presb. Church, Liverpool, 1st Oct. 1930. Marr. 8th Aug. 1931 Margaret Wilson Shaw, daugh. of William Mackay Lennox, Town Clerk, Kilsyth, and has issue—Margaret Lennox, born 18th Oct. 1935; Eva Ann, born 18th May 1938.

NORTH ESK

On 7th June 1649 there was submitted to Parliament a supplication of heritors, members, ministers and kirk session, and inhabitants of Inveresk, to the effect that upon a decision of Synod in Nov. 1648 the Presbytery had visited Inveresk on 5th April 1649, had come to the finding that over 2,000 communicants of the church "was too much for one man." and therefore deemed it necessary that a division of the parish was necessary, and that "the Burgh of Musselburgh and the Fisherrow be erected into a new parish by itself." Having perambulated the bounds, the Presbytery did design the place where a kirk should be built, and it now asked Parliament to ratify the same and "grant an Act for the erection of the said kirk in a paroch by itself, that so with all diligence convenient some course may be taken for building of the same." The matter was remitted to the Commission for the Plantation of Kirks, etc., and the division of 1650 was the outcome.—[*Acts Scott. Parl.*, vi, (2), 393.]

1719 ROBERT BONALY, his son, Robert, apprentice to John More, merchant, Edinburgh, 17th Oct. 1739.

1865 HENRY MONCRIEFF MACGILL, his widow, Janet Seed Whyte, died at Levenhall, 3rd Jan. 1926; his son, Wakefield, died at Manchester 23rd March 1938; his daugh., Jane Whyte, died 23rd Jan. 1942.

JOHN ASHPLANT NICHOLLS, trans. to Cambusnethan, 16th May 1917.
1910

DAVID DUNCAN, trans. from Duntocher (*q.v.*) 17th Oct. 1917; his wife, Jessie McAinsh, died 13th Jan. 1934. He died at Crieff, 20th July 1940; his son, Alastair Jamieson, solicitor, died Sept. 1940.
1917

ORMISTON

There was in the church an altar dedicated to the Virgin Mary.—[*Chart. of Newbattle*, 142.]

ANDREW SIMSON, min. in 1571.—[*Comps. Sub Coll. of Thirds, Linlithgow*, etc.]
1571

NATHANIEL HARLAW, pres. to Borthwick 13th Oct. 1594–5, on death of Nicol Hay.—[*Reg. Sec. Sig.*, lxvii, 75.]
1591

JOHN SINCLAIR, col. 2, lines 8 and 12, for '1662 and 1663'' read "1682 and 1683''; his son Patrick,, rector of Ailmertoun, Norfolk; his daugh., Jean (marr. 17th June 1687 Andrew Hogg, W.S.), died May 1691.
1647

JOHN COCKBURN, marr. Anna Garden.
1688

JAMES BANNERMAN, his daugh., Jemima Margaret, died 25th June 1929.
1833

WILLIAM JOHNSTON, his widow, Mary Mackay, died 4th March 1934.
1880

DAVID CUNNINGHAM GRAHAM, dem. 16th May 1924; died at Bourne, Massachusetts, 11th Oct. 1937.
1911

WILLIAM YOUNG WHITEHEAD, trans. from Law (*q.v.*) 26th Sept. 1924. Ph.D. (1929). Addl issue, William James Bethune, born 19th June 1921. Publication—*History of Ormiston* (1938).
1924

PENICUIK

The present church was built in 1771 and enlarged in the first half of the 19th century. Near it are the ruins of the earlier church, post-reformation and probably 17th century. In April 1251 the Church of Mount Lothian was confirmed as a chaplainry to Holyrood Abbey by David de Bernham, Bishop of St Andrews; and it was attached to the Bishopric of Edinburgh on its erection by Charles I in 1633. The ruins of the church are situated in the churchyard in a wooded enclosure north-north-east of Mount Lothian. Newhalls House is said to have been the site of a Cistercian convent. About 60 yards south-west of the house are fragmentary remains of a chapel, of which in the middle of the 18th century there existed considerable portions of the walls, the east gable showing a pointed window. The ground on the west side of the chapel was termed Chapel Yard. At the close of the 18th century there still remained vestiges of a hospital, termed Back Spittal or Old Spittal House, at the side of the stream on the north of Spittal Hill. There was also a hospital farther south at Spittal Farm. In the same area are Friarstown and Glebe Croft, the latter possibly identical with St Robert's Croft described as situated at the confluence of the Spittal Burn and Monk's Burn. At Polmathorn there was a chapel dedicated to the Virgin Mary.—[*Charters of Holyrood*, 63; *Reg. Great Seal*, viii, 2225, x, 423, 425, 603; Grant's *Call of the Pentlands*, 124; *Report Anc. Monuments Commiss., Midlothian*, 150–1.]

WILLIAM PENYCUKE, son of Sir John P. of Penycuke, parson 1563, and still min. 16th Jan. 1594–5; designated, also vicar of Urr and Provost of the Collegiate Kirk-of-the-Fields; in 1564 he gave a charter of the Parsonage Kirklands and Glebe to his nephew, William P., son of John P. of P.; marr. contract 27th Feb. 1570 Katherine, daugh. of Alexander Wardlaw of Kilbaberton, with issue, including James, eldest son.—[*Cal. of Charters*, ix, 1920, x, 2287; *Acts and Decreets*, xli, 174, xlvii, 404, li, 376, cxcii, 258; *Reg. of Deeds*, xi, 273, 25th Oct. 1570; *Reg. Privy Council*, ix, 501; *Reg. Abbrev. Feu-Charters of Ch. Lands*, ii, 115; *Reg. Great Seal*, 10th Jan. 1507–8; *Reg. Sec. Sig.*, lxvii, 98.]
1556

GEORGE TAIT, min. in 1562, reader 31st March 1566 and 11th Jan. 1575–6.—[*Test. Inventories MS.*; *Test. James Tweedie* 18th Dec. 1575–6, *Coll. Gen. Thirds*, 1562, 102.]
1562

JOHN BARBOUR, exhorter, Mount Lothian, 18th Dec. 1577 and 21st Feb. 1578–9.—[*Edin. Tests.*, vi, 243, 325.]
1577

EBENEZER BROWN, his daugh., Margaret (marr. April 1773 William Braidwood, clerk, Edinburgh).
1746

JOHN HOME, marr. 15th Jan. 1857 Mary Cobden (died 6th May 1920), daugh. of George White, New York.
1856

WILLIAM SCOTT MONCRIEFF, his son, William George, died 2nd Jan. 1927; his daugh., Elizabeth Joanna, died 5th Oct. 1933.
1880

ROBERT THOMSON, died 1st April 1927; his son, John William, Lieut. R.G.A., died 4th Feb. 1919.
1888

WILLIAM MAXWELL LANDALE, pres. by the Presb. *jure develuto* and trans. from Straiton (*q.v.*) 15th Feb. 1928; dem. 30th June 1935; his wife, Anges Frances Anderson, died 9th June 1928. Marr. (2) 30th April 1931 Jessie, second daugh. of Robert Muirhead of Northern Lights Commission, Lasswade. He died suddenly at a football match, Edinburgh, 19th Sept. 1936.
1928

PENTLAND

To the Chapel of Pentland, which belonged to Holyrood Abbey, Alexander II granted 3 acres of land on 25th Aug. 1236. It was a parish church before 1275, the rectory being valued at 8s. in the taxation of that year.—[*Charters of Holyrood*, 46; Theiner's *Vet. Monumenta*, 139.]

GEORGE LUNDIE, son of David L. and Elizabeth, daugh. of Thomas Carkethill, burgess of Edinburgh; had issue—Susanna, born 5th Nov. 1578.—[Stephen's *Inverkeithing*, 187; *Dunfermline Par. Reg.*]
1589

ROSEWELL

JOHN HUNTER, dem. 17th May 1915, died at Edinburgh 4th April 1930; his wife, Christina Bayne Bell, died 26th Oct. 1920.
1876

JAMES MACKENZIE, M.A., ord. 28th Sept. 1915; trans to St Paul's, Perth, 29th Jan. 1919.
1915

JOHN ANDREW INGLIS, ord. 13th May 1919; trans. to Peterhead East, 12th Nov. 1926.
1919

JAMES MATHERS, born 5th June 1873, son of Thomas M., farmer, and Esther Sheldon; educ. at Royal Univ. of Ireland, B.A. (1897), and Univ. of Edinburgh, B.D. (1899); licen. by Presb. of Madras 1915; O.B.E. 1st Jan. 1919; adm. by General Assembly from Congregational Church May 1916; ord. by Presb. of Edinburgh as Secretary for Religious Work and Y.M.C.A. 21st Nov. 1920; app. to Craigmillar Mission 1926; trans. and adm. 3rd Feb. 1927; dem. 30th Sept. 1946. Marr. 29th Aug. 1901 Agnes Malseed, and has issue—Aileen Elizabeth, M.B., Ch.B., born 25th July 1902 (marr. 23rd Aug. 1935 John Edwards, Public Assistance Office, Newport, Monmouth); Agnes Doreen, M.A., born 20th April 1904 (marr. (1) 20th April 1929 Arthur Currie Gordon, min. of Foveran; (2) 2nd July 1947 Malcolm Manford Corner, min. of Drainie); Robert Campbell Malseed, born 14th July 1910, ord. 24th April 1936, min. of Mure Memorial, Baillieston; Amy Lillingston, born 16th Oct. 1912; Joyce, born 3rd Nov. 1914; Alison, born 27th March 1921. Publication—*The Master Builder, a Study of the Life of the Apostle Paul*.
1927

ROSLIN

The Chapel of Roslin, in the old civil parish of Lasswade, is the former Collegiate Church of Roslin founded in 1446 by William St Clair, Earl of Orkney, and Lord of Roslin, in honour of the Holy and Undivided Trinity, Father, Son and Holy Spirit, and the Most Glorious Virgin Mary, Mother of the Lord Jesus, and Matthew, the Apostle and Evangelist. At his death, between 4th Dec. 1476 and 29th March 1482, the building was unfinished; but the work was carried on to some extent by his younger son and successor as baron of Roslin, Sir Oliver Sinclair. The church, however, remained incomplete, the nave never having been begun, and of the transepts the east walls only having been erected. Besides the High Altar of St Matthew, there were in the church altars dedicated respectively to St Matthew, St Pater, St Andrew, and St Mary the Virgin, the last being situated in front of the central pillar, with a figure of the Virgin above it. There was also a lady-chapel which constituted the retrochoir, and contained, in addition to elaborate carving, a representation of the dance of death. The church, with the Castle of Roslin, was pillaged by an unruly mob during the night of 11th Dec. 1688. Dedicated also to St Matthew, there was a church prior to the collegiate church. Remnants of it exist in the cemetery, outside the west wall of which is St Matthew's Well.—[*Chart. Coll. Churches of Midlothian*, xciii-c., 327, 32.]

1877 JOSEPH LOUDON, died 23rd Dec. 1926; his wife, Margaret Mary Campbell Buist, died 23rd Feb. 1924; his daugh., Elizabeth Buist, died 5th April 1948.

1927 SYDNEY SMITH, formerly of Keith (*q.v.*); assistant St Cuthbert's, adm. 30th March 1927; died suddenly when returning from a baptism, 16th Oct. 1932.

STOBHILL

1888 DAVID WILKIE WILSON, died 10th March 1922; his daugh., Edith Agnes (marr. 9th Oct. 1929 Alexander Bache Walker, M.D., Newtongrange).

1922 JOHN ALEXANDER CALDERWOOD, ord. 8th Sept. 1922, trans. to Airdrie 20th May 1927.

1927 ROBERT MACPHERSON, born 23rd May 1892, son of John Forbes M., min. of South Parish, Greenock; educ. at Greenock Academy, Univ. of Glasgow, M.A. (1919); licen. by Presb. of Greenock 1920; assistant Paisley Abbey; ord. to Armadale 7th June 1922; trans. and adm. 23rd Sept. 1927; trans. to Craigrownie 14th July 1932. Marr. 21st Aug. 1922 Jessie Hardie, daugh. of Peter MacColl and Anne Hardie Stewart, and has issue—John Forbes, born 1st July 1923; Stewart MacColl, born 5th Nov. 1925; Anne Hannah, born 13th Nov. 1933.

TEMPLE

The roofless walls of the old church stand in the churchyard on a slope a short distance below the village of Temple and near the bridge which spans the South Esk. The main part appears to belong to the 13th century, but the west end, which shows signs of a heritor's loft, was rebuilt some time after the Reformation. A belfry of the 17th century crowns the east gable, and a weathering at the east end of the north wall may indicate that there a sacristy had existed. The present church occupies a site on the estate of Braidwood on the north side of the road opposite the churchyard. Designed by Thomas Brown, architect, Uphall, it was built by Thomas Creak, Temple, at a cost of £868 in 1831–2, and was ready for occupation in April–May of the latter year. Near the gate an offering house was built. The bell pertained to the old church. In part at least the manse has been built upon the walls of the buildings of the Templar Preceptory; and there have been found on the west side of the manse grounds traces of an old wall running parallel to and near the ravine of the South Esk. The patronage of the Church of Clerkington was granted in 1338 to Newbattle Abbey by Christine Bisset, Lady of Clerkington, widow of Sir John Bisset, Kt., with confirmation in 1359 by her son, Walter Bisset. Later its fruits belonged to the Collegiate Church of Corstorphine. The site of the church, within the grounds of Rosebery, is marked by several old tombstones. The Chapel (or Church) of Moorfoot, now in a very ruinous condition, is situated a short distance from Moorfoot farm. It was linked with the lands of Moorfoot, which in 1142 were granted to Newbattle Abbey by David I.

TEMPLE

Temple was formerly called Balantroda. To the Knights Templars David I gave a grant of the lands of Balantrodach, where they established their first seat. In 1312 their place was taken by the Knights of St John. Friar Thomas was Master of the Hospital of St John of Jerusalem at Balantroda in 1354. The church was dissolved from the collegiate church of Corstorphine in 1634; and that was ratified by Parliament in 1646, "that the samine may remaine as ane several kirke and benefice dismembered thairfrom." How long the church continued to be used for worship is uncertain. On 17th Dec. 1669, when Parliament ratified the Crown Charter whereby Sir John Nicolson of Lasswade acquired the barony of Clerkington including the parsonage and vicarage and the patronage of the church, it was decreed that in time coming Nicolson be "the propper names and designations respective of the forsaids lands, paroch kirk, and Parochine." In 1749 reversion was made to the name Clerkington.—[*Acts Scott. Parl.*, v, 433, vii, 425; *Reg. Great Seal*, i, 326, App., ii, 1173, 1218; *Retours*, iii, 212, xlvi, 166, 170; *Hist. MSS. Commis. Reports*, iii, 414; *Charters of Newbattle*, 292-3, 295; see Corstorphine.]

JOHN BROWN, reader, 1562.—[*Comps. Gen. Coll. of Thirds.*]
1562

JOHN BARBOUR, pres. to vicarage 2nd Jan. 1577 (see under Penicuik) on death of Sir William Henderson. —[*Reg. Pres. Bene.*, ii, (4), 631.]
1577

ROBERT MOWAT, his son, John, apprentice to John Baillie, surgeon, 1st March 1682.
1690

ARCHIBALD WALKER, his daugh., Ann (marr. proc. 7th Nov. 1762 Archibald Walker, merchant, Perth).
1738

JAMES GOLDIE, line 6, for "1897" read "1789." Jointly with the Earl of Roseberry and Robert Dundas of Arniston in 1840 founded and endowed at Toxside a school to provide elementary education for children of the labouring classes in the south-west portion of the parish.—[*Heritors Records*, 25th Jan. 1883.]
1789

THEOPHILUS SMITH, his widow, Roberta Florence Smith, died 19th Nov. 1943.
1843

JAMES WILLIAM BLAKE, dem. 13th June 1935; died at Balerno 4th Jan. 1943; his wife, Beatrix Hewat, died 16th Feb. 1919; his son, Alexander Kirkwood, died of wounds in France 16th June 1916.
1881

PRESBYTERY OF HADDINGTON

ABERLADY

In the churchyard there was a chapel dedicated to the Virgin Mary. At Kilspindie on the north-west side of the village there is said to have been a Culdee settlement. Within the policies of Luffness, a short distance south-west of Luffness House, are the ruins of the church of the Carmelite Friary of Luffness, with its churchyard. In the first half of the 18th century part of the cloisters and portions of the walls of the place still survived. In the north wall of the east end of the church there is an arched tomb with a solid stone coffin and the effigy of a knight with shield on breast and sword in hand. In 1723 it is described as "the tomb of Bickerton," evidently one of the family of that name, who, in the latter part of the 13th century and the first part of the 14th, in the persons of Walter and John de Bickerton, held Luffness off the successive crown vassals, Robert de Pinkeny and his brother and heir, Henry. It may be that the friary was founded by a member of the Bickerton family in the 13th century, the period to which the ruined church appears to belong. In 1361 it received a charter from David II; but no details are available. In 1335–6 it is narrated that from the lands of Luffness there was payable to the friary the sum of ten merks in alms annually as "constituted of old." The friary also held other lands and tenements, including five tenements in the town of Aberlady. At Ballincrieff there was a hospital dedicated to St Cuthbert and said to have been founded in the 12th century. On 23rd Nov. 1296 it is stated that from the two mills of Ballincrieff the hospital received twenty shillings yearly as alms from the late Robert de Pinkeny, as from the foundation of his ancestors, and that by the gift of said ancestors and said late Robert it possessed nine bovates and nine acres of land. At Edinburgh Castle on 29th July 1291 Walter, Master of the Hospital, swore fealty to Edward I; and similar fealty was sworn at Berwick on 28th August 1296 by William Tornall, Guardian of the Hospital. At Gosford there was another hospital, said to have been associated with the Collegiate Church of Dunglass. The site, Red Spittal, may indicate that the house belonged to the Red Friars; and the place may be identical with the establishment of Red Friars in this parish, which is said to have been founded by the Earl of Dunbar (Patrick, 7th Earl, died 1289) in 1286. The vicarage of the church was erected a prebend of Dunkeld Cathedral by Bishop Lauder of Dunkeld 1452–76.—[*Retours*, i, 173; *Cal. of Docs. Rel. to Scotland*, ii, 125, 227, iii, 338, 386; *Reg. Great Seal*, i, 24, App. II, 1381, vii, 258, 1666; *Haddington Sas.*, v, 635, f. 248; *Ragman Rolls*, 19, 147; *Procs. Soc. of Antiquaries*, iii, 299; and *Plate* xxx; Macfarlane's *Geog. Collections*, i, 374, *S.H.S.*; Walcott's *Anc. Ch. of Scotland*, 385; Chalmer's *Caledonia*, iv, 520.]

1567 GEORGE ADAMSON, reader, in office 28th July 1574, when he was called Addesoun.—[*Edin. Test.*, iii, 197.]

1567 WILLIAM KEMP, son of John K., prebendary of Aberlady 10th Oct. 1567.—[*Reg. of Deeds*, vii, 158.]

1577 ROBERT SINCLAIR, pres. to vicarage 27th Feb. 1577 on death of Walter Kemp.—[*Reg. Pres. Bene.*, i, (2), 67,]

1587 JOHN KER, as min. here pres. to vicarage 30th Nov. 1593 on death of Robert Sinclair.—[*Reg. Sec. Sig.*, lxvi, 7.]

ANDREW BLACKHALL, pres. on succession to John Ker.—[*P. S. Reg.*, lxxii, 190.]
1602

JOHN GRAY, eldest son of Andrew G., merchant, Haddington.—[*Reg. of Deeds, Durie*, xxi, 197.]
1684

ADAM GLASS, bapt. 2nd Nov. 1673, youngest son of Alexander G. of Sauchie and Marion, daugh. of James Rae of Cultonhove; marr. 30th May 1698 Helen Hamilton, and had issue—Alexander, born 4th Dec. 1699; Marion, born 5th Aug. 1702; Helen, born 29th Nov. 1704; Thomas, merchant, Stirling, born 3rd March 1706; Adam, born 13th April 1707. —[*Foulis of Ravelstoun Acc. Book*, xxiii; Turnbull's *Diary*, 374.]
1687

THOMAS CALDWELL, app. Depute Clerk of Assembly, 23rd May 1946; D.D. (St Andrews, 27th June 1947.]
1914

ATHELSTANEFORD

The church belonged to the Priory of Haddington. At the Byres there was a chapel dedicated to St Lawrence, which in 1328 David Lindsay, Lord of Crawford, granted to Newbattle Abbey, along with 2½ acres of land beside the chapel for a house to be built, and grazing in the common pasture of Byres, the abbey to supply the chapel with a monk or secular priest, and keep it in repair. The church was dedicated by Bishop de Bernham on 7th April 1244. It was built about the middle of the 12th century by Countess Ada, daughter of the Earl Warrenne and Surrey, and wife of Prince Henry of Scotland, and given by her to the Priory of Haddington. The present church was built in 1784. To Bernard Fraser of Drem Gilbert, Prior of St Andrews 1166-8, granted permission to have a chapel at Drem in return for certain lands and with oblations and obventions for the Church of Haddington which was then the mother church. On the same conditions the permission was repeated by Simon, Prior of St Andrews, who in 1225 resigned the office to become Prior of Lochleven. About 1412 William, Lord Lindsay, founded the Lady Chapel of Drem for himself, Christian, his wife, etc., and endowed it with certain lands and tenements at Drem. In 1483 the chapel was annexed to the "Chaplainrie and Alterage foundit within the paroche kirk of St Andrews at the altar called the Trinity Altar, situat within that part of the said paroche kirk callit the Lord Lindsay's Yle." In the garden west of Drem House are the ruins of the Chapel of St John, probably of the 15th century, which belonged to the Knights Templar. At Fortune there was a hospital with lands attached, which about 1268-70 were given to the House of the Red Friars at Houston, Prestonkirk, by Christina de Moubray, widow of Sir Bernard Fraser of Fortune and Linton.—[*Chart. of Newbattle*, 117-20; *Cal. of Papal Letters*, xii, 114-6; *Reg. Great Seal*, iii, 30, 2569, vii, 71; *Reg. Priory of St Andrews*, 40, 322; *Retours*, xx, 94; *Acts Scott. Parl.*, W, 449; *Proc. Soc. of Antiq.*, 1887-8, 27-8; Fraser's *Haddington Bk.*, ii, 227; Lockhart's *Ch. in Scotland in 13th Century*.]

THOMAS HEPBURN, M.A., min. in 1568.—[*Comps. Sub Coll. of Thirds, Linlithgow*, etc.]
1568

JOHN AUCHINLECK, *alias* John Affleck; was a Friar of the Greyfriars' Friary at Haddington, and became Warden in 1560; reader at "Elstanfurd Jesus" in 1573, the expression meaning, perhaps, that he held as his stipend as reader the revenues of an Altar dedicated to our Lord, St Salvator, in Athelstaneford Church; no trace of him after 27th Nov. 1577.—[Bryce's *Scott. Greyfriars*, 188 and 193.]
1573

JOHN SIMSON, still in office 1590.—[*Comps. Gen. Coll. of Thirds.*]
1578

JAMES CARMICHEAL, min. of Haddington, pres. to vicarage on dem. of John Simson.—[*Reg. Sec. Sig.*, lxii, 4.]
1590

JOHN JENKINSON, marr. (2) Katherine, daugh. of Alexander Cunningham, farmer, Whitekirk; his daugh. Beatrice, is said to have received a diamond
1701

ring from Prince Charles Edward.—[*Soc. of Antiq.*, 19th Dec. 1931.]

ROBERT BLAIR, his son, William, merchant, Edinburgh.
1731

GEORGE GOLDIE, his daughs. Janet died 13th Aug. 1833; Clarissa (marr. 25th Aug. 1824).
1778

WILLIAM RITCHIE, his wife, born 10th Dec. 1799; his son, Andrew, died 9th Nov. 1883.
1805

JOHN MORRISON WHITELAW, line 15, read "Bishop Bree."
1846

THOMAS OGILVY DUNCAN, dem. 5th Nov. 1935; died 20th May 1942; his daugh., Mary Somerville Paterson (marr. 2nd Dec. 1925 Frank Ythol Bethell, Lieut. R.N.); his widow, Jessie Somerville Paterson, died at Moffat 19th June 1943. Publication—*Athelstaneford— A Poet Haunted Parish in East Lothian* (1934).
1912

BOLTON

In the time of William the Lion, apparently about 1200, William de Vipont, eldest son and heir of William de V. and Lady Emma of St Hilary, granted the church to Holyrood Abbey.—[*Holyrood Charters*, 28, 33, 35.]

ANDREW SIMSON, exhorter in 1561, still in office 1572; also at Saltoun.—[*Comps. Gen. Coll. and Sub Coll. of Thirds, Linlithgow*, etc.]
1561

JOHN SINCLAIR, reader at Dumfries; was pres. to the vicarage 29th Sept. 1578 in succession to Andrew Simson and was admitted to the office before 16th Feb. 1578-9 by Patrick Adamson, Archbishop of St Andrews; on the latter date David Forsyth, min. at Bolton, and the parishioners raised an action against the archbishop, who, not possessed of the power of visitation in the region in which Bolton was situated, intruded Sinclair (a "new minister") in the parish; the parishioners, who had for the most part sustained the minister themselves till order
1578

be taken thereanent, had procured a royal order to the archbishop to receive and admit David Forsyth; the archbishop refused because he had given admission to Sinclair, who was still vicar and reader of Dumfries and without standing; and on said admission Sinclair forcibly entered the church, and took institution to the vicarage, and left the burgh of Dumfries, and thus deprived said David Forsyth of a portion of the teind sheaves of Bolton which belonged to the vicarage; the Privy Council referred the matter to the Commissioners of Parliament; before 20th June 1587 Sinclair was deprived for non-residence.—[*Reg. Privy Council*, iii, 95; *Reg. Pres. to Bene.*, ii, 6; *Reg. Sec. Seal*, xlv, 71, lv, 86.]

DAVID FORSYTH, M.A., pres. to vicarage 1st Nov. 1578, on death of Andrew Simson.—[*Reg. Pres. Bene.*, ii, 8.]
1578

JAMES LAMB, pres. to vicarage 27th July 1587 on deprivation of John Sinclair.—[*Reg. Sec. Sig.*, iv, 133.]
1587

JAMES MAITLAND, M.A., pres. to vicarage 20th June 1587, on deposition of John Sinclair for non-residence.—[*Reg. Sec. Sig.*, lv, 86.]
1587

JOHN MANDERSTON, parson 10th Aug. 1573, designated "parson and prebendary" 1599-1600.—[*Yester Writs*, 771, 972.]
1602

JOHN COURTNEY of Trolingshaw, his daugh., Margaret.
1640

WALTER PATERSON, had a son, Francis.—[*Deeds*, 21st Oct. 1706.]
1665

JOHN SINCLAIR, marr. Eupham, daugh. of Alexander Reid, writer, Edinburgh.—[*Burgess Roll*. 11th Dec. 1700.]
1692

WILLIAM HAMILTON, line 3, after wife add Christian Schiell.
1708

JOHN HAMILTON, his son, Robert, died 8th March 1809.
1743

THOMAS DRUMMOND, his daughs.
1843 —Mary Euphemia, died 4th Oct. 1928; Anne Rose, died 15th Jan. 1929; Isabella Sangster, died 15th May 1935.

JOHN BARR SERVICE, dem. 1st June
1883 1928; died 17th May 1936; Davina Shanks, his wife, died 9th Oct. 1923.

ROBERT NINIAN PAISLEY, born
1928 2nd June 1891, son of Robert P., min. of Careston; educ. at Brechin High School and Univ. of St Andrews, M.A. (1911); licen. by Presb. of Brechin 1919; assistant St Matthews, Edinburgh; served in Great War as Lieut. 4 Scottish Rifles; ord. to Ladykirk 11th Jan. 1921; trans. to New Abbey 30th April 1926; trans. and adm. 8th Nov. 1928; died 20th March 1948. Marr. 24th July 1917 Katherine Davidson, youngest daugh. of William Keith, farmer, Westknock, Old Deer, and Elspeth Cummin, and had issue—John Taylor Keith, R.N., born 20th April 1918; Elizabeth Cumming, born 15th June 1923; Robert Ninian, born 27th March 1926.

COCKENZIE

GEORGE HOGG, dem. 21st May 1923;
1885 died 20th June 1927. Marr. (2) 22nd May 1918 Alice Crichton, daugh. of Harry Edward Page, railway inspector, Ashbrittle.

THOMAS OSBORNE, born Motherwell, 29th Nov. 1891, son of William
1923 O. and Mary Twigg; educ. at Hamilton Academy and Univ. of Glasgow; licen. by Presb. of Hamilton March 1921; assistant St Bride's, Glasgow; Middle Parish, Paisley; ord. 27th Sept. 1923; dem. 11th Oct. 1942 on appointment as Town Clerk of Cockenzie, which office he resigned 15th Sept. 1943; re-adm. to charge 23rd Sept. 1943. Marr. 4th April 1921 Mary Cherrie, daugh. of William Gough and Margaret C. Watson, and has issue—Margaret Patricia Frances, born 16th Dec. 1922; Norman Cameron, born 2nd June 1925.

DIRLETON

Beside Dirleton Castle there was a chapel dedicated to St Katherine. Church restored in 1930.

GEORGE HALIBURTON, vicar before Dec. 1576.—[*Edin. Test.*, v,
1576 135.]

ANDREW McGHIE, had issue,
1597 Patrick.

JOHN McGHIE, his son, John; his daugh., Margaret (marr. (1) Robert
1639 Hodge, min. of Inverkeithing, and (2) cont. 24th Nov. 1696 Robert Stewart, shipmaster, Inverkeithing. — [*Stephen's Hist. of Inverkeithing and Rosyth*, 279.]

JAMES GLEN, bapt. 24th Aug. 1692,
1733 son of John G., min. of Stichell; marr. 20th June 1718 Elizabeth Elliot, and had issue—James, bapt. 18th July 1720; Alexander, his successor; William.

ALEXANDER GLEN, marr. Ann,
1769 daugh. of John Blackadder of St Leonards and Catherine Strother Ker of Littledean, and had issue—Walter, died 9th Nov. 1809; James, died 11th Dec. 1828; Katherine, died 1817; Barbara; Elizabeth (marr. 1805 John Finlason of the Admiralty), died 1831; John, died 185–; Robert, died 13th Feb. 1824; Ann, died 23rd Nov. 1859.

LAURENCE CHARTERIS, resident in
1688 Tron Parish, Edinburgh, 3rd Nov. 1694.—[*Tron Poll Tax Roll*, 30.]

JAMES SCOTT, line 2, for "1899"
1843 read "1799"; his daugh., Ann, died 13th March 1915.

WILLIAM LOGIE, his sons—Alexander Graham Spears, Capt. R.A.M.C.,
1864 died 1st Nov. 1919; David Brown, M.B., C.M., died Willington, South Africa, 4th Sept. 1930; his daughs.—Emily Jean (marr. April 1915 Arnold McCaskill, Canadian Forestry Corps); Elizabeth Sarah died at Inverness 17th July 1929; Emily Jean McCaskell, died 27th March 1943.

1878 JOHN KERR, died at Harrogate 8th Dec. 1920; his widow, Marion Groves, died at Keswick 8th April 1942; his daughs.—Winifred Violet (marr. 4th July 1918 Lionel John Willis, R.E.); Constance Ursula (marr. 14th July 1928 Frank Ernest Cole, Dulwich); Edith Kathleen (marr. 9th March 1935 William Dennis Wivell, Keswick).

1915 NORMAN COUTTS KEITH, trans. from Earlston (*q.v.*) 17th May 1915; died 25th Oct. 1927.

1928 HENRY OWENS WALLACE, born Mearns, Renfrewshire, 29th March 1895; son of James W., municipal foreman, and Annie Owens; educ. at Hamilton Academy and Univ. of Glasgow, M.A. (1920); served in 2nd Cameron Highlanders in Salonica and Transcaucasia 1916-19; licen. by Presb. of Hamilton 1921; assistant Barrowfield, Glasgow; ord. to Ladhope 7th Sept. 1922; trans. and adm. 26th April 1928. Marr. 8th Sept. 1919 Sarah McNiven Cameron, second daugh. of William Paterson, and has issue—James, born 4th April 1920; Margaret Paterson, born 20th Oct. 1926.

GARVALD

1568 WILLIAM SANDERSON, min. at Whittingham, also in charge here. —[*Comps. Sub Coll. of Thirds, Linlithgow*, etc.]

1568 THOMAS BROWN, reader 1568-72.— [*Comps. Sub Coll. of Thirds, Dumfries*, etc.]

1570 ALEXANDER CHALMERS, vicar, 3rd Aug. 1570, afterwards vicar of Liberton.

1571-6 PATRICK GALBRAITH, exhorter; designated 1564-7 Patrick and Sir Patrick Galbraith, min. at the Kirk of Garvald.—[*Edin. Tests.*, i, 64.]

1578 JAMES REID, pres. to parsonage and vicarage 20th June 1587 on death of Patrick Galbraith.—[*Reg. Sec. Sig.*, lvi, 153.]

1589 DAVID OGILL, M.A., son of Henry O. of Hartiemurde, pres. to vicarage 8th Aug. 1589 on death of James Reid.—[*Reg. Sec. Sig.*, lx, 43.]

1664 ROBERT FOORD, line 6, for "1667" read "1664."

1685 WALTER GRAY, son of Andrew G., merchant, Haddington, and brother of John G., min. of Aberlady. Had issue—Mr John; Patrick; Robert; Mary; Jean.—[*Test. Mary Blair, Edin.*, 15th Feb. 1737.]

1839 SELBY ORD DODS, marr. only surviving daugh. of John Robertson, merchant, Edinburgh.

1844 JOHN CROSBIE, his daughs.—Jessie, died 30th April 1934; Margaret Renwick, died 7th Sept. 1935.

1876 GEORGE DODS, licen. 6th Dec. 1871; line 24, delete died 14th Nov. 1903. His son, John Erskine, O.B.E., Divisional Food Officer for South-East of Scotland, died at Cultercraigs, Biggar, 22nd April 1940; his daugh., Jane Erskine, D.C.S., died 14th Jan. 1949.

1910 THOMAS LOW, trans. to Newark, Port Glasgow, 3rd Dec. 1925.

1926 VICTOR WILLIAM WANDS, formerly of Nyasaland (*q.v.* and vii, 710); served in Great War for four years, in Gallipoli and France; adm. 14th April 1926; trans to Tweedmouth (*q.v.*) 19th June 1929.

BARO

1563 ALEXANDER CHALMERS, M.A., vicar 17th July 1572.—[*Acts and Dec.*, xxviii, 210; *Reg. of Abbrev. Feu Charters of Church Lands*, i, 118; *Cal. of Charters*, x, 2256.]

1567 THOMAS DUDGEON, reader 1567-8. —[*Comps. Sub Coll. of Thirds, Linlithgow*, etc.]

1594 DAVID OGILL, pres. on dem. of Daniel Chalmers.—[*P. S. Reg.*, lxvi, 193.]

1628 ALEXANDER TROTTER, line 10, for "1643" read "1644."

GLADSMUIR

The first church was built at Thrieplaw in 1650 to serve the west part of Haddington parish. It continued in use till 1695, when it was replaced by the church, built by Sir William Baillie of Lamington, and now a ruin in the churchyard north from the present church, which was opened for worship on 20th Oct. 1839. After 1695 the old church passed to decay, and its walls in part were incorporated in colliers' houses. At a later period four cot-houses there were designated the "Old Kirk"; and the place, about 1½ miles south-east of the present church, is now called "Gladsmuir Kirk." At Samuelston, which prior to the erection of this parish was in the parish of Haddington, there was a chapel dedicated to St Nicolas. In the garden adjoining Longniddry House there is a fragment of a building known as "John Knox House," from its reputed connection with the Reformer.—[*Retours*, xviii, 202; *Report, Royal Comm. on Anc. Monuments, E. Lothian*, 37–8; *Memo*, Rev. W. R. Wiseman.]

MUNGO WATSON, marr. Helen, daugh. of William Young in Groathall, and had issue—Helen; Henrietta.—[*Deeds Mack.*, 1706, No. 199.]
1687

FRANCIS COWAN, his daughs.—Janet (marr. Henry Gillies, writer, Edinburgh; Margaret (marr. proc. 12th May 1796 Joseph Bethune, min. of Renton Chapel).
1759

GEORGE HAMILTON, his son, John James, died 20th Jan. 1831.
1790

JOHN RAMSAY, his daugh., Charlotte (marr. 16th Dec. 1856).
1833

WILLIAM MENZIES, pres. 24th March 1871.
1871

WILLIAM BELL TURNBULL, his widow, Elizabeth Holgate, died 10th Sept. 1918.
1876

WILLIAM REID WISEMAN, had issue—Ewen Reid, born 21st Sept. 1915; Denis Buchanan, born 12th March 1917; Sheina Helen, born 6th July 1918 (marr. 28th Dec. 1940 2nd Lieut. Kenneth Donald Burbridge, architect, son of Leonard B., Surrey); Gladys Brown, born 7th Dec. 1920 (marr. 24th July 1943 Vaughan Mackintosh Shaw, Lieut. K.O.S.B., eldest son of Colonel J. J. M. Shaw, R.A.M.C.).
1914

GULLANE

About 1170 William de Vaux granted the patronage of the church to God and St Mary and the Church of St Nicolas and the Canons of Dryburgh serving God in the said Church of St Nicholas on the island of Elbottle (Fidra), for the soul of King William, etc. There were reserved the rights of the Nunnery of South Berwick in the church, as contained in the "writings" (scriptas) made between said William de Vaux and the nunnery. The grant was confirmed, apparently soon after 1214, by William de Vaux' son and successor, John, for the soul of King Alexander, etc., and by William, Bishop of St Andrews 1202–38. The foregoing rights of the nunnery led to a dispute which was settled about 1221 when Sir Gregory, Master, and Froelina, Prioress of South Berwick, and the convent thereof, surrendered in favour of William de Vaux of Dirleton, and William de Vaux, parson of Gullane, apparently the uncle of William de Vaux, all their rights in the church, with the reservation of what they had when the lawsuit was moved, and also the teind sheaves of the lands of Kingston which they "shall take and hold" after the death of the said William de Vaux, parson. David de Bernham, Bishop of St Andrews, dedicated the church on 8th Oct. 1242, and in the same year he reduced it from a parsonage to a vicarage, to be served by the Canons of Dryburgh, and a priest whose annual payment was 12 merks. Two years earlier Alexander de Vaux had confirmed the patronage of the church to Dryburgh Abbey. About 1220 William de Vaux granted to the Canons of Dryburgh the island of Elbotle itself, and 20½ acres of the lands of Elbotle on the mainland, the lands of Stodfauld, etc. Two canons were obliged to reside and celebrate on the island in the Church of St Nicholas. But about 1240 Alexander de Vaux "in consideration of the imminent dangers of the times present and to come," relieved Dryburgh of the necessity of maintaining that chantry on the island as hitherto, or of building, or sending canons to live on it. Instead a canon was to be provided at Stodfauld on the mainland, and another in Dryburgh, to pray for the souls of his ancestors and successors. It would seem, therefore, that the Church of St Nicholas, whose ruins are on the east side of Fidra about the landing stage, was never really completed. About the same time also Alexander de Vaux confirmed to Dryburgh the grant of the island of Elbotle, etc., made by William his father in 1220. Besides St Nicholas Church, there were other religious foundations in the parish. The Chapel of St Patrick, whose ruins were still visible in the second half of the 18th century, was situated on the shore at the point on the north of Gullane Bay. About 1221 William de Vaux founded at Dirleton a chapel dedicated to All Saints, for the privilege of which he paid a stone of wax annually to Gullane Church, whose rights in other respects were fully conserved. At the same period on behalf of himself and his heirs he conveyed to Gullane Church what services they had to render on their own charges to the Chapel of St Andrew at Dirleton. The chaplain of the chapel had to render fealty to Gullane Church and also pay annually to the same one pound of frankincense. At Congalton, on a site still called chapel, there was founded by a lord of Congalton a chapel, with regard to which there was made in 1224 an agreement between Sir Walter and William de Gullane, rector of Gullane, whereby the said William had to supply a chaplain for the chapel, and in turn was to receive the oblations and offerings made at the same, while Sir Walter and his wife, and the men in the town of Congalton, were to attend at Gullane Church on three festivals, St Andrew's Day, Christmas, Easter, and at penances and the Sacraments. In the 15th century east range of Dirleton Castle there is an apartment which was used as a chapel, with piscina, credence, and benatura. Obviously there was at Stodfauld, somewhere on the mainland not far from Fidra Island, a cell or chapel for the celebrations by a canon of Dryburgh, to which reference has been made. About 1225 a dispute between William de Gullane, rector of Gullane, and the Nunnery of South Berwick, regarding what is called the Chapel of Dirleton, was settled by the arbiter, William, Bishop of St. Andrews, on the basis that the nunnery possess the chapel with the teinds of Elbotle, Dirleton, and Karmuchoc, during the lifetime of the said William, and that the oblations made at the chapel by William de Vaux and other lords of Dirleton pertain to the rector of Gullane. It is uncertain whether the foregoing has reference to the nunnery at Elbotle, a cell of South Berwick, said to have been founded by David I. South Berwick had another cell, described as being near Gullane Church, and also said to have been founded by David I. There was at Dirleton a House of the Red Friars. On 2nd May 1507 Royal Letters of Donation "of the Chapel of St Andrews in Dirleton of the Order of the Trinity, founded by the predecessors of Patrick, Lord Haliburton, the patron," were made to "Friar Alexander Blith of the said Order." The chapel had been vacant for three years through the failure of the Order to supply ministrations, and was at the king's disposal by the death of the said Patrick. Further information regarding the house occurs in 1588 in a charter of "the lands called the Friarlands of Dirleton extending to 10 merks old measure with tenement, land, garden lying in the town of Dirleton, called the Chapelyard, which pertained to the Minister, Prior, and Monastery of Fail, and the Prior of Dirleton, as part of the temporalities of the same, and came to the king by annexation, and which the king incorporated in the tenandry of Craigflat." At Gullane there was a hospital of St John of Jerusalem. On 19th April 1557 Patrick, Lord Ruthven, granted to Janet Stewart, Lady Ruthven, a charter of the provostry, chaplainries, and chapels of Dirleton; and on 19th Dec. 1561 the said Patrick gave to Sir Robert Hoislair, presbyter, the provostry of the Chapel of Dirleton, near the castle, with the lands of Corrige, vacant by the death of Sir Robert Hoppringill. An altar, dedicated to the Holy Trinity, was founded by Sir Andrew Congalton in Gullane Church. The foundation was confirmed by George Dundas, lord of St John's, preceptor of Torphichen, on 18th May 1523, and the patronage was declared to belong to Henry Congalton of the same.—[*Book of Dryburgh*, 15, 16–18, 19–21, 23–6, 27–8, 32–7, 232–7; *Excheq. Rolls*, xii, 693, xlvii, 155; *Reg. Sec. Seal*, i, 1470; *Reg. Great Seal*, iv, 1171, v, 1068; *Cart. Priory of North Berwick*, 82; Keith's *Scott. Bishops*, 461; Walcott's *Anc. Ch. of Scotland*, 379, 385; Armstrong's *Map*, 1773; *Douglas Baronage*, 522; Chalmer's *Caledonia*, iv, 507, 519.]

1567 SIR GEORGE HALIBURTON, vicar in 1567 and 1572.—[*Comps. Sub Coll. of Thirds, Linlithgow, Dumfries*, etc.]

1904 JAMES CAESAR, dem. 31st Aug. 1936; his wife, Wilhelmina, died 26th Dec. 1944. He died 15th Aug. 1945.

HADDINGTON

The church with its chapels was granted to the Priory of St Andrews by David I in 1139. The later building, which is now generally accepted as the church designated "The Lamp of Lothian," seems to have been erected towards the end of the 14th century or early in the 15th. It suffered serious damage in 1548 when the English, who garrisoned Haddington and used the tower of the church for defensive purposes, were besieged by the Scots and French. In a condition of dilapidation it remained till 1562, when work of restoration was inaugurated, the plan being to "byg, beild, and reedyfie sufficiently the fabric extending from the steeple to the west gable, and to roof in the south tufall" (aisle); the north "tufal" to be rebuilt, and "lyhts and glass" provided for the whole building; afterwards the "croce kirk" (transepts) to be proceeded with and "perfittit and byggit with wallis, ruffs, lychts, and utheris necessaris." At that time the choir, which stands roofless, was abandoned. Within the church there were altars as follows: Virgin Mary, St Catherine, Holy Trinity, John the Baptist, Holy Blood, St James, St Peter, St Nicholas, St Ninian, St John, St Michael, Holy Rood, Three Kings of Cologne, St Blaise, St Salvator, and the two brothers Crispin and Crispinanus, patrons of shoemakers, whose altar was upheld by the cordiners of the burgh. There were altars belonging to the Baxters and the Fleshers, but these may be included in the foregoing list. There were chapels with the following dedications: St Laurence; St Anne, situated at what is now St Anne's House; St Catherine, on the south side of the croft of the Franciscans; St Kentigern; and St Ninian in the west area of the town, to the chaplain at which on 9th March 1488 George Kerr of Samuelston granted in pure alms a tenement on the north side of the burgh. The Church or Chapel of St Martin, built probably about the beginning of the 12th century, and situated with its graveyard at the east side of the Nungate, was a dependency of the nunnery, having been granted by Alexander of St Martin's. The nave still survives. At Stevenston there was a chapel, for the erection of which (chantry and oratory) William de Golin (Gullane) received permission from Henry, Prior of St Andrews 1225–35. On 23rd March 1539–40 the church was designated "the Collegiate Church of Haddington," which may indicate that its organisation had something of the collegiate form. On the erection of the Bishopric of Edinburgh in 1633, the church became a prebend of St Giles Cathedral; and by Act of Parliament of 1641 it was separated from the Bishopric of St Andrews and its disposition given to the Earl of Haddington. In 1178 on a site about a mile east of the town a Cistercian monastery or nunnery, dedicated to the Virgin Mary, was founded by the Countess Ada, mother of Malcolm IV and William the Lion. In July 1292 Alicia, the prioress, made homage to Edward I. Similar fealty was declared in Aug. 1296 by Prioress Eve, to whom in consequence the rights of the nunnery were restored. "Destroyed and burned by the calamity of wars between the kings of Scotland and England," involving the loss of its writs, the nunnery in 1359 received a Charter of *Inspeximus* from William, Bishop of St Andrews. In Hertford's expedition in 1544 the nunnery was burned; and it suffered again four years later during the invasion under Somerset. A small part of the graveyard still remains; and the place is also recalled by Abbey Village, Abbey Mill, and the Abbey Bridge. A friary of the Grey Friars, dedicated to St Duthac, and said to have been situated where Elm House now is, was founded prior to 1242. It was given to the flames by Edward III in 1355. Probably some years elapsed before the church at least was rebuilt, for there appears in the Exchequer Rolls on 14th Aug. 1362 the sum of £6 13s. 4d. "given to the Minorite Friars of Haddington for building their Church." The friary further suffered from fire at the hands of Hertford's men in 1544, and also during the siege of 1548. Repair followed; but the church was finally demolished in 1572-3. There were in the church an altar dedicated to John the Baptist, at the north wall of the nave, founded on 22nd July 1389 by Sir William Haliburton, laird of Carlowry, with an endowment of 10 merks annually from the lands of Drem; an altar dedicated to St Clement, founded on 4th Feb. 1494-5 by William Bertram, Provost of Edinburgh, nephew of Sir William Bertram, vicar of Swinton; and an altar dedicated to St Francis. Probably there was also an altar dedicated to the Virgin Mary. There was also a friary of the Black Friars, founded probably in the 13th century. It may be identical with the religious establishment cleared away in 1765 to make room for the Episcopal church. In the Church of the Friary there was an altar called "the Altar of the Holy Rood of Lucanus." About a mile west of the town there was a leper hospital dedicated to St Laurence, founded by Richard Guthrie, Abbot of Arbroath cir. 1450-5, and belonging to the Order of Dominicans. It was refounded in 1480; and in 1532 it was annexed with its lands to the Dominican nunnery of Sciennes, Edinburgh. Its site is at St Laurence House; and its lands are incorporated in the farm of Spittal Rig. Before 11th June 1478 Sir John Haliburton, vicar of Greenlaw, erected in the Poldrait an almshouse dedicated to St Helen. There was also a hospital dedicated to the Virgin Mary, the custody of which on 19th July 1319 was granted by Edward II to Thomas de Gayregrave. A piece of land in the Poldrait was called St Andrew's Land. By charter of 24th March 1566-7 Queen Mary constituted the Royal Foundation of Ministers and Hospitals of Haddington, to maintain ministers and readers and other ecclesiastical burdens, and to provide a hospital for the poor, the mutilated, and miserable persons, and for orphans and other children bereft of their parents. The foundation was granted to the provost, bailies, town council, and community, and was to be administered with the advice and approval of the ministers and Kirk Session. The endowments were all property and annual rents, etc., of chaplainries, altarages, prebends in the burgh, property and annual rents, etc., of monks in the burgh, annual rents levied within the burgh for chaplainries, altarages, and churches elsewhere in Scotland, and dues payable from the Common Good of Haddington to churches outside the burgh. At Garleton (Gamriltoun-Noble) there was a chapel dedicated to St Kentigern. The Hospital of St Laurence near the town for poor men was under the patronage of the Crown, and was served by secular clerics and presbyters. On its becoming vacant in the early part of the reign of James V, that monarch by Letters deprived it of its "hospital nature" and united and incorporated it with the "religious brothers of the Order of St Augustine." None of the Order took up residence there; and indeed no additional accommodation suitable for the friars was provided; and accordingly the king intimated to Pope Leo X (1513-21) that he had appointed his chaplain, Walter Ramsay, to the void house and vacant rectory, and craved the Pope that the house be separated from the Order and restored to its original position. In the Church of Haddington there was an altar dedicated to the Saviour, founded by Mr William Wawane, official of Lothian.—[*Reg. Great Seal*, ii, 610, 1216, 1333, 1836, 2005, 2941, iii, 364, 1616, 1735, 1962, v, 1776, viii, 2225; *Acts Scott. Parl.*, v, 380a; *Retours*, iv, 196, x, 132, xv, 140; *Laing Charters*, 418; *Reg. Sec. Seal*, i, 1710; *Reg. Priory of St Andrews*, 324; *Hist. MSS. Commis. Reports, Earl of Home MS.*, 160; Prynn's *Records of the Tower*, iii, 653; Rymer's *Foldera*, ii, 725, ii, Pt. 1, Ed. 1818, 401; Fraser's *Mem. of the Earls of Haddington*, ii, 226; Chalmers' *Caledonia*, ii, 683, iii, 422, iv, 507, 513–14; Bryce's *Greyfriars of Scotland*, i, 169, 186, ii, 11–21, 170, 172; Millar's *Lamp of Lothian*, 26, 31, 173–4, 175, 176, 177, 179, 388; *Cal. of Yester Writs*, No. 202, 394; *Scott. Rec. Soc.*; *Exchequer Rolls*, ii, 116; *Epistolae Regium Scotorum*, i, 193–4.]

1565 SIR GEORGE REID, perpetual vicar 8th Feb. 1565–6.

1570 JAMES CARMICHAEL, pres. in succession to William Walderstoun; pres. to vicarage 27th April 1581 on dem. of Robert Bonkle.—[*Acts and Decs.*, l, 150; *Reg. Pres. Bene.*, ii, 57.]

1573 WALTER BALCANQUAL, formerly exhorter at Aberdour and Dalgety; On 27th Feb. 1572–3 the Town Council "inducit Mr Walter Balcanqual to read the common prayers in the Kirk at vii hors befor noon in summer, and viii hors in winter, and that on Sunday, Wednesday and Friday, and to be Clerk to the Session and Doctor in the school during the space of one year from the date thereof" (interlined Martinmas next), and resolved annually "to pay sd. reader 5 merks"; adm. to St Giles in 1574.—[*Lamp of Lothian*, 190; Ross's *Aberdour and Inchcolm*, 213.]

1574 ROBERT BONKLE, pres. to vicarage 29th Nov. 1574, vacant by death of Sir William Scott of Balwearie; dem. before 14th Oct. 1580.—[*Reg. Sec. Sig.*, xl, 11, 90; *Reg. Pres. Bene.*, ii, 41.]

1578 HENRY CHAPMAN, reader.—[*Lamp of Lothian*, 190.]

1580 PATRICK BOYLE, pres. to vicarage 14th Oct. 1580 on dem. of Robert Bonkle.—[*Reg. Pres. Bene.*, ii, 41.]

1585 JOHN KER, on 17th Aug. 1582 he was appointed Master of the Grammar School for five years; and he also acted as minister in Mr Carmichael's absence; on 19th Nov. 1585 he received from the burgh 100 merks "in full satisfaction for the parts of the sd. burgh alanerlie of his service done in the function of minister of the Word of God to the hail parishioners there of these divers years bygon."—[*Lamp of Lothian*, 194–5.]

1678 JAMES FORMAN, son of James F., portioner of Inveresk.

1704 JOHN CURRIE, his son, John, apprenticed to David Spence and George Miller, merchants, Edinburgh, 8th May 1734.

1721 PATRICK WILKIE, born 2nd Feb. 1685; marr. (1) 12th Aug. 1719; his daughs.—Janet (marr. proc. 23rd Jan. 1763); Agnes (marr. Henry Hepburn, collector of customs, Prestonpans); his sons—James of Gilchriston, born 24th Sept. 1733, died 9th March 1825; Patrick of Island of St Vincent.

1843 JOHN COOK, his daughs.—Helen, died Haddington 17th May 1933; Martha Mary, died 17th March 1934.

1874 WILLIAM ROSS, his widow, Emilie Alder Fisher, died 11th Jan. 1923.

1880 ROBERT NIMMO SMITH, his widow, Mary Ann Tod, died London 22nd March 1928.

1913 GEORGE WAUCHOPE STEWART, D.D. (Edinburgh, March 1923); licen. 15th May 1887; line 13, for "1912" read "1911"; died at Edinburgh 21st Sept. 1942; was Joint Convener of Public Worship and Aids to Devotion Committee; revision of Church Hymnary and Anthem Book; was one of the greatest

HADDINGTON
SECOND CHARGE

WILLIAM TRENT, his son, Archibald, apprentice to William Hamilton, merchant, 23rd April 1673; his daugh., Marion (marr. Robert Merchiston, min. of Kirkpatrick-Juxta).—[*G. R. Sas.*, 2 Ser., xi, 228.]
1636

EDWARD STEDMAN, his daugh., Martha (marr. proc. 1st June 1766).
1731

ROBERT SCOTT, marr. Jane, daugh. of Andrew Elliot of Howford.
1772

WILLIAM SIBBALD, his wife's mother was Mary Davis, a free negro woman.
1868

WILLIAM PROUDFOOT, born 28th June 1876; his son, Harry Crichton, died at Sydney, N.S.W., 21st July 1933; his daugh., Edith Mary (marr. 26th Aug. 1920 Robert Douglas Osler, M.B., C.M., South Africa).
1891

WILLIAM JOHN FORBES, died 4th Nov. 1946.
1918

HADDINGTON ST MARTIN'S

GEORGE GRIER, his daugh. Isobel.—[*G. R. Sas.*, xii, 69, 4th Nov. 1622.]
1603

HUMBIE

The church was granted to Dunfermline Abbey by Alexander I 1107–24. In the 12th century the parish was described as the Parish of Addockis Ket (Keith) and Siwynis Ket, apparently with the name of the person to whom each district belonged. In a dispute between Dunfermline Abbey and the Church of Crichton, it was decided in 1199, in the time of Pope Innocent III, that the Chapel of Keeth should belong for ever to the Church of Crichton, one merk silver to be paid annually by Crichton Church to the abbey. In the Rental of Kelso Abbey in 1567 Humbie appears under "Lands" and under "Kirkis and Teinds."—[*Reg. of Dunfermline*, 3, 48–69, 96–7; *Reg. of Kelso*, ii, 492–3.]

WILLIAM FRANK, vicar, 1566; still in office 1576.—[*Comps. Gen. Coll. of Thirds.*]
1566

ANDREW SIMSON, min. at Ormiston, had also charge here.
1574

THOMAS CHARTERIS, marr. daugh. of John Byres of Coates.
1646

JAMES HAMILTON, marr. Agnes Swinton, to whom he disponed his estate 14th Dec. 1699 prior to his going north.
1696

GEORGE WEIR, his daugh., Jane Broomfield, died 30th Sept. 1915.
1843

ROBERT BALDOCK SCOTT, trans. to Row, 9th Nov. 1922.
1905

JOHN ANNAND FRASER, born 21st June 1894, son of Charles F., min. of Croy; educ. at Robert Gordon's College, Aberdeen, and Univ. of Aberdeen and Edinburgh, M.A. (1919); served in Gordon Highlanders in Great War; licen. by Presb. of Edinburgh 29th June 1921; Assistant at St Matthew's, Edinburgh; ord. 19th April 1923; trans. to Hamilton Second Charge 14th May 1931; M.B.E. (1940). Marr. 30th Sept. 1925 Leila, eldest daugh. of Colonel Ewen Campbell, Edinburgh, and had issue—Leila Campbell, born 9th Aug. 1926; Charles Annand, born 16th Oct. 1928.
1923

KEITH MARISCHAL

ANDREW SIMSON, min. at Ormiston, had also charge here. See Ormiston.
1574

MORHAM

The church was annexed to the Collegiate Church of Bothans (see Yester).

JOHN WHITE, M.A., reader, parson and minister 1568–9.—[*Comps. Sub Coll. of Thirds, Linlithgow*, etc.]
1565

---

authorities on church music; his daugh., Catherine (marr. 17th Aug. 1926 Ralph Laurence, elder son of Harry Heffer, Cambridge.) Addl. Publication—*Music in the Church.*

ANDREW MELVEN, died Feb. 1689. (P.C., xiv, 257). Marr. Elizabeth, daugh. of Alexander Douglas, W.S., and had issue—Andrew, died young; Jean (marr. Robert Meldrum, min. of Yester); Eliza, killed by a fall of a house in Holland with Lady Dundee; Isobel (marr. George Robertson, Haddington); Margaret; Ann, born 1671 (marr. Gideon Guthrie, min. of Fetteresso); Mary (marr. James Robertson, stationer, Edinburgh).
1663

JAMES MITCHELL PATTULLO, dem. 20th June 1923; died 28th May 1943; his wife, Agnes, daugh. of James Cranstoun of Tinwald House, Dumfries.
1894

NORTH BERWICK

The church was situated on the "Auld Kirk Green" near the harbour. Before 1199 it was granted to the Nunnery of North Berwick by Malcolm, son and successor of Duncan, Earl of Fife. In the church were an altar dedicated to the Virgin Mary, for the support of a chaplain at which Agnes Faulaw, wife of Robert Lauder of the Bass, and daugh. of George F., burgess of Edinburgh, with consent of the said Robert, on 20th Oct. 1491 granted a charter of 10 merks annually and 5 merks annually from tenements in Edinburgh and Leith respectively, for celebrations of the souls of King James IV, etc., and of her late husband, William Carreboris, burgess of Edinburgh; an altar dedicated to St Ninian, in the north transeptal aisle; an altar dedicated to "Our Lady of Peace," erected in St Ninian's aisle with consent of the bailies and community of North Berwick in 1497 by William de Carrick, indweller in Mains of Tantallon; an altar of the Holy Rood; and an altar dedicated to St Sebastion. In addition to St Ninian's aisle there was an aisle of the Lauders of the Bass called "ye lords of bassis yill." About the middle of the 17th century the church was in a decayed condition, and it passed out of use soon after 1656. In 1659 there was begun the erection of a new church on a site on the east side of Law Road, which after considerable delay was completed in 1664 and was used for the first time on 5th June of that year. All that now remains of the earlier church is a small vaulted building which had projected from the south wall. Corrosion by the waves has gradually carried away the graveyard, which does not appear to have been in use after 15th April 1673. During the period between the abandonment of the old church and the completion of its successor, worship was conducted in "the great tenement or Lodgeing" within the burgh, belonging to William Dick of Braid, the site of which is now occupied by the Dalrymple Hotel. In 1770 the church of 1659–64 was in great part rebuilt and at the same time enlarged, and the tower erected; and in 1828 it was re-seated. Forty-six years later attention was turned to the provision of a new church. The last service in the old church was held on 3rd June 1883, and its roofless walls stand in the churchyard. On the south-east corner is a sundial purchased in 1680 and bearing the dates 1660 and 1770. On the east side of the tower in a mutilated condition is another sundial of date 1679. The new church, erected on the site of the old manse in High Street in accordance with a design prepared by Sir Rowand Anderson, was opened for worship on 10th June 1883. The design was completed by the addition of the tower and porch in 1907. In the front of the north gallery is a clock which was in the Luchie Loft of the preceding church, and is said to have been a gift in 1770; and in the vestibule is the bell which was in use in all the three churches, and passed out of use in 1928 when a new bell was given by Mr J. R. Menzies of West Links House, in memory of Mr J. R. Burt, minister of the parish 1904–28. It has this inscription: "Jacobus Monteath me fecit Edinb. . . . gh pro templo de North Berwick Anno Domini 1642, Ipero Meliora." On the Bass Rock are the ruins of St Baldred's Chapel, "newly erected in 1492 by Robert Lauder of the Bass," who himself was the lay rector and patron. Designated the "paris kyrk in the craig of the Bass," it took the place of a cell founded by St Baldred; and it was consecrated and dedicated on 5th June 1542 by Mr William

Gibsone, suffragan of Cardinal David Beton, Archbishop of St Andrews, in the presence of Mr John Lauder, Archdeacon of Tweeddale. The intrusion of this parish church into the parish of St Andrews' Church which belonged to the nunnery led to a dispute between the nunnery prioress and Robert Lauder, the outcome of which is not known. There was also a chapel at Tantallon Castle. Apparently in or about 1150 Duncan, Earl of Fife 1136-54, founded a Cistercian nunnery on the lands called Gillecameston given to the nunnery by himself. To the nunnery Earl Duncan also gave two hospitals, built and endowed by him in connection with the Earl's Ferry. One was situated at the port of landing on the south side, the harbour of North Berwick, and the other at the port of landing on the north side, Ardross, in Fife. The hospitals were for "poor folk and pilgrims." On 10th Oct. 1242 the church of the nunnery was dedicated to the Virgin Mary by Bishop de Bernham. It would appear that at first the nunnery was governed by a prior or master, and a prioress. While we find a sub-prioress acting as the head in 1220, James, Prior, occurs in 1238; and he is probably identical with James, Master, who is mentioned about the same time. Master and prioress are found together representing the nunnery in 1254-9; Master again occurs in 1293; and on 28th Aug. 1296, William, "vicairie de eglise de Laneta," warden of the nunnery, swore fealty to Edward I. Thereafter Prioress alone occurs. An alternative designation in 1383 is abbatess. In addition to lands, etc., the nunnery held the following churches: North Berwick, granted, as we have seen, before 1199 by Malcolm, son of Duncan, Earl of Fife, and himself Earl of Fife 1203-29 in succession to his father; the gift was supplemented by the perpetual vicarage of the church, which was given by Bull of Pope Clement VII 18th Feb. 1383-4, the nunnery being held bound to appoint a chaplain to minister at the church and have the cure of the souls of the parishioners, and also to provide for him a fixed stipend; Logie (Airthrey), confirmed by Simeon, Bishop of Dunblane, about 1178; Kilconquhar, granted about 1200 by Duncan, Earl of Fife 1154-1203, while Adam, lord of Kilconquhar and Earl Carrick, resigned the patronage of the church and ratified Earl Duncan's concession of the same to the nunnery on 16th Feb. 1266-7; Kirkbride in Carrick (now united with Maybole), confirmed by Joceline, Bishop of Glasgow, in 1199, on the petition of Roger de Sealebroc; Largo, granted by Duncan, Earl of Fife 1154-1203, and confirmed by Malcolm, Earl of Fife, 1203-29, and by William, Bishop of St Andrews, 1203-34; Maybole, granted by Duncan, 1st Earl of Carrick, who died on 13th June 1250. Upon the condition of the nunnery in the 14th century light is thrown by a petition presented to Pope Gregory XI by Beatrice the prioress, and "the greater and more sane" portion of the nuns. They narrated that to the nunnery, which was known to occupy a notable and prominent site, resorted nobles and other secular persons, and that this intercourse had increased of late from the building of a number of castles and forts in the neighbourhood. The result was that the nunnery, aiming to render the highest service, had lapsed from devotion, and its sacred cult had suffered great diminution and fallen into contempt; and the said prioress and nuns genuinely feared that greater hurt and more irreparable scandals would follow in the future, unless the remedy suggested by them was applied. It was that, as exit from and entry to the nunnery had been notoriously open from the time of its foundation, the access of such persons as had been mentioned should be prevented by a perpetual enclosure, and that the prioress and nuns should be ordained to live in continual seclusion within the walls of the monastery. The Pope, in reply, on 12th Aug. 1375 gave a mandate to William, Bishop of St Andrews, ordaining an enclosing wall to be built at the expense of the prioress and convent, and that the prioress and nuns reside within the enclosure and continue so to do in all time to come notwithstanding any statutes or practices to the contrary. That, however, was not the only trouble that befell the nunnery. In the Papal Bull 18th Feb. 1383-4 annexing the perpetual vicarage of the Church of North Berwick to the nunnery, there were given as reasons for the annexation the oppressions and hardships caused by the frequent devastations of the plundering of the nunnery possessions through the ravages of war, and the lamentable burning of the church by an invading enemy. The church, however, was rebuilt; and there are records that in it were a chapel of John the Baptist 4th Jan. 1524-5, and an altar of the Holy Rood, of which on 3rd March 1539-40 Sir William Fowlar was chaplain. At the Reformation the prioress and nuns were dispersed, and the buildings, with the exception of the church and cloisters, which still survived at 28th Jan. 1568-9 but had disappeared before 12th Jan. 1587-8, became ruinous. "The Mansion or lodgeing called the Newark" was built on part of the site before 28th Jan. 1568-9, and became the chief residence of Sir Alexander Home, son of Patrick H. of Polwarth, to whom a Crown Charter of 20th March 1587-8 conveyed the possessions of the nunnery, at the same time creating them into a barony. An Act of Parliament of 1592 ratified the infeftments of Sir Alexander Home, and another Act of 1597 dissolved the nunnery. The existing ruins appear to belong to the period immediately after the Reformation. In addition to the Ferry Hospital at the harbour there was a hospital for poor brethren (monks) which was situated on a site now occupied by the Dalrymple Hotel in Quality Street. Described in 1544 as "built by the late Robert Lauder of the Bass," presumably Robert Lauder 1495-1579, it had an endowment of 20 merks annually from lands on the south side of the street of the burgh of Lauder, and other lands, including "Lawrenceland," within the liberty of the said burgh. To the perpetual chaplainry of the shrine or chapel attached to the hospital, Sir Robert Lauder of the Bass, the patron, appointed George Lyall in Sept. 1560 in succession to the late Sir James Cowhen (Cowan), and invested him in possession by presentation of the key of the said chapel and the lodging built over it.—[*Carte Mon. de North Berwic*, xi, xvii, 4-15, 19-20, 31, 37-8, 40, 47, 54-5, 71, 76-7, 84-5; *Reg. Great Seal*, ii, 2068, iv, 55, 382, 1598, 1599, 1919, v, 1492; *Reg. Sec. Seal*, ii, 579; *Acts Scott. Parl.*, iii, 601, iv, 157, vii, 156b, 157a, x, 303; *Excheq. Rolls*, x, 770, xiv, 619-20; *Retours*, xx, 94, xli, 174; *Reg. of Dunfermline*, 131-3; *Cal. of Docs. Rel. to Scotland*, ii, 208; *Cal. Papal Reg., Letters*, iv, 212; *Extractae Variis Cronius Scocie*, 255; Theiner's *Vet. Monumenta*, 355; Dalrymple's *Collections on Scott. History*, 268; Fraser's *Douglas Book*, iii, 165-6; *Miss. Scott. Hist. Soc.*, iv, 309, 334-5; Lockhart's *Ch. in Scot. in 13th Century*, 52; D. B. Swan's *Parish Church of St Andrew, North Berwick*.]

1568 ALEXANDER WOOD, M.A., 1568, also vicar of Largo (*q.v.*).—[*Comps. Sub Coll. of Thirds, Linlithgow*, etc.]

1568 PATRICK CREECH, trans. to Jedburgh 1574.

1569 ROBERT LAUDER, reader 1569-71. —[*Comps. Sub Coll. of Thirds, Linlithgow*, etc.]

1611 WILLIAM GALBRAITH, reader.— [*MS. Min. Book*, 22nd Sept. 1611.]

1628 HENRY AITKENHEAD, his daugh. Isobel, not Helen (marr. Archibald Riddell, min. of Trinity, Edinburgh).

1729 GEORGE MURRAY, had also issue, Jane.

1758 MATTHEW MURRAY, his son, Hugh, died 1846; his daugh., Mary Simpson, died 1876; his son, John, preacher, died 1799; his daugh., Janet, died 25th Oct. 1767.

1792 HENRY DAVID HILL, marr. (1) 1st Oct. 1802; (2) 1818.

1795 GEORGE MURRAY, his daugh., Ann, died 9th Dec. 1867.

1822 ROBERT BALFOUR GRAHAM, his daugh., Christian Mary, died 17th May 1916; his son, Archibald, died at Ballarat; John, died at Barrackpore.

1873 GEORGE WASHINGTON SPROTT, marr. 29th Sept. 1857; his son, Harold George Hill, LL.B., died 18th Jan. 1924; his daughs.—Lilias Harrington, born 4th July 1862, died 27th Nov. 1867; Agnes Jean (Mrs Wylie), died at London 31st Jan. 1939; Mabel (marr. (2) 16th Aug. 1939 Robert Charles Brown, Strone, Bridge of Cally).

1904 JAMES ROBERT BURT, licen. 21st May 1888, dem. May 1927; died 11th Aug. 1935. Marr. 8th Oct. 1919 Anne Calder, second daugh. of Thomas R. Marshall, Edinburgh; she died 20th June 1945.

1928 RITCHIE DOUGHTY LYON, M.A., B.D., trans. from Dunfermline North (*q.v.*) 15th Nov. 1928. Issue—James Doughty, born 27th April 1925; Douglas Ritchie Doughty, born 22nd Dec. 1929.

PENCAITLAND

The greater part of the church was rebuilt in 1631; but the aisle probably belongs to the early part of the 13th century. The church was dedicated by Bishop de Bernham 1st May 1242. About 1343 John de Maxwell, son of the deceased Sir John M. of Pencaitland, Kt., granted to Dryburgh Abbey the patronage of the church with the Chapel of Payston. Subsequent to the Reformation Payston was attached to Ormiston.—[*Book of Dryburgh*, 271; *Reg. Mag. Sig.*, i, App. ii, 944; Lockhart's *Ch. in Scotland in 13th century*, 48.]

1575 ANDREW SYMSOUN, designated min. 18th Oct. 1575; held also Saltoun.—[*Test. Inventories MS.*, *Reg. Ho.*]

1576 DEAN JOHN CHATTO, vicar 1576.—[*Comps. Gen. Coll. of Thirds.*]

1653 ALEXANDER VERNOR, son of Robert V., portioner of Inveresk.—[*Deeds Mack.*, 1704, No. 361.]

1669 ROBERT DOUGLAS, line 38, after "released" add "Feb. 1653"; his son, Archibald, buried at Logie 16th July 1714.—*G. R. Sas.*, xlii, 164; liii, 481.]

1674 JAMES COCKBURN, son of William C., min. of Kirkmichael, Ayr.

1685 WILLIAM DENUNE, his daugh. Christian (marr. James Hepburn Congalton of that ilk).

1705 MATTHEW SIMSON, his son, Adam, apprentice to James Steel, saddler, Edinburgh, 30th Dec. 1730.

1793 DAVID PYPER, his daugh. Caroline (marr. 24th Oct. 1825 James Anderson Berry).

1814 ANGUS McKELLAR, his wife, Helen Stirling, died 27th July 1859.

1872 JAMES COULLIE, dem. 30th Sept. 1924, died 25th June 1927; his daugh., Margaret Evelyn (marr. 18th Sept. 1921 Rev. John William Arthur, M.D., O.B.E., Dunbog); his son, William, Surgeon Lieut.-Commander R.N., died at Southsea 15th Sept. 1924.

1925 GEORGE GRANDISON MORGAN, born 15th March 1894, son of John Morgan and Fanny Miller; educ. at Univ. of Edinburgh, M.A. (1920); licen. by Presb. of Edinburgh 2nd May 1923; assistant, St Mary's, Edinburgh, May 1923; ord. 26th Feb. 1925.

PRESTONPANS

1567 JOHN BARTONE, M.A., Dean of Dunkeld, vicar 1567–71.—[*Comps. Sub Coll. of Thirds, Linlithgow*, etc.]

1595 JOHN DAVIDSON; he founded in Prestonpans "ane schole for teiching Latine grek and hebrew towngis and Language and for Instructing of youth in virtue and learning," and he "dotit to the samin his heretage and all his moveable and frie gudis for ane perpetuall stipend to the maisteris at the said schole." By Act of 11th July 1606 Parliament ratified the erection and all his benefaction to the school.—[*Acts Scott. Parl.*, iv, 302.]

1605 JOHN KERR, had issue—Margaret, bapt. 15th May 1606; Andrew, advocate, bapt. 1607 (delete "died Feb. 1670"); Robert, min. of Haddington;

Margaret, bapt. 16th Jan. 1612; Mary (twin), bapt. 16th Jan. 1612; Elizabeth, bapt. 1st Sept. 1614; John, bapt. 16th Nov. 1615; Thomas, bapt. 2nd Aug. 1618.

JOHN OSWALD, line 1, for "1660" read "1600."
1648

ROBERT RAMSAY, his son, Robert, apprenticed to George Manson, barber, Edinburgh, 27th Feb. 1712.
1682

ROBERT HORSBURGH. MS. volume of sermons in Assembly Library.
1702

MATTHEW REID, his daugh., Margaret (marr. Oct. 1781 James Carmichael, writer, Edinburgh).
1768

GEORGE STUART SMITH, died 7th Jan. 1916.
1889

JOSEPH LOGAN AYRE, trans. from Kirkcowan (*q.v.*), 29th June 1916; died at Lumphanan 11th Oct. 1938; his son, Peter Logan, min. of Kinross; his daugh., Margaret Robertson (marr. 24th Oct. 1946 Harold Edward Mackenzie, Uln Tiram Estate, Johore, Malaya).
1916

SALTOUN

The church was dedicated by Bishop de Bernham on 21st April 1244. Near the Castle of Herdmaston there was a chapel dedicated to St John the Evangelist. About the beginning of the 13th century John de Sant Clair received from the abbot and convent of Dryburgh permission to build the chapel for the use of himself, family household, and guests, the rights of the mother church of Saltoun being reserved. The site with the ruins is in the grounds of Herdmaston House.—[*Retours*, xxxv, 162; *Bk. of Dryburgh*, 135; Lockhart's *Ch. of Scot. in 13th Century*, 58.]

JOHN ABERNETHIE, M.A., vicar 1562–71.—[*Comps. Gen Coll. of Thirds*; *Sub Coll. of Thirds, Linlithgow*, etc.]
1562

JOHN BURNETT, M.A., vicar 1567–71.—[*Comps. Sub Coll. of Thirds, Linlithgow*, etc.]
1567

ARTHUR SIMSON, exhorter in 1568 and 1572; also at Bolton.—[*Comps. Sub Coll. of Thirds, Linlithgow*, etc.]
1568

JAMES GIBSON, pres. to vicarage 9th Dec. 1581, on death of John Abernethie, after his removal to Pencaitland; was fugitive before 1st Feb. 1584–5.—[*Reg. Pres. Bene.*, ii, 63; *Reg. Sec. Sig.*, lii, 1.]
1578

ROGER WILSON, pres. to vicarage 1st Feb. 1584–5, vacant before death of John Abernethie and now vacant through James Gibson, min. of Pencaitland, to whom the vicarage had been assigned as part payment of his stipend, being a fugitive from the country.—[*Reg. Sec. Sig.*, lii, 1.]
1584

ARCHIBALD DOUGLAS, son of John D. of Garvelt.—[*G. R. Inhib.*, 3rd July 1663.]
1646

PATRICK SCOUGALL, line 3, for "1695" read "1659."
1659

ARCHIBALD DOUGLAS, line 11, for "Ewes" read "Mackerstoun."—[*Reg. of Deeds, Durie*, civ, 10th Nov. 1704.]
1684

ARCHIBALD LUNDIE, had issue—John, born 3rd Sept. 1704; Isobel, bapt. 15th Aug. 1706; Andrew, born 14th Dec. 1708, buried 27th March 1716; Archibald, born 3rd Dec. 1710; Cornelius, born 11th Aug. 1716; Katherine, born 9th Jan. 1720, died 13th July 1788; Adam, born 30th July 1722.
1696

ANDREW JOHNSTON, line 8, for "1761" read "1791."
1791

PATRICK FAIRBAIRN, line 15, for "1855" read "1853"; his daugh. Marion died at Tunbridge Wells 8th May 1934.
1840

THOMAS ELLIOT SIMPSON CLARKE, D.D. (Glasgow, 1919), died 28th June 1923; his daugh. Jessie Lothian (marr. 1st Sept. 1920 Capt. James Watt, New York); his son, John Elliot, died 13th Oct. 1943.
1885

JAMES GRAHAM GOODALL NICOLSON, ord. 13th Dec. 1923; trans. to West Linton, 22nd March 1928.

1923

(*Parish united with Bolton* 1928.)

TRANENT

Bishop de Bernham dedicated the Church of Tranent on 11th April 1244, and the Church of Seton on 23rd May 1247. In the parish was a Well of St Clement. At Seton stood the Hospital of St Germain of the Order of Cross-bearers with the Star of Bethlehem, under the rule of St Augustine, alternatively designated in brief, the Order of Bethlehem, the Order of St Mary of Bethlehem, and the Order of St Mary of the Star. The Order, about which some uncertainty exists, was one of Canons Regular of St Augustine, but originally they may have been simple hospitallers. They wore a black mantle on which was a red star with a blue centre, and possibly they also bore a cross. Of the actual founding of the establishment there is no record, but it took place prior to 1222, when Milone Cornet, prior of St Germain, appears as a witness of a Holyrood writ. In 1296 Bartholomew, Master of the Hospital of St Germain, swore fealty to Edward I; and subsequently the head is designated Master or Rector, and sometimes both. The hospital was subject to the Bishop of Bethlehem, who had the right of collation, provision, and disposition. The See of Bethlehem was erected by Baldwin, the first Latin king of Jerusalem, with consent of Pope Paschal II; and the bishop was a suffragan of the Bishop of Jerusalem. After the expulsion of the Latins by the Saracens in 1266 the Bishops took up residence in France, where a hospital was bequeathed to them by William, Count of Nevers, a crusader; and thereafter they were appointed by the Pope on the nomination of the Counts of Nevers, and held a merely titular dignity. To the Hospital of St Germain belonged the churches of Abergairn (Glengairn) and Glenmuick in Aberdeenshire, and Aberlethnott (Marykirk) in Kincardineshire. In addition to the lands of St Germain on which it was situated, the hospital possessed also the lands of Lochhouse in West Lothian; part of the lands of Kinblethmount in Angus, designated "the lands of the Hospital House of St Germain, called the Temple-lands of Kinblackmount"; land in Leith on the south side of the Water of Leith; the lands of Braidleys in the constabulary of Crail in Fife; and the land of St Germain at Inverkeithing. It is likely that to the hospital pertained also St Germain's acre at Inverteil, Kirkcaldy; but in any case the foregoing list canot be regarded as exhaustive. In 1372 Sir John Rollo was master of the hospital. About the beginning of the 15th century John Rollok, Chaplain of the Apostolic See, occupied the same position; and after his death the office was held by various individuals in somewhat rapid succession—Roger de Edinburgh, "a notorious schismatic," deposed in or before 1410; Henry de Ramsay, "of noble birth"; Richard de Maryton, Canon of Scone, in whose favour Robert, Duke of Albany, petitioned Pope Benedict XIII in 1410; John Fleming, secretary of Alexander, Earl of Crawford, "son of a priest and an unmarried woman," and chaplain of the Chaplainries of Kilgeny and St George in the Church of Dundee; and Richard de Langlands, priest of the Diocese of St Andrews, collated and assigned, and provided by John, Bishop of Bethlehem. The right of each of these was challenged; and in reality they constituted claimants and counter-claimants to the office. Later, in Feb. 1434–5, Dominic, Bishop of Bethlehem, claimed that the hospital belonged to the *Episcopa Mensa* of Bethlehem, as against the right of Patrick Rode, who had been collated Master by authority of the ordinary and its ordinance. Patrick Rode resigned his claim, and the Pope ordered the admission of Dominic as Master and granted to him the hospital itself to hold as long as he should be Bishop of Bethlehem. Later Dominic appears to have withdrawn his claim to the hospital, the sentence given in his favour not having been executed. In any case he died soon afterwards; and thereafter the Bishops of

Bethlehem seem to have lost St Germain. In the hands of Dominic's successor as Master, Patrick Piot, the hospital passed under a cloud; and in Dec. 1470 it was charged against him that he "has dilapidated the precious movables of that Church, which is wont to be held by brethern of the Order of the Cross-bearers with Star, and in which there have been wont to be a poor-hospital, and a number of brethern of the said Order, and has kept up no hospitality therein nor kept any brother of the said Order, but on the contrary has profaned the Church, in which there used to be Altars and other Chapels, and the relics of saints, and other ecclesiastical sacraments, and has allowed and still allows laymen to dwell therein with their wives and families, as if it were a private house, with occasional bloodshed, etc., and without the celebration of divine offices." Patrick Piot was deprived of office in or about 1476, and his successor was John de Camera (Chalmers), priest of the Diocese of Aberdeen. The latter ceased actively to hold the office in 1475, and by Papal Bulls of 22nd Dec. of that year he received as an annual pension or in place of a pension 25s. from the teind sheaves of the "vills of de Bernes and de Ecclesmaldeis (Eglismaldie, now Inglismaldie) in the parochial bounds of Aberbthnot (Aberlethnott), belonging to St Germain's Hospital." The next in order seems to have been Thomas Piot, priest of the Diocese of St Andrews, who was certainly in office in 1486. But less than a decade later the condition of the hospital was again revealed as deplorable. The funds had greatly diminished owing to continuous litigation, and not within the memory of man had the institution served the purpose of its founder. The buildings, except the chapel, had become ruinous; and the resources of the hospital were being applied to secular ends. So runs the narrative in the Bull of Pope Alexander VI, 9th Feb. 1495–6, by which on the petition of James IV the hospital was annexed to King's College, Aberdeen. The revenues of the hospital, amounting to £30, were thus devoted to college uses, with the reservation that one "religious person" of the Order of St Augustine should act as chaplain at the hospital, and should uphold and direct the chapel, and that at the hospital three "poor persons" should be maintained. It was also provided that three poor students should be supported at King's College. On 9th Aug. 1497 Thomas Piot resigned the hospital in the hands of William Elphinstone, Bishop of Aberdeen and Chancellor of the University, and received in return on 18th Aug. the Prebend of Cruden and the vicarage of Banff; and on 10th Feb. 1504–5 John Chalmers resigned his right to the hospital and his pension from the teind sheaves of the parish of Aberlethnott, and as part compensation was appointed to the parsonage of Fetterneir and the chaplainry of St Mary Magdalene in St Nicholas' Church, Aberdeen. On 2nd April 1541 Sir Peter Hutchesone was chaplain and preceptor of the hospital; before 12th Aug. 1577 the office was held by Alexander Moresone, alias Moreis, son of late Alexander Moreis, burgess of Edinburgh; and John Smysoun was in possession before 8th Feb. 1585–6.

The Church of Seton was dedicated by Bishop de Bernham on 23rd May 1247. On a petition of George, 3rd Lord Seton, craving that the Church of Seton be erected into a collegiate church for a provost, 6 canons and prebends, and 2 boys and a clerk, Pope Paul II gave mandate on 13th April 1470 to the Bishop of Whithorn and the Abbot of Newbattle to make enquiries and, if they saw fit, to carry out the erection. Delay ensued; and the actual erection was made on 20th June 1493 by George, 4th Lord Seton, following a Bull of Pope Alexander II in 1492. The collegiate church had the cure of souls of the parishioners. In the church there was an altar dedicated to the Virgin Mary, situated in the aisle of that name.—[*Charters of Holyrood*, 49; *Deeds relating to the Homage of Scotland*, 134; *Cal. of Papal Registers, Petitions*, i, 599, 639, *Letters*, viii, 488, 567, 638, xii, 337, 346, 356; *Cal. of Supplications Rel. to Scotland*, 13, 64–5, 83, 85–6, *S.H.S.*; *Fasti Aberdonenses*, 2, 9–11, 15–19, 50–1; *Spalding Club*; *Reg. Great Seal*, ii, 850, v, 2744, vi, 868, 915, vii, 967, 1084, 1568, viii, 197, ix, 289; *Excheq. Rolls*, ii, 445; *The Apostolic Camera and Scott. Benefices*, 165, 181, 256; *Retours*, vii, 312; *Hist. of the Carnegies*, ii, 346; *Scott. Hist. Review*, ix, 110; Lockhart's *Church in Scotland in 13th Century*, 50, 56; Stephen's *Hist. of Inverkeithing and Rosyth*, 332; James Young's *Prot. Bk.*, 450; for details of the church see *The Family of Seton* and Maitland's *Chronicle of the House of Seton.*]

1565 SIR STEPHEN MOFFAT, vicar 11th Nov. 1565.—[*Reg. Sec. Sig.*, xxxiv, 46.]

1568 JAMES SMALL, reader, Longniddry, Oct. 1568.—[*Edin. Tests.*, i, 311.]

1568 ALEXANDER FORRESTER, line 15, for "above" read "after"; his pres. was on the death of John Rowand through Stephen Moffat, present vicar, giving no compearance.—[*Reg. Sec. Sig.*, xlii; *Reg. Pres. Bene.*, i, (2), 28.]

1602 ROBERT WALLACE, his widow marr. (2) Alexander Maxwell of Little Cessnock.—[*Reg. of Deeds, Hay*, ccccix, 22.]

1784 HUGH CUNNINGHAM, his son, Robert Brown, surgeon, Tranent.

1806 JOHN HENDERSON, his daugh. Christina (marr. 26th Jan. 1841 Andrew Brown).

1850 ROBERT STEWART, pres. 3rd May 1850.

1852 WILLIAM CAESAR, pres. by Crown 16th Oct. 1851; his daugh., Lily Walter (marr. Robert Finnie, Riggonhead), died 3rd Nov. 1918; his son, John Alfred Church, died 6th Jan. 1937; his daugh., Felicia Livoni Rose, died 31st March 1945.

1904 ANDREW MIDDLEMASS HEWAT, died 12th March 1942; his son, John Ronald, died at Aberdeen 1st July 1937; his daugh. Margaret Constance Doris (marr. 12th May 1942 George Dudley Hugh, R.A.F., son of W. H. E. Green, Felton, Somerset).

YESTER

The usual name was Bothans; but the church when it was dedicated by Bishop de Bernham in 1241 was designated the Church of Yestrith (Yester). It was also called St Bothans, apparently from a supposed connection with St Bathan or Baithene; but the actual reason for the designation is not clear. In any case the church was dedicated to St Cuthbert. In 1708 the church was removed to Gifford. The old church is near Yester House, and became a mausoleum of the Hay family. On 1st Aug. 1420 William Hay, Kt., Sheriff of Peebles, Thomas Boyd, Lord of Kilmarnock, with consent of his son and heir, Thomas, Eustace Maxwell, and Dougal McDowel of Malcarriston (Makerstoun), co-lords of the Lordship of Yester, and patrons in turn of the Church of St Bothans, petitioned Henry, Bishop of St Andrews, for the erection of the church into a collegiate church; and on 22nd April 1421 the Bishop granted a foundation Charter. The collegiate church was for a provost and four chaplains, for each of whom provision was made, including a manse and garden. The third chaplain had reserved for him the whole land of Kirkbank, and three husband-lands and five cotelands in Duncanlaw; and to the fourth chaplain pertained the fruits of the Church of Morham which was annexed to the collegiate church, the annexation to operate when Morham became vacant, and Morham to be served by a chaplain. Among other details, all furnishings, ornaments, candles, etc., were also to be provided by the founders. There was also a clerk trained to read and sing at the high altar. Subsequently the organisation of the church expanded, and there were the following prebends: prebend of Morham; prebend of the Altar of St Mary the Virgin, on the east side of the church; prebend of Blans; prebend of the Altar of St Ninian; prebend of Kirkbank; prebend of the Altar of the Holy Rood; prebend of the Altar of St Edmund, King and Martyr, in the south transept or St Edmund's aisle. There was also an Altar of our Lord—St Salvator. Probably the first provost of the church was Sir John Richardson, who had been rector of the church and resigned to facilitate the collegiate foundation. At any rate he was provost on 13th Dec. 1432. Succeeding provosts were: Mr Stephen Kerr, in office on 20th Feb. 1442, and died before 28th May 1454; Sir David Ramsay, rector of Keryntoun (Carrington), presented 28th May 1454; Mr Fergus Makdowell, died before 18th March 1470-1; Mr Andrew Hay, Clerk to the Diocese of Glasgow, presented 18th March 1470-1, said to be identical with Mr Andrew Hay, second son of Sir David Hay of Lockerworth, and rector of Biggar, still in office 28th June 1494; Sir Thomas Young, in office 6th Aug. 1496 and 16th Feb. 1504-5; Mr Robert Walterston, in office 23rd May 1513, and still on 12th Dec. 1542, resigned soon after; Mr Thomas Hay, mentioned on 12th Dec. 1542 as future successor of Mr Robert Walterston, provost and usufructurer of the collegiate church, described as Archpriest of Dunbar on 10th Feb. 1542 in a Bull of Paul III allowing him to retain the said archpresbytery resigned by Robert Walterston, along with the provostry of St Bothans, in office as provost 21st March 1542-3, and died before 3rd May 1558; Mr Andrew Hay, chaplain to the provostry, presented 3rd May 1558; Sir William Dobsone, chaplain and prebendary in the church, presented on 29th July 1540 and died before 21st Oct. 1566, when Gilbert Brown, minister of the Church of the Holy Cross, Peebles, received presentation to the emoluments of the office. At Duncanlaw there was a chapel dedicated to St Nicholas. —[*Cal. of Yester Writs*, 16, 40, 53, 54, 55, 59, 79, 85, 86, 87, 92, 110, 116a, 152, 153, 162, 229, 235, 285, 354, 393, 478, 569, 601, 602, 605, 682, 684, 855a, 1001, 1057, 1058; *Reg. Great Seal*, i, App. ii, 1859; *Scots Peerage*, viii, 429; Lockhart's *Ch. in Scot. in 13th Century*, 46-7.]

1567 SIR ANDREW HAY (St. Edmont's) and JAMES TEMPLE, M.A., occur as Prebendaries 1567.—[*Comps. Sub Coll. of Thirds, Linlithgow*, etc.]

1572 WILLIAM MACHAMWELL, in office 1571.—[*Comps. Sub Coll. of Thirds, Linlithgow.*]

1676 JOHN HAY, dep. for fornication with his servant, Margaret Lamb. Was afterwards min. of Dunlop 168?.

1682 ROBERT MELDRUM, marr. Jean, daugh. of Andrew Melvin, min. of Morham.

1720 JAMES WITHERSPOON, his daugh. Susan (marr. proc. 17th Aug. 1760).

1760 JAMES INNES, died Father of the Church; marr. Mary, daugh. of William Hogg, merchant, Edinburgh.

1896 JOHN MUIR, died at Port Bannatyne 13th May 1920.

1920 JOHN CUMMING, M.A., trans. from St Andrew's, Alloa (*q.v.*) 27th Oct. 1920. Marr. 24th July 1923 Mary Graham Herries, daugh. of Thomas Rogerson, Lochmaben, and Anne Boyes Herries, and has issue—Archibald Robert Herries, born 16th Jan. 1926; Ewen Thomas Elder, born 26th April 1927; John Graham Rogerson, born 3rd May 1929; David Patrick Low, born 14th Oct. 1932.

PRESBYTERY OF DUNBAR

BELHAVEN

1840 WILLIAM SORLEY, his son, William Ritchie, died 28th July 1935; his daugh., Mary Simpson, died at London 21st March 1947.

1914 NORMAN MACLEOD, trans. to St. Bride's, Govan, 8th June 1927.

1927 ALEXANDER JOHN CAIRNS RITCHIE, trans. from Orwell (*q.v.*) 7th Oct. 1927; trans. to Culsalmond, 30th Oct. 1947.

COCKBURNSPATH

There was a hospital at Cockburnspath. South of the village is Chapelhill. Cockburnspath and Aldcambus were united by the Lords Commissioners of Teinds before 20th May 1610.

1571 MICHAEL BONKLE, min. at Innerwick, also in charge here.—[*Comps. Sub Coll. of Thirds, Linlithgow,* etc.]

1571 THOMAS LICHTON, reader 1571.—[*Comps. Sub Coll. of Thirds, Linlithgow,* etc.]

1574 DAVID HUME, for "1574" read "1576."

1587 JAMES LAMB, min. here 29th July 1587, when he was pres. to the vicarage of Bolton.—[*Reg. Sec. Sig.,* iv, 133.]

1599 JOHN LAUDER, min. 18th Jan. 1598-9.—[*Presb. Rec. Fraser Papers.*]

1689 DAVID CLUNIE, marr. Grissell, daugh. of Thomas Thomson, burgess of Inverkeithing, and Janet Mitchell. Issue—Helen (marr. cont. 17th April 1711 James Ferguson, burgess of Inverkeithing); Agnes; David, born 1693; John, born 1695; Andrew, born 1696, Christian; Thomas, M.A.; Alexander; merchant, Perth; Mabel.—[*Inverkeithing Burgh Sasines.*]

1789 ANDREW SPENCER, pres. 2nd June 1789.

1869 JOSEPH HUNTER, his widow, Jessie Brand, died 4th Oct. 1935.

1906 GEORGE VICTOR DUNNETT, trans. to Robertson Memorial, Edinburgh, 4th June 1920.

1920 LESLIE DUNCAN, M.A., adm. 28th Sept. 1920; trans. to St George's-in-the-Fields, Glasgow, 17th May 1926.

1926 WILLIAM ERIC KILMORACK RANKIN, born 12th Aug. 1899, son of Ewen Archibald R., D.D., min. of Kilmorack: educ. at Royal Academy, Inverness; Univ. of Glasgow, M.A. (1921), St Andrews, B.D. (26th June 1925); served with Black Watch in Great War; licen. by Presb. of Dingwall 29th April 1925; assistant Paisley Abbey 1925; ord. 28th Sept. 1926; trans. to Second Charge, St Andrews, 21st Feb. 1925; Chaplain to Forces 1939; prisoner of war in Germany June 1940. Marr. 21st June 1927 Irma Mary Lyell, second daugh. of Cuthbert Finch, Ramornie, Ellon, and has issue—Sheila Lois, born 2nd Dec. 1928; John Finch, born 18th Dec. 1934.

ALDCAMBUS

The church, whose ruins are situated on the shore not far from Aldcambus, is said to have been erected in the latter part of the 12th century. At Aldcambus there was a hospital for lepers, belonging to Coldingham Priory. In the time of William the Lion (1165–1214), David de Quinwood, baron of Quinwood, son of Arnold de Quinwood, endowed the hospital by giving to it and the lepers abiding there, a half ploughgate of land at Aldcambus, formerly held by Ralph the Tanner.—[Carr's *Coldingham Priory*, 96–7, 98, 265.]

JAMES LAMB, also min. at Cockburnspath (*q.v.*).
1584

THOMAS BONAR, pres. to vicarage of Simprim on death of Mungo Home, and to Aldcambus on dem. of Alexander Lumsden, 7th Feb. 1599.—[*Reg. Sec. Sig.*, lxxiv, 448.]
1599

DUNBAR

The earliest Christian settlement is said to have been associated both with St Abbs and Old Cambus. Three Northumbrian princesses, having found it advisable to seek refuge in Scotland from a virulent war which had broken out in their father's dominions, set sail for the Firth of Forth in a small vessel along with some friends and domestics. Having been compelled by a contrary wind to land near St Abbs Head, they were entertained by the Prior of Coldingham; and out of gratitude to their respective saints through whose intercession they deemed that they had been preserved, they erected severally a chapel at their own expense, viz. St Abb's (Ebba) on the summit of the "Head"; St Helen's at Old Cambus; and St Bees (Beya) on the shore at Dunbar. Whatever historical value may be attached to the story, certain it is that St Beya was the patron saint of Dunbar. There was a "St Bais Well" which, as indicated in a Charter of 1603, was close to the shore; and the exact locality is denoted by the modern name Bayswell, attached to the area overlooking the sea at the north-east part of the town. But the chapel or cell there must have disappeared at an early date, for the medieval church was situated where the modern church stands. It has been suggested that that church was of Saxon style, and that, when the collegiate church was founded in 1342, to the east end of the Saxon church or parish church of Dunbar were added a Gothic choir and transepts, entrance to the old west portion being by a Saxon arch. As completed, the church was cruciform, with a length of 123 feet, a breadth of 20–25 feet, and the cross-aisle or transepts 83 feet. An altar dedicated to the Virgin Mary was erected anew in 1342 in the nave or old portion of the church, and is described in 1507 as being "in the parish Church of Dunbar." In the church was a chaplainry called *Saulpriestis*. Extensive repairs were carried out on the church in 1779; and forty years later plans were made for a new church on the same site. The last service in the old church was held on 7th March 1819; on 17th April of that year the foundation stone of the new church was laid; and the latter, not quite completed, was opened for worship on 20th April 1821. Patrick, 7th Earl of Dunbar, who died at Whittinghame on 24th April 1289, was interred in the north aisle of the church. At the shore there was a chapel dedicated to St Anne. Hence the modern "St Anne's Court." There was also a chapel dedicated to St John, of which in the Lord High Treasurer's Accounts of 1501 there is this entry: "Item, the xix day of October to Schir Andro Wod to the bigging of Sanct Johne's Chapell in Dunbar, x li." Apparently in 1218 Christian Bruce, 2nd wife of Patrick, 5th Earl of Dunbar, and widow of William Bruce of Annandale, "biggit and foundit ane hous of religioun in the toun of Dunbar, and gave the sammin with all the rentis and profittis thairof to God and the brethern of the Ordour and religioun of the Trinity (Red Friars), the hous to be subject to the cure and reull of the minister of the place and brethern of Trinity at Berwick, the minister to be haldin to sustene and uphold in the said place and hous of Dunbar ane brother of the said Ordour to do divine service therein." In 1473, on account of Berwick having been held for many years by the English, and the Trinity House there "destroyit and put doun," the rents, etc., of that house were transferred by James III to the Red Friars of Peebles. This transfer was held as equivalent to the House of Dunbar and its rents, etc., also being transferred to Peebles; and in Letters of 1st July 1529 to the Ministry and Brethren of Peebles, James V disannulled all dispositions and nominations, etc., to the House of Dunbar that might impede the House at Peebles in the use of Dunbar House and its rents, and ordained Peebles to take all the profits of Dunbar for the sustentation of their place "to the Honour and Glory of God and of the Holy Croce there honorit and kepit." Specially revoked was the gift of the House of Dunbar made by the King to Sir John Scharp, Chaplain, on 8th March 1528-9. On 1st June 1558 Friar Gilbert Brown, Minister of the House of Peebles, set in feu to James Home in Dunbar 52 acres of land at Dunbar, rented 20 merks, that belonged to the House there. The Charter describes the various lands in detail, and includes also *le Masondew* in the north part of the town. By Charter of 31st March 1567 Queen Mary gave the lands, annual rents, etc., of the house to the burgh of Dunbar. The house itself was situated at what is now called Friar's Croft, south of Friar's Vennel, where the tower of the church may still be seen in use as a dovecot. In 1263 Patrick, Earl of Dunbar, founded a House of White Friars (Carmelites). All trace of the building has disappeared, but its situation, according to a Charter of 1576, was on the north side of "3 acres of lands of Newtonleys," in the region of the burgh common. At the head of High Street there was a Maison Dieu which was removed in 1728 to make room for a bowling green. It appears to have been the hospital connected with the collegiate church. Within the burgh there were—Priest's Croft; the lands of the Virgin Mary; the lands of St John; the "Frier-land," called the Kirkhill; and "the lands Franciscan, the Frier-landis," in the vicinity of the churchyard. Queen Mary's Charter of 31st March 1567 to the burgh included also the lands and annual rents that once pertained to the prebends, canons, chaplainries in the collegiate church and choir of the same, with all annual rents of lands in the liberty of the burgh or paid from the burgh common lands.—[*Reg. Great Seal*, ii, 1373, 3145, iv, 1576, 2543, 2978, 3033, 3037, vi, 1418, vii, 442; *Reg. Sec. Seal*, i, 4110, ii, 203; *Lord High Treas. Accounts*, ii, 86; Millar's *Hist. of Dunbar*, 186, 187, 191, 192, 195, with Sketch of Old Church; for account of Collegiate Church, see *Mis. Scott. Hist. Society*, Vol. vi.]

1564 ANDREW SIMSON, M.A., pres. on forfeiture of John Hamilton, M.A., parson (brother of James H. of Samuelston), for crimes of treason.—[*Reg. Pres. Bene.*, i, 26; *Reg. Sec. Sig.*, xxxix, 8; xl, 18.]

1575 ROBERT COLQUHOUN, M.A., parson, 28th April 1575; had a natural daugh., Agnes.—[*Cal. of Charters*, x, 2355.]

1578 WILLIAM KID, vicar and reader, 29th Nov. 1578.—[*Edin. Tests.*, vii, 240.]

1582 ALEXANDER HOME of Houndwood, his son Alexander served heir to his father in Houndwood 19th Feb. 1624, and in Kimmerghame 4th Aug. 1625.

1639 ANDREW STEVENSON, grandson of Andrew S., merchant, Edinburgh; his first wife was widow of Cuthbert Miller, W.S.

1657 RICHARD WADDELL, trans. to Stenton 6th Oct. 1658.

1665 ANDREW WOOD, Bishop of Caithness 1680.

1681 THOMAS WOOD, son of Thomas W., bailie of Maybole.

1733 ALEXANDER PYOTT, his son, James, died in Naples; his daugh., Anna, died unmarr.

1901 WILLIAM BORLAND, D.D. (Edinburgh 1926), died at Hawthorn, Melbourne, 16th Aug. 1945.

1913 JAMES KIRK, served in Seaforth Highlanders in Great War; awarded Military Cross June 1917; died of wounds 1st April 1918; his widow, Elizabeth M., died 3rd Aug. 1943; his only child, Betty Mackay (marr. 12th Oct. 1928 Robert Alastair Cunninghame Macnair, M.B., C.M., Felpham, Sussex).

1918 WILLIAM BROWN, trans. from Campsie (*q.v.*) 9th Oct. 1918; died 2nd Dec. 1940; his daugh., Jean Buchanan (marr. 22nd Sept. 1939 Graeme Matthew Warrack, L.R.C.P.&S., L.D.S., Captain, Royal Scots); his widow, Christina Macnie King, died at Edinburgh 18th Jan. 1947.

INNERWICK

The church was dedicated by Bishop de Bernham 17th Oct. 1242, the patron saint being St Michael. The present church was built in 1784. By Letters of 4th Oct. 1468 Pope Paul II united the perpetual vicarage to the *mensa* of the Collegiate Church of Dunglas. On the shore at Skateraw, at a place still called Chapel Point, there was a chapel dedicated to St Dionysius, the ruins of which still existed in the second half of the 18th century. There was also a chapel dedicated to the Virgin Mary.—[Theiner's *Vet. Monumenta*, 457; Lockhart's *Ch. in Scot. in* 13*th Century*, 52–3; Armstrong's *Map*, 1773; Mackinlay's *Anc. Ch. Dedications, Script.*, 96.]

1562 ALEXANDER CREICHTON, vicar 1562, and may have acted as reader, 14th Feb. 1567–8; died before 3rd July 1573.[*Comps. Gen. Coll. of Thirds*; Sir Thomas Johnsoun's *Prot. Book*, 532; *Reg. Pres. Bene.*, i, 27–8.]

1567 MICHAEL BONCLE, pres. on death of Alexander Creichton.—[*Reg. Pres. Bene.*, i (2), 8.]

1608 DAVID OGIL, M.A., min. at Bara, pres. to vicarage 28th April 1608 on death of Richard Ogil, but he declined.—[*Reg. Sec. Sig.*]

1608 PATRICK HAMILTON, delete "natural son of Thomas, Earl of Haddington" and read "6th son of Hans H., min. of Dunlop." His son Archibald, min. of Wigtown; his daugh., Elizabeth (marr. cont. 26th Dec. 1647 William Cunningham yr., merchant, Edinburgh).

1666 ALEXANDER FOULIS, eldest son of Harry F., commissary of Edinburgh. —[*Reg. of Deeds, Dal.*, xxiv, 531.]

1715 WILLIAM OGILVIE, his eldest son, William, surgeon; his daugh., Henrietta (marr. proc. 25th Dec. 1757 Andrew Hogg, brewer in Pleasance).

1824 ADAM FORMAN, his daugh., Catherine Margaret Martha, died 7th July 1932.

1906 THOMAS WILLIAM GRANT SUTHERLAND, died 13th Jan. 1939; his widow, Elizabeth Grant Cormack, died at Rotherham 21st Feb. 1941; his son, Robert, doctor, Rotherham.

OLDHAMSTOCKS

Before 30th Nov. 1423 Sir Alexander Home of Home and Dunglas founded at Dunglas a chapel dedicated to the Virgin Mary. On that date he granted to the chapel 3 husband-lands with a half land on the east side of Kello in Edrom parish, and an acre of land with "Mansion Place" in the town and territory of Dunglas near the fount called Bryan's Well. By Sir Alexander Home's son and successor, Sir Alexander Home, Kt., the Chapel of the Virgin was erected into a collegiate church for a provost, 3 chaplains, and 4 boys to sing in the choir. The erection was confirmed by Crown Charter of 22nd August 1450, which described the church as "lately founded," and by a Papal Bull of 2nd Jan. 1450–1, which narrates that Sir Alexander's motive for the erection was his desire "by a happy commerce to change earthly things into heavenly and temporal into eternal." The Bull also states that he "of the goods granted him by God caused a church to be built to the honour of Mary the mother of Jesus, and at his own cost to be constructed in a godly manner," which indicates that he had considerably enlarged and embellished the chapel built by his father. Provision for each chaplain was 12 merks annual rent derived as follows: First chaplain, from lands and annual rents of Kello; second chaplain, from lands and annual rents of Balevley and Gourdounshal in Crail in Fife; and third chaplain, from lands and annual rents also of Balevley and Gourdounshall. There was likewise provision for manses for the provost and chaplains. The support of the 4 boys was an annual rent from lands and annual rents of Hutton, Herrsile, Cockburnspath, and Pinkerton in Berwick. The Papal Bull of 2nd Jan. 1450-1, in addition to confirming the erection of the collegiate church, also appropriated, for the purpose of securing full provision for the "Provost and other persons" at the church, the greater and lesser teinds of the "Rectory of the Parish Church of Dunglas" (Oldhamstocks), value £5 yearly, the reasons assigned being that the whole rents provided for the foundation and endowment of the collegiate church were not wholly sufficient, and that the rectory of the Parish Church "so abounds in wealth that the rector for the time can be sufficiently provided for life without the greater and lesser teinds." The scope of the foundation of the church was extended; and there are on record 8 prebends at least—Oldhamstocks —13 merks annually from the lands of the same, given by Patrick Hepburn of Hailes and Oldhamstocks 7th Aug. 1450; Trefontaine or Strafontaine—lands of, in Abbey St Bathans, given on 11th Jan. 1451-2 by James II for the souls of his father and mother, James I and Queen Joan, for his own soul, and for the soul of Marie, his queen; Kello—13 merks annual rent; Chirnside—4 husband-lands, a merk land, and 8 merks annual rent from the Mainslands, all at Chirnside, given by Sir Alexander Home 5th Aug. 1450; Upsettlington—lands of, given by Alexander Benystoun of the same, lord of Upsettlington, 8th June 1460; Dewingham; Barnside—5 acres of land, in parish of Coldingham; Redspittal—lands of, in the parish of Aberlady; and Vigorushauch—lands of, in Roxburgh, and an annual rent of 40s. from Mains of Mordington, given on 16th Sept. 1503 by Patrick Hume or Home of Polwarth and his second wife, Helen Schaw, to a chaplain "celebrating and to celebrate Mass, chanting and to chant, within the Collegiate Church of Dunglas, and principally at the Altar of St Cuthbert on the south side of said Church." By Charter of 26th April 1451 William, Earl of Douglas and Avondale, granted to the church one husband-land in the town and territory of Hutton, and the church and hospital of the same; by Papal Bull of 12th Nov. 1458 the vicarage and tithes of Edrom Church were appropriated to the Provostry of Douglas, which was valued at £5, John Hume, vicar, having resigned; and by similar Bull of 4th Oct. 1468 the perpetual vicarage of Innerwick, not exceeding £12, was appropriated to the capitular *mensa*, the fruits of which were insufficient for the maintenance of the "8 canons and other beneficiaries" of the church. There was in the church an altar of the Virgin Mary, called "Our Lady of Piete" (Pity), to which George Hume of Ayton granted 20 merks annual rent from his lands of Cadschele and his husband-lands of the town of Duns, a Royal Precept of Confirmation being granted on 14th Nov. 1500 "to a perpetual Chaplain to sing at the Altar." The ruins of the church, which in 1711 was used as stables, still stand. Sir Alexander Home also founded near the church a hospital with chapel "under the invocation of the Most Glorious Virgin Mary and St John the Baptist" for the reception and maintenance "of the poor and other miserable persons." For the purpose of fulfilling Sir Alexander's desire to extend the scope of the work of the hospital Pope Sextus IV granted Indulgences to it on 5th Aug. 1480.—[*Reg. Great Seal*, ii, 387, vi, 1559; *Reg. Sec. Seal*, i, 592; *Laing Charters*, 1866; *Retours*, vi, 89; *Cal. Papal Reg., Letters*, xi, 397, xii, 223-4, 363; *Reports Hist. MSS. Comm.*, *MSS. Earl of Home*, 55, 56, 115, 120, 179, 318; Theiner's *Vet. Monumenta*, 457, 487; *The Apostolic Camera and Scott. Benefices*, 166; Walcott's *Anc. Ch. of Scot.*, 409.]

THOMAS HEPBURN, parson, manifestly identical with Mr Thomas Hepburne, rector 12th Aug. 1556, when Alexander Hepburne of Whitsome was described as his brother, and therefore

1547

identical with Thomas Hepburne who is recorded as in the Charge from 1562 onwards, and is described as natural son of Sir Alexander Hepburne of Whitsome; was appointed Master of Requests by Queen Mary on 7th May 1567; summoned for treason 20th Dec. 1567, and was intercommuned by the Privy Council five days later, having along with others held Dunbar Castle and refused to give it up; is called deceased on pres. to his son by James, Earl of Bothwell, 30th June 1584; his daugh. Anne (marr. cont. 24th April 1578 James Murray of Philiphaugh); had also a daugh. Margaret.—[Sir Thomas Dalrymple's *Prot. Bk.*, 12th Aug. 1556; *Acts Scott. Parl.*, iii, 6; *Reg. Privy Council*, i, 510, 552, 565, 576; *Laing Charters*, 2483; *Philiphaugh Charter Chest.*]

1561 GEORGE HEPBURN, M.A., parson and min. 1561-2; probably identical with Thomas H., parson 1556 and 1566.—[*Comps. Gen. Coll. of Thirds* and *Cal. of Charters*, viii, 1679, ix, 2012.]

1563 SIR ALEXANDER ELISOUN, portioner of Oldhamstocks, vicar 28th Jan. 1563-4.—[*Reg. Mag. Sig.*, v, 1217.]

1584 THOMAS HEPBURN, adm. 1584, buried at Oldhamstocks, 28th Jan. 1629; had also issue—Francis; Jean. —[*G. R. Sas.*, 3 Ser., xxxi, 225, xxxv, 266.]

1629 JOHN PATERSON, marr. Margaret, daugh. of William Murray, min. of Dysart; his eldest son, Duncan.— [*Adj.* 27th Sept. 1643.]

1642 THOMAS HEPBURN, his daugh. Margaret (marr. Patrick Hepburn, apothecary burgess, Edinburgh, afterwards Sir Patrick of Blackcastle).— [*G. R. Sas.*, lviii, 9, 2 Ser., viii, 270; xi, 152; xv, 406; 3 Ser., xxxv, 266; *Reg. of Deeds, Mack.*, lxxx, iv, 17th June 1699.]

1706 HARRY ROBERTSON, son of Thomas R., bailie, Edinburgh, was admitted Advocate 2nd July 1690.

1733 JOHN LUNDIE, born 3rd Sept. 1704; his daugh., Isobel (marr. proc. 25th June 1787 Henry Cant, dissenting min. at Spittal, Durham), died 1791.

1844 THOMAS MITCHELL, his daugh., Jemima Wilhelmia, died 26th Dec. 1946.

1876 WILLIAM MENZIES HUTTON, died 3rd Feb. 1915; his son, William, M.D.; his daugh., Janet Georgina, died at Dundee 14th Dec. 1928.

1913 JAMES BRYCE GORDON, died 19th May 1941.

PRESTONKIRK

There is a legend to the effect that at the death of Baldred, the patron saint, which is variously said to have occurred in 607-8 and 756-7, a claim to his body was made by his three churches, Preston (kirk), Aldhame and Tynninghame. In the course of the dispute a pious sage advised a night of prayer, to enable the Bishop in the morning to reach a decision. When the morning came, there were found three biers with three bodies, covered with clothes and alike in every detail. One was sent for interment to each of the claimants. About 50 yards east of the church there is St Baldred's Well, and in the Tyne adjacent is St Baldred's Whirl. There was in the church an aisle of St John the Baptist, for a chaplain of which Patrick Hepburne of Bolton gave on 23rd July 1545 a grant of £10 annually from the lands of Plewlands. The present church, with the exception of the choir, which appears to belong to the middle of the 13th century, was built in 1770. According to one account of St Modevenna or Monenna, an Irish saint, whose period is said to have been the latter part of the 5th century and early part of the 6th, and who left her native land in the company of two handmaidens, Dunpelder Hill (Traprain Law) was one of the sites on which she founded a church or chapel. At Wauchton in the north part of the parish there was a chapel which was subject to the mother church. Another chapel, dedicated to the Virgin Mary, was situated at Markle. In its later stages it had a collegiate organisation with a provostry and prebends, but the erection does not appear to have been confirmed. What remained of the Chapel in the first half of the 19th century is described as the "old ruins of a religious house on the farm of Markle," and under the description "Markle (Ruins of Monastery)" the site is explicitly indicated on the O.S. Map of 1908 in a field on the south side of the railway west of East Linton Station. In her widowhood Christine de Moubray, daughter and heir of Sir Bernard Fraser of Fortune and Linton, and wife of Sir Roger de Moubray of Barnbougle, who died before Jan. 1268-9, founded in the territory of her Manor of Houston in this parish a house of the Order of the Holy Trinity and Redemption of Captives (Red Friars), which was called "The Grace of God." The endowment was the whole land of her Manor of Houston, the whole land called Lyneryngham (Lingeam, Lerigamhill) in the tenement of Houston, the whole land which belonged to the Hospital of Fortune, in the parish of Athalestaneford, the whole land which belonged to the late Thomas of Lessendun, in the territory of Fortune, and the whole land of Crauchot (Crawho, Cracho), with which there appear, at a subsequent date, the Mills of Cracho and fishings. To the foregoing were added later annual rents from lands in the burgh of Haddington. The foundation was confirmed by Alexander II on 26th Jan. 1271-2. In August 1296 John, Master of the Hospital, swore fealty to Edward I, and a little later there was issued to the Sheriff of Haddington a writ to restore the property of the place. By Letter of 2nd Dec. 1531 James V gave the hospital and its endowments to the Red Friars' Convent at Peebles, and the union was made perpetual by a Charter of the same monarch, 8th Jan. 1541-2, which confirmed Christine de Moubray's foundation and its confirmation by Patrick, 7th Earl of Dunbar, and also the resignation made by David Kinloch, Minister at Houston, in favour of Friar James Paterson, Minister at Peebles, of Houston Hospital and its possessions. The exact site of the hospital can hardly be determined. Descriptions of the endowments in the 16th century and later reveal that included in the town and territory of Houston, in the neighbourhood of East Linton, there were, in addition to the lands of Lingeam mentioned in the foundation, Mains of "Houston," the Waulk-Mill of Houston, with 4 acres attached, lands called Hoigsland and Taitlie, the lands of Friarlie, on the east side of Quarrelbog or Quarrybog, in the town and territory of Linton, and salmon fishings in the Tyne, and other fishings, belonging to the said place (of Houston). The Mill of Houston, no longer used as a mill, stands on the right bank of the Tyne, opposite East Linton; and it would appear that somewhere in the region stretching from the mill the Red Friars' hospital was situated.

The patronage of the Chapel of Markles belonged to the Earls of Bothwell. The chaplainry of St John the Baptist in the Church of Prestonkirk was also under the patronage of the said Earls; it was designated the Provostry, and therefore may have been provisionally set aside, probably by the 1st Earl of Bothwell, as the endowment of the provost in a plan to erect the Chapel of Markles into a collegiate church. The endowment included 2 crofts of arable land with house and garden in the territory of the town of Preston or Linton. In the Castle of Hailes there was a chapel dedicated to St Michael the Archangel, the endowment of which was the Waulk-mill of Hailes, with multures, etc., and mill lands, and the lands of Loslett or Lochsleyt. At the Reformation Sir Walter Robesoun, vicar of Aberdour, was chaplain both of the Chaplainry of St John the Baptist and of the Chapel of Hailes.—[*Reg. Mag. Sig.*, ii, 3635; iii, 1220, 2569; v, 759; vi, 64; viii, 570; ix, 1702, 2189; *Reg. Sec. Sig.*, ii, 1069; *Acts Scott. Parl.*, iii, 256, iv, 294; *Retours*, i, 173, xv, 100, 140, xx, 94, xlvii, 291; *Laing Charters*, 499; *Gen. Reg. Sas.*, Vol. 396, f. 104, Vol. 675, f. 63; *Haddington Sas.*, Vol. 402, f. 97, Vol. 465, f. 223, Vol. 692, f. 126, Vol. 893, f. 285, Vol. 900, f. 262;

Prynne's *Recs. of the Tower of London*, iii, 656; Rymer's *Foedera*, ii, 726, i (2), 843, Ed. 1818; *Proc. Soc. Antiq.*, 1887–8, 27–8; *Lamp of Lothian*, 171, 172; Skene's *Celtic Scotland*, ii, 37.]

1561 SIR GEORGE HEPBURN, parson and min. 1561–2.—[*Coll. Gen. Thirds*, 97; *Acts and Dec.*, xxxv, 441; xxxvi, 360; xlii, 403; *Reg. Mag. Sig.*, iv, 2696.]

1562 SIR THOMAS WHITE, designated curate and vicar pensioner, 13th Aug. 1562.—[*Reg. Mag. Sig.*, iv, 2696.]

1569 GEORGE HAMILTON, M.A., parson, 1569.—[*Comps. Sub Coll. of Thirds, Linlithgow*, etc.]

1586 ROBERT HEPBURN, M.A., parson, 22nd July 1586.—[*Cal. of Charters*, xiii, 3016.]

1692 JOHN FOREST, died Dec. 1700; Thomas, his youngest son, 1705.

1702 THOMAS FINDLAY, his daugh., Mary (marr. (2) Oct. 1752 Hercules Lindsay, advocate).

1876 THOMAS STIRLING MARJORIBANKS, died 21st July 1918.

1916 ROBERT CLAYTON CORRIE, trans. from Culsalmond (*q.v.*) (assistant and successor) 19th Jan. 1916.

SPOTT

Spott was at first a dependent Chapel of Dunbar, and probably remained a parochial chapel until the Reformation. The church may have been dedicated to St John, for St John's Well was situated to the west of the church. Of the well, the Old Statistical Account says: "It is carried in pipes two miles to Dunbar for the supply of water to the inhabitants."—[*Scott. Hist. Soc. Mis.*, vi, 82, 102.]

1555 ALEXANDER HOME, second son of Sir John H. of Coldinknowes, was parson before 3rd May 1555, still parson 11th Aug. 1587; marr. Janet Hamilton; had a natural son, John, legitimated 27th Nov. 1582.—[*P. C. Reg., Reg. of Deeds*, xxviii, 44a; *Comps. Sub Coll. of Thirds, Linlithgow*, etc.; *Reg. Mag. Sig.*, v, 478, 1377.]

1574 JOHN MELVILLE, called in 1574, sometime min. of Spott.—[*Comps. Gen. Coll. of Thirds*.]

1631 WILLIAM DOUGLAS, trans. from Whittinghame, 1631.

1683 ARCHIBALD BUCHAN, had issue—Clara.—[*Deeds, Dal.* 1705, No. 233.]

1769 WILLIAM CROMBIE, his daugh., Elizabeth (marr. proc. 5th June 1794 Robert Armstrong, plumber, Edinburgh.)

1799 ALEXANDER GRAHAM, his daughs.—Margaret Aitken (marr. 30th July 1839 William Darling, merchant, Edinburgh); Catherine Hay (marr. 2nd July 1838 William Waddell, merchant, Edinburgh).

1836 ROBERT BURNS THOMSON, his daugh., Charlotte, died 6th Sept. 1923.

1889 LOTHIAN GRAY, died 30th April 1945; his daugh., Christian Isobel (marr. 16th April 1942 George Lloyd Alison Haig, Dylic Tea Estate, Doors, India).

STENTON

There was in the parish a chaplainry of Burnham. Pitcoks was a dependent chapel of Dunbar Church prior to becoming a prebend and was served by a parochial chaplain. The proximity of the Rood Well to the ruins of the old church suggests that the church was dedicated to the Holy Rood. The present church was opened for worship by Dr Chalmers on 4th Oct. 1828. The major part of its construction was borne by Mr H. R. Ferguson.—[*Reg. Mag. Sig.*, viii, 1905; *Miscell. Scot. Hist. Socy.*, vi, 82, 93.]

1568 WILLIAM SANDERSON, min. at Whittinghame, also in charge here.—[*Comps. Sub Coll. of Thirds, Linlithgow*, etc.]

1568 THOMAS DAILL, designated min. in 1568 and also in 1573.—[*Edin. Tests.*, ii, 366.]

1594 JAMES LAUDER, for "1593" read "1594."

1599 PATRICK CARKETTILL, Presb. clerk Jan. to April 1599.—[*Fraser Papers.*]

1658 RICHARD WADDELL, trans. to Kelso 14th May 1660.

1691 ROBERT STARK, born 5th Sept. 1654, son of David S., min. of Stichell. His sons—Robert, min. of Kinross; John, apprentice to George Reid, merchant, Edinburgh, 23rd Aug. 1732.

1849 THOMAS MARJORIBANKS, his son, Alexander, Royal Bank, died 21st Nov. 1923.

1868 GEORGE MARJORIBANKS, died 20th March 1921; his wife, Elizabeth Leslie, died 19th July 1918; his sons—George Erskine, Celtic scholar, died 1st Aug. 1940; James Leslie, M.D., died 25th March 1942.

1916 HUGH SKINNER MACKENZIE, trans. from Mouswald (*q.v.*) (assist. and successor) 16th May 1916; dem. 11th Nov. 1948. Publication—*The Churches of Pitcox and Stenton* (1929).

PITCOKS

1560 PATRICK COCKBURNE, M.A., parson in 1539 and designated parson when he died in 1568; had brothers—William, Adam, Symeon, Alexander.—[*Edin. Test.*, 11th July 1570; *Laing Charters*, 434.]

1578 THOMAS DAILL, min. in 1568.—[*Edin. Test.*, ii, 366.]

WHITEKIRK

On 13th Jan. 1386–7 Papal Relaxation of Penance was given to all who visit and give alms to the fabric of St Mary of Whitekirk, renowned for miracles wrought by Jesus Christ through the intercession and merits of St Mary.—[*Cal. of Papal Reg., Letters*, iv, 253; *Report on Ancient Monuments Commission* for full account of church.]

1592 JAMES KELLIE, pres. to vicarage 27th Oct. 1594 on dem. of James Young, min. at Tyningham.—[*Reg. Sec. Sig.*, lxvii, 108.]

1636 ROBERT LAUDER, his daugh., Margaret (marr. cont. 20th Jan. and 10th Feb. 1664 Alexander Bisset, min. of Melrose).—[*Reg. of Deeds, Mack.*, lxxxiv, 10th Feb. 1699.]

1694 WILLIAM HAMILTON, marr. (1) 24th April 1667.

1732 JOHN CLUNIE, his daugh., Charlotte (marr. James Bigge).

1785 JAMES WILLIAMSON, pres. 21st Jan. 1784.

1853 JAMES LANG, pres. by Crown 9th Feb. 1853.

1867 ADAM INCH RITCHIE, pres. by Crown 23rd Nov. 1867; line 9, for "30" read "13"; line 10, for "11" read "31"; his daugh., Marion Lilias, born 21st July 1862.

1879 PETER HATELY WADDELL, died at North Berwick 22nd Nov. 1922; his widow, Elizabeth Laidlay, died 17th Jan. 1924.—[*Life and Letters of P. Hately Waddell*, by John C. Gibson, 1925.]

1904 EDWARD BLACKMORE RANKEN, drowned while bathing at Scougal Rocks, 22nd Aug. 1916; his widow, Jeannie Mackintosh, died at New Glasgow, Nova Scotia, 31st Aug. 1941.

1917 JAMES TINDAL SOUTTER, trans. from Nairobi (*q.v.*) 8th March 1917; Marr. (2) 1st June 1940 Freda, elder daugh. of Joseph Frederick Pattinson, Fellside, Grange-over-Sands, and has issue, Anna Freda, born 18th April 1941.

ALDHAME

The church, dedicated by Bishop de Bernham on 23rd April 1243, was demolished in 1770. There is a well of St

Baldred. At Scougal, about a mile south-east of Aldhame, there was a chapel founded by one of the Scougal family.—[Chalmer's *Caledonia*, iv, 547; Lockhart's *Church in Scotland in 13th Century*, 53.]

TYNNINGHAME

At Tynninghame there was a Saxon monastery associated with Lindisfarne, to which belonged "the whole land pertaining to the Monastery of St Balthere (Baldred) from Lammermoor as far as Exmouth" (Inveresk). The church and town were burned and destroyed by Anlafus the Dane in 941, shortly before his death. By Bull of Pope Sixtus IV, 24th Feb. 1473, the church became a mensal Church of St Andrews.—[*Chron. of Melrose*, 29; Fordoun, *Scott. Hist.*, i, 134; *The Apostolic Camera and Scott. Benefices*, 173; see Prestonkirk.]

MATTHEW LIDDELL, reader; reader 29th Aug. 1569, and min. Nov. 1572 and 1573.—[*Edin. Test.*, i, 330, ii, 347; *Comps. Sub Coll. of Thirds, Linlithgow*, etc.]
1570

WHITTINGEHAME

Whittingehame was an affiliated Chapel of Dunbar, but it was served by a perpetual vicar. There was also an affiliated Chapel of Dunbar at Penshiel within the bounds. It served the higher part of the parish in the Lammermoors, whereas Whittingehame served the lower. Near the site of Penshiel Chapel are the Chapel Stone on the south, and on the north the Chapel Cleugh with St Mungo's Well, which may indicate the dedication of the Chapel.—[*Misc. S.H.S.*, vi, 82, 92; Chalmers' *Caledonia*, iv, 540.]

THOMAS LYLE, vicar 1560–8.—[*Edin. Tests.*]
1560

WILLIAM SANDERSON, min. in office 2nd Nov. 1571, when he was presented to the parsonage vacant by forfeiture of Claud Hamilton.—[*Reg. Sec. Sig.*, xl, 19.]
1567

WILLIAM STEWART, brother of Thomas S. of Galston, pres. to vicarage 25th Jan. 1570–1 on forfeiture of Claud Hamilton.—[*Reg. Sec. Sig.*, xxxix, 58.]
1570

ABRAHAM HOME, marr. Elizabeth, daugh. of George Hay of Broadhaugh; his daugh. Margaret (marr. James Renton, wine merchant, Eyemouth); his sons—Robert, merchant, Berwick, died 6th June 1812; Abraham, died on passage to London.
1748

JAMES ROBERTSON, died at Edinburgh 27th May 1920; his widow, Elizabeth Mary Scott Moncrieff, died at Edinburgh 15th June 1935.
1865

MARSHALL BUCHANAN LANG, trans. from St John's, Dundee (assist. and suc.) 14th Nov. 1918. D.D. Glasgow (30th June 1930); Moderator of General Assembly May 1935; his daughs.—Margaret Eleanor (marr. 4th July 1925 Robert Holmes Kerr Hope Yr. of Kinnettles, Lieut., Cameron Highlanders); Anne Laurence (marr. 16th April 1932 Capt. Harry Alexander Macdonald, R.E.). Addl. Publications—*The Seven Ages of an East Lothian Parish* (1929); *The Evolution of the Kirk.*—[*Trans. Scot. Eccl. Soc.*, 1932.]
1918

INDEX

North Esk, for "238" read "338."

SYNOD OF MERSE AND TEVIOTDALE

PRESBYTERY OF DUNS

ABBEY ST BATHANS

1563 WILLIAM COLVILLE, reader, 1563-72.—[*Comps. Sub Coll. of Thirds, Roxburgh*, etc.]

1591 MATTHEW LIDDELL, had charge here from 1570. See Cranshaws.

1675 JAMES DUNBAR, his son, David, apprenticed to Thomas Kinnaird, surgeon, 16th Feb. 1676.

1699 GEORGE HOME, marr. (1) Rebecca, daugh. of Robert Pow, notary, Eyemouth; his son, Ninian, apprentice to George Moseman, stationer, Edinburgh, 19th Aug. 1696.

1707 GEORGE HOME, eldest son of Alexander H. of Abbey St Bathans and Ann, daugh. of George Rule, min. of Longformacus. Marr. (1) cont. 14th and 16th July 1692 Eupham, second daugh. of Patrick Hepburn of Nunraw, and (2) cont. 7th Jan. 1700 Rebecca (bapt. 26th Dec. 1670), daugh. of Robert Pow, headmaster of Leith Grammar School.—[*South Leith Reg.; Berwick Sas.*, i, 365, vi, 100, 103.]

1719 JAMES HALL, bapt. Stamfordham, 15th Feb. 1684, son of Thomas H. in Ryall; marr. (1) name unknown, and had issue—Marion, marr. proc. 13th Aug. 1732 (not 1752); (2) proc. 27th May 1722, and had issue—John, bapt. 16th June 1723; George, bapt. 11th April 1725; Janet, bapt. 23rd Feb. 1727; Margaret, bapt. 19th Oct. 1729; James, bapt. 18th May 1732; Jean, bapt. 1st Aug. 1737.

1843 THOMAS DAVIDSON, pres. by Crown, 18th Aug. 1843; his daugh., Christina Simson, died 13th Sept. 1917.

1873 PETER CHRISTIE, pres. 10th May 1873.

1910 WILLIAM WILSON BELL, trans. to Monzievaird 10th May 1918.

1918 ALEXANDER SCOTT BERRIE, trans. from Broughton U.F. Church 19th Sept. 1918; trans. to Berriedale 8th April 1927.

(*Parish united to Cranshaws by General Assembly May* 1927.)

BUNKLE and PRESTON

1563 JOHN BLACK, exhorter at Preston 1563 and Bunkle 1567.—[*Comps. Sub Coll. of Thirds, Roxburgh*, etc.]

1574 WILLIAM SINCLAIR, pres. to vicarage on death of Sir Harry Kinloch; pres. to vicarage of Preston 20th Nov. 1585 on death of John Brisbane.—[*Reg. Pres. Bene.*, iii, 72; *Reg. Sec. Sig.*, lviii, 53.]

1597 JOHN DAVIDSON, min. at Preston, pres. to vicarage 27th Dec. 1597 on death of Alexander Forrester.—[*Reg. Sec. Sig.*, lxix, 181.]

1880 LUDOVIC MAIR, died 20th Dec. 1922; his widow, Jane Barclay Millar, died 14th April 1941; his daugh., Minnie Ronald, died 2nd March 1921.

DONALD WILLIAM MACKAY, born 22nd March 1891, son of Evander Mackay, F.E.I.S., J.P., schoolmaster at Farr, Sutherland, and Isabella McLeod Mackay. Educ. at Farr, George Watson's College, Edinburgh, Univ. of Edinburgh, M.A. (1914), Univ. of Poitiers, France, and Edinburgh Univ. Divinity Hall; Commissioned as 2nd Lieut. R.G.A. (S.R.) Aug. 1914; served in B.E.F. France and Flanders; promoted Major and Battery Commander Oct. 1917; Army of the Rhine 1919; Chief Instructor of Gunnery in II Corps; relinquished commission 1920. Licen. by Presb. of Edinburgh 29th June 1921; Assistant at Lady Glenorchy's, Edinburgh, Oct. 1921 to May 1923. Ord. 10th May 1923; trans. to Scots Church, Rotterdam, 31st March 1935; trans. to Northesk 5th Feb. 1941. Marr. 24th Aug. 1928 Ethel Clair, daugh. of Dr William Symington, V.D., M.B., Ch.B., J.P., of Brampton, Cumberland, and has issue, Iona Clair, born 15th Sept. 1929.
1923

CRANSHAWS

DAVID SWINTON, parson 1561–71.—[*Acts and Dec.*, xxvii, 254; xxxiii, 88; xlvii, 245, 289, 292; *Comps. Sub Coll. of Thirds*, Linlithgow, etc.]
1561

WILLIAM KNOWES, vicar pensioner 1576–7.—[*Comps. Gen. Coll. of Thirds.*]
1563

MATTHEW LIDDELL, adm. after Nov. 1572, continued 1590. See Ellem.
1572

WILLIAM HAY, M.A., son of William H. of Barra; pres. to parsonage and vicarage 27th Jan. 1591–2 on death of David Swinton.—[*Reg. Sec. Sig.*, lxiii, 182.]
1591

ALEXANDER SWINTON, pres. to parsonage and vicarage 2nd June 1593, on death of William Hay.—[*Reg. Sec. Sig.*, lxv, 93.]
1593

JOHN HEPBURN, pres. 21st Feb. 1595–6 on death of Alexander Swinton.
1596

JOHN CAMPBELL, his son, James, apprentice to William Douglas, baxter, Edinburgh, 5th Jan. 1726.
1706

ALEXANDER JOHNSTON, line 4, for "15" read "14."
1792

JAMES HOPE SIBBALD, his daugh., Wilhelmina, died 17th Jan. 1928.
1813

ROBERT BRIDGES SMITH, licen. by Presb. of Edinburgh 11th May 1876; his widow, Mary Ann Pringle, died 23rd May 1923; his son, Robert, died 25th Aug. 1935; his daugh., Christian Kent Bridges (marr. 15th Aug. 1929 Clifford Briggs, Harehill, Leeds).
1879

THOMAS GILLIESON, trans. to St Bride's, Edinburgh, 9th Oct. 1919.
1914

JOHN KENNEDY MACKENZIE, M.A., ord. 19th Feb. 1920; trans. to Stornoway, 26th Nov. 1924.
1920

GEORGE CAMPBELL, trans. from Cartsburn (*q.v.*) 9th April 1925; retired in favour of C. & S.; died at Kirkwall 28th Dec. 1940.
1925

DUNS

ARCHIBALD HOME, M.A., parson 13th Aug. 1562; died in or just before 1572.—[*Comps. Gen. Coll. of Thirds*; *Reg. of Deeds*, vii, 192.]
1562

SIR JOHN RAMSAY, vicar pensioner 28th Sept. 1572.—[*Hist. MSS. Com., Duns Castle Papers*, 40.]
1572

DAVID HOME, parson, 10th Aug. 1573.—[*Yester Writs*, 771.]
1573

PATRICK GAITTES, M.A., pres. to vicarage 26th Jan. 1582 on death of John Bennett.—[*Reg. Pres. Bene.*, ii, 85.]
1582

PETER DANIELSTON, M.A., pres. to parsonage and vicarage 13th Aug. 1585, which had been held by the late Captain David Home of Fishwick.—[*Reg. Sec. Sig.*, xlvii, 16.]
1585

JOHN WEMYSS, line 2, delete "only"; line 19, delete "marr. (2) Janet Murray" to "10th April 1664."
1613

LAURENCE JOHNSTON, father a founder in Edinburgh.
1703

WILLIAM DAVID HERALD, his widow, Florence Elizabeth Renton, died 10th Sept. 1939; his son, Arthur Terrant Ashly, Lieut. 17th Lancers, died from effects of motor accident, Asansol, India, 21st Nov. 1923; his daugh., Agnes Given (marr. 11th Jan 1918 Sir John Fraser, Bart., M.C., M.D.).
1882

ANDREW EWING WALLACE, his mother was Eliza Ewing. He died 18th June 1943.
1907

DUNS BOSTON

WILLIAM COUSIN, his son, William Victor, died 17th July 1918; his daugh., Ann Parker, died 2nd March 1930.
1840

ECCLES

The Church of St Cuthbert of Eccles, with its dependent chapels—Chapel of St Mary the Virgin at Leitholm, Chapel of St John at Mersington, and the Chapel of St Mary Magdalene at Birgham—belonged to the Priory of Eccles. In 1567 there is reference to the parsonage and vicarage of the four kirks and parishes, "Our Lady Parochin, Sanct John's Parochin, and the Magdalene and Sanct Cuthbert's Parochinns," and in 1609 there are "the Parish Church of Eccles called the Lady Kirk, and the Chapels of St John, St Cuthbert, and St Magdalene." It would appear, therefore, that for a time after the Reformation the Lady Chapel at Leitholm was regarded as the parish church. It was situated on a knoll called the Chapel Knowe at the northwest end of the village. The burial ground of the chapel has long since disappeared. The chapel at Birgham was situated in the north end of the existing parish burial ground. In 1649 Parliament ratified a petition of the Presbytery of Duns for disjoining from Eccles the lands east and north of Lamdenburn, and the erection of a new church at East Mersington; but apart from the disjunction of Lamden from Eccles, nothing appears to have been done. In 1774 the old Church of St Cuthbert at Eccles was removed with the exception of the north transept, which appears to have become a burial place and still exists in a ruinous condition; and on a site to the west the present church was then built. The Old Statistical Account states that the old church was Gothic in design, cruciform in shape, vaulted and covered with large flagstones, dedicated to St Andrew in 1248, and ornamented with a cross and a very excellent steeple. It will be observed, however, that in the records of the 16th and 17th centuries there is not only no reference to St Cuthbert having been supplanted by St Andrew, but the name of St Cuthbert is continued. The church was "won" by the English invaders on 27th Sept. 1544. There is a death-bell of 1715 inscribed "For the people of Ekkles." The Cistercian Priory of Eccles, dedicated to the Virgin Mary, is variously stated to have been founded by Gospatrick, Earl of March and Dunbar, in 1154, and a second time by him in 1156, and also to have been founded by the Countess of March. The Church of Eccles and its dependent chapels were granted to the priory by Gospatrick; and the priory held also the Church of Bothkennar. After being burned by the English under Hertford in Sept. 1545, the priory was not rebuilt. By Charter of 28th Jan. 1568–9 Margaret Home, the prioress, conveyed to Alexander Home of North Berwick the mansion called the *Newark*, and the house, buildings of her monastery, with dovecot, gardens, and orchards, belonging to the monastery (except the church and cloisters of the same), which "through turbulent times, chiefly for the cause of religion, when the said Prioress and the Nuns had been dispersed, had fallen into ruins, so that they were in the least degree habitable"; and by Crown Charter of 20th March 1587–8 the King, understanding that "the superstitious monasticism," for which the monastery had been founded, was abolished by the laws of the king, granted to Alexander

Home of North Berwick the place in which the church and cloisters had been situated (foundations now gone), and the *Newark* Mansion, etc. All that remained of the priory in 1834 was "a wall forming part of the East gable of Eccles House," i.e. the Newark Mansion House, "and two vaulted cellars contiguous to the Churchyard." The said wall appears to be identical with what is now the east wall of the rose garden of the present Eccles House built at the site of the former *Newark* Mansion; and the two cells and the fish pond of the priory are situated within the private grounds of Eccles House. In 1939 the church was entirely reconstructed internally and refurnished, a new hall and vestry being added.—[*Reg. Great Seal*, iv, 1919, v, 1492; *Acts Scott. Parl.*, vi, (2) 306; *Report Hist. MSS. Commission, MSS. Duke of Athol and Earl of Home*, 128–9, 131–2, 141, 146–7; *Chron. of Melrose*, 75–6; *Reg. Priory of St Andrews*, 56–60; Chalmers' *Caledonia*, iii, 343; *Memo.*, Rev. J. G. Douglas.]

ROBERT FRENCH, scholar, 1563,
1567 designated min. 1567, Eccles being in his charge after he went to Hume.—[*Edin. Tests.*, v. 80.]

HENRY BLYTH, imprisoned at Blackness 1605, Inverness 1619. His son
1622 by first marr., John, min. of Ochiltree.

JOHN JAMIESON; on 24th July 1654
1654 the Commissioners, under the Commonwealth for visiting Universities and placing and disciplining Ministers, desired the conjoint Sheriffs of Berwick to prevent Mr John Jamieson from preaching in the parish of Eccles; on 1st Feb. 1656 a summons was served upon him by the Commissioners in his "Chalmer in the Tofts" to appear before the Protector's Council on 7th Feb. 1656; and on 8th Feb. 1656 there was issued an Order of Council that in regard Mr Jamieson has preached on the borders of Eccles parish and "taken a libertie to renew the memorie of Charles Stewart (Charles I) to his auditors to stir up their affection to him," the Council require "that he shall not preach any more in the parish or on the border of it."—[*Hist. MSS. Comm. Report, MSS. Earl of Home*, 132–3.]

ANDREW RUTHERFORD; an Order
1655 of the Commissioners under the Commonwealth for visiting Universities and placing and disciplining Ministers, of date at Edinburgh 10th July 1654, narrates that as Mr Andrew Rutherford is elected Minister at Eccles, and "hath a lawfull call by certain Godly and wel affected persons in the said parish to exercise his ministeriall dutyes, the Commissioners approve and authorise him to uplift the stipend, forbidding any one to disturb him in his parish, providing that he shall not revile the Government, nor keep the people disaffected by praying and preaching agt. it."—[*Hist. MSS. Comm. Report, MSS. Earl of Home*, 132–3.]

JAMES RUTHERFORD WATSON,
1846 his daugh., Jessie Rutherford, died at Edinburgh 15th Dec. 1931.

JOHN JOHNSTON, died 26th Nov.
1891 1923; his widow, George Greig, died 25th April 1943.

JOHN LEONARD DOUGLAS, born
1924 2nd June 1899, son of David D., Dundee, and Susanna Alice Fisher; educ. at Harris Academy and Univ. of St Andrews, M.A. (1920), B.D. (1922); served in Cameron Highlanders in Great War; licen. by Presb. of Dundee 8th June 1922; assistant at Riccarton; ord. 8th May 1924. Marr. 22nd July 1932 Mabel Mary Watson, daugh. of John Mackechnie, min. of Edrom, and has issue—David Ogilvy, born 7th May 1933; Iain Mackechnie, born 25th June 1935; Dorothy Elizabeth Susanna Mabel, born 18th July 1938; Margaret, born 9th April 1944; Donald Fisher, born 28th Jan. 1947.

FOGO

DONALD BALFOUR, reader 1571–4.
1571 —[*Comps. Sub Coll. of Thirds, Linlithgow*, etc.]

1591 WILLIAM METHVEN, min. of Langton, pres. to vicarage 8th May 1591 on death of Sir George Manderston.—[*Reg. Sec. Sig.*, lxii, 357.]

1626 JAMES METHVEN, marr. Isobel Dickson.—[*Reg. of Deeds Dal.*, xxvi, 390; *G. R. Sas.*, lx, 286.]

1660 JOHN PRINGLE, line 1, delete "only."

1682 WILLIAM METHVEN, son of James M. in Greenlaw.—[*P. R. Sas.*, Berwick, 2 Ser., iv, 84.]

1785 JOHN TODD, line 5, for "26" read "21."

1843 ANDREW REDMAN BONAR, pres. by Crown 21st July 1843.

1845 ROBERT FORRESTER PROUDFOOT, pres. by Crown 29th April 1845.

1891 WILLIAM HENRY GRAY SMITH, licen. 18th May 1886; his widow, Marion Ellison Somerville Stark, died 17th Feb. 1926; his daugh., Hester Ada (marr. 25th Aug. 1934 Hugh D. R. Davidson, Edinburgh).

1913 ALEXANDER WILSON FINLAYSON, trans. to Campsie 9th April 1919.

1919 HUGH SHIRLAW, M.A., B.D., ord. 11th Sept. 1919; trans. to St Ninian's, Lochee 1st Oct. 1925; trans. to St David's, Crail, 16th May 1949.

1926 JOHN CRABBE TEMPLETON HUNTER, born 21st March 1900, only son of John H., Edinburgh, and Annie Mackenzie; educ. at Univ. of Edinburgh, M.A. (1919), B.D. (1922); Oxford, B.Litt. (1924); licen. by Presb. of Edinburgh 2nd April 1924, assistant West St Giles; ord. 24th March 1926; marr. 31st July 1935 Elizabeth Christina Kennedy, elder daugh. of John McKechnie, min. of Edrom, and has issue—John Rattray Mackechnie, born 20th March 1937; Thomas Mackenzie Douglas, born 19th July 1938; Alisdair David Skene, born 27th March 1940; Elizabeth Marion Mabel, born 3rd July 1942.

GREENLAW

The church was almost entirely rebuilt in the closing years of the 17th century.

1568 WILLIAM SHAW, M.A., parson in 1568 and 1571.—[*Comps. Sub Coll. of Thirds, Dumfries*, etc.]

1569 SIR JOHN AFFLECK, charged to answer for his demerits before the Privy Council 17th Oct. 1569.—[*P.C. Reg.*, ii, 40.]

1573 ROBERT FRENCH, pres. to vicarage on death of Andrew Turnbull.—[*Reg. Pres. Bene.*, ii, (4), 5.]

1645 ROBERT HOME.—[*G. R. Sas.*, liv, 253.]

1674 JOHN HOME of Kello, marr. cont. 17th Sept. 1678 Elizabeth, daugh. of Robert Watson, barber in Eccles.—[*Berwick Sasines.*]

1711 JAMES GILLILAND, his son, James, apprentice to Archibald Ure, goldsmith, 25th Feb. 1730.

1821 ABRAHAM HOME, had issue—George, born 12th Feb. 1823, died March 1858; Patrick Anderson, born 27th April 1824, died June 1874; Susan Hamilton, born 22nd Jan. 1822, died Jan. 1831; Margaret, born 18th Sept. 1825, died 11th Sept. 1907; Ann Mary, born 5th Feb. 1827, died June 1866; Elizabeth Hay, born 15th April 1830, died 20th March 1831.

1844 JOHN HUNTER WALKER, his daugh., Elizabeth, died at Edinburgh 7th Sept. 1925.

1886 HUGH McCULLOCH, died at Portrush 13th Aug. 1937; his widow, Annie Ross, died 2nd Sept. 1937.

1887 THOMAS REID THOMSON, his wife, Henrietta Hamilton Hill, died 11th Nov. 1930. He died at Greenock 30th March 1945 *s.p.*

LANGTON

The church was dedicated by Bishop de Bernham on 6th April 1242.

1570 PATRICK COCKBURN, vicar 1570–1.—[*Comps. Sub Coll. of Thirds, Linlithgow.*]

1584 THOMAS OGILVY, M.A., parson 1584.—[*Comps. Gen. Coll. of Thirds.*]

1810 JOHN BROWN, his daugh., Margaret (marr. 25th July 1855 Colin Brown, Glasgow).

1892 JOHN PEATTIE, licen. 13th May 1887; his wife, Margaret Crombie Grant, died at Alloa 31st Dec. 1917; he died 4th July 1931.

LONGFORMACUS

By Royal Letters of 14th Feb. 1510–11 the church was annexed to the archdeanery of the Chapel Royal of Stirling because the prebend of Glenquhon (Glenholm) within the Chapel Royal "is to be erected in ane Archdeanery within the Chapel Royal," and "the rentis and fruitis of the said prebend as to litill and solur to sustene the honour and expens of the said Archdeanery."—[*Reg. Sec. Seal*, i, 2207.]

1568 ARCHIBALD HOME, vicar 1568.—[*Comps. Sub Coll. of Thirds, Linlithgow*, etc.]

1581 ROBERT DOUGLAS, parson and vicar, died before 6th April 1581; had issue—Robert, was charged to compear before the Privy Council on 26th July 1614, on a charge of having slain Francis Bothwell, brother of John, Lord Holyroodhouse, on 24th July 1614, "with the stock of ane hagbute," failed to appear, and was put to the horn on 8th Sept. following; Patrick, who on 14th Sept. 1614 was grieve to Sir Archibald Douglas of Whittinghame.—[*Reg. Pres. to Benefs.*, ii, 55; *Reg. Privy Council*, x, 255, 269, 271.]

1607 GEORGE RULE, was also min. in charge till 1648. Latterly designated min. of the same; son, Gilbert, identical with Gilbert Rule, M.D., Principal, Edinburgh Univ., and min. of Greyfriars, Edinburgh; Archibald, was merchant in Edinburgh; Isabella, appears to have been unmarr.; Anna was 2nd wife of Alex. Hume of Abbey St Bathans; addit. issue—Robert, portioner, Peelwalls, min., Stirling; George, portioner of Peelwalls (marr. Marie, daugh. of Robert Risley, Peelwalls), died before 27th May 1684.—[*Gen. Sas.*, Ser. 1, 265 (1666), 33–309 (1674), 37–112, 116, 150–268 (1684), 53–284 (1686).]

1715 DANIEL SINCLAIR, son of James S., Thurso, marr. Elizabeth, daugh. of Sir William Hamilton of Airdrie, min. of Bothwell, and had issue—James, born 6th March 1730; Robert, born 21st May 1731; William, born 3rd Jan. 1733.—[*House of Hamilton*, 710.]

1871 GEORGE COOK, his widow, Helen Lorrain, died 6th June 1919.

1916 ROBERT CRANSTON KERR, trans. to Kelso North 14th Nov. 1928.

1929 RICHARD CALLEN, LL.B., born Dunoon 23rd Sept. 1895, son of Richard C., road surveyor, Dunoon, and Isobel Murray; educ. at Univ. of Glasgow, B.L. (1922), M.A. (1925), LL.B. (1926); served in R.A.F.; licen. by Presb. of Glasgow 27th April 1927; assistant Peebles, 1927; ord. 18th April 1929; trans. to Wick North, 30th April 1930; trans. to Westruther, 8th April 1932. Marr. 15th March 1933 Marion Tennant, daugh. of William J. Aitken, and has issue, Richard Murray Aitken, born 14th April 1944.

ELLEM

On 12th Feb. 1507–8 King James IV granted a protection to Mr James Watson, parson of Ellem, "makand mentioun that he is of the King's benevolence and special licence to pass to Sanct Andrie's grafe besyde Napillis and thereafter to remaine in Italy at his study for the space of vi zeris to run," and therefore the King takes his property under his protection.—[*Reg. Sec. Sig.*, i, 1606.]

1574 MATTHEW LIDDELL, had charge here 1574–85. See Cranshaws.

1596 GEORGE REDPATH, returned from Bunkle previous in 1603.—[*Comps. Surplus of Thirds of Benefices.*]

1647 PATRICK HOME, line 3, for "1650" read "before 24th June 1649."

1654 ZACHARY WILKIE, issue by 1st marr.—Mary.—[*Berwick Sas.*, 30th Oct. 1677.]

1684 JOHN BROWN, marr. Margaret, daugh. of John Duns, portioner of Grueldykes.—[*Berwick Sas.*, 15th Dec. 1685.]

POLWARTH

The interior of the church was partially restored in 1928.

1560 ADAM HUME, his wife's name was Dewar, not Stewart; his son, Alexander, described as in North Berwick on 14th Sept. 1614, when he was charged before the Privy Council with having received Robert Douglas, son of late Robert D., parson of Longformacus, after the said Robert had slain Francis Bothwell.—[*Reg. Privy Council*, x, 269.]

1577 PATRICK GALT, min. at Duns, in charge here.—[*Comps. Gen. Coll. of Thirds.*]

1585 DAVID FORSYTH, min. 1581.—[*Comps. Gen. Coll. of Thirds.*]

1652 DAVID ROBERTSON, adm. 28th Jan. 1652.—[*Hist. MS. Com.*, xiv, App. iii, 94.]

1709 ARCHIBALD BORTHWICK, marr. (1) Mary Moore.—[*Poll Tax Roll, Greenlaw*, 12th Dec. 1695.]

1755 ALEXANDER HUME, his daugh., Euphemia (marr. pro. 14th Nov. 1799 Charles Seyman, merchant, Edinburgh).

1882 CHARLES JAMES WATT, dem. 2nd June 1925, died at Edinburgh 5th Dec. 1938; his wife, Margaret Mathie, died at Edinburgh 26th July 1925; his sons—Charles Cecil, killed in action 9th May 1917; Francis Clifford, advocate 1925, M.P. Central Edinburgh 1941–5.

1925 WILLIAM EDWARD GRIMWOOD, born 26th Aug. 1875, son of William Alexander G., warrant officer, R.H.A., and Elizabeth Jones; served as lay missionary at Wallyford; licen. by Presb. of Linlithgow 3rd May 1916, missionary at Wallyford 1907 and Blackridge Nov. 1910; ord. to Carrington 19th Sept. 1916; trans. and adm. 22nd Oct. 1925; died 24th March 1945. Marr. 2nd Nov. 1910 Janet Heugh, daugh. of Colin McLean and Euphemia Ellen Colyer, and had issue—Euphemia Elizabeth, born 25th Sept. 1911; William Edward, born 11th Feb. 1915.

PRESBYTERY OF CHIRNSIDE

AYTON

The patron saint is St Dionysius. The remains of the old church are in the burial ground to the east of the present church. There was in the church an altar dedicated to the Virgin Mary, endowments being various acres and rigs in the Lordship of Ayton, including an acre in *lie wichts-balke*.—[*Reg. Great Seal*, v, 1317.]

1574 JOHN KENT, reader, called vicar-pensioner 1567–8, had conformed.—[*Edin. Test.*, i, 39.]

1601 WILLIAM HOG, born 1570.

1653 WILLIAM HOME, M.A.; on 25th June 1661 he presented to Parliament a petition to the effect that, lawfully admitted to Ayton in 1653, he had been deprived of his stipend for two years by the prevailing usurping power for his loyalty and his opposition to the remonstrating party; the Lords decerned their opinion that he should again be put in possession of the cure, and payment be made to him of the whole stipend which he had formerly enjoyed; Parliament approved and ordained that he be restored to the charge and payment of stipend made to him.—[*Acts Scott. Parl.*, vii, 281–2.]

1667 JOHN BETHUNE, son of Neil B. of Ballichladich, Ross-shire, and Christian Monro.—[*Foulis Writs*, 276.]

1712 THOMAS ANDERSON, son of Robert A., merchant, Edinburgh.

1773 GEORGE HOME, his daughs.—Margaret Ann, born 20th Feb. 1776, died 25th Feb. 1833; Catherine (twin) born 13th Nov. 1779, died 5th Feb. 1782.

1814 GEORGE TOUGH, his daughs.—Margaret Hay Home, born 16th Dec. 1811; Mary Ann, died 6th March 1895.

1882 JAMES JOHN MARSHALL AIKEN, died 27th Nov. 1933.

CHIRNSIDE

The church was dedicated by Bishop de Bernham on 13th April 1242.

1573 JOHN HOME, parson 1573, and prebendary of the Collegiate Kirk of Dunbar.—[*Reg. Abbrev. Feu Charters of Church Lands*, ii, 68.]

1577 ROBERT DENHOLM, pres. to vicarage 31st May 1577 on death of Sir James Gray.—[*Reg. Pres. Bene.*, ii, (4), 55.]

1583 JOHN DOUGLAS, parson and vicar, died Sept. 1583; had a sister Mabel.—[*Edin. Tests.*, xiv, 234, 5th May 1585.]

1607 ALEXANDER SMITH, born 1570.—[*Pitcairn*, ii, 283.]

1690 HENRY ERSKINE, marr. (1) Jean Brown, and had issue—Jean, born in Galashiels 28th June 1653 (marr. 17th Dec. 1686 George Balderston, surgeon, Edinburgh); Elizabeth, born in Wooller 1st May 1655, died 19th June 1657; Philip, born in Wooller 27th Dec. 1657 (rector of Knaresdale, Northumberland); Katherine, born in Cornhill 12th Aug. 1659, died 13th Feb. 1660; Elizabeth, born in Cornhill 4th Feb. 1660–1; John, born in Dryburgh 22nd April 1663; Rachel, born in Dryburgh 11th Nov. 1665; William, born in Dryburgh 8th Oct. 1669; sailed for Caledonia in the *Rising Sun* (Darien expedition) and died on the way 23rd Nov. 1699. First wife died 9th March 1670. (2) 1st Sept. 1674 Margaret (died 14th Jan. 1725), daugh. of Hugh Halcro, Isle of Weir, Rousay, Orkney, and Margaret Stewart of the family of Barscube, and had issue—Henry, born 13th Feb. 1676, died 11th July 1696; James, born 26th May 1677; also sailed in the *Rising Sun* in 1699, fate unknown; Hugh, born 24th Feb. 1679, died 17th June 1679; Ebenezer, born in Dryburgh 22nd June 1680 (min. of Stirling); Margaret, born in Parkrig 17th Jan. 1683; Ralph, born in Monilaws 15th March 1685 (min. of Dunfermline); daugh. born in Rivelaw 31st Dec. 1687, died 2nd Jan. 1688.

THOMAS LOGAN, his daugh. Agnes (marr. 26th March 1832 Abraham Logan, Woodend).
1801

ALEXANDER FORTEATH SMART, died 29th Nov. 1918.
1876

COLDINGHAM

At West Reston there was a chapel dedicated to St Nicholas. It may be that the chapel was identical with the chapel dedicated to "St N., Bishop and Confessor," which, it was proposed about 1540, should be erected into a parish church, with cemetery, baptismal font, bell tower and bells, and all the other rights and insignia of a parish church. The inhabitants of the area had built, founded and suitably embellished and repaired the chapel. The chief reason for the proposal was that at certain seasons the river E. (possibly the Eye) which lay between the towns R. and R. (possibly East and West Reston) on the one hand, and the parish church and churchyard on the other, was difficult of crossing on account of storms, floods, and frost, by the inhabitants who desired to attend the parish church for such services as were beyond the functions of the chapel, and for funerals proceeding to the parish churchyard. It was desired that the rector of the parish church should provide for the vicar of the new church 20 merks annually over and above all the fruits of teind, sheaves and other emoluments which the rector enjoyed from the teinds of grain and goods within the limits of the said towns of R. and R. On the basis that the reference was to this chapel the proposal was not carried out.

St Ebba died in 637, and soon afterwards the monastery was burned through carelessness. It was rebuilt, but was destroyed by the Danes in 870. On a peninsular promontory at St Abbs are the foundations of buildings called "St Abb's Kirk," with a small burial ground—the remains of a cell or chapel attached to Coldingham Priory, and erected at a later date than St Ebba's monastery. King Edgar gave the Priory of Coldingham to St Cuthbert's Canons Regular of Durham, who controlled it and drew the revenues. It was colonised by monks sent by the Abbot of Durham. By Charter of 25th July 1378 Robert II annexed the priory to Dunfermline Abbey, but this did not take effect. Fully a century later, in 1487, James III suppressed the priory and annexed one half of the Chapel Royal at Stirling, the other half to be devoted to the erection of a collegiate church at Coldingham. The King's action induced or precipitated a rebellion which, led by Alexander, Earl of Home, culminated in the Battle of Sauchieburn and the murder of the King. In 1504 the priory was annexed to the Scottish Crown; and five years later, by Order of Pope Julius II, the project of Robert II was carried out and the priory was withdrawn from Durham and annexed to Dunfermline Abbey—a condition that existed till 1560. The priory was under the joint invocation of St Mary, St Cuthbert and St Ebba, but in actual practice the name of the Virgin alone was used. To the priory belonged the following churches: Edrom, with the Chapel of Ercildone (Earlston) and other chapels, granted by Cospatrick, Earl of Dunbar, and confirmed by David I in Sept. 1139; Fishwick and Swinton, confirmed by Robert, Bishop of St Andrews, in 1250; Ednam, with Chapels of Newton, Nenthorn and Nesbit; Earlston, granted by

Walter de Lindsay to Kelso in 1150, and in 1171 given in exchange for Gordon and St Lawrence at Berwick; Stitchell (Chapel); Smailholm, granted by Walter Olifard, justiciary of Lothian, who died in 1242; Holy Trinity at Berwick, granted or confirmed by Bishop Bec 1282–1309; Ayton; Lamberton; Aldcambus. In a Den west of the village there was a Well of St Andrew, whence came the supply of water for the priory. In 1305 Edward I instituted a Fair of St Luke.—[*Acts Scott. Parl.*, ii, 171, 179–82; *Reg. Great Seal*, ii, 839; Carr's *Coldingham Priory*, 131, 227, 235, 238–9, 243, 310, 317, 319, 320, 327; Thomson's *Coldingham Priory and Parish*, 45–6, Appendix VI.]

1622 CHRISTOPHER KNOWES.—[*G.R. Sas.*, xxxviii, 194.]

1677 ALEXANDER DOUGLAS, had seven young children 5th Dec. 1689.—[*P.C. Reg.*, xiv, 542.]

1694 JOHN POW, bapt. 28th March 1669, son of Mr Robert P., headmaster of Leith Grammar School, and his second wife, Jean Learmonth.—[*South Leith Register, Berwick Sas.*, vi, 100, 103.]

1795 JAMES LANDELL, had issue—William, died Glasgow; James, died at Port Antonio; Thomas, died in West Indies; George, died Montreal; Alexander, Lieut. Marines, drowned at Chatham, 31st July 1812.

1827 JAMES HOME ROBERTSON, born 26th May 1801; his sons—John Dickson, Clerk in Holy Orders, died 1915; George Hogarth, Clerk in Holy Orders, died Tasmania, 1900.

1847 DAVID MUNRO, his daugh., Isabella, died 15th Oct. 1929.

1898 HENRY MACLAURIN LAMONT, his daugh. Sheila (marr. 14th June 1938 George Douglas Munro, min. of Reston).

(*Congregations united 6th Oct. 1940.*)

COLDSTREAM

The church at Hirsel was dedicated by Bishop de Bernham 6th Oct. 1248.

1563 ROBERT HOPPRINGLE, M.A., min. 1563.—[*Comps. Sub Coll. of Thirds, Roxburgh*, etc.]

1659 WILLIAM JOHNSTON, died before Dec. 1673.—[*Mack. Warrants.*]

1686 THOMAS BLAIR, his son, Henry, apprentice to Alexander Niven, barber, 15th July 1702.

1735 WILLIAM WILSON, son of John W., stationer, Glasgow.

1830 THOMAS SMITH GOLDIE, marr. Jane Gilloch, daugh. of Donald Morgan, Kirkcaldy.

1860 ARCHIBALD NISBET, his sons—Alexander Allan, died 19th March 1934; Francis Walter, died 18th Jan. 1945.

1912 ROBERT JOHN THOMSON, trans. to Alloa 15th July 1919.

1919 ALFRED ERNEST WARR, adm. 4th Dec. 1919; trans. to Hillhead, Glasgow, 1st March 1923.

1923 WILLIAM BROWN, trans. from Tingwall (*q.v.*) 3rd Aug. 1923. Addl. issue—Agnes Ewing, born 30th Jan. 1933.

EDROM

The church was dedicated to the Virgin Mary. On 1st Dec. 1393 Papal Indulgence was granted for visitors to the "Parish Church of St Mary of Ederham, to which, on account of the miracles which God by the merits and intercession of the said Mary wrought, a great multitude of people of old were wont to flock."—[*Transcripts from the Vatican* i, 344, *MS. Reg. Ho.*]

1570 JOHN COSTRANE, reader, 1570–2.—[*Comps. Sub Coll. of Thirds, Linlithgow*, etc.]

JOHN BARCLAY, eldest son of Adam
B., min. at Perth, etc., probably of
1687 the 1st marriage, and grandson of
Adam B., min. at Alford; was resident at
Peterhead in 1696 with his 1st wife;
assisted Alexander Barclay, formerly min.
at Peterhead, in carrying on Episcopal
services in a meeting house at what is now
No. 3 Port Henry Lane (off the Longate);
probably carried on the work when
Alexander Barclay intruded at Auchterless
cir. 1704–8, and was designated "Episcopal
Minister" at Peterhead in the testament of
his 2nd wife; died after 1714; marr. (1)
Christian, daugh. of Andrew Hay, Bailie
of Peterhead, by his wife, Issobel Dalgarno,
cont. 21st April 1687, with issue, at least,
George, born 25th Aug. 1693, merchant,
Georgia, Jamaica, and later in London,
acquired Cairness, Lonmay, Dec. 1752, and
died 6th June 1756; (2) on 5th June 1703,
Ann, daugh. of William Gordon in Savoch
of Buthlaw, 2nd son of James G. of Buthlaw, with issue—James, also merchant,
Georgia, Jamaica, succeeded his half-
brother, George, in Buthlaw, and died 4th
Jan. 1765; Mary, served co-heiress of her
brother, James, in Cairness, 19th March
1766, and of her sister, Ann, in Cairness,
15th Aug. 1766; marr. her cousin, John
Gordon of Buthlaw (died July 1775), and
died 10th May 1799; Ann, also served co-
heiress to her brother, James, in Cairness,
19th March 1766, marr. Captain James
Thomson, Peterhead, and of Faichfield,
and died June 1766; Jane, also served co-
heiress to her brother, James, in Cairness,
19th March 1766, and of her sister, Ann,
in Cairness, 15th Aug. 1766, marr. Thomas
Gordon (died 28th April 1749), son of
Charles Gordon of Buthlaw, by his wife,
Margaret Gordon, afterwards termed Lady
Findrassie, with issue, including Charles,
who succeeded his uncle, John Gordon, in
the estate of Buthlaw in 1775, and also of
Cairness which in 1776 was transferred to
him by his aunt, Mary, and his mother,
who died after 2nd Feb. 1780; and possibly
also, William, "son of Mr John Barclay,
minister," who on 28th Aug. 1732 was
apprenticed to John Aitoun, wright, Edinburgh; Ann Gordon, widow of John
Barclay, died before 28th Feb. 1766, and
apparently in Jan. of that year.—[*Aberdeen
Test.*, 17th May 1756, 28th Feb. 1766;
Edin. Test., 21st Jan. 1780, cxxvi, 1; *Retours*,
lxxvi, 358–62, 3rd April 1766, Mon. No. 5,
29th Sept. 1766, Mon. No. 10, 26th April
1776, Mon. No. 17; *Reg. of Edin. Apprentices*, 28th Aug. 1732; Burke's *Landed
Gentry*, 1939, 909, 921; *Aberdeen Poll Tax
Roll*, i, 572; *Memo.* E. F. Esson, M.A.,
B.Sc., St Peter's Rectory, Peterhead.]

JOHN HASTLE, his daugh., Elizabeth
1797 (marr. 5th April 1836).

JAMES WILSON, pres. by Crown,
1849 26th July 1849.

GEORGE GIBSON GUNN, pres. 6th
1872 June 1872.

MACDUFF SIMPSON, died 30th June
1925; his widow, Elizabeth Jackson,
1883 died 30th April 1941.

JOHN MACKECHNIE, died 26th May
1944; his daughs.—Mabel Mary
1916 Watson (marr. 27th July 1932 John
Leonard Douglas, min. of Eccles); Nina
(marr. 31st July 1935 John Crabbe Templeton Hunter, min. of Fogo).

EYEMOUTH

In the "town and territory" of Eyemouth there were lands designated the
"four husband lands of Ninewells," a
name that may indicate that here there was
a dedication to the Nine Maidens. In 1581
there are mentioned two tenements of land
in "the place of St Colin," now called the
Loches in the common of Eyemouth. On
account of the distance of Eyemouth from
Coldingham Church, and also because the
prosperity of its harbour had increased its
population, James VI by Charter of 27th
Jan. 1618 dissolved the town of Eyemouth
with its lands, etc., and also the Lands of
Beinryhous from Coldingham, and erected
the Church of Eyemouth into a distinct
parish church, with the foregoing lands as
its parochial area. The Charter, which was
confirmed by Act of Parliament on 28th
June 1633, narrates that the inhabitants

had erected not only a suitable church but also a sufficient manse and glebe for the pastor placed there by John, Archbishop of St Andrews. The stipend was all the vicar's teinds within the above boundaries, along with a chalder of victual formerly assigned to Coldingham.—[*Reg. Great Seal*, vii, 1761; *Acts Scott. Parl.*, v, 143; *Reports of Hist. MSS. Commis.*, *Milne-Home*, 209; *Duns Castle Papers*, 215, 265-6.]

DAVID STIRLING, had a daugh., Ann.—[*G. R. Sas.*, lxxv, 81.]
1687

GEORGE TODD, line 3, for "30" read "22."
1785

JOHN MURDOCH, pres. by Crown 16th Nov. 1843.
1844

STEPHEN BELL, pres. by Crown 29th April 1845.
1845

JOHN DEMPSTER MUNRO, his widow, Agnes Jane Balfour Gregor, died 2nd April 1926, aged 80.
1882

WILLIAM BLACK KENNEDY, dem. 25th April 1933; died at Inveresk 10th Oct. 1946; his wife, Helen Macdonald, died 23rd May 1927; marr. (3) 15th Oct. 1930 Ann, daugh. of Robert Edgar, Eyemouth; his son, Norman Dougall, min. of Friockheim.
1903

FOULDEN

ALEXANDER RAMSAY, parson in office 28th Aug. 1562.—[*Reg. of Deeds*, vi, 97.]
1562

WILLIAM PYLE, M.A., exhorter 1563; designated chaplain 7th June 1542; apparently attached to Jedburgh.—[*Reg. Mag. Sig.*, 7th July 1542; *Comps. Sub Coll. of Thirds, Roxburgh*, etc.]
1563

DAVID HOME, exhorter 1563.—[*Comps. Sub Coll. of Thirds, Roxburgh*, etc.]
1563

THOMAS STORIE, M.A., did return in 1585.—[*Comps. Sub Coll. of Thirds, Roxburgh*, etc.]
1576

OLIVER COLT, adm. advocate 20th Dec. 1606.
1614

THOMAS RAMSAY, had also issue—Alexander and Patrick.—[*Reg. of Deeds, Dal.*, lxi, 90; *G. R. Sas.*, 9th Sept. 1633, 365; xxxix, 185; xlv, 144; lii, 407, lv, 97.]
1630

ALEXANDER CHRISTISON, his daugh., Agnes Montgomery (marr. 15th Sept. 1858).
1821

JOHN REED, licen. 13th May 1884, dem. 21st Dec. 1926, died 24th Sept. 1932; his widow, Martha Craig Gilchrist, died 9th May 1944; his son, John Stewart, Lieut, R.N.R., drowned in submarine in Baltic 4th June 1919; his son, Alexander Chalmers, M.B., Ch.B., Edinburgh. Addl. Publications—Contributions to *Chambers Journal*, and *Good Words*.
1886

JOHN ALEXANDER RUSSELL BROWN MUIR, M.A., born Methil 13th Sept. 1895, son of Thomas M., Ph.D., min. of Skirling; educ. at Biggar High School and Univ. of Edinburgh, M.A. (1923); licen. by Presb. of Biggar 5th April 1926, assistant St. George's, Edinburgh; ord. 2nd Dec. 1927; trans. to Craiglockhart 12th March 1935. Marr. 27th July 1928 Margaret Grant, fourth daugh. of Major Alexander Cumming, Mains of Curr, Strathspey, and has issue, Maud Margaret Russell, born 5th May 1929.
1927

(*Foulden and Mordington were united* 1929.)

HOUNDWOOD

JOSEPH BETHUNE, marr. proc. 12th May 1796 Margaret, daugh. of Francis Cowan, min. of Gladsmuir.
1794

JOHN EDGAR DAVIDSON, died in Western Infirmary, Glasgow, 29th Nov. 1925.
1915

JOHN SCOTT MORRISON, trans. from St Andrew's, Berwick (*q.v.*), 5th Aug. 1926, died at Edinburgh 5th March 1946.
1926

HUTTON

Hutton and Fishwick were united by the Lords Commissioners before 20th May 1610. The church was renovated in 1937.—[*Reg. Mag. Sig.*]

1563 DAVID HOME, exhorter 1563, and at Fishwick.—[*Comps. Sub Coll. of Thirds, Roxburgh*, etc.]

1576 THOMAS WILSON, pres. to vicarage 15th May 1576 on death of Robert Douglas, M.A.

1576 WILLIAM COUTTS, reader here, pres. to vicarage 6th Dec. 1576 on death of Robert Douglas.—[*Reg. Pres. Bene.*, ii, (4), 49.]

1636 JAMES LUNDIE.—[*G. R. Sas.*, lv, 105.]

1649 PATRICK HOME, his son, William, apprentice to George Smailholm, merchant, Edinburgh, 10th Feb. 1669.

1789 ADAM LANDELLS, line 2, for "1st Nov." read "29th Oct."

1821 JOHN EDGAR, his daughs.—Janet (marr. 5th March 1850 Alfred Harris); Alice (marr. 7th June 1844 David Bayne, bookseller, London); Georgina (marr. 28th Oct. 1851).

1858 ROBERT KIRKE, pres. by Crown 1st July 1858.

1906 DAVID SMITH LESLIE, licen. 17th May 1904.

LADYKIRK, UPSETTLINGTON and HORNDEAN

On 5th April 1556 Sir Hugh Hudsoun was admitted to the Prebend of Upsettlington in Dunglass Collegiate Church by Sir William Mustard, a prebendary there, who admitted him by tendering to him the Bible and taking his oath (i.e. by touching the Holy Gospels) to observe the statutes and customs of the church.—[*Reports of Hist. MSS. Commis., Milne-Holme*, 239–40.]

In the village of Horndean there was in 1725 the remains of an old chapel dedicated to the Holyrood, called Rood Kirk.—[*Macfarlane's Geograp. Colls.*, i, 379.]

1574 JAMES ROSS, for "1575" read "1574."

1577 JAMES DOUGLAS, min. here, pres. to vicarage 17th July 1577 on death of John Henrie.—[*Reg. Pres. Bene.*, ii, (4), 58.]

1697 WILLIAM GULLAN, had issue, Andrew.—[*Deeds, Durie*, 1706, No. 508.]

1787 ROBERT PEARSON, pres. 10th Feb. 1787.

1788 THOMAS MILL, pres. 27th Sept. 1788.

1819 GEORGE HOME ROBERTSON, his daugh., Margaret (marr. (1) W. Mitchell, (2) Alexander Macbean, consul at Genoa).

1842 WILLIAM ANDREW McCORKINDALE, pres. by Crown 5th Feb. 1842.

1855 JOHN STEVENSON, pres. by Crown 25th April 1855; his daugh., Marjory Mary, died 23rd June 1917.

1859 WILLIAM DOBIE, pres. by Crown 4th Dec. 1858.

1905 WILLIAM STEVEN MOODIE, died 19th Dec. 1918.

1919 WILLIAM MACKIE LAING, M.A., adm. 13th May 1919; dem 29th Sept. 1920 on appointment to Union Church, Valparaiso (*q.v.*); adm. to Colinton 4th Oct. 1934.

1921 ROBERT NINIAN PAISLEY, M.A., ord. 11th Jan. 1921, trans. to New Abbey 30th April 1926

1926 JOHN TUDOR SCRYMGEOUR, trans. from Caddonfoot (*q.v.*) 27th Aug. 1926; dem. 31st Oct. 1944; died at Edinburgh 26th Feb. 1945.

MORDINGTON and LAMBERTON

In note on Lamberton, line 6, for "Henry VIII" read "Henry VII."

In a description of the liberties of Berwick 20th Jan. 1478–9 there occurs "the place of the Cross of St Mary of Mordington," which may indicate that Mordington Church was dedicated to the Virgin Mary. On the site of the old church there is a burial vault which has on the inside of the west wall a panel with a carved representation of the Crucifixion, an incised inscription IHUS MARIA, and figures of the Virgin Mary and John the Baptist.

The Church of Lamberton, now a burial vault, is situated in the churchyard on the west side of the Dunbar-Berwick road, 4–5 miles from Berwick. Lamberton was united to Ayton by the Lords Commissioners before 20th May 1610, because they were adjacent to each other and formed an "inconsiderable parish." At Charterhouse there was an establishment of the Carthusians, governed by a prior. The Church of St Mary-in-the-Forest, apparently Selkirk, was united to Charterhouse on 22nd July 1439.—[*Monastic Annals of Teviotdale*, 321; *The Apostolic Camera and Scott. Benefices*, lxxivn and 123–4; *Reg. Mag. Sig.*, ii, 1412, vii, 2901.]

1563 DAVID HOME, exhorter at Foulden and also here.—[*Comps. Sub Coll. of Thirds, Roxburgh.*]

1568 ARCHIBALD HOME, M.A., vicar 1568.—[*Comps. Sub Coll. of Thirds, Roxburgh*, etc.]

1573 ROBERT DOUGLAS, parson and exhorter 30th Nov. 1574.—[*Edin. Tests.*, iii, 227.]

1582 ROBERT HISLOPE, pres. to vicarage 14th July 1582 on death of Dean William Learmonth.—[*Reg. Sec. Sig.*, xlix, 17.]

1588 JOHN HOME, M.A., min. of Ayton, pres. to vicarage 23rd May 1588 on res. of Robert Hislope.—[*Reg. Sec. Sig.*, lvii, 120.]

1599 JOHN DOUGLAS, min. of Longformacus, in charge here from 1599.

1607 GILBERT RULE, min. of Longformacus, in charge here.

1648 THOMAS RAMSAY, marr. cont. 9th Jan. 1646, Jean, daugh. of Robert Balcanqual, Tranent.

1833 GEORGE FULTON KNIGHT, his son, Adam Cairns, born 17th Sept. 1845.

1885 HUGH FLEMINGTON, dem. 21st Dec. 1926, died at Leven 25th Aug. 1928.

(*Parish united to Foulden 1927.*)

SWINTON

1595 ANDREW ARBUTHNOTT, line 2, for "1642" read "1612"; died before 1st June 1632, when his testament confirmed.

1691 ROBERT SANDILANDS, trans. to Newbattle 6th May 1695.

1868 ROBERT HOME, pres. by Crown 30th May 1868.

1892 DUNCAN DAVID FARQUHARSON MACDONALD, marr. (2) 11th Oct. 1917 Lizzie Ann, daugh. of John and Elizabeth Morgan, Scone, Perth; line 19, for "1890" read "1900"; Chaplain to Forces at Shorncliffe 3rd Oct. 1919 to 19th April 1920; died at Tayport 12th April 1940.

SIMPRIM

1668 JAMES SANDERSON, son of Robert S., Coldstream.—[*Berwick Sas.*, v, 91, 1689.]

1683 GEORGE IRELAND, min. in 1683, trans. to Lethendry 1687.

1689 JAMES ADAMSON, his son, Samuel, writer in Edinburgh.—[*Reg. of Deeds, Dal.*, 1705, No. 911.]

WHITSOME

1573 THOMAS LYTHTON.—[*Acts. and Dec.*, l, 154.]

WHITSOME—HILTON

1608 ALEXANDER KINNEAR.—[*G. R. Sas.*, xxxviii, 107.]

1656 ANDREW PATERSON, his daugh., Janet (marr. George Paterson of Dunmuire).—[*Berwick Sas.*, 28th July 1683.]

1715 JOHN VEITCH, line 1, for "William" read "John."

1866 JOHN ALEXANDER ROBERTSON, died at Port William, Wigtownshire, 7th July 1918.

1911 HUGH PARK REID, dem. 31st Jan. 1948; died Edinburgh 17th March 1948; his daugh., Kathleen Mary (marr. 9th March 1940 Eric Wallace Forrest, lecturer, Queen Mary's College, London).

HILTON

1562 ARCHIBALD HOME, M.A., vicar 1567–71.—[*Comps. Sub Coll. of Thirds, Linlithgow*, etc.]

1562 JAMES SETON or SEYTOUN, designated parson in 1562, 1569 and 12th Aug. 1589, probably held office before 1560 and conformed.—[*Reports Hist. MSS. Com., Milne-Holme*, 42; *Reg. Mag. Sig.*, iv, 1903; v, 1720; *Comps. Sub Coll. of Thirds, Dumfries*, etc.]

1563 HEW HUTCHISON, reader 1563.— [*Comps. Sub Coll. of Thirds, Roxburgh*, etc.]

1733 GEORGE HOME, trans. to Whittinghame 27th May 1736.

PRESBYTERY OF KELSO

EDNAM

JOHN CLAPPERTON, had issue—
1617 James; William; John, min. of Yarrow.—[*G. R. Sas.*, 2 Ser., xv, 487; *Berwick Sas.*]

THOMAS POLLOK, his daugh., Alison
1723 (marr. cont. 1735 Lieut. John O'Brien, R.N., brother of Marquess of Thomond).

WILLIAM LAMB, pres. 27; his widow,
1844 Christian Archibald MacDougall Yair, died at London 10th July 1921; a daugh. (marr. -. Campbell).

JOHN BURLEIGH, dem. 16th Oct.
1878 1924, died at Edinburgh 2nd Sept. 1937; his son, John Henderson Seaforth, professor of Ecclesiastical History, Edinburgh Univ.; his widow, Agnes Ann Henderson, died at Edinburgh 11th July 1938, aged 79.

WILLIAM SCOTT, M.A., B.D., LL.B.,
1925 served as Trooper in South Africa Police 1909–10; discharged on ground of ill health; taught in Schools, Alberta, Canada; trans. from Bressay (*q.v.*) 17th April 1925.

KELSO

ADAM CLERK, exhorter, designated
1569 reader 5th Feb. 1575–6.—[*Edin. Tests*, viii, 54.]

ALEXANDER THORNTON, M.A.,
1578 min. 24th Feb. 1579–80.—[*Edin. Tests.*, viii, 43.]

ROBERT KNOX, his widow, Elizabeth
1633 Murray; his son, Robert.—[*G. R. Sas.*, 3 Ser., xxxvi, 344, 24th Jan. 1676.]

JAMES RAMSAY, line 1, for "1672"
1707 read "1667."

JOHN GORDON SMITH NAPIER,
1883 licen. 15th May 1879; his widow, Sarah Roberts, died 26th Aug. 1935.

DAVID GORDON HAMILTON, dem.
1916 14th May 1945.

KELSO NORTH

HORATIUS BONAR, his son, Ninian,
1837 died 16th May 1930; his daughs.— Emily Florence, died 1st Feb. 1937; Eliza Maitland, died 16th Nov. 1941.

PETER McKERRON, his widow, Ann
1865 Denholm, died 21st Sept. 1920; his sons—Robert Gordon, died 15th Oct. 1929; George Grant, professor of Law, Rhodes Univ., Grahamstown, South Africa, died 2nd Dec. 1945.

JAMES FERGUSSON McCREATH,
1917 ord. 24th Jan. 1917; trans. to Mertoun 6th Nov. 1918.

WILLIAM JOHN MACFARLAND,
1919 trans. from Craigvad, Co. Down, 30th April 1919; trans. to Borthwick 15th Dec. 1922.

THOMAS CONNELLY, ord. assistant
1923 New Greyfriars, Edinburgh, 13th July 1921, adm. 9th May 1923; trans. to Glassford 2nd Sept. 1925.

CHARLES KEITH MACWILLIAM,
1926 trans. from St Thomas, Leith, 17th Feb. 1926; trans. to Burnbank 10th July 1928.

ROBERT CRANSTON KERR, M.A.
(7th July 1911), trans. from Longformacus (*q.v.*) 14th June 1928; trans. to Smailholm 15th Sept. 1937. Marr. 8th Feb. 1921 Elizabeth Kerr, daugh. of Edward John Smith, Dotham, Northumberland, and has issue—Margaret Elizabeth, born 8th Feb. 1925; Berta Gladstone, born 2nd April 1929; Andrew Edward Cranstoun, born 11th Nov. 1931, died 8th Feb. 1946.

1928

LINTON

There was at Park a chapel dedicated to the Virgin Mary which in 1175–99 Richard de Morville, Constable of Scotland, and Avicia of Lancaster his wife, with consent of their son and heir, William, granted to Melrose Abbey.—[*Book of Melrose*, i, 83, 96–8; *Retours*, xxxix, 248.]

STEVEN SCHILLINGIS, vicar 1563.

1563

MARK KER, parson, 1564.—[*Comps. Sub Coll. of Thirds, Roxburgh*, etc.; *Acts and Dec.*, xxxi, 6.]

1564

JAMES KER, alleged vicar.—[*Acts and Dec.*, xlv, 83.]

1569

WALTER DOUGLAS, marr. Isobel Goldie, who survived him.—[*Reg. of Deeds, Durie*, cxcvi, 1st Aug. 1737.]

1689

GEORGE HALL, delete "grandson of Henry Hall, the Covenanter."

1728

ANDREW OGILVIE, his son, Joseph, died 3rd March 1850.

1781

THOMAS LEISHMAN, his sons— Matthew William Fleming, died at Cubalbogy, West Australia, 20th March 1928; Robert Fleming, died Victor Harbour 2nd Nov. 1936; Thomas Arthur, M.D., Brechin, died 3rd Jan. 1948.

1855

JAMES FLEMING LEISHMAN, died at Edinburgh 9th April 1935; his widow, Jane Leishman, died 24th July 1938. Publication—*Linton Leaves*, edited by his daugh.

1895

MAKERSTOUN

JOHN DAWSON, his daughs.—Margaret Noble (marr. 1st June 1920 William Cuthill, min. of Balmaclellan); Elizabeth Walker, died 16th Jan. 1929.

1869

PHILIP BAINBRIDGE, his daugh., Marion (marr. (1) Thomas Charles Benson, M.B., Ch.B., Perth; (2) 15th June 1927 John Charles Cameron); his widow, Elizabeth McLintock, died at Manchester 9th Dec. 1938.

1880

WILLIAM McCALLUM, Clerk of Presb. 1924; his daugh., Elizabeth, is M.A., LL.B., M.B., Ch.B. (Edin.).

1916

MOREBATTLE

THOMAS MOIR.—[*G. R. Sas.*, xi, 295; xli, 166; lviii, 133.]

1610

CHARLES JAMES COWAN, died at Edinburgh 6th Jan. 1919; his widow, Jane Elizabeth Fleming Leishman, died at Yetholm 4th Jan. 1939.

1876

JAMES JOHNSTONE PRYDE, formerly of Penpont (*q.v.*), army chaplain, adm. 24th April 1919; trans. to Stichell 17th Dec. 1926.

1919

JOHN HARKNESS, trans. from Auchendoir 19th May 1927. Addl. issue—Elizabeth McCulloch, born 29th Feb. 1924; Grace Kerr, born 1st Sept. 1927; Henrietta Margaret, born 21st Aug. 1932; his wife's mother's maiden name was McCulloch.

1927

NENTHORN

DUNCAN WALKER, min. here, pres. to vicarage 23rd May 1584; died before 13th May 1599.—[*Reg. Sec. Sig.*, lxvi, 135; cxiii, 251.]

1584

JAMES ROBERTSON, trans. from Tundergarth 10th June 1664.

1664

JAMES FLETCHER, marr. Margaret Bower, widow of James Wichtoun, notary, Dundee, and Andrew Auchenleck, min. of Dundee. Had issue—

1669

Isabel (marr. Thomas Auchenleck, apothecary in Duns).

1855 MANNERS HAMILTON NISBET GRAHAM, pres. by Crown 3rd Sept. 1854.

1866 JOHN BARCLAY, pres. by Crown 4th Dec. 1865.

1868 HENRY GREY GRAHAM, pres. by Crown 5th Dec. 1867.

1885 DAVID ANDERSON, died 19th May 1936; his widow, Emma Louise Hutchison, died 22nd March 1937; his daugh., Joanna, died 27th Sept. 1937. Publication—*Reminiscences of a Scots Parish Minister* (1937).

1900 GEORGE HISLOP YOUNG, dem. 15th May 1944. His wife, Isabella Kennedy Wilson, died 17th April 1937.

ROXBURGH—ST JAMES'

On a petition by William, Abbot of Kelso, to Pope Martin V, to the effect that in "the Church of St James', Roxburgh, divine office in virtue of a perpetual Chaplainry founded by the late Roger de Alton, layman, had long been celebrated by a chaplain at certain times yearly," but that "on account of the ruin of the said Church in the Border Wars, the saying of the said office had long been neglected and was not likely soon to be resumed," the Pope gave mandate on 25th May 1426 to the Abbot of Dryburgh to grant licence to the said Abbot of Kelso that the office be celebrated in a fit chapel of his monastery by a secular or a regular priest, even a priest of the monastery, appointed by the said abbot, who asserts that to him belongs by ordinance of the founder the appointment of the Chaplain, until the said church returns to its due state and the said chaplainry to its wonted revenues.—[*Cal. Papal Regs., Letters*, vii, 455-6.]

1569 SIR JOHN KER, vicar 7th Oct. 1569, when he was summoned before the Privy Council to answer for his demerits.—[*Reg. Privy Council*, ii, 40.]

1582 SIR THOMAS KER, was vicar before 1582 when he and Thomas Newbie, reader, Hassendean, Archibald Simson, reader, Lilliesleaf, John Scott, reader, Southdean, James Scott, reader, Ashkirk, John McClellan, reader, Kirkandrews, were deprived for abusing the sacraments; they continued in the offence and were excommunicated 26th March 1588, and on 18th June 1590 they were sentenced to act themselves under the pain of death (which they did next day) never to abuse the sacraments nor function in the kirks, and that "they sould be tane to the Mercat Crose of Edinburghe and stand twa houris with paiparis on thair heidis contening the cryme quhairupone Dome wes pronuncait."—[Pitcairn's *Criminal Trials*, i, 190; *Booke of the Univ. Kirk*, ii, 720; *Reg. Privy Council*, iv, 522, xiv, 373.]

1608 WILLIAM WEMYSS.—[*G. R. Sas.*, 2 Ser., x, 178.]

1660 JOHN HALIBURTON, his sons— Andrew, apprentice to John Forrest, surgeon, 21st Feb. 1683; John, apprentice to James Law, skipper, Leith, 10th Sept. 1684.—[*Reg. of Deeds, Mack.*, xxxix, 16th Dec. 1671.]

1897 HENRY ALEXANDER MATHERS, ret. in favour of A. and S. Feb. 1934, died 8th Dec. 1943.

SPROUSTON

1563 PATRICK BALLENDEN, claimed vicarage.—[*Acts and Dec.*, xxviii, 141.]

1655 SAMUEL ROW.—[*G. R. Sas.*, 2 Ser., vii, 466.]

1661 THOMAS INGLIS, his son, Thomas, apprentice to Thomas Borthwick, surgeon, Edinburgh, 1st Jan. 1679.

1689 GEORGE BARCLAY, M.A., resident with three children, eldest seven years, in Lady Yester's Parish 7th Nov. 1694.—[*Lady Yester's Poll Tax Roll*, 10.]

JOHN GOUDIE, his second daugh., Margaret.—[*Reg. of Deeds, Dal.*, clxv, 13th Feb. 1749.]
1691

NINIAN HOME, line 16, for "14th March" read "23rd May"; marr. (2) 1723, not 1725. His mother daugh. of John Trotter of Fogonook.—[*Deeds, Dal.*, 1705, No. 522.]
1704

NINIAN TROTTER, mother Agnes Turner.
1809

DAVID DENHOLM FRASER, died at Kelso 26th March 1948; addl. issue—Helen Lydia, born 18th April 1919; Margaret Jane (marr. 16th June 1927 William Ross Stewart, M.B., F.R.C.S.E.); Dora Denholm (marr. 16th Dec. 1937 Captain Cyril James Mackenzie Martin, R.E.); Katherine Mary (marr. 20th April 1938 Francis Fenwick Pearson, Brant House, Kirkby Lonsdale, Lancashire).
1901

STICHELL and HUME

The parishes of Stichell and Hume were united by the Lords Commissioners before 20th May 1610. The church was dedicated by Bishop de Bernham on 30th March 1242. The patron saint was St Nicholas.—[*Reg. Mag. Sig.*, vii, 290.]

WILLIAM HOOD, called formerly reader, 1577.—[*Comps. Gen. Coll. of Thirds.*]
1577

JOHN FAIRBAIRN, reader 11th Nov. 1578.—[*Edin. Tests.*, vii, 195.]
1578

DAVID COURTNEY.—[*G. R. Sas.*, 3 Ser., ii, 36, 38.]
1613

DAVID STARK, his son, David, has Sasine with his mother of Kirklands of Home, 27th Jan. 1673.—[*G. R. Sas.*, 3 Ser., xxxi, 98.]
1648

JOHN GLEN, died at Dirleton. Marr. cont. 16th Sept. 1691 Helen, daugh. of James Taylor, min. of Greenock and Mearns, and had issue—James, bapt. 24th Aug. 1692, min. of Dirleton; Thomas, bapt. 13th Feb. 1694; John, min. of Stichell, bapt. 22nd Dec. 1695; Elizabeth, bapt. 4th June 1697; Andrew, bapt. 20th Sept. 1699; Samuel, bapt. 31st May 1704.
1691

GEORGE REDPATH, his Diary 1755-61 edited by Sir James Balfour Paul, published by Scottish History Society 1927.
1743

PETER BUCHANAN, born 9th Feb. 1798.
1827

GEORGE GUNN, licen. 11th May 1876.
1878

JOHN LANCELOT CONSTANTINE TULLOCH, trans. to Hamilton 11th Jan. 1917; his son, John Lancelot Hill, C.A., died 16th Dec. 1935.
1900

DAVID JACKSON TWEEDIE, trans. from Riccarton (*q.v.*), died 25th Aug. 1926; his daugh., Ena (marr. 6th April 1925 Flight Lieut. R. Stanley Aitken, M.C., R.A.F.); his widow, Jessie Fleming Allison, died Edinburgh 4th April 1947.
1917

JAMES JOHNSTONE PRYDE, trans. from Morebattle 17th Dec. 1926, died 27th Sept. 1934; his first wife, Annie Elizabeth Drummond Drysdale, died 9th Nov. 1920; marr. (2) 4th July 1922 Jane Baillie Dickson, and had issue—Robert Johnston, born 20th May 1923; James Christison, born 12th June 1926.
1926

HUME

GEORGE HOME, vicar, 1586-8.—[*Comps. Gen. Coll. of Thirds.*]
1586

CHARLES HOME, vicar, 1588.—[*Comps. Gen. Coll. of Thirds.*]
1588

YETHOLM

There was in the parish near the English Border a Chapel of St Ethelbride. The church was entirely renovated in 1934, a chancel being added. Two stained glass windows and a chiming clock were the gift of Andrew R. Blythe, sometime Session Clerk.

1563 JAMES WILLIAMSON, reader 1563 and 1567; excommunicated before 1590 for profaning the Sacraments.—[*Privy Council Reg.*, xiv, 375.]

1568 SIR THOMAS CHRISTISON, vicar 1568 and 1572.—[*Comps. Sub Coll. of Thirds, Dumfries*, etc.]

1579 THOMAS AITKEN, pres. on death of Thomas Christison.—[*Reg. Pres. Bene.*, ii, (4), 64; *Reg. Sec. Sig.*, lxvi, 126.]

1587 WILLIAM DOUGLAS, M.A., parson July 1587.—[*Reg. of Deeds*, xxvii, 221.]

1594 ARCHIBALD OSWALD, M.A., min. at Fishwick, pres. to parsonage and vicarage 3rd May 1594 on dep. of Thomas Aitken on death of William Douglas.—[*Reg. Sec. Sig.*, lxvi, 123, 139.]

1594 ADAM DOUGLAS, M.A., pres. to parsonage and vicarage 7th May 1594 through inability of Thomas Aitken.—[*Reg. Sec. Sig.*, lxvi, 126.]

1604 JOHN BALFOUR, pres. on deprivation of Thomas Aitken and dem. of Adam Douglas.—[*Reg. Sec. Sig.*, lxxiv, 160.]

1699 ROBERT COLVILLE, his son, Walter, apprenticed to John Clarkson, baxter, Edinburgh, 29th Nov. 1723; line 1, for "1677" read "1671."

1862 ADAM DAVIDSON, his son, James Little, died at Broomieknowe 1st May 1933; his daugh., Janet Carlyle, died at Broomieknowe 10th Oct. 1935.

1898 WILLIAM CARRICK MILLER, his widow, Johanna Bonthron, died 30th Dec. 1933.

1916 JAMES WEDDERSPOON, died 24th July 1920.

1921 WILLIAM LINDSAY GORDON, formerly of South Parish, Aberdeen (*q.v.*), adm. here 8th Jan. 1921; dem. 16th March 1925; afterwards Chaplain at Colchester; died 29th Feb. 1940.

1925 OLIVER KENNETH WALLACE McFADDEN, born 19th July 1897, youngest son of Rev. Jackson M., Badoney, Newtown Stewart, Ireland, and Mary Wallace Loudon; educ. at Trinity College, Dublin, B.A., M.A., and Univ. of St Andrews; licen. by Presb. of St Andrews 1922; assistant Abbey, Edinburgh; ord. 20th Aug. 1925. Marr. 4th Dec. 1929 Janet Kay, youngest daugh. of Rev. George Home, Cleland, Glasgow, and has issue—Maureen Margaret May, born 3rd Feb. 1940.

PRESBYTERY OF JEDBURGH

ANCRUM

1560 JAMES THORNTON, parson and vicar in 1561.—[*Comps. Gen. Coll. of Thirds.*]

1569 WILLIAM JOHNSTON, M.A., exhorter in 1563.—[*Comps. Sub Coll. of Thirds, Roxburgh*, etc.]

1578 HECTOR DOUGLAS, pres. to parsonage and vicarage 18th Feb. 1577-8 on death of James Douglas.—[*Reg. Pres. Bene.*, ii, (4), 45.]

1572 GEORGE JOHNSTON, died Father of the Church.—[*G. R. Sas.*, vi, 21.]

1616 JAMES SCOTT, died Father of the Church.

1622 WILLIAM BENNET, his son, William, created a baronet 18th Nov. 1670.—[*G. R. Sas.*, lvi, 67.]

1648 JOHN LIVINGSTON, line 36, add "1727" before "1754"; his son, William.—[*P. R. Sas., Roxburgh*, vi, 186.]

1704 JOHN CRANSTOUN, brother of George C. in Upper Chatto; line 4, for "20" read "1st"; his son, Andrew, apprenticed to John Lennox, skinner, Edinburgh, 15th Nov. 1717.

LANGNEWTON

1647 JAMES COLT, trans. to Roberton about 1663.

BEDRULE

1557 SIR WILLIAM TOD, parson and vicar, 30th Nov. 1557, died before 30th July 1564.—[*Lothian Papers*, portfolio xl, 21; xxv, 359.]

1562 WILLIAM KER, son of John Ker of Ferniehurst, sometime parson.—[*Acts and Dec.*, xxv, 359.]

1562 JOHN STEWART of Traquair, now undoubted parson 1562.

1563 SIR JOHN DOUGLAS, min. 4th Feb. 1563-4.—[*Lothian Papers*, portfolio xi, 42.]

1567 JOHN ALLAN.—[*Acts and Dec.*, xlii, 180; xxv, 359.]

1640 HENRY ELLIOT, marr. Helen, daugh. of John MacGhie of Balmaghie, and had issue—John, Peebles.—[*Lyon Reg.*, i, 138.]

1714 JOHN GILCHRIST, son of Mungo G. in Holm of Dalgarno.—[*Dumfries Tests.*, 29th March 1729.]

1748 GEORGE DICKSON, his daughs.—Margaret (marr. Lieut. William Miller, R.N., Maxwellhaugh); Katherine (marr. Horatio Thomas McGeorge of Langside, Kelso).—[*Roxburgh Services*, 451.]

1875 JOHN STEVENSON, dem. 13th June 1923, died Bonchester Bridge 7th Sept. 1929; his daugh., Mary Farmer, died 24th Dec. 1918.

1923 JAMES DRUMMOND GORDON, trans. from Indian Chaplaincy (*q.v.*) 28th Sept. 1923; died 26th Nov. 1944.

CAVERS

1547 WILLIAM LAMB, parson 24th March 1546-7, sister's son and heir of Patrick Panter, Abbot of Cambuskenneth.—*Acta Dom. Con.*, xxiii, 27.]

WILLIAM CLERK, pres. to vicarage on dem. of Dean John Watson, portioner of Melrose.—[*Reg. Sec. Sig.*, lxxxii, 76.]
1599

HUGH KENNEDY.—[Harvey's *Works*, vi, 408.]
1725

JAMES STRACHAN, his daugh., Janet Dawson, died 21st Dec. 1837.
1809

WILLIAM GRANT, his daugh., Jane Dickson, died Swanage 11th April 1924.
1840

GEORGE BRUCE SCOULAR WATSON, died 30th Dec. 1923; his daughs.—Dorothea Margaret Fleming (marr. 11th Sept. 1919 Robert Calvert Sibbald); Mabel (marr. John James Scott Morrison, min. of John Knox, Aberdeen).
1876

WILLIAM KENNETH GRANT, grandson of William, min. 1840, trans. from Second Charge St Andrews (*q.v.*) 3rd June 1924.
1924

(*The parish church was completely renovated in* 1928.)

CRAILING

On 9th July 1606 the Lords Commissioners appointed a stipend for the minister of Nisbet, Crailing and Spittal, which are joined in one.—[*Acts of Parl.*, iv, 500.]

THOMAS WILKIE, was son of Robert W., min. of Kilmarnock and not as stated. He marr. Euphan Bruce and had issue—Elizabeth.—[*Reg. of Deeds*, *Mack.*, xxiii, 309.]
1621

DAVID BROWN, his daugh., Elizabeth (marr. 30th Aug. 1824).
1789

ADAM CUNNINGHAM, pres. by Crown 21st July 1840.
1840

CHARLES JAMES MORE MIDDLETON, licen. 13th May 1887, died 26th April 1931.
1888

ECKFORD

The church was burned by the English under Sir Rauf Eure 7th Sept. 1544.—[*Hamilton Papers*, ii, 456.]

ROBERT RICHARDSON, vicar, was in office 5th Dec. 1553; Treasurer of Scotland 7th Oct. 1556; Archdeacon of Teviotdale 12th May 1565, and Commendator of the Priory of St Mary of Trayl (St Mary's Isle); acquired various lands, including parts of the Regality of Dunfermline; died in 1571; had 3 natural sons—James, afterwards Sir James of Smetoun, who marr. Elizabeth Douglas, with issue, including Robert, 2nd son, created 1st Bart. of Pencaitland 13th Nov. 1630; Robert; Stephen, in Jedburgh, whose daugh., Alison, marr. Thomas Johnstoun.—[*Reg. Great Seal*, iv, 1041, 1156, 1475, 1817, 1938, 1979, 1982, 2279, 2659, 2843; v, 1730; viii, 2016; *Cal. Laing Charters*, Nos. 975, 976; *Cal. of Charters*, i, 467b, ii, 3; *Cal. of Deeds in Acts and Decreets*, viii, 348; *Reg. of Deeds*, ii, 357; Crawford's *Officers of State*, i, 383; *Complete Baronetage*, ii, 381.]
1560

JOHN CLERK, pres. to vicarage 13th March 1572–3 on death of Sir John Wilson.—[*Reg. Pres. Bene.*, ii, (4), 5.]
1572

ANDREW CLAYHILLS, min. in 1592, pres. to vicarage 30th April 1593 on death of John Clerk.—[*Reg. Sec. Sig.*, lxiv, 45; lxv, 56.]
1593

PATRICK URQUHART, pres. on dem. of Andrew Clayhills.—[*Reg. Sec. Sig.*, lxxi, 137.]
1600

JOHN BOYLE, M.A. (Edin. 1596), blind and discharged by General Assembly from discharging any part of the pastoral office except preaching 19th March 1600; proposed for Second Charge, Jedburgh, 1601 and described as min. there when pres. to vicarage here by James VI 15th March 1605 on dem. of Patrick Urquhart; pres. to Hownam 22nd July 1607; adm. here 5th May 1608; dep. for immoral conduct 11th Jan. 1610; pres. by James, Viscount Clandeboy, to curacy of Kellyleagh, Ireland, and was adm. to rectory there Aug. 1637; denounced the "Black Oath" but afterwards took it, but was arrested and taken to Dublin. He
1608

marr. and had issue—Jean (marr. William Murdoch).—[*Genealogists Mag.*, Sept. 1936, 360; *Reg. Sec. Sig.*, lxxiv, 265.]

1610 THOMAS ABERNETHY.—[*G. R. Sas.*, xli, 475.]

1666 WILLIAM TURNBULL, his son, James, apprentice to Walter Turnbull, surgeon, Edinburgh, 7th Sept. 1670.

1694 JAMES NOBLE, line 8, delete "70."

1829 JOSEPH YAIR, his daughs.—Agnes Archibald MacDougall, died 13th Aug. 1917; Christian Archibald MacDougall, died April 1923.

1897 CHARLES LUCIUS MacLAREN, his mother was Anne Taylor Bell; died 25th July 1944; his widow, Isabella Blyth Dall, died 9th Dec. 1945.

EDGERSTON

1855 JOHN FERGUSSON, his widow, Margaret Richardson, died at Kilmartin, Dumfries, 7th Dec. 1924, aged 88.

1892 THOMAS GORDON, his widow, Adelaide Dobie, died at Kirkcudbright 10th Jan. 1926. He died 5th April 1917.

1917 ARTHUR FRASER, born 21st Aug. 1868, son of John F., min. of Petty; educ. at Univ. of Aberdeen, M.A. (1906); licen. by Presb. of Aberdeen; missionary at Milton of Campsie 1914–17; ord. 21st Sept. 1917; died at Denholm 13th June 1947. Marr. 19th Oct. 1917 Janie Reid, eldest daugh. of James McHardy, min. of Latheron.

HAWICK

The Church of Hawick was erected and created a canonry and free prebend on 30th Jan. 1447–8.

1560 JOHN SANDILANDS, for "1583" read "1563."

1663 ALEXANDER KINNEAR, line 11, for "writer" read "W.S."; resident with his wife, Margaret Rutherford, and three children, eldest 14, in Tron Parish, Edinburgh.—[*Tron Par. Poll Book*, 40.]

1667 JOHN LANGLANDS, his son, John, M.D.

1892 DAVID CATHELS, licen. 17th May 1881; Moderator of General Assembly 1924; died 16th June 1925; his widow, Margaret Agnes Hewat, died at Edinburgh 9th July 1940; his daughs.—Katherine Stuart (marr. 5th Aug. 1917 Harold Mansfield, B.A., M.B., M.R.C.S., Capt. R.A.M.C.); Jane Gardner (marr. 16th April 1917 James Johnston, M.B., Ch.B.); his son, Louis Patrick, Rector of St Peter's, Peterhouse, died 9th April 1939. Publication—*The Permanent and the Transitory* (Moderatorial Address, Edin., 1924).

1925 JOHN ARCHIBALD GLOVER THOMSON, licen. 28th Nov. 1906, formerly of Wallacetown, Ayr (*q.v.*), trans. from Tron, Edinburgh, 19th Nov. 1925; his mother was Anne Dundas Glover; licen. 28th Nov. (not May). Publication—*Roll of the Ministry of Hawick*, 1183 to 1929, *with Notes* (Hawick, 1936).

HAWICK ST JOHN'S

1889 ALEXANDER McINROY THOMSON, licen. 21st May 1888.

1913 ARTHUR HENRY DUNNETT, trans. to Teviothead 1st June 1920.

1920 WALTER GORDON CARTER, B.A., ord. 5th Nov. 1920; trans. to Carluke 21st Aug. 1929.

HAWICK ST MARGARET'S

1905 WILLIAM CUPPLES McCULLOUGH, dem. 1935, died at London 22nd May 1939; his son, William Donald Hamilton, on B.B.C. staff. His wife, Marion Jones, died 2nd Oct. 1934.

HAWICK ST MARY'S

STEWART BURNS, dem. 7th Oct. 1925, died 19th Dec. 1935; his wife, Elizabeth Carruthers Murray, died 17th March 1934.
1880

ERIC MAITLAND KIRK RAFF, born 29th March 1892, son of William Watson R., Melbourne, and Victoria Black, and grandson of William R., Woodlee, Forres; educ. at Scots College, Melbourne, Univ. of Melbourne, B.A. (17th April 1915); Presbyterian Theological Hall; ord. by Presb. of Ormond, North Melbourne, 18th Oct. 1916, to Efate Island, New Hebrides Mission; res. 1923; adm. on probation by General Assembly 22nd May 1924; assistant St Michael's, Dumfries; app. to Rosyth 14th Sept. 1925; adm. here 30th March 1926; died at Bournemouth 22nd March 1927. Marr. 9th Dec. 1916 Ruth (born 30th Oct. 1891), daugh. of John Baird, *s.p.*
1926

WILLIAM SIMPSON, licen. by Presb. of St Andrews, May 1891; trans. from Maud (*q.v.*) 23rd Nov. 1927, dem. 11th Nov. 1933; died from effects of an accident 29th June 1946; his wife, Sarah Dare, died at Bonnyrigg 5th March 1940; his son, William Nightingale, doctor in Stow, born 29th July 1899.
1927

HOBKIRK

JOHN DOUGLAS, pres. to vicarage on death of Sir David Turnbull.— [*Reg. Pres. Bene.*, ii, (4), 537.]
1576

JOHN GORDON, dem. 19th March 1919; teacher, North Berwick; Ph.D. (Edin.) 28th June 1928; reponed June 1926; adm. to Channelkirk 25th March 1927; trans. to Kirkinner 3rd Sept. 1931; dem. 20th Jan. 1943.
1907

JOHN ASHFIELD CLARK, born 1874; educ. at Queen's College, Galway, B.A.; Royal Univ. of Ireland, M.A. (June 1898); Assembly's College, Belfast, and Magee College, Londonderry; licen. by Presb. of Omagh Nov. 1901; assistant at Creevan; ord. to same July 1902; dem. Feb. 1916; assistant South Leith; Craigmillar, April 1916; *locum* Tranent, 31st July 1917; adm. 26th Sept. 1919; drowned by upsetting of boat at Norfolk Broads 28th Aug. 1921.
1919

DAVID LYNEDOCH CATTANACH, trans. from Golspie (*q.v.*) 8th March 1922; Chaplain, Scots Memorial Church, Jerusalem. 1923–4; his daugh., Isobel Mary Lorimer, died 18th Nov. 1929.
1922

ABBOTRULE

JOSEPH TENNANT, pres. to parsonage and vicarage in 1605 on death of Alexander Crichton.— [*G. R. Sas.*, xxx, 1; x, 46; lviii, 433; *Reg. Sec. Sig.*, lxxiv, 390.]
1603

JAMES KER, died Father of the Church.
1624

ROBERT SPOTTISWOOD, his sons, Alexander, apprentice to Alexander Shimster, merchant, Edinburgh, 19th Dec. 1677; Robert, apprentice to Alexander Nicolson, merchant, Edinburgh, 16th Feb. 1681.
1687

THOMAS HARVIE, marr. daugh. of James Ker, min. of this parish.— [*P. C. Reg.*, xiv, 338.]
1687

HOWNAM

JOHN BOYLE, M.A., min. of Christ's Evangel at Jedburgh; pres. to vicarage 22nd July 1607 on death of Andrew Douglas.—[*Reg. Sec. Sig.*, lxx, 134.]
1607

JAMES RUTHERFORD, his son, David Alexander, died at Edinburgh 20th Oct. 1823.
1775

GEORGE WATSON, his widow, Anna Jane Ewen, died at Corpach 16th Aug. 1921; his son, George John Ewen, W.S., died 2nd Nov. 1943.
1865

WILLIAM DRUMMOND MORRIS, died 26th March 1946; marr. (2) 9th Sept. 1919 Jessie Agnes Watson (died 7th Nov. 1941), daugh. of Hugh
1897

McCrostie, Dalcroy, Newhaven Road, Leith. His son, John George Blount Fyfe, doctor, killed in motor accident 19th March 1932.

JEDBURGH

In the church there were an altar dedicated to St Kentigern, to which on 30th Aug. 1479 Mr James Newtoune, rector of Bothrule (Bedrule), granted 10 merks annual rent from a tenement in Jedburgh; an altar dedicated to the Holy Rood, described as in the parish church, probably the nave of the abbey church; an altar dedicated to the Virgin Mary, in the parish church; an altar dedicated to St Ninian, also in the parish church; and an altar also dedicated to the Holy Rood, situated in the "rud loft" of the Monastery of Jedburgh, to the first chaplain (Sir John Quhitlaw) of which, and his successors, Alexander Donaldson, burgess of Edinburgh, mortified certain annual rents from tenements in Edinburgh on 7th Sept. 1493. The last is an instance of an altar situated in the Rood Loft.—[*Reg. Great Seal*, ii, 1432; iv, 1897; *Reg. Sec. Seal*, xxxviii, 107; Young's *Prot. Bk.*, v, va; *Report Hist. MSS. Commiss.*, vii, 729. See *Aberdeen Univ. Chapel (Old Machar)*, and *Dunkeld (Cathedral)* for other instances of altar in Rood Loft.]

1563 ALEXANDER FORRESTER, min. in 1563 and 1566.—[*Comps. Sub Coll. of Thirds, Roxburgh*, etc.]

1593 JOHN ABERNETHY, pres. to vicarage of Oxnam 25th Feb. 1605.—[*Reg. Sec. Sig.*, lxxiv, 248.]

1605 JOHN BOYLE, min. here (probably second min.). See Eckford.

1636 JAMES BURNETT, line 6, for "Feb." read "Sept." He was pres. to Burmarsh, Kent, 19th May and inst. 2nd June 1640, but apparently died shortly afterwards, as his son, James, was inst. 15th April 1641.

1640 WILLIAM JAMESON, his son, Mr Thomas.—[*Burntisland Writs, Reg. Ho.* 1645.]

1661 PETER BLAIR, marr. Mary, daugh. of James Hamilton, min. of Old Church, Edinburgh, and had issue—James, min. of Cranstoun; Margaret (marr. Sir Patrick Davidson, surgeon, London).

1682 WILLIAM GALBRAITH, has sasine to himself and wife of annual rent, 14th Oct. 1672.—[*G. R. Sas.*, 3 Ser., xxx, 259.]

1732 JAMES ROWATT, marr. Agnes (died in Ireland 1763), daugh. of William Mure of Glanderston and widow of William Porterfield of Quarrelton.

1734 JAMES WINCHESTER, marr. Mary, daugh. of Robert Dunbar of Dunphail and Grizel, daugh. of James Brodie, diarist.—[*Duffus Charters.*]

1758 JOHN DOUGLAS, his son, Walter, died 1783.

1843 GEORGE RITCHIE, pres. by Crown 22nd July 1843; his daugh., Margaret Elizabeth, died Edinburgh 30th Sept. 1925.

1877 DONALD MACLEOD, line 2, for "Maxwell Parish, Glasgow" read "St Mark's, Dundee."

1899 JAMES JOHNSTONE DRUMMOND, licen. 4th May 1894, died 28th Nov. 1918; his son, Andrew Alastair Landale, min. of Alva; his daugh., Margaret Louise (marr. 3rd July 1936 Brian Pullen, Northampton).

1919 OSWALD BELL MILLIGAN, B.D., M.C., trans. from St Leonard's, Ayr, 16th May 1919; trans. to Corstorphine 31st March 1827.

1927 GEORGE WILLIAM KINNAIRD MACPHERSON, born Kinnaird 13th April 1891, son of James Rose M., D.D., min. of Dingwall; educ. at Univ. of Edinburgh, M.A. (1912), B.D. (1915); Fellow of Union Theological Seminary, New York, 1919–20; served as Captain 1/4 Seaforths in Great War; was for four years on a mission station in Canada; licen. by Presb. of Dingwall 25th June 1915; assistant St Cuthbert's; ord. 23rd Nov. 1923 to

Carstairs; trans. and adm. 22nd Sept 1927. Marr. 5th Feb. 1924 Irene Colburn, fifth daugh. of Robert C. Buchanan, Mortonhall Road, Edinburgh, and Eliza Russell Macdonald, and has issue—Margery Ann, born 8th Oct. 1926; Robert Buchanan, born 5th July 1929.

KIRKTON

1569 GEORGE DOUGLAS, pres. on death of William Cranstoun.—[*Reg. Sec. Sig.*, xxxvii, 25.]

1616 JAMES SCOTT, trans. to Tongland 1619.

1687 PATRICK CUNNINGHAM, his son, John, probably apprentice to John Walker, skinner, Edinburgh, 9th Aug. 1727.

1758 THOMAS ELLIOT, line 1, for "III" read "II."

1857 GEORGE HUNTER, pres. by Crown 27th May 1857.

1892 JOHN STUART, died 16th Aug. 1930.

MINTO

1575 WILLIAM McGOWAN, line 1, for "1575" read "1574."

1679 JAMES KIRKWOOD. Addl. reference —*History of the Public Library Movement in Great Britain and Ireland*, by John Minto (Allen & Unwin, 1932), in which he is claimed the title of "Father of the Free Libraries" because of his now celebrated "Overture for Founding and Maintaining Bibliotheeks in every Paroch throughout the kingdom."

1865 JOHN PETER McMORLAND, his widow, Elizabeth Macdonald Bradshaw Smith, died 16th June 1917.

1878 ALEXANDER GALLOWAY, died 20th Aug. 1926. Marr. Margaret Rankin, daugh. of William Smith, min. of Douglas; his sons—William G., died at New York 25th June 1936; Alexander, Lieut-.Colonel 1st Cameronians, Instructor Staff College, Camberley.

1927 GEORGE OMOND MACKENZIE, trans. from Methil (*q.v.*) 2nd Feb. 1927; dem. 15th Sept. 1935; adm. to Nicolson Street Church, Edinburgh, 19th Sept. 1939, died 26th Nov. 1943. Addl. issue—Ella Jean Christine, born 14th Jan. 1926.

HASSENDEAN

The church was granted to the Bishopric of Glasgow by David I; and the grant was confirmed by Pope Alexander III in 1170. About twenty years later there was a dispute regarding the patronage of the church between King William the Lion and Joceline, Bishop of Glasgow; and as it appeared impossible otherwise to settle the dispute, they agreed to give the revenues to charity. Accordingly in 1193-4 the Bishop with the consent of the King gave the patronage—lands, tithes, dues—to Melrose Abbey for the purpose of building and maintaining a house at Hassendean for the reception and entertainment of wayfaring poor and pilgrims to Melrose. The hospital was known as Monk's Tower, and its lands were designated Monk's Croft. Some time after 1666 a new church was built at the west end of Roberton parish; and in 1690 Hassendean Church was wholly suppressed. Teviot floods made repeated inroads on the church and churchyard, and in 1796 a specially severe flood completed the destruction.—[*Reg. Epis. of Glasgow*, i, 23-4; *Bk. of Melrose*, i, 112-16; *Chronicle of Melrose*, 100.]

1576 THOMAS NEWBIE, reader 1576, pres. to vicarage 6th Oct. 1576 on dem. of Thomas Westoun, advocate. See under Sir Thomas Ker, *Roxburgh*.—[*Reg. Pres. Bene.*, lxxiii, 40.]

1595 SYMON SCOTT, son of Walter S. of Newton; pres. to vicarage pensionary 17th May 1595 on dem. of Thomas Newbie.—[*Reg. Sec. Sig.*, lxvii, 122.]

1620 JOHN MADDER, pres. on death of Thomas Newbie.—[*Reg. Sec. Sig.*, lxxiii, 40.]

OXNAM

SIR JAMES AINSLIE, reader in 1568; chaplain of the Altar of St Ninian, Jedburgh.—[*Comps. Sub Coll. of Thirds, Dumfries*, etc.]
1574

WILLIAM AINSLIE, min., called parson and vicar 1595-7.—[*Comps. Gen. Coll. of Thirds*.]
1599

JOHN ABERNETHY, min. of Jedburgh, pres. to vicarage 25th Feb. 1605 on depr. of William Ainslie.—[*Reg. Sec. Sig.*, lxxiv, 248.]
1605

THOMAS ABERNETHY, M.A., min. at Hawick, pres. to vicarage of Plenderleith 24th May 1606.—[*Reg. Sec. Sig.*, lxxv, 116.]
1606

ANDREW KIRKTON.—[*G. R. Sas.*, xxxiii, 365.]
1624

ARCHIBALD PORTEOUS.—[*G. R. Sas.*, liv, 175.]
1640

JOHN AINSLIE, marr. Anna Douglas, niece of Thomas Douglas, merchant, Edinburgh, and had issue—Magdalene (marr. Andrew Ker, apothecary, Yetholm); Anne (marr. William Ainslie, vintner, Jedburgh).—[*Reg. of Deeds, Mack.* lxv, 962.]
1682

JAMES RICHARDSON, adm. 8th Nov. not Feb.
1764

JAMES WIGHT, his son, John Rutherford, died 8th Sept. 1919, aged 90.
1820

WILLIAM BARNIE, pres. by Crown 14th June 1859; his widow, Margaret Anne Riddoch, died 18th Dec. 1932; his daughs.—Annie Forrest, died 3rd June 1917; Jessie, died 4th June 1940; his son, Samuel Riddoch, died 28th March 1946.
1859

PETER BRYCE GUNN, died 30th May 1928; his widow, Jessie Turnbull, died 9th May 1939.
1885

GEORGE HENRY GRANT, born 17th April 1905, son of William John G., Rose Villa, Archieston,
1928
and Fanny Calder; educ. at Univ. of Aberdeen, M.A. (1925), B.D. (1928); licen. by Presb. of Aberlour April 1928; assistant Holburn, Aberdeen; ord. 13th Dec. 1928; trans. to West Church, Inverness, 8th July 1936. Marr. 6th Feb. 1929 Kathleen Mary, daugh. of William G. Gilchrist, Campinas, Turriff, and has issue—Sheila Mary, born 8th Dec. 1930; William Niven, born 25th June 1933; Donald Marcus, born 21st Sept. 1945.

SOUTHDEAN

JOHN SCOTT, reader. See under Sir Thomas Ker, *Roxburgh*.
1582

THOMAS THOMSON, died, having been struck by lightning while exorcising a ghost.
1700

JOHN RYRIE SPENCE, date of lic. 10th May 1905; M.A. (1901) and B.D. (1905).
1907

TEVIOTHEAD

THOMAS DYCE, marr. Isobel, daugh. of Alexander Gordon, Fochabers, who died at Aberdeen 5th Sept. 1848.
1792

HENRY SCOTT RIDDELL, marr. 23rd July 1833.
1832

ARCHIBALD HUTTON DINWIDDIE, licen. 13th May 1881; died 7th Oct. 1919.
1887

ARTHUR HENRY DUNNETT, trans. from St John's, Hawick, 1st June 1920; dem. 1st Oct. 1824 on app. as Depute Home Mission Secretary, and on Union of Churches in 1929 became one of the Secretaries of the Home Department; died 28th Aug. 1940. Addl. issue—William Gavin, born 4th Oct. 1919. Publications—*The Child's Prayer Book* (1920); *Book of Prayers* (1925); *The Church in Changing Scotland* (1934).
1920

DAVID SIME STEVEN, ord. 11th Jan., adm. 6th Feb. 1925; trans. to Gilcomiston, Aberdeen, 16th May 1929.
1925

WILTON

1567 THOMAS WESTOUN, parson.

1602 WILLIAM CLARK, pres. to parsonage and vicarage 31st Dec. 1602 on death of John Langlands; his second son, John, 18th Jan. 1634.—[*G. R. Sas.*, xxxviii, 330; *Reg. Sec. Sig.*, lxxv, 156.]

1641 JOHN LANGLANDS, marr. Anna Douglas; his sons—James, apprentice to Robert Blackwood, merchant, Edinburgh, 6th Jan. 1669; Walter, apprentice to Adam Bewcastle, merchant, Edinburgh, 3rd Aug. 1692.—[*Reg. of Deeds, Dal.*, 20th Dec. 1693.]

1887 JOHN RUDGE WILSON, died 27th Aug. 1930; his widow, Georgina Underwood Fiddes, died at Wetheral, Cumberland, 9th July 1947.

1926 CHARLES GUTHRIE COOPER, B.D., trans. from Strathbungo 17th May 1926; trans. to Paisley Abbey 23rd Sept. 1930; D.D. (St Andrews, 18th Feb. 1932); his son, George Douglas, born 4th Nov. 1925, died 17th Oct. 1934.

PRESBYTERY OF EARLSTON

CHANNELKIRK

The chapel at Carfrae was built by John de Sinclair on permission granted by Dryburgh Abbey. About 1200 he gave indemnity that the chapel should not interfere with the rights of the mother church of Channelkirk. The chapel at Glengelt was built by Henry de Mundeville, who about 1400 gave similar indemnity.—[*Book of Dryburgh*, 131-2, 136.]

The bell in Channelkirk has this inscription: "For Channenkirk 1702."

1574 JOHN CHARLES, reader.

1574 GEORGE STRACHAN, vicar in 1576 and 1577.—[*Comps. Gen. Coll. of Thirds.*]

1666 WALTER KEITH, M.A., acted as min. at Guthrie.

1702 HENRY HOME, his eldest daugh., Jean (marr. cont. 15th Nov. 1734 Archibald Campbell, merchant, Edinburgh, late at Crinan).

1862 JAMES WALKER, died at New Westminster, B.C., 15th Oct. 1921.

1891 ARCHIBALD ALLAN, dem. 1924, died at Edinburgh, 29th Oct. 1924; his widow, Jean Christie, died at Edinburgh 16th Dec. 1929.

1925 HENRY McKINLEY, ord. 30th April 1925; trans. to Sinclairtown 2nd Nov. 1926.

1927 JOHN GORDON, formerly of Hobkirk (*q.v.*), adm. 25th March 1927; trans. to Kirkinner 3rd Sept. 1931. Marr. 19th July 1923 Mary Jane, daugh. of Robert Turnbull, solicitor, Edinburgh.

EARLSTON

1571 NINIAN BORTHWICK, reader and exhorter 1571.—[*Comps. Sub Coll. of Thirds, Linlithgow.* etc.]

1575 JAMES FAIRBAIRN, reader 1568, pres. to vicarage 1st Feb. 1577 on death of Christopher Home.—[*Reg. Pres. Bene.*, ii, (4), 123; *Edin. Tests.*, iii, 136.]

1568 JAMES DAES, min. here, pres. to vicarage 20th Dec. 1586, on dem. of James Fairbairn.—[*Reg. Sec. Sig.*, lviii, 185]

1673 JOHN HEPBURN, brother to Patrick H. of Nunraw.—[*Berwick Sas.*, v, 202, 203.]

1694 GEORGE JOHNSTON, son of Patrick J., merchant, Edinburgh.

1869 WILLIAM MAIR, died at Edinburgh 20th Jan. 1920; his widow, Isabella Edward, died at Edinburgh 7th Dec. 1932. Addl. Publications—*Action Sermons* (Edin., 1917); *My Young Communicant* (Edin., 1915).

1915 WALTER DAVIDSON, trans. to Bluevale, Glasgow, 12th June 1929.

1929 PETER WYLIE, born 3rd Sept. 1896; educ. at Congregational Theological Hall, 1922-4; Univ. of Edinburgh; licen. by Ordination 4th July 1924 to Congregational Church, Lanark; dem. 31st Oct. 1926; assistant St Paul's, Leith; adm. on probation for one year by General Assembly 24th May 1928; ord. 28th Aug. 1929, died 4th Dec. 1945. Marr. 2nd June 1926 Jean Watson Muirhead, *s.p.*

(*Charges united 31st March 1946.*)

GORDON

The chapel at Huntlywood was dedicated to the Virgin Mary. The patronage belonged to the Gordon family, a member of whom appears to have been the founder.—[*Reg. Great Seal*, ii, 3416; *Reg. Sec. Seal*, ii, 1696; *Retours*, xiv, 300.]

JAMES STRAITON, line 4, after Oct. add 1662; marr. Jean Craw.—[*Berwick Sas.*, 19th Jan. 1659.]
1662

THOMAS MABON, his daugh., Jean.—[*Hornings*, 11th Dec. 1740.]
1685

JAMES BELL, his son, John, apprentice to Alexander Kincaid, bookseller, Edinburgh, 20th Nov. 1754.
1727

LAUDER

In 1268 the patronage of the Church of Lauder, which was at first a dependent chapel of the Church of Channelkirk, was resigned by John Baliol in favour of Dryburgh Abbey, and like resignation was made by John Baliol's wife, Devorgilla of Galloway, daughter and heir of Alan de Galloway, late Constable of Scotland. Confirmation was given by John de Haddington, Prior of St Andrews. The church stood on the north side of the town, facing Lauder Fort, which now forms part of Thirlestane Castle. The present church, on the south-west side of the town, was built in 1673, and repaired in 1820. The Chapel of Kedslie was dedicated to St John, and though no remains of it now exist, it is perpetuated in the name of the estate and mansion of Chapel-on-Leader. There was a chapel attached to the Hospital of St Leonard. To God, St Mary, St Leonard and the sick brothers of the Hospital of Lauder (St Leonard's), Richard de Morville, Constable of Scotland, for the souls of himself, his wife, his heirs, his father and mother, and his ancestors and successors, gave about 1170 that land where the house of the hospital is situated, according to the boundaries as perambulated by John, Bishop of Glasgow, Avicia, wife of Richard, and William, son of Richard, etc. Evidently the hospital was for leprous monks, and the foregoing date may be approximately the date of its foundation.—[*Book of Dryburgh*, 5–6, 7–9, 267–8, which gives boundaries of the hospital lands; *Procs. of Berwickshire Naturalists' Club*, xiii, 139, which see for details of hospital.]

ANDREW HOME, M.A., son of George H. of Wedderburn and brother of Sir David H. of Wedderburn; parson 17th April 1548, died Sept. 1567.—[*Edin. Tests.*, 7th Jan. 1568; *Reg. Mag. Sig.*, iv, 3rd Feb. 1568; *Reg. Sec. Sig.*, iii, 2725.]
1560

JOHN KNOX, M.A., min. 27th April 1580.—[*Edin. Tests.*, viii, 244.]
1576

DAVID FORRESTER, trans. to Longforgan, 7th Sept. 1684.
1669

JAMES MIDDLETON, his son, James, factor to Lord Howard de Walden, died at Kilmarnock 27th March 1934.
1862

WILLIAM McCONNACHIE, D.D. (Aberdeen, 31st March 1921), died 3rd Oct. 1931. His widow, Ellen Mitchell Douglas, died 6th Jan. 1939.
1906

LEGERWOOD

A church existed here in 1127 when "John, priest of Ledgaresude" signed a charter in connection with Coldingham Priory. In 1164 the church passed by charter into the possession of the Church of St James, St Mirin and St Milburg of Passelet (Paisley) and the priors and monks there till the Reformation.

The church was dedicated by Bishop de Bernham on 30th Oct. 1242. The Hospital of Morriston was at Aldenston. It belonged to Melrose Abbey, and was for "sick brothers," monks afflicted with leprosy. Probably it was founded by Walter, son of Alan, Steward of Scotland. At any rate, towards the end of the 12th century he gave to the hospital and the sick brothers there residing a plough-gate and a half of land, to wit, a plough-gate in the town of Aldenstoun, and a half plough-gate which Dame Emma de Ednaham (Ednam) held, with right of pasture and easements in the forest of Birkenside and Leggardeswude (Legerwood), and liberty to grind at his mills without paying multures. Nichol de Lychardeswode, Chaplain, warden of the hospital, swore fealty to Edward I on 28th Aug. 1296. At Birkenside there was a chapel dedicated to St John.—[*Retours*, iii, 135, xiii, 118; *Bk. of Melrose*, i, 70; *Mon. Annals of Teviotdale*, 265; *Cal. of Docs. Rel. to Scotland*, ii, 211; Lockhart's *Ch. in Scotland in 13th Century*, 52.]

1564 WILLIAM CRANSTOUN, vicar, 5th March 1566-7.—[*Cal. of Charters*, ix, 2079.]

1592 ROBERT FRENCH, min. at Eccles, pres. to vicarage 18th May 1592 on death of William Cranstoun, commissioner of Lauderdale.—[*Reg. Sec. Sig.*, lxiii, 267.]

1859 ARCHIBALD BROWN, died 2nd Dec. 1918.

1899 JOHN ALEXANDER CAMERON, in Great War was Senior Presbyterian Chaplain at Ripon and at Abbeville with 51st Division; in 1929 Joint Clerk of Synod of Merse and Teviotdale; Hon. Sec. Association of General Assembly, Synod and Presbytery Clerks 1927; dem. 15th Nov. 1942; died 24th Jan. 1943. His wife, Elizabeth Farquhar Philip, died by motor accident 19th Dec. 1928; his son, William Marshall Philip, B.Sc. (Edin.), D.I.C. (London), is Entomologist, Khartoum, for Northern Sudan; his daugh., Winifred Mary Elizabeth, A.R.C.M. (London) (marr. 8th July 1930 Ronald Martin Perceval, A.C.A., Monkseaton); his son, John Austen Perceval, F.R.C.S.E., is surgeon in charge of Government Hospital, Penang; his daugh., Ruth Evelyn Philip, is M.S.R. London.

MERTOUN

The present church is situated about a mile north-west of the old churchyard, in which are remains of the early church, the east wall and parts of the north and south walls, probably Norman. The church was dedicated by Bishop de Bernham in 1241.—[*Berwickshire Naturalists' Club*, xiii, 144.]

1560 SIR ANDREW HEGY, vicar; died before 29th Jan. 1582-3.—[*Reg. Pres. to Ben.*, ii, 84v.]

1585 JAMES MENZIES, min., pres. to the vicarage 29th Jan. 1582-3.—[*Reg. Pres. to Bene.*, ii, 84v.]

1594 JOHN HEPBURN, pres. to vicarage 20th Jan. 1594-5 on dem. of James Menzies.—[*Reg. Sec. Sig.*, lxvii, 42.]

1663 THOMAS COURTNEY, marr. Barbara Hamilton, widow of James Hamilton of Stenhouse.—[*Reg. of Deeds, Dal.*, xxii, 633, 23rd March 1667.]

1674 ANDREW MELDRUM, resident with his wife and two children in Tron Parish, Edinburgh, 8th Nov. 1694; his daugh., May, born 9th April 1709 (marr. Robert Morrison, writer burgess of Edinburgh.—[*Tron Poll Tax Roll*, 57.]

1692 JOHN WALLACE, marr. Jane, daugh. of George Hutchison, min. of Irvine.

1697 ROBERT LIVER, marr. Elizabeth, daugh. of James Pillans, Regent, Edinburgh Univ.—[*Deeds, Dal.*, 24th March 1704.]

1718 JAMES INNES, his son, Robert, M.D., died 1798.

1892 ANDREW THOMSON DONALD, his daugh., Edith Armstrong, died 2nd May 1934; his son, George Honey, D.D., min. of St Andrew's and St Paul's, Montreal; his daugh., Dorothy Gray (marr. James Patrick Chrystal), died at Meonstoke, Hants, 24th Feb. 1940.

1908 DAVID GILMOUR MANUEL, died at Edinburgh 1st April 1921; his widow, Agnes Manuel Stenhouse, died at Edinburgh 17th June 1934; his daughs.— Dora Grizel Baillie (marr. 1st Dec. 1931 Andrew Jaffray Dobbie); Agnes Graham (marr. 16th June 1934 Thomas Douglas Vivian Morgan, Shawington Fall, Quebec); Marion (marr. 6th June 1936 David Ritchie Murdoch, Edinburgh).

JAMES FERGUSSON McCREATH,
1918 born 20th Aug. 1883, son of Thomas M., farmer, Challoch, Newton Stewart, and Elizabeth Dunlop; educ. at Univ. of Glasgow, M.A. (1904); licen. by Presb. of Wigtown, April 1907; assistant St Bernard's, Edinburgh; ord. to Kelso North 24th Jan. 1917; trans. (ass. and suc.) 6th Nov. 1918. Marr. 20th Feb. 1917 Marjorie Dennistoun, only daugh. of Thomas Stark Murdoch Riach, Khonikor, Assam, and Christiana Margaret Dennistoun Shaw.

SMAILHOLM

The church was dedicated by Bishop de Bernham on 29th April 1243. Along with the Chapel of Stichell it was granted to Coldingham Priory by Walter Oliford, justiciary of Scotland, who died in 1242.—[Carr's *Coldingham*, 320; Lockhart's *Ch. in Scotland in 13th Century*, 52–3.]

ADAM CLERK, exhorter 1563.—
1563 [*Comps. Sub Coll. of Thirds, Roxburgh.*]

SIR THOMAS GETHERALL, vicar
1563 1563.—[*Comps. Sub Coll. of Thirds, Roxburgh.*]

JOHN HOME of BLACKADDER,
1567 held vicarage 1567–71.—[*Comps. Sub Coll. of Thirds, Linlithgow.*]

GEORGE HOME, son of Alexander
1578 H., fiar of Blackadder and brother german of John H. of Blackadder; vicar in 1578, he had held parsonage in 1548.—[*Reg. Mag. Sig.*, 29th Jan. 1542–3; *Noble British Families*, ii, 28; *Reg. Sec. Sig.*, iii, 2725.]

DAVID FORSYTH, pres. to vicarage
1593 on death of Alexander Home.—[*Reg Sec. Sig.*, lxiii, 184.]

JAMES HUNTER, pres. to vicarage
1598 on death of David Forsyth.—[*Reg. Sec. Sig.*, lxix, 260.]

JOHN BELL, marr. cont. 2nd Sept.
1687 1670 Jean, daugh. of George Murray of Tippermuir, and had issue—Robert and Helen.—[*Deeds, Durie*, 1705, No. 940.]

WILLIAM LAMB SIME, died un-
1887 married 2nd Jan. 1937.

STOW

Stow was anciently called Wedale. Tradition narrates that fragments of the Cross of Christ were brought from the Holy Land by King Arthur, and were preserved with great veneration in the Virgin Mary's Church of Wedale. The early church was situated on the estate of Torsonce, and in the first half of the 19th century a part of one of the walls, three feet thick, was to be seen built in with a common drystone dyke. Near by was the "Lady's Well," and a huge stone, removed in the course of the formation of a new road and subsequently broken up, was said to bear the impression of the Virgin Mary's foot, made on the occasion of one of her descents to visit this favoured sanctuary. The church was dedicated by Bishop de Bernham on 3rd Nov. 1242. A later church, apparently of the late 15th century, but largely rebuilt in the 17th century, with a south aisle added at the same period, stands a ruin at the south end of the village. Here also was a Lady Well.—[*Report Hist. Monuments Comm., Midlothian*, 168; Lockhart's *Ch. in Scotland in 13th Century*, 53; *Chron. of Melrose*, 79.]

GEORGE COOK, vicar 1568 and 1571.
1568 —[*Comps. Sub Coll. of Thirds, Dumfries*, etc.]

JOHN BENNET, M.A., pres. to
1578 vicarage 12th Nov. 1578 on dem. of George Cook.—[*Reg. Pres. Bene.*, ii, 8.]

JAMES MITCHELL, his son, John,
1585 min. of St. Andrew's Church, London.

JOHN CLELAND, his son, Archibald,
1640 apprentice to Alexander Thomson, saddler, Edinburgh, 1st Sept. 1675.

1666 ROBERT KAY, had issue—Barbara, bapt. 4th July 1647; Robert, bapt. 4th Sept. 1648. Marr. (2) 14th Jan. 1658 Janet Brown, Dysart.

1841 DAVID WADDELL, pres. 5th May 1841.

1882 WILLIAM WORKMAN, his widow, Margaret Burrell, died 11th Oct. 1936.

1911 THOMAS WILKIE WILSON, D.D. (Edinburgh, 28th June 1934). Addl. Publications—*Stow in Wedale*; *The Permanence of Christianity*; *St Paul and Paganism*; *The Reform of Health and Life*.

WESTRUTHER

1569 SIR ANDREW CURRIE, charged to answer for his demerits before Privy Council 17th Oct. 1569.—[*P. C. Reg.*, ii, 40; *Edin. Tests.*, ii, 96.]

1595 SYMON SCOTT, son of Walter S. of Newtoun, pres. to vicarage pensionary 17th May 1595 on dem. of Thomas Newbie.—[*Reg. Sec. Sig.*, lxvii, 122.]

1598 THOMAS STORIE, M.A., min. here, presented to vicarage 13th Dec. 1600 in succession to late Sir Andrew Currie.—[*Reg. Sec. Sig.*, lxxi, 236.]

1648 JOHN VEITCH, his son, David, apprentice to John Trotter, merchant, Edinburgh, 14th April 1675.—[*G. R. Sas.*, 3 Ser., xvi, 307.]

1704 WALTER SCOTT, his son, Robert, apprentice to Joseph Gibson, surgeon apothecary, Edinburgh, 2nd Nov. 1737.

1738 FRANCIS SCOTT of Langton, served heir to his uncle, Captain Robert Scott of Langton, 18th April 1749.—[*Roxburgh Services*, 228.]

1838 WALTER WOOD, pres. 25th June 1838; his widow, Margaret G. Brodfoot, died 17th Dec. 1946.

1844 HENRY TAYLOR, pres. by Crown 4th Jan. 1844; his daugh., Elizabeth Robertson, died at Melrose 3rd Oct. 1930.

1904 DAVID SILVER, died 30th Nov. 1921; his widow, Georgina Stephen, died 12th Feb. 1941; his son, George, Captain, 2nd Bengal Lancers, died at Malton, Woodbridge, Sussex.

1927 JOHN JAMES SCOTT THOMSON, M.A., ord. 20th April 1922; trans. to John Knox, Aberdeen, 3rd Sept. 1925.

1926 WILLIAM GILBERT LIMOND, adm. 14th Jan. 1926; trans. to St Leonard's, Lanark, 27th Sept. 1928.

1929 ROBERT ARTHUR, born 31st March 1860, son of William A. and Agnes Carlaw; educ. at Torphichen School, Bathgate Academy, and Univ. of Edinburgh, M.A. (1882); licen. by Free Church Presb. of Linlithgow, 21st April 1886; ord. 26th Jan. 1888 to Free Church, Westruther; adm. 1929; dem. 30th Nov. 1931; died at Edinburgh 12th Feb. 1947. Marr. 8th Aug. 1901 Margaret Isabella (died 18th Aug. 1941), daugh. of James Burnet.

(*A provisional union of the churches was effected* 8*th March* 1928, *confirmed* 13*th March* 1930.)

PRESBYTERY OF SELKIRK

ASHKIRK

1570 JOHN HAMILTON, M.A., pres. to parsonage in 1570 on dem. of John Murie.—[*Reg. Pres. Bene.*, i, (2), 4.]

1574 JOHN SCOTT, was min. here 3rd Nov. 1573.—[*Reg. Pres. Bene.*, ii, (4), 12.]

1574 JAMES SCOTT, reader in 1574, vicar 1586. See under Sir Thomas Ker, Roxburgh.

1579 THOMAS CRANSTOUN, M.A., pres. to vicarage on death of Sir John Muir.—[*Reg. Pres. Bene.*, ii, 29.]

1583 DANIEL CHALMERS, pres. to parsonage and vicarage 19th May 1585 on death of Thomas Cranstoun.—[*Reg. Pres. Bene.*, ii, 126.]

1586 ROBERT SCOTT, pres. to parsonage 15th April 1586 on death of Daniel Chalmers.—[*Reg. Pres. Bene.*, ii, 142.]

1663 THOMAS COURTNEY, min. 7th July 1663.

1685 RICHARD SCOTT, M.A., resident with his wife and daugh. Jean in Lady Yester's Parish 10th Nov. 1694.—[*Lady Yester's Poll Tax Roll*, 31.]

1695 CHARLES GORDON, brother of John G., provost of Aberdeen.—[*Book of Buchan*, 197.]

1711 ROBERT LITHGOW, his son, Robert, apprentice to William Reoch, wright, 20th April 1737.

1780 WALTER STEWART. his sons— Matthew of Barnhill, died 17th March 1782; James died young.

1837 JOHN EDMONDSTON, his daugh.. Elizabeth, died 20th Jan. 1918.

1861 WILLIAM GRIERSON SMITH, his son, Alfred William, born 7th June 1846, died 13th July 1848.

1871 JOHN CHALMERS, his widow, Margaret Steele, died 27th March 1918; his daugh., Louisa Jane, marr. "1893" not "1898"; his sons—Edward Ernest, drowned in Loch Shiel Oct. 1937; Richard Mason, died New Jersey, U.S.A., 1929.

1892 JAMES DAUN, licen. 13th May 1887; dem. 26th May 1926; died at Edinburgh, 24th March 1927, unmarr.

1926 JAMES REEKIE, born Auchtermuchty 8th April 1886, son of Thomas R., Auchtermuchty, and Christina McKay; educ. at Harris Academy, Dundee, and Univ. of St Andrews, M.A. (1910), B.D. (1914); licen. by Presb. of Cupar. 18th May 1914; assistant St Mary's, Dundee, and St Cuthbert's, Edinburgh; ord. to Dean 10th May 1916; trans. and adm. 12th Nov. 1926.

BOWDEN

1508 THOMAS DUNCANSON, pres. to vicarage on death of Sir William Younger.—[*Reg. Pres. Bene.*, i, 6.]

1574 ROBERT KER, reader.

1681 HENRY KNOX, M.A., resident with two children in Old Kirk Parish, Edinburgh, 16th Nov. 1694.—[*Old Kirk Poll Tax Roll*, 18.]

1891 ALFRED MACFARLANE, licen. by Presb. of Dalkeith, 1899; became min. of St Andrews, Niagara, on Lake Ontario; died 4th May 1935.

1899 JOHN BURR, died 27th May 1940; his mother was Mary Smith, daugh. of James Keith, Arbroath; served as Chaplain to the Forces in Great War. His wife, Catherine Mary Knox, died 29th Oct. 1933. He marr. (2) 9th Feb. 1935 Fanny Elizabeth, daugh. of Alexander Beattie, Tunbridge Wells; his daugh., Susan Agnes (marr. 7th Sept. 1933 John Lumley Matthews, Lecturer in New College, London); his son, Robert, banker, born 1905, not 1904; Addl. Publications—*Studies on the Apostles Creed* (London, 1931); *The Lordship of Love* (London, 1932); *The Crown of Character* (London, 1932); *The Prodigal's Progress* (London, 1933); *Studies on the Ten Commandments* (London, 1935); *The Prayer of Prayers* (London, 1937).

CADDONFOOT

1860 JOHN MILNE, missionary here 1860 to 5th Jan. 1864; afterwards Chaplain to Forces (*q.v.*).

1864 JAMES MACKIE, afterwards min. of St Mary's, Partick.

1910 JOHN TUDOR SCRIMGEOUR, adm. as licentiate from Canadian Church 1905; trans. to Ladykirk 27th Aug. 1926.

1926 JAMES MACKENZIE KIRKPATRICK, trans. from St Bride's, Partick (*q.v.*), 9th Dec. 1926; D.D. (Glasgow, 22nd June 1927); dem. 28th Feb. 1940.

ETTRICK

1569 SIR JOHN STEVENSON, vicar 21st Aug. 1569.—[*Reg. of Deeds*, x, 586.]

1641 ALEXANDER CUNNINGHAM, his son, Walter, apprentice to Gideon Schaw, stationer, Edinburgh, 27th Nov. 1667.

1707 THOMAS BOSTON, his daugh., Jane, died 19th March 1782, not 1765.

1772 ROBERT POTTS, dem. 9th May 1780 on app. of an assistant and successor.

1907 ALEXANDER HORN, was missionary at Stormontfield, Scone; dem. 3rd Oct. 1928; died 19th Feb. 1935.

1929 WILLIAM ADDISON, trans. from Kirriemuir (*q.v.*) 22nd March 1929; Ph.D. (Glasgow, 1936).

GALASHIELS

The old parish church having been united with St Paul's, it was sold and St Paul's declared the church of the parish.

1565 JOHN FOTHERINGHAM, reader 1565-7.—[*Edin. Tests.*, i, 38.]

1569 ROBERT KERR, M.A., vicar, died before 18th Aug. 1569; was in office 2nd May 1550, may have conformed and acted as reader.—[*Reg. Pres. Bene.*, i, 27; Grote's *Prot. Book*, 45.]

1569 WILLIAM KER, designated "writtour" and min. 9th Feb. 1575.—[*Test. Inventories MS. Reg. House.*]

1600 PATRICK URQUHART, min. in 1600.

1635 JAMES URQUHART, marr. Elizabeth, daugh. of James Pringle of Buckholm.

1665 THOMAS WILKIE, line 3, for "Jan" read "June."

1672 HUGH SCOTT, trans. to Stow 1689.

1770 ROBERT DOUGLAS. Addl. Publication—*Life of Logan* (Edin., 1912).

1841 KENNETH MACLEAY PHIN, line 3 from bottom, for "1882" read "1862." Addl. publications—*Recent Movements of Scottish Episcopacy in the Counties of Roxburgh and Selkirk* (1856); *The Scriptural Principles of the Solemn League and Covenant in their bearing on the Present State of the Episcopal Churches* (1858).

1871 PATON JAMES GLOAG, line 8, for "27th Sept." read "20th Jan."

DAVID HUNTER, p. 180, line 2, for
1892 "1891" read "1879." His son, Hugh Blackburn, D.S.O.

DUGALD BUTLER, died Peebles 9th
1907 Jan. 1926; his widow, Catherine Christian Barrie Marwick, died Colinton 3rd Feb. 1949. Addl. publication—*Prayer in Experience* (Edin. 1922).

GEORGE HENRY DONALD, D.D.
1918 (Edinburgh, 2nd July 1948); trans. from West Parish, Aberdeen, 5th Sept. 1918; trans. to St Andrew's Church, Montreal, 1925. Addl. issue—Walter Douglas, born and died 12th Nov. 1918.

FREDERICK DAVID LANGLANDS,
1925 trans. from Eastwood (*q.v.*) 30th June 1925 as assistant and successor; Convenor of Christian Life and Work Committee 1936; D.D. (St Andrews, 28th Sept. 1937); his wife, Ruby Agnes Scott, died 21st May 1942. He marr. (2) 16th Aug. 1943 Elizabeth Thomson, daugh. of John T. Forbes, Biggar Bank, Airdrie.

GALASHIELS WEST

WILLIAM DICKSON, his widow,
1909 Edith Jane Hanna, died 10th May 1935.

WILLIAM SUTHERLAND BUCHAN,
1915 trans. to Liff and Benvie 3rd Jan. 1919.

HENRY SHANNON BRISBY, born
1919 Belfast 19th Nov. 1890, son of Rev. James M. B. and Margaret Shannon; educ. at Hutchison's Grammar School, Glasgow, and Univ. of Glasgow, M.A. (1922); licen. by Presb. of Glasgow 25th Aug. 1915; served as Lieut. in Great War, in Royal Enniskillen Fusiliers; assistant, St Mark's, Glasgow; ord. *locum tenens* Dumbarton 10th May 1917; adm. here 24th April 1919. Marr. 2nd July 1919 Helen Campbell, daugh. of William Maxwell, min. of Cardross, and has issue—Desmond Maxwell Shannon, born 9th Sept. 1920; Bryan William James Shannon, born 2nd Sept. 1922.

HEATHERLIE

ROBERT MONTGOMERY BRIGHT,
1916 trans. to Insh, Abernethy, 17th May 1921.

JAMES WILSON, born East Green,
1921 Anstruther, 18th Feb. 1889, son of David W. and Margaret Grubb; educ. at Waid Academy, Anstruther, and Univ. of St Andrews, M.A. (1910), B.D. (1919); served in R.A.M.C. 1915–19 at Aldershot, Malta, Salonica and Northern Italy; licen. by Presb. of St Andrews 22nd March 1919; assistant at Kilconquhar Markinch and St Stephen's, Edinburgh; ord. 28th Sept. 1921.

KIRKHOPE

JOHN SHARPE GIBSON, pres. 16th
1851 July 1851.

HUGH MACMILLAN, dem. 16th May
1876 1918, died at Edinburgh 22nd July 1930; his widow, Emily Jane Mitchell, died 29th Dec. 1940.

GEORGE EDWARD MACKENZIE,
1918 born Inverness 14th Dec. 1887, son of Major George M., Seaforth Highlanders; educ. at Inverness Academy, Lycée de Douai, Nord, France, Univ. of Edinburgh, M.A. (1909), Aberdeen, B.D. (1912); licen. by Presb. of Inverness 1912; served in France as Captain R.F.C., wounded; assistant Dunkeld and Glasgow Cathedral; ord. 19th Sept. 1918; died at Bromley, Kent, 4th Sept. 1934. Marr. 30th Oct. 1930 Mary Rose Murray, elder daugh. of Stanley Greenfield of Marlestan, Bromley, Kent, and had issue—Sylvia Mary, born 13th Aug. 1931; George Murray (post.), born 20th Feb. 1935.

LADHOPE

WILLIAM CORSON CALLANDER,
1884 his widow, Jane May Mason Patterson, died 7th Aug. 1922.

JOHN GEDDES RITCHIE, dem. 13th
1914 Oct. 1916 and served as Army Chaplain in Egypt and Gallipoli; afterwards of Drainie 19th Aug. 1919.

JOHN CAMERON, trans. from Poolewe 5th April 1917; trans to Glassary 2nd March 1922.
1917

HENRY OWENS WALLACE, ord. 7th Sept. 1922, trans. to Dirleton 26th April 1928.
1922

ANDREW REID, assistant Barrowfield; missionary to Nyasaland (*q.v.*); ord. 8th Jan. 1927; adm. to Buckhaven 21st April 1927; trans. and adm. 15th Nov. 1928; ind. to Alexandria, Egypt, 29th Sept. 1933; adm. to Forteviot 28th June 1938.
1928

LILLIESLEAF

ARCHIBALD SIMSON, reader. See under Sir Thomas Ker, Roxburgh.
1582

THOMAS WILKIE, appears from the Kirk Session Records of 30th April 1671 to have been succeeded by two sons, the elder of whom, Thomas, was in 1627 probably reader at Selkirk and the younger, William, min. here.
1588

WILLIAM WILKIE, died suddenly 30th April 1671; his son, Thomas, first min. of the Canongate, Edinburgh.
1640

JOHN CHISHOLM, had issue—William, born 15th Oct. 1682.
1674

DAVID BAXTER, his daughs.—Hariet (marr. 9th Sept. 1857); Helen Frances (marr. 1st July 1845 Dr E. Naysmith Houston).
1816

ADAM GOURLAY, his daughs.—Adamina Herriot, died at Edinburgh 27th Feb. 1924; Margaret Redford, died at Edinburgh 9th May 1925.
1842

ARTHUR POLLOK SYM, D.D. (Edin. 1924), dem. 3rd Oct. 1928; Convener of Committee on Admissions of Ministers of other Churches, 1921-46; Convener of Committee on Proposed Scheme for Superannuation of Ministers, 1933-7; died at Edinburgh 30th April 1946; his wife, Caroline Georgina Simson, died 7th March 1938. Editor of latest edition of Mair's *Digest of Church Laws* (1923); editor of *Year Book of Church of Scotland*, 1914-20. Publications—*The Twenty-Third Psalm: an Anthology of Metrical Versions* (Edin., 1923); Manual on *Marriage in Scotland*, published by authority of the General Assembly (1933; 2nd edition 1936).
1888

JAMES McKENZIE, trans. from St Paul's, Perth, 21st June 1929.
1929

MAXTON

There was a chapel at Murroslaw (Moorhouselaw) belonging to John Haliburton in 1551.—[Corbet's *Prot. Bk.*, 75.]

SIR WILLIAM AINSLIE, he was presented to the vicarage on 28th Aug. 1561 by David Erskine, Commendator of Dryburgh, in succession to the late Sir William Tailfeir, who held the vicarage on 28th Jan. 1551-2.—[*Cal. Laing Charters*, 727; Corbet's *Prot. Bk.*, 75.]
1561

JAMES MENZIES, min. 10th Nov. 1584.—[*Accs. of Exch.*, 1584-98, 15.]
1584

ANDREW DUNCANSON, marr. Mary Knox, who died 15th May 1697, and had issue—Mark of Greatlaws.—[*Roxburgh Services*, 172.]
1640

GABRIEL WILSON, his daugh., Ann, died 19th May 1801; his son, Andrew, M.D., died 4th June 1792, aged 73.
1709

JOHN THOMSON, his daughs.—Beatrice, died 20th Dec. 1918, aged 100; Jane, died 14th May 1842.
1810

MANNERS HAMILTON NISBET GRAHAM, his son, James Ritchie, died Evanston, U.S.A., 3rd Dec. 1935; his daugh., Christian Lawrie, died 17th July 1934; his son, Robert Balfour, M.B.E., Lieut.-Colonel R.A.M.C., died 28th Jan. 1946.
1865

DAVID DENHOLM McKERRON, died 27th June 1948.
1905

MELROSE

The oldest religious building in the parish was burned by the Danes in the seventh century, and what was left of its ruins became a cell of "Solitaries." It was one of the first head places of pilgrimage in Scotland in visiting which wonderful spiritual privileges were obtained. The Cistercian Monks built the later Abbey of Melrose, and part of it was used as the parish church till the beginning of the nineteenth century. The chapel at Blainslie was Chield (= knight) Lyell's.

Originally the church belonged to the Priory of Coldingham, but in 1124–47 the priory conveyed it to David I in exchange for the Church of St Mary of Berwick. Subsequently it belonged to Melrose Abbey. In 1321 the Bishop (Simon) of Whithorn granted an Indulgence of 40 days to all who for the purpose of devotion visited the Chapel of St Cuthbert of Old Melrose, and gave of their means for rebuilding said chapel lately burned by the English. Of the chapel it was further said that it "has led the monastic life and flourished by miracles." "Sanct Robertis' Well," Blainslie, occurs on 5th April 1547.—[*Coldingham Charters*, 5, No. 18; Raine's *North Durham*; *Book of Melrose*, ii, 390–1; Corbet's *Prot. Bk.*, 35.]

The first four ministers mentioned (Vol. ii, 187) were probably never settled at Melrose, John Knox being the first regular minister.

1657 THOMAS FORRESTER.—[*G. R. Sas.*, xlvi, 321.]

1711 ADAM MILNE of BEWLIE, Chaplain at Kersfield 1706; marr. proc. 29.

1898 ROBERT JAMES THOMPSON, dem. 17th Nov. 1946; his daughs.—Dorothy Ann Scott (marr. 15th July 1930 Benjamin Frank McNaughton, surgeon, Montreal); Edith Elizabeth Mary (marr. Rev. W. W. Darke, Congregational min. at Wallasey); his sons—Cyril, on staff of County Council Hospital, London; Robert, secretary, Gresham Trust, London.

(*Churches of Old and St Aidan's united 17th Nov. 1946.*)

ROBERTON

1663 JOHN COLT did penance for immorality in the church of Lilliesleaf 26th March 1682.

1696 JOHN FERGUSON, called 27th May and ord. 23rd Sept. 1696. Having "supplied vacancies in the Shyre of Angus and Mearns" for a quarter of the year 1697, he received calls from Aberbrothock and Montrose, but the Presb. refused translation. Appeal was taken to Synod. On 5th Oct. 1698 a letter was read from the Commission of Assembly blaming the Presb. for not declaring the Kirk of Roberton vacant. F.'s name appears on the Sederunt of that day. He was actually trans. to Aberbrothock (Arbroath) on 20th April 1699.

1786 JAMES HAY, pres. 6th June 1786.

1826 ALEXANDER NIVISON, his daugh., Euphemia Duncan, died at Edinburgh 2nd Feb. 1925.

1845 CHARLES KINNEAR GREENHILL, pres. by Crown 26th March 1845.

1867 MERCER HALL, died 11th March 1927.

1894 AENEAS EDE McINNES, died at Earlston 2nd May 1931.

ST BOSWELLS

1567 JOHN McCLELLAN, reader. See Sir Thomas Kerr, vicar of Roxburgh.

1576 JOHN TURNBULL, reader; was reader and vicar 10th April 1567, when he granted to Andrew Ker of Hersell, Kt., a charter of the 3 merk (church) lands of Allisiden (Lessudden), called Sanct-Boiswellis.—[*Reg. Great Seal*, iv, 2140.]

1661 JOHN SOMERVILLE, line 4, for "1662" read "1661."

1879 ROBERT FISHER, line 11, for "1901" read "1891"; his sons—Frederick Alexander, Engineer of Railways, Patagonia, died at Buenos Ayres 8th Sept. 1919; William White, died 1st Dec. 1918.

ALEXANDER CAMERON WATSON,
1897 died 13th Dec. 1923; res. as missionary 1885; his sons—Alexander Fisher, Lieut. Black Watch, killed in action 23rd April 1917; Henry Steel, missionary in Africa and min. of Lochcraig 1937.

GEORGE THOMAS THOMSON,
1924 trans. from Tain (*q.v.*) 11th June 1924; dem. on app. as Professor of Systematic Theology, Aberdeen, 17th May 1928; D.D. (Edin., 1935).

ALEXANDER WOOD McNAIR,
1929 trans. from Tarves (*q.v.*) 23rd Jan. 1929.

(*Congregations united 3rd March* 1940.)

SELKIRK

The church, which was sometimes called the Church of the Forest, has been claimed to be St Mary's Kirk of the Forest in which in 1297-8 the Scottish Parliament met and gave to Sir William Wallace investiture as Guardian of the Kingdom, though Yarrow Church, St Mary's Kirk of the Lowes, is generally assumed to have been the meeting place. In 1511-12 the church was rebuilt. Apparently there was delay with regard to the steeple, but that it was erected, if not then, certainly at a somewhat later date, is shown by subsequent reference to it as the "high steeple with four turrets." There was in the church an Altar of the Holy Rood. There were two aisles, Ker's Aisle and Brydone's Aisle. The latter aisle, which was repaired in 1617, may have been the aisle for which Sir William Brydone, a vicar of the church, left money to provide a shrine. At dates between 1695 and 1714 extensive repairs were carried out on the church, but in 1735 it had reached an unsatisfactory condition, and in August 1747 its walls were removed down to the ground. Unfortunately the internal woodwork was indiscriminately destroyed, involving two painted panels, one of the Merchant Company's Loft, portraying Justice, blindfolded and holding scales in the hand, with the motto "A false balance is an abomination to the Lord." and the other, on the Tailor's Loft, depicting Adam and Eve in scanty attire, representing their first effort at tailoring. The new church was built in 1748, the congregation having worshipped meanwhile in the Grammar School. In 1858 attention was directed to the internal condition of the church, including its lack of accommodation, and a year later it was resolved to provide a new building. Opposition to that proposal and also a "battle of sites" caused considerable delay, but ultimately the building of a new church was begun in 1861 on a site on the upper portion of the Back Brae Park in the north part of the town, and the church itself was opened for worship on 1st Feb. 1863. It is noteworthy as being constructed of dressed whinstone. On the carved label-stop on the right side of the doorway is a representation of the proverbial "kirk mouse." The roofless walls of the old church, with the aisle of Murray of Philiphaugh on the south side, stand in the churchyard in the Kirk Wynd. In the belfry hangs the bell which, as being the parish bell, was removed from the Council House in 1748. In 1113 Earl David, son of King Malcolm, founded at Selkirk, apparently near his forest castle, a monastery under the invocation of St Mary the Virgin and St John the Evangelist, and in it he placed 13 reformed Benedictine Monks from the Abbey of Tiron in Le Perche, one of their number, Ralf by name, being made first abbot. Thirteen years later Earl David, then David I, with the advice of John, Bishop of Glasgow, and on the ground that Selkirk was "a place unsuitable for an Abbey," removed the monastery and erected it "at the Church of the Blessed Virgin on the banks of the Tweed beside Roxburgh in the place called Calkou" (Kelso). William, also of Tiron, was the 2nd Abbot of Selkirk, 1115-16, and the 3rd was Herbert, in whose time the change took place. The forest castle of Selkirk may have been on the Peel Hill at Haining, near Selkirk.—[Craig-Brown's *Hist. of Selkirkshire*, i, 74-5, ii, 229-32; *Recs. of Selkirk Heritors*, i, 186, 190, 234, 236, 252, 274; ii, 32; *Reg. of Kelso*, i, 4, 5 and vii.]

1563 JOHN GOULD, reader and teacher of youth 1563.—[*Comps. Sub Coll. of Thirds, Roxburgh*, etc.]

1574 THOMAS CRANSTOUN, vicar.— [*Acts and Dec.*, li, 147.]

1577 ALEXANDER DOUGLAS, pres. to vicarage 12th Feb. 1572-3 on death of Sir John Stevenson.—[*Reg. Pres. Bene.*, ii, (4), 69.]

1596 PATRICK SHAW, marr. Ann, daugh. of Sir James Murray of Philiphaugh, and had issue—Hugh of Kelsoland; Marion (marr. 3rd June 1624 Dugald Stewart, merchant, Edinburgh).

1627 THOMAS WILKIE, son of Thomas W., min. of Lilliesleaf, reader here, afterwards of Lilliesleaf.

1634 JOHN SHAW of Newmains and Holmshaw, died before 19th March 1698; marr. Anne, daugh. of Mungo Murray of Ochtertyre, and had issue—Patrick, M.D., buried 7th Nov. 1675; James of Clackmannan; George of Redheugh; Christian (marr. John Rutherford, min. of Yarrow), and others (Vol. ii, 194).—[*G. R. Sas.*, 2 Ser., xiii, 291; 3 Ser., i, 147.]

1678 ALEXANDER COOPER, M.A., died before 6th Nov. 1694, when his widow, Magdalene Watson, was resident with one child aged 16 in Tron Parish, Edinburgh.—[*Tron Par. Poll Tax Roll*, 26.]

1726 DAVID BROWN, marr. (2) cont. 24th Nov. 1735 Janet Scott, widow of Walter H., surgeon; his eldest son, David, apothecary, London.—[*Reg. of Deeds, Dal.*, 175, 2nd April 1754.]

1857 JAMES FARQUHARSON, his widow, Martha Hector, died 10th Dec. 1923; his daugh., Agnes, died 27th Feb. 1946.

1899 GEORGE LAWSON, D.D. (Aberdeen, 27th March 1929), retired in favour of assistant and successor 7th Oct. 1930; died 25th Dec. 1937.

YARROW

The church may have been the meeting place of the Scottish Parliament which invested Sir William Wallace with the guardianship of the kingdom. A fire in the spring of 1922 destroyed all save the walls of the church, but the building was restored on a handsome scale. At Catslacknowe there was a well bearing the name St Philip.—[Craig-Brown's *Hist. of Selkirkshire*, i, 74–5; Mackinlay's *Anc. Ch. Dedications* (script.) 247.]

156– WILLIAM MERITOUN, parson.— [*Acts and Dec.*, xxxv, 277.]

1565 JAMES CASTLELAW, parson.—[*Acts and Dec.*, xxxv, 277.]

1574 THOMAS CRANSTOUN, vicar.— [*Acts and Dec.*, lvii, 147.]

1635 JAMES FISHER, line 2, for "26" read "6."

1666 JOHN CLAPPERTON, was min. of Woodhouse in England 1659; his sons—John, apprentice to William Hume, merchant, Edinburgh, 12th Feb. 1673; Richard, apprentice to James Horne, merchant, Edinburgh, 9th Aug. 1676; James, writer, Edinburgh.

1691 JOHN RUTHERFORD, marr. Christian, daugh. of Gilbert Shaw of Lauriston.

1791 ROBERT RUSSELL, pres. 23rd March 1791.

1841 JAMES RUSSELL, his widow, Janet Margaret Shand, died 30th Dec. 1919; his son, Robert, died Portland, Oregon, 28th March 1944.

1883 ROBERT BORLAND, his widow, Anne Haddon, died 14th March 1922.

1912 ROGER SANDILANDS KIRKPATRICK, licen. 13th May 1881; D.D. (Edinburgh, 1924); died 14th April 1943. Addl. publication—*Playfair in St Andrews* (St Andrews, 1930).

SYNOD OF DUMFRIES

PRESBYTERY OF LOCHMABEN

APPLEGARTH and SIBBALDIE

When Applegarth and Sibbaldie were united on 24th June 1609, it was desired that the church of the united parish should be at Applegarth.—[*Acts of Parl.*, iv, 441.]

1608 JOHN YOUNG, his daugh., Marion (marr. John Maitland of Clontree).—[*Dumfries Sas.*, 31st May 1636.]

1682 THOMAS THOMSON, his widow, Marion, marr. (2) John Kennedy, merchant, Dumfries.

1807 WILLIAM DUNBAR, editor of *Nithsdale Minstrel*.

1862 DAVID LANDALE, his son, David of Dalswinton, died 6th Sept. 1935; his daugh., Jane Jardine, died 28th July 1946.

1900 ANDREW SCOULAR GALBRAITH GILCHRIST, M.C., died suddenly 12th Oct. 1929; his daughs.—Janet Graham, born 11th Dec. 1904 (marr. 23rd Sept. 1933 Leslie James Hastie, accountant, Royal Bank, Meigle).

DALTON

From James VI and the Lords of Council special commission was received by John Spottiswood, Archbishop of Glasgow, to visit in the bounds of Annandale ("in the parts sometyme called the borders") and "take order for building and repairing of the kirks within the samyn." The report of the Archbishop bore that "the povertie of the inhabits in these parts is so great that it is impossible that the said kirks can ather be repaired or yet be sufficientlie planted with ministers in regard of the meannes of the parochines, unless certain of the said kirkis ly and next adjacent to other be united and annexit together." Following upon the report, Parliament by Act of 24th June 1609 effected various unions, one of which was Meikle Dalton, Little Dalton, and Mouswald, with the church at Little Dalton to be the church of the united parish. Later, by Act of July 1615 the Privy Council decreed that the Church of Mouswald be "the place of preaching, etc.," for the parishes of Dalton and Mouswald. A further step was taken on 18th June 1633 when Parliament disjoined the Kirk of Meikle and Little Dalton from Mouswald, and ordained that Meikle and Little Dalton "be ane severall cure and paroche kirk *per se* fra Mowswald." The other unions carried out by the Act were, Cummertress and Trailtrow; Gretna and Redkirk; Kirkpatrich-Fleming and Kirkconnel; Middlebie, Carruthers, and Pennersaughs; St Mungo and Tundergarth; Applegarth and Sibbaldie; Hoddam, Ecclefechan, and Luss (Luce); Hutton and Corrie; also St Leonards and Lanark (*q.v.*).—[*Acts Scott. Parl.*, iv, 441, v, 52a; *Reg. Privy Council*, x, 375; see Little Dalton.]

1563 JOHN LIVINGSTON, reader 1563.—[*Comps. Sub Coll. of Thirds, Dumfries*, etc.]

1715 ROBERT KIRKLAND, probably chaplain to Alexander Murray of Broughton, 1705; marr. Geills, daugh. of James Paton, merchant burgess, Glasgow; his daugh. and heiress, Mary (marr. Robert Drew, portioner of Auchenleck).

ALEXANDER SHEPHERD, his son,
1853 William Alexander, died 5th Aug. 1929; his posthumous daugh., Jane Sophia, born 1868.

JAMES CLOW BRYCE, his widow,
1868 Agnes Smith, died at Edinburgh 29th Nov. 1925 aged 90; his daugh., Marianne Douglas, died 23rd Nov. 1873; Jenny assumed name of Douglas on succession to property, died Moffat 13th Sept. 1947.

CHARLES EDWARD PATERSON,
1870 his widow, Alison Barbara Cruickshank, died 4th March 1924.

ROBERT DONALDSON, his widow,
1875 Rose Emma Coventry, died 18th Feb. 1919. He died 5th Nov. 1917.

WILLIAM ANDREW KNOWLES,
1918 trans. from West Coates (*q.v.*) 21st March 1918, dem. 20th Nov. 1938; died 19th Feb. 1942. He compiled and edited *Prayers for Divine Service* (1923 and 1929).

LITTLE DALTON

JOHN CARRUTHERS, son of John
1565 C. of Holmains; pres. by his father to parsonage 26th Dec. 1565.—[Anderson's *Prot. Book*.]

SIR JOHN BRYCE, vicar of Dumfries
1608 1566; died before 11th Oct. 1608, when he is called last vicar.—[*Reg. Sec. Sig.*]

WILLIAM HAMILTON, M.A., trans-
1611 ferred his residence to Mouswald in 1615, when by Act of Parliament the Church of Mouswald became the church of the united parish, of which he still continued min.

DRYFESDALE

ROBERT HERRIES, his daugh.,
1616 Katherine (marr. John Carruthers, yr. of Dormont), died Dec. 1656.—[*Dumfries Sas.*, 8th April 1639.]

GEORGE BROWN, residing in Dal-
1678 keith 1707; his son, John, apprenticed to Thomas Carruthers, stationer, Edinburgh, 16th April 1707.

JAMES SHORT, son of James S.,
1698 merchant burgess, Edinburgh.

GABRIEL GULLAN, his son, John,
1731 apprenticed to David Home, litster, Edinburgh, 6th Feb. 1744.

MATTHEW CLEGHORN, line 5 and
1765 6, for "18th Aug." read "15th Nov."

ROBERT HILL WRIGHT, pres. by
1843 Crown 28th Aug. 1843.

JOHN ARCHIBALD JOHNSTON,
1887 died Marchmount, Dumfries, 24th Aug. 1931; his wife, Agnes Anderson, died 14th June 1920.

STUART CRAWFORD PARKER,
1914 trans. to Belmont, Glasgow, 9th Dec. 1919.

GEORGE TOD WRIGHT, ord. 6th
1920 April 1920; trans to St Serf's, Edinburgh, 5th April 1927.

JOHN CHARLTON STEEN, born
1927 Kilmarnock 1898; son of James S., teacher, Paisley; educ. at Paisley Grammar School and Univ. of Glasgow; M.A. Served with Argyll and Sutherland Highlanders and later 2/1 Lanarkshire Yeomanry in Great War 1917–19; assistant lecturer in Italian and Comparative Literature, Glasgow Univ., 1922–3; licen. by Presb. of Glasgow, 1926; assistant North Berwick; ord. 3rd Aug. 1927. Marr. 7th Sept. 1927 Jemima Izat, daugh. of Alexander Fletcher, freeman of London, and had issue—Elizabeth Paton Fletcher, born 18th June 1929; Mairi Maclean, born 6th May 1932, died 30th Jan. 1933; James Clement Charlton, born 18th May 1930. Publications—*A Wayside Venture* (an allegory), *The Journal of a Scottish Recluse*.

HUTTON and CORRIE

When Hutton and Corrie were united on 24th June 1689, it was decreed that the church of the united parish should be at Hutton.—[*Acts of Parl.*, iv, 441.]

ROBERT RAYNING, reader at Ruthwell 1571.
1586

GEORGE YOUNG, delete "son of Patrick Y. of Auchensheoch"; he was grandson of George Y., min. of St Mary's, Glasgow; educ. at Univ. of Edinburgh, M.A. (6th Sept. 1699). He had issue—John, physician, Coldstream, born 26th April 1706; George, born 5th Dec. 1708; William, min. of this parish; Elizabeth, born 10th Aug. 1712; Sophia, born 4th Feb. 1715; Christian, born 22nd March 1716 (marr. George Laidlaw in Craikhaugh); Mary, born 4th April 1718; Henry, born 29th April 1720, surgeon, H.E.I.C.S., died St Helena; Margaret, born 4th Jan. 1722 (marr. 1756 William Moffat, merchant, London); Alison, born 11th June 1724 (marr. 1766 John Laidlaw, Galloway), died 30th June 1777.
1702

THOMAS BAIN, licen. 5th Dec. 1871; his widow, Margaret Morton, died 2nd Sept. 1927.
1875

JOHN CHARLES MACK, dem. 2nd March 1934; died 8th Dec. 1939.
1903

JOHNSTONE

ADAM WILKIE, reader in 1576 and 1578.—[*Comps. Sub Coll. of Thirds, Dumfries*, etc.]
1576

STEPHEN JOHN HOWITT, dem. 15th May 1934, died at Moffat 8th Dec. 1939.
1898

KIRKMICHAEL

The old parish of Garrel or Garvald was perhaps united with Kirkmichael in 1662, not 1674.

JOHN KIRKPATRICK, second son of Alexander K. of Kirkmichael, pres. to vicarage and parsonage 22nd Jan. 1604, long vacant since the death of John Thomson.—[*Reg. Sec. Sig.*, lxxiv, 128.]
1604

JOHN BREMNER, died at Edinburgh 28th Aug. 1925.
1876

ROBERT WILSON FORBES, M.A., trans. from Freuchie 11th Oct. 1918; trans. to Methlick 29th Jan. 1925.
1918

ROBERT WILSON TURNBULL, born Hawick 7th May 1893, son of Adam T., schoolmaster, Hawick, and Helen Paterson; educ. at Hawick High School and Univ. of Edinburgh, M.A. (1913), B.D. (1919); served as Lieut., Black Watch and Royal Scots Fusiliers, in France; licen. by Presb. of Edinburgh 1915; assistant Tron Church 1915; assistant Hawick 1919; ord. to Dunsyre 11th March 1921; trans. and adm. 5th June 1925. Marr. 12th Aug. 1916 Catherine Russell, daugh. of Joseph Strang, and has issue—Helen Blair Paterson, born 21st April 1920; Katherine Margaret Strang, born 28th June 1922; Dorothy Annie Wilson, born 15th Jan. 1925; Evelyn Josephine Cathels, born 1st June 1929; Adam Michael Gordon, born 29th Dec. 1935.
1925

GARREL

United to Kirkmichael, 1662.

THOMAS BROWN, reader in 1567–72.—[*Comps. Sub Coll. of Thirds, Dumfries*, etc.]
1567

KIRKPATRICK JUXTA

MUNGO NIVEN, reader in 1563 and 1567.—[*Comps. Sub Coll. of Thirds, Dumfries*, etc.]
1563

JOHN HAMILTON, reader.—[*Acts and Dec.*, lv, 14, 16.]
1574

JOHN COLQUHOUN, clerk of the diocese of Glasgow in 1560, when Sir Humphrey Colquhoun, parson of Kirkpatrick, resigned his parsonage in his favour in the hands of James, Archbishop of Glasgow. In same year Sir Humphrey made a similar resignation in favour of Sir James Laing, chaplain of the diocese of Glasgow, which does not seem to have received effect.—[*Colquhoun Cartulary*, 415.]
1612

1664 ROBERT MERCHISTON, M.A., resident with his daugh., Agnes, in Lady Yester's parish, Edinburgh, 1st Nov. 1694.—[*Lady Yester's Poll Tax Roll*, 31.]

1877 WILLIAM BRODIE, licen. 18th June 1875; dem. 20th May 1918; died at Moffat 15th Feb. 1935.

1918 WILLIAM LOGIE FINLAYSON, born 1st April 1887, son of Joseph Sage F., min. of Burntisland; educ. at Univ. of Edinburgh, M.A. (1909), B.D. (1912); licen. by Presb. of Edinburgh 1912; assistant Glasgow Cathedral; ord. 17th Sept. 1918; killed on railway line near Beattock 5th Feb. 1937; unmarr.

LOCHMABEN

Robert de Brus, son of Robert de Brus, lord of Annandale, whom he predeceased in 1191, granted the church with its lands, teinds, and possessions to the Priory of Giseburn (Guisborough) in Cleveland, Yorks, which had been founded by his grandfather, Robert de Brus, in 1129. By the said Robert de Brus, lord of Annandale, who died in 1194, William, his son and successor, and William the Lion, charters confirming the grant were given apparently about the close of the 12th century. In 1223 the monks of the priory and the Bishop of Glasgow, between whom had arisen differences as to the effect of the grant, reached a settlement whereby the monks retained the tithes of the corn of the church, and received 3 merks yearly from the rector for the maintenance of lights, and the bishop had the right of collation and ordination to the church and the dependent chapel of Rokele. There was in the church an altar dedicated to the Virgin Mary. In 1592 the church was burned by the Johnstones of Annandale, in order to compel the surrender of the Maxwells of Nithsdale, who, defeated in a fight with the Johnstones, had fled to the church for refuge. Its place was taken by a Gothic building with large choir, which was demolished in 1818; and the new church was opened in the following year. In the parish there was a chapel dedicated to St Thomas, apparently the Apostle.—[Dugdale's *Monasticon*, vi, Pt. 1, 266–9; *Reg. Epis. of Glasgow*, i, 105, 106–7, ii, 619–20; *Reg. Great Seal*, ii, 1650; McDowall's *Dumfries*, 318; McKinlay's *Ancient Ch. Dedications*, (script.) 258.]

1561 ROBERT JOHNSTON OF CARRISTAN, 2nd son of John Johnston of that ilk, and his wife Marion or Mariota Maxwell; pres. to the parsonage by his father before 1561, but the appointment may have been a lay one; still parson 13th June 1587.—[*Reports Hist. MSS. Commis.*, xxiv, 33; *Reg. Great Seal*, iv, 2889; *Reg. Sec. Seal*, lxiii, 363; *Annandale Family Bk.*, i, Pref. lxi; *Acts and Dec.*, lvii, 42; *Cal. of Charters*, xiii, 2192.]

1567 JAMES MAXWELL, min. 8th March 1575–6.—[*Edin. Tests.*, vi, 44.]

1595 WILLIAM JOHNSTON, pres. to vicarage in 1592 on death of Robert Johnston of Cariston.—[*Reg. Sec. Sig.*, lxiii, 263.]

1596 JOHN JOHNSTON, successor to above. —[*Reg. Sec. Sig.*, lxviii, 27.]

1675 GEORGE GRAHAM, son of Thomas G., min. of Stronsay. Marr. (1) Christian, daugh. of William Maxwell, Bishop elect of Bath and Wells, (2) Margaret, daugh. of John Teviotdale, and was resident with his wife and children in Tron Parish; had issue—George, merchant, Barbadoes; Margaret (10); James (8); Christian (6); John (2).—[*Tron Poll Tax Roll*, 50.]

1693 WILLIAM STEEL, line 10, for "Margaret" read "Barbara"; his daugh. Juliana (marr. cont. 19th and 21st Oct. 1721).

1850 THOMAS LIDDELL, marr. 16th Nov. 1835.

1881 DAVID NEILL RAE, died 16th Jan. 1923; his widow, Eleanor Alexandrina Mackezie, died at Stonehaven 17th Feb. 1940.

JOHN McCOLL, trans. to Gartsherrie
1915   16th Sept. 1924.

RICHARD GIBB, trans. from Lochee
1925   (q.v.) 17th Feb. 1925; has issue— John Watson, born 21st Oct. 1921; James Craig Scott, born 22nd March 1924; Richard Forbes, born 30th July 1927; Margaret Elizabeth Donald, born 3rd Oct. 1932.

MOFFAT

JOHN WARDLAW, M.A., son of
1561   John W. of Torrie and Elizabeth Beaton; vicar of Peebles 28th March 1557-8; rector here before March 1561-2; also held the perpetual chaplainry of the Chapel of St Andrew in the barony of Brunton, West Lochore; resigned before 16th April 1582.—[*Reg. Mag. Sig.*, iv, 2468; *Reg. Sec. Seal*, xlviii, 146; *Wardlaws in Scotland*, 59-60; *Acts and Dec.*, xlviii, 267.]

DAVID MAYNE, reader 1563.—
1563   [*Comps. Sub Coll. of Thirds, Dumfries*, etc.]

STEPHEN WILSON, parson; pres. to
1583   the parsonage 16th April 1582; designed "domestic servitour to Our Sovereign Lord's deceist spous" 19th Dec. 1590; pres. to H.M. Master Elemozear.—[*Reg. Sec. Sig.*, xlviii, 146; lxi, 105.]

GEORGE BUCHANAN, M.A., was
1637   dep. by the General Assembly at Glasgow 21st Nov. to 20th Dec. 1638 for declining the Assembly, and continuing in his contumacy and refusing to compear before the Commission; and on appeal the Assembly at Edinburgh 26th Aug. 1639 reaffirmed the sentence. On 2nd July 1639 Charles I addressed a letter to James, Lord Johnston, desiring him to see that "Mr George Buchanan, minister at Moffat" be maintained in his place and no other man planted at the church; and by another letter of 13th July the King forbade the Presb. of Lochmaben and Middlebie to proceed further against him or to admit any other man to his church "as they intend to do." Lord Johnston and the Presbytery acted in spite of the royal letters; and as the sentence of the Assembly at Edinburgh 26th Aug. 1639 designates Mr Buchanan as min. at Kirkcudbright, it would appear that he was adm. to the latter charge between 2nd July and 26th Aug. 1639.—[Peterkin's *Recs. of the Kirk*, p. 261; *Reports Hist. MSS. Commis.*, xv, App. ix, 47.]

JOHN LEARMONTH, marr. Jean
1639   Dalziel.—[*G. R. Sas.*, 2 Ser., iv, 425, 25th July 1653.]

GEORGE MILLIGAN, marr. Miss
1695   Johnstone of Corehead.

JOHN GIBSON MACVICAR, his son,
1853   Symon Douglas, died at Invermoidart 27th Feb. 1932; his daughs.—Agnes Gibson, died 24th Aug. 1920; Margaret Macdonald, died 23rd Jan. 1922; Katherine Bickwell of Invermoidart, died 10th March 1939.

DONALD CAMPBELL BRYCE, his
1884   widow, Louisa Wilhelmina Buchan, died at Renwick Manse, Dunscore, 3rd March 1939.

ROBERT SOMERS, died 12th Oct.
1891   1921; his widow, Jane Lamb, died 9th Dec. 1938.

GILMOUR NEILL, adm. 28th Dec.
1921   1921; trans. to Drumelzier 21st May 1926.

JOHN LAURIE FARQUHAR, born
1926   13th Aug. 1894, son of Robert F. and Annie Laurie; educ. at Univ. of Glasgow, M.A. (June 1920); licen. by Presb. of Hamilton, 1921; ord. to Kingston, Glasgow, 19th Sept. 1922; trans. and adm. 5th March 1926. Marr. 17th July 1934 Gunheld Margaretta, daugh. of Chr. Rannestadt, Ekely, Fredrikstadt, Norway.

MOUSWALD

For union of Meikle Dalton, Little Dalton and Mouswald and to the ultimate disjunction, see Dalton.

SIR MARK CARRUTHERS, rector and chaplain 1548; prebendary of Lincluden 1559; vicar and reader 1567–73.—[*Comps. Sub Coll. of Thirds, Dumfries*, etc.; Anderson's *Prot. Book*.]
1567

THOMAS WEIR, exhorter in 1569 and 1672.—[*Comps. Sub Coll. of Thirds, Dumfries*, etc.]
1569

WILLIAM HAMILTON, his daugh., Janet.
1615

ALEXANDER MAKGOWAN, his son, Thomas, provost of Irvine, died 1711.—[*G. R. Sas.*, 2 Ser., ix, 282.]
1637

JOHN GILLESPIE, his widow, Jessie Kirkwood Crichton Patrick, died at Dumfries 5th April 1930; his daugh., Jean Crichton, died Bridge of Allan 12th Nov. 1948.
1865

ALEXANDER MOIR, trans. to Powis, Aberdeen, 24th June 1924.
1916

THOMAS McGINN, born 23rd Dec. 1890, son of John M. and Agnes McLean; educ. at Annbank School and Univ. of Edinburgh; D.C.M. for war service; licen. by Presb. of Edinburgh 19th Dec. 1923; assistant St John's, Edinburgh; ord. 28th Oct. 1924; trans. to Roslin 8th Dec. 1933; trans. to Bedrule 15th June 1945. Marr. 18th July 1919 Joan Ewenson, daugh. of Sinclair Sutherland Spence.
1924

ST MUNGO

St Mungo and Tundergarth were united by Act of Parliament 24th June 1609, the church to be at Tundergarth. The parishes were disjoined, probably in 1650.—[*Acts of Parl.*, iv, 441.]

WILLIAM HOUSTON, M.A., pres. to vicarage on death of Sir James Maxwell.—[*Reg. Pres. Bene.*, ii, (4), 38.]
1575

JOHN McCONZIE, parson 12th April 1585.—[*Sher. Court Books*.]
1585

DAVID MILLAR, M.A., min. of Annan, pres. to parsonage and vicarage 5th Jan. 1591–2 on death of William Houston.—[*Reg. Sec. Sig.*, lxiii, 112.]
1591

WILLIAM BELL, son of B., Blackhattoun, pres. to parsonage and vicarage 3rd March 1601 on death of Sir Robert Maxwell of Castlemilk.—[*Reg. Sec. Sig.*, lxxii, 17.]
1601

JAMES MURRAY, marr. Agnes, daugh. of William Carruthers of Denbie (she marr. (2) James Johnston of Lockerbie) and had issue—John, James and George.
1699

DAVID DICKSON, pres. 6th Dec. 1783.
1784

ANDREW JAMESON, son of Thomas J.
1803

JOHN MEIN AUSTIN, pres. by Crown 26th July 1861; line 11, after "farmer" add "of Dykehead."
1861

JAMES PROPHET, pres. by Crown 27th June 1868; his son, James Maxwell Grant, died at Calcutta 19th Dec. 1924 aged 65, and left £219,000 for tuberculosis and cancer research; Robert Jamieson died 2nd June 1943.
1868

LEE McKINSTERY FLEMING, B.A., adm. by Gen. Assembly May 1888, died 5th Dec. 1925; his widow, Emily Yeates, died 27th Jan. 1937.
1889

JOHN DONALD MACFARLANE BENNY BEATTIE, born 15th May 1896, son of John B., merchant, Montreal, Canada, and Jeannie Elizabeth Alma Macfarlane; educ. at Crichton School, Lower Canada College, McGill Univ., B.A. (1917), and Univ. of Edinburgh. Licen. by Presb. of Edinburgh 28th March 1923; assistant St Cuthbert's, Edinburgh; served during Great War in Canadian Royal Artillery, 1916–18; ord. 11th Jan. 1925; adm. 17th May 1926; trans. to Wilton, Hawick, 23rd June 1931. Marr. 19th April 1934 Mary Elizabeth Wallace, youngest daugh. of Robert Harbiston Gray, Glasgow, and Mary Elizabeth Wallace, and has issue—Jean Elizabeth Mary, born 4th Jan. 1936.
1926

TUNDERGARTH

1586 ANDREW JOHNSTON, parson.—[*P. C. Reg.*, iv, 56.]

1604 JOHN JOHNSTON, slain by David Armstrong 1604.—[*Pitcairn Crim. Trials*, ii, 441.]

1605 WILLIAM JOHNSTON, died before 11th Oct. 1605, when he is called last vicar.—[*Reg. Sec. Sig.*]

1676 JOHN PATERSON, min. in 1676. Marr. 5th April 1667 Rosina, daugh. of James Irvine of East Riggs, whom he divorced.—[*Consist. Process*, 17.]

1717 ANDREW CLERK, nephew of Andrew Bell, deacon of the Weavers, Jedburgh.

1902 HUGH THOMAS SUTHERLAND MORRISON, trans. to Kirkcowan 12th Dec. 1916.

1917 JOHN ALEXANDER KERR, M.A., ord. 20th April 1917; trans. to Ewes 22nd Nov. 1918.

1919 ROBERT KELTIE, M.A., ord. 6th May 1919; trans. to Kemnay 16th May 1924.

1924 ALLAN MANSON NELSON, formerly Indian Chaplain (*q.v.*), adm. 19th Sept. 1924; dem. 11th Nov. 1934.

WAMPHRAY

Was previously united to Johnstone.

1632 JOHN HAITLIE, marr. Alison Stewart.

1697 JOHN TAYLOR, was dep. by the Synod 15th April 1715 for several enormities, and the church was declared vacant in following May, but he continued in the manse and glebe, and intruded in the church by keeping the keys and preaching in it Sept. 1716 to Feb. 1717.—[*Justiciary Recs.*, 1712–17, March 1717.]

1763 WILLIAM BARRON, line 4, for "5th Feb." read "25th April."

1854 GEORGE WIGHT, his widow, Jessie Taylor, died 17th March 1930; his daugh., Helena Mary, died at Moffat 21st March 1941.

1907 RICHARD BELL, dem. on app. as Lecturer in Arabic in Univ. of Edinburgh 5th Dec. 1921; D.D. (Edin.). Publication—*The Origin of Islam in its Christian Environment* (1926).

1922 RICHARD MACKIE CLARK, M.A., trans. from Logie, Dundee, 22nd June 1922; his wife, Jeanie Scott, died 13th April 1932. He marr. (2) 23rd June 1937 Isabella, younger daugh. of James Crawford, Holmwood, Fairlie, Ayrshire; she died 17th Dec. 1938.

PRESBYTERY OF LANGHOLM

CANONBIE

1606 JOHN DOUGLAS, son of William D. of Whittinghame and Elizabeth Maitland.—[*P. R. Sas.*, Edin., xxviii, 200.]

1877 WILLIAM SNODGRASS, his son, John Allan, died 8th July 1929.

1896 ROBERT HOGG KERR, res. as Presb. Clerk Dec. 1927, died 12th Sept. 1930.

CASTLETON

1574 MARTIN ELLIOT, pres. to parsonage and vicarage 11th July 1574.—[*Reg. Pres. Bene.*, ii, (4), 23.]

1883 WILLIAM VASSIE, died at Kingussie 7th Sept. 1917; his widow, Cecelia Pitcairn Playfair, died at Edinburgh 29th Sept. 1917; his son, William Playfair, died at Nottingham 2nd May 1895.

1918 JOHN MORRISON McLUCKIE, trans. from Lady Yester's, Edinburgh, 7th Feb. 1918, died 13th July 1926. His daugh., Joyce (marr. 15th March 1933 Robert Bernard Benson, Natural History Museum, Kensington).

1927 HAROLD ANDREW COCKBURN, born 12th March 1895, son of George Hanna C., schoolmaster, Paisley, and Isabella Brodie Marshall; educ. Univ. of Glasgow, M.A. (1921), St Andrews, B.D. (1924); S.T.M. (Union Seminary of New York, 1925); served in Great War as gunner, R.F.A., 1914-18; licen. by Presb. of Paisley, 1925; assistant St Michael's, Dumfries, 1925; ord. 20th Jan. 1927; trans. to St Michael's, Dumfries, 27th Nov. 1930; liaison officer between Protestant Churches in Britain and United States, Oct. 1942. Awarded the Norwegian Freedom Medal, 1947. Marr. 10th April 1934 Isabella, daugh. of Dr William Henry Manners and Edith Mary Price, and has issue—Eileen Mary, born 30th Aug. 1935; George Hanna Michael, born 13th June 1937.

ESKDALEMUIR

The church was restored in 1907 and further improved in 1936.

1876 JOHN CRAWFORD DICK, his widow, Jane Brown Armstrong, died 27th Nov. 1937.

1904 JAMES RONALD MACDONALD, delete line 5, "St Andrews Univ."; ord. 1st Oct. 1902; retired in favour of assistant and successor May 1933; died 21st Oct. 1937; his widow, Emily Sophia Nichols, died 4th July 1948.

EWES

There were two churches, the Nether Kirk situated at Kirktown, and the Over Kirk, situated at Unthank. In 1296 there swore fealty to Edward I, Robert, son of Randolph, parson of St Cuthbert of Ewesdale, and Mr William Cramond, parson of the Church of Wynchedurres of Dumfries. In a writ of the time of Alexander III, 1249-85, Robert, parson of the Church of St Mark of Ewesdale, appears as a witness; and under Edward I of England warrant was given to John, Bishop or Ely, chancellor, to issue presentation to John de Pontebrugge to the vacant Church of St Martin in Ewesdale in Scotland. Obviously reference in each case is to the Over Kirk; and the probability is that St Mark of the earlier writ is an error for St Martin, whose name here, in view of St Ninian's influence seems appropriate. The Over Kirk was abandoned, apparently soon after the Reformation.—[Rymer's *Fed.*, i, Pt. 3, 35, 1745; *Rotuli Scotiae*, i, 25; *Registrum Honoris de Morton*, ii, 8; *Cal. of Docs. Rel. to Scot.*, iii, 123, No. 653; *Cal. of Papal Regs., Letters*, xii, 540.]

ROBERT MALCOLM, line 14, delete
1717 "11th Sept. 1722."

RICHARD SCOTT, marr. Mary,
1761 daugh. of Hector Turnbull of Cruicksfield; his son, James, died 24th Dec. 1826; his daugh., Janet (marr. 15th June 1791 William Irvine, merchant, Glasgow).—[*Berwick Sas.*, 17th Dec. 1759.]

ROBERT SHAW, his daugh., Marion
1816 Moncrieff, died at Edinburgh 15th July 1925.

DAVID PRESTON, trans to Titwood
1901 27th June 1918.

JOHN ALEXANDER KERR, born
1918 30th Sept. 1884, son of John K., joiner, and Annie Hamilton Kerr; educ. at Univ. of Glasgow, M.A. (1912); licen. by Presb. of Glasgow June 1915; assistant Eastwood; ord. to Tundergarth 20th April 1917; trans. and adm. 22nd Nov. 1918; app. Presb. Clerk Dec. 1927; Chaplain T.A., K.O.S.B. Marr. 1st Aug. 1917 Mary Duff, youngest daugh. of Robert Dawson, Dovehill, Pollokshaws, and Annie Hamilton Dawson, and has issue—Annie Hamilton Duff, born 15th Oct. 1918 (marr. 26th June 1942 Andrew, son of G. S. Easton, Todrig, Ashkirk); Mary Dawson Hamilton, born 14th Nov. 1928; Janet Campbell, born 8th April 1931.

HALF MORTON

WILLIAM BROWN CLERK, pres. by
1839 Crown 26th May 1839.

JOHN CONACHER WILLIAMSON,
1902 dem. 3rd Feb. 1941, died 13th Feb. 1946; his daughs.—Catherine Douglas Conacher (marr. 2nd July 1932 William Harland Coghill, min. of Dalziel North); Mary Ann Conacher (marr. 26th Dec. 1936 Peter Margach, C.A., London); Ethel Isabel Brown (marr. 27th Dec. 1938 Robert Laing, Bredesholm, Baillieston); his wife, Catherine Brown, died 15th Nov. 1940. His father was schoolmaster of Greenlaw.

LANGHOLM

The church was renovated and a magnificent stained window provided in 1925, and in 1928 the hall was extended.

ALEXANDER MEIKLE, his son,
1717 George, apprenticed to Gideon Crawford, bookseller, Edinburgh, 27th July 1748.

JAMES BUCHANAN, died 23rd Oct.
1879 1921; his widow, Maria Vassie, died at London, 26th Jan. 1930; his daughs.—Mary Murray Vassie (marr. 18th Feb. 1921 James Thomson Young, India); Marion Gowans (marr. 8th Aug. 1925 David Williams, B.A., curator of Holy Trinity, Shaw, Lancashire).

WILLIAM LINDSAY, trans. from New-
1922 battle (*q.v.*) 3rd March 1922, died at Carlisle 6th Dec. 1942. Marr. 7th July 1914 Agnes Cowan, elder daugh. of James Young, farmer, Dunning, Perthshire. Publication—*The Church and Parish of Newbattle*; *Heroes of the Great War* (Newbattle, March 1919).

SAUGHTREE

WILLIAM NAPIER BELL, dem. 4th
1910 Nov. 1920 on app. as assistant to Professor of Ecclesiastical History, Univ. of Glasgow.

DAVID SMITH, ord. 31st March 1921;
1921 trans. to Inverkeithing 12th May 1922.

JOHN SCOTT, B.A., trans. from Dal-
1922 keith West 8th Sept. 1922; trans. to Anwoth 26th Aug. 1925.

1925 JOHN WHYTE McGILL, trans. from Inverallochy 23rd Dec. 1925; trans. to Colvend 27th Jan. 1927.

1927 ROBERT DOUGLAS PETTIE, ord. 13th May 1927, trans. to Cleish 14th May 1928.

1929 ROBERT FORSYTH McGARRITY, trans. from Burray (*q.v.*) 15th Feb. 1929, died at Edinburgh 8th May 1933; his widow, Jeanie Gloag, died 13th May 1935.

WAUCHOPE

1685 SYMON WYLD, marr. Rosina, daugh. of John Brown, min. of Westerkirk. He was dead 23rd June 1699.—[*Deeds Dal.*, 1705, No. 1017.]

WESTERKIRK

1668 WALTER DALGLEISH.—[*Reg. of Deeds Dal.*, clviii, 1st July 1745.]

1683 JOHN BROWN, line 6, for "Mownan" read "Mow." His daugh., Rosina, marr. Symon Wyld, min. of Wauchope.

1693 JOHN MEIN. Addl. issue—Isabel (marr. Thomas Mein in Kelso); Janet (marr. Andrew Mein in Newstead); John, surgeon.

1779 WILLIAM LITTLE, his daugh., Elizabeth (marr. Archibald Kean, M.D.).

1910 JOHN GILLIES, dem. 18th Nov. 1948; his daugh., Agnes Grace Thomson (marr. 7th Sept. 1938 Alastair Duncan Cameron, Gourock).

PRESBYTERY OF ANNAN

ANNAN

Robert de Brus, son of Robert de Brus, lord of Annandale, whom he predeceased in 1191, granted the church with its lands, teinds, and possessions to the Priory of Giseburn (Guisborough) in Cleveland, Yorks, which had been founded by his grandfather, Robert de Brus, in 1129 Confirmation charters were granted by the said Robert de Brus, lord of Annandale, who died in 1194, and by his son and successor, William, and King William the Lion, apparently about the close of the 12th century. In 1223 the monks of the priory and the Bishop of Glasgow, between whom differences had arisen as to the effect of the grant, reached a settlement whereby the monks retained the tithes of corn of the church and received 3 merks yearly from the rector for the maintenance of lights, and the bishop had the right of collation and ordination to the church. Early in the 17th century Annan was without a place of worship, and the place being so "miserably impoverished" that the people "nohable to build a kirk to themselves," James VI "granted and disponed to the town and parish the house called the Castle of Annan, the hall and tower thereof to serve for ane kirk and place of convening to heiring of the word and ministrations of the Sacraments." On 24th June 1609 Parliament ratified grant "with power to repair, redifie, flitt, and remove the stones and timber thereof to ony place they think most convenient for building their kirk when they should find themselves thereto." The present church was built in 1790.—[Dugdale's *Monasticon*, vi, Pt. 1, 266-9; *Reg. Epis. of Glasgow*, 105-7, ii, 419-20; *Acts Scott. Parl.*, iv, 441.]

A new church hall was erected and opened in Oct. 1929 and improvements in the church and its furnishings were effected in 1913.—[*The Church of Annan*, by A. Steel, 1934.]

1560 ADAM BARTON, parson July 1560 and 11th March 1582.—[*Dumfries Sheriff Court Books.*]

1580 THOMAS CRANSTON, pres. to the vicarage 29th July 1580 on death of Andrew Rankane.—[*Reg. Pres. Bene.*, ii, 37.]

1584 SIR ANDREW RENTON (? Rankane), parson, vicar 1584.—[*Comps. Gen. Coll. of Thirds.*]

1588 DAVID MILLAR, pres. to St Mungo 5th Jan. 1591-2.—[*Reg. Sec. Sig.*, xxiii, 112.]

1588 JAMES MAXWELL, pres. to parsonage 11th Feb. 1588, on dem. of Sir Andrew Rankane.—[*Reg. Sec. Sig.*, lix, 20.]

1605 JAMES FRENCH, pres. to parsonage and vicarage in 1605 on death of Andrew Renton.—[*Reg. Sec. Sig.*, lxxxiv, 355.]

1607 SIMON JOHNSTON, son of Robert J. of Raecleuch and Barbara Douglas. Marr. (1) Marion Douglas and had issue—Enoch; William; Margaret; Sara or Anna; Elizabeth. He marr. afterwards twice.

1754 WILLIAM MONCRIEFF, son of Andrew M. and Marion Dron.

1783 WILLIAM HARDIE MONCRIEFF, his daugh., Elizabeth (marr. George Rome).

NEIL McCAIG, B.D. (Glasgow, not Edinburgh). Addl. issue—Joyce, born 19th May 1920; Sheila (marr. 12th July 1947 Alexander Irving, Annan). Publication—*The Model Community* (Sermon) (Stockwell) 1912.

1909

BRYDEKIRK

COLIN ARCHIBALD ARTHUR MACVEAN, dem. 3rd Nov. 1930; died from effects of an accident at Edinburgh Royal Infirmary 12th May 1933; his widow, Jane Pollok Heron, died at Glasgow 13th Feb. 1941.

1887

CUMMERTREES

SIR JOHN TAYLOR was in 1561 vicar and reader here and at Penpont, exhorter 1561–72 and 1584, parson 13th Aug. 1565, died before 30th May 1599.—[*Coll. Gen. of Thirds*, 1561–96; *Reg. Mag. Sig.*, iv, 1657; *Reg. Sec. Sig.*, lxix, 271.]

1561

JOHN CARLYLE, for "Keith" read "Kelhead"; pres. to parsonage and vicarage 30th May 1599 on death of Sir John Taylor.—[*Reg. Sec. Sig.*, lxix, 271.]

1599

JAMES FRENCH, M.A.; pres. to parsonage and vicarage 7th Aug. 1605 on death of Sir John Taylor.—[*Reg. Sec. Sig.*, lxxiv, 374.]

1605

JOHN ALEXANDER, min. here in 1683.—[*Reg. of Deeds, Mack.*, lii, 83.]

1683

WILLIAM JOHNSTONE, pres. by Crown 27th July 1870.

1870

ALEXANDER SINCLAIR NICOL, line 8, delete "died at Bournemouth 25th Nov. 1916" and read "died 20th March 1920"; his widow, Dinah Ann McFaden, died at Harrogate 2nd March 1940.

1881

GEORGE WILSON HAMILTON, M.A., B.D., ord. 4th Aug. 1920; dem. 1st Oct. 1925 on app. to Knightswood.

1920

CHARLES FRANCIS McCAUGHEY, born Ballymena, Antrim, son of Thomas Charles M., solicitor, Perth, and Wilhelmina W. McClelland; educ. at Royal Belfast Academical Institution, Trinity College, Dublin, B.A., M.A.; General Assembly College, Belfast; licen. by Presb. of Belfast 30th May 1917; ord. Helen's Bay, Co. Down, 16th March 1920; trans. and adm. 13th Jan. 1926; trans. to St Paul's, Perth, 5th Dec. 1929. Marr. 19th Aug. 1931 Janet Grieve, eldest daugh. of John Wallace, Seafield, Cummertrees.

1926

TRAILTROW

Robert de Brus, son of Robert de Brus, lord of Annandale, whom he predeceased in 1191, granted the church, with its lands, teinds, and possessions, to the Priory of Giseburn (Guisborough) in Cleveland, Yorks, which had been founded by his grandfather, Robert de Brus, 1129. Confirmation charters were granted by the said Robert de Brus, lord of Annandale, who died in 1194, and his surviving son and successor, William, and by William the Lion apparently about the close of the 12th century. In 1223 the monks of the priory and the Bishop of Glasgow, between whom had arisen differences as to the effect of the grant, reached a settlement whereby the monks were to retain the tithes of corn of the church, and the bishop was to exercise the power of collation and ordination to the church. When Cummertrees and Trailtrow were united in 1609, it was decreed that the church of the united parish be at Trailtrow.—[Dugdale's *Monasticon*, vi, Pt. 1, 266–9; *Reg. Epis. of Glasgow*, i, 105–7, ii, 619–20; *Acts Scott. Parl.*, iv, 441. See Dalton.)

ARCHIBALD MENZIES, M.A., parson and exhorter 1561–9.—[*Comps. Gen. and Comps. Sub Coll. of Thirds, Dumfries*, etc.]

1561

JOHN GRAHAM, vicar 1584.—[*Comps. Gen. Coll. of Thirds.*]

1584

DORNOCK

SIR JOHN MORTON, parson 17th Sept. 1583.—[*Cal. of Charters*, xii, 2678.]

1583

GEORGE CLEGHORN, line 4, for
1612 "Clarence" read "Sarah."

JAMES MOFFAT, his daugh., Janet,
1694 died 1734 (marr. Irving of Woodhall).

JAMES HUNTER, assistant at
1715 Sanquhar.

JAMES ALEXANDER ROBERTSON,
1901 died 26th Nov. 1925; his son, Robert Reid, min. of Carriden; his widow, Elizabeth MacKnight Reid, died at Edinburgh 5th March 1945.

CHARLES EDWARD STEWART,
1926 born Downfield, Dundee, 19th Nov. 1896, son of James S., Invertay, Downfield, Dundee, and Jessie Warner; educ. at Harris Academy, Dundee, and Univ. of St Andrews, M.A. (1922); licen. by Presb. of Dundee April 1924; assistant, St Mark's, Dundee, and St Mary's, Dundee; ord. 8th April 1926. Marr. 10th Aug. 1927 Helen Clark, M.A., elder daugh. of James Westwater, 6 Tannadyce Street, Dundee, and Agnes McLeod.

GREENKNOWE

GEORGE GARDNER, his daugh.,
1858 Marion Craig (Mrs Boyd), died 24th Dec. 1937.

JOHN COLQUHOUN THOMSON,
1879 died 27th May 1927; his widow, Jean Maclean, died at Sidcup 31st Dec. 1941, aged 74.

JOHN RODERICK MACPHERSON,
1928 formerly of Evie (*q.v.*); trans. from St Cuthbert's, Glasgow, and pres. by the Presb., *jure devoluto* 27th March 1928; dem. 17th March 1930; trans. to Cummertrees 17th May 1930; adm. to Kinlochleven 15th May 1931; trans. to St Andrew's, Kirkintilloch, 15th Jan. 1936.

(*Parish united with St Andrew's, Annan, March* 1930.)

GRETNA, KINPATRICK or REDKIRK

Robert de Brus, son of Robert de Brus, lord of Annandale, whom he predeceased in 1191, granted the church with its lands, teinds, and possessions to the Priory of Giseburn (Guisborough) in Cleveland, Yorks, which had been founded in 1129 by his grandfather, Robert de Brus. Charters of confirmation were granted by the said Robert de Brus, lord of Annandale, who died in 1194, by his surviving son and successor, William, and by William the Lion, apparently about the close of the 12th century. In 1223 the monks of the priory and the Bishop of Glasgow, between whom differences had arisen as to the effect of the grant, reached a settlement whereby the monks retained the tithes of corn of the church, and received 3 merks yearly from the rector for the maintenance of lights, and the bishop had the right of collation and ordination to the church.—[Dugdale's *Monasticon*, vi, Pt. 1, 266–9; *Reg. Epis. of Glasgow*, i, 105, 106–7, ii, 619–20.]

ARCHIBALD MENZIES, M.A., parson and exhorter 1561–7.—[*Comps.*
1561 *Coll. Gen. and Sub Coll. of Thirds, Dumfries*, etc.]

BLAISE HAMILTON, pres. to parsonage and vicarage of Rinpatrick
1575 20th Oct. 1575, on dem. of Archibald Menzies.—[*Reg. Pres. Bene.*, ii, (4), 37.]

THOMAS MAXWELL, pres. on death of Archibald Menzies.—*Reg. Pres.*
1579 *Bene.*, ii, 19.]

DAVID WOOD, son of James W.,
1608 baxter burgess, Edinburgh.

THOMAS HENDERSON, his son,
1667 Thomas, min. of Morton.

JAMES RODDICK, his son, James,
1828 min. of Lybster.

WILLIAM BELL, his widow, Charlotte
1865 Heathfield, died 17th Jan. 1934.

JOHN OWEN STAFFORD, killed in air raid 7th April 1941; his son,
1906 Kenneth James, Lieut. R.F.A., died of wounds at Rouen 14th Nov. 1918; his widow, Mary Tweedie, died 23rd Jan. 1949.

HODDAM

When Hoddam, Ecclefechan, and Luss (Luce) were united on 24th June 1609, it was decreed that the church of the united parish be at Hoddam, "near the town thereof." It is said that in the parish of Hoddam, St Mungo built churches and placed his see for a time before transferring it to Glasgow.—[*Acts Scott. Parl.*, iv, 441; Watson's *Celtic Place Names*, 169. See Dalton.]

ANDREW LANG, M.A., parson, died before 20th April 1571.
1571

SIR PATRICK LOCH, died before 11th Oct. 1608, when he is called last vicar.—[*Reg. Sec. Sig.*]
1608

JOHN ALEXANDER, son of John A., burgess of Easter Anstruther, and Barbara Balfour.—[*G. R. Sas.*, lvii, 99; 2 Ser., xii, 172; *Acts and Dec.*, cccciii, 210.]
1610

ALEXANDER ORR, his son, William, midshipman in East Indies, 1763.
1729

GEORGE ROSS, his daugh., Christina Laing, died at Bathgate 13th June 1927.
1878

JAMES CHARLES GILLIES COLVIN, was assistant at St Michael's, Dumfries; dem. 31st Oct. 1947.
1899

KIRKPATRICK FLEMING

ROBERT JOHNSTON, pres. on death of Peter Stewart.—[*Reg. Pres. Bene.*, ii, (4), 64.]
1577

JAMES CHALMERS, signs list of parishioners 15th Sept. 1684; resident with his wife and four children in the Canongate 8th Nov. 1694.—[*P. C. Reg.*, 3 Ser., ix, 623; *Canongate Poll Tax Roll*, 1694.]
1684

JAMES GOWANLOCK, his daugh., Agnes (marr. Daniel McClaren, surgeon, in Lorn).—[*Reg. of Deeds, Dal.*, clxi, 18th March 1747.]
1694

ALEXANDER MONILAWS, his daugh., Margaret (marr. 15th March 1830 Dr. John Aitken, Edinburgh).
1784

JOHN MURDOCH, his daugh., Joanna Leonora, died at Calgary, Canada, 13th April 1935.
1845

JOHN WALKER, trans. to Duntocher 1st Oct. 1926.
1906

WILLIAM WILSON FYFFE, born Old Deer 30th Dec. 1900, son of Robert Bullett F., estate factor, and Agnes Wilson; educ. at High School and Univ. of Glasgow, M.A. (1922), B.D. (1925); licen. by Presb. of Perth 5th June 1925; assistant at Airth and St Mary's, Dundee, 1926; ord. 3rd March 1927; died unmarried 30th May 1938.
1927

KIRKCONNELL

Robert de Brus, son of Robert de Brus, lord of Annandale, whom he predeceased in 1191, granted the church with its lands, teinds, and possessions, and the Chapel of Logan, to the Priory of Giseburn (Guisborough) in Cleveland, Yorks, which had been founded by his grandfather, Robert de Brus, in 1129. Confirmation charters were granted by the said Robert de Brus, lord of Annandale, who died in 1194, and his surviving son and successor, William, and by William the Lion, apparently about the close of the 12th century. In 1223 the monks of the priory and the Bishop of Glasgow, between whom differences had arisen as to the effect of the grant, reached a settlement whereby the monks were to retain the tithe of corn of the church and the teinds of the Chapel of Logan, and the bishop was to exercise the power of collation and ordination to the church. When Kirkpatrick-Fleming and Kirkconnel were united in 1609, it was decreed that the church of the united parish be at Kirkconnel.—[Dugdale's *Monasticon*, vi, Pt. 1, 266–9; *Reg. Epis. of Glasgow*, i, 105–7, ii, 619–25; *Acts Scott. Parl.*, iv, 441.] (See Dalton.)

STEVEN CRICHTON, exhorter 1563.—[*Comps. Sub Coll. of Thirds, Dumfries*, etc.]
1563

KIRTLE

1908 ROBERT WILLIAM MALSEED, his wife, Ellen Beatrice Irving, died at Edinburgh 5th June 1926; dem. 2nd Oct. 1945.

MIDDLEBIE

When Middlebie, Carruthers and Pennersaughs were united in 1609, it was decreed that the church of the united parish be at Middlebie.—[*Acts of Parl.*, iv, 441.]

1744 JOHN LAURIE, marr. Ann, daugh. of William Bell of Scotsbrig.

1785 ABRAHAM NIVISON, his daugh., Margaret (marr. 13th April 1830).

1903 ERNEST HAMILTON DUKE, educ. at Rugby School; dem. 22nd Oct. 1947; his daugh., Elizabeth Theodora (marr. 15th June 1929 Seton Steuart Crichton Mitchell, Lieut. R.N.); his son, Walter Derek, Major, Gordon Highlanders, missing at Singapore, March 1942.

RUTHWELL

1563 JOHN IRELAND, reader, designed rector 2nd March 1560 but conformed; parson, vicar and reader 1563–72.—[*Comps. Gen. Coll. and Sub Coll. of Thirds, Dumfries*, etc.; *Laing Charters*, 717.]

1675 ROGER LAWSON, had issue, Elizabeth; Janet; Sara; Grizel.—[*Reg. of Deeds, Durie*, 1706, No. 671.]

1799 HENRY DUNCAN, nephew of Thomson, author of *The Seasons*; Dumfries erected a statue to him.

1890 JOHN LINTON DINWIDDIE, D.D. (Edinburgh, 28th June 1935); died 21st Jan. 1936. His wife, Agnes Margaret Melville, died 14th Dec. 1923; his sons—James Linton Norris, M.B., Ch.B., died 23rd Oct. 1932; Melville, D.S.O., min. of St Machar, Aberdeen, Regional Director, B.B.C. for Scotland; Noel Alexander Williamson, M.A., B.Com. (Edinburgh, 1925), bookseller, Dumfries. Publications—Editor of *Gallovidian*.

PRESBYTERY OF DUMFRIES

CAERLAVEROCK

The church belonged to the Collegiate Church of Lincluden. There was in the church an altar dedicated to the Virgin Mary.—[*Reg. Mag. Sig.*, vi, 777.]

1558 JOHN PATERSON, vicar 16th Dec. 1558, continued as vicar and reader to at least 1572.—[*Comps. Sub Coll. of Thirds, Dumfries*, etc.; *Reg. of Abbrev. of Feu Charters of Church Lands*, i, 203; *Chronicles of Lincluden*, 28.]

1574 NINIAN DALZELL, died 21st April 1587. See Colvend.

1578 EDWARD MAXWELL, pres. to vicarage 26th Nov. 1578 on dem. of Sir John Paterson.—[*Reg. Pres. Bene.*, ii, 28.]

1605 DAVID ROGERS, was min. of Dalgarnock when pres. here in 1605.—[*Reg. Sec. Sig.*, lxxiv, 407.]

1611 HERBERT GLEDSTANES, line 2, for "1612" read "1611."

1613 WILLIAM McGEORGE, line 6, for "son" read "nephew"; his son, William, was of Ingliston.

1833 ROBERT GILLIES, marr. Margaret Anne, daugh. of William Irvine, Soultra.

1846 JOSEPH CURRIE LORRAINE, his daugh., Helen Scott, died 17th May 1923.

1892 THOMAS DALE McILVEAN, dem. 1st Oct. 1930; died 16th March 1932.

COLVEND

1562 NINIAN DALZELL, vicar, reader, 1562, probably trans. to Dalgarnock.

1562 WILLIAM LOGAN, vicar 1562.—[*Reg. of Abbrev. of Feu Charters of Church Lands*, i, 214.]

1567 JOHN LOGAN, reader, afterwards of New Abbey (*q.v.*).

1571 ARCHIBALD MENZIES, M.A., reader 1571-6, also at Morton (*q.v.*).

1579 JOHN TAYLOR, pres. to vicarage 1st July 1579 on death of Archibald Menzies. On 30th July George Oliver, parson and vicar of Southwick, was ordered to give him possession of the vicarage and exercise of the office of reader.—[*Reg. Pres. Bene.*, ii, 19; *Cal. of Charters*, x, 2523.]

1598 WILLIAM TAYLOR, pres. to vicarage on death of Sir John Taylor, his brother.—[*Reg. Sec. Sig.*, lxix, 266.]

1598 DAVID MURRAY, son of Sir Charles M. of Cockpool, pres. to vicarage 9th May 1598 on death of Sir John Taylor.—[*Reg. Sec. Sig.*, lxix, 262.]

1671 ROBERT STRACHAN, delete father's name, as he could not have been son of min. of Kincardine o' Neil.—[*Forfar Sas.*, xv, 16.]

1715 JOHN WATSON, his MS. Sermons in Museum at Thornhill.

1844 JAMES FRASER, his widow, Jessie Ker Pagan, died at Dalbeattie 19th May 1922; his son, Malcolm, died 31st Dec. 1928; his daugh., Annie McDiarmid, died at Edinburgh 2nd Feb. 1922.

1902 JOHN CHALMERS, died at Edinburgh 4th March 1917; his widow, Janet Mitchell, died 6th May 1919.

JAMES GARROW BERRY, B.D., trans. from Leslie, Aberdeen (*q.v.*), 2nd Aug. 1917; dem. 16th June 1926 and became min. of Presb. Church, Fredericton, New Brunswick (*q.v.*).
[1917]

JOHN WHYTE MACGILL, formerly of Inverallochy (*q.v.*); trans. from Sauchtree 27th Jan. 1927; died 1st Jan. 1937; his widow, Edith Sarah Luxton, died Edinburgh 19th Jan. 1947.
[1927]

DALBEATTIE

JOHN MACKIE, licen. 16th May, 1877; line 8, add before "1885" "29th Oct."; died at Ichbesham, Coonan, India, 3rd July 1929; his widow, Elizabeth Smith Brown, died 14th Oct. 1930.
[1877]

LEWIS McGLASHAN, trans. to Menmuir 12th July 1929.
[1907]

ST MICHAEL'S, DUMFRIES

The church, with the Chapel of St Thomas, a toft belonging to the chapel, and 5 acres of land given by William the Lion to the church and chapel, was granted to Kelso Abbey by William the Lion, 1165–1214. There were in the church an Altar of Our Lady of Pity, an Altar of the Holy Blood, founded by William Cunninghame, burgess of Dumfries, in the aisle of the Virgin Mary, apparently on 15th Nov. 1506, an Altar of St Gregory, founded apparently on 5th Nov. 1508 by Sir Herbert Gladstone, Rector of Dornock, an Altar of St Andrew founded 24th July 1547 by Sir David Wallace, son and heir of late Adam Wallace, burgess of Dumfries, and a Chapel of St Nicholas. Doubtless there were an Altar of the Virgin Mary in the aisle bearing her name, and an Altar of St Nicholas in the chapel bearing his name. In St Nicholas' Chapel there was a chantry in honour of God, the Virgin Mary, and All Saints, the erection of which was confirmed by David, Earl of Carrick, on 27th Dec. 1394, the endowment being two stone houses on the east side of the Market Cross of the burgh. In or near the Gallowgait of the burgh there was a Chapel of St Mary of Willies; and in the liberty of the burgh there was the Chapel of St Mary of Casteldykis, to which pertained ¼ acre of the lands of Kingisholme near the chapel. In the territory of the burgh there was a Chapel of the Virgin Mary, commonly called *lie Casteldikis*. On 8th May 1537 Roger Macbrair, Provost of the burgh, and Herbert Cunningham and Edward Johnstone, bailies, on behalf of the community, granted to John Makilreve, custodier and administrator of the chapel, and his heirs male, 4 acres of land called the *Chapelland*, held by the late Duncan Ferguson, Andrew Ferguson, and Patrick Ferguson, custodiers and administrators in the said chapel, with houses, buildings, gardens, and orchards, lying at the said chapel, bounded by the High way, the rivulet flowing from the well of the chapel, a piece of the common land occupied by Thomas Welsche, and the common lands, the custodier being held bound to provide for the celebration of certain masses.—[*Reg. Sec. Seal*, i, 3998, 1302, liv, 55; *Reg. Great Seal*, ii, 3010, 3335; iii, 862, 2083; iv, 2246; *Spalding Mis.*, v, 250–2.]

SIR PATRICK WALLACE, min. 21st Jan. 1561–2; son of John W. and Marieta Forrester; chaplain 1543, curate of Dumfries 1543–59; reader 15th Dec. 1570.—[*Trans. Dumfries and Galloway Antiq. Socy.*, 1936, 111; *Edin. Tests.*, vii, 156.]
[1561]

ALEXANDER AUCHENLECK, M.A., min. in 1563.—[*Comps. Sub Coll. of Thirds, Dumfries*, etc., 173.]
[1563]

SIR JOHN BRYSON or **BRYCE** vicar 17th May 1566, 23rd March 1572–3, 3rd March 1578.—[*Acts and Dec.*, lxii, 9; *Edin. Tests.*, vii, 149.]
[1572]

JOHN SINCLAIR, formerly chaplain of St Ninian's Altar; reader, pres. to vicarage of Bolton 16th Aug. 1575.—[*Reg. Sec. Sig.*, xlv, 71.]
[1578]

THOMAS MAXWELL, reader in 1585.—[*Reg. of Assig.*, 44.]
[1580]

THOMAS RAMSAY, marr. Elspeth Johnston, relict of Matthew Poole, merchant and burgess of Edinburgh.—[*G. R. Sas.*, xxxi, 28, 7th June and 25th July 1631.]
1605

HUGH HENDERSON, his son, Alexander.—[*Kirkcudbright Sher. Court Deeds*, 2233.]
1648

WILLIAM VEITCH, line 14, for "Hanamhall" read "Harnamhall"; line 15, for "Seaton" read "Stanton"; col. 2, line 2, for "sent" read "sentenced, but not sent 28th July 1674"; line 12, after "Scotland" add "2nd Nov. 1687." Publications, line 2, for "*Commons*" read "*Commissioner*"; add a *True copy of the last sermon*, etc. (Edin., 1720).
1694

ROBERT PATON, trans. to Second Church 13th Nov. 1727; his daugh., Mary, died 23rd May 1788.
1715

ROBERT WIGHT, his daughs.—Jean, born 6th Jan. 1728; Mary, died 1st June 1815; Janet (marr. Walter Murray); Belle, died 24th Jan. 1789.
1732

JOHN DUNCAN, pres. by Crown 7th Feb. 1865.
1865

JAMES FRASER, pres. by Crown 29th Oct. 1866.
1867

ALEXANDER BRYSON, pres. by Crown 8th Oct. 1867.
1868

JAMES BARCLAY, pres. by Crown 18th Oct. 1870.
1871

JOHN PATON, pres. by Crown 30th July 1874; his daugh., Catherine Isabella, died 8th Sept. 1932.
1874

JAMES MONTGOMERY CAMPBELL, licen. 3rd. Moderator of General Assembly 19th May 1928; dem. 16th May 1930; died at Edinburgh 13th Feb. 1937; his wife, Agnes Grey, died 28th Nov. 1935.
1908

SECOND CHARGE

PATRICK LINN, marr. 2nd July 1724 Alison, daugh. of William Charteris of Brigmuir and widow of John McMurdo, min. of Torthorwald.
1715

GREYFRIARS

ANDREW GRAY, pres. by Crown 18th June 1858.
1858

MALCOLM CAMPBELL TAYLOR, pres. by Crown 13th Sept. 1862.
1862

DONALD MACLEOD, pres. by Crown 26th Oct. 1865.
1866

ROBERT WALTER WEIR, pres. by Crown 20th Jan. 1868, died at Colinton 23rd Sept. 1925; his widow, Jessie Macdonald Macvicar, died at Colinton 8th Sept. 1933. Addl. publication—*Notes on the History of the Christian Unity Association of Scotland* (Edin., 1917).
1868

JAMES BRYCE JAMIESON, trans. to Dalziel 26th July 1929.
1911

ROBERT ALEXANDER KING, D.D., K.I.H., born 30th April 1873, son of Robert K., Edinburgh, and Janet Blair; educ. at Winnipeg Collegiate School and Manitoba College, B.A. (1895), M.A. (1911) Univ. of Edinburgh, B.D. (1900), D.D. (Toronto, 1910); licen. by Presb. of Winnipeg 1898; Member of Canadian Church College, Indore, India, 1902; Fellow of Univ. of Allahabad; Member of Council, Univ. of Agra; adviser on education to British Administration of Central India and Inspector of High Schools for Central India; adm. 14th Nov. 1929; died at Edinburgh 30th Jan. 1947. Marr. 14th Aug. 1902 Annie Kidston (died 1st Feb. 1947), daugh. of John Murray, Brandon, Manitoba. Publications—*Lecture Notes on Economics and Logic*; various articles on Missions and Religious Types, in Canadian and Scottish papers.
1929

ST MARY'S, DUMFRIES

The endowment granted by Robert I to the Chapel of the Holy Rood was 100s. sterling annually from the revenue due to him from the barony of Caerlaverock. It was given for perpetual celebration for the soul of Sir Christopher Seton, "our beloved kinsman slain in our service," on account of the good will and affection which the King had entertained for him.—[*Reg. Great Seal*, i, App. i, 61, ii, 318.]

ANDREW FYFE, line 2, delete "born 1796."
1840

ALEXANDER CHAPMAN, died at Chorley Wood, Herts, 12th June, 1919.
1877

ROBERT GORDON MILLAR, killed in action 11th May 1917.
1915

WALTER McINTYRE, ord. 18th Oct. 1917; trans. to Logie 24th Jan. 1922.
1917

DAVID BROWN, ord. 30th June 1922; trans. to West St Giles, Edinburgh, 24th Sept. 1925.
1922

ROBERT PAUL FAIRLIE, trans. from New Ardrossan (*q.v.*) 14th Jan. 1926. Addl. issue—Margery Christine Carrick, born 5th Aug. 1919; Joyce Florence Wilson, born 11th Feb. 1924; Archibald Robin Paul, born 7th March 1933.
1925

DUNSCORE

Among the witnesses of a charter of Edgar, son of Donald, in the time of King William the Lion, is Murchereach, priest of St Capre of Dunescor (Dunscore). There were four saints named Cairbre (Cairpre, Coirpre), but there is nothing to show which was associated with Dunscore. On 18th March and 8th April 1645 the Synod decerned that a new church be built by the heritors and parishioners at Dalgonar, near the centre of the parish; and that was ratified by Act of Parliament on 13th Feb. 1647. The church, manse and churchyard dykes were completed before 16th March 1649. The church was rebuilt in 1823.—[*Acts Scott. Parl.*, vi, (1), 697, vi, (2), 345, 719a; *Reg. Great Seal*, viii, 127; *Charters of Holyrood*, 213.]

SIR JOHN WELSH, superior of the Monastery of Holyrood; pres. to the perpetual vicarage 27th Nov. 1562 by Thomas, Commendator of Holyrood, and acted as reader at least to 1572 both parsonage and vicarage.—[*Cal. of Charters*, ix, 1896; *Comps. Sub Coll. of Thirds, Dumfries*, etc.]
1562

JOHN JAMESON, reader 1574-5, son of a laird in the parish and formerly, 31st Dec. 1543, chaplain of Dumfries and vicar here 1545.—[Anderson's *Prot. Book.*]
1574

GEORGE HERIOT, pres. to vicarage on death of Alexander Gardiner.—[*Reg. Sec. Sig.*, lxxiii, 105.]
1602

WILLIAM BENNET, read "Burnet."
1664

ALEXANDER MELDRUM, became min. of Glendevon 1688.
1683

JAMES GILCHRIST, excommunicated 14th March 1718.
1701

ROBERT BRYDON, his mother, Margaret Meickeson.
1822

JOHN HOPE, presented by Crown 29th July 1843.
1843

ROBERT SIMPSON, his widow, Agnes Campbell Stout, died at Glasgow 12th July 1933; his daugh., Margaret Hilda, M.A., died 3rd March 1920.
1886

ALEXANDER MASTERTON, died 30th March 1930.
1904

HOLYWOOD

At Berwick-on-Tweed on 28th Aug. 1226 Dugald, Abbot of Holywood (St Bryce) swore fealty to Edward I. The reference to the saint is not clear.—[*Cal. of Docs. Scot.*, ii, 196.]

MUNGO MacGHIE, was vicar pensioner in 1537 and reader in 1567.—[*Reg. Mag. Sig.*, v, 115; *Reg. of Abbrev. Feu Charters of Church Lands*, i, 117.]
1567

JAMES BETOUN, min. at Glencairn, reader here.
1574

JOHN SINCLAIR, reader at Kirkmahoe (*q.v.*), also in charge here.
1579

HERCULES STEWART, pres. to vicar-pensionary 4th May 1580 on death of Mungo MacGhie.—[*Reg. Pres. Bene.*, ii, 357.]
1580

1582 JOHN MAXWELL, reader, pres. to vicar-pensionary 29th Jan. 1582–3.—[*Reg. Pres. Bene.*, ii, 84.]

1584 JAMES MAXWELL, son of John M., min. of Glencairn, pres. to vicar-pensionary 1st Feb. 1584–5 on dem. of Robert, son of Archibald Newall, burgess of Dumfries, with consent of his father and vacant by dem. of John Maxwell, sometime vicar or by death of Hercules Stewart. Under Lochmaben he is described as son of James M., min., whereas he himself was min. of Lochmaben (*q.v.*).—[*Reg. Sec. Sig.*, lii, 22.]

1633 JAMES MAXWELL, son of George M., min. of Mearns, pres. 11th Feb. 1633; afterwards of Kirkgunzean.—[*Pres.*, vi, 123.]

1665 JOHN MALCOLM, buried at Dumfries 20th March, 1716; marr. (1) Agnes Charteris; (2) Janet, buried 20th Jan. 1732, and had issue—Agnes, buried 4th Aug. 1690; John, buried 16th Aug. 1690; Anna, buried 10th Aug. 1691; Jean, buried 17th Oct. 1695; Alexander, merchant, buried 3rd April 1708; Isobel, buried 13th Dec. 1730; William; his daugh., Marion, marr. (2) John Kennedy, merchant, Dumfries.

1899 JOHN McCOMBIE, died at Dumfries 10th Oct. 1947.

1928 JOHN WATT, born Tynron; educ. at Royal Univ. of Ireland, Magee College, B.A.; trans. from Bucklyvie (*q.v.*) 8th June 1928, died 26th Dec. 1933.

KIRKBEAN

The church was built in 1776 and rebuilt in 1825.

1563 CHARLES HUME, reader 1563.—[*Comps. Sub Coll. of Thirds, Dumfries*, etc.]

1566 WILLIAM SOMERVILLE, vicar before 1566 and in 1585.—[*Acts and Dec.*, xxx, 333; lviii, 328; lxi, 165.]

1637 ROBERT BROWN, min. at Weshingtoun 28th May 1648.—[*P. R. Sas., Dumfries*, v, 235.]

1640 CHARLES ARCHIBALD, his widow, Jean Porteous, marr. (2) George Gledstanes, min. of Urr.

1660 ANTHONY MURRAY, son of Thomas M., advocate, and Jean Murray.

1687 HUGH CLANNY, M.A., performed irregular marriages and baptisms at New Abbey Sept. 1714, July 1715 and Oct. 1716.—[*Justiciary Records*, 1712–17.]

1733 WILLIAM STEWART, was latterly Collector of Customs at Dumfries 3rd March 1753.—[*Reg. of Deeds, Mack.*, 468.]

1745 JAMES HOGG, line 2, for "1st" read "3rd"; line 3, for "19" read "8."

1912 JOHN DOUGLAS COCHRANE, was assistant at Inveresk; died 25th Nov. 1941. His wife, Isabel Cochrane Martin Mackenzie, died 12th March 1930; He marr. (2) 2nd Sept. 1937 Mary, daugh. of Alexander Wright and Jane Hyslop.

KIRKGUNZEON

The patron saint is Findbarr of Moyville, who was for some time in Whithorn, and whose death is recorded in 579. The alternative name of the church in the 12th and 13th centuries, Kirkwynnin, contains the Welsh form of *Finnan* or *Finnen*, which is a diminutive of the name of Findbarr. By Bull of 3rd Feb. 1216 Pope Innocent III confirmed to the Abbey of Holm-Cultram in Cumberland the Chapel of Kyrkewynnin, which the abbey had held for forty years in peace by concession or confirmation of Jocelin, Bishop of Glasgow 1175–99. In the time of Pope Honorius III, Walter, Bishop of Glasgow, challenged the right of the abbey to the chapel, complaining that the monks of Holm-Cultram had usurped churches in his diocese and expelled the clergy, and craving that the chapel should be restored, but eventually on 27th May 1222 he agreed that the abbey should hold the chapel in accordance with the confirmation of Pope Innocent and Bishop Jocelin. In the latter part of the 14th century and early part of the 15th, the wars between Scotland and England rendered somewhat precarious the abbey's hold upon the chapel, now a church, with the result that the church was "of little profit" to the abbey, and its services suffered from neglect, being carried out, not by a monk of the abbey as formerly, but "now by one priest, now by another"; and on 17th June, 1391, Pope Clement VII (anti-Pope), on a petition of the Abbot of Holm-Cultram, committed the church temporarily to Thomas de Glenluce, of that monastery. Subsequently the church was granted in *commendam* to various persons; and later still, on a petition of Patrick Leche, Clerk, of the Diocese of Glasgow, M.A., which stated that on account of the commends which had gone on for forty years, it would be difficult for the union of the abbey and the church to take effect, and that the church had been so long void that there was no certain knowledge of the mode of voidance. Pope Martin V on 27th Sept. 1424 gave mandate to the Official of Glasgow to summon the interested parties and make enquiries, and, if he found the facts as stated, to suppress both the commends and the alleged union, and collate said Patrick to the church. What emerged is not clear; but before 20th April 1447 the abbey had ceased to have any right to the church, which was then in lay hands, possibly the family of Herries of Terregles. Towards the close of the 18th century the medieval church was almost a ruin. Its roof, of peculiar construction, is said "to have been formed at Holm-Cultram in Cumberland, and brought hither when the parish of Kirkguneon belonged to the Abbey." In 1790 it was replaced by the present church.—[*Reg. and Recs. of Holm-Cultram Abbey*, 21, 48, 49, 51, 53–4; *Cal. of Papal Regs., Petitions*, i, 385, 576, *Letters*, vii, 67, 344, x, 280, xi, 261, 625, xii, 45, 225; *Reg. Great Seal*, i, 282, App. ii, 1574, ii, 3446; Watson's *Celtic Place Names*, 165; Johnston's *Place-Names of Scot.*, 223, 228.]

1563 NICOL EDGAR, reader 1563.—[*Comps. Sub Coll. of Thirds, Dumfries*, etc.]

1643 JAMES MAXWELL, trans. from assistant at Kingarth 1643; was trans. to Holywood but perhaps not settled there.

1865 JAMES EWER GILLESPIE, died 9th March 1918; his widow, Agnes Isabel Murray, died at Dumfries 15th July 1923, aged 75; his sons—Garnet, died 21st April 1917; Hope Murray, died at Eastwood, Notts, 18th May 1927; Angus died 5th Oct. 1932; his daugh., Mary Charlotte, died 30th Jan. 1946.

1918 JAMES TAYLOR LORNIE, trans. from Cawnpore (*q.v.*) 20th Aug. 1918, died 24th Jan. 1923; his widow, Marjorie A. Jackson, died 7th April 1945.

1923 JOHN WILSON BAIRD, M.A., ord. 8th June 1923; trans. to St Andrew's Second Charge 3rd Sept. 1925.

1926 ROBERT LOVE HUNTER, trans. from Townhead, Glasgow (*q.v.*), 15th Jan. 1926; dem. 11th Nov. 1932, died 12th Dec. 1933; his widow, Annie Mackay Macmillan, died 20th Feb. 1934.

KIRKMAHOE

The church was restored at its centenary in 1926. The saint is Mo-Choe, evidently Mocha of Clendrium on Loch Cuan (Strangford Loch).—[Watson's *Celtic Place Names*, 162.]

1564 WALTER STEWART, M.A., parson 1564, rector 10th Jan, 1567–8.—[*Reg. Sec. Sig.*, xxxvii, 31; *Reg. Abbrev. Feu Charters of Church Lands*, i, 293.]

1579 JOHN SINCLAIR, reader, declared an apostate 11th Aug. 1590.—[*Reg. Privy Council*, xiv, 373.]

1605 GEORGE HERIOT, marr. (2) cont. 9th March 1631.—[*Prot. Book Walter Logan*, 7th June 1632.]

KIRKMAHOE—KIRKPATRICK IRONGRAY

1666 JOHN WALLACE, said to be 50 years of age and unmarried 8th Aug. 1684.—[*P. C. Reg.*, 3 Ser., ix, 271.]

1682 JAMES HUME, line 11, for "Auchenson" read "Aucherson."

1687 FRANCIS IRVING, a prisoner in Dumfries prison 20th April 1685.—[*Fraser Papers*.]

1696 JAMES HENDERSON, for "James" read "John."

1716 DAVID GRAHAM, marr. Margaret, daugh. of William Graham of Mossknowe, and had issue—William; Archibald; David; John; Mary; Isobel.—[*Reg. of Deeds, Dalrymple*, cix, 19th Dec. 1718.]

1725 EDWARD BUNCLE, probably son of James B., merchant, Linlithgow, and Margaret Jervie; marr. (1) proc. 28th Jan. 1728 Margaret (bapt. 28th Aug. 1695).

1750 ARCHIBALD LAWSON, his wife, Mary Guthrie, died 4th March 1820.

1879 MAXWELL HUTCHISON, line 2, for "John" read "George."

1907 JOHN MACKENZIE FORBES, Ph.D. (Edin., 1928), died 26th Jan. 1939; his widow, Mary Watson Main McTaggart, died 3rd April 1945.

min. at Haltwhistle in England.—[*Edin. Burgess Roll*, 13th Aug. 1656.]

1673 ALEXANDER SANGSTER, vicar 24th July 1673.—[*P. R. Sas., Dumfries*, i, 234.]

1699 JAMES HILL, had other issue—Agnes; Jean; Isobel; Helen; Sarah.

1744 ROBERT MACMORINE, his daugh., Elizabeth, died at Dumfries 2nd March 1789.

1843 GEORGE GREIG, pres. by Crown 28th Aug. 1843.

1870 ANDREW LAIDLAW, pres. by Crown 26th March 1870.

1876 WILLIAM ADAM STARK, licen. 1st Dec. 1871; died 22nd Feb. 1927. Marr. (2) 1st June 1917 Effie Jane, youngest daugh. of Maxwell Palmer, Lochpark, Dalbeattie; she died at Castle Douglas 23rd May 1921.

1916 WILLIAM ADAM, trans. to Stanley 15th Oct. 1924.

1925 WILLIAM MACKEAN CAMPBELL, trans. from Boquhanran (*q.v.*) 15th May 1925; his wife, Margaret Magdalen Ramsay, died 10th Aug. 1929. He died 28th March 1945.

KIRKPATRICK-DURHAM

1563 ANDREW EDGAR, reader 1563.—[*Comps. Sub Coll. of Thirds, Dumfries*.]

1575 WILLIAM TURNER, M.A., vicar in 1559 and 20th March 1560–1; reader; pres. to vicarage 1st Dec. 1575 on death of Thores.—[*Reg. of Pres. Bene.*, ii, (4), 308; *Reg. Abbrev. Feu Charters of Church Lands*, i, 214; *Laing Charters*, 167, 217; *Kirkcudbright Sheriff Court Deeds*, 1146.]

1641 ADAM BROWN, line 2, for "James B. min. of Kirkpatrick Irongray" read "Adam B. of Gorgiemylne." He marr. (2) Janet McMillan. In 1670 he was

KIRKPATRICK IRONGRAY

There was a chapel and a well called the Angel's Well situated at the east side of the lands of Barnesoul, called Drumdrynie. There was also a chapel designated the Chapel of the Chapel-Yard.—[*Anderson's Prot. Book*, 21; *Retours*, xxvii, 325; *Reg. Great Seal*, ii, 3446.]

1565 SIR JAMES BRYCE, vicar 1565–6.—[*Reg. Abbrev. Feu Charters of Church Lands*, i, 182, 276.]

1571 MICHAEL WIGHTMAN, reader 3rd Dec. 1577.—[*Edin. Tests.*, viii, 35.]

1601 JAMES BROWN, delete from issue—Adam, min. of Kirkpatrick-Durham.

1646 PATRICK BROWN, min. here in 1646. —[*Dumfries Sas.*, v, 164.]

1653 JOHN WELSH, his mother, Martha Pont.

1694 JAMES GUTHRIE, his daugh., Janet, marr. 21st Nov. 1763 James Crocket in par. of Holywood.

1822 DAVID DOW, born 29th March 1798; his daugh., Ann, died 11th May 1917, aged 72.

1843 JAMES WILSON, marr. 26th Oct. 1841 Isabel, daugh. of Robert Clark, S.S.C. His son, Thomas Jackson, S.S.C., died 20th Feb. 1932.

1857 THOMAS UNDERWOOD, his widow, Agnes Stewart McGill, died 16th June 1922.

1895 SAMUEL DUNLOP, licen. 4th; trans. to Old Greyfriars, Edinburgh, 17th May 1917.

1917 JOHN MIDDLETON, LL.D., trans. from Kemback (*q.v.*) 2nd Nov. 1917, died at London 21st Oct. 1927.

1928 WILLIAM ROCK, M.A., born Glasgow 21st Nov. 1899, son of William R., steelworker, and May Taylor; educ. Newlands School, Hutchison's Grammar School and Univ. of Glasgow, M.A. (1922); served in Great War; licen. by Presb. of Glasgow March 1925; assistant Greenhead and Bluevale; ord. to St James, Kirkcaldy, 13th May 1925; trans. and adm. 18th May 1928. Marr. 2nd Sept. 1925 Helen Heughan, daugh. of Andrew Irving Kerr, Millerston, and has issue—William Gordon, born 10th Oct. 1928; Helen Cochrane Henderson, born 26th Feb. 1930; Joycelyn Patricia Kerr, born 2nd Nov. 1937.

LOCHRUTTON

1558 GEORGE ARNOT, vicar, 8th May 1558, parson of Essie and vicar here 1566.—[Anderson's *Prot. Book*.]

1563 NINIAN DALZIEL, M.A., min. in 1563.—[*Comps. Sub Coll. of Thirds, Dumfries.*]

1563 WILLIAM LAING, reader 1563.—[*Comps. Sub Coll. of Thirds, Dumfries.*]

1567 JOHN LITTLE, exhorter 1567 and 1572. —[*Comps. Sub Coll. of Thirds, Dumfries*, etc.]

1589 ROBERT DOUGLAS, M.A., parson 9th April 1589, Provost of Lincluden.—[*Cal. of Charters*, xii, 3003.]

1606 JOHN CURROUR, his pres. here when reader, 28th June 1606, was on death of (George) Arnot.—[*Reg. Sec. Sig.*, lxxv, 103.]

1618 ALEXANDER TRAIN.—[*G. R. Sas.*, lxi, 373.]

1728 GEORGE DUNCAN, left a journal.

1884 THOMAS CROSBY, dem. 13th June 1923; died 6th Aug. 1948; his daugh. Isobel Helen Murray (marr. 31st May 1918 John Rae, master mariner).

1923 ANDREW LOW McGREGOR MACKENZIE, born 27th Feb. 1890, son of Alexander M., schoolmaster, and Agnes Dryburgh Mackenzie; educ. at Woodside School and Glasgow Univ., M.A. (1911), B.D. (1920); licen. by Presb. of Glasgow 1920; assistant Rutherglen; ord. 11th Oct. 1923; trans. to Crailing 24th Sept. 1931. He marr. 10th Dec. 1923 Sarah, daugh. of James Carson, and has issue—Margaret Logan McTaggart, born 21st April 1925.

MAXWELLTOWN

1863 WILLIAM VILANT GRAHAM, his widow, Watson Allan Smith, died 19th July 1923; his daugh., Robina Williamson, died 19th Feb. 1924.

1897 DUNCAN MORRISON SLESSOR, died 20th April 1937.

NEW ABBEY

1563 PATRICK COULL, reader in 1563, when designated "Dene."—[*Comps. Sub Coll. of Thirds, Dumfries*, etc.]

JOHN LOGAN, formerly monk here, reader in 1569, charged with profaning the Sacraments 11th Aug. 1590.—[*Comps. Sub Coll. of Thirds, Dumfries*, etc.; *Reg. Privy Council*, iv, 375.]
1569

ARCHIBALD HAMILTON CHARTERIS, line 2, for "nephew" read "grand nephew"; pres. by Crown 21st March 1859.
1859

JOHN STEWART WILSON, pres. by Crown 30th June 1863; his daugh., Jane Ewing, O.B.E. (marr. Robert Kerr Hannay, Historiographer Royal for Scotland and Professor of Ancient History, Univ. of Edinburgh), died 14th April 1938.
1863

JOHN MURRAY WOODBURN, trans. to Beith 25th Sept. 1919.
1911

WILLIAM SUTHERLAND, M.A., D.D., M.C., ord. 9th April 1920; trans. to Eastwood 8th Jan. 1926.
1920

ROBERT NINIAN PAISLEY, trans. from Ladykirk 30th April 1926; trans. to Bolton and Saltoun 8th Nov. 1928.
1926

GEORGE GORDON DUNDAS STEWART DUNCAN, formerly of St Cuthbert's, Edinburgh, trans. from St Paul's, Montreal, to Govan 13th May 1921; trans. and adm. 1st March 1929; died 19th Oct. 1932. Marr. 10th Oct. 1914 Catherine Louise, only daugh. of Robert Hunt White, Castle Park, Prestonpans, and had issue—Alastair, born 14th Oct. 1915, died 29th March 1916.
1929

SOUTHWICK

15.. **SIR MICHAEL DYSART**,

SIR JOHN CORSWELL.—[*Acts and Dec.*, xxxv, 155.]
1565

GEORGE OLIVER, reader 1567–79.—[*Comps. Sub Coll. of Thirds, Dumfries*, etc.; *Cal. of Charters* xi, 2537.]
1567

ARCHIBALD SINCLAIR, M.A., parson 1572 and 4th May 1577.—[*Cal. of Charters*, xi, 2439.]
1572

JOHN THOMAS PATTERSON, dem. 9th Jan. 1918; was afterwards chaplain to Glasgow City Hospitals; died at Bearsden 14th Nov. 1943; his widow, Ann Black Morison, died 21st April 1946.
1900

JAMES ANDERSON LOW, B.D., trans. from Glengairn (*q.v.*) 28th June 1918; dem. 11th Nov. 1933.
1918

TERREGLES

On the petition of Archibald, Earl of Douglas, lord of Galloway, Papal Commission was given on 7th May 1389 to the Bishop of Glasgow to convert the Nunnery of Lincluden into a collegiate church. The Earl narrated that the nunnery had been founded by his predecessors for eight or nine nuns and a prioress, that only four nuns and a prioress remained, that these were living disgracefully and insolently, that by their carelessness and negligence the buildings had become unsightly and ruinous, that they had no wish to repair them, and that to the repair of the vestments and ornaments they gave no attention. He asked that the prioress and nuns be transferred to another monastery or place either of the Benedictine or the Cluniac Order. The collegiate church was to be for a provost, 8 prebends, extended later to 12, and 24 bedesmen; and for the support of the establishment there were set apart the revenues of the nunnery and of the Hospital of the Sacred Grove (Holywood), situated near the nunnery and annexed to the collegiate church. The hospital, which was dedicated to St John the Baptist, had its origin in a house and chapel founded and built by Edward Bruce, brother of Robert I, within the bounds and limits of the Monastery of Holywood, and founded anew by Archibald, Earl of Douglas, whose charter was confirmed by Robert II on 2nd June 1372, for the reception of poor, weak, and sick people to the number of 18, the endowment being the lands of Crossmichael and Troqueer in the lordship of Galloway. The churches belonging to the collegiate church included Caerlaverock; Kirkbean; Preston; Colvend;

Terregles; Lochrutten; Kirkanders, made a prebend by Alexander, Bishop of Glasgow, 16th Jan. 1447–8; Lochmaben, made a prebend by William, Bishop of Glasgow, confirmed by Pope Nicholas V, 3rd March 1449–50; Kirkpatrick in Nithsdale, made a prebend before 9th Aug. 1453; Kirkbride, annexed before 23rd June 1487. On 22nd Sept. 1429 Margaret, Duchess of Turaine, widow of Archibald, Duke of Turaine, Earl of Douglas, for the souls of Robert III and Queen Annabella, her father and mother, etc., founded a chaplainry in the church, the endowment being the lands of Estwood, Barschryve, Le Bank, Carvorland, Dummokhead, le Maynys, Suthake, and de Barnes, in the Constabulary of Kirkcudbright and lordship of Galloway. By Bull of 11th Dec. 1482 Sextus IV annexed the provostship to the Episcopal Mensa of Moray, during the lifetime of Andrew Stewart, Bishop of Moray; but in 1488 Parliament declared the annexation to be null and void, the patronage to remain with the King, and the pretended annexation in favour of Andrew, Bishop of Moray, to be of no effect. By James IV the provostship was annexed to the Chapel Royal of Stirling, confirmation being granted by Pope Julius II on 2nd June 1508; and on 11th July 1527 James V declared "that his mynde and will is that the foundation of his Chapell riale of Striveling and the unions of Inchmahomo (Inchmahome) and Lincluden be observit and kepit in tyme to cum efter the form of the erection and union maid tharupon by his mest noble fader . . . and that supplication be direct to our haly fader tharupon."—[*Acts Scott. Parl.*, ii, 209; *Cal. Papal Regs., Letters*, vii, 143, 493, 526, 630; *Transcripts from Vatican*, i, 288–97, iii, 163–74, *MS., Reg. Ho.*; *Reg. Privy Council*, xii, 445; *Acts Lords of Council in Public Affairs*, 259, 325; *The Apostolic Camera and Scott. Benefs.*, 221, 308; *The Douglas Bks.*, i, 348–9; For lands of Lincluden Church, see *Acts Scott. Parl.*, iii, 436ab, 587b, v, 570–1, and *Reg. Great Seal*, i, 483, ii, 130, iv, 1652, 1653, 1685, 2488, 2661, 2734, 2889, v, 17, 32, 42, 234, 820, 1232, 1506, 1507, 1891, 1981; for details of Nunnery and Church, see *The Chronicles of Lincluden*.]

1563 NINIAN DALZIEL, M.A., min. in 1563.—[*Comps. Sub Coll. of Thirds, Dumfries.*]

1563 PATRICK LOCH, reader in 1563.—[*Comps. Sub Coll. of Thirds, Dumfries.*]

1567 WILLIAM THOMSON, M.A., pres. to vicarage 26th Nov. 1580 on death of John Row. His son, John, pres. to vicarage of Urr 1602.

1619 THOMAS MELVILLE, his son, Thomas, min. of Cadder; his daughs.—Bessie (marr. (1) William Taylor, wright, Dumfries, (2) Andrew Hunter, merchant, Dumfries); Margaret (marr. John Thomson, portioner of Kirkland of Terregles); Jean (marr. Thomas Cunyngham, glover, Edinburgh); Lilias.—[*Dumfries Sas.*, 2nd March 1659.]

1690 ROBERT PATON, line 4, for "1691" read "1690."

1899 JAMES STEWART, his son, James Main, min. of Balgay and John Street, Glasgow; his wife, Margaret Waddell Main, died 28th July 1942. He died 24th Nov. 1944.

TINWALD

There was in the church an altar dedicated to the Virgin Mary.

15.. CHARLES GEDDES, died before 1604.

1604 ALEXANDER THOMSON, pres. 27th Jan. 1604.—[*Pres.*, iii, 386.]

1777 JOHN WILLIAMSON, lines 1–3, for "probably son," etc., read "son of David W., overseer to Messrs Crawford at Wanlockhead."

1847 JAMES VALLANCE, pres. by Crown 24th Oct. 1846; his daugh., Margaret Rebecca, died at Gorebridge 1st Sept. 1923.

1889 GEORGE SCOTT KERR, died 22nd Jan. 1937; his wife, Lucy Edmondson, died 16th Dec. 1946; his son, Hugh George, M.B., Ch.B., Eccleshall, Stafford.

TRAILFLAT and DUNGRIE

1566 SIR JOHN SINCLAIR, pres. to vicarage pensionary 8th April and 20th May 1566 by William, Commendator of Kelso, vacant by death of David Welsh; died before 5th Aug. 1591.—[*Reg. Sec. Sig.*, xxxv, 46; lxii, 123.]

1591 JOHN GLOVER, son of Martin G. in Woodsyde of Hempisfield, reader, pres. to vicarage of Dungrie 5th Aug. 1591 on death of Sir John Sinclair.—[*Reg. Sec. Sig.*, lxii, 123.]

1627 GEORGE REDDICK or RODDICK, marr. Barbara Spottiswoode.—[*G. R. Sas.*, xxi, 138; 21st May 1627.]

TORTHORWALD

1586 JAMES RAMSEY, pres. to vicarage April 1582 on death of James Wallace.—[*Reg. Pres. Bene.*, ii, 72.]

1883 GEORGE LAURIE FOGO, licen. 18th Nov. 1870; his widow, Fanny Elizabeth Blagden, died 18th Sept. 1930.

1894 JAMES MARJORIBANKS CAMPBELL, died 12th Jan. 1949; his wife, Edith Leonora Gillott, died 21st June 1932, and in her memory Mr Campbell erected a bell-ringers' shelter.

TROQUEER

The church was dedicated to St Convellus, the Welsh Conguell, like Convill, Cynwell, Irish Connall, a disciple of St Mungo.—[Watson's *Celtic Place Names*, 168.]

1563 NINIAN DALZIEL, min. in 1563.—[*Comps. Sub Coll. of Thirds, Dumfries*, etc.]

1570 JOHN HALLIDAY, reader 1570–2.—[*Comps. Sub Coll. of Thirds, Dumfries*, etc.]

1574 JOHN FULLARTON, vicar.—[*Acts and Dec.*, liii, 557.]

1577 ADAM MURRAY, pres. to vicarage on death of Robert Martin; was nephew of William Somerville, vicar of Kirkbean.—[*Reg. Pres. Bene.*, ii, (4), 59.]

1615 HERBERT GLEDSTANES, probably schoolmaster, Kirkcudbright, 9th Feb. 1592. Marr. Janet Cunningham and had issue—Thomas, writer, Edinburgh.—[*Dumfries Sas.*, 15th Feb. 1637.]

1668 JAMES MAIR, marr. Margaret, daugh. of John Crichton of Crawfordston and widow of William Lawrie of Ingliston, merchant in Dumfries; she remarr. Walter Gledstanes, min. of New Abbey.

1683 JAMES GLENDINNING, amanuensis to James, Bishop of Galloway, 17th Dec. 1680; died August 1713.

1876 JAMES ALEXANDER CAMPBELL, died at Edinburgh 19th June 1924.

1918 JOHN WILSON, awarded the Norwegian Freedom Medal 1947; trans. assistant and successor from St Paul's, Perth; his daugh., Margaret Craig (marr. 20th Oct, 1937 John Harry Whittaker Glover, Newhaven, Edinburgh).

URR

Situated in the Diocese of Glasgow, the church, called the Church of St Constantine of Hur, was confirmed to Holyrood Abbey by William de Bondington, Bishop of Glasgow, on 20th April 1250. There was in the parish another church, dedicated to St Bride, and called the Church of St Brigit of Blacket and Loublaket. About 1160 it was granted to Holyrood Abbey by Uchtred, son of Fergus, lord of Galloway, with confirmation by Ingelram, Bishop of Glasgow, Alan, son of Rolland the Constable, Eustache Baliol, and others. Little is known of the church but it was independent of Urr.—[*Charters of Holyrood*, 28, 41–2, 56–7, 61, 68, 69; *Cal. Papal Regs., Letters*, x, 547, xi, 304.]

1563 JOHN BROWN, reader, 1563-8, vicar and reader.—[*Comps. Sub Coll. of Thirds, Dumfries*, etc.]

1573 WILLIAM PENNYCUICK, M.A., vicar 31st July 1573, when he was also rector of Pennycuik (*q.v.*) and Provost of the Collegiate Church of Kirk of Fields.—[*Cal. of Charters*, x, 2287.]

1602 JOHN THOMSON, M.A., son of William T., vicar of Terregles, pres. to vicarage 1602.—[*Reg. Sec. Sig.*, lxxii, 73.]

1641 GEORGE GLEDSTANES, marr. Jane Porteous, widow of Charles Archibald, min. of Kirkbean.—[*Dumfries Tests.*, Daniel Wallace, 20th May 1690.]

1666 JOHN LYON, adm. 1st May 1665; marr. (1) –. Leslie and had issue—John, min. of Old Greyfriars; (2) Emilia Nisbet and had issue—Thomas, chyrurgeon in Shaws, died 1st July 1736; William, probably apprenticed to George Langland, surgeon apothecary, Edinburgh, 29th July 1724.

1770 JAMES MUIRHEAD, line 27, for "Vacceram" read "Vacerram."

1855 JOHN MACRAE SANDILANDS, pres. by Crown 17th May 1855.

1892 DAVID FREW, LL.D. (St Andrews, 28th Sept. 1937); retired in favour of assistant and successor, June 1937; died 4th May 1946; his wife, Jeanie Lymont, daugh. of John Boyd, Coltness, died 28th Oct. 1938. Addl. publication—*A Young Borderer* (a Memoir of Captain A. S. Young Herries), (Edin., 1928).

PRESBYTERY OF PENPONT

At the union of the Churches in 1929 this Presbytery ceased to exist, the parishes being transferred to the Presbytery of Dumfries, except Wanlockhead, which was transferred to the Presbytery of Lanark.

CLOSEBURN

The name has other forms, Kylosbern, Killcosburne, and is held to commemorate Osbern, an English saint. There is another saint, Osbran, anchorite and bishop of Cluain Creamha in Roscommon, who died in 752.—[Watson's *Celtic Place Names*, 167.]

1612 ALEXANDER FLEMING, his son, Malcolm.—[*G. R. Sas.*, 23rd Nov. 1643, liii, 429.]

1815 CHARLES ANDERSON, ord. to Gask 22nd April, not Aug.

1872 DAVID OGILVY RAMSAY, his son, David, died from the effects of an accident at Dumfries 20th Dec. 1925; his daugh., Anne Maxwell, died 22nd Jan. 1937.

1910 CHARLES ROLLAND RAMSAY, M.A. (Edinburgh, 1886), died at Abbey Town, Cumberland, 28th Aug. 1939. His sons—Norman and Ian, both Captains; his daugh., Ellen Margaret Sibbald (marr. 7th Feb. 1927 John Hubert Graham, farmer, The Gale, Cumberland); his widow, Agnes Maud Campbell, died 26th June 1940.

DALGARNO

The church was granted to Holyrood by Edgar, son of Deferald, in the time of William the Lion.—[*Holyrood Charters*, 43.]

1568 JAMES WILLIAMSON, designated min. 1567–8.—[*Edin. Tests.*, i, 11, Jan. 1567–8.]

DURRISDEER

There was in the church an altar dedicated to the Virgin Mary.

1567 JAMES HAMILTON, seems to be identical with John Hamilton, M.A., sub-chanter of Glasgow, who was parson in 1567 and died 1570.—[*Comps. Sub Coll. of Thirds, Dumfries*, etc.]

1567 LYON BROWN, pres. to parsonage and vicarage 25th Jan. 1574–5 on dem. of Peter Young.—[*Reg. Pres. Bene.*, ii, (4), 29.]

1570 PETER YOUNG, M.A., his pres. to parsonage and vicarage and sub-chanter of Glasgow 5th Aug. 1570 on death of John Hamilton.—[*Reg. Pres. Bene.*, ii, (2), 1.]

1575 JAMES LINDSAY, pres. to parsonage and vicarage 18th Dec. 1575 on dem. of Peter Young.

1579 JAMES BRYSON, pres. on dem. of Peter Young.—[*Reg. Pres. Bene.*, ii, 22.]

1656 ALEXANDER STRANG, his son, Patrick, apprenticed to Paul Meldrum, corset-maker, Edinburgh, 14th Sept. 1670.

1683 JOHN ALEXANDER, resident in St Cuthbert's parish, Edinburgh, 17th Nov. 1694.—*St Cuthbert's Poll Tax Roll.*]

1771 JOHN McKELL, his diary in Museum, Thornhill.

DAVID LITTLE JARDINE, died Bournemouth 14th Feb. 1929. Marr. (2) 9th Oct. 1917 Violet (died 26th March 1944), eldest daugh. of Henry Candlish, M.A., Alnwick, Northumberland; his daugh., Helen, M.B., Ch.B., London.
1894

GAVIN KERRILL MACKAY, M.A., ord. A. and S. 1st June 1920; trans. to Dalziel 24th June 1924.
1920

THOMAS HARPER, born Glasgow 30th May 1893, son of Alexander R. H., J.P., and Agnes Murray; educ. at High School and Glasgow Univ., M.A. (1916), B.D. (1920), Ph.D. (1928), and at New York Theological Seminary, S.T.M. (1923); licen. by Presb. of Perth May 1920; assistant Partick; ord. 20th Oct. 1924; trans. to Eastwood 6th Feb. 1930. He marr. 23rd June 1931 Margaret Simpson, daugh. of John M. Ross, and has issue—Alexander Murray, born 31st May 1933; John Ross, born 20th March 1935.
1924

GLENCAIRN

JOHN JAMESON, exhorter; designated vicar-pensioner 10th April 1574; seems therefore to have been in office prior to 1560 and to have conformed; probably identical with John Jameson who was presented to the vicarage of Dunscore in 1573, was reader there 1574–85, and became min. there in 1586.—[*Laing Charters*, 890; *Comps. Sub Coll. of Thirds, Dumfries.*]
1567

SIR ROBERT HOUSTON, vicar 22nd June 1574.—[*Reports Hist. MSS. Commiss.*, App. 9, 26.]
1574

JOHN JAMESON, min. at Dunscore, had also charge here in 1586; may be identical with foregoing John Jameson.
1586

JOHN BROWN, line 9, delete "John of Ingliston"; his daughs.—Mary (marr. Robert Maitland of Eccles); Sarah (marr. (2) James Grierson of Capenoch).—[*Dumfries Sas.*, 30th Nov. 1642.]
1589

WILLIAM BROWN, servitor to Thomas, Earl of Haddington; line 10, for "James" read "John"; line 12, for "uncle" read "father." See *Douglas of Morton*, 314.
1632

1692 GEORGE BOYD. He marr.

PATRICK BORROWMAN, his daugh., Sophia Patricia, died 23rd July 1936.
1837

ROBERT HOME, line 3, for "Dec." read "Oct."
1864

JOHN AGNEW FINLAY, dem. 4th Oct. 1921; was min. at Cairo; D.D. (Edinburgh, 2nd July 1931); died 25th Aug. 1941.
1914

JAMES CAMPBELL, trans. from Kingston, Glasgow (*q.v.*), 15th May 1922; trans. to Durrisdeer 5th June 1930. His son, William Craigie Drysdale, born 2nd Nov. 1917, Missionary, Assam, under Colonial Committee.
1922

KEIR

WILLIAM MENZIES, licen. 29th Aug. 1821.
1827

DAVID BAYNE JARDINE, his son, Brigadier Christian West, C.B.E. (1944); his widow, Helen Octavia Tapson, died 8th Jan 1948, aged 92.
1870

KIRKCONNEL

The church was dedicated to St Convallus, Old Welsh *Conguall*, later *Cinvall*, *Cynwall*, Irish *Conall*, a disciple of St Mungo. The ruins of the old church, with the Well of St Conal near at hand, are situated about 2 miles from Kirkconnel village. On the farm of Rig there is a field called Libry Park, which may denote that it was the site of a hospital for lepers.—[Watson's *Celtic Place Names*, 169; Wilson's *Annals of Sanquhar*, 40, 42, 43.]

WILLIAM BLACKADDER, M.A., vicar and exhorter 1561–89.—[*Reg. Sec. Sig.*, lx, 74; *Comps. Sub Coll. of Thirds, Dumfries*, etc.]
1560

1569 JOHN FULLARTON, reader 1568, exhorter 1568–72, vicar and min. 1576; pres. on death of Sir David Maxwell; mentioned as at Troqueer in 1574; died 27th April 1595; had issue—William and Bessie.—[*Comps. Sub Coll. of Thirds, Dumfries*, etc.; *Reg. Pres. Bene.*, i, 19; *Acts and Dec.*, liii, 557; *Edin. Tests.*, 5th Jan. 1596.]

1579 SIR WILLIAM BROWN, vicar pensioner, died at Edinburgh 24th Nov. 1579.—[*Edin. Tests.*, vii, 208.]

1605 ROBERT BIGGERT, his pres. in 1605 was upon the death of John Fullarton.—[*Reg. Sec. Sig.*, lxxiv, 403.]

1732 PETER RAE, his son James, farmer, Nether Farding, was agent for Queensberry and not Buccleuch.

1899 CHARLES FORBES CHARLESON, licen. 1st May 1895; his son's name Conal, not Connell. Publication—"Notes on the Site of a Pre-Norman Chapel of St Conal in Upper Nithsdale," *Trans. Scot. Eccl. Socy.*, ix, part iii, 1929–30.

MORTON

1560 ARCHIBALD MENZIES, M.A., acted as exhorter and reader, holding parsonage and vicarage 1563 and 1572; also at Colvend 1572.—[*Comps. Sub Coll. of Thirds, Dumfries*, etc.]

1572 ROBERT CUSSANE, reader.—[*Comps. Sub Coll. of Thirds, Dumfries*, etc.]

1579 ARCHIBALD DOUGLAS, pres. to vicarage 1st July 1579 on death of Archibald Menzies.—[*Reg. Pres. Bene.*, ii, 19.]

1608 SIR JOHN MORTON, died before 11th Oct. 1608, when he is called last vicar.—[*Reg. Sec. Sig.*]

1687 THOMAS HENDERSON of Broomfield, son of Thomas H., min. of Gretna.—[*Dumfries Sas.*, v, 447.]

1691 PATRICK FLINT, his son, William apprenticed to Andrew Torrance, wright, Edinburgh.

1809 DAVID SMITH, son of William S., farmer, Gatehills, Kirkpatrick-Fleming. He was at presentation Governor of George Watson's Hospital, Edinburgh. Left in MS. a memoir of James Galt, min. of Gretna 1730–87.

1885 JAMES HONEYMAN OSWALD, licen. April 1883, died 15th April 1939; his widow, Mary Grace Ramsay, died 20th Nov. 1943; his son, John Alexander Ramsay, died 11th Feb. 1933, Lieut. K.O.S.B.

PENPONT

1541 SIR ROBERT WELSH, vicar 1541, afterwards reader 1567.

1561 JOHN TAYLOR, vicar, reader and exhorter 1561–9.—[*Comps. Coll. Gen. of Thirds*, 94.]

1578 WILLIAM TAYLOR, vicar, designated min. 27th July and 26th Dec. 1578.—[*Edin. Tests*, vi, 219, 285.]

1636 SAMUEL OUSTANE, his son, Samuel, afterwards merchant in Virginia; his daugh., Mary (marr. Francis Herries of Lambholm).—[*Acts and Dec., Dal.*, lxxxvii, 25th Jan. 1683.]

1693 JAMES MURRAY, marr. Isabel, daugh. of John Laurie, schoolmaster, Kirkcudbright.—[*Deeds*, 1st Nov. 1706.]

1736 JOHN COLLOW, his son, James, died in Tobago 1795.

1845 JAMES GRAHAM, his daughs.—Elizabeth, died 14th Oct. 1920; Isabella, died Cummertrees 13th Jan. 1924; Margaret, died at Cummertrees 21st March 1925.

1870 ANDREW PATON, died at Alstonlea, Kinross, 21st July 1921.

1909 JAMES JOHNSTONE PRYDE, became Chaplain to the Forces; adm. to Morebattle 24th April 1919.

1917 WILLIAM COCHRAN CONN, trans. and adm. (assist. and suc.) from Coylton (*q.v.*) 13th July 1917; died 13th Aug. 1945.

SANQUHAR

Line 6, after "Logan" read "vicar of Colvend."

The present church was built in 1823–4 on the site of the medieval church whose foundations have been outlined by flagstones. In the church there were an altar dedicated to the Virgin Mary; an altar dedicated to the Holy Rood; and an altar dedicated to the Holy Blood, founded in 1519 by John Logan, vicar of Colvend, a native of Sanquhar. In the south-west corner of the present church there is the effigy of a churchman, which bore the name of "The Saint of the Choir." St Bride's Well was situated in the midst of a grove called Welltrees behind the knowe at Broomfield. It is now covered by the railway, but its waters have burst forth in another direction. In the vicinity of Newark there was a chapel dedicated to St Nicholas, at the site of which about twenty years ago there was discovered the sculptured effigy of a bishop, in robes and with crozier, and at his feet a figure presenting a scroll. The head and arms are missing. Near the farmhouse of Dalpeddar there is an old burial ground called Chapel Yards, the site of a chapel which is said to have been dedicated to St Peter. There was another chapel in Eliock House which was in existence till in the middle of the 18th century extensive alterations to the house led to its disappearance; and still another was situated at the farmstead of Tower, where there survives the Chapel Well. The Chapel Hill at Carco on Crawick Water, and the Chapel Rig and Our Lady's Well at Knockenstob, indicate two other chapels. Tradition tells of a chapel and religious house for women at the farmhouse of Orchard, and of a religious settlement at Goosehill, formerly Olive Hill. In the burgh, on the site behind the town hall, there was a house designated the Mansion House of St John the Baptist, but of its exact nature nothing appears to be known. Sanquhar Hospital, said to have been dedicated to St Mary Magdalene, was situated near the farmhouse of Newark. It was in existence before 28th Aug. 1296, when Bartholomew de Eglisham, chapeleyn, warden of "the new Place at Senerwar" (Sanquhar), swore fealty to Edward I.—[Wilson's *Annals of Sanquhar*, 9–10, 36–7, 39–40, 41–2; *Cal. of Docs. Rel. to Scotland*, ii, 206.]

SIR THOMAS FLEMING, was chaplain of the Chaplainry of the Holy Cross, 13th May 1559.—[*Reg. of Abbrev. of Feu Charters of Church Lands*, ii, 207.]
1559

ROBERT CRICHTON, M.A., parson 17th Jan. 1554 and 20th Dec. 1565; was chaplain of St Nicholas called the Newark; died 15th June 1570.—[*Reg. of Deeds*, i, 56; xii, 261; *Edin. Tests*, ii, 159.]
1560

JOHN YOUNG, reader, called vicar pensionary in 1574; died before 20th April 1583.—[*Reg. of Abbrev. of Feu Charters of Church Lands*, ii, 135.]
1567

JAMES BLACKWOOD, app. before 28th March 1576, but a year later was accused of "brooking" both Sanquhar and Saline, and serving "not ane"; pleaded that he dared not go to Sanquhar for fear of his life to work there, and asked to be allowed to serve at Saline till he got security of Sanquhar and not compelled to resign either; ord. by Assembly to "travell" at Saline till next Assembly and meantime John Fullarton to support Kirk of Sanquhar upon his costs, and the Commissioners of the County ordained to admonish the tutor of Sanquhar (William Crichton) to make no impediment or trouble to Blackwood in using his office and serving Sanquhar; still "brooked" Saline 11th June 1578, when he was ordered by Assembly to demit the same; entered at Sanquhar probably soon after and was deprived some time before 16th Dec. 1594 for diverse treasonable causes.—[*The Book of the Universal Kirk*, i, 386, 397, 424, 465, 472; *P. C. Reg.*, 30th June 1574, 23rd March 1576–7; *P. S. Reg.*, lxvii, 23, 36; *Reg. Abbrev. of Feu Charters of Church Lands*, ii, 133.]
1577

ROBERT HUNTER, pres. by the church to parsonage and vicarage 16th and 28th Dec. 1594 on dep. of James Blackwood, the patron, Lord
1594

Crichton of Sanquhar, having failed to present a lawful person in due time.—[*Reg. Sec. Sig.*, lxvii, 28, 36.]

1666 JAMES KIRKWOOD, adm. before 1666, left at Revolution; adm. Rector of Magheracross and Prebendary of Kelskeery, Co. Fermanagh, 1692. Marr. daugh. of George Ker, provost of Sanquhar and Chamberlain of Queensberry.—[Simpson's *History of Sanquhar*; Leslie's *Clogher Clergy*; *Gleanings among the Mountains*.]

1738 JOHN SANDILANDS, son of John S., min. of Dolphinton, and Margaret Johnston.

1785 WILLIAM RANKEN, marr. Margaret, daugh. of Robert Barker in Castlemains.

1845 JOHN INGLIS, schoolmaster, Maybole; his daugh., Agnes Hutchison, died 24th Feb. 1930.

1881 ARCHIBALD EDMISTON DEWAR, born 2nd Oct. 1856.

1888 JAMES RICHMOND WOOD, licen. 9th June 1880, died 1st May 1929.

KIRKBRIDE

1560 THOMAS WEIR, reader 1560.—[*Comps. Sub Coll. of Thirds, Dumfries*, etc.]

1563 JOHN DOUGLAS, rector 30th Oct. 1563.—[Sir T. Johnson's *Prot. Book*, 685.]

1652 THOMAS SHIELS, Chaplain or student of divinity to William Douglas of Morton.

TYNRON

1561 ROBERT WELSH, reader designated "Dene" and held the vicarage in 1560 and conformed, died in June 1568; had a brother, Sir William W.—[*Comps. Coll. Gen. of Thirds*, 1561; *Edin. Tests*, i, 344; *Reg. Sec. Sig.*, xxxvii, 72.]

1589 WILLIAM TAYLOR, pres. to vicarage 28th June 1568 on death of Robert Welsh; min. 27th July and 24th Nov. 1578.—[*Edin. Tests*, vi, 219, 285.]

1664 ROBERT RAMSAY, his widow, Katherine Alexander, buried in Greyfriars, Edinburgh, 13th Dec. 1697.

1871 DAVID COUPAR, his widow, Christina Jane Clark, died 26th Feb. 1925; his daughs.—Evelyn Susanna, died at Traquair 29th Oct. 1927; Edith Hylda Hope, died at Traquair 8th June 1930.

1902 SAMUEL GILFILLAN CARMICHAEL, died 11th March 1938.

WANLOCKHEAD

1732 ALEXANDER HENDERSON, min. in 1732.

1734 JOHN LAWRIE, preacher 1734, received £5 for pastoral duties there.—[*Trans. Dumfries and Galloway Antiq. Society*, xviii, 94.]

1800 JAMES RITCHIE, dep. 25th May 1802.—[*Diary of Rev. John Wightman of Kirkmahoe*, unpublished.]

1848 JAMES LAIDLAW, his daugh., Isabella Sutton, died at Kippen 26th Jan. 1932.

1886 CHARLES PATRICK BLAIR, died 8th Nov. 1923.

1924 NORMAN FARQUHAR ORR, trans. from Stanley 16th May 1924; dem. 6th July 1926; afterwards min. at Buncrana, Donegal.

1926 ROWELLYAN RAMSAY, B. Comm., ord. 21st Oct. 1926; trans. to Ruthrieston, Aberdeen, 8th Nov. 1928.

1929 THOMAS EDMUND HILL JONES, formerly min. of Deerness (*q.v.*), trans. from Portsoy 29th March 1929; dem. 25th Oct. 1932 and went to Belfast; died 23rd Feb. 1943. Marr. (2) 25th Nov. 1931 Charlotte Rowe. He had issue—Arthur, born May 1902; Gladys Eleanor Agnes, born 1st Sept. 1912; Edmund, S. S., born 1st March 1934; Norman Charles Patten, born 27th April 1935; Marjory Elizabeth Lucy, born 27th June 1936, died 30th April 1937; Harold Douglas Theodore, born 30th Dec. 1938.

SYNOD OF GALLOWAY

PRESBYTERY OF STRANRAER

ARDWALL

1902 ANDREW MUIRHEAD BARR, died 22nd Nov. 1933; his widow, Rachel Morris, died 30th July 1944.

ARNSHEEN

1863 THOMAS JARDINE, his son, William Hugh, died Coatbridge 8th Oct. 1942.

1895 WILLIAM GORDON, dem. 1937, died 24th Feb. 1944; his son, Arthur Currie, min. of Kells; his daugh., Mary, M.B., Ch.B.; his widow, Alison Jollie, died 9th Nov. 1945.

BALLANTRAE

1571 JOHN CUNNINGHAM, pres. to vicarage 23rd April 1571 on death of Andrew Oliphant; trans. to Dailly 1573.—[*Reg. Pres. Bene.*, i, (2), 16].

1658 JOHN CROOKS, marr. Margaret, daugh. of James Simson, min. of Bathgate, and had issue—Patrick; Catherine.—[*G. R. Sas.*, vi, 75.]

1687 JOHN WHITE, intruded at Aberdour, Deer, 1694; see also Coylton.

1830 JOHN MILROY, his daugh., Euphemia Catherine (marr. 6th Nov. 1863).

1913 ROLLO RUSSELL GRANT SUTHERLAND, trans. to Skelmorlie 11th Feb. 1921.

1921 JAMES HOUSTON BAXTER, M.A., B.D., ord. 21st July 1921; app. to Chair of Ecclesiastical History, St Andrews, and adm. 10th Nov. 1922.

1923 MUNRO SOMERVILLE, trans. from Newhaven 5th April 1923; trans. to Garvock 13th Dec. 1928.

1929 JOHN CHISHOLM COCKBURN, born at Mansewood, Glasgow, 6th Dec. 1903, son of William Allan C. and Jeanie Paul Chisholm; educ. Hutcheson's Boys' Grammar School and Univ. of Glasgow, M.A. (1925), B.D. (1928); licen. by Presb. of Paisley, 2nd May 1928; assistant Cambuslang; ord. 2nd May 1929; min. of united charge, former parish of (Innertig) and U.F. (Ardstinchar) from 21st Dec. 1930; trans. to Jordanhill 26th April 1944.

COLMONELL

The church along with the Chapel of St Constantine and a caracute of land was granted to Holyrood Abbey by Uchtred, son of Fergus, lord of Galloway, *cir.* 1161–74. On 28th Aug. 1467 Pope Paul II granted indulgence to those visiting the Chapel of St Ninian near Ardstinchar Castle, and giving for the conservation of its buildings and the better supply of its books, chalices and other ecclesiastical ornaments. There was also a chapel at Mains of Carleton.—[*Cal. Papal Regs.*, xii, 580; *Charters of Holyrood*, 19, 42; *Retours*, v, 25.]

1568 JAMES GREIG, min. here, pres. to parsonage and vicarage 1568; died before 21st July 1585.—[*Reg. Pres. Bene.*, i, 13; *Reg. Sec. Sig.*, ii, 178.]

1570 JOHN DAVIDSON, principal of Glasgow University, held the vicarage 6th May 1570.—[*Monumenta Univ. Glasgow*, i, 82.]

1585 JAMES GRAHAM, pres. to parsonage and vicarage 21st July 1585.—[*Reg. Sec. Sig.*, ii, 178.]

1850 WILLIAM DILL, his daughs.—Elizabeth, died at Seble, Hedingham, Essex, 1st July 1918; Euphemia Maclagan (Mrs Johnston), died at Glasgow 7th May 1940.

1884 JAMES McFADZEN, died 9th May 1925; his wife, Anne Templeton, died same day; his daugh., Kathleen Constance (marr. 4th July 1936 Alexander John Gibson, D.S.O., M.B., Ch.B.).

1925 JAMES BROWN, born Rosewell 20th Dec. 1896; son of James B., Largs, and Janet Reid; educ. at Lasswade H.G. School, Univ. of Edinburgh, M.A. (1918), B.D. (1921), and Oxford; licen. by Presb. of Dalkeith May 1921; assistant Peebles; ord. 17th Sept. 1925. Served in Great War with Highland Light Infantry and Scottish Rifles.

GLENAPP

1894 EWEN MACDONELL MACGREGOR, died 17th Dec. 1940; his widow, Wilhelmina Fisher, died 16th March 1947.

INCH

1567 CUTHBERT ADAIR, exhorter 1563, designated min. 1568.—[*Comps. Sub Coll. of Thirds, Dumfries*, etc.; *Edin. Tests.*, i, 10th May 1568.]

1568 SIR WILLIAM MacDOWALL, vicar 20th Aug. 1559 and 6th Feb. 1566, may have conformed. See Dalmeny.—[Grote's *Prot. Book*, 155; *Reg. Mag. Sig.*, iv, 1763; *Comps. Sub Coll. of Thirds, Dumfries*, etc.]

1601 JOHN WATSON, died 31st Dec. 1639; John, his son; a daugh. (marr. Alexander Blair).

1680 J. ROSS, parson of Saulsett, signs an Episcopal Charter as a member of Chapter of Whithorn 17th Dec. 1680.

1695 WILLIAM WILSON, his daugh., Agnes (marr. Gilbert Adair, merchant, Stranraer).—[*Reg. of Deeds Dal.*, clvii, 2nd May 1745.]

1762 ANDREW ROSS, his son, James.

1788 PETER FERGUSSON, pres. 24th Dec. 1787.

1862 JOHN McCALMAN, pres. by Crown 26th Jan. 1862; his widow, Mary Melville, died 15th Jan. 1929; his daugh., Ursula, died 5th March 1931.

1872 JOHN SERVICE, pres. by Crown 29th Feb. 1872.

1879 JAMES AIKMAN PATON, licen. 16th May 1878; his wife, Katherine Ann Malcolm, died 26th Oct. 1919.

1916 BRODIE SMITH GILFILLAN, trans. to Wallacetown, Ayr, 5th Nov. 1924.

1925 ALEXANDER WRIGHT STEVENSON, trans. from Balshagray (*q.v.*) 12th March 1925; died 24th Dec. 1925; his son, John Alexander, min. of Coulter, editor of *Life and Work* 1946.

1926 JOHN YOUNG CLARK, born Cambuslang 22nd Dec. 1882; son of Robert C. and Ann Young; educ. at Kirkhill Public School and Univ. of Glasgow; served in Royal Marine Engineers in Great War (one of six brothers with the colours); licen. by Presb. of Hamilton 31st March 1919; ord. to Buenos Ayres 12th April 1920; adm. to Laurieston, Glasgow, 3rd June 1924; trans. and adm. 23rd Sept. 1926; trans. to Braemar 14th May 1931; trans. to Colonsay 3rd Nov. 1943. Marr. 2nd Oct. 1919 Edith Graham (died Nov. 1948), daugh. of William Abercrombie and Margaret Edith Sims.

(*Charges united 2nd Aug.* 1931.)

SAULSEAT

1567 JAMES THOMSON, reader, in office 1563.—[*Comps. Sub Coll. of Thirds, Dumfries*, etc.]

KIRKCOLM

The church was granted to Sweetheart Abbey in 1275 by Devorgilla, lady of Galloway, and about 1401 by Archibald, 4th Earl of Douglas. The chapel at Killiemaccuddican was dedicated to St Mochuter, the name being Cill-Mo-Chudagon, Mochutu's Church, Mochester of Rathan and Lismore, who died in 637.—[*Maxwell Monuments*, 13; *Book of Caerlaverock*, ii, 417; Watson's *Celtic Place Names*, 166.]

1684 JAMES NASMYTH, his son, James, apprenticed to John Hepburn, apothecary, Edinburgh, 21st June 1693.

1862 THOMAS BARTY, his widow, Katherine Gray Allan, died at Edinburgh 10th Dec. 1928.

1898 ALBERT TARBETT, his daugh., Dorothy Allan (marr. (1) 28th Feb. 1934 John Carlyle Conn, insurance broker, Ayr, (2) 22nd April 1947 Alastair James Clark).

KIRKMAIDEN

The patron saint was St Medana, whose day was on 5th July. The name may be taken, therefore, as the Latinised form of M'Etain, for Mo'-Etain, the virgin of Tuam Noa, whose day is the same. Near Maryport there was a chapel dedicated to the Virgin Mary.

1563 JOHN TROUGHTON, exhorter 1563.—[*Comps. Sub Coll. of Thirds, Dumfries*, etc.]

1562 JOHN WHITE, held vicarage 1568, called Dene 1562 when reader.—[*Comps. Sub Coll. of Thirds, Dumfries*, etc.]

1579 SYMON JOHNSTON, pres. to vicarage 3rd March 1579–80 on death of Dean John White.—[*Reg. Pres. Bene.*, ii, 31; *Comps. Sub Coll. of Thirds, Dumfries*, etc.]

1593 ADAM THOMSON, pres. to vicarage 24th Nov. 1593 on death of George Niven.—[*Reg. Sec. Sig.*, lxvi, 18.]

665 JAMES McGILL, his widow, Elizabeth Inglis, resident with her son James in Lady Yester's par. 7th Nov. 1694.—[*Lady Yester's Poll Tax Roll*, 17.]

1881 DAVID RITCHIE WILLIAMSON, died 23rd Jan. 1940.

1915 JAMES MACMORLAND, trans. to Tarbat 11th Nov. 1920.

1921 JACKSON LOUDON McFADDEN, M.A., ord. 7th April 1921; trans. to Fearn (Ross) 2nd June 1925.

1925 ROBERT HILL RICHMOND, trans. from Shapinsay (*q.v.*) 29th Oct. 1925; trans. to Coull 4th July 1928.

1928 JOHN ADAMSON HONEY, born 26th March 1900, son of John Adamson H., min. of Inchture; educ. at Univ. of St Andrews, M.A. (3rd Oct. 1924); licen. by Presb. of St Andrews 1927; assistant at St Michael's, Dumfries, 1927; ord. 27th Sept. 1928; trans. to Cargill 9th Nov. 1933. Marr. 2nd Aug. 1933 Marion, daugh. of John Boog Colledge, Cairngaan, Drummore, and has issue—John Sime Colledge, born 9th March 1940; Margaret Elizabeth Cochrane, born 9th April 1942.

(*Charges united 9th Aug.* 1931.)

LESWALT

1561 SIR WILLIAM MacDOWALL, vicar 1561–72; also at Dalmeny (*q.v.*).—[*Comps. Sub Coll. of Thirds, Dumfries*, etc.]

1563 THOMAS MACALEXANDER, reader 1563–9. — [*Comps. Sub Coll. of Thirds, Dumfries*, etc.]

1567 WILLIAM BARBOUR, adm. exhorter 26th May 1567; pres. 21st May 1568 to two prebends of Collegiate Kirk of Restalrig, on death of Melville Spittal and Sir Archibald Ellam.—[*Reg. Sec. Sig.*, xxxvii, 62; *Reg. Pres. Bene.*, i, 10.]

1574 NICOL McCLELLAN, M.A., in office 1591.—[*Reg. Abbrev. Feu Charters of Church Lands*, ii, 91.]

RICHARD VAUSS (Wauss), son natural of Patrick V. of Barnbarroch, pres. to vicarage 3rd March 1578–80 on death of Sir William MacDowall.—[*Reg. Pres. Bene.*, ii, 31.]
1579

JOHN MOFFAT, yr., reader 1584, as min. of Kirkcowan pres. to vicarage here 22nd April 1586 in succession to late Sir Nicol McClellan; as min. pres. to vicarage of Tostertoun and Kirkmaiden Kirk and parish on death of Sir Michael Hawthorn.—[*Reg. Pres. Bene.*, ii, 31; *Comps. Sub Coll. of Thirds, Dumfries.* etc.; *Reg. Sec. Sig.*, liii, 68.]
1590

WILLIAM SOMERVELL, had issue—William, born 1688; Thomas, rector of Myross, Co. Cork, born 1689; Judith (marr. William Cameron of Lochbar, Dean in Church of England).—[Burke's *Landed Gentry, Ireland*.]
1668

THOMAS ELDER, marr. (1) Sara Grierson (died 1707), sister of Homer G., surgeon apothecary in Dumfries.—[*Wigtoun Tests.*]
1731

THOMAS BLIZZARD BELL, his daugh., Isabella Ross, died at Worthing 19th July 1937.
1841

FREDERICK JOHN BOUTEVILLE JOHNSTON, assistant Burntisland; pres. by Crown 3rd Dec. 1873.
1874

JOHN BALFOUR ROBERTSON, dem. 2nd June 1923; died Edinburgh 3rd Jan. 1944; his widow, Jessie Robertson Longmuir, died 1st April 1946.
1878

MATTHEW ROBERT DRYSDALE, born 26th June 1889; son of Robert Ringland D., min. of Creggan, Antrim, and Elizabeth Johnston; educ. at Sandymount Academical Institution, Dublin, Univ. of Dublin (Trinity) and Univ. of Edinburgh, B.A. (1911); served in Great War in Forth R.G.A. 1915–19; licen. by Presb. of Edinburgh 1921; assistant St Bernard's, Edinburgh; ord. 1st Nov. 1923; trans. to St John's, Kirkcaldy, 12th Nov. 1931; drowned in river Leven, near Leslie, 18th Sept. 1940. Marr. 23rd Oct. 1918 Lily, daugh. of Thomas Small. *s.p.*
1923

LOCHRYAN

JOHN McGUFFIE, his son, John, died 28th Jan. 1922.
1878

ALEXANDER MURRAY MACGREGOR, died 1st Nov. 1935; his widow, Margaret Campbell, died 14th Sept. 1937.
1886

NEW LUCE

ALEXANDER PEDEN, born 1626, licen. by Presb. of Biggar. Col. 2, line 29, for "Colinswood" read "Columwood or Colyumwood, now Coilshelm"; line 33, for "Ayr" read "Lugar"; 36, for "Sorn" read "Tenshillingside"; 37, for "28" read "6."
1659

JAMES CADDELL, line 4, for "Ballochmyle" read "Ballochyle."
1770

ANTHONY STEWART, line 2, for "2nd" read "27th."
1792

WILLIAM KERR, pres. by Crown 31st Aug. 1854.
1854

WILLIAM FORSYTH, pres. by Crown 11th Dec. 1862; his daugh., Elizabeth Isabella, died 17th Aug. 1934.
1863

JAMES FRANCIS GRAHAM, died 20th July 1948; his son, Gerard Francis, M.C., M.D., died 7th Oct. 1932.
1909

OLD LUCE or GLENLUCE

The church was dedicated to St Michael.

JOHN SANDERSON, exhorter 1563, styled Dean 1563, vicar pensioner before 1560, reader in 1574.—[*Comps. Sub Coll. of Thirds, Dumfries*, etc.]
1563

NINIAN McCLENOCHAN, pres. to vicar pensionary 12th Jan. 1592 on death of Dean John Sanderson.—[*Reg. Sec. Sig.*, lxv, 4.]
1578

ROBERT WALLACE, vicar and min., Jan. 1567, pres. to vicar pensionary 11th Feb. 1599–1608 vacant by deaths of Ninian McClenochan and Dean
1599

John Sanderson; pres. to vicarage of Girvan 5th Jan. 1602 but did not take office.—[*Reg. Sec. Sig.*, lxxii, 229, lxxi, 154.]

1684 JOHN INNES, adm. 1684, resident with his wife, Christian Walker, in Tron Parish, Edinburgh, 9th Nov. 1694.—[*Tron Poll Tax Roll*, 32.]

1694 ROBERT CAMPBELL, adm. 19th Dec. 1694.

1699 ROBERT COLVILLE, marr. Katherine, daugh. of Robert Westwood, burgess of Edinburgh.

1858 BRYCE FROOD, his widow, Agnes Bell, died 2nd Feb. 1918.

1881 JAMES FARQUHAR SMITH, his widow, Isabel Aitken, died 1st Aug. 1932.

1909 ALEXANDER TAYLOR HILL, dem. 6th Dec. 1926; adm. to Leswalt 5th Jan. 1933; dem. 1935; died 27th Jan. 1939. Marr. (2) 1st Jan. 1935 Euphemia, daugh. of –. Young, retired butcher, Scone.

1927 DAVID GALLOWAY, born 15th Dec. 1898; licen. by Presb. of Irvine 1926; assistant Irvine; ord. 11th May 1927. Marr. 30th April 1934 Helen Margaret McEwan and has issue—David Robert, born 28th April 1935; John Finlay, born 6th March 1944.

PORT PATRICK

1666 JOHN CALDWELL, son of John C., cordinar burgess of Glasgow; his daugh., Janet (marr. John Glen, tailor, Glasgow).

1832 ANDREW URQUHART, his daughs. —Elizabeth Morris, died 4th June 1918; Martha Hawthorn, died 19th July 1929; Sarah Comrie, died at Dumfries 3rd Feb. 1940.

1880 JAMES RUSSELL KENNEDY, licen. 5th July 1882; dem. 2nd Dec. 1931; died 11th Nov. 1933; his sons—Frederick, min. of Strathblane; Major-General Sir John Noble, K.C.V.O., K.B.E., Governor of Southern Rhodesia 1946; his widow, Sarah Maud Noble, died 20th Nov. 1941.

(*Charges united* 14*th Dec.* 1930.)

SHEUCHAN

1916 WILLIAM PORTER, trans. to Ordiquhell 31st May 1918.

1918 THOMAS FERGUSSON, born Kinbuck, Dunblane, 23rd Feb. 1874, son of John Bryden F. and Barbara McAllister; educ. at Kinbuck School, Stirling High School, Univ. of St Andrews, M.A. (1898), Edinburgh, B.D. (1900); licen. by Presb. of Edinburgh 19th May 1908; assistant Liberton, Kilsyth, St Thomas, Glasgow, Dalserf and Dalmarnock; ord. 6th Nov. 1918; died 21st June 1946.

STONEYKIRK or STEPHENKIRK

Kilasser in Stoneykirk is "Lassair's Church," Laisre, Lasrach, Lassar. There are various female saints of those names, and there is nothing to show which is intended here. In 1420–7 Alexander, Bishop of Galloway, appropriated the Church of Clayshant to the Capitular Mensa; and on 9th Aug. 1427 Pope Martin V gave mandate to the Provost of Lincluden to confirm the appropriation if he deemed it fit.—[Watson's *Celtic Place Names*, 167; *Cal. Papal Regs., Letters*, vii, 526.]

1556 SIR ROBERT WATSON, was vicar of Clayshant 26th Feb. 1556-7, and in office June–July 1573 and died before 18th Feb. 1580-1; may have conformed and acted as reader.—[*Reg. Great Seal*, iv, 1160; *Edin. Test.*, i, 309; *Reg. Sec. Seal*, xlvii, 83.]

1561 SIR NEILL McDOWELL, parson, vicar 1563.—[*Comps. Coll. Gen. Thirds.*]

1563 –. THOMSON, reader at Clayshant.—[*Comps. Sub Coll. of Thirds, Dumfries*, etc.]

1563 JOHN GIBSON, called min. 1563; exhorter 1568–71.—[*Comps. Sub Coll. of Thirds, Dumfries*, etc.]

1565 DONALD McCULLOCH, reader 1565.—[*Comps. Sub Coll. of Thirds, Dumfries*, etc.]

1574 JAMES LAW, reader at Clayshant.

1580 ARCHIBALD EGLINTON, pres. to vicarage 18th Feb. 1580–1.—[*Reg. Sec. Seal*, xlvii, 83.]

1584 PATRICK STIRLING, pres. to vicarage 5th May 1584 in succession to Sir Robert Watson.—[*Reg. Sec. Seal*, xlvii, 83.]

1585 ARCHIBALD ADAIR, son of Ninian Adair of Kinhilt, pres. to the vicarage of Torkingtoun 8th June 1585, vacant by dem. of Sir Michael Hawthorne.—[*Reg. Sec. Seal*, iii, 180.]

1588 JOHN MOFFAT, min. of Leswalt, pres. to vicarage of Tosterton and Kirkmaiden 7th Dec. 1594 on death of Sir Michael Hawthorn.—[*Reg. Sec. Sig.*, lxvii, 36.]

1595 HEW McDOWALL, parson 1595–7.—[*Comps. Sub Coll. of Thirds, Dumfries*, etc.]

1605 GILBERT POWER.—[*Gen. Reg. Sas.*, xliv, 50.]

1684 ROBERT BOWES (or Bowie), M.A., late min. at Stoneykirk, resident with his wife and child in Tron Parish, Edinburgh, 8th Nov. 1694.—[*Tron Poll Tax Roll.*]

1697 ROBERT CAMPBELL, delete sons Thomas and William; had issue—Robert; Hugh, apprenticed to William Blackwood, merchant, Edinburgh.—[*Edin. App. Reg.*]

1757 JOHN HUNTER, his daugh., Margaret (marr. pro. 16th April 1795 Alexander Leslie, flax dresser, Edinburgh).

1840 ROBERT McNEIL, pres. by Crown 11th Oct. 1939.

1844 JOHN JAMES CAMPBELL, pres. by Crown 18th Dec. 1843.

1858 JAMES DOUGALL, his son, James Julius, died at Aberdeen 13th June 1926.

1895 WILLIAM JAMES LOWRIE, died 27th April 1941.

TOSTERTOUN

1563 JAMES McCULLOCH, reader 1563.—[*Comps. Sub Coll. of Thirds, Dumfries*, etc.]

1576 JOHN GIBSON, min. of Stoneykirk, also in charge here 1576.

STRANRAER

1638 JOHN LIVINGSTON, line 3, for "3rd Aug." read "25th April."

1649 JOHN PARK, second son of Robert P., merchant, Glasgow.—[*Burgess Roll*, 23rd June 1647.]

1695 WALTER LAURIE, by Deed of 29th July 1736 because the charge was "destitute" of manse and glebe, and the stipend small, he mortified certain lands and houses by way of provision of a manse and glebe, subject to the life rent of himself and his wife, the trustees being the minister and elders and their successors.—[*Books of Council and Session*, 15th June 1742.]

1846 WILLIAM MUNGALL SIMPSON, pres. by Crown 3rd Dec. 1845; his son, James Nicolson, died Glasgow 20th March 1929.

1867 THOMAS LITTLE, pres. by Crown 18th June 1867.

1872 ROBERT SHARP WARREN, pres. by Crown 16th April 1872.

1879 HARCOURT PETER CHARLTON, his son, Henry Lyons, died at Dedza, Nyasaland, 31st May 1925; his daugh., Margaret O'Brien, died 9th Jan. 1935.

1915 ANSON ROBERTSON CRAIK WOOD, trans. to Cupar First Charge 16th May 1924.

1924 RUSSELL WALKER, trans. from Torphins (*q.v.*) 25th Sept. 1924. Marr. 10th Aug. 1926 Nelly, youngest daugh. of John Kirkland, Glasgow, and Agnes Dempster.

PRESBYTERY OF WIGTOWN

BARGRENNAN

1907 GEORGE MUIR, trans. to Houston 18th May 1917.

1917 JOSEPH CAMPBELL, formerly of Lugar (*q.v.*), ord. 20th Sept. 1917, died 12th Nov. 1924; his widow, Marion McKinlay Park, died 28th Sept. 1944.

1925 ANDREW HAMILTON, born 1870, son of James H. and Margaret Edwards; educ. at George Watson's College, Mansfield College, Oxford, Univ. of Edinburgh, M.A. (1890); licen. by Presb. of Hawick 1925; assistant at Lyndhurst Road Church, Hampstead; ord. to Congregational Church, Leek, Staffordshire 1896; trans. to Pollokshields Cong. Church 1897; dem. 1920; adm. by General Assembly on probation 1921; adm. 24th April 1925; dem. 25th Jan. 1933. Marr. (1) Aug. 1897 Wilhelmina Wood (died 1918), daugh. of William and Bella Anderson, and had issue—James Russell, born 1899, killed in war at Passchendaele 1917; William Anderson, born 1900, Colombo; Marie Anderson, born 1901 (marr. Drew McClymont, Ourbank, Bargrennan); (2) March 1921, Catherine Doig, daugh. of William and James Crookston.

GLASSERTON

1561 RODOLPH PEARSON, reader and vicar of Kirkmaiden in Farines in 1561.—[*Coll. Gen. of Thirds*, 96.]

1563 HENRY SMITH, reader 1563.—[*Comps. Sub Coll. of Thirds for Dumfries*, etc.]

1569 JOHN KAY, reader in 1569 and 1570.—[*Comps. Sub Coll. of Thirds, Dumfries*, etc.]

1569 GEORGE STEVENSON, vicar and reader in Kirkmaiden in Farines 1569–81.—[*Comps. Sub Coll. of Thirds, Dumfries*, etc.]

1574 JOHN LIVINGSTON, pres. to vicarage 20th Jan. 1574 on death of Raulf Pierson.—[*Reg. Pres. Bene.*, ii, (4), 29.]

1584 SIR WILLIAM McLELLAN, vicar, probably died 1584.—[*Comps. Gen. Coll. of Thirds.*]

1584 ROBERT STEWART, vicar, also vicar of Galston; marr. Geillis Murray, died in or just before 1590.—[*Comps. Gen. Coll. of Thirds.*]

1587 JOHN WATSON, pres. to vicarage 12th Feb. 1587–8 on death of George Stevenson.—[*Reg. Sec. Sig.*, lvii, 27.]

1591 JAMES DAVIDSON, M.A., pres. to vicarage 19th Jan. 1591–2 on death of Robert Stewart.—[*Reg. Sec. Sig.*, lxiii, 130, 161.]

1626 GEORGE GALLOWAY, son of Patrick G., min. of St Giles, Edinburgh, and brother of Lord Dunkeld; died before 1664, when his wife marr. (2) Robert Stewart of Tonderghie; his daugh. Jean (marr. James Stewart in Balliewhir).—[*Reg. of Deeds, Mack.*, xi, 243.]

1761 JAMES LAING, line 5, for "III" read "II."

1848 ARCHIBALD STEWART, pres. by Crown 17th March 1849; his son, Henry Goodsir, agent, British Linen Bank, Wooler, died at Glasgow 1st Jan. 1928; his daugh., Elizabeth Magdalene, died 15th June 1929.

JOHN GORDON, died at London 24th
1876 Sept. 1920.

JOHN GREENSHIELDS SCOULAR,
1914 licen. by Presb. of Cupar 3rd May 1910; dem. 26th June 1945. Marr. 18th Sept. 1923 Mabel, only daugh. of James Alexander, Isle of Whithorn, and has issue—Mabel Alexander, born 22nd June 1924; John Richard, born 27th June 1931.

(*The charges of Glasserton and Isle of Whithorn united 13th Jan. 1946.*)

KIRKCOWAN

The saint appears to be Eoghan, probably Eogan of Ard-Strathe, of the first half of the 6th century, who is stated to have been trained at Whithorn. The present church was built in 1834.—[Watson's *Celtic Place Names*, 164.]

JOHN MOFFAT, was min. here when
1586 he was pres. to the vicarage of Leswalt.—[*Reg. Sec. Seal*, liii, 168. See Leswalt.]

BENJAMIN DENOON, his widow,
1883 Mary Jane Abel, died at Dumfries 14th June 1926.

ANDREW FALLAS MITCHELL, his
1886 widow, Grace Gow Anderson, died 5th Jan. 1939.

HUGH THOMAS SUTHERLAND MORRISON, trans. to Dysart 2nd
1916 Charge 16th Dec. 1925.

LEWIS HERBERT WATSON, ord. 1st
1926 June 1926, trans. to Cults 7th April 1929.

KIRKINNER, formerly CARNESMOLL

The early name was Carnesmoll or Carnismole. Before 1326 it was granted to Whitern Priory by Edward Bruce, Lord of Galloway, brother of Robert I. By Papal Bull of 4th June 1504 the church, which belonged to the Prior and Chapter of Candida Casa, was annexed and appropriated to the Mense of the Chapel Royal of Stirling.—[*Cal. Papal Reg., Letters* xi, 39, 113; *Rymers Foedera*, ii, (1), 401; *Reg. Mag. Sig.*, i, App. I, 20; *Transcripts from the Vatican*, iii, 77; *MS. Reg. Ho.*]

ALEXANDER HUNTER, exhorter.—
1563 [*Comps. Sub Coll. of Thirds, Dumfries*, etc.]

ROBERT CHAMPARE, pres. to
1569 vicarage 13th Sept. 1569 on death of James Makaloun.—[*Reg.Pres.Bene.*, i, 29.]

JAMES KNOX, pres. to vicarage 2nd
1569 Jan. 1569–70 on death of David Gibson.—[*Reg. Pres. Bene.*, i, 34.]

MICHAEL or NICOL DUNGALSON,
1574 reader, exhorter in 1565, min. in 1572.—[*Comps. Sub Coll. of Thirds, Dumfries*, etc.]

ANDREW LAMB, M.A., min. of the
1602 Evangel, pres. to parsonage and vicarage 4th Jan. 1602 on deaths of William Duncanson, Min. of the Evangel, and Dean John Angus.—[*Reg. Sec. Sig.*, lxxii, 207.]

GEORGE WAUGH, line 5, for "Leu-
1647 chars" read "Edinburgh."

WILLIAM CAMPBELL, second son of
1702 Robert C., maltman burgess, Glasgow.—[*Burgess Roll*, 20th March 1713.

ROBERT PATON, his widow, Susan
1865 Dawson Reid, died 26th Nov. 1930.

JOHN CUNNINGHAM WALKER,
1900 licen. 20; died 16th March 1931.

LONGCASTLE

GEORGE STEVENSON, reader 1563.
1563 —[*Comps. Sub Coll. of Thirds, Dumfries*, etc.]

DENE JOHN MARTIN, vicar in office
1565 1565—[*Comps. Sub Coll. of Thirds, Dumfries*, etc.]

WILLIAM VANS, reader and school-
1568 master 1568, vicar before 22nd April 1581.—*Comps. Sub Coll. of Thirds, Dumfries*, etc.; *Reg. Pres. Bene.*, ii, 57.]

NICOL or MICHAEL DUNGALSON.
1574 —[*Reg. Pres. Bene.*, ii, (4), 27.]

JOHN YOUNG, min. here, pres. to vicarage in 1577 on death of Nicol Dungalson.—[*Reg. Pres. Bene.*, ii, (4), 67.]
1577

KIRKMABRECK and KIRKDALE

PATRICK GRANT, reader of Kirkdale 1563.—[*Comps. Sub Coll. of Thirds, Dumfries*, etc.]
1563

JOHN MOFFAT, was min. here 8th April 1583, when he was presented to the vicarage and pensionaire in succession to deceased Thomas Regnall.—[*Reg. Sec. Seal*, xlix, 115.]
1585

JOHN CALLANDER, pres. to vicarage by King James VI in succession to Edward, Commendator of Dundrennan, Lady Lamington, the patron, having failed to present a qualified person within six months.—[*Reg. Sec. Sig.*, lxxiii, 170.]
1603

DAVID McQUERNE, marr. Sara, daugh. of David McQuorne, min. of Straiton.
1668

ROBERT EDWARD, M.A., resident with his wife and son in Tron parish, Edinburgh, 9th Nov. 1694. —[*Tron Poll Tax Roll*, 59.]
1684

JOHN COLVIN, pres. by Crown 20th Jan. 1859.
1859

CHARLES STUART WALLACE, served as Chaplain to Forces in France 1916–18, and Macedonia 1918–19 with Royal Scots; died suddenly in hotel in Edinburgh 8th Nov. 1932. Marr. 5th Nov. 1918 Barbara Erica, younger daugh. of Johnston Stephen, Woolmet, Midlothian, and Helena Kitto, and had issue—Diana Helena Barbara Stuart, born 16th Feb. 1920; Robert James Stuart, born 29th Jan. 1921, min. of Brydekirk 1947; Charles Stuart, born 6th July 1930.
1904

MOCHRUM

LEWIS FRASER, designated min. 1569 but subsequently as reader 7th Aug. 1572.—*Edin. Tests*, ii, 154.]
1567

ANTHONIE STEWART, vicar 1584.— [*Comps. Sub Coll. of Thirds, Dumfries*, etc.]
1584

HENRY WALLACE, M.A., resident with his wife, Isabel Cook, 8th Nov. 1694.—[*Tron Poll Book*, 30.]
1683

JOHN STEVEN, pres. 26th April 1787.
1787

ROBERT JAMES CRAIG, pres. by Crown 8th May 1863.
1863

WILLIAM ALLAN, pres. by Crown 9th June 1869; his widow, Isabella Milne Wright, died 22nd Dec. 1942.
1869

ANDREW ROBERTSON, trans. to Prestonfield, Edinburgh, 6th Oct. 1926.
1926

JAMES THOMSON, trans. from Martyrs, Paisley (*q.v.*), 21st July 1927; dem. 30th June 1947; his daugh., Mary Farquhar (marr. 5th Jan. 1940 David Jones, Scotstoun); his son, Ivan Samson Durham, born 18th Jan. 1917.
1927

MONIGAFF

JOHN STEWART, exhorter 1563 and 1572.—[*Comps. Sub Coll. of Thirds, Dumfries*, etc.]
1567

ANDREW MENZIES, min., reader here before June 1576.—[*Edin. Tests*, v. 263,]
1576

ALEXANDER HAMILTON, marr. Margaret, daugh. of Abraham Henderson, min. of Whitern; his daughs. Margaret, mentioned in a divorce case 8th Aug. 1622; Mary, born March 1619.— [*G. R. Sas.*, xi, 10, 1st July 1622; xx, 184.]
1620

THOMAS CAMPBELL, eldest son of Robert C., maltman burgess of Glasgow.—[*Burgess Roll*, 20th March 1713.]
1699

JOHN GARLIES MAITLAND, pres.
1789   24th Oct. 1788.

MICHAEL SHAW STEWART JOHNSTON, his daugh., Harriet Stewart
1836   Hamilton, died 4th Jan, 1921; his son, Dunlop Stewart, died 28th July 1922; his daughs.—Lilias Alice, died 14th Oct. 1927; Edith Augusta Octavia, died 9th April 1933; Elizabeth McLeod, died at Stirling 24th Aug. 1943.

LOUIS EDMOND McVICKER, trans.
1915   to Macduff 4th July 1929.

PENNINGHAME

MARTIN GIB, reader, holding vicarage
1561   from 1561, portioner of Penninghame.—[*Coll. Gen. of Thirds*, 96.]

ANTHONE STEWART, son of Alexander S. of Garlies, pres. to par-
1566   sonage 22nd April 1566 on dem. of Sir Andrew Arnott. Marr. Barbara, daugh. of Alexander Gordon, titular Bishop of Athens, a son of John Master of Huntly, and was ancestor of Castle Stewart family.—[*P. S. Reg.*, xxxvii, 70.]

WILLIAM THOMSON, mentioned as
1651   min. 23rd June 1651.—[*Reg. of Deeds, Dal.*, xxv, 624.]

JAMES COLQUHOUN, Archdeacon
1666   of Whitern, 17th Dec. 1680.—[*Reg. of Deeds, Dal.*, lxxxviii, 23rd July 1703.]

WALTER BOYD, delete "born
1760   1718."

JOHN McDONALD INGLIS, assistant
1880   South Leith; died 30th Oct. 1929.

SORBIE, KIRKMADRYNE and CRUGILTON

About 1200 Ivo de Vipont granted to Dryburgh Abbey the Church of St Foylen (Fillan of Greater Sorbie), and about 1220 Robert de Vipont granted similarly the Church of St Michael of Lesser Sorbie. In the latter case confirmation was made by Alan, father of Robert. At the request of Dryburgh Abbey, Gilbert, Bishop of Whithorn, about 1250, on the ground that the two churches were sufficient only for the support of one man, consolidated the two, and decerned the Church of St Michael of Lesser Sorbie to be the mother church of each place. Before the middle of the 19th century there remained no traces of the churches, but their sites were pointed out, one at Culnorg in the north-west, and the other at Gilfillan near the centre of the parish. The church in the village of Sorbie was rebuilt about 1750, and thoroughly repaired in 1824. A new church was built at Millisle in 1874–6.—[*Book of Dryburgh*, 53, 56, 59–60.]

Kirkmadryne. The saint is *Draigne, Draighne*, which, with *gh* silent in med. and mod. Gaelic, becomes *Drine* in English. *Draigne* is said to have been one of the ten sons of Dina, daugh. of the King of the Saxons, and Bracan, King of Brachineoc, of the Britons. To the Priory of Trallesholm (St Mary's Isle of Trail) William the Lion granted the Church of Egarnesse (Kirkmadryne) given by Rolland, son of Uchtred.—[*Cal. of Charters*, i, 14; Watson's *Celtic Place Names*, 162–3.]

Crugilton. In 1420–7 Alexander, Bishop of Galloway, appropriated the church to the Capitular Mensa; and on 9th Aug. 1427 Pope Martin V gave mandate to the Provost of Lincluden to confirm the appropriation if he deemed it fit.—[*Cal. Papal Regs., Letters*, vii, 526.]

WILLIAM TELFER, reader, held the
1561   vicarage, was designated "Dene" and therefore was apparently pre-Reformation vicar and conformed.—[*Reg. Sec. Seal*, xlix, 64.]

JOHN McPHAIL, reader 1563.—
1563   [*Comps. Sub Coll. of Thirds, Dumfries*, etc.]

SIR GILBERT OISLAR, was vicar,
1566   apparently at and before 1560; died June 1566.—*Reg. Sec. Seal*, xxxvi, 28.]

ROBERT BLINSCHELL, min. at Wig-
1566   town, was collated vicar in succession to Sir Gilbert Oislar 10th Dec. 1566; ratification by Crown 20th Feb.

1566-7; he appears to have held Sorbie along with Wigtown at that time.—[*Reg. Sec. Seal*, xxxvi, 28.]

PETER GOWAN, reader, pres. to vicarage 21st Jan. 1576 on death of Robert Blinshell.—[*Reg. Pres. Bene.*, ii, (6), 51.]
1579

ARCHIBALD NORVELL, pres. in conjunction on death of Peter Gowan (MacGowan).—[*Reg. Pres. Bene.*, ii, 94.]
1583

NICOL McBLANE, pres. to the vicarage 17th Jan. 1582-3 in succession to Dene William Telfer.—[*Reg. Sec. Seal*, xlix, 64.]
1588

JOHN KAY, min. and reader, pres. to vicarage 2nd Aug. 1591 on death of Sir Nicol McLellan.—[*Reg. Sec. Sig.*, lxii, 123.]
1590

ALEXANDER RYNE, line 4, for "James VI" read "Charles I."
1633

ROBERT KAY, pres. to vicarage of Crugelton 26th May 1594 on dem. of John Kay.—[*Reg. Sec. Sig.*, lxvi, 134.]
1594

ANDREW AITKEN, his son, John, apprenticed to Robert Freebairne, bookbinder, Edinburgh, 27th Nov. 1706.
1684

ARCHIBALD HADDEN, son of Archibald H., weaver, Glasgow.
1700

JAMES MAITLAND, marr. Agnes, daugh. of John Dempster, min. of St Madoc's.
1738

ALEXANDER FORRESTER, line 25, for "Rutlan" read "Rutlain."
1835

ALEXANDER MURDOCH, pres. by Crown 21st June 1869; his daug., Martha Bowman, died 22nd March 1944.
1869

OLIVER SHAW RANKIN, educ. at George Watson's College and Univ. of Berlin; adm. Professor of Old Testament Language, Literature and Theology, New College, 5th Oct. 1937; D.Litt.
1912
(Edinburgh, 1928); D.D. (Glasgow, 27th June 1938). Addl. issue—Kenneth Walker, born 5th April 1920. Publications—*Origins of the Festival of Hanukkah* (Edinburgh, 1935); *Israel's Wisdom Literature, its Bearing on Theology and the History of Religion* (Edinburgh, 1936).

WHITERN

The Augustinian priory of St Mary's Isle was a dependent cell of Holyrood Abbey.

In 1324 King Robert I confirmed to Whithorn Priory the following churches—Church of St Kenere of Carnesmoll (Kirkinner) and the Church of St Mathew of Wigton, the gift of Edward Bruce, "our brother," lord of Galloway; Church of St Brigid in Lair in Man, the gift of Thomas Randolph, Earl of Moray; Church of St Columkill in Kintyre, the gift of Patrick McSciling and Finlach, his wife; and the Church of St Michael of Gemelston (Gelston), the gift of John de Gemelston, son and heir of late John de G., Kt. In a letter of Edward I of England, 21st Sept. 1301, William de Dorem narrated that his spy told him that these Scots (who had retreated from Nithsdale towards Galloway) heard that my lord, your son, was on pilgrimage of St Ninian (Rineyan), and they removed the imagine (of the same ?) to New Abbey, and on the morning they hoped to find it, and it had gone back to St Ninian. The reference is to the image of the Saint at Whithorn.—[*Reg. Great Seal*, i, App. I, 20; *Cal. of Docs. Rel. to Scot.*, ii, 311; *Cal. Papal Regs., Letters*, vii, 368.]

ADAM FOULIS, M.A., min. in 1563.—[*Comps. Sub Coll. of Thirds, Dumfries*, etc.]
1563

DENE JOHN JOHNSTON, reader 1563, vicar-pensioner apparently at and before 1560; died before 4th Nov. 1566.—[*Reg. Sec. Seal*, xxxvi, 8.]
1563

DENE ADAM FLEMING, was canon of Whithorn; collated vicar-pensioner by the Commendator of Whithorn 4th Nov. 1566; Crown ratification 14th Feb. 1566-7.—[*Reg. Sec. Seal*, xxxvi, 8.]
1566

WHITERN—WIGTOWN

DENE JOHN HAY, his collation as vicar-pensioner in succession to Dene John Johnston in 1566 was ratified by the Crown 20th Feb. 1566–7, Dene Adam Fleming apparently not having actually assumed duty.—[*Reg. Sec. Seal*, xxxvi, 27.]
1566

ADAM FLEMING, reader 1572.—[*Comps. Sub Coll. of Thirds, Dumfries*, etc.]
1572

JAMES ADAMSON, master of Wigton Grammar School; pres. in 1582 on death of Adam Fleming.—[*Reg. Pres. Bene.*, ii, 66.]
1582

ABRAHAM HENDERSON, his daugh. Margaret (marr. Alexander Hamilton, min. of Monigaff).
1605

ANDREW LAUDER, died before 1669; his son, William, apprenticed to Laurence Graham, furrier, Edinburgh, 20th Jan. 1669.
1638

ROBERT GRAY, had issue—William, bapt. 14th May 1687.—[*Aberdeen Reg.*]
1686

ALEXANDER DUNLOP, marr. Katherine, sister to Gavin Dunbar of Cathkin.
1697

THOMAS ELDER, marr. Sara Grierson (died 1707), sister of Homer Grierson, surgeon apothecary, Dumfries.
1704

CHRISTOPHER NICHOLSON, his daugh., Margaret, marr. (2) 21st June 1854.
1811

MATTHEW JARDINE, his widow, Mary Gourlay, died 11th June 1830; his daugh., Grace Broadfoot, died Newton Stewart, 19th Jan. 1947.
1864

DONALD MACINTYRE HENRY, died 18th Aug. 1920; his daugh., Dorothea (marr. 6th July 1920 John Taylor Wyllie, Dumfries).
1886

WILLIAM ARNOLD REID, born Alva 20th Dec. 1890, second son of William R., Eastbank Academy, Shettleston and Jessie Hunter; educ. at Alva Academy, High School and Univ. of Glasgow, M.A. (1911); licen. by Presb. of Glasgow 1914; served in Great War as Captain and Adjutant, Northumberland Fusiliers, 1914–19; assistant Hamilton 1914; Springburn 1919–20; ord. 16th Feb. 1921; app. Presb. Clerk 25th June 1929; trans. to St Mary's, Selkirk, 4th June 1931; trans. to Holywood, 13th May 1948. Marr. 15th June 1917 Marion Baillie Darling Wilson, M.B., Ch.B., elder daugh. of Dr George Wilson, Shettleston, and Jeanie Darling, and had issue—Margaret Jean Garth, B.Sc., born 3rd July 1919 (marr. 7th Jan. 1946 Frederick Tidd, Chaplain to the Forces); Kathleen Arnold, born 15th March 1923 (marr. 1st Nov. 1949 Charles William Younger, son of William Drummond, Newlands, St Boswells); Alastair Arnold, born 22nd March 1926; Marion Lesley, born 5th July 1930.
1921

WIGTOWN

The church was granted to Whitern Priory before 1326 by Edward Bruce, Lord of Galloway, brother of Robert I. On 9th Feb. 1541–2, "Sanct Laurence day, quhilk the nynt day of August" is described as the principal fair day at Wigtown.—[*Reg. Mag. Sig.*, i, App. i, 20; *Acts of the Lords of Council on Public Affairs*, 513.]

PATRICK McCULLOCH, reader.—[*Comps. Sub Coll. of Thirds, Dumfries*, etc.]
1563

ROBERT BLINDSHIEL, M.A., min. in 1563, also held Sorbie.—[*Comps. Sub Coll. of Thirds, Dumfries*, etc.]
1567

JAMES FALCONER, reader 1572–3.—[*Comps. Sub Coll. of Thirds, Dumfries*, etc.]
1572

ARCHIBALD HAMILTON, son of Patrick H., min. of Innerwick.—[*Hamilton MSS.*, 166.]
1654

ANDREW DONNAN, his daugh., Janet, died 19th Nov. 1847.
1785

JAMES CULLEN, his daugh., Rose Elizabeth, died 7th Dec. 1933.
1863

GAVIN LAWSON, marr. 2nd April 1924 Janet Broadfoot; dem. 18th Dec. 1947.
1910

(*Churches united 1st Jan. 1948.*)

PRESBYTERY OF KIRKCUDBRIGHT

ANWOTH

The church, along with the Chapel of Culenes, was granted to Holyrood Abbey by David, son of Terr, confirmation being given by John, Bishop of Whithorn, 1189–1209.—[*Charters of Holyrood*, 38, 40.]

1563 WILLIAM MOSCROP, M.A., min. in 1563, had also charge of Girthon, St Mary's Isle, Kirkandrews, Sennick and Borgue.—[*Comps. Sub Coll. of Thirds, Dumfries*, etc.]

1563 JAMES WYLIE, reader 1563.—[*Comps. Sub Coll. of Thirds, Dumfries*, etc.]

1569 ALEXANDER YOUNG, reader in 1569 and 1570.—[*Comps. Sub Coll. of Thirds, Dumfries*, etc.]

1577 DAVID MURRAY, reader, pres. on death of Malcolm McCulloch; still in office 1590.—[*Reg. Pres. Bene.*, ii, (4), 64.]

1577 ELIAS McCULLOCH, pres. to vicarage 17th Jan. 1577–8 on death of Malcolm McCulloch.—[*Reg. Sec. Sig.*, xlv, 5.]

1601 ISAAC PATERSON, pres. in 1602, on deprivation of David Murray for not serving the cure and residing at the kirk.—[*Reg. Sec. Sig.*, lxxiii, 12.]

1643 JOHN MEIN, line 6, delete "probably deprived in 1662." He marr. Barbara Dickson.—[*Reg. of Deeds*, 1671, p. 295.]

1665 JOHN RICHMOND, min. in 1665. Marr. Jean Lauder.—[*Kirkcudbright Sheriff Court Deeds*, 190.]

1668 JAMES SHAW, had six children.—[*P. C. Reg.*, 29th July 1685.]

1804 THOMAS TURNBULL, his daugh., Agnes (marr. 3rd Dec. 1833 John Craig, Edinburgh).

1839 THOMAS JOHNSTONE, his daugh., Lilias, died at Dalbeattie 10th April 1934.

1876 WILLIAM MACMILLAN BLACK, his widow, Amy Greenshields, died at Oldcolwyn 8th May 1920.

1907 FRANK WILLIAM SAUNDERS, enlisted as a private in Great War, Lieutenant Argyll and Sutherland Highlanders, served in Palestine; killed in action 1st Aug. 1918; his widow, Janet Cochrane Meiklejohn, died 17th Oct. 1933; his daugh., Katherine Helen (marr. 28th April 1936 John Porter, Dalmarnock, Bute.)

1919 FRANKLIN ROSS TAYLOR LORNIE, ord. 13th Feb. 1919; trans. to Buccleuch, Glasgow, 26th March 1925.

1925 JOHN SCOTT, B.A., formerly of Dalkeith West (*q.v.*); trans. from Saughtree 26th Aug. 1925; dem. 2nd Dec. 1931.

AUCHENCAIRN

Note. Line 5, for "Auchenatary" read "Auchenabony."

1856 DAVID WARK, his widow, Jessie Morton Crosbie, died 19th April 1917.

1900 WALTER ROBERTSON HENDERSON, marr. 18th June 1919 Margaret, second daugh. of David Johnston of Linkens, Castle Douglas; she died 20th May 1948.

(*Charges united 9th Nov.* 1932.)

BALMACLELLAN

1562 SIR GEORGE GRAY, prebendary and vicar 1562.—[*Reg. Abbrev. Feu Charters, Church Lands*, i, 187.]

1563 ELIAS McCULLOCH, reader in 1563 and 1567.—[*Comps. Sub Coll. of Thirds, Dumfries*, etc.]

1625 ROBERT MURRAY, was dep. by the Commission of Kirkcudbright appointed by the General Assembly at Glasgow 1638 for oppression, drunkenness, railing, selling the sacraments, sacrilege, bribery, etc., which sentence was approved by the General Assembly at Edinburgh 27th Aug. 1639.—[Peterkin's *Records of the Kirk of Scotland*, 261.]

1668 JOHN ROW, for an account of an assault on him see *Privy Council Reg.*, 3 Ser., iii, 100.

1685 PATRICK GEDDIE, his son, Andrew, min. at Farnell.

1689 THOMAS WARNER, line 5, delete "1691." Marr. (1) Mary Grier and had issue—Thomas; (2) Jean Gordon and had issue—Agnes.—[*Privy Council Reg.*, 3 Ser., iii, 100.]

1747 WILLIAM McKIE, line 5, for "1747" read "1746."

1791 JAMES THOMSON, line 3, for "6th" read "1st."

1851 GEORGE MURRAY, pres. by Crown 15th July 1851; his daugh., Margaret (marr. James J. R. Hope, M.D.), died at New Galloway 25th Sept. 1930.

1881 WILLIAM CUTHILL, died at Edinburgh 12th Dec. 1927. Marr. 1st June 1920 Margaret Noble, daugh. of John Dawson, min. of Makerstoun.

1915 GEORGE MURRAY, died at Lennoxtown 26th July 1925; his widow, Elizabeth Lumsden, died 22nd April 1945; his son, John, 2nd Lieut. K.O.S.B., killed 16th Aug. 1917; his daugh., Evelyn Hope (marr. Thomas Kennedy Johnston, his successor).

1920 THOMAS KENNEDY JOHNSTON, born 20th March 1890, son of David J., min. of St Columba's Gaelic Church, Paisley; educ. Paisley Grammar School and Univ. of Glasgow, M.A. (1914); licen. by Presb. of Hamilton June 1919; assistant Pollokshields; ord. 23rd Sept. 1920; trans. to East Kilbride 26th Oct. 1932. Marr. 26th Aug. 1924 Evelyn Hope, younger daugh. of George Murray of Troquhain, min. of this parish, and has issue—Elizabeth Kennedy, born 4th March 1926; David, born 4th July 1927, died 4th Feb. 1934; George Murray, born 3rd March 1930; Evelyn Kennedy, born 21st Nov. 1933; William, born 6th May 1936.

BALMAGHIE

1563 ROBERT CHAPMAN, reader in 1563 and 1567.—[*Comps. Sub Coll. of Thirds, Dumfries*, etc.]

1565 GEORGE CRICHTON, vicar and dean.—[*Acts and Dec.*, xxxiv, 392.]

1574 JAMES CARRUTHERS, for "trans. from Crossmichael" read "min. also at Crossmichael."

1588 JOHN ADAMSON, M.A., pres. to vicarage 22nd May 1588 on death of Robert Chapman.—[*Reg. Sec. Sig.*, lvii, 120.]

1588 JOHN HILTON, pres. to vicarage 15th July 1588 on death of Sir Robert Chapman.—[*Reg. Sec. Sig.*, lvii, 135.]

1594 JAMES MAXWELL, son of Alexander M. of Ingliston, or Balgreden, pres. to vicarage 7th Jan. 1594-5, on depr. of John Charters.—[*Reg. Sec. Sig.*, lxvii, 42.]

1601 JOHN FAIRFOUL, pres. on dep. and dem. of James Maxwell.—[*Reg. Sec. Sig.*, lxxii, 20.]

1605 WILLIAM DALZIEL, M.A., pres. on 25th June 1605 on death of John Fairfoul.—[*Reg. Sec. Sig.*, lxxiv, 239.]

1605 GAVIN MAXWELL, M.A., pres. to vicarage 4th July 1605 on death of John Fairfoul.—[*P. S. Reg.*, lxxiv, 349.]

1664 JAMES KIRK, born 25th Feb. 1634, resident with a son aged 12 in Lady Yester's parish, Edinburgh, 1st Nov. 1694.—[*Lady Yester's Poll Tax Roll*, 18.]

1904 WILLIAM ALEXANDER MOWAT, marr. 14th June 1917 Frances Rosa, daugh. of George Holmes, County Inspector, Royal Irish Constabulary, Dublin, and has issue—Magnus, born 28th April 1918; George Holmes, born 7th May 1920.

BORGUE

About 1170 the church, under the name of the Church of Worgis, was granted to Dryburgh Abbey by Radulphis de Campania. It was dedicated to St Nicholas.—[*Bk. of Dryburgh*, 49.]

1563 WILLIAM MOSCROP, M.A., min. of Anwoth, also in charge here.

1563 JAMES SCOTT, reader 1563.

1568 JOHN STRUDGEON, exhorter 1568–72.—[*Comps. Sub Coll. of Thirds, Dumfries*, etc.]

1574 WILLIAM STRUDGEON, reader.

1584 SIR MICHAEL HAWTHORN, vicar 1584.—[*Comps. Gen. Coll. of Thirds*.]

1590 JOHN AIKMAN, min. here, pres. to vicar-pensionary 30th May 1590 on death of Robert Blenshell.—[*Reg. Sec. Sig.*, lx, 137.]

1596 ABRAHAM HENRYSON, pres. on dep. of John Aikman.—[*Reg. Sec. Sig.*, lxix, 51.]

1607 GAVIN MAXWELL, line 6, for "Hawick" read "Ancrum."—[*G. R. Sas.*, xxviii, 293.]

1649 ADAM KAE, died 1665. Marr. Grizel Cairns, who survived him and marr. (2) William MacMillan of Caldew. Publication—*A Sermon concerning the Believers sitting under Christ's Shadow.*—[*Kirkcudbright Sher. Court Deeds*, 250, 251, 1349.]

1669 JAMES MURRAY, adm. before 18th May 1669.

1680 ROBERT MONTEITH, min. before 17th Dec. 1680.

1683 PATRICK HASTIE, marr. Rebecca Higgins and had issue—Patrick.

1843 WILLIAM REID, pres. by Crown 27th July 1843; his widow, Anna Tomlinson, died 16th Feb. 1923.

1867 GEORGE COOK, pres. by Crown 3rd Jan. 1867; his daugh., Charlotte Stewart, died at Corstorphine 5th Sept. 1922.

1899 WILLIAM JOSEPH PENNELL, dem. 2nd Dec. 1942. Publication—*History and Modern Religious Thought* (London, 1924).

(*Charges united* 14*th Dec.* 1933.)

KIRKANDREWS

On 14th Jan. 1447–8 Pope Nicolas V granted mandate to confirm the erection of the Church of Kirkandrews into a Prebend of Lincluden by William, Earl of Douglas.—[*Cal. Papal Regs., Letters*, x, 342.]

1563 WILLIAM MOSCROP, M.A., min. of Anwoth, in charge here.—[*Comps. Sub Coll. of Thirds, Dumfries*, etc.]

1563 DONALD MacALLAN, reader.—[*Comps. Sub Coll. of Thirds, Dumfries*, etc.]

1582 JOHN McCLELLAN, reader. See under Sir Thomas Ker, Roxburgh.

SENNICK

At Kessoktoun in the parish there was a church dedicated to St Kessoc or Kessog.—[Scott's *The Pictish Nation, its People and Church*, 140.]

1563 WILLIAM MOSCROP, M.A., min. of Anwoth, also in charge here.—[*Comps. Sub Coll. of Thirds, Dumfries*, etc.]

JOHN McCLELLAN, reader.—[*Comps.*
1563 *Sub Coll. of Thirds, Dumfries.*]

ANDREW DAVIDSON, M.A., vicar
1566 7th Aug. 1566; parson of Kinnettles 1573.—[*Reg. of Deeds*, viii, 406; Grote's *Prot. Bk.*, 377.]

BUITTLE and KIRKENNAN

The Church of Buittle was granted to Sweetheart Abbey by Thomas de Dalston, Bishop of Whithorn, 1296–1311.—[*Maxwell Monuments*, 6.]

SIR JOHN PARKER, vicar-pensioner
1562 and reader 1562, still in office 1565. —[*Reg. Abbrev. Feu Charters of Church Lands*, i, 100.]

JAMES PARKER, vicar in 1567, died
1567 before 10th July 1587.—[*Reg. Sec. Sig.*, lv, 98.]

DAVID (JOHN) AIKMAN, pres. to
1587 vicarage 10th July 1587 on death of James Parker; murdered 2nd Sept. 1593 by John Muir, son and heir of John M. of Hallmuire, and his brothers Adam and George and their servant.—[*P. C. Reg., Reg. Sec. Sig.*, lv, 98.]

PATRICK ADAMSON, for "his in-
1614 sufficiencie for the Ministrie, frequent drunkenness on the Sabbath, and dancing in his drunkenness, and disobedience of the Presbyterie" he was dep. by the Commission of Kirkcudbright appointed by the General Assembly at Glasgow 1638; the sentence was approved by the General Assembly at Edinburgh 27th Aug. 1639.—[Peterkin's *Recs. of the Kirk*, 261.]

ROBERT FERGUSON, imprisoned at
1645 Edinburgh 1663.

JAMES WALKER, M.A., resident with
1676 three young children in Tron parish, Edinburgh, 9th Nov. 1694.—[*Tron Poll Tax Roll*, 59.]

WILLIAM TOD, marr. (1) 9th May
1699 1697 Anna Hepburn, widow of Hugh Rose, writer, Edinburgh.— [*Deeds Dal.*, 1705, Nos. 23, 24.]

JOHN DAVIS, enlisted in R.A.M.C.,
1907 died of heat stroke at Amara, Mesopotamia, 22nd July 1917.

JAMES MURRAY HADDOW, born
1918 Glasgow 9th Nov. 1890, son of Alexander H. and Isabella Murray; educ. Hutcheson's Boys' Grammar School and Univ. of Glasgow; licen. by Presb. of Dunbarton 1916; assistant St Giles, Edinburgh; ord. 25th Jan. 1918; trans. to Oatlands-St Bernards 30th March 1936; died 3rd May 1940. Marr. 12th Dec. 1918 Margaret Elizabeth, daugh. of Thomas Gillespie, 109 Gt. Western Road, Glasgow, and had issue—Alexander, born 3rd July 1921; Thomas Gillespie, born 10th July 1923; James Murray, born 24th Sept. 1925.

CARSPHAIRN

On 25th Jan. 1633 there was laid before the Commission for the Plantation of Kirks a supplication from heritors and inhabitants of lands in the parishes of Kells and Dalry situated 12–16 miles from each of the two parish churches, to the effect that they were defrauded of the comfort of the Word and the benefit of the Sacraments, while poor people were oftentimes buried in the fields, having none to carry them the long distance to the churchyard, and craving that said lands be erected into a separate parish. The Commission ordered the supplication "to be insert in their books qill (till) the erection should be passed." Thereafter at a village called Tantallocholme which on 31st July 1635 was erected by Charles I into a Burgh of Barony under the name of the Burgh of Kirkton a church called the Church of Carsphairn (Scarefernhome) was built by voluntary subscription by the heritors and inhabitants and opened for worship in or just before 1636, and a minister was settled whose stipend was also provided by the same means. On 15th Dec. 1638 a supplication from the church, which then had 500 communicants, was presented to the General Assembly, craving help from Presbyteries towards the provision of "competent means" for a minister, and this was renewed on 27th Aug. 1639, when the Assembly commended the appeal to "the bounds there designed for that contribution." The position was regularised when, after approval of the erection of the parish by the General Assembly on 4th Feb. 1645 and by the Committee of Parliament on 7th Feb. 1645, the erection was ratified by Parliament on 8th March of the same year. The church was rebuilt in 1815 and thoroughly repaired in 1837.—[*Acts Scott. Parl.*, v, 596b, vi, (1), 398, vii, 159; *Reg. Great Seal*, ix, 374; Peterkin's *Recs. of Kirk of Scot.*, 184, 262.]

1669 THOMAS COLDEN, line 3, for "1657" read "2nd Dec. 1664."—[*G. R. Sas.*, 3 Ser., xxx, 9.]

1881 PETER CHARLES FINDLAY, died at Edinburgh 10th March 1924; his wife, Barbara Stuart Macleod, died 13th Dec. 1919.

1913 GEORGE FERRIER ANDERSON MACNAUGHTON, ord. 6th Nov. 1890, dem. 16th May 1925; died at Stansted, Essex, 11th April 1933. Line 19 for "Finlay" read "Findlay."

1925 WILFRED ROBERT SIEVEWRIGHT, born Glasgow 18th March 1891, son of Andrew S. and Agnes Clark; educ. at Hutcheson's Grammar School and Univ. of Glasgow; licen. by Presb. of Glasgow 4th May 1921; assistant Govan Parish Church and St Marnoch's, Kilmarnock; ord. 17th July 1924 to West Wemyss; trans. 16th Sept. 1925. Marr. 23rd June 1926 Anna M., daugh. of John and Marjory Stewart.

(*Charges united* 6*th July* 1930.)

CASTLE DOUGLAS

1874 GEORGE WALKER, died at Aberdeen 22nd May 1919.

1915 LUKE McQUITTY, trans. to Monkton 28th June 1923.

1923 MATTHEW McPHAIL, ord. 7th Nov. 1923; trans. to St Luke's, Lochee, 12th Oct. 1927.

1928 DAVID EASTHAM AUTY, B.D., trans. from St Clement's, Dundee (*q.v.*), 22nd March 1928; his daugh., Eunice Mary (marr. 14th June 1940 Colin Rea Duncan Brown, 2nd Lieut. Argyll and Sutherland Highlanders, son of Peter B., Cliff Lodge, Greenock).

CORSOCK

The laird of Corsock, John Neilson by name, was one of the martyrs of the "killing time." The site of his castle is still visible, and here the first conventicle was held. The circumstances were these. In the year 1662 a throng of men and women fugitives from the neighbouring parish of Kirkpatrick Durham came with their minister, Gabriel Temple. The hospitality and protection of Neilson having been given, services were held in the hall of the manor. Large numbers flocked to them and, the accommodation being limited, the congregations assembled at length on the green, and in this way the first of the "Field Meetings" or "Conventicles" was held. Later Neilson was taken prisoner at Rullion Green and eventually put to death after being tortured on "the boot."

1104 JOHN PAUL, adm. by General Assembly 1899; dem. 27th Oct. 1930; adm. to Ayton West 23rd April 1931, died at Edinburgh 7th Aug. 1933. Marr. 5th Jan. 1921 Jessie Hutcheson Millar (died at Edinburgh 31st March 1931), eldest daugh. of James McGregor, Dunella, Stonehaven.

(*Charges united* 1930.)

CROSSMICHAEL

1668 JOHN WAUGH, marr. (1) and had issue—Barbara, John; (2) 1675, Helen, daugh. of William Gordon of Airds.—[*Kirkcudbright Sher. Court*, 221.]

1837 JOHN WHITSON, his daugh., Euphemia Dick of Essendy (marr. William Fraser, min. of Tradeston U.F. Church), died at Edinburgh 19th Oct. 1923.

1871 JOHN DOUGLAS STEWART, dem. 10th Dec. 1918; died 16th Feb. 1919; his widow, Ann Craig Allison, died 9th Feb. 1939; his son, John Douglas, died 16th Nov. 1928.

1912 JAMES ANNETT FISHER, marr. 30th Nov. 1918 to Marjory, daugh. of Kingsford Pawling, Barnet, and has issue—Michael Joseph Pawling, born 6th June 1920; Pauline Margaret Clara, born 23rd April 1924.

DALRY

1563 JAMES DODDS, min. in office 1563.—[*Comps. Sub Coll. of Thirds, Dumfries*, etc.]

1563 FRANCIS HOME, reader 1563.

1569 CUTHBERT ADAIR, exhorter 1569-72.—[*Comps. Sub Coll. of Thirds, Dumfries*, etc.]

1690 WILLIAM BOYD, marr. (1) 11th March 1691, Isabel Anderson, Glasgow, and had issue—William, bapt. 2nd Dec. 1694; Andrew, born 1697; by second marriage—Edward; Robert; David; Isabel and Barbara.—[*Dumfries Tests*, *Edward Maxwell of Hills*, 22nd Feb. 1723.]

1753 ALEXANDER MACGOWAN, his daugh., Mary (marr. 24th June 1923 James Glover, writing master, Liverpool).

1907 JOHN ANDERSON, trans. to St. Kenneth's, Govan, 18th May 1927.

1927 HAROLD GEORGE MULLO WEIR, born Edinburgh 29th Sept. 1899, son of James Mullo Weir, S.S.C., Edinburgh, and Minnie Augusta Wilkins; educ. at Royal High School and Univ. of Edinburgh, M.A. (1923); licen. by Presb. of Edinburgh 1st Dec. 1924; student assistant North Berwick 1924; Greenock West 1925; ord. 28th Sept. 1927.

GIRTHON

1563 WILLIAM MOSCROP, M.A., min. of Anwoth, also in charge here.—[*Comps. Sub Coll. of Thirds, Dumfries*.]

1563 ROBERT MUIR, vicar, exhorter and reader from 1565 to 1574.—[*Cal. of Charters*, x, 2326.)

1664 LEWIS LAWSON of LEUCHOLD, "late min. at Girthon," mentioned 9th April 1664. Marr. Lucy Moodie.—[*Reg. of Deeds, Mack.*, xiv, 888.]

1666 SIMON KNOX, his son, William, min. of Dairsie.

1684 ROBERT CHEYNE, resident in Greyfriars parish, Edinburgh, 9th Nov. 1694. Marr. (2) Jean Orrok, widow of Alexander Ramsay, min. of Old Kirk, Edinburgh.—[*Poll Tax Roll*, 54.]

1699 PATRICK JOHNSTON, son of James J., merchant, Edinburgh.

1737 ROBERT THOMSON, son of Andrew T., min. at Ansell.

1848 GEORGE MURRAY, pres. by Crown 23rd July 1843.

1852 HUGH MORTON JACK, pres. by Crown 27th Nov. 1851; his daugh., Marianne Louisa, died 23rd March 1936.

1901 JOHN STEWART, died 24th June 1937.

(*Charges united* 21*st March* 1932.)

KELLS

1586 CHARLES McCULLOCH, pres. to vicar pensionary 13th July 1586 on death of Sir Donald Mure.—[*Reg. Sec. Sig.*, liv, 35.]

1636 JOHN DICKSON, his sons, Robert of Buchtrig, advocate 1666, M.P. New Galloway 1661-74, died 10th Jan. 1674; George of Buchtrig, advocate 1674.

1659 JOHN CANT, p. 412, line 10, for "1694" read "1674."

1685 JAMES BROWN, M.A., described as "a poor man with five children" when resident in Lady Yester's parish, Edinburgh, 7th Nov. 1694.—[*Lady Yester's Poll Tax Roll*, 4.]

1879 PIRIE PHILIP, dem. 7th Nov. 1921, died 18th Aug. 1945. Publication—*A New Interpretation of the Cross* (1942).

1826 JAMES MAITLAND, his daugh., Jane Agnes, died 21st Feb. 1940.

1922 SAMUEL WOOD CAMERON, ord. 30th March 1922; dem. on appointment as Indian Chaplain 29th Oct. 1925.

1926 JOHN ARTHUR CAMERON, born 5th April 1894, son of Nicol F. C., solicitor, Glasgow; educ. at Glasgow Academy and Univ. of Glasgow, M.A. (1914); became a solicitor in Glasgow; licen. by Presb. of Edinburgh 26th Dec. 1924; assistant St John's, Edinburgh; ord. 25th March 1926; died 31st Jan. 1928. Marr. 16th June 1921 Agnes May, daugh. of John Gavin Dickson, min. of St John's Edinburgh, and had issue—Ian Nicol Ferguson, born 6th Aug. 1922, Flight Navigator, R.A.F., killed on active service 1943; Mary Henderson, born 11th May 1925; Agnes Eleanor, born 29th Dec. 1927.

1928 ARTHUR CURRIE GORDON, born Edinburgh 1st Feb. 1904, son of William G., min. of Arnsheen, and Alison Jollie; educ. at George Watson's College and Univ. of Edinburgh, M.A. (1924), B.D. (1928); licen. by Presb. of Edinburgh April 1927; assistant St Bernard's, Edinburgh 1927; ord. 7th June 1928; trans. to Foveran 20th April 1932; killed in action in France June 1940. Marr. 30th April 1929 Agnes Dorien, daugh. of James Mathers, O.B.E., min. of Rosewell, and Agnes Malseed, and had issue—Maureen Agnes Elizabeth, born 24th Nov. 1934; Arthur William Norman, born 6th Feb. 1937; his widow marr. (2) Malcolm Manford Corner, min. of Drainie.

KELTON

In the 12th century the church was designated Cheletun and Lochelletun. It belonged originally to Iona, and was granted to Holyrood Abbey in 1161–74 by Uchtred, son of Fergus, lord of Galloway.—[*Charters of Holyrood*, 38, 40, 41.]

1567 SIR HERBERT ANDERSON, vicar 3rd Feb. 1567-8.—*Cal. of Charters*, 2108.]

1567 SIR JAMES PAINE, reader, still in office 1572.—[*Comps. Sub Coll. of Thirds, Dumfries*, etc.; *Edin. Tests*, iii, 120.]

1590 DAVID BLYTH, M.A., min. at Kirkcudbright, pres. to vicarage 30th Sept. 1590 on death of Sir Herbert Anderson.—*P. S. Reg.*, lxi, 52.]

1627 ROBERT McCLELLAN, for "insufficiencie, intemperat drinking, and disobedience to the Presbyterie" he was dep. by the Commission of Kirkcudbright appointed by the General Assembly at Glasgow 1638; the sentence was approved by the General Assembly at Edinburgh 27th Aug. 1639.—[Peterkin's *Recs. of the Kirk*, 261.]

1642 JAMES FERGUSON, his son, James, apprenticed to Andrew Brown, surgeon, Edinburgh, 2nd March 1670.

1695 WILLIAM FALCONER, his second son, Gilbert.—[*Sas.* 1727.]

1916 DONALD MacINTYRE HENRY, marr. (1) 3rd Feb. 1920 Agnes (died 22nd May 1922), second daugh. of Stewart Nicolson, Bombie, and had issue—Donald MacIntyre, born 23rd Feb. 1921; Malcolm Nicholson, born 13th May 1922; (2) 12th Aug. 1931 Barbara, youngest daugh. of William Jamieson, min. of St Ringan's, Castle Douglas, and has issue—Alastair, born 27th June 1932.

GELSTON

The Church of Gelston, called also Gemilston and Gevellestoune, was dedicated to St Michael. It was granted to the Priory of Whithorn by John de Gelston, son and heir of (late) John de Gelston, Kt.; confirmation charter by Robert I, 1306–29; annexed to Kells 1618.—[*Reg. Great Seal*, i, App. I, 20; ii, 460.]

1563 JOHN WRIGHT, reader.—[*Comps. Sub Coll. of Thirds, Dumfries*, etc.]

1571 DEAN JOHN MARTIN, vicar and reader in 1571.

1581 MICHAEL HENDERSON, pres. to vicarage and as min. 1st April 1581 on death of Dean John Martin.—[*Reg. Sec. Sig.*, xlvii, 103.]

1591 JOHN TAYLOR, M.A., pres. to vicarage 5th Jan, 1591–2 on death of Robert Stewart.—[*Reg. Sec. Sig.*, lxiii, 111.]

KIRKCORMACK

There were several saints of the name Cormac. One was Bishop of Armagh, who died in 496. Another was Cormac Ua Liathain, a contemporary of Columba and Abbot of Durrow, who voyaged to the Orkneys. He may be the saint here commemorated. The church belonged originally to Iona, and along with the Chapel of Balnacross it was granted in 1161–74 to Holyrood Abbey by Uchtred, son of Fergus, lord of Galloway.—*Charters of Holyrood*, 38, 40, 41; Watson's *Celtic Place Names*, 167.]

1563 SIR MICHAEL DUNN, "ane auld blynd man," vicar in 1563 and 1572, natural son of Sir Herbert D., min., legitimated 23rd Aug. 1550.—[*Kirkcudbright Sher. Court Deeds*, 82; *Comps. Sub Coll. of Thirds, Dumfries*, etc.]

1573 ROBERT FORRESTER, vicar in 1580.—[*Kirkcudbright Sher. Court Deeds*, 108.]

KIRKCUDBRIGHT, GALTWAY, DUNROD

The Church of Kirkcudbright, designated in the 12th and 13th centuries the Church of Desnesmor and Denesmor, and in the 14th century the Church of Kirkcudbright of Denesmor, was granted to Holyrood Abbey by Uchtred, son of Fergus, lord of Galloway, *cir.* 1161–74. On a request by the General Assembly 29th June 1564, Queen Mary granted the Church of the Grey Friars for use as the parish church instead of St Cuthbert's. The latter church stood in the churchyard about quarter-mile east of the town. On 24th Dec. 1580 Sir Nicol McClellane, Sir Herbert Anderson, Mr. Edward Forrester and Ninian Anderson, prebendaries and Stallaris of St Andrew's Church, Kirkcudbright, with consent of the patron of the church, Thomas McClellane of Bombie, disponed the lands, etc., pertaining to the church to Robert Forrester, burgess of Kirkcudbright. The Church of Galtway belonged to Holyrood Abbey before 29th July 1163, and appears to have been granted by Fergus, lord of Galloway, who died in 1161. It was situated about two miles from the town.

The Church of Dunrod, dedicated to St Mary and St Brioc, was granted to Holyrood Abbey by Fergus, lord of Galloway, with confirmation by Christianus, Bishop of Galloway, 1154–86. It stood in the churchyard in the south-east part of the parish, about six miles from Kirkcudbright. On 5th May 1555, at the instance of Mr John Stevenson, precentor of Glasgow, vicar of Dunrod, and first provost of Biggar Collegiate Church, the perpetual vicarage of the church, with fruits and rents, was added, with consent of the patrons, the Canons Regular of Holyrood, and of the Ordinary of the Diocese of Galloway, to the said Collegiate Church of Biggar, on condition that there be provided for a vicar-pensioner of the Cure of Dunrod 20 merks Scots, with house and garden and an acre of arable land. The Charter of Collation of the Bishop of Galloway bears that the vicarage was granted in consideration "of the singular zeal and pious affection towards God and the Catholic Church, which were shown in these unhappy days of Lutheranism by a sometime mighty and noble Lord, Malcolm Fleming, in found the Church of Biggar at his own expense." The collation was on the supplication, 5th March 1555, of James, Lord Fleming, who had right to the patronage and right of the vicarage of Dunrod, and was ratified by Queen Mary on 14th May 1556.—[*Charters of Holyrood*, 19, 20, 22–4, 38, 40, 61, 95–6, 294–8; *Reports Hist. MSS. Commiss.*, iv, 539; *Reg. Great Seal*, v, 86; *Charter Chest, Earl of Wigton*, 540, 546; *Scott. Rec. Soc.*]

1563 ALEXANDER ALLARDYCE, M.A., min. 1563.—[*Comps. Sub Coll. of Thirds, Dumfries*, etc.]

1563 MICHAEL DUNN, exhorter 1563.—[*Comps. Sub Coll. of Thirds, Dumfries*, etc.]

1569 JAMES DODDS, marr. Eupham Kirko.—[See Grant's *Burgh Schools*; *Kirkcudbright Sher. Court Deeds*, 98.]

1575 THOMAS ANDERSON, vicar, reader 1568-9, died before 30th July 1580.—[*Acts and Dec.*, lxi, 335; *Reg. Sec. Sig.*, xlvii, 133; *Comps. Sub Coll. of Thirds, Dumfries*, etc.]

1580 JOHN MEIKLE, pres. to vicarage 30th July 1580 and 11th May 1591.—[*Reg. Sec. Sig.*, xlvii, 133, lxii, 50.]

1589 DAVID BLYTH, son of George B., burgess of Edinburgh, and Margaret Blackburn; pres. to Kelton 30th Sept. 1590; appointed schoolmaster *ad interim* of Kirkcudbright on 12th Oct. 159–; murdered 2nd Sept. 1593 by John, Adam and George, sons of John Muir of Halmuir, and their servants.—[Grant's *Burgh Schools*; *Reg. Sec. Sig.*, lxi, 523; *P. C. Reg.*, 1593; *Reports Hist. MSS. Commiss.*, iv, 539.]

1601 ROBERT GLENDENYNG, line 5, for "1602" read "1601"; his pres. to Dunrod vicarage 15th May 1605 on death of Mungo Carmichael; his son James banished for slaughter of Peter Duncan 21st June 1638.—[*P. C. Reg.*, 2 Ser., vii, 23; *Reg. Sec. Sig.*, lxxiv, 263.]

1638 JOHN McCLELLAN, adm. before 21st Nov. 1638; accompanied Livingston on his voyage to New England in 1636.—[Peterkin's *Records of the Church*, 109.]

1638 GEORGE BUCHANAN, adm. between 2nd July and 26th Aug. 1639 and in defiance that John McClellan held office. (See Moffat.)

1723 GEORGE GARTSHORE, his daugh., Ann (marr. 23rd Oct. 1742 Thomas Gordon of Kenharvie).

1820 GEORGE HAMILTON, his son, John James, died 1917; his daugh., Rose, died 25th Feb. 1917.

1837 JOHN McMILLAN, line 9, for "1877" read "1876"; his daugh., Anne Marshall, died at Janefield, Kirkcudbright, 8th Aug. 1932.

1843 JOHN UNDERWOOD, pres. by Crown 14th July 1843.

1879 ALEXANDER DUNCAN CAMPBELL, licen. 28th Sept. 1870; his widow, Mary Jane Muir, died 23rd Sept. 1931.

1914 WILLIAM BARCLAY, dem. 30th Sept. 1926 on appointment to Custron Church, Hamilton, Ontario.

1927 JOHN ELMORE MOTHERSILL, born 29th Sept. 1890, son of Joseph M. and Eleanor Dobson Mothersill; educ. at Univ. of Toronto, B.A. (1910), and Knox College, Toronto; licen. by Presb. of Toronto 10th April 1913; ord. to Knox Church, Galt, Ontario, Nov. 1913; trans. to Taylor Church, Montreal, March 1915; served in war in R.A.M.C.; assistant Govan 1924; Superintendent, Pearce Institute, Govan; adm. by General Assembly 3rd July 1926; adm. 3rd Feb. 1927. Marr. 21st Sept. 1920 Eleanor Oughtred, and has issue —Alan Keith, Lieut. R.A.F., born 27th Aug. 1921, killed in action, Tunisia, March 1943; Donald Joseph, born 28th May 1923; Eleanor Daintry, born 6th Nov. 1926.

DUNROD

1571 WILLIAM McLELLAN, reader 1571-2.—[*Comps. Sub Coll. of Thirds, Dumfries*, etc.]

1595 JAMES DONALDSON, min. 1595; trans. to Kirkmabreck 1597.

ST. MARY'S ISLE

1563 WILLIAM MOSCROP, M.A., min. of Anwoth, also in charge here.—[*Comps. Sub Coll. of Thirds, Dumfries.*]

1571 THOMAS ANDERSON, exhorter 1571-2.—[*Comps. Sub Coll. of Thirds, Dumfries*, etc.]

PARTON

1562 CHARLES GEDDES, parson in office 13th April 1562, reader 14th May 1566.—[*Reg. Abbrev. Feu Charters of Church Lands*, i, 223; *Reg. Sec. Sig.*, xxxv, 23, 456.]

1563 JOHN DURY, exhorter 1563.—[*Comps. Sub Coll. of Thirds, Dumfries.*]

1574 NINIAN McCLENNOCHAN, afterwards of Glenluce.

1620 JAMES IRVING, marr. Margaret Gordon.—[*G. R. Sas.*, xxxiii, 228, 3rd May 1632.]

1692 SAMUEL SPALDING, marr. cont. 16th April 1693 Elizabeth, daugh. of Gilbert Brown of Templeton; his sons—Alexander, apprenticed to John Speirs, merchant, Edinburgh, 13th Jan. 1720, purchased Holm 1750, died 24th March 1776; William, died before 1731; Samuel, died 1774.

1859 HENRY ALEXANDER PATTULLO, his widow, Maria Mitchell, died at Musselburgh 4th Oct. 1925.

1886 HARVEY NICHOLS, died at Newport, Monmouth, 5th April 1930; his widow, Isabella Blair Sandilands, died at Newport 9th March 1938; his daughs.—Irene Blair (marr. 23rd Sept. 1924 John Alexander Douglas, M.B., Ch.B., Johannesburg); Ruby (marr. 21st Dec. 1922 Frank William Bannister).

RERRICK

One cannot now definitely locate the site of the parish Church in years before the Reformation. There seems to have been at that time not only a parish church, but some chapels in the parish. There was a church, perhaps the parish church, at Kirkcarswell (which is a corrupt form of Kilkoswald); there was also in close proximity to a holy well, known as St Glassin's Well, a chapel at Kirkland, and the names Chapelton and Chapelhill appear to point to some chapel as being located in their neighbourhood. The Abbey Church of Dundrennan was the church of the monks and of the parishioners generally. Soon after the founding of the monastery in the 12th century, the parish church was "appropriated to" the abbey; that is to say, its endowments were transferred to the abbey as part of its revenues and henceforth the duty of ministering at its altar would devolve upon the monks, who would perform other parochial duty. When the Reformation took place in 1560, the parish church once again came into its own, but no certainty exists as to its site at that time, and not until the early part of the 18th century have we definite knowledge that the old chapel at Kirkland was now constituted the parish church. It continued as such till 1865, and on a part of its wall still left standing in the centre of the kirkyard there was on its demolition affixed an inscribed stone with this inscription: "This Church, originally a chapel, was enlarged in 1743 and taken down in 1865." On the demolition of this old church at Kirkland, a new church was erected in the village of Dundrennan and was opened for public worship in 1866.

1580 JAMES HUTTON, formerly Dean and Prior of Dundrennan.—[*Kirkcudbright Sheriff Court Deeds*, 27.]

1590 JOHN BROWN, min. of Glencairn, pres. to vicar pensionary 13th July 1590 on death of William Cutlar.—[*Reg. Sec. Sig.*, lxvi, 197.]

1594 JOHN CALLENDAR, pres. to parsonage and vicarage 5th Aug. 1594 on death of David Blyth.—[*Reg. Sec. Sig.*, lxvi, 197.]

JOHN DUNCAN, his son, Andrew, charged to enter heir 1676.—[*Edinburgh Burgh Writs.*]
1655

WILLIAM JAMIESON, line 7, delete "Father of the Church."
1731

TONGLAND

In 1161-74 the church was granted to Holyrood Abbey by Uchtred, son of Fergus, lord of Galloway. The Cell of St Salvator, near the monastery, and its garden called the Chapel Yard, pertained to the vicarage. The Church of Balnacross was originally a chapel dependent upon Kirkcormack and belonging to Iona. In 1161-74 it was granted to Holyrood Abbey by Uchtred, son of Fergus, lord of Galloway.—[*Charters of Holyrood*, 22-4, 38, 40, 41.]

WILLIAM SHARP, vicar at the Reformation; reader in 1563, exhorter in 1567; pres. to vicarage of Lanark 24th June 1588; his son, Roger.—[*Reg. Sec. Sig.*, lvii, 125; *Dumfries Sas.*, 1st Oct., 1628; *Cal. of Charters*, 2126; *Reg. Mag. Sig.*, v, 782.]
1563

JAMES SCOTT, for "sacriledge, intromitting with penalties and contributions, disobedience to the Presbyterie, tableing, conversing with excommunicat Papists, and declyning the General Assembly" he was dep. by the Commissioners of Kirkcudbright appointed by the General Assembly at Glasgow 1638; the sentence was approved by the General Assembly at Edinburgh 27th Aug. 1639.—[Peterkin's *Recs. of the Kirk of Scot.*, 261.]
1619

GEORGE RUTHERFORD, marr. Margaret Gordon and had issue—Barbara; David; Jean; Marion; Martha.—[*Dumfries Sas.*, 20th Nov. 1630, 31st Dec. 1654.]
1640

ALEXANDER BROWN, line 3, for "22" read "26."
1745

WILLIAM DOW, born 9th Feb. 1800.
1826

WILLIAM LECKIE McFARLANE, pres. by Crown 20th April 1859.
1859

ANDREW EDGAR, pres. by Crown 18th Nov. 1862.
1868

GEORGE McINNES, pres. by Crown 18th Dec. 1874 (last presentation); his widow, Margaret Hamilton, died 15th Aug. 1928.
1875

WILLIAM IRELAND GORDON, died 29th Jan. 1927.
1881

BRYCE MACFARLANE, died 25th July 1931.
1898

(*Charges united 3rd Feb.* 1932.)

TWYNHOLM and KIRKCHRIST

The parishes were united after 31st July 1643. The Church of Twynholm was granted to Holyrood Abbey by Uchtred, son of Fergus, lord of Galloway, whose time was *cir.* 1161-74. It was rebuilt in 1730 on a new site about quarter-mile from the earlier building. Portions of the walls of the Church of Kirkchrist stand in the churchyard on the west bank of the Dee opposite Kirkcudbright. At Kirkeoch in the Parish of Kirkchrist there was a nunnery, the existence of which is recalled by place names of the neighbourhood, High Nunton, Nun Mill, Low Nunton. Manifestly this is the nunnery cited in a Papal Bull of 22nd May 1423 giving assent to a petition by John of Inverkeithing, Canon of Holyrood, who craved that the Cistercian Priory of St Evoca the virgin, situated in the Diocese of Whithorn, value not exceeding 10 libs., be given to him in commendam for five years. The priory had been governed by "holy nuns and matrons," but on account of the meagre amount of the fruits had long since been deserted by them, and was now empty and derelict, and he was desirous that goods set apart to God and religion should not be devoted to lay and secular uses. About forty years later, the nunnery, designated "the Church or Chapel of Kirkeoch" where "a nun or otherwise religious woman used to dwell of old," was the subject of a petition of Robert de Colston, Rector of Kirkchrist, which narrated that his predecessor held as united to the said Parish Church of Kirkchrist, the church or chapel called Kyrknok or Kyrkenok (Kirkeoch) situated in the bounds of the parish, took its tithes, etc., and exercised the cure of souls of the parishioners who dwelled thereby, and that he had continued the said possession for about eight years, that there was no further proof of the said union, and therefore his use of the tithes and his possession might be interfered with, that no nun or religious woman had for thirty years lived a regular life in the said church or chapel, and that its buildings had fallen, and it had been so long void that there was no certain knowledge of its voidance. Pope Pius II on 10th Jan. 1463-4 gave mandate to the Bishop of Brechin, etc., to make enquiries, and if they found the facts as stated, to confirm the said union.—[*Vatican Transcripts*, 1421-59, 90, MS. Reg. Ho.; *Cal. Papal Register, Letters*, xi, 507; *Reg. Great Seal*, viii, 127, ix, 1416; *Charters of Holyrood*, 31, 38, 40.]

RICHARD BALFOUR, parson.—
1562   [*Coll. of Thirds*, 1562, 101.]

ALEXANDER COLE, pres. to vicarage
1580   18th Oct. 1580 on death of John Row.—[*Reg. Sec. Sig.*, xlvii, 31.]

JOHN AIKMAN, pres. to vicarage in
1582   1582 on death of John Row and again 19th Oct. 1592.—[*Reg. Pres. Bene.*, ii, 72; *Reg. Sec. Sig.*, lxv, 256.]

THOMAS IRELAND, marr. Agnes
1672   Burd, widow of William Menzies, min. of Kenmore; resident with his wife at Inveresk in 1694.—[*Inveresk Poll Tax Roll*, 8.]

LEO WRIGHT, signs an episcopal
1680   charter 17th Dec. 1680.

ROBERT ALLARDYCE, died 7th
1899   Sept. 1939.

KIRKCHRIST

JOHN MOFFAT, reader, 1563.—
1563   [*Comps. Sub Coll. of Thirds, Dumfries.*]

ROBERT FORRESTER, reader
1568   1568.

THOMAS MAKCULTRIE, reader 1569
1569   -72.—[*Comps. Sub Coll. of Thirds, Dumfries.*]

DAVID BLYTH. M.A., pres. to
1591   vicarage 9th Oct. 1591 consequent on James McCulloch, vicar, being non-resident.—[*Reg. Sec. Sig.*, lxii, 192.]

SYNOD OF GLASGOW AND AYR

PRESBYTERY OF AYR

ALLOWAY

Preliminary paragraph, line 5 from end, for "right bank" read "left bank."

JOHN LOCHHEAD, born 18th Nov. 1833, died 12th Nov. 1913; marr. (1) 1867 Mary Anne, daugh. of John McLean, Glasgow, and Anne Niven (died July 1900), and had issue—John McLean, born 1867, medical practitioner, Indianapolis, Indiana, U.S.A.; Anne Niven McLean, born 1869; Thomas McLean, born 1871; (2) 1901, Eliza, daugh. of John Houston, Sandyhills, Shettleston; she died at Cheltenham 24th Oct. 1937.
1859

SAMUEL MARCUS DILL, died at Edinburgh 23rd Jan. 1924; his widow, Agnes Graham Rowe, died 2nd April 1934 aged 85; his daughs.— Hessy Foster (marr. 19th Sept. 1924 William John Jackson, Croydon); Rosa (marr. 22nd Feb. 1922 Edward Wickham Jones, M.C., Norwood, London), died 4th Dec. 1927.
1881

JOHN MACFARLANE HAMILTON, marr. 21st April 1925 Mary Hamilton, daugh. of Gavin Crawford, min. of Fauldhouse, and has issue—Gavin Crawford, born 26th Sept. 1926; Margaret Macfarlane, born 30th Oct. 1929.
1918

ANNBANK

ROBERT SMITH MACKINTOSH, delete "M.A."
1913

GEORGE LINDSAY STEWART, trans. to St. Paul's, Leith, 9th Dec. 1920.
1917

GEORGE ANDREW JOHNSTON, born Chapel of Garioch 1st Dec. 1889, son of Alexander J., farmer, and Jane Durno; educ. at Chapel of Garioch Public School, Gordon's College and Univ. of Aberdeen, M.A. (1911); licen. by Presb. of Garioch 1914; served in Mountain Gun Battery R.G.A. in Great War; ord. by Presb. of Paisley, Chaplain to Forces 27th July 1917; assistant Arbroath 1920; adm. 20th April 1921; trans. to Kirkmichael, Ayr, 26th Sept. 1930; marr. 1st Dec. 1921 Frances Hardy, daugh. of Albert Ping, Excise Officer, and Christina Miller, Auchtertool, and has issue—Alexander Durno, born Oct. 1926; Jack Miller, born Oct. 1928.
1921

AUCHENLECK

The interior of the church was destroyed by fire on 3rd April 1938 and has since been restored. The mission chapel at Dargonner is closed.

JOHN GRANT, marr. cont. 2nd Dec. 1712 Henrietta, daugh. of Donald Campbell of Boghall and Elizabeth Innes.
1712

JAMES HILL, died 27th Sept. 1940. Issue—Alexander, B.Sc., Electrical Engineer; Hugh Blair McLellan, B.Sc., Lecturer Mechanical Engineering; Alison Irene, diploma in Physical Instruction; Eric Alan, diploma in Art.
1893

AYR

(Contributed by Rev. Archibald MacKenzie, Minister of Ayr (2nd Charge).)

It is uncertain as to when a Christian church was first planted at Ayr, but that a Christian church existed at Ayr at the beginning of the 13th century can be authenticated, and indeed it may even date from the latter part of the 12th century. The earliest reference to this church is 1233 in the Chartulary of the Abbey of Paisley. It was a prebend of Glasgow, and of the Chapel Royal at Stirling. The Ayr church in pre-reformation days was never collegiate; it was only a parish church of the larger type with its twelve altars at least and its numerous clergy staff.

In 1652 Cromwell had his citadel built at Ayr with stones which, it is said, were taken from the old castle at Ardrossan. The church, which was included in the fortifications, was utilised as a military store, the chancel being kept as a place of worship for the soldiers. In 1660 the citadel was abandoned and gradually demolished, but the church remained intact. At the Indulgence it was purchased by John Moor of Park, and the Rev. Wm. Eccles, who had been "outed" for refusing to sign the Test Act, was brought back and ministered within its walls from 1687 and 1689, while the curates occupied the present old parish church. In 1690 it was once more derelict until 1706, when the structure was bought by four burgesses of Ayr. One of these gave his fourth share of the stones to build a steeple to the Tolbooth, and the remainder of the stones were in time used to build dykes in and about the town. The tower, which was left, has been restored by the Marquis of Bute and is open to visitors. It contains four apartments.

1559 ROBERT ACHESOUNE, min. 1559–61. —[*Ayr Burgh Accounts.*]

1560 JAMES DALRYMPLE, pres. to vicarage in 1571 on death of Sir Robert Leggett.—[*Reg. Pres. Bene.*, i, (2), 19.]

1561 DAVID GIBSON, parson 1561.

1561 ROBERT DENNISTOUN or DANIELSTON, parson in 1541–2; dem. before 16th Feb. 1573–4, when he was parson of Dysart and Canon of Chapel Royal of Stirling.—[*Reg. of Deeds*, v, 209; vi 104; x, 102; xi, 26.]

1573 JAMES COCKBURN, son of Patrick C. of Clerkington, pres. to parsonage and vicarage 16th Feb. 1573, on dem. of Robert Danielston.—[*Reg. Pres. Bene.*, i, (4), 17.]

1573 HEW KENNEDY, reader, pres. to vicarage 23rd March 1573–4 on dem. of James Dalrymple promoted to Alloway.—[*Reg. Pres. Bene.*, i, (4), 18.]

1574 ROBERT HERBERTSON, was parson in 1563 and still in office 21st May 1576; had issue—John.—[*Cal. of Charters*, xi, 2395; *Reg. Abbrev. Feu Charters of Church Lands*, ii, 88.]

1580 JOHN PORTERFIELD, pres. in 1581 upon death of James Dalrymple and in 1582 on death of Robert Herbertson.—[*Reg. Pres. Bene.*, i, 57, 58.]

1582 WILLIAM MONTGOMERIE, pres. to parsonage 20th June 1582 on death of Robert Herbertson.—[*Reg. Pres. Bene.*, i, 75.]

1594 ROBERT MONTGOMERIE, M.A., parson 9th Nov. 1594.—[*Cal. of Charters*, xiv, 3296.]

1607 GEORGE DUNBAR, marr. Margaret Wallace.—[*Reg. of Deeds*, cxcviii, 407.]

1638 ROBERT BLAIR, M.A.; on 19th Dec. 1638, on a supplication in name of the town of St Andrews for his transportation to the church there, "for the good of their Universitie," the General Assembly called upon Mr Blair, who answered, "I confesse I am in the hands of this Assembly; but I protest heir, in God's presence, that I had rather lay downe my life nor be separat from my flock at Air." The matter was referred to a committee, who reported on 20th Dec., and after a prolonged discussion the Assembly by a majority of 4 or 5 decerned that he be transported to St Andrews.—[Peterkin's *Recs. of the Kirk*, pp. 187, 189.]

JOHN FERGUSHILL, graduated M.A.,
1639 1611, not 1612.

ALEXANDER GREGORIE, marr.
1683 Anna, daugh. of Alexander Ross, merchant burgess of Aberdeen.—[*Aberdeen City Sas.*, 2nd July 1680.]

JOHN HUNTER, line 15, delete
1701 "Father of the Church."

THOMAS DYKES, pres. by Crown 24th
1863 Jan. 1863; his widow, Margaret Shedden, died 18th Nov. 1922.

WILLIAM CAIRNS DUNCAN, died
1909 3rd May 1926.

WILLIAM PHIN GILLIESON, M.C.,
1926 trans. from 2nd Charge 22nd July 1926; died 30th March 1942; his daugh., Margaret Marion Phin (marr. 19th Dec. 1939 James Macpherson Jolly, elder son of James J., New York). Addl. Publication—*Letters from Sudan* (1936).

SECOND CHARGE

WILLIAM WATERSTON, his son,
1682 Alexander, apprenticed to William Thomson, periwig-maker, 23rd Aug 1710.

JOHN McDERMETT, probably matri-
1716 culated at Glasgow 1st March 1698.

WILLIAM SHAW, pres. by Crown 27th
1853 May 1853.

ARCHIBALD MACKENZIE, trans.
1926 from Balfron (*q.v.*) 23rd Nov. 1926; served in Great War as Captain, H.L.I., and Staff Captain R.A.F.; acted as min. of St Andrews, Georgetown, Demerara and Commissioner from the Home Church in that Colony 1937–8. Publications—*William Adair and his Kirk; The Old Kirk of Ayr, 1639–84 (Ayr Advertiser,* 1933); *An Ancient Church: the Pre-Reformation Church at Ayr (Ayrshire Post,* 1935); *An Old Church and Burns' Memories (Ayrshire Post,* 1934).

NEWTON-UPON-AYR

WILLIAM RAINIE, dem. 11th June
1881 1928, died 27th Nov. 1928.

DAVID ALBERT MURDOCH, line 3,
1928 for "Benter" read "Baxter"; served in Great War with Seaforth Highlanders on Salonica Front and on Intelligence Staff of B.M.R. in Sophia; trans. from Dingwall (*q.v.*) 14th Nov. 1928; died 14th March 1945. Addl. issue—Kenneth Lyle Stewart, born 1st Aug. 1928; Dorothy Margaret, born 29th April 1933.

AYR, ST. JAMES

JOHN HENDERSON, M.A. (Glasgow,
1889 1879).

MUIR ANDREW, dem. 17th May
1919 1921.

THOMAS REID ALLISON, born
1921 Paisley 20th Feb. 1889, son of Matthew A. and Margaret Reid; educ. at John Neilson School, Paisley, and Univ. of Glasgow, M.A. (1910); licen. by Presb. of Paisley Jan. 1920; ord. 7th Sept. 1921; trans. to Helensburgh Old 6th Aug. 1930. Marr. 30th Aug. 1921 Margaret Gemmell, daugh. of James Graham and Rachel Graham, and had issue—Thomas Reid, born 20th Aug. 1924; Margaret Graham, born 26th March 1927.

AYR, ST. LEONARD'S

"St Leonard's Chaplainrie without the Port of Ayr" occurs in 1585.—[*Comps. Gen. Coll. of Thirds.*]

WILLIAM GRANGER, licen. 4th June
1886 1884.—[*Memoir by James Millar.*]

WILLIAM WALKER, afterwards min.
1898 of Foss 23rd Nov. 1926.

JOHN ELLIS, trans. to Rubislaw, Aber-
1919 deen, 5th Sept. 1930; died 21st Sept. 1939.

AYR, WALLACETOWN

GEORGE JOHN CHALMERS
1865 SCOTT, his daughs.—Ethel Agnes Watson, born 30th May 1866 (marr. 7th Oct. 1893 Captain Thomas Josiah

Clugston Boyd, of S.S. *Lord Rosebery*), died 12th Jan. 1931; Lilian Anna (marr. 26th Oct. 1895 Charles Frederick Pfeiffer, merchant, London), died 18th May 1906; Jessie Helen (marr. 7th April 1897 Robert Brewster Cowan, insurance inspector); Amy Constance, died 13th July 1935; Bertram Watson, died 1st Feb. 1913.

1917 JOHN MARTIN, trans. to Dalmuir 17th June 1924.

1924 BRODIE SMITH GILFILLAN, trans. from Inch (*q.v.*) 5th Nov. 1924; dem. 15th Nov. 1944; his son, John Brodie Smith, born 7th April 1921; his wife, Helen Johnston Smith, died 21st Nov. 1931.

BARR

1665 HERCULES LINDSAY, designed preacher at Monkton 1st June 1678.—[*Regs. of Deeds*, lxxxv, 971, 26th April 1698.]

1843 JAMES MACMASTER, pres. 21st Aug. 1843.

1859 WILLIAM MUNGALL, pres. 21st Sept. 1858.

1873 CHARLES GOODALL, pres. 1st Mar. 1873; his widow, Jane Watson, died 18th Sept. 1941; his son, Dr Charles, died 6th Oct. 1941.

1889 GEORGE DODS, died 31st May 1922; his daughs.—Ida Mary Homan, died at Karachi 13th March 1921; Edith Jane (marr. 18th Aug. 1896 Rowland, 6th Baron Headley); his widow, Eliza Mary Homan, died 18th June 1942.

1922 ANDREW DOUGLAS McMURRAY, born Castle Douglas 18th July 1890; son of Andrew McM. and Margaret Affleck; educ. at Whitehaven Ghyll Bank College and Univ. of Edinburgh, M.A.; licen. by Presb. of Edinburgh 30th June 1920; assistant Glasgow Cathedral; ord. 18th Oct. 1922; LL.B. (London); L.V.C.M. (London).

CATRINE

1899 WILLIAM JOHN, appointed Clerk of Presb. 3rd Sept. 1930; dem. 31st May 1948; his son, Graham Taylor, headmaster, Coldingham school, Berwickshire; his daughs.—Marjorie Patricia (marr. 22nd Sept. 1941 William McCreath, 2nd Lieut. R.A.S.C., Dalruaine, Troon); Kathleen (marr. 27th June 1946 Leslie Richard Leonard Parry, South Woodford, London).

COYLTON

1581 MATTHEW WYLLIE, pres. to vicarage in 1582 on death of Alexander Scott.—[*Reg. Pres. Bene.*, i, 57.]

1654 WILLIAM RICHARDSON, has sasine of glebe 8th March 1654.—[*Ayr Sas.*, i, 144.]

1700 WILLIAM BOYD, his mother was Margaret Naismith.

1866 JAMES GLASGOW, his widow, Margaret Macfarlane Maitland, died 29th Jan. 1929.

1917 WILLIAM CRAWFORD, trans. to Uphall North 24th Feb. 1932; dem. 6th Nov. 1946; marr. 4th Sept. 1935 Elizabeth Fleming, third daugh. of Peter Watson of Drumsine, and has issue—Gavin Fleming, born 14th Sept. 1936; Elizabeth Jane, born 12th April 1938.

CRAIGIE

1548 THOMAS MARJORIBANKS, M.A., pres. to vicarage 16th Nov. 1548 vacant by death of his brother Robert, who had received a presentation on 2nd May same year in succession to John Hamilton, M.A.; still vicar 1572, a prebendary of Corstorphine (*q.v.*) in succession to his said late brother Robert.—[*Comps. Gen. Coll. of Thirds*; *P. S. Reg.*, ii, 2026, 2027, 2756.]

1806 JOHN STIRLING, line one, for "John" read "James."

1843 ROBERT INGLIS, his daugh., Margaret Ann, died at Troon 23rd March 1930.

DAVID STIRLING, his widow, Agnes Maria Fairlie, died at Largs 9th Feb. 1925.
1859

WILLIAM CAMPBELL, died 6th June 1920; his widow, Janet Burns Lindsay, died at Edinburgh 10th Oct. 1926, aged 75; his son, Gavin Lindsay, died Davidsons Mains 5th Jan. 1938.
1883

ROBERT JOHN PAUL, trans. from Elder Park, Glasgow, 25th Nov. 1920; died 7th June 1929.
1920

CROSSHILL

ROBERT STEWART, licen. 1887; dem. 5th Aug. 1925; died 18th Jan. 1926; his widow, Jane Stewart, died 4th Dec. 1943; his daughs. Elizabeth Margaret (marr. 1st June 1927 Louis Herbert Watson, min. of St Luke's, Edinburgh); Agnes McFadzean, died Edinburgh 24th Nov. 1941.
1888

JAMES STORRY BARROWMAN, trans. from Carntyne (*q.v.*) 14th Jan. 1926, died 30th Oct. 1930; his widow, Mary Leitch Anderson, died 10th March 1937; his daugh., Dorothy Freda (marr. 2nd Aug. 1933 William R. Eadie).
1926

(*Charges united 25th Feb. 1931.*)

CUMNOCK

JOHN DUNBAR, designed parson and vicar, also Canon of Glasgow, 13th Aug. 1561.—[*Cal. of Deeds*, iv, 300.]
1560

JOHN RAMAGE, reader 1573.—[*Comps. Gen. Coll. of Thirds.*]
1573

GEORGE CAMPBELL, pres. to vicarage on death of John Ryhnd.—[*Reg. Pres. Bene.*, i, (4), 43.]
1579

WILLIAM HAMILTON, M.A., parson 2nd April 1584.—[*Cal. of Charters*, xii, 2720.]
1578

JOHN SPENCE ROBERTSON, died at Axminster, Devon, 1st June 1934; his wife, Catherine Forbes Sharp, died 12th July 1928; his sons—Robert, a barrister; Rev. Edmund Downing, died at Sidmouth 14th Jan. 1942; his daugh., Lillian Mabel Forbes (marr. 25th March 1936 Robert Edward Campion, Oldham).
1875

JOHN DOUGLAS McCLYMONT, born Glasgow 30th Nov. 1903; son of John Douglas McC. (died Feb. 1924), Glencaple and Glasgow, and Margaret Murray (died Jan. 1937); educ. North Kelvinside Secondary School and Univ. of Glasgow; M.A. (1924); B.D. (1927); licen. by Presb. of Glasgow April 1927; assistant St Bernard's, Glasgow, New Kilpatrick, and Glasgow Cathedral; ord. (ass. and suc.) 23rd Nov. 1927. Contributor to *Chambers's Journal* and other periodicals.
1927

NEW CUMNOCK

HUGH CRAWFORD, his second daugh.—[*Reg. of Deeds, Durie*, 194, 23rd Dec. 1736.]
1653

JAMES MILLAR, died 5th March 1921.
1886

WILLIAM BODIN, ord. (ass. and suc.) 12th May 1920; trans. to New Ardrossan (*q.v.*) 31st May 1926.
1920

ANDREW BURNETT, trans. from Martyrs, Glasgow (*q.v.*), 25th Nov. 1926; marr. 28th Aug. 1945 Meta Louisa, daugh. of Alfred Hitchcock, F.E.I.S., Edinburgh.
1926

DAILY

The alternative name of the parish, Dalmakeran, Dalmakerane, or Dalmulkerane, is *Dail Mhaoil-Chiaran*, "Holme of St Ciaran's servant." The church was granted to Paisley Abbey by Duncan, son of Gilbert, Earl of Carrick, and himself Earl of Carrick, on condition that the abbey erected in Carrick a monastery of the Cluniac Order, and gave the church to the said monastery. The grant was confirmed by Florence, Bishop-Elect of Glasgow, in 1202, and by Alexander II 5th Aug. 1236. In terms of that condition the church was given to Crossraguel Abbey on its foundation soon after 18th July 1244. In 1696 the church was removed to a central position, and was rebuilt in 1766.—[*Reg. of Paisley*, 427-8; Watson's *Celtic Place Names*, 417; see Kirkoswald.]

1590 ALEXANDER BOYD, vicar, deprived before 17th March 1590-1 for absence from his charge.—[*Miscel. Eccles. Documents*, 23; *Reg. Sec. Seal*, lxii, 35.]

1590 DAVID BARCLAY, M.A., pres. to vicarage 16th April 1591 on dep. of Alexander Boyd, non-resident.—[*Reg. Sec. Sig.*, lxii, 35.]

1660 ANDREW MILLAR, M.A. (Glasgow 1650.)

1665 THOMAS SKINNER, was 51 years of age Oct. 1684.—[*Reg. Sec. Sig.*, 3 Ser., ix, 538.]

1691 PATRICK CRAUFORD, his sons—Hew (eldest); James.—[*Deeds Mack.* 1705, No. 818.]

1724 WILLIAM PATON, marr. Janet, daugh. of Alexander Kennedy of Drummellan.

1841 WILLIAM CHALMERS, pres. by Crown 12th March 1841; his son, William Bryce, died 10th April 1922.

1843 DAVID STRONG, pres. by Crown 12th July 1843. Line 21, add "of Kilmarnock" after parish.

1855 CORNELIUS GIFFEN, pres. by Crown 9th June 1855.

1869 GEORGE TURNBULL, pres. 27th June 1869; his widow, Elizabeth Steel Colledge, died at Glasgow 27th Feb. 1921; his daugh., Elizabeth, died 5th June 1921; his son, John Colledge, died 13th June 1942.

1908 CHARLES GOODALL, trans. to St Oswald's, Edinburgh, 15th Jan. 1924.

1924 DAVID ALEXANDER DUNCAN, ord. 30th April 1924; trans. to Kilmadock 17th May 1929.

DALMELLINGTON

1562 RANKEN DAVIDSON, pres. in 1569 on death of Sir John Dunlop.—[*Reg. Pres. Bene.*, i, 28.]

1572 DAVID CATHCART, pres. in 1572 on death of Sir John Dunlop.—[*Reg. Pres. Bene.*, i, (3), 24; *Cal. of Charters*, xi, 2475.]

1591 JOHN McQUORNE, pres. to vicarage 20th Dec. 1591 on death of David Cathcart.—[*Reg. Sec. Sig.*, lxiii, 87.]

1621 GAVIN STEWART, son of Hector S., merchant burgess of Glasgow; marr. Rachel, daugh. of Patrick Sharpe, min. of Govan. Addl. issue—John, M.A. (Glasgow 1651).

1880 GEORGE SMITH HENDRIE, line 6, add "Univ. of Leipzig"; line 11, for "Gairdner" read "Aitken"; dem. 25th Nov. 1924, died at Edinburgh 18th May 1945; his son, John Gairdner White, min. of Dunnottar and Colombo.

1925 JOHN SHEDDEN, M.A., trans. from Haggs 30th April 1925; trans. to St Clement's, Dundee, 11th Sept. 1928.

1929 WILLIAM RUTHERFORD MELROSE, born 3rd Sept. 1900, son of George M. and Agnes Loudon, St Boswells, Roxburghshire; educ. at Galashiels Academy and Univ. of Edinburgh, M.A. (1923); licen. by Presb. of Edinburgh 1st April 1926; assistant Goven; ord. 27th March 1929; dem. 1st Feb. 1933; adm. to St Donan's, Kildonan, Arran, 2nd Aug. 1935; trans. to Rutherglen West 26th April 1938; trans. to Eassie and Nevay 24th June 1943; trans. to Tewchar 8th Oct. 1947. Marr. 6th July 1929 Mary McAnally, daugh. of John Brown and Agnes Ramsay, and has issue—James Henderson Loudon, born 24th March 1930.

WATERSIDE

1907 JOHN MACKINTOSH, line 3, for "June" read "Jan."

1915 JOHN CADENHEAD, died 4th March 1929, unmarried.

ROBERT NICOLSON TULLOCH ANDERSON, born 16th June 1878, son of Robert Henry A., Standard Life Assurance Co., Edinburgh, and Annie Mathieson Humphray; educ. Royal High School, Edinburgh, and Univ. of Glasgow; became missionary and came here from Invergordon 4th Aug. 1929; licen. by Presb. of Ayr 2nd July 1930; dem. Nov. 1930; ord. to Dunrossness 9th Dec. 1930; dem. 1st July 1948. Marr. 3rd July 1916 Rose Emily, younger daugh. of George Lloyd Fountain of Greenford, Middlesex.
1929

DALRYMPLE

JOHN ADAMS, M.A., Moderator of General Assembly 1744.
1727

ROBERT STEVEN, son of Hugh S. of Barransmill, Girvan, and Agnes, daugh. of John Brown of Littleton.
1798

GEORGE ALLAN SEATH, died at Ayr 6th March 1945; his widow, Agnes Jane McCosh Hammond, died at Ayr 3rd May 1948.
1902

DUNDONALD

In or about 1221 the church, along with the Chapels of Crosbie and Riccarton, was granted to the Convent of St Mary of Dalmullin by Walter (II), son of Alan, Seneschal of Scotland. In 1238, when the said convent became a cell of Paisley Abbey, the church with its chapels also became part of the abbey possessions—confirmed by William, Bishop of Glasgow, in 1239. The Chapel of St Ninian, situated near the Royal Castle of Dundonald, where Robert II died in 1390, was termed the Chapel Royal of Dundonald. On 9th July 1511 Sir John Leith was indicted for breaking into the chapel and the chest of ornaments, and carrying off "the book, chalice, and ornaments of said chapel."—[*Reg. of Paisley*, 18, 22, 225–6; *Diocesan Reg. of Glasgow*, i, 493, 495, 511; ii, 23–4, 369, 383–4, 415, 500; *Excheq. Rolls*, iii, lxxii, xcv–vi, 242, 279, 280.]

HUGH MONTGOMERY, M.A., vicar 6th Jan. 1562–3 and 1568.—[*Cal. of Charters*, ix, 1901; *Comps. Sub Coll. of Thirds, Stirling*, etc.]
1562

ROBERT RAMSAY, sometime schoolmaster at Irvine.
1625

GABRIEL MAXWELL, his son, Robert, apprenticed to Hugh Cunningham, merchant, Edinburgh, 2nd July 1684.—[*G. R. Sas.*, 2 Ser., vi, 245.]
1642

THOMAS WALKER, marr. (1) Mary Montgomery, died 3rd April 1741, and had issue—Jean; (2) Jean Robertson; (3) Ann Shaw. Clerk of Synod.
1732

JOHN MACLEOD, son of Alexander M., who emigrated to North Carolina.
1816

ALEXANDER WILLISON, his son, Alexander Stewart, min. of Saline.
1841

JAMES HOGG GILLESPIE, marr. (2) 21st Dec. 1944 Jean, eldest daugh. of Rev. William Campbell, Kilmarnock; his daughs.—Kathleen Barbara (marr. 30th June 1933 William Barclay, min. of Trinity Church, Renfrew); Alison Drysdale (marr. 14th Aug. 1936 Lachlan McLean Robertson, min. of Macmillan Church, Glasgow); Elspeth Taylor, M.A. (marr. 1st July 1937 Andrew Murray Richmond Martin, M.A., C.A., Glasgow); Marjorie, M.D., Glasgow, 1931. Publications—*James Brown, a 'King o' Men'* (Church of Scotland Committee on Publications, 1939); *Dundonald, a Contribution to Parochial History* (John Wylie & Co., Glasgow, 1939), two volumes.
1902

FISHERTON

WILLIAM MURDOCH, his widow, Sarah Davidson McCracken, died 7th March 1940.
1870

JOHN AITKEN SPENCE, trans to Norrieston 18th Nov. 1927.
1918

DAVID GRANT MILNE, trans. from Stronsay (*q.v.*) 20th April 1928.
1928

FULLARTON

1837 DAVID WILSON, his son, William Cunningham, solicitor and bank agent, Irvine, died 29th Sept. 1931.

1876 JOSEPH THOMSON PATON, his widow, Maggie Charles Ward, died 14th Jan. 1936.

1903 JOHN PATERSON, res. in ill health 1937; died 18th Oct. 1938.

GALSTON

The parsonage as well as the vicarage belonged to the Red Friars of Fail.—[*Cal. Papal Letters*, xii, 377.]

1559 SIR JAMES DOUGLAS, vicar 26th Aug. 1559.—[*Reg. Mag. Sig.*, v, 998.]

1566 JOHN DOUGLAS, M.A., vicar 26th March 1566-7.—[*Cal. of Charters*, ix, 2024.]

1568 RANKEN DAVIDSON, exhorter at Loudoun (*q.v.*).

1578 JOHN WALLACE, son of Adam W., burgess of Glasgow; pres. to vicarage 1st Jan. 1578-9 on dem. of Sir John Cunningham.—[*Reg. Pres. Bene.*, ii, 10; *Comps. Gen. Coll. of Thirds.*]

1582 JOHN MARTINE, pres. to vicarage 8th March 1582 on death of Michael Henryson.—[*Reg. Pres. Bene.*, i, 86.]

1591 JOHN TAYLOR, M.A., pres. to vicar. 5th Jan. 1591-2 on death of Robert Stewart.—[*Reg. Sec. Sig.*, lxiii, 111.]

1592 ALEXANDER WALLACE, M.A., pres. parsonage 17th Jan. 1592 on death of John Wallace.—[*Reg. Sec. Sig.*, lxxv, 7.]

1648 ALEXANDER BLAIR, his son, Alexander, merchant, Edinburgh.

1672 ADAM ALASOUN, his marriage cont. dated 27th Jan. 1659.—[*Kirkcudbright Sher. Court Deeds*, 125.]

1687 ROBERT SYMSON, residing with his wife, Margaret Hamilton, in Tolbooth Parish, Edinburgh, 8th Nov. 1694. Addl. issue—James, bapt. 18th July 1695.—[*Aberdeen Reg.*]

1887 JAMES ALLAN HOGG, his son, Robert Blacklock, M.C., Lieut. Border Regiment; his daughs.—Helen Arthur (marr. Sydney H. R. Warnes, min. of Buckie); Mary Allan, died April 1925. Publication—*Jesus which is called Christ*, a pamphlet on the Fourth Gospel; numerous pamphlets, including *The Wonder in Darkness* (1938).

GIRVAN

1578 ALEXANDER BOYD, pres. to vicarage 6th March 1578-9 on death of Robert McNeil.—[*Reg. Pres. Bene.*, ii, 13.]

1601 ANDREW BOYD, son of Quinten B. of Allerthew, pres. to vicarage 2nd April 1601.—[*Reg. Sec. Sig.*, lxxii, 35.]

1674 ALEXANDER GADERER, set up a meeting house at Keith 1706, died 1714.

1848 WILLIAM CORSON, his son, Lockhart Dobbie, S.S.C., died 5th June 1926.

1888 SAMUEL CAMPBELL FRY, died 31st Dec. 1922; his daughs.—Janet Ranken Campbell (marr. 8th March 1924 William Shairp, M.C., Oban); Jane Ranken Campbell, died 24th Oct. 1942.

1923 ROBERT SMITH MACKINTOSH, trans. from St Margaret's, Arbroath (*q.v.*) 27th June 1923; had addl. issue—Athole Spalding, born 16th June 1926; Fiona Martin Ancell, born 10th April 1924. Publications—Contributions to periodicals.

GIRVAN SOUTH

1907 THOMAS GOURLAY SINCLAIR, dem. 30th March 1947.

GLENBUCK

1895 COLIN ARCHIBALD MACKENZIE, died 27th March 1935.

KIRKMICHAEL

In 1370–80 the church is described as the Parish Church of St Michael of Munthyrduffy, with the variation Menterduff in 1386–1400; and in 1470 there is the Parish of Munterduff. The designation "Parish of Kirkmichael" occurs on 3rd July 1443 and 30th July 1564. On 26th Oct. 1545 John Kennedy, son of Hugh K. of Girvan Mains, was instituted in the office of Clerkship of the Church by Sir Hugh Crawe, vicar, who in confirmation delivered to him a bell and stoup of holy water, as is usual in like cases.—[*Laing Charters*, 64, 72, 73; *Reg. Mag. Sig.*, ii, 1810, iv, 1548; *Cal. Papal Letters*, ix, 4; Colville's *Prot. Book*, 5, (8a)].

ANDREW CHARTERIS, sometime parson.—[*Acts and Dec.*, xxiv, 937.]
1564

SIR THOMAS McGUDE, vicar.—[*Comps. Sub Coll. of Thirds, Stirling*, etc.]
1568

ROBERT PEEBLES, his mother was Marion, daugh. of Robert Hunter of Hunterston. Addl. issue—Patrick, M.A. (Glasgow 1653); Robert, M.A. (Glasgow 1653).
1635

JOHN HUNTER, described as late of Kirkmichael and Ireland; went to Coylton 1692.—[*Deeds, Durie*, 1705, No. 471.]
1691

JAMES GILCHRIST, marr. Margaret Aird.—[*Reg. of Deeds, Durie*, 27th April 1710.]
1691

JAMES LAURIE, delete "M.A. Glasgow 1707."
1711

JOHN RAMSAY, his father, a weaver; adm. burgess of Glasgow 12th Jan. 1792. Marr. Margaret, daugh. of John McFadzean; his daughs.—Janet (marr. Adam Thomson); Margaret (marr. Robert McDermeit, Fergushall).
1766

HENRY ALEXANDER FAIRLIE, pres. 26th June 1866.
1866

WILLIAM HENRY RANKINE, died 11th July 1921; his son, George, died Diamantina Hospital, Brisbane, 25th Sept. 1935.
1918

GEORGE CHARLES SMITH, born Shettleston, Lanarkshire, 24th Dec. 1889, son of Henry S. and Anne Martha Thomson; educ. at Eastbank Academy and Univ. of Glasgow, M.A. (1915); served in War 1914–19, Military Cross; licen. by Presb. of Glasgow 28th June 1920; assistant Cathcart; ord. 8th Dec. 1921; trans. to Dunoon High Church 16th May 1930; trans. to Lochwinnoch 18th Feb. 1948. Marr. 19th April 1919 Catherine, daugh. of Alexander Burleigh and Jessie Malcolm, and has issue—Dorothy Kathryn Malcolm, born 17th June 1933; Harry Charles Thomson, born 28th July 1936.
1921

KIRKOSWALD

Under the designation the Church of St Oswald of Turberry, the church was granted to Paisley Abbey by Duncan, son of Gilbert, Earl of Carrick, and himself Earl of Carrick, on condition that the abbey founded in Carrick a monastery of the Cluniac Order, and gave the church to the said monastery. The grant was confirmed by Florence, Bishop-Elect of Glasgow, in 1202, and by Alexander II on 5th Aug. 1236. In terms of that condition the church was given to Crossraguel Abbey on its foundation soon after 18th July 1244. The church was also called the Church of Turnberry. There was a Chapel of Turnberry which likewise pertained to Paisley Abbey.—[*Reg. of Paisley*, 113, 309, 427–8; *Reg. Epis. of Glasgow*, i, 121, 124. See *Charters of Crossraguel* for an account of the abbey.]

JOHN CUNNINGHAM.—[*Acts and Dec.*, I, 453.]
1573

HEW KENNEDY, in office 1603.—[*Comps. Surplus of Thirds.*]
1576

JOHN OSBURNE, his sons—William, min. of Tarbolton; Anthony.—[*Deeds Dal.*, 1706, No. 1399.]
1687

JAMES MUIR, dem. 5th Oct. 1931, died 17th Sept. 1933; marr. 20th Jan. 1925 Elizabeth Coventry, daugh. of Alexander Cunningham, Gullane. Publication—*Burns till his Seventeenth (Kirkoswald) Year* (Kilmarnock, 1930).
1890

LUGAR

JOHN SKEOCH CLELLAND, licen. by Presb. of Glasgow 6th Dec. 1871.
1876

JAMES MOROGH YOUNG, killed on railway near Grantown 23rd July 1925.
1912

JAMES MAWER WALLACE, born Edinburgh 2nd Jan. 1891; son of Alexander W. and Helen Maxwell Mawer; educ. Fossoway Public School and Dollar Academy, Manitoba Univ. and Glasgow Univ.; served in Canadian 11 Field Ambulance 1916–18; student missionary in Canada 1919–23; licen. by Presb. of Dunbarton May 1925; assistant Dunbarton Aug. 1924; ord. 17th Dec. 1925; trans. to Thornton 24th Oct. 1929. Marr. 3rd Feb. 1926 Ann McKendrick, daugh. of George McKendrick King and Jessie Manson Russell, and has issue—Eileen Margaret, born 19th Oct. 1927; James Victor Bryden, born 19th Dec. 1929.
1925

MAUCHLINE

(*Note by Rev. D. E. Easson*)

There was no monastery at Mauchline, and the frequently repeated statement that there was a monastery here (it goes back at least to Habakkuk Bisset) rests on nothing better than conjecture. Melrose had evidently something in the nature of a grange there; and in the sixteenth century a *hospitium* was erected. But the only ecclesiastical building, properly so called, was the Parish Church of St Michael, which was appropriated to Melrose.—[*Reg. Mag. Sig.*, ii, 3514, iii, 1369.]

About 1204–14 Walter, son of Alan, and 3rd High Stewart of Scotland, and his wife Beatrice, daugh. of Gilchrist, Earl of Angus, granted to Melrose Abbey the territory of Mauchline and the Church of St Michael situated thereon. On 30th June 1315 Robert Wishart, Bishop of Glasgow, for himself and his successors, granted to the Abbey of Melrose, and specially permitted the said abbey to hold, the chapel or church in the territory of Mauchline, already built, the said church to have the insignia of a parish church, to hold all teinds great and small, and be equipped with cemetery, etc.; and this was confirmed by John Lindsay, Bishop of Glasgow in 1326. There was at Mauchline a hospital belonging to Melrose Abbey.—[*Book of Melrose*, i, 64, ii, 368–9, 371–4; *Reg. Great Seal*, iii, 2567.]

ANDREW MICHELL, chaplain, curate.—[*Acts and Dec.*, xxiv, 250.]
1562

WILLIAM AULD, second son of William A. in Underwood and Margaret sister to Robert Campbell of Townhead of Newmills.
1742

ANDREW EDGAR, his widow, Mary Sybilla Cowan, died at St Andrews 14th Jan 1928, aged 82; his daughs. —Jean Violet (marr. 21st Dec. 1922 Rev. John Manisty Hardwick, assistant master, Rugby School); Mary Campbell, poetess (marr. 12th Sept. 1895 George Smith, M.A., headmaster, Merchiston Castle, afterwards Master of Dulwich College); his sons—Campbell Cowan, D.Litt. (Dublin), Department of Antiquities, Cairo, died 10th May 1938; Charles Samuel, professor of Greek, Stellenbosch, South Africa; his daugh., Magdalen Grace, died 18th May 1943.
1874

JOSEPH MITCHELL, Moderator of General Assembly, dem. 1st Oct. 1930, died at Bridge of Allan 18th March 1931; his wife, Helen Honeyman Litster, died 25th June 1921; marr. (2) 31st Oct. 1924 Jean Walker, J.P., eldest daugh. of William Brown Robertson, 20 Albany Street, Dundee.
1890

NEW MAUCHLINE

The division of the Parish of Mauchline and the erection of a "new kirk" were approved by the Presbytery on Aug. 15th 1649; and on Nov. 7th 1649 the Presbytery decided upon a site for the new kirk (as well as a kirkyard, manse and glebe) on part of the land of Gilmilnscroft. The New Kirk of Mauchline had a minister, John Blair, whose career is given in the "Fasti." But he seems to have been the first and last minister of the "new" parish; and although the Parish of New Mauchline is mentioned in 1672 [*Privy Council Register*, 3 Ser., iii, 443, 445], its separate existence must have terminated in the last quarter of the 17th century, a period for which the Presbytery records are unfortunately missing. There is no trace on the lands of Gilmilnscroft of any church, nor has the factor been able to find any record of it. Most of the lands which are mentioned as included in the "New" parish are now in the Parish of Sorn.

MAYBOLE

On 29th Nov. 1371 Sir John Kennedy of Dunure, for the souls of himself, Marie, his wife, and their children, founded beside the churchyard of the parish church a chapel dedicated to the Virgin Mary, for a clerk and three chaplains. The endowment for the support of the chapel, chaplains, and clerk was 18 mercates of land beside the chapel, 18 bolls of meal of day multure yearly from said lands, 10 merks stg. yearly from the lands of Balmaclewhane, 5 mercates of the lands of Barrycloych, 6 mercates of the lands of Treuchan. Later he granted to the chapel the lands of Glenap and others which his ancestors had given to the Abbey and Canons of Bangor, Ireland, but which the Scottish King had regarded as forfeited. On 1st March 1383–4, with the approval of Pope Clement VII, Sir John erected the chapel into a collegiate church for three chaplains, one of whom was to be provost, and a clerk. The provision for the provost was the whole lands of Barclach, Barcley, Over Balmaclawnathan, to wit, Archylone and Ardowray; he was to pay 20 sh. stg. to one of the chaplains as hereafter stated; he was also to have one mercate of the lands of Kynach. For the second chaplain there were provided 3 mercates of the lands of Maybole, with the mill situated there, 1 mercate of the lands of Knokneby, 4 mercates of the lands of Treuchan, 2½ merks annual rent of the lands of Nether Balmaclathane, and 1 mercate of the lands of Kynach. The third chaplain's provision was 4 mercates of the lands of Pennyglen, 3 mercates of the lands of Knyleteycowyn, 3 mercates of the lands of Maybole, 1½ merks annual rent from the lands of Nether Balmaclathane, and 20 sh. stg. from the provost as foresaid, and also 1 mercate of the lands of Kynach. For the maintenance of the clerk there was set apart one mercate of the lands of Kynach near the church. Two additional chaplainries were forthcoming. One was founded by Gilbert Kennedy of Dunure on 18th May 1451, for celebrations at the Altar of the Virgin Mary in the church, for the souls of himself, Katherine Maxwell, his wife, and their children, the endowment being the lands of Larginlen and Broklach, in the Earldom of Carrick. The other was founded by Ergidie Blair, widow of James Kennedy of Row, on 24th April 1516, when for the souls of King James V, Gilbert, Earl of Cassilis, and his consort, Elizabeth Campbell, and for the soul of her late husband, herself, and their fathers, mothers, brothers and sisters, she granted to God, and the Virgin Mary, and Sir James Douglas, Chaplain, and his successors as chaplains, 10 merks annual rent from the lands and barony of Dunure, which she had purchased from the said Gilbert, Earl of Cassilis. On 17th July 1516 she also gave 1 acre with a rood of land near the church; and to the chaplainry there likewise pertained 2 acres of land in the same area, resigned by Sir John Kennedy, chaplain of the third stall, on 17th July 1516. There were thus at least five chaplainries or prebends. Each chaplain had a manse and garden. Apparently further endowments were made, as evidenced by a Crown Charter of 1586, which contains the following possessions of the provostry—4 mercates of the lands of Barlach, 1 mercate of the lands of Harkagstoun, 2 mercates of the lands of Auchinernie, 40 sh. of the lands of Barclay, 9 sh. of the lands of Rowestoun, 8 sh. of the lands of Knokinche (or Knokinlard), 8 sh. of the lands of Holmheid, 16 sh. of the lands of Balliecullie, 8 sh. of the lands of Clunloch, 26 sh. of the lands of —————, 2 mercates of the lands of Gilberstoun, 2 mercates of the lands of Balsayrt, 1 mercate of the lands of Little Enoch, 2 mercates of the lands of Artreis—set in feu to Elspit

McGill, wife of Thomas Kennedy of Culzean, and their son and heir, Thomas, the combined *reddendo* being 40 lib. Scots. The same charter contains the following endowments of the second prebend—2 mercates of the lands of Ballefatownes, 1 mercate of the lands of Whitefauldis, 3 mercates of the lands of Drummorane, Knokune, and Broichhill, called the 40 sh. lands of Drummorane, with the mill called Deanis-mylin, with dry multures, etc., in the Bailery of Carrick—*reddendo* 22 merks 40 pence. A charter of 1598-99 contains 5 sh. of the lands of Smythstoun as pertaining to the third prebend. There was a *Maisondeu* in the burgh, possibly attached to the collegiate church.—[*Reg. Great Seal*, i, 378, 428, ii, 466, iv, 2377, 2746, v, 992, vi, 860; *Reg. Epis. of Glasgow*, i, 285, 286-8, ii, 526-7, 527-8; *Charters of Crossraguel Abbey*, i, 33-4; *Scots. Peerage*, ii, 446.]

1565 JOHN DOUGLAS, parson.—[*Acts and Dec.*, xxxiii, 196.]

1569 ARCHIBALD HERBERTSON, pres. to vicarage 7th Dec. 1569 on death of Sir John Hamilton.—[*Reg. Pres. Bene.*, i, 31.]

1599 DAVID BARCLAY, trans. to Dumfries after 15th July 1605.—[*Reg. of Deeds*, clxviii, 129, 14th Jan. 1609.]

1608 JAMES BONAR, pres. to kirk and parsonage by Thomas Kennedy of Bargennie before 14th Jan. 1609.—[*Reg. of Deeds*, clxviii, 129; clxx, 407; *G. R. Sas.*, x, 101.]

1655 JOHN HUTCHESON, his daugh., Agnes (marr. cont. 29th April 1690 John Wallace of Camsiscan).

1667 JOHN JAFFRAY, his son, William.—[*Kirkcudbright Sheriff Court Deeds*, 987.]

1720 ROBERT FISHER, his daugh., Jean, died 1817.

1770 JAMES WRIGHT, born 6th July, 1739; 2 col., line 3, for "Balony" read "Ballony"; his son, John of Dalquharn and Ballony.

1840 ANDREW THOMSON, pres. 17th July 1840.

1843 WILLIAM MENZIES, pres. 12th Sept. 1843.

1870 GEORGE PORTER, pres. by Crown 25th June 1870.

1902 DAVID SWAN, died 12th Feb. 1944.

MAYBOLE WEST

1905 WILLIAM ALEXANDER REID, died 18th Jan. 1946.

1916 ALEXANDER WILLIAMSON. Publications—*Guide to Maybole; Crossraguel Abbey*. Papers on *Maybole Collegiate Church* and other subjects.

MONKTON

The Chapel of the Virgin of Grace, situated in the common pasture of Admanton, was founded just prior to 13th Aug. 1446 by John Blar of Admanton.—[*Reg. Great Seal*, iii, 1845; *Cal. Papal Regs., Letters*, ix. 548.]

Note. Line 16, read "The well and ruined chapel still remain."

1591 JOHN MUIRHEAD, M.A., pres. to vicarage 2nd June 1591 on death of Andrew Lockhart.—[*Reg. Sec. Sig.*, lxii, 67.]

1594 NINIAN YOUNG, min. here, pres. to vicarage on depriv. of William Chisholm, bishop of Dunblane, 4th Jan. 1591-2.—[*Reg. Sec. Sig.*, lxiii, 108].

1600 JOHN LINDSAY, M.A., son of Robert L., min. of Lanark; pres. to parsonage and vicarage 4th June 1600 on dem. of John Swinton.—[*Reg. Sec. Sig.*, lxxi, 230.]

1676 ALEXANDER CUNNINGHAM, had also David and John.—[*Deeds, Dal.*, 1706, 208, 211.]

1888 DAVID ALLAN REID, died 3rd Jan. 1923.

1923 LUKE McQUITTY, trans. from Castle Douglas (*q.v.*) 28th June 1923; died 5th Feb. 1947. Marr. 14th Oct. 1908 Floranna Thompson (died 26th July 1942), daugh. of Isaac Harvey, headmaster, Rosetta Academy, Belfast, and Flora Louisa Thompson; his son, George, born 5th died 8th Jan. 1913.

PRESTWICK

1563 ROBERT HOGGART, reader.—[*Comps. Sub Coll. of Thirds, Stirling*, etc.]

MUIRKIRK

1568 WILLIAM KINROSS, M.A., 1568 and 1569.—[*Comps. Sub Coll. of Thirds, Stirling*, etc.]

1879 ROBERT MONTGOMERY, his widow, Annie Vallance Bardner, died 22nd Jan. 1931.

1910 JOHN HENDERSON, died 26th Jan. 1946; his daugh., Ina Noble (marr. 25th July 1944 Dr George Howie, B.Sc., Rutherglen).

OCHILTREE

The patronage of the church was granted to Melrose Abbey, apparently in 1316 by Lady Eustace de Colville, Lady of Ochiltree and widow of Reginald le Chene.—[*Book of Melrose*, ii, 360-1, 364, 366.]

About 1296 Symon de Spalding was parson and his brother, John de Spalding, was reader here.

1571 ADAM LANDETHS, exhorter 1571; marr. Helen Wilson.—[*Accs. Sub Collector of Benefices*, 1571.]

1661 ROBERT MILLER, his daugh., Euphame.—[*Reg. of Deeds Dal.*, 139, 5th March 1736.]

1705 SAMUEL LOCKHART, his son, Alexander, apprenticed to George Cowan, wright, Edinburgh, 10th Sept. 1729.

1844 WILLIAM MONTGOMERY WALKER, his daugh., Margaret Laird, died 1st Feb. 1912; Jane, died 19th April 1930; his sons—William Hugh, died 25th June 1913; Josiah Charles, died 28th April 1882; his daugh., Frances Hunter, writer of poems and prose sketches, died 17th June 1933; his son, Patrick Hunter, died 14th Sept. 1939.

1880 NIEL MACKAY, died 19th July 1930; his widow, Teresa Kossuth Forbes, died 29th June 1935.

1923 DAVID SINCLAIR RUTHERFORD, ord. A. and S. 3rd May 1923; trans. to Biggar 20th June 1928.

1928 ANGUS MacLEOD, born 6th July 1893, son of Angus M., slate quarryman, and Annabella Gillies; educ. at Univ. of Glasgow, M.A. (1919); licen. by Presb. of Glasgow Dec. 1923; assistant Martyrs, Glasgow; ord. to Salen 10th July 1924; trans. to Kilcalmonell 25th Nov. 1925; trans. and adm. A. and S. 30th Nov. 1928; died 3rd March 1945. Marr. 28th Dec. 1923 Helen Cowan, daugh. of John Ranken Macintyre and Margaret Cowan Wilkinson, and has issue—Angus Iain, born 8th Dec. 1924; Kenneth Gillies, born 11th Sept. 1928.

PATNA

1919 DOUGLAS DICKSON ROBERTSON, trans. to Dalkeith West 21st April 1927.

1927 WILLIAM PAUL MONTEATH, trans. from St Andrews, Johnston (*q.v.*), 14th Sept. 1927; dem. 1st Oct. 1930; died 28th Nov. 1937; had issue—William Paul, M.A., min. of Viewpark, Uddingston.

PRESTWICK, ST. NICOLAS

1909 JAMES MONTGOMERY CRAWFORD, died at Glasgow 27th Dec. 1926.

1927 GEORGE MacLEOD DUNN, formerly of West Wemyss (*q.v.*); trans. to Kelvinhaugh 13th March 1924; trans. and adm. 8th June 1927; has addl. issue—Grace Catherine MacLeod, born 29th Dec. 1924.

RICCARTON

The church was at first a dependant chapel of Dundonald (*q.v.*).

1876 EMMANUEL MORGAN, died 8th Feb. 1929.

1917 BERRY PRESTON, trans. to Peebles 24th March 1926. Addl. issue—Thomas Russell, born 2nd April 1923.

1926 CHARLES JAMES DONALDSON, trans. from Battlefield (*q.v.*) 24th Nov. 1926; died 27th Jan. 1946. Addl. issue—Dorothy Dobie, born 7th Jan. 1923 (marr. 9th July 1948 Frederick Richard Benson, South Kensington, London).

ST QUIVOX, formerly SANCHUR IN KYLE

On 7th Jan. 1434–5 the church is termed the Parish Church of St Quivox (Sancti Kevoci). Kevoc is regarded as a form of Mo Choemoc, later Mo Chaomhog of Liath Mor or Liath Mo Choemoc in Tipperary, whose day was 13th March; he died in 656. It may be noted, however, that apart from the Aberdeen Breviary, which records St Kevoca the Virgin, there was a St Evoca the Virgin.—[*Cal. Papal Regs., Letters*, viii, 492-3; Watson's *Celtic Place Names of Scot.*, 189–190; *Transcripts from Vatican*, 1421–59, 90.]

1572 JOHN LEVERANCE, min.—[*Acts and Dec.*, xlix, 40.]

1618 PATRICK HAMILTON, son of George H., of Bogwood, and Jean Lockhart.

1633 ROBERT MONTGOMERY, line 2, for "Adam M. of Macbiehill, Ayrshire" read "Hew M. of Auchenhood." Line 5, for "1636" read "1633."

1820 STAIR PARK MACQUHAE, line 9, for "St Croix" read "St Evox." He was active in the Church Extension movement in Ayrshire and in 1850 was president of the Glasgow Society of the Sons of Ministers of the Church of Scotland. His first wife, Louisa Georgina, was daugh. of Captain Lewis Mackenzie, Seaforth Highlanders; his son, William, educ. at Haileybury, Madras Civil Service, died 26th Oct. 1930. His second wife, Louisa Georgine, was daugh. of Assistant Commissary General John Mackenzie, 5th Regiment; his daughs.—Caroline, died 3rd April 1937; Mary Laura, died 26th Dec. 1936; Louise, died 31st Oct. 1930; his son, John Mackenzie, C.B., Captain R.N., died 1900.—[Information from Messrs. Mackenzie, St Evox, Newnham.]

1859 JAMES WILSON, line 4, for "Scoonie" read "Leven."

1906 JAMES PETER WILSON, marr. 29th April 1925 Margaret Whiteford, daugh. of John Hamilton and Isabella Steedman and sister of John Macfarlane Hamilton, min. of Alloway; educ. at Ayr and Kelvinside Academies; ord. to Dalbeattie 25th Feb. 1897, not 1899. Publications—Articles in *Expository Times*.

SORN

1843 JOHN RANKINE, his sons—Sir John, died 8th Aug. 1922; James, died 10th April 1927.

1919 DAVID FYFE McMATH, trans. to St David's, Kirkintilloch, 15th Oct. 1924.

1925 WILLIAM LOWYS DAVIES, adm. 12th March 1925; trans. to Auchendoir 16th May 1928.

1928 JAMES GEGG, born Motherwell 1896, son of James Gegg and Jane Moffat; educ. Dollar Academy and Glasgow Univ.; licen. by Presb. of Hamilton May 1926; assistant South Dalziel 1926; ord. to Menmuir 12th May 1927; trans. and adm. 19th Sept. 1928.

STAIR

1785 JOHN STEELE of Palmone.

1899 WILLIAM HENRY SHANNON, died 18th Dec. 1942; his wife, Hilda Meikle, died 31st Aug. 1929. Marr. (2) 30th Aug. 1941 Betty S. Thomson, daugh.

of Alexander Robb, bank manager, Edinburgh; his daugh., Hilda Helen Elizabeth (marr. 10th June 1936 Hugh Richmond Thom, min. of Corsock). Addl. issue—William Henry, born 23rd Jan. 1918; his daugh., Constance Eileen (marr. 5th July 1938 Thomas Hughes, teacher, Ardrossan).

STRAITON

The church was granted to Paisley Abbey by Duncan, son of Gilbert, Earl of Carrick, and himself Earl of Carrick, on condition that the abbey erected in Carrick a monastery of the Cluniac Order, and gave the church to the said monastery. The grant was confirmed by Florence, Bishop-Elect of Glasgow, in 1202, and by Alexander II 5th Aug. 1236. In terms of that condition the church was given to Crossraguel Abbey on its foundation soon after 18th July 1244.—[*Reg. of Paisley*, 427–8.]

1565 JOHN McQUORNE, had issue, John, his successor.—[*Reg. Sec. Sig.*, lxix, 271.]

1644 HEW ECCLES.—[*Reg. of Sas.*, 3 Ser., xxxvi, 30, 25th Aug. 1675.]

1844 JOHN BLAIR, pres. 4th May 1844.

1899 WELLWOOD MAXWELL LANDALE, trans. to Penicuik 15th Feb. 1928.

1928 JOHN FOSTER McCALLUM, trans. from Dunnichen (*q.v.*) 15th Aug. 1928.

SYMINGTON

1563 JOHN LINDSAY, exhorter and reader 1563–8.—[*Comps. Sub Coll. of Thirds, Stirling*, etc.]

1592 JOHN SYMINGTON, son of William S. of Ryhills, pres. to vicarage 5th Feb. 1592–3 on dem. of Robert Symington, but may not have entered.—[*Reg. Sec. Sig.*, lxv, 13.]

1592 JOHN LINDSAY, pres. to vicarage 14th Feb. 1592–3 on death of Robert Symington.

1598 JOHN CUNNINGHAM, M.A., pres. to vicarage 27th May 1598 on death of John Miller.—[*Reg. Sec. Sig.*, lxix, 269.]

1685 WILLIAM BLAIR, it may have been his widow and two children, Jean and Margaret, who were resident in the Canongate, Edinburgh, 14th Nov. 1694.—[*Poll Tax Book.*]

1687 JOHN GEMMELL, his daughs.—Agnes (marr. Thomas Stewart of Gabrochill); Margaret.—[*Deeds. Dal.*, 1706, No. 1399.]

1840 GEORGE ORR, his daughs.—marr. Professor T. B. Kirkpatrick, D.D., Toronto, and James Martin, C.A., Edinburgh.

1906 JOHN GAGE BOYD, died Edinburgh 31st May 1947; his widow, Mary Reid, died 22nd Oct, 1947.

TARBOLTON

In 1335 John de Graham, lord of Tarbolton, granted the patronage of the Church of Tarbolton, with the lands of Unthank, to his kinsman, Robert de Graham of Walston. Subsequently John de Graham conveyed the patronage to Friar John, Minister of Fail, in exchange for a white horse, which the said Friar John later took back. On 21st Feb. 1340, on the plea that he had been led astray by the wiles of Friar John, John de Graham revoked the gift of the patronage to Fail, conceding that Robert de Graham was the patron; and on 11th July 1342 Robert de Graham bestowed the patronage upon Melrose Abbey. A vacancy in the rectory of the church in 1404 brought forward three claimants to the patronage, Melrose Abbey, the Ministry of Fail, and John Seneschal, lord of Tarbolton; and ultimately the claimants by Notarial Instrument of 14th Dec. 1414 agreed to keep their dispute in abeyance by constituting King James I their procurator in making a presentation to the vacant living. What steps were subsequently taken to arrive at a settlement is not clear; but it is on record on 22nd July 1422 that the patronage of the church was "of Laymen," showing that Melrose and Fail had been eliminated. In 1426-37 the church was erected into a Prebend of Glasgow by John Cameron, Bishop of Glasgow, with the consent of Sir John Stewart, Kt., lord of Darnley and Tarbolton, who was obviously the patron of the church. Prior to that, on 22nd Feb. 1422, the said Sir John Stewart presented a supplication to the Pope, stating that he proposed to found and partly endow a college for six priests with church and offices in his domain of Darnley and craving the Pope to incorporate, annex, and perpetually unite the Parish Church of Tarbolton to the said college. The project was not carried out. The Red Friars' Monastery at Failford, on the right bank of the Fail, already noted, was founded by Andrew Bruce in 1252. The monastery held the churches of Barnewell, Symington, Galston, Torthorwald, and Inverchaolain. In answer to a petition by James II and his queen, Mary of Gueldres, Pope Calixtus III decerned on 3rd Nov. 1459, that the monastery be suppressed, and the house and church and their revenues be assigned as a hospital for poor infirm from the same erection. The superior or minister of the house was Provincial of the Order of the Red Friars in Scotland, and sat in Parliament among the abbots.—[*Book of Melrose*, ii, 414–15, 417, 420, 421, 422–4, 425, 510–12; *Reg. Great Seal*, ii, 3691; *Cal. Papal Regs., Letters*, vii, 210; *Reg. of Glasgow*, ii, 430; *Scott. Supplics. to Rome*, 203–4; *Acts Scott. Parliament*, ii, 447a, 525b; Walcot's *Anc. Ch. of Scotland*, 349; Keith's *Cat. of Scott. Bishops*, 396–7.]

1571 JAMES CHISHOLM, M.A., parson and perpetual vicar 19th March 1571–2, Archdeacon of Dunblane.—[*Cal. of Charters*, x, 2239.]

1571 DAVID CURLE, reader, in office 26th Dec. 1573.—[*Edin. Tests*, iii, 21.]

1695 HENRY OSBURNE, son of John O., min. of Kirkoswald.

1829 DAVID RITCHIE, line 10, for "1832" read "1882"; his daugh., Susan Alexis, died 24th Sept. 1935.

1883 JAMES CRAIG HIGGINS, died at Ayr 28th Nov. 1930; his wife, Mary Ann Macleod Campbell, died 16th March 1926.

1927 ARCHIBALD MORTON PATERSON, born 23rd March 1892, son of Robert P. and Mary Morton; licen. by Presb. of Glasgow 1919; assistant Elgin; ord. to Slamannan 28th Feb. 1923; trans. 15th Dec. 1927. Marr. 23rd Oct. 1923 Marion Fotheringham Forrest, daugh. of James Allan, and has issue—Lorraine Mary, born 24th June 1925; Robert Archibald, born 6th Dec. 1929.

BARNWELL

The church was dedicated to the Holy Rood. In or about Oct. 1459 James II and his queen, Mary of Gueldres, presented a petition to the Pope, Pius II, stating that the ministers and friars of the Trinitarian House of Fail (in this parish) were neglecting their duty and living in uncleanness, etc., to great public scandal, and that on account of their exemption from episcopal control and dangers from sea and land, and the negligence of their superiors, their enormities and shameful life were not corrected, and further that they had become so involved in evil that they could not be brought back to decency and the observance of their rule. The petition craved the suppression of the house and its annexation to "a certain great Hospital, with Church, houses," etc., which the Queen had erected and endowed. On 3rd Nov. 1459 the Pope gave mandate to the Bishops of Glasgow and Whithorn and the Archdeacon of Glasgow to make enquiries, and if they found the statements were true, to remove the said ministers and friars to other houses of the same Order in the country, suppress said Order in said house, and unite and appropriate the said house and annexes to said church and hospital in perpetuity. The appropriation was not carried out. Manifestly the reference is to the Trinity Collegiate Church and Hospital, Edinburgh.—[*Cal. Papal Regs., Letters*, xi, 403; *Diocesan Reg. of Glasgow*, i, 305, ii, 67.]

WILLIAM WALLACE, "His Majestie's belovit clerk," brother of John W. of Craigie and son of John W. of Craigie, pres. to the min. of Fulfurde 18th April 1576 on the death of Robert Cunningham; still min. 18th June 1587.—[*Reg. of Pres. Bene.*, i, 42; *Reg. Mag. Sig.*, 31st Dec. 1575; *Reg. Sec. Sig.*, lv, 84.]

1576

TROON

A new church was built at Troon and opened for public worship 29th Dec. 1925. It is situated beside the old one, which now forms part of a suite of church halls.

JAMES FLEMING, his daugh., Rebecca Maxwell, died at Troon 31st Aug. 1922.

1836

ROBERT SMITH, D.D. (Glasgow 19th June 1935); died 20th Nov. 1937; his wife, Janet Gilmore, died 16th June 1924. Marr. (2) 22nd Nov. 1927 Margaret Brown Guthrie (died 20th Nov. 1937), widow of David Moore. His son, Robert James, C.E., M.A. (Edin.), B.A. (Cantab), Irrigation Department, Sudan.

1887

PRESBYTERY OF IRVINE

ARDROSSAN

There were in the church an altar dedicated to the Virgin Mary to which pertained 5 merks annual rent from the lands of Bar, and an altar dedicated to St Peter. There was also in this parish a chapel dedicated to All Saints.—[*Reg. Mag. Sig.*, iv, 1674.]

1568 JOHN PORTERFIELD, pres. to vicarage 29th April 1568 on dem. of Sir Allan Porterfield.—[*Reg. Pres. Bene.*, i, 8.]

1574 GEORGE BOYD, pres. to vicarage 23rd March 1573 on dem. of John Porterfield.—[*Reg. Pres. Bene.*, i, (4), 17.]

1591 ALEXANDER CAMPBELL, pres. to vicarage on death of George Boyd.—[*P. S. Reg.*, lxv, i.]

1830 JOHN CAMPBELL BRYCE, his daugh., Elizabeth, died 19th March 1931.

1858 DAVID EVAN McNAB, his sons—Richard Bein Hagart, died 10th Jan. 1937; William Brown, vicar of Hadley, Shropshire, 1903–17, St Michael's, Shrewsbury, 1917–31, died at Shrewsbury 28th Feb. 1936; Radstock Bein Hagart, town clerk, Cape Town, died 12th Aug. 1938.

1888 WILLIAM ROSSIE BROWN, his widow, Mary Jane Fullarton, died 5th Jan. 1937.

1908 DAVID DANIEL REES, his first wife, Grace Evelyn Emlyn Jones, died 31st May 1921; marr. (2) 27th Feb. 1924 Jessie Turner (died 13th Sept. 1935), daugh. of Capt. Hugh Wylie. He died 26th Jan. 1940. His daugh., Catherine Grace (marr. 12th Aug. 1931 William McCallum Clyde, M.A., Ph.D., lecturer in English, St Andrew's University).

NEW ARDROSSAN

1854 JOHN DRENNAN McCALL, his widow, Mary Williamson Blackwood, died 7th Feb. 1924; his son, David, died at Regina, Canada, 30th April 1931; his daughs.—Margaret Mary Williamson, died at Aberfeldy 19th Sept. 1930; Elizabeth Buchanan, died at Aberfeldy 15th Feb. 1937.

1917 ROBERT PAUL FAIRLIE, trans. to St Mary's, Dumfries, 14th Jan. 1926.

1926 WILLIAM BODIN, born Kilmartin, Argyll, 7th March 1891, son of Hugh B. and Annie Hastie; educ. at Bellahouston and Albert Road Academies, Glasgow, and Univ. of Glasgow, M.A. (1916); licen. by Presb. of Glasgow Dec. 1919; student assistant Govan, assistant Maxwell, Glasgow; ord. (A. and S.) New Cumnock 12th May 1920; trans. and adm. 31st May 1926; trans. to St Luke's, Lochee, 16th Oct. 1929; dem. 23rd March 1948. Marr. 8th June 1920 Elizabeth Patterson, daugh. of John Marr, Captain, Mercantile Marine, and Martha Seaton, and has issue—Hugh Alexander Andrew, born 11th May 1921, died 2nd Sept. 1944; Ian Marr, born 26th Jan. 1924; Cyril William, born 10th Nov. 1926; David Seaton, born 10th April 1936.

NORTH CHURCH, SALTCOATS

1873 JOHN GAULD SMITH, ord. to Natal by Presb. of Edinburgh 5th March 1877.

JOHN CLARK, licen. 9th June 1875.
1877

JOHN ROBERT SPOTTISWOODE, dem. 30th Nov. 1939.
1899

BEITH

The Church of Beith was situated near Lochwinnoch, and from it "most of Beith" was distant three to four miles. Because of that and "by reason of storms of weather and of deep and evell wayes adjacent thairto," Parliament passed an Act on 28th June 1633 for a new church and manse to be built in the middle of the parish, the old buildings to be applied to the use of the builders and for the provision of a new manse and glebe. On the site of the new church a chapel seems to have stood prior to 1560. There was in the parish a chapel with burying-ground, dedicated to St Bride. Near at hand was a well of the same name. There was also a chapel called Chapel of Trearne (Treehorn), in existence in the first quarter of the 13th century, to which belonged 2 acres of land on the south side of the chapel.—[*Acts Scott. Parl.*, v, 52, 161; *Reg. Great Seal*, v, 341; vi, 207.]

JOHN YOUNG, line 10, John Campbell, his brother-in-law.
1589

PATRICK COLVILLE.—[*G. R. Sas.*, 2 Ser., 20th May 1655.]
1645

ANDREW BROWN, his daugh., Helen Mary, died at Dolgelly 10th Sept. 1944.
1852

CROSSHOUSE

WILLIAM WHITE, born Dalgarven, Kilwinning, 10th Jan. 1866, fourth son of Matthew W., grain merchant, miller and farmer, Partick and Kilwinning, and Marion Kennedy; educ. at Kilwinning Public School, Irvine Royal Academy, Univ. of Glasgow, M.A. (1887), B.D. (1889); studied at Tübingen and Berlin; licen. by Presb. of Glasgow 1890; assistant at Dunblane Cathedral and Motherwell; ord. 10th Jan. 1895; app. clerk of Presb. of Irvine and Kilmarnock 8th Oct. 1929; app.
1895

clerk of Synod of Ayr 11th Oct. 1938; died Glasgow 29th Dec. 1943. Publications—*Addresses on the Future Life*; *Sermons on the Shepherd and the Sheep*; *Thoughts on Prayer for the Departed* (1940).

DALRY

There were originally two churches in the parish, one on the east of the village, and the other on the west. The latter, situated "near to ground called the Old Glebe," appears to have been the parish church which was dedicated to St Margaret of Antioch. St Margaret's Fair was held in the parish on 31st July, St Margaret's Day, Old Style, when it was customary to kindle a bonfire, called a "tannel." Early in the 17th century, apparently 1600–8, a single church was built to take the place of the two old churches. In 1771 a new church was built. It was repaired in 1821 and rebuilt 1871–3. Up to about the middle of the 18th century remains of the church to the east of the village still existed.—[*Cal. Papal Regs., Letters*, ix, 144–5.]

GEORGE HEPBURN, natural son of Patrick Hepburn, Bishop of Moray, and grandson of Patrick Hepburn of Beynstoun; legitimised 4th Oct. 1545; rector here 20th Dec. 1567, when he was summoned for treason.—[*Acts Scott. Parl.*, iii, 6; *Reg. Great Seal*, iii, 3169; *Scots Peerage*, ii, 142–3.]
1565

ARCHIBALD CRAWFORD, min. of Stevenston in charge here 1574–9.
1574

SYMON PRESTON, vicar.—[*Acts and Dec.*, lvii, 515.]
1575

GEORGE BOYD, designated vicar 16th May 1577.—[*Edin. Tests.*, ix, 265.]
1577

ARCHIBALD BLACKBURN, M.A., pres. to vicarage 2nd Sept. 1593 on death of Archibald Crawford.—[*Reg. Sec. Sig.*, lxv, 253.]
1593

MATTHEW HAMILTON, M.A., pres. to parsonage and vicarage 12th March 1602 on trans. of Archibald Blackburne, but apparently not found qualified.—[*Reg. Sec. Sig.*, lxxii, 273.]
1602

1602 WILLIAM DUNLOP, M.A., one of the regents of the College of Glasgow, pres. to parsonage and vicarage 22nd May 1602, vacant by non-qualification of the person lawfully provided and the lawful transport. of Archibald Blackburne.—[*Reg. Sec. Sig.*, lxxiii, 12.]

1604 JOHN CUNNINGHAM.—[*G. R. Sas.*, xxxvi, 235; xiii, 267; 2 Ser. viii, 40.]

1916 ANDREW BALD THOMSON, dem. 16th March 1933; died 21st May 1934; his daugh., Jessie, born 4th Oct. 1919.

WEST DALRY (Q.S.)

1910 JAMES JOHNSTON, educ. Gracehill Academy, Methodist College, Queen's College and Assembly's College, Belfast; assistant Lissura, Co. Down, and St Enoch's, Belfast; died 22nd July 1943. Addl. issue—Noel, born 25th Dec. 1916, died 3rd Jan, 1917; James Hastings Chambers, born 18th Jan. 1918, died 26th May 1942.

(*United with St Andrew's, Dalry, 30th Dec.* 1945.)

DARVEL

1889 JOHN WATSON JACK, died 16th March 1937.

DREGHORN

1567 GAVIN NAYSMITH, pres. to vicarage 28th Nov. 1572 on death of Andrew Laing.—[*Reg. Pres. Bene.*, i, (4), 2; *Cal. of Charters*, xii, 2697.]

1590 WILLIAM FULLARTON, M.A., pres. to vicarage 15th Sept. 1589, on death of Gavin Naysmith.—[*Reg. Sec. Sig.*, lx, 57.]

1621 WILLIAM LINDSAY, his father, merchant burgess of Glasgow; pres. by Lord Kilmarnock 10th Aug. 1620; banished to Hamarade Kirk, Ireland. Marr. Elizabeth, not Margaret, and had issue—James, matric. Glasgow Univ. 1643. —[*G. R. Sas.*, xlii, 346.]

1687 JAMES STEWART, line 4, for "1688" read "before 30th Aug. 1687."

1695 ALEXANDER CUNNINGHAME, his son, Alexander, apprenticed to James Ogstoun, bookseller, Edinburgh, 2nd Dec. 1713.

1914 WILLIAM JAMES JAMIESON, marr. 28th June 1927 Martha, daugh. of David Walker and Margaret Latta.

PIERSTON

1577 ROBERT BARCLAY, vicar 1577-90.— [*Comps. Gen. Coll. of Thirds.*]

DUNLOP

The church was rebuilt about 1766, and again in 1835, being opened in December of that year. The Chapel of the Virgin Mary was situated at Chapelton, about ½ mile distant from the village. The writer of the Old Statistical Account suggests that the chapel was really the pre-Reformation church of the parish, and that later its place was taken by a church on the present site.

1560 JOHN HOUSTON, vicar 1560.—[*Reg. Abbrev. Feu Charters of Church Lands*, i, 67.]

1563 HANS HAMILTON, pres. to the vicarage 16th Dec. 1569 in succession to Mr John Hamilton; he was the great-grandfather of William Carstares, Principal of Edinburgh Univ., and of William Dunlop, Principal of Glasgow Univ., whose mother was Elizabeth Mure, daugh. of William Mure of Glanderston, by his wife, Jean, daugh. of Hans Hamilton. In the south-east corner of the churchyard there is a marble monument in memory of Hans H. and his wife. Erected by their son John, Viscount Clanderboyes, in the peerage of Ireland, it consists of a vaulted chamber under which they are buried, and is called the "Picture-House." His son, Patrick, min. of Innerwick.—[*Reg. Pres. to Benefs.*, i, 33.]

1569 JOHN HAMILTON, M.A., may be identical with John Hamilton, reader and exhorter in 1567; in any case he was vicar, and he died before 16th

Dec. 1569, when he was succeeded in the vicarage by Hans Hamilton.—[*Reg. Pres. to Benefs.*, i, 33.]

1566 ARCHIBALD BETOUN, servitor of the Sovereign's Privy Chamber, received on 9th Feb. 1566–7 a Royal Letter of Presentation to the vicarage vacant by the death of John Houston; it is doubtful if the presentation took effect.—[*Reg. Sec. Seal*, xxxvi, 8.]

1607 JAMES MONTGOMERY, his widow, Elizabeth Montgomerie, marr. (2) Robert Brown, town clerk of Irvine.

1615 HUGH EGLINTON, his son, George, by first marriage.

1734 ROBERT BAIRD, his daugh., Helen (marr. Thomas McGowan of Smithston).

1834 MATTHEW DICKIE, his daugh., Janet Barbour, died Edinburgh 3rd Dec. 1925.

1884 ROBERT GRAHAM, his widow, Georgina Agnes Gunn, died 30th April 1925; his daugh., Margaretta Maria Lothian, died 24th Nov. 1921.

1886 JAMES SYMON, his widow, Mary Wilson, died 4th Oct. 1921.

1915 JAMES McCARDEL, trans. to Shettleston 5th June 1923.

1923 DAVID BROOK BAXTER, ord. 1st Nov. 1923; trans. to Largs 2nd Oct. 1928.

1929 JOHN BAYNE, born Greenloaning, Perthshire, 16th Feb. 1892, son of Henry B., Denny, and Barbara Campbell Ferguson; educ. at Webster's Seminary, Kirriemuir, Forfar Academy and Univ. of St Andrews, M.A. (1915), B.D. (1920); war service—1916, joined Black Watch (R.H.), sergeant instructor; 1917, commissioned R.G.A.; active service with the Royal Siege Artillery in France, Belgium and the Rhine; licen. by Presb. of Stirling 1920; assistant Tron and St Andrews', Edinburgh; ord. to St Ninian's, Glasgow, 8th April 1924; trans. and adm. 14th Feb. 1929; trans. to Bo'ness 29th July 1937. Marr. 9th April 1925 Euphemia Adam Bell, daugh. of William Shirran, 17 Spottiswoode Street, Edinburgh, and has issue—Ian Fergus, born 13th Jan. 1926, died 4th June 1930; Rosemary Agnes, born 12th May 1931; Yvonne Barbara, born 31st June 1934. Publications—*Dunlop Parish*; newspaper articles.

FENWICK

1829 JOHN GEDDES CROSBIE, joined Catholic-Apostolic Church, London.

1887 ANDREW BURNS, dem. 1931; died 5th Feb. 1932; Mary Retson, his widow, died 4th Jan. 1939; his son, Andrew, doctor in London; his daugh., Agnes (marr. William Archibald, Lanark)

FERGUSHILL

1880 WILLIAM MACALPINE, died 19th Dec. 1924; his daugh., Rose (marr. 5th Oct. 1926 Philip, son of Philip William Lilley, min. of Trinity Church, Irvine).

1925 THOMAS BARR VALLANCE, trans. from Creich, Fife (*q.v.*), 16th May 1925; trans. to Townhead, Glasgow, 16th Jan. 1936. Issue—James Alexander, born 26th June 1927.

HURLFORD

1911 JAMES WILSON MUGGOCH, trans. to Logie, Dundee, 13th Dec. 1922.

1923 JAMES WAUGH, B.D.; ord. 10th May 1923; trans. to Glenmuick 26th Oct. 1928.

1929 WILLIAM SERIGHT, born 20th Feb. 1891, educ. Univ. of Glasgow, M.A. (1914); licen. by Presb. of Glasgow; assistant St George's in the Fields, Glasgow, 1920; ord. to Milton, Glasgow, 27th June 1922; trans. and adm. 28th Feb. 1929. Marr. 7th Nov. 1922 Margaret Thomson Ramsay, M.D., and has issue—William, born 23rd Sept. 1923; Gavin Ramsay, born 12th June 1928.

IRVINE

There were in the church an altar dedicated to the Virgin Mary in the north aisle, an altar dedicated to St Catherine in the south aisle, an altar dedicated to St Nicholas, an altar dedicated to St Peter in the north aisle, between the Altar of the Virgin Mary on the north and the Altar of St Ninian on the south, and an altar dedicated to St Michael, described 16th Nov. 1446 as situated "in the new aisle of St Mary the Virgin." The Altar of St Ninian and St Katherine was founded by Mr William Cunningham of Dundonald on 1st March 1418-19. The Altar of St Salvator and St Thomas the Martyr was situated in the aisle described on 17th Nov. 1506 as "built by Rankine Brown (then alive), burgess of Irvine, in the nave of the Church on the north side." The Altar of St Conval, St Stephen the Martyr, and St Sebastian the Martyr was situated in the south aisle. At the Altar of St John the Baptist, St Cristopher the Martyr, and St Ninian the Pontiff, situated in the nave of the church, a perpetual chaplain was founded on 4th Oct. 1540 by Alexander Scott, Provost of Corstorphine Collegiate Church.—[*Monuments of the Burgh of Irvine*, i, Pref. xxxiv-v, 125, 136, 145, 149, 158, 161, 166, 198, 199, 202.]

1569 THOMAS ANDREW, reader 1569.—[*Comps. Sub Coll. of Thirds, Stirling*, etc.]

1583 WILLIAM STRANG, marr. 17th May 1575 Agnes, daugh. of George Borthwick of Nether Lenie.

1584 WILLIAM ANDREW, vicar 31st July 1584.—[*Reg. Sec. Sig.*, l, 169.]

1589 ALEXANDER SCRIMGEOUR, pres. to vicarage 6th March 1591 on death of William Fullarton; marr. Jean Hunter, widow of William Cunningham of Woodhead, and had issue—Hugh; Jean; Margaret.—[*Reg. Sec. Sig.*, lxii, 8; *Ayr Sas.*, 3rd April 1602, 28th Dec. 1599, 21st Dec. 1603.]

1676 JOHN STIRLING, his widow, Christian Forbes, buried 24th Aug. 1687.

1709 WILLIAM McKNIGHT, marr. (1) Agnes Cunningham and had issue—James, born 8th Aug. 1714; John, born 9th Sept. 1717.

1751 CHARLES BANNATYNE, his daugh., Jean, died at Kilmarnock 24th Dec. 1789.

1891 HENRY RANKIN, retired 1928, died 31st Aug. 1937; his wife, Helen Martin, died at Clackmannan Manse 24th June 1929.

1929 ALEXANDER MACARA, born 15th Oct. 1900, son of Alexander M., min. of Denny; educ. at Denny and Stirling High School, Univ. Glasgow, M.A.; licen. by Presb. of Stirling April 1927; assistant Shettleston; ord. A. and S. 20th Sept. 1928. Marr. 16th April 1929 Marion Wiseman, younger daugh. of James Mackay, Buckie, Banffshire, and has issue—Alexander Wiseman, born 4th May 1932; Ann Elizabeth, born 18th Oct. 1936.

KILBIRNIE

1565 JAMES SCOTT, provost of Corstorphine, vicar by Royal Letters on or before 4th April 1565.—[*Reg. Sec. Sig.*, xxxiii, 32.]

1567 ARCHIBALD HAMILTON, designated rector of Kilbirnie 1567 and on 3rd July 1572.—[*Privy Council Reg.*, ii, 155; *Cal. of Charters*, x, 2332.]

1571 ROBERT CRAWFORD, pres. to vicarage 9th Sept. 1571 on forfeiture of Archibald Hamilton.—[*Reg. Pres. Bene.*, i, (3), i.]

1586 JOHN HERIOT, pres. to parsonage 7th Aug. 1581 on death of Alexander, Commendator of Kilwinning.—[*Reg. Sec. Sig.*, cxii, 156.]

1604 MALCOLM HAMILTON, marr. Margaret Wilkie.—[*Ayr Sas.*, 28th June 1604 and 29th Jan. 1607.]

1688 JOHN GLASGOW, line 14, for "344" read "354."

1723 JAMES SMITH, his daugh., Elizabeth (marr. 7th Jan. 1756).

1886 HENRY RITCHIE BUCHAN, his widow, Jessie Blackwood Orr, died 22nd Jan. 1942.

1918 HUGH CLARKE McCOLL, trans. to St Matthew's, Dundee, 9th Oct. 1924.

1925 COLIN CECIL PITCAIRN HILL, formerly Indian Chaplain (*q.v.*); adm. 12th March 1925. Marr. (2) 5th Oct. 1927, Rosamund Annie, daugh. of Frederick Roome Lumsden, schoolmaster, Newburn, Fife, and has issue—Frederick Charles, born 17th Nov. 1930; Cecilia Rose, born 18th Jan. 1932. His son, Acting Flight Lieut. James Anderson, D.F.C., D.S.O., killed in action Sept. 1940.

KILMARNOCK LAIGH

FIRST CHARGE

1564 ROBERT HAMILTON, vicar.—[*Acts and Dec.*, xxxii, 147.]

1580 ROBERT WILKIE, min. 1574, pres. to parsonage and vicarage 7th Aug. 1591 on death of Alexander, Commendator of Kilwinning.—[*Reg. Sec. Sig.*, lxii, 146.]

1608 WILLIAM WHITEFORD, M.A., regent of the College of Glasgow when pres. to parsonage and vicarage 1608.—[*Reg. Sec. Sig.*, liv, 150.]

1610 MICHAEL WALLACE, M.A. (Glasgow 1601), regent, Univ. of Glasgow 1601.

1699 FRANCIS FINLAYSON, studied arts at Glasgow Univ., matric, 1692.

1843 JAMES BUCHANAN HAMILTON, his daugh., Mary Anne Dunlop, died at Helensburgh 19th Sept. 1930.

1881 WILLIAM DUNNETT, retired 1923, died 18th Feb. 1928; his widow, Jane Inglis, died 29th Jan. 1938; his sons—Sir James McDonald, K.C.I.E., Indian Civil Service, retired 1936; George Victor, adm. to Flisk 1937; Hamilton David Forrester, trans. to Ellon 1923; Arthur Henry, secretary to the Home Board; his daugh., Charlotte Inglis, head of School of Domestic Science, Aberdeen, died 18th Oct. 1933.

1923 JOHN HENRY DUNCAN, trans. A. and S. from St Madoes (*q.v.*) 19th July 1923; trans. to St Mary's, Dundee (C. and S.), 17th May 1937; D.D. (St Andrews, 30th June 1944). Addl. issue—Kenneth Playfair, born 1924. Publication—Sermons on *Messages from Scots* (Angus and Robertson, Sydney, N.S.W.).

SECOND CHARGE

1711 GEORGE PEDEN, his son, George, born 1716, died at Paisley 13th March 1789.

1916 DAVID PORTER HOWIE, trans. to First Charge 5th May 1938; has issue—Jean Daveena Ogilvy, born 28th Jan. 1925.

KILMARNOCK HIGH

1915 DAVID CRAWFORD WATSON, trans. to Lenzie 19th Jan. 1926.

1927 DAVID NORMAN MASSON, trans. from Slains (*q.v.*) 23rd June 1927. Addl. issue—Norman Guthrie, born 5th Aug. 1928; William David, born 26th Sept. 1931.

KILMARNOCK, ST ANDREWS

1885 JAMES LINDSAY, died 25th March 1923; his widow, Margaret Dykes Cook, died 14th June 1942.

KILMARNOCK, ST MARNOCH'S

1863 JOHN THOMSON, his widow, Agnes S. Nisbet, died 12th July 1938.

1912 WILLIAM JAMES SMITH, trans. to Bo'ness 1st Sept. 1925.

1926 ROLLO RUSSELL GRANT SUTHERLAND, formerly of Ballantrae (*q.v.*); trans. from Skelmorlie 18th Feb. 1926; dem. 16th Dec. 1929 on admission to Queen's Road, Brighton; dem. 1941;

chaplain to Forces; adm. to Guernsey 1946. Addl. issue—Ian Douglas, born 2nd Jan. 1920. His marr. with Helen J. T. Laurie dissolved by Court of Session 25th Nov. 1933; marr. (2) 18th Dec. 1933, Jessie Morton.

KILMAURS

Prebends of the collegiate church included Cherickeheuch, Bellahill, and Fluris and Bankhead. On 13th July 1670 Parliament granted to Sir John Cunningham of Lambrochtoun the vacant stipend for one year for repair of the church and manse, "ruinous through the carelessness of the incumbent and the vacancy."—[*Reg. Mag. Sig.*, iv, 2221; *Acts. of Parl.*, viii, 23–4.]

1568 JOHN HERVY, vicar 1568–9.—[*Comps. Sub Coll. of Thirds, Stirling*, etc.]

1569 JOHN COLWYN, parson 1569.—[*Comps. Sub Coll. of Thirds, Stirling*, etc.]

1598 DAVID HENDERSON, pres. on depr. of his father Alexander H.; his son, Frederick, M.A. (Glasgow 1647).—[*Reg. Sec. Sig.*, lxx, 6.]

1641 WILLIAM CROOKES, marr. cont. 28th April 1660 Anna, daugh. of Henry Kelso, bailie in Largs.—[*Baill. Cunningham, Deeds*, 11th Aug. 1680.]

1685 GEORGE BROWN, his wife was widow of Archibald Menzies of Culdares.—[*Deeds Mack.*, 1705, No. 398.]

1806 JOHN ROXBURGH, born 14th Dec. 1780; his mother, Margaret Wilson.

1858 ALEXANDER INGLIS, his sons—James Macfarlane, died 15th July 1937; Daniel Macfarlane, a leading churchman and Chairman of the General Trustees of Church of Scotland, died 3rd Oct. 1944.

1903 JOHN KNOX THOMSON, severely wounded in action 1917. Addl. issue—Marion Forrest, born 10th Oct. 1919 (marr. 8th March 1946 Flying Officer I. E. W. Stewart, Gifford).

KILWINNING

Wynnen, the Welsh form of Finnan, a diminutive of the name of Findbarr of Mayville, whose death is recorded in 579. At Eglinton there was a Chapel of Reviseyn.—[*Retours*, xxvii.]

1567 WILLIAM KIRKPATRICK, had also issue—Marion.—[*Edin. Tests*, ix, 265.]

1866 WILLIAM LEE KER, his widow, Janet Caldwell, died 28th Nov. 1923; his sons—James Campbell C.I.E. (1924), C.S.I. (1928), Indian Civil Service, ret. 1930, M.P. West Stirlingshire 1931–5; Findlay Caldwell, died 27th Oct. 1942.

1903 ARCHIBALD HUNTER, died 23rd Nov. 1945; his son, Archibald McBride, B.D., Ph.D., min. of Old Comrie 1934–7, Yates Professor of New Testament, Mansfield College, Oxford, min. of Kinnoul 4th Dec. 1942, Professor of Biblical Criticism, Aberdeen, 1945; his daughs.—Crissie Swan (marr. 1933 James Nairn Young, bank agent, Ballantrae); Janet Winning (marr. 1934 Harry Whyte, accountant, Commercial Bank, Ayr).

LOUDOUN

1567 RANKIN DAVIDSON, exhorter, one of the readers approved by the General Assembly 20th Dec. 1560, afterwards min. at Galston (*q.v.*).

1574 ROBERT WILKIE, trans. from Cupar Fife about 1573.

1685 JOHN CAMPBELL, issue by 1st marriage—Jean; Elizabeth. Marr. (2) Anne Bannatyne and had issue—William; James; Isobel; Margaret; Anne; Maryanna; Dorothy.—[*Deeds Mack.*, 115, 3rd Nov. 1714].

1793 ARCHIBALD LAWRIE, marr. Anne, daugh. of James McKittrick Adair of the family of Maryport; his daugh., Frances Wallace (marr. 7th Sept. 1826 Thomas Carlyle, advocate).

HAMILTON MOORE, died 16th Aug. 1927; his father min. of Elmwood Church, Belfast; his widow, Anne Kinnear Stephen, died 19th Jan. 1940.
1891

JOHN GARDNER MACLEOD THOMSON, born Chapelton, Lanarkshire, 2nd June 1902, son of William T., min. of Chapelton, and Helen Macleod; educ. Chapelton, Hamilton Academy, Univ. of Glasgow, M.A. (1922), B.D. (1927), Ed.B. (1935); trained as teacher, Jordanhill College 1923; licen. by Presb. of Hamilton 1927; assistant Avondale; ord. 15th Dec. 1927; dem. 30th Dec. 1939. App. Director of Religious Education at St Andrews, Dundee Training College, May 1939. Marr. 26th June 1929 Helen Craig, youngest daugh. of Alexander Torrance, Crookedstone, Quarter, and has issue—William Paterson Loudoun, born 9th May 1933; Elizabeth Helen Torrance, born 5th June 1936.
1928

STEVENSTON

JAMES WALKER, M.A., vicar and min., 1562, also in charge of Inniscailleoch.—[*Comps. Gen. Coll. of Thirds.*]
1562

ARCHIBALD CRAWFORD, M.A., pres. in 1569 on death of James Walker, and to parsonage on death of Alexander, Commendator of Kilwinning; had Dalry also in charge 1579.—[*Reg. Pres. Bene.*, i, 27; *Reg. Sec. Sig.*, lxii, 155.]
1569

1641 JOHN BELL.—[*G. R. Sas.*, xv, 217.]

ROBERT STIRLING, his son, John, min. of Ballyhelly 1699–1752 (see Ireland).
1689

ROBERT JOSEPH KYD, delete lines 1 and 2; died 3rd May 1921.
1886

ALEXANDER MACDONALD, trans. from Glassary (*q.v.*) 28th Sept. 1921; trans. to Alloa 22nd June 1927.
1921

JOHN GEDDES RITCHIE, trans. from Drainie (*q.v.*) 24th Nov. 1927.
1927

STEWARTON

THOMAS HAMILTON, M.A., brother of John Hamilton of Stanehouse; vicar 7th July 1566, and still in office 16th Feb. 1578-9.—[*Reg. of Deeds*, vii, 298; *Reg. Great Seal*, iv, 2839; *Cal. of Charters*, xi, 2446.]
1576

ROBERT MONTGOMERY, his daugh. Katherine.—[*Ayr Sas.*, 23rd July 1601, 30th Nov. 1606.]
1589

JAMES MONTGOMERY, M.A., son of Neil M. of Langschaw, pres. 18th June 1600 on dep. of Robert Montgomery.—[*Reg. Sec. Sig.*, lxxi, 228.]
1600

WILLIAM CASTLELAW, had issue by second marriage with Marion Geddes—John; Thomas; Eupham; Elizabeth and Ann.—[*Reg. of Deeds, Mack.*, xviii, 29th July 1665.]
1645

JAMES CORNWALL BRYCE, his widow, Eliz. C. Brown, died 29th Nov. 1925.
1879

WILLIAM FALCONER OGILVIE, died 6th June 1939; his daugh., Lorna Falconer (marr. 26th Dec. 1941 Alexander Stewart Borrowman, min. of Torthorwald).
1908

WEST KILBRIDE

By Charter of 5th June 1509 John, 1st Lord Semple, for the souls of the King and Queen, his own soul, and the soul of his wife, Margaret Creichton, granted to a chaplain to celebrate perpetually in the Chapel of St Anand to be built by him within the cemetry of said chapel within the domicile lands of Suthennane, an annual rent of 10 merks from the lands of Mekle and Little Kyll-niskan, and two "soums" of grass in the pasture of the lands of Suthennane, with an acre of land on the north side of the said cemetry for building a chaplain's manse. The chapel was erected before 13th May 1510.—[*Reg. Great Seal*, ii, 3354; *Reg. Sec. Seal*, i, 2066.]

SIR JOHN MAXWELL, exhorter 1567
1567 and 1568.—[*Comps. Sub Coll. of Thirds, Stirling*, etc.]

JOHN HARPER, pres. in 1601 to
1594 vicarage on death of Archibald Crawford, parson of Eaglesham and last vicar here; line 9, for "Mary" read "Margaret."—[*Reg. Sec. Sig.*, lxxii, 180.]

GILBERT HAMILTON of Braehead of
1672 Raploch, died Sept. 1672; marr. Margaret Baillie and had issue—William of Braehead; James in Glasfoird.—[*House of Hamilton*, 180; *Gen. Reg. Sas.*, 2 Ser., xiv, 52, 9th Oct. 1657.]

THOMAS FINDLAY, his daugh., Isa-
1832 bella Donaldson of Warriston, died 19th Sept. 1935, aged 99.

ANDREW FORRET SCOTT PEAR-
1914 **SON**, F.R. Hist. Socy. (1922); D.Litt. (Glasgow 1927); dem. 30th Sept. 1929 on appointment as Professor of Church History, Presbyterian College, Montreal; adm. to High Church, Johnston, 16th May 1934; app. Professor of Church History, Presbyterian College, Belfast, June 1942. Addl. issue—Muriel Paxton Corbett, born 6th Jan. 1922; Doris Nancy Forrest, born 25th April 1926. Publications—*Thomas Cartwright and Elizabethan Puritanism* (Cambridge Univ. Press, 1925); conducted correspondence column in the *Scots Observer*, 1928–9; *Church and State: Political Aspects of 16th Century Puritanism* (Cambridge Univ. Press, 1928); introductory essay on *Die Puritanische Bewegung* in volume of *Ekklesia*, published at Zurich, on British Free Church (1937).

PRESBYTERY OF PAISLEY

BARRHEAD

1914 JOHN CHARLES CONN, trans. to Elgin, Second Charge, 10th May 1922.

1922 GEORGE MURRAY DAVIDSON SHORT, adm. from Benholm (*q.v.*) 20th Sept. 1922; dem. on app. as Indian Chaplain 17th Nov. 1924.

1925 THOMAS CROMBIE, born 4th March 1900, son of Robert C. and Magdalen Hodge Lyall; educ. at Hutcheson's Grammar School and Univ. of Glasgow, M.A. (1920), B.D. (1925); licen. by Presb. of Hamilton 1923; assistant Airdrie, Barony 1924; ord. 1st May 1925; trans. to St Andrews, Glasgow, 22nd Sept. 1930. Marr. 15th Sept. 1926 Elizabeth Guthrie, daugh. of Alexander Thomson and Sarah McFarlane, and has issue—Morag McFarlane, born 18th Sept. 1934. Publications—*Short History of the Parish Church of Barrhead*; *Training the Citizens of To-morrow*.

BRIDGE of WEIR

1899 ALEXANDER MASON SHAND, dem. 30th Nov. 1939; died at Aberdeen 24th Jan. 1949.

CALDWELL

1891 DAVID STEWART, dem. 14th Dec. 1925; died 25th Sept. 1931; his wife, Jane Kidney, died 19th Dec. 1930.

1926 JOHN FAITHFUL IRVINE FORTESCUE, born 6th June 1883, second son of William Archer Irvine F. of Kincausie and Swanbister, M.B., C.M., and Edith Virginia, daugh. of John Robert Duguid of Gibraltar; educ. at Grammar School, Aberdeen, univs. of Edinburgh and Aberdeen; in mercantile business; ord. to Congregational Church, Oban, 18th July 1920; trans. to Thurso 16th Oct. 1921; dem. 18th Dec. 1923; assistant East Church, Aberdeen; held commission in A.S.C. during war; adm. on probation by General Assembly 22nd May 1924; licen. by Presb. of Aberdeen 30th June 1925; ord. 12th April 1926. Marr. 14th April 1917 Annie, daugh. of Joseph Brockhurst Souter, and had issue—Edith Caroline, born 28th May 1921; Francis John, born 10th Oct. 1926, died 15th Jan. 1929; Hugh William, born 14th Sept. 1930.

CARDONALD

1889 WILLIAM ALEXANDER LISTON, his widow, Patricia Napier, died 29th Aug. 1947, aged 100.

1915 DUNCAN FINLAY McLEAN, trans. to St Paul's, Fairlie; dem. 10th Jan. 1945.

EASTWOOD

St Convallus, the patron saint, a disciple of St Mungo, is said to be buried at Inchinnan. In the church there were altars as follows: Virgin Mary, Gwallis, Holy Rood, St Ninian. At the manse there is a stone with this inscription in Old English letters: "Ecclesiae Dei construendum curavit Thomas Jackaeus 1577." Evidently the manse had been rebuilt then under the ministry of Thomas Jack.—[*The Maxwells of Pollock*, i, 119, 120n, 251; *Celtic Place Names*, 193.]

1563 JOHN CARNESS, exhorter, 1563.— [*Comps. Sub Coll. of Thirds, Stirling,* etc.]

EASTWOOD—GIFFNOCK

1567 JAMES CARRUTHERS, exhorter, 1567–8.—[*Comps. Sub Coll. of Thirds, Stirling*, etc.]

1568 SIR WILLIAM BANE, vicar, 20th July 1568, died before Sept. 1570.—[*Reg. Mag. Sig.*, iv, 2411.]

1569 THOMAS KNOX, reader and exhorter in 1569 and 1573.—[*Comps. Gen. Coll. of Thirds.*]

1570 THOMAS JACK, pres. on death of Sir William Bane.—[*Reg. Pres. Bene.*, i, (2), 2.]

1599 JOHN GIBSON, Henry, his nephew.— [*Gen. Reg. of Sas.*, xii, 158.]

1606 WILLIAM WALLACE, graduated 1595, not 1599.

1652 HUGH SMITH, marr. Elizabeth Colquhoun, who survived him.—[*Deeds Dal.*, 1706, No. 561.]

1703 ROBERT WODROW, marr. 15th Nov. 1708 and had issue—Mary, born 26th Sept. 1709; James, born 18th Oct. 1710; Robert, born 21st Dec. 1711; Patrick, born 8th March 1713; Ebenezer, born 12th May 1714; Alexander, born 20th Nov. 1715; Margaret, born 24th Feb. 1717; William, born 20th April 1718; Marion, born 21st Sept. 1719; Janet, born 24th March 1721; John, born 30th May 1723; Lilias, born 28th Oct. 1724; Martha, born 22nd Sept. 1726; William, born 11th Jan. 1729; James, born 21st March 1730; Alexander, born 20th Sept. 1731. There are seven volumes of his in MS. in Church of Scotland Library.

1858 GEORGE CAMPBELL, his daugh., Edith Graham (marr. Maxwell James Wright, min. of St Ninian's, Aberdeen); his sons—John Maxwell, died at Manchester 29th Jan. 1942; George Graham, died 22nd Jan. 1944; his daugh., Alice Mary, died 13th Nov. 1948.

1909 FREDERICK DAVID LANGLANDS, trans. to Galashiels 30th June 1925; his son, Frederick Peters, born 4th April 1914, died 30th July 1915.

1926 WILLIAM SUTHERLAND, M.A., B.D., born 1891; served in war 1914, M.C.; licen. by Presb. of Caithness 1914; assistant St Stephen's, Edinburgh; ord. to New Abbey 9th April 1920; trans. and adm. 8th Jan. 1926; died at Glasgow 21st July 1929.

ELDERSLIE

1920 JOHN MEIKLE GRAY, ord. 4th May 1920; dem. on appointment to St Andrew's, British Guiana (*q.v.*), 16th May 1923.

1923 WILLIAM WILSON MORRELL, ord. 17th Sept. 1923; trans. to Battlefield, Glasgow, 7th July 1927.

1927 WILLIAM POLLOK MORRISON, born Glasgow, 24th Feb. 1885; son of John M., ironworker manager, Maryhill, Glasgow, and Janet Pollok; educ. at Royal Technical College, Glasgow; Baptist Theological College; Univ. of Glasgow and Edinburgh 1926–7; served in war as Engineer Inspector, Tank Department of Mechanical Warfare; ord. to Baptist Church, Lochee, Oct. 1912; trans. to Kelvinside, Glasgow, 1915; trans. to Grantown-on-Spey 1920; adm. on probation as licentiate by General Assembly 3rd June 1926; assistant St Stephen's, Edinburgh, 1926; ord. 27th Sept. 1927; trans. to Stair 15th April 1942. Marr. 26th June 1916 Margaret, daugh. of Thomas Somerville, builder, Prestwick, Ayrshire, and has issue—Fairlie Pollok, born 26th July 1917.

GIFFNOCK

1919 ALBERT McCLUGGAGE, died 7th Aug. 1921; was for ten years min. of York Street Congregational Church, Dublin; chairman of Congregational Union of Ireland.

ERNEST ORMROD RODGER, trans. from Aberfoyle (*q.v.*) 16th Feb. 1922; dem. 9th Oct. 1948.
1922

GREENBANK

JAMES FRASER, died 16th Feb. 1921.
1883

JAMES ARTHUR COWLEY, trans. from St Columba's, Oban (*q.v.*), 8th Sept. 1921; had addl. issue—Ruth Margaret, born 11th Jan. 1924 (marr. 9th Oct. 1947 Rev. William Bryce Johnston, B.D., C.F.); Joyce Katherine, born 20th May 1926.
1921

HOUSTON

LAURENCE DUNCAN, reader, died 1563.—[*Comps. Sub Coll. of Thirds, Stirling*, etc.]
1560

ROBERT ALLAN, app. reader 1563.—[*Comps. Sub Coll. of Thirds, Stirling*, etc.]
1563

ANDREW MARTIN, vicar 1571.—[*Comps. Gen. Coll. of Thirds.*]
1571

ROBERT CARRICK, marr. 13th Jan. 1724 Margaret, daugh. of John Paisley, min. of Lochwinnoch.
1720

GEORGE MUIR, died 27th June 1939; his son, George Bruce, in Civil Service, Malaya.
1917

HOWWOOD

JOHN GILBERT, dem. 11th Nov. 1939, died 14th Feb. 1946; his widow, Alice B. Guthrie, died 25th March 1946.
1887

KILLELLAN

St Fillan seems to be identical with Faelan of Clurain Moesena in Meith, whose day was 9th Jan.—[Watson's *Celtic Place Names*, 193.]

ROBERT COOK, exhorter 1563, pres. on death of Robert Maxwell.—[*Reg. Pres. Bene.*, i, (4), 11; *Comps. Sub Coll. of Thirds, Stirling*, etc.]
1563

ROBERT MAXWELL, M.A., pres. on death of Robert Cook.—[*Reg. Sec. Sig.*, 24th Jan. 1575.]
1575

JOHN MONTEATH, line 4, for "1754" read "1759."
1748

INCHINNAN

It may be that Inchinnan contains the name of (St) Finnan, Findbarr of Maghbhile. St Convallus is said to be buried here. There was in the Place of Inchinann a chapel with an image of the Babe Jesus, of Our Lady and a great image with an image of St Anne.—[*Rep. Hist. MSS. Com.*, iii, 394.]

WILLIAM JACKSON, reader 1567 and 1568.—[*Comps. Sub Coll. of Thirds, Stirling*, etc.]
1567

SIR BERNARD PEEBLES, vicar in 1566, died after 27th July 1587.—[*Comps. Sub Coll. of Thirds, Stirling*, etc.; *Reg. Sec. Sig.*, lv, 153.]
1566

GABRIEL MAXWELL, pres. on dem. of Sir Bernard Peebles.—[*Reg. Pres. Bene.*, i, 40, 93.]
1580

THOMAS LAW, his eldest son, James, M.A., Glasgow (1646).
1626

LAURENCE LOCKHART, his son, James Somerville, died 5th Jan. 1922.
1822

FREDERICK ALEXANDER STEUART, died 2nd Nov. 1930; his widow, Marie Louise Dickenson, died 29th Aug. 1948.
1919

JOHNSTONE

JOHN LENNOX HOWAT, trans. to Queen's Park, Glasgow, 9th Sept. 1928.
1919

GAVIN KERR MACKAY, born 28th July 1891; son of David M., master baker, and Elizabeth Dewar Brown, educ. at Univ. of Glasgow, M.A. (1913); licen. by Presb. of Glasgow May 1915; assistant St Michael's, Dumfries; ord. to Durisdeer 1st June 1920; trans. to Dalziel
1929

24th June 1924; trans. and adm. 16th Feb. 1929; trans. to Balshagray 16th Nov. 1933; C.F. 156th Scottish Infantry Brigade, 5th Cameronians. Marr. 6th July 1920 Jeanette, daugh. of George Dunsmore and Elizabeth Kirkwood, Glasgow, and has issue— Ronald Kirkwood, born 28th Aug. 1922, died 18th April 1923; Gavin Kirkwood Kerr, born 16th Nov. 1924.

JOHNSTONE, ST ANDREW'S

1888 ARCHIBALD HALLIDAY, his widow, Grace Beaumont, died 6th Aug. 1933.

1917 WILLIAM PAUL MONTEATH, trans. to Patna 14th Sept. 1927.

1928 JOHN WILLIAMSON, formerly of Rousay (*q.v.*); trans. from Kirkfieldbank 30th Jan. 1928; trans. to St James, Kirkcaldy, 30th Oct. 1928.

1929 COLIN MACPHERSON, born Skye 13th Oct. 1883, son of Archibald M., landholder, and Flora Macrae; educ. at Glasgow High School and Univ. of Glasgow, M.A. (1921); licen. by Presb. of Glasgow Jan. 1924; ord. to Glencoe 6th June 1924; trans. and adm. 3rd June 1929. Marr. 20th Nov. 1925 Jean Tennant Ramsay, daugh. of John McKail and Isabella Stevenson Forbes, and has issue— Isobel Stevenson Forbes, born 17th Oct. 1928.

KILBARCHAN

The Chapel of St Catherine in the churchyard was founded in 1401 by Thomas Crawford of Auchenames. At the same time he founded in the church an altar dedicated to the Virgin Mary. For the support of a chaplain to serve both in the chapel and at the altar he gave Lynnernocht and other lands. At Ranfurly of Prieston farm, a little to the east of the castle, there was a Chapel of St Mary, founded by a member of the Knox family. St Bride's Chapel was situated at the village of Kenmuir in the south-west corner of the parish. On 12th Dec. 1564 David Coull, chaplain of the Chapel of St Katherine, conveyed the glebe and chapel lands of the chapel to John Chalmers, brother of James C. of Gadgirth.—[*Reg. Abbrev. Feu Charters of Church Lands*, i, 10, 14; *Origines Parochialis Scotiae*, i, 84.]

1560 JOHN McQUEEN, vicar 1560 and 1569, died after 24th April 1575.—[*Comps. Gen. and Sub Coll. of Thirds, Dumfries*, etc.; *Reg. Mag. Sig.*, iv, 2070, 2412.]

1563 ADAM WATSON, exhorter and reader 1563.—[*Comps. Sub Coll. of Thirds, Stirling.*]

1572 JOHN METHVEN, vicar, died before 18th March 1572-3.—[*Reg. Pres. Bene.*, i, 91.]

1572 ALEXANDER CUNNINGHAM, reader, pres. to vicarage 15th March 1572-3; res. before 16th Nov. 1573. —[*Reg. Pres. Bene.*, i, 91, 143.]

1573 ROBERT CRAWFORD, reader, pres. to vicarage 16th Nov. 1573.—[*Cal. of Charters*, xii, 2780; *Reg. Pres. Bene.*, i, 143.]

1585 GAVIN HAMILTON, vicar 1585-90. Marr. Catherine Cumming, who died 20th June 1604, and had issue— a son and three daughters.—[*Test.*, May 1606; *Comps. Gen. Coll. of Thirds.*]

1593 ROBERT STIRLING, had issue— Robert.—[*G. R. Sas.*, 3rd Sept. 1618.]

1701 ROBERT JOHNSTON, his daugh., Anna (marr. 13th Nov. 1741 and died 7th Aug. 1786).

1847 ROBERT GRAHAM, D.D., his widow, Margaret Ann, daugh. of Archibald Glen, merchant, Glasgow, died 16th Jan. 1925.

1895 ROBERT DUNBAR MACKENZIE, D.D. (St Andrews 26th June 1925), died 27th July 1939; had addl. issue —William Scott, born 15th Nov. 1920; Janet Elsie, born 26th Nov. 1932.

LEVERN

1894 THOMAS COOK, died 2nd Feb. 1940.

(*United with Nitshill* 21*st April* 1940.)

LINWOOD

1880 JOHN ADAMSON ABERNETHY, dem. 15th Nov. 1926, died 3rd Aug. 1936; his wife, Margaret Arniel Gray, died 31st March 1929; his daugh., Margaret, died 25th March 1926.

1927 ALEXANDER REAPER, trans. from Rayne (*q.v.*) 17th March 1927; trans. to Barony, Kirriemuir, 11th July 1935. Marr. 12th July 1927 Elizabeth Nicol Shepherd, M.A., daugh. of James Shepherd, farmer, and Susan Lamb, and has issue—Isabel Shepherd, born 4th May 1929.

LOCHWINNOCH

On 21st April 1504, John, 1st Lord Sempill, founded in his park near Castle Sempill, for his own soul, for the soul of Margaret Colville, his wife, and for the souls of his progenitors and successors, and all the faithful departed, the Collegiate Church of Lochwinnoch, to the Most High God and the Glorious Virgin, the Mother of Jesus Christ, for a provost, six chaplains, two singing boys, and a sacrist, the chaplains to include a clerk in Holy Orders, a precentor, and a schoolmaster. The provost was to wear on feast days a lawn surplice, a scarlet hood, and an almuce on the arm. The chaplains, the singing boys and the sacrist were each to wear a linen surplice at the daily service; and in addition the chaplains were to wear red hoods lined with black lamb's wool. The duties of the sacrist were to take charge of the porch, the copes, and the altar ornaments; array the altar itself; regulate the clock; ring the bell for the church services, with double ringing on feast days; sweep the church, and decorate it with leaves and flowers. General endowment of the church was the fruits and revenues of the Church of Glassford; and particular endowments were as follows: Provost, the teind sheaves of Glassford, extending to 45 lib. Scots, with the whole glebe except a piece of ground and the manse attached to the vicarage; First Chaplain, the teind sheaves of Nether Schelis, Schavtounhill, Ridrane, and the hill of Drumtall, and Gruderland, in the parish of Glassford, extending to 10 and 8 merks Scots; Second Chaplain, the teind sheaves of the village of Chapelton and Nether Schavtoun, West Ridrane of Drumbow, and *de flat*, extending to 10 and 8 merks Scots; Third Chaplain, the fruits and emoluments of the parish clerkship of Lochwinnoch, extending to 10 and 8 merks Scots, the chaplain to provide for the support of the clerk; Fourth Chaplain, all the lands of Upper Pennale occupied by Archibald Reid, and the place, dwelling, garden, and orchard, and 40 sh. of pension from East Bryntschellis and West Bryntschellis in the parish of Kilbarchan, extending to 10 and 8 merks Scots; Fifth Chaplain, all and whole the lands of Nether Pennale, with the mill, extending to 20 and 4 merks, and the emoluments of the parish clerkship of Kilbarchan; he was to act as organist and in the singing school teach the boys in the Gregorian Chant plain or pointed; he was also to make provision for the support of the boys and of the parish clerk of Kilbarchan; Sixth Chaplain, all the fields of Auchinlodmond, with the mill and mill lands, extending to 22 merks Scots; he must be learned in grammar and skilled in the Gregorian Chant plain or pointed, and instruct the boys in the first and second parts of grammar; Sacrist, the fruits, revenues, and emoluments of the parish clerkship of Glassford, extending to 6 merks Scots; he had to make provision for the support of the parish clerk of Glassford. There were granted also to the provost and chaplains 10 roods in Lochwinnoch Park for building manses and for gardens near the church; and for entertainment and fellowship, for bread, wine, and wax, 5 merk lands of Easter Welland in the parish of Kilbarchan, and the lands formerly annexed by the founder's progenitors to St Brigit's Chapel in Kenmuir Village in the Parish of Kilbarchan, the lands which pertained to the founder's chapel in Kilbarchan, and the lands annexed to the Chapel of St Conal in Paisley Parish, situated in the village of Ferans.—[*Reg. Epis. of Glasgow*, ii, 505–16.]

1691 JOHN PAISLEY, son of Robert P., bailie of Paisley; his daugh., Margaret (marr. Robert Carrick, min. of Houston).

1873 ROBERT ZUILLE GILFILLAN, his widow, Agnes Brodie Smith, died 12th May 1933.

1893 WILLIAM SINCLAIR STEVENSON, his wife, Isabella Black, died 20th June 1943; he died at Edinburgh 6th Aug. 1946.

MEARNS

In addition to the Altar of St Bridget, there was in the church an altar to the Virgin Mary.—[*Maxwells of Pollok*, i, 251.]

1563 JOHN HAMILTON, claimed vicarage. —[*Acts and Dec.*, xxviii, 35.]

1575 WALTER STEWART, reader.—[*Acts and Dec.*, lvii, 491.]

1665 JAMES TAYLOR, his daugh., Helen (marr. John Glen, min. of Stichell).

1691 JAMES McDOUGALL, his daugh., Katherine (marr. William Thomson, bailie of Irvine).

1868 MUNGO REID, died at Edinburgh 19th Jan. 1924; his widow, Isabella Hamilton Pearson, died 28th Dec. 1927.

1915 DAVID SCOTT, served as Chaplain in France and Flanders with 15th Scottish Division; dem. 20th May 1929 on app. to Knox Crescent Presbyterian Church, Montreal; D.D. (St Andrews, 29th June 1945). He had issue—Hew Ferguson, born 6th Oct. 1923; Charles Findlay, born 30th May 1926; Elspeth Patricia Mary, born 2nd July 1928.

NEILSTON

1560 SIR STEVEN WILSON, vicar, probably in 1560 or soon thereafter; described 4th March 1579–80 as "mass priest of Neilston mony years and rebel put to the horn for continual disobedience in abusing the sacraments, saying mass, and dissolving marriage at pleasure, and still in prison till his trial."—[*Reg. Privy Council*, iii, 273.]

1578 JAMES DAVIDSON, reader, in office 4th March 1579–80.—[*Reg. Privy Council*, iii, 273.]

1632 JOHN LAW was son of Andrew L. by his second marriage. He had only one son, called William, the two sons of that name given were one and the same. He had a daugh., Margaret.

1687 JOHN KINNEAR, M.A., was resident with his wife and three children in Tron Parish, Edinburgh, on 9th Nov. 1694.—[*Tron Poll Tax Roll*, 6.]

1703 JOHN MILLER, line 6, delete "of Divinity."

1873 THOMAS MILLER, his sons—Thomas of Auchenheath, died 18th April 1935; Hugh, M.B., Ch.B., Dundee, died at Edinburgh 22nd July 1930.

PAISLEY

1610 ARCHIBALD HAMILTON, Archbishop of Cashel, M.A. (Glasgow 1599); delete second marriage and read "marr. (2) Anna, daugh. of Balfour of Burleigh, and had issue—John, matriculated Univ. of Glasgow 1631; Malcolm, matriculated 1633.

1653 ALEXANDER DUNLOP, had also issue—Elizabeth.—[*Reg. of Deeds, Dal.*, 1705, No. 378.]

1667 JAMES CHALMERS, marr. (1) pro. 1st March 1660 Elspeth Petrie.— [*Aberdeen Reg.*]

1669 MATTHEW RAMSAY, had issue— John.—[*Reg. of Deeds Mack.*, xli, 562.]

JOHN BAIRD, eldest son of John B. of Selvadge, burgess of Inverkeithing; had issue—Margaret, born 1689, died Nov. 1695; Janet.—[*Hist. of Inverkeithing and Rosyth*, 476–8.]
1669

JOHN FULLARTON, marr. (3) Isobel Sinclair.—[*G. R. Sas.*, 3 Ser., xxviii, 256; *Sas. Argyll*, lix, 36, 21st June 1688.]
1684

THOMAS GENTLES, his widow, Cecilia Wernicke, died at Edinburgh 5th Jan. 1922 aged 82.
1878

ALEXANDER MILLER MACLEAN, died 6th March 1925; his widow, Mary Brown, died 25th May 1931; his daugh., Alice Mary Jane, marr. (2) 4th July 1935 John McKellar Robertson of Noddesdale, Largs, Captain R.N.V.R., C.B.E.
1910

WILLIAM MAIN, D.D., trans. from Trinity, Edinburgh, 11th Sept. 1925; died 15th Oct. 1929; his wife, Anne Macnaughton, died 22nd Dec. 1919. He had addl. issue—John St John, born 11th Aug. 1896, died 4th June 1897; Margaret Mary (marr. 2nd Nov. 1944 James Dunbar Michael, O.B.E., Indian State Railways).
1925

SECOND CHARGE

JAMES STIRLING, brother of Robert S., student, Glasgow. Marr. Elizabeth, daugh. of John Lennox of Woodhead.—[*G. R. Sas.*, xv, 260, 15th Oct. 1658.]
1654

JAMES SMITH, youngest son of James S., weaver, Glasgow, adm. burgess of Glasgow 22nd Oct. 1806.
1798

PATRICK BREWSTER, his daugh., Margaret Mary Crawford, died 30th July 1935.
1818

JAMES BOATH DALGETY, his widow, Jane Balfour, died 21st Feb. 1924.
1878

JOHN WALLACE, his widow, Mabel Blanche Powell, died at Reading 23rd Feb. 1945.
1916

ALEXANDER RUTHERFORD HOWELL, Senior President of Edinburgh University Dialectic Society 1894–5. Licen. 1895, he was first a reader and then an assistant in St Giles Cathedral; during the war (1914–18) he served for a time in France as General Superintendent of the Scottish Churches Huts. It was during his ministry in the abbey that the restoration of that church was completed, involving the entire rebuilding of the choir and many other alterations. Into this work Mr Howell threw himself with characteristic energy, and the exquisitely restored building owes much to his artistic genius and comprehensive knowledge of church architecture. The stately and appropriate form of service observed in the abbey is also largely his work. He resigned his charge in Paisley 13th April 1937 owing to ill health and retired to St Andrews; died at Edinburgh 2nd Dec. 1943. In the wider work of the Church of Scotland Mr Howell took a considerable share. For a year he acted as Organising Secretary for the Foreign Mission Committee. At the invitation of the Colonial Committee he ministered for a period in 1907 at Homburg, and in 1927–8 at Cairo. He was on the Council of the Church Service Society and in 1935–6 was President of the Scottish Ecclesiological Society. Publications—*Paisley Abbey: its History, Architecture and Art*. To the devotional literature of the Church he contributed a book of *Church Prayers for War-Time*, which has had a large circulation. On artistic questions his judgment was fine and his advice greatly valued. On the Executive Committee of the Scoto-Russian Fellowship of St Andrew, a member of the Executive Committee for the Restoration of the Church of the Holy Rude, Stirling, and was convener for some years of the Ceremonials Committee of the Presbytery of Paisley. An enthusiastic student of antiquity, he was a trustee of the Dalrymple Archaeological Fund. His sons—Edward Alexander, in the R.A.F., O.B.E. and D.F.C.; David Logan, Navigator in a Bomber Squadron. The daughs.—Anne served in the A.T.S. and Isabella in the
1918

W.A.A.F. (marr. 3rd Sept. 1945 Flight Lieut. Leslie Shepherd, Sevenoaks).

(*Charges united* 14*th April* 1937.)

GREENLAW

1907 GEORGE NISBET DODS, died 14th June 1921.

1914 JOHN CHAMBERS, M.B.E. Addl. issue—Evelyn Robertson, born 5th Sept. 1916, died 3rd March 1917; Mary Manson, born 4th April 1918.

HIGH KIRK PARISH

1910 JOHN MUIR, died at Glasgow 19th Oct. 1947.

ST GEORGE'S

1882 ALEXANDER FYFE BURNS, his widow, Isabella Martin Ritchie, died 10th Nov. 1931; line 19, for "Wentworth" read "Waitworth."

MARTYRS

1897 JAMES THOMSON, trans. to Mochrum 21st July 1927.

1928 JAMES WILSON MUGGOCH, trans. from Logie, Dundee, 18th Jan. 1928; trans. to Heriot 3rd Sept. 1936; his daughs.—Helen Milne Lawson (marr. 21st Dec. 1939 James C. P. Logan, M.B., Ch.B.); Dr Edith Mary (marr. 5th July 1947 Dr John White, Airdrie).

MOSSPARK

1923 GEORGE SCOTT, M.A., trans. from Meldrum (*q.v.*) 30th Sept. 1923; trans. to Holburn, Aberdeen, 24th March 1933; trans. to Langside Hill, Glasgow, 27th Sept. 1940. Marr. 19th April 1927 Mary Cunningham, daugh. of William Clark Hamilton and Christina Martin Paterson, and has issue—Christina Mary, born 9th June 1930.

PAISLEY, MID.

1882 GEORGE PARK, died 30th May 1927.

1924 WILLIAM GEORGE JOHNSTON, trans. from Kirn (*q.v.*) 10th Dec. 1924; dem. 31st May 1947. Addl. issue—Margaret Helen Wotherspoon, born 9th Feb. 1917; William James Simpson, born 13th Feb. 1921.

PAISLEY, NORTH

1883 JAMES YOUNG, D.D. (Glasgow, 24th June 1925), died 25th June 1925.

1926 JOHN REEVIE JOHNSTON MERRY, trans. from Calderhead (*q.v.*) 7th Jan. 1926; wife's mother's name, Jane Jamieson. He had issue—Jane Hislop, born 22nd Sept. 1918; Janette Alexander, born 7th April 1920; John Leech Johnston, born 11th Sept. 1926; William Adam Johnston (twin), born 11th Sept. 1926.

PAISLEY, ST COLUMBAS

1880 DONALD MACKAY, his widow, Catherine Morison, died at Stirling 10th April 1925; his daugh., Jane Georgina, died 17th Jan. 1944.

1883 DAVID JOHNSTONE, his widow, Janet Kennedy, died 26th Oct. 1929.

1903 JOHN McNIVEN, dem. 16th May 1928.

1928 GILLESPIE MACGREGOR CAMPBELL, trans. from Muckairn (*q.v.*) 13th Nov. 1928; died 21st March 1946.

PAISLEY, SOUTH

1879 WILLIAM MUSHAM METCALFE, his widow, Cecilia Simpson, died 23rd Oct. 1928.

1917 FRANK HENDERSON, trans. to Sandyford, Glasgow, 16th May 1930; dem. 11 Jan. 1938; died 27th June 1940. Addl. issue—Henry David Christopher, born 13th April 1921; Alistair Lowson, born 26th Feb. 1929.

POLLOKSHAWS

1845 ALEXANDER ROBERTSON WATSON, marr. and had issue—a son died in infancy 15th Oct. 1849.

1913 JOHN MACFARLANE, dem. 30th Sept. 1927, on app. to Brussells; his wife, daugh. of George Barker. Addl. issue—Margaret, born 12th Sept. 1928.

1928 ARCHIBALD EWING MacINTYRE, trans. from Innellan (*q.v.*) 7th March 1928; trans. to Buittle 22nd April 1948.

RENFREW

There were also in the church altars dedicated respectively to the Virgin Mary, St Andrew, and St Bartholomew. To a perpetual chaplain at the Altar of St Thomas in the church there was granted by Papal Bull of 20th May 1475 the Chapel of St Thomas the Martyr outwith and near the city of Glasgow.—[*Acts Scott. Parl.*, v, 546; *The Apostolic Camera and Scott. Benefices*, 181.]

1560 ANDREW HAY, called parson 21st May 1576.—[*Cal. of Charters*, xi, 2395.]

1563 ROBERT HERBERTSON, chaplain to the Chapel of St Ninian, Darnlie.—[*Reg. of Abbrev. of Feu Charters of Church Lands*, i, 14.]

1568 WILLIAM JACKSON, reader Sept. 1568 and 20th July 1569.—[*Edin. Tests*, v, 310.]

1589 JOHN HAY, pres. to the parsonage and vicarage 30th May 1589 on dem. of his father; his son, George, student in arts at Glasgow 1628.

1628 JOHN HAY.—[*G. R. Sas.*, xli, 497, 3 Ser., x, 386.]

1683 FRANCIS ROSS, had issue—Margaret, bapt. 17th March 1690; Mary, bapt. 15th Aug. 1692.—[*Old Machar Reg.*]

1790 THOMAS BURNS, pres. 22nd April 1790.

1843 JAMES GRAY WOOD, pres. by Crown 21st July 1843.

1850 GEORGE ALEXANDER, pres. by Crown 6th Sept. 1850.

1858 ROBERT STEPHEN, pres. by Crown 2nd June 1858.

1916 DAVID YOUNG, died 30th March 1933; his widow, Minnie d'Esterre Macleod, died 13th March 1935; his daugh., Minnie Aileen d'Esterre (marr. 19th Oct. 1937 Rev. Hugh Legh Beauchamp McCarthy, St Mary's, Banbury).

SHAWLANDS

1882 JOHN SLOAN, line 3, for "Rankin" read "Bankier."

1933 JAMES EDWARD HOUSTON, dem. 13th Aug. 1935, died 26th Nov. 1935; his wife, Effie Terras Yule, died 23rd Sept. 1927.

THORNLIEBANK

1890 JOHN CHARLSON, licen. by Presb. of Linlithgow 1889; died at Dunranion Billericay, Essex, 30th June 1942.

1902 ROBERT HARVIE SMITH, died at Kyle of Lochalsh 14th Nov. 1926.

1927 REGINALD FREDERICK WHITELEY, trans. from Brechin East (*q.v.*) 7th June 1927. Had issue—Beverley Frederick, born 4th April 1928.

PRESBYTERY OF GREENOCK

CUMBRAE

In 1325–35 the church, then a chapel annexed to the Church of Largs, was confirmed to Paisley Abbey by John, Bishop of Glasgow. The Church of Cumbrae is mentioned apart in 1561. On 20th Nov. 1510 Mr. Patrick Shaw, vicar of Monkton, was "farmer of the fruits of the Churches of Largs and St Kenote"; and that, in view of the conjunction of Largs and Cumbrae Churches, may indicate that the Church of Cumbrae was dedicated to St Kenneth. The church was rebuilt at the Kirktown in 1612 and again in 1802.—[*Reg. of Paisley Abbey*, 238–9, 240–2; *Original Parishes of Scot.*, i, 90; see Largs.]

1623 THOMAS MOORE or MURE, M.A., in office 15th Aug. 1617.—[*Yester Writs*, 1180.]

1668 ALEXANDER SANGSTER, trans. to Kirkpatrick Durham before 24th July 1673.—[*P. R. Sas.*, *Dumfries*, i, 234.]

1867 JAMES SIMPSON MACNAB, his son, James, died at Ruthen, North Wales, 7th Jan. 1921.

1889 ARCHIBALD GRIERSON, died at Rothesay 7th March 1940, unmarried.

ERSKINE

1561 SIR HOMER FRASER, vicar 1561–2.—[*Comps. Gen. Coll. of Thirds.*]

1561 GAVIN DUNBAR, parson 1561.—[*Acts and Dec.*, xxii, 333.]

1562 DAVID STEWART, parson 1562, Canon of Glasgow 1565.—[*Reg. Abbrev. Feu Charters of Church Lands*, i, 15, 141.]

1561 ROBERT SEMPILL, vicar and reader 1561–79; conformed; died Dec. 1606 and had a son, George.—[*Comps. Gen. Coll. and Sub Coll. of Thirds, Stirling*, etc.; *Glasgow Tests*, 2nd Oct. 1612.]

1571 JAMES HILL, parson 1571–9; rector 30th May 1580. Had issue—Thomas.—[*Comps. Gen. Coll. of Thirds*; *Reg. Mag. Sig.*, v, 581.]

1586 DAVID STEWART, parson, died before 16th Jan. 1586-7; his daugh., Jean (marr. Abraham Abercrombie).—[*Reg. of Deeds*, xxvii, 155a.]

1592 WILLIAM BRISBANE, his pres. in 1592 was on the death of William Cranstoun; his sons, William and John.—[*Reg. Sec. Sig.*, xiv, 9.]

1642 MATTHEW BRISBANE, his son, Matthew, M.D., Utrecht, Holland, M.A. (Edinburgh 1656); Rector of Glasgow Univ. 1677 and 1679–81; Town Physician of Glasgow; surgeon to H.M. Life Guards; died 1699.—[*Gen. Reg. Sas.*, xiv, 333.]

1705 WALTER MENZIES, marr. Isabel, daugh. of Alexander Clark, merchant, Edinburgh.

1851 THOMAS McKIE, his sons—Henry Bannerman, died 14th June 1927; John McMillan, died at Poulton le Fylde, Lancashire, 17th June 1925; Walter Dunlop, died at Buxton 19th Oct. 1920.

1871 JOHN McILRAITH, line 24, for "1889" read "1881."

1913 DAVID MELVILLE STEWART, died 18th Jan. 1936.

DONALD FERGUS FERGUSON,
1921 born 16th Oct. 1896, son of Donald Fergus F. and Mary Dunn; educ. at High School and Univ. of Glasgow; licen. by Presb. of Dunbarton 1920; assistant New Kilpatrick; ord. Colleague and Successor 14th July 1921; dem. 1928 on app. to St Andrew's Church, Selangor; adm. to Abernethy North 17th Feb. 1933; app. Chaplain to Forces in Middle East March 1941. Marr. 31st July 1928 Edith, daugh. of Alexander Rae and Jean Moir and has issue—Joyce Fergus, born 7th Feb. 1930; Norman Douglas, born 7th Aug. 1933; Fergus, B.Sc., died off Liberia, 1st Feb. 1949.

DAVID YOUNG ROBERTSON, M.A.,
1929 S.T.M., trans. from Dingwall (*q.v.*) 6th March 1929; Chaplain at Simla 1935; trans. to Dulnain Bridge 7th May 1941; dem. 21st Sept. 1947.

FAIRLIE

ARTHUR ALLAN, dem. 15th Nov.
1884 1934.

GOUROCK

ALEXANDER MILNE, his wife, Helen
1884 Elizabeth Kirke, died 9th Aug. 1920; his daugh., Margaret Elizabeth (marr. 25th July 1923 Harry Steel Watson, min. of Lochcraig).

GEORGE BENNET THOMSON
1907 MICHIE. He enlisted in Gordon Highlanders 1915, Private O.T.C. Inns of Court 1916, commissioned 31st Jan. 1917, trans. to M.G.C. Tank Corps, served in France 1917-18, retired as Captain; drowned 22nd March 1938. Marr. 5th June 1920 Agnes May Kirkland, daugh. of William Stewart, M.B., C.M., D.P.H., Benview, Gourock.

GREENOCK, AUGUSTINE

CHARLES CHRISTIE, licen. by Presb.
1887 of Edinburgh 13th May 1887; died 2nd Aug. 1920; his widow, Elizabeth Arthur Shaw, died 15th Dec. 1938.

DAVID WILSON BAIRD, trans. from
1920 St James Presb. Church, Sunderland; adm. 15th Dec. 1920; trans. to Whiteness 7th Feb. 1923.

WILLIAM WILSON, ord. 19th July
1923 1923; trans. to Glenisla 21st March 1928.

(*United with Cartsburn* 1929.)

CARTSBURN

KENNETH ALEXANDER MAC-
1913 LEAY, line 16, for "1903" read "1902"; line 18, for "23" read "21"; he was adm. to Delting 27th Sept. 1920.

JAMES FRANCIS, died 30th April
1919 1943.

GREENOCK EAST

JAMES HUTCHESON, his widow,
1844 Annie Scott Brown, died 8th Feb. 1924.

GEORGE DAVID HENDERSON,
1916 trans. to St Mary's, Partick, 30th Nov. 1922.

STEPHEN GREEN, ord. 14th May
1923, dem. 4th June 1928 on ap-
1923 pointment to Nyasaland (*q.v.*) 10th March 1928.

IAN McCULLOCH, trans. from Tealing (*q.v.*) 27th Nov. 1928; trans. to
1928 Grahamston 2nd April 1937.

GREENOCK GAELIC

JOHN STEWART McCALLUM, his
1913 widow, Isabella Leitch Thomson, died 27th Nov. 1919.

DUNCAN MACARTHUR, his wife's
1919 mother, Catherine Fraser; trans. to Lochbroom 28th Sept. 1927.

GEORGE MACKENZIE, trans. from
Kilmore 17th May 1928; trans. to
1928 Dores and Bona 11th Sept. 1946; dem. 15th Oct. 1947.

LADYBURN

1919 GEORGE HOPE JAMIE, res. 24th Nov. 1920 on commission as Navy Chaplain to Atlantic Fleet; adm. to Craigrownie 31st Aug. 1926.

1921 ROBERTSON McCALLUM MILLAR, trans. from Glengarry 4th May 1921; trans. to Twechar 7th April 1927.

1927 JOHN FLEMING, born 9th Oct. 1902, son of Gavin F. and Isabella Patience McClymont; educ. at Univ. of Glasgow, M.A. (1924), B.D. (1927); licen. by Presb. of Glasgow 1927; assistant Ferniegair and Prestwick; ord. 28th July 1927; trans. to Kells 4th Oct 1932; trans. to Skirling 25th Sept. 1936; trans. to Kincardine in Menteith 16th Oct. 1942. Marr. 29th June 1927 Williamina Mary Watt, daugh. of William Twaddle of Ferniegair House and Marion Logan.

GREENOCK MIDDLE

1769 JOHN ADAM, marr. Elizabeth, daugh. of William Parker of Barleith.

1877 DAVID SMITH PETERS, died 28th Feb. 1924.

1924 JAMES LAWSON MacCURRACH, trans. from Gilcomston (*q.v.*) 18th Sept. 1924, died 4th Sept. 1944.

GREENOCK NORTH

1898 ADAM CURRIE, dem. 16th May 1934. Marr. (2) 4th Feb. 1938 Catherine Poole; his son, Adam, born 22nd May 1894.

GREENOCK ST PAUL'S

1879 THOMAS FRANCIS JOHNSTONE, his widow, Florence Mary Cowley, died at London 27th Feb. 1939.

1918 CHARLES LAING WARR, line 12, for "Tulloch" read "Tatlock"; trans. to St Giles, Edinburgh, 11th Feb. 1926.

1926 MALCOLM MUNRO MACPHERSON, born 30th Jan. 1892, youngest son of Robert M., D.D., min. of Elgin; educ. at Univ. of Edinburgh, M.A. (1919); served as Captain in European War, O.B.E. (1st June 1919); licen. by Presb. of Elgin 1920; assistant St Giles, Edinburgh; ord. A. and S. to Helensburgh 25th Oct. 1922; trans. and adm. 8th July 1926; dem. 6th Nov. 1945. Marr. 11th Aug. 1931 Jessie Mary, daugh. of Alexander Fleming, jun., Greenock.

GREENOCK SOUTH

1881 JOHN FORBES MACPHERSON, his wife, Jessie Ewart, only daugh. of John Hannah of Girvan and Auchenvale, Ayrshire, died 4th July 1928; he died 13th April 1929.

1920 JOHN YOUNGSON THOMSON, son of John T., Beverley Hall, Chicago; trans. from Leadhills (*q.v.*) 18th Dec. 1920; trans. to Annbank 1st May 1931, unmarried.

WELLPARK

1879 WILLIAM WILSON, died at Kirn, 12th Feb. 1925.

1916 CHARLES PETER GRANT, trans. to Dalbeattie 19th Dec. 1929. Marr. 11th Dec. 1929 Grace Gill Orr.

GREENOCK WEST

1598 PATRICK SHAW, pres. 28th Nov. 1598 on death of Andrew Murdo.—[*Reg. Sec. Sig.*, lxvi, 6.]

1904 WILLIAM JACK NICHOL SERVICE, his wife, Amy Margaret Angus, died 16th June 1943. He died Glasgow 16th Feb. 1945.

INVERKIP

There was in the parish a chapel dedicated to the Holy Trinity. Manifestly this is identical with the chapel designated the "Holy Trinity of Cristelwell" or "Castelwell." Other designations were Cristiswell and Chrystswell. It was under the patronage of the Crown, and therefore was in all likelihood the chapel to which the following reference is made in a record of Charters of Robert III, 1390-1406, "Charter for ane foundation of a Chapel att Chrystswell." If the first part of the name refers to Christ, the Holy Trinity may have been a later dedication. The endowment of the chapel included the £5 lands of Auchymillin and mill in the bailery of Cowell and the Forty-Penny lands of the "prebend of chaplainry of Crystiswell called the Chapelands of the said Chapel of Crystiswell."—[*Transcripts from the Vatican*, i, 341, *MS. Reg. Ho.*; *Reg. Great Seal*, i, App. ii, 1848; iii, 938, 1227, 1533; v, 2051; *Reg. Sec. Seal*, i, 400, ii, 1896, 1898 and *n; Retours*, xliii, 83.]

1563 JAMES SCOTT, exhorter 1563.—[*Comps. Sub Coll. of Thirds, Stirling.*]

1567 DAVID CHRISTISOUN, vicar 1567.—[*Acts and Dec.*, xxiv, 454.]

1565 JOHN STEWART, M.A., in Stirling, pres. to vicarage 12th April 1565 on death of Sir David Christison.—[*Reg. Sec. Sig.*, xxxiii, 3; *Comps. Sub Coll. of Thirds, Stirling*, etc.]

1591 ANDREW MURDO, M.A., pres. to vicarage 9th Jan. 1591-2 on death of John Stewart.—[*Reg. Sec. Sig.*, lxiii, 119.]

1592 THOMAS YOUNGER, M.A., had also a son, Tobias.—[*Test Dougal Bannatyne, Glasgow Tests*, 28th Nov. 1623.]

1869 ALEXANDER McQUISTEN, his daugh., Henrietta Mary, O.B.E. (marr. 22nd April 1896 Sir Robert Campbell Mackenzie of Edinbarnet), died 26th Feb. 1930; his son, Alexander, died 29th Feb. 1940.

KILMACOLM

1562 UMPHRA CUNNINGHAM, vicar in 1562.—[*Comps. Gen. Coll. of Thirds.*]

1563 ARCHIBALD CRAWFORD, M.A., min. 1563.—[*Comps. Sub Coll. of Thirds, Stirling*, etc.]

1563 ROBERT MAXWELL, reader in 1563.—[*Comps. Sub Coll. of Thirds, Stirling*, etc.]

1630 NINIAN CAMPBELL, second son to Colin C. of Ormidale.—[*Gen. Reg. of Sas.*, xxxiii, 37.]

1875 JAMES MURRAY, died Father of the Church 25th Nov. 1939; his wife, Margaret Anne Darling, died 21st March 1935.

1918 WILLIAM BLACK was ord. to army and not to this parish.

1921 FOSTER FRANKLIN, born Ayr 14th Sept. 1889, son of Foster F., H.M. Customs, and Annie C. F. Scott; educ. at Hull Grammar School and Hutcheson's Grammar School, Glasgow, Univ. of Glasgow, M.A. (Hons.); Captain, 3rd Highland Light Infantry; licen. by Presb. of Glasgow 1919; assistant Douglas 1919, Kilmacolm 1920; ord. (assistant and successor) 9th Feb. 1921; trans. to Corstorphine 30th Sept. 1940. Marr. 1st Sept. 1921 Mary Maclean, M.A., M.B., Ch.B., daugh. of John Weir, Catford, and Mary Maclean, and has issue—Anne Mary, born 29th July 1922 (marr. 18th Sept. 1947 Alan Hugh Dermid, M.B., Ch.B.); John Weir, born 26th July 1925, died 7th April 1926; James Murray, born 5th Aug. 1927. Publication —*This Thing Today* (1932).

LANGBANK

1867 ROBERT CRAWFORD, his widow, Margaret Kirk Stewart, died at Edinburgh 14th Nov. 1925; his daughs.—Janet Campbell (marr. 12th Feb. 1921 Robert Macfarlane, M.A., B.Sc., Dunbarton); Margaret Stewart, died 30th May 1927; Jane Blackwood (marr. 24th Nov. 1937 Alexander G. Macmillan, Port Albirnie, British Columbia); Marjory Stewart, parish sister, Tolbooth, Edinburgh, died 10th June 1941.

1893 JOHN KNOX BROWN, his widow, Katherine Macgregor, died 20th May 1936.

1896 WILLIAM ALEXANDER, dem. 7th June 1932, died 15th Oct. 1936.

LARGS

In 1316 Walter, Seneschal of Scotland, granted the church to Paisley Abbey for the souls of himself and Marjory, his late wife, etc.; and the grant with the addition of the Chapel of Cumbrae was included in confirmation Charters by John, Bishop of Glasgow 1325-35; and others. In 1832 "cross aisles" were added to the "eastern extremity" of the church by means of funds belonging to the poor, seat-rents being levied for the benefit of the funds.—[*Reg. of Paisley*, 237-44.]

1563 DAVID NEILL, exhorter 1563.— [*Comps. Sub Coll. of Thirds, Stirling*, etc.]

1748 PATRICK WALLACE, M.A. (Glasgow, 1736).

1910 ROBERT OSWALD, died 8th Feb. 1928; his daugh., Helen Dorothy (marr. 25th June 1932 Dr L. N. A. Harrison, London.)

1928 DAVID BROOK BAXTER, born 12th June 1898; son of Fred Walker B., F.R.C.O., organist and choirmaster, and Laura Brook. Educ. at Univ. of Glasgow, M.A. (1920), B.D. (1923); licen. by Presb. of Irvine 9th Jan. 1923; assistant at Stevenston and Lady Glenorchy's, Edinburgh, 1923; ord. to Dunlop 1st Nov. 1923; trans. and adm. 2nd Oct. 1928. Marr. 27th April 1926 Margaret Maitland, third daugh. of John Barclay, Dalry, Ayrshire, and Jessie Cowan Macdougall, and has issue—Winifred Margaret, born 22nd Aug. 1928; John Barclay Walker, born 20th Jan. 1931; Fred Walker, born 2nd Feb. 1935.

NEWARK

1882 THOMAS HARKNESS GRAHAM, dem. 18th May 1925; died 19th June 1927; his widow, Isabella Rankin Brooks, died 9th Feb. 1941.

1925 THOMAS LOW, son of Andrew L., The Rectory, Peebles; trans. from Garvald 3rd Dec. 1925; trans. to Charteris Memorial, Edinburgh, 4th Oct. 1934. Marr. 6th Sept. 1933 Mary Evelyn (died 1944), daugh. of Richard Edwards, 54 Warrender Park Road, Edinburgh.

PORT GLASGOW

1877 JOHN REID, his widow Margaret Birkmyre Laird, died 15th March 1934.

1907 DAVID JOHN MOIR PORTEOUS, died 31st Jan. 1942; his widow, Edith Lucy Bertram, died at Edinburgh 15th Sept. 1942.

SKELMORLIE

1911 DAVID BRUCE NICOL, trans. to St Margaret's, Edinburgh, 3rd Aug. 1920.

1921 ROLLO RUSSELL GRANT SUTHERLAND, trans. from Ballantrae (*q.v.*) 11th Feb. 1921; trans. to St Marnock's, Kilmarnock, 18th Feb. 1926.

1926 DUDLEY STUART HOPKIRK, B.D., B.Litt., ord. 5th Aug. 1926; trans. to Greenside, Edinburgh, 26th April 1929.

PRESBYTERY OF HAMILTON

AIRDRIE, EAST

1792 ALEXANDER BOWER, a licentiate of the Irish Presb. Church; was Relief min. at Shiprow, Aberdeen, 1799–1806; died 1837.

AIRDRIE, WEST

1881 DAVID HOWAT PATERSON, granted an A. and S. 21st Dec. 1920; died at Cathcart 11th June 1925.

1921 JOHN FORSYTH MARSHALL, M.A., M.C., ord. 28th April 1921; trans. to Helensburgh West 17th Jan. 1927.

1927 JOHN ALEXANDER CALDERWOOD, born Barrhead, Renfrewshire, 25th April 1893, son of John Alexander C. and Agnes Muir; educ. at Morrison's Academy, Crieff, and Univ. of Glasgow, M.A. (1915); licen. by Presb. of Paisley June 1920; assistant Monkton (June 1921 to Sept. 1922); ord. to Stobhill 8th Sept. 1922; trans. and adm. 20th May 1927; dem. 14th Nov. 1933 on adm. to Madeira. Marr. (1) 6th March 1923 Mary Brough, daugh. of Rev. Alexander Gibson, Prestwick (whom he divorced 22nd Dec. 1933), and has issue—John Alexander, born 13th April 1924; Gordon Gibson, born 10th May 1928; (2) 24th Jan. 1935 Margaret, daugh. of James and Margaret Gilbert.

AVENDALE

1563 DAVID CUNNINGHAM, M.A., min. in 1563.—[*Comps. Sub Coll. of Thirds, Stirling*, etc.]

1567 SIR JOHN ANDERSON, apparently vicar before 1560 and conformed, vicar and reader 1561 and 30th Aug. 1575.—[*Comps. Gen. Coll. of Thirds*; *Glasgow Tests.*, ii, 93, 175.]

1574 JOHN HAY, vicar.—[*Acts and Dec.*, lviii, 174.]

1648 HUGH ARCHIBALD.—[*G. R. Sas.*, 2 Ser., ii, 257, vii, 265.]

1672 JAMES HAMILTON, delete M.A. (Glasgow, 1638).

1850 ROBERT REID RAE, marr. 27th Sept. 1852 Jessie Croil, and had issue—Jessica, born 27th May 1853; Jane Donaldson, born 20th July 1854.

1904 JOHN MUIRHEAD, app. clerk of Presb. of Earlston 1899; app. clerk of Presb. (assistant and successor) 25th June 1929; received assistant in clerkship 1st Feb. 1938; died 2nd May 1938.

EAST STRATHAVEN CHAPEL

1887 THOMAS HILL, licen. by Presb. of Glasgow 4th June 1884.

BAILLIESTON

1892 ALEXANDER ANDREW, D.D. (Glasgow Univ. 1929); Convener Education Committee 1929; dem. 8th Nov. 1940; died 8th March 1942; his wife, Isabella Lumsden Allan, died 4th April 1941.

BARGEDDIE

1917 ALEXANDER LYON BENNETT, trans. to Bridgeton 11th Oct. 1923.

1924 JAMES RAMSAY THOMSON, born Dunbarton 14th Oct. 1898, son of Peter T., J.P., and Isabella Drysdale; educ. at Dunbarton Academy and Univ. of Glasgow, M.A. (1920), B.D. (1928); served in Highland Cyclist Batt. in Great War; licen. by Presb. of Dunbarton 1922; assistant at Cambuslang 1922 and Glasgow Cathedral 1923; ord. 28th Feb. 1924; trans.

to Applegarth 4th April 1930; trans. to St Andrews, Carluke, 3rd July 1942; trans. to St Margaret's, Barnhill, 1st May 1947. Marr. 12th July 1933 Joanna, daugh. of Rev. John Hunter, M.A., and Jenny Allan, and has issue—James Drysdale, born 6th July 1935.

BELLSHILL

JAMES MILLAR KILLEN, assistant at Partick, died 22nd July 1928; his widow, Annie Gilbert, died 26th June 1934.
1878

HUGH WILSON, his widow, Margaret Josephine Taylor, died 16th May 1942.
1882

GAVIN WARNOCK, trans. to Kirkcowan 24th July 1930; dem. 12th June 1932; died 21st Aug. 1932; his daugh., Annabella Janet May Louise (marr. 29th June 1940 –. Simpson); his son, Gavin David Ross, Captain, R.A.M.C.
1901

BLANTYRE

RICHARD HENDERSON, his son, Robert, born 18th Jan. 1730.
1722

STEWART WRIGHT, born Inveraray 15th Oct. 1829, son of James W., provost of Inveraray, and Maria Brooks; educ. at Inveraray, Irvine Academy and Univs. of Glasgow and Edinburgh; licen. by Presb. of Glasgow; assistant at St Matthews, Glasgow, 1855; ord. to St George's-in-the-Fields 23rd May 1855; Chaplain at Madras 1858–65; Bangalore 1865–71; adm. 3rd Aug. 1871, died 29th Nov. 1887. Marr. 3rd Jan. 1856 Alice, eldest daugh. of Colin Smith, D.D., min. of Inveraray, and had issue—James Stewart born 29th Nov. 1856, died 11th Sept. 1857; Annie Campbell, born 28th Dec. 1857, died at Glasgow 26th Aug. 1932; Mary Harriet, born 25th Dec. 1859, died at Glasgow 17th Aug. 1928; Alice Narcissa, born 26th March 1861, died at Carluke 20th May 1930; Elizabeth Stewart, born 12th Oct. 1862, died at Bangalore, 1866; Jeanie Shaw Stewart, born 9th Jan. 1864; John Brooks Stewart, born 2nd Jan, 1865, died at Madras 1868; Colin Stewart, born 26th Jan. 1867, died in infancy; William Norman Stewart, analytical chemist, born 10th April 1868, died 20th April 1944; Elizabeth Stewart, born 19th April 1869, died at Blantyre 1886; Flora Montgomery Stewart, born 19th April 1870 (marr. 22nd June 1894 John Craig Millar of Waygateshaw, Carluke); Dora Stewart, born 25th May 1872, died at Glasgow 8th June 1931.
1871

CHARLES SCRIMGEOUR TURNBULL, dem. 7th Nov. 1933, died 16th July 1924, unmarried.
1888

BOTHWELL

On the petition of Archibald, Earl of Douglas, Papal Mandate was given on 21st Feb. 1397–8 to Matthew, Bishop of Glasgow, to erect the church into a collegiate church for a provost and six chaplains or prebendaries. For the collegiate church the Earl assigned two parish churches of which he was patron, and a chapel having Masses for his progenitors in the territory of Orbenistoun—the Chapel of St Catharine, Orbiston. To this chapel Walter Olifard, Justiciar of Lothian, granted in 1242 an endowment of 10 lib. annual rent from the lands of Oberniston, which failing from the Mill of Bothwell. On 18th May 1410 there was given Papal Validation of the erection of the collegiate church in spite of an incorrect statement in the Papal Commission thereanent. The prebends of the church, increased to eight, were—Kittymuir, Stonehouse, Hessildene, Netherfield of Strathaven, Overtoun of le Newtoun, Cruikburnie, the Church of Hawick, and the Church of Bertram-Shotts. The Churches of Stonehouse and Strathaven were included. The Church of Hawick was erected into a prebend on 4th Oct. 1447 by the Dean and Chapter of Glasgow, with the consent of Gavin, Provost of Glasgow Collegiate Church, and William, Earl of Douglas, lord of Hawick. On 15th Nov. 1457 and on 21st May 1471 the provost of the church is described as "Provost of St Mary's, Bothwell," and on 30th April 1476 the church is designated the "Parish Church of St Mary of Bothwell." It would appear, therefore, that in all likelihood, when the church was made collegiate, the name of the Virgin was added to that of St Bridgit. In 1719 the porch of the choir which constituted the church was taken down "to admit of a modern addition to accommodate the congregation." About 1779 the church was repaired; and in 1795 it is described as "an old structure in the Gothic style, of excellent workmanship . . . near the outer base of the spire the name of the Master-Mason is writ in Saxon Characters, Magister Thomas Tron." In 1833 there was added a new church or nave "in Gothic style corresponding to the old fabric," with a tower 120 ft. high between the old work and the new. But the old and the new were separate and at different levels, the new being used as the place of worship. But a scheme of renovation carried out in 1933 at a cost of £10,000 united the buildings into an harmonious whole, comprising nave, choir, and transepts. The interior of the church of 1833 was completely cleared out, including the plaster on the walls and gallery and ceiling; and the floor was lowered to a common level with that of the ancient choir. For the support of the tower there was introduced a massive steel structure encased in freestone, and beneath the tower a large central arch was constructed to lead into the crossing. The vestibule formerly separating the nave and choir was opened up by four arches to form transepts, and the wall that filled the choir-arch was taken down to open up the interior from end to end. The roof of the nave was lined with timber; and an old vestry at the west end was transformed into a vestibule with pillared arcade. New flooring, seating accommodation, and furnishings completed the scheme. Niches in the walls of the nave were made to contain architectural fragments of a 12th century Norman church discovered during the course of the reconstruction. In 1939 the north transept was converted into a suitably appointed baptistry. On 15th Aug. 1529 the Chapel of St Lessert—Lasrach or Lassert—was in the King's hands on account of the death of James, Earl of Arran. On 22nd Sept. 1300–1 Edward I made an offering of 7 sh. "in his Chapel of Bothwell" in honour of St Mauricius.—[*Transcripts from the Vatican*, ii, 30, 199, *MS. Reg. Ho.*; *Reg. Great Seal*, ii, 2453; *Reg. Epis. of Glasgow*, ii, 366; *Reports Hist. MSS. Commis.*, xi, 48; *Cal. Papal Regs.*, xi, 334, xii, 379; *Cal. of Docs. Rel. to Scot.*, iv, 449; Watson's *Celtic Place Names*, 307; Memo. Rev. R. J. Thomson, B.D., Bothwell.]

1568 JOHN HAMILTON, pres. to vicar pensionary 30th March 1568 on death of Sir James Rae.—[*Reg. Pres. Bene.*, i, 8; *Reg. Sec. Sig.*, xxxvii, 55.]

1574 MUNGO BAXTER, reader 1574 and 1590.—[*Comps. Gen. Coll. of Thirds.*]

1608 ROBERT BOYD.—[*G. R. Sas.*, xxxiii, 254.]

1649 MATTHEW McKELL, M.A. (Glasgow 1631), his son, Matthew, M.A. (Glasgow, 1661), apprenticed to Robert Douglas, merchant, Edinburgh, 24th June 1668.

1709 SIR WILLIAM HAMILTON, his daughs.—Grizel, died 1783; Elizabeth (marr. Daniel Sinclair, min. of Longformacus).

1865 JOHN PAGAN, his widow, Margaret Wiseman Lang, died at Largs 15th Aug. 1933.

1916 SAMUEL JOHN HAMILTON, died from effects of bicycle accident near Kirkcaldy 3rd Sept. 1926; his daugh., Dorothy Poll (marr. 19th Nov. 1938 Orto Ferdinand Stiltner, Maklatz, Pomerania).

1927 ROBERT JOHN THOMSON, M.A. (1907), B.D. (Glasgow, 1910), formerly of Coldstream (*q.v.*), trans. to Alloa 15th July 1919; trans. and adm. 16th Feb. 1927. Marr. 11th Sept. 1917 Isabel Margaret Ann, only daugh. of Alexander Paterson, Burnside, Tain, and Euphemia Margaret Finlayson, and had issue—David Alexander, born 6th June 1918; Euphemia Isabel, born 27th Aug. 1919; Robert Paterson, born 6th June 1922; John Kenneth, born 11th April 1925.

BURNBANK

ANDREW SMITH DINGWALL SCOTT, 1894 died 25th July 1920.

JOHN SMITH SIEVWRIGHT, M.A., ord. 2nd Feb. 1921; trans. to Ballingry 11th Jan. 1928.
1921

CHARLES KEITH McWILLIAM, 1928 born Aberdeen 29th Jan. 1896, son of Charles McW. and Jane McWilliam Keith; educ. Robert Gordon's College and Univ. of Aberdeen, M.A. (1919), B.D. (1920); licen. by Presb. of Aberdeen April 1920; assistant Holburn, Aberdeen; ord. to Leadhills, 17th Sept. 1920; trans. to St Thomas, Leith, 11th April 1923; trans. to Kelso North, 17th May 1926; trans. and adm. 10th July 1928. Marr. 5th Nov. 1933 Margaret, daugh. of John and Margaret McDonald, Aberdeen.

CADZOW

THOMAS FOREST HARKNESS GRAHAM. Addl. publications—
1919 *Scenes on the Avon, Lanarkshire; Tributaries on the Avon, Lanarkshire; Muttonhole Road and other Poems; Culzean Castle* (short history).

CALDERBANK

WILLIAM BUCHANAN STRACHAN
1884 his widow, Helen Shaw Munro Fleming, died 8th Sept. 1921.

WILLIAM HENDERSON ADAM, died 28th Feb. 1923; his widow,
1919 Margaret Wallace, died 19th July 1946.

JAMES MacGILLIVRAY, M.A., formerly of Lochcarron (*q.v.*), adm. 4th
1923 July 1923; died 2nd Dec. 1924.

JAMES WALLACE SIMPSON, M.C., ord. 22nd April 1925; trans. to
1925 Crimond 5th April 1928.

(*Charges united* 1930.)

CALDERCRUIX

WILLIAM BLACK JACK, died 29th
1896 March 1938.

CALDERHEAD

JOHN REEVIE JOHNSTON MERRY,
1918 trans. to Paisley North 7th Jan. 1926.

DUNCAN CONACHER, trans. from Kilmorie, Arran (*q.v.*), 2nd June
1926 1926; his wife, Elsie Robertson Gordon, died 26th March 1935; his son, Duncan Gordon, Captain, R.A.M.C.

CAMBUSLANG

DAVID CHRISTISON, sometime parson.—[*Acts and Dec.*, xxiv, 454.]
1562

WILLIAM HAMILTON, parson, 1564, 1568 and 1572.—[*Acts and Dec.*,
1564 xxxii, 436; xxxiv, 371; xlix, 30; *Comps. Gen. Coll. and Sub Coll. of Thirds, Dumfries*, etc.]

JAMES LINDSAY, called min. 1563, still in office 13th Feb. 1581-2.—
1567 [*Comps. Sub Coll. of Thirds, Stirling.*]

ADAM FOULIS, pres. on death of William Hamilton, 1572.—[*Reg.*
1572 *Pres. Bene.*, i, (8), 20.]

JOHN HOWIESON, M.A., pres. to vicar pensionary 2nd Dec. 1591 on
1579 death of Thomas Lindsay.—[*Reg. Sec. Sig.*, lxiii, 30.]

JOHN DRUMMOND, pres. to parsonage and vicarage 23rd Aug. 1580.
1580 —[*Reg. Pres. Bene.*, i, 387.]

ROBERT FLEMING, line 5, delete "who was James Fleming's first
1653 wife."

WILLIAM McCULLOCH, marr. Janet, daugh. of Robert Dinwoodie, mer-
1731 chant, Glasgow.

JAMES MEIK, son of John M. of Fortisset, born 12th March 1740.
1774 Publication—*Reply to Mr Ewing's Animadversion of Lay Preaching Indefensible*, Glasgow, 1800.

JOHN ROBERTSON, his daugh., Sarah
1797 (marr. John Whitehead, S.S.C.).

JAMES STEWART JOHNSON, his
1843 daugh., Helen Isabella (marr. Archibald Russell, son of Archibald

Russell of Auchenrath, Boithwell), died at Moffat 28th Feb. 1938.

1908 ROBERT SIBBALD CALDERWOOD, D.D. (Glasgow, 1928), granted A. and S. 11th June 1935; his son, Walter Macfarlane, min. of St Mary's, Hawick; his daugh., Mary Sibbald, died 28th Aug. 1940.

CAMBUSLANG WEST

1903 ARTHUR STANLEY MIDDLETON, trans. to Dean, Edinburgh, 15th March 1927.

1927 ROBERT JAMES STEELE DICKEY, trans. from Beath (*q.v.*) 29th Sept. 1927; M.A. (St Andrews, June 1938); trans. to Firth 11th Jan. 1946; his wife, Helen Russell, daugh. of Thomas Ritchie and Catherine Anderson, St Andrews (marr. 20th Nov. 1915), died 18th May 1941. He marr. (2) 7th Oct. 1942 Flora, daugh. of Charles MacGregor, Kirkwall, and widow of Alexander Andrew Moir, M.A., rector of Dornoch Academy.

CAMBUSNETHAN

Cambusnethan is "Neighton's bight' or "bend." At this bend stood the old Church of Cambusnethan; and the name doubtless commemorates a Welsh saint of that name; may be identical with Nathalan, Nechtan, whose day was 8th Jan. and who died in 679 and was buried, it is said, at Tullich, Upper Deeside.—[Watson's *Celtic Place Names*, 329-30.]

1588 ALEXANDER ROWATT, min., pres. to parsonage and vicarage 4th Jan. 1591-2.—[*Reg. Sec. Sig.*, lxiii, 107.]

1592 THOMAS MUIRHEAD, had a son, John.—[*Glasgow Tests.*, 12th Nov. 1635.]

1851 ROBERT SHAW HUTTON, his daughs.—Ella (marr. 24th Jan. 1925 John F. Williams, Overdale, Wishaw); Ada Nichol, died Edinburgh 26th May 1946.

1900 GILBERT ALEXANDER KENNEDY, his widow, Mary Bryars, died Kenya 26th Dec. 1935; his daugh., Adelaide Margaret (marr. 26th July 1923 Gordon Alfred Lyns, London).

1917 JOHN ASHPLANT NICHOLLS, convicted of assault and found insane; died at Montrose 20th July 1934; his sons—John, in Malay Police; William, in London; his daugh., Christian (marr. 4th March 1939 Geoffrey Charles, son of Captain F. G. White, R.F.A.).

CHAPELTON

1891 WILLIAM THOMSON, dem. 15th June 1930; died 27th Oct. 1933; his widow, Helen Macleod, died 29th Dec. 1939; his son, John Gardner, B.D., B.Ed., ordained to Loudoun Parish 15th Dec. 1927; his daugh., Jane Duncan, died 5th July 1923.

CLARKSTON

1872 JAMES BRANDER, his widow, Jessie Lorimer, died 24th Dec. 1926.

1889 WILLIAM OGILVY DUNCAN, born 23rd Jan 1858, not 1850 as in print; dem. 31st Dec. 1933, died 2nd Feb. 1936.

CLELAND

1891 DUNCAN CAMERON, born 18th May 1853; his wife, Agnes Jack Lang, died 10th Sept. 1935. Retired for sake of Union, 3rd Dec. 1929; died 10th Feb. 1938.

COATDYKE

1905 JAMES CROMARTY SMITH, D.D. (Edinburgh, 28th June 1929, and Montreal, April 1929); dem. 31st May 1939, died at Airdrie 22nd Dec. 1944. His wife, Emma Mary Philip, died same day.

COATS

1882 WILLIAM HUTCHISON, his widow, Elizabeth Dinwoodie, died 5th Nov. 1935; his daugh., Mary Macdonald (marr. 3rd March 1927 Walter Douglas Dykes Jones).

1907 GEORGE MACKENZIE, D.D. (Aberdeen, 29th March 1933); his daugh., Joan Noble, author of *The Homeward Tide* (marr. 5th Dec. 1934 James Beattie Burnett, son of James Beattie Burnett, min. of Fetteresso). A. and S. granted 6th April 1937. Publications—Edited *Alma Mater* (Aberdeen Univ. Magazine) 1885–6; Church of Scotland Jewish Mission Quarterly, 1924–33; *The Few Things through the Ages*; *At the Old Sea Gate of Jerusalem*; *Sermons* in Christian World Pulpit; Articles in *Expository Times*, *Life and Work*, etc.

COLTNESS MEMORIAL CHURCH

1879 JAMES ROBERT CHRYSTAL, died at Melrose 27th Jan. 1930; his daugh., Alice Margaret Wilkie, died at Elie 6th Aug. 1948.

1892 WILLIAM ROBERTSON, dem. 11th Nov. 1920; died at Edinburgh 29th May 1936.

1921 DONALD MACDONALD, ord. 22nd April 1921; dem. on app. as Indian Chaplain (*q.v.*) 10th Dec. 1924.

1925 HAMILTON RUSSELL FERGUSON, born Ollaberry, Shetland, 25th June 1900, son of Gilbert Young F., schoolmaster, and Mary J., daugh. of Henry Mouat of North Hammersland, Shetland; educ. at Anderson Institute, Lerwick, and Univ. of Glasgow, M.A. (1922); served in Gordon Highlanders in Great War 1918; licen. by Presb. of Glasgow 1924; assistant, Calton and St Georges-in-the-Fields, Glasgow; ord. 24th April 1925; dem. 1945; Director, Scottish Religious Film Society. Marr. 25th Aug. 1926 Brenda Morag, daugh. of James Bannatyne, solicitor, Glasgow, and has issue—Ian Russell, born 3rd Feb. 1929; Sheila Morag, born 4th Sept. 1930; Rosemary Jean, born 9th Oct. 1936.

CRAIGNEUK

1906 ROBERT GEDDES BRODIE, died at Glasgow 16th June 1924.

1924 PETER JOHN McIVER, trans. from Cross and Burness 10th Dec. 1924; trans. to Inchture 17th Feb. 1928.

1928 WILLIAM WILSON BELL, formerly of Abbey St Bathans (*q.v.*); trans. from Monzievaird and Strowan 10th Oct. 1928; died 13th July 1948.

DALSERF

1563 JOHN RAMAGE, reader 1563–9.—[*Comps. Sub Coll. of Thirds, Stirling*, etc.]

1646 FRANCIS AIRD.—[*G. R. Sas.*, lix, 14.]

1672 THOMAS KIRKCALDY, his son, William, apprentice to George Smailholm, merchant, 13th Oct. 1680.

1681 JOSEPH CLELAND, wife, was widow of David Liddell, Prof. of Divinity, Glasgow.—[*Deeds, Dal.*, 1705, No. 352.]

1805 JAMES CRAIG, son of James C., Chaplain to Duke of Hamilton; dem. and went to Shrewsbury 1816. Marr. (1) Sara Dixon (born 1781, died 1830) and had issue—James, born Dec. 1812, died June 1873; John, born Dec. 1814; Elizabeth, born 1816 (marr.); Charles, born 1818, died 1890; Alexander, born 1819, died 1884; Robert Wallace, born April 1821, died 1884; Anne (twin), born April 1821, died Oct. 1821; Mary, born 1823, died 1875. He marr. (2) June 1832 Elizabeth Brayne (died 11th July 1884), Shrewsbury, and had issue—Agnes Wallace, born 1836 (marr. Thomas Burd); Catherine, born 1838 (marr. Wakefield Dixon); Donald, born 1842, died 1934.

1907 ALEXANDER BARCLAY, Ph.D. (Edinburgh, 1926), died 24th April 1937. Publication—*The Protestant Doctrine of the Lord's Supper*, 1926.

DALZIEL

In the Barony of Dalziel there was land called Saint Laurence Land.—[*Laing Charters*, 695.]

1567 JOHN ROBESON, pres. to vicar-pensionary 18th Feb. 1569 on death of Sir Alexander Walker.—[*Reg. Pres. Bene.*, i, 38.]

1607 DAVID MAYNE, his son, Thomas, merchant, Glasgow; his daugh., Jean (marr. John Weir, maltman, Glasgow).—[*Glasgow Burgess Roll*, 4th Aug. 1636.]

1874 DAVID SCOTT, died at Edinburgh, 21st Sept. 1924; his wife, Elizabeth Christian Ritchie, died 4th July 1922; his daugh., Mary Elizabeth Bradfute (marr. 6th April 1938 Sir James MacIver Macleod, K.B.E., C.M.G., Consul-General, Tunis).

1919 THOMAS BENTLEY STEWART THOMSON, trans. to St Stephen's, Edinburgh, 20th Dec. 1923.

1924 GAVIN KERR MACKAY, M.A., trans. from Durisdeer 24th June 1924; trans. to Johnstone High 21st Feb. 1929.

1929 JAMES BRYCE JAMIESON, trans. from Greyfriars, Dumfries (*q.v.*), 26th July 1929; D.D. (Edinburgh, 2nd July 1948); his son, George Thomson, min. of Viewfield, Erskine, Stirling, B.A. (Cant.); his daugh., Jean McGill, M.A. (Hons.), Teacher, Blyth, Northumberland; his son, Henry Moncrieff, M.A. (Hons.).

DALZIEL, ST ANDREW'S

1904 JAMES GELLATLY, died 28th June 1932.

DALZIEL, ST MARY'S

1902 WILLIAM SMITH, died 13th March 1923; his widow, Maria Hatelie, died 19th May 1935.

1923 ALEXANDER MAUCHLINE, formerly of St Matthew's, Dundee (*q.v.*), and missionary at Blantyre, Nyasaland; adm. 12th Sept. 1923; trans. to St Thomas, Leith, 22nd Sept. 1926.

1927 WILLIAM BUCHANAN, trans. from Menmuir (*q.v.*) 23rd Feb. 1927; trans. to Belhavie South 3rd April 1946; had issue—Elaine Helen Margaret, born 20th Dec. 1926; Gwynneth Ann Stuart, born 16th Dec. 1930.

DALZIEL SOUTH

1883 DUFF MACDONALD, D.D. (Aberdeen) 1923, died 20th Jan. 1929. Marr. (2) 27th July 1920 Christina Gourlie Reid.

1929 JOHN MAUCHLINE, born Glasgow 5th July 1902, son of John M. and Christina Morton; educ. at Hutcheson's Grammar School and Univ. of Glasgow, M.A. (1923), B.D. (1926); licen. by Presb. of Glasgow 28th April 1926; assistant at St Bride's, Glasgow, and Carluke; ord. 26th June 1929; dem. 30th June 1934; app. to Chair of Old Testament Language and Literature, Glasgow, 8th Oct. 1934; D.D. (Edinburgh, 2nd July 1948). Marr. 17th Sept. 1930 Helen Brisbane, M.A., daugh. of John B. Paterson and Mary Dawson, and has issue—John, born 1st July 1933; William Morton Paterson, born 19th Nov. 1935; Robert Lawman, born 22nd Oct. 1938. Publications—Articles in various learned magazines.

DUNDYVAN

1905 ANDREW ROBERTSON, his widow, Marea Christina Sieberg, died 22nd Jan. 1939.

1917 CHARLES MACKINNON, trans. to St Paul's, Glasgow, 8th March 1922.

1922 JAMES MUDGE, ord. 26th July 1922; resignation accepted 18th Jan. 1926; app. to Scots Kirk, Rangoon (*q.v.*), Feb. 1926.

1926 DUNCAN SMITH HENDERSON, trans. from Sinclairtown (*q.v.*), 24th June 1926; trans. to St Stephen's, Glasgow, 19th March 1931; died 17th April 1945. Addl. issue—Duncan Smith, born 24th June 1926; Shiena Frances McAdam, born 26th Nov. 1927; Aileen Ishbel McCombie, born 3rd Sept. 1929.

FLOWERHILL

ROBERT HENDERSON, dem. 16th June 1926, died 28th Jan. 1941; his wife, Isabella Wright, daugh. of Alexander Gibson, town clerk, Kirkcaldy, died 28th Dec. 1935.
1889

JAMES STRATHEARN McNAB, served as Lieut. in 7th Cameronians in France and Belgium in Great War; trans. from Bannockburn (*q.v.*) 20th Oct. 1920; trans. to St Leonard's, Ayr, 11th March 1931. Marr. 17th Oct. 1922 Dorothy Mary, eldest daugh. of John Moir, The Mount, Montrose, and Isabella Pirie, and had issue—Isabel Moir, born 30th July 1925; Dorothy Marion Joyce, born 3rd Dec. 1928. Publications Translated—*The Christian Life and Credo*, by Karl Barth; *Cross and Swastika; The Ordeal of the German Evangelical Church*, by Dr Arthur Frey.
1926

GARTSHERRIE

JOHN ALEXANDER IRELAND, licen. 2nd Nov. 1870; his daugh., Charlotte, died 7th Aug. 1928; his widow, Charlotte Chalmers Reid Falconer, killed in motor accident, Newark, 22nd Aug. 1939.
1891

ROBERT WILLIAM RUTHERFORD, died at Bournemouth 12th March 1924; his son, David Sinclair, min. of Biggar.
1917

JOHN McCOLL, trans. from Lochmaben 10th Sept. 1924. Marr. 28th April 1917 Mary Gwendoline, daugh. of Henry Edgar Molyneux ffennell, Woodlands, Brighton, and has issue—Alexander Browning, C.A., born 27th Jan. 1918; Moira Huntly, born 10th Jan. 1921.
1924

GARTURK

HUGH DUNCAN, died 21st Nov. 1934; his wife, Mary Alice Swallow, died 4th March 1927; his daugh., Mary Elizabeth, died 16th April 1933.
1890

GLASFORD

JOHN HAMILTON, reader 1576 and 1577.—[*Comps. Gen. Coll. of Thirds.*]
1576

ALEXANDER HAMILTON, M.A., called min. 1581–5; pres. to vicarage by Robert, Lord Sempill, on death of Sir John Hamilton; evidently identical with above. Marr. Janet Hamilton, and had issue—James (eldest); John.—[*Comps. Gen. Coll. of Thirds; Cal. of Charters*, xii, 2820; *House of Hamilton*, 369.]
1585

JAMES HAMILTON, M.A., min. in 1589 when parsonage held by Mr Robert Sempill.—[*Comps. Gen. Coll. of Thirds.*]
1589

PETER CAMERON, M.A. (Glasgow, 1593).
1594

WILLIAM HAMILTON, marr. 1646 Margaret, daugh. of James Hamilton of Barnecleuch and widow of Alexander Durham of Muirhouse, merchant in Edinburgh.
1644

GAVIN LANG, his son, Alexander, C.M.G., died 29th June 1930.
1832

ROBERT PATERSON, died 3rd Aug. 1920; his daugh., Edith Maud (marr. 1st Nov. 1922 John Annan, Bearsden.)
1871

ROBERT DALY, trans. to St James', Glasgow, 18th March 1925.
1918

THOMAS CONNOLLY, born Rutherglen 25th Dec. 1873, son of Edward C. and Janet Strathearn Jackson; educ. Rutherglen Public School, Baptist Colleges at Dunoon and Glasgow, Univs. of Glasgow and Edinburgh, M.A. (1922), and Manchester; ord. to Hopeman Baptist Church Jan. 1904; trans. to Inskip 1907; to Oldham 1909; Ancoats, Manchester, 1912; Old Cumnock 1916 and to Dumfries, March to July 1918; app. to Robertson Memorial Mission, Grassmarket, June 1918; adm. by General Assembly on probation 1920 and as licentiate 26th May 1921, and by Presb. of Edinburgh 29th June 1921; assistant, South Leith; ord. 13th July 1921; adm. 9th May 1923 to Kelso North; trans. and adm. 2nd Sept. 1925; dem. 3rd Sept. 1947. Marr. 31st Aug. 1905 Mary McFarlane Brown (died 26th Aug. 1941),
1925

daugh. of James Daly and Marion Morrison Brown. Marr. (2) 8th Sept. 1943 Helen Glennie Livingstone.

GREENGAIRS

1916 JAMES RUSSELL, died 24th Feb. 1931; his widow, Mary Keddie, died 3rd Feb. 1946.

HALLSIDE (now FLEMINGTON)

1918 WILLIAM CONWAY, trans. to Raith 11th May 1927.

1927 THOMAS RAMSAY KEARNEY (see vii, 697), trans. from Charteris Memorial Church, Edinburgh, 21st Sept. 1927; granted A. and S. 7th July 1936. Publication—*The Jubilee of our China Mission.*

HAMILTON

To Pope Nicholas V a petition was presented by James, 1st Lord Hamilton, to the effect that he, considering that the Church of Hamilton, otherwise called of old "Cadzow," whose Rector is Dean of Glasgow, was wont to be governed by only one vicar, and had, as it now has, a wide parish, with many inhabitants of both sexes, beside a multitude of souls, men making daily journey by land or water, and coming to the church for masses and to hear other divine offices, and that the cure of souls could not be conveniently exercised nor the church duly served by the vicar alone, granted and gave to the said church 20 lib. worth of lands and annual rents within his lordship for divine service and the cure of souls, and support of the said parish church, that he desired the erection of the church into a collegiate church for a provost and 6 chaplainries for as many chaplains, in addition to the rector, who was non-resident, and that he had also given 4 chaplainries founded by his ancestors and of his patronage, the Chapel of Machan, the Chapel of Hamilton within his lordship, the Chapel of St Thomas near Glasgow, and the Chapel of Lanark, to be erected and incorporated for the chaplains, the present vicar to be installed as provost, and for the erection he proposed to enlarge and adorn the said church. The Pope gave mandate to William Turnbull, Bishop of Glasgow, on 4th Jan. 1450-1 to make due enquiries and carry out the erection. On 9th Aug. and 18th Sept. 1451 the Bishop, "being occupied daily about the King in arduous and necessary business of the realm," gave commission to Thomas Spens, Bishop of Galloway, and Archibald, Abbot of Holyrood, to carry out Lord Hamilton's wishes; and on 15th March 1452-3 the Abbot of Paisley was given Papal Mandate to confirm the erection carried out by the said bishop and abbot. But a dispute arose as to the patronage of the provostry, George de Graham, vicar of the church, being presented by Lord Hamilton, and Martin Waus by Thomas Waus, Dean of Glasgow. Appeal was made to Rome, and by Bull of 10th April 1462 Pope Pius II gave decision for Lord Hamilton, confirmed the collegiate erection, and directed the Archdeacon of Glasgow and the Provost of St John the Baptist's Church, Corstorphine, to induct and install George de Graham as provost of "the new College." The fruits of the perpetual vicarage of the church were appropriated to the provostry. On 5th Jan. 1450-1 Relaxation of Penance was given by the Pope to all visiting and giving alms on the Assumption and Annunciation of the Virgin for the building, enlargement and conservation of the "Collegiate Church of St Mary, erected by Lord Hamilton"; and it is on record that Lord Hamilton "built new the parish kirk of Hamilton, the queere, and two cross isles, and steeple, all of polished stone." The church, as noted, was dedicated to the Virgin Mary. By deed of gift in 1552 the Abbot and Convent of Paisley united the Church of Carmunnock to the collegiate church, and made supplication to the Archbishop of Glasgow to confirm the union. But it appears that the confirmation did not take place. On 12th Oct. 1538 Sir David Hamilton is recorded as Rector of Kilbride and Prebendary of Hamilton, which may indicate that the Rectory of Kilbride was a prebend of Hamilton Collegiate Church.—[*Cal. Papal*

Regs., *Letters*, x, 75–6, 85, 97, xi, 438–9; Theiner's *Vet. Mon.*, 438; *Hist. MSS. Commis. Report*, xi, 20, 49.]

FIRST CHARGE

JOHN DAVIDSON, M.A., min. in 1563.—[*Comps. Sub Coll. of Thirds, Stirling*, etc.]
1563

JOHN RAYES, exhorter and teacher of the young, 1563.—[*Comps. Sub Coll. of Thirds, Stirling*, etc.]
1563

ARCHIBALD BARRIE, M.A., vicar pensioner 1571–7, probably did not conform.—[*Comps. Gen. Coll. of Thirds.*]
1571

JAMES HAMILTON, on 27th Aug. 1639 the General Assembly at Edinburgh "upon his humble supplication and confession" declared him capable of the Ministry. Marr. Katherine, daugh. of James Hamilton of Torrens.—[*House of Hamilton*, 855; Peterkin's *Record of the Kirk*, 261.]
1609

ROBERT DOUGLAS, line 5, for "that year" read "1682."
1675

ROBERT SCOTT, had issue—Marie, bapt. 31st July 1678; Anna, bapt. 2nd May 1680 (marr. William Lyell, Dysart), died 21st April 1753. He marr. (2) cont. 1st Nov. 1701 Barbara, daugh. of George Martin, min. of Dundee South, and widow of Dr Charles Carnegie, min. of Farnell, Dean of Brechin, and had issue—William, died March 1703, aged 11 months.
1686

JOHN INGLIS, line 21, for "John" read "Alexander"; resident with his wife and three children, including Christian, in Lady Yester's parish, Edinburgh, 10th Nov. 1691.—[*Lady Yester's Poll Tax Roll.*]
1687

ALEXANDER FINDLATER, born 1666, son of Alexander F. of the parish of Dyke, and Christian Brodie. Issue—Alexander, born 23rd Dec. 1695; Thomas, min. of West Linton, born 2nd July 1697; Elizabeth, born 10th June 1699; Robert, born 1st May 1702; Ann, born 25th Sept. 1705; Basil, born 8th March 1707; Joan, born 16th May 1709; Charles, born 14th Aug. 1711; Christian, born 18th Dec. 1713 (marr. Alexander Strang of Burnhouse); James, born 7th March 1716, died 6th April 1769.
1715

EDWARD LITTON THOMSON, died 17th Sept. 1923; his widow, Ella Gunn Russell, marr. (2) 29th Jan. 1934 Robert Gordon Watt Brown, Dundee.
1900

NORMAN MACLEOD CAIE, granted A. and S. 11th June 1930, died 2nd May 1937; his son, Norman, died 4th Aug. 1931; his daugh., Annabel Hyndman (marr. 31st Aug. 1934 Ronald John, son of William Rankine, Portkel, Kilcreggan); his widow, Mary Rennie Mathers Wood, died at Stewarton 24th Dec. 1947.
1917

SECOND CHARGE

WILLIAM ROBERTSON, his daughs.—Elizabeth Margaret, died 11th Jan. 1924; Agnes Fraser, died 22nd Jan. 1931.
1858

JOHN LANCELOT CONSTANTINE TULLOCH, died 2nd Feb. 1926; his widow, Janet Richmond Macdonald, died at Edinburgh 13th June 1932; his son, John Lancelot Hill, C.A., died 10th Dec. 1935; his daugh., Jean Margaret Richmond (marr. 17th Oct. 1936 Alexander Edward Turnbull, M.B., Ch.B., Yetholm).
1917

MATTHEW STEWART, trans. from Keith (*q.v.*) 3rd Sept. 1926; trans. to First Charge, A. and S., 10th Nov. 1930; D.D. (Glasgow, 1944); Moderator of General Assembly May 1947; dem. 15th Nov. 1948. Issue of 2nd marriage—Frances Mary, born 17th Feb. 1927; Norah Evelyn, born 17th Feb. 1930.
1926

HARTHILL

ALEXANDER WATT, died at Polmont 21st March 1928; his wife, Sarah Alice Mahon, died 19th Jan 1922; his daugh., Agnes Mary Stewart (marr. Mr McDonald, Turduff).
1877

KENNEDY ADAMS, dem. 31st Dec.
1919 1937, died Ayr 14th Aug. 1942, *s.p.*

(*This parish transferred to Presb. of Bathgate after Union 1929.*)

HOLYTOWN

JOHN DALZIEL DYKES, died 28th
1906 March 1936.

CARFIN

WILLIAM NOTMAN NEILL, died 7th
1919 Oct. 1925.

JOHN HENDERSON MACKENZIE,
1929 formerly of Nesting (*q.v.*), trans. from St Andrews, Berwick, 30th July 1929; appointed by Home Mission 19th Nov. 1929, dem. 31st Dec. 1945.

KENMUIR

GEORGE ALEXANDER STALKER,
1910 dem. 18th Jan. 1926; his wife, Gavina Elizabeth Young, died 3rd Dec. 1934. Marr. (2) 11th July 1942 Edna Rachael Ratcliffe.

ROBERT LAURIE KILGOUR, born
1926 4th Oct. 1893 at Darjeeling, India, son of Robert K., D.D., and Agnes Elizabeth Horn; educ. Morrison's Academy, Crieff; St Paul's School, London; and Univ. of Glasgow, M.A. (1921); served in Great War in France and Mesopotamia, 1914–19 (wounded, despatches); licen. by Presb. of Glasgow 1924; assistant, Hillhead, Glasgow, and Dunblane Cathedral 1924; ord. 3rd June 1926; trans. to Elie Old, 22nd July 1931. Marr. 18th Jan. 1939 Elsie Johnston, daugh. of W. J. Christian, Ealing; dem. 15th July 1943 and became Missionary at Lovedale. Publication—*The Scottish Universities' Mission*.

EAST KILBRIDE and TORRANCE

The right to have a chapel in the Castle of Kilbride was granted to Roger de Valons by Joceline, Bishop of Glasgow, 1175–99—ratified by Parliament 1182–9. By charter of 11th June 1618 James VI mortified to Glasgow University the Church of Kilbride, and also, on the resignation of the Archbishop of Glasgow, the Church of Torrens, "a small parish and least of all able to sustain a ministrie" and "inseparably united to Kilbride." The Charter further narrated that Torrens had "always been a pendicle of Kilbride, and that the entire parishioners through diverse years have frequented Kilbride."—[*Reg. of Glasgow*, i, 48; *Acts Scott. Parl.*, i, 386; *Reg. Great Seal*, vii, 1840.]

JOHN STEVENSON, M.A., parson
1563 and vicar, was dead 1563.—[*Comps. Sub Coll. of Thirds, Stirling*, etc.]

ALEXANDER LINDSAY, M.A., in
1567 Auldhouse, reader before 14th July 1568, died 1589; had issue—Archibald; James.—[*Comps. Sub Coll. of Thirds, Stirling*, etc.; *Edin. Tests.*, vii, 142.]

JOHN COLWYER, M.A., min. in 1569.
1569 —[*Comps. Sub Coll. of Thirds, Stirling*, etc.]

JAMES FLEMING, son of John F.,
1580 merchant, Glasgow.—[*House of Hamilton*, 621.]

ROBERT DARROCH, min., pres. to
1584 parsonage of Torrens.—[*Reg. Sec. Sig.*, lxix, 221.]

DAVID SHARPE, M.A. (Glasgow,
1608 1596).

JAMES CRICHTON, (2) marr. cont.
1663 24th Jan. 1674 Jean, daugh. of Sir Robert Elphinstone of Quarrell.—[*Deeds, Mack.*, 1705, No. 325.]

SIR HENRY WELLWOOD MON-
1837 CRIEFF, line 19, for "Glasgow" read "Edinburgh"; col. 2, line 12, for "characters" read "Churches."

WILLIAM CARRICK, pres. by Crown
1843 21st July 1843.

WILLIAM JACK, granted A. and S.
1894 3rd May 1932, retired to Colinton, died 30th March 1935; his widow, Margaret Gilmour Giffen, died 5th Dec. 1937.

(*Parish transferred at Union 1929 to Presb. of Glasgow.*)

LARKHALL

JOHN CRICHTON, his widow, Mary
1856   Ann Slater Giffen, died 6th Nov. 1926.

JOHN DONALDSON McCALLUM,
1885   Moderator of General Assembly 1926; dem. 30th Nov. 1929; died at Moffat 7th Oct. 1930.

MEADOWFIELD

NEIL LIVINGSTONE THOMSON,
1893   licen. 14th May 1890; dem. 15th May 1932; died at Hamilton 13th Feb. 1937.

(Parish transferred to Presb. of Bathgate 1929.)

NEW MONKLAND

LUDOVIC SOMERVILL, marr.
1653   Marion, daugh. of Alexander Hamilton of Haggs.

THOMAS FREEBAIRN, his daugh.,
1794   Margaret Molyson (marr. 1815 Robert Monteith).

ROBERT ARCHIBALD, his daugh.,
1846   Marion Birkmyre, died 24th Aug. 1924.

JOHN McGAVIN BOYD, his widow,
1876   Janet Fulton Brown, died 7th Jan. 1930; his daugh., Eleanor Brown (marr. 18th June 1930 Henry Tod Robertson, Meadowbank, Airdrie).

OLD MONKLAND

DAVID HAMILTON, exhorter 1568,
1568   reader 14th Sept. 1579.—[*Comps. Sub Coll. of Thirds, Stirling,* etc.; *Edin. Tests.,* vii, 280.]

JAMES HAMILTON, Bishop of Argyll,
1574   held parsonage of Monkland and Cadder 21st May 1574.—[*Coll. of Charters,* xi, 2379.]

JOHN BELL, pres. to vicarage of Cad-
1594   der and Monkland 25th Nov. 1594 on dem. of Michael Chisholm.—[*Reg. Sec. Sig.,* xlvii, 97.]

JOHN LOTHIAN, his daugh., Eliza-
1636   beth (marr. Matthew Ramsay, min. of Paisley.)

HUGH WEIR, marr. after 5th Dec.
1653   1653 Janet, daugh. of Thomas Bogle, maltman and burgess, Glasgow.—[*G. R. Sas.,* 2 Ser., vi, 389.]

PETER CAMERON BLACK, his
1864   widow, Jane Brown, died 21st June 1932.

MATTHEW SCOTT DICKSON, D.D.
1894   (Glasgow, 6th June 1932), vice-chairman of General Trustees of the Church of Scotland, died 19th April 1938

OVERTOWN

DAVID LIVINGSTON THOMSON,
1888 died 8th Aug. 1922.

THOMAS MILLER McKENDRICK,
1922   ord. 13th Dec. 1922; trans. to Laurieston, Glasgow, 24th Feb. 1927.

HECTOR McLENNAN MacLEOD,
1927   born Glasgow 31st Dec. 1901; son of Hector MacL. and Elizabeth Taylor; educ. at Hyndland School and Univ. of Glasgow, M.A. (1923), B.D. (1926); licen. by Presb. of Glasgow April 1926; assistant Barony May 1925 to May 1927; ord. 8th June 1927; trans to Killearn 24th June 1931.

QUARTER

GEORGE BLAIR, died at Blantyre
1881 23rd Jan. 1929.

THOMAS MURRAY INGLIS, trans.
1920   from Twechar (*q.v.*) 14th Sept. 1920; trans. to Birnie 26th June 1929.

SHOTTS

Before 1476 James Hamilton, lord of Bertram-Shotts and Hamilton, founded and built at Bertram-Shotts a chapel dedicated to St Catharine, which the Bishop erected into a parish church. At the church he also built a hospital to receive the poor of Christ. The reason that he assigned for the church was that "the desert-place of Bertram-Shotts is distant about 8 miles from the Parish Church of St Mary of Bothwell, and is remote and like a desert though inhabited; and it is an infertile and cold mountain region, on account of which cold and the distance of the place many of the inhabitants there die without receiving the sacraments, and incur many other dangers," to avoid which he had founded the chapel. He further stated that as the rector of the church for the time being, and the poor of the hospital were alike without means of sustenance, he proposed to endow the church and hospital, and to provide to the said parish certain new possessions reclaimed by him at great cost from the sea by permission of the King. In a petition to Pope Sixtus IV he narrated the foregoing, and asked the Pope to confirm the foundation and to declare the possessions reclaimed or to be reclaimed from the sea, which are new and have never paid teinds or first fruits to any church, to belong to the said church and the hospital, although the lands are situated in the bounds of the Parish of Kinneil (on the Forth), and to provide the teinds and first fruits to the church and the rector for the time. On 30th April 1476 a Bull in terms of the prayer of the petition was issued by Pope Sixtus. Before 13th Oct. 1488 the patronage of the church belonged to the Collegiate Church of Bothwell. It would appear that St Catherine gave place to the Virgin Mary, for in 1552 there is reference to the "Church of the Blessed Virgin Mary in Bertram-Shottis."—[*Reports Hist. MSS. Commis.*, xi, 48; *Reg. Great Seal*, ii, 1784; *Descriptions of Sheriffdom of Lanark and Renfrew*, 43n.]

JOHN ROBESOUN or ROBERTSON, reader; vicar and reader in 1569.—
1571 [*Edin. Test.*, ii, 108.]

THOMAS HAMILTON, described as vicar 13th Aug. 1576, 10th Sept.
1574 1579; marr. Katherine Bailie; "was in Shotts" 8th Jan. 1551-2.—[*Reg. Great Seal*, iv, 1869, 2899.]

JAMES CURRIE, his son, William, apprenticed to William Grierson,
1649 merchant, Edinburgh, 18th June 1673.

GEORGE CLELAND, his sons Robert, apprenticed to Robert Sel-
1688 krig, merchant, Edinburgh, 22nd Aug. 1705; William, apprenticed to William Johnston, skinner, Edinburgh, 29th May 1706.

WILLIAM MARTIN WATT, his daugh., Helen Elizabeth, died 22nd
1844 June 1935.

JOHN McNICOLL RAMSAY, line 2, for "1863" read "1857"; died 27th
1892 Sept. 1934. Marr. 4th July 1923 Janet Williamson, eldest daugh. of John Dunn, schoolmaster, Netherby, Harthill.

STONEFIELD

THOMAS PRYDE, died at Cardonald
1880 20th Oct. 1925.

JAMES LAMONT, born Ulster 7th July 1870, son of John L., farmer,
1920 and Elizabeth Jane Wylie; educ. at Univ. of Glasgow and Queen's College; ord. to Belalie and Clare, Australia, 1901; adm. to West Scotland Street, Glasgow, 1904; trans. to Park Terrace, Gateshead, 1908; trans. to Augustine U.F. Church, Glasgow, 1911; trans. and adm. 13th May 1920; dem. his status 16th May 1923; adm. to Martyrs U.F. Church, Dundee, 1924; trans. to Hope Church, Wamphray, 23rd Nov. 1934. Marr. 28th April 1896 Charlotte (died 7th May 1939), daugh. of Robert Ralston, and has issue Jessie Caroline Adelaide, M.A., born 2nd Aug. 1901 (marr. 29th Dec. 1938 Jacob Morrison, M.A., teacher, Glasgow).

WILLIAM HUTCHISON MAC-DIARMID, B.D., trans. from Bal-
1923 ingry (q.v.) 10th Oct. 1923; trans. to Lowson Memorial, Forfar, 26th June 1925.

STONEHOUSE

JOHN OLIPHANT, trans. to Carluke
1654 1689.

JAMES WYPER WILSON, dem. 29th Sept. 1925, died 10th May 1936.
1887

THOMAS McCAUGHAN, M.A., trans. from Douglas Water (*q.v.*) 11th Feb. 1926. Granted an A. and S. 5th Feb. 1935; his daugh., Elizabeth Maude, died 20th Jan. 1943.
1926

UDDINGSTON

JOHN MACKINTOSH, died at Edinburgh 15th June 1921; his widow, Annie Alexandra Lindsay, marr. (2) 20th Jan. 1927 Thomas Winn Boyce of Hill House, Ely, Cambridgeshire.
1874

GUY STEEL PEEBLES, trans. to Birnie 29th March 1933; his daughs.—Margaret Eleanor (marr. 11th April 1928 Claude Hilary Taylor); Mary Agnes (marr. 25th April 1939 Arthur Paul Barry, Old Court House, Lempsfield, Surrey).
1918

WISHAW

ALEXANDER HARPER, his widow, Mary Thomson, died 26th Feb. 1922; his son, Alexander Bain, min. of Monzievaird.
1870

WILLIAM CLARK, died 20th Dec. 1924; his son, Frank Davidson, died at Fettes College 11th April 1938.
1911

DONALD CHISHOLM WHITELAW, born Auchterarder 29th Jan. 1886; son of Robert W. and Isabella Mailer; educ. at Camelon Public School, Univ. of Glasgow, M.A. (20th June 1923); licen. by Presb. of Glasgow, Jan. 1925; assistant So. Dalziel 1924–5; ord. 29th April 1925. Marr. 2nd July 1912 Agnes Mirk, daugh. of George Fotheringham and Margaret Henderson, and has issue—Robert George, M.A. (Hons.), born 29th April 1913, medical student, Glasgow; Margaret Henderson, born 30th Nov. 1914, domestic science student; Ian Chisholm, born 26th May 1919, Bank of Scotland, Motherwell.
1925

PRESBYTERY OF LANARK

CARLUKE

DAVID FORREST, reader 16th Nov. 1578.—[*Edin. Tests.*, vii, 42.]
1574

DANIEL McLAREN, his daugh., Alexandrina Grace Janet (Mrs Goldsmid), died East London, South Africa, 9th March 1942; his son, Herbert Wroughton, C.A., died Guildford 10th March 1947.
1874

FRANCIS MARMADUKE HAUXWELL, died 20th Feb. 1929; his wife, Helen Stalker, died 4th March 1927.
1888

WALTER GORDON CARTER, born Hastings, Ontario, Canada, 30th Oct. 1889, son of John C. and Janet Fife; educ. at Norwood High School and Queen's College, Kingston, B.A. (1914); licen. by Presb. of Edinburgh 1920; ord. to St John's, Hawick, 5th Nov. 1920; trans. and adm. 21st Aug. 1929; died 5th Dec. 1936. Marr. 29th Dec. 1917 Agnes Mildred, daugh. of Duncan James and Esther Mitchell, and had issue—Esther Muriel Fife Carter, born 14th May 1922. His widow re-marr. 25th Sept. 1945.
1929

CARMICHAEL

GEORGE DOUGLAS, parson 1568.—[*Comps. Sub Coll. of Thirds, Stirling,* etc.]
1568

NINIAN SWANE, reader 1568.—[*Comps. Sub Coll. of Thirds, Stirling,* etc.]
1569

JOHN CUNNINGHAM, vicar.—[*Acts and Dec.*, liv, 22.]
1573

JOHN SYMONTON, line 4, for "Jean" read "Isobel."
1597

LACHLAN ROSS was vicar of Ardagh.
1687

JAMES DUNCAN WALKER GIBSON, died 16th May 1924; his widow, Jessie Blackburn Craig, died 14th July 1933.
1884

THOMAS WATT McANDREW, his wife, Christina Mackie Wilson, died 8th April 1939; his daugh., Margaret Craig Wilson (marr. 28th Feb. 1924 Alexander Murdoch).
1918

CARNWATH

THOMAS KING, exhorter in 1568 and 1569; in 1578 he held the chapel of Muirhall.—[*Comps. Gen. Coll. of Thirds; Comps. Sub Coll. of Thirds, Stirling,* etc.]
1567

JOHN CUNNINGHAM, vicar and parson.—[*Acts and Dec.*, liv, 22.]
1573

HEW SOMERVILLE, held "the haill chaplainrie of the yle of Carnwath."—[*Comps. Gen. Coll. of Thirds.*]
1579

THOMAS MAXWELL, pres. to vicarage pensionary 11th Jan. 1590–1 on death of Sir John Cunninghame and again 24th May 1594.—[*Reg. Sec. Sig.*, lxi, 114; lxvi, 137.]
1588

THOMAS LIVINGSTONE, M.A., parson and vicar in 1568.—[*Comps. Gen. Coll. and Sub Coll. of Thirds, Dumfries,* etc.]
1594

PATRICK SCOTT, his son, James, apprenticed to Archibald Punton, baxter, 29th Nov. 1738.
1718

ROBERT JACK, line 11, for "Sept." read "Oct." Addl. issue—Mary, born 28th April 1740.
1749

LEWIS BEATON, his daugh., Patricia, died 27th Dec. 1929.
1878

DAVID HAY SAWERS, dem. 7th Aug. 1938; his wife, Agnes McKean, died 16th Feb. 1947.
1905

AUCHENGRAY CHAPEL

WILLIAM RICHMOND SCOTT, trans. to North Ronaldshay 1st Dec. 1920.
1908

CARSTAIRS

JOHN SCOTT, vicar 1563.—[*Acts and Dec.*, xxxvii, 364; *Comps. Sub Coll. of Thirds, Stirling*, etc.]
1563

THOMAS RUSSELL, reader 1563.—[*Comps. Sub Coll. of Thirds, Stirling*, etc.]
1563

JAMES STIRLING, was excommunicated by the Bishop of Glasgow 24th April 1576.—[*Book of the Universal Kirk*, 357.]
1571

JOHN KINNAIRD, son of Patrick K. of that ilk, pres. to vicarage 26th April 1572 on death of John Scott; was before General Assembly as a delinquent in 1575 and was excommunicated by the Bishop of Glasgow.—[*Reg. Pres. Bene.*, i, (3), 16; *Comps. Gen. Coll. of Thirds*.]
1572

WALTER HALDANE, min. here, pres. to parsonage 21st Feb. 1574 on dem. of James Stirling.—[*Reg. Pres. Bene.*, i, (4), 30.]
1574

GEORGE MOSMAN, pres. to vicarage 3rd Sept. 1580.—[*Reg. Pres. Bene.*, i, 39.]
1580

WILLIAM GRAHAME, son of James G., burgess of Edinburgh, as reader here pres. to vicarage 8th March 1580–1 and 9th Dec. 1581 vacant by deposition of John Kinnaird for slaughter of John Ramsay, for which he was declared a rebel. —[*Reg. Pres. Bene.*, i, 51, 63.]
1580

JOHN LINDSAY, min. here, pres. in 1581 to parsonage on dem. of Richard Weir.—[*Reg. Pres. Bene.*, i, 61.]
1581

ALEXANDER LIVINGSTONE, line 2, for "1639" read "1640."
1672

ALAN JOHNSTONE, resident with his family in Lady Yester's parish 10th Nov. 1694; his son, Andrew, apprenticed to John Law, goldsmith, 17th Feb. 1692.—[*Poll Tax Roll*.]
1685

JOHN OLIPHANT, his son, James, apprenticed to James Borthwick of Stow, surgeon, 31st March 1675.
1693

ROBERT MEREDITH SHARPE, died 5th June 1923; his widow, Helen Russell Orr, died 8th Nov. 1944.
1888

GEORGE WILLIAM KINNAIRD MACPHERSON, B.D., ord. 23rd Nov. 1923; trans. to Jedburgh 22nd Sept. 1927.
1923

JOHN SMART, trans. from Carmunnock (*q.v.*) 15th March 1928; had issue—John Daniel Arthur Mardon, born 1st Aug. 1918, surgeon lieutenant, R.N.; Helen Isabel, born 26th Oct. 1924.
1928

CRAWFORD

In 1327 David Lindsay, Lord of Crawford, granted to Newbattle Abbey for the souls of himself and Marie, his wife, the Chapel of St Thomas the Martyr beside Crawford Castle, with the old manse for a dwelling and garden, etc., the abbey being bound to supply the chapel with a monk or secular priest, and keep it in repair.— [*Chart. of Newbattle*, 117–20.]

JAMES DOBBIE, reader.—[*Comps. Sub Coll. of Thirds, Stirling*, etc.]
1563

JAMES FOTHERINGHAM, reader in 1568 and 1569.—[*Comps. Sub Coll. of Thirds, Stirling*, etc.]
1568

ROBERT LANDELLS, as min. pres. to vicarage 17th Feb. 1588–9 on death of William Livingstone.— [*P. S. Reg.*, lix, 28.]
1588

JOHN ROSS, his mother, Elizabeth Pursell; he marr. Mary, daugh. of John Clerk, W.S.; his daughs.— Agnes Colquhoun (marr. John Bower,
1807

surgeon, R.N.); Helen Campbell, died unmarr. 1917; Eliza Fletcher (marr. 1849 John Craw Richardson of Pont-y-Gwyder and Glanbrydan Park); his son, Archibald Campbell, died of cholera at Madeira 6th Sept. 1856.

1870 JAMES ALEXANDER BURDON, pres. by Crown 30th May 1870.

1876 CHRISTOPHER McKUNE, died 20th Sept. 1921; his widow, Elizabeth A. Chute, died 21st Jan. 1945.

1922 THOMAS LOGAN DOUGLAS, trans. from Gorbals (*q.v.*) 21st Feb. 1922. Addl. issue—Dr Laetitia Janet Williams, born 2nd Dec. 1918 (marr. 10th July 1942 Flying Officer Atholl Gordon Forbes, M.B., Ch.B., son of J. Grant Forbes, min. of Forteviot).

CRAWFORDJOHN

1579 JOHN HAMILTON of Gilkerscleuch, son of Sir James H. of Crawfordjohn, and Helen Cunyngham of Caprington; parson in 1577, died 13th July 1628; marr. (1) cont. 1583-4 Agnes, daugh. of William Baillie of Lamington, from whom he was divorced for adultery, and had issue—Mary; (2) Margaret, daugh. of James Hamilton of Neilsland, and had issue—John of Gilkerscleuch; William, died 13th Nov. 1621; James, burgess and guild burgess of Edinburgh 4th Aug. 1630; Thomas; Mary (marr. Hugh Weir of Clowburn); Ann (marr. John Weir, min. of Morton).—[*House of Hamilton*, 282; *Comps. Gen. Coll. of Thirds; Laing Charters*, 1347; *Reg. Mag. Sig.*, iv, 119, v, 1698.]

1816 WILLIAM GOLDIE, his daughs.— Margaret, died 3rd May 1930; Isabella, died 14th Sept. 1937.

1866 JAMES COWAN, his daugh., Mary Murray Grace, killed in motor accident, Queensferry Road, 20th Oct. 1934.

1893 GEORGE McWILLIAM, died at Troon 9th Feb. 1933; his wife, Mary Inglis, died 7th July 1932. Publication—*A Poem, The Evolution of a Dominie* (*Alma Mater*, Aberdeen University Magazine).

DOUGLAS

By Papal Bull of 27th March 1423 assent was given to a petition by Archibald, Earl of Douglas, for the erection of the church into a collegiate church, and the annexation of the Churches of Crawford and Carmichael to the same. The fruits of the church were to be devoted to the provision of a perpetual vicar and also of canons and prebendaries. On 7th Aug. 1448, in response to a petition by William, Earl of Douglas, Pope Nicholas V granted mandate to William Turnbull, Bishop of Glasgow, to erect the church into a collegiate church for a provost and 13 prebendaries. The Earl had assigned for the purpose various rents and goods, and the fruits of the Churches of Foresta (Carluke), Culter, and Glenquhon (Glenholm), said churches to be united and appropriated to the capitular *mensa*. The Bishop was authorised to create and institute the provost from the fruits of Douglas Church, and from the said other fruits to create the 13 prebendaries. The Churches of Carluke, Culter and Glenholm were to be served each by its corresponding prebendary. On 1st Feb. 1450-1 relaxation of penance was granted to all who "visit and give alms for the completion, conservation, and maintenance of the Parish Church of Douglas erected by Papal authority into the College Church of St Bride, which William, Earl of Douglas, has by wonderful and expensive work caused to be built anew"; somewhat earlier, on 15th Jan. 1450-1, there occurs, unnamed, "the Provost of the College Church of St Bride of Douglas"; and on 31st Jan. 1488-9 George Douglas, son and heir apparent of Archibald, Earl of Angus, received a charter which included the "patronage of the Provostship of Douglas." The erection, however, was not completed. On 7th March 1483-4 Archibald, Earl of Angus, granted to a chaplain at the Altar of the Virgin Mary in the church, 2 oxgates of land in le Scrogtoun, and this was repeated on 16th June 1506;

and on 11th March 1535–6 Sir John Purvis, chaplain, was presented to the Altar of St Thomas in succession to the late Sir John Inglis. Barbour (*the Bruce*) narrates that the bones of "The Good Sir James Douglas" were brought back from Spain, whence he had gone for the purpose that is set forth in a Bull of Pope John XXII, 6th Aug. 1331, granting absolution on the petition of Thomas, Earl of Moray, "to those who at the King's bidding took out his heart to be carried into Battle against the Saracens," and "richt honorabilly / Intill the kirk of Douglas war / Erdit with dule and mekil car, /" and that by his son, Archibald, there was erected there an alabaster tomb, which is considered to be identical with a tomb in a still existing portion of the old church. The present church was erected in 1781. By charter of 22nd June 1531 James V granted to Sir George Eirmare and his successors as chaplains in the Chapel of the Blessed Virgin Mary of Parrockholm the 4 merk lands of Parrockholm, with enclosures of the same, in the Lordship of Douglas. This may refer to the foundation of the chapel. At Crookbat of Douglas Hugh, Earl of Douglas, who died after 1347, founded a chapel, dedicating it to St John the Baptist, the endowment including fees from the ferry boat, with provision for keeping the boat in repair.—[*Reg. Great Seal*, ii, 1586, 1827, 2974, iii, 1036, iv, 2180; *Reg. Sec. Seal*, ii, 1978; Theiner's *Vet. Mon.*, 251; *Papal Warrants* 1421–59, 78–81, 86, *MS. Reg. Ho.*; *Cal. Papal Letters*, x, 84, 429; *The Douglas Bk.*, iii, 242–4.]

1561 WALTER KENNEDY, parson, deceased.—[*Acts and Dec.*, xxiii, 186, xxiv, 288.]

1563 WILLIAM COLHERD, reader, 1563.—[*Comps. Sub Coll. of Thirds, Stirling*, etc.]

1567 JOHN LIVERANCE, designated min. and parson 4th Sept. 1589.—[*Cal. of Charters*, xiii, 3023.]

1621 THOMAS BANNATYNE, his son, William, born 1618, educ. at Edinburgh Univ., became a Roman Catholic while travelling in France, entered Scots College at Rome 1641; ord. priest 1646; app. Prefect Apostolic of Scotland 1653, died 1661.

1686 ANDREW SIMSON, resident with wife and two children, the elder not 14, in Lady Yester's parish, 9th Nov. 1694.—[*Poll Tax Roll*, 31.]

1858 WILLIAM SMITH, died 22nd Sept. 1921.

1922 ALEXANDER SALMOND SMITH, B.D., trans. from Pathhead (*q.v.*) 20th April 1922. Addl. issue—Alexander Salmond, born 3rd Feb. 1920; Moira May Robertson, born 11th June 1929.

DOUGLAS WATER

1892 ANDREW HUTTON GILRUTH, died at Edinburgh 30th Sept. 1925.

1919 THOMAS McCAUGHAN, trans. to Stonehouse 11th Feb. 1926.

1926 RHODERICK JAMES WILSON, born 15th March 1897, son of Sir Courthope W., K.C., Vice-Chancellor of the Duchy of Lancaster; educ. at Royal High School, Edinburgh, Birkenhead School, and Edinburgh Univ., M.A. (1922); licen. by Presb. of Edinburgh 19th Dec. 1923; assistant at St Andrew's, Edinburgh, and Glasgow Cathedral; ord. 24th June 1926.

FORTH

1884 WILLIAM PATERSON BROCK, died at Rothesay 16th Dec. 1920.

1921 JOHN TORRENS DOUGHARTY, B.A., adm. 29th June 1921; trans. to Kingston, Glasgow, 17th Nov. 1926.

1927 CHARLES HEUGHAN, trans. from Carntyne (*q.v.*, and Vol. I, 336) 3rd June 1927; died 8th April 1934, aged 49. Addl. issue—Ruth Mary, born 15th Jan. 1914 (marr. 24th Feb. 1942 William Farrer, R.A.F.V.R.); Hazel Elizabeth, born 16th Sept. 1918; Miriam Margaret, born 13th Jan. 1920.

HAYWOOD

GILBERT CLARK, dem. 5th June 1923, died 24th May 1930.
1884

PETER CARMICHAEL MARR, formerly min. of Strachan (*q.v.*), assistant Linlithgow; adm. 27th Nov. 1923. Being charged with murder of J. M. Dalgleish, house painter, Leith, Aug. 1930, was found insane and confined in criminal lunatic asylum 17th Nov. 1930; died 15th July 1937.
1923

(*This Charge was united with Wilsontown on 8th May* 1938.)

KIRKFIELDBANK

JOHN ARNOTT HAMILTON, trans. to Newbattle 14th July 1922.
1917

JOHN WILLIAMSON, trans. from Rousay (*q.v*) 5th Dec. 1922; trans. to St Andrew's, Johnstone, 30th Jan. 1928.
1923

JAMES LYON AINSLIE, born Leeds 24th July 1873, son of William A.; educ. at Woodhouse Hall and at Leeds Grammar School, Westminster Col., Cambridge, and Glasgow Univ., B.D. (1913), Ph.D. (1935), and Edinburgh; licen. by Presb. of Yorkshire; ord. 1904 to Harbottle Presb. Church, Northumberland; trans. and adm. 12th July 1928; dem. 31st Aug. 1944.
1928

LANARK

To Dryburgh Abbey David I gave the church and, along with it, the Chapel of Pedynana (Pettinain) and the Chapel of Imbristoun. The gift was confirmed by Herbert, Bishop of Glasgow 1147–64. Walter, Bishop of Glasgow 1208–32, confirmed to Dryburgh the Chapel of Clegern (Cleghorne), granted by Bishop Herbert. In the church there were altars dedicated respectively to the Virgin Mary and the Holy Rood; and probably the "Altarage of Sorrowflat," described as in the burgh, referred to an altar also situated in the church. To the Altar of the Virgin, James IV on 18th Oct. 1500 granted a tenement in the Burgh of Lanark which had fallen to the Crown through the bastardy of the late owner. To the building of "the Church of St Nicholas of Lanark" Andrew Allan, Lanark, bequeathed 5 merks in 1550, which may indicate that the Chapel of St Nicholas, as it is usually designated, underwent extensive repairs or rebuilding at that time. In the chapel there were altars dedicated respectively to the Virgin Mary, St Catherine, the Holy Blood, and St Michael. On 7th March 1491–2 James IV, for the use of the lieges and for his favour towards Sir Stephen Lockhart of Cleghorne, Kt., patron of the Altar of St Catherine, granted to the chaplain of the said altar to have and hold a passage-boat across the Clyde at Clydsholm for the transportation of the lieges and goods, with free passage, entry and exit, and right to the profits arising therefrom. The boat had been placed there by the said chaplain, to meet the needs of the lieges who converged upon that place in great numbers, and in the absence of a bridge or other means of transportation were liable to be exposed to danger and to perish in the waters. On 1st Aug. 1526 James V by letter ratified and approved the gift made by Thomas Newton, Sub-Prior of Dryburgh and the convent of the same, to Sir Thomas Mudy, chaplain, of a chaplainry founded in St Nicholas Chapel by the predecessors of the said sub-prior and convent. Apparently the revenue of the Altar of the Virgin Mary in the chapel was derived from the barony of Jerviswood. The church or chapel at Nemphlar was united by King William the Lion to Lanark Church, of which it became a dependent chapel. It was situated on temple lands called Oldmanis-Apletree or Almansapletree, which were part of East Nemphlar. The Hospital and Chapel of St Leonard, founded before 1319, were situated beside the east well of the burgh. After the Reformation the church or chapel seems to have had an attached area; and on 24th June 1609, under the designation of "Kirk of St Leonard's," it was united to the Kirk of Lanark, "wheir the samin hes bene continwalie servit in tymes bypast." The friary of the Greyfriars was founded by

Robert I either towards the close of 1328 or in the early part of 1329, the site granted by the King within the burgh being a manor and orchard enclosed by a wall, which by excambion he had acquired from Elene Quarantlay. In response to a petition by David II and his queen, Johanna, confirmation was granted on 29th Nov. 1346 by Pope Clement VI. In 1550 Andrew Allan, Lanark, who desired that his body be buried in the "Aisle of St Mary" in the Church of the Friary, made bequests to the Church of the Friars of Lanark 40 sh., to the Church of the distinguished Friars (fratrum egregiorum) 40 sh., to the Church of the Friars 2 merks. Probably the various sums were bequeathed to the Greyfriars for different purposes, the scribe who copied the testament considering that he did enough if he stated merely the sum and the legatee; and the term "egregiorum" would be used not in regard of another Order of Mendicants, but as appreciative of the Greyfriars.—[*Reg. Great Seal*, i, 76; ii, 2093, 2549, 3809; iii, 1036; *Reg. Sec. Seal*, i, 3461, ii, 111; *Excheq. Rolls*, i, 163–4; *Transcripts from the Vatican*, i, 14, *MS. Reg. Ho.*; *Retours*, ii, 116, xxxi, 212, xxxii, 8, 40, 250; *Acts Scott. Parl.*, iv, 441; *Bk. of Dryburgh*, Pref., lxix, 34–5, 39–40, 250; *Test. of Andrew Allan*, 8th June 1550, *Glasgow Commis.*; *Extracts from Recs. Burgh of Lanark*, 15, 326, 354; *Rymer's Foedera*, ii, 401.]

1562 DAVID CUNNINGHAM, marr. Margaret Dalzell, who survived him.—[*Comps. Sub Coll. of Bene.*, 1571.]

1576 ROBERT LINDSAY, M.A., as min. pres. to vicarage 9th Feb. 1587–8 on death of John Weir. His son, John, vicar of Monkton.—[*Reg. Sec. Sig.*, lvii, 12, lxxi, 230.]

1582 JOHN WEIR, vicar.—[*Reg. Abbrev. Feu Charters of Church Lands*, ii, 195.]

1588 WILLIAM SHARP, M.A., min. of Tongland, pres. to vicarage 21st June 1588 on death of Andrew Davidson.—[*Reg. Sec. Sig.*, lxvii, 152].

1597 WILLIAM BIRNIE, pres. in succession to Robert Lindsay.—[*Reg. Sec. Sig.*, lxix, 188.]

1643 ROBERT BIRNIE.—[*G. R. Sas.*, 2 Ser., vi, 145, 3 Ser., xxxiii, 117, 25th Dec. 1673.]

1688 JOHN BANNATYNE, p. 308, line 3, for "1685" read "1684"; line 22, for "1695–9" read "1695–1700."

1708 JOHN ORR, son of John O., factor to Sir Robert Denholm of Westhall. Marr. cont. 1st Sept. 1714 Susan Hall, daugh. of Eupham Christie; col. ii, line 5, delete *s.p.*—[*Reg. of Deeds, Mack.*, clviii, 17th Nov. 1735.]

1872 THOMAS LITTLE, pres. by Crown 21st Nov. 1871; his son, Thomas Gavin Steel, died Bombay Feb. 1927.

1905 ROBERT MARCUS DICKSON, dem. 30th Sept. 1948.

NEW LANARK

1876 JAMES FRENCH, died 30th June 1927.

ST LEONARD'S, LANARK

1915 ROBERT LANG PINKERTON, trans. to Ecclesmachen 17th Sept. 1924.

1925 NINIAN ELLIOT, M.A., ord. 19th Feb. 1925; trans. to Slamannan 11th April 1928.

1928 WILLIAM GILBERT LIMOND, born 15th April 1889, son of John L., Maybole, and Mary Hayle; educ. Ayr Grammar School and Edinburgh Univ.; licen. by Presb. of Edinburgh 26th March 1924; ord. assistant South Leith 1st March 1925; adm. to Westruther 14th Jan. 1926; trans. and adm. 27th Sept. 1928. Marr. 22nd Dec. 1925 Agnes Fairlie, elder daugh. of Charles Thom, Lagura, Ayr, and has issue—John Charles, born 16th Feb. 1928.

LAW

1914 WILLIAM WHITEHEAD, trans. to Ormiston 26th Sept. 1924.

1925 WILLIAM ANGUS WALLACE, adm. 11th Feb. 1925; trans. to Fairmuir, Dundee, 15th Dec. 1926.

1927 WEILD ANDERSON, born Pollokshields 30th Nov. 1885, son of James C. A., Glasgow, and Mary Hutchison; educ. Blair Lodge and St Andrews Univ.; licen. by Presb. of Abernethy; ord. 20th April 1927; dem. 7th July 1940; died 18th Nov. 1940.

(*Charges united 7th July 1940.*)

LEADHILLS

1843 GEORGE RUSSELL, ord. 1843; trans. to Cromarty 27th Aug. 1846.

1878 JAMES SYMINGTON, died at Kirn 23rd Sept. 1921; his widow, Elizabeth Kenny, died 8th Dec. 1939.

1917 JOHN YOUNGSON THOMSON, born 29th July 1877 (not 1878), son of John T., Beverley Hall, Chicago; adm. 18th Dec. 1917; trans. to Greenock South 22nd June 1920.

1920 CHARLES KEITH McWILLIAM, ord. 17th Sept. 1920; trans. to St Thomas, Leith, 11th April 1923.

1923 ROBERT CONDIE HUNTER, born Bathgate 1861, son of Henry H.; educ. Wemyss and Univ. of Edinburgh; formerly of Annbank, Asquith, Canada, 1910; Westport 1913; St Paul's, Invercargill, 1914; Queenstown, New Zealand, 1917 (*q.v.*); adm. 17th July 1923; dem. 1936; died 18th Sept. 1939. Marr. 1913 Mary Ann Ellen, daugh. of Joseph Tyler, who died 14th March 1941. *S.p.*

LESMAHAGOW

FIRST CHARGE

Between 1315 and 1321 Robert I granted to God, the Blessed Virgin Mary, and St Machutus, and the monks of Lesmachu, 10 merks stg. annual rent from his mills of Carneluk (Carluke) to provide eight tapers of a pound of wax each to be burned round the tomb of St Machutus on Sundays and festivals, as the custom is in cathedral and collegiate churches.—[*Reg. Great Seal*, i, 75.]

1839 ANDREW BORLAND PARKER, his son, William, marine insurance broker, died 29th Dec. 1921; his daugh., Mary, died 31st Dec. 1923.

1873 THOMAS HARDIE TURNBULL, licen. by Presb. of Glasgow 6th Dec. 1871.

1894 JAMES GILLIES, died 15th March 1934; his daughs.—Isobel (marr. 27th April 1932 Robert McGeachy, Toorak, Melbourne); Helen, marr. 9th Nov. 1924 Captain Thomas Eastoun, Bombay.

SECOND CHARGE

1648 ROBERT SEMPLE, M.A. (Glasgow, 1649).

1708 ROBERT BLACK, marr. cont. 22nd April 1703 Mary, daugh. of John Bryson, merchant, Glasgow.—[*Reg. of Deeds, Durie*, 194, 21st Dec. 1736.]

1740 THOMAS LINNING, eldest son of James L., cordiner, Glasgow; adm. burgess of Glasgow 9th April 1752.

1796 JOHN WILSON, his daugh., Agnes Clarke (marr. 31st Jan. 1828).

1842 THOMAS BURNS, his daugh., Agnes, died at Edinburgh 21st Dec. 1930.

1869 THOMAS WILSON, his son, Captain Douglas Hamilton, died at Rangoon July 1938.

1913 ROBERT ROBERTSON LINDSAY, Ph.D., died 21st Feb. 1941; his daugh., Margaret Wilson Robertson (marr. 20th April 1938 Archibald MacLellan Beaton, min. of Lochgilphead).

PETTINAIN

1569 ROBERT FISHER, pres. to vicarage 8th Dec. 1569 on death of John Tweedie.—[*Reg. Pres. Bene.*, i, 32.]

1583 JOHN WEIR, vicar, 19th May 1585.—[*Cal. of Charters*, xii, 2791.]

1600 WILLIAM LAWRIE, pres. in 1600 on dem. of John Weir.—[*Acts and Dec.*, clxvii, 251.]

1679 WILLIAM FYFE, M.A., resident with his wife and two children, 12 and 10, in Canongate 10th Nov. 1694.—[*Poll Tax Book*.]

1684 ALEXANDER CARMICHAEL, had issue—Frederick; William, died 24th Feb. 1703; Lilias; Anna; Cecil (marr. Robert Honyman, min. of St Andrews.—[*Scot. N. and Q.*, 3 Ser., vi, 37; Turnbull's *Diary* (*Scot. Hist. Socy.*), 427-8.]

1689 JOHN BRADFUTE, son of James B., Culter and Helen Mitchell. Marr. Janet, daugh. of James Mure, merchant, Edinburgh.

1710 CHARLES HUNTER, son of James H., baxter burgess of Edinburgh.

1881 JAMES MACMEIKAN, his widow, Agnes Peebles, died 19th Oct. 1924.

1908 JAMES BAIRD, died 4th Feb. 1925.

1925 THOMAS BOYD MILLAR, born Larkhall 5th April 1900, son of James M. and Margaret Lohoar Boyd; educ. at Larkhall Academy, Glasgow High School and Univ. of Glasgow, M.A. (1922), B.D. (1925); served in Royal Garrison Artillery in Great War 1918-19; licen. by Presb. of Hamilton 1925; ord. 23rd June 1925; died 11th April 1948.

WISTON

1563 WILLIAM SIMSON, reader in 1563, died before 1568.—[*Comps. Sub Coll. of Thirds, Stirling*, etc.]

1568 ROBERT ALLAN, reader in 1568.—[*Comps. Sub Coll. of Thirds, Stirling*, etc.]

1579 THOMAS LINDSAY, son of John L. of Covington, pres. as a student to vicarage 26th Nov. 1579, in succession to John Weir, and to parsonage 4th Jan. 1580-1.—[*Reg. Pres. Bene.*, i, 47, ii, 24.]

1592 MATTHEW WILSON, as min. pres. in 1592, on deprivation of Thomas Lindsay.—[*Reg. Sec. Sig.*, lxiv, 188.]

1678 THOMAS HARPER, M.A., resident with his wife, Katherin Rae, and children, James and Rachel, the eldest not 8, in Tron Parish, Edinburgh, 8th Nov. 1696.—[*Poll Tax Roll*, 25.]

1694 PATRICK EASON, his son, Alexander, apprenticed to Jerome Robertson, wigmaker, Edinburgh, 1st June 1707.

1786 JOSEPH HENDERSON, pres. 28th June 1785.

1839 DAVID BURNESS, pres. 1st Oct. 1838.

1880 HENRY LITTLEDALE DICK, died at Southport 16th Dec. 1932; his widow, Louisa Jane Schrader, died 29th Oct. 1944.

1907 ROBERT BOYD, dem. 27th June 1946; died 5th Sept. 1946; his wife, Bertha Matilda Hunter, died 9th July 1931; his son, Gavin Charles Hunter, min. of Larbert West, succeeded his father as min. here 1946.

(*Charges united* 3rd *April* 1938.)

ROBERTON

1563 CUTHBERT BAILLIE, exhorter 1563.—[*Comps. Sub Coll. of Thirds, Stirling*, etc.]

1654 THOMAS LAURIE, adm. before 1st July 1654.

1682 JAMES LEIPER, M.A., resident in Lady Yester's parish, Edinburgh, with four children, the eldest not 14, 12th Nov. 1694.—[*Poll Tax Book*.]

PRESBYTERY OF DUNBARTON

ALEXANDRIA

1844 WILLIAM KIDD, his daugh., Catherine, died 22nd Jan. 1932 (marr. Dr J. F. Cullen Brown).

1916 WILLIAM GORDON MACLEAN, dem. 9th Feb. 1932 on app. to First Presbyterian Church, Winnipeg. Marr. 28th Sept. 1920 Christina Macqueen, B.Sc., daugh. of Ex-Provost John Pearson, Alloa, and had issue—Kathleen Deas, born 20th July 1921; William Gordon, born 9th April 1924; John Pearson, born 3rd Aug. 1926; Donald Neil, born 24th Nov. 1930.

ARROCHAR

1658 ALEXANDER McLACHLAN, died Father of the Church.

1782 JOHN GILLESPIE, marr. Bethia, daugh. of John Erskine, hammerman, Glasgow.—[*Burgess Roll*, 26th Dec. 1838.]

1889 JAMES DEWAR, his daughs.—Jessie Edmiston, died 6th Feb. 1935; Alice, died at Crieff 15th Feb. 1943.

1913 HUGH SINCLAIR WINCHESTER, dem. 28th Nov. 1935. Publication—*God in the World* (1937).

(*Charges united 10th June 1947.*)

BALDERNOCK

1568 JOHN LANDALLS, parson and vicar 1568.—[*Comps. Sub Coll. of Thirds, Stirling*, etc.]

1838 JOHN POLLOCK, his son, James Innes Wright, F.C. Min., Mauchline, 1878, Arbroath High, 1887–96.

1843 WILLIAM HUNTER, pres. by Crown 28th Aug. 1843.

1885 MORRISON BRYCE, dem. 12th July 1926, died at Rosneath 11th March 1929. Marr. 16th Aug. 1926 Mary Alice Alderson, who survived him.

1878 JAMES SMITH, his widow, Jemima Aikman Thomson, died 3rd Sept. 1944.

1927 ANDREW SNADDEN KIDSTON, born Falkirk 16th April 1894, younger son of Richard K., Falkirk, and Mary Forbes Sneddon; educ. at Falkirk High School and Univ. of Glasgow, M.A.; licen. by Presb. of Linlithgow 30th March 1920; assistant Carndow; Arbroath 1921; Inveresk 1924; served in European War; ord. 14th Jan. 1927. Marr. 6th June 1927 Allison, youngest daugh. of William Doig, papermaker, Eskside, Musselburgh, and Ann Millar, and has issue—Richard Allister Millar, born 6th Jan. 1929; Alan William Kidston, born 22nd March 1933.

BALFRON

Apparently in 1303 the patronage of the Church of Bruthbren (Balfron) was granted to Inchaffray Abbey by Sir Thomas Cromennane, and on 3rd Oct. of the same year Robert, Bishop of Glasgow, granted power to the abbey and convent, on the death of the rector of the church, to convert the church to their own use, the church to be served by a vicar, or a secular chaplain, or one of the canons of the abbey. The power was granted "in compassion for the plunderings, burnings, and innumerable afflictions which the Abbot and Convent of Inchaffray had suffered through wars, and desirous of relieving, so far as he could, their poverty and low estate."—[*Charters of Inchaffray Abbey*, 113.]

1846 JAMES LINDSAY, died Father of the Church.

BALFRON—BUCHANAN

1919 ARCHIBALD MACKENZIE, trans. to Ayr Second Charge 23rd Nov. 1926.

1927 THOMAS HUTCHISON BURNS-BEGG, born 7th Oct. 1897, son of Robert Burns-B., Sheriff Clerk of Kinross, and Jane Isabella Hutchison, and grand-nephew of Robert Burns, poet; educ. at Dollar Academy and Univ. of Edinburgh, M.A.; licen. by Presb. of Kinross, April 1924; assistant Scoonie 1924; ord. 1st April 1927.

BONHILL

1560 PATRICK REID, reader 1560–3.—[*Comps. Gen. Coll. and Sub Coll. of Thirds, Stirling*, etc.]

1568 MALCOLM STEVENSON, reader and vicar 1568, adm. before 29th Jan. 1577–8.—[*Prot. Book*, David Watson, 225, *penes Duke of Argyll*; *Comps. Gen. Coll. and Sub Coll. of Thirds, Stirling*, etc.]

1587 JAMES CUNNINGHAM, M.A., schoolmaster, Dunbarton, pres. to vicarage 13th Aug. 1587 on death of Malcolm Stevenson.—[*Reg. Sec. Sig.*, lvi, 4.]

1639 JOHN STEWART, had issue, John.

1674 WILLIAM McKECHNIE, M.A., resident with his wife, Janet Edmonstone, in Tron Parish, Edinburgh, 9th Nov. 1694.—[*Tron Poll Tax Roll*, 9; *Deeds, Dal.*, 5th July 1704, 103, 127.]

1878 WILLIAM SIMPSON, his widow, Margaret Wilson, died 27th April 1921.

1913 JOHN ROLLAND McNAB, died at Lossiemouth 18th July 1931; his widow, Marion Johnston, died 4th Dec. 1943; his daughs.—Marion Rolland Johnston (marr. 24th Oct. 1923 Capt. Ralph Juanrenaud Smith, Indian Forestry Service); Winifred Elizabeth (marr. 29th Jan. 1926 James Crawford Shaw, farmer); Doris Maud Jane (marr. 20th April 1927 Tom Osborne Howie, medical practitioner); his son, James Strathearn, min. of Bannockburn, Flowerhill, and St Leonard's, Ayr.

BOQUHANRAN

1907 WILLIAM MACKEAN CAMPBELL, trans. to Kirkpatrick-Durham 15th May 1925.

1925 WILLIAM ROY, born Glasgow 5th March 1900, son of John R., motorman, and Annie Browning Potter; educ. at Univ. of Glasgow, M.A. (1920), B.Sc. (1923); served in H.L.I. in Great War; licen. by Presb. of Glasgow 1925; assistant Irvine; ord. 23rd Sept. 1925; trans. to St Stephen's West, Glasgow, 10th Sept. 1931. Marr. 3rd Nov. 1926 Isabella Downe, daugh. of James Wyllie McCrossan, and Margaret Gardiner Wyllie, and has issue—Margaret Wyllie, born 10th Aug. 1928.

BUCHANAN

The sacred bell of St Kessog was here preserved, indicating that in the parish there had been a chapel dedicated to that saint. On 20th Jan. 1566–7 George Buchanan of that ilk received a confirmation charter of the lands of Buchanan with the bell and alms of St Kessog.—[*Reg. Mag. Sig.*, iv, 1757.]

1561 JAMES WALKER, still in office in 1568.—[*Comps. Sub Coll. of Thirds, Stirling*, etc.]

1567 JOHN MacEACHRAN, vicar.

1567 DAVID CUNNINGHAM, son of William C. of Cunynghamhead, had letters of collation from Andrew Hay, commissioner of Superintendent of Glasgow, of parsonage and vicarage 6th Oct. 1571; line 2, delete "afterwards Bishop of Aberdeen."—[*Prot. Book*, David Watson, *penes Duke of Argyll*, 39; *Cal. of Charters*, xi, 2395.]

1613 ARCHIBALD CAMERON, his son, Archibald, M.A. (Glasgow, 1647).

1892 WILLIAM HOULDSWORTH MACLEOD, dem. 16th May 1922, died at Fuinary, Shandon, 24th March 1935. Publication—*The Beginnings of the Houldsworths of Coltness* (Glasgow, 1938).

WILLIAM ROLAND LACEY, M.A. (1935); trans. from Hillhead 11th Sept. 1922; dem. 20th April 1944; his wife's mother was Henrietta Alexander Kirkpatrick; had issue—Ellen Mary Henrietta, born 11th April 1920; Walter Kirkpatrick, born 25th May 1921; Ruth Sharlaw, born 18th Jan. 1923, died 18th Aug. 1932; Elizabeth Kirkpatrick, born 26th May 1927. His wife, Ellen Bryce Paterson, died at Melrose 13th April 1948.

CARDROSS

On 3rd May 1357 David II granted to William Napier ½ caracute of the lands of Kilmahew in which the Chapel of Kylenchak is situated.—[*Reg. Mag. Sig.*, i, App. i, 129.]

1563 JOHN COOK, reader, 1563.—[*Comps. Sub Coll. of Thirds, Stirling*, etc.]

1596 JAMES CUNNINGHAME, pres. on death of Thomas Archibald.—[*Reg. Sec. Sig.*, xix, 18.]

1603 JAMES CUNNINGHAM, M.A., son of Donald C. of Aikenbar, pres. to parsonage and vicarage in Feb. 1603 on death of James Cunninghame, but may not have entered.—[*Reg. Sec. Sig.*, lxxiii, 208.]

1603 JOHN BLACKBURN, M.A., pres. to parsonage and vicarage 10th May 1603 on death of James Cunningham.—[*Reg. Sec. Sig.*, lxxiv, 11.]

1688 HUGH GORDON, his wife called Elizabeth Cove.—[*Deeds, Dal.*, 1706, No. 191.]

1727 JOHN EDMONSTON of Warroxhill, eldest son of John E., merchant, Glasgow; adm. burgess of Glasgow, 21st Sept. 1752.

1881 WILLIAM MAXWELL, died 18th Feb. 1931; his daugh., Margaret Dunn (marr. at Calcutta, Jan. 1916, Andrew Walter Matthew, jute manufacturer, whom she divorced 1925); his widow, Helen Buchanan Lawson, died 13th May 1940.

(*Charge united with Burns Church 17th May* 1945.)

CLYDEBANK, ST JAMES

1901 WILLIAM STEVENSON BROWNLIE, died 12th Dec. 1930.

CRAIGROWNIE

1887 KENNETH ALEXANDER MACLEAY, adm. min. of Delting 27th Sept. 1920.

1920 JOHN FORD McLEOD, trans. to Tron Church, Edinburgh, 5th May 1926.

1926 GEORGE HOPE JAMIE, formerly of Ladyburn (*q.v.*), assistant Barony, adm. 31st Aug. 1926; dem. 14th Dec. 1931; adm. to Garngad 19th Oct. 1933; dem. 1935.

DALMUIR

1920 JAMES PITT WATSON, M.A., B.D., ord. 14th Oct. 1920; trans. to Sandyford 18th Dec. 1923.

1924 JOHN MARTIN, trans. from Wallacetown (*q.v.*), Ayr, 17th June 1924.

DALREOCH

1873 JAMES McBAIN, his widow, Margaret Cowan, died 17th March 1931.

1910 ROBERT ALEXANDER ORR, dem. 31st Dec. 1945; his son, Lieut. R. A., missing 1942.

DRYMEN

There was also a chapel at Easter Mayis. —[*Reg. Mag. Sig.*, vii, 1168.]

1560 THOMAS ARCHIBALD, M.A. designated parson and vicar pensioner 6th Nov. 1567 and 30th March 1581. —[*Reg. of Abbrev. Feu Charters of Church Lands*, i, 311; *Cal. of Charters*, xi, 2586.]

1562 ROBERT GRAHAM, vicar pensioner. —[*Acts and Dec.*, xxiv, 52.]

1648 ALLAN FERGUSON.—[*Gen. Reg. of Sas.*, 2 Ser., iv, 401.]

1878 JOHN ROY, his daughs.—Margaret Anderson, died 28th Aug. 1921; Cecilia Buchanan (marr. 11th June 1925 John Moffat); his widow, Margaret Norrie, died 4th Dec. 1947.

1918 JAMES TAYLOR MONTEITH, has issue—Jeannie Gordon, born 12th Oct. 1920; Bethia Mary, born 12th Oct. 1920; James Taylor, born 9th Jan. 1928. Publication—*The Training of a Nation* (1929–30).

(*Charges united 27th Feb.* 1935.)

DUNBARTON

In the church there were also the following altars: St Mary the Virgin on the south side; St Peter; St Sebastian; and the Holy Rood. In 1519–20 Andrew Danielston, natural son of Robert Danielston of Culgrane, acquired from Robert Feriar of Fareland the office of custodier of the light of the Holy Rood in the church. On 11th May 1453 the Town Council conveyed to Mabel, Countess of Lennox and Duchess of Albany, the Chapel of St Mary the Virgin, of which the Council was patron, with its lands, rents and patronage, to enable the Countess to erect the chapel into a collegiate church. To the Pope, on 3rd Jan. 1453–4, the Countess addressed a petition to the effect that "some years ago her late husband, Murdoch, Duke of Albany and Earl of Fife and Menteith, and her father (Duncan) Earl of Lennox, and their children, namely the sons and brothers of the said Countess, were, by order of the late James, King of Scots, who was evilly counselled or informed, disinherited and put to death (on the Heading Hill at Stirling Castle in 1425), leaving no successor in the right line excepting the said Countess, a solitary widow and very poor, who succeeded by paternal right to her father," and that "for the welfare of their souls and in lasting memory of them" she desired to erect into a collegiate church for a provost and chaplains the said Chapel of the Virgin Mary, which "she is to enlarge, build and repair for the purpose." The Pope on 4th Feb. 1453–4 remitted to the Bishop of St Andrews and the Prior of Inchmahome with power to make enquiries, and to erect the collegiate church for a provost and such perpetual chaplains "as they deemed reasonable." At the same time, likewise on the crave of the Countess, the Hospital of Polmadie, with its annexed Church of Strathblane, and also the Church of Fintry, were assigned to the collegiate church. The Bishop and Prior were also granted faculty to "collate and assign for this turn the Provostship" to George Abernethy, Clerk of the Diocese of Glasgow, rector of the said Hospital of Polmadie, "a son of the sister (Maria ?) of the said Countess," by her husband, Sir William Abernethy of Saltoun. George Abernethy was still provost on 6th March 1468–9. Further endowments granted by the Countess to the church were the following lands—Strathblane; Stuckroger and Ferkinch or Forkinch in Lues; Balernicbeg in Cardross; Knockdouriebarber in Rosneath; and Ladytown in Bonhill. The Church of Bonhill, which also pertained to the collegiate church, appears likewise to have been her gift. The collegiate church was dedicated to the Virgin Mary. The Bedesmen Hospital was probably attached to the church. By Crown Charter of 12th March 1551–2 there was conveyed to Paisley Abbey the patronage of the collegiate church and of the chaplainries of the hospital and the begging poor, *lie bedemen;* and a further Crown Charter of 1st Feb. 1552–3 to the same effect described the gift as "the Patronage of the Provostry, prebends, prebendaries, and chaplainries of the Collegiate Church of the Virgin of Dunbarton, with the Hospital and the Wayfarer's Inn (or Hospitium) and the poor, *lie bedemen*, of the same." The Fair of St John the Baptist was instituted by Crown Charter of 11th March 1225–6.—[*Cal. Papal Regs., Letters,* x, 623–4, xii, 670; *Reg. Great Seal*, i, 760, iii, 188, iv, 683, 747, 811, v, 188, vii, 190; *Reg. Sec. Seal*, ii, 809; *Book of Assumptions of Benefices.*]

1568 PATRICK WODDEROW, M.A., pensioner, 1568.—[*Reg. Abbrev. Feu Charters of Church Lands*, ii, 103.]

1574 ROBERT GLATTISBERRIE, reader.—[*Acts and Dec.*, lvii, 229.]

1593 PATRICK WEMYSS, M.A., min. pres. to vicarage 22nd March 1595 on dem. of George Moncrieff.—[*Reg. Sec. Sig.*, lxix, 81.]

1601 WILLIAM SYMSON, died 1620.

1620 WILLIAM BLAIR, born Irvine; marr. Barbara, daugh. of –. Robertson of Orbieston.

1681 JAMES DONALDSON of Murroch, son of James D., probably min. of Rerrick, died 25th April 1722. Marr. 3rd April 1681 Anna, only daugh. of John Stirling of Bankell and Elizabeth Dick, and had issue—Henry, born 22nd Jan. 1683, died young; Elizabeth, born 22nd Dec. 1684 (marr. 1707 John Colquhoun of Ennistrossan); James, born 10th June 1686, died young; William of Murroch, Sheriff Depute, Dunbarton, died 22nd Aug. 1764; George, born 17th Aug. 1689; Nicolas, born June 1691; Grizel, born 8th Nov. 1692; Margaret, born 25th Dec. 1693; John, born 17th July, died 3rd Aug. 1695; James, born 3rd Aug. 1696; Archibald, born 13th June 1698; Henry, born 3rd June 1700; Alexander, born 18th June 1702; Anna, born 4th June 1704; Thomas, born Oct. 1705. Two of these daughs. marr. Colin Maclachlan, Luss, and Archibald his brother.

1843 ANDREW GRAY, his daugh. died at Cove 2nd Dec. 1925.

1882 GEORGE ALPINE, his daugh., Mary Turner (marr. James A. Latta), died 25th March 1946.

1915 WILLIAM WALKER REID, died 25th Feb. 1946; his wife, Mary Scott, died 28th Nov. 1937; his daugh., Mary Helen Isabel, born 10th Aug. 1919.

SECOND CHARGE

1689 ROBERT ANDERSON, returned to Rhu 1704.

DUNTOCHER

1918 NEIL MacGILL, trans. to Tomintoul 21st April 1926.

1920 JOHN WALKER, trans. from Kirkpatrick-Fleming (*q.v.*) 1st Oct. 1926; trans. to Johnstone 21st Dec. 1934; his daugh., Edith Isobel (marr. 17th Jan. 1942 Capt. James Strathearn Dundas, K.O.S.B.).

FINTRY

By Papal authority on 4th Feb. 1453-4 the church was annexed to the Collegiate Church of Dunbarton.

1560 GEORGE WATSON, exhorter, "entered to Service" Candlemas 1560, being elected and adm. with a "sober and small stipend" and manse and glebe belonging to the vicarage which the vicar brooked; on 18th March 1567-8 the Privy Council ordained James Galbrayth of Kilcrewth who had withheld the glebe, manse and yard since 1560, to desist and grant possession to the said George.—[*Reg. Privy Council*, i, 615.]

1571 ANDREW KEMP, adm. before 1571. Marr. Isobell Anderson who survived him.—[*Accs. Sub Coll. of Bene.*, 1571.]

1573 THOMAS FLEMING.—[*Acts and Dec.*, 1, 95.]

1907 MATTHEW BARCLAY, died 30th July 1938.

GARELOCHHEAD

1848 JOHN PAISLEY, born 20th Nov. 1814; line 3, for "Mary Catherine Russell" read "Elizabeth Lang"; his second daugh., Eupham, died 29th Oct. 1928; George, his son.

1906 JOHN PATTERSON, died 28th Sept. 1934; his widow, Jane Templeton Couper, died 5th Jan. 1946.

1919 CHRISTIAN ARTHUR ROBERTSON, dem. 3rd June 1924 on app. to St Andrew's Church, Alexandria, Egypt; adm. to Greenock, Wellpark West, 14th May 1930; trans. to Avondale 22nd Feb. 1939.

1924 ALEXANDER HASTIE BODIN, born 24th May 1887, son of Hugh B. and Annie Hastie; educ. at Univ. of Glasgow, M.A. (16th Nov. 1912); licen. by Presb. of Glasgow 30th June 1920; assistant Barony and St Matthew's, Glasgow and Dalziel; ord. 18th Sept. 1924; died 1st Feb.

1948. Marr. 10th Jan. 1929 Eliza Margaret, daugh. of Thomas Alexander Boyd and Jane Finlayson Govan, and has issue—Hugh Arthur Boyd, born 6th June 1930; Michael Alexander, born 20th April 1932.

(*Charges united* 15*th March* 1938.)

HELENSBURGH

1895 JOHN GEORGE CROCKET CHRISTIE, died at Clarkston 8th Dec. 1925; his widow, Emily Agnes Jones, died 8th June 1948.

1922 MALCOLM MUNRO MACPHERSON, O.B.E., ord. A. and S. 25th Oct. 1922; trans. to St. Paul's, Greenock, 8th July 1926.

1926 THOMAS JAMES CAMPBELL CRAWFORD, born 3rd April 1890, son of John C., builder, and Sarah Louise Waters; educ. at Univ. of Glasgow, M.A. (1921); licen. by Presb. of Glasgow 1920; assistant, Barony; ord. assistant 19th Feb. 1922; adm. 15th May 1922 to Twechar; trans. and adm. 10th Nov. 1926; trans. to West Kilbride 19th Feb. 1930. Marr. 6th July 1922 Isobel Sharpe Hastings, and has issue—Eileen, born 8th Jan. 1924; Elma Louise, born 18th March 1926; Isabel Campbell, born 31st Aug. 1928.

HELENSBURGH WEST

1889 JOHN BAIRD, died 14th Sept. 1932; his daugh., Jean (marr. 6th June 1922 Neil Conley, M.A., min. of U.F. Church, Mortlach); his son, John Logie, inventor of television, managing director of Baird Television, Television Station, Alexandra Palace, July 1936; died 14th June 1946.

1919 WILLIAM HARVEY LEATHAM, dem. on app. to St Andrew's Church, Ottawa, 4th Oct. 1926; died at Montreal 26th Feb. 1937; his son, George Rendle, min. of St Bride's, Edinburgh.

1927 JOHN FORSYTH MARSHALL, born 8th Dec. 1893, son of Archibald Millar M., min. of U.F. Church, Cowie, and Christina Frere Forsyth; educ. at Univ. of Edinburgh, M.A. (1915), and Oxford, M.A. (1920); served in War with Highland Light Infantry, M.C.; licen. by Presb. of Edinburgh June 1920; assistant St Cuthbert's; ord. 28th April 1921 to Airdrie; trans. and adm. 17th Jan. 1927; trans. to Renfrew Old 30th Nov. 1933. Marr. 26th July 1921 Anne Pringle, daugh. of Alexander Pringle Davidson, min. of Skirling U.F. Church, and Mary Gemmell Duke, and has issue—Archibald Humphrey Miller, born 25th May 1922; Doris Mary Christine, born 30th June 1924; Jean Margaret Miller, born 22nd April 1926.

JAMESTOWN

1876 DANIEL JACK MILLER, died 23rd Jan. 1925; his son, John Russell, min. of Kilsyth; his daughs.— Elizabeth Roxburgh (marr. 1st Aug. 1935 George Garland, Falkirk); Marion, M.A. (marr. 13th Feb. 1934 James Gibson, Glasgow).

1925 MALCOLM BLAIR MACGREGOR, born Glasgow 22nd Feb. 1900, son of John Malcolm M. and Margaret Gardner Morrison; educ. at Whitehill School and Univ. of Glasgow, M.A. (1922), Ph.D. (1929); licen. by Presb. of Glasgow 19th Dec. 1923; assistant St Andrew's, Glasgow, 1924, Cambuslang; ord. 29th May 1925. Marr. 22nd Sept. 1925 Lily, youngest daugh. of John Downie and Catherine Stewart, and has issue—Catherine Stewart, born 9th April 1928; Margaret Morrison, born 21st May 1937. Publications—*The Sources and Literature of Scottish Church History* (Glasgow, 1934); *Jamestown Parish Church* (Historical Sketch) (Dunbarton, 1934).

KILLEARN

1566 WILLIAM GRAHAM, parson in 1566. —[*Comps. Sub Coll. of Thirds, Stirling*, etc.]

1572 PATRICK PATERSON, pres. to vicar-pensionary 15th Sept. 1572 on death of Sir John Snell.—[*Reg. Pres. Bene.*, i, (3), 21.]

KILLEARN—OLD KILPATRICK

1586 JOHN GRAHAM, Lord of Council, parson 1586.—[*Lamont Papers*, 328, 105.]

1658 JAMES CRAIG, had issue—James of Costerton, W.S., died 5th Aug. 1743.

1883 JAMES DICK, died at Kirknewton 1st May 1930.

1898 ALEXANDER GORDON MITCHELL, dem. 2nd Feb. 1931, died 2nd Nov. 1943; his wife, Edith Rebecca Gillies, died 5th Nov. 1925; his son, John William Forrester Gordon, died 21st June 1938; his daughs.—Jessie Murray Graham, died 7th Feb. 1926; Elizabeth Edith (marr. 6th Oct. 1942 Lieut. Roy Greer Donnan, Pioneer Corps). Addl. Publications—*Original Latin Dramas of George Buchanan in English Verse*; *Odes of Horace in English Verse*.

(*Charges united 2nd July* 1931.)

KILBOWIE

Services were begun in a hall purchased in 1896 by the Kirk Session of Old Kilpatrick. The church was built in 1904 and tower built and bell instituted in 1933. A hall was built in 1928.

1898 JOHN HAMILTON, died 29th Jan. 1947; line 8, for "Jane" read "Janet."

KILMARONOCK

The patronage of the church was granted to Cambuskenneth Abbey 1306–29.—[*Reg. Mag. Sig.*, i, App. ii, 105.]

1574 GEORGE McGLEISS, reader, pres. to vicarage pensionary 25th May 1574 on death of Sir James Hunter.—[*Reg. Pres. Bene.*, i, 21.]

1581 ARCHIBALD CRAWFORD, M.A., vicar pensioner 20th Sept. 1581, also parson of Eaglesham (*q.v.*).—[*Reg. Privy Council*, ii, 421–2.]

1601 LUKE STIRLING, M.A., min. pres. to parsonage and vicarage on dep. of Robert Alexander.—[*Reg. Sec. Sig.*, lxxiv, 175.]

1836 WILLIAM BERRY SHAW PATERSON, his daughs.—Janet Shaw, died at Edinburgh 1st June 1923; Margaret, died at Edinburgh 4th Dec. 1927.

1879 WILLIAM BOYD, his daugh., Isobel McCulloch, died 18th Aug. 1938.

1920 WILLIAM McLAUCHLAN GOLDIE, dem. 7th April 1948; his daugh., Winifred Maud (marr. 15th Oct. 1926 Walter Bilsland, farmer, Gartenbantrick, Kilmaronock); his wife, Matilda Maud Barr, died 2nd Aug. 1943.

KNIGHTSWOOD

1925 GEORGE WILSON HAMILTON, born 17th May 1891, second son of Thomas H., Drumcross, Bathgate; educ. at Peebles High School, Univ. of St Andrews, M.A. (1913), B.D. (1916); student missionary at Elvanfoot 1914–15; licen. by Presb. of Peebles 1916; assistant Inveresk; served in R.A.S.C. in France, Egypt and Palestine; ord. to Cummertrees 4th Aug. 1920; trans. and adm. 1st Oct. 1925; trans. to Comrie 1st Dec. 1937. Marr. 4th Aug. 1921 Elizabeth Tyler, youngest daugh. of John Bruce, St Margaret's, Loanhead.

OLD KILPATRICK

Attached to the lands of Kilbowie, there was a chapel with chapel lands.—[*Retours*, xxxiii, 36.]

1563 ROBERT HOUSTON, exhorter.—[*Comps. Sub Coll. of Thirds, Stirling*, etc.]

1573 WILLIAM HAMILTON, pres. on dem. of Archibald Berne "not able to travel or supply."—[*Reg. Pres. Bene.*, i, (4), 127; *Edin. Tests*, 12th May 1575.]

1587 WALTER STEWART.—[*G. R. Sas.*, xxiv, 97.]

1667 THOMAS ALLAN, his sons—Andrew, buried 9th Aug. 1687; John, buried 27th Dec. 1689.

1916 HARRY SMITH, trans. to Heriot 7th June 1928.

JOHN KENNEDY, born 21st Jan. 1897, son of Andrew K. and Barbara Helen Kennedy; educ. at Hutchison's Grammar School and Univ. of Glasgow, M.A. (1922), B.D. (1925); served with R.A.F. in Great War, 1918; licen. by Presb. of Glasgow 1924; assistant St Mungo, Glasgow; ord. to Lowson Memorial, Forfar, 15th Sept. 1925; trans. and adm. 19th Dec. 1928; trans. to Cambuslang 11th March 1936. Marr. 21st Oct. 1925 Ellison Bryson, daugh. of John Gilchrist, and has issue—John Gilchrist, born 9th Nov. 1926; Margaret Alison, born 27th Jan. 1929; Alan Gordon, born 31st March 1936. Publications—*Thrums and the Barrie Country*; *A Quiver of Arrows*; *Worry, its Cause and Cure*.
1928

NEW KILPATRICK

At Balvie-Logan there was a chapel dedicated to St Kessog.—[*Reg. Mag. Sig.*, ii, 2648.]

JOHN LOGAN, his son, Walter, comptroller of customs, Perth Amboy, New Jersey.
1716

JAMES WATERS KING, his daugh., Amy Mary Waters, died Versailles 15th Jan. 1943.
1870

JOHN HENRY DICKEY, died in Glasgow Royal Infirmary 30th Jan. 1926.
1907

WILLIAM WHITE ANDERSON, M.C., D.D. (Glasgow, 23rd June 1943), trans. from Bellahouston (*q.v.*) 9th Sept. 1926; trans. to St Cuthbert's, Edinburgh, 23rd April 1931; Vice-Convener Business Committee 1946; Convener Home Board.
1926

DRUMCHAPEL

JOHN EASTON BLACK, adm. first min. of parish 3rd Nov. 1923; died 17th Feb. 1942; his daugh., Jean Bethia Naismith (marr. 28th June 1933 Robert Montague Lloyd Puckeridge, Midstead, Hants). His father was J.P., Stonehouse, Lanarkshire.
1910

KNOXLAND

JOHN SMITH, licen. by Presb. of Glasgow 1884.
1886

JAMES LITTLE, died 31st March 1946.
1910

ARCHIBALD MONTGOMERY, trans. to Condorrat 22nd March 1927.
1916

NORMAN GOTTFRIED KESTING, born 22nd June 1885, son of Ernest K., organist and teacher of music, and Isabella Thornwaite Rigg; educ. at Univ. of Edinburgh, M.A. (1906); licen. by Presb. of Edinburgh April 1909; assistant, St Margaret's, Edinburgh, 1909, Selkirk 1911, Newington 1913; ord. to Drumelzier 20th April 1917; trans. and adm. 29th Sept. 1927; trans. to Kirkhope 17th May 1935. Marr. 26th July 1917 Maud, second daugh. of Hugh Cameron, min. of Newington, and has issue—Hugh Morrison, born 25th May 1918, died 14th Nov. 1940; John Rigg, born 10th Oct. 1919; Norman Douglas, born 20th Sept. 1921; Elizabeth Maud, born 12th April 1923; Isabel Margaret, born 19th Jan. 1925. Publication—Chapter on Drumelzier in *History of Peeblesshire*.
1927

LUSS

On 8th March 1315–16 Robert I granted to God and St Kessog the privilege of gyrth round the church for three miles on every side, both land and water.—[*Hist. MS. Commiss.*, iii, 387.]

Sir Thomas Henderson was on 12th April 1556 presented and invested at the Altar of the Blessed Virgin Mary of Luss in the south part of the church, and to the office of clerk of the parish by delivering to him a missal book, cup, and other vestments of the altar.—[*Chiefs of Colquhouns*, i, 117.]

JOHN LAYING (LAING), M.A., parson in Feb. 1555–6, having succeeded Mr James Colquhoune, son of Walter C., 3rd son of Sir John C. of Luss by his first wife, Elizabeth Stewart;
1555

designated prebendary of Luss in 1561, and parson and vicar in 1563, when it is narrated that he has been possessed of "the parsonage and vicarage years bygone and his furneist and sustenit ministeris for reading and edifeing of the parochinaris thairof yeirlie sen the alteratioun of the religioun conforme to ordour taken thairanent lyke as he yiet dois"; parson of Kirkpatrick-Juxta 1539–53, perpetual vicar of Dreghorn 1553, Canon of Glasgow 1564, Dean of the Faculty of Glasgow Univ. 1552–5, and Judge-Commissary of the Archbishop of St Andrews 1564; died in Sept. 1571.—[*Chiefs of Colquhoun*, i, 89, 97, 118, 123, 124, ii, 82, 247, 262, 345; *Acts and Dec.*, xxiv, 73, xxvii, 32, xxviii, 143, xxix, 79, xl, 153; *Notes on the Black Book of Paisley*, 93, 95; *Edin. Tests.*, ii, 232.]

1560 JAMES COLQUHOUN, M.A., min. in or soon after 1560; parson 28th April 1566; died before 1st Nov. 1572; had issue—John, James. He was nephew of Mr Archibald Colquhoun, parson of Stobo.—[*Reg. of Deeds*, viii, 201, x, 222; *Chiefs of Colquhoun*, i, 222; *Edin. Tests.*, viii, 311.]

1567 JAMES LAYING, reader; Clerk of the Diocese of Glasgow in 1534, and Chaplain of the Diocese 1550; conformed and became reader here in 1560; dem. apparently in 1572; later was parson. —[*Chiefs of Colquhoun*, ii, 336, 96; *Notes on the Black Book of Paisley*, 96; *Compts. Sub Coll. of Thirds, Stirling*, etc.]

1572 WILLIAM CHIRNSYDE, min., and also parson in succession to Mr John Laying; on Jan. 10th 1572–3 he set in feu to Sir Humphrey Colquhoun, son of Sir John C. of Luss, the parsonage manse, place, and yard, situated at the south side of the Rotten Row of Glasgow; trans. apparently before 27th April 1576.— [*Notes on the Black Book of Paisley*, 96; *Colquhoune Cart.*, i, 397–400; *Chiefs of Colquhoun*, ii, 435.]

1576 JAMES LAYING, above mentioned, parson 27th April 1576.—[*Chiefs of Colquhoun*, ii, 435. See Kirkpatrick-Juxta.]

1585 MALCOLM STEVENSON, Chaplain of the Diocese of Glasgow; vicar-pensioner here at the Reformation; his claim for his pension of 20 merks for 1561–2 was refused in 1563 by Mr John Laying, parson, because he "his maid na service thairintill this lang time bypast as he aucht to have done," and "he is bot ane feall and pensioner"; subsequently, in 1563, he is designated exhorter, and he appears to have continued to discharge that duty.—[*Comps. Sub Coll. of Thirds, Stirling*, etc.; *Chiefs of Colquhoun*, i, 83; *Acts and Dec.*, xxvii, 32; *Edin. Test.*, ii, 232.]

1594 WILLIAM CHIRNSYDE, had issue at least—Archibald and David; died before 1st March 1600.—[*Chiefs of Colquhoun*, i, 148, 180, ii, 435.]

1599 DUNCAN ERROLL, on 1st March 1600 he was presented by Alexander Colquhoune of Luss to the parsonage and vicarage, vacant by the death of Mr William Chirnsyde; by act of Assembly 1605 he was deprived of the living, and on 26th Feb. 1606 the Synod ordained the presb. to put into execution against him the Act of Assembly, and that they should make provision, before his deposition from the ministry, for the maintenance of himself, his wife, and bairns, seeing he had served so long in the ministry. He was, however, supported by Alexander Colquhoune of Luss and the parishioners, and in spite of his deprivation he continued in full possession till his death, administering the Word and Sacraments and receiving the stipend. He marr. –. Buchanan.— [*Chiefs of Colquhoun*, i, 180, 218.]

1607 JOHN CAMPBELL, the patron, Alexander Colquhoune of Luss, made a presentation in favour of Mr Malcolm Colquhoune, but the presb. presented Mr Campbell, *jure devoluto*, on the ground that Mr Erroll had been lawfully deprived, and that a successor had not been timeously presented by the patron; objections to the presbytery's procedure were set aside and Mr Campbell was settled.—[*Chiefs of Colquhoun*, i, 218–20.]

1685 WILLIAM ANDERSON, his sons—Robert, min. of Row, Alexander; Charles.—[*Deeds, Dal.,* 1705, No. 503.]

1698 DANIEL McGILCHRIST, second son of Donald M., writer, Rothesay, and Janet, daugh. of William Yair, town clerk, Glasgow. Marr. proc. 5th April 1707 Margaret McDougal, Dunblane.—[*Reg. of Deeds, Dal.,* 21st Aug. 1721.]

1723 JAMES ROBERTSON, line 5, delete "Father of the Church."

1908 ALEXANDER SLATER DUNLOP, trans. to St Andrews Second Charge 7th Oct. 1924; line 5, for "Edinburgh" read "Glasgow."

1925 ALISTAIR CAMPBELL, trans. from Kilninver (*q.v.*) 26th Feb. 1925; Chaplain to Lord High Commissioner 1932. Marr. 9th Feb. 1922 Elizabeth M., daugh. of Matthew H. Craig and Margaret Craig, and has issue—Margaret Elizabeth, born 10th Nov. 1922; William Alexander, born 29th April 1927; Donald George Craig, born 27th Aug. 1931.

MILNGAVIE ST PAUL'S

1898 JOHN EDGAR, died 3rd July 1925.

1925 DUNCAN McCORKINDALE, trans. from Bonnybridge 22nd Dec. 1925 (*q.v.*); line 1, for "29" read "28"; dem. 1st Oct. 1940.

RENTON

1913 JOHN MACLEAN, trans. to Liff and Benvie 25th March 1925; his son, John, born 13th Nov. 1919.

1925 GEORGE NEILSON DUFF, born 12th April 1896, son of William Butler D. and Janet Neilson; educ. at Hutcheson's Grammar School and Univ. of Glasgow, M.A. (1918); served in Great War; licen. by Presb. of Glasgow 4th May 1921; assistant, St Ninian's, Glasgow, 1922, St Paul's 1924; ord. 26th Aug. 1925; trans. to Abbotsford-Chalmers, Glasgow, 5th April 1934; trans. to Albert Drive, Pollokshields, 23rd Oct. 1946. Marr. 9th Feb. 1926 Fanny, daugh. of Edward McRoberts and Fanny Phelps, and has issue—William Butler, born 8th Jan. 1928; Frances McRoberts, born 30th June 1932.

ROSNEATH

The church was granted to Paisley Abbey by Anlay or Amelec, brother of Maldouin, Earl of Lennox, with confirmation by said Maldouin, and by Alexander II, 12th March 1225-6. It was dedicated to St Nicholas. Traditionally, however, the dedication is said to have been to the Virgin Mary, but the probability is that that was the dedication of the Chapel of Kilcreggan—hence the popular interpretation of Rosneath "isle" as the Virgin Promontory. On 1st June 1621 the parishioners unsuccessfully petitioned Parliament for the removal of the church from the "island" to the mainland at Ardinconnel, where Rhu Church was subsequently built. Besides the chapel at Kilcreggan, there were in the parish the Chapel of St Modan in the churchyard where the relics of the saint were kept, the Chapel of St Bean at Fasslane, and a chapel at Port Kill, "harbour of the Chapel." The chancel of the church was extended in 1922 by H.R.H. Princess Louise, Duchess of Argyll, in memory of her husband, John, 9th Duke, and of George, 8th Duke. The reredos was erected by her in 1931.—[*Reg. of Paisley Abbey,* 209; *Acts Scott. Parl.,* iv, 407b; Fraser's *Lennox,* 230; Watson's *Celtic Place Names,* 289, 312.]

1567 MALCOLM STEVENSON, exhorter 1563.—[*Comps. Sub Coll. of Thirds, Stirling,* etc.] (See Luss.)

1614 GEORGE LINDSAY of Blackscolme.—[*G. R. Sas.,* ix, 140, 10th Dec. 1621.]

1651 NINIAN CAMPBELL, second son of Colin C. of Ormidale (first family); had issue—William; Colin, matric. Glasgow 1647.—[*G. R. Sas.,* 2 Ser., xiii, 41.]

1665 ALEXANDER CAMERON, dem. 2nd June 1680.

1682 JAMES GORDON, third son.—[*G. R. Sas.*, 3 Ser., xxix, 341.]

1682 JAMES GORDON, had issue—Robert.—[*Deeds, Dal.*, 1706, No. 260.]

1689 ROBERT CAMPBELL, min. at Stephenkirk in Ireland 1710; his son, Hugh, apprenticed to William Blackwood, merchant, 13th Dec. 1710.

1887 ALFRED WARR, his widow, Christian Grey Laing, died 27th Feb. 1945; his daugh., Agnes Christian Constance (marr. 28th Oct. 1931 Stuart Kindersley Turnbull).

1916 ALEXANDER BROWN GRANT, dem. 10th April 1939; his wife, Agnes Bryden Mackendrick, died 13th Dec. 1925. Marr (2) 3rd Jan. 1928 Mabel Symon, second daugh. of David Low, Bearsden, Glasgow; his daugh., Juanita Turner (marr. 1st July 1936 Robert McHarg, merchant, Glasgow).

ROW or RHU

1684 ROBERT ANDERSON, son of William A., min. of Buchanan.—[*Deeds, Dal.*, 1705, Nos. 503, 504.]

1825 JOHN MACLEOD CAMPBELL, his daugh., Margaret Duncan, died at Stewkley Ham, Bucks, 25th Jan. 1933.

1832 JOHN LAURIE-FOGO, his daughs.—Jane, D.C.S., died 25th Nov. 1929; Bertha Margaret, died 12th March 1930.

1877 JOHN McKESSER WEBSTER, his daugh., Winifred Mary (marr. 1908 Lt.-Col. Sir James Forest Halket Carmichael, C.M.G.); his widow, Mary Jane Dennistoun, died 22nd March 1941.

1914 VINCENT CASSELS ALEXANDER, trans. to Rubislaw 14th June 1922.

1922 ROBERT BALDOCK SCOTT, trans. from Humbie (*q.v.*) 9th Nov. 1922, died 7th May 1924; his widow, Alexa Evelyn Macleod, died 18th March 1937.

1924 DONALD McGREGOR GRANT, trans. from Newport (*q.v.*) 16th Oct. 1924; drowned at Granton 11th Dec. 1929. Addl. issue—Espeth Catherine, born 13th June 1926. His daugh., Helen McGregor (marr. 7th Aug. 1946 Robert, younger son of Robert Aitken Dunbar).

STRATHBLANE

The church belonged to the Hospital of Polmadie, and with the hospital became a prebend of Glasgow in 1425–6 and in 1453–4 was annexed to the Collegiate Church of Dunbarton.

1650 JOHN COCHRANE, his daugh., Anne (marr. cont. 31st May 1679 Archibald Macgregor of that Ilk); died 24th June 1725.—[*Stirling Sas.*, 10th March 1680.]

1748 JAMES GRAY, marr. Agnes, daugh. of William Fogo, merchant, Glasgow.

1835 HAMILTON BUCHANAN, born 13th June 1805.

1874 DANIEL JOHN FERGUSON, his widow, Henrietta Hamilton Montgomery, died 21st Dec. 1941.

1886 WILLIAM BEGBIE MOYES, dem. 5th Sept. 1933; died 8th March 1946. Marr. (2) 12th Oct. 1932 Catherine Renwick Watson.

(*United with Blanefield 9th Feb.* 1934.)

STRATHFILLAN

Part of the endowment granted by Robert I to the Chapel of St Fillan, which he founded in 1314, was the 5 lib. Lands of Wichtertiry (Uchterteris) in Glendochart. On 26th Feb. 1317–18 he granted the patronage of the Church of Killin to the Abbey and Convent of Inchaffray on condition that the abbey provided a canon to serve at the chapel; and the grant was repeated on 18th April 1318 without condition. Apparently the original design of the King was a chapel with a canon, but soon after the foundation the chapel was converted into a priory, as is shown by a charter of William Sinclair, Bishop of

Dunkeld, dated 28th Oct. 1318, granting to the Prior of Inchaffray and to the canons the Church of Killin (whose patronage, as just stated, had been granted by Robert I), and all the teinds, fruits, revenues of the same, to be converted to the use of the prior and canons living at the said chapel for the worship of God, provided that according to the capabilities of the place a sufficient number of canons should be settled there by the Abbot of Inchaffray. The Prior of St Fillan's Chapel, on the occurrence of a vacancy, was to be presented by the abbot and convent, and instituted by the Bishop. It may be that to the enlargement of the place, in order to render it fitting for a priory, there has reference an entry in the Exchequer Rolls in 1329 to the following effect—Payment through Sir Robert de Bruce, natural son of King Robert, of a sum of 20 lib. for the building of the Church of St Fillan. In 1543-4 the church was repaired at a cost of 300 merks.—[*Charters of Inchaffray Abbey*, 116–20; *Reg. Great Seal*, i. App. 2, 658, ii, 347, 2458, iii, 2705; *Excheq. Rolls*, i, 214.]

1846 ALEXANDER MACKINNON, his son, Duncan Archibald, M.A., min. of U.F. Church, Marykirk, died at Cromdale 22nd March 1922; his daugh., Jessie Elizabeth, died 22nd March 1932.

1894 GEORGE CALDER, D.D. (Glasgow 1936), died 1st April 1941; his daughs.—Helen Edith (marr. 26th April 1922 Andrew Davidson, M.B., Ch.B.); Margaret Evelyn Campbell (marr. 12th Nov. 1930 George Stanley Gillies, Travancore, India). Addl. Publications— *The Scholar's Primar* (1917); *Togail na Tebe. The Bard of Statues* (1922); *Gaelic Grammar* (1923); *Gaelic Songs by William Ross* (1937).

1913 NEIL DUNCAN MACKINNON, dem. 31st May 1920.

1920 JAMES GOURLAY, M.A., B.D., licen. by Presb. of Dunfermline 1916, assistant South Leith; ord. 21st Dec. 1920; dem. 30th Sept. 1930; assistant at Larbert; died 24th Dec. 1939.

TEMPLE

1890 JAMES STUART CARSWELL, died 22nd Oct. 1940.

YOKER

1917 JAMES SMITH, dem. 1st June 1920 on app. of Director of Religious Instruction, St Andrews and Dundee Training College; his wife, Ruth Lindsay Morrison, died 3rd Oct. 1945. Marr. (2) 2nd Sept. 1947 Margaret Helen Kemp, elder daugh. of George Birnie, min. of Speymouth. Publications—*The Book of the Prophet Ezekiel*; *The Teacher's Handbook to the Syllabus of Religious Instruction*.

1920 JOHN SIMPSON AGNEW, M.A., born 30th June 1888; licen. by Presb. of Paisley 1912; enlisted as private in Scots Guards, officer in H.L.I., three times wounded; assistant, East Wemyss, Kirkcaldy; ord. 11th Nov. 1920; died at Paisley 28th Dec. 1920. Marr. 12th Feb. 1910 Eliza Jane Campbell, and had issue— William Craigie, born 14th April 1911.

1921 WILLIAM WALLS, born 13th Oct. 1889, son of David W., farmer, East Hillhouse, Riccarton, Ayrshire, and Agnes Stark; licen. by Presb. of Glasgow 20th Dec. 1920; assistant Calton; ord. 20th April 1921; dem. 30th June 1935. Marr. 27th March 1918 Mary Louisa, daugh. of William Jackson, and has issue—Phyllis Mary, born 24th March 1919; Ian Gascoyne, born 28th April 1922. Publications —*Life, Love and Light* (Edinburgh, 1926); *Inescapable Questions* (Govan, 1927).

PRESBYTERY OF GLASGOW

BANTON

1915 JOHN ARCHIBALD DRON, trans. to Colintraive 8th July 1932, died 26th July 1939; his wife, Ethel Margaret Walworth Hutchison, died 14th June 1935.

CADDER

1576 JAMES HAMILTON, Bishop of Argyll, held parsonage 1576.—[*Cal. of Charters*, xi, 2395.] (See Monkland.)

1583 JOHN SPOTTISWOOD, M.A., yr., parson 8th Oct. 1583; John S. of Cadder is mentioned at the same time.—[*Cal. of Charters*, xii, 2685.]

1594 JOHN BELL, M.A., pres. to vicarage of Cadder and Monkland 25th Nov. 1594 on dem. of Michael Chisholme. —[*Reg. Sec. Sig.*, lxvii, 9.]

1650 THOMAS MELVILLE, son of Thomas M., min. of Terregles. Marr. Christian Rae, daugh. of Katherine Inglis.

1882 JOHN BUCHAN ADAM WATT, his widow, Margaret Annie Edith Sprague, died 21st May 1945.

1911 JAMES WOODSIDE ROBINSON, died 21st Aug. 1948.

1929 ALASDAIR ROBERT ELLIS MACINNES, born Tayvallich 4th Oct. 1897, son of Alexander McI., min. of New Liston U.F. Church, and Margaret Ellis; educ. Dingwall Academy and Univ. of Edinburgh; licen. by Presb. of Bathgate (U.F.) 1926, assistant Buenos Ayres 1927; adm. by General Assembly as licentiate 24th May 1928; assistant Mauchline; ord. A. and S. 5th June 1929, dem. 30th Sept. 1941; adm. to Rodney Street, Liverpool, 12th Dec. 1946; dem. 1949. Marr. 8th April 1930 Jane Seton Normansell Kyd, only daugh. of William Ingram, K.C., advocate (divorced for desertion 23rd Oct. 1936).

CAMPSIE

On 6th June 1508 John Stirling of Craigbernard, Kt., founded a perpetual chaplainry at the Altar of the Virgin Mary in a cell or chapel in the church, and in a cell or chapel, also dedicated to the Virgin Mary, within the Place and Manor of Craigbernard, the endowment being 6 merks 10 sh. from the lands of Craigbernard, and 6 merks from the lands of Glorat.—[*Reg. Great Seal*, ii, 3240; *Dioc. Reg. of Glasgow*, ii, 413–14.]

1563 SIR WILLIAM ERSKINE, Knight, parson in 1563, second son of James E. of Little Sauchie, Commendator of Kinloss, Archbishop of Glasgow, a layman, had issue—Robert; Adam; Janet (marr. William, Earl of Stirling); Catherine (marr. 19th Dec. 1594 John, son of John Blair of Westkirk, Culross).—[Stephen's *Inverkeithing and Rosyth*, 528; *Reg. of Deeds*, ix, 103, xix, 194; *Comps. Sub Coll. of Thirds, Stirling*, etc.]

1563 JOHN ARTHUR, reader in 1563.— [*Comps. Sub Coll. of Thirds, Stirling*, etc.]

1574 JOHN STODDART, min.; held the prebend of Castlehill; pres. to vicarage pensionary 20th June 1589 on death of Archibald Douglas. He mortified to the poor of Campsie 40 sh. annual rent from two houses and ½ acre of land at the Kirk of Campsie, the property to be sold and the feu of 40 sh. administered by the min. and elders.—[*Hist. MSS. Commis. Reports*, iii, Duntreith, 113; *Comps. Gen. Coll. of Thirds*; *Reg. Sec. Sig.*, lx, 20.]

1576 ARCHIBALD DOUGLAS, servitor to James, Earl of Morton; his pres. on death of William Kincaid.—[*Reg. Pres. Bene.*, i, (4), 45.]

1578 WILLIAM ERSKINE, marr. Janet Erskine.

1649 ARCHIBALD DENNISTOUN, M.A.; his second wife, Katherine Stirling, with her son, George, a writer's servant, was resident in Tron Parish, Edinburgh, 12th Nov. 1694.—[*Tron Poll Tax Roll*, 11.]

1783 JAMES LAPSIE, pres. 6; line 26, add "pension of £50."

1844 THOMAS MONRO, pres. by Crown 6th Jan. 1844; his son, James Berkeley Stevenson, died at Adelaide, South Australia, 1st Aug. 1923; his daugh., Eliza Alice Stevenson, died 14th May 1934.

1919 ALEXANDER WILSON FINLAYSON, licen. by Presb. of Edinburgh May 1909, died 26th June 1940. Marr. 23rd June 1914 Evelyn Violet Emily, daugh. of James Oliver and Adeline Moubray, and had issue—Evelyn Adeline Margaret, born 3rd June 1917 (marr. 3rd June 1941 Robert Wark Jenkins, R.N. Pay Corps); Marjory Edith Winifred, born 20th Feb. 1926; Geoffrey Beauchamp Alistair Moubray, born 17th July 1934.

CARMUNNOCK

1559 ARCHIBALD HAMILTON, vicar in 1559.—[*Reg. Abbrev. Feu Charters of Church Lands*, i, 81.]

1563 ROBERT KERR, reader 1563.—[*Comps. Sub Coll. of Thirds, Stirling*, etc.]

1568 PETER PATERSON, his pres. in 1568 was consequent upon the dem. of James Hamilton.—[*Reg. Pres. Bene.*, i, 9.]

1585 ANDREW HAMILTON, pres. to vicarage 14th Aug. 1575 on death of William Hamilton.—[*Reg. Pres. Bene.*, i, (4), 38.]

1608 ARCHIBALD GLEN.—[*G. R. Sas.*, xxvii, 37.]

1614 ROBERT GLEN, his wife, Jean Sharp, may have been a daugh. of Patrick Sharp, min. of Govan, for Patrick's son, Mr David Sharp, min. of Kilbride, appears as a witness of Robert Glen's will.—[*Glasgow Test.*, 13th March 1622.]

1633 JAMES HUTCHESON, his son, James, M.A. (Glasgow, 1645).

1650 ANDREW MORTON, line 27, for "1685" read "1683"; son of Andrew M., min. of Lundie.

1692 ANDREW TAIT, his son, William, went to Virginia.—[*Reg. of Deeds, Dal.*, 6th Sept. 1745.]

1744 JOHN KERR, his daugh., Isobel, died 30th Oct. 1788.

1888 GEORGE GREEN GILLAN, his widow, Agnes Wedderburn, died 10th Jan. 1930; his son, Sir Robert Woodburn, died 2nd July 1943.

1913 JOHN SMART, trans. to Carstairs 15th March 1928.

1928 JOHN ANDERSON, born at Millerhill 28th May 1901, son of Thomas A., Wester Millerhill, Dalkeith, and Helen Mathieson; educ. at Newton (Dalkeith), and Broughton, Edinburgh, and Univ. of Edinburgh, M.A. (1923), B.D. (1926); Union Theological Seminary, New York, S.T.M. 1927; licen. by Presb. of Edinburgh 12th May 1926; assistant St Matthews, Edinburgh, 1927–8; ord. 21st Sept. 1928; trans. to Old Monkland 12th Oct. 1938. Marr. 29th July 1929 Dorothy Mary Elizabeth, B.A., daugh. of David Gall Cromb, 14 Eyre Crescent, Edinburgh, and Eleanor Rankin, and has issue—David Mathieson, born 22nd July 1930; twin sons stillborn 12th Sept. 1933; Elspeth Eleanor Margaret, born 4th May 1935; Marjorie Isabel Helen, born 28th June 1939.

CATHCART

A new church, the last in Scotland to be built by the heritors, was opened in June 1929.

GLASGOW] CATHCART—CUMBERNAULD 287

1563 JOHN COLVILLE, reader 1563.—[*Comps. Sub Coll. of Thirds, Stirling*, etc.]

1568 JAMES HILL, line 5, for "1572" read "1571."

1574 JOHN RATTRAY, vicar pensioner.—[*Acts and Dec.*, liv, 229.]

1577 ROBERT HAMILTON, son of James H. of Garyn, pres. in 1577 when reader here, on death of John Rattray. Marr. Isobel, daugh. of James Hamilton of Torrance.—[*House of Hamilton*, 364.]

1652 WILLIAM MUIRCROFT, adm. to Ardstraw, Ireland, 1655; dep. for nonconformity 1661, but continued to minister to 1672.

1788 DAVID DOW, his daugh., Janet, died 21st June 1840.

1896 ARTHUR EUGENE CLAXTON, licen. 1st May 1889.

1910 JOHN ALEXANDER COULL MACKELLAR, D.D. (Glasgow, 22nd June 1938); Convener, Jewish Committee, 1922; Joint Convener 1929–33; his wife, Jessie Kirkwood Semple, died 18th May 1927. Marr. (2) 22nd July 1931 Margaret Stevenson, daugh. of John Anderson and Mary Dunlop. His son, Ian Coull Semple, chartered masseur.

CHRYSTON

1875 WILLIAM DAVIDSON, dem. 4th June 1929; died at Bridge of Weir 9th April 1933; his daugh., Jane Beattie, died 15th Aug. 1929.

(*Charges united 5th March 1950.*)

CONDORRAT

In Oct. 1929 transferred to the Presbytery of Linlithgow and Falkirk.

1920 DONALD MACPHERSON, delete entry, as he did not accept.

1921 CHARLES HEUGHAN, trans. from Hutchesontown (*q.v.*) 7th Dec. 1921; trans. to Carntyne 16th Sept. 1926.

1927 ARCHIBALD MONTGOMERY, trans. from Knoxland (*q.v.*) 24th March 1927; trans. to Buccleuch, Glasgow, 2nd July 1929.

1929 GEORGE MARTIN, born Glasgow 29th March 1899, son of David M. and Jean Lafferty; educ. at Skerry's College, Glasgow, and Univ. of Glasgow; licen. by Presb. of Glasgow 4th June 1929, assistant Barony; ord. and adm. 18th Sept. 1929; trans. to Chapelton 14th Oct. 1936. Marr. 8th Oct. 1929 Christina, daugh. of J. P. Crosbie, and has issue—David Clinton, born 2nd Aug. 1930; James Gordon, born 4th Feb. 1932; Morag Christine, born 25th Dec. 1934.

CUMBERNAULD

The church was repaired in 1810. Within the parish are the ruins of the old Parish Church of Lenzie (Kirkintilloch). There was a chapel at Chapelton on the farm of Achinkill. Transferred to Presb. of Linlithgow and Falkirk Oct. 1929.

1666 GILBERT MUSHET, on account of the opposition of the parishioners he was compelled to "leave home and Church" before 21st Jan. 1692, with "no hope of returning"; and on that date John Paterson, "Bishop of Glasgow," imprisoned in Edinburgh Castle, sent to "All Archbishops, Bishops, Presbyters, and other Clerics of Churches of England and Ireland" a letter commending Mushet in the hope that "he may be admitted to the ministry."—[*Cal. Laing Charters*, 2894.]

1848 HUGH PARK, his son, Sir Maitland, died at Cape Town 15th March 1921.

JOHN OGILVIE, died 7th Dec.
1900 1948.

CUMBERNAULD, EAST

JOHN COCHRANE, had issue—
1839 Georgina Isabella Waddell, born 24th June 1846 (marr. 1st Aug. 1873 William Thomson Henderson, Bo'ness).

EAGLESHAM

HENRY SINCLAIR, Bishop of Ross,
1561 described as parson, vicar and min. in 1561.—[*Comps. Gen. Coll. o, Thirds.*]

ARCHIBALD CRAWFORD, M.A.,
1563 second son of John C. of Crawfordland; secretary and almoner to Mary of Lorraine; app. Lord of Session 26th April 1566, but depr. 2nd June 1568; was parson 12th June 1558, in 1563, and still in office 1580.—[*Acts and Dec.*, xxxiii, 404; xli, 323, 337, 360; *Reg. Abbrev. Feu Charters of Church Lands*, i, 5, ii, 160; *Reg. of Deeds*, iii, 3014, vi, 272, xii, 149.] (See West Kilbride and Kilmaronock.)

ROBERT BROWN, reader 19th Aug.
1580 1580.—[*Edin. Tests.*, viii, 277.]

ANDREW BOYD, M.A. (Glasgow,
1589 1584), natural son of Thomas, first Lord Boyd of Kilmarnock.—[*Reg. of Deeds*, clxxxiii, 176, 15th June 1603.]

JAMES HAMILTON, his sons—
1648 Robert, apprenticed to Archibald Hamilton, merchant, Edinburgh, 13th Jan. 1675; William, apprenticed to John Day, surgeon apothecary, 22nd April 1692.

JOHN HOUSTON, intruded at Lonmay
1685 before 1696, died 1707.

ALEXANDER DOBIE, line 8, for
1786 "Carfin" read "Greenholm"; his son, David, surgeon, H.E.I.C.S.

JAMES BUCHANAN, died 4th Aug.
1881 1924.

DAVID LANGLANDS SEATH, born
1917 Dundee; marr. 12th Aug. 1925 Janet, daugh. of James Gemmell and Agnes Wallace, and has issue—Joyce Gemmell, born 27th Feb. 1926.

GLASGOW
ABBOTSFORD

JAMES McNAUGHT, his wife, Janet
1877 Kinnear Beatson, died 18th June 1876; his daughs.—Jane Helen (marr. P. Nisbet, C.A.), died at Perth 5th June 1921; Elizabeth Barclay Campbell, died at Droitwich 4th Feb. 1932.

ROBERT NELSON, dem. 15th June
1904 1933 on union of Abbotsford with Chalmers (formerly U.F.) Church. Became senior assistant, South Leith, 1st Oct. 1936; his son, Robert Arthur, tweed manufacturer, Earlston.

(*United with Abbotsford-Chalmers 15th June* 1933.)

ANDERSTON
(now Anderston Old)

JOHN LOVE, father a weaver, mother
1800 Margaret Lang. Marr. Janet McKillop, *s.p.*; line 25, add "2 vols. (1929)."

ALEXANDER NEIL SOMERVILLE,
1837 his son, James Ewing, died at Crieff 20th Dec. 1923; his daugh., Eliza (marr. Major-General J. Keir), died 6th Feb. 1921.

JAMES ROBERTSON, his widow,
1904 Anne Gordon, died at Croy 31st Aug. 1944.

ALEXANDER MOFFATT, son of
1920 Alexander M. and Jane McClymont, trans. from St Stephen's, Perth (*q.v.*), 15th June 1920; trans. to Second Charge, Campbeltown, 9th July 1930; dem. 8th May 1945; adm. to Lethnot and Navar 14th Oct. 1945. Marr. Margaret Moffat, daugh. of William Morris, and has issue—Ninian, schoolmaster, born 14th April 1913, died 23rd June 1942; Claire, born 22nd Aug. 1916.

BALSHAGRAY

1909 ANDREW WATT, his wife, Mary Campbell Burns, died 12th March 1937.

1910 ALEXANDER WRIGHT STEVENSON, trans. to Inch 12th March 1925.

1925 PETER CARMICHAEL MILLAR, O.B.E., trans. from Balmerino (*q.v.*) 1st Oct. 1925; trans. to St Nicholas's West, Aberdeen, 27th March 1933; D.D. (Glasgow, 26th June 1945); trans. to Fintray, 2nd Oct. 1947. Marr. 28th April 1926 Ailsa Rose Brown, daugh. of Colonel Ewan Campbell, Edinburgh, and has issue—Peter Carmichael, born 19th Feb. 1927; Jessie, born 9th Dec. 1929.

BARONY

1623 ZACHARY BOYD.—[*G. R. Sas.*, xxv, 85.]

1699 JAMES STIRLING, line 3, for "3000" read "300."

1750 LAWRENCE HILL, p. 394, line 12, for "John" read "James."

1851 NORMAN MACLEOD, his son, William Mackintosh, died at London 30th June 1931; his daughs.—Ann Campbell (Lady Wilson) died at Crieff 13th April 1921; Jane, died at Edinburgh 8th Feb. 1939; Mary Rhoda, died 28th Feb. 1947.

1873 JOHN MARSHALL LANG, pres. by Crown 23rd Sept. 1873.

1911 JOHN WHITE, D.D., born Glasgow 16th Dec. 1867, son of Matthew W., grain merchant, Kilwinning and Partick; educ. at Univ. of Glasgow, M.A. (1891); licen. by Presb. of Dunbarton in 1892; missionary at Drumchapel; ord. to Shettleston 14th March 1893; built churches in Carntyne and Tollcross and a new parish church at Shettleston; trans. to South Leith 27th Sept. 1904; trans. and adm. 7th June 1911; Secretary and afterwards Convener of General Assembly's Committee for Conference on Union with United Free Church; Convener of Business Committee of the General Assembly of the Church, 1926–40; Chairman of the Church and Nation Committee; first President of the Scottish Churches Council; Convener of Special Committee on Teinds and Church Property, leading to legislation in 1925; Convener of Home Mission Committee and afterwards Convener of the Home Board; Convener of the special "Church Extension Committee" 1933; Chaplain to the Forces in France 1914–17; Convener of Church and Nation Committee; Joint Convener of Committee to confer with Representatives of Anglican Church; Commissioner to the Church in Australia and representative to the Church in Tasmania on occasion of its centenary; Chaplain to His Majesty King George V 4th Aug. 1924, to King Edward VII, to King George VI; Chairman of the Church of Scotland Trust; Moderator of the General Assembly 1925; first Moderator of the General Assembly of the United Church Oct. 1929; received Freedom of the City of Edinburgh 1929; D.D. (Glasgow, 1920); LL.D. (Glasgow, 1929); LL.D. (Edinburgh, 1929); D.D. (St Andrews, 28th Sept. 1937); honoured by King George with the Companionship of Honour, C.H., 1936. Marr. (1) 5th Sept. 1893 Margaret (died 20th Sept. 1942), elder daugh. of John Gardner, Muirpark, Partick, and has issue—Matthew Kennedy, born 29th May 1895, Captain Vth Cameronians (Scottish Rifles); John Gardner, born 17th May 1897, Lieut. Vth Cameronians (Scottish Rifles), attached Royal Flying Corps; fell at La Bruyère Ferme, France, 26th Aug. 1917; Lilias Paton, born 8th Feb. 1899 (marr. Captain John K. Tullis Glen, Caldercruix); James Bishop, born 30th July 1901; Margaret Gardner, born 27th July 1903, died 26th Dec. 1914; (2) 24th April 1945 Anne May Calderwood, only daugh. of David Woodside, D.D., min. of Newlands U.F. Church, Glasgow. Publications—*With the Cameronians* (Glasgow, 1917); *Memorandum on Church Properties with a View to Legislation*; *The Church and Reunion in Scotland*; *Efficiency* (Assembly closing address, 1925); *Reunion and its Tasks* (The Union Assembly address, 1929); *Burge Memorial Lecture; Reunion and International Friendship* (1930); *The New World Situation.*

BARROWFIELD
(now St Francis in the East)

1883 ROBERT TURNBULL, his widow, Kate Anderson Smith, died 27th March 1924.

1919 WALTER SHAW, dem. 28th Nov. 1928; died 4th Jan. 1929.

BATTLEFIELD
(now Battlefield West)

1919 CHARLES JAMES DONALDSON, trans. to Riccarton 24th Nov. 1926.

1927 WILLIAM WILSON MORRELL, M.B.E., born Glasgow 11th July 1898, son of David Alexander M., assistant inspector, Glasgow Parish Council, and Eliza Wilson; educ. John Street H.G. School, Glasgow, and Univ. of Glasgow; licen. by Presb. of Glasgow 20th Dec. 1922; assistant Greenhead 1923; Neilston; ord. to Elderslie 17th Sept. 1923; trans. and adm. 7th June 1927; trans. (C. and S.) to Trinity College and Moray-Knox, Edinburgh, 28th Oct. 1936. Marr. 21st Nov. 1923 Grace, daugh. of James Reid and Wilhelmina Liddell, and has issue—Grace Wilhelmina Reid, born 18th Feb. 1928; David William James, born 26th July 1933.

BELLAHOUSTON

1887 JOHN BROWN, his daughs.—Margaret Romanes, died 4th March 1922; Jean, died at Edinburgh 24th Feb. 1929; his widow, Margaret Romanes Rankine, died at Edinburgh 25th Oct. 1943, aged 95.

1919 WILLIAM WHITE ANDERSON, trans. to New Kilpatrick 9th Sept. 1926; line 10, for "Doo" read "Dud."

1927 HENRY COULTER, trans. from Holburn 9th Feb. 1927; his daughs.—Sylvia Lucinda (marr. Robert Duncan Fairbairn, Midland Bank, England); Dorothy Ruth, born 10th Sept. 1924; Marjorie Iona Bride, born 27th Jan. 1929; his son, John Aitken, agricultural student; his daugh., Dorothy Ruth (marr. 15th April 1947 James Gordon, son of Thomas Macpherson, M.P., Great Wagley, Essex.)

STEVEN MEMORIAL, BELLAHOUSTON

1915 ROBERT CHALMERS ANDERSON, dem. 6th July 1923; adm. to Dulnain Bridge 1925; trans. to Culsalmond 15th July 1927; died 25th Nov. 1931.

1925 GEORGE WILLIAM WALKER, trans. from Ceres (*q.v.*) 8th Dec. 1925; trans. to Dailly 28th Nov. 1929; died Ayr 4th May 1946.

BELMONT

1886 JOHN FRASER GRAHAM, died 14th Sept. 1937; his wife, Helen Taylor Thomson Hume, died 29th Sept. 1934; his daughs.—Katherine (marr. (2) 16th July 1930 James John Ainslie); Helen Thomson (marr. Colin Macfarlane, Glasgow), died 17th March 1939.

1919 STUART CRAWFORD PARKER, dem. 28th March 1923; went to St Andrews, Toronto, died 15th Jan. 1950.

1923 WILLIAM LARNOCH TENNYSON LEVACK, trans. from Leuchars (*q.v.*) 9th Oct. 1923; D.D. (Glasgow, 19th June 1929); died 8th Dec. 1935. His son, William Larnoch, min. of Mauritius.

BLACKFRIARS

1636 JOHN BELL, line 2, for "John B., min. of Tron Parish, Glasgow" read "third son of James B., merchant, Glasgow."—[*Burgess Roll*, 23rd March 1633.]

1845 PETER NAPIER, his daugh., Isabel, died Bridge of Allan 13th June 1943.

1865 JAMES MACKAY, his son, Herbert James Hay, died 22nd Jan. 1937.

1873 THOMAS SOMERVILLE, his widow, Agnes Dawson, died at Edinburgh 28th Jan. 1926; his daugh., Agnes Naysmith, died 6th Feb. 1940.

DAVID FRANCIS LIDDLE, died 17th Oct. 1936; had issue—Louise Pinckney, born 29th Nov. 1919; Catherine Fraser, born 4th May 1921.
1916

BLUEVALE

ANDREW MILLER, his widow, Janet Agnes Kirke, died 3rd Nov. 1935; his daugh., Jane Johnstone (marr. 22nd June 1929 Andrew, son of Andrew Yardley, Stafford).
1885

JAMES AITKEN BOAG, served as officer in Royal Scots Fusiliers; Chaplain to Duke Street Prison; died 3rd Nov. 1928.
1919

WALTER DAVIDSON, trans. from Earlston (*q.v.*) 12th June 1929; trans. to Galston (C. and S.) 30th Sept. 1931; trans. to Elie Old 23rd March 1944; has issue—Lorenzo Douglas, M.A., B.Sc., schoolteacher, died 1st July 1933; Frances Mary; William Leslie Beaumont, British Linen Bank; Phyllis Margaret, born 25th July 1918.
1929

BLYTHSWOOD

(*United to St Matthew's* 11*th June* 1920.)

BRIDGEGATE

JOHN STEWART, dem. 28th May 1931, died 17th Dec. 1932; assistant St John's, Glasgow, before 1875; his son, Joseph, died 1st June 1891; his daughs.—Margaret, died 4th May 1890; Elfledamacuaria, died 11th Nov. 1909.
1882

(*United to Hutchinsontown* 28*th May* 1931.)

BRIDGETON

GEORGE SIMPSON, his widow, Rachel Grace Weir Thomson, died at Lesmahagow 26th March 1939.
1852

THOMAS HISLOP, died 11th Jan. 1929.
1877

ALEXANDER LYON BENNET, trans. A. and S. from Bargeddie (*q.v.*) 11th Oct. 1923; trans. to Chryston East 9th Jan. 1930; trans. to Lasswade Old 4th Sept. 1935; died 19th Feb. 1940. Marr. 30th April 1929 Margaret Elizabeth, daugh. of John Findlay.
1923

BUCCLEUCH

JOHN MACKINTOSH, died 12th Oct. 1924; his widow, Eugenie Fairweather, died 21st Oct. 1938.
1912

FRANKLIN ROSS TAYLOR LORNIE, M.A., trans. from Anwoth 26th March 1925; trans. to Fyvie 20th Feb. 1929.
1925

ARCHIBALD MONTGOMERY, educ. at Dalintober and Grammar School, Campbeltown; Royal Bounty Missionary at Cairndow, Argyll, 1908; Darconner Mission, Auchinleck, 1914; ord. to Knoxland 30th March 1916; trans. to Condorrat (*q.v.*) 24th March 1927; trans. 2nd July 1929; dem. 14th Oct. 1945; died 29th June 1947. Marr. 3rd May 1927 Margaret Oliver (died *s.p.* Oct. 1938), daugh. of William Oliver Chisholm.
1929

(*Charge united with St Stephen's* 14*th Oct.* 1945.)

CALTON

The church was transported to a new site within the parish at Newbank, opened 6th Dec. 1935, as part of the scheme for church extension.

JOHN JACK, pres. by Crown 30th Nov. 1861.
1861

JOHN MURRAY, son of Henry M., farmer, and Janet Petrie; pres. by Crown 17th June 1864.
1864

WILLIAM CHALMERS SMITH, died 7th Aug. 1937; his widow, Elizabeth Dorothea Lyness, died 21st May 1944; his children—Dorothea Stewart, died 15th June 1916; George Cruickshank Lyness, engineer; William Courtland Bannatyne, min. of Clousta; Helen Stewart, doctor; Anne Lindsay Stewart, medical student.
1898

CARNTYNE, ST MICHAEL'S

A chapel was built here in 1900 by the Rev. John White, min. of Shettleston, and the parish of Carntyne was disjoined from Shettleston on 14th Jan. 1914.

JAMES STORRY BARROWMAN, trans. to Crosshill, Ayr, 19th Jan. 1926.
1910

CHARLES HEUGHAN, trans. from Condorrat 16th Sept. 1926; trans. to Forth 3rd June 1927.
1926

DONALD JOHNSON, born at Knockbain 13th Aug. 1884, son of Donald Johnson, F.E.I.S., schoolmaster, and Catherine McDonald; educ. Dunskellor P.S., North Uist, and Glasgow High School; Univ. of Glasgow; licen. by Presb. of Glasgow 27th April 1927, assistant Chalmers, Glasgow; ord. 15th Nov. 1927.
1927

CHALMERS

JAMES COLLIER, his widow, Agnes Learmonth Davidson, died 2nd Aug. 1929.
1876

ROBERT JACK, died 16th April 1941. Marr. 28th Oct. 1919 Euphemia Amelia Nightingale, younger daugh. of E. J. Mozart Allan, music publisher, Glasgow, and had issue—Robert, born 21st Sept. 1920; David Allan, born 13th Sept. 1923; Christina McKenzie, born 20th Jan. 1926.
1897

COLSTON WELLPARK

ALEXANDER MACLELLAN, died 14th Oct. 1934; his widow, Isabella Spence, died 11th Dec. 1944.
1904

COWLAIRS

JOHN GIBB DUNCAN, died 28th March 1934; his widow, Catherine Reed Arthur, died 17th Feb. 1946.
1899

DALMARNOCK

JAMES KELLY, had issue—James, born 31st Aug. 1880, Principal of Aitchison (Chief's) College, Lahore, India; Isabella F., born 28th Nov. 1881, teacher of Domestic Science; Margaret S., born 8th March 1883, shorthand typist; Ellie A., born 15th March 1885, Church of Scotland Mission, Madras (marr. S. H. Pugh, M.B., Ch.B., F.R.C.S. (Edin.), London Missionary Society, Neyyoor, Travancore, India); Katherine, born 15th March 1885, Church of Scotland Mission, Madras, now at Arkonam; William A., born 19th March 1888, incapacitated through accident while student at Brasenose College, Oxford; Thomas, born 10th April 1889, engineer, Babcock & Wilcox, London; John Tannahill, born 4th March 1895, student, Glasgow University, killed in action, Ypres 31st July 1917 (25th Machine Gun Corps).
1877

CHARLES WILLIAM KENNEDY, died 8th March 1927.
1900

PETER HILL NICOLL, B.D., formerly of Abbey, Arbroath, and All Saints, Demerara (*q.v.*); adm. 27th Sept. 1927; trans. to Garvock 11th July 1944. Marr. 14th Jan. 1915 Margie Vivien, daugh. of Michael Kennedy, and has issue—Freda Cecilia Jean, medical student, born 23rd Oct. 1915; James, C.A., born 6th July 1917; Ivan Kennedy, C.A., born 14th Jan. 1921. Publication—"Argentine Memories—the Royal Road," *Blackwood's Magazine*, Sept. 1917, Jan. 1918.
1927

DEAN PARK

JAMES THOMAS GRAHAM, his widow, Annalexa Macmaster, died 3rd Aug. 1940; his son, William, min. of Ardersier.
1878

CHARLES SCOTT BURDON, born 3rd Nov. 1862, died 4th March 1930.
1919

JOHN MOREL McWILLIAM, trans. A. and S. from Craigmore (*q.v.*) 17th May 1928; adm. to united charge of St Kiarans and Dean Park 19th Nov. 1931; trans. to Tynron 8th Sept. 1938; had issue—Hester Lowry Douglas, born 14th April 1918 (marr. 9th Aug. 1939 George Patrick Henderson, M.A.). Publications—*The Birds of Bute* (London, 1927); *The Birds of*
1928

the Firth of Clyde (London, 1935), and many papers on ornithology and natural history in *Zoologist, Scottish Naturalist, British Birds*, etc.

(*United to St Kiarans 1st June* 1932.)

ELDER PARK

Parish erected 11th July 1892.

DAVID ORR, his daughs.—Elizabeth Anna (marr. 27th Jan. 1922 Sir John Auld MacTaggart, Bart.); Elinor Liddell (marr. 22nd Jan. 1924 Stuart Phillip McCreadie).
1890

ARCHIBALD GRAHAM STUART, trans. from Ardler (*q.v.*) 19th May 1921, died 24th Jan. 1936; his daugh. Ann Bruce Mackenzie (marr. 21st March 1929 Arthur John de Burgh Persse Hetherington, min. of Melville Church, Montrose).
1821

GARTCOSH

DONALD STEWART MACKENZIE, formerly of Kildrummy, adm. 3rd April 1926; trans. to Aberlour 25th June 1930. His daugh., Muriel, M.B., Ch.B. (marr. 24th June 1948 Benjamin Henry Dawson, M.B., Ch.B.).
1926

GORBALS

WILLIAM ANDERSON, born 30th June 1728, eldest son of John A., tenant in Bickramside of Nether Kinneddar in parish of Saline, Fife; educ. at Univ. of Edinburgh; app. Schoolmaster, Precentor and Session Clerk in the parish of Carnock, Fife, in 1748; licen. by Presb. of Dunfermline 11th Dec. 1760; app. as preacher at Gorbals, Glasgow, in 1770; pres. by Univ. of Glasgow in March, and ord. first min. of the parish 9th May 1771; died 11th Dec. 1792, and buried in Gorbals Burial Ground. He marr. Elizabeth (born 17th April 1723, died 19th April 1795), youngest daugh. of John Stobie, portioner of Wester Luscar in the parish of Carnock, and of Grisel Stobie, and had issue— Grisel, born 24th Dec. 1753 (marr. 15th Feb. 1790 Bailie John Smith), died *s.p.*
1771

5th Feb. 1791; Janet, born 11th April 1755, died 11th April 1851; Margaret, born 22nd Dec. 1757, died 28th Oct. 1784; Elizabeth, born 15th June 1759, died 28th May 1836; John, born 19th March 1761, merchant, Glasgow; William, born 17th Feb. 1765, died 1765; William, born 2nd July 1766, died 1819; surgeon, Glasgow. (*Glasgow Past and Present*, etc.).—[Ex. inform. H. L. Anderson, 18 Rosary Gardens, London, S.W.7.]

JAMES McLEAN, father a flesher.
1793

THOMAS LOGAN DOUGLAS, trans. to Crawford 21st Feb. 1922.
1915

WILLIAM FULTON, ord. 5th Dec. 1922; trans. to Canisbay 18th July 1928.
1922

EDWARD ARTHUR NEIL SINCLAIR, born 23rd June 1894, son of Archibald S., Tiree, and Catherine Mackinnon; educ. Bellahouston Academy, Glasgow; Univ. of Glasgow, M.A. (1919); licen. by Presb. of Lorn, 1920; assistant Wallyford (Inveresk) and Largs, 1921; ord. 29th Nov. 1928; trans. to Cortachy 26th Nov. 1942. Marr. 3rd June 1929 Jane, daugh. of James Campbell, Ayr, and Helen Neil, and has issue—Maureen Campbell, born 20th Jan. 1931; Lorna Jean, born 4th March 1939. Publications— *Legend of Kilchurn*; *Songs of Ivar* (1921).
1928

(*United with John Knox's 30th March* 1943.)

GOVAN

There was in the church a chapel dedicated to the Virgin Mary, of which the parishioners were patrons.

At Polmadie there was a hospital, in existence in the time of Alexander III, 1249–85, dedicated to St John, and, according to a statement in 1453 by Isabel, Countess of Lennox, widow of Murdoch, Duke of Albany and patron of the hospital, "founded and endowed by her predecessors." By Bull of Pope Martin of 12th Jan. 1426-7 the hospital with its attached Church of Strathblane was erected into a prebend of Glasgow. The prebendary had to give 16 merks for the support of four boys to sing in the choir of Glasgow Cathedral, and also had to make provision for a vicar to serve the Church of Strathblane. In 1453 the foresaid Countess of Lennox declared that the hospital was so remote from Lennox that her "predecessors could not conveniently visit and reform it, so that it is neglected and forgotten, and is turned from its original purpose"; and on her petition at that date the Pope decreed that the hospital with its annexes, including the Church of Strathblane, be attached to the Chapel of St Mary of Dunbarton, the future collegiate church of that town, and that in it "shall be observed the same hospitality as has been wont to be observed in the said hospital from the time of its foundation."

In the parish at "the Bridge of Glasgow" there was also a leper hospital, with chapel, founded by Marjory Stewart, daughter of Robert, Duke of Albany, and wife of Sir Duncan Campbell of Lochow, afterwards Lord Campbell, and dedicated to St Ninian the Confessor and Pontiff. For the rebuilding and endowment of the chapel William Stewart, Prebendary of Killearn and Rector of Glasford, by Charter of 31st May 1494 granted a tenement in Glasgow and also various annual rents.—[*Reg. Mag. Sig.*, v, 599; *Cal. of Papal Registers, Letters*, x, 623–4; *Reg. Epis. of Glasgow*, i, Pref., cl, 223, 225; ii, 326–7, 341, 488–90; *Excheq. Rolls*, iv, Pref. clxxxvi; Rymer's *Foedera*, ii, Pt. i, 401, edition 1818; see Dunbarton and Strathblane.]

1560 STEPHEN BEATON, M.A., designated parson and vicar 1563.—[*Comps. Sub Coll. of Thirds, Stirling*, etc.]

1566 THOMAS ARCHIBALD, M.A., parson 1566.—[*Comps. Sub Coll. of Thirds, Stirling*, etc.]

1567 JAMES GIBSON, exhorter 1567 and 1569.—[*Comps. Sub Coll. of Thirds, Stirling*, etc.]

1585 PATRICK SHARP, his daughs.—Mary (marr. Thomas Muir, merchant); Rachel (by second marriage) (marr. Gavin Stewart, min. of Dalmellington).

1650 HUGH BINNING, his widow marr. (2) 30th Aug. 1660.

1688 JOHN PETTIGREW, his daugh., Margaret (marr. Robert McBrayer, merchant, Glasgow).

1875 JOHN MACLEOD, the acknowledged leader of the important movement in doctrine, ritual, and church order of which the Scottish Church Society was a principal exponent; his sons—John Norman, C.M.G., C.I.E., died at Nice 16th Jan. 1932; William Arthur, Canon and Rural Dean of Wakefield, died 8th Nov. 1932.

1913 JOHN McGILCHRIST, licen. 24th April 1894; trans. to Old Machar 23rd Nov. 1923.

1924 GEORGE GORDON DUNDAS STEWART DUNCAN, formerly of St Cuthbert's, Edinburgh (*q.v.*); trans. from St Paul's, Montreal, 13th May 1924; trans. to New Abbey 1st March 1929; died 19th Oct. 1932.

1929 DAVID BRUCE NICOL, M.C., formerly of Skelmorlie (*q.v.*), trans. from St Mark's, Dundee, 5th Sept. 1929; died 23rd March 1930. His son, Thomas James Trail, Chaplain to Forces. Addl. issue—David Wotherspoon, born 19th July 1926; Kenneth Mair, born 11th Dec. 1928.

GOVANHILL
(now Govanhill South)

1875 JOHN MUIR, died 16th Jan. 1931; his widow, Margaret Picken Pollock, daugh. of Robert Sim, Stewarton, died 2nd Feb. 1933.

1916 THOMAS STOBO GLEN, trans. to Dollar 14th Feb. 1929.

1929 WILLIAM DARLING GUTHRIE, born at Leven 23rd Sept. 1900, son of William G. and Janet Baynes; educ. Leven H.G. School, Univ. of St Andrews, M.A. (1922), and Edinburgh; licen. by Presb. of St Andrews 1924;

assistant Kingsbarns 1924; St Matthew's, Edinburgh, 1925; ord. to Thornton 17th Dec. 1925; trans. and adm. 18th June 1929.

GREENHEAD

EDWARD GILLESPIE, born 13th Aug. 1859; ord. to Ardeer Free Church 1909, adm. with his congregation from Free Church by General Assembly 1915; pres. by Presb. of Glasgow *jure develuto*; adm. 28th Sept. 1920; dem. on union with Greenhead East 19th Nov. 1937; died 18th June 1939. Marr. 2nd June 1882 Jane —— and had issue—Margaret C., born 30th Nov. 1883; John M., born 8th Dec. 1887; Agnes A., born 22nd Dec. 1891.
1920

HILLHEAD

DAVID STRONG, died 25th June 1923; his widow, Barbara Jane Hamilton Thomson, died 9th Dec. 1931.
1872

WALTER ROLAND LACEY, M.A. (1895), trans. to Buchanan 11th Sept. 1922.
1914

ALFRED ERNEST WARR, born 29th July 1889, elder son of Alfred W., min. of Rosneath; educ. at Glasgow Academy, Univ. of Edinburgh, M.A. (1911), B.D. (1914); licen. by Presb. of Dunbarton 1914, assistant at Hamilton; served in 16th Royal Scots and as Major taken prisoner at Armentières in April 1918; *locum tenens* High Church, Inverness; ord. to Coldstream 4th Dec. 1919; trans. and adm. 1st March 1923; chaplaincy at Simla and Lahore in India under General Assembly's Overseas Committee 1932–3; trans. to St Mary, Dundee, 8th Nov. 1933; died at London 13th Sept. 1936. Marr. 24th June 1915 Hilda Smallpage, youngest daugh. of John Bayley Lees, Oaklands, Handsworth, and Emilia Smallpage, and had issue— Hilda Nevyth Sheila, born 7th Aug. 1916 (marr. 15th June 1945 Wing Commander George E. B. Christie, O.B.E., R.A.F.V.R.); Jean Audrey Lascelles, born 4th Nov. 1920 (marr. 15th Nov. 1946 Robert Stanley Norim, Fleetwood, Knutsford, Cheshire); Charles Alfred Wellesley, born 21st July 1933, Major, Black Watch.
1923

HUTCHESONTOWN

CHARLES HEUGHAN, trans. to Condorrat 7th Dec. 1921.
1917

DUNCAN MacGILLIVRAY, trans. from Benbecula (*q.v.*) 17th May 1921; dem. 28th May 1931; died 2nd Dec. 1938. Addl. issue—Esther Evelyn, born 14th March 1920; Elizabeth, born 25th April 1923; Agnes, born 7th March 1926; Mary, born 8th Feb. 1929; George Alexander, born 11th Aug. 1936; his sons— Archibald, died 10th Aug. 1895; Alexander, died 10th July 1900; his daugh., Mary Webster, died 8th Feb. 1929.
1921

(*United to Bridgegate 28th May 1931.*)

HYNDLAND

JOHN SERVICE, his widow, Jessie Bayne, died 5th May 1921; his son, John, died 27th March 1943.
1878

HENRY GREY GRAHAM, his widow, Alice Carlyle, died at London 4th April 1928, aged 82.
1884

MATTHEW GARDNER, died at Edinburgh 20th Dec. 1939; his wife, Marion Plumer Semple, died 1st Nov. 1939, aged 77; his daugh., Florence Marguerite (marr. 7th April 1920 William Hugh Hamilton of Cairns Castle, W.S.).
1906

JOHN LAMB, trans. from Fyvie (*q.v.*) A. and S. 3rd Oct. 1923; trans. to Crathie 6th May 1937; M.V.O. (Jan. 1947); Domestic Chaplain to H.M. the King; has issue—Catharine Beatrice Howden, born 23rd Feb. 1915 (marr. 3rd June 1938 George Speirs); John, architect, born 16th June 1917.
1923

KELVINHAUGH

Now incorporated with St Enoch's, Kelvingrove (formerly U.F.), to form St Enoch's, Kelvinhaugh, 8th March 1935.

DONALD MACMILLAN, dem. 3rd Oct. 1923, died at Knapdale, Forest Row, Sussex, 27th March 1927. Addl. publications—*Life of Professor Hastie* (Paisley, 1926); *Representative Men of the Scottish Church* (Edinburgh 1928).
1891

GEORGE MACLEOD DUNN, trans. from West Wemyss 13th March 1924; trans. to St Nicholas, Prestwick, 8th June 1927.
1924

ARCHIBALD BELL, born Aberlour 3rd June 1892, son of Neil Bell and Mary Sinclair; educ. Islay and Kingussie Schools, Univ. of Glasgow, M.A. (1920), and Edinburgh; licen. by Presb. of Edinburgh 1920; app. assistant Northern Suburbs, Beunos Aires, 1921; adm. 1st Nov. 1927; trans. to Broomknoll, Airdrie, 24th Jan. 1933; trans. to Resolis 28th June 1945. Marr. 5th June 1928 Elizabeth, daugh. of James Nicol, and has issue—Elizabeth A., born 2nd April 1929; Mary Sinclair, born 12th March 1931; Aluinn Neil, born 5th June 1934.
1927

KELVINSIDE
(now Kelvinside Old)

JOHN ANDERSON, dem. 10th April 1930, died 21st June 1933. Marr. (1) April 1878 Margait Hamilton (died 23rd June 1879); his wife, Margaret Stevenson Paton, died 22nd Feb. 1927.
1877

ALEXANDER DOUGLAS FRASER, born Glasgow 27th July 1898, son of James Fraser and Helen Steedman Douglas; educ. Albert Road Academy, Glasgow, Univ. of Glasgow, M.A. (1922); licen. by Presb. of Glasgow Dec. 1923; student assistant Govan 1922–3; assistant St Nicholas, Prestwick, 1924, St Andrew's, Glasgow; ord. A. and S. 23rd June 1925; trans. to Skelmorlie 29th Oct. 1929, and to The Park, Glasgow, 3rd March 1938.
1925

KINGSTON

(19th Dec. 1938 united with Union (formerly U.F.) Church.)

JAMES GIBSON, his sons—Robert, born Aug. 1844, died 17th Feb. 1846; John Campbell, born 10th Jan. 1849, died 25th Nov. 1919; his daughs.—Jane Kinnear, born Feb. 1840 (marr. James McNaught, D.D., min. of Abbotsford); Isabella, born 17th April 1842 (marr. Oct. 1889 James Main, M.A.), died 24th Feb. 1913; Elizabeth, born 7th Dec. 1845 (marr. 21st Jan 1881 Rev. George Smith), died 15th Feb. 1891.
1839

JOHN GUNSON, died at Garelochhead 15th June 1926.
1882

JAMES CAMPBELL, trans. to Glencairn 15th May 1922.
1916

JOHN LAURIE FARQUHAR, ord. A. and S. 19th Sept. 1922, trans. to Moffat 5th March 1926.
1922

JOHN TORRENS DOUGHERTY, M.A., born 29th Jan. 1887; ord. 1908; adm. by General Assembly from Presb. Church of Ireland 1915; assistant Dalziel 1920; adm. to Forth 29th June 1921; trans. and adm. 17th Nov. 1926; dem. 19th Dec. 1938; died 12th April 1940.
1926

KINNING PARK

WILLIAM EDGAR, B.A. (1905); B.D. (1908); Ph.D. (Glasgow), 1934; died 28th Jan. 1940; his wife, Rosa Elizabeth Cullen, died 7th Dec. 1933. Publication—*Thesis on Ideas of Life; Religion in Scotland, with special reference to Mediterranean Sources.*
1911

LANGSIDE
(now Langside Old)

JOSEPH McNEILL FRAZER, dem. 2nd June 1926; died at Edinburgh 7th Jan. 1929.
1897

JAMES ANDERSON, born at Springburn, Glasgow, 5th Aug. 1896, son of John Johnston A. and Isabella Cowan; educ. at Hanley High School and Univ. of Glasgow, M.A. (1922), B.D. (1926); licen. by Presb. of Glasgow 1924; student assistant at Queen's Park, Glasgow, 1919–24; assistant at Langside 1924–6; ord. 5th Oct. 1926; trans. to South Leith 17th May 1938; trans. to Brechin Cathedral 30th Sept. 1942. Marr. 5th Feb. 1936 Catherine Wilson, daugh. of David Alexander and Agnes Arbuthnot Porteous.
1926

LAURIESTON

1905 AUGUSTINE WENTWORTH SCUDAMORE FORBES, line 4, for "Dec." read "Sept."

1920 WILLIAM EWART GLADSTONE MILLER, trans. to St Margaret's, Arbroath, 1923.

1924 JOHN YOUNG CLARK, adm. 3rd June 1924; trans. to Inch 23rd Sept. 1926.

1927 THOMAS MILLER McKENDRICK, born 27th March 1871; educ. at South Kennington College, Univ. of Glasgow, Evangelical Hall; licen. Oct. 1896; ord. to E.U. Innerleithen Nov. 1896; trans. to Masson Memorial, Clydebank, Nov. 1900; served in France in war; adm. on probation May 1921; licen. by Presb. of Dunbarton 1922; ord. to Overton 13th Dec. 1922; trans. and adm. 24th Feb. 1927; dem. 12th Nov. 1934; died 31st Dec. 1935. Marr. 30th March 1897 Agnes Macdonald (died 1st March 1921), and had issue— William, born 6th March 1894; Elizabeth, born 16th March 1899; Jemima, born 28th Jan. 1901; James, born 10th April 1904; Thomas George, born 8th March 1906; Agnes Jennie, born 26th May 1908; Ethelwyn, born 22nd Sept. 1912.

MACLEOD

1881 EDWARD WALTERS, line 9, for "May" read "9th June"; his wife, Mary Rue, died 8th Feb. 1937.

1919 FRANCIS GILBERT GEDDES, dem. 31st Oct. 1929 on appointment as Chaplain to the Glasgow Infirmaries; his daugh., Emily Alison Dorothy (marr. 12th July 1935 Neville Gordon Sutton); his son, Francis Lennox, Civil Engineer.

(*United to Brunton March 1930, and to Barony 7th Jan. 1944.*)

MARTYRS

1859 THOMAS GRAHAM, his daugh., Mary Mathers Nairn (marr. Dr William Skinner, Ballindalloch), died 2nd April 1932.

1879 JAMES FORFAR, died 21st Oct. 1931.

1917 ANDREW BURNETT, trans. to New Cumnock 25th Nov. 1926.

1927 JAMES MILLER, trans. from Inverarity 17th May 1927 (*q.v.*); trans. to Orwell 11th April 1935; his daugh., Naomi (marr. 27th March 1943 Captain T. Swinbank, R.A.); his son, Colin Finnie, min. of Auchtergaven.

(*United with Robertson Memorial 3rd June 1945.*)

MARYHILL

1854 JOHN COLVIN, pres. by Crown 26th Nov. 1853.

1859 WILLIAM SPEIRS SHANKS, pres. by Crown 25th May 1859.

1888 JOHN OLIVER, dem. 16th May 1922, died at Edinburgh 3rd Jan. 1925; his widow, Isabella Kellie Dunlop, died at Boscombe 17th Oct. 1942.

1922 PETER COWAN, born Larbert 17th Sept. 1896, son of Alexander C. and Euphemia Muir; educ. Falkirk High School and Univ. of Glasgow, M.A. (1920); licen. by Presb. of Glasgow 1922; assistant New Kilpatrick; ord. 12th Dec. 1922; dem. 30th Sept. 1940; adm. to Raploch, St Mark's, Stirling, 31st Jan 1943. Marr. 17th Jan. 1923 Marion Annie Grice, daugh. of Egbert Piers Sumner, Stony Park, Aberfoyle, and Agnes Yuill Watt, and has issue —Alexander, born 2nd Feb. 1924; Agnes Yuill Watt, born 30th March 1926; Effie Muir and Marion Sumner (twins), born 8th Feb. 1928; Peta Ruth, born 20th Nov. 1934.

MAXWELL

1877 WILLIAM WEIR TULLOCH, his widow, Esther Procter Hamilton Adamson, died at Greystones, Wicklow, 28th Aug. 1929.

1912 ALFRED BROWN, dem. 31st Aug. 1942. Lecturer in Practical Theology 1943 ; McNeill - Fraser, Lecturer 1943-4; Lecturer in Pastoral Theology

(Glasgow, St Andrews and Aberdeen); his wife, Petrina Marion Campbell, died 30th April 1928; Hon. T.C.L. (1940); D.D. (Glasgow, 1944); his daugh., Marion (marr. 29th June 1937 William Ian Gordon, M.B., Ch.B., F.R.C.S., Edinburgh); his son, William died 16th Nov. 1938; Alfred Finlay, M.B., Ch.B., F.R.C.S.E.

MERRYLEA

1919 JOHN MACLAGAN, D.D. (Edinburgh, 8th July 1949); his wife, Mary Chilton Lind Smith, died 12th July 1927; his son, Ian Addison, Lt. 1st Battn. Seaforth Highlanders. Marr. (2) 23rd April 1941 Roberta Helen, widow of Thomas Miller of Auchenheath House, Lanarkshire.

MILTON

1836 JOHN DUNCAN, his daughs.—Annie (marr. ——————— Lochee of St Thomas); Maria (marr. Adolph Spaeth of Philadelphia).

1920 THOMAS ROBERTSON, born Balthayock, Perth, 9th Sept. 1868, son of David R. and Annie Brough; educ. at Kinnoull Public School, Perth Academy, and Univ. of Edinburgh; U.P. College, Edinburgh; licen. by U.P. Presb. of Perth, June 1900; assistant Paterson U.F., Kirkwall, 1902; Cowcaddens U.F., Glasgow, 1903-4; ord. 29th June 1904 to Ashington, Northumberland; trans. to Burnbank U.F., Hamilton, 5th Sept. 1917; adm. 17th Feb. 1920; dem. 25th Jan. 1922; Kirkcowan U.F., 13th Nov. 1922; adm. to Bower U.F. 1927; dem. 30th Sept. 1940. Marr. 9th Aug. 1906 Anne, daugh. of Ebenezer Shepherd and Jean Chalmers, and has issue—Jean Chalmers, born 18th Jan. 1911; Alice Brough, born 7th July 1914.

1922 WILLIAM SERIGHT, ord. 27th June 1922; trans. to Hurlford 28th Feb. 1929.

NEWHALL

1903 JOHN NELSON MACDONALD, dem. 2nd April 1940, died 31st Jan. 1942.

NEWLANDS

1890 GEORGE ALLAN, died 15th Sept. 1930; his widow, Jeanie Walker, died 29th July 1937.

NORTH ALBION STREET CHAPEL

1782 JOHN MACLEOD, younger son of Malcolm M., merchant; his son, John, merchant burgess of Glasgow 22nd Nov. 1811.

OATLANDS

Incorporated with St Bernard's to form Oatlands St Bernard's 28th May, 1932.

1883 ARTHUR WELLESEY WOTHERSPOON, dem. 31st Oct. 1923; died at Edinburgh 15th March 1936.

1924 JOHN THOMSON WOTHERSPOON, born Glasgow 28th April 1897, son of Alex. Baird W. and Ann Thomson; educ. at Whitehill H.G. School, Glasgow, and Univ. of Glasgow; licen. by Presb. of Glasgow, 1923; assistant, St Paul's; ord. 12th Feb. 1924; adm. to united charge of Oatlands and St Bernard's 28th May 1932; trans. to Kinglassie 9th Oct. 1935; dem. 20th Nov. 1948. Marr. 24th July 1935 Evelyn Margaret (died 30th Jan. 1937), daugh. of John Anderson, min. of St Kenneth's, Glasgow, and had issue—Margaret Ann Evelyn, born 6th May 1936; died 30th Jan. 1937. Marr. (2) 18th April 1945 Flora Macdonald Barbour.

PARKHEAD

1905 DUNCAN HUNTER BRODIE, died 23rd Dec. 1930; his widow, Margaret Gibb Gray, died 8th Nov. 1940.

PARTICK

1886 JOHN SMITH, Moderator of General Assembly 1922, died suddenly at a meeting at Glasgow 9th June 1927; his son, John Sydney, died at West Kilbride 27th Sept. 1928; his daugh., Jane Briggs Burns, died 21st April 1919. A distinguished educationist, for many years Chairman of Govan School Board.

JOHN ANTHONY MACRAE, trans. from St John's, Dundee (*q.v.*), 10th Jan. 1928; trans. to Redgorton 30th April 1946. Publication—*For Kirk and King* (Edinburgh, 1911).

1928

ST MARY'S, PARTICK

WILLIAM ROSS, dem. 26th April 1922; died at Dulnain Bridge 8th July 1929.

1893

GEORGE DAVID HENDERSON, trans. from East Parish, Greenock, 30th Nov. 1922; dem. 29th Oct. 1924 on app. to Chair of Church History, Univ. of Aberdeen, 1st Oct. 1924.

1922

SYDNEY HERBERT RUTT WARNES, M.A., born London 18th Sept. 1892, son of Henry George Charles Alexander Rutt W. and Sarah Clara Mary Page; educ. at Giggleswick School and Univ of Glasgow; M.A. (1922); licen. by Presb. of Glasgow 1924; assistant Riccarton 1924; ord. 12th May 1925; trans. to St Francis in the East 22nd Jan. 1930, and to South Church, Buckie, 29th Aug. 1934; dem. 22nd July 1941; Chaplain to Forces 1941; adm. to Creich, Cupar, 16th Aug. 1945. Marr. 15th April 1914 Helen Arthur, daugh. of James A. Hogg, min. of Galston, and has issue—Helen Arthur, born 22nd Feb. 1915; Clara Page, born 4th Nov. 1916; David MacMath Rutt, born 3rd Oct. 1925. Publication—"Scottish Herring Fishing Industry," *Scots Independent*, Nov. 1937.

1925

PLANTATION

JAMES WALLACE, his widow, Christina Macfarlane, died 1st April 1929.

1872

JOHN MAIR HUTCHEON, trans. to Stromness 7th Jan. 1925.

1916

JOHN COOPER, born Cambuslang, 1st April 1886, son of John C. and Isabella McNeil; educ. at Allan Glen's School, Glasgow, and Univ. of Glasgow, M.A. (1916); licen. by Presb. of Glasgow June 1918; assistant at St Andrew's, Glasgow; ord. 23rd June 1923, as Associate Minister of Central Presb. Church, Brooklyn; adm. 12th May 1925. Marr. 8th Jan. 1934 Jenny, daugh. of George Russell Dick Gilchrist and Janet McNaughton Wiseman.

1925

POLLOKSHIELDS

The Mission Chapel in Tradeston was closed before 1911.

THOMAS BROWN WILLIAM NIVEN, his son, Thomas Brown William, died 21st Jan. 1930.

1876

SAMUEL JAMES RAMSAY SIBBALD, D.D. (Aberdeen 1926), extra Chaplain to King Edward VII 1907, Chaplain in Ordinary 1908–10; to King George V 1910–36; to King Edward VIII 1936; and to King George VI 1936; Examiner in Divinity, Univ. of Edinburgh, 1905–8, Aberdeen, 1915–18, and Glasgow 1930–4; Lecturer in Divinity, Univ. of Aberdeen, 1915, and New Testament Language and Literature, Univ. of Glasgow, 1932–3. Marr. 14th July 1898 Elizabeth (died 29th June 1946), daugh. of Henry Farquharson Begg of Tillyfour, and has issue—Samuel James Ramsay; Edward Ramsay.

1918

(*United with Titwood* 15th June, 1941.)

POSSILPARK

WILLIAM McCULLOCH STEVEN, dem. 10th Jan. 1933, died 26th June 1935, unmarr.

1902

QUEEN'S PARK

DONALD MacCORQUODALE, his widow, Elizabeth Colville, died 24th May 1921; his daugh., Eleanora Emma (marr. 22nd June 1921 George Herbert, Bearsden).

1868

ADAM MACKAY, trans. to Huntly 24th July 1924, died 25th Jan. 1931.

1915

DONALD DAVIDSON, trans. from Campbeltown 20th Jan. 1925; trans. to South Leith, Feb. 1928.

1925

JOHN LENNOX HOWAT, trans. from Johnstone (*q.v.*) 7th Sept. 1928; died 26th Aug. 1946. Marr. 5th Aug. 1915 Christina Lennox, daugh. of Alexander Bennie, J.P., and has issue—William Prentice (B.D., Glasgow), ord. C.F. 4th June 1940, min. of Chalmers, Bridge of Allan, 1947, born 21st May 1916; Marie Roberton, born 21st Nov. 1921; Alastair John, born 5th April 1926.
1928

RENFIELD

MICHAEL WILLIS, father a Burgher min.
1839

ROBERTSON MEMORIAL

JOHN POTTER, his widow, Mary Young Thomson, died 13th March 1928.
1892

JAMES ANDERSON, trans. to Ruthven 20th July 1927.
1919

ALEXANDER ANDERSON, trans. from Mains and Strathmartin (*q.v.*) 12th Jan. 1928; dem. 15th May 1929.
1928

(*United with Martyrs 3rd June 1945.*)

ST ANDREW'S

JOHN GEDDES, line 8, for "June" read "Jan."
1832

FREDERICK LOCKHART ROBERTSON, his daugh., Flora Isabella Douglas, died 30th April 1948, aged 85.
1878

JAMES THOMSON, died 19th July 1926; his widow, Anne Dundas Glover, died 14th Nov. 1942.
1894

ARTHUR JOHN HOWISON GIBSON, trans. (A. and S.) from St Stephen's, Inverness (*q.v.*), 18th May 1922; dem. 12th Dec. 1929 on appointment as Secretary of Church and Ministry Department. Addl. issue—Marjorie Waugh, born 6th July 1926.
1922

ST BERNARD'S

ROBERT NICHOLSON THOMSON, dem. 28th May 1931; died 7th March 1940; his widow, Margaret Chisholm, died 22nd Oct. 1944.
1895

(*United with Oatlands 28th May 1931.*)

ST BRIDE'S, PARTICK

JAMES MACKENZIE KIRKPATRICK, trans. to Caddonfoot 9th Dec. 1926.
1897

NORMAN MACLEOD, trans. from Belhaven (*q.v.*), 8th June 1927; died 26th Jan. 1942. Addl. issue—Norman, born 6th Sept. 1920; his daugh., Mary Lyon Campbell (marr. 21st June 1934 Frederick Neville Davidson Kelly, LL.B., S.S.C.).
1926

ST CLEMENT'S

DAVID WATSON, born 7th Nov. 1859; dem. 31st Dec. 1938; died 5th Nov. 1943; his wife, Janet Martin, died 12th Nov. 1932; his son, David Crawford, min. of Lenzie; his daughs.—Florence Jean Crawford (marr. 17th Sept. 1929 Professor William Lillie, M.A., B.D., Murray College, Sialkot); Janetta Martin (marr. Dr Thomas Anderson, Norwich). He was a recognised authority on all matters affecting social welfare, particularly among the depressed and criminal classes. Gunning Lecturer, Univ. of Edinburgh, 1910; Lecturer, Queen's College, Belfast, 1917; Chaplain, Barlinnie Prison, 1910-14; Convener of General Assembly's Committee on Social Work, 1929-35; Founder and President, Scottish Christian Social Union, 1901-38; Chairman, Scottish Council for Women's Trades, 1914-15; Vice-President, Scottish Churches' Council, 1938. Addl. Publications—"Hooliganism" (*Hastings Dictionary of Ethics*); *Chords of Memory* (Edinburgh, 1935); *Memorial of A. D. Ross of Laurieston* (1938).
1886

THOMAS SMITH, trans. A. and S. from Anstruther Easter (*q.v.*) 4th Oct. 1928; dem. 31st May 1942.
1928

ST COLUMBA'S

ALEXANDER McKINNON, trans. to Kilmonivaig 20th Feb. 1925.
1918

JOHN MALCOLM MUNRO, trans. from West St Giles, Edinburgh, 18th June 1925; trans. to Kilmartin 4th Jan. 1928.
1925

ALEXANDER MACDONALD, formerly of Glassary (*q.v.*); trans. from Alloa 6th June 1929; D.D., Glasgow (1944); Moderator of General Assembly May 1948. His sons—William Uist, min. of St Nicolas, Carntyne; Donald Macaulay, M.A., assistant Dunblane Cathedral, min. St Paul's, Milngavie, 1941.

1929

ST CUTHBERT'S

FINLAY McCULLOCH, dem. 28th May 1924; his wife, Anna Taylor, died 10th March 1935; *s.p.*, died 29th Sept. 1949.

1919

JOHN RODERICK MACPHERSON, trans. from Evie 9th Dec. 1924; trans. to Greenknowe 27th March 1928.

1924

SAMUEL IVAN BELL, born Ballynagilly, Omagh, Co. Tyrone, 12th Aug. 1878, son of John Armstrong B. and Catherine Mayne; teacher in Mayne National School, Omagh, Ireland, 1897-9; local preacher; studied Arts and Theology under Wesleyan Conference; student of Free Church 1905; Congregational Hall, 1906-8; Univs. of Aberdeen and Glasgow; min. of Stead Memorial Congregational Church, Newcastle-on-Tyne, 1908; Kilsyth Congregational Church, June 1909 to 1917; Bon Accord Church, Aberdeen, 1917; White Street Congregational Church, Glasgow, July 1924; adm. on probation as licentiate 26th May 1927; assistant at Old Monkland and Kirkintilloch; ord. 11th Sept. 1928; died 23rd Nov. 1936. Marr. 1908 Agnes Janet, daugh. of John Banks, and had issue—Kathleen Lillian Bell, born 5th Dec. 1908 (marr. L. R. Beesly); Raymond McKean, doctor, born 2nd Oct. 1910; Leonard John Armstrong, min. of Laurieknowe (Maxwelton), born 31st Oct. 1912.

1928

ST DAVID'S, RAMSHORN

JOHN MacLAURIN, of the marriage of his daughter with Andrew Craig, surgeon, Glasgow, was born Agnes Craig, who married James Maclehose, writer, Glasgow, and was "Clarinda" of Burns' songs and correspondence.—[*Glasgow Test.*, lxix, No. 28; *Poetical Works of Robert Burns*, 382-3, W. M. Rossetti's Ed.]

1723

JOHN GORDON LORIMER, his son, Alexander Gordon, born 12th July 1843, died 30th May 1845; his daughs.—Joanna Gordon, born 6th May 1845 (marr. 21st July 1875 William Wright), died 9th April 1910; Agatha, born 5th Sept. 1847, died 18th Sept. 1931.

1832

ROBERT DICKSON, his widow, Agnes Smith, died 22nd Aug. 1927; his daugh., Agnes Margaret, died 26th June 1948.

1880

JOHN ARBUCKLE SWAN, wife's mother Helen Buchanan; his son, John Herbert St David, born 7th March 1922; Helen Isobel Sinclair, born 19th Feb. 1927; Donald, Officer, Mercantile Marine (R.N.R.).

1917

ST ENOCH'S

JAMES HENDERSON, his son, Archibald, died 16th April 1927.

1832

ARCHIBALD MACLAREN, died 15th July 1923.

1899

WILLIAM McCAIG WIGHTMAN, D.D. (St Andrews 30th June 1937); trans. from Boharm (*q.v.*) 17th June 1924; dem. 26th Oct. 1927 on app. as Director of Religious Instruction.

1924

(*The decrees erecting parish of 17th July 1782 and 7th June 1820 were annulled and a new parish at Hogganfield erected 12th Jan. 1885 as St Enoch's-Hogganfield; St Enoch's Church was demolished.*)

ARCHIBALD COWAN KENNEDY, trans. from Arbirlot (*q.v.*) 8th May 1928; trans. to Chair of Hebrew, Aberdeen, 16th May 1932; D.D. (Edinburgh, 23rd June 1944).

1928

ST GEORGE'S

JAMES CRAIK, his daughs.—Margaret, died 2nd Feb. 1929; Jane Paterson, died Kensington 1st Aug. 1932; his son, Sir Henry, died 16th March 1927.

1843

1882 GEORGE GIBSON GUNN, his widow, Elizabeth Robertson Kinnoch or Wilson, died 8th July 1928.

1907 DUNCAN ALEXANDER CAMERON REID, Convener of General Assembly's Committee on Chaplains to H.M. Forces, died 16th Sept. 1941.

ST GEORGE'S IN THE FIELDS

1859 THOMAS SLATER, his widow died at Edinburgh 17th Jan. 1921.

1865 PETER SINCLAIR MENZIES. Publication—*Sermons* (1875).

1875 ANDREW LAIDLAW, died 25th Aug. 1921; his widow, Lilias Jane Anderson Dickson, died 15th March 1929.

1922 COLIN MACKAY KERR, trans. from Kettins (*q.v.*) 16th May 1922; dem. 24th Dec. 1925; app. to St Andrew's Church, Halifax, Nova Scotia, 1926.

1926 LESLIE DUNCAN, born at Fyvie 26th April 1886, son of William Duncan, millwright, and Agnes Mackinlay; educ. at Robert Gordon's College, Aberdeen, and Univs. of Aberdeen, M.A.(1909), and Edinburgh; served with Balkan Ex. Force 1916–17; Service Officer, North West Persia; Captain, Cameron Highlanders, 1917–19; licen. by Presb. of Edinburgh April 1919; ord. *locum tenens* Liberton 24th Aug. 1919; adm. to Cockburnspath 28th Sept. 1920; trans. and adm. 17th May 1926; app. Organising Secretary, Foreign Mission Committee, 10th July 1928 and dem. 31st Oct. 1928. Marr. 12th April 1913 Jean, daugh. of Alexander Anderson, schoolmaster, Aberdeen, and Charlotte Cockerill, and has issue—Alastair Robert Campbell, Lecturer in Philosophy, Univ. College, London, born 12th July 1915; Elizabeth Charlotte Mackinlay, student, Univ. of Edinburgh, born 28th July 1920.

1929 JAMES CHALMERS GRANT, born Glasgow 14th March 1903, son of James Grant, M.P.S., and Isabella Smith; educ. at Glasgow High School, Univ. of Glasgow, M.A. (1925), B.D. (1928); licen. by Presb. of Glasgow May 1928; assistant St Mungo's, Glasgow, 1928; ord. 9th April 1929; trans. to Uddingston 19th Oct. 1933; to Queen's Park, St George's, Glasgow, 18th May 1939; trans. to Dunblane Cathedral 26th Sept. 1945. Marr. 31st July 1931 Alexandra Brown, daugh. of David Baird and Martha Brown and has issue—James Gordon, born 5th July 1932; David Norman, born 31st Dec. 1934.

ST GILBERT'S, POLLOKSHIELDS

1916 THOMAS JOHN BUNTING, trans. to St Andrew's, Dundee, 11th Feb. 1942; had issue—Thomas, born 25th died 26th June 1920; Marie, born 13th Dec. 1922; John Smith Gilbert, born 19th Aug. 1927.

(*United with Sherbrooke* 20*th Nov.* 1942.)

ST JAMES

1890 JOHN PARKER, previously min. of South Shields Presbyterian Church.

1910 JOHN DALL GLASS, died 25th Sept. 1924; his eldest son, John Knox.

1925 ROBERT DALY, trans. from Glasford (*q.v.*) 18th March 1925; died 29th Sept. 1948; his son, Allan Sinclair, Lieut. Anti-tank Regiment, Glasgow Yeomanry.

ST JOHN'S

1819 THOMAS CHALMERS, p. 447, line 1, for "23" read "18."

1909 ANDREW JAMES CAMPBELL, D.D. (Glasgow, 31st June 1933), Hastie Lecturer, Univ. of Glasgow, 1924; Depute Clerk of Presb. of Glasgow 27th Feb. 1929; Joint Clerk Oct. 1929; dem. 30th Nov. 1936; trans. to Evie 3rd Dec. 1936; dem. 15th May 1948; Moderator of General Assembly 20th May 1945; his wife, Caroline Cumming, M.A., daugh. of Robert Spence, died 8th Jan. 1924. Marr. (2) 7th March 1927 Anna Mary, M.A., daugh. of William Robertson, Lerwick. Publications—*The Things which cannot be Shaken, a Sermon* (Lerwick, 1914); *Two*

Centuries of the Church of Scotland (Paisley, 1930); *Fifteen Centuries of the Church in Orkney* (Kirkwall, 1938); *Christianity in History* (Bible Class Textbook) (Edinburgh, 1931); *The Story of the Church* (joint author with J. Aulay Steele) (Edinburgh, 1934).

ST KENNETH

1901 GEORGE BELL, died 6th March 1923.

1923 NORMAN MACLEOD WRIGHT, adm. 15th May 1923; trans. to Kilmory, Arran, 23rd Sept. 1926.

1927 JOHN ANDERSON, trans. from Dalry, Galloway (*q.v.*) 18th May 1925; app. Joint Presbytery Clerk 3rd Nov. 1936; D.D. (Aberdeen, 1944); his daugh., Evelyn Margaret (marr. 24th July 1935 John Thomson Wotherspoon, min. of Oatlands), died 30th Jan. 1937.

ST KIARAN'S

1879 DUNCAN MACNAIR CONNELL, his daughs.—Jessie, died 4th Dec. 1937; Laura, died 7th Oct. 1943.

1904 DUNCAN MACLEAN, his three sons, Duncan, Hector and Norman, served with Canadians in Great War.

1919 JOHN MacCALLUM, trans. to Dores 11th April 1924.

1924 ALEXANDER MACDONALD, ord. 5th Aug. 1924; trans. to Ardchattan 20th July 1926.

1928 JOHN McKECHNIE, born 2nd March 1897, son of Donald M. and Katherine McNeill; educ. at Copland Road Academy, Glasgow, Univ. of Glasgow, M.A. (1921), B.D. (1927); M.A. National Univ. of Ireland, M.A. (1937); licen. by Presb. of Glasgow May 1927; assistant at Govan, St George's-in-the-Fields, Linwood, and Paisley Abbey; ord. 17th Jan. 1928; trans. to Newlands East 3rd March 1931. Marr. 25th Nov. 1921 Ailie Muriel Mackenzie, daugh. of William Lucas and Ella Macdonald, and has issue—Donald Kenneth Macdonald, born 11th May 1923; Elizabeth Eilidh, born 10th March 1928; Ailie Muriel Katherine Susanna, born 1941. Publications—*Instructio Pie Vivendi* (Irish Texts Society) (London, 1933); *The Owl Remembers* (Stirling, 1933); *Gaelic without Groans* (Stirling, 1934).

(*United to Dean Park by General Assembly 1st June* 1932.)

ST LUKE'S

1871 DAVID DICKIE, D.D. (Glasgow, 1919), died 12th May 1924.

1922 ALEXANDER MACKENZIE, born Old Deer 27th Nov. 1891; son of Alexander M., Baker, and Laura Elizabeth Mackie; educ. at Old Deer School, Robert Gordon's College, Aberdeen, and Univ. of Aberdeen, M.A. (1914), B.D. (1919); licen. by Presb. of Deer 1919; assistant South Dalziel; ord. A. and S. 24th April 1922; served in R.A.M.C. with the British Expeditionary Force at Salonika 1916-19.

ST MARGARET'S, POLMADIE

1902 FRANCIS DAVID BROUN, dem. 21st Dec. 1927; died at Ayr 17th Aug. 1946.

1928 JOHN BELL, trans. from Rathen (*q.v.*) 23rd April 1928; trans. to Amsterdam 10th May 1936; dem. and joined Scottish Episcopal Church, deacon 1938, curate of St John's Church, Dumfries.

ST MARK'S

1916 MURDOCH LAMONT, trans. to Rothiemurchus 10th Feb. 1925.

1925 JOHN LIVINGSTON, born 30th Nov. 1883, son of John L., engineer, and Mary Duggan; licen. by Presb. of Glasgow May 1923; assistant Barrowfield 1922; ord. 10th June 1925. Marr. 23rd Dec. 1919 Elizabeth, daugh. of James McKenna and Sarah Gillespie; *s.p.*

ST MATTHEW'S

United to Blythswood by Court of Teinds 11th June 1920.

ALEXANDER SPARK, ind. to united charge 29th June 1920. Addl. issue —Margaret Enid Hendry, born 12th March 1924; Alexander Graham Oatt, born 12th Oct. 1926.

1914

ST MARGARET'S, TOLLCROSS

Mission work was begun here in 1898 by the Min. of Shettleston—Rev. John White. A chapel was built shortly thereafter and the parish was disjoined from Shettleston and erected on 25th June 1920.

DAVID ALEXANDER MILLER. Addl. issue—Christian Mary, born 17th May 1921; David Alexander Ramage, born 18th Feb. 1925.

1919

ST MUNGO or HIGH CHURCH

On 31st March 1464 Pope Pius II granted plenary indulgence to people dying within the poor Hospital of St Nicholas the Confessor, in Glasgow, founded near the Episcopal Houses by Andrew Muirhead (de Durrisdeer), Bishop of Glasgow, who "proposes" to endow the hospital and chapel. On 20th June 1506 the Chapel of St Roche, situated "without the north gate" of Glasgow, was described as "founded and about to be built." The founder was Mr Thomas Muirhead, Canon of Glasgow and Prebendary of Stobo, and also Prebendary of Govan, who died before 24th Nov. 1512. On or about 11th June 1511 he founded a chaplainry in the chapel, or church as it was sometimes called. On 18th March 1506-7 there is reference to the lands of the Chapel of St Mungo founded in the Church of the Gallowgate—generally called "St Mungo's Kirk without walls" or "Little St Mungo" in contradistinction to the cathedral.—[*Cal. Papel Reg., Letters*, xi, 662; *Diocesan Reg. of Glasgow*, i, 349, 365, 505, 509, 537, 539.]

HENRY SINCLAIR, Bishop of Ross, held parsonage 1561 and vicarage 1563.—[*Comps. Gen. Coll., and Sub Coll. of Thirds, Stirling*, etc.]

1561

JAMES HAMILTON, M.A., app. reader 1561, still in office 1566-7.—*Privy Council Reg.*, i, 188.]

1561

JOHN HOUSTON, vicar 1563 and 1566.—[*Comps. Sub Coll. of Thirds, Stirling*, etc.]

1563

DAVID WEMYSS, M.A., designated parson 8th June 1581; his pres. in 1601 was on dem. of Archibald Douglas; his son, William, advocate and commissary of St Andrews, father of David, min. of Scone.—[*Cal. of Charters*, xi, 2588; *Reg. Sec. Sig.*, lxxii, 187; *Gen. Reg. of Sas.*, 1 Ser., xix, 336, xxviii, 317.]

1565

ALEXANDER LAUDER, M.A., parson 5th Oct. 1566, on which date he was charged by the Privy Council to furnish bread and wine for Communion "conforme to use and wont"; Henry (Sinclair), Bishop of Ross, last parson, had furnished the same "sen the Reformation of religion within this realme"; Lauder died before 20th Aug. 1571.—[*Reg. Privy Council*, i, 492; *Reg. Pres. to Benefs.*, i, (2), 19.]

1566

ARCHIBALD DOUGLAS, his pres. in 1571 was on death of Alexander Lauder.—[*Reg. Pres. Bene.*, i, (2), 19; *Cal. of Charters*, xi, 2395.]

1571

ROBERT BOYD, son of James B. of Hutterhill; pres. to vicarage pensionary 2nd Sept. 1571 on dem. of David Wemyss.—[*Reg. Pres. Bene.*, i, (2), 20.]

1571

JOHN ALLANSON, M.A., reader 1603.—[*Comps. Surplus of Thirds.*]

1603

ROBERT SCOTT, his eldest son, John.—[*Reg. of Deeds*, 492-142, 1629.]

1616

ST MUNGO'S NORTH

ADAM GORDON, line 1, for "Adam" read "James."

1680

ST MUNGO'S EAST

JOHN GLENDIE.—[*Books of Council and Session*, 6th Sept. 1676, 4th Oct. 1678, 8th Jan. 1672; Inventory of Fordel Writs.]

1664

ST MUNGO'S WEST

ROBERT CRAIGHEAD, for "1690"
1689 read "1689."

ST MUNGO'S SOUTH

ALEXANDER LAUDER, parson 1567.
1657 —[*Acts and Dec.*, xl, 299; xlii, 401; xliv, 141, 222, 424; xlvii, 93, 170.]

ROBERT SCOTT, his eldest son, John.
1616 —[*Reg. of Deeds*, dxcii.]

JAMES DURHAM, son of Sir James
1651 D.; his daugh., Grizell, bapt. 31st Dec. 1644; line 17, for "1st May" read "30th April."

WILLIAM TAYLOR, marr. Anne,
1780 daugh. of Matthew Stewart and Jean Galt Arnot of Lochrig, Stewarton.

JOHN ROBERTSON, pres. by Crown
1858 25th Jan. 1858.

GEORGE STEWART BURNS, pres.
1865 by Crown 13th March 1865.

PEARSON McADAM MUIR, died at
1896 Manse of Cambuslang West 13th July 1924; his son, John Joseph Johnston, died at Aberdeen 28th Oct. 1945.

JAMES McGIBBON, died 16th Nov.
1919 1922.

LAUCHLAN MacLEAN WATT, born
1923 Grantown 24th Oct. 1867, son of Andrew and Margaret Gillanders M. W. (Skye); educ. various parish schools and Edinburgh Univ., M.A. (1893), B.D. (1897), D.D., Edin. (1920), LL.D., Glas. (21st June 1933), F.R.S.E., F.S.A. (Scot.); J.P. of the County of the City of Glasgow; missionary, Lochcarron, 1894; Mission Church, Lochinver, 1895; Church work, Dalkeith, 1896; licen. by Presb. of Dalkeith 1896; assistant, Lady Glenorchy's Parish Church, 1896; ord. to Turriff Parish 7th April 1897; Alloa and Tullibody 12th May 1901; St Stephen's, Edinburgh, 16th Feb. 1911; Glasgow Cathedral 26th June 1923; Moderator of General Assembly 1933; retired 15th May 1934 to Kinloch, Lochcarron, Ross-shire. In Iceland representing *The Times, Scotsman, Manchester Guardian* and *Daily Graphic* during visit of the King of Denmark, 1907; Chaplain, Great War, 1914-17, retired Hon. Lt.-Col.; Commissioner from H.M. Gov. to U.S.A. and Canada 1918; President, Pan-Celtic Congress, London, 1930; Grand Chaplain, Grand Lodge of Scotland, 1933; Murtle Lecturer, Aberdeen Univ.; Warrack Lecturer and McNeil Frazer Lecturer on Pastoral Theology, Univs. of Glasgow, Edinburgh and St Andrews, 1930; in Australia as Turnbull Preacher, Melbourne, and visited churches and colleges in Victoria, New South Wales and New Zealand, 1932; created Bard at Welsh Eisteddfod, Amonsford—title "Gwylan yr Ynys" ("Seagull of the Islands"). Marr. 8th June 1897 Jennie Hall (died 8th March 1927), daugh. of John A. Reid of New Kelso, Strathcarron, and had issue—Hector, B.A. (Oxon), Order of the Nile, Sudan Political Service (marr. Gwynydd, granddaugh. of Chief Justice Sir Wm. Grantham, died at Khartoum 9th June 1943). Publications—*God's Altar Stairs; The Communion Table; By Still Waters; Prayers for Public Worship; The Saviour of Men; The Minister's Manual; Gates of Prayer; The Soldier's Friend; Life and Religion*; (Verse) *The Tryst, a Book of the Soul; In Poet's Corner; In Love's Garden; The Grey Mother and Songs of Empire; The Land of Memory; Britannia's Answer;* (Fiction) *Edragil 1745; Moran of Kildally; The House of Sands; The Advocate's Wig; By the Christmas Fire; Oscar;* (History) *Scottish Life and Poetry; Burns; Carlyle; Great Britain, for Schools*—1714-1914; *Alloa and Tullibody; In the Land of War; In France and Flanders with the Fighting Men; The Heart of a Soldier; Scottish Covenanters;* (General) *Attic and Elizabethan Tragedy; Douglas's Aeneid; The Scottish Ballads and Ballad-Writing; The Book of the Beloved; While the Candle Burns; The Minister's Life and Work (Pastoral Theology Lectures); Literature and Life.* Edited the *Dunedin Magazine*. Smith's *Summer in Skye*, Mrs. Stowe's *Dred*, etc. Contributor to *Spectator, Westminster Gazette, St James's Gazette, Scribner's Magazine, Chambers's Journal, Temple Dictionary of the Bible* and leading

newspapers and magazines in prose and verse, on folklore, antiquities and history, especially Celtic and Gaelic.

ST NINIAN'S

1877 JAMES BRYCE, his daugh., Margaret Williamson (marr. 25th July 1895 Alec Leiper Mackay); his son, John, died 16th Aug. 1935; his daugh., Leggat Watson (marr. Alan Cant, min. of Creich).

1887 WILLIAM SEATH PROVAND, Hastie Lecturer, Univ. of Glasgow, 1914; Depute Clerk of Presb. 30th April 1919 to 1st Oct. 1929; Clerk of Synod of Glasgow and Ayr 14th April 1924, res. 8th Oct. 1929; dem. his charge 31st Dec. 1923; D.D. (Glasgow, 24th June 1925); died 12th June 1943; his son, Ninian, electrical engineer, born 2nd Dec. 1897. Publication —*Puritanism in the Scottish Church* (Paisley 1923); Editor *St Andrew*, 1903–6.

1924 JOHN BAYNE, ord. 8th April 1924; trans. to Dunlop 14th Feb. 1929.

1929 ALEXANDER McCLYMONT ADAMS, trans. from Sauchie (*q.v.*) 11th June 1929; dem. 12th; adm. to Arngask 26th June 1934; trans. to Aberdour, Deer, 26th Nov. 1936.

(*Incorporated* 23rd Nov. 1934 *with Wynd* (*formerly U.F.*) *to form St Ninian's Wynd.*)

ST PAUL'S
(now St Paul's Outer High)

1691 ALEXANDER HASTIE, in the company of the Earl of Argyle he landed from Holland at Campbeltown on 20th May 1685 and preached in the church there four days later; he returned to Holland before 2nd Jan. 1686, and after visiting various places, including Rotterdam, Delft, Leyden, Utrecht and Haarlem, he came back to Scotland soon after 8th Jan. 1687; had issue—Alison.—[Erskine of Carnock's *Journal*, 110, 119, 172, 185, 189, 196, 219; *Deeds, Durie*, 1705, No. 1205.]

1713 JOHN SCOTT, marr. Grizel Kid.

1844 ROBERT JAMIESON, his son, William Andrew, died 12th Jan. 1935.

1913 GORDON QUIG, trans. to Monifieth 28th Sept. 1921.

1922 CHARLES MACKINNON, M.A., trans. from Dundyvan (*q.v.*) 8th March 1922; died 15th June 1940.

Collegiate Ministers

1656 ROBERT McCUARD, born Glenluce. His letter to my Lord Warriston in Prison in Edinburgh in Assembly Library, 1662.

ST PETER'S

1886 MALCOLM MACLELLAN, died 15th June 1921; his widow, Jane Emily Robinson, died at London 11th April 1929.

1921 JOHN FAIRLIE, trans. from Inverkeithney 16th Dec. 1921; trans. to Wallacetown, Dundee, 18th May 1931. Addl. issue—Andrew Addison, born 6th March 1925.

ST STEPHEN'S

1892 JAMES BELL GRANT, dem. 30th Sept. 1922, died Edinburgh 22nd March 1943.

1923 THOMAS WYLIE SHARP, born Glasgow 30th April 1893, son of Robert S. and Mary Auld Wylie; educ. at Woodside School, Glasgow, and Univ. of Glasgow, M.A. (1914); licen. by Presb. of Glasgow 1920; assistant St Ninian's, Glasgow, 1920, Springburn 1921; ord. 20th Feb. 1923; trans. to St Machan's, Larkhall, 10th Sept. 1930, to High Ch., Paisley (C. and S.), 16th Sept. 1937. Marr. 9th June 1925 Janet Fulton, daugh. of Thomas Rodger and Jessie Leckie, and has issue— Jessie Leckie, born 1st Nov. 1926; Robert Wylie, born 24th Oct. 1930. Publication— *The Centenary Book, Larkhall*, 1935.

(*United with Buccleuch* 14th Oct. 1943.)

ST THOMAS
(CHAPEL OF EASE)

Retained by Free Church in 1843, afterwards sold to Wesleyan Methodist Church and now used by them.

ST THOMAS

ANDREW BRYSON, dem. 3rd March 1938; died at Prestwick 10th Nov. 1940.
1920

(*United 3rd March 1938 with Gallowgate (U.F.) Church.*)

ST VINCENT

Incorporated 1934 with Kent Road (formerly U.F.) Church, to form Kent Road-St Vincent's.

JAMES BELL HENDERSON, licen. by Presb. of Edinburgh 18th May 1886.
1899

THOMAS SMITH MACPHERSON, trans. to Highland Charge, Campbeltown, 23rd Dec. 1925.
1916

JOHN AULAY STEELE, trans. from Mannofield (*q.v.*) 17th June 1926; trans. to Lerwick 11th April 1934; dem. 12th Jan. 1944; adm. to Cleish 4th July 1945.
1926

SANDYFORD

Incorporated with Henderson Memorial (formerly U.F.) Church to form Sandyford-Henderson Memorial 8th June 1938.

JOHN ROSS MACDUFF, his first wife, Annie Joan Seton, died 1st Sept. 1847 and had issue—Alexander Ross, born 27th Jan. 1845.
1855

JAMES ELDER CUMMING, his daughs.—Janet Parker, died 27th April 1925; Ella Stead, died at St Andrews 5th Dec. 1930.
1871

WILLIAM STEVENSON STUART, trans. to East Church, Stirling, 6th June 1923.
1903

JAMES PITT WATSON, trans. from Dalmuir 18th Dec. 1923; trans. to Alloa 12th Sept. 1929.
1923

SPRINGBURN

DAVID ANDREW ROLLO, his widow, Lizzie McConachie, died 25th Dec. 1943.
1907

DUGALD CLARK, assist. West Church, Aberdeen, 1900–1; died 24th Nov. 1925.
1918

JOHN STUART CAMERON, trans. from St Clement's, Aberdeen (*q.v.*) 17th May 1926; dem. 1936 to become min. of Malone Presbyterian Church, Belfast, 6th Oct. 1936.
1926

DENNISTOUN

ROBERT WALKER MUIR, first min. of parish on erection, 19th March 1920; trans. to Stewart Church, Whiting Bay, 8th Feb. 1933; died 24th June 1941; Lily Craig, first wife, died 17th Nov. 1917, leaving issue—James Laurence, in Manchester; Campbell Craig, clerk; Ruby Walker (marr. 1st July 1937 Hugh McKenzie, M.A., teacher); Norman Dennistoun, ship's sick berth attendant; marr. (2) 10th Sept. 1919 Martha Cameron, daugh. of James McMunn and Agnes Scouler; she re-marr. 18th Dec. 1945.
1908

STRATHBUNGO

ROBERT McMILLAN, died 1st July 1920.
1876

CHARLES GUTHRIE COOPER, trans. to Hawick Wilton 17th May 1926.
1917

JOHN MACLAINE MUNRO, trans. from Ferryport on Craig (*q.v.*) 16th Nov. 1926; issue—Catherine Livingston, born 7th Sept. 1925; served with R.A.M.C. and Argyll and Sutherland Highlanders at Salonica in Great War. Publication—*Strathbungo and its Church, 1833–1933*.
1926

THE PARK

DONALD MACLEOD, his widow, Isabella Anderson, died at Caputh 7th Oct. 1923.
1869

JAMES ALAN CAMERON MURRAY, Chaplain to the Forces, 15th and 51st Divisions, 1917–18; marr. Ellen, only daugh. of Sir John Mackintosh Macleod, Bart., M.P., C.A., Glasgow, and
1915

Edith Fielden; dem. 2nd Feb. 1932; adm. to Kerse 31st May 1935; trans. to Tolbooth, Edinburgh, 15th Oct. 1943. Issue—Ellen Catriona Cameron, born 3rd Feb. 1922 (marr. 22nd Sept. 1942 Rev. Lumir Soukup, Ph.D., Prague); Alan Norman Macleod, born 30th Nov. 1925. Publication—*Introduction to Christian Psycho Therapy* (Edinburgh, 1938).

ST OSWALD'S WOODSIDE

Erected as Woodside Parish by Court of Teinds 1921.

1877 DAVID WATSON, died 12th Feb. 1934.

1922 JOHN MITCHELL KERR, adm. first min. of parish 28th Jan. 1922; trans. to Whiting Bay 27th May 1942. Marr. 29th Nov. 1922 Isabella Black, daugh. of John Morrison; his daugh., Jessie, died 31st July 1933.

TITWOOD

1918 DAVID PRESTON, Convener of Colonial and Continental Committee, 1935.

(*United with St Kentigern's 15th June 1941.*)

TOWNHEAD

1879 ROBERT PRYDE, died at Morebattle 11th Jan. 1925; his wife, Margaret Drysdale, died 9th Jan. 1924; his daugh., Crichton Jane Isobel (marr. W. Weir Breen, Newport).

1915 ROBERT LOVE HUNTER, trans. to Kirkgunzeon 15th Jan. 1926.

1926 CHARLES WHITEHEAD HUTCHESON, trans. from Aberfeldy (*q.v.*) 17th May 1926; dem. 16th May 1935; died 17th Sept. 1935; his widow, Isabella Martin, died 31st May 1946.

TRON

1594 JOHN BELL, line 17, delete "John, Min. of Blackfriars, Glasgow."

1628 JOHN BELL, delete parentage.

1644 HEW BLAIR, line 9, for "1657" read "1651."

1730 JOHN ANDERSON, marr. (2) Marion, daugh. of Walter Menzies, min. of Erskine.

1833 ROBERT BUCHANAN, his daugh., Charlotte Elizabeth, died 29th March 1932.

1903 WILLIAM RATTRAY, died 29th Nov. 1942; his daugh., Catherine (marr. 1925 John Boyd, Trinidad); his widow, Catherine Stevenson, died 1st Aug. 1947.

WHITEINCH

Disjoined 1875, not 1865.

1872 QUINTIN JOHNSTON, assistant at Duffus 1857.

1894 DONALD NESS, trans. to Savoch 16th Aug. 1928.

1928 WILSON SIMMS LESLIE, trans. from Macduff (*q.v.*) 13th Dec. 1928; trans. to Falkirk Old 22nd Nov. 1940.

WILTON

1912 JOHN LIVINGSTON, trans. to Teviothead 12th Nov. 1929. Addl. issue—Stewart Kennedy, born 18th Jan. 1919; Robert H. D. (third son), now a C.A.; his wife, Janet Brackenridge Mary McCallum, died 26th April 1948.

HOGGANFIELD

1887 JOHN FERGUSON ANDISON, died 18th Jan. 1938.

KILSYTH

1560 ALEXANDER LIVINGSTON, parson before 1560 and 18th May 1584.—[*Cal. of Charters*, xii, 2728; *Reg. Abbrev. Feu Charters of Church Lands*, i, 105.]

1568 SIR GILBERT LAW, parson and vicar 1568–72.—[*Comps. Sub Coll. of Thirds, Dumfries*, etc.]

ARCHIBALD GRAHAME.—[*G. R. Sas.*, 2 Ser., vii, 259.] — 1615

GABRIEL CUNYNGHAME, son of William C. of Craigends and Elizabeth Napier.—[*G. R. Sas.*, 2 Ser., vii, 332, vi, 156.] — 1637

JAMES HAY, his daugh., Marian (marr. James Anderson of Dowhill, provost of Glasgow.) — 1682

ROBERT RENNIE, pres. 13th June 1789. — 1789

HENRY DOUGLAS, pres. by Crown 14th July 1843. — 1843

ALEXANDER HILL, pres. by Crown 29th Aug. 1849. — 1849

ALEXANDER SPIERS, pres. by Crown 29th Nov. 1860. — 1861

ROBERT HOPE BROWN, pres. by Crown 25th March 1871; his widow, Agnes (died 11th Aug. 1923), only child of Adam Duncanson, bank agent, Enniskillen. — 1871

PETER ANTON, his widow, Mary Alice Heggie, died 3rd July 1927; his daugh., Florence Heggie (marr. 19th Jan. 1920 Sir Thomas Guthrie Russell, K.C.B., K.C.). — 1881

DUNCAN CAMERON, app. Assistant Clerk of Assembly May 1928; died 30th July 1929; his son, Donald Ewen, M.B., Ch.B.; his daugh., Aileen Isabel (marr. 7th Oct. 1930 Dr William McC. Harrowes, Glasgow). — 1912

KIRKINTILLOCH

Before 1195 William, son of Thorald, Sheriff of Stirling, gave the Church of "Kirkintulach" to Cambuskenneth Abbey. The grant was confirmed by Alexander II 27th March 1226-7. On 23rd July 1451 Robert Fleming of Biggar founded a chaplainry at the High Altar of St Ninian's Church of Kirkintilloch, alias Lenzie, the endowment being the 10 merk lands of Auchinrivoch in the lordship of Auchtyrmoyne in Stirling, 6 merks annual rent from the lands of Panmure in Forfar, 2 merks from the lands of Kirkintilloch, and a tenement in Kirkintilloch. It will be noted that at that date Lenzie appears as an alternative name to Kirkintilloch; and in 1530 the church is designated St Ninian's Church of Lenzie. There was also in the church an altar dedicated to the Virgin Mary. In 1621 the Earl of Wigton and the parishioners petitioned Parliament for licence to transport the church from the west end of the parish to the middle of it; but at that time nothing was done. The church, however, was included in Cumbernauld when that parish was erected in 1649; and thus it lost its parochial status. The church has disappeared. Its precincts, situated in the churchyard, are designated "The Old Aisle." By Charter, confirmed by Robert III on 17th Aug. 1399, David Fleming, Lord of Biggar, mortified to the Chapel of the Virgin Mary at Kirkintilloch his whole lands of Drumtieblae in Lenzie. On the site of the chapel there was built in 1644 a church which became the church of the parish of Kirkintilloch five years later. Alterations were made to the church in the early part of the 19th century, when galleries were introduced; but it is still a good example of a 17th century attempt to revive the Gothic tradition in architecture. It stands in the old churchyard, on the line of the Roman fortifications.—[*Reg. Epis. of Glasgow*, ii, 309; *Diocesan Reg. of Glasgow*, ii, 406-7, 421; *Acts Scott. Parl.*, iv, 607*b*; *Reg. Pres. to Benefs.*, i, 68; *Chart of Cambuskenneth*, 175-6, 195; *Charter Chest of the Earl of Wigton*, Nos. 12, 13, *Scott. Rec. Society*.]

ALEXANDER DRYSDALE, M.A., vicar 1568-72.—[*Comps. Sub Coll. of Thirds, Dumfries*, etc.] — 1568

NINIAN DREW, M.A., min. in 1589; pres. to vicarage 29th Sept. 1594 on death of Richard Herbertson.—[*Reg. Sec. Sig.*, lxvi, 217; *Comps. Gen. Coll. of Thirds.*] — 1574

JOHN FORSYTH.—[*G. R. Sas.*, xx, f. 1, 2 Ser., ii, 25.] — 1620

ROBERT FLEMING OF BALLOCH, his sons—Charles, apprenticed to Alexander Murray, merchant, Edinburgh, 18th Feb. 1708; Robert, apprenticed to Andrew Simpson, sometime min. at Kirkinner, 8th Feb. 1710, afterwards bookseller and printer, Edinburgh.—[*Edin. App. Roll.*]
1681

SAMUEL TELFER, his son, John, apprenticed to William Carmichael, merchant, Edinburgh, 4th Sept. 1728.
1709

THOMAS ANGUS MORRISON, died 21st June 1941; his daughs.—Janet Galloway Angus (marr. (1) 7th Sept. 1921 Arthur Poole, M.B., Ch.B., Manchester; (2) 21st April 1934 Rev. John Whitehead Cheshire, B.A., C.F., Rector of Utrecht, Natal); Mary Bethia Galloway (marr. 9th April 1937 Robert McInnes, advocate).
1893

KIRKINTILLOCH ST DAVID'S

FRANK ROBERTSON, trans. to Monquhitter 6th June 1924.
1919

DAVID FYFE McMATH, M.C., trans. from Sorn (*q.v.*) 15th Oct. 1924. Addl. issue—Margaret Cargill, born 4th April 1922.
1924

TEWCHAR

Disjoined from Kirkintilloch and erected Jan. 1922.

WILLIAM DEANS, died at Alexandria, Egypt, 11th Nov. 1934; his wife, Minnie Scott, died 8th Jan. 1930. He marr. (2) 5th Sept. 1933 Nurse Agnes Daffa, Jaffa, Palestine; she died at Hamburg 8th June 1935; his daugh., Minnie Hunter, died 30th Oct. 1922.
1911

THOMAS MURRAY INGLIS, trans. to Quarter 14th Sept. 1920.
1917

THOMAS JAMES CAMPBELL CRAWFORD, ord. 15th May 1922; trans. to Helensburgh 10th Nov. 1926.
1922

ROBERTSON McCALLUM MILLAR, trans. from Ladyburn, Greenock, 7th April 1927; dem. 30th Oct. 1928; adm. to Stronsay 6th Feb. 1929.
1927

GORDON MILNE EWAN, born Glasgow 30th May 1896, son of James Gordon E. and Kate Nelson Twaddle; educ. Albert Road Academy, Glasgow, and Univ. of Glasgow; licen. by Presb. of Glasgow 26th March 1924; assistant Campsie 1924; ord. to Forgandenny 17th May 1926; trans. and adm. here 12th June 1929; trans. to St Peter's, Glasgow, 2nd May 1939. Marr. 17th Sept. 1929 Annie Mitchell, daugh. of Daniel Duncan and Anne Mitchell, and has issue—Audrey Mitchell Duncan, born 10th Aug. 1930.
1929

LENZIE (now Lenzie Old)

WILLIAM BROWNLIE, dem. 30th June 1926; died 1st Jan. 1933; originally a teacher at Castle Douglas and Dundonald; his widow, Isabella Anderson Simpson, died 23rd Aug. 1946.
1891

DAVID CRAWFORD WATSON, trans. from High Kirk, Kilmarnock (*q.v.*), 19th Jan. 1927; dem. 31st Dec. 1948. Addl. issue—David George Martin, born 29th July 1923; his daugh., Lorna Martin Turnbull (marr. 10th Aug. 1943 Fred Young, son of Rev. Alexander Frazer). Wife's name—for "Mary" read "May, daugh. of George Turnbull, shipowner, and Janet Govan."
1927

RUTHERGLEN

There were in the church Altars of the Holy Rood and St Nicholas.—[*Reg. Sec. Sig.*, 1, 67.]

THOMAS INCH, exhorter, 1563 and 1568, called min. 1569.—[*Comps. Sub Coll. of Thirds, Stirling*, etc.]
1563

JOHN MUIRHEAD, his pres. in 1586 was on death of Robert Herbertson. —[*Reg. Pres. Bene.*, i, 75.]
1586

ROBERT YOUNG, son of a burgess of Glasgow.—*Burgess Roll*, 27th May 1643.]
1611

JOHN DICKSON.—[*G. R. Sas.*, 2 Ser., 188.]
1635

HEW BLAIR, M.A. It may have been his widow, Ann Blair, and her children, Jean and Marjorie, resident in the Canongate, Edinburgh, 14th Nov. 1694.—[*Canongate Poll Tax Book*.]
1642

JAMES FURLONG, father a merchant.
1780

WILLIAM FERRIE STEVENSON, his widow, Anne Paterson, died 20th Nov. 1921.
1862

GEORGE SIMPSON YUILLE, died 20th May 1932.
1909

WALLACE NEWMAN JAMES, born Welshpool, Montgomery, 7th Nov. 1877, son of Thomas J. and Julia Elvina Keeling; educ. at Stonehouse School and Collegiate Academy, Welshpool, Didsbury Theological College (affiliated to Univ. of Manchester); entered as candidate for Wesleyan Ministry 1900; ord. in Wesleyan Church 1907; held the following charges — Hamstreet, Ashford, Kent; Thrapston, Northants; Kettering, do.; Burnley, Lancashire; St John's Wesleyan, Glasgow (12 years); adm. by General Assembly, 24th May 1928; licen. by Presb. of Glasgow June 1927; assistant Barony; ord. A. and S. 12th Dec. 1928; trans. to St George's in the Fields, Glasgow, 16th May 1934; died 8th Aug. 1946. Marr. 1st Aug. 1916 Lilian, daugh. of Thomas Andrew Hayward and Jennie Hamar. Publications —Contributions to *Scottish Pulpit*.
1928

RUTHERGLEN WEST

WILLIAM VALLANCE, died 17th Jan. 1923.
1896

ANDREW VEITCH, trans. to East Church, Tarbert, 15th Sept. 1937; dem. 15th May 1945; has issue— Thomas, born 10th July 1912, M.A. Glasgow, student of Divinity, assistant (student) at Kirkintilloch.
1917

SHETTLESTON

Was disjoined from the Barony; a new church was built and opened during the ministry of Rev. John White, 1903.

MATTHEW RODGER, pres. by Crown 18th Sept. 1861.
1861

GILBERT JOHNSTON, pres. by Crown 14th Sept. 1864; his son, George Burns, died 28th April 1921.
1864

ALEXANDER (also ALISTAIR) MACLEAN, trans. to Daviot and Dunlichity 1st Dec. 1922.
1913

JAMES McCARDEL, trans. from Dunlop (*q.v.*) 5th June 1923; trans. to New Kilpatrick 19th Nov. 1931. Marr. 4th April 1916 Agnes, daugh. of Philip Mackie, marine engineer, Burma, and Janet Watt, and has issue—James Dunlop, born 3rd Nov. 1919; Philip Mackie, born 3rd June 1922.
1923

STEPPS

GEORGE CONDIE, line 4, for "July" read "Dec."
1904

MALCOLM SHENNAN, born Glasgow; dem. 24th Jan. 1948.
1913

WARDLAWHILL

DAVID JACK, dem. 30th Sept. 1922, died at Hornchurch, Essex, 1st Aug. 1925; his wife, Isabella McLean Finlayson, died 28th Oct. 1920.
1886

CHARLES McARTHUR, trans. from Gardenstown 21st March 1923; dem. 16th Dec. 1925; became Chaplain to Fleet; adm. to St Fittock's, Aberdeen, 28th Dec. 1928.
1923

WILLIAM WRIGHT, born Paisley, 5th Sept. 1890, son of Walter W. and Mary Scott; educ. at Paisley Grammar School and Univ. of Glasgow, M.A. (1914), B.D. (1921); licen. by Presb. of Paisley, 1920; ord. to Mills and Steamers Chaplaincy, Calcutta, 28th March 1920; assistant Barony, Glasgow, 1925; adm. to Wardlawhill 25th March 1926. Marr. 9th July 1930 Elizabeth Jamieson, daugh. of James Branagan and Alison Scott Jamieson, and has issue—Alison Scott, born 6th July 1931; Walter Andrew, born 18th July 1933; James William, born 1st Aug. 1938.
1926

SYNOD OF ARGYLL

PRESBYTERY OF INVERARAY

ARDRISHAIG (Q.S.)

JOHN McRORIE KAY, trans. to Lochlee 19th May 1922.
1918

JOHN PAUL GLEN, trans. to Strone 6th Nov. 1925.
1920

WILLIAM McPHAIL, trans. from Kilbrandon (*q.v.*) 3rd March 1926; dem. 15th April 1945; died Oban 3rd Dec. 1948.
1926

(*Charge united with North Church 15th April* 1945).

CRAIGNISH

NEIL CAMPBELL, son of Archibald, son of John C. of the Melfort family, parson of Luing, 20th Dec. 1558; rector and vicar 24th July 1580; chaplain at the Altar of the Virgin Mary in Kilmartin Church; died between 1591 and 1602. His daugh., Bessie (marr. 6th Jan. 1587–8 James, son of Alexander Kincaid, maltman, Stirling).—[*Reg. Mag. Sig.*, v, 131; *Cal. of Charters*, x, 2303; xii, 2796.]
1571

COLIN CAMPBELL, after his deposition the church was vacant till at least 10th Oct. 1649.—[*G. R. Sas.*, xlv, 294.]
1617

JOHN MACLACHLAN, son of John M., min. of Kilninver.
1669

FRANCIS STEWART, his daugh., Grace, died at Carlisle 24th Aug. 1891, aged 82.
1795

NEIL MACMICHAEL, his daugh., Elizabeth Davina Colville, died at Edinburgh 9th Sept. 1923.
1860

JAMES KEITH WILKIE, dem. 15th May 1945; died 14th Feb. 1947. Marr. 30th April 1925 Janet Riddell, daugh. of John Pendreich, Park Road, Trinity, and Elizabeth Riddell.
1909

CUMLODDEN

In 1840 the presbytery resolved to build a church at Cumlodden for the people in that area of Inveraray and in the adjacent part of Glassary parish. The church was built in the following year at a cost of £548, towards which contributions were made by General Assembly's Committee on Church Extension, £225; Duke of Argyle, £200; Sir Archibald Campbell of Garscube, £100.

"**MR JACKSON**," a probationer, was appointed in 1841, to "preach and visit"; his salary was forthcoming from the General Assembly's scheme for the employment of probationers £20, from Sir Archibald Campbell £10, and contributions from other individuals in the district and presbytery; apparently he was identical with Donald Jackson who was ordained to Lochgilphead in 1843.
1841

WILLIAM EADIE, died 25th Nov. 1926; his widow, Mary Danks, died 29th Nov. 1945.
1917

DONALD MACKINNON, trans. from Assynt 19th Aug. 1927; died 10th Nov. 1939.
1927

GLASSARY

1575 **JOHN WHYTE**, rector.

ARCHIBALD McCALLUM, his sons, Duncan and Donald.—[*Argyll Sas.*, xxxii, 68, 15th Feb. 1672.]
1639

ARCHIBALD CAMPBELL, his son, Nigel.—[*Argyll Sas.*, iv, 294.] **1687**

DONALD CAMPBELL, his son, Colonel Donald Graham, died at Balerno 14th Dec. 1928; his daugh., Jessie Campbell Graham, died at Guildford 7th Nov. 1940. **1852**

ALEXANDER MACDONALD, his son, William Uist, min. of St Nicholas, Cardonald. **1914**

JOHN CAMERON, his sons—James, killed on Campsie Hills 7th June 1936; Gilleasbuig, died 3rd Aug. 1942; his daugh., Jessie Russell, marr. 18th Dec. 1948 Terence Laurie, only son of Rev. William Monaghan-Combs, Egham, Surrey. **1922**

GLENARAY

On 27th Dec. 1651 the Commissioner for the Plantation of Kirks modified stipends for the respective Irish (Gaelic) and English Churches of Inveraray.—[*Recs. of Synod of Argyll*, 251, S.H.S.]

DONALD MACILVORICH or McILVORIE; on 1st May 1650 his widow, Janet Campbell, represented to the Synod of Argyle that she was "in great necessity, and that through the burning of Mr Donald's parish, houses and dwellings (by the Irish under Alexander McDonald in 1644) she is disappointed of that composition which ministers' wifes get either from Ann or for contentation of glebe and manse, and so left very poor and indigent"; the Synod granted to her the share of her husband from the money granted by the Estates for distressed mins. of Argyle. His daughs.—Anna (marr. cont. 22nd March 1624 Alexander MacIver or Campbell of Pennymore); Katherine (marr. Niall Malcolm, min. of Kilchrenan).—[*G. R. Sas.*, xxii, 36; xxix, 328; *Records, Synod of Argyll*, 181.] **1595**

NEIL MACPHERSON, his sons—Malcolm, died 4th May 1939; Godfrey, died 18th Dec. 1932. **1867**

PETER NEIL MACKICHAN, his daugh., Muriel Gladys (marr. 15th Oct. 1922 Frank Macdonald Holman of Pen Harbour, Hurstpierpoint, Sussex); his widow, Harriet Kathleen Whitfield, died at Edinburgh 7th March 1940, aged 85. **1897**

JOHN MACLACHLAN, trans. from Lochcarron 4th Jan. 1923, died at Glasgow 17th Oct. 1927; his daugh., Margaret Morris (marr. 19th July 1933 Hugh McLure, son of James McArdle, Airdrie). **1923**

(*Charge united to Inveraray, March* 1930.)

INVERARAY

The saint of the old Church of Glenaray at Kilmalew, Kilmaliew, is said to have been Liubha or, in its earlier form, Liba, Kilmalieu being *Cill Mo Liubha*, "my Liubha's Church." There are various saints of that name. Another view is that Kilmalew is "Church of St Maluog" or "Moluoc," probably a friend of Columba, and equivalent to "my dear little Leu" or St Lupus. The site was at the old town on the north shore of the bay where the river Aray joins the sea. About 1778 the old town was removed and the present town of Inveraray built. The church was demolished at the same time as the town; and for fifteen years there were only temporary places of worship. Eventually in 1794 the existing two churches, with a steeple 107 ft. high, were built at Inveraray from a design by Mr Milne, London. They were repaired in 1838, having suffered serious damage from lightning in the previous year. The steeple, having become dangerous, had to be taken down in 1941. The name Kilmalew remained with the churchyard. Mundu or Munnu is an affectionate form of the name of St Fintan. Hence Kilmun, the name of the place on the west side of Glen Aray, where stood the chapel dedicated to that saint.—[Watson's *Celtic Place Names*, 304–5, 307; Johnston's *Place Names of Scotland*, 220.]

ALEXANDER GORDON, one of the leading characters of Neil Munro's "John Splendid." It is stated that he was min. of a church at Tynemouth, Northumberland, now Howard Street Church, North Shields. He had sasine in the lands of Knock in Ayrshire on adjudication 16th April 1670.—[*Brit. Weekly*, 11th Jan. 1931; *G. R. Sas.*, 3 Ser., xxiv, 310.]
1650

ALEXANDER McTAVISH, marr. Margaret, daugh. of John Campbell of Lerags; his son, John, went to Jamaica.
1775

JOHN FINLAY DAWSON, dem. 21st Nov. 1930; died 24th June 1941; his wife, Flora, daugh. of John Thomson, burgh chamberlain, Inveraray, died 21st July 1939; he dem. to facilitate union 21st Feb. 1930.
1904

(*Both charges united March* 1930.)

KILMARTIN

There was in the church an altar dedicated to the Virgin Mary, the endowment of which included the lands of Pennykill and Darrok in the barony of Craignish, 3 merks of the lands of Auchafyne, and the 40 sh. lands of Aithaned in the barony of Ardskeodenis.—[*Reg. Great Seal*, v, 131, 2249.]

NEILL CAMPBELL, son of Neill C., Bishop of Argyll, became Bishop of Argyll in 1580, rector 8th July 1585, on which date his natural son, Nigel, received letter of legitimation, apparently identical with Mr. Nigell, rector of Craignish.—[*Reg. Mag. Sig.*, v, 839.]
1574

DONALD CAMPBELL, had issue— Neill, Robert.—[*G. R. Sas.*, 2 Ser., viii, 33, 6th June 1654.]
1628

WILLIAM MACLACHLAN, his sons —Archibald; William of Fearnoch. —[*Auchendarroch Writs*, 16th July 1696.]
1669

DONALD CAMPBELL, marr. Isobel Campbell, who survived him.
1699

HECTOR CAMERON, trans. to Oban 12th Oct. 1922.
1912

ALEXANDER MACKENZIE, trans. from Duirinish (*q.v.*) 11th April 1923; trans. to North Bute 25th Nov. 1927.
1923

JOHN MALCOLM MUNRO, son of John M., Chief Officer, Clyde Training Ship, and Jane Mitchell; trans. from St Columba's, Glasgow, 4th Jan. 1929; dem. 19th May; died 16th June 1942. Marr. (2) 16th Jan. 1929 Adelaide Mary Louisa Fletcher, daugh. of James Bapty and Anne Renton; his daugh., Margaret (marr. 3rd Aug. 1926 William Christopher Miller, M.R.C.V.S., Edinburgh).
1929

NORTH KNAPDALE

In the second quarter of the 15th century there occur references to the Perpetual Vicarage of St Ferchanus's in Knapdale, probably Kilberry, Ferchan being an erroneous form of Bearchan, Saint of Kilberry. The writer of the new Statistical Account states that the mother church of the two Knapdales, built by Cormaig Mac O'Charmaig, was called Kilvic O'Charmaig. The saint may be either Baetan Maccu Cormaic, abbot of Cluain mac Nois, who died 1st March 664, or Abban Maccu Cormaic of Magh Arnaide, whose day was 27th Oct. The Church of Kilmichael Inverlussay was built in 1820, and the Church at Tayvallich in 1827.—[*Cal. Papal Regs., Letters*, viii, 596, 625; Watson's *Celtic Place Names*, 282.]

DUNCAN MACPHAIL, vicar.—[*Acts and Dec.*, 25th July, 1567–8, 113, 149.]
1567

PATRICK MACQUEEN, parson, grants a tack of teinds to Campbell of Auchenbreck, 1595.
1595

DUGALD CAMPBELL, his daughs.— Elizabeth (marr. cont. 15th July 1655); Mary (marr. cont. 10th Dec. 1659), alive 18th Dec. 1670.—[*G. R. Sas.*, xxxviii, 217; 3 Ser., vii, 247; xxxiii, 102.]
1620

JOHN McGILCHRIST, son of John M., writer, Kilmichael-Glassary.
1715

JOHN CAMPBELL, M.A. (King's College, Aberdeen, 1782.)
1811

DUNCAN CAMPBELL, pres. by Queen Victoria 26th April 1846; his sons—John Archibald, born 9th April 1844, died Jersey 25th Oct. 1906; Francis Stewart, born 1846; his daughs.—Catherine, born 1841, died 3rd Oct. 1910; Eugenia (marr. Roderick Maclaren, M.D.); Jane Macdiarmid, died at Bath 30th Aug. 1926, aged 75.
1846

DONALD MACLACHLAN, pres. 15th June 1871.
1871

LACHLAN MACLEAN, his widow, Annie Miller, died 4th Aug. 1928; his sons—Lachlan, died Makalapye, Bechuanaland, 18th June 1934; Thomas Finlay, died 27th Nov. 1934.
1878

DONALD McDONALD LAMONT, his wife, Sarah Lamont. died 5th Feb. 1940.
1914

DONALD GRANT, dem. 31st May 1944.
1921

SOUTH KNAPDALE

The Churches at Achahoish and Inverneil were both built about 1775. For the saint of Eilan-mor-vic-O'Charmaig, see North Knapdale.—[Watson's *Celtic Place Names*, 282.]

ALEXANDER MACKENZIE, pres. by Crown 30th Dec. 1842.
1843

DONALD ALLAN CAMERON, trans. to Westray 10th May 1922.
1896

ANGUS MACDONALD, born North Uist; licen. by Presb. of Glasgow, 1921; assistant St Michael's, Dumfries; served in Navy during war for three years; ord. 27th Sept. 1922; dem. 16th May 1925.
1922

HECTOR CAMERON, trans. from Small Isles (*q.v.*) 12th Nov. 1925; trans. to Kilfinan, 23rd Dec. 1930.
1925

LOCHGILPHEAD

DONALD JACKSON, pres. by Crown 10th May 1842.
1843

JOHN MACKAY, pres. 30th Sept. 1844.
1844

JOHN MACFARLANE, pres. 8th June 1847.
1847

PETER NEIL MACKICHAN, pres. by Crown 1st Jan. 1863.
1863

ALEXANDER CAMERON ROBERTSON, D.D. (Aberdeen 1923), died 18th Jan. 1933 unmarr.
1876

TARBERT

A mission with a missionary was established here about 1775.

DONALD MacINTOSH LOGAN, trans. to Arisaig 27th April 1927.
1914

JOHN MACDONALD GILLIES, born Laggan, Kingussie, 10th Dec. 1894, son of James G., grocer, and Jane Mackintosh; educ. at Kingussie School and Univ. of Aberdeen, M.A. (1918); licen. by Presb. of Abernethy, 12th May 1921; assistant Wemyss 1921; ord. to Murthly 12th May 1925; trans. 31st Aug. 1927; trans. and adm. 31st Aug. 1927; trans. to South Knapdale 4th Nov. 1931. Marr. 28th April 1932 Chrissie, only daugh. of Lauchlan Scott, Burrelton, Coupar Angus.
1927

PRESBYTERY OF DUNOON

ARDENTINNY

1855 JAMES PATTERSON, born Kilsyth 26th Jan 1830; ord. to Hemmingford 8th Sept. 1865; D.D. (Montreal Presb. College, 1915); was chaplain of prisons for Montreal for 35 years; Clerk of Presbytery 1858–1917; died April 1932, aged 102. Marr. 8th April 1863 Rosina, daugh. of F. W. Sherriff of Huntingdon, and had seven children.

1860 ROBERT CRAIG, his daugh., Jean Sarah, M.A. (marr. 26th Oct. 1932 Malcolm Smith, rector of St Paul's Episcopal Church, Rothesay).

1903 ALEXANDER WILLIAM MITCHELL, dem. 2nd June 1932, died 20th July 1935; his wife, Janet McGibbon Stalker, born 4th Aug. 1887, died 22nd April 1924.

(*Charge united to Strone 1st June 1932.*)

CRAIGMORE

1903 THOMAS NELSON ALLEN, adm. to Savoch of Deer 22nd Feb. 1924.

1916 JOHN MORELL McWILLIAM, trans. to Dean Park, Govan, 17th May 1928.

1928 JOHN DUNLOP BROWN, trans. from Whiting Bay (*q.v.*) 25th Oct. 1928; died 16th July 1948.

DUNOON

On 12th March 1439–40 Lord Duncan Campbell of Lochow gave ½ merk from the lands of Ardenslate for the maintenance of lights and wax candles before the image of the Virgin Mary in the church. The church was dedicated to St Mary; and by Bull of Pope Pius II 4th March 1461–2 it was united to the *mensa* of Lismore. In the church there was an Altar of the Holy Rood, founded on 21st Aug. 1420 by John Campbell, inhabitant of Dunoon. The church was enlarged in 1911 by addition of transepts and the flat ceiling opened up and supported with transverse beams of pitch pine at a cost of £5,200.—[*Cal. of Scottish Supplications*, 226 *S.H.S.*; Theiner's *Vet. Monumenta*, 434–5.]

1560 JOHN CAMERON. Delete entry.

1610 JOHN CAMERON, probably Treasurer of diocese.

1626 EWEN CAMERON of Dunloskin, had also issue—Margaret (marr. cont. 24th June 1686 Edward Gillespie, merchant, Edinburgh).—[*Deeds, Mack.*, 1705, No. 1241.]

1666 HECTOR McLAINE, line 2, for "5th Aug. 1666" read "20th March 1665."

1740 ALEXANDER MACKAY, marr. cont. 18th and 19th Aug. 1725 Elizabeth, daugh. of John Campbell, Captain of Dunoon.

1844 JOHN CLARK, line 7, for "1818" read "1828"; line 8, for "ord." read "adm."

1873 JOHN CAMERON, his daugh., Williamina Buchanan, died at Vancouver 9th Sept. 1932.

1901 WILLIAM HOWIE, died 1st Nov. 1929; his wife, Mary Catherine McNeill, was born at Entre Rios, Argentina, 22nd May 1881. Addl. issue—William Bruce, M.B., Ch.B., born 20th Jan. 1924.

INNELLAN

ARCHIBALD EWING MacINTYRE,
1919 trans. to Pollokshaws 7th March 1928.

DOUGLAS GORDON McLEAN, born 19th Dec. 1893, son of William
1928 George Green M., min. of Cullen; educ. at Boddam School, Fordyce Academy and Univ. of Aberdeen, M.A. (1920); served with Gordon Highlanders in Great War, wounded at Hooge 1915, Company Commander and Brigade Bombing Officer 1917-18; tutor in Glasgow; licen. by Presb. of Edinburgh 16th March 1928; assistant Lady Glenorchy's; ord. 7th June 1928. Marr. 22nd June 1918 Jessie Cormack Shaw, M.A., daugh. of James Shaw, auditor, Indian Railways, and has issue—William James, born 28th May 1920, died 26th Nov. 1943; Wendy Moira, born 1st Jan. 1926. Publications—*The History of Fordyce Academy* (1936); *Life at a Banffshire School*, 1592-1935.

TOWARD CHAPEL

RONALD MACDOUGALL, died 4th
1885 Feb. 1942.

WILLIAM GRAHAM BROWN, went
1918 to Canada, died 13th Dec. 1928.

JOHN ALEXANDER, app. 15th Jan.
      1922, died 29th March 1926, aged
1922 73.

(*St Bride's Church was rebuilt and restored Aug.* 1935.)

INVERCHAOLAIN

The Churches of Inverchaolain and Kilmorie in Strathlachlan were united, apparently some time after the Reformation; on 27th Dec. 1651 the Commission for the Plantation of Kirks dissolved the union, made Inverchaolain "a distinct kirk" and modified to the same a stipend with manse and glebe. The church was rebuilt in 1745. At Toward Point there was a chapel dedicated either to St Fillan, but which of that name is uncertain, or, as the designation Kyllenane also occurs, to St Finan.—[*Recs. of Synod of Argyle*, 250, *S.H.S.*; Watson's *Celtic Place Names*, 285, 518.]

DUGALD CAMPBELL, his pres. in
      1574 was on the death of John
1574 Lamond.—[*Reg. Pres. Bene.*, i, (4), 24.]

JOHN SCOULAR THOMSON, dem.
      11th Nov. 1938; died at Edinburgh
1918 30th March 1939; his son, Ian Alastair Cameron, min. of Latheron 11th May 1946. Addl. issue—Roland Malise Fraser, born 16th March 1923; Madeline Ruth Veronica, born 11th March 1930. Publications—Editor *British Students Song Book*, and Editor *Glasgow University Magazine*.

KILFINAN

The church was granted to Paisley Abbey by 1230-40 by Duncan, son of Ferchar or Ferhard, and Laumann, son of Malcolm and nephew of Duncan—confirmation by Angus, son of Duncan, 9th July 1270; in 1253 the church was designated "the Church of St Finan which is in Kethromecongall" (in the quarter of Cowal), and at that time it was known as "Kerry or Caathramh," i.e. "the fourth part." Of a Charter of 6th July 1452 Sir Robert Dewar, "vicar of St Serf's of Kilfinnan," is a witness; but of this dedication nothing further is known. There was in the church an altar dedicated to St Fynnan, to which pertained the 4 lib. lands of Awchingyle. Whether this was a second altar to St Finan is not clear. At Ardmarnock, St Marnock's Field, there was a chapel dedicated to that saint. A small portion of the chapel still exists. A short distance above the chapel there was a cell, to which St Marnock was wont to resort for fasting, penance and devotion.—[*Reg. Great Seal*, iv, 791, v, 2095; *Reg. of Paisley*, 132-3, 137-9.]

JOHN McNEIL, min. in 1614.—[*G. R.*
1614 *Sas.*, x, 204.]

DONALD McVICAR, died before 12th
      Jan. 1637.—[*G. R. Sas.*, xlv, 258;
1637 xlvi, 13.]

AENEAS McLAINE, trans. to Kilninian in Mull, 1673.
1666

ANGUS MACPHEE, dem. 30th Sept. 1924, died 1st March 1926; his widow, Margaret Ferguson Russell, died at Paisley 11th June 1927.
1876

ARCHIBALD ANDERSON, trans. from Kilcalmonell (*q.v.*) 6th May 1925; trans. to Kilmore 11th Feb. 1930; dem. 28th May 1945.
1925

KILMODAN

WALTER LAMONT, died before 12th Aug. 1595.
1575

ROBERT LAMONT, son of Walter L., natural son of Sir John L. of Inneryn, Kt., pres. to parsonage 12th Aug. 1595 on death of Walter Lamont, his father.—[*P. S. Reg.*, lxvii, 184.]
1595

DONALD MACVICAR, died before 12th Jan. 1637; his son, Gilbert.—[*G. R. Sas.*, xlv, 253.]
1598

DONALD McCLOY, marr. Elizabeth Crawford; his daugh., Beatrice (marr. cont. 16th March 1637 Donald Campbell of Kilmichael); had also issue, a son John.—[*Prot. Book* of Donald McGilchrist; *Reg. of Deeds*, 10th July 1652.]
1611

JOHN CAMPBELL, his daugh., Marianna (marr. 18th July 1737); line 12, for "1738" read "18th July 1737."
1699

DUNCAN MACLEAN, line 16, for "Georgina" read "George; died 1901." See Vol. VII, 44, for family.
1838

JOHN CAMERON, dem. 31st Dec. 1933; died at Corstorphine 31st Oct. 1935.
1908

KILMUN

The Church of St Columba, Kyllemine (Kilmun), is mentioned on 24th Aug. 1391. To the Glory of God and in honour of St Mundus and all saints, Sir Duncan Campbell of Lochow erected the church into a collegiate church for five chaplains, one of whom was to be provost, and another was to serve the cure of the parishioners; and by Charter of 4th Aug. 1442, confirmed by James II, 12th May 1450, for the souls of James I and Joan, his consort, James II himself, Marjorie (Stewart), his late wife, Margaret (Stewart), his wife, and the late Celestine, his eldest son, he gave an endowment to the church—the 3 merk land of Auchinlochir in the barony of Kilmun, the 6 merk land of Blairmore and Garronletter in said barony, the 2 merk land of Craghawas in the barony of Cowal, the 2 merk land of Cafflade and Clogyne in the barony of Kilmun, the 1 merk land of Kilmolew in the barony of Lochow; 2 merks Scots annual rent from the lands of Dalmeloncharde, 1 merk Scots annual rent from the land of Auchingar, 2 merks Scots annual rent from the lands of Greghane and Gawane. He also gave the Church of St Conan of Dysart (Glenorchy) and the Church of the Three Holy Brethren (Lochgoilhead). By mandate to the Archdeacon of Argyle Pope Eugenius IV confirmed the erection. In answer to a petition by the provost and chapter of the collegiate church, which stated that after the erection by the Archdeacon, George (Lauder), Bishop of Argyle, united the parsonage of Kylmalew (Inveraray), with the consent of the patron, to the Capitular *Mensa* of the collegiate church. Pope Paul II, by Bull of 26th March 1466, gave mandate to the Official of Argyle to make enquiry and confirm the erection and the appropriation and union of the parsonage of Kylmalew. Among the witnesses of a Charter of 6th July 1452 are the provost and seven chaplains, which serves to show that to the original foundation three chaplains were added.—[*Reg. Great Seal*, ii, 346, iv, 791; *Cal. Papal Regs.*, *Letters*, xii, 242–4.]

ALEXANDER ROBINSON, his son, Nigel Alexander Watt, died Monzie, Crieff, June 1930.
1894

ALEXANDER WALLACE McKINLAY, dem. 13th June 1922; died 19th March 1929.
1897

ALEXANDER BAIN HARPER, ord. 26th Sept. 1922; trans. to Monzievaird 3rd Feb. 1929.
1922

ALEXANDER GILLAN, born Larkhall 15th Jan. 1896, son of Alexander G. and Elizabeth Millar; educ. at Larkhall Academy and Univs. of Glasgow and Edinburgh; licen. by Presb. of Dalkeith 14th May 1928; assistant Inveresk; ord. to Inverallochy 26th June 1928; trans. 16th Aug. 1929. Marr. 26th Oct. 1926 Margaret, daugh. of Henry Chalmers and Jean Brackenridge.
1929

KINGARTH

On 21st April 1529 mention is made of the late Sir Patrick McConnoquhay, "Ladyprest of the Kirk of Kyngarth," indicating that there was in the church an altar dedicated to the Virgin Mary.—[*Reg. Sec. Sig.,* ii, 52.]

SIR JAMES McVERITIE, alleged vicar pensioner.—[*Acts and Dec.,* xxix, 337.]
1564

ARCHIBALD SINCLAIR, died before 25th Feb. 1595.
1572

JAMES McQUIRRTIE, vicar, called "excommunicat apostet" 24th April 1593.—[*Book of the Universal Kirk,* 803.]
1593

PATRICK STEWART, pres. to vicarage 25th Feb. 1595 on death of Archibald Sinclair.—[*P. S. Reg.,* lxviii, 139.]
1597

DONALD OMEY, trans. from Ardnamurchan 1625; trans. to Campbeltown before 4th June 1631.
1625

JOHN BUCHANAN, born 19th Oct. 1794.
1827

JOHN SAUNDERS, dem. 15th Dec. 1925; died 8th Oct. 1926; his widow, Katherine Evans Begg, died 2nd May 1943.
1879

DANIEL STEWART, born Muthill, Perthshire, 19th Dec. 1899, son of John S. and Euphemia McIlvride;
1926
educ. at George Heriot's School and Univ. of Edinburgh, M.A. (1922); licen. by Presb. of Edinburgh 19th Dec. 1923; assistant, Lady Glenorchy's, Edinburgh, Jan. 1924; St Paul's, Leith; ord. 12th May 1926; dem. 20th March 1931; re-adm. by General Assembly 25th May 1940; adm. to Craigside, Innerleithen, 10th Dec. 1940; trans. to Invergarry, 17th Nov. 1943; trans. to Benholme 20th Nov. 1947. Marr. 9th April 1930 Dorothy, daugh. of John Phillip and Helen Kirkhope.

(*United with Kilchathan Bay* 5th May 1931.)

KIRN

WILLIAM GEORGE JOHNSTON, trans. to Paisley Mid, 10th Dec. 1924.
1918

THOMAS COOK, born 18th April 1900, son of Thomas C., min. of Levern; educ. at High School and Univ. of Glasgow, M.A. (1921), B.D.; served with 6th Batt. Argyll and Sutherland Highlanders, 1919; licen. by Presb. of Paisley, 1924; assistant, Barony; ord. 24th April 1925; trans. to Rutherglen Old, 10th Jan. 1935; dem. 1st April 1947. Marr. 7th Sept. 1925 Lily, daugh. of John Griffin, Newton, Kirkpatrick-Fleming.
1925

LOCHGOILHEAD

The parish was variously termed Kenlochgilpe and Lochgilpe. The church was dedicated to the "Three Holy Brethern," whose identity is uncertain. It was granted by Sir Duncan Campbell of Lochow to the Collegiate Church of Kilmun on its foundation in 1442. At Kilmore there was a chapel dedicated to the Virgin Mary, which *cir.* 1230–40 was granted along with the land of Kilmore to Paisley Abbey by Duncan, son of Ferchar or Ferkard, and Laumann, son of Malcolm and nephew of Duncan. The grant was confirmed by Duncan's son, Angus, on 9th July 1270.—[*Reg. of Paisley,* 132–3, 137–9, 309; *Cal. Papal Reg., Letters,* xii, 242–4.]

Kilmorich. About 1246 the church was granted to Inchaffray Abbey by Gilchrist, son of Malcolm MacLauchlan, for the souls of himself and Betrice his wife.—[*Inchaffray Charters*, Bk. 65.]

1575 ROBERT MONTGOMERIE, archdeacon of Argyll.

1604 JAMES KIRK, his son, George.—[*G. R. Sas.*, 26th June 1631, fo. 314.]

1614 ARCHIBALD McLAUCHLAN, line 2, for "1618" read "1614."

1629 ARCHIBALD McLAUCHLAN, his son, Donald.—[*G. R. Sas.*, xxxix, 273, 11th March 1634.]

1641 COLIN McLAUCHLAN.—[*G. R. Sas.*, xlii, 233.]

1674 ARCHIBALD McLAUCHLAN, was Synod Bursar 11th Feb. 1648.

1915 DONALD MATHESON MACLEAN, his son, Hayward Gillian Carruthers, LL.B., 2nd Lieut. Seaforths, killed in action in France 4th June 1940.

NORTH BUTE

1881 PETER DEWAR, dem. 16th May 1927; died 20th Nov. 1927; his widow, Marion Lizzie Maund, died 27th Feb. 1929.

1927 ALEXANDER MACKENZIE, trans. from Kilmartin 25th Nov. 1927; trans. to Collieston 6th Aug. 1930.

ROTHESAY

1580 CUTHBERT HENDERSON.—[*Acts and Dec.*, lxxxii, 97.]

1589 PATRICK MacQUEEN, pres. to vicarage 20th June 1589 on dem. of David Cumming, prebendary of Restalrig, and Patrick Dunbar, last vicar.—[*Reg. Sec. Sig.*, lx, 22.]

1595 ROBERT STEWART, pres. in 1595 on depriv. of Patrick MacQueen.—[*Reg. Sec. Sig.*, lxvii, 112.]

1618 PATRICK STEWART, adm. before 15th Aug. 1617.

1642 ROBERT STEWART of Skerrels, marr. Jean Colquhoun and had issue—Janet (marr. Duncan Campbell of Ashfield).

1658 JOHN STEUART, his widow, Anne Gordon, marr. (2) Robert Moor.—[*G. R. Sas.*, lx, 19.]

1691 JOHN MONRO, marr. Jean Baillie.

1754 HUGH CAMPBELL, his daugh., Elizabeth (marr. John Blain, Commissary of the Isles).

1884 JAMES KING HEWISON, dem. 1924, died at Thornhill, Dumfriesshire, 23rd Jan. 1941. He gifted his valuable collection of Covenanting books and relics to the Church of Scotland Library. Addl. publications—*The Romance of Dumfries and Galloway in Early Caledonia* (Dumfries, 1939).

1907 JOHN DALL, his widow, Agnes F. G. Cowper, re-marr. 4th Aug. 1945.

1925 WILLIAM THOMAS SMELLIE, O.B.E. (1918), trans. from Lowson Memorial, Forfar (*q.v.*), 6th April 1925; trans. to St Andrew's, Dundee, 5th March 1936; trans. to Pollokshields-Titwood 1st Aug. 1941. Publications—*The Tombstones of Rothesay Churchyard and The Kirk Session Records of Rothesay* (1658–1750); *The Kirk Session Records of Kingarth* (1641–1703) (*Trans. of Buteshire Natural History Society*, x, xi, xii).

NEW ROTHESAY

1911 JOHN McAUSLAND DICKIE, died 18th Jan. 1942; his daugh., Janet Reid Inglis (marr. 17th April 1936 Denis Anthony Frank Butter, textile manufacturer, London).

(*Church united with Brigend, 6th Sept.* 1942.)

ROTHESAY GAELIC CHAPEL

1905 NEIL McDOUGALL, his widow, Agnes Macrae Sandilands Brown, died 2nd May 1929.

SANDBANK

1915 ANGUS MACDONALD, trans. to Ardrossan Barony 20th March 1930; dem. 9th Sept. 1948; died at Greenock 13th Dec. 1948.

(*Charges united 6th Sept.* 1936.)

STRACHUR or KILMOGHLAS and STRATHLACHLAN

Kilmoghlas or Kilmaglas may mean "Church of the Sons of Glas," but no details are known. The Church of Strathlachlan was also called the Church of Kilmorie in Strathlachlan. At first it was united with Inverchaolain; but on 27th Dec. 1651 the Commission for the Plantation of Kirks dissolved the union and united Kilmorie in Strathlachlan with the Church of Kilmoglas in Strachur.—[Watson's *Celtic Place Names*, 305; *Records of Synod of Argyle*, 471.]

1661 DONALD MORRISON, depr. by Act of Parliament 11th June and Act of Privy Council 1662.

1911 WILLIAM GILLIES, dem. 15th May 1937; died 16th Jan. 1942; his wife, Catherine Colville Blyth, was born 1st April 1868.

(*Charges united 21st July* 1937).

STRONE

1883 ALEXANDER MACARTHUR, dem. 16th May 1925; died 10th May 1931.

1925 JOHN PAUL GLEN, trans. from Ardrishaig (*q.v.*) 6th Nov. 1925; dem. 30th Nov. 1936; died 13th June 1938; his widow, Agnes Wardrop, died 29th Oct. 1943.

(*Strone and Ardentinny united 1st June 1932 and Kilmun united 11th April* 1937.)

TIGHNABRUAICH

1919 PATRICK HAMILTON BORROWMAN, dem. 4th Feb. 1930 and adm. to Nyasaland; died 20th Jan. 1948; his wife, Maude Helen Dickson, was born 23rd April 1885. Addl. issue—Philip Ronald, Lieut. R.E., born 30th Dec. 1923. His daugh., Margaret Helen Grierson (marr. 25th Jan. 1947 Hilary William King, Fowey).

(*Charges united 8th June* 1930.)

PRESBYTERY OF KINTYRE

BRODICK

The church was opened for worship second Sunday of December 1839 and was served by a missionary.

MALCOLM MACLEAN, died at Milngavie 25th April 1931.
1875

MALCOLM MACKINNON, dem. 13th Oct. 1932; died at Glasgow 16th Sept. 1939.
1919

CORRIE

JAMES BROWN, adm. first min. of parish 21st July 1923; dem. 18th Dec. 1934; died at Alyth 15th Feb. 1941.
1900

CAMPBELTOWN

Kilchiaran. The Church of St Queran (Kiaran) was granted to Paisley Abbey by Angus, son of Donald. The grant was confirmed by Alan, Bishop of Argyll, 1250-61 and by Laurence, Bishop of Argyll, 23rd Oct. 1269.—[*Reg. of Paisley*, 7, 27-9, 132, 136.]

Kilchuslan. St Constantine is "Constantin the Briton" of lasting grace, whose conversion is recorded in 588. He is said to have been King of Cornwall and to have left his kingdom to become Abbot in succession to Mochertu. It is further stated that he passed over to Scotland and suffered martyrdom in Kintyre. The church was a canonry and prebend of Lismore before 23rd June 1433.—[Watson's *Celtic Place Names*, 188-9; *Cal. Papal Reg., Letters*, viii, 468.]

MALCOLM McOSONAGE, min. of Kilcheran before 24th Nov. 1620.— [Campbell's *Argyll Sas.*, i, 120.]
1620

DONALD OMEY, probably descended from Duncan O., principal surgeon to James V in 1526 and Customar of Perth; adm. to Ardnamurchan before 12th Feb. 1624; trans. to Kingarth 1626; trans. and adm. before 9th June 1631. On 30th Dec. 1632 he received from James, Earl of Kintyre, a charter of a piece of land in Lochhead (Campbeltown), with "full and free power to market," to buy and sell a tun (252 gallons) of wine annually, and liberty to buy and sell all kinds of merchandise within the said town of Lochhead and all the bounds of Kintyre—which involved trading usually forbidden to a min. by the Church; he had also a son, Duncan, to whom on 11th Oct. 1648 the Synod of Argyle made an education grant.—[*P. C. Reg.*, xiii, 427-8; *G. R. Sas.*, xxxv, 237, 11th Jan. 1633; *Argyle Sas.*, 2 Ser., ix, 452; *Recs. of Synod of Argyle*, 123, S.H.S.]
1631

NEIL CAMPBELL, line 5, delete "but was probably never settled." On sederunt Synod of Argyle May 1643.
1642

JOHN CAMERON.—[*Reg. of Deeds, Dal.*, lxxx, 18th Jan. 1697.]
1669

LAUGHLAN CAMPBELL, friend and correspondent of Wodrow.
1703

WILLIAM MACLEOD, his daugh., Anne (marr. Angus McNeill, min. of Barra).
1767

JAMES CURDIE RUSSELL, died at Edinburgh 18th March 1925; his daugh., Margaret Huison, died 6th March 1937. He bequeathed £1,000 to Kirk Session for augmentation of stipend from 1925, of Second Charge.
1854

NORMAN MACKENZIE, trans. to Moy 28th Aug. 1925.
1918

THOMAS SMITH MACPHERSON, trans. from St Vincent's, Glasgow, 23rd Dec. 1925; dem. 3rd Dec. 1946; died at Langholm 26th March 1947. Addl. issue—John Cook, born 5th May 1922; Robert, died 19th Sept. 1944.
1925

(*Charges uncollegiated 8th May 1945.*)

CAMPBELTOWN
LOWLAND CHARGE

EDWARD KEITH, marr. Jean, daugh. of Major William Campbell of Ballygregan; his daugh., Margaret (marr. cont. 7th May 1687 Henry, son of Robert Gardyne, merchant, Montrose).
1655

JOHN McALPINE, son of David M., schoolmaster, Dunbarton; his son, Walter, min. of Culross.
1750

GEORGE ROBERTSON, son of William R. of Teaninich, Alness, and Catherine Ross.
1763

HECTOR McNEILL, his sons—Duncan, died at Bridlington 9th Jan. 1925; Hector, died at Edinburgh 26th April 1933; Godfrey Alexander, died at Lasswade 4th April 1943; his daugh., Jessie Elizabeth, Lady Paulin, died 29th Aug. 1933.
1841

GEORGE WALTER STRANG, his widow, Janet Fleming Calderwood, died 10th Aug. 1931.
1874

CHRISTIAN VICTOR AENEAS MacECHERN, dem. 23rd Oct. 1922 on app. to Scots Church, Kandy, Ceylon; trans. to Aberdeen North and Trinity 3rd June 1929.
1919

DONALD DAVIDSON, M.A., B.D., ord. 4th April 1923; trans. to Queen's Park, Glasgow, 20th Jan. 1925.
1923

JOHN RUSSELL MILLER, born 26th April 1900, son of Daniel Jack M., min. of Jamestown; educ. at Vale of Leven Academy and Univ. of Glasgow; M.A. (1920), B.D. (1923); served with 4th Argyll and Sutherland Highlanders 1918–19; licen. by Presb. of Dunbarton 1923; assistant Dunbarton and St Mungo, Glasgow, 1924; ord. 13th May 1925; trans. to Kilsyth 12th Feb. 1930. Marr. 3rd Aug. 1933 Phyllis, daugh. of Arthur John Whiston, Ton-y-Pandy, Cardiff, and has issue—Madeline Ruth, born 23rd Sept. 1938.
1925

KILCHIEVAN

See under Campbeltown, First Charge.

GIGHA

JOHN DARROCH, min. in 1632; marr. cont. 29th and 31st Oct. 1632 Margaret, daugh. of George Campbell of Ballochlavan.—[*Craignish MS.*, 283.]
1632

DONALD MACFARLANE, died 10th Feb. 1923.
1907

KENNETH MACLEOD, trans. from Colonsay 24th July 1923; D.D. (St Andrews, 28th June 1932); dem. 9th Sept. 1947.
1923

KILBRIDE IN ARRAN

The church was rebuilt in 1773. The New Statistical Account states that on Holy Island at the entrance of Lamlash Bay there was a religious house or monastery. The saint of the island was St Malise, Malios, Molios, Mo-Laisse, Mo-Laise, a reduced form of Laisren, with *Mo* (my) prefixed. On the island was his cave, on the roof of which was a runic inscription with the name of the saint. Lamlash is *Eilean M' Laise* (Mo-Laise's isle), and the name was primarily that of Holy Island.—[*New Stat. Acc.*, v, *Bute*, 24, 33; Watson's *Celtic Place Names*, 24, 33. See Kilmorie and Brodick.]

JOHN KNOX, was min. in 1623.—[*G. R. Sas.*, xiv, 192.]
1623

ANDREW WILLIAM KENNEDY died 9th Sept. 1948.
1914

KILBERRY

St Berach, whose day was 15th Feb., was the son of Remnann, and Abbot of Cluain Coirpthi, and was contemporary with Columba. Here his bell is said to have been preserved.—[Watson's *Celtic Place Names*, 301.]

KILCALMONELL

1580 HECTOR McALLISTER, pres. in 1580 on dem. of Alexander McAllister.—[*Reg. Pres. Bene.*, ii, 38. See Kilmorie.]

1614 MAURICE DARROCH, min. in 1614. Marr. Finuall Carmichael, who survived him.—[*G. R. Sas.*, 24th Feb. 1634, xxxix, 266.]

1680 SWEYN McSWEYNE, his daugh. (marr. Hector Maclean of Kinloch); line 4, for "Glenlirk" read "Glenelg, which at this time was in the Presb. of Lorn."—[*Memo*, Rev. J. McK. Campbell, Lochgilphead.]

1844 JAMES ROBERTSON CAMPBELL, his daughs.—Christian Eliza, died at Cargill 10th Aug. 1929; Harriet, died 6th Dec. 1935.

1885 JOHN DOWNIE, marr. (2) 21st Aug. 1925 Maude Trowbridge; she marr. (2) 23rd June 1938.

1917 ARCHIBALD ANDERSON, trans. to Kilfinan 6th May 1925.

1925 ANGUS MACLEOD, trans. from Salen 25th Nov. 1925; trans. to Ochiltree 30th Nov. 1928.

1929 WILLIAM URQUHART MACNAB, M.C., Legion of Honour, Croix de Guerre; trans. from Ullapool (*q.v.*) 17th May 1929. Has issue—Mairi Campbell, born 26th May 1929, died at Glasgow 8th Jan. 1947; Evan John, born 28th Aug. 1934. His mother-in-law was Mary Campbell.

KILLEAN

The Church of Kilmarubh belonged to the Priory of Ardehattan.—[*Reg. Mag. Sig.*, vi, 881.]

1629 MURDOCH McWHIRRIE, M.A. (Glasgow, 1621).

1639 MALCOLM OSENOG, brother of Murroch; min. of Kilchievan or Campbeltown before 24th Nov. 1620; trans. before 24th April 1639.—[*G. R. Sas.*, xi, 63.]

1852 DONALD MACFARLANE, his daugh., Jessie Margaret, died 30th May 1938.

1880 DONALD JOHN MACDONALD, dem. 1st March 1926, died 27th Dec. 1930; his widow, Margaret Colvill, died 18th Feb. 1936.

1926 DONALD MACDONALD, trans. from Benbecula (*q.v.*) 29th Dec. 1926, died 13th Feb. 1928.

1928 ANGUS MACMILLAN, born Lewis 4th March 1886, son of Kenneth M., Captain, steam yacht, and Margaret MacIver Macmillan; served with Seaforth Highlanders 1904-11 and 1914 in Great War, as Major Cameronians, 1920-7, in France and Belgium; wounded, twice mentioned in despatches; awarded Military Cross, D.S.O. and Legion of Honour avec palme, Croix de Guerre; licen. by Presb. of Glasgow 28th March 1928; ord. 5th June 1928; trans. to St Columba's Church, Edinburgh, 18th June 1931; Chaplain to Forces 12th Jan. 1939; trans. to Gigha 9th March 1948. Marr. 1st June 1909 Catherine, daugh. of Robert Drummond and Annie Bowie Drummond, and has issue—Kenneth, born 5th March, died 2nd May 1910; Robert (twin), born 5th March, died 5th May 1910; Annie Isabella Bowie, born 28th March 1911; Kenneth, born 16th March 1913; Margaret MacIver, born 8th April 1918; Catherine Drummond, born 6th Dec. 1919; Ruth Duncan, born 2nd Feb. 1923; Drummond Hope, born 20th Dec. 1927.

(*Charges united 7th March* 1944.)

KILMORIE IN ARRAN

The church was rebuilt on the original site in 1785, an aisle with a gallery was added in 1810, and in 1881 complete renovation was carried out by the Duke of Hamilton. The Chapel or Church at Shisken, which was the place of worship of the district, was rebuilt in 1805, and the min. of Kilmorie conducted a service there every third Sunday. It was the Pre-Reformation Chapel of St Malise or St Molios,—Mo-Laisse, Mo-Laise, a reduced form of Laisren, with *mo* (my) prefixed. He died in 639, and his grave is said to have been in the middle of the ground at Shisken.—[Watson's *Celtic Place Names*, 305. See Lochranza and Kilbride.]

1580 HECTOR McALLISTER, pres. 13th Aug. 1580 on death of Alexander McAllister.—[*Reg. Pres. Bene.*, ii, 38.]

1617 JAMES McKIRDIE, adm. before 15th Aug. 1617; appears to have been removed in 1643 from the charge, which was reported on 11th Oct. 1649 to have been vacant five years.—[*Synod of Argyll*, 150; *G. R. Sas.*, dii, 222.]

1687 AENEAS MORRISON, pres. to Contin 5th Sept. 1687.—[*Deeds Dal.*, 1706, No. 1762.]

1876 DUNCAN BLACK, his widow, Susanna McDougall, died 26th Dec. 1925.

1914 DUNCAN CONACHER, trans. to Calderhead 2nd June 1926.

1926 NORMAN MACLEOD WRIGHT, born Glasgow 1872, son of Alexander Macmillan W.; educ. at High School and Univ. of Glasgow, and U.P. College, Glasgow; licen. by U.P. Presb. of Glasgow Jan. 1895; ord. by Berwick Presb. in English Presb. Church May 1897, to Ancroft Moor, Northumberland; trans. to Goodmayes, London, 1907; app. Chaplain to Forces Sept. 1914; went to France March 1915; mentioned in despatches; Chaplain to Bellahouston Hospital 1921; adm. to St Kenneth's, Govan, 15th May 1923; trans. and adm. 23rd Sept. 1926; died 14th Oct. 1941. Marr. 1900 Mima, daugh. of William Wood, Duddo, Northumberland, and has issue—Janet Richmond, born 18th Sept. 1901; Margaret Elma, born 24th June 1904; Ronald Campbell, born 21st Oct. 1906; Elizabeth Proctor, born 18th Oct. 1907; Jessie Macleod, born 14th June 1912.

LOCHRANZA

On 26th Dec. 1651 the Commission for the Plantation of Kirks, in view of the largeness of the parish of Kilmorie, 24 miles long, ordained that a new kirk be erected beside Lochranza for all the lands between the Water of Irsay and the north end of Arran, and dismembered the lands of the laird of Skelmorlie, within the parish of Kilbride, from that parish, and annexed them to the said new kirk which was to be served *per vices* with Kilmorie. A stipend was modified for the min. of the two kirks, with manse and glebe at Kilmorie. To what extent the decreet was put into effect is not clear. The present church was built in 1795 and seated in 1830 for 300 people. The work was then carried on by a licentiate who acted as assistant to the mins. of Kilmorie and Kilbride and whose remuneration was in part the annual revenue of a mortification made for the purpose by Anne, Duchess of Hamilton, about 1700. A condition of the mortification was that the min. at work should not possess ordained status. The "Convent" of St Bridget at Lochranza is associated with the "Nunnery" of Sir Walter Scott, where for a time lived the "Maid of Lorn." It does not appear that there actually was a convent here. The building in question seems to have been a chapel.—[*Recs. of Synod of Argyle*, 247, S.H.S. See Kilmorie.]

1893 JOHN COLVILLE, died at Glasgow 9th July 1930.

SADDELL

1639 MURDOCH McWHIRRIE or MURRIE, died before 11th Oct. 1648; his son, Donald, to whom Synod made an education grant on that date.—[*G. R. Sas.*, xlviii, 317; *Accounts of the Regality of Argyll; MSS. Gen. Reg. House.*]

1864 JOHN GRANT LEVACK, his widow, Margaret Jane Isabella Larnach, died at Partick 8th May 1924.

1907 JAMES ARCHIBALD ARGYLL BAKER, marr. (1) 15th Jan. 1924 Catherine Macpherson, second daugh. of Keith Campbell, Post Office, Carradale, and Janet Currie, (2) 12th Nov. 1946 May Fisher Maclachlan.

SKIPNESS

1892 JOHN MACLACHLAN, dem. 12th Dec. 1921, died 1930.

1922 JOHN MACNAB, born 23rd April 1874; licen. by Presb. of Edinburgh 1919; ord. 1919 (assistant); adm. 18th April 1922; died 5th Sept. 1939, unmarr.

SOUTHEND—KILCHOLUMKILL

The Church of Kilcholumkill was granted to the Priory of Whithorn by Patrick Macseillinges and Finlach, his wife. There does not appear to be any authority for the statement that the Church of Kilblaan belonged to the said priory. It is not included among the churches pertaining to the priory in James II's Confirmation Charter of 1st July 1451; and on 25th Sept. 1538 the rectory is recorded as belonging to the Crown.—[*Reg. Great Seal*, i, App. i, 208, ii, 460–1; *Reg. Sec. Seal*, ii, 2724.]

1629 DUNCAN OMEY, on 1st Oct. 1640 he declared himself "through age and infirmitie unable to execute the function of the ministeriall calling," and "out of tenderness of conscience least the people should want services" he "voluntarily and freely resigned his office and benefice in the Assemblie's hands, reserving to himself yearly all that the stipend will exceed fyve hundred marks"; he appears to have dem. before 7th Oct. 1641.—[*Recs. of Synod of Argyle*, 19, 23, S.H.S.]

1641 JOHN DARROCH, M.A., trans. from Jura between 6th May and 7th Oct. 1641; on 8th Sept. 1644 he, having confessed himself guilty of "very grosse complyance and that he hath been for a long time a preacher to the rebells" (Montrose's men), was "*simpliciter* deposed *tam a beneficio quam ab officio*"; he appears to have applied for reinstatement to his status as a min., and on 11th March 1648 he was app. by the Synod "afternoon at next Session to give in his declaration in writ seconded with his unfeigned sorrow for his miscarriage in being with the rebels"; and on 11th Oct. of the same year it is recorded that "he has been licensed to preach, and given proof of repentance in life and doctrine," and accordingly the Synod appointed him "to repair to Aran to Kilmorie Kirk now vacant and preach there and to receive a chalder of victual, and also to preach at Gya (Gigha) and receive the teinds thereof"; his death took place about that time, for under the same date (11th Oct. 1648) Henry, "son of the late Mr John Darroch," appears among a list of boys to whom the Synod awarded grants from their special fund for education; on 9th May 1649 his widow, Margaret Campbell, for "herself and her fatherless children," was ordained by the Synod to get a chalder of victual of the vacant stipend of Arran, apparently Kilmorie, for crop 1648, and on 15th Oct. 1651 the Synod awarded her 12 bolls of the meal of Gigha.—[*Recs. of Synod of Argyle*, 21, 26, 29, 39, 101, 106–7, 122–3, 133, 224.]

1672 DAVID SIMSON, marr. 20th Nov. 1656 Jean Thomson.—[*St Andrews Reg.*]

1742 DAVID CAMPBELL, his daugh., Elizabeth, died 17th July 1797.

1910 ANGUS JOHN MACVICAR, his mother was Isabell Maclean and his wife's mother Mary Cameron. Addl. issue—John, born 6th Nov. 1927.

WHITING BAY

1910 JOHN DUNLOP BROWN, trans. to Craigmore 25th Oct. 1928.

1929 CALLUM MACKENZIE, born Lochinver, Sutherland, 16th March 1902, son of Hector M. and Jean Maclean; educ. at Golspie School and Univ. of Glasgow; M.A. (1921); licen. by Presb. of Paisley April 1928; assistant Paisley Abbey; ord. 11th June 1929; trans. to Leswalt 5th March 1937. Marr. 2nd July 1936 Janet Mackenzie, only daugh. of John Taylor, J.P., Burlington House, Whiting Bay, and has issue—Margaret Joan Janetta, born 17th March 1937; Christine Mackenzie, born 15th April 1939.

PRESBYTERY OF ISLAY

COLONSAY

KENNETH MACLEOD, trans. to Gigha 24th July 1923.
1917

ANGUS MACFADZEAN, born 4th Oct. 1878, son of Angus M., blacksmith, and Margaret Livingston Macphail; licen. May 1925; ord. 5th Aug. 1925; trans. to Duror 8th July 1930. Marr. 1st Oct. 1914 Catherine Ferguson, daugh. of Allan Cameron, J.P., Bowmore, Islay, and has issue—Alina Cameron, born 14th Oct. 1916 (marr. 29th Sept. 1939 Elis Victor Karlssen, Vardo, Aland, Finland); Catherine Margaret, born 15th Dec. 1919; Angus Donald, born 4th Dec. 1925.
1925

JURA

Church renovated and reopened 28th Dec. 1922.

JOHN DARROCH, min. in 1632. Marr. cont. 29th and 30th Oct. 1632 Margaret, daugh. of George Campbell of Ballochlavan.—[*Craignish Writs*, 283.]
1632

JOHN DARROCH, M.A., trans. to Southend between 6th May and 7th Oct. 1641.
1635

ANGUS McCUAIG, his widow, Jane Macdonald, died 7th Jan. 1933.
1876

DONALD JOHN ROBERTSON, licen. 4th May 1898; died 16th July 1947.
1903

KILARROW

The church belonged to the Priory of Ardchattan. Kilbrannon in the parish suggests a dedication to St Brendan. At Cill Sleibhein are the ruins of a chapel dedicated to St Slebhine; and near the Laggan river there once stood Tighlagh Chill ma-Cheallich, the law-house of the Chapel of St Calloch. In Loch Finlagan near the centre of the parish there is St Finlagan's Isle, on which there was a chapel dedicated to that saint. The chapel was associated with the Chapel of St Columba in the services of a single chaplain. On 5th April 1661 there was presented to Parliament in name of the parishioners a supplication to the effect that "the scarcity of honest and able ministers haveing the Yrish tongue, and the Remotenes of the place hath keept their congregation desolate and without a satled minister for some tyme bypast, and being necessitat to make use of ane expectant Mr Robert Campbell who can only preach to these who understand the English and for want of the Yrish tongue cannot be admitted to be their minister, Thairfor humbly desyreing that a compitent mantenance furth of the stipend of Yla might be appointed for the said Mr Robert his paines." Parliament answered the supplication by modifying "300 merks to be paiyed to said Mr Robert Campbell for his bygone service at the Kirk of Yla and ordainis the same to be payed to him out of the said stipend of Yla for this crop and year 1661." The alternative name, "Kirk of Yla," will be noted.—[*Reg. Sec. Seal*, i, 911, 3882, ii, 4546; *Reg. Great Seal*, ii, 2887; *Acts Scott. Parl.*, vii, 128; *Orig. Parochiales Scotiae*, ii, 261; Skene's *Celtic Scot.*, ii, 408; Mackinlay's *Anc. Ch. Dedications*, (non-script.), 67, 143–4.]

ALEXANDER STEWART, pres. by Crown 10th Aug. 1842.
1843

JOHN McGILCHRIST, pres. by Crown 23rd July 1859.
1859

NEIL ROSS, licen. May 1899; his wife's to mother, Finguel Mackenzie; adm. united charge 3rd May 1931; dem. 15th July 1947; died at Dunvegan 24th Oct. 1947.
1913

KILCHOMAN

ARCHIBALD CAMPBELL, parson of Melfurde, pres. to parsonage 3rd May 1593 on death of Duncan Mackilwray.—[*Reg. Sec. Sig.*, lxvii, 54.]
1593

ARCHIBALD McALISTER, M.A., on 9th May 1649 the Synod relaxed him from his suspension and permitted him again to preach, and ord. him to attend the charges of Kilcalmonell, Skipness, Tarbert and Gigha by convenient courses for a year and to have their tithes for his maintenance.—[*Synod Reg.*, 132.]
1630

DAVID SIMSON, his daugh., Margaret (marr. Archibald Campbell of Askomel).
1692

JOHN CAMPBELL, had issue—Ninian; Isobel.—[*Tombst.*]
1702

ALEXANDER CAMERON, his daugh., Elizabeth, died at London 17th May 1935.
1824

ALEXANDER MACNAB, pres. by Crown 29th July 1843.
1844

JAMES DEWAR, pres. by Crown 11th May 1846; his daugh., Helen Jane, died at Edinburgh 23rd March 1932.
1846

JOHN MACLEAN, pres. by Crown 15th Nov. 1866.
1867

GEORGE MACKENZIE, trans. to Kilmore 28th Sept. 1923.
1921

ALEXANDER MACBEAN, trans. from Hylipol 9th April 1925; died 3rd June 1928.
1925

KILDALTON

At Cill Cathain west of Port Ellen there was a chapel dedicated to St Chattan.—[Mackinlay's *Ancient Church Dedications*, (non-script.), 110.]

MARTIN McLACHLAN, had to flee for his life during Royalist rebellion and afterwards returned to his charge; still min. in 1661.—[*G. R. Sas.*, xxxi, 55.]
1630

ARCHIBALD ROBERTSON, line 6, for "30" read "18."
1789

JAMES MACFADYEN, pres. by Crown 1st Sept. 1859; his widow, Margaret Smith, died 14th Jan. 1928.
1860

JAMES MACKINNON, dem. 16th May 1938, died 19th June 1939; his daugh., Sheila Margaret Sillars (marr. 18th April 1923 John Winter Tulloch, B.A.).
1894

KILMENY

The old parish church was dedicated to St Columba.—[*Cal. of Papal Reg., Petitions*, i, 574.]

DONALD McDONALD, pres. by Crown 31st Jan. 1844.
1844

HUGH LAMONT, pres. by Crown 25th June 1870.
1870

ALEXANDER JAMES WISHART TANT, pres. by Crown 27th Feb. 1872.
1872

KENNETH SMITH, trans. to Duror 6th April 1926.
1918

OA

ANGUS MACUAIG, pres. by Crown 12th June 1871.
1871

DONALD F——— MACLEAN, died 5th Dec. 1930.
1887

HUGH LIVINGSTON, trans. to Torosay 4th May 1927.
1919

(*Charge suppressed* 1930.)

PORTNAHAVEN

DAVID McFIE, pres. by Crown 17th June 1845; his daugh., Jessie Ann, died 8th March 1938.
1845

JOHN ALEXANDER CAMPBELL, his daughs.—Mary Ealnor (marr. 30th March 1939 Robert John Henry Carter, Lodge, Montrath); Margaret Drysdale Robertson (marr. 6th April 1937 Colin Sherwin, 2nd Lieut. R.G.A., elder son of Donald Alexander Macleod, Mosman, Sydney); his widow, Agnes Jane Cockburn, died 29th July 1948.
1882

NEIL GILLIES MACDONALD, trans. to Tiree 9th May 1923.
1920

DONALD HENRY MACDONALD, born Dec. 1873; educ. at Dunoon Theological College; R. B. Missionary, Obbe, July 1902, Kilfinichen, Dec. 1904, Glencreren, July to Sept. 1917, Glenetive, Oct. 1917 to Sept. 1920, Melness, St. Columba's, Glasgow, April 1921; studied at Univ. of Glasgow; adm. licentiate for Gaelic Charges 24th May 1923; ord. 20th Dec. 1923; trans. to Hylipol 24th Oct. 1934; died 16th Nov. 1936. Marr. Dec. 1905 Jessie Ann Mactavish (died 3rd Feb. 1940).
1923

PRESBYTERY OF LORN

APPIN

A "new Church" was built at Appin by Sir Donald Campbell of Ardnamurchan before 7th Oct. 1641, on which date he petitioned the Synod to ordain Mr Duncan McCalman, min. at Lismore, to conduct services *per vices* at the said new church. The Synod left the matter to the discretion of the min. On 10th Oct. 1642 the Synod, regarding Lismore and Appin as an unsuitable charge for one min., and considering that there was a sufficient maintenance for two charges, deemed it expedient that Lismore be constituted a charge by itself, that Appin and Duror be erected into a parish, with a min. at Appin Church, and that Elen-Mun, including Glencoe and Mamore, be annexed to Appin, and that the preaching every third Sunday be at Elen-Mun. On 7th Oct. 1643 it was intimated to the Synod that Sir Donald Campbell of Ardnamurchan, who was tackman of one half of the teinds of Lismore, aided by others, fearing that the erection of Appin into a separate parish with provision from the teinds of Lismore would be to his prejudice, sought to bar the project by locking the door of Appin Church, thus refusing the min. entrance, and even seeking to hinder the people from attending worship in the churchyard by the min. as enjoined every third Sunday. The Synod ordained the Presb. of Lorne to cite parties, and, if they pleaded guilty, to ordain them to make repentance at Appin Church, and, if not, to proceed further against them. On 5th Dec. 1657 the Commission on the Plantation of Kirks dismembered and disjoined Appin and Duror from Kilmaluag in Lismore, and Glencoe from Illanmoun, Appin, Duror and Glencoe to be erected into a new parish with a church to be built at Kilcollumkill in Duror. A stipend was also modified for a min. at said new church, with a sufficient manse and glebe. The decreet of the Commission was not ratified by Parliament, and therefore would take effect only if all parties interested were agreed. Though the min. of Lismore acquiesced, it does not appear that the opposition disclosed at the Synod was waived; and apparently the decreet was without result. The Recissory Act of 1661 had no bearing upon this case. Appin Church was rebuilt in the district of Strath and was repaired prior to 1791.—[*Records, Synod of Argyll*, 26, 57, 83, 237.]

1903 CHARLES MACDONALD, trans. to Enzie 6th Oct. 1926.

1927 JOHN MACLEAN, formerly of Kilmuir (*q.v.*); trans. from Strontian 12th April 1927; dem. 15th May 1933; adm. to Inverkeithny 18th Feb. 1938; trans. to Kilmeny, Islay, 28th July 1948. Has issue—Fiona M., born 15th May 1927.

ARDCHATTAN

The patron saint was not Modan, but Baodan, Baetan, the earlier name of the place occurring in several forms, Balivedan, Balliebodane, Ballebadin, Ballibodan, Ballebhodan, which is *Baile Bhaodain*, the town or dwelling of Baodan. There were at least five saints bearing the name Baetan, late Baodan, but it is not clear which saint of that name was the patron here. In Glen Salach in the parish there was a large block of stone, called *Suidhe Bhoadain* (Baodan's Seat). It was broken up long ago. Of the church, which has been long a ruin, it was said in the early part of the 18th century that it "is above the bigg church a litle on the syd of ane hill in a pleasant place where the sunn useth daylie to rise upone when it ryseth upone one pairt of the country, and this is called Kilbedan." The present church was built in 1836. The Priory of Ardchattan was dedicated to John the Baptist. The seal of the priory has a figure of the Baptist holding on a plaque the Agnus Dei, and bears the inscription SIGILL. CONVENTUS DE ARDKATTAN IN ARGADIA. In addition to the Church of Balivedan (Ardchattan), which had an early dependence on the Bishop of Dunkeld, the priory held also the Churches of Kilniniver, Kilbrandon, Kirkapol (Tiree), Kilmonivaig and Kilmarow (Kilarrow). In a clan feud the Church of the Priory was burned by the Macdonalds in 1644, and all that now remains is some ruins. The prior's dwelling constitutes the mansion house of the local estate.—[Skene's *Celtic Scotland*, ii, 408; *Origines Parochiales Scotiae*, ii, (1), 148, 149; Watson's *Celtic Place Names*, 122–3, 262, 300–1; Mackinlay's *Anc. Ch. Dedications, Script.*, 324, 326.]

1618   JOHN CAMPBELL, min. in 1625 and 1628; had issue—Archibald.—[*G. R. Sas.*, xix, 7, 9th June 1619.]

1639   JOHN McILVORIE, had a son, John, to whom the Synod made an education grant 11th Oct. 1648.

1667   COLIN CAMPBELL, adm. Presb. Clerk 1667. Line 14, delete "Father of the Church."

1817   HUGH FRASER, his daugh., Mary Jane Cadogan, died 1st Aug. 1922, aged 90.

1874   HUGH MACLACHLAN, his widow, Anne MacIntyre or Elphinstone, died 6th Aug. 1928.

1903   JOHN ARCHIBALD MacCORMICK, died 9th Jan. 1926.

1926   ALEXANDER MACDONALD, born Hosta, North Uist, 25th April 1897, son of Malcolm M., crofter, and Mary Ann Macaulay; educ. at Kingussie School and Univ. of Glasgow; licen. 14th Dec. 1924; assistant, St Columba, Glasgow, 1924; ord. 5th Aug. 1924 to St Kiarans, Govan; trans. and adm. 20th July 1926; served in Great War with R.A.F. in France. Marr. 3rd Oct. 1945 Alexandrina, S.N.F.W., younger daugh. of M. C. Cowper, Gogar Mains, Edinburgh, and has issue—a son born 17th July 1946; a daugh. born 8th Feb. 1948.

CONNELL

1894   CHARLES DOUGLAS MACINTOSH, died 19th Nov. 1923.

1924   JOHN McINNES, born Glendale, Skye, 30th Nov. 1893, son of John McI. and Catherine MacLean; educ. at Portree School and Univ. of Edinburgh; M.A. (1920); Ph.D. (Edin., 1941); served in Great War in Cameron Highlanders in the ranks and as an officer; twice wounded; licen. by Presb. of Edinburgh 1922; assistant Galashiels; ord. 4th April 1924; was Planters Chaplain in Western Duars, 1930; trans. to Halkirk 27th April 1934.

DUROR

In 1826 there was built at Duror a parliamentary church 9 miles from Appin; and to it were attached the districts of Duror and Glencoe, *quoad sacra*. A Royal Bounty Missionary served Glencoe and Glencreran in Appin as well as Glenetive in Ardchattan. Prior to the appointment of the missionary the min. of Lismore preached four times annually at Glencoe. (See Lismore, Appin, Glencoe.)

1844   NEIL MACKENZIE, pres. by Crown 5th July 1844.

1871   JAMES MACDOUGALL, pres. by Crown 30th June 1871; his widow, Agnes, daugh. of Cuthbert Cowan, banker, Ayr, died 1st May 1940, aged 91.

1921   DUGALD COWAN MACRAE, dem. 3rd Dec. 1924.

1926   KENNETH SMITH, trans. from Kilmeny (*q.v.*) 6th April 1926; died at Dundee 5th April 1929; his daugh., Isabella (marr. John Alexander Mackay, min. of Chapelton); his widow, Sophia Christina Macdonald, died 18th June 1930.

GLENCOE

The parish of Eil Munde embraced Glencoe and the adjacent parts of the braes of Appin on the south side of Lochleven, and the districts of Mamore and Onich on the north side towards Fort William. The church was reported to the Synod on 11th Oct. 1649 as having been vacant for five years.—[*Recs., Synod of Argyle*, 150, S.H.S.]

1916 ALEXANDER BOYD, trans. to St Mary's, Inverness, 6th Feb. 1924.

1924 COLIN MACPHERSON, ord. 6th June 1924; trans. to St Andrew's, Johnstone, 4th June 1929.

GLENORCHY and INISHAIL

The parish was sometimes called Dysart. The church was granted by Sir Duncan Campbell of Lochow to the Collegiate Church of Kilmun on its erection in 1442. It was rebuilt in 1811. The Church of St Findoc of Inchealt (Inishail) was granted to Inchaffray Abbey on 29th June 1257 by Ath, son of Malcom Macnauchton. The saint is Findoc, Findoca, the virgin whose day is 13th Oct. The Church of Inishail was removed to the mainland in 1736.—[*Cal. Papal Regs., Letters*, xii, 242-4; *Charters of Inchaffray Abbey*, 75-6; Watson's *Celtic Place Names*, 286-7.]

1562 JOHN McCALLUM, min. in 1562, 1592, and rector of Lochawe 1622; probably father of Neil McCallum or Malcolm, min. of Kenmore.

1632 JOHN MALCOLM, min. of Kenmore, parson of Lochawe.

1894 FARQUHAR MACRAE, dem. 31st Dec. 1930; died 20th Aug. 1943.

(*Charges united 20th Feb. 1931.*)

INISHAIL

1572 DONALD CARSWELL, brother to Bishop of Isles; died *s.p.*

NEIL MALCOLM, parson of Lochow.

JOHN BANE McKELLAR, residing at Fernoch, Lochow.

1607 JOHN MALCOLM, parson of Lochow, served fortnightly until 1607, and before 1614 desisted from the cure.

1614 JOHN CAMPBELL, min. of Ardchattan, served cure fortnightly.

KILBRANDON

The church belonged to the Priory of Ardchattan.—[Skene's *Celtic Scot.*, ii, 408.]

1579 PATRICK DENISON, vicar of Seill.— [*Acts and Dec.*, lxxix, 57.]

1597 NEIL MACLACHLAN, vicar in 1597, had wadset of teinds; his son, Patrick, renounced same 1621.— [*G. R. Sas.*, 16th March 1621.]

1852 ARCHIBALD CAMPBELL, his daugh., Catherine, died at Winnipeg 14th July 1931.

1902 WILLIAM MACPHAIL, trans. to Ardrishaig 3rd March 1926.

1927 ADAM ERNEST ANDERSON, born 22nd June 1902, son of Arthur MacGregor A., schoolmaster, Boat of Garten, and Davina Porter; educ. at Univ. of Edinburgh, M.A. (Hons. Celtic) (1924); licen. by Presb. of Abernethy May 1927; ord. 27th Sept. 1927; trans. to Glenorchy 23rd July 1931; Chaplain to Forces 12th April 1940; dem. 11th Nov. 1943. Marr. 29th Nov. 1928 Elsie Grant, daugh. of John McInnes and Mary Grant, and has issue—John Brendan, born 25th Dec. 1930; Adam Connan, born 11th April 1933.

(*Charges united 17th Dec. 1930.*)

KILCHRENAN

There were chapels dedicated to St Mundu or Munnu at Kilmun on the shore of Loch Avich, and at Kilmun north of the river Avich between Loch Avich and Loch Awe. The latter was the old Church of Dalavich. The two existing churches at Kilchrenan and at Dalavich, in the latter case situated on the shore of Loch Awe opposite Inischonnel, were built about 1771–5.—[Watson's *Celtic Place Names*, 307.]

1570 NEIL MALCOLM, probably son of John M., min. of Glenorchy.

1610 JOHN MALCOLM or McCALLUM, probably son of preceding. Marr. Eupham Campbell and had addl. issue—Dugald.—[*G. R. Sas.*, 13 Jan. 1618, 371; xxxviii, 219.]

1631 NEIL McCALLUM, trans. from Kenmore before 24th June 1631. Marr. Katherine, daugh. of Donald McIlvorie, min. of Glenaray.—[*G. R. Sas.*, 8th May 1618, i, 324, 325; xxxi, 309.]

1852 NEIL MACKENZIE, his son, Nigel Banks, died 4th Nov. 1924; his daugh., Eleanora Alexandrina, died 17th Feb. 1940.

1905 NEIL DONALD CAMPBELL MACKINNON, died 15th April 1939.

(*United with Kilchrenan West and Portsonachan.*)

KILMORE and KILBRIDE

The Church of Kilmore was dedicated to St Bean.

On 10th Oct. 1649 Mr Archibald Campbell of Dunstaffnage made a claim to the Synod for "better accommodation" for the parishioners, and suggested a central church for both parishes. The Synod referred the matter to the Commission on Plantation of Kirks, and on 15th April 1651 that body decreed that instead of Kilmore and Kilbride there be built at Oban a new church, to be called the Church of Oban, with manse and glebe there. The min., Mr Nicol McCalman, was to have the choice of continuing to live in the manse at Kilmore or transferring to the new manse at Oban. The decreet did not take effect. Kilbride Church is of the 15th century, and Kilmore Church was rebuilt in 1740.—[*Recs. of Synod of Argyle*, 243, S.H.S.; *Cal. Papal Regs., Letters*, vii, 407.]

1561 JOHN COCKBURN, parson 3rd July 1561.—[*Acts and Dec.*, xxi, 282.]

1598 NEIL MACLACHLAN, vicar.

1608 NICOL McCALMAN, removed from Kilbride to Kilmore before 18th Oct. 1637; his sons—Archibald; Alexander, to whom the Synod made an education grant 11th Oct. 1648.—[*G. R. Sas.*, 1st March 1639, xlviii, 250; *Synod Reg.*, 123.]

1666 ALEXANDER CAMPBELL OF AUCHNACLOICH, only son of Archibald C. of Auchnacloich and Katherine Stewart; died 1698. Marr. (1) 1669 Margaret, daugh. of John Campbell of Dunstaffnage, and had issue—James, of Stonefield, sheriff depute of Argyll, died 22nd Aug. 1729; (2) Elizabeth, daugh. of Sir John Campbell of Glenorchy and sister of John, first Earl of Breadalbane and widow of John Campbell of Lochnell family, and had issue—Archibald, of Stonefield, born 1696, advocate, sheriff of Argyll, died 19th Aug. 1777.

1700 DANIEL CAMPBELL, marr. Isobel Campbell, and had issue—Janet, Betty and Archibald.—[*Argyll Sas.*, v, 149; *Argyll Tests.*, 9 and 11.]

1891 JOHN MACNAB MACGREGOR, dem. 15th May 1923; died at Auchtertool Manse 22nd Sept. 1925.

1923 GEORGE MACKENZIE, trans. from Kilchoman 28th Sept. 1923; trans. to Greenock Gaelic 17th May 1928; trans. to Dores and Bona 11th Sept. 1946; dem. 19th Oct. 1947.

KILNINVER

The church belonged to the Priory of Ardchattan.—[Skene's *Celtic Scotland*, ii, 408.]

1560 SIR JOHN McPAUL, portioner of Ardchattan, was parson some years prior to and after 1561.—[*Orig. Paroch. Scot.*, ii, (1), 149.]

1580 ALEXANDER CAMPBELL, rector 8th May 1580; he and his brother John and his sister Margaret received Letters of Legitimation on 12th Sept. 1580; was Commendator of Ardchattan, and Commendator and Abbot of Iona 6th June 1581.—[*Reg. Great Seal*, v, 13, 93, 208, 441.]

1580 SIR NIGEL REID, vicar 8th May 1580.—[*Reg. Great Seal*, v, 13.]

1599 JOHN REID, min.

1618 ARCHIBALD CAMPBELL, may have been identical with Archibald C., pres. to parsonage of Kilchrenan 5th May 1593.—[*Reg. Sec. Sig.*, lxvii, 54.]

1639 PATRICK MACLACHLAN, had a son, Nigel, to whom the Synod made an education grant 11th Oct. 1648.—[*Synod Reg.*, 123.]

1650 JOHN McLACHLAN, marr. (2) Elizabeth Campbell, widow of John and wife of Donald, son of Dougald Campbell of Kenmore; his daugh., Isobel (marr. cont. 27th Jan. 1671 John McDougall, fiar of Ardencaple); his sons—John, min. of Craignish; Martin; Neil, drover.—[*G. R. Sas.*, 3 Ser., xxvi, 449.]

1702 JAMES CAMPBELL, his daugh., Anne (marr. Archibald Campbell, Glenfeochan).

1798 DONALD CAMPBELL, son of John C., tacksman of Corlaroch, and Margaret Macleod.

1917 ALASTAIR CAMPBELL, trans. to Luss 26th Feb. 1925.

1925 DUGALD BELL, trans. from South Uist (*q.v.*) 30th July 1925; trans. to Lismore 1st Aug. 1928.

LISMORE

On 5th Dec. 1651 the Commission on the Plantation of Kirks dismembered and disjoined Appin and Duror from Kilmaluig in Lismore and decerned Lismore with the lands of Kingarloch to be a distinct parish, and the kirk to be removed from Kilmaluig to the most central part of the parish, the Presbytery of Kilmoir to visit the parish and determine whether the church should be removed or not. The decreet apparently did not take effect. In 1791 there were in the parish four places of worship, Lismore, Appin, Glencoe, and Kingarloch, and the min. had the assistance of a missionary.—[*Recs. of Synod of Argyle*, 237. See Appin, Duror, Glencoe.]

1619 DUNCAN McCALMAN, min. in 1619.

1645 DUNCAN McCALMAN, formerly of Ardnamurchan (*q.v.*).

1650 ARCHIBALD REID, M.A.; adm. after 10th Oct. 1649, when the church was noted by the Synod of Argyle as vacant, and had been so for five years.—[*Recs. of Synod of Argyle*, 150, S.H.S.]

1660 ALEXANDER McCALMAN, apparently son of Nicol M., min. of Kilmore; has sasine of ½ merk land of Darrenaneach 22nd Nov. 1672.—[*G. R. Sas.*, 3 Ser., vi, 246; xxx, 389.]

1886 WILLIAM TORRIE, his widow, Mary Wright Clark, died at Edinburgh 4th June 1930.

1911 LACHLAN MACKINNON, died 10th Sept. 1927.

1928 DUGALD BELL, trans. from Kilninver 1st Aug. 1928; died 30th Sept. 1936; his wife, Emily Blanche Sykes, died 3rd Jan. 1905. Marr. (2) 10th April 1929 Flora Beaton Campbell.

MUCKAIRN

Another form of the old name *Cladh Choireil*, and Kilespikural, indicating that the cell or chapel in the graveyard was dedicated to St Cyrillus, St Cyril. At first the chief place was Kilmaronag in the east part of the parish, where there was a church dedicated to St Cronoc, a name borne by thirty saints. Shortly before the Reformation the church was removed from Kilmaronag to Muckairn and took the place of the chapel in the graveyard there, the walls of which still existed at the close of the 18th century. It is said that the bishopric was at Muckairn prior to its removal to Lismore; and for a time Muckairn Church was a possession of the Bishops of Dunkeld and was a mensal church. The present church was built in 1829. On a small island in a lake called Kilvarie or Kilmorie Loch, in the west part of the parish, there was a chapel dedicated to St Maelrubha. Near it is Ballindeor, the town of the Dewar or hereditary keeper of a relic of the saint, called in a manrent of 1518 Arwachyll, maybe a *bachull* or pastoral staff.—[Skene's *Celtic Scotland*, ii, 408, 412; Watson's *Celtic Place Names*, 303.]

1583 JOHN McKELLAR, had pres. to vicarage of Cilleasbuig Earaild in 1583 on death of Angus McPhail. He had no issue and was succeeded by his nephew, John.—[*Reg. Pres. Bene.*, ii, 92; *G. R. Sas.*, xxx, 306.]

1619 ARCHIBALD McCALMAN, died before 22nd Nov. 1672. Had issue, John.—[*G. R. Sas.*, 3 Ser., xxx, 389.]

1843 LACHLAN MACKENZIE, pres. by Crown 26th Dec. 1837.

1851 DONALD MACFARLANE, pres. by Crown 4th Oct. 1850.

1852 JOHN SINCLAIR, pres. by Crown 19th April 1852.

1859 DONALD McCAIG, pres. by Crown 13th July 1859.

1886 MALCOLM MACCALLUM, dem. 14th Dec. 1921, died at Oban 30th Oct. 1928; his son, Nathaniel Cameron, killed by fall from cliff near Oban 10th Nov. 1928; his widow, Christina Cameron, died 9th Nov. 1939.

1921 GILLESPIE MACGREGOR CAMPBELL, trans. from Glenaray 17th May 1922; trans. to St Columba's, Paisley, 13th Nov. 1928.

1929 JOHN MACPHERSON, born Qu'appelle, Saskatchewan, Canada, 24th June 1902, son of Angus M., Balnain Street, Inverness, and Ann Stewart; educ. at Inverness High School, Kingussie Secondary School and Univ. of Edinburgh; M.A. (Oct. 1925) and Hons. Celtic Languages (Oct. 1927); licen. by Presb. of Inverness 7th May 1929; ord. 15th Aug. 1929; trans. to Daviot and Dunlichity 24th Feb. 1943. Marr. 20th April 1943 Jane Watson Wallace, and had issue—Sheena, born 22nd April 1944.

(*Charges united* 17*th Dec.* 1930.)

OBAN

1891 ALEXANDER DUFF, dem. 16th May 1922; died at Edinburgh 26th Nov. 1930; his widow, Helen Baillie Drummond, died 17th July 1937.

1922 HECTOR CAMERON, trans. from Kilmartin (*q.v.*) 12th Oct. 1922; trans. to Moy 20th May 1932; died 8th May 1940. Issue—Hector Alexander, in merchant service, born 30th Jan. 1917; Alastair Ross, born 27th July 1918; Anna Edith Agnes, born 28th Jan. 1920; Martin Argyll, born 24th May 1921; Ewen Mackenzie, born 19th Jan. 1923. Publications —*Handbook of Tiree* (1938); edited *The Tiree Bards* (1932).

OBAN, ST COLUMBA'S

1922 MALCOLM MACKERACHER, died Edinburgh 31st July 1942.

PRESBYTERY OF MULL

All the charges in the Island of Mull were noted by the Synod on 10th Oct. 1649 as having been vacant since the Reformation.—[*Recs. of Synod of Argyle*, 150, S.H.S.]

ACHARACLE

1840 SAMUEL CAMERON, pres. by Crown 14th March 1840.

1843 HUGH MACDIARMID, pres. by Crown 24th Sept. 1843.

1844 ROBERT STEWART, pres. by Crown 2nd Jan. 1844.

1856 DONALD McFADYEN, pres. by Crown 12th June 1856.

1861 DONALD MURRAY SIMPSON, pres. by Crown 7th March 1861.

1873 DUNCAN MACNAUGHTON, pres. 27th Jan. 1873.

1887 NEIL MACKINNON, died 14th Nov. 1928; his widow, Margaret Campbell, died 30th July 1943; his daugh., Agnes (marr. (1) Captain William Douglas; (2) 6th April 1946 Alexander Wallace, Perth).

ARDNAMURCHAN

The patron saint is Comgan, said to have been the brother of Kentigern, a daughter of Callach Cualann of Leinster, who died in 734.—[*Cal. of Papal Regs. Letters*, viii, 10; *Cal. of Scottish Supplies*, 457; Watson's *Celtic Place Names*.]

EILEAN FINAIN. The island, named Eilean Fhionain, on Loch Shiel, was the burial place of the Clan Ranalds until the close of the 16th century. On the island are the ruins of St Finan's Chapel, which is said to have been built by Alan MacRuairidh, one of the Clan Ranald Chiefs. There survives the altar of rough stone; and upon it is St Finan's bell, said to have been brought from Ireland by St Finan himself. Noteworthy is the face of Christ on the stone crucifix.—[Seton Gordon's *Highways and Byways of the West Highlands*, 168–70.]

1613 JOHN RONALDSON, parson of Eilean Finain, had letters of tack from John McRonald of Moydart, Captain of Clanranald, to him, Allan McRonald, his brother's son, and the heir male of Allan, for nineteen years of twenty shilling land of Deniles, etc., in barony of Moydart, April 1625.—[*Clan Donald*, iii, 649.]

1624 DONALD OMEY, afterwards of Kingarth, 1626.—[*P. C. Reg.*, xiii, 427–8.]

1629 DUNCAN McCALMAN, son of Duncan M., min. of Lismore, app. schoolmaster of Lismore 17th April 1659. On 1st May 1650 and on 16th Oct. 1650 it was laid to his charge by the Synod that though justly dep. and excommunicated, "he does dayly in the barbarouse and remote highlands baptise children and mary pairties coming to him to that effect''; the Synod remitted him to the Marquis of Argyle, "Justice in the bounds," for apprehension and punishment; the Marquis seems to have delayed action.—[*Recs. of Synod of Argyle*, 171, 184, S.H.S.]

1635 DONALD DOUGALSON, vicar 2nd Oct. 1635, and may have acted as reader.—[*Clanranald Papers*.]

LACHLAN FRASER, min. at Kilmallie and Eilan Finain 23rd April 1678.
1678

JOHN McCALLUM, had issue—Neill; Archibald.—[*Argyll Sas.*, lxxviii, 107.]
1700

ANGUS MacLAINE, born at Ardtornish 24th Feb. 1800, son of Allan M. and Marjory, eldest daugh. of Angus Gregorson of Ardtornish.—[*Tombst.*, Warriston.]
1827

JOHN SMITH, dem. 11th Nov. 1924; died at Ardrishaig 29th Sept. 1927; his daugh., Amelia Helena (marr. 23rd Dec. 1924 James Christian Hall, M.B., Ch.B., son of James H., min. of Banchory Ternan); his widow, Amelia Isabel Fraser McIntyre, died 15th Oct. 1937.
1890

NEIL GILLIES MACDONALD, trans. from Tiree 6th May 1925. Marr. 26th June 1929 Mary, daugh. of Duncan Cameron and Sarah MacEachran, and has issue—Ian Uist, born 21st March 1932; Cameron MacEachran (twin), born 21st March 1932.
1925

COLL

The church belonged to the Augustinian Priory of St Mary in Iona. On 27th Feb. 1450-1 it was designated St Finnoga's, Cill Fhionnaig. The saint is Findsech, Findoca, Latin, Findoca, whose day was 13th Oct. A Parliamentary church, served by a resident missionary, was built in 1802.—[*Cal. Papal Regs.*, *Letters*, x, 501-2; Watson's *Celtic Place Names*, 286-7.]

NEIL McKILLOP, dem. 3rd Feb. 1925; line 3, p. 110, for "Ritchie" read "Kitcher"; died 14th Feb. 1935, aged 68.
1917

GEORGE ALEXANDER SELBIE, formerly of Clatt (*q.v.*) and Gillingham, 1909-14; Army Chaplain, 1914-19; missionary at Craigellachie 1920-3; adm. 14th Dec. 1927; dem. 19th Oct. 1930; died at Lethendy 22nd May 1935, aged 76.
1927

HEYLIPOL

ALEXANDER GRANT, his widow, Christina Grant Miller, died 23rd Feb. 1943.
1913

ALEXANDER MACBEAN, trans. to Kilchoman 9th April 1925.
1914

HUGH MACKENZIE, ord. 16th Sept. 1925; trans. to Cabrach 9th Sept. 1927.
1925

MALCOLM MACDONALD, born 23rd March 1862; ord. to Kinlochewe U.F. Church 6th Feb. 1901; trans. to Duirinish 10th Nov. 1908; Shieldaig 19th Sept. 1912; trans. to U.F. Church, Benbecula, 22nd Oct. 1915; trans. 24th April 1929; dem. 30th June 1933; died 9th April 1935. Marr. 30th Dec. 1902 Margaret Fraser, and had issue—Greta Mackinnon, born 15th March 1905.
1929

SOROBIE

JOHN FRASER, M.A.; on 8th Nov. 1677 a Letter of ordination and admission by Alexander Young, Bishop of Edinburgh, was granted to him as min. of Sorobie.—[*Cal. Laing Charters*, 2774.]
1677

IONA

FINGON MACMILLAN, still min. in 1623.—[*G. R. Sas.*, xiv, 192.]
1573

HEW MACLEAN, his son, Ewen.—[*G. R. Sas.*, 2 Ser., xii, 289.]
1630

DONALD McVEAN, his sons—Colin Alexander, died 18th Jan. 1912; Archibald Arthur, died at Edinburgh 21st Jan. 1933; his daugh., Mary Helen, born 2nd June 1843.
1835

ALEXANDER MACGREGOR, pres. 18th Oct. 1843.
1843

ARCHIBALD MACMILLAN, dem. 30th Sept. 1930; died at Dollar 23rd Feb. 1938; his wife, Georgina Ritchie, died 21st Jan. 1936.
1890

KILFINICHEN and KILVICHEOAN

According to Dr Watson, the saint of Kilfinnichan, Cill Fhionnachain, is Findchan, a contemporary of Columba, who founded the Monastery of Artchain in Tiree. The same authority gives Kilvicheoun, Kilviceuen, as *Cill Mhic Eoghain*, Church of the son (*Mhic*) or of the sons (*Mhac*) of Eoghain, probably the latter, for Gorman gives "the three sons of Eoghain," whose day is 19th May. A further suggestion is "Church of the son of Ewen," i.e. Ernan Mac Eoghain, son of Cumad, sister of Columba. In Papal records the saint is erroneously given as St Ouen (St Eugenius). On the petition of Donald, Lord of the Isles, nephew of the late Robert III, on behalf of his chaplain, Adam Dominicus, Perpetual Vicar of the Parish Church of St Eugenius (Kilvicheoan), which stated that "by reason of wars in the Western Highlands of the King of Scotland, ecclesiastical benefices are for the most part so poor and slender that a single priest can hardly be sustained respectably on the fruits of any one benefice, especially because custom is in these parts for every beneficiary continually to hold free hospitality for God's sake," Papal dispensation was granted for two years to the said Adam on 24th Nov. 1421 to hold another benefice along with Kilvicheoan; and a little later this was extended for life. Papal dispensation was also given to the said Adam on 9th Jan. 1428-9 to hold along with Kilvicheoan the Perpetual Vicarage of St Kenithus. This may mean Inchkenneth, Isle of St Kenneth, where, according to Fordun, there was a parish church. There was, however, a Church of St Kenneth at Lochbuie.—[*Cal. of Scottish Supplications*, 268-9, 275; *Cal. Papal Regs., Letters*, viii, 25; Watson's *Celtic Place Names*, 304, 305; *Highland Papers*, iv, 165, 166 and n, 167.]

1623 JOHN CAMPBELL, adm. min. before 11th Oct. 1623.—[*G. R. Sas.*, xiv, 142.]

1667 JAMES FRASER, min. before 6th July 1667, when he was adm. burgess of Rothesay.

1677 DUNCAN BETHUNE, son of John B. of Skeabost and a daugh. of Macleod of Gesto; min. here 11th Aug. 1677.

1756 NEIL MACLEOD, brother of Donald M. of Swordale, had issue—Norman, born 17th Oct. 1757, died 25th May 1759; Donald, born 15th Feb., died 17th May 1761; Florence, died 12th Dec. 1869 (marr. (1) James Roy, adjutant, Military Depot, Aberdeen; (2) Major Robert Watson, Ceylon Rifles); John; Charles; Mary, died 9th March 1853; Susanna; Archibald Norman; Alexander; Roderick, born 29th Aug., died Sept. 1776; Donald; Anne, born 19th Jan. 1778.

1917 NEIL MACPHAIL, died 3rd Nov. 1929.

KILNINIAN

1650 MARTIN McILVRA, had issue—Donald; Finguella (marr. 1657 Donald McLean).—[*G. R. Sas.*, 20th July 1642, li, 359, 371; xliii, 109, 111; 2 Ser., xiii, 194.]

1673 AENEAS McLAINE, trans. from Kilfinan (*q.v.*) 1673; died July 1675. Marr. cont. 19th June 1668 Isabella Hamilton, who survived him.—[*Argyll Hornings*, i, 127; 31st July 1675.]

1766 ARCHIBALD McARTHUR, had issue—Helen, bapt. 28th July 1768.

1914 MARTIN MACRAE, trans. to Trossachs 3rd Feb. 1926.

(*Charges united 24th April* 1931.)

KINLOCHSPELVIE

1914 IAN CARMICHAEL, D.S.O., M.C., afterwards adm. to Martin Memorial, Stornoway, 22nd Jan. 1936; trans. to Lismore 26th Oct. 1945. Marr. 8th Aug. 1917 Dorothy Mary Chard, and had issue—Neil, born Nov. 1916, died 10th Jan. 1935; Betty, born 6th Oct. 1923; Sine, born 23rd Sept. 1925 (marr. 17th Sept. 1947 Ian McGregor Millar, farmer,

Bailuachdaraich, Lismore); Seumas, born 10th April 1928. Publication—*Lismore in Alba* (1948).

PETER HECTOR MACLEAN, died 17th April 1924.
1919

JOHN MacINTYRE, born 12th Sept. 1872, son of William M., quarrier, and Ishbel Rankin; licen. by Presb. of Mull; ord. 18th Nov. 1926; dem. 31st Jan. 1949. Marr. 19th March 1923 Catherine Robertson, and has issue—William, born 15th Jan. 1924; Margaret MacLure, born 19th March 1925; Ronald Robertson, born 23rd March 1928; Ishbel Rankin, born 6th Sept. 1932.
1926

MORVERN

Killundine in the parish is *Cill Fhionntain*, Church of Fintan, evidently St Fintan or Finten, a follower of St Columba. On 27th Dec. 1651 the Commission for the Plantation of Kirks ordained that a new church be built on the lands of Finarie instead of the two churches at Kilcolumkill and Kilintach, the parish to be called the Parish of Finarie, and modified a stipend with a manse and glebe beside the church; it does not appear that the order took effect.—[Watson's *Celtic Place Names*, 93, 304; *Recs. of Synod of Argyle*, 251, S.H.S.]

ANGUS MACLAINE, died before 13th Nov. 1635, when his son, John, was served heir to him in the lands of Knock.—[*Retours*, xvi, 17.]
1611

JOHN MACLEOD, line 20, for "Donald" read "John."
1824

JOHN KENNETH MACLEAN, trans. to Olrig 17th Jan. 1929.
1908

(*Charges united 30th Nov. 1930.*)

SALEN

ALEXANDER KENNEDY, ord. 17th June 1816; trans. to Jura 11th Sept. 1823.
1814

ALEXANDER FERGUSON, trans. from Ulva June 1924; trans. to Tobermory 28th Aug. 1828.
1824

MUNGO CAMPBELL, pres. 17th Jan. 1847.
1847

JOHN DEY, pres. by Crown 30th July 1873.
1873

JOHN MATHESON MACLEOD, trans. to Erchless 26th Dec. 1923.
1919

ANGUS MACLEOD, ord. 10th July 1924; trans. to Kilcalmonell 25th Nov. 1925.
1924

TIREE

The Church of Sorobie was dedicated to St Columba. At the ancient burial ground at Kirkapol there are two sculptured slabs of the West Highland type, and also a portion of a shaft and one arm of a cross. There are two monasteries founded in the time of St Columba. One was at Artchain, "The Fair Cape (or Height)," founded by St Findchan. The other was on Campus Lunge, or Campus Navis, "Ship's Plain" (*Magh Luinge*), founded by St Columba, and ruled for a time by St Baithene, St Columba's cousin and his successor as abbot of Iona. *Brigit Maigi Luinge* is one of the fifteen saints named Brigit in Rawl. At Kilchainie are the walls of a chapel that was dedicated to St Cainnech, probably St Cainnech, who was the honoured guest of St Columba at Iona and accompanied him on his visit to King Brude. Among the rocks beside Ben Kenavara, near the south-west shore, are the foundations and east gable of a chapel, dedicated to St Patrick and called Temple-Patrick. In the rocks on the shore below are several round holes, one of which is called St Patrick's Vat. Close to the ruins are some stones with incised Latin crosses. At Kilmoluag about half a mile north-west of Loch Bharapol there was a chapel dedicated to St Mo-Luoc, who died in 592 and whose day was 25th June. All trace has disappeared, and the burial ground has been ploughed up. In the latter part of the 6th century St Congal founded a monastery, of which there is no information.—[Watson's *Celtic Place Names*, 92, 188, 292; Mackinlay's *Anc. Ch. Dedications*, (non-script.), 62, 63,

70, 72, 83, 145, 159; *Cal. of Supplications Rel. to Scot.*, 271.]

Kirkapol. The church belonged to the Priory of Ardchattan.—[Skene's *Celtic Scot.*, ii, 408.]

MARTIN McILVRA, min. here before 11th Oct. 1623.—[*G. R. Sas.*, xiv, 192.]
1623

FARQUHAR FRASER, on 11th Oct. 1648 he was charged by the Synod with having gone to Lochaber with Sir Lachlan McLean and his men in April 1645 when they went to join Montrose, and with having permitted in his church at Tiree the said Sir Lachlan when under sentence of excommunication. The Synod suspended him *ab officio et beneficio* till next Synod, and warned him of absolute deposition if anything further occurred. On 15th Oct. 1651 the Synod continued him under the sentence of suspension till next Synod. In 1662 the Privy Council awarded him £100 stg. from vacant stipends of Coll and Tiree for his loyalty and as a preacher in Sir Lachlan McLean's Regiment, and for the loss of all his goods and plenishing at the hands of Sir Donald Campbell of Ardnamurchan.—[*Recs. of Synod of Argyle*, 121, 217; *Recs. Privy Council*, 3rd Ser., i, 222-3.]
1633

JOHN FRASER, on 8th Nov. 1677 a Letter of Ordination and Admission was granted to him as min. of Sorbie by Alexander Young, Bishop of Edinburgh.—[*Cal. Laing Charters*, 2774.]
1678

WILLIAM MORRISON, his widow marr. (2) Farquhar McIlmun in Tiree.
1717

ARCHIBALD McCOLL, his daugh., Flora (marr. 1828 Captain Duncan Innes, 42nd Highlanders).
1780

DONALD MACPHERSON, born 1876. Marr. (1) 29th Dec. 1898 Annie Campbell, who died 1st Aug. 1900; and (2) Flora Ann McEwan Wilson; had issue—two children—born 29th Dec. 1899; born 2nd Jan., died 3rd July 1901.
1900

JOHN STEWART, trans. to Halin-in-Waternish 20th Oct. 1922.
1917

NEIL GILLIES MACDONALD, trans. from Portnahaven (*q.v.*) 9th May 1923; trans. to Ardnamurchan 6th May 1925.
1923

ALLAN MACKENZIE, trans. from Rogart 16th Sept. 1925; died at Uig Manse 15th June 1926.
1925

KENNETH MACKAY, born Lewis 11th April 1880, son of John M., fisherman, and Marion Morrison; licen. by Presb. of Glasgow 1927; ord. 22nd June 1927; trans. to Robertson Memorial, Glasgow, 24th April 1930; trans. to Knoydart 6th Dec. 1944; dem. 21st May 1948. Marr. 10th Oct. 1914 Jean Mackay, daugh. of Donald McNeill and Christina Macinnes and has issue—Catriona, born 18th July 1915; Neil, born 13th Nov. 1917.
1927

TOBERMORY

DONALD STEWART, pres. 25th Sept. 1839.
1839

DAVID ROSS, pres. by Crown 29th Jan. 1844.
1844

MALCOLM MacINTYRE, pres. by Crown 27th July 1855.
1855

NEIL McNEIL, pres. by Crown 12th March 1859.
1859

PETER THOMSON, pres. by Crown 9th Nov. 1869.
1870

JOHN MENZIES MENZIES, dem. 31st Dec. 1944; died Wishaw 8th Dec. 1948; his daugh., Margaret Dean (marr. 5th June 1940 Allan Davidson, youngest son of R. J. Brown, Stonsaule, Tobermory).
1919

TOROSAY

On 30th May 1393 Papal Indulgence was granted to visitors to the Parish Church of St John the Evangelist in Ard of Mull (Torosay) who contributed to the repair of the said church, "to which for the cause of devotion a multitude of people are wont frequently to resort with fitting honours." When the parish lost its status as such is not clear. But in 1720 Murdoch McLean, yr. of Lochbuie, in name of himself and other heritors, applied to the Synod of Argyle, praying them to erect Torosay into a parish out of the parishes of Kilvicuen and Kilninian, and to allow part of the Synod funds for a stipend to the min. The Synod approved of the plan, and granted £300 Scots £25 stg.) of their teind duties for promoting it. Apparently the said teind duties were the grant made by Queen Anne in 1705 to the Synod of Argyle, of the haill rents, revenues, casualties, and emoluments of the Bishopric of Argyle and the Isles for crop 1705, and of all former years resting owing, and in time coming, during Her Majesty's pleasure, and for the uses therein expressed.—[*Transcripts from the Vatican*, i, 328; Ninian Elliot's *Teinds in Story's Church of Scotland*, vi, 569.]

1879 WILLIAM MACKINTOSH, dem. 15th May 1926, died at Edinburgh 11th July 1927.

1927 HUGH LIVINGSTON, adm. from Oa 4th May 1927; adm. to united charge 14th Jan. 1930; his son, John, died 6th Sept. 1912.

ULVA

1812 ARCHIBALD MACTAVISH, ord. 13th Sept. 1810; trans. to Jura 6th May 1812.

1814 DONALD CAMPBELL, ord. 30th March 1814; trans. to Kilfinichen 25th Jan. 1816.

1817 ALEXANDER FERGUSON, ord. 23rd June 1817; trans. to Salen June 1824.

1918 DONALD WILLIAM MACKENZIE, trans. to Kilninver 3rd Dec. 1929; dem. 31st May 1938; died at Stirling 26th Oct. 1943; line 18, for "*Uirsgeulam*" read "*Uirsgeulan*."

(*The Church united to Salen* 1938.)

PRESBYTERY OF ABERTARFF

ABERTARFF

1574 JAMES DUFF, M.A., his pres. in 1580 was on the dem. of Patrick Dunbar.—[*Reg. Pres. Bene.*, ii, 33.]

1579 PATRICK DUNBAR, M.A., pres. to vicarage 12th Dec. 1579 on death of –. Brown.—[*Reg. Pres. Bene*, ii, 27.]

ARDGOUR

Kilbedane or Kilbodane in Ardgour is Cill Bhaodain, the church of St Baodan or Baetan.—[Watson's *Celtic Place Names*, 300.]

1910 ALEXANDER DUNCAN MACLEAN. Addl. issue—Sine Henretta, born 15th April 1926.

ARISAIG

The Church of Kilvoury (Arisaig) was noted by the Synod on 10th Oct. 1649 as having been vacant since the Reformation.—[*Reg. Synod of Argyll*, 150.]

1919 JAMES ALEXANDER DONALD, JOHN MACDONALD, dem. 18th May 1925; adm. to Lowick 9th Sept. 1932; dem. 17th April 1945; died 13th Feb. 1947; his wife, Harriet Emma Corderay, died 24th Jan. 1932.

1926 EDMUND STUART RUSSELL, trans. from Poolewe 29th March 1926; trans. to Inverkeithny 12th Aug. 1926.

1927 DONALD MACINTOSH LOGAN, trans. from Tarbert 27th April 1927. Addl. issue—Gertrude Margaret Charmian, W.R.N.S., born 4th June 1923; his daugh., May Louise (marr. 12th April 1944 Rev. Alick Hugh Macaulay, chaplain to the Forces).

MALLAIG

1909 WALTER JOHN MATHAMS, died at Swanage, Dorset, 29th Jan. 1931; his son, Robert Millan, M.A., died at London 13th April 1924.

1926 DUNCAN MACNAB SINCLAIR, born Glasgow 29th Jan. 1884, son of John S., cabinetmaker, Oban, and Anne Macnab; licen. by Presb. of Lochaber 20th Aug. 1926; assistant Scotstoun, Glasgow 1915; Blair Athol 1919; ord. 11th Oct. 1926; ind. to united charge 30th Jan. 1931; trans. to Longriggend 27th April 1933; trans. to Tenandry 6th June 1935. Marr. 1st Jan. 1908 Catherine Scott, daugh. of James Lambert, Tillicoultry, and Jane Wood and has issue—John James Lambert, born 21st Aug. 1910.

(*Charges united 30th Jan. 1931.*)

BALLACHULISH

1843 ALEXANDER MACKELLAR, pres. by Crown 18th Oct. 1843.

1847 JOHN McLEOD, pres. by Crown 6th Feb. 1847.

1851 ALEXANDER STEWART, his mother was Isabella Hogarth; pres. by Crown 10th Feb. 1851.

1901 JOHN NORMAN MACLENNAN, dem. 7th Nov. 1938; his wife, Margaret Grant Mackenzie, died 28th Jan. 1928.

DUNCANSBURGH

1752 JOHN COOPER, ord. 11th Aug. 1752.

1919 JOHN MACDOUGALL, trans. to Aberfoyle 27th June 1922.

DAVID COLVILLE MACMICHAEL, formerly of St Andrew's Church, Colombo (*q.v.*); adm. 15th Dec. 1922; dem. 16th May 1932; died 15th Aug. 1937; his widow, Jane Grace Marion Govan, died 15th April 1939.
1922

FORT AUGUSTUS

GEORGE ROSS MONRO, app. 26th March 1800; ord. assistant at Beltie 28th Aug. 1800.
1800

WILLIAM CRAIG FLINT, ord. 1878; died 1st Nov. 1933; his widow, Katherine Maud Byam Menzies, died Prestwick 5th Jan. 1942.
1885

NEIL LOUIS ARTHUR CAMPBELL, trans. to Chapel of Garioch 19th June 1925.
1922

AUGUST JOHN KESTING, trans. from Mossgreen (*q.v.*) 12th Nov. 1925; dem. 15th May 1939; died at Edinburgh 25th Sept. 1947; his wife, Maude Cumming Grant, died 4th Aug. 1939.
1925

GLENGARRY

JAMES HILL, trans. to Teviothead 23rd Feb. 1940.
1921

KILMALLIE

On 10th Oct. 1649 the church was reported to the Synod as having been vacant since the Reformation. The church was rebuilt in 1783.

ROBERT STEWART, ed. ii, line 1, for "Dugald" read "Donald."
1714

DUNCAN MacINTYRE, born 22nd June 1757; had issue—John, min. of Kilmonivaig, born 10th Jan. 1794; Ann, born 5th Feb. 1795, died 15th Dec. 1864; Margaret, born 16th Oct. 1796, died 17th April 1861; Marion, born 1798; James, born 5th Nov. 1799, missionary at Laggan, Loch Lochy, died 20th March 1873; Jane, born 21st Dec. 1800 (marr. 5th Oct. 1827 Capt. John MacPhee, 79th Highlanders), died at Melbourne 31st Jan. 1896; Donald, born 1802; Mary, born 10th June 1804 (marr. John Maclachlan, farmer, Blairich, Lochiel), went to Australia; Angus, born 16th Aug. 1805, died 1883; Frances, born 29th Jan. 1807, went to Tasmania; Duncan, born 1808, went to Australia; Catherine, born 9th July 1810 (marr. Archibald MacIntyre), went to Tasmania; Duncan Alexander, born 10th Feb. 1815, went to Australia; Ewen, born 11th July 1817, went to Australia; Martin, licentiate, born 8th March 1821, died 1847.
1816

ARCHIBALD CLARK, his daughs.—Margaret Carmichael, died at Rhu 27th Aug. 1929; Mary Ann Robina, died at Rhu 15th Jan. 1926.
1844

ROBERT BROWN CRAWFORD, died 2nd Aug. 1931; his wife, Emma Isabella Brown, died 29th Aug. 1930; his son, Robert Macalpine, died 4th Sept. 1916.
1887

KILMONIVAIG

The church was called variously the Church of St Munengs, St Monewog, St Monevog, St Monawk, St Moneiveg and Moneweg Church. On 13th Nov. 1393 Benedict John of the Diocese of Argyle prayed Anti-Pope Clement VII for a dispensation to hold, in addition to another living, "the Church of St George of Monewog." Of this dedication nothing further is known. The church belonged to the Priory of Ardchattan. On 10th Oct. 1649 it was reported to the Synod that the church had been vacant since the Reformation. On 27th Dec. 1651 the Commission for the Plantation of Kirks decreed that there be two kirks in Lochaber, Kilmallie and Kilmonivaig, and that both continue as before. It was further ordained that a kirk "be bigged" on the lands of Kilfinen and Auchadrome, to be served *per vices* with Kilmonivaig, that the lands of Glengarie and Auchadrome be transferred from Kilmallie to the said new Kirk of Kilfinan, and the lands of Mamore from Illan Moune to Kilmallie, and the lands of Garviche, Gleneves, and the two Achitors from Kilmonivaig to Kilmallie. A stipend was also modified for each kirk with manse and glebe. The church was rebuilt in 1812.

The name is Cill. Mo. Naomhaig, the church of Naemoc, now Naomhag, "Little saint."—[*Cal. Scott. Supplics.*, 143, 147, 171, 172, 173, S.H.S.; *Cal. Papal Regs. Petitions*, i, 573, 678; *Recs. Synod of Argyle*, 150, 249, S.H.S.; *Reg. Great Seal*, vi, 891; Skene's *Celtic Scotland*, ii, 408; Watson's *Celtic Place Names*, 307.]

1750 WILLIAM GRANT, his daugh., Grizel (marr. Miles McInnes of Camuscross, Sleat, and had issue—General John McInnes).—[*Scot. N. and Q.*, Feb. 1929, 32.]

1828 JOHN MACINTYRE, his daugh., Isabella (marr. 29th March 1859).

1871 DONALD CAMERON, his widow, Sarah Hume Gentle, died at London 13th Nov. 1923.

1901 JOHN WALKER MACINTYRE, died 25th Oct. 1924; his wife, Eliza Scott-Thomson, died 8th July 1923.

1925 ALEXANDER McKINNON, trans. from St Columba's, Glasgow, 20th Feb. 1925. Chaplain to Glasgow Highlanders 1921–5. Publication—*The Atonement in the Light of Christ's Teaching and Ministry*.

STRONTIAN

1850 ROBERT STEWART, pres. by Crown 11th Oct. 1849.

1854 JOHN WILLIAM TOLMIE, pres. by Crown 16th May 1854.

1856 JAMES McFADYEN, pres. by Crown 19th April 1856.

1860 JOHN ROBERTSON, pres. by Crown 29th March 1860.

1865 DUNCAN CAMERON MACVEAN, pres. by Crown 30th June 1865.

1895 DONALD MACDONALD, died 31st March 1924; his widow, Jeannie W. Campbell, died 30th July 1931.

1924 JOHN MACLEAN, formerly of Kilmuir, Skye; adm. 2nd Sept. 1924; trans. to Appin 27th April 1927.

SYNOD OF PERTH AND STIRLING

PRESBYTERY OF DUNKELD

AUCHTERGAVEN

The present church was erected in 1812-13.

1567 THOMAS ROBERTSON, alias McGibbon, still in office 1572, also of Logiebride and Moneydie.—[*Comps. Sub Coll. of Thirds, Perth*, etc.]

1567 DAVID MURRAY, reader 1567 and 1571.—[*Comps. Sub Coll. of Thirds, Perth*, etc.]

1782 ANDREW WILLIAMSON, line 5, for "14" read "12."

1784 WILLIAM CHALMERS, marr. Margaret, daugh. of George Ross, provost of Montrose.—[*Montrose Deeds, Protests* 374, 12th Oct. 1786.]

1856 DAVID LANDALE, pres. by Crown 5th May 1856.

1862 WILLIAM FERGUSON WIGHT, pres. by Crown 2nd Aug. 1862.

1871 DAVID WINTER, pres. by Crown 5th Sept. 1871; his daugh., Mary Latham (marr. 28th March 1924 David Aitchison Coates, solicitor, Perth).

1904 ALEXANDER MATTHEW WYLIE, died 3rd Oct. 1936.

(*Charges united* 28*th July* 1931.)

LOGIEBRIDE

In 1510 Bishop Brown of Dunkeld added the church to the Hospital Prebend of Fordieschaws of Dunkeld Cathedral.

1567 THOMAS ROBERTSON, alias McGibbon, min. 1567-71. (See Auchtergaven.)

1564 ALEXANDER CRICHTON, reader, in office 1564.—[*Comps. Sub Coll. of Thirds, Fife*, etc.]

1569 JAMES LAUDER, M.A., his pres. to the Prebend of Fordeschaw and parsonage of Logiebride was on the death of Michael Balfour; and it was provided that he should make his residence at the said kirk, exhort and instruct with the Word of God by himself, and minister at the Sacraments and continue honest in life and conversation, also answer to the bedesman founded at St George's Chapel for their yearly living out of said prebend and parsonage; he was inst. 20th May 1569.—[*Cal. of Charters*, x, 153.]

1580 WILLIAM MARTIN, pres. to vicarage 3rd May 1580 on death of George Martin.—[*Reg. Pres. Bene.*, ii, 34.]

BLAIR ATHOLL

The chapel at Little Lude was dedicated to St Columba. The chaplainry of the Chapel of Tillypowrie was held by John, Earl of Atholl, in 1569.—[*Comps. Sub Coll. of Thirds, Perth*, etc.]

Lude. The parsonage was held by John, Earl of Atholl, in 1569.—[*Comps. Sub Coll. of Thirds, Perth*, etc.]

Kilmoveonaig. According to Forbes, the church was dedicated to John Scot, Bishop of Dunkeld, who died 13th July 1203. There was here a fair called Feill Espog

Eon, the Fair of Bishop John. The patron saint may be Beoghand, second Abbot of Bangor, who died in 606, the name being Cill Mo Bheoghana. The parsonage and vicarage were held by John, Earl of Atholl, in 1569.—[*Cal. Scott. Saints*, 360; Watson's *Celtic Place Names*, 310; *Comps. Sub Coll. of Thirds, Perth*, etc.]

1565 SIR ARCHIBALD LOWNIE, vicar 1565 and 1567-9.—[*Edin. Tests*, i, 57.]

1593 DUNCAN MACAULAY, trans. to Kenmore before 1st Aug. 1607.

1673 ROBERT CAMPBELL, line 10, for "1716" read "1715."

1709 DUNCAN STEWART, his son, James, apprenticed to Robert Stewart, litster, Edinburgh, 15th May 1706.

1726 ROBERT BISSET, had also issue—James; Robert.

1843 ALEXANDER ROBERTSON IRVINE, his daugh., Elizabeth (marr. 7th May 1861).

1876 JAMES FRASER, his daugh., Katherine Maclean, died 5th Feb. 1936.

1908 DONALD LAMONT, D.D. (Edinburgh 28th June 1929); adm. to united charge 18th Jan 1934; dem. 28th Nov. 1946.

CAPUTH and LOGIE MACHED

Malcolm, Earl of Athole, *c*. 1153-89 or 1198, granted to Scone Abbey the Church of Logie-Machedd, with its dependent Chapels of Kilcherni or Kilkenry, Dunfalontyn, Kilkassin, Kilmichall or Kilmichilde, and Tulemath or Tulechmat.— [*Book of Scone*, 21, 35-6.]

1572 THOMAS CRUICKSHANK, min. in 1572, in charge also of Lethendrie, Lundeiff and Blairgowrie.—[*Comps. Sub Coll. of Thirds, Perth*, etc.]

1604 JAMES BANNERMAN, pres. on death of George Crichton.—[*Reg. Sec. Sig.*, lxxiv, 136.]

1681 ROBERT GORDON, M.A. (Marischal College 1654).

1783 WILLIAM INVERARITY, line 4, for "1st April" read "20th March."

1869 THEODORE MARSHALL, pres. by Crown 3rd Dec. 1868; his widow, Anna Nicholson, died at Edinburgh 29th Sept. 1939.

1911 KENNETH OLUNS MACLEOD, dem. 17th Dec. 1948.

CARGILL

At one time Cargil was designated the "West Parish." In 1754 the church was thoroughly repaired and in 1794 was described as "very old"; in 1831 it was rebuilt.

1561 SIR WILLIAM DRUMMOND, reader, was vicar and reader in 1561, still in office 1572.—[*Comps. Sub Coll. of Thirds, Perth*, etc.]

1569 THOMAS CRUICKSHANK, min. in 1569.—[*Comps. Sub Coll. of Thirds, Perth*, etc.] (See Caputh.)

1571 WILLIAM EDMONSTON, held Chancellary of Dunkeld.—[*Reg. Sec. Sig.*, lxxiv, 404.]

1605 GEORGE PATULLO, M.A., pres. to Chancellery of Dunkeld 20th Nov. 1605, and to vicarage here 2nd Dec. 1605 on death of William Edmonston.— [*Reg. Sec. Sig.*, lxxiv, 404, 407.]

1784 JAMES PATRICK BANNERMAN, his family—David, born Nov. 1794, died 1795; Janet or Jessie (marr. Colonel Harry Burney, H.E.I.C.S.), died 1844; Jean, died 1830; Anne, died 1846; Robert, died July 1851; William, died 1851.

1843 WILLIAM CHARLES ROSE, pres. by Crown 4th Aug. 1843.

1870 ROBERT NIMMO SMITH, pres. by Crown 3rd May 1870.

1875 WILLIAM ALBERT CAMPBELL, died 7th Dec. 1930.

CLUNIE

The church was built in 1840, taking the place of the church erected in 1732 and repaired in 1788. Besides the Chapel of St Catherine on the island of the loch there were in the parish four other chapels, of all of which at the close of the 18th century remains with cemeteries existed, and, in the case of three, vestiges are recorded in 1845. They were situated, respectively: within the manor of Little Gourdie; at Chapelton; at another site called Chapelton; at Chapelhill in a park called Laighwood, a little north of the church. Dedicated to the Holy Ghost, the chapel at Little Gourdie was built by David Scrymgeour of Fardill, who died between 2nd July 1527 and 27th Oct. 1528; and by charter of the latter date Mr James Scrymgeour, precentor of Brechin, brother-germane of David Scrymgeour, and his heir of tailzie and testamentary executor, granted to a chaplain to make perpetual celebrations in the chapel daily, and in winter in the Church of Cluny, where the said David was buried, 5 merks annually of the lands of Ards, 4 merks of the lands of Easter Fardill, 4 merks of the lands of Wester Fardill, 3 merks of the lands of Drummadirte, in the barony of Fardill, and a piece of land at the Manor of Little Gourdie near the fount called *le Gryis-well*. Further endowments were a tenement on the south side of Argyle-gait, Dundee, and an annual rent of 4 merks from lands also on the south side of Argyll-gait at Sereis-Wynd. The Scrymgeours of Fardill retained the patronage of the chapel. In 1575 it was called Cluny Kilmarenock. There was in the church an Altar of the Virgin Mary.—[*Reg. Great Seal*, iii, 759, 2441, vi, 142, 1421, 1855; *Book of the Universal Kirk*, 336.]

1561 WILLIAM SALMON, vicar in 1561.—[*Comps. Sub Coll. of Thirds, Perth; Reg. Sec. Sig.*, xxxv, 24.]

1569 PATRICK LAYNG, vicar 1569.—[*Comps. Sub Coll. of Thirds, Perth*, etc.]

1574 JOHN BARTANE, M.A., in 1568 became Dean of Dunkeld in succession to James Hepburn.—[*Comps. Sub Coll. of Thirds, Perth*, etc.]

1576 ARCHIBALD HENRY, pres. to vicarage 7th Nov. 1576 on death of William Salmon.—[*Reg. Pres. Bene.*, i, (4), 49.]

1691 ROBERT GORDON, M.A. (Marischal College, 1654).

1839 GEORGE MILLAR, his daugh., Jessie Jane (marr. 9th Sept. 1890 William Christopher, son of Sir John Leng, Dundee).

1890 ALEXANDER AYTOUN YOUNG, died 19th Aug. 1927.

1928 LAUCHLAN MACPHERSON, born 12th March 1891, son of Archibald M., Waverley Hotel, Fort William, and Mary Campbell; educ. at Univ. of Toronto and Glasgow, M.A. (1922); was sometime a banker; served in Great War in France, Italy, Salonika and Asia Minor; licen. by Presb. of Lochaber March 1924; assistant Alloa; ord. to Ardoch 19th March 1925; trans. and adm. 18th Jan. 1928; died 6th Aug. 1940. Marr. 4th Aug. 1926 Jean (died 19th July 1945), daugh. of Thomas Macpherson, Saughton, Edinburgh, and Jane Macpherson, and had issue—Archibald Cameron, born 23rd Oct. 1927; Jean Wight, born 14th Aug. 1930.

DUNKELD

By Malcolm IV, 1153–65, the Church of the Holy Trinity, Dunkeld, was granted to Dunfermline Abbey, the grant to take effect on the death of Andrew, Bishop of Caithness, who had been a monk of Dunfermline and held the fruits of the church. Of the grant there were various confirmations, Episcopal, Papal, Royal, but of the church nothing more appears to be known. The choir of the cathedral was built by Bishop Sinclair 1312–38. On 27th April 1406 the nave was founded by Bishop Cardny, who built it to the second arches or *blyndstoriis*. It was completed by Bishop

Lauder, who dedicated the church in 1464. He also laid the foundation of the west tower on 5th March 1469–70 and completed it in 1476; and by him also was carried out the building of the chapter house, whose erection began in 1457. The Altar of the Virgin Mary was endowed out of property in Cluny by Bishop Macknachtane; the Altar of St Katharine, Virgin and Martyr, was built by Bishop Livingstone 1476–83; and about 1506 Bishop Brown founded a second Altar of the Virgin Mary, called *S. Marie Libera nos a Penis Inferni*, to which pertained 4 bolls of "white and good meal called *twyce schelit meil* from the lands of Easter-Eschindy," for the purpose of annual distribution to "the poor of Christ" at the hands of the chaplain of the altar. Bishop Brown further chose seven vicars for altars not yet founded —St Martin, St Nicholas, St Andrew, Holy Innocents, All Saints, St Stephen the Proto-Martyr, and St John Baptist. Of these the Altar of All Saints was set up and painted by Master John Donaldson, Chancellor of Dunkeld. There were also in the cathedral an altar dedicated to St Adamnan, of which the patron was Scott of Balweary: an altar dedicated to St Peter, founded before 2nd April 1490 by James Laicok, Sub-Dean of Dunkeld; and an altar dedicated to St Thomas. The Altar of the Holyrood was in the Rood Loft. On the top of an eminence called Hillhead, east of Dunkeld, there was a chapel dedicated to St Jerome. On a site now occupied by buildings in Athol Street there was founded about 1420 by Bishop Cardny a chapel dedicated to St Ninian, which became the place of interment of the bishop, who died 16th Jan. 1436–7. The foundation of the Hospital and Chapel of St George by Bishop Brown in 1510 was actually the restoration of a hospital prebend of the cathedral, the revenues of which, from the lands of Ferdischawe, had been applied by his predecessors to their own table. As the fruits were insufficient for the purpose, he added the Church of Logybride to the prebend and instituted a hospital with master, for seven old men who had a free house, 5 bolls of meal, and 5 merks Scots. The hospital was burned in 1689 and was replaced by small cottages, and later by substantial buildings. In connection with the Chapel of St George, Bishop Brown founded in honour of the Blessed Virgin of Consolation a scholastic perpetual chaplain who was to celebrate in the chapel and rule a grammar school. In 1490 Bishop Brown also restored a house at Guay which, about 1340, had been erected by a Bishop of Dunkeld, but which subsequent bishops had closed, with consequent misapplication of rents.—[*Reg. Great Seal*, ii, 429, 1056, 1942, 3482; iii, 97, iv, 200, 1208; v, 205, 1189, 1611; vi, 1227, 1542; vii, 416; *Acts Scott. Parl.*, i, 407a; *Reg. Sec. Seal*, iii, 861, 1312; *Reg. of Dunfermline*, 22; Myln's *Lives of the Bishops of Dunkeld*, 13–16, 18, 23–4, 26, 43–4.]

JOHN MONCRIEFF, exhorter 1561.—
1561 [*Comps. Gen. Coll. of Thirds.*]

THOMAS CLARK WILSON, his daughs.—Jane Macfarlane, died 6th May 1927; Mary (Mrs Angus), died 16th Feb. 1939.
1846

THOMAS RANKEN RUTHERFORD, died 11th June 1926; his daughs.—Margaret, died at Dunkeld 28th March 1939; Isabella Christina, died at Edinburgh 21st April 1940; Edith, died 14th Jan. 1944.
1877

ROBERT GEORGE JAMIESON, formerly Indian Chaplain (*q.v.*); adm. 15th Oct. 1926; trans. to Newton 27th Feb. 1931; died at Perth 22nd Jan. 1934; his widow, Jean Ainslie Gordon Watson, died 27th Feb. 1935; his son, George Bryce, C.A., died 22nd July 1933; his daugh., Marjorie Hamilton (marr. 22nd June 1940 Thomas Bissett Crombie, Dooars, India, second son of Thomas Crombie, Dunkeld); his son, Robert Ainslie, F.R.C.S.E.
1926

DOWALLIE

St Muireach or Mhuirich, Muireadhach. Of that name there were Muireadhach, Bishop of Cell Alad, whose day was 12th Aug., and Muireadhach, Abbot of Hi, who died in 1011. Near the public road some distance east of Ballinluig is a praying-stone associated with St Moroc's (Muireach) Chapel on the terrace above. On the top of the bank above Dalshian, not far from Pitlochry, is the site of a chapel dedicated to St Catherine, apparently of Alexandria. It is situated in the centre of an old Pictish fort, known as the "Fourich"—the place of watching.—[Watson's *Celtic Place Names*, 293; Mitchell's *Pitlochry District*, 84–5.]

1573 DUNCAN McLELLAN, M.A., pres. to vicarage 11th Aug. 1573 on death of Dean David Guthrie.—[*Reg. Pres. Bene.*, i, (4), 10.]

1574 WALTER STEWART, pres. to vicarage 8th May 1572.—[*Reg. Sec. Sig.*, xl, 92.]

1885 DAVID RUSSELL KYD, died at Edinburgh 26th June 1926.

LITTLE DUNKELD

The old church, 130 ft. long, 20 ft. wide, described in 1793 as "ruinous and uncomfortable," was replaced by the present church in 1798. At Kinnaird there was a chapel with well dedicated to St Laurance. In the burgh and town of Little Dunkeld there were lands called the crofts of St Thomas the Apostle, pertaining to the Chaplainry of St Mary the Virgin of Inver in Dunkeld Cathedral, and also the lands of St Mary the Virgin and the lands of St Katharine the Virgin. The Church of Laggan-Allochie was added to the Archdeanery of Dunkeld, for the purpose of increasing the revenues of the latter, by Bishop Sinclair 1312–38. The church was rebuilt just prior to 1793.—[*Reg. Great Seal*, v, 1138, 1189; Myln's *Lives of the Bishops of Dunkeld*, 16–18.]

1573 DUNCAN McNAIR, pres. to the Treasury of Dunkeld, which is the vicarage of Little Dunkeld, Dowally and Caputh, vacant by Act of Parliament, in default of Robert Abercrombie, last vicar, being "ane Jesuit beyond the say"; competent not before the Bishop of Dunkeld 19th Dec. 1573.—[*Reg. Pres. Bene.*, i, 14.]

1769 JOHN ROBERTSON, educ. at Marischal College.

1851 DANIEL McBRIDE, pres. by Crown 22nd Oct. 1850.

1866 JAMES SKINNER MACKENZIE, pres. by Crown 6th April 1866; his widow, Evelyn Rachel Woodman, died 14th April 1930; his son, William Hector, M.D., died 26th Oct. 1939.

1914 CHARLES MONCRIEFF ROBERTSON, trans. to Ferryhill, Aberdeen, 15th May 1924.

1924 THOMAS ROGER GILLIES, born Bridge of Glassary, Argyll, 21st March 1893, son of Robert G., tailor and clothier, and Agnes Loney Rodger; served in 2nd Fife and Forfar Yeomanry 1915–19; educ. at High School and Univ. of Cambridge and Glasgow; licen. by Presb. of Glasgow 1923; assistant at Govan 1922–3, Springburn 1923–4; ord. 23rd Oct. 1924. Marr. 26th Dec. 1923 Nanie Thomson, fourth daugh. of Robert Leishman, Laurieston, Falkirk.

LAGGAN (LOGIE) ALLACHIE

The church was annexed by Bishop Sinclair 1312–28 to the Archdeanery of Dunkeld for the purpose of increasing the emoluments.—[Myln's *Lives of Bishops of Dunkeld*, 16–18.]

1576 MICHAEL GREIG, pres. to vicarage 12th Aug. 1568 on the death of William Cowny (Cownic).—[*Reg. Sec. Sig.*, xxxvii, 82.]

1590 ALEXANDER IRELAND, pres. to parsonage and vicarage with manse and yard on death of David Spens. —[*Reg. Sec. Sig.*, lxiv, 35.]

GLENSHEE

Prior to the concluding part of the 18th century there was a chapel here in which the minister of Kirkmichael conducted services every four or five weeks. The present church was built in 1831.

1881 THOMAS CRAWFORD, his widow, Elizabeth Carmichael, died at Davidson's Mains 4th Nov. 1928.

1908 JOHN THOMSON, dem. 15th May 1941, died 10th Jan. 1943.

KINCLAVEN

The Church of Kinclaven was granted to Cambuskenneth by King William the Lion before 13th May 1195. In the following century a letter of Richard, Bishop of Dunkeld, dated 2nd Nov. 1260, stated that the Church of Kinclaven had been divided into two parts, one of which belonged to the Dean and Chapter of Dunkeld, and the other to the Abbot and Convent of Cambuskenneth, a position that caused great danger to the souls of the people of Kinclaven from the church not being well served. Therefore, with consent of the respective parties, the granters ordained that the Church of Kinclaven, with its cure and possessions, should henceforth belong to the precentory of the Kirk of Dunkeld, the precentor to pay 6 merks annually to the abbot and convent, and to serve the Church of Kinclaven by a qualified chaplain.—[*Chartulary of Cambuskenneth*, 43-4, 267.]

1568 PATRICK DAWSON, vicar 6th Oct. 1568.—[*Reg. of Abbrev. Feu Charters of Church Lands*, ii, 242.]

1571 THOMAS ROBERTSON, alias McGIBBON, min. in 1571 and 1572. See also Auchtergaven.—[*Comps. Sub Coll. of Thirds, Perth*, etc.]

1590 SIR JOHN SALMON, vicar 1590, but may be identical with Patrick Salmon, 1567-91.—[*Comps. Gen. Coll. of Thirds.*]

1594 ALEXANDER IRELAND, pres. to vicar pensionary 15th July 1595 on death of Patrick Salmon, and to parsonage and vicarage 11th Dec. 1595 on death of James Currle.—[*Reg. Sec. Sig.*, xlvii, 147; lxviii, 39.]

1687 THOMAS MURRAY, Patrick probably his son, apprenticed to Patrick Murray, goldsmith, Edinburgh, 10th Sept. 1718.

1883 HENRY KILGOUR REEKIE, dem. 30th Sept. 1929, died at Uddingston 17th Dec. 1929; his widow, Agnes Mary Wemyss, died 17th May 1934; his son, Andrew, D.P.H., M.O.H., Lanark.

(*Charges united 23rd March 1937.*)

KIRKMICHAEL

Kirkmichael is said to have been an Abthane (see Dull). The Church of Strathardil was granted to Dunfermline Abbey by King William the Lion in 1165–89.—[*Reg. of Dunfermline*, 39.]

1564 WILLIAM EVEATT, designed reader in Strathardail and Glenshee 1564, 1569 and 1572.—[*Comps. Sub Coll. of Thirds, Fife*, etc.; *Sub Coll. of Thirds, Perth*, etc.]

1790 ALLAN STEWART, marr. Jean, daugh. of Captain Lachlan Macpherson, barrack master, Ruthven.

1884 JAMES CUNNINGHAM MACKAY, dem. 6th Oct. 1924; died at Edinburgh 3rd Jan. 1940; his wife, Isabella Smith Small, died 12th May 1924.

1925 JAMES WILLIAM RENWICK ROUTLEDGE, ord. 28th Jan. 1925; adm. Indian Chaplain 15th and dem. 26th Dec. 1927.

1928 ROBERT MONTGOMERY BRIGHT, trans. from Inch, Abernethy (*q.v.*), 19th July 1928; trans. to Kinclaven 12th May 1930; dem. 26th March 1938; died at Kincraig 12th Jan. 1947.

LETHENDY and KINLOCH

In the parish there was a tenement of land called St Katharine's land, indicating a dedication to that saint. There is mentioned also "a tenement with yard and croft foundit and left to our Lady Altar in the Church." This was an altar dedicated to the Virgin, and situated apparently in an aisle or transept.—[*Book of Scone*, 230; *Reg. Great Seal*, viii, 65, 553; *Retours*, xv, 10.]

1569 JOHN CURROUR, reader 1569 and 1571-2.—[*Comps. Sub Coll. of Thirds, Perth*, etc.]

1571 THOMAS CRUICKSHANK, min. in 1571.—[*Comps. Sub Coll. of Thirds, Perth*, etc.] (See Caputh.)

1585 JOHN STRATHANNAN, in 1585; still reader 17th Oct. 1604.—[*P. S. Reg.*, lxxv, 188.]

1607 WILLIAM BALNEAVES. (See Kinloch.)

1639 JOHN STRACHAN, educ. at Marischal College.

1847 DAVID SMITH RAE, pres. by Crown 9th Oct. 1846; his daughs.—Helen (marr. Frank Martin, min. of St Matthew's, Edinburgh), died 30th May 1939; Eliza Margaret Ponton, died 19th Sept. 1935.

1890 THOMAS MILNE, died 9th March 1941; his wife, Alexandria Watson, died 3rd Feb. 1926; his son, James Ian Hood, M.A., B.Sc., mathematical master, Ardrossan Academy, died 1st March 1936.

LUNDEIFF

An alternative name of the parish was Strogyhill.—[*Reg. Mag. Sig.*, vi, 1615.]

1566 ALEXANDER CRICHTON, held parsonage, died before 3rd July 1573.—[*Reg. Pres. Bene.*, i, 94.]

1567 THOMAS CRUICKSHANK, min. in 1567, pres. to parsonage and vicarage in 1573 on death of Alexander Crichton.—[*Reg. Pres. Bene.*, i, (3), 8; *Comps. Sub Coll. of Thirds, Perth*, etc.] (See Caputh.)

1591 WILLIAM BALNAVES, pres. to parsonage and vicarage on death of Thomas Cruickshank 14th May 1591; held charge of Lethendy and Lundeiff till 1629. Had issue—Walter, burgess of Perth.—[*G. R. Sas.*, xiii, 1; *Reg. Sec. Sig.*, lxii, 53; *Reg. Mag. Sig.*, vi, 1513.]

MOULIN

The fair, *feill mo-Cholmoig* ("My Colmoc's Fair"), was held at the end of February, and this indicates that the saint was Colman (one of many saints of this name), whose day was 18th Feb. At Chapelton of Cluny there are the ruins of a chapel with praying-stone, probably of 7th century, and at Faskally land called Dysart, which indicates a Culdee retreat or place of contemplation. On a neolithic burial mound at Old Faskally, beyond the Pass of Killiecrankie, there are the remains of a chapel with the socket of a praying-stone a short distance to the north. At Pitlochry there was a spring called St Fergan's Well, *Tobar Fheargain*, probably Fergna ("the Briton"), who was fourth Abbot of Iona, and died in 623. His day was 2nd March.—[*Retours*, vii, 335; *Reg. Great Seal*, ii, 2814; Mitchell's *Pitlochry District*, 85; Watson's *Celtic Place Names*, 322, 278.]

1574 GEORGE DOUGALSON, reader and vicar 1574, died before Nov. 1578.

1575 ALEXANDER HARVIE, vicar, died before 26th March 1575–6.—[*Reg. Pres. Bene.*, i, 127.]

1577 DUNCAN MACLAGGAN, pres. on death of George Dougalson 30th July 1580.—[*Reg. Pres. Bene.*, ii, 38.]

1578 WILLIAM CRARER, pres. to vicarage 16th Nov. 1578 on death of George Dougalson, but may not have accepted.—[*Reg. Pres. Bene*, i, 10, ii, 8.]

1702 JAMES STEWART, line 10, for "John" read "Colin," and before "daugh." "second."

1668 WILLIAM BALNAVIS, had also issue —James.—[*Deeds Dal.*, 1706, No. 596.]

1887 DUNCAN MACALISTER DONALD, dem. 29th June 1926; died 24th Jan. 1936; his wife, Frances Elizabeth Strathy, died 15th May 1932. He marr. (2)

15th Aug. 1934 Sarah Isabella Brewis, widow of R. F. Galloway of Viewfield, Pitlochry; his daugh., Dorothy (marr. 5th Dec. 1926 Patrick William Barty, Sudan); his son, Ian, died 7th Aug. 1916.

CHARLES MICHAEL HEPBURN, born 5th May 1894, only son of James H., Gaberston Park, Alloa, and Georgina Erskine; educ. at Univ. of Edinburgh, M.A. (1915), B.D. (1920); served in Argyll and Sutherland Highlanders in Great War; licen. by Presb. of Stirling 1920; assistant Pollokshields; ord. to Dalkeith West 4th Jan. 1923; trans. and adm. 25th Nov. 1926; trans. to St Michael's, Crieff, 26th April 1939. Marr. 3rd June 1924 May Calder, only daugh. of Robert Chapman, Johnston House, Gartcosh, and Elizabeth Main, and has issue—James Hepburn, born 11th Aug. 1926.
1926

MURTHLY

GEORGE EDDIE THOMSON, res. 13th Jan. 1925; app. min. of Newcastle-on-Tyne 1925; trans. to Monquhitter 23rd Oct. 1929.
1914

JOHN MACDONALD GILLIES, ord. 12th May 1925; trans. to Tarbert 31 Aug. 1927.
1925

LOUIS CLARENCE DUNCAN DOUGLAS, formerly of Walls, Orkney (*q.v.*), adm. 17th Feb. 1928; died 12th March 1937.
1928

RATTRAY

ANDREW ABERCROMBY, parson.— [*Acts and Dec.*, xxxvi, 12.]
1565

DONALD CARGILL of Kirklands of Rattray, reader in 1574; adm. notary public 28th April 1583; styled vicar 1606–21; died between 21st May 1622 and 5th June 1624. Marr. Margaret Blair and had issue—Janet (marr. John Blair of Pittendreich); John of Haltoun of Rattray, N.P.; Grizeld (marr. George Drummond, portioner of Kirktoun of Rattray and brother of John D. of Blair); Laurence of Bonytoun of Rattray, N.P.— [*Rattray Parish Register; Banff Charters; Perth Sas.*, 4th July 1607, 4th Nov. 1606, 11th July 1603, 10th March 1606; iii, 240; v, 113; 29th June 1624.]
1574

JOHN CURROUR, reader 1569–72.— [*Comps. Sub Coll. of Thirds, Perth,* etc.]
1578

SILVESTER RATTRAY, marr. cont. 4th June 1609 Mary, daugh. of George Stewart, fifth of Cardney and Arntullie.
1591

JOHN RATTRAY, brother of David R. of Craighall and grand-nephew of preceding.—[*Perth Sas.*, iii, 232, 406; iv, 10th March 1606.]
1629

THOMAS LUNDIE.—[*G. R. Sas.*, 2 Ser., xiv, 160.]
1637

FRANCIS COWAN GILLIES, his son, Rev. James Robertson, died 26th March 1938.
1837

WALTER SIMPSON, trans. to Nigg, Aberdeen, 12th Dec. 1928.
1922

MILLAR OGILVIE, trans. from Dunrossness (*q.v.*) 16th May 1929; trans. to Covington 16th Nov. 1932. Has issue—Jean, born 23rd Nov. 1937.
1929

TENANDRY

WILLIAM GOLDIE BOAG, his widow, Elizabeth Gilmour Johnson, died at Moffat 11th Feb. 1941.
1903

JOHN LAMB, dem. 12th Nov. 1922; app. to Grassmarket Mission, Edinburgh, 1924; died at Duddingston 14th March 1936.
1913

DONALD MACBEAN, born Tarbert, Loch Fyne, son of Donald M. and Agnes Pollock; licen. by Presb. of Edinburgh 1920; assistant West St Giles; ord. 1st March 1923; trans. to Logie Easter 20th Dec. 1934; trans. to Rosehall 21st Nov. 1945.
1923

PRESBYTERY OF WEEM

ABERFELDY

1887 WILLIAM BALLANTINE CAMPBELL, died at Perth 23rd May 1924.

1912 CHARLES WHITEHEAD HUTCHESON, line 2, read "second son"; trans. to Townhead, Glasgow, 17th May 1926.

1926 DAVID RUSSELL MITCHELL, formerly Chaplain at Alexandria (vii, 557, *q.v.*); adm. 27th Aug. 1926; trans. to Penninghame 18th Feb. 1930; dem. 14th June 1947.

AMULREE

1838 JOHN LAMONT, afterwards of Hallin in Waternish.

1843 DUNCAN McINTOSH, afterwards of Kilfinan.

1889 ALEXANDER DEWAR, dem. 26th Nov. 1925; died 5th Oct. 1932.

1926 JAMES HIGGINS, trans. from Orphir 10th June 1926 (*q.v.*); dem. 15th Nov. 1946.

(*United with Strathbraan 30th Jan.* 1947.)

BRAES OF RANNOCH

1885 ALEXANDER McGREGOR, his widow, Elizabeth McDonald, died 9th Sept. 1935.

1907 ARCHIBALD AENEAS ROBERTSON, Chaplain Astley Ainslie Institution, Edinburgh; his wife, Catherine Clason Macfarlane, died 17th Dec. 1935. Marr. (2) 7th Dec. 1936 Winifred Dorothy, only daugh. of Henry Hutcheson, Glasgow.

1918 WILLIAM MARTIN, trans. to Kinnell 15th Oct. 1925.

1926 WILLIAM DUNLOP, formerly of Buckhaven (*q.v.*); adm. 23rd Feb. 1926; dem. 27th Nov. 1930; died at Edinburgh 22nd Dec. 1937; his widow, Mary Grant Watson, died 13th Jan. 1943.

DULL

Dull was one of three Abthanes, Dull, Kirkmichael, Madderty, which King Edgar granted to his youngest brother, Ethelred, Abbot of Dunkeld. About 1159–89 Malcolm, Earl of Athol, granted the church with its chapels and lands to St Andrews. This was confirmed by King William the Lion, and the Chapter of Dunkeld, the latter including the Chapel of Fossach (Foss), and reserving the Church of Branboth in Glen Lyon and an annual rent of 20s. payable to the chapter and their clerics from the Abthane of Dull. In a burial ground on a rocky mound, called Chapelton, near the head of Glenfincastle are the ruins of a church or chapel in use till about 1770; and another chapel is indicated by Chapelton, the name of a house near a burial ground, a short distance beyond Borenich on the way to Loch Tummel. Another chapel was situated at Duntanlich on the east side of a field opposite the Queen's View.—[*Reg. Priory of St Andrews*, 230, 245, 296; Mitchell's *Pitlochry District*, 83–4, 87–8; *Reg. Mag. Sig.*, ii, 12th Aug. 1471.]

1564 DUNCAN MACAULAY, in office 1570.—[*Comps. Sub Coll. of Thirds, Fife*, etc.]

1565 DAVID GUTHRIE, M.A., perpetual vicar 14th Feb. 1561, vicar 25th Jan. 1565–6.—[*Reg. Sec. Sig.*, xxxiv, 91; *Reg. Mag. Sig.*, iv, 1730.]

1583 DUNCAN McLAGLAN, trans. and adm. before 6th May 1583.

1624 JOHN CUNISON, died Father of the Church.

1699 JOHN McKERCHAR, marr. Jean Campbell and had issue—Alexander, bapt. 3rd July 1706; Daniel, apprenticed to John Blair, periwig-maker, Edinburgh, 19th March 1712.

1839 DUNCAN DEWAR, line 8, for "1863" read "1868."

1903 WILLIAM ALEXANDER MACFARLANE, died 8th Nov. 1943.

FORTINGALL

At Coshieville (Cois a Bhile) there was held on 9th Aug. old style "My Coeddie's Fair."—[Watson's *Celtic Place Names*, 314.]

1564 WILLIAM RAMSAY, M.A., pres. to parsonage and vicarage, which pertained in common to the Channerery of the Cathedral Kirk of Dunkeld, before 1564; was min. at Kenmore before 1st Oct. 1566; died before 18th Feb. 1568–9; his wife survived him.—[*P. S. Reg.*, xxxvii, 81; *Reg. of Pres. Bene.*, i, 18.]

1569 DUNCAN MACAULAY, pres. to parsonage and vicarage 15th Feb. 1568–9 on death of William Ramsay. —[*Reg. Pres. Bene.*, i, 18.]

1687 ALEXANDER ROBERTSON, his daugh., Janet (marr. Duncan Campbell of Milton of Glen of Glenlyon).

1754 DUNCAN MACNAB, son of Patrick M., tenant in Conachan, and Janet Henry.

1897 WILLIAM CAMPBELL, licen. by Presb. of Glasgow 1891; B.D. (1891); dem. 4th Dec. 1935 to facilitate union; died at West Linton 8th June 1940, unmarr.

(*Charges united 5th Jan.* 1940.)

FOSS

The Church of Foss was at first a dependent Chapel of Dull. It is said to have been founded by St Chad in or about 650. Here was a fair of St Patrick; and the Atlas of Scotland, 1832, gives the Well of St Peter, the name being probably a mistake for St Patrick.—[Mitchell's *Pitlochry District*, 84.]

1842 JAMES ARMSTRONG, pres. by Crown 19th July 1842.

1920 REGINALD IAN DAVIDSON, trans. to Kingoldrum 17th May 1926.

1926 WILLIAM WALKER, formerly of St Leonard's, Ayr, adm. 23rd Nov. 1926; dem. 7th June 1932; died at Edinburgh 14th Nov. 1941; his wife, Marion Jane Mackenzie, died at Colinton 7th March 1933.

GLENLYON

On 5th Feb. 1500–1 there was made an agreement between the Dean and Chapter of Dunkeld, with consent of the Bishop (George Brown), and Sir Donald Maiknachtane, vicar of Fortingall (anent a controversy between them in and upon the pension of the said vicar given and assigned by the Chapter, and a portion assigned by the vicar), whereby Sir Donald renounced for all time his right and claim to said portionary of Fortingall, so that for the future he and his successors shall have the old erection of the vicarage, 13 merks Scots, with manse, etc., and the chapter shall pay yearly to the vicar for his time 12 merks Scots for sustenance of a chaplain of Bambrow, otherwise Glenlyon, to have care of the souls of Glenlyon and answer to the ordinary for such souls; and after his death the chapter shall have a perpetual chaplain at Glenlyon who shall have a yearly pension of 12 merks Scots, with all the rights which the chapter had to the glebe of the said chapel, commonly called Fybart of Brabo, etc. On 11th Sept. 1639 Parliament referred to the Commission for Augmentation of Stipends, etc., the desire of the General Assembly to have the lands of Glenlyon dismembered from Fortingall and erected into a separate parish. Objections were raised and nothing was done then.—[*Reports, Hist. MSS. Commis.*, vii, 710b; *Acts Scott. Parl.*, v, 597a.]

1842 CHARLES STEWART, pres. by Crown 26th March 1842.

1844 DAVID DRUMMOND, pres. by Crown 20th April 1844.

1904 GEORGE DRUMMOND, adm. to united charge 1930; dem. 15th May 1940; died at Luss 23rd Sept. 1942.

GRANTULLY

The Chapel of St Mary was the Parish Church of Grantully. On 3rd June 1533 Alexander Stewart of Grantully, with consent of his son and heir, Thomas, gave to God, the Blessed Mother Mary, St Andrew, St Adamnan, and Bean the Confessor, Croft Dawe, for a suitable chaplain-curate personally residing at and making divine celebrations in the Church of St Mary of Grantully, sasine being given to Alexander Young, Sub-Prior of St Andrews, as representing the curate. The church was for a time the burial place of the barons of Grantully. The decorative paintings executed in 1636 comprise scriptural subjects, armorial bearings, and monograms. Among the first are figures of the four evangelists and a representation of the Day of Judgment—the graves giving up their dead, the redeemed ascending, and the condemned falling into eternal night.—[*Reg. Book of Grantully*, i, Pref. xxii–xxiii, 73; Mackinlay's *Anc. Ch. Dedications, Script.*, 117.]

1564 WILLIAM RAMSAY, min. at Weem, had also charge here, holding the vicarage 1564.—[*Comps. Sub Coll. of Thirds, Fife*, etc.]

1564 WILLIAM CRAIGIE, reader.—[*Comps. Sub Coll. of Thirds, Fife, Perth*, etc.]

1909 DUNCAN MACRAE, he died Edinburgh 28th May 1943; his wife, Elizabeth Paterson, died 23rd March 1906; his son, Ian, B.Sc.

1919 ALEXANDER ANDREW, his daugh., Elizabeth Grant (marr. 4th Aug. 1939 Henry Campbell, eldest son of W. F. MacAusland, Windy Knowe, Scotstounhill).

KENMORE

It is uncertain whether the earlier name of the parish, Inchadney, or Inchadin, indicates St Aidan as the patron saint. In Gaelic Inchadney is *Innis Chailtnidh* ("Keltney Haugh"). The principal fair at Inchadney was called "the Nine Maidens"; and it might be conjectured that that was the dedication of the church. The present church was built in 1760, and a new wing was added in 1832.—[Watson's *Celtic Place Names*, 517–18.]

1561 WILLIAM RAMSAY, graduated M.A., St Andrews Univ., 1537; became chaplain at Finlarig 1555; settled at Inchadny 20th May 1561; had gift of vicarage vacant by death of William Lumsden 1st Oct. 1566; trans. to Kilmany, Fife, 27th June 1564.

1564 DUNCAN McLAGGAN, reader in 1564 and 1571.—[*Comps. Sub Coll. of Thirds, Fife*, etc.]

1574 WILLIAM SPIERS, reader.

1595 GEORGE GRAHAM, Dean of Dunkeld, parson and vicar of Inisadain and Cluny.

1607 DUNCAN MACAULAY, trans. before 1st Aug. 1607.

1627 NEIL MALCOLM, trans. to Kilchrenan 1629. See also Glenorchy.

1636 WILLIAM MENZIES, his widow, Agnes Burden, marr. (2) Thomas Ireland, min. of Twynholm.

1660 PATRICK CAMPBELL, his son, Colin, bapt. 17th Oct. 1669, died Jan. 1699; his daugh., Anna (marr. Duncan Campbell, son of Colin Campbell of Edramuckie).

1676 ALEXANDER COMRIE, his son, John, bapt. 18th Dec. 1677; his wife, Jean Campbell, died 7th Feb. 1701.—[*Information for Breadalbane*, 270.]

1794 COLIN McVICAR, son of Wadsetter of Tiray.

1912 WILLIAM ALEXANDER GILLIES, D.D. (Glasgow, 23rd June 1943); adm. to united charge 15th May 1931; his daughs.—Barbara Sinclair (marr. 18th Oct. 1933 Thomas Calvert, min. of Braes of Rannoch); Margaret Mackenzie St Clair (marr. 27th March 1940 Norman David, son of David Richardson, Eskbank); his son, Kenneth Alastair, Captain, Black Watch, killed in Middle East Jan. 1943. Publication—*In Famed Breadalbane* (Perth, 1938).

KILLIN

On a small promontory on the south side of Loch Tay, called now *Ard-Eodhnaig*, formerly Ard Eodhnain ("Adamnan's Cape"), there is an ancient site called *Cill Mo-Charmaig* ("My Cormac's Church"), the inference being that the church was founded from Iona in Adamnan's time and that the land was gifted to Adamnan and to Cormac, the cleric in charge.

On 26th Feb. 1317–18 Robert I granted the patronage of the church to the Abbey of Inchaffray, the vicarage of the church to be served by a canon, or if more agreeable to the Abbey, by a secular chaplain. There is a tradition that the site of the earliest church was near the village, beside what is called Fingal's Grave, which is marked by a stone. It is more likely, however, that it was situated in the churchyard wherein stood the medieval church. The ruins of the latter existed in 1842. The present church was built in 1744, which date along with the name of the builder, Thomas Clerk, appears on a stone built into the wall. It was repaired in 1832. Killin is said to be Gaelic *cill fhiom* ("White Church"). But there is at Garve in Ross-shire a Killin which is regarded as *Cill Fhinn*, and, as Loch Garve is still called *Loch Maol-Fhinn* ("Fionn's servant's loch"), it may be that there is involved in Killin a Saint Fionn. No saint of that name, however, is on record. New churches were also built in 1744 at Strathfillan and Ardeonaig; and it was customary for the min. to preach alternately in them and the parish church. Later, a missionary was appointed to each of the two chapels. The salary of the missionary at Strathfillan accrued from a sum mortified for a chaplain in that district by Lady Glenorchy, under the management of the S.P.C.K., and there were also manse, glebe, hill pasture. The salary of the Ardeonaig missionary was paid in equal portions by Lord Breadalbane and the S.P.C.K., and there were also manse and glebe.— [*Charters of Inchaffray Abbey*, 116–19; *Reg. Great Seal*, i, App. ii, 658; *In Famed Breadalbane*, 54, 282, 286; Watson's *Celtic Place Names*, 149, 283, 523.] (See Strathfillan.)

1567 JOHN McCORCADILL, pres. 18th April 1569 to the Priory of Strathfillan, which is the parsonage and vicarage of the annexed Kirks of Strathfillan and Killin, on the death of Sir John Paterson; pres. to Logy 1585.—[*Reg. Pres. Bene.*, i, 19.]

1585 SIR MAKTOR WHITEHILL, vicar in 1585, was prior of Strathfillan.—[*Reg. Pres. Bene.*, ii, 129.]

1606 GREGOR McGILLIECHALLUM, min. in 1603.—[Gavin Hamilton's *Prot. Book*, 303.]

1617 DUNCAN McAULAY, adm. before 1617.

1618 WILLIAM MENZIES, adm. 1618.

1637 COLIN McLAUCHLAN, adm. before 1637.

1677 ALEXANDER RIDDOCH, M.A., Schoolmaster, Inverkeithing, which office he resigned Oct. 1675, having got a kirk next Candlemas, min. here 4th Feb. 1677.—[Stephen's *Inverkeithing and Rosyth*, 390; *Testificate* 26th Feb. 1677, *Breadalbane Papers*.]

COLIN ARCHIBALD McVEAN, his son, Patrick, doctor R.N., Bradford; his daugh., Elizabeth Jane, died at Edinburgh 11th Jan. 1931.
1869

GEORGE WILLIAM MACKAY, D.D. (St Andrews), died at Cairnhill, Dunblane, 18th March 1931.
1888

(*Charges united* 18*th Oct.* 1931.)

KINLOCH RANNOCH

THOMAS GLASS, reader, 1567–9, also at Moneydie.—[*Comps. Sub Coll. of Thirds, Perth*, etc.]
1567

JOHN MENZIES, reader at Weem, held vicarage in 1569, pres. to parsonage and vicarage of Rannoch on death of Charles Michelson.—[*Reg. Sec. Sig.*, lxii, 193; *Comps. Sub Coll. of Thirds, Perth*, etc.]
1591

DUNCAN MACFARLANE, pres. by Crown 15th Nov. 1848.
1849

JOHN WALKER McINTYRE, pres. by Crown 3rd Dec. 1868.
1869

JOHN SINCLAIR, his widow, Margaret Ballingall, died at Muirhead of Liff 6th Feb. 1925, aged 73.
1878

JOHN CAMPBELL MacLELLAN, died at Glasgow 22nd Sept. 1923.
1917

ALLAN MUIRHEAD, born 7th March 1888, son of Allan M., portioner, and Martha Robertson Muirhead; educ. at Univ. of St Andrews, M.A. (1914), B.D. (1918), B.Phil. (1916), and Union Theological Seminary, New York, M.Th. (1921); licen. by Presb. of St Andrews; Scripture Reader in City Churches, Dundee, assistant at Blair Atholl; ord. 13th Feb. 1924. Marr. 21st April 1931 Ethel Jane, daugh. of Henry Gore Wright, I.C.S., Dunbar, and Emma Turnbull.
1924

LOGIERAIT

Under the name of Logy Makedd or Mekedd, the church, with the Chapels of Kilchemy (Killiechangie), Dunfoluntyn (Dunfallandy), Kilcassy or Kilkasam, and Kilmichel or Kilmichell of Tulichmet or Tulimat, was granted to the Abbey of Scone by Malcolm, Earl of Athol, *circa* 1154–89. Lands belonging to the church were "Rath which is the head of the Caddom, all the Thanage of Dulmonych, and all the Thanage of Fandufuith."—[*Book of Scone*, 21, 35.]

WILLIAM CRAIGY, pres. to vicar-pensionary 9th May 1569 on death of Sir Robert Robertson; vicar in 1571–2.—[*Reg. Pres. Bene.*, i, 23.]
1569

SIR WALTER ROBSONE (Robertson), was vicar at Aberdour (*q.v.*), adm. reader here before 6th March 1573–4 by James, Bishop of Dunkeld; within twenty days of his admission he passed "with a dead corps to the Kirk, having the supercloath upon him in Popish manner"; the Bishop was ordained by the Assembly on the foregoing date to try "the said Sir Walter's alledgance touching the smelling of Papistry"; pres. to the vicarage 19th Oct. 1580 in succession to Henry Abercrombie.—[*Book of the Universal Kirk*, 287; *Reg. Sec. Seal*, xlvii, 27.]
1573

JOHN MARSHALL, pres. to vicarage 24th Aug. 1590 on death of Sir Walter Robertson.—[*Reg. Sec. Sig.*, lxi, 33.]
1590

HENRY ABERCROMBY, vicar, died before 19th Oct. 1580.—[*Reg. Sec. Sig.*, xlvii, 27.]
1580

JAMES BANNERMAN, M.A.—[*Reg. Sec. Sig.*, lxi, 260.]
1600

ADAM FERGUSON, line 19, p. 189, for "1887" read "1867."
1714

SAMUEL CAMERON, his daughs.—Alexandra Helen (marr. William Edward Townsend), died 8th Sept. 1929; Flora, died 10th Feb. 1938.
1842

COLL ARCHIBALD MACDONALD, D.D. (Glasgow, 21st June 1933); dem. 30th Sept. 1946; his sons—Colin Lorne, Sudan Defence Force and Political Service, died 1st April 1941; Angus, O.B.E. 1942.
1913

WEEM

It is said that in the course of his missionary journeys, 651–61, St Cuthbert came to a town called Dul, and for a time gave himself to a solitary life in the woods of a height in the district called by the inhabitants Doilweme (Rock of Weem). There he brought a fountain of water out of the hard rock, erected a large stone cross, built an oratory of wood, and out of a single stone near the cross, fashioned a bath, in which it was his habit to immerse himself and spend the night in prayer. Accused by the daughter of the king of a base action, he had resort to prayer, whereupon at a place called Corruen the earth opened and swallowed her up. On this account he never permitted a female to enter a church —a practice adopted by the Picts. Later he left the district. To the hollow stone called St Cuthbert's Bath people were wont to go in search of health. In the Newhalls district were Cill Daidh, St David's burying ground, and Feill Daidh (St David's Fair), which, held in March, was removed to Kenmore. St David was also associated with a spring about the middle of the Rock of Weem. If, it was said, anyone made a suitable offering in the spring, at the same time "wishing a wish," St David, the patron, would grant the fulfilment of the desire. According to tradition, also, he had a chapel on a shelf of rock called Craig an-t'Sheepail. At Killiechassie there was a chapel with a graveyard in which are buried descendants of the Wolf of Badenoch. The saint's name is from Cass, which along with its derivatives Cassan, Cassin, Caissin, constitutes the names of various saints. West of Killiechassie House is *Tom a Chanoin*, "the Canon's Knoll," and in the Tay opposite Aberfeldy is *Poll a Chanoin* ("the Canon's Pool").— [Watson's *Celtic Place Names*, 312–13; Skene's *Celtic Scotland*, ii, 206.]

1560 SIR JOHN DUNCANSON, still vicar 1569.—[*Reg. Abbrev. Feu Charters of Church Lands*, ii, 125.]

1567 WILLIAM RAMSAY, M.A., before 1st Oct. 1566 he was min. of Kenmore (*q.v.*).

1567 THOMAS ROBERTSON, alias McGIBBON, min. at Moneydie, held the parsonage and vicarage 1567–9. —[*Comps. Sub Coll. of Thirds, Perth*, etc.]

1570 JOHN MENZIES, had parsonage in 1590.—[*Comps. Gen. Coll. of Thirds.*]

1590 ALEXANDER MENZIES, also had parsonage in 1590.—[*Comps. Gen. Coll. of Thirds.*]

1603 JOHN MENZIES, rector.—[Gavin Hamilton's *Prot. Bk.*, 296.]

1635 THOMAS IRELAND, marr. Agnes Burden, relict of William Menzies, min. of Kenmore.

1663 JAMES STRACHAN, described as min. at St Fillans.—[*Deeds Dal.*, 26th July, 1705.]

1871 ROBART GRANT DUNBAR, his widow, Isabel Stewart, died at Aberfeldy 19th Oct. 1923.

1921 FINLAY MACKINNON, trans. to Edderton 10th Feb. 1924.

1924 IAN MacLELLAN, born 17th Sept. 1894, son of John McL. and Mary Anderson; served as combatant 1914–18 with 8th Argyll and Sutherland Highlanders (lost left arm); educ. at Univ. of Glasgow, M.A. (1921); licen. by Presb. of Glasgow 20th Dec. 1922; assistant at Irvine 1923; ord. 14th May 1924. Marr. 3rd Sept. 1924 Netta, only daugh. of Peter McLellan, Torrenich, Dalnottar Hill, Old Kilpatrick, and has issue—Annie, born 10th May 1926; Mary Anderson, born 30th May 1928; Margaret Mactaggart, born 11th Aug. 1930; Janette Eila, born 28th Dec. 1932.

PRESBYTERY OF PERTH

ABERDALGIE

1564 WILLIAM GIBSON, reader 1564 and 1572.—[*Comps. Sub Coll. of Thirds, Fife and Perth*, etc.]

1574 ROBERT SIMPSON, was parson of Dupplin 15th Sept. 1604; marr. Dorothy Burdon.—[*Perth Sas.*, iii, 264.]

1611 PATRICK PLAYFAIR.—[*G. R. Sas.*, xxxviii, 196.]

1843 MAITLAND THOMSON, pres. by Crown 17th July 1843.

1848 JOHN SHARP, his son, John, died at Trinity 12th July 1926.

1919 ROBERT SCARTH VALENTINE LOGIE, his wife, Ethel Margaret Theresa Masson, died 26th Feb. 1920; he died at Perth 9th Nov. 1948.

ABERNETHY

The church is said to have been founded in 460 by Nectan, King of the Picts, who gave Abernethy, whose boundaries are described, to God and St Bridget till the Judgment Day. Another story is to the effect that the "Collegiate Church of Abernethy" was founded and built by Garnald, son of Dompnach or Makdompnach, who reigned 584–96, and that after St Patrick brought St Bridget and her Nine Maidens to Scotland, Garnald conveyed to God and the Blessed Mary and St Bridget and her Maidens all the lands and teinds of Abernethy which the priory and canons possessed of old. Still another story ascribes the foundation to another King Nectan who was subsequent to Garnald. Apparently there is a confusion of facts; but it may be that Abernethy was originally a nunnery which later became a collegiate establishment of monks. In any case, in or about 1173 Laurence, son of Orm of Abernethy, apparently Lay Abbot of Abernethy, granted to the Abbey of Arbroath the Church of Abernethy with its pertinents, the Chapels of Dron, Dunbog, and Errol. Subsequently there arose a question as to Abernethy Church between Clement, Bishop of Dunblane, and the Abbot of Arbroath; and in 1239 this was settled by an ordinance of Papal delegates, in accordance with which the abbey ceded to the Bishop the whole altarage of Abernethy and certain lands, the Bishop to provide, from the fruits of the altarage, for the service of Abernethy and for a vicar of the choir to serve at Dunblane, while the abbey was to retain certain lands and the teinds of the church, with the rights and emoluments of the chapels, and the abbot was to be installed a Canon of Dunblane Cathedral and granted a toft at the Cathedral for a manse. Up to the first half of the 15th century the church was designated the "secular and Collegiate Church of Abernethy," and it was governed by a prior and canons. On 8th Feb. 1364 the secular prior and chapter, with consent of Margaret, the elder Countess of Angus, patron of the church, petitioned to the effect that the church was founded in honour of St Mary the Virgin and St Bridget by lay patrons, the lords of Abernethy, ancestors of the said Countess, for a prior and five canons, that upon the express desire of some patrons to augment the rents of the church the number of canons was, upon such hope, raised to ten, that the augmentation of rents did not take place and that in consequence of wars, fire, and ruin, the prior and chapter were brought to straits, and accordingly Walter, Bishop of Dunblane, with the advice of the said patrons and David II, reduced the canons to the original number, five. To the Bishop of St Andrews, Pope Gregory XI gave mandate to make enquiries, and on the Bishop's report that the net revenue did not exceed 200 gold florins per annum, 50 merks Stg.—a sum insufficient if the prior and canons did not add to it by their industry, the Pope confirmed the reduction by Bull of 30th Oct. 1375. Apparently after 1450, and before 1456, George Earl of Angus founded anew the collegiate church; and after 1456 the head of the church is designated provost, which indicates a regular collegiate constitution. The number of prebends appears to have been six. At least that number is on record—Forevenschip (Flisk), Balmanno Pettinbrog, Petmeddin, Colsy and Balmanno, Colsy. Abernethy Church was itself a Prebend of Dunblane, the Abbot of Arbroath being the prebendary. Of the collegiate church it was narrated in 1722 that "yet the ruins of it remain. Likway there is in it a great Church with pillars which yet remain in its noble fabric; it was destroyed from its primitive magnificence by Kenneth, King of Scots."—[*Chronicles of the Picts*, Skene, 6, 7, 28, 201, 389; Fordun's *Scotichronicon* (*Scott. Historians*), ii, 407; *Reg. of Arbroath*, Vetus 1–8, 5–6, 25–6; *Cal. Papal Regs., Letters*, iv, 214–15, viii, 100–1, x, 1, 306, 579, xii, 607, *Petitions*, i, 89, 579; *Exchequer Rolls*, x, 167; *Charters of Coll. Churches of Midlothian*, Pref. iv; *Reg. Great Seal*, iii, 148, 315, v, 2125, 2737; Macfarlane's *Geog. Colls.*, i, 117.]

1567 PATRICK GALT, min. in 1567 and 1572.—[*Comps. Sub Coll. of Thirds, Perth*, etc.]

1586 ARCHIBALD MONCRIEFF, pres. to vicarage 5th Sept. 1585 on death of John Wemyss.—[*Reg. Sec. Sig.*, xlvii, 203.]

1587 JOHN WEMYSS, M.A., son of Patrick W., min. of Abernethy, reader 1569 and 1577, pres. to vicarage 9th Oct. 1587 on dem. of John Wemyss of Petlurgy (probably J. W. of 1572).—[*Reg. Sec. Sig.*, lvi, 49; *Comps. Sub Coll. of Thirds, Perth*, etc.; *Edin Tests*, vi, 125.]

1672 ROBERT JUNKENE, had issue—Robert.

1691 ALEXANDER DUNNING, his son, Alexander, apprenticed to James Davidson, bookseller, Edinburgh, 8th Aug. 1722.

1871 WILLIAM GORDON, his widow, Octavia Rosa Watson, died at Levenhall 18th Dec. 1935, aged 99; his sons—James Montagu Dickson, died 30th June 1940; Robert Murray, died 14th Aug. 1941.

1903 GEORGE MACDOUGALL, died 26th Feb. 1932; his widow, Christina Powrie, died at Scone 9th Jan. 1948; his son, George, B.Sc., died 26th Feb. 1949.

COLLACE

1564 JAMES THAFT, reader 1564–72.—[*Comps. Sub Coll. of Thirds, Fife and Perth*, etc.]

1569 JAMES ANDERSON, in charge 1569.—[*Comps. Sub Coll. of Thirds, Perth*, etc.]

1582 HENRY GUTHRIE, pres. in 1582 on dem. of James Anderson.—[*Reg. Sec. Sig.*, xlix, 50.]

1852 THOMAS LEISHMAN, pres. by Crown 17th Jan. 1852.

1855 THOMAS BROWN, pres. by Crown 9th Aug. 1855; his daughs.—Janet, died 10th April 1936; Helen Elizabeth Ponder, died 3rd Dec. 1937.

1908 GEORGE VEITCH, dem. 9th May 1933; died Coupar Angus 29th Sept. 1944.

DRON

The Church of Pottie belonged to St Giles, Edinburgh. In the Act of Parliament of 1592 ratifying the patronage of the Church of Dunbarney to Edinburgh for the endowment of the college, it is described as a pendicle of Dunbarney. A lead seal of a Papal Bull (Nicolas IV, 1288–92), discovered in what was the burial ground of Pottie Church about the middle of last century, was given to the Museum of the Society of Antiquaries of Scotland.—[Lees' *St Giles*, 85; *Acts Scott. Parl.*, iii, 582; Laing's *Lindores Abbey*, 432.]

1569 JOHN LENNOX, reader 1569 and 1572.—[*Comps. Sub Coll. of Thirds, Perth*, etc.]

1593 ALEXANDER JUSTICE, pres. in 1593 on depos. of George Moncrieff.—[*Reg. Sec. Sig.*, lxv, 75.]

1605 PATRICK RYND, delete from line 3 "succeeded" to line 13 "Beith," and line 15 from "He" to line 19, "books."

1656 ALEXANDER PITCAIRN, marr. (3) before 1678 Mary Anderson; his sons—Alexander, bapt. 13th Jan. 1650; George, bapt. 12th Feb. 1652.—[*St Andrews Reg,*.]

1844 CHARLES GOODALL, pres. by Crown 7th May 1844; line 9, for "Jan." read "June."

1897 WILLIAM ALEXANDER SHEPHERD, died 2nd Aug. 1929.

ECCLESMOGHRIDAIN

The church belonged to Lindores Abbey, and was served by a chaplain. After the Reformation it had no parochial status; and in view of that, and the further fact that of old divine worship had been performed by a chaplain, King James on 31st March 1600 granted power to Patrick Leslie, son of Patrick L., Commendator of Lindores, to appoint a reader for the church or chapel at an annual payment of 40 merks.—[*Acts Scott. Parl.*, iii, 582.]

DUNBARNEY

The church belonged to St Giles, Edinburgh; and when St Giles was made a collegiate charge in 1466 it was decreed that in addition to his "pension" the provost should receive certain fruits, rents, and profits from the Church of Dunbarney, with the adjacent manse or parsonage and glebe of the church, and that he should appoint a curate to whom he was to allow 25 merks annually, with a house beside the church. Moncrieff Church also belonged to St Giles, and is described as a pendicle of Dunbarney in the Act of Parliament of 1592 ratifying the patronage of Dunbarney Church to Edinburgh for the endowment of the college.—[Lees' *St Giles*; *Acts Scott. Parl.*, iii, 582.]

1561 JOHN MONCRIEFF, M.A., vicar and exhorter 1561 and 1572. Marr. Jean Stewart and had issue—George.—[*Acts and Dec.*, lxxxi, 125; *Comps. Sub Coll. of Thirds, Perth*, etc.]

1569 ALEXANDER DYSART, reader 1569–72.—[*Comps. Sub Coll. of Thirds, Perth*, etc.]

1579 GEORGE MONCRIEFF, pres. to vicarage 17th Dec. 1579 on death of John Moncrieff.—[*Reg. Pres. Bene.*, ii, 27.]

1665 JOHN WEMYSS, line 8, for "1648" read "1668."—[*Perth Reg.*, 18th Feb. 1668.]

1691 JOHN TULLIDELPH, marr. (2) Katherine, daugh. of Walter Ranken of Orchardhead; his sons—Walter, apprenticed to John Knox, surgeon, Edinburgh, 6th Aug. 1718; David, apprenticed to James McQueen, bookseller, Edinburgh, 4th May 1720.

1834 ALEXANDER CUMMING, his son, James, died 28th Sept. 1925; line 9, for "Dron" read "Dunbarney."

1843 THOMAS DUNCANSON KIRKWOOD, his son, Thomas Adam, died at Blundellsands, Liverpool, 16th June 1925.

1893 JOHN SINCLAIR CLARK, died at Dundee 6th Nov. 1929; his widow, Mary Cameron Blyth, died at Perth 26th Dec. 1933; his daugh., Jean (marr. 30th June 1934 John, elder son of ———, Proven, Wallacetown, Bridge of Earn).

(*Parish united with Bridge of Earn* 1930.)

ERROL

At Polcak there was a chapel dedicated to St Nicholas, Bishop and Confessor. Gilbert de Hay, Lord of Errol, Constable of Scotland (died 1333), gave to the Abbey of Cupar the right of patronage of the Parish Church of Errol, founded by his ancestors and situated within his Barony of Erroll. The church was dedicated by Bishop de Bernham on 9th Aug. 1243. In 1430, on the resignation of Richard de Crech, the church was united to Charterhouse, Perth. On 6th Dec. 1495 Sir David Ogilvie of Inchmartin gave to Sir John Simon, Chaplain of the Chapel of the Virgin Mary of Carsgrange, 2 acres of Langland of Carsgrange beside the lands of Carsgrange, in augmentation of the service.—[*Reg. Great Seal*, i, App. 2, 1296; iv, 1163, 2290; *The Apostolic Camera and Scott. Benefices*, 101; *Lockhart's Ch. in Scot. in 13th century*, 57.]

1564 ALEXANDER ALLARDYCE, min. in 1564.—[*Comps. Sub Coll. of Thirds, Fife*, etc.]

1576 SIR ALEXANDER BAWNE, sometime curate, died 20th Jan. 1576-7. May not have conformed.—[*Edin. Tests*, vii, 186.]

1573 WILLIAM POWRIE, M.A., reader 20th Feb. 1577-8, pres. to vicarage in default of Edmond Hay.—[*Reg. Pres. Bene.*, i, (4), 15; *Edin. Tests*, vi, 35.]

1581 JAMES SMYTH, had addl. issue—Helen.

1583 JOHN MOUBRAY, M.A., parson of Inchmartin 15th May 1583.—[*Reg. Sec. Sig.*, xlix, 121.]

1626 ALEXANDER OMEY, his son, James, died 24th July 1633.

1725 LAUCHLAN McINTOSH, son of Robert M. and grandson of John M. of Dalmunzie; his son, John, apprenticed to James Mansfield, merchant, Edinburgh.

1858 ROBERT GRAHAM, his son, John Thomas, died 20th May 1925.

1914 KENNETH DANIEL MACLAREN, his wife, Martha Stephen Berry, died 14th March 1935.

FORGANDENNY

There was in the church an altar dedicated to St Katherine, founded probably about 1494, by Sir John Myrtoun, Canon of Dunkeld and Prebendary of Forgandenny.—[*Reg. Mag. Sig.*, ii, 2569.]

1569 SIR ROBERT OSTLAIR was chaplain of the chapel of St Katherine.—[*Comps. Sub Coll. of Thirds, Perth*, etc.]

1569 GEORGE CREICHTON, reader 1569-71.—[*Comps. Sub Coll. of Thirds, Perth*, etc.]

1569 JOHN ROW, M.A., min., had also Muckersie in charge.—[*Comps. Sub Coll. of Thirds, Perth*, etc.]

1589 WILLIAM ROW, pres. to vicarage 22nd Dec. 1591 on depos. of George Hering. Addl. issue—Marjorie.—[*Reg. Sec. Sig.*, lxiii, 77; *G. R. Sas.*, vii, 328.]

1624 WILLIAM ROW, his son, Thomas, apprenticed to Hugh Blair, merchant, Edinburgh, 6th Feb. 1677; his daugh., Isobel (marr. Gilbert Miller, apothecary, Haddington).—[*Reg. of Deeds Mack.*, xxxi, 212; *G. R. Sas.*, xlix, 126.]

1843 JOHN WILSON, pres. by Crown 12th July 1843.

1861 JOHN PAGAN, pres. by Crown 27th July 1861.

1866 JAMES JOHNSTON, pres. by Crown 29th Dec. 1865.

1867 DAVID WILLIAMSON, pres. by Crown 22nd May 1867.

1909 JAMES PATERSON BROWNLIE, dem. 29th Dec. 1925; died 17th Feb. 1943.

1926 GORDON MILNE EWAN, ord. 17th May 1926; trans. to Twechar 12th June 1929.

FORTEVIOT

Forteviot was a residence of the Pictish kings and later monarchs. To Forteviot, according to the legend of St Andrew, Regulus and his followers proceeded with the relics of the apostle after they had landed at Kilrimont (St Andrews) in 736 according to one view, and according to another, in 761. There they met in residence the three sons of Hungus, King of the Picts, who himself had gone on an expedition into Argyle. To God and St Andrew the three princes gave a tenth of the "town" of Forteviot, whereupon Regulus gave them his blessing, and in commemoration of the gift he and his followers erected a cross. Regulus and his retinue then proceeded to Kindrochet in Braemar, where they met Hungus on his return from Argyle. Before the relics of the apostle exhibited to them, the King and his nobles prostrated themselves; and thereafter the monarch gave the place to God and St Andrew, and there built a church. Proceeding southward over the Mounth, he and the holy men came to Monichie (Monikie) where he also built a church in honour of God and the apostle; and then they passed to Forteviot, where Hungus built a church ("basilica") to God and St Andrew. The site of the church is considered to be the Halyhill (Holy Hill), upon which also in all probability stood the royal residence. About 1830 there was discovered under the Holy Hill in the bed of the river May a semicircular arched stone cut in the form of an arch of 4 ft. span and 21 ft. in height, and carved in relief on the front with a cross standing on a pedestal over the centre of the arch, and having on one side the *Agnus Dei*, and on the other a robed figure in a sitting posture, bareheaded, and his feet resting on an animal; and on the opposite side of the cross below the *Agnus Dei* three figures habited in the same manner, but with helmets on their heads and swords in their right hands. It would appear that the stone is the superportal of a church belonging to an early period; and while it can hardly be regarded as of the time of Hungus, it may still be a very early representation of that monarch, the founder of the church, and his three sons who made a gift of one-tenth of that town to God and St Andrew. About 1165 King William the Lion gave the Church of Forteviot to his chaplain, Richard de Stirling; and eleven years later he decreed that the church with its chapels, etc., should pass to Cambuskenneth Abbey after the death of the said Richard, in excambion for the king's teinds, pleas, and profits of Stirling, and Stirlingshire and Callander. The church was dedicated by Bishop de Bernham in 1241. In the reign of James III (1460-88), and probably before 1465, it was annexed to St Salvator's College, St Andrews, "for sustaining a prebendary to serve and sing in the Choir." By Bull of Pope Sixtus IV, 26th Feb. 1473-4 the church was made a mensal church of St Andrews; and by Act of Parliament of 1592, conform to a letter of James VI under the Privy Seal, it was annexed anew to St Salvator's for "the sustentation of the provest, maisteris, regentis, bursaris and foundit persons therein."—[*Acts of Scott. Parl.*, iii, 551; *Chart. of Cambuskenneth*, 132; *The Apostolic Camera and Scott. Benefices*, 173; *Procs. of Soc. of Antiqus.*, xxvi, 1891-2, 435-7; Skene's *Celtic Scot.*, i, 297.]

1585 JOHN LAYNG, vicar in 1585 and 1588; vicar of Panbride and chancellor of Brechin.—[*Comps. Gen. Coll. of Thirds.*]

1586 JAMES MARTIN, parson in 1586.—[*Comps. Gen. Coll. of Thirds.*]

1917 NEIL MELDRUM, trans. to St George's in the West, Aberdeen, 3rd June 1925.

1925 JAMES FORREST KELLAS, ord. 18th Sept. 1925; trans. to Mannofield, Aberdeen, 15th Dec. 1926.

1927 JAMES GRANT FORBES, trans. from Monymusk (*q.v.*) 17th May 1927; died 22nd Jan. 1938; his daughs.—Mary Margaret (marr. 10th Nov. 1931 Robert C. Anderson, B.Sc., The Meadow, Lenzie); Caroline Marion Storry (marr. 4th

May 1935 William Hume Maxwell, eldest son of Dr Dawson, Buckhaven); Mabel, died 19th April 1911.

MUCKERSIE

The church is included in a list of churches conferred and confirmed by David I and Malcolm IV to the Priory of St Andrews. The church was made a Prebend of Dunkeld Cathedral by Bishop Lauder of Dunkeld (1452–76).—[*Reg. Priory of St Andrews*, 59, 64; Mylne's *Lives of Bishops of Dunkeld*, 23–4.]

The church became the burial place of the Invermay family.

1564 LAWSON, min. in 1564.—[*St Andrews Kirk Session Register*, 228.]

1569 ANDREW ABERNETHY, formerly a friar, parson and vicar 1569–72.—[*Comps. Sub Coll. of Thirds, Perth*, etc.]

1570 JOHN THOMSON, reader in 1570 and 1572.—[*Comps. Sub Coll. of Thirds, Perth*, etc.; *Edin. Tests*, vi, 22.]

1572 JOHN ROW, min. in charge 1572.—[*Comps. Sub Coll. of Thirds, Perth*, etc.] (See Forgandenny.)

1576 GEORGE MORRISON, reader before 15th Aug. 1576.—[*Edin. Tests.*, vi, 22.]

1585 JOHN LINDSAY of Dowhill and Kinloch, second son of James L. of Dowhill and Janet, daugh. of James Ross of Craigton; min. in 1585; appears to have dem. after 27th April 1592 and before 1599; died Nov. 1629. Marr. (1) cont. 19th May 1601 Christian, daugh. of John Schaw of Lethangie, and had issue—James of Dowhill, died Oct. 1638; Elizabeth (marr. John, eldest son of Harry Guthrie of Halkertoun); (2) cont. 16th and 22nd July 1609 Jean, daugh. of George Ramsay of Bamff and widow of James Nicolson, Bishop of Dunkeld, and had issue— William of Kinloch; Mr Laurence; David; John.—[*Clan Lindsay Magazine*, ii, 259; *Reg. Mag. Sig.*, v, 2330, vi, 1494, vii, 1336; *Retours*, xi, 43; *St Andrews Tests*, 4th April 1668; *Gask Papers*, xxviii, 606; Stephen's *Inverkeithing and Rosyth*, 200; Hall's *Kirk of Cleish*, 149–52.]

MAILOR

There was in the church an altar dedicated to St Ann of which Sir Constance Millar was chaplain at the Reformation.— [*Reg. Pres. Bene.*, i, 139.]

KILSPINDIE

The church was confirmed to Scone Abbey by Walter, Bishop of St Andrews, on 10th June 1395. The saint may be Pesandus, a disciple of Boniface.—[*Book of Scone*, 153–4; Johnston's *Place Names*, 222.]

Raitt. As a dependent of Scone Church, the Chapel of Raitt was confirmed to Scone Abbey by Richard, Bishop of St Andrews 1163–77. It was a church before 7th May 1411.—[*Reg. Great Seal*, ii, 2031.] (See Scone.)

1564 ALEXANDER DUNMURE, Min. in 1564 and 1572.—[*Comps. Sub Coll. of Thirds, Perth*, etc., *and Fife.*]

1569 SIR MARK JAMIESON, vicar pensioner 14th June 1561 and 1569–71. —[*Comps. Sub Coll. of Thirds, Perth*, etc.; *Reg, Mag., Sig.*, iv, 1744.]

1569 PATRICK LAYNG, vicar-pensioner 1569–71.—[*Comps. Sub Coll. of Thirds, Perth*, etc.]

1571 ANDREW STEWART, reader 1571.— [*Comps. Sub Coll. of Thirds, Perth*, etc.]

1623 DAVID WILLIAMSON, imprisoned for assault and fraud 1619.

1667 JOHN BLAIR, his son, John, graduated at Leyden Univ. 22nd Oct. 1696; was Physician at Dundee; joined the Jacobites 1715, and was at Sheriffmuir, where he aided Lord Panmure to escape; was at Avignon in 1716, when he was appointed Physician-in-Ordinary to James III; returned to Dundee, and acquired the estate of Balmyle, Perth.—[*English-Speaking Students of Medicine at Univ. of Leyden*, 24.]

WILLIAM LANG WOTHERSPOON,
1850 pres. by Crown 5th June 1850; his daugh., Anne, died 30th March 1930.

JAMES McTURK STRACHAN, died at Dundee 2nd Aug. 1936; his wife, Elizabeth Walker Bell Irvine, died 25th Oct. 1935, aged 73; his son, Thomas Eric, died 8th Sept. 1939.
1888

KINFAUNS

As a dependent of Scone Church, the Chapel of Kinfauns was confirmed to Scone Abbey by William, Bishop of St Andrews, 1202–38. The chapel was a church prior to 1560. At Seggieden, near the Castle, there was a St Augustine Hospital, the Master of which, Friar William, swore fealty to Edward I at Berwick on 28th Aug. 1296. There was also in the parish a chapel dedicated to St Ninian. On 27th Oct. 1419 Papal assent was given to a crave that, "since on Friday of every week a multitude of the faithful, on account of the devotion to St Ninian, flock to the Chapel of St V (Ninian), St Andrews Diocese, in the Parish of Kinfaunis—in order that the devotion of the people may be augmented, and the fabric and ornaments of the chapel be fittingly preserved, may the Pope grant relaxation of 7 years and as many quarantines to all Christ's faithful visiting that Church and stretching out a helping hand to its fabric and ornaments on the feasts of the said St V and the above Fridays." On 31st Jan. 1420–1 Papal Assent was given to a further crave that "since a multitude of the devout flock to the Chapel of St Ninian within the Parish of Kinfawyns in St Andrews Diocese, which is endowed with no possessions whereby it can be fittingly repaired in its edifices and ornaments, may therefore the Pope grant an indulgence of 4 years and as many quarantines to all Christ's faithful stretching out helping hands to the fabric and ornaments, or visiting the Chapel in honour of St Ninian on the more important double feasts of the year and in their octaves."—[*Cal. of Docs. Rel. to Scot.,* ii, 208; *Cal. of Scott. Supplications,* 114, 159, S.H.S.; *Book of Scone,* 216.]

WILLIAM EDMONSTON, min. 1564.
1564 —[*Comps. Sub Coll. of Thirds, Fife,* etc.]

ROBERT DUFFUS, reader 1569.—
1569 [*Comps. Sub Coll. of Thirds, Perth,* etc.]

JAMES MACLAGAN, his sons—John Maclagan Wedderburn, died at Braidwardine, Manitoba, 9th March 1929; Joseph Robert, died 17th May 1936.
1821

LACHLAN McLEAN, pres. by Crown
1843 27th July 1843.

GEORGE SMYTTAN DAVIDSON, pres. by Crown 25th Sept. 1852; his widow, Mary Gammell Stewart, died 30th Sept. 1923.
1853

KINNOUL

JOHN BLAIR, reader 1564.—[*Comps.*
1564 *Sub Coll. of Thirds, Fife,* etc.]

WILLIAM RYND, min. in 1564; delete line 6 "became" to line 9 "1599";
1564 line 21 from "having" to "geir," line 23; line 27 "William" to "dollars," line 34; pres. to third of parsonage 24th Sept. 1587 and to parsonage and vicarage 12th Jan. 1597–8 on death of Robert Carnegy.—[*Reg. Sec. Sig.,* lvi, 38; lxxvii, 213.]

ROBERT CARNEGY, M.A., parson
1592 in 1592.—[*Reg. Sec. Sig.,* lxv, 38.]

NINIAN DRUMMOND, his daugh.,
1611 Jean (marr. (1) cont. 19 and 25).

JOHN ANDERSON, his daughs.—
Margaret (marr. 12th Oct. 1886
1852 Robert Hope Moncrieff, W.S.), died 30th May 1931; Lucy (marr. 13th April 1898 James Henry Peter of Kirklands, Leven); Jane Hope, died 4th Dec. 1908. (There is a long reference to him in the Life of Sir John E. Millais, whom he married, and also John Ruskin.)

JOHN WILLIAM HENDERSON, died
1897 14th June 1942.

LOGIEALMOND

PATRICK MACGREGOR, his widow, Barbara Miller, died 17th Aug. 1926.
1859

GAVIN MILLAR, his son, Malcolm, M.D., D.Peych.
1904

JAMES GRIEVE, died 25th Aug. 1928; his son, Malcolm, M.A., vicar of Satterthwaite.
1916

ANDREW SCOULLAR, born 24th Aug. 1870, son of Andrew S. and Marion Cook; educ. at Univ. of Glasgow; Congregational Church Hall 1893-7; U.F. College, Glasgow; licen. May 1897; ord. to Dalmellington 21st April 1898; trans. to Avonbridge 26th May 1901; trans. to Cleland 27th Jan. 1907; Chaplain, Omoa Poorhouse, 1917-23; adm. to Wanlockhead U.F. Church 27th June 1923; adm. by General Assembly on probation 26th May 1927; assistant at Larbert; adm. 14th Feb. 1929; trans. to West Wemyss 10th April 1930; dem. 31st Dec. 1940. Marr. (1) 18th April 1893 Mary, daugh. of John Sommerville and Helen Downs (died 10th Oct. 1907), and had issue—Helen Downs Sommerville, born 8th Oct. 1894; Minnie Cook, born 14th March 1898; Andrew John, born 27th Aug. 1900; (2) 26th Nov. 1912 Catherine (died 24th July 1932), daugh. of Gavin Adamson and Margaret McCallum.
1929

METHVEN

The church was dedicated by Bishop de Bernham on 25th Aug. 1247. It would appear that the saint was St Mernoc the Confessor, whose name appears in the dedication of the collegiate church. By letter sealed on 1st May 1433 Walter Stewart, Earl of Athole, Caithness, and Stratherne, and lord of Methven, founded at the parish church of which he was patron, the collegiate church in honour of God and Jesus Christ, the Blessed Virgin Mary, St Mernoc the Confessor, and All Saints. On 4th May of the same year confirmation of the erection of the church was given by Henry, Bishop of St Andrews. The collegiate church was for a provost, five perpetual chaplains, and four boys. Each chaplain was to have 14 merks annually of current money with a dwelling near the church, and each boy 5 merks annually from the tithes and fruits of the said church. For the provost there were the remainder of the tithes, together with the following lands, namely 8 merks worth of land to be chosen by him from the Earl's lands adjoining the Church of Salchope, Petterley, Pettrevy, Drumcarne, with common pasture and firing, and other appurtenances etc., and with 12 merks worth of lands of Campsie, situated within the Earl's laid demesne of Methven, the provost to bear all the burdens of the provostry, and to pay 12 merks annually to the vicar-pensioner of the church. The Chapel of Auldbar, subsequently united to Aberlemno, also belonged to the provost, a chaplain being appointed to serve at the chapel. On 15th Oct. 1510 appears an annual rent of 14 merks from the lands of Easter Busbye and Wester Busbye to a chaplain singer in the church, but that may be included in the foregoing allowances to the five perpetual chaplains. A significant stipulation of the erection of the church was "that no Chaplain shall publicly keep a concubine, under pain of deposition by the Bishop after being thrice warned by the Provost." Culdeesland is traditionally said to have been the site of an early religious foundation.—[*Cal. Pap. Reg., Letters*, viii, 460-1; *Reg. Great Seal*, ii, 3510; *The Provostry of Methven*, i; Lockhart's *Ch. in Scot. in 13th century.*]

ALEXANDER YOUNG, min. in 1571, had "twa barellis salmond given and assignit at quomand of the Kirk in consideratioune of his grait familie and houshould."—[*Comps. Sub Coll. of Thirds, Perth*, etc.]
1567

EDWARD MONCRIEFF, reader 1569-72.—[*Comps. Sub Coll. of Thirds, Perth*, etc.]
1569

JOHN MURRAY, his widow, Isobel Scrymgeour (marr. (2) 29th March 1670 Robert Alexander of Corschyra).
1648

1694 WILLIAM MONCRIEFFE, had issue —John, min. of Rhynd; Robert, bapt. 8th Jan. 1708; Bethia, bapt. 23rd Nov. 1701; Nicolas, bapt. 17th Feb. 1704; Mary, bapt. 12th May 1706.

1750 JAMES OSWALD. Publication—*Hypocrisy Detestable and Dangerous* (1791).

1841 THOMAS BUCHANAN, born 8th July 1802.

1904 JAMES ROBERTSON, died 19th Nov. 1929. Marr. (2) 6th Aug. 1914 Mary C. Glendinning, born 3rd Feb. 1877, died 1928.

MONEYDIE

1564 PATRICK LAYNG, reader 1564–9.—[*Comps. Sub Coll. of Thirds, Fife,* etc.]

1567 THOMAS ROBERTSON, alias Macgibbon, min. of Foulis, Madderty and Kinkell; pres. in 1567 on death of Michael Walker.—[*Reg. Pres. Bene.,* i, 1.]

1568 THOMAS GLASS, reader in 1568 and 1569.—[*Comps. Sub Coll. of Thirds, Fife,* etc.]

1571 ALEXANDER CREICHTON, reader in 1571–2.—[*Comps. Sub Coll. of Thirds, Perth,* etc.]

1596 GEORGE GRAHAM, M.A., brother of Patrick G. of Inchbrakie, pres. to parsonage 19th Aug. 1596 on death of Thomas Robertson.—[*Reg. Sec. Sig.*, lxvii, 212.]

1655 DAVID DRUMMOND, M.A., died before 8th Nov. 1694, when his widow, Katherine Smith, was resident in Tron Parish, Edinburgh.—[*Tron Poll Tax Book.*]

1717 JOHN GARDINER, his son, James, apprenticed to Patrick Lindsay, merchant, Edinburgh, 20th Dec. 1738.

1899 DAVID GOWANS YOUNG, Clerk of Synod Oct. 1929 to 22nd Feb. 1937; dem. 11th Nov. 1933; died at Newtyle 9th Sept. 1938; his wife, Elizabeth Grainger Hart, died 22nd Feb. 1937; his daugh., Elizabeth (marr. 26th July 1928 Kenneth John, son of David Cuthbertson, sub-librarian, Edinburgh Univ.); his son, Archibald, died Blairgowrie 20th Dec. 1943.

PERTH

The Church of the Priory of the Charterhouse was dedicated to the Virgin Mary and St John the Baptist. The lands of Magdalene were among the possessions of the priory. The Church of the Blackfriars' Monastery was dedicated to the Virgin Mary. It was dedicated by Bishop de Bernham on 13th May 1240. There was in the church an Altar of St Andrew. The Church or Chapel of Our Lady of Loretto was founded by Sir Edward Gray, Rector of Lundie. To him and his successors, the Chaplains, James V on 28th Dec. 1528 granted a tenement of land with houses on the south side of Argyle-gait, and also a tenement of land on the north side. There were also in the church altars dedicated respectively to St Nicholas and St Catherine. The Chapel of the Holy Rood was situated at the Bridge of Tay. Additional altars in the Church of St John were St Mark, St Mary of Consolation; and the Visitation of our Lady, which belonged to the fleshers. The Altar of St Blaise was situated in the choir, and the Altar of St Fillan the Abbot on the "east side behind the High Altar." To the Monastery of the Blackfriars Robert III on 3rd Dec. 1405 granted the Chapel of St Laurance in the town of Perth for the souls of his father, and especially of Elizabeth Muir, his mother, who "rests in the Church of the Friars." On 2nd Feb. 1433–4 Archibald, Duke of Touraine, for the honour and praise of God, the Virgin Mary, and St John the Evangelist, and for the souls of himself, Euphame his wife, etc., granted to the Priory of Charterhouse certain lands in the Barony of Sprouston. The "Booth of St Sebastian the Martyr" in Perth occurs in 1534. The Chapel of the Holy Rood was "beyond" the bridge at Perth. —[*Reg. Great Seal*, iii, 722, iv, 1729, v, 740, 1816; Milne's *Blackfriars of Perth*, Pref., xvi and 4, 175; Lockhart's *Ch. of Scotland in 13th century*, 46–7; Mackinlay's *Anc. Ch. Dedications, Script.*, 75; *Reports Hist. MSS. Commiss.*, vi, 714, xiv, 24; xiv Report, App., iii, 243; Sir Robert Pollock's *Prot. Bk.*, 7, 13, 14, 81, 143.]

EAST CHURCH

1570 GEORGE OUKE, vicar in 1570 and 1574; was in office 1554.—[*Edin. Tests*, ii, 119; *Colleg. Churches of Midlothian*, 221; *Book of Assumptions*.]

1580 JAMES SMITH, reader 22nd Sept. 1580.—[*Edin. Tests*, viii, 250.]

1608 ALEXANDER BALNAVES, reader 24th May 1608. Marr. Elspeth Robertson.—[*Perth Sas.*, vi, 411.]

1605 WILLIAM COUPAR, M.A., pres. to vicar pensionary and to be min. on death of Patrick Galloway.—[*Reg. Sec. Sig.*, lxvii, 327.] (See Samual Clark's *Lives of the Fathers*.)

1630 HENRY ADAMSON, reader. Marr. Jean Lethame.—[*Perth Sas.*, 2 Ser., iv, Pt. 2, 28th Oct. 1630.]

1688 ADAM BARCLAY, died after 15th Dec. 1698 and before 8th Feb. 1703; his marriage contract with Marjorie Forbes Sept. 1663; he marr. (2) before 1698, –. Irvine. His sons—John, by first marriage, min. of Edrom; Adam, probably notar in Aberdeen, and Mr Charles, died before 10th June 1735; Alexander, born 1689, died at Grammar School, Aberdeen, buried 7th March 1701.—[*Aberdeen Tests*, 10th June 1735; *Aberdeen Sas.*, 24th Sept. 1694; *Old Machar Reg.*]

1705 THOMAS BLACK, marr. Jean, daugh. of James Drummond of Comrie.

1741 HENRY LINDSAY, student of divinity and schoolmaster of Carnock, probably son of John L., elder, Carnock. There was no John L., min. of Carnock.— [*Hist. of Carnock*, 1871, 662–5.]

1871 WILLIAM GEORGE HAYWARD CARMICHAEL, his widow, Isabella Gray Sidey, died 26th April 1932.

1901 WALTER EDWARD LEE, D.D. (Glasgow, 23rd June 1927), his daughs.— Janet Margaret (marr. 5th Aug. 1925 Robert Service Kinloch, Greenbury, Pennsylvania, U.S.A.); Rosa Masson Bethia (marr. 24th Oct. 1933 James Paton Watson); Bethia Edghill Dalgety, his wife, died at Edinburgh 17th Sept. 1938.

ST MARK'S

1905 ROBERT STEPHEN BARCLAY, son of James B., ship's carpenter, Fraserburgh, born 20th Nov. 1868.

1923 PETER ROBERT LANDRETH, died 31st July 1945.

(*United with West Church*, q.v. 1919.)

WEST CHURCH

1679 ALEXANDER SKENE, marr. Christian Forbes and had issue—Mary and Helen, twins, born 20th April 1672. —[*St Andrew's Reg.*]

1836 ANDREW GRAY, marr. Barbara, second daugh. of Alexander Cooper, manufacturer, Grandholm. Publications—*Lecture on Means of Promoting a Return to the Parochial Economy of the Church of Scotland* (Edinburgh, 1835); Lecture xii, *Establishment* (in Assembly Library).

1857 ROBERT MILNE, his daugh., Jane Ramsay Stormont, died 12th March 1924.

MIDDLE CHURCH

1903 JAMES MacGLASHAN SCOTT, died 24th Jan. 1933.

PERTH ST ANDREW'S

1919 JOHN FREELAND, trans. to Keith 4th March 1927.

ROBERT WILSON, trans. from Udny (q.v.) 30th Sept. 1927; trans. to Eskdalemuir 14th Nov. 1933; has issue—Margaret Montgomery, born 25th Dec. 1923 (marr. 17th Dec. 1948 James Murdoch, elder son of Oswald J. Bell, Largs Bay, South Australia); Elsie Rose, born 26th April 1926; Robert Douglas, born 22nd Dec. 1929; Gladys McLean Watt, 4th April 1934. His wife obtained decree of divorce against him for cruelty Oct. 1944.

PERTH ST LEONARD'S

1862 JAMES WILSON, his daugh., Marie Atkinson, died 21st May 1935.

1888 JOHN SCOTT MACNAUGHTON, D.D. (Edinburgh, 28th June 1946); his daughs.—Margaret Cromarty (marr. 2nd June 1913 Arthur Owen Warren, London); Anna Hepburn (marr. 24th Jan. 1934 Henry Davies Kingsley Davies, London); his wife, Mary Munro Keir, died 23rd July 1947.

PERTH ST PAUL'S

1856 ARCHIBALD FLEMING, his son, Maxwell, died at Hyères, France, 28th Feb. 1935.

1919 JAMES MACKENZIE, trans. to Lilliesleaf 21st June 1929.

REDGORTON

1564 ALEXANDER COLT, exhorter in 1564; pres. in 1577 on death of Dean Walter Abercrombie.—[*Reg. Pres. Bene.*, i, (4), 62; *Comps. Sub Coll. of Thirds, Fife*, etc.]

1865 ALEXANDER NEILSON, pres. by Crown 2nd Feb. 1865.

1916 DAVID GRAHAM, born 10th Jan. 1868, educ. Univ. of Glasgow; line 2, for "1904" read "1894"; died Perth 12th July 1940. Marr. 2nd Jan. 1891 Jessie Greig Whiteford (she died 11th Sept. 1939) and had issue—David, born 5th April 1891, died 16th May 1930.

LUNCARTY

In this parish there was a stream designated in 1597 Sanct Phillanus burn.—[*Reg. Mag. Sig.*, vi, 586.]

1564 ALEXANDER MONCUR, reader in 1564.—[*Comps. Sub Coll. of Thirds, Fife*, etc.]

1582 WILLIAM YOUNG, pres. in 1582 on dem. of William Balfour.—[*Reg. Pres. Bene.*, ii, 85.]

(*United with Redgorton 26th Jan. 1941.*)

RHYND

Apparently in the early part of the 17th century the church was rebuilt on the old site in the south-east corner of the parish. The present church was erected in a more central situation in 1842. In 1214–38 the Cistercian Nunnery of Elcho at Orchardneuk was founded by David Lindsay of Glenesk and his mother, Aleonora de Limesay or Limassi, daugh. of Gerarde de L. It was dedicated to the Virgin Mary. To the nunnery a charter of certain liberties was granted by David II; and a Papal Bull of 26th May 1418 confirmed the places of Elcho, Kynhard, Benyn, Standartlands, the places called the villages, with their rights, whole teinds, meadows, lands, knowes, pastures, fishings, woods, mills, possessions, and other places and goods wherever existing. Subsequently there occur fuller details of the possessions of the nunnery—the lands of Easter Binning, Wester Binning, Braidlaw, *alias* Middle Braidlaw, called the Nunlands, the lands of the vicarage and the patronage of the vicarage of the Parish Church of Binny, the lands of Braidlaw and Hunganside, *alias* Middle Binning, with the manor, with the church lands of Binny extending to 40 acres or thereby, in the County of Linlithgow; the lands of Wester Elcho, with the teind sheaves and great and small teinds, called *lie* Mains, the lands of Westerton of Elcho with the teinds, the lands of Cotis with *lye outsettis* called Cauldcottis, in the County of Perth; the lands called Standartlands or Standarts in Lothian (East); the lands of

Kinniard with manor and dovecot, in Fife, granted by Madoch (Malise ?), Earl of Strathearn; the Church of Dun in Angus; and an annual rent of 8s. from land in the Castlegait, in Perth. In the 16th century misfortunes overtook the nunnery. Apparently about 1524-5 a Papal Bull granted the office of prioress to Dame Euphame Leslie on the resignation of Dame Elizabeth Swinton, who was stated to have been deprived because of excesses, but who herself affirmed that she had been compelled through fear to resign by Athol (John, third Earl) and the Bishop (Andrew Stewart) of Caithness, who at the head of 80 armed men had forced entrance into the Monastery and confined her in a chamber. For three or more years Dame Swinton, by various pleas against the monastery, uplifted the fruits and possessions "by force and arms," with the result that, to sustain and protect the monastery, cups and other precious things had to be sold and deposits contracted. By Robert Leslie of Innerpeffry, apparently the brother of Dame Euphan, help was rendered in various ways, including the redemption of the cups and the sustenance of the monastery, for two years; and in return for the money which he had thereby expended Dame Eupham granted him a charter of the lands of Kinnaird and the "feu-farm" of the same and also the fermes of the lands of Binning amounting respectively to 50 and 21 merks. Some years later financial stringency was again experienced; and on 22nd April 1540 the lands of Cotis were set in feu to Alexander Bruce of Fingask and his wife, Elizabeth Bruce, for the repair of the monastery and the regular houses, and for the relief of creditors. Further misfortune followed. In 1548 a party of the English garrison of Broughty Ferry Castle plundered and burned the monastery, thereby reducing the inmates to poverty and debt. From John Wemyss of Wemyss, who was appointed bailie of the monastery, help then and later was forthcoming towards relieving debts and charges, rebuilding the monastery, supplying food for prioress and nuns, and providing seed for tilling the mains and grange of Elcho. The debts brought the place near to being laid under "process of cursing," which would have arrested religious worship within its precincts. Unable to pay the debt of 400 merks thereby incurred to John Wemyss, the prioress and chapter granted to him in feu on 20th Aug. 1558 24 acres of the cottar lands in Elcho, and on 26th Sept. and 25th Oct. of the same year the mains and grange of Elcho. Subsequent to the Reformation the possessions of the monastery were constituted a lordship; and on 21st Sept. 1570 Mr Andrew Moncrieff, son of William Moncrieff of Moncrieff, was appointed commendator. On 6th Nov. of the same year he conveyed the fee to his son and heir, William, who seems to have predeceased his father; and on 20th Jan. 1601, following the death of Mr Andrew, the commendatorship was granted to Mr Alexander Moncrieff, min. of Abernethy. On 20th Feb. 1610 James VI suppressed the monastery and conveyed to David, Lord Scone, the Monastery and the Place of Elcho, and all the possessions save the nunlands, etc., in the County of Linlithgow, which had been granted in 1606 to Sir Thomas Hamilton of Monkland.—[*Acts Scott. Parl.*, iv, 339; *Reg. Great Seal*, i, App. ii, 1250; ii, 1648; iii, 2746; iv, 1396, 1939; v, 882; vi, 724, 1135; vii, 248; *Acts Lords of Council in Public Affairs*, 273; *Retours*, ii, 105; *Transcripts from Vatican*, ii, 334; *MS. Reg. Ho.*; *Reg. Pres. to Benefs.*, i, 40; *Lives of the Lindsays*, i, 26; *Scots Peerage*, iii, 6; Chalmer's *Caledonia*, vii, 181; *Weymss Bk.*, i, 134-5, 135-6; ii, 188, 192-7, 279-80, 281-2, 289, 290-1, 294-5, 295-6.]

1561 JOHN LOGIE, reader in 1561, died in or just before 1590.—[*Comps. Gen. Coll. of Thirds.*]

1569 SIR JOHN LAMB, vicar in 1569 and 1572.—[*Comps. Sub Coll. of Thirds, Perth*, etc.]

1569 ANDREW YOUNG, exhorter in 1569.—[*Comps. Sub Coll. of Thirds, Perth*, etc.]

1632 ALEXANDER PETRIE.—[*Scot. Notes and Queries*, Oct. 1933.]

1678 WILLIAM PAPLAY, marr. (2) Margaret, relict of George Drummond, min. of St Madoes.

1731 JOHN MONCREIFFE of Tippermalloch, had issue—........, bapt. 24th Jan. 1746, died 13th Feb. 1816; Hugh, bapt. 2nd Feb. 1747; Archibald, bapt. 17th Oct. 1749; John, bapt. 4th June 1751; Robert, bapt. 16th Oct. 1758; Katherine, bapt. 22nd March 1748; Bethia, bapt. 2nd July 1752; Nicolas, bapt. 5th Feb. 1754, died 22nd April 1806; Helen, bapt. 19th Sept. 1755.

1878 JAMES BALLINGALL, dem. 29th Nov. 1921, died 3rd Oct. 1926.

ST MADOES

The name in the vernacular is Semmidoes or Semmidores, and it appears as St Medoc, St Modoc, St Madois. The patron saint was Docus, a shortened form of Cadog of Llancarvan, an eminent Welsh saint of the 6th century. There was in the parish a chapel dedicated to St Lawrence.—[Watson's *Celtic Place Names*, 327 and n. Gaw's *Prot. Book.*, 46]

1571 WILLIAM EDMONSTON, min. at Kinfauns, also in charge here 1571–2; may be identical with William E, chancellor of Dunkeld.—[*Comps. Sub Coll. of Thirds, Perth*, etc.]

1574 DAVID BALVAIRD, min. in 1569.— [*Comps. Sub Coll. of Thirds, Perth*, etc.]

1591 ALEXANDER LINDSAY of Evelick, marr. (1) cont. 15th July 1575 Barbara, daugh. of Bruce of Fingask.

1640 JAMES CAMPBELL, pres. 1st Oct. 1640; app. to Lord Couper's Regiment in England 7th Feb. 1645; died 26th Nov. 1667.—[*Scot. Hist. Review*, xxv, 257.]

1668 JOHN OMEY, pres. by James, Bishop of Dunblane, 6th May 1668.

1676 GEORGE DRUMMOND, his widow marr. (2) William Paplay, min. of Rhynd.

1706 JOHN DEMPSTER. Addl. issue— Agnes (marr. proc. 13th May 1789 James Maitland, min. at Sorbie); Elizabeth.—[*Edin. Services*, 1745.]

1796 THOMAS KENNEDY, his son, Robert, W.S., died 17th March 1840.

1856 WALTER TAIT, his widow, Jane Eliza Campbell, died 15th May 1924; his son, Adam Duncan, W.S., died at Oxford 4th Nov. 1946.

1920 JOHN HENRY DUNCAN, trans. to Kilmarnock 19th July 1923.

1923 RONALD HERBERT RAMSAY LIDDELL, born 19th Nov. 1898, son of John L., min. of Advie; educ. at Fordyce Academy, Univ. of St Andrews, M.A. (1920); served in war in Royal Field Artillery, M.C.; licen. by Presb. of Abernethy 27th March 1923; ord. 8th Nov. 1923; trans. to Rangoon 10th Dec. 1929; trans. to St Andrews, Calcutta, 1944; app. to St George's Presb. Church, Johannesburg, March 1946.

ST MARTIN'S

To Holyrood Abbey William the Lion, 1165–1214, granted the church with all its just pertinents and with the land which in Scots (Gaelic) is called Abthane, and with the land which is called Petfrethin which lies on the west side of the church, as set forth in the charter of John, Bishop of Dunkeld, either John Scott, Bishop 1178–1203, or John of Leicester, Bishop 1200–1213. The Church of Cambusmichael was confirmed to Scone Abbey by William, Bishop of St Andrews 1202–38, being one of a group of churches described as granted to the abbey by Alexander I, Malcolm IV, William the Lion. Apparently from the Reformation the Churches of St Martin's (Megginch) and Cambusmichael were conjoined and served by one minister who preached in the Churches "per vices" every Sabbath. But there does not seem to have been any actual union, and each congregation kept apart from the other and attended worship only when it took place in their own church. Realising the unsatisfactory position, the Presbytery of Perth in 1644 resolved to take steps to have the churches disjoined, each to have a separate minister, and a competent stipend provided for Cambusmichael from Scone. It was further proposed to disjoin Friarton, Gardrum and Boghall from Scone and be attached to St Martin's, Balbeggie from Kinfauns and be attached to Scone, and Nether Colm from Scone and be attached to Cambusmichael. Efforts continued till at least 1650, but the proposed disjunction failed. The actual union of the parishes took place cir. 1690-3. The Church of St Martin was rebuilt in 1776, and again in 1842. The Church of Cambusmichael was situated in the churchyard beside the Tay, and, along with a chapel also in the churchyard, was described in 1794 as ruinous. The Abthane included in the Charter of William the Lion denotes that there had existed in the parish an early religious settlement governed by an abbot. Bauchland for Bacnall-land, that is "crozier-land" in the vicinity of the church, probably was so called because it belonged to this ancient monastery. The name was revived in "St Martin's Abbey," the designation of the Mansion House for a period in modern times.—[Holyrood Charters, 38; Chart. of Scone, 31; Hunter's Diocese of Dunkeld, i, 332-4; Watson's Celtic Place Names, 266-7.]

1564 ALEXANDER GRAY, reader in 1564 to 1572.—[Comps. Sub Coll. of Thirds, Fife, etc., and Perth, etc.]

1569 THOMAS MORRISON, M.A., min. at Scone, also in charge here, called vicar and min. 1571-4.—[Comps. Sub Coll. of Thirds, Perth, etc.]

1677 PATRICK STRACHAN, regent in Marischal College, Aberdeen, 1663-5.

1844 JOHN PARK, pres. by Crown 1st Dec. 1843.

1863 WILLIAM MURRAY SMYTH HAMILTON, his daugh., Susan Isabella, died 20th Aug. 1935 (marr. Dr J. Holmes Morrison).

1896 ALEXANDER INGLIS SCOTT, died 16th Aug. 1947.

CAMBUSMICHAEL

In Cambusmichael there was a piece of land called Chapelfield.—[Reg. Mag. Sig., v, 2273.]

1567 THOMAS MORRISON, M.A., min. at Scone, also in charge here 1567 and in 1574; held vicarage of Melginche (Cargill).—[Comps. Sub Coll. of Thirds, Perth, etc.]

SCONE

It is thought by Skene that Nectan, King of the Picts, who died in 732, founded at Scone a church dedicated to the Holy Trinity. Certainly there was at Scone a Culdee settlement which bore the foregoing dedication. It was a *Muinnter*, later known as a Celtic Abbacie—a church governed by an Ab who directed the affairs of the daughter churches. This church Alexander I re-formed in 1114-15, placing in it a colony of Canons Regular of the Augustinian Order, and adding to the original dedication of the Holy Trinity, the Virgin Mary, St Michael, St John, St Laurence, and St Augustine. To the abbey thus established Robert I, on 7th April 1313, gave the Thanage of Abthane of Scone—the lands which had pertained to the Celtic Abbacie. The Church of Scone, along with its Chapels of Kinfauns, Crag, and Rait, was confirmed to Scone Abbey by Richard, Bishop of St Andrews 1163-77. In a confirmation charter of William, Bishop of St Andrews 1202-38, it is the first-named of a group of churches described as granted to the Abbey by Alexander I, Malcolm IV, William I. There were in the church altars dedicated to the Holy Trinity and to the Virgin Mary, the latter being situated on the north side of the church and called the "Quhyte-Ladye-Ile." It is said that the church was situated on the Chapel-hill near the Palace. However, there is uncertainty about the matter. In any case the Abbey Church seems to have been the Parish Church from the Reformation till 1624, when the abbey or what remained of it fell, and David, 1st Viscount Stormont, built a handsome church on the Mote Hill or Hill of Faith (Collis Credulitatis), 60 or 70 yards north of the old Abbey Church. In the latter part of the 18th century that church was in need of repairs, and, being otherwise inefficient, it was replaced by a new church built in 1784 in the village of Scone between the Palace and the Lodge Gate. All that was left of the old church was an aisle devoted to the purpose of a mausoleum of the Scone family. In 1804–5 the village was transplanted to New Scone, and with it was removed the church, taken down stone by stone and carefully rebuilt. In 1834 the village feuars increased the accommodation of the church by an abutment which lines north and south and gives the building the form of a T. Connected with the lands of Balquhorm or Balformach, situated on the west side of Scone, there was a chapel dedicated to St Marnoc, with chapel yard, croft called "Sanctmernok Croft," and dovecot. There were also at Scone the Croft of St James, Trinity Croft or Trinity-Land, a croft and garden called "Our-Lady-Petie-Land," St Katharine's Land, probably pertaining to the Altar of St Katharine in the Abbey Church, and land called Sanct Augustine's Land.—[*Book of Scone*, 1–2, 13–16, 31, 34–5, 41, 65–6, 97, 226, 229, 230, 231; *Reg. Great Seal*, v, 928, 947, 948, 1011; Skene's *Celtic Scot.*, ii, 233, 368, 375, iii, 59; Fordoun's *Scotichron.*, i, 227, *Scott. Historians*; Dalrymple's *Colls.*, 238–9, Ed. 1705; Scott's *Pictish Nation*, 128; *Chron. of Melrose*, 65 *and* n; *Procs. Soc. of Antiq.*, viii, 89, 90, *and* n; *Procs. Aberdeen Eccles. Society*, 1897, 78–9.]

1564 JAMES PITCAIRN, reader 1564–72.— [*Comps. Sub Coll. of Thirds, Fife*, etc. and *Perth*, etc.]

1575 HENRY ABERCROMBY, dean.— [*Acts. and Dec.*, lxi, 24.]

1620 DAVID WEMYSS, grandson of David W., merchant, Glasgow.—[*G. R. Sas.*, xix, 83; lvi, 204.]

1793 JOHN WRIGHT, College Chaplain, Glasgow, 1773.

1844 JOHN CROMBIE, pres. by Crown 6th Jan. 1844.

1873 ANDREW BENVIE, pres. by Crown 21st Feb. 1873.

1908 DAVID LOGAN BLAIR, D.D. (Glasgow, 21st June 1939); dem. 30th Sept. 1948.

STANLEY

1858 ANDREW JAMES BURT BAXTER, died at Comrie 5th Aug. 1924; his widow, Eliza Pullar, died at North Berwick 15th Dec. 1931.

1866 GEORGE MURRAY, his widow, Margaret Anne Graham, died 7th Nov. 1927.

1918 NORMA FARQUHAR ORR, trans. to Wanlockhead 16th May 1924.

1924 WILLIAM ADAM, trans. from Kirkpatrick Durham (*q.v.*) 15th Oct. 1924; trans. to Portmoak 18th Feb. 1927.

1927 JOHN DEAS LOGIE, formerly of Farr (*q.v.*); trans. from Glenisla 8th Sept. 1927; died 10th Aug. 1932.

TIBBERMORE

In the church there were two altars founded on or about 4th Feb. 1532–3 by Sir James Cuthbertson—the Altar of St Cuthbert, of which he was chaplain, and the Altar of St James the Greater and St Ninian. There was in the churchyard a chapel dedicated to the Virgin Mary, and at Ruthven Castle an altar dedicated to St Peter, to each of which on 14th June 1509 Sir William Ruthven of Ruthven, Kt., fiar of the same, and Sir William Ruthven, Kt., life rent granted an annual rent of £10 from lands in the barony. At Huntingtower there was a chapel which, it may be presumed because of the proximity of a spring called St Conwall's Well, was dedicated to that saint. In the part of the parish north of the Almond there was a Chapel of St Serf, deserted, it is said, because a child of Lord Ruthven of Huntingtower, who had been baptised in it, was drowned in the Almond when the members of the family were returning home. Bishop George Brown of Dunkeld, 1485–1514, rebuilt and restored the chapel, appointed a vicar for it, and gave him a vicarage and glebe lands.—[Mackinlay's *Ancient Ch. Dedications of Scotland*, Non-Scrip., 189, 488; *Reg. Mag. Sig.*, ii, 3357, iii, 1341.]

1564 EDMOND MONCRIEFF, reader 1564–72.—[*Comps. Sub Coll. of Thirds, Perth*, etc., and *Fife*, etc.] (See Methven.)

1565 ANDREW ABERCROMBIE, M.A., pres. to vicarage 24th Feb. 1565–6 on death of William Cranstoun.—[*Reg. Sec. Sig.*, xxxiv, 57.]

1593 ROBERT SINCLAIR, reader 26th Nov. 1593.—[*Reg. Sec. Sig.*, lxvi, 28.]

1612 ALEXANDER BALNEVIS of Cairnbaldie.—[*Deeds, Mack.*, 1706, Nos. 289, 290, 292.]

1845 EDWARD ROBERTSON, pres. by Crown 25th March 1845.

1869 CHARLES SMITH ADIE, pres. by Crown 9th Nov. 1869.

1916 JAMES CAMERON CAMPBELL, his wife, Sarah Large Cameron, died 11th May 1947.

PRESBYTERY OF AUCHTERARDER

ARDOCH

SAMUEL GRANT, marr. 1st March 1847 Williamina, daugh. of William Clark, ironmonger, 12 Union Terrace, Aberdeen, and had issue—Margaret Ann Alice, born 23rd July 1849 (marr. (1) ———— Gage, (2) ———— Binnie), died at Glasgow 30th Oct. 1934; Williamina Jessie, born 25th July 1851, died at Dumfries 5th Jan. 1940.
1840

JOHN ROBERT CAMPBELL, pres. by Crown 20th June 1858.
1858

WILLIAM MAIR, pres. by Crown 16th Dec. 1864.
1865

CHARLES MACGREGOR, pres. by Crown 3rd March 1869.
1869

GEORGE DONALD MACNAUGHTON, pres. by Crown 18th March 1874.
1874

ALEXANDER COSKERY, dem. 13th Nov. 1924; died at Bude 20th Dec. 1931.
1904

LAUCHLAN MACPHERSON, ord. 19th March 1925; trans. to Clunie 18th Jan. 1928.
1925

JAMES HAMILL MACONACHIE, born Moss-side, Antrim, 1872. Educ. at Queen's College, Belfast, B.A.; Presb. College, Belfast, B.D.; ord. to Ahogill, Antrim, 1900; trans. to Trinity Church, Newcastle-on-Tyne, 1908; adm. 28th June 1928; died 11th May 1929. Marr. 19th June 1903 Jeannie Shannon Rea, and had issue—John Christie, born 4th April 1904; Bessie Hamill, born 8th Aug. 1905; Aileen Wallace, born 14th March 1909; James Drew, born 5th March 1911; Margaret G., born 10th April 1918.
1928

AUCHTERARDER

In 1200 the Church of "Mackessog of Auchterarane" (Auchterarder) was granted to Inchaffray Abbey by Gilbert, Earl of Strathearn. The church was situated about half a mile east of what was said to have been a hunting-seat of Malcolm Canmore. Its remains were designated "St Mungo's Chapel" in each Statistical Account. The present church was built in 1784, and in 1811 it was enlarged by "setting back" the front wall.—[*Charters of Inchaffray Abbey*, 6–8.]

DAVID MURRAY, reader in 1564–72. —[*Comps. Sub Coll. of Thirds, Fife,* etc.]
1564

JOHN HAMMYL, M.A., pres. to vicarage in 1568 on death of Robert Arkersyne; had Dunning and Aberuthven also in his charge.—[*Reg. Sec. Sig.*, xxxvii, 77; *Reg. Pres. Bene.*, ii, 86; *Comps. Sub. Coll. of Thirds, Perth*, etc.]
1568

WILLIAM BLACKWOOD and **JAMES BLACKWOOD**, his brother, received Royal Confirmation of gift to them 6th Jan. 1571–2 of vicarage, by Dean and Chapter of Dunblane Cathedral. —[*Reg. Pres. Bene.*, i, (2), 21.]
1571

JAMES MITCHELL, his son, John, apprenticed to John Osburne, merchant, Edinburgh, 15th May 1717.
1700

DAVID SHAW, his son, Thomas, apprenticed to John McGill, surgeon apothecary, Edinburgh, 12th Dec. 1711.
1718

ROBERT YOUNG, his son, Robert, died 5th March 1938; his daugh., Jane Wylie, born 1862.
1843

ARCHIBALD JAMIESON, died at Edinburgh 23rd May 1929; his widow, Marcia Maziere Jameson, died at Edinburgh 25th Dec. 1935; his daugh., Janet May Maziere (marr. 14th April 1936 Gordon Edward Small, Edinburgh).

1888

HUGH MITCHELL JAMIESON, his widow, Ethel Levinson, marr. (2) 22nd Nov. 1924.

1899

ROBERT GARDNER, Ph.D. (St. Andrews, 1934); his daugh., Nancy (marr. 12th Jan. 1939 Alexander James Haggart, Crieff).

1917

ABERUTHVEN

About 1200 the church was granted to Inchaffray Abbey by Gilbert, Earl of Strathearn.—[*Charters of Inchaffray Abbey*, 2–3.]

ROBERT HARBESOUN or HERBERTSON, M.A., vicar, died 1563–4.—[*Cal. of Charters*, ix, 1901; *Reg. Abbrev. Feu Charters of Church Lands*, 205, 219.]

1562

THOMAS DUNNING, reader 1564.—[*Comps. Sub Coll. of Thirds, Fife*, etc.]

1564

JOHN MAXWELL, min. 1st March 1582–3.—[*Reg. Sec. Sig.*, xlix, 81.]

1582

JAMES ELPHINGSTON, parson 1596.—[*Comps. Gen. Coll. of Thirds.*]

1590

BLACKFORD and STRAGEITH

On 23rd May 1572 Sir Henry Oswald was chaplain of the Chaplainry of the Kyldees in the Kirk of Tullibardine.—[*Reg. Abbrev. Feu Charters of Church Lands* ii, 154.]

Strageith. In 1200 the church was granted to Inchaffray Abbey by Gilbert, Earl of Strathearn. The church was rebuilt in 1738, and the present church was built in 1850. The Church or Chapel of Tullibardine was built in 1446 by Sir David Murray of Tullibardine, for the purpose of a collegiate church. To what further extent Sir David proceeded with his scheme is not clear. In any case, in furtherance of the declared purpose of William Murray of Tullibardine, son and successor of Sir David, to endow and infeft certain chaplainries in the "Chapel" of Tullibardine, James II, by charter of 31st Oct. 1455, transferred to the chapel and to the patronage of the said William, a chaplainry which had been founded in the Church of Muthill, with the lands of Kildeis as endowment, by the king's predecessors, Earls of Strathearn, which apparently had fallen into desuetude. There are subsequent references to chaplainries in the church or chapel, two in number, Kildais (Culdees) and Tullibardine. It may be that the full collegiate erection was not completed. The dedication is variously given as the Holy Trinity and the Blessed Saviour.—[*Charters of Inchaffray Abbey*, 6–8; *Reports Hist. MSS. Commis.*, vii, 708; *Reg. Great Seal*, v, 278, vii, 886; *Eccles. Architecture of Scot.*, iii, 337.]

WILLIAM DRUMMOND, min. in 1572.—[*Comps. Sub Coll. of Thirds, Perth*, etc.]

1572

ALEXANDER CRISTISON, reader in 1572.—[*Comps. Sub Coll. of Thirds, Perth.*]

1572

JAMES GOVAN, had issue—William; Katherine; Janet, bapt. Montrose 7th July 1622.—[*Perth Sas.*, vi, 379.]

1618

DAVID MORAY, line 6, for "1687" read "1689."

1683

ARCHIBALD MONCRIEFF, line 2, for "Monzie" read "Moonzie."

1697

PETER MILNE, had issue—Peter, born 31st Jan. 1924; Robert Hally, born 6th Sept. 1927.

1910

COMRIE and TULLICHETLE

The present church was built in 1805. Under the name of the Church of St Serf of Tulliedene, the Church of Tullichetle was granted to Inchaffray Abbey by Gilbert, Earl of Strathearn, in 1219, confirmation being given in 1220 by Gilbert's son,

Robert. Apparently in this parish were the lands of Barnseles, Barnachills, or Barnahillis (Church-hill), with the chapel and sacred bell of St Kessog, belonging to the lordship of Drummond.—[*Inchaffray Charters*, 32, 34, 41; *Reg. Mag. Sig.*, iii, 1895, 2504.]

1561 DUNCAN COMRIE, reader in 1561.—[*Comps. Sub Coll. of Thirds, Fife*, etc., and *Perth*, etc.]

1574 WILLIAM DRUMMOND, min. at Crieff, also in charge here. (See Crieff.)

1585 ALEXANDER CHISHOLM or CHISHOLME, M.A., was rector 12th May 1566, and so recorded in various years up to 10th July 1587; was also in charge here along with Muthill in 1576; it is not clear that he was min. at Lecropt; died before 6th June 1598; marr. Janet Buchanan; he had a natural son, Malcolm, who received Letters of Legitimation on 12th May 1566.—[*Reg. Great Seal*, iv, 2912, v, 425, 1288; *Reg. Sec. Seal*, xxxv, 23, lxx, 5.]

1586 DAVID GRAHAM, vicar 1586–9.—[*Comps. Gen. Coll. of Thirds*.]

1591 ANDREW GRAHAM, pres. to vicarage 2nd Nov. 1591 on death of John Sinclair.—[*Reg. Sec. Sig.*, lxiii, 3.]

1598 JOHN MONTEITH, pres. to parsonage 6th June 1598 on death of Mr Alexander Chisholm.—[*Reg. Sec. Sig.*, lxxx, 5.]

1841 JAMES CARMENT, pres. by Queen Victoria 13th May 1841; his sons—William Maxwell, died at Victoria, B.C., 23rd Jan. 1929; James, died at Perth 18th May 1931; John, died at Comrie 1st Feb. 1933; David, died at Sydney, N.S.W., 29th April 1934; his daugh., Isabella Ann, died at Blairgowrie 9th July 1927.

1843 JOHN MACDONALD, pres. by Crown 15th July 1843.

1875 JOHN MACPHERSON, his daughs.—Isabella Macdougall, died at Brandon, Manitoba, 4th April 1929; Mary Grieve, died at Cairo 29th Aug. 1934; Christina Ann, died 4th June 1938.

1911 ANDREW BLAIR WANN, D.D., died 28th June 1923. His daughs.—Ruth (marr. 7th Nov. 1923 Alexander Munro, Puerta Ainas, Chile), died 31st May 1935; Mary (marr. 21st Dec. 1926 Joseph Russell), died 22nd March 1941; his son, Thomas, missionary, Kalimpong; his widow, Mary Wann, died 7th Nov. 1946.

1924 CHARLES WILLIAM FARISH, M.C., trans. from Bothkennar (*q.v.*) 19th Dec. 1924; trans. to Muirton-Marykirk (Aberbuthnott) 27th Oct. 1933; dem. 11th Nov. 1946. Marr. 2nd Oct. 1923 Agnes, daugh. of James Fraser, Leslie Place, Edinburgh, and has issue—Margaret Merry, born 27th July 1927.

TULLICHETLE

1564 JOHN WHITE, reader in 1564 and 1572.—[*Comps. Sub Coll. of Thirds, Fife*, etc., and *Perth*, etc.]

CRIEFF

Apparently in addition to the high altar there was in the church another altar dedicated to St Michael, called Pittenteane, the designation probably denoting the endowment of the altar. In May 1776 a petition was presented to the Presbytery of Auchterarder by several heads of families in the parish, setting forth the inadequacy of the church and the rent condition of its walls, and craving that the heritors be compelled to provide a new church. Protracted litigation ensued as to the liability for the cost of the new church and the division of the area among the heritors. At last, in 1787, the church was built; but the allocation was not finally settled till 1828. In the previous year the church had required repairs. In 1882 the present church in Strathearn Terrace was erected, and the church of 1787 became a hall.—[Macara's *Guide to Crieff*, 30–4; *Reg. Pres. to Benefs.*, i, 122.]

ALEXANDER CRISTISON (Christie), pres. to 24 merks of the vicarage 10th July 1568 on death of Sir Andrew Dawson.—[*Reg. Sec. Sig.*, xxxvii, 81.] — 1560

THOMAS DRUMMOND, his relict, Nicolas Murray, mentioned 1569.— [*Comps. Sub Coll. of Thirds, Perth.*] — 1563

WILLIAM DRUMMOND, exhorter 1564, as min. here, pres. to prebend of Crieff on death of George Cook. —[*Comps. Sub Coll. of Thirds, Fife*, etc.; *Reg. Pres. Bene.*, i, 19.] — 1564

SIR WILLIAM ANGUS, clerk to the Chapel Royal, pres. to vicarage 27th Feb. 1565, on death of James Gordon, chancellor of Moray.—[*Reg. Sec. Sig.*, xxxvii, 57.] — 1565

GEORGE COOK, prebendary of Crieff and Chaplain of the Lady Altar of Dunkeld.—[*Comps. Sub Coll. of Thirds, Perth*, etc.] — 1571

SIR HUGH CURRIE, parson 1572.— [*Reg. Mag. Sig.*, 11th Aug. 1572.] — 1572

JOHN KINLOCH, vicar in 1585, died before 1590.—[*Comps. Sub Coll. of Thirds, Perth*, etc.] — 1585

DAVID DRUMMOND, pres. 26th Sept. 1592 to vicarage, with houses, biggings, yards, manse, glebe, merklands, on death of William Drummond, and on 10th March 1596–7 to parsonage on death of Dean John Angus.—[*Reg. Sec. Sig.*, lxiv, 45; lxix, 65.] — 1592

JOHN DRUMMOND, marr. 18th Dec. 1697 Grizel, daugh. of Patrick Moag, portioner of Scone; his son, John, apprenticed to John Cleavland, merchant, Edinburgh, 27th Jan. 1731. — 1699

ANDREW CAMPBELL, died 8th Aug. 1938; his daughs.—Flora Colquhoun (marr. 12th July 1934 James Ranald Alexander, M.A., B.Sc., Ph.D.); Letitia May Macrae, born 16th Feb. 1924 (marr. 2nd Aug. 1944 Squadron Leader Allan Anderson, son of David A., Hally, Crieff); Jessica Maxwell (marr. 16th Jan. 1937 William Robert Ashcroft, D.A., A.R.I.B.A.); Jean Hope (marr. 11th Sept. 1937 J. Clark Taylor, M.B., Ch.B.); Dorothea Jeanna (marr. 26th March 1939 William Clark Taylor, B.Sc., C.E., Kai, Sudan); Frances Helen (marr. 20th Sept. 1939 Charles Kennedy Airth, Inverness); his son, William Andrew, W.S. Publication—*Crieff in the Great War* (1925). — 1895

CRIEFF WEST

ARCHIBALD HART, his daughs.— Rebecca Young, died at Edinburgh 8th Jan. 1932; Barbara Jane, died 1st Aug. 1940. — 1862

JOHN HEGGIE, trans. to Kildrummy 9th Sept. 1926. — 1918

CHARLES GORDON MACKENZIE, formerly of Methlick (*q.v.*) and Ceylon; assistant at Mauchline; adm. 24th Feb. 1928; trans. to Cowdenbeath 15th April 1931; trans. to Logie Colstone 24th Jan. 1934; died 19th July 1943. Publications—*Back to God* (volume of sermons); Pamphlets—*The Titanic Disaster*; *God's Building*; *Facts for Oor Folks*; *The Unforgivable Sin*. — 1928

DUNDURN

THOMAS ARMSTRONG, his son, Arthur, died at Paris 23rd July 1947. — 1895

ADAM WYLIE HEMPSEED SCOTT, died 29th July 1929. As he had no heirs, half his estate fell to the Crown. — 1908

DUNNING

There was a chapel of St Serf in the village of Dunning, with chapel lands called the lands of Granto, Sir John Leirmonth being chaplain apparently at the Reformation. The church was granted to Inchaffray Abbey by Gilbert, Earl of Strathearn, 1200–3.—[*Laing Charters*, 803; *Reg. Sec. Sig.*, ii, 2463; *Charters of Inchaffray Abbey*, 19–21.]

JOHN HAMMILL, M.A., min. in 1564. —[*Comps. Sub Coll. of Thirds, Fife*, etc.] — 1564

WILLIAM BANNERMAN, pres. to vicarage (prebend of Kippen) April 1566 on death of Sir John Hammill.—[*Reg. Sec. Sig.*, xxxiv, 72.]

1566

JOHN GRAY, reader in 1567 and 1572.—[*Comps. Sub Coll. of Thirds, Perth.*]

1567

ANDREW SMYTH, was Royal Bounty Missionary in 1725 at Braemar.

1728

JOHN WILSON, his son, Sir James, died at Crieff 22nd Dec. 1926. Line 25, for "Helen Maclean" read "Hector Maclean, M.D., B.Sc., Inspector of Rivers, West Riding of Yorkshire."

1861

PETER THOMSON, died at Glasgow 17th Oct. 1935; his wife, Margaret Thomson Mackay, died 20th April 1923; his son, Sir John Mackay, K.B.E., secretary, Scottish Education Department; his daugh., Agnes Irene (marr. Alastair G. Bell, stockbroker, Glasgow.)

1873

EDWIN MAXWELL MURRAY DAVIDSON, trans. to Inveravon 9th May 1924.

1917

JOHN CAMPBELL McKINNON, born 15th May 1894; educ. Univ. of Edinburgh, M.A. (1917); licen. by Presb. of Edinburgh 12th May 1920; assistant Holborn, Aberdeen; ord. 10th Sept. 1924. Marr. 22nd March 1939 Jenny Maxwell, daugh. of Hugh J. Ferguson, Burnside, Rutherglen.

1924

FOULIS WESTER

About 1210 the church was granted to Inchaffray Abbey by Gilbert, Earl of Strathearn. St Mavarie's Well was situated near the Almond in the neighbourhood of Buchanty and appears to be identical with "Holy Mill" on Pont's map and the present mill at Buchanty near Findoch Burn. The pre-Reformation church was restored in 1927.—[*Reg. Mag. Sig.*, iii, 2832; *Inchaffray Charters*, 25.]

DAVID MURRAY, reader 1564 and 14th April 1578.—[*Comps. Sub Coll of Thirds, Fife*, etc.; *Edin. Tests.*, vi, 12.]

1564

ROBERT RIND, M.A., min. in 1585.—[*Comps. Gen. Coll. of Thirds.*]

1585

JOHN DRUMMOND, died after 8th Oct. 1721.—[*Note Book of an Episcopal Parson.*]

1674

ALEXANDER TURCAN, his son, Alexander, apprenticed to Antonius Wright 16th April 1736.

1718

JOHN MURRAY, educ. at Marischal College.

1768

THOMAS HARDY, his daugh., Robina Forrester, killed in accident at Luton 7th Oct. 1934.

1852

JAMES CHRYSTAL MUIR, dem. 24th Oct. 1923; adm. to Tullynessle and Forbes 18th May 1928.

1909

THOMAS CHALMERS SHERRIFF, born 30th Nov. 1889, son of James Cousin S., Dunfermline, and Catherine Wilson McKenzie; educ. at Univ. of Edinburgh, M.A. (1919); served in Royal Artillery in Great War; licen. by Presb. of Edinburgh 26th Jan. 1920; assistant at St Columba's, London, Jan. 1921; Larbert; ord. 16th April 1924; died 10th April 1941. Marr. 12th Nov. 1928 Charlotte Mary, daugh. of John Baird, Craigie House, Crieff, and has issue—Charlotte Baird, born 5th Sept. 1929; James Cousin, born 23rd Dec. 1931; Catherine McKenzie, born 29th Sept. 1933; John Baird, born 1st March 1936.

1924

GASK or FINDO-GASK

Alternative names of the church were Nesgasc and Gasknes. The saint was Findoca, described in the Martyrology of Aberdeen at 13th Oct. as "a virgin who has a Church in the diocese of Dunblane." The 13th Oct. is the day of "Findsech, a virgin from Sliabh Guaire in Gailenga," now part of Meath—*Findseck, Findoc,* Latin *Findoca*. In 1210-18 Seher or Seyr de Quincey, Earl of Winton, granted the church to the Hospital of St James and St John of Brackley in Northampton, for the souls of his father, Robert, his mother, Orable, his eldest son, Robert, his son,

William, and his wife, Margaret. At Whit-Sunday 1266 the master and brethren set the church *ad firmam* for five years to Robert, Bishop of Dunkeld, for an annual payment of 24 merks sterling, with provision that if the Bishop desired the church *ad firmam* for a further five years, the agreement would be renewed, and so on for successive periods of five years. The agreement appears to have been periodically renewed, for in 1358 the church was the patrimony of the Archdeanery of Dunblane, being termed "His (Archdean) Church of Nesgask." The church was rebuilt in 1800.—[*Charters of Inchaffray Abbey*, 53, 55–6, 124–5, 155–7; Watson's *Celtic Place Names*, 286–7.]

1564 THOMAS SCOTT, reader in 1564 and 1567.—[*Comps. Sub Coll. of Thirds, Fife*, etc.]

1572 ROBERT MATHESON, vicar pensioner, died before 12th Aug. 1572.—[*Reg. Pres. Bene.*, i, 80.]

1572 WILLIAM MELROSE, exhorter in 1567 and 1569; pres. to vicar-pensionary 12th Aug. 1572.—[*Reg. Pres. Bene.*, i, 80.] (See Dupplin.)

1593 ALEXANDER GAW had charge here 1576 and 12th April 1577 when min. of Trinity Gask.—[*Edin. Tests*, vi, 50.]

1853 JAMES MARTIN, pres. by the Crown 8th Feb. 1853.

1906 JOHN DODS, died 22nd Oct. 1947.

GLEN DEVON

1568 SIR THOMAS HUTSOUN, reader, designated vicar pensioner 1571–2. Marr. Katherine Henderson, who was his widow in 1572.—[*Comps. Sub Coll. of Thirds, Perth*, etc.]

1576 STEVEN WILSON, marr. Grizel, daugh. of James Moutray of Markinch.—[*Reg. Mag. Sig.*, iv, 1344, 2354.]

1585 ADAM MARSHALL, pres. 29th Aug. 1588 on death of Symon Patoun.—[*Reg. Sec. Sig.*, lviii, 14.]

1591 ADAM KIRK, reader at St Ninian's; pres. to vicarage 28th Jan. 1591–2 on deposition of Adam Marshall. Addl. issue—Agnes (marr. Thomas Keith, younger of Shirdrum).—[*Reg. Sec. Sig.*, lxiii, 148.]

1639 ANDREW KIRK, his widow, Elizabeth Holiday, marr. (2) James Kid in Fossaway.—[*Dunblane Com. Dec.*, ii, 134.]

MADDERTY

The church was granted by Gilbert, Earl of Strathearn, to the Monastery of Inchaffray, which he founded in 1200. The parish was formed out of Earl Gilbert's new manor of Madderty, forfeited by Gillecome Marescall, who was slain 30th Sept. 1185. Madderty was the seat of an early Celtic monastery, the lands of which, called the Abthane of Madderty, were also bestowed by Earl Gilbert upon Inchaffray Monastery. At Williamston there was a chapel dedicated to St Anne, with lands called "Sanct-Annis-lands," and moor called "Sanct-Annis-Mos." The churches belonging to the Abbey of Inchaffray were—Aberuthven, Auchterarder, Madderty, Strageith, Kinkell, Wester Foulis, Dunning, Monzievaird, Kilbride (Dunblane), Trinity-Gask, Inishail, Strowan, Killin, Kilmorich, Balfron, Tullichetil and Cortachy, granted in 1257, but the grant may not have taken effect. To the abbey also belonged the Chapel of the Holy Trinity Teampul-na-Trianade, with the lands of Karynche (Carinish), in North Uist. Cells of the abbey were Abernethy Priory, and Strathfillan Priory, "Scarinche Priory, Isle of Lewis" has also been recorded as a cell of Inchaffray, but this may be due to confusion with Carinish in North Uist. In the first part of the 13th century the Abbot of Inchaffray was assigned a canonry, the precentorship, in Dunblane Cathedral.—[*Reports Hist. MSS. Commis.*, iv, 515;

Charters of Inchaffray Abbey, xxxvii, xli, 2, 3, 4, etc.; *Book of the Isle of Masses*, viii, Pref.; *Reg. Great Seal*, viii, 1342; *Retours*, xxxiv, 6.]

1564 JOHN HUME, exhorter 1564–72.—[*Comps. Sub Coll. of Thirds, Fife*, etc., and *Perth*, etc.]

1567 THOMAS ROBERTSON or MACGIBBON, min. here 2nd Jan. 1567, when pres. to Moneydie (*q.v.*).

1741 ANDREW RAMSAY, M.A. (Marischal College, 1724).

1734 JAMES RAMSAY, M.A. (Marischal College, 1747).

1830 WILLIAM STODDART, M.A. (Marischal College, Oct. 1812).

1891 JAMES BROWN, died 17th May 1935; his daugh., Winifred Helen Douglas (marr. 3rd June 1930 George William Newton Nicholls, Southport).

MONZIE

The church, in which there was a pulpit with the date 1617, was rebuilt in 1685, repaired shortly before 1795, and rebuilt in 1830–1. The Church of Innerpeffray, dedicated to the Virgin Mary, was situated in a detached portion of the parish of Monzie, which by Decreet of the Court of Session in 1702 was transferred to the parish of Muthill. By charter of 3rd Feb. 1506–7, John, Lord of Drummond, for the souls of the King and Queen, of Elizabeth Lindsay, his wife, and of Margaret, his daughter, granted to four chaplains to celebrate at four altars in the church an annual rent of 40 merks from the lands of Innerpeffray and Dunfallis, with houses, manses, gardens, etc. Manifestly these chaplains were intended to constitute the prebendaries of the collegiate erection, which, it is stated, was carried out by the said John in 1508. The church is designated a collegiate church in a charter of 25th Oct. 1542; and on 3rd Jan. 1581–2 there occurs "William Lindsay, Provost and Chief or Perpetual Chaplain of the Church of the Virgin of Innerpeffray," who at that date set in feu to James Drummond of Innerpeffray 6 acres of lands, 6 acres lying together in the lands of Logan beside the Gellie-burne, four gardens between Pethis-Manis and the Royal Way, and the lands of Kirkhill between Pethis-Manis and the Water of Erne. These are in the main "the Church lands, acres, houses and gardens of the Provostry of the Collegiate Church of Innerpeffray, with teinds of the same, viz., the lands of Burnesyde, *lie* Priestes aikers, 6 acres of land, other 6 acres, 4 gardens, lands of Kirksyde (vel. Kirkhill) with teinds of the same," in Monzie parish, occurring in a Retour of 1624. Several references also occur to the patronage of the Collegiate Church of Innerpeffray and Chaplainries of the same. In 1602–3 and at other dates reference is made to the "Church lands or glebe called *lie* Ibert of the Parish Church of Monzie." Ibert is the Gaelic Iobairt, an offering or gift land to the Church.—[*Reg. Mag. Sig.*, ii, 3048; iii, 2825; v, 442; vi, 1304; ix, 1058; *Retours*, viii, 307, xxvi, 299.]

1569 WILLIAM SCOTT, reader 1569 and vicar 1574; charged with abusing the Sacraments; dep. 1582 and excommunicated 26th March 1588; on 18th June 1590 acted himself under pain of death never to abuse the Sacraments or function of the Kirk.—[Pitcairn's *Criminal Trials*, i, 190; *Reg. Privy Council*, iv, 521; xiv, 578.]

1574 HECTOR CRANSTON, reader 16th May 1574.—[*Test. Inventories MS. Register House.*]

1574 WILLIAM DRUMMOND, min. at Crieff, also in charge here.

1592 JOHN CLERK, pres. to parsonage on removal of William Chisholm, Bishop of Dunblane.—[*Reg. Sec. Sig.*, lxiii, 84.]

1691 WILLIAM CHALMERS, educ. at Marischal College.

ARCHIBALD BOWIE, his sons—
1710   Archibald, merchant, Edinburgh; Patrick, merchant, Edinburgh.

THOMAS BARTY, line 2, for "27"
1780   read "22."

JOHN REID OMOND, his daugh.,
1836   Helen Mary, died 2nd April 1926.

GEORGE BLAIR, pres. by Crown 22nd
1843   July 1843.

GEORGE HUTCHISON, pres. by
1845   Crown 13th Jan. 1845.

JAMES TAYLOR, pres. by Crown 26th
1847   March 1847.

HOTCHKIN HAYNES MURRAY,
1899   dem. 1st July 1938; died 17th June 1940; his daugh., Elspeth Maclean (marr. 11th June 1931 Ian Menteath Cairns Macnaughton, Auchterarder); his wife, Agnes Wright Knox, died 17th July 1938.

MONZIEVAIRD and STROWAN

In 1219 the Church of Monzievaird was granted to Inchaffray Abbey by Gilbert, Earl of Strathearn. Alternate services were held in the Churches of Monzievaird and Strowan till 1804, when the present church was built in a central position for the united parish. The old Church of Monzievaird was situated in the old churchyard within the grounds of Ochtertyre, and its site is now occupied by a mausoleum. In 1490, as a result of a feud between the Murrays and Drummonds, there was fought a battle in which the latter suffered a reverse. The former, with their wives and children, proceeded to Monzievaird Church to give thanks for their victory, and thither they were followed by the Drummonds, who had been reinforced by McRobbies and Campbells. Surrounding the church, the Drummonds and their allies set fire to the building, which had a roof of thatch; and the Murrays, with one exception, were either burned to death or slain when attempting to escape. Evidence of the deed was found in the discovery of the bones of the victims when the site was cleared for the foundations of the mausoleum. In 1556, and at other dates, reference is made to "the Glebe and Church Lands of the vicarage of Monywaired (between the Water of Turret, the Burn *lie* Kelak, and the lands of the Lord of Monywaird, called Ballintra), called *lie* Yburd." Yburd, Ibert, is the Gaelic Iobairt, and denotes an offering or gifts made to the Church. In 1282–3 Malise, son of Malise, Earl of Strathearn, granted to Inchaffray Abbey the Church of Struy (Strowan), with the ground on which the church was founded, and the portion of land with which the Church was dowered by him at its dedication. The ruins of the church are situated in the churchyard nearly opposite Strowan House. The saint here is evidently St Ronan, Abbot of Cann Garadh, Kingarth in Bute, who died in 737.—[*Charters of Inchaffray Abbey*, 32, 33, 104, 170–2; Watson's *Celtic Place Names*, 254, 309; Macara's *Crieff*, 88, 89, 116; *Reg. Mag. Sig.*, iv, 2061; ix, 1199.]

ALEXANDER CRISTISON, reader
1564   1564 and 1567.—[*Comps. Sub Coll. of Thirds, Fife*, etc.]

THOMAS GLASS, reader 1569 and
1569   1574.—[*Comps. Sub Coll. of Thirds, Perth*, etc.]

WILLIAM DRUMMOND, min. of
1572   Crieff, in charge here.—[*Comps. Sub Coll. of Thirds, Perth*, etc.]

JOHN MALLOCH, reader 1576–7.—
1576   [*Comps. Gen. Coll. of Thirds.*]

GEORGE CALLUM, min. at Comrie,
1608   in charge here.

JOHN CAMPBELL, master of Grammar School of Glasgow in 1683.—
1692   *Reg. of Deeds, Mack.*, 10th Jan. 1701.

WILLIAM DUNCAN, educ. at Mari-
1721   schal College.

WILLIAM ROBERTSON, his daugh.,
1843   Charlotte Sarah (marr. Nicoll McNicoll, naval architect, Glasgow), died at Largs 29th Jan. 1923.

JOHN ROBERT CAMPBELL, his daugh., Jane McConachie, died at Oxford 12th June 1941; his son, Dr Ian, died at Harrogate 7th Jan. 1942.
1864

HON. ARTHUR GORDON, line 25, for "Plain" read "Plaint"; his daugh., Helena Constance Strathearn (marr. 11th Sept. 1943 Colonel John Hugh Mackenzie, C.M.G., D.S.O., Royal Scots).
1895

DAVID HEGGIE, his widow, Rosina, daugh. of Thomas William Clements, died at Edinburgh 27th Sept. 1922; his daugh., Rosanna (marr. 21st Aug. 1934 Douglas Percy Dowe, L.M.S.).
1903

WILLIAM WILSON BELL, trans. to Craigneuk 10th Oct. 1928.
1918

ALEXANDER BAIN HARPER, born 24th Oct. 1886, son of Alexander H., min. of Wishaw; educ. at Univ. of Glasgow, M.A. (1907), B.D. (1910); served in Royal Field Artillery and Royal Flying Corps, Balloon Observer and Balloon Commander, in Great War; licen. by Presb. of Hamilton 1910; assistant at Tarves, Shettleston, 1920; ord. to Kilmun 26th Sept. 1922; trans. and adm. 26th Sept. 1929. Marr. 4th April 1923 Eileen Margaret, daugh. of James Hope, Lenzie, and granddaughter of Senator the Hon. John Ferguson, Queensland, and has issue—Alexander James Hope, born 11th Aug. 1924; Aileen Hope, born 16th April 1928; William George Hope, born 3rd July 1933.
1929

STROWAN

JAMES MURRAY, reader in 1564 and 1567.—[*Comps. Sub Coll. of Thirds, Fife*, etc.]
1564

ALEXANDER GALL, min. at Muthill, in charge here.—[*Comps. Sub Coll. of Thirds, Perth*, etc.]
1572

ALEXANDER CHISHOLM, min. at Muthill, in charge here.
1576

NORMAN LESLIE, parson, 1586–90. —[*Comps. Gen. Coll. of Thirds.*]
1586

MUTHIL

The remains of the old church include the early Norman tower and portions of the rebuilding scheme carried out in or soon after 1425 by Dean Michael Ochiltree of Dunblane, afterwards Bishop of Dunblane. A sketch from the north-east by John Claude Nattes about 1799 shows that the nave and aisle had a roof of one span with no clerestory over the nave arcade. On the north side of the chancel is a tomb with two recumbent figures much defaced, which, according to a tablet placed there by their descendants, the Drummonds of Megginche, late of Lennoch in Strathearn, in 1880, are those of Ada, daughter of Henry, Seneschal of Strathearn, and of Sir Muriel Drummond, first knight of Concraig, who died in 1362. There was also a Chapel of St Patrick at Strageath which lies in a north-easterly direction from Muthil. Near it is the farm of Dalpatrick. According to the Breviary of Aberdeen, St Fergus, with a few companions, settled for a time in Strathearn near Strogeth, now Strageath in Muthil, where he founded three churches and dedicated them to St Patrick. The Chapel of St Patrick at Struthill is described by Macfarlane in the first part of the 18th century as "ane old ruinous popish cheaple where superstitious people used to bind distracted persons upon a large stone in the middle of it, and it has been reported that they have been loos'd and restored to their right wits in the morning." The well near by was regarded as having curative properties; and people visiting it left "a penny, a clout, a pairte of the beastis hair, or any such trifle as ane offering to the Sanct." So seriously did the Presbytery of Auchterarder regard the superstitious practices that in 1650 it ordered the walls of the chapel to be thrown down. But portions at least remained till 1846, when they were removed and the burying-ground levelled, and the well drained into a trough. The foundation stone of the present church was laid on 14th March 1826, and the building was completed in August 1828.—[*Macfarlane's Geog. Collections*, i, 132, S.H.S.; *Ross's Eccles. Architecture*, i, 196–7, 203.]

ALEXANDER GALL, called reader 1564 and 1567.—[*Comps. Sub Coll. of Thirds, Fife*, etc.]
1564

JOHN DAVIDSON, pres. to vicarage 10th Aug. 1590 on death of James Drummond and to parsonage on 4th Jan. 1591-2 on removal of William Chisholm, Bishop of Dunblane.—[*Reg. Sec. Sig.*, lxi, 40; lxiii, 105.]
1590

JAMES SCOTT, educ. at Marischall College.
1735

JAMES RANKEN, pres. by Crown 20th March 1868; his daugh., Arabella Louisa, died 28th April 1943.
1868

ANDREW MUTCH, his wife, Petrus Dow Young, died 12th Aug. 1940.
1902

GEORGE CONDIE, his widow, Mary Calvert Walker, died 15th Nov. 1928.
1912

ALEXANDER CROSS, his daugh., Jean (marr. 20th Aug. 1934 Hamish Sharp, min. of Kilbowie).
1919

TRINITY-GASK

The church was also designated Gask Christ or Gascrit, which might indicate an alternative dedication to the Saviour. In 1220-3 Gilbert, Earl of Strathearn, granted the church to the Abbey of Inchaffray. The church was rebuilt in 1770. At the farm of Cow or Coul Gask there was a chapel, the site of which, designated the Chapelhill, was trenched over in the early part of the 19th century.—[*Charters of Inchaffray Abbey*, 39.]

WILLIAM MELROSE, exhorter 1564-72, was curate prior to 1560.—[*Comps. Sub Coll. of Thirds, Fife*, etc., and *Perth*, etc.]
1564

SIR THOMAS SCOTT, reader 1564-71, also at Findogask.—[*Comps. Sub Coll. of Thirds, Perth*.]
1564

1574 THOMAS LUMSDEN.

WILLIAM OSWALD, pres. in 1584 on death of Sir William Ruthven.—[*Reg. Sec. Sig.*, lii, 2.]
1596

JOHN MURRAY, his son, Mungo, macer of Justiciary, 1662.
1639

JAMES BRUGH, son of John B. of Forwell Mill and Catherine, daugh. of John Campbell, supervisor of excise, Inverness.
1794

DAVID JOHN MACLAREN, trans. to Dundurn 16th May 1930.
1916

KINKELL

In 1200 the church was grated to Inchaffray Abbey by Gilbert, Earl of Strathearn. The bell, sold apparently in 1708 to Cockpen Church, to which it belongs, has the inscription: "This Bel Bellongs to the Church of Kinkail. Jasper van Erpecour me fecit 1680."—[*Charters of Inchaffray Abbey*, 6-8, 13-14.]

ALEXANDER MURRAY, reader in 1564.—[*Comps. Sub Coll. of Thirds, Fife*, etc.]
1564

WILLIAM MELROSE, exhorter here 1567. (See Findo Gask, Foulis Wester and Dupplin.)
1567

WILLIAM DRUMMOND, min. at Crieff, also in charge here.—[*Comps. Sub Coll. of Thirds, Perth*, etc.]
1574

ADAM SIBBALD, pres. to vicarage 2nd March 1587-8 on death of Dean George Spiers, monk of Inchaffray.—[*Reg. Sec. Sig.*, lvii, 71.]
1587

PRESBYTERY OF STIRLING

AIRTH

The church was granted to Holyrood Abbey by David I, apparently soon after 1128. The ruins of the medieval church stand in the churchyard near Airth Castle. On the south side of the nave is the Airth Aisle, called "Our-Ladeis-eyle of Airth," probably of the 15th century; and west of it is the Elphingston Aisle erected about 1600. There is also the Bruce Aisle of date 1414. The date of the tower is 1647. The present church was opened for worship on 20th Feb. 1820. The Lady Well is described in the 18th century as near the Abbeytown bridge. There was a chapel at Carnock in the barony of Plean.—[*Charters of Holyrood*, 7; *Reg. Great Seal*, iii, 762, viii, 1022; *Procs. Soc. of Antiq.*, iii, 165-8.]

1679 PAUL GELLIE, his son, John, apprenticed to Joseph Young, merchant, Edinburgh, 9th Sept. 1702.

1763 ROBERT URE, *primus*, his son, John, died Nov. 1793.

1900 FREDERIC HENDRY, died at Craigellachie 13th July 1937.

1928 THOMAS DONALDSON, trans. (ass. and suc.) from St Mary's, South Ronaldsay (*q.v.*), 14th Nov. 1928. Marr. 5th Aug. 1927 Katherine Mary, daugh. of Donald Maclennan, Dingwall, and has issue—Katherine Mary, born 27th Feb. 1929; Elizabeth Alexandra, born 31st Aug. 1931.

ALLOA

On 21st Oct. 1497 Alexander, Lord Erskine, granted an annual rent of 24 sh. from his land and croft in Alloa called Croft-Angrie, to a qualified chaplain to celebrate at the Altar of St Kentigern "which is called 'the great and authentic Altar' in the Church of Alloa." The remains of the old church, which was repaired and enlarged in 1680, are situated in the churchyard. The present church was erected in 1819. The interior redecoration of the church, at a cost of £8,000, was completed in Sept. 1937.—[*Reg. Mag. Sig.*, ii, 2377.]

1589 JAMES DUNCANSON, in 1579 he received a grant, renewed in 1580, of "the haill chaplainry of the Chapel Royal in Stirling, qlk p. tent of before to Sir George Maxwell."—[*Comps. Gen. Coll. of Thirds.*]

1758 JAMES FORDYCE, marr. 2nd May 1771 Henrietta Cummyn, sister to James C., Lyon Clerk Depute.

1863 WILLIAM SHAW, pres. by Crown 27th Aug. 1862; his daugh., Christian Margaret, died 7th Feb. 1936.

1870 ALEXANDER BRYSON, pres. by Crown 21st May 1870.

1911 AUGUSTINE SCUDAMORE WENTWORTH FORBES, for "Wentworth" read "Waitworth."

1919 ROBERT JOHN THOMSON, trans. to Bothwell 16th Feb. 1927.

1927 ALEXANDER MACDONALD, trans. from Stevenston 22nd June 1927; trans. to St Columba's, Glasgow, 6th June 1929.

1929 JAMES PITT WATSON, born 9th Nov. 1893, son of John W., Church of Scotland Social Work Committee, and Margaret Robertson; educ. at George Heriot's School and Univ. of Edinburgh, M.A. Hons. (1917), B.D. (1920); licen. by Presb. of Edinburgh 1919; assistant Tron

Church, Edinburgh; ord. to Dalmuir 14th Oct. 1920; trans. to Sandyford 18th Dec. 1923; trans. and adm. 12th Sept. 1929; dem. 14th July 1945; adm. to Chair of Practical Theology in Trinity College, Glasgow, 14th July 1946; D.D. (Edinburgh, 4th July 1947). Marr. 28th Jan. 1918 Margaret Munro, daugh. of Robert Munro Ritchie, H.M. Register House, Edinburgh, and Margaret, daugh. of Lieut. Thomas Ross Smith, and has issue—Marjorie Ritchie, born 11th Dec. 1918 (marr. 20th April 1945 Edmund, son of A. Barton, Rosside, Ulverston); Eileen Louise, born 10th April 1920 (marr. 17th Aug. 1946 Gerald F. S. Brian, Lieut.-Com. R.N.); Ian Pitt, born 15th Oct. 1923. Publication —Skirving Lecture: *The Christian Law of Liberty*.

TULLIBODY

The old church consists of bare walls, the roof and windows having been removed in 1916. More than three and a half centuries earlier it had suffered a somewhat similar fate at the hands of a French army, which, in 1560, had marched into Fife from Edinburgh by way of Stirling. Compelled to retreat on the same track, they found their passage blocked by the action of Kirkcaldy of Grange in breaking down the bridge across the Devon at Tullibody, and they had resort to removing the roof of the church and utilising the timbers to provide a substitute bridge.—[Beveridge's *Between the Ochils and the Forth*, 309.]

1571 ALEXANDER FARGY, min. at Logie, held the vicarage.—[*Comps. Sub Coll. of Thirds, Perth*, etc.]

ST ANDREW'S ALLOA

1882 GEORGE MITCHELL, his daugh., Janet, died 4th April 1946, aged 83.

1921 JAMES SMITH CLARK, served in Great War, 1914. Marr. 2nd Sept. 1930 Ann Vaughan (died 12th Nov. 1943), daugh. of John Gilchrist, and had issue—Robert Vaughan, born 16th Jan. 1933; John Gilchrist, born 20th Nov. 1934.

ALVA

1566 ROBERT MONTEITH, min. in 1566. —[*Comps. Sub Coll. of Thirds, Perth*, etc.]

1675 ROBERT FORBES, educ. at Marischal College.

1884 JAMES ALEXANDER WILLIAMSON, D.D. (St Andrews); dem. 1929; died 12th June 1930; his daugh., Mary Ann Winter Conacher (marr. 10th Nov. 1931 William Christie, son of J. Belfrage, J.P., Durham House, Portobello).

BANNOCKBURN

1884 WILLIAM BLACKLEY RITCHIE, his widow, Annie Louisa Hodson, died Edinburgh 6th June 1945.

1921 JAMES STRATHEARN MACNAB, trans. to Flowerhill 20th Oct. 1926.

1927 NEILL McNEILL, born 11th Nov. 1894, son of Hugh M., J.P., Dublin, and Emma Lucy Gregg; educ. at MacCrea-Magee College, Londonderry, Trinity College, B.A. (June 1917), M.A. (June 1921); Assembly's College, Belfast; licen. by Presb. of Dublin June 1920; assistant, Agnes Street, Belfast; ord. to Chalmers Church, Ardwick, Manchester, 21st Sept. 1921; assistant Cambuslang 1st July 1925; adm. by General Assembly 3rd June 1926; adm. 23rd March 1927; trans. to Steven Memorial Church, Glasgow, 30th May 1930. Marr. 14th Sept. 1927 Euphemia Williams (died 28th Feb. 1937), daugh. of David Alexander Morrell and Eliza Jane Wilson, and had issue—Hugh Morrell, born 5th July 1929; David Wilson Gregg, born 19th April 1933.

BONNYBRIDGE

1878 JAMES STEEL, his wife, Annie B. Ure, died at Stirling 14th June 1932; he died 13th April 1946, aged 94.

1919 DUNCAN McCORKINDALE, trans. to Milngavie 22nd Dec. 1925.

BARTY DANIEL SINCLAIR, born
1926 24th Nov. 1890; educ. at Univ. of Glasgow, M.A. (1923); assistant Shettleston 1924; ord. 5th May 1926.

BOTHKENNAR

The patron saint was Cainer, daughter of Caelman, otherwise Cainder and Cainner. The church belonged to the Priory of Eccles. —[Watson's *Celtic Place Names*, 276.]

JOHN GALBRAITH, his son,
1629 Humphry, probably min. of Dollar. —[*G. R. Sas.*, 2 Ser., ix, 163.]

JOHN SKINNER, his son, George,
1676 apprenticed to Joseph Young, merchant, Edinburgh, 13th Dec. 1697.

WILLIAM MUNRO, his son, William,
1766 died at Whitacre, 5th July 1794.

GEORGE DICKSON HUTTON, died
1893 at Edinburgh 3rd Dec. 1929; his son, William Menzies, Royal Corps of Signals, died prisoner of war Aug. 1944.

CHARLES WILLIAM FARISH, trans.
1919 to Comrie 19th Dec. 1924.

PETER CRAIG MacQUOID, ord.
1924 (ass. and suc.) 22nd April 1924; trans. to Turriff 20th April 1927.

WILLIAM THOMSON, trans. from
1927 Kelty (*q.v.*) 30th Sept. 1927 (ass. and suc.); died 18th Jan. 1943.

CLACKMANNAN

The church was dedicated by Bishop de Bernham 24th Aug. 1249. It belonged to Cambuskenneth Abbey, having been granted to the same by David I prior to 1153, along with 40 acres of land and the priest's toft in the town of Clackmannan. About 1160 the grant was confirmed by King David's son, Malcolm IV. The church was served by a parish chaplain from the Abbey. Alloa Church was a dependent chapel of Clackmannan—a position that was not without friction. In a dispute between Sir Thomas Erskine, Kt., of that ilk, and the Abbot of Cambuskenneth, regarding the services of Alloway (Alloa) Chapel, which, Sir Thomas affirmed, should be performed by the Abbot as perpetual vicar of Clackmannan, a Decreet Arbitral was pronounced on 4th April 1401 to the effect that the Abbot and Convent should consent that the canon or priest serving at Clackmannan should serve in the chapel on the Lord's Day and festival days, in the manner hitherto, if the licence of the Bishop of St Andrews was procured by Sir Thomas and the inhabitants and others frequenting the chapel. Eight years later the matter in dispute was the repair of Clackmannan Church, to which the parishioners at Clackmannan declined to contribute on the ground that the inhabitants of the Lordship of Alloway were refusing so to do; and in a letter of 20th May 1409 Henry Wardlaw, Bishop of St Andrews, found that Alloway was bound to make contribution, instructed the parish chaplain of the Church of Clackmannan to warn the parishioners, and especially those in the Lordship of Alloway, to begin repairs in thirty days and carry them to completion, on pain of excommunication, and directed that, in the event of the recreants lying under excommunication for nine days, with hardened hearts, the Church of Clackmannan, and the chapels and oratories within the parish, should be placed under ecclesiastical interdict, and that no divine service should be performed or sacraments administered in the same excepting the absolution of the dying and the baptism of infants. There were in the church an altar dedicated to St Ninian and in the barony of Sauchie a chapel dedicated to St Blane.—[*Chart. of Cambuskenneth*, 29–30, 31–3; Lockhart's *Ch. in Scot. in 13th Century*, 63; Gaw's *Prot. Book*, 34; *Exch. Rolls*, xvii, 583.]

ALEXANDER FARGY, min. at Logie,
1571 in charge also here.—[*Comps. Sub Coll. of Thirds, Perth*, etc.]

JOHN GILCHRIST, his daugh., Isa-
1862 bella Jane, died 7th Nov. 1941.

**ALEXANDER IRVINE ROBERT-
1877 SON**, died at Stirling 21st Feb. 1925; his daugh., Charlotte Stewart (marr. at Shanghai 18th Aug. 1933 Mervyn Armstrong, son of Rev. E. A., Ebbw Vale).

ROBERT ANDREW AGNEW, trans. to Cardross 19th May 1932; Ph.D. (Edinburgh 1935); died 22nd May 1936. Marr. 25th Oct. 1929 Gladys Campbell, second daugh. of Matthew Greenlees, Aberdona House, Clackmannan.

1921

DENNY

By Act of Parliament in 1641 the church, which "some fourtie years" earlier "had been dismembered from the parsonage of Falkirk with the consent of the patron and the parson" of that parish, was erected into a parish and was granted the privileges, liberties, emoluments, and endowments competent to a parish. Enclosed within the waters of Carron and Boyne, and situated four miles from Falkirk, the inhabitants of Denny could not possibly have the benefit of Divine Service at Falkirk, and for the space foresaid, forty years, they had been served "be thair owne pastores upon meanes within themselffis."—[*Acts Scott. Parl.*, v, 473; *Stewarton Case*, 115.]

ALEXANDER CALANDER.—[G. R. Sas., 2 Ser., xii, 12.]

1627

JOHN WINGATE of Chartershall, his son, John, apprenticed to Patrick Murray, goldsmith, Edinburgh, 17th Sept. 1703.—[*Deeds, Mack.*, 1705, No. 386.]

1681

JAMES TURNBULL, son of Robert T., bailie of Linlithgow.—[*Services of Heirs*, 7th April 1752.]

1750

COLIN McCULLOCH, pres. by Crown 5th Aug. 1843.

1843

WILLIAM ANDERSON, pres. by Crown 2nd Feb. 1854.

1854

ALEXANDER FALCONER, pres. by Crown 5th March 1856.

1856

ALEXANDER MACARA, died at Woburn, Bucks, 5th April 1944; his son, Alexander, min. of Irvine.

1904

DOLLAR

The church was dedicated to St Columba, and belonged to Inchcolm Abbey, being apparently a mensal church of the abbot. A scheme of restoration or rebuilding of the church by the abbot is said to have been in process in 1336, when valuable woodwork about to be used in the scheme was carried off by English raiders from ships in the Firth of Forth. According to the tale, the vessel containing the timber and the raiders sank in a storm in deep water off Inchcolm, the tempest being due to the intervention of St Columba. The church was rebuilt in 1775, and again in 1841.—*Book of Pluscarden*, 281, Scott. Historians; *Scotichronicon*, Goodall's Ed., xiii, cxxxvii; *Extracta Variis Chron. Scotia*, 170; *Chart. of Inchcolm*, 56, Scott. Hist. Soc.]

SIR HENRY BALFOUR, vicar in 1561–72, removed for non-compearance before 19th Dec. 1573.—[*Laing Charters*, 849; *Reg. of Pres. Bene.*, 19th Dec. 1573; *Acts and Dec.*, xxx, 111, 170; xxiv, 152; *Comps. Sub Coll. of Thirds, Perth*, etc.]

1561

SIR ROBERT BURR, curate in 1561, reader in 1567; pres. to vicarage 19th Dec. 1573 on non-compearance of Sir Henry Balfour; still in office 1590.—[*Acts and Dec.*, xxiv, 152; xxx, 170; *Reg. Pres. Bene.*, i, (4), 14; *Comps. Gen. Coll. of Thirds*.]

1561

GAVIN DONALDSON, pres. to vicarage 12th Feb. 1588–9 on depriv. of John Burne.—[*Reg. Sec. Sig.*, lix, 28.]

1589

PATRICK SMYTH, M.A., pres. to parsonage and vicarage 11th May 1596 on dem. of Henry Guthrie.—[*Reg. Sec. Sig.*, lxviii, 127.]

1596

HUMPHREY GALBRAITH, probably son of John G., min. of Bothkennar.

1664

ROBERT FINDLAY, educ. at Marischal College.

1757

JOHN WATSON, educ. at Marischal College.

1792

ROBERT SCOTT McCLELLAND, trans. to Burnside, Rutherglen, 8th Oct. 1928.

1920

THOMAS STOBO GLEN, trans. from Govanhill (*q.v.*) 14th Feb. 1929; trans. to Kildonan 2nd July 1948.
1929

GARGUNNOCK

JOHN EDMONSTONE, his son, Patrick, apprenticed to Archibald Fisher, barber, Edinburgh, 21st Feb. 1694.
1666

JOHN STARK, his son, Matthew, died at Westertown, Doune, 26th July 1912.
1844

ROBERT STEVENSON, dem. 6th Jan. 1927; his wife, Agnes Jeannie Dodds, died 25th July 1938; he died Melrose 14th Jan. 1947.
1888

JOHN HENRY HORTON McNEILL, trans. from Indian Chaplaincy (*q.v.*) 12th May 1927; trans. to Rosebank, Dundee, 11th Oct. 1933; dem. 9th Sept. 1939.
1927

HAGGS

ALEXANDER ROBERTSON, his widow, Jeanie Hunter Henderson, died 2nd Oct. 1938.
1877

JOHN SHEDDEN, trans. to Dalmellington 29th April 1925. Line 1, for "James" read "John."
1922

JOHN JACKSON, son of John J., quarryman, and Martha Bryson Jackson; educ. at Univ. of Glasgow; licen. by Presb. of Hamilton; min. at Collie, Western Australia, 1910; served in Army; missionary at St Machan's, Larkhall, 1919; ord. 9th Sept. 1925. Marr. 8th Dec. 1909 Christina, daugh. of Thomas Strachan Purden and Isabella Macfarlane, and has issue—Christina Purden, born 22nd Oct. 1910; Margaret Isabel Macfarlane, born 13th March 1912, died 6th Dec. 1918.
1925

LARBERT and DUNIPACE

Larbert and Dunipace were described as chapels or chapel kirks on 11th July 1606, when the Chapel of Larbert was erected by Parliament into a separate parsonage. They were also described on 1st June 1621 as "formerlie united," but there does not appear to be any record of the actual date of union. On 4th Aug. 1621 there were before Parliament two warrants under the King's hand "concerning the appointing and determinating wche of the two Kirks of Larbert and Dunipace formerlie united should be the ordinarie place of publick divine service of the said two parishes." In the Parish of Dunipace there were a chapel dedicated to St Helen, the mother of Constantine the Great, situated near St Helen's Loch now extinct, and a chapel dedicated to St Alexander. To the latter, vestiges of which existed in 1723, there pertained lands called the Kirklands. A short distance from the chapel was St Alexander's Well, "famous in old times for several cures." In the neighbourhood there were also St Alexander's Hill, St Alexander's Cuthill, evidently a grove, a retreat in a wood, and the Cuthill Burn. As a dependent chapel of St Ninian's, Larbert was granted, probably about 1130, to Cambuskenneth Abbey by Robert, Bishop of St Andrews 1124–58.—[*Acts Scott. Parl.*, iv, 346b, 407b; *Reg. Great Seal*, iii, 2879, iv, 815, xi, 323; *Retours*, vii, 220, xxvii, 247, xxviii, 136, A, 201; Macfarlane's *Geog. Coll.*, i, 332; *Chart. of Cambuskenneth*, 108; Jamieson's *Dictionary*, i, 554, Ed. 1879; *Chart. of Cambuskenneth*, 43–4.]

ALEXANDER NORIE, son of Alexander N., min. of Fern. Addl. issue—Jean, died 1683; his son, James, Notary and Town Clerk, Stirling, died 1674.
1619

THOMAS HOG, had issue—William, advocate, 1680.
1650

FRANCIS MACGILL, pres. by Crown 12th July 1843.
1843

JOHN McLAREN, pres. by Crown 21st June 1847.
1847

JOHN FAIRLEY, died 1st April 1931; his son, Norman Alexander, died 27th Feb. 1916; his daugh., Agnes Stevenson, died 27th March 1924; his
1902

widow, Janet Muir, died 8th March 1941; his son, John Macdonald, R.A., died Sept. 1943.

DUNIPACE

As a dependent Chapel of St Ninian's, Dunipace was granted, probably about 1130, to Cambuskenneth Abbey by Robert, Bishop of St Andrews 1124–58. In 1163 Pope Alexander III confirmed to Dunfermline Abbey the Chapel of the Castle of Dunipace; and there was a similar confirmation in 1184 by Pope Crucius III. Subsequently there arose a dispute regarding the chapel between the Abbot and Convent of Dunfermline and the Abbot and Canons of Cambuskenneth, and on 24th Oct. 1215 there was confirmed an agreement between the parties, whereby the Abbot and Canons of Cambuskenneth gave up all right to the church in favour of the Abbot and Convent of Dunfermline. Subsequently, and before 21st Jan. 1426–7, Dunipace became a parish. The old church, situated near the "Hills of Dunipace," was replaced by the present church, opened on 29th June 1834. There was in the parish a Chapel of St Alchenter (Alexander), who is said to have been the son of a Scottish king. The well of the chapel also bore the saint's name, and was famous for reputed cures. At the close of the first quarter of the 18th century vestiges of the chapel still remained. In the latter part of the 13th century an uncle of Sir William Wallace served the cure of Dunipace. His house Sir William frequently made his home; and he was the author of the following lines, which the famous patriot oft repeated:

"*Dico tibi verum, libertas est optima rerum, Nunquam servili sub nexu vivito fili.*"

("I will tell you the truth, of all things liberty's the best,
O never be, my son, with slavery opprest.")

In Torwood was Wallace's oak-tree, said to have been twelve feet in diameter, in the hollow trunk of which Sir William secreted himself after his defeat in the north.—[*Chart. of Cambuskenneth*, 43–4, 112, 114–16, 148, 149–57; *Chart. of Dunfermline*, 152, 157; Macfarlane's *Geograph. Collections*, i, 332.]

PLEAN

1900 WILLIAM THOMSON PONTON MACDONALD, dem. 25th Nov. 1923; died at Stirling 7th Dec. 1932.

1925 ROBERT CRAWFORD, ord. 26th April 1925; trans. to Alford 17th June 1927.

1927 DAVID WILLIAMSON, trans. from Edzell (*q.v.*) 12th Oct. 1927; trans. to Garvock 29th Nov. 1935; dem. 31st Dec. 1943; died at Coupar Angus 24th Sept. 1948; his daugh., Olive (marr. 24th Dec. 1938 Hugh Wotherspoon, Tillicoultry).

ST NINIAN'S

The church was also sometimes called the Parish Church of Kirketoun and the Parish Church of St Ninian of Kirketoun. Probably in or about 1130, the church with its Chapels of Dunipace and Larbert and its other chapels and oratories was granted to Cambuskenneth Abbey by Robert, Bishop of St Andrews 1124–58. Kirk O' Muir, dedicated to the Virgin Mary, was situated at Dundaff. In 1458, and again in 1468, it is designated "the Chapel of St Mary of Garvald in Dundafmoor." On 8th Feb. 1458–9 King James II granted to the chaplain and his successors in the chapel 2 merks of the lands of Ernbeg "in which is situated the Cross of Kippen" in the Lordship of Menteith. At one time it was a charge apart from St Ninian's, and was termed "the Church of Dundaffmure." The Lord's Supper was served in it after the Reformation. Before the middle of last century all trace of the church had gone; but a small burial-ground remained. The patronage of the church was in the hands of the Grahames of Montrose. Among the possessions of the Chapel of the Virgin Mary of Skeoch (Bannockburn) was *lie Cuthill*, a grove, a special place of residence, a retreat among trees, possibly the abode of "the hermit of the Chapel of Bannockburn," to whom on 16th May 1496 James IV gave an offering of 4 sh. The same monarch gave alms to the priests of the chapel on 26th Aug. 1505, and to the chapel a Mass Book on 20th Jan. 1506–7. On 14th Aug. 1533 James V made a payment of £3 6s. 8d. to Sir James Inglis, chaplain, "that sings for the King's soul at Bannockburn."—[*Chart. of Cambuskenneth*, 43–4; *Reg. Great Seal*, ii, 672, iv, 1630, v, 188; *Retours*, ix, 185; *Excheq. Rolls*, vii, 575, 625; *Lord High Treasurer's Acc.*, i, 324, iii, 63, 206, vi, 102.]

1556 ROBERT AUCHMOWTIE, vicar of Stirling, was chaplain of Blessed Virgin Mary at Skeoch or Bannockburn.—[*Reg. Abbrev. Feu Charters of Church Lands*, i, 42.]

1591 ANDREW KIRK, reader; pres. to vicarage of Glendevon 28th Jan. 1591–2.

1684 JAMES FULLARTON, had issue—probably William, a divinity student who died at Old Aberdeen, buried 7th March 1701.

1687 JAMES FORSYTH, his sons—David, born 13th May 1678; James, min. of Craig; his daugh., Margaret, born 1675.

1843 ROBERT PAISLEY, father's name "James," not "John."

1913 EDWARD ROWLAND JONES, born 21st Aug. 1876, son of Captain Jones, R.N., and nephew of James Alexander Crichton, D.D., min. of Annan; educ. at Annan Academy, Dumfries Academy and Univ. of Edinburgh, M.A. (1907), St Andrews, B.D.; travelled on Continent and studied at Univs. of Vienna, Breslau, Paris and Berlin and received high commendation for his research work in church history; licen. by Presb. of St Andrews 30th Nov. 1910; assistant at Clackmannan and in this parish 1911. On outbreak of war he joined the Army as a combatant and was known as "the Fighting Parson," was wounded by shrapnel in the spine, from which he never recovered; ord. 4th June 1913. He was a brilliant linguist and had command of twelve languages and assisted his uncle, Dr Crichton, in the preparation of his works on Syriac and Ethiopiac grammar; died 29th April 1939, unmarr. Publication—*The Book of Poets*, a hitherto unknown work of the Arabic scholar Mohamed Ibu Habil.

SAUCHIE

1915 ALEXANDER McCLYMONT ADAMS, trans. to St. Ninian's, Glasgow, 11th June 1929.

1929 JAMES MUDGE, formerly of Rangoon (*q.v.*); adm. 5th Sept. 1929. He had issue—Eva Lyon, born 1st Jan. 1926; Nancy Esther, born 20th May, 1929; Eleanor Isobel, born 7th Aug. 1934.

STENHOUSE

1900 DAVID SCRIBNER MERROW, B.D., dem. 31st Oct. 1941, died at St Andrews 5th Nov. 1947.

STIRLING

On 21st Jan. 1361–2 Sir Robert de Erskine, Kt., Chamberlain of Scotland, granted to Cambuskenneth Abbey the patronage of the Church of Kinnoull for the repair of the abbey, which had suffered "by reason of divers incursions of the English and others who have taken away gold and silver chalices, linen and woollen cloths, and Church ornaments, charters and instruments," and through the bell tower being struck by lightning and burned, and the choir thereby also "greatly destroyed." By charter of 10th March 1402–3 Robert III conveyed to the abbey the Hospital of St James at "the Caleyard of the Brig of Stirling." Before 24th Jan. 1488 James IV founded a chaplainry at the Altar of the Virgin Mary in the abbey for the singing of masses for the souls of his father, James III, and his mother, Queen Margaret. Other altars in the abbey were St Andrew, St John the Evangelist, St John the Baptist, St Laurence, St Nicholas, St Ninian, St Catharine, and All Saints. The Altar of St Ninian is described as "in the Parish Church of Cambuskenneth," and therefore in all likelihood it was the parochial altar with the chaplain serving the parochial cure.—[*Chart. of Cambuskenneth*, 224-5, 297, 307; *Reg. Great Seal*, i, App. i, 151, App. ii, 1797; *Reg. Sec. Seal*, i, 2040; *Lord High Treas. Accs.*, i, 102, ix, 449; *Cal. Papal Regs., Petitions*, i, 475, 539, *Letters*, iv, 234.]

1560 JOHN DUNCANSON, died Father of the Church.

1564 ROBERT AUCHMOUTY, vicar in 1564; he was in office 24th April 1556, and was also chaplain of the Chapel of the Virgin Mary of Skeoch, *alias* Bannockburn; died 1st July 1587.—[*Lord High Treas. Accs.*, xi, 317; *Reg. Great Seal*, iv, 1630; *Edin. Test.*, 1st Aug. 1587.]

1650 JAMES GUTHRIE, on the petition of his widow, Jean Ramsay, and his daugh., Sophia, that they might be transferred to the Continent "for the more convenient managing their household virtue, the only means of their lyviehood," the Privy Council in Feb. 1661 remitted to the Lord Commissioner his Grace "to alter and change their place of confinement as his Grace shall think expedient."—[*Reg. Privy Council*, 3 Ser., i, 333.]

STIRLING, THE ROOD CHURCH EAST

1563 THOMAS DUNCANSON, reader in 1563.—[*Book of the Universal Kirk*, 44.]

1649 JAMES GUTHRIE, son of William G. of Memes and brother of Alexander G. of Memes.—[*G. R. Sas.*, 2 Ser., 30th April 1659.]

1661 MATHIAS SYMSON, marr. (3) proc. 24th May 1657.

1676 WILLIAM PIERSON, had issue—Agnes, born 7th Sept. 1667; Thomson, born 28th Jan. 1669; David, born 3rd May 1670; James, born 17th Jan. 1672; John, born 17th Dec. 1673.—[*Dunfermline Register*.]

1694 ROBERT RULE, marr. (1) Barbara Bonar (died after 23rd April 1674) and had issue—Barbara; (2) before 19th May 1682, Elizabeth Campsie; his son, Robert, M.D., of Peelwells.—[*Glasgow Sas.*, xxxiii, 209; xxxvii, 1,112; 268.]

1726 ALEXANDER HAMILTON, eldest son of James H. of Balderston.—[*Deeds Dal.*, 21st Feb. 1704.]

1770 THOMAS RANDALL, marr. 28th Sept. 1742; had issue—David; Thomas, born 11th June 1747; William, born 27th Nov. 1748, died 11th Nov. 1759; Janet, born 14th July 1750; Mary, born 14th Feb. 1752, died 17th July 1766.

1793 JAMES SOMERVILLE, p. 322, line 2, for "1793" read "1803."

1839 ALEXANDER BEITH, had six sons and eight daughters; his daugh., Julia (marr. Rev. James Alexander George, Montrose), died 18th Feb. 1926; his son, John Alexander, J.P., Manchester and Altanacraig, Oban, died Oct. 1896, father of Major-General John (Ian Hay), C.B.E., M.C.

1858 GEORGE ALEXANDER, his daugh., Jane Edith, died at Hythe 5th April 1948.

1873 JAMES PAISLEY LANG, dem. 1922, died at Dunkeld 28th Dec. 1939; his widow, Frances Ann Holbrow, died at Dunkeld 2nd Jan. 1934; his daugh., Frances Marion Marshall, died at North Palmerston, New Zealand, 16th May 1941.

1923 WILLIAM STEVENSON STUART, trans. from Sandyford, Glasgow (*q.v.*), 6th June 1923; his wife, Steuart Stewart Gordon, died 19th March 1928. Marr. (2) 15th Sept. 1930 Janet, daugh. of W. A. Young of Abbey Park Craig; dem. 1934.

STIRLING WEST

1650 DAVID BENNET.—[*G. R. Sas.*, 2 Ser., i, 232.]

1682 JAMES HUNTER, son of Thomas H., W.S., indweller in Monkton, Musselburgh.

JOHN FORRESTER, line 1, for "James" read "Alexander"; his widow, Marion Hay, and James, only son (minor).—[*Deeds Mack.*, 1704, No. 525.]
1696

ROBERT MACAULAY, marr. daugh. of Andrew Burnett of Warriston, advocate.
1706

CHARLES MOORE, son of Captain James M., an officer in King William's Army, descended from Rowallan; his daughs.—Charles, died 9th April 1787; Mary (marr. George McIntosh); Barbara (marr. William Todd, Stirling).
1718

WILLIAM FINDLAY, his daugh., Elizabeth Smith, died 14th April 1934; his sons—John Smith, died 16th July 1938; William Frederick, assessor and collector for Midlothian, died 24th Feb. 1932.
1855

GEORGE MURE SMITH, his widow, Margaret Wright Spence, died 13th Oct. 1942.
1876

ARCHIBALD JAMES MILLER, died 7th May 1928.
1907

JOHN DOUGLAS GLENNIE, born Balmedie, Aberdeen, 16th Oct. 1896, son of Charles Emslie G., M.A., F.E.I.S., schoolmaster, and Elizabeth Johnstone Milne; educ. at Gordon's College and Univ. of Aberdeen, M.A. (1921), B.D. (1925); licen. by Presb. of Aberdeen 27th March 1923; served in Great War with Gordon Highlanders and Machine Gun Corps and in European War as Chaplain to Ayrshire Yeomanry and a base hospital in France 1939; assistant at Nigg, missionary at Hunton, Orkney; assistant Pollokshields; ord. to Ladybank 17th Sept. 1925; trans. 26th Sept. 1929; dem. 15th April 1935, preparatory to restoration of the ancient church of the Holy Rude; *locum tenens* St Peter's, Thurso, 1935; adm. to Kirkpatrick Durham 7th April 1938; died at Gleneagles Hospital 30th Sept. 1940. Marr. 1st July 1927 Margaret Murison, daugh. of William MacWhirter, warehouseman, Glasgow, and had issue— a son stillborn 4th April 1931; Rosemary
1929

Margaret Diana, born 31st March 1933. Publication—*The Rev. Ebenezer Erskine, M.A.*, paper read to Stirling Archaeological Society, March 1936.

STIRLING NORTH

EBENEZER ERSKINE, his son, Ebenezer, apprenticed to Thomas and Walter Ruddiman, printers, Edinburgh, 4th June 1740.
1731

ARCHIBALD BRUCE, his daugh., Eliza Banks (marr. 23rd April 1846 David Thomson).
1817

DAVID PATRICK McLEES, dem. 12th Nov. 1934; died 7th June 1939; his son, Alexander Gray, English Master, Kirkcaldy High School; his widow, Jessie Gray, died 18th Nov. 1949.
1895

CHAPEL ROYAL OF STIRLING

The parsonage and vicarage of Glenholm was a chaplaincy of the Chapel Royal.— [*Reg. Sec. Sig.*, xxxix, 114.]

JOHN DUNCANSON, pres. in 1567 on death of Sir William Younger.— [*Reg. Pres. Bene.*, i, 77.]
1567

RICHARD WRIGHT, reader, pres. to vicarage 25th Jan. 1574–5 on dem. of John Duncanson.—[*Reg. Pres. Bene.*, i, (4), 29.]
1574

JOHN CRAIG, his daugh., Barbara (marr. William Watson, min. of Markinch).
1579

MARYKIRK

THOMAS SKEOCH, dem. 8th July 1948.
1901

CAMBUS KENNETH

There appears to have been a parish of Cambus Kenneth, with the cure served by a parochial chaplain at the Altar of St Ninian in the Abbey.—[*Cart. of Cambus Kenneth*, 297.]

JAMES DALMAHOY, exhorter in 1567 and 1571, designated min. 24th Aug. 1580.—[*Comps. Sub Coll. of Thirds, Perth*, etc.; *Edin. Tests*, viii, 304.]
1567

PRESBYTERY OF DUNBLANE

ABERFOYLE

There was an Autumn fair of St Barquhan. The saint is St Bechan, whose day was 4th Aug.—[Watson's *Celtic Place Names*, 194.]

HENRY SEYTOUN, son of Alexander S. of Northrig, vicar on 21st Dec. 1567, dep. for non-compearance and non-compliance before 6th July 1573.—[*Reg. Mag. Sig.*, v, 143; *Acts and Dec.*, lvii, 469; *Reg. Pres. Bene.*, i, (3), 9.]
1567

ALEXANDER SEYTOUN of Northrig, vicar 1569-72, possibly a lay holding.—[*Comps. Sub Coll. of Thirds, Perth*, etc.]
1569

ROBERT (or **JOHN**) MacEACHERN, exhorter and reader 1571.—[*Comps. Sub Coll. of Thirds, Perth*, etc.]
1571

MALICE or **MALISE GRAHAM**, reader here 1573; was pres. by the King to the vicarage in succession to Henry Seytoun 6th July 1573, with Letters of Collation of 10th July to John Winram, Superintendent of Fife.—[*Reg. Pres. to Benefs.*, i, (3), 9; *Reports Hist. MSS. Commiss.*, iii, 398-9; *Acts and Dec.*, lxxxiii, 240.]
1573

JAMES KENNEDY, parson.—[*Acts and Dec.*, 1, 305.]
1573

WILLIAM STIRLING, pres. on death of James Kennedy; died before 9th Feb. 1622; his son, William, had sasine of annual rent from lands of Easter Feddels in Perthshire; there is apparent obscurity as to his actual residence here. On 17th Sept. 1622 there is a "narrative of the desolate congregation of Aberfule for want of a pastor, where never in no man's memory living there was any resident minister to preach the Word of God and minister His Holy Sacraments, wherethrough the most part of the parishioners thereof remains in great blindness and ignorance," and that William, Earl of Menteith, Lord Kilpunt and Kilbryde, had made contract on the foregoing date "obliging himself and his heirs for the weal of the souls of his tenants and vassals in the parish of Aberfoil to provide a competent stipend to the minister who shall serve the cure in the said parish in all time coming, and to make the Glebe and Manse 'void and rid' of the present possessors." On the above narrative Adam Bellenden, Bishop of Dunblane, granted on the same date a Bond of Dissolution of the patronage of the Church of Aberfoyle from the Bishopric of Dunblane, and gave a Procuratory for resigning the same into the King's hands in favour of the said Earl William.—[*Reports, Hist. MSS. Commiss.*, iii, 399; *Reg. Pres. Bene.*, i, (2), 19; *G. R. Sas.*, v, 166, 4th Feb. 1620, vii, 208; ix, 190.]
1574

JAMES KIRK, marr. 4th June 1633; his son, Alexander, apprenticed to John Liston, yr., cordinar, Glasgow, 2nd Nov. 1666.
1639

ROBERT KIRK, inscription on his tombstone "Hic sepultis ille Evangelli Promulgator accuratus et Linguae Hiberniae lumen M. Robertus Kirk, Aberfoile pastor, Obiit 14 Maii 1692, aetat 48," and beneath are cut figures of dagger and crook, insignia of the true soldier and shepherd of Christ, being the arms of Kirk family.
1685

ARCHIBALD FRANCIS STEWART, his son, Col. Thomas Brown, died at Dover 30th Dec. 1924.
1845

WILLIAM MONCRIEFF TAYLOR, his widow, Jessie Macdonald, died 11th March 1933.
1880

395

1922 JOHN MACDOUGALL, trans. from Duncansburgh 27th June 1922; trans. to West Calder 17th June 1927.

1927 WILLIAM GREIG STRACHAN, trans. from Tullynessle 23rd Nov. 1927 (*q.v.*). Addl. issue—Dorothy Burton, born 5th Aug. 1928.

BALQUHIDDER

The site of a chapel near the church was called *Cirrinn* Aonghus (Angus offering), that is, the offering made to Angus. The fair bearing the saint's name was held on the first Wednesday after the second Tuesday of August.—[Watson's *Celtic Place Names*.]

1546 JAMES ROLLAND, M.A., parson in 1546; died Sept. 1570; had brothers, Robert and Thomas; he ordained that he be "layd wtin ye paroche Kirk of Forgund callit St Fyllan's kirk wtn. Fyfe."—[*Reg. Great Seal*, v, 1274; *Edin. Test*, ii, 108.]

1567 JOHN BURDOUN, reader 1567 and 1572.—[*Comps. Sub Coll. of Thirds, Perth*, etc.]

1687 WILLIAM CAMPBELL, his daugh., Elizabeth (marr. Colin Campbell of Bragleen).

1806 ALEXANDER MacGREGOR, son of John M. in Little Fanderis in Strathbraan, of the family of Dunan, and a daugh. of Gregor More MacGregor or Drummond.

1879 DAVID CAMERON, dem. 4th Dec. 1930, died at Edinburgh 4th July 1944.

BRIDGE OF ALLAN

1865 JOHN REID, his daugh., Christian Brown, died at Edinburgh 22nd March 1929.

1913 JAMES ALEXANDER SUTHERLAND WILSON, trans. to Tealing 13th June 1929.

BUCHLYVIE

1919 JOHN WATT, trans. to Holywood 8th June 1928.

1929 CONSTANTINE SINCLAIR, born 27th Jan. 1898, son of John Henry S., solicitor and procurator fiscal, Dunbar, and Mary Jane Constantine; licen. by Presb. of Edinburgh 19th Dec. 1923; assistant at Wilton and St Matthew's, Edinburgh; ord. to Burghead 4th Nov. 1926; trans. and adm. 1st Feb. 1929; dem. 30th May 1931, joined Scottish Episcopal Church; adm. deacon St Peter's, Edinburgh, 1931-3; ord. priest 22nd May 1932, trans. to Wanstead 1933, Witham 1934, Foots Cray 1937; Precentor and Assistant Vicar, St George's, Perry Hill, London, 14th June 1937. Marr. 2nd June 1931 Bethia Hay Hamilton, third daugh. of William Cassels, Coalmaster, Airdrie.

CALLANDER

The church belonged to the Bishopric of Dunblane, from which it was dissolved by James VI on 8th July 1594, the patronage being then united to the barony of Callander. About 1773 the church was rebuilt in the centre of the town. It had a "pavilion roof," a spire over the pediment at the front, a bell which, provided by public subscription, was cast in Glasgow, and is said to have been heard at a distance of up to 12-14 miles. The present church was built in 1881-2. The circular mount, Tom-na-Chessaig, adjoined the churchyard, and the fair, Feill-na-Chessaig, was held on 21st March, 10th in the old style. The Church of Kilmachog is doubtless the "Church of St Maghot" in the Diocese of Dunblane, which occurs in 1275. The "Church of St Mathocus" (Mathoc), which appears in the same year and in the same diocese, seems to be another form of the name. The saint may be St Hog or St Chug, Kilmachog being *Cill Mo-Shug*, whose festival was on 26th Nov. The parish of Kilmachog appears to have been united to Callander after 16th June 1620. The church, in whole or in part, was in existence in 1723. On 15th Sept. 1572 Donald Dewar received a

Crown Charter of the 40 penny lands of Garrindewar or Carnedewar in Strathgartney in the Seneschalship of Menteith, "which formerly were mortified for the ringing of a bell before corpses on thir way to interment in the parish of Kilmahog in papal times." At Little Leny, a short distance west of Callander, there was a chapel called Norie's Chapel, with a graveyard which was the burial-place of the Buchanans. Here also was a conical mount similar to the eminence at Callander Churchyard. At Anie on the east side of the road opposite the lower end of Loch Lubnaig there was a chapel with graveyard, dedicated to St Bridgit. Before 10th April 1615 the Commissioners united part of the parish of Leny to the parish of Port of Menteith, another part of the parish of Kincardine, and the remainder with the manse and glebe to the parish of Callander. —[*Reg. Great Seal*, iv, 2092; vi, 118, 414, 1277, vii, 222; *Retours*, xvi, 70; Theiner's *Vet. Mon.*, 112, 115; Macfarlane's *Geog. Colls.*, i, 133–4, S.H.S.; Watson's *Celtic Place Names*, 315; Johnstone's *Scott. Place Names*, 220.]

1569 SIR JOHN WRIGHT, vicar 1569–72; was chaplain of St Michael's chapel, Dunblane.—[*Comps. Sub Coll. of Thirds, Perth*, etc.]

1668 JAMES MENZIES, his son, Robert apprenticed to William Dunbar, periwig-maker, Edinburgh, 27th Aug. 1707.

1709 JOHN McCALLUM, his sons— Andrew, apprenticed to William Tod, merchant, Edinburgh, 28th Jan. 1730; Archibald, apprenticed to James Heriot, wright, Edinburgh, 18th Feb. 1736.

1843 HUGH McDIARMID, pres. by Crown 19th July 1843.

1911 ALEXANDER RUSSELL, elected M.P. for Tynemouth 1923.

1916 THOMAS BURNETT PETER, died at Edinburgh 30th March 1946; his daugh., Mary Helen (marr. 23rd April 1933 W. Nimmo Allan, M.C., B.Sc., Sudan, son of Rev. G. Allan, Callander).

KILMACHOG

By Act of 17th Dec. 1669, Parliament transferred to Doune "a Fair anciently kept at the Kirk of Kilmahony (Kilmachog) on St Mahans' or Mahon's Day, 15th November." The actual transference had been effected between 1633 and 1639. St Mahan or Mahon may be regarded as indicating the patron saint of the church.— [*Acts Scott. Parl.*, vii, 663]. (See Kilmadock)

1567 GILBERT YALILEE, reader in 1567–72.—[*Comps. Sub Coll. of Thirds, Perth*, etc.]

LENY

1580 ALEXANDER DRYSDALE, vicar 1580 and 20th Dec. 1581; was servitor to David Erskine, Commendator of Dryburgh.—[*Reg. Mag. Sig.*, v, 752.]

DUNBLANE

1692 MICHAEL POTTER, his son, Walter, apprenticed to Hugh Somervell, surgeon, 9th Dec. 1691.

1844 JAMES BOE, pres. by Crown 8th Nov. 1843; his daughs.—Margaret, died at Edinburgh 8th Nov. 1940; Agnes Caroline, died 10th Sept. 1942.

1861 JAMES INGRAM, pres. by Crown 4th Dec. 1860; his daugh., Maria Petronella de Boij, died at Brooklyn 29th Feb. 1932.

1870 JAMES BARCLAY, pres. by Crown 13th Oct. 1869.

1872 DAVID MORRISON, pres. by Crown 30th Oct. 1871.

1886 ALEXANDER RITCHIE, died at Edinburgh 3rd July 1931; his wife, Jane Baillie Cairns, died at Edinburgh 30th March 1927.

1918 JAMES HUTCHISON COCKBURN, D.D. (Glasgow, 20th June 1934); Clerk of Union Committee 1927-9; Convener of Committee on Church and Nation 1929–35; Moderator of General

Assembly May 1941; Chaplain to the King Nov. 1944; app. as Senior Secretary, Department of Reconstruction of Christian Institutes in Europe, 1945. His daugh., Emily Robinson (marr. 28th March 1940 Robert Dermit McMahon Williams, M.A., Administrative Service, Northern Nigeria).

KILBRIDE

In 1219–23 the church was granted to Inchaffray Abbey by Gilbert, Earl of Strathearn.—[*Charters of Inchaffray Abbey*, 19–20, 32–3.]

1564 JAMES LEARMONTH, reader 1564.— [*Comps. Sub Coll. of Thirds, Fife.*]

GARTMORE

1899 JAMES CHRISTIE JOHNSTON, dem. 15th May 1936; died 5th March 1938; his wife, Emma Gilkes, died 18th Oct. 1933; his son, Alister Christie, ord. to Kikuyu 24th April 1930; adm. min. of St Peter's, Glasgow, 18th Aug. 1933; trans. to North Yell 18th May 1938; dem. 30th April 1943; adm. to Forres High Church 23rd July 1943; trans. to Walls and Sandness 7th May 1947; his daugh., Elizabeth (marr. Dr James Moir Crombie, Queen's Park, Glasgow).

KILMADOCK

The patron saint was Docus (Madoc), a shortened form of Cadog of Llancarvan, an eminent Welsh saint of the 6th century, one of the sons of Cannton, king of the Britons. The church was situated at the junction of the Annat Burn with the Teith. According to the Old Statistical Account it was transferred to Doune in 1756. That, however, is contested in the New Statistical Account, which further affirms that the church was taken down in 1744 and a new church built in Doune two years later. By Act of Parliament 17th Dec. 1669 there were transferred to Doune "the Fair anciently kept at the Kirk of Kilmadock on St Mettan's Day, 31st January," and "the Fair anciently kept at the Kirk of Kilmahoug (Kilmahog) on St Mahan's or St Mahon's Day, 15th November." The Act was in reality the ratification of what had taken place in each case between 1633 and 1639. There was a Chapel of St Fillan inside Doune Castle; and near the Castle there was another chapel with the same dedication. The latter may have been identical with the chapel which existed at Newton a short distance from Doune. Other chapels were situated respectively at Annat, on the Annat Burn, Lanrick, Torry, Walton, and probably also at the Bridge of Teith. One of those chapels may have been identical with the Chapel of Cristis Well in the parish, of which on 5th Dec. 1519 Sir Dionysius Row was appointed chaplain in succession to late Sir John Done. The former was succeeded on 10th March 1536–7 by Robert Arnot. It may be noted that a short distance to the east of the Annat Burn is Loch Mahaick, *Loch Mo-Thathaig*, from *Mo-Thatha*, the form assumed in Scottish Gaelic by the Irish name Tua, "the silent one," whose day was 22nd December. But there is no definite proof of a connection between Tua and the Annat Chapel.—[*Reg. Great Seal*, viii, 1239; [*Reg. Sec. Seal*, i, 3056, ii, 2226; *Acts Scott. Parl.*, vii, 663; Watson's *Celtic Place Names*, 251, 298, 327n.]

1571 ALEXANDER FARGIE, pres. in 1571 on death of James Kennedy.—[*Reg. Pres. Bene.*, i, (2), 21; *Acts and Dec.*, xlix, 105.]

1590 MALCOLM HENDERSON, min., pres. to vicarage 17th March 1591–2 on death of Alexander Fargie, min. at Logie.—[*Reg. Sec. Sig.*, lxiii, 218.]

1838 GORDON MITCHELL, his daughs.— Marion Hay Murray, died at Kippen 8th Jan. 1940; Marjorie Helen Harvie (Mrs Ballingall), died 4th Jan. 1946.

1894 JOHN CHALMERS PEAT, died 19th Nov. 1928; his widow, Amelia Mitchell, marr. (2) 28th Dec. 1932 David Ramsay Henderson, min. of Lecropt.

1929 DAVID ALEXANDER DUNCAN, born Forfar 18th May 1890, son of Alexander D., Forfar, and brother of Principal George, D.D., St Andrews;

educ. at Forfar Academy, Harris Academy, Dundee, Univs. of St Andrews, Edinburgh, M.A. (1911), B.D. (1921), and Union Theological Seminary, New York, S.T.M. (1920); served in Great War with Y.M.C.A. in France 1914–19; licen. by Presb. of Forres 28th Aug. 1920; assistant Peebles 1922–4; ord. to Dailly 30th April 1924; trans. and adm. 17th May 1929. Joint author of *The Way of Revelation* (Bible Class Teacher's Notes) (1929).

KINCARDINE IN MENTEITH

In or about 1199 King William the Lion granted to the Abbey of Cambuskenneth the Church of Kincardine with its chapels . . . and a toft with garden pertaining to the bell of St Lolan, and a toft with garden pertaining to the staff of St Lolan. In 1612 and again in 1675 the Holy Bell of St Lolan appears as a pertinent of the Barony of Kincardine. It is said that at Kincardine St Lolan was buried. Among the church lands were the Croft of St Lolan and the Croft of St Lawrence, but it may be that the latter is identical with the former, Lawrence being an error for Lolan.—[*Chart of Cambuskenneth*, 166–7; *Retours*, 128, xxxii, 184; *Reg. Great Seal*, vii, 301, 2125, ix, 1072.]

1682 JOHN CAMERON, resident with his wife, son and three daughters, all under 10 years, in Tron Parish, Edinburgh, 3rd Nov. 1694; his wife, Janet Barclay, buried 15th Sept. 1700. Marr. (2) 12th Jan. 1701.—[*Tron Poll. Tax Roll*, 12.]

1858 BIOT EDMONDSTON, his widow, Adelaide Annette Gray, died 1st Nov. 1939.

1919 GEORGE NEAVE LESLIE, dem. 27th Nov. 1928 and trans. to St Andrew's, Demerara, 1928; died 8th Aug. 1937.

1929 DAVID SMITH, formerly of Inverkeithny (*q.v.*); trans. from Ceres 10th May 1929; dem. April 1940; adm. to Oldhamstocks 9th Jan. 1942; dem. 31st Jan. 1946.

KIPPEN

About 1286 Walter (Stewart), Earl of Menteith, and Alexander, his son and heir, for the safety of their own souls and of the soul of Matilda, wife of Alexander, and for a selected burial place for them in the Abbey of Cambuskenneth, granted to the said abbey the Church of Kippen with the patronage of the same. By charter of 6th April 1496 James IV, patron of the church, in view of the fact that the church and its patronage had been out of the possession of the abbey for a long time, confirmed the Earl's donation, granting the church and its patronage and also its parsonage and vicarage after the demission or decease of Mr John Mayson, the rector. Meantime— and at what date does not appear—the church was also a Canonry and Prebend of Dunblane Cathedral, and was administered by the cathedral as such. Each party laid claim to the church; and ultimately there was made, on 13th March 1510, an agreement between James Chisholm, Bishop of Dunblane, and Andrew, Abbot of Cambuskenneth, whereby the vicarage of the church, with its fruits, rents, revenues, and £20 from the fruits, rents, and profits of the rectory, along with the manse of the prebend, constituted a canonry and prebend of Dunblane Cathedral, and the fruits of the rectory, subject to the payment of the said £20, were granted to the Abbey in pure alms. In terms of this agreement, on 21st July 1510 Andrew, Abbot of Cambuskenneth, was instituted in the said rectory with all its sundry rights, etc., by the delivery to him of the book, chalice, and other ornaments before the High Altar in the choir of the church. The successive canons and prebends were held bound either by themselves or by fit and sufficient chaplains to minister all services to the Church of Kippen. The early church was situated on the knoll, called Kirkhill, in a field near Kirkhill Cottage. On 12th Oct. 1489, James IV, returning to Stirling from the field of Gartalunane in the neighbourhood of Aberfoyle, where the rebel force led by the Earl of Lennox had been defeated, made an offering of an angel (23s.) in the church for the said victory.

By Act of 8th Feb. 1665 the Commissioners for the Plantation of Kirkis decerned the removal of the church to a site more commodious for the parish, the building being then described as ruinous. Difficulties developed, and the matter was deferred, probably till 1691, when a church was built. The Latter was repaired in 1777, and now stands a ruin in the churchyard close to the village. The present church was built in 1827. It is embellished internally by the art of Sir D. Y. Cameron, R.A., R.S.A., etc.—[*Cal. Papal Reg., Letters*, vii, 252-3, viii, 438; *Reg. Sec. Seal*, i, 2233; *Reg. Great Seal*, ii, 2306; *Lord High Treas. Accs.*, i, 122; *Reg. of Cambuskenneth*, 167-70, 173; *Reg. of Diocesan Synod of Dunblane*, 22, 24-5.]

1561 DONALD STEVENSON, curate.—[*Acts and Dec.*, xxxii, 196.]

1563 SIR JOHN HAMMILL, prebendary of Kippen 1563; died 2nd April 1566. —[*Comps. Sub Coll. of Thirds, Stirling*, etc.; *Edin. Tests*, i, 51.]

1595 ANDREW FORRESTER, pres. in 1595 on death of Alexander Chisholme.—[*Reg. Sec. Sig.*, lxviii, 83.]

1619 HENRY LIVINGSTONE, his son, Henry, M.A. (Glasgow, 1651).

1666 EDWARD BLAW, for "Blair" read "Blaw."

1908 PETER GEORGE SMITH, assistant at Ollaberry, Killean and Whiting Bay. Marr. Jessie, daugh. of Walter Borland, Stonehouse, and Margaret Barclay, and had issue—Walter Peter; Ian Russell Grant; Peter George, 2nd Lieut. H.L.I., killed in action June 1940.

1920 JOHN MILNE YOUNIE. Addl. issue —David Young Cameron, born 17th March 1924, died 1st March 1942; Edward Milne, born 9th Feb. 1926.

LECROPT

The saint is said to have been Moroc, Abbot of Dunkeld, and to have been buried here. An alternative form claimed as having been in use here is Maworrock, which, however, indicates *Mo-Bharroc*, the affectionate diminutive of Barrfind, son of Aed, who was a brother of Findbarr (St Barr). In terms of a letter of Richard (of Inverkeithing), Bishop of Dunkeld, of date 2nd Nov. 1260, the said Bishop and Chapter of Dunkeld ordained that the Church of Lecropt in which the Abbot and Convent of Cambuskenneth previously had no right, should on the granter's collation pertain to said abbot and convent, who were held bound to supply the church with a qualified chaplain.—[Watson's *Celtic Place Names*, 329; *Chart. of Cambuskenneth*, 267.]

1567 ANDREW ROW, exhorter 1567 and 1572; also vicar of Foulis.—[*Comps. Sub Coll. of Thirds, Perth*, etc.]

1569 SIR JOHN KEMP, reader and vicar 1569.—[*Comps. Sub Coll. of Thirds, Perth*, etc.]

1627 JOHN CUNYNGHAME.—[*G. R. Sas.*, xxxiv, 33, xlviii, 369.]

1667 WILLIAM WEMYSS, line 10, for "1655" read "1665."—[*Perth Sas.*]

1697 HUGH WALKER, his son, John, apprenticed to Robert Drummond, barber wigmaker, Edinburgh, 2nd Dec. 1724.

1893 DAVID RAMSAY HENDERSON, his wife, Evelyn Leslie Smith, died 26th March 1924; died 13th Feb. 1946. Marr. (2) 25th Dec. 1932 Amelia, daugh. of James Mitchell, Greenock, and widow of John Chalmers Peat, min. of Kilmadock; his daugh., Lois Marjorie Ramsay, died 29th March 1936.

LOGIE

The parish was a prebend of Dunblane. Its church was dedicated to St Serf and was originally Logie-Atheron (Airthrey). It belonged to the priory of North Berwick.

1566 ROBERT MENTEITH, min. at Alva, held vicarage.—[*Comps. Sub Coll. of Thirds, Perth*, etc.]

1571 ALEXANDER BALVAIRD, in office 1571.

1585 JOHN LOGIE, vicar in 1585 and 1588.—[*Comps. Sub Coll. of Thirds, Perth*, etc.] (See Rhynd.)

1604 ROBERT SEYTOUN, reader; perpetual vicar of Logie and Prebendary of Dunkeld 17th March 1567 and 24th Aug. 1569; son of Walter Seytoun of Tullibody and his wife, Elizabeth Erskine.—[*Reg. Great Seal*, iv, 1472, 1903, 2378.]

1617 HENRY SHAW.—[*Gen. Reg. Sas.*, xli, 38.]

1649 GEORGE SHAW. Addl. issue—Alexander; Margaret (marr. Robert Bruce, yr. of Kinglassie); his widow marr. William Elphinston, min.—[*Reg. of Deeds, Decree*, lxxxiii, 252.]

1844 ROBERT JOHN JOHNSTON, his son, Henry Buist, died 24th Oct. 1907.

1885 ROBERT MENZIES FERGUSSON, his daugh., Mary (marr. 4th June 1926 Frederick Hay Ellis, late of St John's, Newfoundland, and of New York); his widow, Isabella Fergusson, died 9th May 1944.

1922 WALTER McINTYRE, died 16th Feb 1949; had additional issue—James Campbell, born 23rd Dec. 1922; William Henry Rankine, born 24th June 1926.

MENSTRIE

1900 JOHN BOYD, D.D. (St Andrews, 30th June 1933), died 28th Jan. 1940.

NORRIESTON

On 7th June 1649 the parishioners and ministers of Kilmadock and Kincardine, and the Moderator of the Presbytery of Dunblane, presented to Parliament a petition to the effect that "qr they have taken in thair considerasun of that part of the cuntrie whair they reseid the dangerous conditioune thairof by reason of Ignorance and the want of the power of godlines among the most pairt of the Inhabitants, They conceave this great evill not only to aryse from poucitie of kirk among them and consequent penurie of the menis, but also from the inconvenient and dissordorlie situasun of these that are espeallie of the parishes of Kincardine and Kilmadock the boundis of thair residence that lye so promiscouslie in a dismembered and disjointed way as will be found strange to thais who shall perambulat the bounds and diligentlie consider of the same Whairfoir it coms to pase that many of the comouns are strangers not onlye to the preaching of the Word but discipline and uyr means tending to the promoving of personall and domesticall reformasun, being far distant from their awne parish kirk and not subject to the censor and ordor of that kirk to the which the place of yr residence is nearest Whence libertie Ignorance and profanitie is much cherished and puritie wt the promoving of reformasun much hindered and obstructed in these pairts. For remead of which evils they have resolved upon building a Church and the erectioun of a new parish, and are content and willing to build the same upon their own chairgis and to provyd a Manse and gleab yrto provyding they may have a competent maintinance out of the teinds of the sd parish for him who shall be appointed to serve at the said kirk Thairfoir humblie supplicating the Comissrs of the General Assembly That they wold be pleased to give thair concurrance for promoving of the said work and give thair best advyce to the Parliament for thair erectioun of the said kirk and provyding of the same wt ane competent stipend and that they wold show Him what may be the most compendious course for them to chuse Whereby this work may tak some speedie effect without any longer delay which they trust will be a service very acceptable to God and conducing much for the reformsun of these bounds As at mair lenth is conteinet in the said supplicsun Quhilk being recommendit by the saids Comissionars of the General Assemblie to the estaits of Parliament and thairefter being red and considerit be them

They have recomendit and seriouslie recomends the forsaid supplicsun and the desyre of the supplicants therein contenit to the Comissrs appointit for plantation of kirkis that some short and speidie course may be takine thairanent without delay.''
In the following year the church was built, Mr Gabriel Norrie of Norrieston giving both the site of the church and the churchyard. But for the stipend no such provision was made as suggested by the petition. Later, however, we learn that the stipend was paid from a fund raised in part from contributions by the people of the district; and in part by collections made in five Synods under the authority of the General Assembly of 1730. The money thus provided, called the Norrieston Fund, was utilised for the purchase of land which was managed by the Presbytery of Dunblane, the net income being paid to the minister. There were also a glebe of six acres and a manse with garden built in 1774. At the closing period of the 18th century the stipend is stated—"£30 stg. and 40 bolls of meal or bear." A new church was built in 1812; and it gave place in 1879 to the present church outside the churchyard. At first the minister was assistant to the minister of Kincardine, who had the power of nomination for the office. But in 1771, on a petition from the congregation, the General Assembly allowed the post, then vacant, to be filled by a majority of the examinable persons attached to the church. As early as 1853 steps were taken to secure the erection of the parish *quoad sacra*, but difficulties about the title to the properties caused delay.—[*Acts Scott. Parl.*, vi, (2), 400.]

1879 JAMES GORDON MITCHELL, dem. 11th June 1926; died at Kippen 3rd Jan. 1933.

1927 JOHN AITKEN SPENCE, trans. from Fisherton (*q.v.*) 18th Nov. 1927; dem 16th May 1934; died at Edinburgh 5th Nov. 1945; his widow, Margaret J. Mitchelhill, died at Edinburgh, 10th Aug 1948.

PORT OF MENTEITH

1638 THOMAS HENDERSON, his daughs. —Maria (marr. Archibald Graham in Seviack); Janet (marr. Thomas Henderson, merchant, Stirling).—[*Deeds, Durie*, 1705, No. 32.]

1843 ALEXANDER TURNER, his daughs. —Anita, died 14th Sept. 1928; Isabelle, died at Palmyra, New Jersey, 14th March 1922.

1916 DAVID JAMES MACQUEEN, his wife, Annie Minto Cheyne, died at Glasgow 2nd Dec. 1928. Marr (2) 5th Feb. 1930 Helen, daugh. of John Milligan, Langholm.

TILLICOULTRY

1566 ROBERT MENTEITH, min. at Alva, also in charge here 1566 and 1569.— [*Comps. Sub Coll. of Thirds, Perth*, etc.]

1881 JOSEPH CONN, his widow, Christina Caldwell, daugh. of Findlay Caldwell, Glasgow, died 26th July 1941.

1923 GEORGE LYALL, born 13th March 1897, youngest son of James L., 31 Lixmount Avenue, Edinburgh, and Euphemia Brown; educ. at Univ. of Edinburgh, M.A. (1916), licen. by Presb. of Edinburgh 1920; assistant St Cuthbert's, Edinburgh; ord. 20th Feb. 1923. Marr. 29th March 1923 Agnes, daugh. of William McLelland, Rocklands, Elie, and Elizabeth Baxter, and has issue—James Farquhar, born 14th April 1924; William McLelland, born 25th Nov. 1927. Publication— *History of Tillicoultry Parish Church* (Tillicoultry, 1929).

TROSSACHS

1884 WILLIAM WILSON, died at Edinburgh 11th Oct. 1925; his widow, May Isabella Macpherson, died 15th Nov. 1948.

1926 MARTIN MACRAE, trans. from Kilninian (*q.v.*) 3rd Feb. 1926.

TULLIALLAN

The earliest church stood within the grounds of Tulliallan; the second, roofless but well preserved, stands in its churchyard on the slope on the north side of Kincardine and built in 1675, is an excellent example of the secondary Episcopacy period architecture. Sir John Mudge was parson on 14th Jan. 1448-9.—[Stephen's *Inverkeithing and Rosyth*, 515.]

1559 PATRICK BLACKADDER, second son of Patrick B. of Tulliallan and his wife, Margaret Halkerston, received parsonage from his father in 1559; died May 1599.—[*P. C. Reg.*, iv, 350; *Laing Charters*, 788, 1065; *Edin. Tests*, 28th July 1599.]

1571 WALTER MILLAR, exhorter 1571-2. —[*Comps. Sub Coll. of Thirds, Perth*, etc.]

1631 JOHN WOOD, his daugh., Sarah (marr. (2) James Hay of St Martin's in the Fields, Middlesex.)

1673 ALEXANDER WILLIAMSON, educ. at Marischal College; had issue—Elizabeth, bapt. 2nd Oct. 1684; Margaret, bapt. 27th Aug. 1686; Eleanora, bapt. 31st July 1688; Anna, bapt. 21st Aug. 1689.

1714 GEORGE MAIR, his son, Thomas, min. of Orwell, born 27th April 1697; Catherine, born 17th May 1698; Patrick, born 27th July 1699; Veronica, born 4th Sept. 1701; Margaret, born 20th May, 1703; Mary, born 4th Sept. 1704; John, born 29th Nov. 1705; Ann, born 4th Oct. 1709.—[*Culross Reg.*]

1719 THOMAS THOMSON, son of James T. in Pardovan, and Helen Dawson.—[*Linlithgow Sheriff Court Decreets*, 23rd March 1722.]

1758 ROBERT BROWN, marr. Magdalen, daugh. of John Stein of Kennetpans, and Margaret Caldom (born 11th April 1737), and had issue—Malcolm, died 20th Dec. 1832; Margaret (marr. James Reid); Isabella, died 17th April 1850 (marr. David Murray, Whitehouse, Musselburgh.)

1848 JOHN SMEATON, ord. 5th Jan. 1844, to Abernyte; his son, John, died 11th Aug. 1928; his daugh., Jane Davidson, died 26th Sept. 1932.

1888 JOHN MACLAREN, dem. 2nd June 1931, died 15th May 1945.

SYNOD OF FIFE

The Register of the Synod of Fife begins in 1610. The first volume is Diocesan, and the first entry is of date 7th Sept. 1610 on page 5, pages 1–4 being missing. This volume extends to 27th April 1636. The next volume begins 2nd April 1639, and extends to 9th April 1657. The third volume, like the first, is also Diocesan and extends from 14th Oct. 1662 to 6th Oct. 1687.

PRESBYTERY OF DUNFERMLINE

ABERDOUR

Comparison of dates shows that the church was granted to Inchcolm Abbey 1123–4—donor unknown. The south aisle was added in the early part of the 16th century; and there is on the north side a small transeptal 17th-century aisle. In 1796–8 a new church was built in Wester Aberdour; and the old church was left roofless. An effective scheme of restoration, rendered possible by the munificence of the Misses Lawrie of Starleyburn, was carried out in 1925–6; and services in the church were resumed in July of the latter year. On 13th April 1927 the Presbytery reaffirmed the status of the church as the church of the parish. The church in Wester Aberdour has been converted into a church hall. Sir Henry Ramsay was vicar of the parish 5th June 1551, when Letters of Legitimation were granted to his natural sons—John, Alexander, James. Dalgety and Beath were united with Aberdour 1611–43 (see Beath) and history in part repeated itself on 21st June 1940, when Aberdour and Dalgety were united along with St Colme's, Aberdour, the former U.F. Charge, under the name of Aberdour and Dalgety. Near Bowprie, a short distance south of Aberdour, there was a chapel dedicated to St Martin, belonging to Inchcolm Abbey. On 22nd July 1474 the hospital in Easter Aberdour was founded by Sir John Scott, Canon of Inchcolm and Vicar of Aberdour, in honour of the Omnipotent God, His Most Blessed Mother, Mary, our Lady, ever-virgin, and the Blessed Martha, the hostess of our Lord Jesus Christ, for the support, maintenance and entertainment of poor pilgrims and wayfarers who visited St Fillan's Well in the village. The foundation was based upon a gift of 1 acre of land and a free manse for the vicar by James, Earl of Morton. On 22nd June 1474 Michael, Abbot of Inchcolm, had granted to the said Sir John Scott the cure of the hospital. An additional 3 acres of land were given by the Earl of Morton on 1st Sept. 1479. But, finding in 1486 that the scheme had not been completed, the Earl, with the place given over to him by Sir John Scott, added a further 4 acres, and by Charter of 16th Oct. 1486 placed the hospital under the charge of the Third Order of St Frances. This was confirmed by Bull of Pope Innocent VIII, 23rd June 1487, granting the hospital with its chapel, gardens, fields, rights, goods, and all pertinents, to Isobel and Jean Wight, Frances Henryson and Jean Dross, sisters of the Third Order of St Frances called *de paenitentia*, and to John Scott, Canon of Inchcolm and Vicar of Aberdour, Master and founder of "the Hospital of St Mary the Virgin." Authority was also given to the Bishop of Dunkeld to "altogether and utterly suppress and extinguish in the said Hospital the name and title of Hospital and all the rights of a Hospital"; the buildings were to be

ABERDOUR

altered and enlarged with dormitory, refectory and cloister, after the pattern of other hospitals of the Order in France, etc.; and the sisters were to receive maidens and other women fleeing from the world, and to retain and instruct therein young maidens of honourable parentage, willing to be instructed in literature and good arts. The effort to make the dedication entirely to the Virgin was not successful; and the place continued to be called St Martha's Hospital of Aberdour. There was in the church an altar dedicated to St James, of which at the Reformation Henry Davidson was chaplain.—[*Chart. of Inchcolm*, 5, 8, 32, 251, S.H.S.; *Reg. Great Seal*, 5th June 1551; Theiner's *Vet. Monumenta*, 500; *Reg. Hon. de Morton*, 235-8, 238-40; *The Apostolic Camera and Scott. Benefices*, 22; *Memo*, Rev. Dr Johnston; *Book of Assumptions*, Reg. House.]

SIR WALTER ROBESOUN (Robertson) or Downie; had a brother, John Robertson, in Aberdour, and may have been of the family of Robertson of Downie in the parish of Meigle, and possibly also belonged to the family with which was connected Walter Robertson, who, as heir of his brother, John Robertson alias McDonchie in Cousland, was infeft in Oct. 1623 in ¼ lands of Hilhead of Fongarth; was designated Vicar of Aberdour on 24th July 1556, when he ministered and executed the office anent the handfasting between Robert Lawder, Yr. of the Bass, and Jean, daugh. of Patrick, Earl of Bothwell, and held office at and subsequent to the Reformation; at the Reformation he was also Chaplain of the Chapel of St Michael the Archangel in Hailes Castle, and also of the Chaplainry called the Provostry in the Church of Preston (East Linton); he was a confident of James, Earl of Bothwell, and was one of those present with the Earl at Norham on 23rd March 1563, prior to the latter setting out for France after he had escaped from Edinburgh Castle and was shipwrecked on the coast of England; at Edinburgh on 30th Oct. 1563 Jeane Hepburn, Lady Wedderburn, acting on the Earl's instructions, gave
1556

to Sir Walter the custody of "Reversions and other evidents" belonging to the Earl; on 10th June 1561 he appears as one of the chaplains and choristers of the choir of Dunkeld Cathedral, where he had a house belonging to the Sub-dean, and on 6th Jan. 1562-3 as a notar at Dunkeld; he ceased to be vicar at Aberdour in 1570-1, and, according to one source, he died at that time; but probably he was identical with Sir Walter Robesoune, adm. reader at Logierait *cir.* 1572-3 by James, Bishop of Dunkeld, and with Walter Robesoun pres. to the vicarage of Logierait 19th Oct. 1580. Sir Walter Paterson, designated vicar 24th Oct. 1560, appears to be the same individual with an error in name.—[*Reg. Great Seal*, iv, 1529, v, 759, 1138, 1189, vi, 1227; *Reg. Sec. Seal*, xxv, 212; *Reg. of Deeds*, xxix, 412; *Comps. Sub Coll. of Thirds, Fife*, etc.; *Bannatyne Mis.*, iii, 306-8; *Reg. Kirk Session of St Andrews*, 55, S.H.S.; *Cart. of Nunnery of North Berwick*, 72.] (See Logierait and Prestonkirk.)

PETER BLACKWOOD, his pres. to vicarage in 1571 was consequent upon the death of Sir Walter Robesoun; *Minutes of Synod of Fife* err in stating that he removed to Aberdeen; adm. notary 16th May 1583.—[*Reg. Pres. to Benefices*, 19, Sept. 1571; *Reg. Sec. Seal*, xl, 6.]
1566

JOHN PATERSON, in executing a summons on 22nd Dec. 1560 he is described as min.—[*Reg. Kirk Session of St Andrews*, 54, S.H.S.]
1567

JOHN PATERSON, his pres. to vicarage in 1573 was consequent upon the death of Peter Blackwood. —[*Reg. Pres. to Benefices*; *Reg. Sec. Seal*.]
1567

ANDREW KIRK, his pres. to vicarage, 20th May 1587, was consequent upon the death of Peter Blackwood. —[*Reg. Pres. to Benefices*.]
1587

PATRICK CARMICHAEL, pres. to vicarage 17th Dec. 1606, vacant by the death of Sir Walter Downie or "Roberston."—[*Reg. Sec. Seal*, lxxv, 212.]
1602

1611 WILLIAM PATON. (See Dalgety.)

1695 JOHN WHITE, formerly of Coylton, Ballantrae, described as sometime min. at Aberdour 1695; died before 1705. Marr. Helen Cruickshank, who survived him.—[*Deeds, Durie,* 1706, No. 137.]

1701 ALEXANDER MARSHALL, licen. by Presb. of Dunfermline; app. by Earl of Morton to serve here from Marts 1701 to Whitsunday 1702.—[*Deeds, Mack.,* 1705, No. 885.]

1914 ROBERT JOHNSTONE, D.D. (St Andrews, 23rd June 1935), colleague and successor, adm. 23rd Nov. 1940, died at Edinburgh 5th April 1944; his second daugh., Isobel Thorburn (not Mabel T.) (marr. 10th June 1939 John, son of late David Cunningham, Aberdour, and Mrs C., Cheadle, Cheshire); his second son, Robert Lawrence, licen. by Presb. of Dunfermline and Kinross 12th April 1938, assistant St George's Parish, Edinburgh, 1938–40; Chaplain to the Forces 1940; adm. min. of Clyne and Brora 1948; his elder son, Alistair Thorburn, Nigerian Forest Service, died at Edinburgh, 1st Feb. 1940.

BEATH

The Chapel of Beath, subsequently annexed to Dalgety, was granted to Inchcolm Abbey before 1178, and probably in the period 1170–8. There was a well of St Margaret near Lassodie House. On 24th March 1546–7 Mr John Bannatyne was pres. to the chaplainry of the chapel in succession to the late Sir Alexander Guthrie. After the Reformation Beath continued to be attached to Dalgety till 17th Jan. 1611, when by an order of the Commissioners for Modification of Stipends, etc., approved by Crown Charter of 7th March 1618, the Church of Dalgety and Beath were united to Aberdour. Unsatisfactory results followed; and, consequent upon a resolution of the Synod of Fife of 9th April 1641 to refer the matter to Parliament, the Committee of Parliament in January 1643 disjoined the three parishes. (For Beath, see Dalgety and Aberdour up to 1643.)—[*Cart. of Inchcolm,* 2, S.H.S.; *Cal. of Supplications Rel. to Scotland,* 195, S.H.S.; *Cal. of Papal Regs.,* vii, 144; *Reg. Sec. Seal,* iii, 2215; *Reg. Great Seal,* 7th March 1611; *Minutes Synod of Fife;* Ross' *Aberdour and Inchcolm,* 227–8.]

1644 HARRY SMITH, as Robert Bruce, min. at Aberdour, maintained his right to the emoluments, including manses and glebes, of the three parishes, which were ratified to him by Parliament in 1646; neighbouring congregations contributed to Mr Smith's support; and in 1650 the sum of £1,200, contributed by the four Presbyteries of Fife—St Andrews £400, Cupar £250, Kirkcaldy £300, Dunfermline £250—was mortified to provide a stipend; had issue, John, born 4th June 1643.—[*Acts Scott. Parl.,* vi, (1), 607; *Minutes of Synod of Fife,* April 1648, 2nd April 1650.]

1691 ALEXANDER STEEDMAN, his son, Alexander, apprenticed to Robert Steedman, merchant, Edinburgh, 19th June 1717.—[*Reg. of Edin. Apprentices.*]

1915 ROBERT JAMES STEELE DICKEY, trans. to Cambuslang West 29th Sept. 1927.

1928 JAMES MARSHALL, from Buenos Ayres, and earlier, Rosyth (*q.v.*); adm. 25th Jan. 1928; dem. 4th Feb. 1929, and went to Canada.

1929 GEORGE PORTEOUS McWILLIAM, trans. from Towie (*q.v.*) 16th Oct. 1929; issue—Isobel Helen, born 24th Jan. 1923; Charles Campbell, born 11th June 1924; George Thomas, born 30th Dec. 1925; Margaret Eugenie, born 5th Feb. 1933.

KELTY

1919 WILLIAM THOMSON, line 4, for "St Andrews" read "Glasgow"; trans. to Bothkennar 30th April 1927.

1928 DAVID KINNEAR BOGIE, born 19th April 1873, son of John Francis B., 17 Lauriston Place, Edinburgh; educ. Edinburgh Univ., M.A. (1899), and

New College; licen. by U.F. Presb. of Edinburgh 17th June 1902; ord. to Polmont U.F. Church 30th July 1907; trans. and adm. to Fossoway U.F. Church 18th Oct. 1923; app. by the Presby. *jure devoluto* 4th April 1928; and adm. 4th May same year; died suddenly in his study 30th Aug. 1929.

CARNOCK

1567 RICHARD BROWN, was reader 1563. —[*Comps. Sub Coll. of Thirds, Fife*, etc.]

1592 JOHN ROW, his daugh., Margaret, marr. (1) Stephen Tullidef; and (2) David Robertson.—[Webster's *Hist. of Carnock*, 127–8.]

1679 THOMAS MARSHALL, had issue, Christian; Margaret, bapt. 12th Dec. 1685.—[*Carnock Reg.*; *Memo.*, Rev. J. M. Webster.]

1699 JAMES HOG, marr. Janet Pyper; various MSS. of his in Assembly Library.—[*Aberdeen City Sas.*, 6th Feb. 1756.]

1730 DAVID HUNTER, his son, James, apprenticed to Archibald Davie, merchant, Edinburgh, 18th Nov. 1747.

1827 WILLIAM GILSTON, his wife was Graham, daugh. of David Arrot and Janet Cargill; she died 8th May 1842 (*Tombst*; *Memo.*, Rev. J. M. Webster); his daughs.—Jessie, died 1st Sept. 1880; Isabella, died 30th Jan. 1916.

1880 WILLIAM AULD, died at Liberton 20th June 1936; his wife, Emily Wallace, died there 19th Nov. 1936.

1920 JAMES MOIR WEBSTER, dem. as Presb. Clerk 7th Sept. 1948. Marr. (2) 14th May 1924 Helen, third daugh. of Adam Main, Woodside Cottage, Fetternear, Kemnay, with issue—Christine Margaret, born 11th Feb. 1925; his daugh., Mary Paterson, died 29th Oct. 1919. Publication—*History of Carnock* (Blackwood, 1938).

COWDENBEATH

1914 ROBERT MUIR, his widow, Charlotte Cook, died 12th Feb. 1944.

1922 JOHN WATSON ELMSLIE, dem. 20th Oct. 1926 and went to Pictou, Nova Scotia; returned and was assistant at Dysart, and was inducted to Duntocher 19th Dec. 1935; in Sept. 1939 volunteered as a combatant, and was awaiting appointment as a commissioned officer when he died 6th Oct. following. Marr. 19th May 1926 Margaret Wills, daugh. of John Laing and Margaret Wills, and widow of William McLean, Old Inn, Cowdenbeath, with issue—Isabella Jean Galloway, born 16th Aug. 1927.

1927 JAMES MacMORLAND, trans. from Tarbat (*q.v.*) 24th March 1927; trans. to St John's, Glasgow, 4th Sept. 1930.

CULROSS

A narrative of 1420 bears that the monastery "unhappily in the not distant past has been burned by the English enemies of the said realm" (Scotland); and the Pope at Florence on 10th June 1420 gave effect to a crave "to grant to all Christ's faithful visiting the Monastery upon the first of July, the feast of the said confessor (St Serf), or giving pious alms for its restoration, an indulgence of six years and as many quarantines, as often as they do so." Probably the depredation of the English occurred in their invasions 1384–5. By Act of Parliament 28th June 1633 there were ratified Crown Grants of the vicarage and small teinds of the benefice as the endowment of the Grammar School which existed within the Abbey "in all tyme bygane," and "in whilk the youth of the burgh and land of Culross weis instructit in grammar and traint in virtue and letters in ye commoun weill of ye haill communitie." There was a chapel called the Bar Chapel, situated at what is called the Chapel Barn, close to the west Abbey lodge. The ground plan of St Mungo's Chapel was laid bare by excavations in 1926. By Charter of 20th June 1589 James

VI erected the Rectory and Vicarage of Culross, the emoluments of the Rector who was to reside continually at Culross being 200 merks from the readiest of the fruits of the church, with manse and glebe.—[*Cal. of Supplications Rel. to Scotland*, 208, S.H.S.; *Acts Scott. Parl.*, v, 909; *Reg. Sec. Seal*, lix, 116–17, lxxiii, 195; *Reg. Great Seal*, 10th Nov. 1546, v, 1675.]

FIRST CHARGE

ROBERT WRIGHT, his son, Robert, apprenticed to David Fyfe, surgeon-apothecary, Edinburgh, 29th Dec. 1703.—[*Reg. of Edin. Apprentices.*]
1684

ALLAN LOGAN, son of George L. of that ilk; his son, Hugh, died 1759.
1717

WALTER McALPINE, marr. Janet (died 21st April 1747), daugh. of John Stein of Kennetpans, and Margaret Caldom, with issue—James, died 27th Nov. 1847; Mary, died at Edinburgh 9th Jan. 1860; Margaret, died at Edinburgh 6th April 1881; Helen, died at Edinburgh 16th June 1881, all three unmarr.
1816

ANDREW BETHUNE DUNCAN, his son, John William, manufacturer, of Duncan & Don, Lochee, Dundee, died 9th March 1931.
1824

DAVID McHARDY HAMPTON, dem. 28th May 1924 and died at Pittenweem 14th July 1926; his widow, Margaret H. B. Hogg, died there also, 16th June 1927.
1904

SECOND CHARGE

ROBERT EDMONSTONE, his son, James, apprenticed to William Maisson, merchant, Edinburgh, 21st June 1676.
1649

JOHN GEDDES, his sons—Robert, apprenticed to John Rutherford, merchant, Edinburgh, 28th May 1729; William, adm. N.P. 16th Feb. 1732.
1719

ALEXANDER SMITH ALLAN, his daugh., Maggie Bertha, died 28th Dec. 1940.
1881

JOHN MILLER GOW, became sole min. on the union of the Charges by the Court of Teinds, 16th Dec. 1925.
1921

DALGETY

The church was granted to Inchcolm by William the Lion, 1170–8. At the west end of the old church are the burial vault and heritors' loft built by Alexander Seton, first Earl of Dunfermline. There is also a burial vault under the floor of the chancel, with a stone on the north wall, carrying a shield with the arms quarterly of Abernethy and Moultrie of Seafield, and narrating that here lies William Abernethy of Dalgety, who died 1540. The chapel at Fordell, near which on the south side is the chapel well, was dedicated to St Thereot, Terott, Cereot. (See Beath for the union of the Churches of Dalgety and Beath with Aberdour in 1611.)—[*Cal. of Supplications Rel. to Scotland*, 195, S.H.S.; *Cart. of Inchcolm*, 103, S.H.S.; Stephen's *Inverkeithing and Rosyth*, 139.]

SIR JOHN MURRAY, vicar; on 6th Aug. 1559 he granted a feu charter of the church lands to Henry, third son of Sir James Stewart, first of Beath; he died in 1574.—[*Reg. Great Seal*, 13th Jan. 1575-6; Sept. 1561; 6th March 1563-4.]
1559

JOHN PATERSON, reader; reader also at Aberdour 1568.—[*Comps. Sub Coll. of Thirds, Fife*, etc.]
1567

JOHN BROWNHILL (Dene), in office before 1570.—[*Edin. Tests*, ii, 227.]
1570

JOHN BURNE, min. at Inverkeithing, had also charge here, at least in 1572-3, when he received £30 out of the Thirds of Inchcolm.—[*Rep. Hist. MSS. Commission*, vi, 636.]
1572

ALEXANDER STEVEN, pres. to vicarage of Dalgety and Beath 14th June 1574, 1st May and 14th June 1575, vacant by death of Sir John Murray. —[*Reg. Sec. Sig.*; *Reg. Pres. Bene.*]
1574

WILLIAM PATON, M.A.; on 21st March 1600 the Presbytery of Dunfermline appealed to the General Assembly anent a decision of the Synod of Fife at Cupar 6th March 1598 which found that the Presbytery had done wrong in planting the Kirk of Dalgety with hurt and prejudice to the Kirk of Aberdour, the latter being the most great and populous congregation and the haill stipend but a mean stipend, and therefore ordained the haill stipend to remain with the Kirk of Aberdour; the Assembly ordained Mr Paton, min. at Dalgety, to be min. at both and to have the haill stipend of both before division thereof for crop and year 1599 and so on.—[*Booke of the Univ. Kirk*, 961-2; *G. R. Sas.*, 2 Ser., ix, 125.]
[1598]

ANDREW DONALDSON, adm. consequent upon the disjunction of the parishes of Aberdour, Dalgety, Beath, and the re-erection of Dalgety into a separate charge, in 1643.
[1644]

JOHN CORSAIR, his son, Mr John, described as eldest son, was writer in Edinburgh, and died 22nd Feb. 1730; he marr. Anne (died 26th June 1746), daugh. of Sir William Drummond of Hawthornden; Marie, bapt. 5th Aug. 1655; David, bapt. 5th Nov. 1657.—[*Edin. Test*, 8th and 12th Nov. 1746; Douglas's *Bar.*, 573; *S. Leith Reg.*]
[1669]

ARCHIBALD CAMPBELL, his son, Charles, apprenticed to Thomas Stantain, merchant, Edinburgh, 14th March 1716.—[*Reg. of Edin. Apprentices.*]
[1696]

WILLIAM HENDERSON, his son, Charles, died 1st Feb. 1734; his son, John, apprenticed to Alexander Brown and Thomas Hepburn, merchants, Edinburgh, 5th July 1752.—[*Reg. of Edin. Apprentices.*]
[1717]

ALEXANDER WATT, his wife was daugh. of Alexander Campbell, in the Army, and –. Maitland.
[1828]

DONALD STEWART ROSE, dem. 21st June 1940; died 14th May 1947; his daugh., Ella Stewart (marr. 16th April 1938 Will West Machin, C.E., Ruthin, North Wales, younger son of William M., Hoylake); his wife, Christian Blair, died 26th Jan. 1947.
[1899]

(*United to Aberdour 21st June 1940.*)

DUNFERMLINE

In the Abbey there were the following altars: Parish Kirk, the Outer Kirk, "Sanct Margaretis Kirk Wytr"; the High Altar, probably dedicated in the name of the Holy Rood; the Rood and Our Lady, sometimes described as "situat at the Hee Altar"; Our Lady, St Michael, and St Katherine; St Margaret; St Mary of Pity; St Nicholas; St Ninian; St Salvator; Holy Blood; Conventual Kirk, the Inner Kirk, the High Altar, dedicated to the Holy Trinity, and after 1250 to St Margaret also; Our Lady, in St Mary's Aisle or St Mary's Chapel; St Andrew; St Benedict; St Cuthbert; St John; St Katharine; St Katharine and St Margaret; St Laurence; St Mary Magdalene; St Mary of Pity; St Michael; St Peter; St Stephen; St Ursula; and Corpus Christi and the Relic Altar (Relic Almery), both probably also in the Conventual Kirk. The site of the residence of the Abbot is indicated in an action by David Fergusson, min., against the Commendator, for the provision of a manse, in which the Lords of Session on 29th Oct. 1574 pronounced a decreet giving the min. "the house that pertained to the Abbot as manse," bounded "by the kirk at the east, the kirkyard at the north, the Abbey place and close yrof at the south, the commont entres to said Abbey at the west."—[Beveridge's *Dunfermline Burgh Records*, xxiv, ff.; *Acts and Dec.*, lvi, 419.]

JOHN BURNE, reader 1563; min. at Inverkeithing 1570.
[1563]

WILLIAM LUMSDEN, M.A., monk of Dunfermline, held the vicarage; also parson of Cleich (*q.v.*).— [*Comps. Sub Coll. of Thirds, Fife*, etc.]
[1564]

JOHN CRISTISON, M.A., reader, and in 1574; became min. at Logie, Dundee.—[*Comps. Sub Coll. of Thirds, Fife*, etc.]
[1570]

WILLIAM SMYTH, reader, 8th Oct.
1590 1590.—[*Reg. Sec. Seal.*]

JAMES THOMSON, died Father of
1743 the Church.

ROBERT STEVENSON, died 14th
1880 Aug. 1931.

SECOND CHARGE

JOHN STENHOUSE, probably successor to Samuel Row.—[Henderson's *Annals of Dunfermline*, 302.]
1640

JAMES WILLIAM BAIRD, adm. to First Charge 17th March 1932; became sole min. when Scheme of Unification was adopted by the Presbytery, 6th June 1933; his daugh., Isabel (marr. 24th Dec. 1938 James Muir, M.A., B.Sc. (St Andrews), Teacher of Science, High School, Dunfermline); his daugh., Mary (marr. 30th Dec. 1937 Andrew Gibb, cashier, Sugar Beet Factory, Cupar, Fife).
1903

TOWNHILL

JACOB PRIMMER, his son, John Boyd (marr. 10th March 1903 Jane Reid, daugh. of Archibald S. Robertson, Dunfermline).
1876

JOSEPH JAMES LORRAINE, licen. 8th June 1886; died 22nd March 1931; after his resignation in 1917 the charge was served by a layman till May 1930, when the General Assembly annulled the Chapel of Ease Constitution, and the Charge was merged in the former United Free Charge.
1908

ST ANDREW'S

ANDREW SUTHERLAND, his daugh., Joanna Julia, died at Glasgow 21st May 1943.
1839

WILLIAM ANDREW HUTCHISON, Chairman, Fife Education Authority, 1925; Vice-Chairman, Carnegie Dunfermline and Hero Fund Trusts, 1936; Life Member, Carnegie United Kingdom Trust, 1914; dem. 11th Nov. 1947.
1903

NORTH

RICHARD DOUGHTY LYON, trans.
1920 to North Berwick 15th Feb. 1928.

JOHN FRASER, trans. from Kintore (*q.v.*) 4th July 1928; trans. to St Ninian's, Grange, 18th March 1937. Issue—Shiela, born 11th July 1923; John Milner Ross, born 20th Aug. 1924; Isabel Mary, born 4th Oct. 1927; Jean McHardy, born 9th Feb. 1930 and died 8th May 1936.
1928

ST LEONARD'S

CHARLES EDWARD HOULSTON,
1904 born 11th April 1876.

WILLIAM McMILLAN, Ph.D. (Edinburgh, 1925); D.D. (Glasgow, 15th June 1932); Associate of the College of Preceptors (A.C.P.), London, 1909; joined 3rd (V.B.) K.O.S.B. Sept. 1899; Territorial Efficiency Medal (T.E.M.) 1912, being the only Church of Scotland min. to hold this medal; served with the Forces in France 1915–16, in Egypt and Palestine 1916–17; Chaplain (4th Class), Divisional Troops 52nd (Lowland) Division; appointed Chaplain to the Forces (Reserve of Officers) April 1928. Addl. Publications —*The Worship of the Scottish Reformed Church, 1550–1638* (London, 1931); *One Hundred Scottish Prayers* (Edinburgh, 1933); *John Hepburn and the Hebronites* (London, 1934); *Book of Common Order for use in Sunday Schools* (Dunfermline, 1928), second edition (Edinburgh, 1932); *Worship in Covenanting Times* (Dumfries, 1932); *Sanquhar in Covenanting Times* (Dumfries, 1936); *The Story of the Scottish Flag* (Glasgow, 1925), joint author with John A. Stewart; *The Annals of Sanquhar* (Dumfries, 1931), joint author with Tom Wilson. Smaller Works—*Guide to Dunfermline Abbey* (Dunfermline, n.d.); *St Leonard's Hospital and Chapel* (Dunfermline, 1928); *Ministerial Titles in Scotland* (Dunfermline, 1926); *Armorial Gallery in St Leonard's Church* (Dunfermline, 1924); *The Scottish Coronation Stone* (Dunfermline, 1924); *Presbyterianism and the Revised Prayer Book* (Dunfermline, 1928), second edition (Dundee, 1928); *Commemoration Service at*
1917

Whithorn (15th Centenary of St Ninian), *Order of Service with Notes* (n.p. 1932); *St Cuthbert's Day, Order of Service with Notes* (Edinburgh, 1934); *Commemoration Service at Inchcolm, Order of Service with Notes* (Aberdour, 1929); *Form and Order of Divine Service for Commemoration of St Aidan and Venerable Bede, compiled from Scottish Sources* (Edinburgh, 1935); *Hymn for St Ninian's Day* (Dunfermline, 1934); *Records of the Scottish Church History Society*: Vol. iii, "Festivals and Saints' Days in Scotland after the Reformation"; Vol. iv, "The Anglican Book of Common Prayer in the Church of Scotland"; Vol. v, "The Hebronites"; Vol. vi, "The Lord High Commissioner to the General Assembly"; *Transactions of the Dumfries and Galloway Natural History and Antiquarian Society*, Third Series: Vol. xii, "The Pre-Reformation Clergy of Sanquhar"; Vol. xiv, "The Celtic Church in Upper Nithsdale"; Vol. xvi, "The Church of Sanquhar"; Vol. xviii, "The Post-Reformation Ministers of Sanquhar, The Church of Sanquhar after the Revolution"; Vol. xix, "Sanquhar Kirk Session Records"; *Scottish Ecclesiological Society Transactions*: Vol. ix, "Argyll Prayer Book, Lecterns"; *Church Service Society Annual*: No. 1, "Concerning Lectionaries"; No. 4, "Mediaeval Survivals in Scottish Worship"; No. 5, "Knox's Berwick Communion Service 1549-51"; No. 6, "The Lifter Controversy"; No. 7, "George Wishart's Communion Service"; No. 9, "Euchologion"; *Burns Chronicle*: No. 29, "Burns and Uppermost Clydesdale. The Heraldry of Burns"; No. 31, "Burns as Employer"; No. 32, "Burns and Shelley"; No. 33, "Gilbert Richardson and his Family"; No. 34, "Robert Burns the Third"; Second Series: No. 2, "Burns the Royal Archer"; Editor, *The Scottish Service Book for the Use of His Majesty's Forces* (Edinburgh, 1935).

INVERKEITHING and ROSYTH

St Erat's Well, under the pavement on the east side of Heriot Street, near the church, indicates an earlier dedication than St Peter. Other holy wells were the Lady Well in the hollow across which passes the railway embankment south of the Ferry Toll; St John's Well on the west side of Church Street, adjacent to the Temple Lands, a portion of which was designated St Germain's; St Mary's Well on the west side of Dhuloch; and the Priest's Well at North Dhuloch, still in use for farm supply. A fire in the burgh in 1420 had the effect of diminishing the rents of the Altars of the Holy Cross and the Virgin Mary, that they were incapable of sustaining the chaplains; and in response to a crave by the "baillies and community" of the burgh, who had founded and partly endowed the altars, the Pope on 26th Aug. 1420 granted "to all who, truly penitent and confessed, shall visit the aforesaid Altars in any year in the feasts of the Holy Cross and the Assumption and Nativity of the Blessed Virgin, and who stretch out helping hands to the augmentation and endowment of the chaplaincies, as often as they do so, three years and as many quarantines of indulgence to last in perpetuity or at least until the rents of the said Altars are raised to 20 merks sterling annually; granting faculty to the priests ministering at the Altars, to give a simple blessing, and imposing excommunication upon all who alienate the lands or steal the possessions of the Altars." In the burgh there are the Hospitium restored by the Town Council in 1935, and portions of foundations of other buildings of the Grey Friars' Friary, founded in the third quarter of the 14th century. The Chapel of Inverkeithing, of which there is now no trace, was granted to Dunfermline Abbey by Malcolm IV in 1159. At North Queensferry, disjoined from Dunfermline and attached to Inverkeithing *quoad sacra* about 1642, there are the ruins of the Chapel of St James the Apostle, which belonged to Roger de Moubray, Baron of Inverkeithing, and on his forfeiture in 1320 was granted to Dunfermline Abbey by Robert I. The Church of Rosyth was granted to Inchcolm about 1162-9—donor unknown. It is mentioned 1251-72, in conjunction with its annexed Chapel of Logie and the lands attached thereto.—[Stephen's *Inverkeithing* and Rosyth, 263, etc.; *Chart. of Inchcolm*, 1, 2, S.H.S.; *Calendar of Supplications Rel. to Scotland*, 228, S.H.S.]

1560 WILLIAM BOSWELL, vicar at 1560.— [*Book of Assumptions.*]

1562 JOHN ANGUS (Dene), was still vicar 1568.—[*Comps. Sub Coll. of Thirds, Fife*, etc.]

1563 JOHN RATTRAY, exhorter, and in 1564.—[*Comps. Sub Coll. of Thirds, Fife*, etc.]

1567 JOHN BURNE, reader at Dunfermline, also reader at Rosyth.—[*Comps. Sub Coll. of Thirds, Fife*, etc.]

1568 SIR ADAM ANGILL, reader 1568, and apparently from 1560; succeeded in 1593 by John Bonar; Adam Angill had been a chaplain at one of the altars in the church at 1560.—[*Comps. Sub Coll. of Thirds, Fife*, etc.; Stephen's *Inverkeithing and Rosyth*, 273.]

1570 GEORGE DURY, reader at Rosyth, and in 1574; he had been chaplain of the Altar of St Catharine in Inverkeithing Church at 1560.—[*Reg. of Ministers*, etc., Maitland Club; Stephen's *Inverkeithing and Rosyth*, 235.]

1570 JOHN BURNE, probably a son of John B. of Bowprie, Aberdour; pres. to vicarage of Rosyth 12th Jan. 1587-8, vacant by death of Sir James Chalmers, who on 9th Feb. 1544-5 had been presented to the vicarage-pensionair in succession to Sir Andrew Masson, with emoluments £10 Scots and a manse; his wife was daugh. of David Towris, burgess of Edinburgh; he died after July 1611, but some time prior to that date he had been "tyed to the bed through age and infirmitie, and nawayes abill to discharge the functioun and cuir of the said kirk." Addl. issue—Mr John, min. at Langton.—[Stephen's *Story of Inverkeithing and Rosyth*, 151; *Reg. of Deeds, Scott.*, 16th July 1611.

1611 ROBERT ROCHE, in virtue of a contract between him and the Town Council of the burgh as representing the community, the Council pledged themselves to pay to him "320 merkes yeirley and ilk yeir during the lyfetime of Jon Burne and during the space of ane yeir and ane half yeir immediately following his deceis."—[*Reg. of Deeds, Scott.*, 16th July 1611.]

1673 ROBERT SCOTT, his daugh., Anna (marr. (2) Mr Charles Erskine of Edinshead).—[*Edin.Tests*, 7th March 1764.]

1792 ANDREW ROBERTSON, born 1758, son of Andrew R., Kinghorn Mill, and Jean Gilchrist.—[Stephen's *Story of Inverkeithing and Rosyth*, 151.]

1897 WILLIAM STEPHEN, D.D. (Aberdeen, 1st April 1931); died at Blackhall, Edinburgh, 27th Jan. 1946 (C. and S. Rev. John Johnstone, B.D., St Mary's, Old Aberdeen, ind. 26th Jan. 1938); Member, Scottish Records Advisory Council, 1938; Vice-Chairman, General Trustees of Church of Scotland, 1944; his sons—William D. M., Engineer (Signals), L.N.E.R.; Graham M., manager, Elgin Motors, Elgin; Ranald D., with Luke, Thomas & Co., shipping agents, Aden. Addl. publications—*The Story of Inverkeithing and Rosyth* (Moray Press, 1938); Editor, *The Register of Consultations of Ministers of Edinburgh*, etc., 1652-7, ii, S.H.S., 1930.

ROSYTH

The church, built from plans by Hugh Motram, A.R.I.B.A., F.I.Arch.Scot., was opened and consecrated on Saturday, 11th July 1931, by Right Rev. J. A. Graham, D.D., C.I.E., Moderator of the General Assembly; the Mission became an Extension Charge in Oct. 1928; and the parish *quoad sacra* was erected by the General Assembly, 25th May 1935.

1560 DAVID HENRYSON, vicar 1560.— [*Book of Assumptions.*]

1925 ERIC MAITLAND KIRK RAFF, app. 16th Sept. 1925; ind. to St Mary's, Hawick, 30th March 1926.

1926 REGINALD INNES MORRIS, born 5th Jan. 1889, son of Octavius Fitz Morris and Jane Kerr Munro, of Hay, New South Wales, Australia; educ. at

Barmedan Public School and Newington College, Sydney, and Melbourne Univ., B.A., with Honours, and M.A.; Theological training at Ormond College, Melbourne, and Edinburgh Univ.; licen. by Presb. of Melbourne 1923, and ord. Jan. 1924, Merbein, Victoria; app. to Rosyth 1st April 1926 and res. 28th Feb. 1928; returned to Australia and ind. to Cavendish June 1928; returned to Scotland and adm. min. of Church of Scotland by General Assembly May 1931; ind. to St Andrew's Presbyterian Church, Chatham, Presb. of London South, April 1932; ind. to Millport West 18th May 1938. Marr. 14th Feb. 1928 Elsie Ellen, daugh. of Rev. Robert Thomson Louden, B.D., min. of Cockpen U.F. Church, and Alice Wood Mutter, with issue—twin girls, stillborn, 28th Feb. 1930.

1928 ARNOLD BOYD, born at Bombay 17th Sept. 1870, son of Dugald Cameron B., min. of Free Church of Scotland, Bombay, and afterwards of F.C., Portsoy; educ. at Bombay, Portsoy, Fordyce Academy, and Banff, and Univ. of Aberdeen, M.A. (1890); teacher, Fordyce Academy, 1890-2; Theological Course, Free Church College, Glasgow, 1892-6; licen. by F.C. Presb. of Fordyce 1896; assistant, Kelvinside F.C., Glasgow, 1896-7; ord. to St Andrew's F.C., Dalry, Ayrshire, 17th March 1897; min. of U.F.C., Mussoorie, N.W.P., India, 1902; and Lahore, 1902-6; U.F. Church, now East Church, Kinross, 1908-13; Narrandera, New South Wales, 1914; St Peter's, Adelaide, 1923-6; adm. to Church of Scotland 1926; assistant, Alloa Parish Church and St George's Parish Church, Edinburgh; app. to Rosyth Extension Charge Oct. 1928; dem. 31st March 1942. Marr. 12th April 1899 Mary Lucas (died 20th June 1947), daugh. of Francis Baird, Postmaster Surveyor, Glasgow, and Emma Gladman.

MOSSGREEN

1854 JAMES YOUNG, his son, William Moir, died at San Francisco 3rd Jan. 1933.

1870 ROBERT ROBERTSON, marr. Isabella Simpson.

1878 JOHN CLARKE, died 29th Sept. 1937; his wife, Margaret Mitchell, died 3rd Aug. 1936; his daugh., Margaret, wife of Andrew Wilson, quarry master and contractor, Rosyth, died 21st Nov. 1938.

1918 AUGUST JOHN KESTING, trans. to Fort Augustus 12th Nov. 1925.

1926 WILLIAM MURRAY, trans. from Burghead (*q.v.*) 17th May 1926; trans. to Saline 21st March 1928.

1929 ALEXANDER DOUGLAS BROWN, born 13th March 1900, younger son of Archibald B., B.A., schoolmaster, Dunlop; educ. at Hutchison's Grammar School, Glasgow, and Glasgow Univ., M.A., B.D.; licen. by Presb. of Irvine, 4th May 1928; assistant at Larkhall Parish Church, now St Machan's; ord. 23rd Jan. 1929; trans. to St Andrew's, Greenknowe, Annan, 8th March 1934. Marr. 3rd Aug. 1932 Mary, eldest daugh. of Samuel Yates, Sandyknowe, Crossgates, with issue— Archibald Haworth, born 10th May 1938.

SALINE

Bishop Geoffrey of Dunkeld, 1236-49, app. the church for the allowance of resident canons. The existing church was built in or before 1809; and the materials of the old church, situated in the churchyard, were sold by public auction on 22nd Feb. 1811. Adam, Commendator of Dundrennan, and son of Adam Blackadder of Inzievar, and grandson of Sir Patrick B., first of Tulliallan, received from the Crown, on 10th Oct. 1547, the gift of the parish clerkship, vacant by the death of his brother, John Blackadder, slain at the Battle of Pinkie.—[*Rental of Dunkeld*, 335, S.H.S.; Mercer's *Notes on the Early History of Saline Kirk*, *Dunfermline Press*, 20th July 1889; *Reg. Sec. Seal*, xxi, 43; Stoddart's *MS*., 1089, Lyon Office.]

1567 PETER BLACKWOOD, following his presentation to parsonage in 1568, he was on 18th July 1568 instituted by David Ferguson, min. at Dunfermline, in actual and real possession by exhibiting of the Bible and placing him in the pulpit. —[*Dunfermline Burgh Sas.*, i, 116.]

JAMES BLACKWOOD, adm. to vicarage 26th Dec. 1567 by Royal Letters in succession to Sir John Fargy; pres. to parsonage of Sanquhar in or before early part of 1575, but continued to "brook" both charges till 1578; it is doubtful if he did return to Saline. Issue, James, vicar here later.—[*Reg. Sec. Seal*, xxvii, 21, li, 15; *Book of the Universal Kirk*, i, 386, 424.]

THOMAS BROWN, app. reader 1571.—[Mercer's *Notes on Early History of Saline Kirk*.]

JOHN PATTOUN, reader; pres. to vicarage 31st May 1575, vac. by translation of James Blackwood to parsonage of Sanquhar; his claim to the emoluments was successfully opposed by James Blackwood.—[*Reg. Pres. Bene.*, 31st May 1575; *Acts and Decreets*, lx, 199.]

JOHN SEMPLE of Beltrees, described in 1579 as "the late parson."—[*Reg. Pres. Bene.*, ii, 22.]

JAMES STEWART, his pres. to vicarage 18th Nov. 1584 was consequent upon the deposition of James Blackwood, sometime reader, "fra the office and function of the ministrie or through ony oyer crime or offence"; and his pres. to the parsonage 17th May 1587 followed the death of Peter Blackwood.—[*Reg. Sec. Seal*, li, 117, lv, 62.]

JAMES BLACKWOOD, younger, pres. to vicarage 11th Dec. 1584, vac. by the demission of James Blackwood, last vicar; it may have been he who appears in the list of offenders in Aug, 1590.—[*Reg. Pres. Bene.*, 11th Dec. 1584; *Reg. Privy Council*, 11th Aug. 1590.]

WILLIAM PATOUN, M.A., pres. to vicarage 18th Nov. 1592, vac. by demission of Mr James Stewart.—[*Reg. Sec. Seal*, lxiii, 15.]

ANDREW LEARMONTH, was min. apparently before 10th Oct. 1624.—[*Dunf. Reg. Baptisms*.]

THOMAS COUPER, was min. prior to 19th Oct. 1632; trans. to Menmuir before 29th Aug. 1634.—[*Dunf. Reg. Baptisms*; *Reg. of Brechin*, ii, 321–2.]

WILLIAM MARSHALL, trans. before 29th Aug. 1639.—[*Reg. of Brechin*, 321.]

JAMES LINDSAY, his son, John, apprenticed to John Falconer, litster, Edinburgh, 25th Jan. 1681.

WILLIAM STEWART, was min. at 29th Nov. 1678, and probably for some time prior thereto.—[Mercer's *Notes on Early History of Saline Kirk*.]

ALEXANDER STEWART WILLISON, his widow, Isabella Stewart, died 15th May 1926.

JOHN MACARA, dem. 15th July 1927 on appointment to Kandy, Ceylon; ind. to Kiltarlity 20th Sept. 1932; dem. 26th June 1943.

WILLIAM MURRAY, formerly of Burghead (*q.v.*); trans. from Mossgreen 21st March 1928; dem. in favour of Union, when Union with the former U.F. Charge was accomplished, 25th Sept. 1935; adm. to Gartmore 1st Dec. 1936. Issue, Muriel, born 9th Oct. 1929. Publications—*Notes* (*Teaching of our Lord*) *for Teachers*, 1925-6; Church of Scotland Bible Class First Course; Various Articles in *The Sunday at Home*.

TORRYBURN and CROMBIE

The Church of Torryburn was rebuilt in 1616. On 6th June 1647 it is recorded "that the Kirk was too little to contain the people of the parish," and that "hundreds were constrained to ly in the kirkyard in time of sermon about the doors and windows"; and the heritors, on a petition being presented to them, enlarged the building by the addition of an aisle. That building was replaced by the present church in 1800; and a chancel was added in 1928, when the interior of the church was also remodelled.

The land of Crombie was designated Abercromby; and under that name the Chapel of Crombie was granted to Dunfermline Abbey by Malcolm IV, 1153-63. Between 1203 and 1214 Malcolm, seventh Earl of Fife, granted to Dunfermline Abbey the Church of Abercromby, with the teinds of Quichts, i.e. land near Outh in the north part of Dunfermline parish, and others, for his own soul and the souls of his father and mother, and of all his predecessors and heirs. The church is described as the *new Church of Abercromby* in a Deed between William (II), Abbot of Dunfermline, and William, apparently William de Ramsay, Abbot of Culross, dated Paschal 1227, dealing with a dispute between the two abbeys, which was settled on the basis of Culross Abbey continuing to enjoy the teinds of fruits, trees, etc., in their own territory of Abercromby which had been included in Earl Malcolm's foundation charter of the "new Abbey" at Culross in 1217, and Dunfermline Abbey receiving from Culross an annual payment of 15 marks silver—a settlement confirmed by Pope Gregory IX in 1230. It may be assumed that the designation *new Church* is due to the church having taken the place of the chapel; and the church may have been built by Earl Malcolm himself. The remains of triple lancet-windows in the east gable of the ruined church, which stands on an eminence overlooking the shore of the Forth about a mile east of Torryburn, and constitutes the burial-place of the Colvilles of Ochiltree, are suggestive of 13th-century construction. By Charter of 20th June 1589 James VI erected the Rectory and Vicarage of Crombie, the emoluments of the rector, who was to reside continually at Crombie, being 100 merks from the readiest of the fruits of the church, with manse and glebe.—[*Reg. of Dunfermline*, 23-4, 83, 126-7, 168; *Royal Commission on Ancient Monuments*, etc., *Fife*, etc., 272; Douglas's *Culross Abbey and Its Charters*, reprinted from *Proceedings of Soc. of Antiquaries*, xii, 5 Ser., 1925-6, 67-94; *Reg. Great Seal*, v, 1675.]

1567 JOHN HUTCHISON, had still charge of Crombie also in 1572.—[*Comps. Sub Coll. of Thirds, Perth*, etc.]

1574 EDWARD BRUCE, dem. before 19th Feb. 1606.—[*Reg. Great Seal.*]

1585 WILLIAM HOME, he held the vicarage of Culross as Master of Culross Grammar School.—[*Reg. Sec. Seal*, lix, 168.]

1668 JAMES AIRD, the record of his admission is: "Mr Willm. Persone preacht and after sermone and prayer Mr James Aird was entred to ye exercise of his ministrie at ye sd. (Torrieburne) Kirk, and the byble was delyvered to him as the rule of his life and doctrine, and the kyes of the kirk doores as ane testimonie of his power under the King's majestie and my Lord Arch. to open the sd. doores for divine service and ye moderator and brethren gave him the right hand of fellowship." The date of his deposition was 4th Sept. 1689.—[*Presbytery Records*; *Reg. Privy Council*, 3 Ser., xiv, 472.]

1695 ALAN LOGAN, he was chosen Professor of Divinity in King's College, Aberdeen, on 28th April 1703; but the Presbytery refused transportation, and the Assembly adhered.—[*King's College Officers and Graduates*, 70-1.]

1832 THOMAS DOIG, his sons—John, M.D., Bathgate; Thomas, engineer, Glasgow; Robert Fleming, captain in Army, killed by tiger.

1918 WILLIAM PITCAIRN CRAIG, dem. 31st Oct. 1944.

(*Charge united with Newmills, 19th Sept. 1945.*)

PRESBYTERY OF KINROSS

ARNGASK

It is said that the church was originally a chapel for the family of Balvaird. That may just mean that one of the line of that family was the founder of the church. In 1281 William, Bishop of St Andrews, confirmed to Cambuskenneth Abbey the gift of the patronage of the church made by Gilbert de Frisly, lord of Forgy, and also granted the fruits of the church, the grant being made effective in 1282 on the resignation of the rector, Radufus, Lord Symmersburn, who had been presented by the late Duncan, lord of Forgy. In 1282 John, Prior of St Andrews, also confirmed Gilbert de Frisly's gift of the patronage. By Charter of 1st Oct. 1527, Margaret Barclay, lady of Arngask, Sir Andrew Murray, her husband, and their son, David, founded a chaplainry in the church "for the praise, glory and honour of the indivisible Trinity, Father, Son, and Holy Ghost, and the most glorious virgin, and St Columba, abbot, patron of our Parish Church of the Parish of Arryngrosk." The charter also conveyed 2 acres of land on the south side of the graveyard, for a manse, garden, and buildings for the chaplain, then Sir William Melville. The present church was built in 1806, enlarged in 1821, and restored in 1879, and of the old church the writer of the *Old Statistical Account* says, "Part of the Church is Pre-Reformation, as there is a place in the wall for a font, and the statue of the foundress (Mrs Barclay ?) has the beads used by Catholics hanging round the hands." The statue was removed to Balvaird Castle when the church was rebuilt in 1806.—[*Chart. of Cambuskenneth*, 3, 4, 5, 20, 34–5; Millar's *Hist. of Fife*, i, 268.]

GEORGE MONCRIEFF, line 13, for
1635 "Elizabeth" read "Helen."

ROBERT GEDDIE, line 13, for "Eliza-
1665 beth" read "Helen."

ROBERT KIRKWOOD MON-
1877 CREIFFE, died 4th April 1930.

JAMES CAMPBELL, trans. to Cairney
30th March 1933. Marr. Annie,
1920 daugh. of John Stuart, farmer, Succoth, Glenrinnes.

BALLINGRY

In the 13th century the church was a dependent chapel of Auchterderran. The church was partly rebuilt and enlarged in 1831. On the north side there is the Malcolm burial aisle, containing a two-light window of Renaissance design, with mullions and transoms, and the date 1661. The keystone has a cherub's head, and the soffit a skull; and beneath the cherub's head is the inscription, "O Death, where is thy sting?" The belfry is of 17th-century type; and the bell has inscribed on the upper part, MALCOLME OF LOCHORE, with the initials I.H.C. in monogram below; while round the skirt there is in Latin: "Blessed are they who know the joyful sound of these Church bells of Ballingry." There was a chapel at Inchgall, Chapel Farm. The chapel at Lochore was dedicated to St Andrew. On the south side of Lochleven at the west end are the lands of Navitie and Navitie Hill with Dunmore "great fort." Navitie or Navity, Nevody in 1477, and Navaty in 1550–1t is akin to the Gaulish word *nemeton*, sacred place, an institution, originally pagan, taken over by the Christian Church. It is the same as *Neamhaidigh*, Navity, at Cromarty.
—[Sievwright's *Kirk of Ballingry*; *Reg. Great Seal*, 8th Dec. 1477, 5th Feb. 1550–1, iv, 3; Watson's *Celtic Place Names*, 246–9; Mackenzie's *Scott. Place Names*, 225.]

SIR JAMES STANIS, inst. vicar-pensioner 31st Oct. 1549, and continued till 1573.—[*Prot. Book of Sir Alexander Gaw*, 30; *Comps. Sub Coll. of Thirds, Fife*, etc.]
1549

WILLIAM BRAIDFUTE, pres. to the parsonage and vicarage, with the glebe, manse, house, park, and yards by Andrew Wardlaw of Torrie, and adm. 13th Nov. 1580 by David Ferguson, min. at Dunfermline, "visitor in the bounds of Fife be west Leven," after trial "in doctrine, teaching, in oppen pulpit qualifications, conversation, manners, life."—[Kingorne's *Prot. Book*, 1580-97, 5, Dunfermline.]
1580

DAVID ANDERSON, M.A., in the autumn of 1609 one Forrester, son of James Forrester, falconer, "cuttit his airme from him"; the assailant took refuge with Sir Robert Forrester of Stratherne, who on 3rd Nov. 1609 was ordered by the Privy Council to give him up.—[*Reg. Privy Council*, xiv, 612.]
1595

JAMES PENNELL, his daughs.—Julia Oriana (marr. Captain John Black Peters), died 9th April 1934; Blanche died at Otley 5th Jan. 1941; his son, James Henry Leslie, died 31st Oct. 1943.
1857

DAVID JAMIE, his daugh., Anne Macgregor, died at Glasgow 7th May 1931; his son, William Dallas, C.A.; his widow, Sarah Jane, died 16th March 1947.
1882

GEORGE SCANLAN, trans. to Strathmiglo, 12th May 1927.
1924

JOHN SMITH SIEVWRIGHT, born 6th June 1882, son of James S. and Mary Smith; educ. at Glasgow Univ., M.A. (1907); licen. by Presb. of Glasgow 30th April 1919; assistant at St George's, Glasgow, 1919-20, and at St Paul's, Glasgow, 1920; ord. to Burnbank 2nd Feb. 1921; trans. and adm. 11th Jan. 1928. Marr. 25th Aug. 1925, at Burnbank, Margaret, daugh. of Samuel Porter and Catherine Agnew. Publication—*The Kirk of Ballingry* (David Brown & Son, Kinross, 1931).
1928

BLAIRINGONE

The constitution of the church was approved by the subscribers on 28th Oct. 1839, and after an appeal it was fixed by the Presbytery in Dec. 1840 on remit from the General Assembly.—[*New Stat. Account, Perth*, 1022.]

JOHN FAWNS CAMERON, dem. 15th Jan. 1930, and died 2nd May 1931; his widow, Margaret Janet Mowbray, died 19th March 1933.
1885

CLEISH

The church was dedicated to the Virgin Mary. It was rebuilt in 1775, and again after a fire in 1832.—[Hall's *Kirk of Cleish*, 1, 74.]

WILLIAM LUMSDEN, was parson in 1564.—[*Comps. Sub Coll. of Thirds, Fife*, etc.]
1567

JOHN ANDERSON, v., described as reader 1570 to 1573.—[*Comps. Sub Coll. of Thirds, Fife*, etc.]
1567

JOHN HENDERSON, one of the Conventual Brethren of Dunfermline Abbey; pres. to vicarage 30th April 1575, vacant by death of John Anderson.—[*Reg. Sec. Seal.*]
1575

CHARLES ROSS, his son, Rev. Charles Beveridge R., died at Silton, Sask., Canada, 1st June 1926.
1843

WILLIAM COWPER ROBERTSON, dem. 12th Oct. 1927 on appointment to Paris.
1907

ROBERT DOUGLAS POTTER, born 28th Nov. 1888 at Larkhall, son of William P. and Elizabeth Naismith Douglas; educ. at Larkhall Academy and Edinburgh Univ.; lay missionary at St Ninian's, Edinburgh, 1912-14, Mallaig (St Columba's) 1919-22, and St Fothad's, Auchterderran, 1922-7; licen. by Presb. of Kirkcaldy 21st April 1927; ord. to Saughtree 13th May 1927; trans. and adm. 14th May 1928; trans. to Cairn's Church, Cowdenbeath, 10th June 1931; trans. to
1928

Uyeasound 16th Feb. 1948; war service—Lieutenant, Northumberland Fusiliers, 1914–18. Marr. 29th Jan. 1916 Alice (died 28th Feb. 1941), daugh. of Robert Sharp, Edinburgh and Comrie, and had issue—William Douglas, born 4th Oct. 1916; Amelia Roberta, born 26th Jan. 1919; Rhoda Alice, born 12th Feb. 1922; Jacobus Louw, born 21st Nov. 1925.

FOSSOWAY

The old church, represented now merely by foundations, stood in the kirkyard on the north side of the road leading from Yetts of Muckhart to Milnathort, about half a mile east of the Old Fossoway Bridge over the Devon. Two acres of land with the patronage of the church were granted to Cupar (Angus) Abbey by Gilbert de Hay, Kt., lord of Errol, Constable of Scotland, confirmation charters being given by Malice, Earl of Strathearn, and by Robert I on 5th Oct. 1309. The modern church at Crook of Devon in the old parish of Tullibole was built in 1806.—[*Reg. of Cupar Abbey*, 11, 286–7.]

1659 ALEXANDER IRELAND, he was summoned before the Estates, and the Estates having received satisfaction from him that he had not seen the Proclamation emitted by the Estates, nor known the nature of it till he came to Edinburgh, and upon consideration of it he was satisfied anent his scruples and would read it next Sunday, ordained him to continue in the peaceable exercise of the ministry and enjoyment of the kirk and benefice, and ordained the parishioners and Sir William Bruce, Sheriff, to make open the kirk doors to him and maintain him in possession thereof, 7th May 1689.—[*Acts Scott. Parl.*, ix, 11–12.]

1854 WILLIAM FERGUSON, his son, James Haig, M.D., LL.D., died at Edinburgh 2nd May 1934.

1889 PATRICK BAEDA THOM, died at London 2nd Jan. 1939; his wife, Madeline McInroy, died at Aberdeen 16th April 1925; his daugh., Patricia Madeline (marr. 2nd June 1925 Kenneth, son of Charles Davis, Kew Gardens).

1918 WILLIAM WILSON BOYLE, died 15th Dec. 1939; his daugh., Eileen Skinner Wilson, Mus.B. (marr. Ralph Langdon, Mus.B.).

TULLIBOLE

The foundations of the church may be traced in the kirkyard situated outside the north-east corner of the policies of Tullibole Castle, about a mile east of Crook of Devon. The church belonged to Culross Abbey, appearing in the rentals of that abbey subsequent to the Reformation. "Church of Tulybothwyn" occurs in Earl Malcolm's foundation Charter of Culross Abbey in 1217; and that has been regarded erroneously as signifying Tullibody, which, however, pertained to Cambuskenneth Abbey. It refers to Tullibole.—[Douglas' *Culross Abbey and Its Charters*, 14, 6, reprinted from the *Proceedings of Society of Antiquaries of Scot.*, xii, 5 Ser., 1925–6, 67, 94.]

1589 PATRICK HOLBURNE, reader, 24th March 1589, of the family who held lands at Tullibole and were the progenitors of Holburne of Menstrie.—[Stephen's *Hist. of Inverkeithing and Rosyth*, 171.]

KINROSS

The church was dedicated by Bishop de Bernham 27th June 1246; and on 14th Nov. 1315, along with the Chapel of Orwell, it was granted to Dunfermline Abbey by Robert I. In a ruined condition, it stands in the old churchyard on the east shore of Lochleven. Both church and churchyard passed through a strange experience when in Lent 1335 an English force under Sir John Stirling laid siege to Lochleven Castle. "They took up a position at Kinross in the sacred cemetery whereof they fortified a position and strengthened it by walling it in with sods of earth and surrounding it with a stockade; and thus, not having God before their eyes, sacrilegiously despising and making light of the judgment of God, they lay there as in a robber's cave, and laid waste the whole country round." In 1742 the church at the loch side was abandoned, and a new church was opened on a site which was then at the west side of the town, a steeple being added in 1751. But the town rapidly extended, and thereby "put the Church in the centre and opposite a big public house"; and accordingly the church was replaced by the existing church, which, built farther to the west, was opened on 11th March 1832. The steeple survived, and is now the tower of the Townhouse. There was a Chapel of St Ninian at and associated with the lands of Brunthill, Cavelstone, and Colden, on the west of Lochleven, and alongside the Great North Road about two miles south of Kinross. Included in those lands is the small farm of Goudierannet; and it may be regarded as certain that on it was the site of the chapel. The second part of the name is *annaid*, old Irish *andoit*, Annat, a patron saint's church, or a church containing the relics of the founder. Here, then, there is an instance of what prevails throughout the country, that wherever there is an annat, there are records or traces of an ancient chapel or cemetery, or both; there is also an instance of what is rare, the known association of a particular saint with the Annat. It may be, therefore, that St Ninian himself, about the details of whose work there is singularly little available knowledge, actually visited this district and founded the chapel. —[*Cart. of Dunfermline*, 229; *Bk. of Pluscarden*, 272-3; *Reg. Great Seal*, 12th Feb. 1639; Watson's *Celtic Place Names*, 170, 250-1; Mackenzie's *Scott. Place Names*, 226.]

1563 ALEXANDER WARDLAW, reader 1563.—[*Comps. Sub Coll. of Thirds, Fife*, etc.]

1572 WILLIAM BALFOUR, M.A., exhorter at Orwell, also exhorter here 1572. —[*Comps. Sub Coll. of Thirds, Fife*, etc.]

1679 HENRY CHRISTIE, his son, George, apprenticed to William Brydon, baxter, Edinburgh, 12th Aug. 1719; his son, William, is Mr William, 29th July 1715.—[*Reg. of Edin. Apprentices; Fife Sas.*, 29th July 1715.]

1782 ROBERT STARK, of his sons, Robert was a writer; William, surgeon, 44th Foot; Adam, writer, Kinross; David, major, 44th Foot.

1845 WILLIAM PETERS, his daugh., Jessie Ann, died 4th May 1923.

1895 FREDERICK HUNTER WILLIAMSON, died 14th June 1944; his son, John, M.A., First Class Hons. in Mathematics, and D.Sc. (Edin.); Ph.D. (Chicago Univ.); Fellow of Royal Society of Edinburgh; Commonwealth Scholarship, U.S.A., in Mathematics; Lecturer in Mathematics, St Andrew's Univ.; and in 1928 app. Assistant Professor in Mathematics at the Johns Hopkins University, Baltimore, U.S.A.

MUCKHART

1479 JOHN ANDREW, was rector 2nd Sept. 1479.—[*Charters Rel. to Burgh of Stirling.*]

1555 JOHN SEMPILL, Clerk to the Diocese of St Andrews; was pres. to the parsonage by John, Archbishop of St Andrews, 23rd March 1555-6, vac. by death of Sir Alexander Ramsay, Presb. Archdean of St Andrews; held office till 1577, when he suffered "forfaulture . . . for certain crimes."—[*Cal. of Charters*, viii, 1676.]

1577 HARRY COLVILLE, min. here, pres. to parsonage and vicarage 24th Oct. 1577 in succession to John Sempill. —[*Reg. Pres. Bene.*, 24th Oct. 1577.]

1583 THOMAS SWINTON, was min. 11th March 1579; he marr. Elizabeth Salmond, relict of John Matthew, burgess of Perth.—[*Acts and Dec.*, lxxx, 165.]

1585 HEW INGLIS, M.A., pres. to the parsonage 21st July 1585, vac. by dem. of Harry Colville.—[*Reg. Sec. Seal*, lii, 163.]

PATRICK DAVIDSON, pres. to the parsonage and vicarage 22nd April 1594, vac. by deprivation of Mr James Cokburne.—[*Reg. Sec. Seal*, lxvi, 109.]
1594

JAMES THOMSON, his son, Alexander, died 3rd Aug. 1932.
1832

GEORGE PAULIN, his daugh., Jane Wright, died 14th Nov. 1936.
1870

JOHN EDGAR CAIRNS, died at London 7th Nov. 1933; his son, John Douglas, B.Sc., C.A.; his daugh., Alice Norah (marr. Henry Charles Wright Westwood, B.A.Hons. (Cantab), eldest son of D. Westwood, Gorakhpur, India); his sons—John, died 23rd Oct. 1898; Charles Albert, died 3rd April 1931.
1907

ORWELL

The Chapel or Orwell was associated with the Church of Kinross when Robert I granted a Charter of both the church and the chapel to Dunfermline Abbey, 14th Nov. 1315. Orwell may have had the status of a parish before 7th April 1506, when Mr James Simson was "vicar of Kinross and Orwell," and certainly at 25th Aug. 1551, when George, Commendator of Dunfermline, pres. Sir John Mowss to the vicarage-pensionary of the two parishes. The old church stood at Bell's Brae on the north shore of Lochleven in the kirkyard, where a mound seems to indicate foundations. A modern mausoleum occupies part of the eastern extremity of the site of the church. The existing church, situated on rising ground north-west of Milnathort, took the place of the old church in 1729.—[*Reg. of Dunfermline*, 229, 398; *Reg. Great Seal*, 7th April 1506; *Cal. of Papal Reg., Letters*, xii, 670; *Edin. Tests*, vi, 372.]

JOHN McCRATHANE, reader 1568. —[*Comps. Sub Coll. of Thirds, Fife*, etc.]
1568

WILLIAM (or WALTER) BALFOUR, M.A.; called exhorter 1568.— [*Comps. Sub Coll. of Thirds, Fife*, etc.]
1580

JOHN SPENCE, MS. volume of sermons in Assembly Library.
1774

ALEXANDER JOHN CAIRNS RITCHIE, trans. to Belhaven, Dunbar, 7th Oct. 1927.
1911

THOMAS NELSON ALLEN, trans. and adm. from Savoch (*q.v.*) 22nd March 1928; died at Dunfermline 18th July 1931; his widow, Thomasina Buchanan Macfarlane, died at Craigmore 28th March 1941.
1928

PORTMOAK

The church was situated in the old burying ground at Portmoak farm near the south-east shore of Lochleven, and was associated with St Moan, called also Moach or Moak. Hence the name of the church and parish. It has also been called the Monastery of Lochleven and Portmoak, and as such is said to have been founded by Eogachman, King of the Picts, may be Eoghane, son of Fergus, and also by Rogasch, King of the Picts. Manifestly there is some confusion in those statements; but at least they may indicate that there was a Christian settlement of some kind at the place prior to the time when it became the church. About 1103 the church was bestowed the Culdee Priory of St Serf's Island; but it does not appear that the grant included the church. The latter, however, may have been closely associated with St Serf's Priory. In any case it was bestowed upon the Priory of St Andrews by Bishop Arnold or Ernald of St Andrews 1158–9; and it was dedicated or rededicated to St Stephen and St Moan by Bishop de Bernham of St Andrews on 23rd July 1243. The church was removed to the present site near Scotlandwell in 1659–61, and it was rebuilt a few years prior to 1839. A corner of the old church was still in existence at the close of the 18th century, but no portions now remain above ground. A few years ago the ancient baptismal font, considerably mutilated, was discovered by representatives of the Presb. of Dunfermline and Kinross in use as a feeding-trough at Portmoak farm; and at present it is in the custody of the Presb. at Cleish Church. The well adjacent to the old churchyard and now used by Portmoak farm may be the former Holy Well of the church. The name of St Moan was further perpetuated, up at least to the 18th century, by "a concavity like to a seat" on the hillside above Scotlandwell, "where the abbot for his recreation sometimes used to solace himself, the top of the adjoining rocks giving umbrage to the place." It was popularly called St Moucum's Seat, that is, St Moak's Seat. In the narrowest part of Glenvale between the Bishop Hill and the West Lomond there is situated "John Knox's Pulpit"—a large cavity in a sandstone rock which serves as a sounding-board. There the Reformer is said to have addressed the people. The glen is also sometimes called the Covenanter's Glen; and the "pulpit" may have been the rallying-place of conventicles.

The Hospital of the Red Friars was situated in the old churchyard at the southeast side of Scotlandwell. The church of the hospital was dedicated to St Mary the Virgin on 2nd Oct. 1244 by Bishop de Bernham, who about the same time gave the adjacent wood of Kelgad (Kilmagad) for the endowment of the church. There may have been an earlier settlement at or near the same site, for a confirmation charter of Hugo, Bishop of St Andrews cir. 1178, to the Priory of St Andrews, includes "the Hospital of St Thomas at the bridge of Portmoak," for the reception of the poor, the gift of Bishop Richard, 1163-77. Such an earlier settlement might in turn indicate something of fact in Sir James Balfour's statement about a hospital and chapel at Scotlandwell, founded by Madocus, Earl of Ernewell. At the close of the 18th century remains of a church and house were still to be seen; but all traces have now disappeared. Archibald Arnot, son of Walter A. of Arnot, was "minister" of the hospital 24th Jan. 1545-66, having been presented in succession to his brother, Robert, 8th Jan. 1542-3; and Andrew Arnot was "Minister" 24th March 1574-5.

The Celtic Priory on St Serf's island was given, according to the Register of the Priory of St Andrews, by King Brude (died 843), son of Dergard, with the isle to God and St Serf and the hermit Culdees dwelling and serving God there. But Andrew de Wynton, who was Prior there from 1395 and there may have written his *The Orygynal Cronykil of Scotland*, identifies the donor with Brude (died 706), son of Dirle. Apparently about 1146-8 Robert, Bishop of St Andrews, conveyed the priory to the Canons Regular of St Andrews; and about 1150 a Charter of David I repeated the gift with the stipulation that the Culdees were to be allowed to remain only on condition that they submittted to the rule of the canons. Remains of the priory include portions of a 12th-century church. —[Lockhart's *Ch. of Scotland in the 13th Century*, 56, 59; *Cal. of Charters*, i, 26, B; *Reg. Priory of St Andrews*, 115, 215, 348; *Reg. Sec. Seal*, xvii, 9; Sibbald's *Hist. of Fife* (Ed. 1803), 282.]

1564 JOHN HIMMELL, M.A., min. here 1564, and also at Kinglassie.—[*Comps. Sub Coll. of Thirds, Fife*, etc.]

1565 JOHN RENTOUN, reader, 1565.—[*Cal. of Charters*, ix, 2015.]

1573 HENRY FORSYTH, his pres. to the vicarage in 1573 was consequent upon the death of Mr Robert Winrahane.—[*Reg. Pres. Bene.*, i, 16.]

1844 JOHN STEELE, his daugh., Martha, died at Comrie 12th April 1942.

1908 JAMES FERRIER POLLOCK, trans. to Grahamston 1st Oct. 1926.

1927 WILLIAM ADAM, formerly of Kirkpatrick-Durham (*q.v.*); trans. to Stanley 15th Oct. 1924; trans. 18th Feb. 1927; his daugh., Florence Elizabeth Taylor (marr. 23rd Sept. 1938 George Temple, Milnathort).

PRESBYTERY OF KIRKCALDY

AUCHTERDERRAN

The church was granted, about 1059, to Serf's Priory, Lochleven, by Fothad II, Bishop of Alban, who is called Modach, son of Malmykel. He is said to have been the patron saint of the church, which was dedicated by Bishop de Bernham 27th Sept. 1243. Of the church, which gave place to another in 1676, all that remains is part of the chancel, incorporated in a mausoleum in the churchyard. The existing church, adjacent to the churchyard, was built in 1700 and enlarged in 1891. Keir Chapel may denote the site of the chapel associated with the church at an early period. St Fothad's Mission Church was opened on 3rd April 1910. In the 13th century Ballingry Church was a dependent chapel of Auchterderran.—[*Reg. Priory of St Andrews*, 33, 117; Houston's *Auchterderran*, 35, 37, 40, 41, 67, 203; *Reg. of Dunfermline*, 202.]

1567 GEORGE BOSWELL, described as parson 1561, reader 1563, parson and min. 1564.—[*Comps. Sub Coll. of Thirds, Fife*, etc.; *Comps. Gen. Coll. of Thirds*.]

1638 JOHN CHALMERS, his first wife, Isabel, was a daugh. of John Scrymgeour of Wester Bowhill, min. at Kinghorn; his daugh., Elizabeth (marr. John Paton).—*Gen. Reg. Sas.*, 2 Ser., xv, 358; Houston's *Auchterderran*, 149.]

1668 THOMAS KINNINMONTH, his daugh., Margaret, born 12th July 1669.

1889 ARCHIBALD McNEIL HOUSTON, D.D. (St Andrews, 1926), died 6th June 1933.

AUCHTERTOOL

The church is included among the possessions of Inchcolm Abbey in the Bull of Pope Alexander III in 1178. There are indications that the church has been altered or rebuilt several times, and carved stones exist that belong to the Norman period. An aisle that existed on the north side appears to have had a groined roof. On the lines of this aisle, a new aisle with Norman arcade was added in 1906. At Lochhead on the north border of the parish and formerly in Ballingry, there was a Chapel of St Fillan—hence Lumphinnans, not far distant.—[*Cart. of Inchcolm*, xx, *S.H.S.*; Stevenson's *Parish of Auchtertool*, xviii-xix, 99.]

1563 THOMAS THALLAND, reader 1563-8.—[*Comps. Sub Coll. of Thirds, Fife*, etc.]

1574 WILLIAM THALLAND, dep. 20th June 1587 for performing a marriage on 14th Feb. 1586-7, secretly and without proclamation three several days, and after lawful impediment offered in the Kirk of Glamis, within a private house in another min.'s bounds; the complaint was made by Elizabeth Learmonth (daugh. of Sir Patrick L. of Dairsie), who had also offered the impediment at Glamis Kirk, and the contracting parties were William Kirkcaldy, alias Kerr, laird of Grange, and Elizabeth Lyon, daugh. of John, 8th Lord Lyon of Glamis, and formerly wife of Patrick, 6th Lord Gray; he was afterwards in the service of William Kirkcaldy.—[*Book of the Universal Kirk*, 695; *Scots Peerage*, vii, 291; *Reg. Great Seal*, 8th June 1591.]

JAMES TULLIS, pres. to the vicarage 13th May 1594, consequent upon the demission of David Creighton.—[*Reg. Sec. Seal*, lxvi, 126.]
1594

HENRY MOIR, his daugh., Jean, died 17th Sept. 1792.
1746

WILLIAM STEVENSON, his widow, Isabella Walker Gibb, died 30th Sept. 1929.
1891

JAMES STEWART WATT IRVINE, died 27th Aug. 1936; studied at Marbourg and Oxford Univs.; served as Chaplain to Royal Scots, Nov. 1916 to June 1918; app. Presb. Clerk 1929; Ph.D. (Edinburgh, 1930).
1908

BUCKHAVEN

WILLIAM DUNLOP, was missionary here prior to being at Coltness as assistant; adm. to Braes of Rannoch 23rd Feb. 1926.
1911

JOHN W. SPENCE, dem. 23rd Nov. 1926; adm. to Symington, Biggar, 26th Jan. 1928.
1923

ANDREW REID, ord. 21st April 1927; trans. to Ladhope 15th Nov. 1928.
1927

WILLIAM COULTHARD, born at Perth 4th Dec. 1902, son of George C. and Margaret A. Lyall; educ. at Dundee High School and Univ. of St Andrews, M.A. (1925), B.D. (1928); lic. by Presb. of Dundee 12th May 1928; assistant at Eastwood 1928–9; ord. 25th April 1929; trans. to St Leonard's, St Andrews, 27th July 1933. Marr. 5th Sept. 1929 Janet Freebairn, younger daugh. of Thomas Tully, M.A., min. of Muirhead of Liff, Dundee, with issue—Margaret Ruby, born 12th June 1938.
1929

BURNTISLAND

The church appears in a confirmation Charter of Richard, Bishop of St Andrews 1163–77, to Dunfermline Abbey, and in other similar deeds; in the Charter of Bishop David in 1240 it is narrated that the revenue of the church is so small that if a vicar were instituted there, virtually nothing would accrue to the monks, and therefore the bishop decreed that the church be served by fit and proper chaplains. The "New Kirk at Burntisland" was declared and ordained to be the parish church on 14th May 1594. The church was dedicated by Bishop de Bernham 19th May 1243.—[*Reg. of Dunf.*, 58, 71, etc.; *Book of the Universal Kirk*, 835.]

JOHN BROWN, exhorter, 1563–72.—[*Comps. Sub Coll. of Thirds, Fife*, etc.]
1563

WILLIAM SYMSON, when he was given liberty by the Assembly on 21st March 1600 to transport himself from Burntisland, he was described as having served there "many yeirs bygane but any stipend," "the Queen and her chamberlain refusing payment who used to pay to ministers." The stipend, no doubt, was paid from the Lordship of Dunfermline, which was held by Anne, Queen of James VI.—[*Book of the Univ. Kirk*, 961–2.]
1597

WILLIAM WATSON, the sum of 500 merks assigned to him as stipend and as "constant stipend to the ministers serving the cure" was payable "from the readest of His Majestie's Thirds" and was prompted by the King's recollection of "the grit extraordinar and exorbitant expenss sustanit and debursit be thame (the burgesses) in the erecting, edifieing and beilding of ane new paroche kirk within thair said burgh, albeit it be destitute altogidder of ony certaine stipend for thair minister serving the cure."
1601

JOHN MICHAELSON, his son, John, father of John, rector of St Laurence, Chelmsford.
1616

JAMES ADAMSON, reader, 15th March 1630.—[*Reg. Great Seal*, viii, 1572.]
1630

JAMES INGLIS, had issue, James.—[*Berwick Sas.*, 20th July 1703.]
1693

HENRY ROBIN, his second wife, Annabell Livingston, died 16th April 1706.—[Turnbull's *Diary*, 481, S.H.S.]
1714

ROBERT SPEARS, his son, Robert, buried at Linlithgow 31st Mar. 1737.
1743

JOHN ROBIN, his daugh., Mary, died at Windsor 11th July 1932.
1849

ROBERT JAMES CAMERON, marr. Sara (died 15th July 1928, aged 85), daugh. of Hon. James Fraser, Nova Scotia.
1877

JOHN MACALISTER THOMSON, his widow, Frances Ann Robertson Paterson, died 8th May 1928. Addl. issue—Charles Macalister, born at Calcutta 29th Oct. 1860, died May 1911; Walter Alexander John, born at Calcutta 1864, died at Camberley, Surrey, 27th Aug. 1925; George James Aiken, born 25th July 1867, died at Longniddry 3rd Dec. 1939; Frances Ann Macalister, born 8th Sept. 1876 (marr. 1907 Vincent Theodore Carruther, M.D., F.R.C.S.E., who died 4th June 1928); Jean Macalister, born 9th Aug. 1880; his son, Donald Sinclair, was born at Calcutta and died there 27th Oct. 1897.
1880

JOSEPH SAGE FINLAYSON, his widow, Jamesina Macdonald, died 3rd April 1937; his son, William Logie, min. of Kirkpatrick-Juxta, died 5th Feb. 1937.
1880

JOHN ROGAN, trans. to Lundie and Fowlis 14th June 1929, and died 22nd Dec. 1929; his son, William Henry, B.D. (marr. 6th April 1940 Norah Violet Henderson, daugh. of late Harry Thomas H. and of Mrs H., Hapland, Helensburgh); ord. to Priory Church, Whithorn, 3rd Sept. 1932, and trans. to St Bride's, Helensburgh, 3rd Sept. 1936; his daugh., Elizabeth Agnes (marr. William Stevenson, min. at Kinghorn); his son, John McGhie, M.B., Ch.B., 1935, M.D. (19th July 1938), Edinburgh.
1910

JOHN HENRY MICHELL DABB, born 1889, son of John D.; educ. at Scotch College and Univ. of Melbourne, B.A. (17th April 1915), and Ormond College, Melbourne, B.D. (13th May 1919); lic. by Presb. of Launceston, Tasmania, 1917; ord. to Devonport 1918; Moderator, State Assembly Presbyterian Church, Tasmania, 1919; Repatriation Secretary, Tasmania, 1918; *locum tenens,* Chalmers Church, Adelaide, 1920; min., St Andrew's Church, Perth, W.A., Nov. 1920, and of Cairn's Memorial Church, Melbourne, 18th April 1922; dem. latter 30th Sept. 1927; Lecturer to Junior Divinity Students, Ormond College, Melbourne; post-graduate course, Edinburgh Univ., and assistant, South Leith Parish Church; adm. by General Assembly on probation for one year 24th May 1928; ord. 30th Oct. 1929. Marr. (1) 3rd May 1916 Flora Gladys (died 13th Nov. 1920), daugh. of William Scott Graham, with issue—Rosina Given, born 23rd May 1918, awarded the Jane Paterson Medical Scholarship (1936) at Edinburgh Ladies' College; and (2) 22nd April 1924, Anne, daugh. of Robert Ormiston Stow, with issue—Ruth Ormiston, born 16th April 1928.
1929

DYSART

The church was dedicated by Bishop de Bernham 26th March 1245, but what remains of the pre-Reformation structure indicates a scheme of rebuilding probably in the early part of the 16th century. There were in the church altars dedicated to St James, St John, and the Holy Trinity, and a cell dedicated to St Catharine. The Chapel of St Denis (Dionysius), situated in the south part of the town, and converted into a smithy long prior to 1836, when part of a wall was still in existence, was the Chapel of the Blackfriars' Friary. Mr Alexander Colville was parson 4th Sept. 1515.—[*Gleanings from the Records of Dysart,* 14–15; *Fife Sheriff Court Bk.,* 16–18, S.H.S.]

ROBERT DANIELSTON, also designated Sir Robert Dennistoun, parson 1551 and 28th July 1553, still rector 27th Sept. 1569; was also parson of Ayr and Canon of the Chapel Royal, Stirling; died before 25th May 1574; had a natural son, George.—[Sir Thomas Johnsoun's *Prot. Bk.,* 376, 491, 492, 804; *Gleanings from Records of Dysart; Reg. Sec. Seal,* 25th May 1574; *Reg. of Deeds,* v, 209, vi, 104, x, 102, xi, 26.]
1560

1564 GEORGE STRACHAN, vicar-pensioner 1564 and prior to 28th July 1553; designated vicar July 1571.—[*Acts and Dec.*, xxx, 158, xlii, 167, 188; *Edin. Tests.*, vi, 69.]

1565 ANDREW FORRESTER, still in office 1571-2.—[*Edin. Tests.*, ii, 216.]

1570 ROBERT WILLIAMSON, reader 1570-3.—[*Comps. Sub Coll. of Thirds, Fife*, etc.]

1574 GEORGE SCOTT, pres. to the prebend of the Kirk Heugh, St Andrews, which is the parsonage and vicarage of Dysart, 25th May 1574, vac. by the death of Mr Robert Danielston; he was dead in 1582, when collective reference is made to his widow and children.—[*Reg. Pres. Bene.*, 25th May 1574; *Comps. Gen. Coll. of Thirds*.]

1582 JOHN YOUNG, min., and in 1583.—[*Comps. Gen. Coll. of Thirds*.]

1584 WILLIAM MURRAY, a cadet of the Murrays of Ochtertyre.

1586 PATRICK SCOTT, son of Thomas Scott of Abbotshall, pres. to parsonage and vicarage 25th Oct. 1586, vac. by the demission of his uncle, George Scott.—[*Reg. Pres. Bene.*, 25th Oct. 1586.]

1601 ANDREW PEEBLES, M.A., vicar 7th Feb. 1601.—[*Reg. Mag. Sig.*, vi, 151.]

1610 ALAN LAMONT, son of Alan L., min. at Scoonie (*q.v.*); reader in 1610 and still in office 1629, but res. before 1632.—[*Invent. of Lamont Papers*, 140, etc.]

1617 WILLIAM NAIRN, brother germane of Mr Robert Nairn of Bannockburn.—[*Reg. Sec. Sig.*, xxiv, 211.]

1664 JOHN ANDERSON, marr. (2) Isabel Riddoch; his son, Andrew, Clerk of Exchequer in 1698.—[*Fife Sas.*, xvi, 173, 15th March 1694.]

1708 DAVID PITCAIRN, his son, David, apprenticed to Patrick Crichton, saddler, Edinburgh, 10th March 1734.—[*Reg. of Edin. Apprentices*.]

1850 WILLIAM MUIR, marr. (1) Christian, daugh. of James Bain, factor on Dysart Estates, and Margaret Thomson (born 6th Dec. 1807, died 10th Jan. 1846.]

1874 JOHN WAUGH GIBSON, his widow, Catherine Elizabeth Polson, died at Bearsden 17th Sept. 1931.

1907 HUGH MENZIES, became sole min. when the second charge was united with Sinclairtown 20th May 1928; died 1st July 1941; his daugh., Margaret Skeoch (marr. 22nd April 1925 Wilfrid H. Babington, R.N.).

SECOND CHARGE

1904 DAVID ALEXANDER MORRISON, died 12th Sept. 1923.

1925 HUGH THOMAS SUTHERLAND, formerly of Tundergarth (*q.v.*); trans. from Kirkcowan 16th Dec. 1925; became min. of the United Charge at Sinclairtown on union with Sinclairtown 20th May 1928, and adm. 20th June 1928; died 6th May 1935. Addl. issue—Walter, born 3rd Sept. 1912; his daugh., Jean Scouller (marr. 17th Sept. 1938 William Wardrop, son of late Robert Black, 75 John Street, Penicuik).

KENNOWAY

In connection with the festival of St Kenneth, 11th Oct., there are six lessons in the *Breviary of Aberdeen* where he is described as "St Kenneth the Abbot who in Kennoway in the Diocese of St Andrews is held as patron." On 14th Jan. 1552–3, James Hamilton, clerk of the Diocese of Glasgow, who had been presented to the perpetual vicarage by John, Archbishop of St Andrews, vac. by the death of David Ballingawe, was inducted, on the command of the Archbishop, by John Sinclair, Provost of the Collegiate Church of Roslin; and the curate of Kennoway, Sir Robert Bute, placed and conducted Alexander Gourlay, as procurator of James Hamilton, in possession of the vicarage, and by delivery of the missel book, cups, and ornaments of the high altar invested and instituted him. There was a chapel at Chapel Brae, near Kilmux House.—[Mackinlay's *Church Dedications* (nonscript.), 63; Colville's *Prot. Bk.*, 45, 52a.]

1560 JOHN ROW, held the vicarage in 1564, and was still vicar in 1572.—[*Comps. Sub Coll. of Thirds, Fife,* etc.; *Reg. Abbrev. Charters of Church Lands,* 11, 314.]

1573 ALEXANDER SAUCHIE, reader here and at Scoonie and Methil 1565; pres. to the vicarage 28th Jan. 1573-4, vac. by dem. of Mr John Row.—[*Reg. Pres. Bene.*]

1575 JOHN SYMSON, his presentation, 18th Dec. 1575, was consequent upon the death of Alexander Sauchie.—[*Reg. Pres. Bene.*]

1585 ALLAN LAMONT, M.A., min. 1585–9. —[*Comps. Gen. Coll. of Thirds.*]

1588 CHARLES WALWODE, M.A., reader at Scoonie; was pres. to vicarage 7th Dec. 1588, vac. by dem. of Mr Robert Wood.—[*Reg. Sec. Seal.*]

1592 JOHN ELPHINGSTON, M.A., son of John E., pres. to vicarage 13th Nov. 1592, vac. by death of Mr Robert Hamilton.—[*Reg. Sec. Seal.*]

1690 THOMAS RUSSELL, his son, Alexander, apprenticed to William Rankin, wright, Edinburgh, 15th Nov. 1721.—[*Reg. of Edinburgh Apprentices.*]

1716 ROBERT PONTON, MS. vol. of sermons in Assembly Library.

1865 DAVID STEWART, his son, Philip, died 28th March 1934.

1888 JAMES SMITH SIMPSON, died 1st Dec. 1924; his daugh., Annette (marr. 17th July 1937 Harry Brooks Rose, Thornhill, Ilkley); his widow, Emily Frances Stewart, died 31st Dec. 1945.

1925 WILLIAM ROBERTSON SMART, trans. from Tannadice 19th May 1925; issue—Norman Sanderson, born 27th Aug. 1924; Elizabeth, born 30th Jan. 1930 and died same day; Alice Elizabeth Margaret, born 23rd April 1932; Thomas Kenneth, born 18th June 1935.

KINGHORN EASTER

The church was dedicated to All Saints before 1290. It was granted to Holyrood Abbey by King William the Lion between 1165 and 1177, Charters being given also by Richard, Bishop of St Andrews 1163-77, and others. Some time afterwards, apparently in the first part of the 13th century, at the instance of the parishioners, and as the church lay outside the town, the Abbot of Holyrood caused a new church to be built in the town, and to be consecrated by the Ordinary, and the parochial insignia to be taken there. This was apparently the church dedicated by Bishop de Bernham 17th May 1243, and of which there still survives a rectangular east portion, aisled on the south, at the east end of the present church on the Kirk Craig. Allusions to the fabric in the Kirk Session Records indicate that the building was cruciform in chape and possessed two aisles. The present church was built in 1774 and renovated in 1894. The site of the original church outside the town is not definitely known. But there are indications that it was at Tyrie or Grange some distance north of the burgh. There, not far from the manor of the barony, there was a church popularly called Eglismaree, but in its oldest and most frequent and probably correct form, Eglismalie, Malin, Maling, Malinus. It is mentioned in the Bull of Pope Alexander III to Inchcolm Abbey, 6th March 1178–9, which confirms to the Abbey "the half-ploughgate of land, lying beside the Church of St Malin, with the Chapel of the same"; and the statement is amplified in a Retour of 1642 and a Crown Charter of 1611–12, each of which deals with the former possessions of Inchcolm, and contains "the half-ploughgate of land, beside the Church of St Maleing, now called Inchkerie, with the Chapel of Buthadlach (or Buchadlach), now called Eglismalye." It may be that the Chapel of Buthadlach, which, with the land of Inchkerie, belonged to Inchcolm Abbey, had the same dedication as the church. But in any case the church was distinct from the chapel; and it is most probable, if not absolutely certain, that here we have the original Church of Kinghorn. Additional support is given to the probability not only from the proximity of the church to the Manor of Grange, but also from the fact that in this neighbourhood were the vicar's lands, still called Vicarsgrange, from which was delimited the original post-Reformation glebe of the parish, later excambed for land near the burgh. Malie or Malee, the name of the saint who on the foregoing probability was displaced by the dedication "All Saints," almost certainly when the parish church was transferred to the burgh, may be identical with St Moling, otherwise St Malin, founder of Tighmoling, now St Mullens, in County Carlow, and Bishop of Ferns from 691 till his death in 697. Another view is that the saint is Maillie, *Maillidh*, a saint not mentioned in the Calendars. The churchyard of St Malin's Church, which has long since ceased to exist, is the reputed burial place both of Sir James Kirkcaldy of Grange, and of his son and successor, Sir William Kirkcaldy, whose body, eight years after his execution on 3rd Aug. 1573, was brought from its original place of interment in Edinburgh. Part of a gable of the church was still in existence in 1843. The Church of Kinghorn was served by a rector till 1418–19, up to which time the Abbey of Holyrood held only one-half of the teinds. At that date the whole of the teinds became the possession of the Abbey, who thereafter supplied the church with a vicar. At or near the burgh was a piece of land called the "Reud-Aiker," which may indicate that in the church there was an Altar of the Holy Rood. Within the burgh was situated St Leonard's Chapel, which after the Reformation was converted into the burgh Townhouse and jail, and in 1822 gave place to the present Townhouse. The chapel apparently was of great antiquity, and that, with its situation within the burgh, may be regarded as explaining the presence of the figure of St Leonard on the burgh seal. Situated also in the burgh was a hospital with chapel dedicated to St James, founded on 20th July 1478 by Robert Pierson, burgess of Kinghorn, the endowment being twelve particles of land at Kinghorn, and an annual rent of 10 merks, 5 of which were to be devoted to supplementing the necessities of the poor and sustaining readers, and 5 for a chaplain to celebrate three Masses. The name and site of the hospital are perpetuated in St James' Place. On the east side of Kinghorn Bay, above the Kirk Craig, are the lands of Abden. The name is a corruption of Abthanrie or Abbacie, which denotes lands that belonged to an abbey or monastery of the Columban Church, and had fallen to the Crown either through the monastery having become extinct or having fallen into the hands of lay abbots. Of the particular story of the lands and their monastery nothing is known. A place in the parish, designated St Ninian's Chapel, indicates that there had existed a chapel dedicated to that saint—probably identical with the chapel which was situated at Chapelflat, North Glassmount.—[*Cal. of Papal Regs., Letters*, i, 512, x, 711; *Petitions*, i, 137; *Chart. of Holyrood*, 37, 129, 193, 195; *Cal. of Supplic. Rel. to Scot.*, 7, 92, S.H.S.; *Chart. of Inchcolm*, 2, S.H.S.; *Reg. Great Seal*, ii, 1407, vi, 1394, vii, 440; *Retours*, xxix, 9; Stevenson's *Parish of Auchtertool*, 26, 31; Mackinlay's *Anc. Ch. Dedications* (nonscript.), 130; Watson's *Celtic Place Names*, 290; Skene's *Celtic Scot.*, iii, 261; Reid's *Kinghorn*, 31; *Test. Efram. Gibbon*, 7th April 1614, *St Andrews Tests.*]

DENE JOHN WILSON, vicar 8th Feb. 1549, also Canon of Holyroodhouse; on a Sunday in Feb. 1559, within the parish Church of St Andrews, he renounced "the Pope, his authoritie, power, and jurisdiction, all maner of idolatrie, superstitions, and hypocrisie, and espetial the mass, veneration of Saints and purgatory" and accepted Christ as the only head, ruler and guide of the Church. He died before 18th July 1570.—[*Reg. of Kirk Session of St Andrews*, 11.]

JOHN BROWN, apparently the reader whom, as narrated by the bailies of Kinghorn in their complaint to the Privy Council in 1564, John Moultrie, laird of Seafield, had in the most cruel manner ejected furth of his house which he had "peccabillie broukit be a large space." The laird was ordered by the Council on 8th May 1564 to restore the reader to his house under pain of escheat and being put to the horn.—[*Reg. Privy Council*, i, 277.] *1562*

ANDREW KIRKCALDIE, exhorter 1563-5.—[*Comps. Sub Coll. of Thirds, Fife*, etc.] *1563*

THOMAS BIGGAR, he may have been in office in 1564, for his tombstone bears that he died in 1605, in the 41st year of his ministry at Kinghorn; his presentation on 18th July 1570 was consequent upon the death of Dene John Wilson. —[*Reg. Pres. Bene.*] *1566*

STEVEN WILSON, vicar in 1572.— [*Acts and Dec.*, xlix, 162, lxi, 353.] *1572*

DAVID COUPAR, reader here, pres. to vicarage 2nd July 1576.—[*Reg. Pres. Bene.*] *1576*

JOHN YOUNG, M.A., pres. to vicarage 24th Oct. 1595, vac. by death of David Coupar.—[*Reg. Pres. Bene.*] *1595*

JOHN SCRYMGEOUR, pres. to vicarage 20th April 1606; his daugh., Isabella, was the first wife of John Chalmers, min. at Auchterderran.—[*Reg. Sec. Seal*, lxxv, 12.] *1604*

GILBERT LYON, his son, Alexander, apprenticed to Thomas Henderson, surgeon-apothecary, Edinburgh, 15th Dec. 1695.—[*Reg. of Edin. Apprentices.*] *1663*

PATRICK LYON, his son, Robert, bapt. 24th Nov. 1690.—[*St Andrews Reg.*] *1686*

FERGUS JARDINE, his children— Agnes, died 7th March 1887; Jessie (marr. William Cooper); Harriet Bruce, died 29th July 1894; Ann Irvine *1831* (marr. Rev. W. Will); John Martin, died 12th Nov. 1912; Isabella, died 3rd May 1921.

WILLIAM JARDINE DOBIE, line 3, for "min. of" read "licentiate"; line 14, insert comma after "Russell"; died 31st Oct. 1932; his widow, Margaret Hamilton Veitch, died 25th May 1933. *1867*

ALEXANDER HANNAY McILWRAITH, died at Endiburgh 14th Dec. 1926. *1908*

WILLIAM STEVENSON, born at Bannockburn 3rd Dec. 1901, son of John S. and Helen Chalmers; educ. at Stirling High School and Univ. of Glasgow, M.A. (1922), B.D. (1925); lic. by Presb. of Stirling April 1925; studied at Union Theological Seminary, New York, 1925-6; assistant, Eastwood, 1926; ord. 12th May 1927; trans. to Grange Parish, Edinburgh, 14th Dec. 1933. Marr. 27th Dec. 1929 Elizabeth Agnes, daugh. of John Rogan, min. of Burntisland and later of Lundie and Fowlis, with issue—Marjorie Henrietta, born 9th Nov. 1930; Laura Christian, born 23rd April 1933; Anthony John Maxwell, born 6th July 1939. *1927*

KINGLASSIE

The church was dedicated by Bishop de Bernham 27th May 1243. Sir Thomas Boswale was vicar in 1551.—[*Gleanings from Records of Dysart*, 18.]

SIR MATTHEW VALLANGE, vicar 5th Dec. 1563.—[*Cal. of Charters*, ix, 1932.] *1563*

JOHN HIMMEL, M.A., min. 1563 and also 1564, with charge likewise at Portmoak.—[*Comps. Sub Coll. of Thirds, Fife*, etc.] *1563*

DAVID STARK, reader; on 17th Feb. 1562 he was charged before the Kirk Session of St Andrews with having administered baptism in Kinglassie Church without lawful admission, and having no office in the Kirk interponed himself to read the common prayers there and interrupted *1567* the lawfully admitted reader; he admitted the charge and was ord. by the Superintendent to abstain, and to acknowledge his offence next Sunday in Kinglassie Church, and ask the congregation's forgiveness.—[*Reg. of Kirk Session of St Andrews*, ii, 179-80.]

1568 DENE ALEXANDER AITKEN, had been one of the monks of Dunfermline Abbey; vicar in 1568 and in 1573.—[*Comps. Sub Coll. of Thirds, Fife*, etc.]

1568 PETER WATSON, min. at Markinch; had also charge here 1568-9.—[*Comps. Sub Coll. of Thirds, Fife*, etc.]

1569 JOHN RYND, M.A.; called exhorter 1569-70; pres. to the Chapel of St Blais the Martyr, Perth, 3rd Feb. 1570-1; min. of Old Cumnock (*q.v.*).—[*Comps. Sub Coll. of Thirds, Fife*, etc.; *Reg. Pres. Bene.*, 3rd Feb. 1570-1.]

1569 ANDREW ANGUS, reader 1569.—[*Comps. Sub Coll. of Thirds, Fife*, etc.]

1571 GEORGE RAMSAY, pres. to vicarage 31st March 1571, vac. by death of Sir Matthew Vallange, and to the office of reader.—[*Reg. Pres. Bene.*]

1571 THOMAS METHVEN, M.A., parson, 27th June 1571.—[*Cal. of Charters*, ix, 2225.]

1590 JAMES WILSON, M.A., min. here, pres. to vicarage 11th May 1590, vac. by death of Alexander Aitken.—[*Reg. Sec. Seal*, lxix, 126.]

1897 JOHN FRASER, colleague and successor, ind. 9th Oct. 1935; died at Kirkcaldy 2nd May 1944; his wife, Helen Weir, died 2nd Nov. 1939; his daugh., Helen Macdonald (marr. 19th Oct. 1934 Robert Millar Nisbit, Limekilns). Publications—Dramas, *Conriel and Olina* (Paisley, 1901); *A Royal Tragedy, James I of Scotland* (Paisley, 1920); *A Royal Pair, James IV and Margaret Drummond* (Kirkcaldy, 1924); *A Royal Feud, or The Gowrie Conspiracy* (Kirkcaldy, 1930).

KIRKCALDY

ABBOTSHALL

At Wester Bogie there was a chapel dedicated to St Ninian.—[Mackinlay's *Ancient Church Dedications* (non-script.), 30.]

1650 PATRICK WEYMSS, had issue, Harry, born 25th Feb. 1656; Eupham, born 29th Oct. 1657; George, born 19th Aug. 1660.

1710 THOMAS NAIRNE, marr. 14th Aug. 1712 Janet Ramsay, with issue—Samuel, bapt. 8th July 1713; Margaret, bapt. 16th Oct. 1715; Jean, bapt. 5th April 1724; Mary, bapt. 23rd July 1727; John, born 21st April 1735.

1839 ALEXANDER OSWALD LAIRD, his daugh., Emily Christine, died at Mentone, France, 20th Jan. 1937.

1865 BRUCE BEVERIDGE BEGG, his widow, Magdaline Currie, died 8th Feb. 1928.

1911 JOHN MERCER HUNTER, O.B.E., D.D. (St Andrews, 25th June 1948). Line 9, delete "Captain, Black Watch"; served as Chaplain in France, attached to the Black Watch, and was mentioned in Dispatches; trans. to Legerwood 23rd Feb. 1949. Addl. issue—Eunice Christian, born 27th June 1927.

INVERTIEL

The Chapel of St Katharine is mentioned along with "St Katharine's toun called the Brigland, and the pendicle called St German's acre."—[*Retours*, xx, 16.]

1861 JAMES SMEATON, his daugh., Margaret Wallace, died at Edinburgh 20th July 1931.

1915 JOHN BARBOUR, his mother, Mary McKay; his wife, Charlotte Smith, daugh. of James Dawson and Elizabeth McHardy, died 6th July 1933. Marr. (2) 30th June 1937 Alice Laird, daugh. of Allan Law and Margaret McPolland Laird, Kirkcaldy.

ST BRYCE

The church was dedicated by Bishop de Bernham 21st March 1244–5. It was enlarged and repaired in 1643 and was rebuilt in 1807, only the tower, probably of the early part of the 16th century, being left. In 1554 it is designated the "College Kirk of Kirkcaldy," indicating that the cure was then served by two or more clergy. Other altars in the church, besides that of St Katharine, were the Holy Blood (St Sanguin), the Holy Cross, and St Ninian, the patrons of the last being the bailies and community of the burgh. About 1127–30 the Shore of Kirkcaldy, including the church, which had been held by Constantine the King, was granted to Dunfermline Abbey. The "lands of St Brice" are mentioned in 1579.—[*Cal. of Charters*, ii, 6; *Reg. of Dunfermline*, 16, 383; *Acts and Dec.*, viii, 569; *Laing Charters*, 977; *Reg. Mag. Sig.*, iv, 2499; *Reg. Pres. Bene.*, ii, 133.]

1560 JAMES MOULTRAY, vicar 1560; dem. 3rd Feb. 1565, and died before 28th May 1576.—[*Comps. Sub Coll. of Thirds, Linlithgow*, etc.; *Acts and Dec.*, xxvi, 264, 357, 423; *Reg. Sec. Seal*, xl, 40; *Reg. Pres. Bene.*, i, (4), 42.]

1567 STIVEN WILSON, alleged vicar; had left at Jan. 1571–2, but on 28th May 1576 was confirmed in the vicarage, vac. by dem. of James Moultray on 3rd Feb. 1565.—[*Reg. Sec. Seal*, xl, 40; *Reg. Pres. Bene.*, i, (4), 42.]

1578 JAMES MORRISON, reader, 3rd Oct. 1578.—[*Edin. Test.*, vii, 80.]

1601 THOMAS WARDLAW, M.A., brother of Henry Wardlaw of Balmule (1st of Pitreavie), pres. to vicarage by Queen Anne prior to 1601, vac. by death of Stiven Wilson—probably a lay appointment.—[*Acts and Dec.*, cxcviii, 11, 11th Jan. 1601.]

1619 JAMES MILLAR, reader 13th Oct. 1619.—[*Reg. Mag. Sig.*, viii, 136.]

1726 JAMES DRYSDALE, marr. Ann, daugh. of William Ferguson, provost of Kirkcaldy, and Elizabeth Henderson, sister of one of the slayers of Archbishop Sharp, with issue—William, merchant, Kirkcaldy, purser, H.M.S. Sloop *Syren and Porcupine*; Robert, Town Clerk, Kirkcaldy; John, min. of the Tron Church; George, provost and collector of Customs, Kirkcaldy; Andrew, apprenticed to James Carmichael, cordiner, Edinburgh, 21st Jan. 1738; his portrait is at Kilrie.

1807 JOHN MARTIN, his daugh., Anne, died 7th Nov. 1885.

1838 JOHN ALEXANDER, his daugh., Joanna Haddo Lang, died 10th April 1880.

1881 JOHN CAMPBELL, his father was schoolmaster at Fortingall; dem. 21st Oct. 1926, and died at Newtonmore 21st Oct. 1935; his wife, Elizabeth Renwick, died 27th Jan. 1927; his daugh., Phyllis Carruthers (marr. 28th March 1925 Donald Charles MacArthur, Nareen, Winston, Queensland); his daugh., Mabel, died at Allendale, Northumberland, 3rd Nov. 1939.

1927 EVELYN GALL, trans. from St Luke's, Lochee (*q.v.*), 27th April 1927; died 12th Oct. 1946; his daugh., Evelyn Graham, was app. to the Calabar Mission May 1940.

PATHHEAD

1909 JOHN YUILL WALKER, his daugh., Noreen Christian May (marr. 22nd July 1939 John Kellwick Wright, Lieut. R.N.).

1922 THOMAS GILLESPIE SNODDY, issue—Margaret Lawson, born 2nd May 1925; Elizabeth Whitehead Roper, born 19th Nov. 1926; James Beresford, born 11th Sept. 1929.

RAITH

1888 DAVID LAWRENCE FRANCIS, dem. 4th Jan. 1927; died 18th Jan. 1928.

WILLIAM CONWAY, trans. from Hallside (*q.v.*) 11th May 1927; his wife, Mary Anderson, died 7th Oct. 1920, and he marr. (2) 14th March 1922 Grace Beattie Calderwood, with issue—Grace Beattie, born 4th Sept. 1924.
1927

ST JAMES

DAVID BRUCE MILLARD, died 12th May 1940.
1902

DAVID GRANT MILNE, trans. to Stronsay 12th Feb. 1925.
1918

WILLIAM ROCK, ord. 13th May 1925; trans. to Kirkpatrick-Irongray 18th May 1928.
1925

JOHN WILLIAMSON, trans. from St Andrew's, Johnstone (*q.v.*), 31st Oct. 1928.
1928

ST JOHN'S

ROBERT BROWN WISEMAN, trans. to Dolphinton 1st June 1928.
1909

JAMES YOUNGSON, adm. from Nelson, British Columbia (*q.v.*), 19th Sept. 1928; became min. of First Presbyterian Church, Nelson, B.C., Aug. 1931; ind. to St Andrew's South, Dunfermline, 20th May 1935; trans. to Tullynossle and Forbes 30th May 1941; dem. 12th June 1947; died 16th July 1947.
1929

SINCLAIRTOWN

AENEAS NELSON CRAIG, date of marriage 12th Oct. 1900, with issue—Agnes Mary, born 12th March 1902, died 13th June 1918; James Howard, born 25th Dec. 1904, died 3rd Sept. 1907; his widow, Edith Grace Kennard (born 9th Dec. 1878), became an evangelist and went to the United States, where she was min. at Hossick, New York, from 1926 to 1938; she marr. 4th Jan. 1928 Marcus T. Reynolds, and is now Mrs Craig Reynolds, The Parsonage, Hossick, N.Y.—[*Memo*, Mr Jas. T. Davidson, Westerlea, Kirkcaldy.]
1918

DUNCAN SMITH HENDERSON, trans. to Dundyvan 24th June 1926.
1922

HENRY McKINLEY, trans. from Channelkirk 2nd Nov. 1926; dem. 27th Dec. 1927; adm. to St Ninian's, Edinburgh, same year; adm. colleague and successor, Cambusbarron, 13th June 1934; died 24th May 1945.
1926

HUGH THOMAS SUTHERLAND MORRISON, Second Charge, Dysart (*q.v.*); adm. 20th June 1928, consequent upon the union of Sinclairtown and Second Charge, Dysart, 20th May 1928; died 6th May 1935.
1928

LESLIE

The church is called Christ's Kirk-on-the-Green, which indicates dedication to our Lord. Leslie Green has been claimed to be the scene of the poem, "Christ's Kirk on the Green," ascribed to James VI. A controversy in 1239 regarding the patronage of the church, between the Bishop and Chapter of Dunkeld and Merleswain of Ardross, son of Waldene, was settled on the basis of the church becoming a prebend of Dunkeld, Merleswain being patron of the prebend—an arrangement that was not carried out. In 1263 Geolastica, daughter of the late Merleswain, and Richard her husband, gave the patronage to Inchcolm Abbey, in favour of which about the same time Alexander Comyn, Earl of Buchan, on his own behalf and that of Thomas Meldrum, gave up his claim to the patronage. That was followed by a confirmation charter of Richard, Bishop of Dunkeld, which gave the church to the Canons of Inchcolm for their proper use. There was within the churchyard a chapel dedicated to the Virgin Mary, probably a chantry chapel. The church was rebuilt in 1820.—[*Cart. of Inchcolm*, 15–16, 24–6, 31, 127, 145, 151, xxvii, S.H.S.]

PATRICK COUSTANE, M.A., min. 1566.—[*Comps. Sub Coll. of Thirds, Fife*, etc.]
1566

ANDREW ANGUS, reader in 1561 and also at Kinglassie 1568.—[*Comps. Gen. Coll. of Thirds*; *Comps. Sub Coll. of Thirds, Fife*, etc.]
1567

1568 PETER WATSON, min. at Markinch, had also charge here.—[*Comps. Sub Coll. of Thirds, Fife*, etc.]

1585 JAMES WILSON, M.A., min. at Kinglassie, had also charge here; dem. before 6th Oct. 1592.—[*Reg. Sec. Seal.*]

1592 JOHN ELPHINGSTONE, M.A., min. here, pres. to parsonage and vicarage 6th Oct. 1592, vac. by death of James, Abbot of Inchcolm, and the dem. of Mr James Wilson.—[*Reg. Sec. Seal*, 6th Oct. 1592.]

1759 GEORGE WILLIS, his son, George, died 18th Oct. 1846.

1825 JAMES NICOL, his daugh., Eliza Hunter (marr. 1867 Alexander Marjoribanks of that ilk).

1864 DAVID WILLIAM RUNCIMAN, his son, Leslie, died at La Cumbrie, Argentine, 22nd Dec. 1924; his daugh., Jane Elizabeth Boog, died at La Cumbrie, Argentine, 20th March 1948.

1878 ANDREW RUSSELL, his widow, Emily Cecilia Davies, died 11th Nov. 1928.

1907 JOHN ROBERTSON MACGREGOR, his wife, Mina Grandison, died 4th May 1926; and he marr. (2) 27th June 1934 Amina Mary, daugh. of Rev. A. G. Danielson, D.D., Chindwara, India; he died 11th Oct. 1938, a colleague and successor, William Henry Drummond Page, having been ordained 25th March 1931.

LOCHGELLY

1863 THOMAS DEWAR, died at Lumley, Durham, 9th Dec. 1933.

1918 ROBERT NICOL PATON, trans. to Chapelshade, Dundee, 20th June 1934; his daugh., Esther Margaret (marr. 28th June 1941 Herbert Harry Wills, 2nd Lieut. R.A.O.C.).

MARKINCH

Maeldum, Bishop of Alban, at St Andrews 1028–55, son of Bishop Gillandris, gave the church with all its land to God and St Serf and the Culdees of Lochleven; and Duncan, sixth Earl of Fife 1154–1203, gave the church to the Priory of St Andrews. The patron saint was St Drostan, and later, apparently when the church was dedicated by Bishop de Bernham on 19th July 1243, St John the Baptist was joined with St Drostan. The 12th-century tower is attached to the modern church. The ruins of Kirkforthar Church stand on a tree-enclosed mound not far from Kirkforthar farm.—[*Reg. Priory of St Andrews*, 116, 348; *Reg. Pres. Bene.*]

1561 DAVID MYRTON, M.A., vicar 4th Jan. 1561–2, and prebendary of St Catharine's Chaplainry in Crail Parish Church.—[*Reg. Great Seal*, 16th Feb. 1578–9; *Reg. Kirk Session of St Andrews*, 106n, S.H.S.]

1572 JOHN RYND, M.A., exhorter 1572–3. —[*Comps. Sub Coll. of Thirds, Fife*, etc.]

1572 ANDREW ANGUS, reader at Leslie and also here 1572.—[*Comps. Sub Coll. of Thirds, Fife*, etc.]

1580 ARCHIBALD FRASER, pres. to vicarage 6th Nov. 1580, vac. by death of Mr David Myrton.—[*Reg. Pres. Bene.*, ii, 43.]

1585 JOHN RENTOUN, reader 1585–9.— [*Comps. Gen. Coll. of Thirds.*]

1619 ANDREW LAMONT, his pres. to parsonage and vicarage of Kirkforther, 16th May 1626, was consequent upon the death of Mr Thomas Lumsden, Provost of Kinkell.—[*Reg. Sec. Seal*, xc, 45.]

1640 FREDERICK CARMICHAEL.— [*Scot. N. and Q.*, 3 Ser., vi, 36.]

1684 JOHN MIDDLETON, had issue— Robert, bapt. 16th Feb. 1666; Isobel, bapt. 28th Oct. 1670; Margaret, bapt. 28th Nov. 1678; Alexander, bapt. 12th May 1680; John, bapt. 1st June 1681; George, bapt. 25th Sept. 1682; Alexander, bapt. 7th Feb. 1684 and apprenticed to Andrew Law, goldsmith, Edinburgh, 10th Feb. 1697.—[*Reg. of Edin. Apprentices; Fife Sas.*, 10th March 1684.]

1889 JAMES HENDERSON BRYDEN, died at Birklea, Dumfries, 18th Sept. 1939. Publications—*Memories of Holywood and Markinch* (Dumfries, 1935); *Some Old Parish Customs and other Papers* (Dumfries, 1936); Article in the *Gallovidian, Humour in the Kirk and outside it.*

KIRKFORTHAR

1560 HENRY LUMSDEN, M.A., son of Andrew L. in Wester Ellon; parson of Kinkell; was parson and vicar 1560.—[*Comps. Sub Coll. of Thirds; Reg. Sec. Seal*, xxxv, 108; *Acts and Dec.*, cxxxvi, 309.]

1560 SIR DONALD DONALD, parson and vicar soon after 1560.—[*Book of Assumptions.*]

1575 THOMAS LUMSDEN, M.A., son of Andrew L. in Wester Ellon; parson of Kinkell; parson and vicar 1575; died before 16th May 1626.—[*Comps. Gen. Coll. of Thirds; Acts and Dec.*, cxxxvi, 309; *Reg. Sec. Seal*, xc, 45.]

METHIL, METHKYLL, METHKAL

It was a pre-Reformation parish; and the church with the lands is mentioned in 1207. The church was dedicated by Bishop de Bernham, 28th March 1245. The benefice belonged to the Priory of St Andrews. Situated at Methilmill, north of the town and near the river Leven, with the Kirklands in the vicinity, the pre-Reformation church existed till about 1738; but the parish was incorporated with Wemyss some time after 1561. [*Papal Letters*, i, 30; *Papal Petitions*, i, 618; *Reg. Great Seal*, i, 1444; *Reg. Kirk Sess. of St Andrews*, 282; *Memo.*, Rev. A. H. Forbes; *Pontificale Ecclesiae S. Andreae.*]

1561 WILLIAM BLACKADDER, M.A., parson 1561.—[*Comps. Gen. Coll. of Thirds.*]

1566 ALEXANDER SAUCHIE, reader, Kennoway; also reader here.—[*Edin. Tests.*, iii, 60.]

1574 ROBERT SWYNE, reader in 1574; a priest of St Andrews, he had been installed rector, 22nd and 28th June 1545, on the resignation of Mr William Blackadder, who was vicar 1533-4 and rector 1539.—[*Reg. Kirk Sess. of St Andrews*, 282n; *Reg. Great Seal*, iii, 259, 1339.]

1907 ALEXANDER ROBERTSON, his widow, Ann Shepherd, died 30th April 1924.

1923 GEORGE ORMOND MACKENZIE, trans. to Minto 2nd Feb. 1927.

1927 ALEXANDER HAY FORBES, trans. from Cawdor (*q.v.*), 8th Sept. 1927.

MILTON OF BALGONIE

1843 WILLIAM BAIN, had by first marriage six other children, who died in infancy; he marr. (2) Jessie Urquhart, with issue—Jessie Strachan (marr. Alexander Strachan Wood); William Urquhart, M.D., died 1892; Jessie, died 17th Nov. 1926.

1921 JAMES FAULDS, trans. to Clyne 15th Dec. 1926.

1927 JAMES RAE, trans. from North Yell (*q.v.*) 7th July 1927; dem. 16th May 1932, and died at Edinburgh 8th Aug. 1932; his wife, Annie Sykes, died 12th March 1929.

PRINLAWS

1884 JAMES NIVEN HILL, his widow, Marion Josephine Hatch, died 29th June 1935; his son, Colin Cecil, min. of Kilbirnie (*q.v.*).

1920 ARNOLD GRAY SMITH, dem. 16th May 1935; died at Perth 19th Oct. 1940; his daugh., Margaret Euphemia Mortimer, born 28th Nov. 1909.

SCOONIE

Tuthald, Bishop of Alban at St Andrews 1055–9, gave the church to St Serf and the Culdees of Lochleven; and Duncan, Earl of Fife 1154–1203, gave it to the Priory of St Andrews. The church was dedicated by Bishop de Bernham 30th May 1243. The patron saint, St Memma the Virgin, has been identified with St Modwena at Longforgan, and also, but unlikely, with St Memmie, whose memory is perpetuated at the village of Memmie in France. The church was situated in the old churchyard; and a portion of it is said to survive as the burial vault of the Durie family. A new church was built at Leven in 1775, which is the date on the weather-vane of the steeple. The present church, which is incorporated with the 18th-century steeple, was built in 1902–4.—[*Reg. Priory of St Andrews*, 116, 244, 348; Mackinley's *Ancient Ch. Dedications* (non-script.), 132–3, 501; *Memo.*, Rev. G. I. Edwards.]

1564 GEORGE BALFOUR, vicar 1564.—[*Comps. Sub Coll. of Thirds, Fife*, etc.]

1566 ALEXANDER SAUCHIE, reader at Kennoway, was also reader here and at Methil.—[*Edin. Tests.*, iii, 60.] (See Kennoway.)

1566 JOHN SYMSON, was min. 1565.—[*Cal. of Charters*, ix, 2015.]

1588 CHARLES WALWODE, M.A.; reader before 1588, when he was pres. to vicarage of Kennoway (*q.v.*).

1591 JAMES BALFOUR, Dean of Glasgow, vicar before 27th Feb. 1591–2; died before 9th Feb. 1602, when Alan Lamont, min. here, was pres. to the vicarage.—[*Comps. Gen. Coll. of Thirds*; *Invent. of Lamont Papers*, iii; *Reg. Sec. Seal*, lxii, 249.]

1643 ALEXANDER MONCRIEFF, his daugh., Anna (marr. 15th Dec. 1681 Sir Hugh Cunningham).

1860 WILLIAM LOGIE, min. of Firth and Stennes, Orkney; pres. by the Crown, but objections to his pulpit ministrations were upheld by the General Assembly, May 1860.

1861 JAMES BLACKWOOD, assistant at Ceres; pres. by Queen Victoria 22nd Aug. 1860 and ord. 20th June 1861.

1881 CHARLES DURWARD, died 29th Dec. 1924; his son, Eric Stanley, died at Houston, Texas, 16th July 1943; Charles Walker, M.B., Ch.B., died 19th Feb. 1946.

1925 GEORGE JEHU EDWARDS, trans. from Inverallan (*q.v.*) 4th June 1925.

THORNTON

1877 DUNCAN MACFARLANE WILSON, died 10th Aug. 1925.

1925 WILLIAM DARLING GUTHRIE, ord. 17th Dec. 1925; trans. to Govanhill 18th June 1929.

WEMYSS

The church was dedicated to St Mary. If there was a dedication to St Cuthbert—and no evidence has been given in support of that view—it was an early dedication and was superseded some time prior to 1239–40, when John de Methill or de Wemyss, son of Michael de Wemyss, granted the "Church of St Mary of Wemyss" to the Hospital of the Holy Trinity of Soutra. This grant was confirmed in 1261 by Bishop Gamelin of St Andrews, the confirmation stipulating the provision for honourable sustenance for the vicar of Wemyss serving on behalf of the Soutra, and also for the payment of a pension due annually by the Church of Wemyss to Dysart Church. The church passed to Trinity College and Hospital, Edinburgh, in 1460–2, when Soutra was annexed to the latter by Mary of Gueldres, Queen of James II, confirmation being made by Bull of Pope Pius II, and Episcopal Charters; and after the

Reformation it became the property of the provost, magistrates and community of Edinburgh, when by various Crown grants of 1563 and later years, ratified by Acts of Parliament of 1587 and 1592, there were conveyed to them Trinity College and its possessions. In 1528 it is recorded that Sir Patrick Jackson, Chaplain of the Chapel of St Mary at West Wemyss, "was 'biggand' the Church, and purposed to 'big' and continue." It may be assumed that the church at and subsequent to 1560 was the church as rebuilt in whole or in large part at that time. It appears to have consisted of a nave and choir. In 1659 transepts with lofts were added on the north and south sides; and these with the central portion of the old church became the nave, while the choir became the east transept, and the west portion of the old nave became the west transept, each of them being fitted with a loft. Before 1640 the east part of the choir with its pre-Reformation Gothic window had become the burial vault of the Wemyss family; and the vault is separated from the rest of the east transept by a wall erected probably when the vault was constructed. The old Gothic window in the west end of the old nave, now the west transept, was curtailed in height by the insertion of the corresponding loft. The existing galleries may have been constructed in 1792, when the church was "repaired and much improved." The belfry on the existing west gable bears the date 1693. In 1705 George, Earl of Cromarty, in memory of his wife, Margaret, Countess of Wemyss and Countess of Cromarty, mortified the annual sum of 100 merks Scots to the Church of East Wemyss for the provision of a catechist, the Wemyss family to be patron, and the Kirk Session the right of trial and appointment of the catechist. Through accumulations the annual revenue is now £137, which at present constitutes part salary of a probationer-assistant.—[*Memo.*, Rev. John Kennedy, B.D.; *Wemyss Bk.*, i, 112-13, 219, 232, ii, 276; *Charters of the Collegiate Churches of Midlothian*, 34-5, 57-60, 62-3; *Reg. Great Seal*, 29th July 1587; *Acts Scot. Parl.*, iii, 499, 582.]

1568 ROBERT ADAMSON, reader 1568.—[*Comps. Sub Coll. of Thirds, Fife*, etc.]

1585 JAMES TULLOS, M.A.—[*Cal. of Charters*, xiii, 2921.]

1623 ADAM BLACKWOOD, reader 5th to 27th Dec. 1623.—[*Reg. Great Seal*, 1620-33, 623.]

1678 ALEXANDER MUNRO, D.D., pres. to parsonage and vicarage of Methil by David, Earl of Wemyss, 1678.—[*Wemyss Bk.*, ii, 253.]

1686 ALEXANDER KER, deprived 29th Aug. 1689.

1711 JOHN CLEGHORN, marr. Janet, daugh. of Matthew Selkirk, min. of Crichton.

1894 JOHN KENNEDY, his wife, Elizabeth Rollo, died 15th Jan. 1939; his elder son, David, of Wemysshop, Lady Nairn Avenue, Kirkcaldy, a major in the 8th Black Watch; in 1914-18 he was a pilot in the Air Force, with the rank of Lieut.; his younger son, George, M.B., Ch.B. (Edin.), is in practice at Claverley, Shropshire.

WEST WEMYSS

In the gardens at Wemyss Castle, called the Chapel Gardens, there was a chapel, of which no trace now remains, dedicated to St Mary the Virgin. To it pertained a manse and salt-pan, with coals and dovecot. It is on record in Feb. 1536 that upon the chapel and manse Sir Patrick Jackson, chaplain from 1515, had expended £1,000.—[*Memo.*, Rev. John Kennedy; *Wemyss Bk.*, i, 112-13, 117.]

1906 SAVILLE MIDDLEMAS, his widow, Jessie Baxter Stark, marr. (2) 21st Aug. 1923 Robert Duncan Ross, Nigeria, and died 30th April 1946.

1921 GEORGE MACLEOD DUNN, trans. to Kelvinhaugh 13th March 1924.

1924 WILFRID ROBERT SIEVEWRIGHT, ord. 17th July 1924; trans. to Carsphairn 16th Sept. 1925.

1926 GEORGE DRUMMOND SUMMERS, born Markinch 31st March 1899, son of Robert S. and Margaret Philp; educ. at Bell Baxter Academy, Cupar, and Univ. of St Andrews, M.A. (1922); licen. by Presb. of St Andrews 6th May 1925; assistant, Arbroath; ord. 4th Feb. 1926; trans. to Parton, 14th Nov. 1929.

PRESBYTERY OF CUPAR

ABDIE

The church was dedicated by Bishop de Bernham 5th Sept. 1242. The patron saint was St Adrian; but it would appear that there was a later dedication to the virgin, for the sasine of an annual rent of 27th June 1555 contains an obligation that a reversion be delivered upon "the High Altar of our Lady of Abdie." In 1661 an aisle was added on the north side of the church by Sir Robert Balfour of Denmylne. There were in the church Altars of St Ninian and St Lawrence. The church ceased to be used for worship on 11th Nov. 1827, the year in which the present church was built; and its roofless walls stand in the churchyard on the west shore of Loch Lindores. The Chapel of Dundemore occurs in 1198 in Pope Innocent III's confirmation of the foundation Charter of Lindores Abbey, 1178. There was another chapel at Lindores Castle, built by William de Brechin of Lindores, which had to render canonical obedience to the parish church. There were an Abbot's Well and a Monk's Well, and a Well of St Andrew at the foot of Lindores Bank.—[*Chart. of Lindores*, 68, S.H.S.; Laing's *Lindores Abbey*, 46, 69, 196, 433; Sir Alex. Gow's *Prot. Bk.*, 146; *Exchequer Rolls*, viii, 187.]

1561 JOHN SYMMER, pres. to vicarage-pensionary 5th May 1561; still in office 22nd Nov. 1569.—[*Reg. Pres. Bene.*]

1564 WILLIAM SCOTT, M.A., vicar 1564. —[*Comps. Sub Coll. of Thirds, Fife*, etc.]

1568 JOHN WEMYSS, reader 1568-73.— [*Comps. Sub Coll. of Thirds, Fife*, etc.]

1572 PATRICK GALT, min. 1572-3.— [*Comps. Sub Coll. of Thirds, Fife*, etc.]

1574 ALEXANDER GARDEN, min. at Monimail, had charge here.

1574 THOMAS ASHON, pres. 28th Aug. 1574.—[*Acts and Dec.*, lx, 109.]

1839 JOHN DUNCAN, his wife, Agnes Boswell Walker, died 24th July 1933; his daughs.—Euphemia Catherine, died 10th June 1928; Agnes Boswell, died 24th Oct. 1933.

1897 ALEXANDER ALLISON, dem. 1st March 1945; his son, Donald, M.B., Ch.B.

AUCHTERMUCHTY

The church was dedicated by Bishop de Bernham 31st March 1245. Lockhart's *Church of Scotland in the 13th Century* gives the dedication as Holy Trinity. That, however, seems to be an error. St Serf is generally regarded as the patron saint, and that finds support in the annual July observance of St Cyre's or St Sair's Day in the burgh. There was also in the parish a piece of land designated "Paitmyre de Sanct Serf." On 17th March 1350, Duncan, Earl of Fife, granted the Church to Lindores Abbey in fulfilment of a vow which he made when taken captive by the English at the Battle of Durham (Neville's Cross), 17th Oct. 1346. The existing church was built in 1780. There was near the burgh a spring called St Brydeswell—St Bridget.—[Lockhart's *Church of Scotland in the 13th Century*, 59; Laing's *Lindores Abbey*, 453; Turnbull's *The Story of the Lomond Vale*, 19; *Reg. Great Seal*, 28th Oct. 1591.]

1574 ALEXANDER GARDEN, min. at Monimail, had Auchtermuchty also in charge. (See Monimail.)

1575 SIR WILLIAM SCOTT OF BALWEARY, Kt., held the vicarage prior to 2nd June 1575; probably identical with Mr William Scott, pres. to the vicarage on 28th Oct. 1547, in succession to his kinsman, Sir William Lacheris or Latheris, slain at the Battle of Pinkie.—[*Reg. Sec. Seal*, iii, 2516, 2669.]

1575 GEORGE LESLIE, reader; pres. to vicarage 2nd June 1575, vac. by the death of Sir William Scott.—[*Reg. Pres. Bene.*]

1579 JAMES LESLIE, reader; pres. to vicarage 1st Aug. 1579, vac. by dem. of Mr George Leslie.—[*Reg. Pres. Bene.*]

1701 THOMAS THOMSON, his son, Francis, apprenticed to John Dunsmuir, merchant, Edinburgh, 29th April 1747.—[*Reg. of Edinburgh Apprentices.*]

1905 JOHN GILMOUR, died 9th Feb. 1945, unmarr.

BALMERINO

By indenture of 8th Feb. 1435–6 between Bishop Wardlaw of St Andrews and John de Haylis, Abbot of Balmerino Abbey, the latter was granted the privilege of having a baptismal font and administering the sacraments in the Chapel of St Ayle (Agilus ?), possibly for the benefit of the people at large. For some time subsequent to the Reformation, the chapel, designated "Sanct Talis Kirk," was used as the church of the parish; and in the second half of the 17th century the parish was called "Sanct Teal's parrochin." Possibly, therefore, the site of the chapel may have been in the present churchyard. The existing church was built in 1811.—[*Reg. of the Kirk Sess. of St Andrews*, 180 and *n*, 242, 300; Campbell's *Balmerino and its Abbey*, 156, 212, 215, 618, 2 Ed.]

1568 ANDREW KEMP, reader 1568–9.—[*Comps. Sub Coll. of Thirds, Fife*, etc.]

1573 HENRY LEITCHE, reader 1573; and also at Logie.—[*Comps. Sub Coll. of Thirds, Fife*, etc.]

1578 THOMAS DOUGLAS, pres. to vicarage 8th Oct. 1591, vac. by death of Dene James Herrat.—[*Reg. Sec. Seal.*]

1824 JOHN THOMSON, his daugh., Mary Janette, died 20th July 1936.

1857 JAMES CAMPBELL, line 10, for "1908" read "1876."

1907 JOHN THOMAS ARNOTT, his daugh., Christine Isobel Syme (marr. 14th Sept. 1939 John Belford Wilson Christie, advocate).

1920 PETER CARMICHAEL MILLAR, line 2, for "1867" read "1886"; trans. to Balshagray, Glasgow, 1st Oct. 1925.

1926 WILLIAM JOHN McFARLAND, born at Castlederg, County Tyrone, 30th Dec. 1880, son of Thomas McF. and Margaret Kerr; educ. at Bangor Grammar School, Queen's College, Galway, and Royal Univ. of Ireland, B.A.; lic. by Presb. of Donegal 10th Nov. 1908; Chaplain to Clandeboy Camp 1915; ord. to Ballygilbert, County Down, 21st Sept. 1909; adm. to Kelso North 30th April 1919; trans to Borthwick 15th Dec. 1922; trans. and adm. 6th May 1926; died 25th June 1937. Marr. 10th June 1913 Sara (born 7th April 1885), daugh. of Robert Gilmer and Agnes Adair, Glenside, Crawfordsburn, County Down, with issue—Donald Keith, born 21st Nov. 1914, apprentice C.A., Sergeant Pilot R.A.F., killed June 1941; Kenneth Adair, born 13th May 1916, with Thomas Hedley & Co., Newcastle-on-Tyne; Norman Kerr, born 24th Oct. 1918, dental student; Roderick Gilmer, born 28th Sept. 1921, died 28th Nov. 1922; Ian Robinson, born 25th Jan. 1926.—[*Memo.*, Mrs. McFarland.]

CERES

On the south side of the old church, which is said to have been dedicated to St Cyr or Quiricus, there was an aisle that belonged to the Craighall family, containing an altar or chapel dedicated to St Ninian. "Ye prebendarie" called St Ninian's Altar is mentioned in 1620. In later days the revenues of the altar formed at least part of the emoluments of the parochial schoolmaster. There was also an Altar of St Mary the Virgin. The present church was built in 1806 on the site of the old church. In the vestibule there is the recumbent effigy of a knight, apparently of the 15th century.—[*Gen. Reg. Sas.*, 5th April 1620; Walker's *Pre-Reformation Churches*, iii; James Anderson's *Prot. Bk.*, 22nd July 1537.]

1560 PATRICK COUSTON, was one of those within the bounds of St. Andrews adjudged fit by the General Assembly on 20th Dec. 1560 for "ministering and teaching."—[*Booke of the Universal Kirk*, 4.]

1564 DAVID CUNNINGHAM, M.A., prebendary of Ceres 1564.—[*Comps. Sub Coll. of Thirds*, Fife, etc.]

1578 THOMAS BUCHANAN, was one of those within the bounds of St Andrews adjudged fit by the General Assembly on 20th Dec. 1560 for "ministering and teaching."—[*Booke of the Universal Kirk*, 4.]

1599 ROBERT BUCHANAN, on 21st March 1600 an appeal was brought before the General Assembly by James, Lord Lindsay of Byres, and others, parishioners of Ceres, against the Presbyteries of Cupar and St Andrews regarding the admission of Mr Robert Buchanan to the ministry of the Kirk of Ceres and his transportation from Forgan; on report the Assembly ordained Mr Buchanan to remain at the Kirk of Ceres, and gave power to James Melville and others to choose a discreet man, with consent of the parishioners of Ceres, "to be adjonit to Robert as minister and fellow helper," and to arrange a proportion of the stipend for said helper; the Assembly further recommended Mr William Simsone, Minister, Burntisland, as helper.—[*Booke of the Universal Kirk*, 960.]

1837 JOHN DUNCAN, his wife, Margaret Henrietta Somerville or Johnston, died 3rd Oct. 1851.

1910 GEORGE WILLIAM WALKER, trans. to Steven Memorial Church, Glasgow, 3rd Dec. 1925. Publications—*A Sevenfold Claim*; Editor, *Church and Parish* (Historical Papers of the Parishes of Cupar Presbytery).

1926 DAVID SMITH, trans. from Inverkeithing (*q.v.*) 14th May 1926; trans. to Kincardine-in-Menteith 10th May 1929.

1929 IAN GRINDLAY SIMPSON, born at Bathgate 2nd April 1899, son of Alexander Petrie S., W.S., Linlithgow, and Helen Brown; educ. at Stramongate Quaker School, Kendal, and Edinburgh Univ., M.A. (25th July 1924), and New College; lic. by U.F. Presb. of Aberdeen 29th June 1925; assistant, Kelvinside U.F. Church, Glasgow, 1925; ord. to Ceres and Strathkinnes U.F. Church, 7th July 1926, and became min. of United Charge of Ceres 11th Aug. 1929; served as pilot R.N.A.S. and R.A.F. during the Great War; dem. 30th June 1943. Marr. 12th Oct. 1926 Elenora Howie, M.B., Ch.B. (Edin.), daugh. of Hugh H. and Elenora Law, Ripponden, Yorks, with issue—Faith Elenora Helen, born 6th Sept. 1929; Hugh Walter, born 4th April 1931; Anne Ceres, born 3rd Jan. 1933. Contributor to *The Expositor*, *Scotsman*, and *Yorkshire Post*.

COLLESSIE

The church was dedicated by Bishop de Bernham 30th July 1243. The patron saint was St Andrew. There was in the church an altar dedicated to St Laurence. On a tree-covered eminence north-west of the village there is the site of a chapel, maybe the Chapel of St Thomas, which existed in the parish; and in the vicinity is a passage across the stream, called Chapel-Ford.—[*Chart. of Lindores*, 98; *Exchequer Rolls*, viii, 177; *Reg. Great Seal*, 11th Feb. 1591-2, 18th June 1593.]

1561 JOHN WEBSTER, reader, in office 10th Dec. 1560 and onwards to 1569.—[*Reg. Kirk Sess. of St Andrews*, 132 and *n*; *Comps. Sub Coll. of Thirds, Fife*, etc.]

1563 JOHN PATERSON, exhorter 1563.—[*Comps. Sub Coll. of Thirds, Fife*, etc.]

1574 ALEXANDER GARDEN, min. at Monimail, had also charge here.

1688 JOHN OGILVIE, was residing in Kirkcaldy 1695.

1888 JOHN HENDERSON, died at Perth 20th June 1925.

1925 JOHN TAYLOR, trans. from Golspie (*q.v.*) 10th Dec. 1925. Issue—Eileen Margaret Strathern, born 7th Dec. 1927.

CREICH

By Bull of Benedict VI, 23rd April 1414, the church was annexed to Lindores Abbey, on account of the abbey buildings being ruined and the rents diminished by nearness of the wild (Silvestrium) Scots. The ruins of the old church stand in the churchyard, in an isolated part of the parish. A chapel or shrine was founded on the south side of the church by Mr Gilbert Strachen, Canon of Aberdeen and Moray, before 20th Dec. 1538, on which date his nephew, Mr James Strachan, Canon of Aberdeen and Moray, his testamentary executor, granted a charter of certain annual rents to the chaplains at the Altar of the Holy Trinity, the Blessed Virgin, and St Andrew, situated in the chapel. A few feet of the walls of the chapel may still be seen. Associated with the church in the 12th century is a chapel, which may be the chapel that existed at Parbroath farm, and the foundations of which are said to have been dug up somewhat more than a century ago. The last service was held in the church on 8th Dec. 1832, at which date the present church in Luthrie village was ready for use.—[*Reg. Great Seal*, 24th Dec. 1538; *Reg. of Dunf.*, 208; Laing's *Lindores Abbey*, 456; Leighton's *Hist. of Fife*, ii, 137; *Cal. Papal Reg., Petitions*, i, 601.]

1560 JOHN SEYTOUN, M.A., designated vicar and reader 26th Aug. 1547, and vicar and min.; died in 1569.—[*Comps. Gen. Coll. of Thirds*; *Comps. Sub Coll. of Thirds, Fife*, etc.; *St Andrews Tests.*, i, 170.]

1567 ROBERT WILLIAMSON, reader 1567; and also at Flisk, 1570.—[*Comps. Sub Coll. of Thirds*, etc.]

1570 ROBERT PATERSON, M.A., min. here before 6th Nov. 1566; pres. to vicarage 21st Oct. 1570, vac. by death of Mr John Seytoun.—[*Reg. Pres. Bene.*; *Reg. Kirk Sess. of St Andrews*, 283.]

1583 ANDREW BENNET, min. here before 1583; his pres. to vicarage was consequent upon the death of James Carie.—[*Reg. Pres. Bene.*]

1585 THOMAS BAXTER, his pres. in 1592 consequent upon the death of John Kinloch.—[*Reg. Pres. Bene.*]

1605 ALEXANDER STRACHAN, apparently related to James S., min. of Logie-Coldstone, died after 14th March 1607 when he was at Campvere.—[*Kincardine Sas.*, ii, 233.]

1685 JAMES SETON, ord. to Desertoghill and Errigal (Garvagh) 1658; dep. for non-conformity 1666, and imprisoned in Scotland for holding conventicles.

1815 ALEXANDER LAWSON, died Father of the Church.

1875 JOHN RITCHIE, his son, Frederick Johnston, died in Canada 6th Nov. 1936; his son, John, tea-planter, Assam, died 25th Oct. 1925; his younger daugh., Elizabeth Clark (marr. 14th Sept. 1916 Thomas Lionel Hardy, M.A., M.D.).

THOMAS BARR VALLANCE, trans.
1922 to Fergushill 16th May 1925.

ALAN CANT, formerly Chaplain, Indian Army Establishment (*q.v.*);
1925 adm. 12th Aug. 1925; D.D., St Andrews (26th June 1936); his wife, Mary Leggat Watson, daugh. of James Bryce, min. of St Ninian's, Glasgow; his son, Ronald Gordon, app. Lecturer on Mediaeval History and Sub-Librarian, St Andrews Univ., in 1936; his daugh., Marjorie Stuart (marr. 24th May 1940 James Lockhart Mitchell, N.A.J.A.).

CULTS

The church was dedicated by Bishop de Bernham, 8th Aug. 1243. The present church was built in 1793 and enlarged in 1835. On the foundation of the College and Collegiate Church of St Salvator, St Andrews, by Bishop Kennedy in 1451, the Church of Cults was granted to the same by the founder, and was assigned to the Provost.—[Theiner's *Vet. Mon.*, 383–5, 428–9.] (See St Andrews.)

JOHN BALFOUR, probably identical with John Balfour, reader at Kettle,
1563 1573. (See Kettle.)

JOHN RUTHERFORD, M.A., second son of Andrew or Archibald Ruther-
1563 ford, canon of Jedburgh, and grandson of George Rutherford of Hunthill; his mother is said to have been a daugh. of Douglas Bonjedward; he was "professor of philosophy, divinity, and medicine in Conimbrica in Sorben and other places abroad," and "professor and rector of the Universities" of St Andrews, "graduat in all the saidis sciences"; was Principal of St Salvator's College before 25th June 1563, when he complained to the General Assembly that Mr John Balfour usurped the ministry at Cults, being unqualified to discharge the same, and seeing the kirk pertained to him as Principal, he offered himself to minister according to his talents; the Assembly ordained him to accept the same, which he did; he had also a son, William, "Skipper of his own ship at Leith," whose son, William Rutherford of Quarrelwood, was the father of Andrew, Lord Rutherford and Earl of Teviot.—[*Scots Peerage*, vii, 371; *Reports Hist. MSS. Commis.*, vii, 736; *Booke of the Universal Kirk*, i, 31–2.]

PATRICK PEAT, M.A., at the meeting of Synod at Dysart on 30th Sept.
1595 1595 it was deemed expedient and ordained that Mr James Martine, Provost of St Salvator's College and min. of Cults, have a helper to reside at Cults for the better serving of the cure, because Mr Martine's ordinary function did not permit him to reside at Cults, and also because of the distance of St Andrews (where he resided) from Cults. An agreement was made between Mr Martine and the other masters of St Salvator's on the one side, and Mr Peat on the other, whereby Mr Peat should become assistant, on a proposal by Mr Martine to that effect. Mr Peat was adm. assistant by Cupar Presbytery with emoluments, the "minute" and small teinds of the parish, with occupancy of croft and yard, the use of the dovecot and house, and also an amount of victual teind.—[Laing *Charters*, 1303.]

JOHN KEIR, marr. Catherine, daugh. of Patrick Lentron, St Andrews, and
1686 Margaret Keir.—[*Commis. St Andrews Act Book*, xiv, 74.]

JAMES FORBES, his daugh., Agnes
1879 Hope, died 7th Feb. 1941.

WILLIAM HENRY PORTER, dem.
1900 10th Dec. 1935.

CUPAR

FIRST CHARGE

The church was dedicated to St Christopher, and later, probably on 15th May 1233, when the *Chronicle of Melrose* records the dedication of the Church of St Mary of Cupar, the Virgin Mary took the place of St Christopher. Originally the church stood some distance north-west from the burgh, in the grounds of Springfield, now called Kinloss. But in the 15th century a transference took place. In 1415 it is recorded that in Cupar of Fife there was founded the new parish church which before was distant from the burgh on the north side. But considerable delay resulted; and not till 1431 is there any record of the work being carried on. In that year John Haldenstone, Prior of St Andrews, and the canons made protest that they should suffer no detriment in all time coming from the new parish church "which the burgesses in Cupar have rashly and contumaciously began to erect in that burgh without the consent of the said Prior and Canons, patrons of the Church." Clearly that protest determines the actual date of the erection of the church, towards which the prior apparently content with his protest, gave aid, "not because it was incumbent upon him, but as a favour." That church, situated in the Kirkgate, was for the most part rebuilt in 1785, the tower and certain other parts alone surviving. Altars in the church included St Andrew, founded on 12th June 1510 by John Fouty, burgess of Cupar, the endowments being annual rents from Cupar and elsewhere, St James the Apostle, and St Colme; and in addition to the High Altar, the Virgin Mary had an altar in an aisle or chapel. Subsequent to 1431 the Church of St Christopher, along with its site which was within the royalty, continued to be called "the old Church and Churchyard of the burgh of Cupar." It was served by a chaplain; and successive holders of the office on record, along with their dates of presentation, were—Sir John Lamb, 12th April 1498; Sir Walter Kersane, 2nd Dec. 1509; Sir Alexander Cowper, 3rd Dec. 1541; Sir John Lowklaw, 12th April 1542. On 17th Feb. 1532 Sir Walter Kersane granted to Sir John Spens of Maristoune (Mairstoun) a charter of "those my 4 acres of arable land called lie Maryfauld," lying in the "town" of Pettblathow (Pitblabo) which pertained to the "Church or Chapel of the Blessed Cristopher." In post-Reformation times the site of the church was included in the glebe, till by contract of excambion in the first part of the 19th century it passed to the proprietor of Springfield. The foundations of the church were dug up in 1759, and an elevation alone now indicates the site. At Kilmarrn in the north part of the parish was a chapel dedicated to St Ronan.—[*Extracta en variis Cronicis Scocie*, 1842, 217; *Reg. Great Seal*, 9th March 1505-6, 12th June and 11th Aug. 1510; *Chronicle of Melrose*, 143; *Cal. Laing Charters*, 429, 596; *Copiale Prioratus Sancte Andree*, 120; Lyon's *Hist. of St Andrews*, ii, 313; *Reg. Sec. Seal*, i, 188, 1967, ii, 4315, 4576, 1510; *Retours*, vi, 11, xxvii, 52; MacKinley's *Ancient Ch. Dedications* (non-script.), 151.]

The church of Tarvit was dedicated by Bishop de Bernham, 3rd April 1245. It was situated with its burial-ground on a conical eminence on the east side of the river Eden, known as St Michael's Mount, and now traversed by the railway near the north end of Cupar Station. Originally the river constituted the boundary between Cupar and Tarvit; but the diversion of the river in this locality into a straight course early in the 19th century placed a small part of Tarvit on the west bank. On 10th Nov. 1546 Sir Robert Robertoun, Chaplain, was pres. to the parsonage of Tarvit, vacant by the forfeiture of Mr John Gray for his participation in the slaughter of Cardinal Beaton.—[*Reg. Sec. Seal*, iii, 1985; *Lord High Treasurer's Accounts*, ix, 30, 45.]

At the foot of the south side of Castlehill, later Schoolhill, was situated the Black Friars' Friary, founded by Malcolm, 7th Earl of Fife, early in the 13th century, and dedicated to St Catharine. By charter 4th Oct. 1519 of Friar John Anderson, Professor of Theology, Provincial Friar of the Black Friars, the settlement, described as bounded by the Eden, the east gate of the burgh, the Castlehill, and the tenement of the late Thomas Steill, was incorporated with the Black Friars of St Andrews. Included in the charter were 4 acres of arable land belonging to the settlement, called "Sanct Katherine's Hauch," lying opposite the settlement on the east side of the Eden, between the Eden on the north and west, the lands of Little Tarvit, called Hipplehill, on the east, and the way which leads from the bridge over the Eden to

Ballas and the Church of St Michael on the south. The Convent of the Blackfriars was founded by Duncan, Earl of Fife, who on 21st Nov. 1348 received from Pope Clement VI "faculty to found a Convent of Friars Preachers in his Castle of Cupar, and to build an oratory, offices, and other necessaries." On the same date Papal Licence "was granted to the Vicar-General of Scotland of the Prior-Provincial of the Friars Preachers of the Provence of England, to found a Home in Scotland for 12 Friars," and also "to receive the land called 'le Bayllyard' in the Castle of Cupar, given them by Duncan, Earl of Fife, and erect thereon an oratory with tower and bells and necessary offices."

By charter of 14th June 1572, James VI constituted "The Royal Foundation of the Ministry and Almshouse at Cupar," by which there were conveyed to the magistrates, councillors and community of the burgh, the friary and all property pertaining thereto in the burgh, for founding an almshouse for the poor, lame, deformed, and incapacitated, and orphans and other children without parental care, to be administered by the ministers and elders, and for the support of ministers and readers, and defraying other ecclesiastical charges. The almshouse, locally called almshouses, was situated near the church, and was administered by the Kirk Session till taken over by the Parish Council. It was demolished in the latter part of last century. In 1836 steps were taken by the Kirk Session to let or feu the yard of the almshouse for a burial ground; and it is now included in what is called St James' Churchyard. In 1796 considerable portions of the chapel of the friary, "built of cut free-stone," still survived.—[*Cal. Papal Regs.*, *Petitions*, i, 144, *Letters*, iv, 304; Mackinley's *Ancient Ch. Dedications* (nonscript.), 149; *Reg. Great Seal*, 23rd Jan. 1520, 14th June 1572; *Laing Charters*, 395, 495; *Reg. Great Seal*, 7th March 1600.]

1562 ROBERT MONTGOMERY, min., was among those thought fit by the General Assembly on 20th Dec. 1560 to be ministers and commissioners.

1564 JOHN ACHESON, parson at Tarvit 1564.—[*Comps. Sub Coll. of Thirds, Fife.*]

1567 ALEXANDER SPENS, was min. 1564, and in 1568 had charge also of Moonzie.—[*Comps. Sub Coll. of Thirds, Fife*, etc.]

1576 ROBERT FLESCHER, M.A., vicar 8th June 1576, and died in 1588.—[*Cal. of Charters*, xi, 2402; *Comps. Gen. Coll. of Thirds.*]

1585 THOMAS ANDERSON, reader, 21st June 1585.—[*Reg. Sec. Seal.*]

1915 ROBERT FRIZELLE, died at Crieff 6th Sept. 1935.

1924 ANSON ROBERTSON CRAIK WOOD, died suddenly 14th Feb. 1936.

SECOND CHARGE

1665 WILLIAM WILSON, his son, Robert, apprenticed to David Boswell, glazier, Edinburgh, 21st June 1693. —[*Reg. of Edin. Apprentices.*]

1712 JAMES GREIG, for "James" read "John."

1844 JAMES WORDIE, line 17, delete "marr. . . . Glasgow."

1916 ROBERT ALEXANDER, became sole min. on the union of the two charges, Old and St Michael's, 10th July 1938; his son, Andrew Roy, lic. by Presb. of Cupar 8th Dec. 1936; Assistant, Dunfermline Abbey, and app. Colonial Chaplain at Rawalpindi and Murree 10th April 1938; adm. to Law 11th Dec. 1940 and to Kildrummy 10th March 1944.

(*Charges united* 10*th July* 1938.)

DAIRSIE

The church was dedicated by Bishop de Bernham 2nd Aug. 1243.

1565 ROBERT WINRAM, M.A., vicar 6th May 1565.—[*Laing Charters*, 1094.]

JOHN WILLIAMSON, reader, pres. to vicarage 24th Nov. 1577, vac. by death of Mr John Winhrane.—[*Reg. Pres. Bene.*, i, (4), 62.]
1577

DAVID BARCLAY, of Easter Touch in the Parish of Kirkcaldy; his first wife, Alison Melville, died before 24th Nov. 1606, at which date he granted the life rent of Easter Touch to his second wife, Issobel Morris; at that date he was still at Maybole.—[*Reg. Great Seal*, vii, 1340.]
1630

WILLIAM KNOX, his son, Henry, apprenticed to William Robertson, merchant, Edinburgh, 19th Aug. 1724.—[*Reg. of Edin. Apprentices.*]
1704

GEORGE SCOTT, his sons—Sir James George, died 7th April 1935; Sir Robert, died 1933.
1850

ROBERT WRIGHT, his widow, Margaret Anderson, died at Corstorphine 25th Nov. 1927, aged 86.
1861

DUNBOG

The existing church was built in 1803. There is included in the charter of King William the Lion to Arbroath Abbey the Chapel of Dunbog, maybe the precursor of the 17th-century ruined chapel in a wooded enclosure near Ayton farmhouse. The Preceptory or Priory of Eadvan was situated at Dunbog House. In 1603 there is mentioned the lands of Eadvan, with manse, meadow, and chapel.—[*Report Royal Commis. on Ancient Monuments, Fife*, 100; *Reg. of Arbroath*, 25; *Reg. Great Seal*, 20th Dec. 1603.]

SIR ROBERT MELVILLE, apparently of the Kirkhill family; vicar in 1550, and died in or just before 1570; probably did not conform.—[*Gleanings from Record of Dysart*, 12; *Comps. Sub Coll. of Thirds, Fife*, etc.]
1550

ROBERT PATERSON, M.A.; pres. to vicarage 2nd Sept. 1570, vac. by death of Sir Robert Melville.—[*Reg. Pres. Bene.*]
1567

ROBERT WILLIAMSON, reader 1568-9.—[*Comps. Sub Coll. of Thirds, Fife*, etc.]
1568

JAMES CARIE, reader 1572-3.—[*Comps. Sub Coll. of Thirds, Fife*, etc.]
1572

WILLIAM THOMSON, reader; pres. to vicarage 18th April 1574, vac. by death of Robert Paterson.—[*Reg. Pres. Bene.*]
1574

THOMAS BAXTER, died Father of the Church.
1585

JOHN MURRAY, his son, C—— N——, papermaker, killed in motor accident at Asansol, India, 8th Feb. 1932.
1838

WILLIAM MIDDLETON TOCHER, dem. 6th Feb. 1938, died at Carnbo, Kinross, 13th March 1942.
1896

FALKLAND

The church of the parish of Kilgour, afterwards Falkland, was dedicated by Bishop de Bernham 26th July 1243. Early forms of the name are Kilgoueri, Kylogour, Kilgouririn, and Kylgoverin; and Prof. W. J. Watson suggests that the patron saint may be St Gabrien or Gobran, a bishop of the Britons, and a contemporary of St Columba, Kil(Cill)gour being the Church of Gabrien or Gobran. The church was situated 1-2 miles west of Falkland. About 1425-31 it was accidentally burned, and was rebuilt after 1431 by John Haldenstone, Prior of St Andrews, 1417-43. In the latter part of the 16th century a church, termed "the new Church of Falkland," was built in the town. The old church survived in part at least till about 1825, when the foundations were dug up, the stones being used for drains, and a stone coffin utilised as a drinking-trough. The churchyard was ploughed up at the same time, and only the site now remains. Near by is the rock upon which the bell was swung. At a Diocesan Synod visitation of Falkland on 9th Aug. 1611 the "new Church," a rectangular building, was "ordaint to be repaired, My Lord of Scone (David Murray of Gospetrie, afterwards Viscount of Stormont, 16th Aug. 1621) promesit to big ane isle at ye south side of ye kirk, and to help to contribute with ye toun for bigging ane isle to be biggit at ye north syd of ye kirk directly opposite to ye isle to be biggit by my Lord of Scon, be qlk maines ye kirk slabe ane cross kirk; the gentlemen of ye landward ordinit to big ye uyr half or third part of ye said north isle; qlk iles salbe biggit wtin ane yeir . . . ye north isle to have lofts.'' On the carved oak front of the north aisle lofts were the Arms of Viscount Stormont. The date 1620 that was on the church may indicate additional work. In 1850 the church, which had been thoroughly repaired in 1772, was superseded by the present building, the gift of O. Tyndall-Bruce of Falkland, and his wife, Margaret, heir of her brother, John Bruce of Falkland. At the Chapel of the Virgin, situated "near the Palace and town" and called the "Lady Chapel of Birkensyde," frequent offerings were made by James IV. In the Palace there was a Chapel of St Thomas which about 1530 gave place to the present Palace Chapel. The existence of an acre in the burghal area, called "Croft angrie or Crystiscroft," indicates that there had been a dedication to our Lord.—[*Copiali Prioratus Sancti Andree*, 120; *Reg. Great Seal*, 2nd Jan. 1528, 24th May 1595, 30th May 1606; *Laing Charters*, 2123; *Reg. Sec. Seal*, i, 4018, ii, 636, 773; *Min. of Synod of Fife*, 45; Watson's *Celtic Place Names*, 323, 519; *Retours*, xxviii, 1; *Lord High Treas. Accs.*, 1502-6, 74, etc.; *Story of the Lomond Vale*, 44-5; *Retours*, 20th June 1826, Mon. No. 30; *Gen. Reg. Sas.*, 1506-83.]

1565 ALEXANDER MURE, called min. also, 16th Jan, 1571, and exhorter in 1573.—[*Bk. of the Universal Kirk*, i, 222; *Comps. Sub Coll. of Thirds, Fife*, etc.]

1571 ALEXANDER FAIRNEY, reader; on 27th Sept. 1571 he was pres. to the chaplainry of the Chapel of the Virgin Mary, Birkenside.—[*Reg. Pres. Bene.*, i, 62.]

1589 JAMES PITCAIRN, his pres. to vicarage 28th Oct. 1595 was consequent upon the death of David Cowper.—[*Reg. Pres. Bene.*]

1635 WILLIAM BARCLAY, formerly factor to William, Lord Balvaird. Had issue—Katherine (marr. 1665 Alexander Orme, surgeon, Perth); Alexander; Marjorie (marr. Egerton Snow, merchant, Edinburgh).—[*Gen. Reg. Sas.*, lii, 123, lxxiii, 379, 4th Oct. 1697.]

1673 JOHN HAY, died before 4th Aug. 1718. Had issue—Elizabeth (marr. 25th Nov. 1712 William Wardlaw of Abden, with issue), died 23rd March 1749, aged 73.—[*Scroll Sas., Fife*, 1716-19, Nos. 88, 296; *Scots Magazine*; *Wardlaws in Scotland*, 177.]

1726 ALEXANDER STODDART, his son, James, apprenticed to James Stuart and Archibald Walker, merchants, Edinburgh, 13th June 1753.—[*Reg. of Edinburgh Apprentices.*]

1770 THOMAS SPANKIE, probably son of James S., min. of Coupar Angus; his second son, Robert, became Serjeant Spankie, and was a distinguished member of the English Bar; was in India for a time, and on 23rd May 1825 spoke before the Privy Council in defence of the Regulations of the Bengal Press; in 1833 was designated of Serjeants' Inn, Chancery Lane, Home Circuit; died before 1845; had at least two sons, Robert and John, both of Oxford Univ., and the former apparently identical with Hon. Robert Spankie, one of the judges of the High Court of Agra, East Indies.—[Clark's *English New Law List*, 1833, 46; *Asiatic Journal*, xx, 636; Foster's *Men at the Bar*, 439; *Alumni Oxonienses*, 1331.]

1784 ANDREW BROWN, D.D.; his wife, Anne, youngest daugh. of Thomas Gordon, Professor of Philosophy, King's College, Aberdeen, was a noted collector of ballads, and is classified with Lord Hailes and other Scottish copyists who, from the fact that they "possessed some poetic taste and were to a certain extent experts in traditional beliefs and in ballad phraseology," contributed much to account for "the superior poetic excellence of many Scottish versions of traditional ballads to the English versions." In the Minstrelsy of the Scottish Border, Sir Walter Scott makes acknowledgment of the very material assistance that he received from "2 MS. Books of Ballads" described by him as a "curious and valuable collection," and cited under the name of "Mrs Brown of Falkland, the ingenious lady to whose taste and memory the world is indebted for the preservation of the tales which they contain." As a girl, Mrs Brown heard "the songs and tales of chivalry" from an aunt who "spent the best part of her life amid flocks and herds" in upper Deeside, and there learned "from nurses and countrywomen" the songs which her tenacious memory retained. Enthralled by her aunt's recitals and equally tenacious in memory, Mrs Brown learned the songs by heart; and they ultimately were recorded in the MS. books to which reference has been made and which contained also "many beautiful legendary poems apparently the exclusive property of bards of Angus and Aberdeen." These books were in the keeping of Mrs Brown's father, who through a friend placed them at the disposal of Sir Walter. —[*The Minstrelsy of the Scottish Border*, i, Pref. xiv, xx, xxi; Intro. 170–1.]

1867 JOHN BARRACK, his widow, Margaret Jane Dunn, died at Yealmpton, Devon, 2nd Jan. 1942.

1912 JAMES KEDDIE RUSSELL, became sole min. on union with Falkland East Church 13th Dec. 1938. Had issue—Dolina Elizabeth Mairsali, born 2nd March 1923.

FLISK

The church was dedicated by Bishop de Bernham 7th Sept. 1242. It is mentioned along with its chapel in 1176. On Fliskmill Hill there still existed in 1838 a few stones, placed as arms of a chair and called "Muggin's Seat," Muggin being a corruption for Magridin (Adrian), the reputed place of the meditations of the patron saint of the church and parish. The existing church was built in 1790. On the upper floor of the south portion of Balmbreich Castle there was a chapel, probably of the 14th century, of which, in the living room into which it was converted about the end of the 15th century, various traces may still be seen—a large Gothic window in the east gable, upper parts of three sedilia in the south wall, the back of a piscina, and portions of two long Gothic windows. To the east of the castle is Chapel Hill, with foundations of a chapel still visible. There was still another chapel at Flisk Wood. Traces of the foundations of its walls and its enclosing wall may still be seen. It is probably identical with Glenduckie Chapel. —[*Reg. Priory of St Andrews*, 34; *Reports of Ancient Monuments Commission, Fife*, 148; *Retours*, xxxvi, 165.]

1504 DAVID SPENS, parson, 14th July 1504, and rector of St Andrews Univ.; son of Murdo Spens of Wormiston; died between 26th July 1519 and 12th April 1520.—[*Reg. Great Seal*, 14th July 1504, 12th June 1513; *Fife Sheriff Court Book*, 49, 153, 169, S.H.S.; *East Neuk of Fife*, 452.]

1561 JAMES BALFOUR, M.A., parson 1561, and at least up to 1573; Sir James Balfour of Pittendreich, Lord President of College of Justice 6th Dec. 1567; joined the assassins of Cardinal Beaton and was a slave in the same galley as John Knox; suffered forfeiture for being implicated in the murder of Darnley.—[*Acts and Dec.*, xxiii, 179, 334, xxxi, 393, 401; *Reg. Sec. Seal*, 7th March 1563–4; *Comps. Gen. Coll. of Thirds*; *Comps. Sub Coll. of Thirds, Fife*, etc.; *Reg. Great Seal*, 9th July 1582.] (See *Scots Peerage*, i, 533, and Brunton and Haig's *Senators of College of Justice*, 110, for fuller details.)

1564 ROBERT PATERSON, min., and in 1568.—[*Comps. Sub Coll. of Thirds, Fife*, etc.]

1568 ROBERT WILLIAMSON, reader 1568–73.—[*Comps. Sub Coll. of Thirds, Fife*, etc.]

1572 WILLIAM GLEN, exhorter 1572.—[*Comps. Sub Coll. of Thirds, Fife*, etc.]

1574 JOHN HENRYSONE, reader here, pres. to vicarage 30th April 1574, vac. by death of Mr Robert Paterson.—[*Reg. Pres. Bene.*]

1697 WILLIAM THOMSON, had also a son, John, burgess of Lanark.—[*Reg. of Drem*, 1732–9, 77, 20th June 1737.]

1843 ROBERT FINDLAY FISHER, his daugh., Jane, died at Inveresk 7th March 1927.

1886 GEORGE JOHNSTONE, his widow, Agnes Madeline Lawson Sharp, died 14th Sept. 1935.

1908 CHARLES ROBB McMURRAY, licen. 1894; died 17th July 1936; his son, James, ord. to Tannadice 1st Sept. 1930; his widow, Catherine M. Hardie, died 2nd April 1946.

FREUCHIE

1877 CHARLES FRASER, his widow, Janet Balfour Matthew, died at Aberdeen 14th March 1944.

1922 WILLIAM GEMMELL MITCHELL, line 13, for "1923" read "1922"; trans. to Buccleuch, Edinburgh, 16th May 1929.

1929 FREDERICK ANGUS SIMPSON, born at Crieff 15th Oct. 1903, son of Frederick John Leslie S., bookseller, and Mary Angus; educ. at Morrison's Academy, Crieff, and Univ. of St Andrews, M.A. (1924); licen. by Presb. of Auchterarder 15th April 1927; assistant at Stirling April 1927 to Sept. 1928, and Paisley Abbey Sept. 1928 to Sept. 1929; ord. 30th Sept. 1929; trans. to Tron, Edinburgh, 30th June 1941. Marr. 7th July 1934 Elizabeth Brown, daugh. of Walter McNicoll and Cecilia Stewart Ross, with issue—Leslie Ninian, born 18th April 1935; Walter Adrian, born 5th Nov. 1937.

KETTLE

The Church of Lathrisk was dedicated to St Ethernasc (Athernasc) and re-dedicated by Bishop de Bernham 28th July 1243 to St John the Evangelist and St Ethernasc. Its site is near Lathrisk House. It was granted to the Priory of St Andrews before 1181, along with its lands and chapels, by Nesius, son of William, and Orabile his daugh.; and this was ratified by Roger de Quency, Earl of Wintone, who designates Nesius "our predecessor." Roger de Quency also granted the patronage of the church to the Priory. The chapels given to the Priory along with the church were Katel or Catel (Kettle) and Fordin. The latter may have been the chapel which is reputed to have existed at a barrow in Forthar ground, where, it is also said, there was too a regular place of burial. The Chapel of Catel was dedicated to St Catallus, identified with St Cathcan, bishop of Rathderthaige, who is commemorated in the *Martyrology of Donegal* on 20th March. There was also a chapel at Clatto. In 1238–51 John, Prior of St Andrews, with consent of David, Bishop of St Andrews, granted Duncan de Ramsay permission to have a chapel in his lands of Claytin (Clatto). The church was removed to Kettle in 1636 and rebuilt in 1834–5.—[*Reg. Priory of St Andrews*, 59, 81, 85, 244, 254, 256, 336, 337, 348; Mackinlay's *Anc. Ch. Dedications* (non-script.), 138–9; Walker's *Pre-Reformation Churches*, v.]

1568 ALEXANDER MURE, exhorter 1568.—[*Comps. Sub. Coll of Thirds, Fife*, etc.]

1569 WILLIAM BRAIDFUTE, min. at Strathmiglo, had also charge here 1569.—[*Comps. Sub Coll. of Thirds, Fife*, etc.]

1573 DAVID METHVEN, vicar; dep. before 30th Oct. 1573.—[*Reg. Pres. Bene.*, i, 96.] (See Forgan.)

1573 JOHN BALFOUR, pres. to vicarage Oct. 1573, vac. by deprivation of Mr David Methven, for refusal to assent to the Articles of Religion.—[*Reg. Pres. Bene.*, i, 96.]

WILLIAM REID, his daugh., Ann Morrison, died at Edinburgh 25th Dec. 1926.
1842

AENEAS GUNN GORDON, dem. 23rd Nov. 1930 and died 23rd Nov. 1931; his wife, Christine Moncur Stewart, died 29th Sept. 1927.
1878

KILMANY

It has been suggested that the church was dedicated to St Monan (Moinenn). St Eithne is regarded as probable by Dr Watson, Kilmany being *Cill M'Eithne*, "my Eithne's Church." In 1768 the church was rebuilt. On 10th Oct. 1547 Michael Balfour received Letter of Presentation to the parish clerkship, vacant by the death of his cousin, Patrick Balfour, and his brother, Mr David Balfour, slain at the Battle of Pinkie. On the foundation of the College and Collegiate Church of St Salvator, St Andrews, by James Kennedy, Bishop of St Andrews, in 1451, the Church of Kilmany was granted to the same by the founder.

WILLIAM RAMSAY, on 27th June 1565 complaint was made by the Superintendent of Fife to the General Assembly "for want of a preacher" at Kilmany, "ane common kirk of St Salvator." The Assembly made remit to the Superintendent of Angus and Fife, etc., to consider the complaint and make a decision. Probably Ramsay's duties at St Salvator's College interfered with his pastoral work at Kilmany.—[*Booke of the Universal Kirk*, 62.]
1564

JAMES FORSYTH, M.A., clerk, pres. to vicarage 26th Sept. 1570, vacant through forfaulture of Robert Balfour, son of Andrew of Montquhany.—[*Reg. Pres. Bene.*]
1570

ROBERT HYNDSCHAW, his pres. to vicarage 1st Dec. 1578 was consequent upon forfaulture of Robert Balfour, brother of Sir James B. of Pittendreich.—[*Reg. Pres. Bene.*]
1574

GEORGE THOMSON, marr. Bessie, daugh. of John Duncan, min. of Culross, and had issue—John, bapt. 8th April 1652.
1640

ROBERT THOMAS MARSHALL, died at Kirkcaldy 11th June 1936; his widow, Jeannie Thomson, died at Kirkcaldy 23rd Jan. 1943; his daughs.—Jeannie Thomson Kirk (marr. 17th March 1942 Charles William Alexander, only son of C. Young, Ballater); Mary Lily (marr. 19th July 1947 Angus Macdonald, only son of John Sutherland, Barnhill, Dundee); Margaret Peattie, district nurse, Crail, died 5th April 1948.
1898

LADYBANK

On 8th March 1247–8 Roger de Quincey granted to Lindores Abbey 200 cartloads of heather from Kyndeloch, and leave to dig as many peats in his peat moss, which is called Monegro, as they needed for their wants. He gave also a free road through the middle of the wood of Kyndeloch as far as the moor of Eden for heather, and through the middle of the moor itself as far as the peat moor called Monegrey for peats. Hence the original name of the place, Monksmoss, or Monkston, which is still applied to some houses on the west side of Ladybank. The monks themselves used the designation "Our Lady Bog," in view of the name of the Virgin appearing in the dedication of Lindores Abbey; and that subsequently gave place to Lady Bog, which in turn, shortly before the railway station was opened, became Ladybank.—[Laing's *Lindores Abbey*, 78, 175, 178, 499; Turnbull's *Story of the Lomond Vale*, 62.]

ROBERT HAGART KERR, dem. 18th May 1925; died at Southampton 2nd Dec. 1927; his son, Thomas Edward, died at Southampton 14th Oct. 1928.
1882

JOHN DOUGLAS GLENNIE, ord. 17th Sept. 1925; trans. to Stirling West 26th Sept. 1929.
1925

LOGIE-MURDOCH

The modern church was built in 1826.

1564 THOMAS FORRET, M.A., vicar 1564–75.—[*Comps. Sub Coll. of Thirds, Fife*, etc.; *Comps. Gen. Coll. of Thirds*; *Reg. Pres. Bene.*, ii, 54.]

1577 JOHN FORRET, M.A., vicar 1577; but may be identical with foregoing Thomas.—[*Comps. Gen. Coll. of Thirds.*]

1573 HENRY LEITCHE, reader, 1573, and at Balmerino.—[*Comps. Gen. Coll. of Thirds.*]

1580 THOMAS DOUGLAS, M.A., pres. to vicarage 21st March 1580; also min. Balmerino.—[*Reg. Pres. Bene.*, ii, 54.]

1590 WILLIAM METHVEN, min. here, pres. to parsonage and vicarage 4th Feb. 1590–1, vac. by resignation of Henry Cramond.—[*Reg. Sec. Seal.*]

1700 JOHN STARK, his son, Henry, apprenticed to William Crookes, merchant, Edinburgh, 26th June 1723.—[*Reg. of Edin. Apprentices.*]

1803 ANDREW MELVILLE, his second wife, Anne, was the elder daugh. of William Gordon of Dundee, Woodhaven (Fife), and Blelack (Aberdeenshire), by his wife, Barbara Stark, daugh. and heiress of William Syme of Dundee and Woodhaven.—[Michie's *Logie-Coldstone and Braes of Cromar*, 164–6.]

1874 DAVID PITCAITHLY FENWICK, his daugh., Janet Maxton, died at Edinburgh 27th Oct. 1925; his son, William, F.F.A., died 9th Jan. 1945.

1922 ALEXANDER AITKEN MORTON, trans. to Armadale 14th March 1928.

1928 FRANCIS McHARDY, trans. from Garvock (*q.v.*) 26th July 1928; dem. 30th Nov. 1942, died at Yarrow 23rd June 1944; his son, Francis, min. of Blackhill 1936.

MONIMAIL

Nothing remains of the old church except a small part of the east end, practically rebuilt as a burial enclosure. The existing church was built in 1796. All that survives of the Palace of the Bishops and Archbishops of St Andrews, ascribed to Cardinal Beaton, 1539–46, is Monimail Tower. Adjacent to it is Cardan's Well. It is said that by means of the healing virtues of the well John Hamilton, Archbishop of St Andrews 1549–71, when residing at the Palace, was cured of a dangerous malady—phthisis, it has been conjectured by Jerome Cardan, the famous Italian physician. The name of the well has been suggested as indicating that the church was dedicated to St Cardan, an unknown saint. There was in the parish a chapel dedicated to St Leonard.—[Fraser's *The Melvilles*, i, xlviii and *n*, iii, 79; McKinlay's *Ancient Ch. Dedications* (non-script.), 506.]

1563 GEORGE COOK, M.A., vicar; on 12th Feb. 1563–4 he gave a charter of the Kirklands of the vicarage, called Montagrat and Brewlands, to John Clapan, Burntisland, and Alison Orrok, his wife.—[*Reg. Abbrev. Charters of Ch. Lands*, i, 16.]

1573 JOHN WEBSTER, exhorter 1753; evidently identical with John Webster, exhorter, Collessie.—[*Edin. Test.*, ii, 341.]

1577 ROBERT RYND, M.A., min. 1577.—[*Comps. Gen. Coll. of Thirds.*]

1585 ANDREW BENNET, min.; in office 1584, and min. at Creich; died Father of the Church.—[*Comps. Gen. Coll. of Thirds.*]

1641 DAVID ORME, had issue—David, min. of Forgandenny; George, apothecary, Cupar; Alexander, surgeon-apothercary and Town Clerk of Perth, born 25th Aug. 1683.

1679 WILLIAM ORME, died before 1694; had issue—Katherine.—[*Forfar Sas.*, 19th Dec. 1694.]

1686 JAMES ROSS, died 4th April 1733; had issue—Arthur, apprenticed to George Stewart, bookbinder, Edinburgh; Charles, Bishop of Dunblane; Clementina (marr. John Carmichael of Baiglie); Margaret; Stewart; Arthur.—[*Reg. of Edin. Apprentices.*]

1776 SAMUEL MARTIN, born "7," not "17"; his widow died, aged 75; his son, David, died 3rd Feb. 1863.

1905 ALEXANDER JAMES MARSHALL, born at Aberchirder; died 3rd Dec. 1927.

1928 JOHN MONTGOMERY McQUITTY, trans. from Gilcomston, Aberdeen (*q.v.*), 29th Nov. 1928; killed in motor accident 15th Feb. 1943; his daugh., Frances Jean (marr. 12th Feb. 1944 Captain Alistair Campbell, Royal Dental Corps); his son, Eoin Leonard, Captain, R.A.M.C.

(*United with Bow of Fife 2nd Jan. 1944.*)

MOONZIE

The church was dedicated by Bishop de Bernham 5th April 1245.

1563 THOMAS LAWSON, min. 1563-4.—[*Comps. Sub Coll. of Thirds.*]

1564 PATRICK CONSTANE, M.A., min. 1564.—[*Comps. Sub Coll. of Thirds.*]

1568 ALEXANDER SPENS, min. at Cupar, had also charge here.—[*Comps. Sub Coll. of Thirds.*]

1577 ROBERT RALDSON, vicar pensioner 26th Feb. 1577-8.—[*Book of Assumptions.*]

1588 ROBERT ARNOT, vicar 1588-90.—[*Comps. Gen. Coll. of Thirds.*]

1678 THOMAS HONEYMAN, M.A., designated min. of Moonzie, may have held office in the period 1678-85; he marr. Helen, daugh. of John Alexander, Procurator Fiscal of Commissariot of St Andrews; she marr. (2) William Gray, St Andrews.—[Macfarlane's *Gen. Colls.*, ii, 201, S.H.S.]

1685 WILLIAM MONCRIEFF, marr. pro. 3rd Aug. 1680 Eupham Alexander.—[*St Andrews Reg.*]

1847 ALEXANDER FORBES, his posthumous daugh., Susan Grace Devon, died 19th Jan. 1925.

1871 GEORGE MIDDLETON, his daugh., Jane (marr. Fritz Behrend, Ph.D., Berlin), died in Berlin 9th Feb. 1935; his daugh., Anne Forbes, died 10th Nov. 1936.

1909 SAMUEL SOMERVILLE SANDERSON, trans. to Garvald 19th Nov. 1929, died 3rd July 1939.

1929 The Charge was served by a lay missionary under the supervision of Creich till 1939, when a modified ministry was granted.

NEWBURGH

The Chapel of St Katherine was rebuilt 1508-13, and dedicated to St Duthac, Katherine, and Mary Magdalene. On 19th Aug. 1513 St John Malcumsone, chaplain at the Altar of St Dionysius in Lindores Abbey, made resignation of an annual rent of 5 sh. from the tenement in the burgh of Newburgh, belonging to Archibald Carno, burgess of Newburgh, for a chaplain to serve in the "new kirk" of the burgh; and Bailie Kawe, by laying a penny in the hand of the image of St Katherine "then present" at the tenement, "gave heritable possession to the said image in name of St Katherine, and seised and infeft the said image." Newburgh was erected into a parish on 1st Oct. 1622, and ratification was made by Act of Parliament 28th June 1633. The chapel, which served as the parish church, was taken down in 1832 to make room for the present church, then being erected. There was a well of the Nine Maidens, situated in the burgh common.—[Laing's *Lindores Abbey*, 202, 299, 511-12, 514, 187; *Acts Scott. Parl.*, v, 152-3; *Report of Commiss. on Ancient Monuments, Fife*, 222.]

1578 ROBERT SIM, reader of the burgh 8th Nov. 1578.—[*Edin. Test.*, vii, 101.]

1785 THOMAS STUART, his father, Alexander S., who was of Loinmarestock, near Blair Athol, and was a cadet of the Stuarts of Urrard, lineal descendants of the "Wolf of Badenoch," for a time was a companion of Prince Charlie in his wanderings after Culloden, and often lulled the Prince to sleep by playing on a Jewish harp, besides on occasions making "crowdie" for him in the heel of an old shoe; at their parting the Prince gave Stuart a coat of brown satin with buttons of beautifully chased steel, which was retained by his descendants till it came to the maternal grandmother of Rev. Dr Stirton, Crathie, after whose death the nurse of her children thoughtlessly cut it up to make corsets for herself, only the buttons surviving; Stuart subsequently wandered in the wilds of Aberdeenshire, where in Glengairn he met other fugitives, Lawrence Oliphant of Gask and his son; with them he travelled to Birkhall, and then to Braedownie in Glen Clova, whence, with a letter or recommendation to Lady Gask from her husband, he passed to Gask, where he settled as a farmer; a cherished possession of Dr Stuart, now in possession of his descendant, Rev. Dr Stirton, was the gold watch and seal of his fiancée, Helen Euphame Clephane, the seal bearing the skeleton of a leaf and the motto in French: "I change not, though dying."—[*Memo.*, Rev. Dr Stirton.]

1864 ROBERT EDGAR, his widow, Helen Russell, died at Blair Atholl 24th June 1931; his daughs.—Eleanor Russell (marr. David Mitchell, 63 Wardie Avenue, Edinburgh), died 18th Oct. 1932; Janie Russell, of Dallantsagart, died 23rd Feb. 1939.

1895 HUGH YOUNG ARNOTT, his wife, Christian Dandie Clark, died 17th June 1942; he died 21st Nov. 1943.

SPRINGFIELD

1919 DAVID LAIRD, has issue—Thomas Cowan, born 20th March 1925; Elizabeth Fleming, born 5th July 1927; Jane Allan, born 31st July 1932.

STRATHMIGLO

An alternative name was Eglismartine. The church was a mensal church of Dunkeld. On 5th Nov. 1506 there is noted 53s. 2d. spent on the repair of the choir; and in 1513–14 a chalice, 63½ oz. in weight, was provided for the church at a cost of £7 8s. 2d., being 2s. 4d. per ounce. On 4th March 1508 the Bishop of Dunkeld assigned the fruits of the church to Sir William Scott of Balweary. Possibly that was in view of Sir William's project to convert Strathmiglo into a collegiate church, for the furtherance of which an agreement was made on 31st March 1527 between Sir William for himself and in name of most of the parishioners on the one hand, and, on the other, Henry Sibbald, parish clerk, whereby in return for a victual pension, said Henry resigned the clerkship to Sir William and the parishioners, the profits of the office to be assigned to "the childer to sing divyne service in the kirk with the prebendar of the said College," Sibbald's son being one of the "childer." Already, by arrangement between Sir William and Henry, the former "hes devoted in past years the profits of the clerkship to certain young childer singers in said college." That seems to indicate that to some extent the plan was in operation; and tradition affirms that certain houses adjacent to the church, possibly those mentioned in 1605 and 1606 as situated on the north and west sides of the churchyard, constituted the residences of the clergy. The pedagogy, described on 31st May 1601 as "the old ruinous house *lie auld scoolhous*," stood on the north side of the churchyard. In charters of 5th March 1528–9 and 30th April 1548, and in a Retour of 20th Jan. 1579, the patronage of the Provostship and the Prebendaries of the College of Strathmiglo is included among the Balweary possessions. It would seem, however, that the project, probably owing to lack of endowments, was not carried to completion. The church, consisting of a nave and choir, stood in the churchyard; and the present church, built in 1787, is situated on the glebe at the east end of the town. St Mary's Chapel, which, with St Mary's Well and attached lands, was at the west end of Gateside, was in all likelihood built by the Abbot of Balmerino for the abbey's tenants and servants. There was a Friarmill in the parish.—[*Rental of Dunkeld*, 9, 198, 208, 239, S.H.S.; *Acts of Lords of Council and Session in Public Affairs*, 257; *Reg. Great Seal*, 27th Feb. 1509-10, 5th March 1528-9, 30th April 1548, 20th March 1606, 14th July 1632; *Retours*, A.87, H.186, ix, 106; *Balmerino and its Abbey*, 156; Millar's *Hist. of Fife*, i, 162; Leighton's *Hist. of Fife*, ii, 184.]

1562 GEORGE LESLIE, on 29th June 1562 he was a member of the Convention of the Kirk; on 28th June 1563 complaint was made against him by the superintendent that he did not execute his summons against some person in Auchtermuchty where he was also min., and that he did not administer the sacraments since December last.—[*Book of the Universal Kirk*, i, 13, 36.]

1563 JOHN MASON, reader 1563.—[*Comps. Gen. Coll. of Thirds.*]

1568 JOHN BALFOUR, reader 1568-70.—[*Comps. Sub Coll. of Thirds, Fife,* etc.]

1572 ROBERT SCOTT, reader, pres. to the vicarage 26th Nov. and 6th Jan. 1572, vac. by the death of Mr Gilbert Seytoun; on 6th March 1572 he made complaint against Mr John Winrame, Superintendent of Fife, for refusing to give him his letters testimonial of the vicarage, and for not admitting him reader conform to the Regent's presentation; the matter was remitted to the Kirk Session of St Andrews, but no further steps are recorded. —[*Reg. Pres. Bene.*, 26th Nov., 6th Jan. 1572; *Book of the Universal Kirk*, i, 264; *Acts and Dec.*, liii, 291, lvii, 206.]

1572 WILLIAM BRAIDFUTT, M.A.; his pres. to vicarage, 26th Jan. 1572-3, was consequent upon the death of Mr Gilbert Seytoun.—[*Reg. Pres. Bene.*]

1580 ROBERT SCOTT, "lang time providit to the Parish Church of Strathmiglo," is presented to what is called "the pettie vicarage," 1st March 1580-1, probably in succession to Mr William Scott who had been presented to "lie petty vicarage" 1st Oct. 1545, vac. by the resignation or demission of Sir Simon Younge; Robert Scott "has been reader in tymes bygane, and the kirk is now provydit with a ministrie"; obviously he is identical with Robert Scott, 1572.—[*Reg. Sec. Seal*, 1st March 1580-1, iii, 1348.]

1588 JAMES BALCANQUALL, pres. to vicarage 3rd Jan. 1591-2, vac. by the deprivation of Robert Scott for treasonable conspiracy against the person of the King.—[*Reg. Sec. Seal.*]

1655 JOHN RIGG, his son, David, apprenticed to Andrew Bruce, merchant, Edinburgh, 1st Aug. 1677.—[*Reg. of Edin. Apprentices.*]

1686 DAVID BARCLAY, adm. before 29th Nov. 1685.

1889 JAMES RANKIN, his widow, Elizabeth Ford, died 9th Jan. 1937; his sons— William Humphry Ford, died 14th Dec. 1926; James, licentiate, assistant, St Bernard's, Edinburgh, died 26th Feb. 1930.

1923 ROBERT FORRESTER VICTOR SCOTT, trans. to St Andrews, Dundee, 26th Jan. 1927.

1927 GEORGE SCANLAN, trans. from Ballingry (*q.v.*) 12th May 1927; died 26th Jan. 1936; his son, William Cunningham, killed in motor-cycle accident 5th April 1928; his daugh., Jean Margaret (marr. 24th Nov. 1933 David Dryborough, M.A., F.F.A.).

PRESBYTERY OF ST ANDREWS

ABERCROMBIE or ST MONANS

The Church of Abercrombie was dedicated by Bishop de Bernham 24th Oct. 1247 to St Mary and St Margaret. Its ruins stand in the grounds of Balcaskie.

The Church of St Monans was originally a chapel in the Parish of Kilconquhar, and is said to have been founded by Sir Alan Durward, probably about the middle part of the 13th century, though possibly an early place or earlier places of worship on the spot had enshrined the relics of St Monan; in or before 1362 it was founded anew by David II, and endowed by him in 1369; about 1473 it was given to the Dominican Friars, and in 1579 it was incorporated with the same Friars of St Andrews; it was burned by the English in 1544; by Act of the Presbytery of St Andrews July 1647, ratified by Act of Parliament June 6th 1649, St Monans was disjoined from Kilconquhar and attached to Abercrombie, St Monans to be the Kirk and Abercrombie to be the name of the parish. Near the church is St Monan's Cave, and about a mile eastward along the shore is a Spring called St Monan's Well. From 1477 to 1519 there was a small priory in existence, and it continued afterwards to be the residence of two friars but was suppressed in 1550. In 1319 William Lamberton, Bishop of St Andrews, granted the church to increase the lighting of the High Altar of the Cathedral.—[*Transactions of Aberdeen Ecclesiological Society*, 1897, 181, 185, 191, 192, 193, which see for full details; *Fifeana*, 224–5; *Acts Scott. Parl.*, vi, (2), 434b; *Reg. Priory of St Andrews*, xxxv.]

1563 JOHN STEVENSON, reader, deprived of office 15th March 1563–4 for fornication, and to give satisfaction to Anstruther Kirk.—[*Reg. Kirk Session of St Andrews*, 189.]

1576 THOMAS YOUNG, reader, with the vicarage, 1567 or 1568, and in 1574.—[*Reg. of Kirk Sess. of St Andrews*, 189.]

1587 JAMES MELVILLE, M.A., pres. to vicarage 8th May and 4th Dec. 1587, vac. by death of Alexander Borthwick.—[*Reg. Sec. Seal.*]

1593 ALEXANDER FORSYTH, his pres. in 1593 was consequent upon the dem. of Mr James Melville.—[*Reg. Sec. Seal.*]

1704 JOHN CRAIGIE, his son, James, apprenticed to Thomas Fenton, merchant, Edinburgh, 2nd Dec. 1724.—[*Reg. of Edin. Apprentices.*]

1882 JOHN TURNBULL, D.D. (St Andrews, 1926); died 30th Sept. 1933.

ANSTRUTHER, EASTER

In 1592 steps were taken towards the planting of a church at East Anstruther. Nothing further resulted till 1639, when the General Assembly, with consent of the bailies and council, disjoined it from Kilrenny. That received effect by Act of Parliament in the same year; and by a further Act of Parliament in 1641 the erection of the separate parish was decreed. The steeple of the church, a Dutch model, was added in 1644. After the erection of the separate charge, a house in Pend Wynd became the manse; by transaction of 1713 it passed to Sir John Anstruther in exchange for Melville's house in 1590, which in 1637 had been acquired from James Melville's grandson, Ephraim, only son of Ephraim Melville, min. of Pittenweem. On the highest window, chiselled in stone, are the words "Watch Tower." There was a

Chapel of St Ayle (Aylus, Agilus), designated in 1632 "the tenement called Sanctcyldus Chapel in East Anstruther."—[*Acts Scott. Parl.*, v, 472, 596b; *East Neuk of Fife*, 361, 362–3, 377; *Retours*, xii, 61.]

1677 EDWARD THOMSON, his son, James, bapt. 23rd Oct. 1673.—[*St Andrews Reg.*]

1717 JAMES NAIRN, had issue—John, born 1707, died 1709; James, born 1709, died 1712; Janet, born 1714, died same year.

1876 THOMAS MURRAY, his widow, Mary Jane Christie, died at Edinburgh 11th Aug. 1927.

1917 THOMAS SMITH, trans. to St. Clement's, Glasgow, 4th Oct. 1928.

1929 GEORGE OGG, formerly Principal of Training Institution of Scottish Universities' Mission, Kalimpong (see Vol. vii, 704); *locum tenens* Tighnabruaich, 1928; adm. 27th Feb. 1929.

ANSTRUTHER, WESTER

The church was dedicated by Bishop de Bernham 28th June 1243, St Nicholas being patron saint. In the Lord High Treasurer's Accounts is: "In Anstruther when the king came on land to the priests of Anstruther to say ane trentale of Masses of St Nicholas XXS," 3rd June 1503. The tower of the church, which has undergone considerable alterations, appears to belong to the 16th century.—[*East Neuk of Fife*, 343; *Lord High Treasurer's Accs.*, ii, 261.]

1563 JOHN FORMAN, M.A., vicar 1563–73; also at Kilrenny.—[*Comps. Sub Coll. of Thirds, Fife*, etc.]

1592 ROBERT DURIE, his pres. to vicarage in 1592 was consequent upon the dem. of William, Commendator of Pittenweem; was at Campvere 14th March 1607.—[*Reg. Sec. Seal*; *Kincardine Sas.*, ii, 233.]

1668 DAVID TAYLOR, his eldest daugh., Isabella (marr. John Fogo, writer, St Andrews).—[*Fife Sas., Warrant*, 107.]

1689 THOMAS AUCHENLECK, min. in Dundee 1704.

1799 JAMES MACDONALD.—[*Scott. Notes and Queries*, Sept. 1933, 27.]

1908 JAMES ALEXANDER PATERSON. Addl. issue—Christian Gordon Cargill, born 16th May 1932.

BOARHILLS

Inchmurthac, on the banks of the Kenly, near the village, was a residence of the Bishops of St Andrews as early as the time of Bishop de Bernham, 1239–53. At the beginning of the 18th century there still remained ruins and the walls of a chapel. The dovecot there, now also in ruins, is said to have been built of stones from the Bishop's "palace." During a year's vacancy in the see after the death of Bishop Lamberton, the revenues were assigned to the Earl of Carrick, afterwards David II, and his countess, Johanna, daugh. of Edward II; and they are said to have resided for a time at Inchmurthac, where King David's second marriage—to Margaret, daugh. of Sir John Logie—took place.—[Sibbald's *Hist. of Fife*, 348; Fleming's *Guide to St Andrews*, 132.]

1903 ROBERT HENRY MACKAY, died 9th April 1935.

CAMERON

The Act of Parliament erecting the parish was passed 24th Feb. 1645, when the church was almost completed. That church was removed in a very ruinous condition and the present church built in 1808.—[*Acts Scott. Parl.*, vi, (1), 332.]

1678 ANDREW FLOCKER, died before 8th May 1719; had issue—Ninian, bapt. 2nd March 1684; Ninian, bapt. 19th Feb. 1685; Cecil, bapt. 20th July 1688 (marr. Robert Lyon, surgeon-apothecary).—[*Fife Sas., Warrant*, 412; *St Andrews Reg.*]

1877 WILLIAM LANG BAXTER, died at Crieff 26th Jan. 1937, Father of the Church. Addl. publication—*Moses or Moffat*.

1924 ANDREW WARREN, formerly Professor of Scottish Church's College, Calcutta (see Vol. vii, 710); adm. C. and S. 4th July 1924; his father was Rev. Thomas W., and his wife's father Rev. Joseph Arthur Lambert; assistant min. Portobello Parish Church, 1921-2; *locum tenens*, Errol Parish Church and St Mark's, Dundee, 1922-4.

CARNBEE

Under the designation Kellyn, the Church of Kellie in this parish was dedicated by Bishop de Bernham 19th June 1243. It was granted to Dunfermline Abbey by Malcolm, 1153-65. Either it was suppressed at a later period, or it was the earlier name of what became Carnbee Church. The existing church was built in 1793.—[*Reg. of Dunfermline*, 24; Sibbald's *Hist. of Fife*, 207.]

1564 WILLIAM SCOTT, M.A., min. 1564, was one of the List of the General Assembly 20th Dec. 1560 for "ministering and teaching."—[*Book of the Univ. Kirk*, 4; *Reg. Kirk Sess. of St Andrews*, 229.]

1565 ANDREW OLIPHANT, son of Walter O.; vicar 1565.—[*Comps. Sub Coll. of Thirds, Fife*; *Reg. Great Seal*, 2nd Jan. 1565-6.]

1567 DAVID SPENS, his pres. to vicarage was consequent upon the death of Mr Andrew Oliphant.—[*Reg. Pres. Bene.*]

1576 THOMAS WOOD, M.A., as min. here his pres. to vicarage in 1576 was consequent upon the death of Mr David Spens; he is not identical with Thomas Wood, St Andrews (*q.v.*).—[*Reg. Pres. Bene.*; *Reg. Kirk Sess. of St Andrews*, 727n.]

1864 THOMAS PETER JOHNSTON, D.D. (St Andrews, 28th June 1929); died, Father of the Church, at Crail 20th Feb. 1932; his daugh., Mary Matthew (Mrs Mackinnon), died at Crail 20th Oct. 1940; his son, Thomas Evans, died 13th Sept. 1945.

1905 GEORGE SPEED THOMSON, died 8th May 1929; his daugh., Isabel May (marr. 3rd Aug. 1938 Edward Mills, M.B., Ch.B.)

CELLARDYKE

1883 JAMES RAY, died at Harrogate 12th June 1933; his son, James Forrest, died 15th May 1930.

CRAIL

The church is virtually the ancient collegiate edifice. It was dedicated by Bishop de Bernham 21st June 1243, probably soon after the earlier nave was almost completely taken down and rebuilt with aisles and the present western tower. After various disputes it was confirmed to the burgh by Act of Parliament in 1633. There was a Chapel of St Maelruba, sometimes designated St Rufus, within the Castle of Crail; and there was also a priory dedicated to the same saint. A ruined gable with a Gothic window stood till 1801, when it was overthrown by the sea, leaving only foundations to mark the priory's site. Near by were the Prior's Croft and the Briery (Priory) Well.—[*East Neuk of Fife*, 414; *Reg. Great Seal*, 31st Aug. 1458, 21st June 1512; *Acts Scott. Parl.*, v, 99.]

1562 THOMAS SKIRLING, reader; was summoned on 20th Jan. 1562-3 for administering baptisms and marraiges without being adm.—[*Reg. Kirk Sess. of St Andrews*, 176.]

1575 THOMAS KINNEAR, M.A., min., pres. to the Provostrie 17th Dec. 1575, vac. by the non-compearance of Mr Patrick Mortoun.—[*Reg. Pres. Bene.*, i, (4), 39.]

1576 PATRICK MORTOUN, M.A., min., pres. to the Provostrie 6th April 1576.—[*Reg. Pres. Bene.*, i, (4), 42.]

1593 DAVID MAXWELL, reader 30th Aug. 1593.—[*Reg. Kirk Sess. of St Andrews*, 757.]

1600 WILLIAM MURRAY.—[*Fife Sas.*, iv, 16, 10th Jan. 1603.]

ALEXANDER EDWARD. Addl. issue
1663 —Alexander.

JOHN REID, his son, John, Calcutta,
1865 died 27th May 1925.

WILLIAM MURRAY MILNE. Addl.
1915 issue—Kathlene Barbara, born 9th Jan. 1925.

DUNINO

On the foundation of the College and Collegiate Church of St Salvator, St Andrews, by Bishop Kennedy in 1451, the Church of Dunino was granted to the same by the founder. The present church was built in 1826.

ROBERT SMYTT, vicar 1560; reader
1568 1568-9, when he appears as witness of the Testament of Alexander Norrie, burgess of St Andrews; Sempill, not Smyt, appears in the early part of the Testament narrative, but it is probably an error for Smyt.—[*Edin. Test.*, i, 257, 24th April 1569.]

JOHN RUTHERFORD, was parson
1578 4th Nov. 1577.—[*Cal. of Charters*, xi, 2456.]

JAMES WOOD, was one of the Com-
1640 mission who brought Charles II from the Continent in 1660; had issue—John, bapt. 16th Feb. 1654; Anna, bapt. 1st Nov. 1652.

ALEXANDER MACDONALD, D.D.
1911 St Andrews, 28th Sept, 1937); died 28th Feb. 1949. Marr. 2nd Sept. 1936 Maud Alexander, eldest daugh. of Joseph Hutchinson Wilson, LL.D., solicitor, Carlisle, and has issue—Alexander William Barlas, born 9th Oct. 1942.

ELIE

The steeple was built by Sir John Anstruther of Anstruther in 1726. On Earlsferry point there was a hospital or hostel to which probably a chapel was attached, founded by Duncan, Earl of Fife, who died in 1154.—[*East Neuk of Fife*, 192.]

ROBERT WEMYSS, only son of James
1649 Wemyss, merchant, St Andrews, and his wife, Euphemia Findlaw (Findlay), and grandson of John Wemyss, merchant, St Andrews, and his wife, Judith Nairne, daugh. of Alexander Nairne; was also of Cuttlehill, Aberdour; died May 1675; his son, William, of Cuttlehill.—[*St And. Tests.*, James Wemyss, 16th July 1627, John Wemyss, 1st April 1615, etc.; *Gen. Reg. Sas.*, xi, 398 (2 Ser.), cvii, 435, 438 (2 Ser.), xii, 18 (1 Ser.); *Retours*, i, 82.]

JOHN ARTHUR, probably identical
1692 with John, born 1675, son of Patrick Arthur of Ballone, surgeon, Wemyss and Elie.—[*East Neuk of Fife*, 202.]

JAMES CHALMERS, his son, John,
1701 apprenticed to James Beveridge, litster, Edinburgh, 8th Feb. 1727.—[*Reg. of Edin. Apprentices.*]

ROBERT HAMILTON DUNLOP,
1887 line 2, for "Baillieston" read "Edinburgh"; died at Edinburgh 16th Sept. 1931; his son, James Weir, died at Toronto 31st Aug. 1941; daugh. (marr. John Irwin Scott, M.A., headmaster, Kettering Grammar School).

DAVID MATHIESON BELL, trans. to
1920 Woodside, Aberdeen, 2nd Oct. 1930, and to Forfar Old Church 4th June 1935. Addl. issue—John Ramsay, born 5th Feb. 1925; Josephine Margaret Elizabeth Anne, born 3rd July 1929; Ruth Allison, born 27th Feb. 1936.

FERRYPORT-ON-CRAIG

The name was formerly Portincraig, Southferrie of Portincraig, and East Ferry of Portincraig. In the Act of Parliament of July 1606, erecting the parish, the church is described as "laitlie biggit." There was an aisle with burial vault underneath, added, it is said, by Sir John Buchanan of Scotscraig. The church was rebuilt in 1825. On the western face of the tower there is built in a lintel on which are two coats of arms, one that of Margaret Hartsyde, and the other that of her husband, Sir John

Buchanan. Manifestly the lintel had belonged to the doorway or a doorway of the former church; and it indicates that the aisle had been built by Sir John, who died before 8th Sept. 1641, and his wife, Margaret Hartsyde, who died June 1642. Also on the tower, below the lintel, are two panels, one with the arms of Sir John Buchanan and Margaret Hartsyde, impaled, and flanked by the date 1644, and the other with the arms of Sir Arthur Erskine of Scotscraig, fourth son of John, Earl of Mar, by his second wife, Marie Stewart, and his wife, Margaret Buchanan, one of the two daughs. and heiresses of Sir John B. and Margaret Hartsyde, impaled, and flanked by the date 164–. On the north gable of the church is a stone with date 1607, also taken from the former church, and probably indicating the year when that church was completed for worship. There was a chapel at Chapeltoun in the barony of Scotscraig, dedicated to St John.—[*Reg. Sec. Seal*, 6th Dec. 1606; *Reg. Pres. Bene.*, 4th Nov. 1609; *Reg. Great Seal*, 25th July 1622, 8th Sept. 1641; *Retours*, xvii, 83–4; *Acts Scott. Parl.*, iv, 302; *Scots Peerage*, v, 621–2; *Reg. Great Seal*, 8th Feb. 1594–7.]

1605 SIMEON DURIE, pres. to vicarage 6th Dec. 1606, vacant by death of Andrew Allan.—[*Reg. Sec. Sig.*, lxxv, 212.]

1666 ROBERT WHITE, issue bapt.—Helen, 3rd Sept. 1669; James, 10th Aug. 1670; Robert, 14th Sept. 1671; Charles, 30th March 1680; Elizabeth, 29th Nov. 1684. Addl. issue—William, bapt. 3rd April 1676.—[*Ferryport-on-Craig Reg.*]

1697 PATRICK TULLIDELPH, his daughs. bapt.—Elizabeth, 21st May 1699; Helen, 4th May 1703. Addl. issue bapt.—William, 26th May 1700; John, 3rd Feb. 1706; Patrick, 8th Feb. 1708.—[*Ferryport-on-Craig Reg.*]

1716 WILLIAM VILANT. Issue bapt.—Christina, 13th May 1718; Jessabil, 13th Sept. 1724; Ann, 7th Aug. 1726; Walter, 23rd March 1729; Eupham, 29th Dec. 1732; Bethia, 13th April 1734.—[*Ferryport-on-Craig Reg.*]

1739 WILLIAM DALGLEISH, his daugh. buried at Linlithgow 17th Oct. 1773.

1820 WILLIAM DALGLEISH SWAN, marr. Susannah, younger daugh. of William Gordon of Woodhaven, Dundee, and Blelack, Aberdeenshire, and his wife, Barbara Stark, daugh. and co-heiress of William Syme of Dundee and Woodhaven, Fife, but had no issue.—[Michie's *Logie Coldstone and Braes of Cromar*, 164.]

1855 DAVID ROSE, his widow, Elena Cameron, died at Haddington 29th Oct. 1925.

1879 CHRISTOPHER HALLIDAY, his widow, Freda Paxton Martin, died 8th Aug. 1945; his daugh., Sybil Mary Freda (marr. 24th April 1940 James Henry Brownlee, M.B., Ch.B.]

1923 JOHN MACLAINE MUNRO, adm. 29th June 1923; trans. to Strathbungo 16th Nov. 1926.

1927 CHARLES WALKER STOBIE, trans. from Forgue 27th April 1927.

FORGAN

The parish was also called St Fillan, and, once, Adhenachthen. About 1150 David I granted the church, with a full mensal toft, to the Priory of St Andrews. That was confirmed by charter of Malcolm IV, who added half a caracute of land, called Chingothe. In the concluding part of the 12th century Alan de Lascelles, patron of the church, son of Alan de Lascelles and Julian Somerville, in accordance with his own desire and that of Amable, his wife, granted to the priory, the mother church of his land of Adhenachthen, namely the Church of Forgun, along with the Chapel of Adhenachthen, and a caracute of land, both adjoining the church. Adhenachthen, is now Naughton. The patron saint was St Fillan, but St Andrew was substituted before 1154–9. The ruins of the old church are situated in the churchyard at Kirkton. Besides the Chapel of Adhenachthen, there was a Chapel of St Thomas at "Sea-Mylns of Innerdovat." Nine Wells in the east part of the parish may indicate that there was a chapel dedicated to the Nine Maidens.—[*Reg. Priory of St Andrews*, 51, 107-8, 187, 198-9, 205, 274; *Reg. Great Seal*, 26th March 1618, 31st July 1637; *Reg. Pres. Bene.*, i, (4), 10.]

1571 JOHN SMYT, reader Feb. 1571 and 24th July 1573.—[*Edin. Tests.*, ii, 322.]

1573 DAVID METHVEN, vicar; dem. or dep. before 12th Sept. 1573.—[*Reg. Pres. Bene.*, i, 96.]

1573 ANDREW BENNET, reader; pres. to vicarage 12th Sept. 1573, vac. by removal of Mr David Masson.—[*Reg. Pres. Bene.*, i, 96, (4), 10.]

1589 WILLIAM BALFOUR, M.A., pres. to vicarage 21st May 1589, vac. by the demission of Mr James Tullis.—[*Reg. Sec. Seal*, 21st May 1589.]

1590 ROBERT BUCHANAN, M.A., pres. to vicarage 25th Sept. 1590, vac. by the demission of Mr James Tullis.—[*Reg. Sec. Seal*, xli, 38.]

1599 WILLIAM MARCHE, his presentation 28th June 1598 was consequent upon the deprivation of Mr Robert Buchanan.—[*Reg. Sec. Seal*, 28th June, 1598.]

1674 WILLIAM SCOTT, marr. Susanna Gratwick, who survived him.

1718 JAMES RUSSELL. Addl. issue—Patrick, bapt. 10th Dec. 1727.

1836 CHARLES NAIRN, his son, Boswell Laird, ship and insurance broker, Dundee, died 28th April 1942.

1891 THOMAS MUNN, died suddenly on Craigmillar Golf Course 31st Oct. 1934. Line 12, for "Ayr" read "Glasgow"; his mother-in-law was Jessie Lewars Kissock; his widow, Jessie Lewars Findlay, died 13th Jan. 1948.

1921 HUGH FULTON FRAME, trans. to Lesmahagow 17th Jan. 1942. Issue —Marjorie, born 8th April 1921; Hugh Forgan, born 28th May 1925; Robert Laird, born 24th April 1930. Publications—*Wonderful Counsellor*; *The Ivory Idol*; *Salvage*; *Roll on, Wagon Wheels*.

KEMBACK

The church was dedicated by Bishop de Bernham 6th Sept. 1244. Its ruins are situated in the churchyard a short distance south-west of the present church, which was opened for worship in May 1814. The lintelled entrance doorway near the west end of the south wall of the old church has the date 1582. On the foundation of the College and Collegiate Church of St Salvator, St Andrews, by Bishop Kennedy in 1451, the Church of Kemback was granted to the same by the founder.

1730 ROBERT MELDRUM, bapt. 4th Aug. 1688, son of Robert M., tenant of Balmullo, and Janet Shepherd. Marr. Anne, sister of John McCormack, min. of St Andrews, with issue—Anne.—[*Fife Sheriff Court Books*, 24th Feb. 1723.]

1888 JOHN HENRY, his son, Robert Alexander, M.B., Ch.B., died at Nelson, Lancashire, 15th May 1932; his widow, Patricia Barty Barran Gloak, died 30th March 1938.

1911 JOHN MIDDLETON, son of James M., engineer, Greenock.

1918 RODERICK JOHN FRASER MACDONALD, died 5th Aug. 1932. Marr. 3rd July 1929 Isabella Richardson C., M.A.(Hons.), St Andrews, daugh. of Benjamin C. Calcott, Montrose, and Catherine C. Phimister.

KILCONQUHAR

The church was dedicated by Bishop de Bernham 12th July 1243. St Monan has been suggested as having been the patron saint, also St Concad, an obscure Irish saint, and likewise the Irish St Chonchobar, Conquhar or Connacher, pronounced Conneuchar. In 1499 Patrick Dunbar, lord of Kilconquhar, founded in the church an altar of "Our Ladie of Pitie" (Pity) for the souls of himself, Christian Home, his mother, Janet Dunbar, evidently his grandmother, and Isabella Dishington, his wife. By Act of Parliament, 1597, Kilconquhar was dissolved from North Berwick and made a separate rectory. Of the old church only a part of a nave arcade is now visible. The existing church was built in 1820–1. In a field at Rires stood the Chapel of "Our Lady of Rires," or "the Chapel of Marie, Rires." On 1st Sept. 1404 John Wemyss, Kt., Lord of Rires, endowed the chapel with various lands and annual rents from his barony of Leuchars and his lands of Rires, and extensive pasture privileges, for the souls of Robert III, Queen Annabella, etc. Rires is now part of Elie parish. There is a roofless Renaissance Chapel within the grounds of Balcarres House.—[Mackinlay's *Ancient Church Dedications* (nonscript.), 493; *East Neuk of Fife*, 118, 155, 162; Johnstone's *Place Names*, 217; *Acts Scott. Parl.*, iv, 137; *Wemyss Bk.*, ii, 266; *Report Ancient Monuments Commission, Fife*, 163.]

1564 JOHN HAMILTON, M.A., vicar 1564. —[*Comps. Sub Coll. of Thirds, Fife*, etc.]

1567 GEORGE LESLIE, his pres. to the vicarage in 1568 was consequent upon the deprivation of Mr John Hamilton, convicted of treason by Parliament; trans. to Mortlach 30th Sept. 1573. —[*Reg. Pres. Bene.*]

1574 WILLIAM BELLENDEN, youngest son of Sir John B. of Kilconquhar; reader 1571; pres. to vicarage 30th Sept. 1573; still in office 1587, and in 1606 designated vicar of William Scott of Elie. Marr. Anabel Pearson, with issue, at least Thomas, who in 1625 marr. Euphemia, daugh. of Stephen Duddingston of Sandford.—[*Reg. Pres. Bene.*; *East Neuk of Fife*, 155–6, 165; *Fifeiana*, 295.]

1646 DAVID FORRET, marr. 30th Jan. 1645 Elizabeth, daugh. of Ebenezer Borthwick, St Andrews.

1735 THOMAS AYTON, had issue—Janet, bapt. 6th Aug. 1726.

1866 WALTER IRVING, his widow, May Julia Kay, died 31st May 1926.

KILRENNY

The church was dedicated by Bishop de Bernham 26th June 1243. It has been suggested that the patron saint is St Ethernanus, Ethernan, Ernan, uncle of St Columba, and St Ringan. St Ninian also finds favour. A third suggestion is St Irenaeus of Lyons. Land near the church bore the name Rinniehill, Irniehill; there is said to have been a St Irnie's Well, and the church tower was called St Irny by the fishermen, who used it as a landmark. Further, a tradition exists or existed "that the devotees at Anstruther, who could not see the Church of Kilrenny till they travelled up the rising ground to what they called 'the hill,' when they pulled off their bonnets, fell on their knees, crossed themselves and prayed to St Irnie." Prof. W. J. Watson, however, considers that St Irnie is fictitious, and that what we have to do with is *irnaide, urnaidhe*, middle Gaelic form of mod. G. *urnuigh*, meaning (1) Prayer; (2) Oratory; the name, therefore, would arise from the ancient oratory, and Irniehill would likely be designated of old *Cnoc Irnaidhe*, "the hill of prayer" or "the hill of the oratory," mod. G. *Cnoc na k-Urnuighe*. All that remains of the old church is the tower, probably early 15th century, at the north-west angle of the present church, which was built 1806–8. The old church had a nave and two aisles. —[Watson's *Celtic Place Names*, 519–20; *East Neuk of Fife*, 222.]

1563 WILLIAM CLERK, min. at Anstruther, Abercrombie, Pittenweem, had also charge here.—[*Comps. Sub Coll. of Thirds, Fife*, etc.]

1563 ANDREW KEMP, reader 1563.— [*Comps. Sub Coll. of Thirds, Fife*, etc.]

1563 JOHN FORMAN, M.A., vicar 1563–72, and also at Anstruther; may have held the vicarage as exhorter or as reader.—[*Comps. Sub Coll. of Thirds, Fife*, etc.]

1564 ALEXANDER SPENS, M.A., min. 1564.—[*Comps. Sub Coll. of Thirds, Fife*, etc.]

1567 WILLIAM CLERK, min. of West Anstruther, in charge here.

1574 JOHN ANSTRUTHER, son of John A. of that ilk 1516-47; his presentation on 17th Feb. 1579 was consequent upon the demission of Mr John Forman; still held office 20th Oct. 1591, probably as exhorter or as reader. Marr. *cir.* 1570 Jean Lindsay, widow of John Melville of Carnbee and Granton, and daugh. of Lord Lindsay of the Byres, probably John, fifth Lord Lindsay.—[*Reg. Pres. Bene.*, 17th Feb. 1579; *East Neuk of Fife*, 331, 354-5; *Writs of Pittenweem Priory.*]

1835 GEORGE DICKSON, his daugh., Janet, died 21st June 1926.

1875 GEORGE STRANG ANDERSON, died 16th Nov. 1925.

1925 JOHN MARSHALL PRYDE, formerly of St Modan's, Falkirk (*q.v.*); trans. from Ruthrieston, Aberdeen, 29th May 1925; Chaplain to the Forces at Salonika in the Great War; dem. 8th Oct. 1947; his son, George, Squadron Leader, R.A.F., killed in action 18th June 1940; his daughs.—Helen (marr. 4th Sept. 1935 James Robert Grant); Jean (marr. 4th April 1938 William Crew, Rossie Mills, Montrose). Addl. issue—John Marshall, born 22nd March 1915; William Symington, born 21st Jan. 1917, Flying Officer, R.A.F., killed by aircraft accident 24th Sept. 1939; David Douglas, born 17th April 1918, D.F.C., Flying Officer, killed June 1942. Publications—*Livingstone and the Slave Trade* (gained the Livingstone Gold Medal) (Oppenheim and Longman, Glasgow, 1920); "Joseph Mazzini," Lecture, in *Britannia* magazine (Brett, 1905); various articles in magazines.

KINGSBARNS

The church was built in 1631, and enlarged, apparently to the extent of being in most part rebuilt, in 1811. The lower portion of the bell tower is of the 17th century. There was a chapel at Chesterhill.—[*Report, Royal Commission on Ancient Monuments, Fife*, 176, 178.]

1663 GEORGE PATULLO, his son, George, was of Balhouffie.—[Macfarlane's *Gen. Collections*, ii, 168; *East Neuk of Fife*, 338-9.]

1678 GILBERT SIMSON, his son, William, apprenticed to Charles Duncan, goldsmith, Edinburgh, 25th March 1713; he had also a daugh., Jean, bapt. 15th Dec. 1690.—[*Reg. of Edin. Apprentices*; *Parish Reg.*]

1869 ALEXANDER TODD, died 24th Dec. 1932; his son, Rear-Admiral George James T. of Burncrook, Moffat, D.S.O., died at Edinburgh 7th March 1927, having distinguished himself in Naval operations in the Near East, and in 1916 received authority from King Victor Emmanual to wear the insignia of a Commander of the Crown of Italy.

1926 DOUGLAS GEORGE BISSET, born 18th April 1900 at Oyne, son of Peter Smith B., min. of Oyne and then of Craig; educ. at Montrose Academy and Edinburgh Univ., M.A. (1921); lic. by Presb. of Brechin 6th May 1924; assistant, East Church, Stirling, 1924-6; ord. C. and S. to Dr Todd, 4th June 1926. Marr. 27th Aug. 1930 Helen, daugh. of Robert Geddes, Bithnie, Alford, with issue—Elizabeth Margaret, born 16th Jan. 1932; Peter Douglas Geddes, born 6th June 1934; Sheila May, born 22nd May 1939.

LARGO

The church was dedicated by Bishop de Bernham 17th July 1243. It appears to have been rebuilt in the early part of the 17th century, for the chancel and the tower now existing belong to that period, and bear respectively the dates 1623 and 1628. A further rebuilding scheme was carried out in 1817, "and in 1826, there was taken into the new building an aisle belonging to the old, by which the spire is supported, bearing date 1623." That evidently refers to the chancel. The "Chaplainries of Strathairlie in the barony of Lundie" are mentioned, without any details, in 1600, and "Sanct Androc's landis" in Lundie in 1593. In the church was an altar, dedicated to St John the Baptist and St John the Evangelist, founded in Nov. 1510 by Sir John Lundin of Lundin in the new aisle built by him on to the church, the endowment including the Temple Lands of Balcormo, the Temple Lands on the south side of Lundin Orchard, and a Rig of Temple Lands in the Persflat of Lundin.—[*Retours*, ii, 34; *Reg. Great Seal*, iii, 78, 6th April 1593.]

1550 ALEXANDER WOOD, M.A., second son of Sir Andrew Wood of Largo, of Naval fame, and his wife, Elizabeth Lundin; was vicar in 1550; dem. in 1576, and died in 1592; was also vicar-pensionary of North Berwick. Marr. Elizabeth Creichton, widow of William Dishington, friar of Ardross, who was killed at the Battle of Pinkie; his natural daugh., Alison, marr. Alexander Carrick, burgess of North Berwick, brother of Thomas C., burgess of the same—contract 10th May 1559; in 1550 he and Margaret Home, prioress of North Berwick, were replegiated by the official of St Andrews "to underly the law for waylaying and murderously assaulting Alexander Oliphant of Kellie," that is, taken out of the hands of the criminal authorities under pledge that they would be tried by the ecclesiastical courts, on the ground that they were ecclesiastics. The quarrel evidently concerned the lands of Grange, which Alexander Wood acquired from the nuns of North Berwick in 1560.—[*East Neuk of Fife*, 72, 183, 184, 215, 238, 259; *Reg. Great Seal*, 24th April and 31st May 1565; *Reg. Pres. Bene.*, i, (4), 41; *Carte Monialuni de Northbervie*, 75.]

1576 JAMES WOOD, was of Coulston; was reader in 1568, and as such was pres. to vicarage 1st April 1576, in succession to Mr Alexander Wood.—[*Comps. Sub Coll. of Thirds, Fife*, etc.; *Reg. Pres. Bene.*, i, (4), 41.]

1588 ANDREW MONCRIEFF, min. at Kilconquhar; had also charge here, 1588.—[*Comps. Gen. Coll. of Thirds.*]

1665 JOHN AUCHENLECK, had issue—Mr Thomas, Mr James; Grizel (2); Barbara (3), Janet.—[*Deeds, Mack*, 1704, Nos. 580, 1446.]

1904 DUNCAN MACMICHAEL, died 29th Nov. 1943; his wife, Mary Elizabeth Wishart, died 14th April 1934; his son, Neil, M.B., Ch.B.

LARGOWARD

The church was opened for worship in Sept. 1835.

1916 GEORGE WHITE, dem. 31st Oct. 1948.

LEUCHARS

The church was dedicated by Bishop de Bernham 4th Sept. 1244. In modern times the site of the Chapel of St Bonoc was occupied by the parish school. There was a well of the same name. Our Lady Well was on the north-east side of the village. According to tradition there was a chapel on the east side of the road opposite Ardit House; and there were at East Dron a chapel and burying ground. Sir Thomas Wemyss was chaplain of the chaplainry of St Bonit (Bonoc) 3rd May 1586.—[*Reg. Sec. Seal.*]

1566 SIR ROBERT OGILVY, vicar 30th April 1566; was in office 29th April 1548; died before 25th Feb. 1576-7. —[*Reg. Great Seal*, iv, 220; *Reg. Pres. Bene.*, 25th Feb. 1576-7.]

1576 ROBERT ARTHUR, reader here, pres. to vicarage 25th Feb. 1576-7, vac. by death of Mr Robert Ogilvy.—[*Reg. Pres. Bene.*]

1568 ANDREW ALLANE, M.A., pres. to vicarage 20th Dec. 1586 in sucession to Robert Arthur; still in office 8th July 1600.—[*Reg. Sec. Seal*, liv, 161; *Reg. Kirk Sess. of St Andrews*, 940.]

1587 DAVID INGLIS, M.A., pres. to vicarage 26th May 1587, vac. by deprivation of Robert Arthur by the Provincial Assembly for certain offences and crimes.—[*Reg. Sec. Seal.*]

1684 ROBERT LUNDIE, deprived 21st Aug. 1689; his son, Charles, apprenticed to James Peacock, periwig-maker, Edinburgh, 24th Oct. 1705.—[*Reg. of Edin. Apprentices.*]

1706 JAMES ROBERTSON, his daugh., Jean, died at Edinburgh 9th June 1794.

1907 WILLIAM LARNACH TENNYSON LEVACK, his son, John Grant, M.A., B.D., ord. to Dornoch 12th March 1936, and marr. Oct. 29th 1936 Jessie Fairley, daugh. of Walter M. Paterson, min. of West Church, Garelochhead.

1924 WILLIAM BORTHWICK, trans. from Huntly (*q.v.*) and adm. 9th April 1924; his daughs.—Margaret Janet (marr. 27th Dec. 1939 Alistair Gilbert Steven Rae, M.A., min. of Craigmillar Castle Church, Edinburgh, son of late Alexander Steven Rae, Southampton, and Charlotte Crowe); Elizabeth died 26th July 1922.

NEWBURN

The church was dedicated by Bishop de Bernham 15th July 1243. It was rebuilt by James Beaton, Archbishop of St Andrews 1522–39, and its ruins stand at the south side of the road near Little Dumbarnie. The existing church was built in 1815. At Balchristie there was a Chapel of the Culdees belonging to Serf's Priory, Lochleven. The town of Balchristie was given to Serf's Priory by King Malcolm and Queen Margaret 1070–93. Old foundations dug up in the last decade of the 18th century by the proprietor of Balchristie near the west wall of his garden may have been those of the chapel. In the *New Statistical Account* Rev. Dr Laurie states that the ancient name of the parish was Drumaldry, and that Newburn was subsequently adopted; and in a bequest by John Wood of Orkie in 1659 for a free grammar school within the parish, and the maintenance of several poor scholars, the designation is "the parish of Drumalry *alias* Newburn." The name Newburn, however, is found applied to both the parish and the church in the 12th century and the 13th; and at subsequent dates up to the Reformation, and thereafter to the present time, whereas Drumaldry is applied to lands in "the parish of Newburn." In or shortly before the closing year of his reign (1153) David I granted the town of Nithbren with its appendages to Dunfermline Abbey. This was confirmed by Bull of Pope Alexander III on 5th June 1163, and Bull of Pope Lucius on 28th April 1182, each of which included not merely the town but also the Church of Nithbren. It would appear, therefore, that the church was built between the date of David I's charter and 1163, or it may have been in existence at an earlier period and have been granted to the Abbey by an unrecorded charter prior to 1163. It was rebuilt by James Beaton, Archbishop of St Andrews 1524–39.—[*Reg. Great Seal*, iv, 1469, 1477, 1608; *Reg. of Dunf.*, 8, 33, 52, 55–7, 59, 63, 154, 156, 387, 428; *Reg. of Arbroath*, *Vetus*, 234; Macfarlane's *Gen. Coll.*, i, 6; *Reg. Priory of St Andrews*, 115.]

1574 DAVID BAXTER, reader, 5th Aug. 1574.—[*Book of Assumptions.*]

1787 JAMES MITCHELL, son of James M. in Burrance.

1880 GEORGE GEEKIE, his widow, Anna Mary McEwan, died 18th April 1947; his daughs.—Margaret Mann, died at Leven 23rd Jan. 1926; Janet Crawford Anderson, died at Wakefield 26th Aug. 1941.

1914 WILLIAM NEIL, dem. 15th May 1943.

NEWPORT, ST THOMAS

1920 DONALD MACGREGOR GRANT, trans. to Rhu 16th Oct. 1924.

JOHN SIMPSON MUTCH, trans. from Arbuthnott (*q.v.*) 18th May 1925. Issue—Margaret Helen, born 6th March 1923; a daugh., born and died 15th Oct. 1926; Alexander James, born 28th March 1929.

1925

PITTENWEEM

Up to 1588 no church existed; but some kind of place of worship had been secured, for in 1588 William Scott of Abbotshall, in giving the community a grant of the west portion of the priory buildings, to provide a "decent, honest, and comely kirk," set forth that "the house which they have coft, ordered, and plenished at their great expense, and which presently serves them for a kirk, cannot conveniently be enlarged, having rather the form of a private house than of a kirk." The church, however, was ultimately built on the north side of the priory settlement, near the site of the Priory Church. The tower of 1588 still remains, but the rest of the church is virtually modern, having been completely restored. The Well of Mary Magdalene was near the churchyard, and that might indicate that to her the priory was dedicated. At the north-west corner of the priory buildings stood the Lady Chapel. Hence the names of *Mary Gate* and *Lady Wynd*.

By deed of gift of 30th June 1589, which bears that the church had lately been erected into a parish church, King James VI granted to Mr Nicol Dalgleish, min. of the church, and his successors in office certain quantities of victual and salt; and by signature under his hand (16th Aug. 1611) the same monarch "ratified and approved the erection of the said Kirk into ane paroche kirk and sua ratified in the preceding Parliament." But by the negligence of those entrusted with the management of the town's affairs the said Act of Erection was amissing, and "be the lyk slaknes of thes quha wer imployit thairine" the said signature "was never prosecute nor exped." Accordingly by Act of 28th June 1633 Parliament anew erected and reconstituted the said church into a parish church, and dissolved from West Anstruther parish the Burgh of Pittenweem between Anstruther West on the east, the lands of St Monans and Abercromby on the west, and the lands of Balcaskie and Grangemuir on the north, except 80 acres of the feuars of Anstruther and Myltoune be east of the march stones in the parish of West Anstruther. At the same time Parliament ratified a bond of security by Alexander, Lord Fenton, to the Bailies and Council of Pittenweem for 400 and 500 merks Scots respective out of the parsonage and vicarage of the Lordship of Pittenweem of date 6th June 1632, and also a contract of 12th July 1632 between the Bailies and Council of Pittenweem and the min., Rev. John Melville, by which they provided him and his successors in office a yearly duty of 120 merks Scots from the maills, customs, and common good of the Burgh.—[*Acts Scott. Parl.*, v, 142; *East Neuk of Fife*, 301, 302, 303, 304; *Rep. Royal Commission on Ancient Monuments, Fife*, 224; *Reg. Mag. Sig.*, 21st and 24th May 1593, 3rd Aug. 1592.]

WILLIAM CLERK, min. at Abercrombie, Anstruther, Kilrenny, also in charge here at his death in 1583 and almost certainly a good many years prior thereto.—[*East Neuk of Fife*, 300.]

1583

ROBERT WOOD, min. Anstruther, had also charge here 1583–6.—[*East Neuk of Fife*, 301.]

1583

JAMES MELVILLE, min. Anstruther; min. here also 1586–9.—[*East Neuk of Fife*, 301.]

1586

NICOL DALGLEISH, on his admission in 1589, by letters of provision issued by James VI, there was settled on him and his successors in office a yearly stipend out of the funds of the priory and the old assumption of the third thereof, in part money, in part victual, ultimately converted into a money payment of £300 Scots.—[*East Neuk of Fife*, 301; *Reg. of Inhibitions*, i, 18.]

1589

EPHRAIM MELVILLE, his daugh., Christian (marr. William Lamb, Skipper in Kirkcaldy).

1617

JAMES NAIRNE, his son, John, R.N., fought under Nelson at the Battle of Copenhagen, and was the father of Rev. Spencer Nairne, rector of Lutton in Herefordshire, who, by his wife, a daugh. of Lord Curriehill, Scottish Lord of Session, had — Rev. Alexander Nairne, D.D. (St Andrews), Regius Prof. of Divinity at Cambridge Univ., and Canon of St George's Chapel, Windsor.

JAMES GRAHAM GOODALL, died at Edinburgh 24th Oct. 1931.

1776

1893

ST ANDREWS

The following seven churches are said to have existed in St Andrews at an early date —St Regulus, St Aneglas the Deacon, St Michael the Archangel, St Mary the Virgin, St Damianus, St Brigid the Virgin, St Muren the Virgin.

The College of St Salvator and the Collegiate Church of St Salvator, one and the same foundation, was founded by James Kennedy, Bishop of St Andrews, confirmation being granted by Pope Nicholas V on 5th Feb. 1451-2. The foundation was for thirteen persons "after the number of Apostles," the first of whom was to be the Provost and S.T.M., the second to be a Licentiate of Theology by examination, the third to be a completed Bachelor of Theology, four of the rest to be M.A. and priests, and the remaining six to be poor clerks. To the foundation were granted the Churches of Kilmany, Cults, Kemback and Dunino, all prebends. Cults was assigned to the Provost and Kemback to the Licentiate. By Bull of 4th April 1458 Pope Pius II confirmed the reformation of the statutes and foundation anew of the college and church by Bishop Kennedy; and on 4th Dec. 1460 the same Pope granted indulgence to all visiting and contributing for the completion of the buildings and ornaments of the church and its fortification, "that it may be safe from the attack of its enemies." The foundation was then described as for thirteen masters, scholars studying theology, and certain chaplains. Other prebends included Balbithie and Pitmilly for one chaplain; "the parsonage called of old Chalmoure's Chaplainry," being the rectory of Kinnell Church; the vicarage of the Church of Cranston, and the lands of Balgonar, Saline, for two Chaplains, granted by the King as tutor of his brother, the Earl of Mar, on 28th April 1464, and confirmed by Crown Charter on the following day. Altars in the church were—St Mary, probably the Virgin; Holy Spirit; St Olave the Martyr; St Olave and St John the Baptist; St Catherine in St Catherine's Aisle; St John; and St Michael, at which on 10th April 1528 Gavin Dunbar, Bishop of Aberdeen, in accordance with the last will and testament of Edward Stewart, Bishop of Orkney, founded in honour of the Holy Trinity, the Virgin Mary, St Michael, and All Saints, three perpetual chaplains for the souls of the said Bishop Edward and of John, Bishop of Orkney. On 28th Jan. 1475-6 James III confirmed a charter of John Thom, Rector of Inverarity, founding two chaplainries in the church in honour of the Holy Trinity and St John the Evangelist. In a Templar writ of 10th July 1547 mention is made of a chaplainry of St John and St Coill in St Salvator's. Coill appears to be a mutilated form of the name of a saint. St Salvator's was burned in 1546 by Norman Leslie and his accomplices.

There was a chapel dedicated to St Anne, with houses, enclosure, well and garden, situated in the North Street. The Chapel of "Sanct Gormos," whose chaplain, Sir John Stephen, was summoned by the superintendents on 25th Oct. 1564 for ministering the Sacraments, and solemnising marriages in "Papisticall fashion," may be the Chapel of St Cormac.

ST ANDREWS

FIRST CHARGE

The Kirk-heugh may have been the site of the monastery founded by St Cainnech, a friend of St Columba, in the latter part of the 4th century; and of that monastery, it is said, Tuathalan, who died in 747, was

Abbot. Skene's statement is that St Cainnech appears to have founded a *Recles* or monastery at a place in East Fife called Rig-Monadh or Royal Mount, which afterwards became celebrated as the site where the Church of St Andrews was built, and as giving to that church its Gaelic name of Kilrimont. Professor Watson regards *Recles* as a "cell" or "oratory," and holds the view that the interpretation is that in Cell Rigmonaid, i.e. in the Church of St Andrews, there was an oratory or chapel named in honour of St Cainnach. The Blackfriars' monastery in South Street was founded by Bishop Wishart 1272-9. Permission to build the aisle, which still exists, was given by Archbishop James Beaton in 1529. The body of Cardinal Beaton, brought from the Bottle Dungeon in the Castle, was interred in the monastery. To the monastery there was annexed, apparently in the first half of the 16th century, a hospital for "brethren" or "brothers" (monks, friars, priests) afflicted with leprosy. Situated near St Andrews, on the shore of the East Sands, the hospital was in existence in the second half of the 12th century, and was dedicated to St Nicholas. Following the annexation, James V, on 22nd April 1540, granted to the monastery a confirmation charter of the endowments of the hospital—the right to have a wagon for fuel from the king's moss at Crail for the use of the house, granted by King William the Lion; two bovates of land in Polagwin, with pasture of 20 animals (cattle, sheep) and 6 horses, granted by Hugh Gifford about 1178; land of Putekin, granted before 1188 by Roger, Bishop-Elect of St Andrews; relief of rights and services due to the king in respect of a ploughgate of land which the hospital held, granted by Alexander II, 1214-49; a toft and croft in Lundin, which John Melville had held, an acre of land on the west side of Gamell hill, and common pasture for 40 sheep, 6 oxen, and 3 horses and a sow with six porklings, granted, probably about 1220, by Thomas de Lundin, grandson of Philip de Lundin, and probably son of Walter de Lundin who succeeded his father, Philip. The Convents of St Monance and Cupar were also annexed to the monastery. In 1546 the church of the monastery was burned by Norman Leslie, Friar of Rothes, and his "accomplices," of whom the following are given as escheated in 1547— Mr Andrew Whitelaw, parson of Aberdour (Aberdeenshire), who died in the latter year; John Leslie; Mr Henry Balnavis of Halhill and his wife, Christina Scheves; James Kirkcaldy of Grange; John Kirkcaldy of Firthfield; Peter Carmichael of Balmedie; and John Carmichael, his brother. They had joined Leslie both in his deeds at the Castle, and also "in burning Sanct Salvatoris College, and the Blak and Gray Freris Kirkis," variations with regard to the kirkis being "burning and destruction of the Kirkis of the Gray and Blak Friaris," and the "destruction and douncasting of the Blak and Gray Friaris." According to Father Hay, the Greyfriars' monastery was founded by Bishop Kennedy of St Andrews in 1458; and on 21st Dec. 1479 James III confirmed to the friars the site of the place pertaining to them, and the ground and lands lying there, given by Bishop Kennedy and his successor, Bishop Graham. As already stated, the church of the monastery was burned in 1546. The well of the settlement is at No. 4 Greyfriars Gardens. It may be noted that on 29th March 1466 Pope Paul II gave a mandate to the official of St Andrews to the following effect: "The recent petition of the vicar and friars of the Order of Friars Minor of Scotland contained that the late Henry, Bishop of St Andrews, granted to them the place of Bertheon in the diocese of St Andrews, after which the said friars had a house with a Church and other necessary offices built in the said place, and have therein more than 40 years served the Most High. At their petition to the Pope to confirm the said grant, and to grant that they may receive the said house anew, and to absolve from excommunication those of them who received it without papal licence, and have inhabited it, etc., the Pope hereby orders the above official to absolve all those friars who received the said house, and also those who have inhabited it, as above, enjoining a salutary penance, etc.; dispense them on account of irregularity contracted, if any, and rehabilitate them, and, moreover, if they find that the said grant was lawful, to approve and confirm it and its consequences by papal authority. In the event of such approbation and confirmation the Pope grants to the said vicar and friars indult to receive the said house anew for their use (and) habitation." Obviously the mandate imparts fresh information about one of the Greyfriars' settlements in the Diocese of St Andrews; but the description of the locality of that settlement does not suffice for identification.

The Hospital of St Andrews for poor pilgrims was a Culdee institution, and, passing to the Bishopric, it was granted to the Priory of St Andrews by Bishop Robert in his foundation charter of the priory in 1144. The endowments of the hospital included a ploughgate of land in Chatalach or Cathelai, granted by Simon, son of Michael, and confirmed by Simon's son, Alan, and Kings Malcolm IV and William the Lion; lands of Kenlakin, one portion of what belonged to the Altars of St Andrews, and a half of the Bishop's cane (customs or rents paid in kind) of the Parish Church of the Holy Trinity, and a whole tenth of the Bishop's cane from Bladebolg, granted by David I; the right for the cattle of the hospital to have commonty in the pasture of the prior and convent, granted by Malcolm IV; the lands of Petmulin which Malisius held, and land at Crail which was occupied by Radulf of Aluerbas, granted by Countess Ada, mother of Malcolm IV and William the Lion; and the lands of Upper and Lower Kinlochquay or Kinnochy. In 1158–9 the "New Hospital" is mentioned in a charter of Bishop Arnold; and in a confirmation charter of King William the Lion in 1165–70 both the hospital and the "New Hospital" occur. In the time of Bishop de Bernham, 1239–53, there appears the Hospital of St Leonard which with its dependent "grange of Kellakin" is also included among the possessions of the priory in a Bull granted to the priory in 1243–54 by Pope Innocent IV. There are indications that the "New Hospital" and St Leonard's Hospital were identical. In any case the Hospital of St Andrews came to be associated with St Leonard. As time passed, pilgrims ceased to frequent the hospital, which in consequence was converted into a residence for aged women. These, however, proved disappointing in that they displayed little or nothing of good fruits in life and conduct, and on 15th Feb. 1512–13 Prior John Hepburn and Archbishop Alexander Stewart joined the hospital and its lands, teinds, and annual rents to the Church of St Leonard, and converted the hospital and church, "newly built in a proper manner at the expense of the Church of St Andrews," into a college to be named "The College of the Poor Clerks of the Church of St Andrews"—St Leonard's College. In a charter of Simon, son of Simon of Kyner, in or before 1250, there is mentioned land at St Andrews called the "acre of the brothers of St Lazarus." That may indicate a house of that name at St Andrews; but there is no information on the matter.

In Theiner's *Vetera Monumenta*, the Register of the Priory of St Andrews, and Balfour's *Collection of Charters*, there are various writs which throw light upon the struggle between the provost and canons of St Mary's Church of the Kirkheugh and the Prior and Convent of St Andrews, which ended about the beginning of the 14th century in the subjugation of St Mary's to the contention of the prior and convent that in the direction and management of St Mary's they had the precedency and superiority. As Chapel Royal, St Mary's gave place to Restalrig before 1486–7, when in the Exchequer Rolls there occurs a payment for slates "for the King's Chapel near the Parish Church of Restalrig"; but the designation continued to be applied to St Mary's. On 2nd May 1501, when the Chapel Royal at Stirling was erected by James IV into a collegiate church, it was decerned that the Provostry of St Mary's be the deanery of the church, and that the provost as dean preside over the people in the church, and have the cure of the souls of the king and his household. But by a rescript of 3rd July 1504, Pope

Julius II restricted the provost to his former function, and confirmed the office of Dean to the Bishop of Whithorn (Galloway). The prebends of St Mary's were—Church of Strabrok (Uphall); Church of Fetteresso; Church of Arbuthnot; Church of Dysart; Church of Ceres, attached to the Altar of St Ninian; Church of Benholme; Kinkell; Kingask; Dura; Idwie; Kinglassie (St Andrews); 10 merks of the lands of Kinaldie and Kernes; Lammalethin and Kyninnes (formerly Carnegour), described in *cir*. 1290 as Lethin and Kyninnis when William Comyn, provost, confirmed a charter of Adam de Malkirwistun, who was provost in 1250, granting the land to John, son of William of Lambere, the name Lambere evidently explaining the later designation Lammalethin; Kernes and Cameron. Lands acknowledged about the close of the 12th century by Gilbert, Prior of St Andrews, as belonging to St Mary's "without question" were—Kingask, Kinkell with Petsforgin, Petkennin, Lethem with Kininnis, Kermes with Camberum. Manifestly those lands, and probably most, if not all, of the other lands comprising the prebends, belonged to the church as the Culdee Monastery. By Act of Parliament of 1621 the provostry of the Kirkheugh, exclusive of the six churches, was annexed to the Archbishopric of St Andrews. It may be noted that the Provost of St Mary's had a seat in Parliament on 3rd Feb. 1489-90. The Chapel of St Peter was situated near the shore and the road leading to the Castle; and on the shore at Kinkell, east of St Andrews, there was a Chapel of St Ann, built, it is said, by Kellack, Bishop of St Andrews about 875.

At St Andrews there was an altar dedicated to St Eloy (Eligius, Eloi, Loye), apparently in the parish church. "Trinity bred" in the same church, at which James IV made an offering of 14 sh. in 1497, may denote that there was there a subsidiary altar dedicated to the Holy Trinity. At the west port there was a chapel dedicated to St Ninian, demolished before 3rd Oct. 1562. About 1178 the priory was designated the "Church of St Andrew the Apostle," and in 1202 it was called the "Church of the Blessed St Andrew."—[*Lord High Treasurer's Accs.*, i, 332, 333; *Nicol Thounis' Prot. Bk.*, No. 100; *Cal. of Charters*, i, 7, 16; *Chronicle of Picts and Scots*, 187; *Misc. Spalding Club*, 25-7, 75; *St Andrews Kirk Session*, 227; *Reg. Mag. Sig.*, ii, 793, 794, 1039, 1157, 1221, 1434, 1444, 2132, 2601, 2850, 2971, 3812, iii, 2132, iv, 2498, v, 883, 1825, 1909, vi, 533, 1450, vii, 1434; *Reg. Sec. Seal*, ii, 1694, 4550, iii, 198, 660, 661, 700, 1343, 1716, 1884, 2248, 2345, 2354, 2363, 2381, 2472, 2485, 2515, 2575, 2683, 2817; *Laing Charters*, 15, 348, 943; *Acts Scott. Parl.*, ii, 216a, iv, 634; *Reg. Priory of St And.*, pref. xxxvii, 53, 56, 103, 122-3, 127, 133, 144-7, 150, 189-91, 193-5, 208, 209, 210-11, 212, 213-16, 233, 281, 292, 318-19, 407; *Cal. Papal Reg., Letters*, i, 293, 578, ii, 60-1, 72, 301, iii, 150, ix, 83, x, 88, 400, xi, 371, 417, xii, 538-9; *Petitions*, i, 52, 634; *Excheq. Rolls*, ix, 540; Skene's *Celtic Scot.*, ii, 137; Watson's *Celtic Place Names*, 276-7; *Theiner*, 59-60, 383-5, 428-9, Note; *Cal. Supplic. Rel. to Scot.*, 96, S.H.S.; Bryce's *Greyfriars of Scot.*, ii, 175; *Hist. of Chapel Royal of Stirling*, pref. xxxiii, *Register*, 15, 18; *Retours E.*, 149; Sibbald's *Hist. of Fife*, 348, Ed. 1803; Fleming's *Guide to St Andrews*, 13-14, 110.]

ADAM HERIOT, the Christian Reformed Church and congregation of the City of St Andrews was in existence before 16th March 1559, with him as min. and twelve elders and eight deacons. On 2nd June 1565 he conveyed to Patrick Lermont of Dairsie, Kt., Provost of St Andrews, the tenement belonging to the vicarage with the teinds of fish and herring taken by hook and net by fishers within the parish for 10 merks Scots annually, on the ground "that by the change of religion the fruits and profits of all vicarages and of his own vicarage had been reduced within narrow, over-meagre bounds"; of him it is recorded that he was "greatly beloved of the citizens for his humane and courteous conversation, and of the poorer sort much lamented, to whom he was in his life very beneficent."—[*Cal. of Charters*, ix, 1993; *Reg. Kirk Sess. of St Andrews*, 2, 3 and *n*, 45, 47.]

CHRISTOPHER GOODMAN, min. app. July 1560.—[*Kirk Session Record*, 3n.]
1560

ROBERT HAMILTON, seventh son of Gavin H. of Orbieston and Marion Wallace; educ. at St Andrews Univ. 1552. Marr. Elizabeth (Elspeth) Traill.—[*Acts and Dec.*, l, 255.]
1566

THOMAS WOOD, reader, pres. to vicarage on death of Adam Heriot 24th March 1574–5, but John Winram, superintendent, refused to admit him and on 21st May 1575 was charged by the Privy Council to do so; was one of the Convent of Lindores, and joined the Reformers in 1562; the Scottish Psalter, still in MS., suggested by the Prior of St Andrews, afterwards Regent Moray, was carried through by Wood, the harmonising being the work of David Peebles, one of the canons of St Andrews; died probably in 1592.—[*Reg. Pres. Bene.*; *Reg. of Deeds*, Pt. 2, 415–17; *Reg. Kirk Sess. of St Andrews*, 727n, 40n, S.H.S.]
1574

GEORGE BLACK was one of the deacons of St Andrews Reformed Church and congregation constituted before 16th March 1559–60 and continued to serve as such at least till 1584; he was reader before 31st May 1564, designated exhorter 27th Sept. 1580 and reader 14th March 1581, 11th April 1582, and 27th Feb. 1582–3; during the vacancy in the ministry 1581–4 he "ministered" the Sacraments and performed marriages.—[*Reg. of St Andrews Kirk Session*, 1–3, lxvii, 35, 45, 47, 75, 78, 197, 450, 473, 478, 488n, 500, 512.]
1579

ROBERT PONT, it is doubtful if he was actually min. at St Andrews; the church was vacant on 7th June 1581; on 30th Oct. 1581 representatives were appointed to see the Earl of March, Commendator of Pittenweem, regarding provision of a stipend for Mr Robert Pont, "whom the Session thinks meet to be minister of this parish"; on 20th Dec. 1581 it was intimated that the Town Council was to meet next day to appoint a representative to take the Council's letter to Edinburgh to Mr Robert Pont to be pastor, that they may know his attitude; a min. was mentioned, but not by name, on 14th March 1581–2. On 9th May 1582 representatives were again appointed to confer with the Earl of March "for gude ordour to be taken for Mr Robert Pont, minister, for his stipend, that he may be hastit to cum hame." On 12th April 1582 he was a member of Edinburgh Presbytery. On 31st Oct. 1582 the charge was without a min., and in April 1583 he intimated to the Assembly that "he had proponit to sitt down in St Andrews, and had served on his own chairges a whole year, but had left through lack of provision of stipend," and he prayed the kirk "not to lay the Charge upon him against his will"; apparently, therefore, he served at the most only part of a year at St Andrews, and was never actually settled as min. During the vacancy George Black, reader and exhorter, and Thomas Wood, reader, carried out such duties as were open to them, and teaching was overtaken by James and Andrew Melville, and Patrick Adamson, Archbishop of St Andrews. It was suggested that the Earl of March deliberately prolonged the vacancy that he might have the stipend for his own personal use.—[*Reg. of St Andrews Kirk Session*, lxvii, 453, 460, 461, 463, 473, 481, 488n; *Booke of the Universal Kirk*, 574, 620.]
1581

JOHN RUTHERFORD, his father was also min. of Cults (*q.v.*).
1584

ROBERT BLAIR. Issue bapt. as follows—Samuel, 20th June 1640; John, 19th June 1642; Andrew, 29th July 1644; Hugh, 6th Feb. 1652; Katherine, 27th April 1654.—[*St Andrews Reg.*; *G. R. Sas.*, 2 Ser., v, 352, viii, 44.]
1639

WILLIAM MOORE, was Archdeacon of St Andrews 29th Feb. 1667.—[*St Andrews Reg.*]
1664

ANDREW BRUCE, was Archdeacon of St Andrews 7th March 1674.
1673

JOHN ANDERSON, called by the whole session which resolved to that effect on 6th June 1698.
1699

WILLIAM HARDIE, his daugh., Catherine, bapt. 4th Dec. 1703; his son, William, apprenticed to Duncan Campbell, merchant, Edinburgh, 15th June 1711.

1712

ANDREW KENNEDY HUTCHISON BOYD, his daugh., Agnes Mary, died at Hatfield, Perveral, Essex, 1st March 1935.

1865

PATRICK MACDONALD PLAYFAIR, his widow, Eliza Anna Walker, died 25th March 1946.

1899

ALEXANDER SLATER DUNLOP, trans. from Second Charge 16th April 1925; awarded Norwegian Freedom Medal 1947; dem. 30th Sept. 1947.

1925

SECOND CHARGE

JAMES WOOD, formerly min. of Dunino; at a meeting of the Kirk Session on 16th April 1646, Mr Blair "motioned" that Mr James Wood, "now ane of the Masters of the New College," be appointed "ane helper to our ministerie pair in yes toune" having "willingie consented" to be the same, and the Session approved "with on voyce"; he was adm. 7th May 1646; became Provost of St Salvator's in 1657.—[*Reg. of St Andrews*, Sec. Vol., vii, 411.]

1646

ROBERT HONEYMAN, his daughs.—Nicholas, bapt. 29th May 1653; Margaret (marr. Robert White, merchant, Dundee); Mary.—[*St Andrews Reg.*]

1681

JOHN INNES, reader, 1687. Marr. Grissel Kerr, and had a child bapt. 25th Dec. 1687—[*St Andrews Reg.*]

1687

JOHN WOOD, M.A., his son, Patrick, bapt. 13th April 1688.—[*St Andrews Reg.*]

1686

ALEXANDER SHIELDS, in the Kirk Session Records of 4th Aug. 1701 there is a copy of a letter by him to the Session, dated from the *Rising Sun*, Caledonia Bay, 2nd Feb. 1700. After personal references he recounts the "wicked society of monsters" he was thrust in among during the voyage, and how near he was brought to the gates of death by a long and severe fever which raged among them all the voyage, which few escaped, and whereby about 150 persons were cut off by death besides what had died since; their arrival on 30th Nov. 1699, and their sad disappointment in finding the colony deserted instead of the comfortable settlement that they had expected, nothing being left but a howling wilderness with all the circumstances of impassable woods and vast desolations never frequented by mankind, and dangers and difficulties: a land pleasant, fruitful, rich, if only they had the means to subdue it, and the skill to improve it; no shelter except the ships, or under trees, or little huts made by tree branches; no provisions except what had been brought from Scotland, and these now musty, rotten, old, salt, and near to exhaustion, which, if it occurred, would mean the break-up of the colony. However, in spite of the discouragements, difficulties, and apparent hopelessness of the situation, mindful of the promises that he had made at home, and in dependence upon God, he would stay on till it was seen what would become of the colony, and "some weak endeavours be made to lay the foundations of a Church"; he would return home with all expedition as soon as his "year was out," or sooner if the colony broke up because of the lack of provisions.—[*St Andrews Reg.*]

1697

WILLIAM KENNETH GRANT, trans to Cavers 3rd June 1924.

1916

ALEXANDER SLATER DUNLOP, trans. from Luss (*q.v.*) 9th Oct. 1924; adm. to First Charge 16th April 1925.

1924

JOHN WILSON BAIRD, born 29th March 1891 at Mauchline, son of William B., min. U.P. Church, Mauchline, and Caroline Henderson Rollo; educ. at Mauchline School, Kilmarnock Academy, and Glasgow Univ., M.A.

1925

(1913); lic. by Presb. of Glasgow 31st March 1920; assistant, Inveresk Parish Church 1920-3; ord. to Kirkgunzeon 8th June 1923; trans. and adm. 3rd Sept. 1925; trans. to St Machar's Cathedral, Aberdeen, 24th March 1934; D.D. (Glasgow 1946). Marr. 18th Oct. 1923 Elizabeth Watson, daugh. of William Smith, Governor of Mossbank Industrial School, with issue—Elizabeth Caroline, born 6th May 1925; John Wilson, born 31st May 1929.

THIRD CHARGE

ROBERT YULE, M.A., pres. to vicarage 25th Oct. 1592, vac. by death of Thomas Wood. On 2nd Nov. following he produced to the Presbytery two Presentations, and desired to be adm. as (1) reader, (2) min., and on 16th Nov. he was adm. reader and to use the gift of exhortation; and on 23rd Nov. he was ord. "as Reader to solemnize the banns of mariage"; on 5th Oct. 1603 he was chosen moderator because he was a Presbyter, but declined to accept office; it seems that his status was that of exhorter. —[*Reg. Sec. Seal*, 25th Oct. 1592; *Reg. Kirk Sess.*]

1592

ST LEONARDS

ROBERT WILFRID WALLACE, died 5th Nov. 1932; his widow, Mary Josephine, died 2nd June 1946.

1898

STRATHKINNES

WALTER MacLEOD, died 26th April 1935; his wife, Isabel Forgan Arthur, died 17th Oct. 1932.

1897

WORMIT

HARRY LEGGATT, dem. 30th July 1923; adm. to Corgarff 16th Feb. 1928.

1917

ROBERT MORRIS, trans. to St Enoch's, Hogganfield, Glasgow, 31st Jan. 1933. Issue—Barbara Monica, born 19th Oct. 1924; Margaret Simpson, born 18th Feb. 1928; Colin McKenzie, born 21st Aug. 1933.

1923

SYNOD OF ANGUS AND MEARNS

PRESBYTERY OF MEIGLE

AIRLIE

The church was dedicated by Bishop de Bernham on 27th Aug. 1242. At Baikie there was a chapel dedicated to St John the Baptist. On 26th Feb. 1361–2 David II confirmed a charter by William Fenton of Baikie, granting the lands of Kinrosse (Lunross) to the chaplain celebrating in the chapel.

1890 WILLIAM WILSON, D.D. (Glasgow, June 1926); adm. to united Charge 2nd Feb. 1931; dem. 14th Oct. 1931; died at Coatbridge 4th Nov. 1936.

ALYTH

The church was erected a Prebend of Dunkeld by Bishop Thomas Lauder 1452–76. In 1727 the church was described as 49½ feet broad, 50 in length, "abstracting from the quire," and "stands on two rows of pillars," and at the close of the 18th century as "an old Gothic building." On the north side of the churchyard there was a chapel dedicated to St Ninian, to which were attached the lands of Balwhyn. There was also a chapel at Inverqueich.—[*Reg. Great Seal*, i, 126; iii, 494; Macfarlane's *Geograph. Colls.*, i, 266; Myln's *Lives of the Bishops of Dunkeld*, 23–4; *Retours*, xiv, 319; Lockhart's *Ch. in Scotland in 13th Century*, 50–1.]

1561 ROBERT GRAHAM, vicar 1561.—[*Comps. Gen. Coll. of Thirds.*]

1567 JAMES SANDEMAN, reader 1567, 7th Jan. 1579–80.—[*Edin. Tests.*, vi, 118; vii, 308.]

1567 LAURENCE DUNCAN, reader 1567 and 1569.—[*Comps. Sub Coll. of Thirds, Perth*, etc.]

1569 JAMES GRAHAM, vicar in 1569.—[*Comps. Sub Coll. of Thirds, Perth*, etc.]

1572 DAVID GRAHAM, for "Graham" read "Ramsay"; see also Meigle.

1602 THOMAS LUNDIE, his sons—Thomas, min. of Rattray; Robert, died before 1634; Robert, bapt. June 1634.

1610 JOHN STEWART, son of James S., Commissary of Dunkeld, pres. to the prebend of Alyth 9th Feb. 1610 on death of James Graham.—[*Reg. Pres. Bene.*, iv, 36.]

1637 JOHN RATTRAY. Addl. issue—Alexander (second son).

1686 JOHN LAWSON, died 1693; his only daugh., Jean (marr. Mr Blair, session clerk).

1702 JOHN THOMSON, line 2, for "24th July 1690" read "23rd July 1697"; line 8, for "43" read "41"; line 15, for "transite nocte" read "tramsite noctee." Addl. issue—Marjorie (marr. Dec. 1737 George Scott in Borrington, Kylse, Northumberland); Jean, died 1771; George, bapt. Feb. 1719, died in infancy.

1886 JOHN REID MACLAREN, his wife, Mary Jane Wylie, died 28th Oct. 1924; his son, William Richard, D.S.C., chief engineer, Henderson Line, died in Islay 10th July 1939.

JAMES MEIKLE, dem. 12th Oct. 1932; died at Edinburgh 9th Feb. 1947; his son, Robert, died Jan. not June. Publications—*The History of Alyth Parish Church* (1933); *Places and Place Names round Alyth* (1925); *The Seventeenth Century Presb. of Meigle* (Scottish Church Hist. Society, 1934.)

1897

ARDLER

DAVID ANTON MORRISON, Chaplain to Forces, B.E.F., 1914; Senior Chaplain, 9th Division, 1915, 55th Division 1916–18; D.P.C., VI Corps, 1918–19; died at Dundee 12th Nov. 1948. His wife, Agnes Richmond, died 2nd Dec. 1932; his son, Alexander Abercromby, ord. Min. of Innerwick 20th July 1939; his daugh., Jean Gemmell (marr. 19th Oct. 1940 Hugh Hamilton Maxwell); his son, James, died 22nd Sept. 1925.

1921

BENDOCHY

Originally the parish was made up of two portions, the Lowland and the Highland, or the East and West. The Lowland division was intersected by the river Ericht in the north and the river Isla in the south, and the Highland division, separated from the Lowland by the parishes of Rattray and Blairgowrie, consisted of two portions, Persie and Cally, situated between the Ardle and the Blackwater, and Drimmie, separated from Persie and Cally by a part of Blairgowrie. Probably that part of Blairgowrie may have been "the town of Persie (Parsyos)" of old, belonged to the Church of Blairgowrie, but by amicable arrangement between the Abbots of Scone and Cupar was transferred to Bendochy. Before 1st July 1429 the arrangement was amicably annulled, and "the town of Persie" reverted to Blairgowrie. The Highland division ultimately became part of the parish of Persie, and the portion of the Lowland division south of the Isla was erected into the parish of Coupar Angus. About 1214 the Church of Bendochy was confirmed to Dunfermline Abbey by Hugh de Sigillo, Bishop of Dunkeld. In a dispute regarding Bendochy between Abbeys of Dunfermline and Cupar, Pope Honorius III decerned on 29th Oct. 1219 that the Church of Bendochy be held off Dunfermline Abbey by the Abbey of Cupar— reddendo 2½ silver merks per annum. The church was repaired in 1803 and again in 1842, when "the old grey slates" were removed and were replaced by "blue slates." Inside there is a Sacrament House, defaced but still beautiful, having at the foot the arms and initials of William Turnbull, Abbot of Cupar *cir.* 1506–26. Other features are a pulpit of 17th-century panelling and a series of sepulchral monuments about the early part of that century. In the north part of the parish, beyond the Ericht, there was a chapel dedicated to St Fincana or Findoce, belonging to Cupar Abbey. The saint is St Findeach the Virgin, whose day is 13th Oct., Findoce being the Latin form of Findeoch. The name survives locally in St Fink or St Phink, the designations of lands and a hill in that region. Dedicated to the Virgin Mary, the Chapel of Cally was situated at Monk's Cally or Monkstown on the east side of Glen Ardle, some distance above Bridge of Cally, and also belonged to Cupar Abbey. The churchyard attached to it was still in use in the first half of the 19th century.—[*Reg. of Cupar Abbey*, ii, 207; *Reg. of Dunfermline*, 76, 133–5; *Reg. Great Seal*, vii, 1956; *Cal. of Charters*, ii, 279; Watson's *Celtic Place Names*, 286–7; *Trans. Scott. Eccles. Soc.*, ii, 1909, 301.] (See Coupar Angus and Persie.)

ROBERT DRYSDALE, reader 1563–72. —[*Comps. Sub Coll. of Thirds, Perth*, etc.]

1563

DAVID WHITE, M.A., min. in 1582.— [*Comps. Gen. Coll. of Thirds.*]

1582

JAMES STRACHAN BARTY, his daugh., Agnes Margaret, died at Winnipeg 24th Aug. 1934.

1829

BLAIRGOWRIE

The church, called the Church of Blair in Gowrie, was confirmed to Cambuskenneth Abbey by Bull of Pope Innocent III, 6th May 1207; and in or about 1215

William, Bishop of St Andrews, granted to the Abbey 100 sh. from the church, payable by the parson. On the renunciation of the Church of Kerinton (Carrington) by the Abbey of Scone, William, Bishop of St Andrews, on 12th Feb. 1356, granted to Scone Abbey the Church of Blair in Gowrie, the gift to take effect on the death or demission of Sir John Lyill, parson of Blair, 100 merks stg. being assigned by the abbey for a perpetual vicar to minister at Blair. The church was dedicated by Bishop de Bernham 13th Sept. 1243.—[*Book of Scone*, 130-3; *Chart. of Cambuskenneth*, 47-8, 65, 66.] (See Carrington.)

1569 THOMAS CRUICKSHANK, min. at Caputh, also in charge here 1569.—[*Comps. Sub Coll. of Thirds, Perth*, etc.]

1576 ANDREW MONCUR, pres. to vicarage pensionaire 30th April 1576 on death of John Hepburn.—[*Reg. Pres. Bene*., i, (2), 42.]

1586 WILLIAM RATTRAY, son of Walter R. in Little Blair, reader here, pres. to the vicarage 24th Sept. 1586. Marr. Sibell Halyburton.—[*Reg. Pres. Bene*., ii, 157; *Perth Sas*., i, 196; iv, 344.]

1916 JOSEPH EDWARD RICHERS, dem. 11th Nov. 1948; his daughs.— Margaret Colling (marr. 7th Nov. 1928 James Stevenson Fenton, District Commissioner, Sierra Leone, son of James F., min. of Wallacetown U.F. Church, Dundee); Elena (marr. 12th June 1934 George, son of George Kidd, Parker Cottage, New Rattray).

BLAIRGOWRIE, ST MARY'S

1878 ROBERT STEWART, licen. 16th May 1877; dem. 16th May 1929; died 18th Feb. 1931; his widow, Jessie Jane Lunan, died 11th Nov. 1944.

COUPAR ANGUS

Coupar Angus is called Cupermaccultin in 1150-3, and Tybermackotus (Coupermaccouty) on 24th July 1382, when a Papal Bull confirmed the collation of John Wernock by the Bishop of St Andrews to the perpetual chaplainry of St Ninian there. As the parish of Bendochy was divided in the middle by the river Isla which constituted a danger in winter time so that the inhabitants of the parish on the south side of the Isla could not cross to the church without loss and danger of life, James, Lord Coupar, at the special desire of James VI and the Commission for the Plantation of Kirks, consented to build a new church within the precincts of the Abbey of Coupar, to be called the Church of Coupar, for service of the parishioners in the town of Coupar and on the south side of the Isla, and to dispone for a min. of the church a sufficient manse and glebe with stipend of 500 merks; and accordingly the King by charter of 24th Dec. 1618 erected the said new church into a separate parish, and dissolved the town of Cupar and the lands on the south side of the Isla from the old Church and Parish of Bendochy, and annexed the same to the said new church, with Lord Coupar as patron. The church was in great measure rebuilt in 1780, added to in 1831, and rebuilt in 1859.—[*Reg. Great Seal*, vii, 1956; *Reg. of Dunfermline*, 74; *Cal. Papal Reg., Petitions*, i, 56, 57.]

1571 ROBERT FISHER, pres. to vicarage 6th April 1571.—[*Reg. Pres. Bene*., i, (2), 15.]

1647 GEORGE HALIBURTON, delete from "D.D." to "Bishop of Aberdeen."

1659 GEORGE HALIBURTON, adm. to Parish and Archdeaconry of Dunkeld about 14th June 1659, afterwards Bishop of Brechin (*q.v.*).

1703 THOMAS OGILVIE, line 2, for "Turfandry" read "Turfauchie"; educ. at St Andrews (divinity); line 8, for "3" read "13."

1742 THOMAS SPANKIE, for "Thomas" read "James." Marr. Margaret, daugh. of William Inglis, surgeon, Lanark; his son, Thomas, probably min. of Falkland.

1881 FINLAY ROBERT MACDONALD, min. at Newcastle, New Brunswick, 1689–74.

1902 CHARLES STEWART, dem. 26th Oct. 1947; his wife, Edith Susan Kerr, died 19th Aug. 1946; his daugh., Mary Elizabeth Murray (marr. 12th June 1928 William Todd Bruce, Meigle), died 10th May 1930; his son, Charles, M.B., Ch.B. (Edinburgh); Edith (marr. 24th Feb. 1937 George Lightbody).

EASSIE and NEVAY

The church was dedicated by Bishop de Bernham on 13th May 1246. There was in the parish at Balgowny a hospital with chapel dedicated to the Virgin Mary. To the hospital pertained the lands of Balgowny, with mill and mill lands, of which on 17th July 1565 Patrick Lyon, preceptor of the hospital, granted a charter to John Lyon, son and heir apparent of John L. of Haltoun.—[*Reg. of Panmure*, ii, 236; Lockhart's *Ch. in Scot. in 13th Century*, 61–2; *Reg. Great Seal*, iv, 1786; *Scott. Supplications to Rome*, 16, S.H.S.]

1563 JOHN NEVAY, min. at Newtyle 1564, also in charge here; min. of Glamis also, in charge 1571.—[*Comps. Sub Coll. of Thirds, Forfar*, etc.]

1564 MATTHEW MONCUR, reader in Aug. 1564 and 1574, also reader at Nevay. —[*Edin. Tests.*, iv, 181; v, 279, 286–8, 306.]

1568 GEORGE ARNOT, parson 18th July 1564, 1568 and 15th June 1577.— [*Acts and Dec.*, lxviii, 219; *Reg. of Deeds*, vii, 11; *Cal. of Charters*, x, 2137.]

1569 HEW CURRIE, parson 11th Aug. 1572. —[*Acts and Dec.*, xlvi, 75; *Reg. Sec. Sig.*, 11th Aug. 1573.]

1606 WILLIAM MURRAY, M.A., parson and reader 1606.—[*Reg. Mag. Sig.*, vi, 1726.]

1844 DAVID LINDSAY, his sons—James Ainsworth, architect, Edinburgh, died 19th Oct. 1928; Robert Archibald, S.S.C., Edinburgh, died 29th June 1938; David, died 18th July 1938.

1901 ALEXANDER WADDELL, dem. 30th Nov. 1942; died 3rd Oct. 1944; his widow, Effie Morrison Anton, died 19th Feb. 1946.

NEVAY

1563 JOHN NEVAY, in charge here. (See Newtyle.)

1563 ALEXANDER TYRIE, reader.— [*Comps. Sub Coll. of Thirds, Forfar*, etc.]

1568 MATTHEW MONCUR, pres. to vicarage 14th June 1572; reader here Nov. 1562 and also at Eassie.— [*Edin. Tests.*, v, 120, 288; *Reg. Pres. Bene.*, i, (3), 18.]

1570 GEORGE SWINTON, M.A., rector 1570, died after 20th March 1606.— [*Edin. Tests.*, ii, 88; *Reg. Mag. Sig.*, iv, 2825; vi, 1726.]

1577 THOMAS MONCUR, M.A., reader 18th Feb. 1577-8.—[*Edin. Tests.*, vi, 25.]

1582 ALEXANDER TYRIE, min. 8th May 1582; had issue—Alexander; John. —[*Reg. of Deeds*, xxi, 42.]

GLENISLA

The church was granted to Cambuskenneth Abbey by William the Lion 1165–1214. On 11th Sept. 1311 Fergus, Abbot of Cambuskenneth, gave the church to Cupar Abbey, subject to an annual payment of £10 by the latter to Cambuskenneth. In or soon after 1469 the church was repaired or rebuilt.—[*Chart. of Cambuskenneth*, 137–9, Pref. liii; *Reg. of Cupar*, i, 150–1.]

1563 JOHN SMYTH, reader 1563.—[*Comps. Gen. Coll. of Thirds.*]

1849 GEORGE GIBB, his daughs.—Christina, died 20th Jan. 1937; Mary, died 21st March 1945.

1913 WILFRED JOSEPH LEWIS, dem. 21st April 1926 on app. to Rosedale Presb. Church, Toronto; died 5th Jan. 1929.

1926 JOHN DEAS LOGIE, trans. from Farr 15th Sept. 1926; trans. to Stanley 8th Sept. 1927.

1928 WILLIAM WILSON, born 20th Dec. 1867, son of Hugh W., grocer, and Elizabeth Robb; became a cashier and bookkeeper; educ. at Manchester College, Oxford, and Univ. of Glasgow; was a missionary in London 1900; adm. min. of Unity Church, Gateshead, 1908; Waterloo Place Congregational Church, Dumfries, 1913–17; *locum tenens* Applegarth Feb. 1918 to Jan. 1919; assistant St. Luke's Church, Glasgow, Aug. 1920; adm. probationer May 1921; asistant South Dalziel; ord. to Augustine, Greenock, 19th July 1923; trans. and adm. 21st March 1928; dem. 21st Sept. 1941. Marr. (1) 30th June 1892 Sarah Philip (died 6th March 1933), daugh. of James Graham, timber merchant, and Sarah Philip, and had issue —Dorothy, born 14th Aug. 1895 (marr. 14th Aug. 1919 William Boyd, M.A., B.Sc., Ph.D., Lecturer on Education, Univ. of Glasgow); Arthur William, born 6th Jan. 1899; Helen Mary Graham, born 27th June 1903 (marr. 28th May 1931 Dr Maurice Rosenfield, Qualified Psychotherapist, London); (2) 26th June 1947 Isabel Beck Burton.

(*Charges united* 21*st Sept.* 1941.)

KETTINS

Kettins was the seat of a Celtic monastery to which may have been attached the following six chapels situated respectively at—the village of Pettie, the site being marked on the O.S. one-inch map; South Costoun or Corstoun; Piteur; Mairyfaulds; Denhead; and the south side of Kettins village. In the majority of cases there were burial grounds. By charter of 1292–3 Hugh of Over, lord of Kettins, granted to Cupar Angus Abbey his well in his lands and Abthanage of Kettins, called Bradwell (St Bride's Well) with its aqueduct and servitude of water gauges; and in a Retour of 1658 there occur "the lands called the Abden of Kettins comprising lands in the west of the village of Kettins, Over Corstoune, Greenbarns, Mill of Kettins, and the Chapel of Kettins." The *Atlas of Scotland* 1832 gives a site on the north of Kettins village as "Greenburn Abbey in Ruins"; but its actual significance has not been ascertained. The Church of Kettins, dedicated by Bishop de Bernham on 18th April 1249, was granted "of old"—so it is narrated in 1391–2—along with its fruits, to the Red Friars Monastery of Berwick, and was to remain annexed thereto so long as the Burgh and Castle of Berwick continued faithful to and at peace with the Scottish Crown, thus permitting the said monastery to be "fortified" with monks carrying out divine celebrations in peace according to use and wont. But in 1391–2 Robert III, on account of the English occupation of Berwick rendering the foregoing conditions impossible of fulfilment, granted the church with its fruits and offerings to the Red Friars' Hospital and House of Dundee, to amplify its alms, for his own soul, the soul of his Queen, Anabella, and the souls of his ancestors and successors. How long that grant continued operative is not clear. But, at any rate, on 3rd Feb. 1473 the church was annexed to the Red Friars of Peebles. In 1768 the church was rebuilt, or, as is narrated, was "heightened by stones from Cupar Angus Abbey." There was in the church an altar dedicated to the Virgin Mary, founded by Alexander Rattray at Petcur, of which in 1533 Sir David Jak was chaplain. The bell bears the date 1519, and the inscription, mainly in Roman capitals, "Maria Troon es minen naem Meester Hans Popen Reider gaf mi." Maria Troon may refer to the Virgin Mary, the expression denoting one of her attributes as Queen of Heaven, "Mary of the Throne."—[*Reg. Mag. Sig.*, i, 838; iii, 1279; iv, 2232; *Retours*, xxiii, 223; Jervise's *Epitaphs and Inscriptions*, ii, 99; Lockhart's *Church in Scot. in 13th Century*, 61–1.] (See Peebles, Dunbar, Dundee.)

1563 JAMES JAMIESON, reader in 1563 and 1567.—[*Comps. Sub Coll. of Thirds, Forfar*, etc.]

1568 ARCHIBALD KEITH, min. at Lundie, in charge here 1568.—[*Comps. Sub Coll. of Thirds, Forfar*, etc.]

1650 DAVID PATON, had addl. issue—George.

1922 CHARLES NEILSON RUTHERFORD, trans. to Huntly 3rd Sept. 1931; trans. to St Michaels, Linlithgow, 15th Nov. 1939; has issue—Elizabeth Melville, born 24th Aug. 1925; John Quintin, born 6th March 1929.

KINGOLDRUM

1563 JOHN YOUNG, min. at Kirriemuir, also in charge here.—[*Comps. Sub Coll. of Thirds, Forfar*, etc.]

1563 JAMES STEILL, reader 1563 and 1567.—[*Comps. Sub Coll. of Thirds, Forfar*, etc.]

1580 DAVID HALIBURTON, M.A., exhorter, held vicarage; excommunicated before 30th July 1580.—[*Reg. Sec. Seal*, xlvii, 27.]

1580 DAVID BLACK, min. Kirriemuir; pres. to vicarage 30th July 1580.—[*Reg. Sec. Seal*, xlvii, 27.]

1589 ROBERT HEPBURN, M.A., vicar 1589–90.—[*Comps. Sub Coll. of Thirds, Forfar*, etc.]

1590 WILLIAM FORBES, pres. to vicarage 28th Dec. 1588 on death of William Malcolm.—[*Reg. Sec. Sig.*, lxix, 267.]

1606 JOHN OGILVY, for "trans. from Bervie" read "trans. from Inchture Kinnaird and Bervie."—[*Reg. Sec. Sig.*, lxxv, 211.]

1656 WILLIAM RAIT, marr. Margaret Symmer and had issue—Margaret (marr. John Ogilvie of Braesyde).—[*Forfar Sas.*, i, 360, 19th Feb. 1664.]

1887 JAMES CRAIG JACK, died 17th Nov. 1925.

1926 REGINALD IAN DAVIDSON, trans. from Foss (*q.v.*) 17th May 1926; trans. to Maryton 16th March 1933; had issue—Robert Cunningham Foss, born 22nd June 1921; Isobel Evelyn Parker, born 3rd July 1925; Ian Murray Pollock, born 14th March 1928; Susan Porteous Murray Cunningham, born 1st Oct. 1933.

LINTRATHEN

The Vicarage of Lintrathen belonged to the Priory of St Colmoc of Inchmahome. A house near the church pertained to St Madan's Bell.—[*Cal. Papal Regs., Letters*, viii, 203; *Misc. Spalding Club*, iv, 118–19.]

1560 SIR JAMES ARCHIBALD, vicar 27th May 1560, at which date a letter of Darnley and Queen Mary, charging "the parishioners to pay arrears of his stipend for diverse years," stated that "he had been vicar divers years" and "hes causit the common prayeris and homilies be red owlkilie (weekly) to the parrochinaris of the said parrochin, and otherwise is content to abyde sik reformatioun as the lordis of our Secreit Counsale pleais mak thairintill." On 14th Nov. 1580 the said Sir James, designated Burgess of Stirling and Vicar of Lintrathen, in contract with James, Lord Airlie, agreed, in consideration of payment of 400 merks to him, to demit the vicarage and to obtain a presentation of the same directed to the Superintendent of Angus in favour of David, son of said James, conform to the new order now observed in such cases.—[*Misc. Spalding Club*, iv, 120–2.]

1571 JOHN NEVAY of that ilk, min. at Glamis, etc., also in charge here.

1571 ADAM FOULIS, parson 27th June 1571.—[*Cal. of Charters*, x, 2225.]

1572 ROBERT STEWART, reader, pres. to vicarage 29th July 1587 on death of David Ogilvie.—[*Reg. Sec. Sig.*, lv, 122.]

1580 DAVID OGILVIE, son of James, Lord Airlie, died before 29th July 1587.—[*Misc. Spalding Club*, iv, 120; *Reg. Sec. Sig.*, lv, 123.]

1603 WILLIAM FORBES, M.A., min. of Kingoldrum and Lintrathen, pres. to vicarage 18th Aug. 1603 on death of Robert Stewart.—[*Reg. Sec. Sig.*, lxxiv, 72.]

1664 THOMAS OGILVY, dem. 1716.

1717 LAURENCE BROWN, probably younger son of Sir John B., second Baronet, of London and Danzig. Marr. Elizabeth, daugh. of George Lyon of Wester Ogil and Jean Nisbet; delete "son, John."

1855 CHARLES CHREE, his sons—Charles, died 12th Aug. 1928; Sir William, LL.D., Dean of the Faculty of Advocates, knighted June 1934, died 10th Jan. 1936.

1893 JOHN ROBERT STRACHAN, died 5th April 1925; his son, George, in Union Bank of Scotland.

1925 RODERICK FRASER, trans. from Rousay 30th Sept. 1925; trans. to Dingwall 26th Sept. 1929.

(*United with Lintrathen 2nd Oct.* 1938.)

MEIGLE

The church with its chapel was granted to the Priory of St Andrews by Simon de Meigle, confirmation being granted by William the Lion, *cir.* 1178–87. On 25th April 1474, David, Earl of Crawford, endowed a chaplainry in the church with various annual rents and lands; and on 22nd June 1504 Walter Tyry of Lunan, on behalf and in name of late Mr Gilbert Tyry, vicar of Cargill, his uncle, granted to the Altar of St Paul in the church an annual rent of 10 libs. from the lands of Lunan.—[*Reg. Great Seal*, ii, 2797; Lyon's *History of St Andrews*, ii, 205.]

1562 SIR ALEXANDER MONCRIEFF, vicar 1562.—[*Comps. Gen. Coll. of Thirds.*]

1569 SIR ALEXANDER IRVINE, vicar 1569.—[*Comps. Sub Coll. of Thirds, Perth*, etc.]

1575 DAVID RAMSAY, min. of Alyth, Meigle and Glenisla, min. 11th Nov. 1575.—[*Clan Campbell*, viii, 677.]

1586 ROBERT HALDANE, vicar 1586–90. —[*Comps. Gen. Coll. of Thirds.*]

1679 ANDREW BRUCE, Bishop of Dunkeld, also min. here 1679.

1808 JAMES MITCHELL of Auchinrath, eldest son of Matthew M. in Mid Dargavel, Dumfriesshire, and Mary Johnston.

1853 JOHN NICOLL, his daugh., Jessie, died 3rd Aug. 1938; his son, John, died at Ottawa 19th Jan. 1941.

1897 HUGH CLIMIE, dem. 31st May 1948.

NEWTYLE

The church was dedicated by Bishop de Bernham 29th Aug. 1242.

1563 JOHN NEVAY of that ilk, min. (See Meathie.)—[*Comps. Sub Coll. of Thirds, Forfar*, etc.]

1566 SIR ANDREW LINDSAY, vicar 20th Aug. 1562 and 28th July 1581; was tutor of David Lindsay of Lenoll 1562.—[*Reg. Privy Council*, v, 218; *Reg. Mag. Sig.*, v, 237.]

1571 ROBERT BOYD, pres. in 1571 on death of Sir Andrew Lindsay.—[*Reg. Pres. Bene.*, i, (2), 17.]

1919 ROBERT WOOD, his daugh., Catherine Grant (marr. 15th Aug. 1934 Dr David W. F. Hardie, Ivy Bank, Ladebraes, St Andrews).

(*Charges united 4th Sept.* 1938.)

PERSIE

1831 JOHN BAXTER, missionary 1831–8, afterwards min. of Hiltown, Dundee.

THOMAS SMITH, dem. 30th Sept. 1939, died at Blairgowrie 16th March 1941. Line 2, for "Donhead" read "Hillhead Denman."
1885

(*United with Netherton 1st Oct. 1939.*)

RUTHVEN

A Fair of St Munn or Mundu at Ruthven is mentioned in 1542. Mundie or Munnu is for Mo-findu, an affectionate form of Finten, Finton, Finntain, Fionntain, who died in 635.—[Watson's *Celtic Place Names*, 307; *Reg. Mag. Sig.*, iv, 1442, 2166, 2798.]

GEORGE HAY, parson.—[*Acts and Dec.*, xxiii, 112, lx, 290.]
1561

JAMES FLEMING, reader 1563.—[*Comps. Sub Coll. of Thirds, Forfar*, etc.]
1563

WALTER LINDSAY, pres. to vicarage 22nd July 1569 on death of Patrick Blair.—[*Reg. Pres. Bene.*, i, 27.]
1574

DAVID CUMYNG, pres. to vicarage 17th March 1574–5 on death of Patrick Blair.—[*Reg. Pres. Bene.*, i, (4), 31.]
1574

ROBERT CARRINGTON, reader here, pres. to vicarage 30th Oct. 1576 on death of David Cumyng.—[*Reg. Pres. Bene.*, i, (4), 48.]
1576

DAVID RAMSAY, still in office 1590.—[*Comps. Sub Coll. of Thirds, Forfar.*]
1582

ROBERT HAMILTON, sixth son of John H. of Orbiston and Janet Hamilton.
1595

JOHN GORDON McPHERSON, his daugh., Christina Gordon, died 17th Sept. 1933.
1879

ALEXANDER KIDD WATT, died at Dundee 10th Dec. 1926.
1910

JAMES ANDERSON, trans. from Robertson Memorial, Glasgow (*q.v.*), 20th July 1927; died 3rd Jan. 1941. Marr. 28th March 1922 Alice Lilian, daugh. of Harry Smith and Mary Ann Toone (born 12th June 1877, died 20th Oct. 1937).
1927

PRESBYTERY OF FORFAR

ABERLEMNO

The church was dedicated by Bishop de Bernham 21st Aug. 1242.

1572 WILLIAM GARDYNE, vicar on 2nd Dec. 1558, brother of Alexander G. of Brakinto.—[*Reg. of Deeds*, iii, 109, 206.]

1597 HENRY STIRLING, pres. to Treasureship of Brechin in 1597 on death of John Hepburn.—[*Reg. Sec. Sig.*, lxxi, 5.]

1910 DAVID NELSON, his daugh., Margaret Catherine (marr. 4th June 1937 Andrew Carmichael Bennet, Edinburgh).

ALDBAR

The church was dedicated by Bishop de Bernham 27th Aug. 1243.

1563 DAVID FOWLER, reader in 1563.—[*Comps. Sub Coll. of Thirds, Forfar*, etc.]

CLOVA

A chapel is said to have stood at Lethnot, a short distance south of the church, perhaps the Chapel of Clova which was annexed to Glamis Church on 5th Sept. 1486.—[*Reg. of Arbroath, Nigrum*, 246; *Land of the Lindsays*, 282.]

1563 THOMAS LOVE, reader in 1563.—[*Comps. Sub Coll. of Thirds, Forfar*, etc.]

1568 JAMES OGILVY, min. in 1568.—[*Comps. Sub Coll. of Thirds, Forfar*, etc.]

1900 ROBERT MATTHEW WATSON, trans. to Careston 17th March 1926.

1926 ARCHIBALD JOHN DARLING SCOTT, trans. from Northmaven (*q.v.*) 14th July 1926; died 15th Nov. 1945.

(*United with Glenprosen 31st March 1946.*)

CORTACHY

On 12th Dec. 1257 Maliseus, Earl of Strathern, granted the Church to the Abbey of Inchaffray. On 20th Oct. 1429 the patronage of the church was bestowed upon Brechin Cathedral by Walter, Earl Palatine of Strathearn, Athol, and Caithness. By John, Bishop of Brechin, the patronage was appropriated to the Capitular Mensa, and this was confirmed by Bull of Pope Martin V 8th May 1430, £10 annually being reserved for a perpetual vicar to serve Cortachy. By another Bull, of 5th May 1430, the same Pope had confirmed a gift of £40 annually from the lands of Cortachy by the said Walter for two chaplains and six boys for perpetual celebrations of divine offices in the cathedral, a fourth chaplain to be provided by the Bishop.—[*Charters of Inchaffray*, 76; *Cal. Papal Regs., Letters*, vii, 162, 164.]

1563 JAMES RAIT, reader in 1563.—[*Comps. Sub Coll. of Thirds, Forfar*, etc.]

1563 ALEXANDER RAY, vicar pensioner 1563.—[*Comps. Sub Coll. of Thirds, Forfar*, etc.]

1571 JAMES OGILVY, min. in April 1568. —[*Comps. Sub Coll. of Thirds, Forfar*, etc.] (See Clova.)

1580 JAMES NICOLSON, pres. to parsonage and vicarage 7th May 1580, vacant by dem. of James Ogilvy.—[*Reg. of Brechin*, ii, 340.]

DAVID RAMSAY, his daugh., Janet, alive June 1696.
1628

JAMES ADAM, adm. to Olrig 19th June 1656; his daugh., Matilda (marr. David Guthrie, apothecary, Dundee).
1659

ALEXANDER LINDSAY, line 2, delete "about 1700."
1687

JOHN STRACHAN, died 20th March 1927; his widow, Catherine Anderson, died 22nd Jan. 1941.
1894

DAVID CRAWFORD, trans. from Midmar (*q.v.*) 24th Aug. 1927; died 23rd March 1930; his daugh., Vida Olive Monica, nurse, died at Glasgow 24th Feb. 1940.
1927

DUNNICHEN

The Church of Dunnichen, in 1220 Dunnachtyn, seems to be identical with the Church of Strathechtyn which with its chapel was granted to Arbroath Abbey in 1201-7 by Gillechrist, Earl of Anegus (Lenegos).—[*Reg. of Arbroath, Vetus*, 31.]

JAMES COCHRANE, vicar 1563-8.— [*Comps. Sub Coll. of Thirds, Forfar*, etc.]
1563

JOHN RIGG. Marr. (1) Jean Gairden; his daugh., Elizabeth (marr. Alexander Barbour, servitor to Alexander Gibson of Durie, Principal Clerk of Session).
1589

HENRY LINDSAY, his son, George, merchant, Dundee, tenant in Invereighty.
1682

JOHN FOSTER McCALLUM, trans. to Strontian 15th Aug. 1928.
1923

JOSEPH McKENZIE McPHERSON, trans. from Rickarton (*q.v.*) 27th Feb. 1929; trans. to Forglen 17th April 1931; D.D. (Aberdeen 26th March 1930); dem. 30th Nov. 1939; died 26th June 1944. Marr. (2) 4th Nov. 1930 Jean Cattanach, daugh. of James Stirling, Letham. His daugh., Margaret (marr. 7th July 1934 Thomas Hugh Russell, Royston, Edgeware, Middlesex). Publications— *Primitive Beliefs in the North East of Scotland* (1929); *Extracts from the Records of Forglen; The Famines of the North East*.
1929

(*Dunnichen, Letham and Kirkden united 6th Sept.* 1931.)

FORFAR

The Chapel of St Margaret belonged to Cupar Abbey. Situated apparently in or near the town of Forfar was the Chapel of St Biternan (Ethernan) in the Diocese of Brechin, in which David, Earl of Crawford, who died probably in Feb. 1403-4 and certainly before 7th July 1404, founded a chaplain in memory of his grandfather, Sir John Stirling, etc., with an endowment of 10 merks annually from the fermes of Forfar. The church was dedicated by Bishop de Bernham 23rd Aug. 1242.— [*Excheq. Rolls*, iii, 606, iv, 30; *Reg. of Cupar*, i, 272, ii, 68-71; Jervise's *Memo. of Angus and Mearns*, 24, 466.]

DAVID LINDSAY, min. in 1563, had charge also of Restennet and Aberlemno.—[*Comps. Sub Coll. of Thirds, Forfar*, etc.]
1563

ROBERT WOOD, reader in 1563.— [*Comps. Sub Coll. of Thirds, Forfar*, etc.]
1563

ROBERT STEVENSON, his daugh., Marion Scott, died 14th June 1930.
1843

GEORGE JOHNSTONE CAIE, his widow, Margaret Matthew Myles, died 18th March 1932; his daughs. —Anne Whitson, died 22nd Dec. 1935; Mary Richardson, died at Edinburgh 17th Feb. 1940.
1875

WILLIAM GALLOWAY DONALDSON, died suddenly in pulpit 25th Nov. 1934.
1901

RESTENNET

The church was dedicated by Bishop de Bernham 30th Aug. 1243. Within the priory was buried a Prince of Scotland, John, infant son of King Robert Bruce; and in his memory King David II granted the monks an annual rent of 20 merks from the customs of Dundee.—[*Hist. MSS. Commission Fourteenth Report*, 49–50; *Excheq. Rolls*, i, cxxvi.]

1563 DAVID LINDSAY, min. in 1563. (See Forfar.)

FORFAR, ST JAMES

1866 JOHN WEIR, died at Paisley 13th March 1925.

1917 JAMES AITKEN, trans. to Livingston 14th Sept. 1928.

1929 JOHN STRACHAN, born 31st Oct. 1897, son of John S., coachsmith, Dundee, and Ann Marr Kidd; educ. at Univ. of St Andrews, M.A. (1925); licen. by Presb. of Dundee Oct. 1928; assistant at Clepington and Arbroath; ord. 28th Feb. 1929; trans. to Collace 5th Oct. 1933; trans. to Dores 1st Sept. 1943; died 19th Feb. 1946. Marr. 24th July 1929 Agnes Laird, daugh. of William and Agnes Annan, Belfast.

LOWSON MEMORIAL

1921 WILLIAM THOMAS SMELLIE, trans. to Rothesay 7th April 1925.

1925 JOHN KENNEDY, B.D., ord. 15th Sept. 1925; trans. to Old Kilpatrick 19th Dec. 1928.

1929 WILLIAM HUTCHISON MACDIARMID, formerly of Ballingry (*q.v.*); trans. from Stonefield 26th June 1929; died 3rd Nov. 1939; his widow, Marion Barclay, died 4th July 1944.

GLAMIS

The church was dedicated by Bishop de Bernham 25th Aug. 1242. The old Celtic cross at Glamis Manse does not belong to the earliest period of Christian art in Scotland as stated in Vol. v, 289. Its ornamentation and general character prove it to be of the third period of Celtic Christian art, namely the ninth century. There are two other Celtic crosses in the parish of the same period—the Thornton stone on the Hunter's Hill and the Cossius stone on the north side of the parish. A portion of another Celtic cross was also found when the churchyard was being dug, and several other portions have been found beside the foundations of the present church—all of the third period of Celtic work and contemporary with the life of St Fergus, the founder of the Celtic community in Glamis. A good many years ago the cave associated with him disappeared because of the rock, which enclosed it, having fallen in. The well is still there and is near the church in the romantic Den of Glamis.

The Celtic cross slab at the manse is usually designated "King Malcolm's Gravestone" from the fact that King Malcolm II died at Glamis in A.D. 1034, but on the face of it the stone is of older date, and probably is the gravestone of St Fergus himself.

No remains of the medieval church are extant except the south transept, beneath which is the vault of the Strathmore family. It is a beautiful specimen of 15th-century Gothic and is in excellent preservation and contains the altar-shaped tomb of Patrick Lyon, first Lord Glamis, who died in 1459.

The endowment of the Altar of St Thomas in the aisle of St Thomas on the south side of the church by John, Third Lord Glamis, on 20th Oct. 1487 was an annual rent of 12 merks from Nelstoun, which failing, from the whole thanage of Glamis, and 1 acre on the west side of the orchard of Glamis, with toft, etc. On 26th Oct. 1492 Walter Ramsay of Denoune founded on the north side of the church an altar dedicated to the Holy Trinity, with an endowment of 10 merks annual rent from the lands of Denoune, in warrandice of 6 merks annual rent from the lands of Petpoynt in Forfar, and also of 4 merks annual rent from the lands of Bahaglis in Perth. To the same altar John, Lord Glamis, on 20th Oct. 1492 gave 2 acres of the barony of Glamis, with toft, fodder in the marshes on the north side of Doune Water, herbage for a horse, and pasture for two cows.—[*Reg. Great Seal*, ii, 2158, 2223; *Reg. Sec. Seal*, ii, 4351.]

1564 JAMES ROLLAND, vicar.—[*Acts and Dec.*, xxxiii, 136.]

1570 PATRICK LYON, M.A., son of James L., burgess of Dundee, pres. to vicarage 11th Oct. 1570 on death of James Rolland.—[*Reg. Pres. Bene.*]

1571 JOHN NEVAY of that ilk. (See Meathie.)

1575 ROBERT RAMSAY, reader, pres. to vicarage 30th Oct. 1575 on dem. of Patrick Lyon.—[*Reg. Pres. Bene.*, i, (4), 37; *Reg. Sec. Sig.*, xlii, 123, xliii, 36; *Edin. Tests.*, v, 238.]

1601 DAVID BROWN, pres. in 1601 on dem. of Robert Ramsay.—[*Reg. Sec. Sig.*, lxxii, 218.]

1674 WILLIAM CHALMERS, had issue—Patrick; Grizel; Helen.—[*Forfar Sas.* 23rd Aug. 1698; *St Andrews Com. Act Book*, xii, 160, 165.]

1873 JOHN STEVENSON, LL.D., his widow, Elizabeth Valentine, died at Brechin 11th Dec. 1926.

1919 MATTHEW BABINGTON, died at Dundee 7th June 1942. Marr. 5th May 1927 Anna Arnot Bell or Whyte.

GLENPROSEN

1907 JAMES DALGETY, dem. 30th Sept. 1943; died 2nd June 1945.

INVERARITY

The church was dedicated by Bishop de Bernham 4th Sept. 1243.

1561 SIR HEW LINDSAY, vicar 1561-3, Chaplain of Denside 1566.—[*Comps. Sub Coll. of Thirds, Forfar*; *Reg. Mag. Sig.*, v, 1704.]

1563 JAMES BLINDSCHALL, reader 1563. —[*Comps. Sub Coll. of Thirds, Forfar*, etc.]

1563 JAMES FOTHERINGHAM, min. in office 1563-8, with charge also of Meathie and Kinnettles.—[*Comps. Sub Coll. of Thirds, Forfar*, etc.]

1713 ROBERT YOUNG, his son, William, probably apprenticed to Samuel Graham, bookbinder, Edinburgh, 13th June 1733.

1715 JOHN GRUB, M.A., intruded here Sept. 1715 to Feb. 1716.—[*Justiciary Records.*]

1921 JAMES MILLER, trans. to Martyrs, Glasgow, 17th May 1927.

1927 WILLIAM KILGOUR BLACK, trans. from Kirriemuir South (*q.v.*) 11th Aug. 1927; dem. 30th June 1945.

MEATHIE

The church was dedicated by Bishop de Bernham 3rd Sept. 1243. It was granted to Coupar Abbey by Sir Alexander Abercrombie *circa* 1290–1315.—[*Frasers of Philorth*, ii, 21.]

1567 JAMES FOTHERINGHAM, min. (See Inverarity.)

1577 JOHN NEVAY of that ilk, min. 27th April 1577.—[*Edin. Tests.*, vi, 248.]

KINNETTLES

The church was dedicated by Bishop de Bernham 11th Nov. 1241.

1563 JOHN (? JAMES) SCOTT, parson 1563, died before 22nd May 1566.—[*Comps. Sub Coll. of Thirds, Forfar*, etc.; *Reg. Sec. Sig.*, xxxv, 46.]

1566 ANDREW DAVIDSON, preacher, pres. to parsonage 22nd May 1566; also held vicarage; died before 4th Dec. 1587.—[*Reg. Sec. Sig.*, xxxv, 46; *Reg. of Deeds*, viii, 406; *Grote's Prot. Book*, 377.] (See Sennick.)

1587 ALEXANDER LINDSAY, M.A., regent, St Andrews, pres. to parsonage 4th Dec. 1587 on death of Andrew Davidson.—[*Reg. Sec. Sig.*, lvi, 107.]

1587 JAMES DAVIDSON, M.A., min. here, pres. to vicarage 15th Dec. 1587 on death of Andrew Davidson.—[*Reg. Sec. Sig.*, lvi, 115.]

1588 JAMES RAIT, min. here, pres. to parsonage and vicarage 10th Sept. 1588 on death of Andrew Davidson.—[*Reg. Sec. Sig.*, lviii, 24.]

1899 MAUNSEL GRANT MACKINTOSH DONALD, died 7th May 1941.

KIRRIEMUIR

In 1201-7 the church was granted to Arbroath Abbey by Gillechrist, Earl of Anegus (Lenagos). There was at Kirriemuir a Chapel of the Holyrood; and in the churchyard there was a chapel dedicated to St Colmoc, to which pertained crofts and buildings in the town. Colmoc is apparently Mo-Cholmoc of Druim Mor in Ulster, whose day is 7th June.—[*Reg. Great Seal*, v, 1170; *Retours*, xlviii, 881; Watson's *Celtic Place Names*, 279.]

1561 GEORGE FLETCHER, vicar 1561-6.—[*Comps. Gen. Coll. and Sub Coll. of Thirds, Forfar*, etc.]

1563 JOHN YOUNG, min. in 1563, had charge also at Kingoldrum.—[*Comps. Sub Coll. of Thirds, Forfar*, etc.]

1564 GEORGE CLEPEN, vicar.

1571 DAVID BLACK, pres. 20th July 1580 to Kingoldrum (*q.v.*).

1574 ABRAHAM CRICHTON, reader.—[*Acts and Dec.*, lv, 1, 2.]

1586 ALEXANDER KYNNINMONTH, pres. to vicarage 15th Dec. 1587.—[*Reg. Sec. Sig.*, lvi, 116.]

1669 SILVESTER LYON, his son, David, merchant, Dundee.

1715 JAMES RAIT, M.A., formerly at Inverkeilour, intruded here from 15th Sept. 1715 to Jan. 1716.—[*Justiciary Records.*]

1873 JOHN BOYD, his widow, Charlotte Josephine Ramsay, died 14th Feb. 1939; his son, Angus, died at Hong Kong 24th Jan. 1931.

1913 GEORGE JOHNSTON CHREE, died at Cults 29th Sept. 1935; his widow, Helen Robertson Hay Arthur, died 9th Dec. 1947. Publication—*Handbook of the Church in India.*

1921 WILLIAM ADDISON, trans. to Ettrick 22nd March 1929.

1929 ARCHIBALD HENDERSON MITCHELL, trans. from Chapelshade, Dundee (*q.v.*), 22nd Aug. 1929; trans. to Mortlach 9th Jan. 1935; died 10th Dec. 1941.

KIRRIEMUIR SOUTH

The church was refloored and restored in 1928 and further improvements made in 1936.

1915 WILLIAM KILGOUR BLACK, trans. to Inverarity 11th Aug. 1927; his son, Douglas Andrew Kilgour, B.Sc., St Andrews 1933, M.B., Ch.B. (June 1936).

1927 JOHN CALLANDER GRIERSON, born 1883, son of John G. and Janette Callander; educ. at West of Scotland College of Pharmacy, M.P.S. (1910); became missionary in Canada; educ. Presbyterian College, Saskatoon; B.A. Milton Univ., Baltimore (1926); licen. by Presb. of Saskatoon 6th April 1923; ord. to Pontax, Westerleigh and McKnight in Saskatchewan; adm. on probation by General Assembly 3rd June 1926; ord. 8th Dec. 1927; dem. 30th June 1946; died 16th Aug. 1947. Marr. 14th Oct. 1910 Isobel Tripney, daugh. of Robert Cowan, Bathgate, and Mary Clark, and has issue—Mabel Cowan, born 2nd April 1912.

OATHLAW OR OLD FINHAVEN

The Church of Finhaven was frequently called the "Kirk of Aikenholt." In 1380, before going abroad, Sir Alexander Lindsay of Glenesk rebuilt the church and erected it into a Prebend of Brechin Cathedral. The prebendary had a stall in the choir, and was to say mass for Sir Alexander's safe return. The return, however, did not materialise, for he died in Canada in 1382. Probably in the early part of the 17th century and before 1618, which is the date on the bell, the church was removed to Oathlaw. The foundations of the old church, called the "Kirk of Aikenauld," occupy a site at the junction of the Esk and the Lemno, a little below the ruins of Finhaven Castle. A spring called "Nine Well," on the hill above the old church, may mean that the church was dedicated to the Nine Maidens. St Mary's Well at Oathlaw suggests that a pre-Reformation chapel with that dedication may have been there situated. There was in the parish a Chaplainry of St Leonard, apparently attached to Brechin Cathedral.—[*Reg. of Brechin*, i, 196–7, ii, 361; *Land of the Lindsays*, 132, 135, 161–2, 165–7; *Lives of the Lindsays*, i, 73.]

1696 JOHN GRUB, M.A.; he preached in a meeting house at Gairden in the parish of Kirkden in June–July 1712 and intruded in the Church of Kirkden June 1714, and in Inverarity Church from Sept. 1715 to Feb. 1716; conducted services in a meeting house at Arbroath Nov. 1713, and performed marriages and baptisms at various places, including Guthrie, 1712–15. —[*Justiciary Records*, 1712–17, 15th March 1715.]

1880 ALEXANDER RITCHIE, dem. 28th Dec. 1926; died 30th Jan. 1929.

1927 THOMAS HENRY WRIGHT, trans. from Paris (*q.v.*) 12th May 1927; died at Brechin 24th June 1942.

RESCOBIE

1563 THOMAS CORMACK or GORMACK, min. in 1563.—[*Comps. Sub Coll. of Thirds, Forfar*, etc.]

1641 THOMAS LYON, present parson 12th Nov. 1641.—[*Deeds, Dal.*, 1705, No. 571.]

1677 PATRICK LYON, his daugh., Grissell (marr. Robert Straton of Warburton); died 11th Oct. 1765.

1843 DAVID ESDAILE, his daugh., Agnes (Mrs Thom), died at Minho, Portugal, 1937.

1850 ALEXANDER WALKER, his widow, Mary Mowbray Esdaile, died 4th March 1925.

1899 ROBERT HALL, dem. 16th May 1937; died 25th May 1938.

TANNADICE

The church, dedicated by Bishop de Bernham on 11th Aug. 1242, was made a Mensal Church of St Andrews by Bull of Pope Sextus IV, 26th Feb. 1473. A cairn-crowned hill is called St Arnold's Seat, but formerly was known as St Eunandi's Seit or St Eunan's Seat—forms of St Adamnan. In 1744 the min. designated it St Ernan's Seat, and stated that the church was St Ernan's.—[Macfarlane's *Geograph. Colls.*, i, 286–7; S.H.S.; *The Apostolic Camera and Scott. Benefices*, 173; Lockhart's *Ch. in Scot. in 13th Century*, 50–1.]

1560 JAMES KINLOCH, reader in 1560.— [*Comps. Sub Coll. of Thirds, Forfar*, etc.]

1563 JAMES MELVILLE, M.A., min. in charge 1563, and at Fearn and Menmuir.—[*Comps. Sub Coll. of Thirds, Forfar*, etc.]

1575 EDWARD CHISHOLM.—[*Acts and Dec.*, lx, 395.]

1724 JOHN OGILVIE of Queich, marr. (1) pro. 14th Oct. 1714 Margaret Lidderdale, Montrose.

1921 WILLIAM ROBERTSON SMART, trans. to Kennoway 18th May 1925.

1925 DONALD MacGILLIVRAY BEATON, trans. from Leslie (Garrioch) (*q.v.*) 24th Sept. 1925; trans. to Glenrinnes 31st May 1929.

PRESBYTERY OF DUNDEE

ABERNYTE

1858 ROBERT MACKAY LEITCH, his widow, Edith Mary Smith, died 12th Nov. 1926.

1890 WILLIAM LISTON MILROY, died 26th Dec. 1925; his widow, Jessie Stobo Haining, died 11th March 1939.

1926 HENRY REID CHALMERS, trans. from Duffus (*q.v.*) 15th June 1926; dem. 15th Jan. 1933.

AUCHTERHOUSE

On 21st June 1460 Papal Indulgence was granted for those who contributed to the building and repair of the Church of the Most Glorious Virgin of Auchterhouse.—[*Transcripts from Vatican*, iii, 28; *MS. Gen. Register House.*]

1563 SIR DUNCAN GRAY, vicar and reader 1563, 1565 and 5th June 1579.—[*Edin. Tests.*, i, 32; *Reg. Mag. Sig.*, v, 1170.]

1563 ALEXANDER TYRIE, min. in 1563 and 1568; pres. to parsonage and vicarage 3rd July 1564.—[*Reg. Sec. Sig.*, lxvi, 166; *Comps. Sub Coll. of Thirds, Forfar*, etc.]

1568 JAMES MELVILLE, M.A., pres. to parsonage and vicarage 29th July 1568.—[*Reg. Pres. Bene.*, i, 15.]

1844 HUGH ARBUTHNOTT LYELL, his son, David John Stewart, died at Coupar Angus 2nd Nov. 1931.

1912 JOHN KIRKLAND CAMERON, served as Chaplain to Argyll and Sutherland Highlanders, 2nd K.O. S.B. and XI Corps Troop in Great War; dem. April 1942; died 12th March 1947. His daugh., Jessie (marr. 3rd Dec. 1930 John Stirling, East Mains, Auchterhouse). Publication—Joint Author of *Auchterhouse, an Historical and Social Record.*

BROUGHTY FERRY

1827 DAVID DAVIDSON, marr. 15th Jan. 1828. Line 13, for "1827" read "1828."

1921 WILLIAM DAY FYFE, died at Aberdeen 21st Sept. 1924.

1926 ALEXANDER SMART, trans. from Daviot (Garioch) (*q.v.*) 24th March 1926; Ph.D. (Aberdeen, 1938); trans. to St Cuthbert's, Saltcoats, 11th Dec. 1940 and has issue—Aileen Elizabeth, born 28th April 1925; Lois Marjory, born 11th Feb. 1928.

BEACH

1906 JAMES BURGESS, died 11th Nov. 1924; his widow, Harriet Louise Bartlett, died 13th Nov. 1939.

1925 CHARLES SYDNEY FINCH, born 25th July 1891, son of Zeph. F., butcher, and Eliza Killington; educ. at Univ. of Edinburgh, M.A. (1923); licen. by Presb. of Edinburgh 28th March 1923; assistant St Matthew's, Edinburgh, 1923; ord. 3rd April 1925; trans. to Wilton, Glasgow, 4th June 1930; trans. to St George's, Hawick, 23rd Sept. 1936. Marr. 25th Dec. 1915 Annie Bethune (died 27th March 1937), daugh. of James Whitehead and Annie Robertson, and has issue—Muriel Annie Sydney, born 15th April 1928.

BROUGHTY FERRY ST JAMES

DOUGLAS WILLIAM BRUCE, dem. 16th Feb. 1925 on app. to Buenos Aires.
1919

JAMES CHARLES CONN, Ph.D. (St Andrews), trans. from Elgin 4th Aug. 1926; dem. 30th Sept. 1946; had issue—Janet Sorley, born 13th May 1917; Agnes Kirkland, born 27th June 1919. Publication—Thesis: *The Contribution of Thomas Erskine of Linlathen to Scottish Theology.*
1926

DUNDEE ST MARY'S

There was a Chapel of St Mary Magdalene between Dundee and Broughty of which Sir Walter Brugh, who died 1582–3, Chaplain of St Ninian's in Dundee, was also chaplain. There was also a chapel dedicated to St Clement in which there was an altar dedicated to the Virgin Mary and under the patronage of the provost and bailies.

Apparently in 1391 Sir James Lindsay of Crawford founded the Hospital and House of the Red Friars. He gave certain buildings at the foot of South Tay Street, and some annual rents, for the maintenance of the said Friars, weak old people, and diseased folk. Robert III granted confirmation by charter of 1391–2, and at the same time gave Kettins Church to the House. Within the "Great Lodging" of the Lindsays of Crawford, on the south side of the Parish Church, there was a chapel or oratory dedicated to St Michael.—[*Reg. Great Seal*, i, 838; *Reg. of Brechin*, App., 372; *Lives of the Lindsays*, i, 97, 110; *Cal. of Papal Reg., Letters*, xii, 722; *St Andrews Tests.*, 7th Jan. 1583–4.]

WILLIAM CHRISTISON, pres. to vicarage 1569 on forfaulture of John Hamilton.—[*Reg. Pres. Bene.*, i, 30.]
1560

JOHN HAMILTON, reader 1561.—[*Comps. Gen. Coll. of Thirds.*]
1561

JAMES HAMILTON, vicar 1563.—[*Comps. Sub Coll. of Thirds, Forfar*, etc.]
1563

WILLIAM KYDE (KIDD), reader 1563; pres. to vicarage 5th Aug. 1570 on forfeiture of John Hamilton.—[*Reg. Pres. Bene.*, i, (2), 1; *Comps. Sub Coll. of Thirds, Forfar*, etc.]
1563

ROBERT STIBBLES, reader 29th April 1623.—[*Reg. Mag. Sig.*, viii, 644.]
1623

ANDREW AUCHINLECK, his children—Thomas, Charles, Isabel, Margaret, Eupham and Lilias, were by Margaret Bower, his fourth wife.—[*Decreets, Durie*, cxiii, 132.]
1642

ARCHIBALD WATSON, his daugh., Robina, died at Edinburgh 21st Oct. 1931; Archibald, his son, died in Natal 23rd Aug. 1938.
1862

COLIN CAMPBELL, died at Callander 20th June 1931; his widow, Jessie Taylor, died at Edinburgh 29th July 1944.
1882

ADAM WIGHTMAN FERGUSON, died at Yarrow 21st July 1943; his daugh., Beatrice Mair (marr. 10th Sept. 1931 Alexander William Sawyer, min. of Inchinnan).
1911

SOUTH CHURCH
SECOND CHARGE

GEORGE MARTIN, his daugh., Helen, bapt. 3rd Jan. 1656; Dean of Faculty 3rd Jan. 1656.—[*St Andrews Reg.*]
1658

DUNDEE ST CLEMENT'S

JAMES MUIRHEAD BENSON, died unmarr. 5th Nov. 1925.
1894

DAVID EASTHAM AUTY, trans. to Castle Douglas 22nd March 1928.
1922

JOHN SHEDDEN, formerly of Haggs (*q.v.*), trans. from Dalmellington 11th Sept. 1928; trans. to Trinity, Edinburgh, 18th May 1932; trans. to Cardonald 18th Sept. 1935; died 4th Aug. 1947.
1928

BALGAY

WILLIAM HALL, dem. 16th May 1924,
1898 died at Dundee 28th March 1925.

CYRUS MAXWELL MORTIMER, born Edinburgh 14th March 1897,
1924 son of Alfred M. and Anne Watt Chalmers Pryde; educ. at Royal High School and Univ. of Edinburgh, M.A. (1922); served in Great War as Lieut. R.F.A., R.F.C. and R.A.F., Air Force Cross; licen. by Presb. of Edinburgh 20th Dec. 1922; assistant St Leonard's, Edinburgh, and Dunblane; ord. 3rd Sept. 1924; trans. to Roberton 6th May 1930. Marr. 26th Dec. 1918 Dorothy Aileen, daugh. of Edward Elliot, and has issue—Aileen Marion, born 14th Feb. 1921; Dorothy Anne Elliot, born 23rd Dec. 1928.

CHAPELSHADE

ARCHIBALD HENDERSON MITCHELL, born 1st Oct. 1897, son of
1924 George M., farm overseer, and Agnes Henderson; educ. at Univ. of Aberdeen, M.A. (1919), B.D. (1922); licen. by Presb. of Aberdeen, 1922; assistant Kirkcaldy; ord. 17th Dec. 1924; trans. to Kirriemuir 22nd Aug. 1929; trans. to Mortlach 9th Jan. 1935; died 10th Dec. 1941. Marr. 28th July 1926 Jean Fraser, daugh. of J. Farquhar McRae, factor, Kirkton of Rayne, Meikle Wartle, Aberdeenshire, and has issue—Ian McRae, born 13th April 1927; Evelyn McRae, born 13th April 1927; Isabel Henderson, born 19th Dec. 1933.

CLEPINGTON

DAVID RAE ROBERTSON, his widow, Jane Morris Galloway, died
1875 27th Sept. 1928; his daugh., Elizabeth Mary, died at Broughty Ferry 19th May 1925.

GEORGE MacWILLIAM, trans. to
1918 Audlearn 14th April 1926.

DAVID DICK, born 8th Aug. 1896,
1926 son of John D. and Thomasina Smith; served in Argyll and Sutherland Highlanders in France and Macedonia; retired Lieut. 1919; educ. at Univ. of St Andrews, M.A. (1921), B.D. (1924); licen. by Presb. of St Andrews 1924; assistant at Dunblane; ord. 1st Sept. 1926; Chaplain to Forces Territorial Army 1930; trans. to Torthorwald 16th May 1935; trans. to St Ninian's, Stirling, 12th June 1940. Marr. 25th Feb. 1931 Ella Margaret Torrance, daugh. of William Steele Nicoll, J.P., and Isabella Orrick Birrell, and has issue—David Douglas, born 11th May 1933; Dennis John, died 1st Oct. 1934; Doreen Ella Margaret Nicoll, born 24th April 1937. Publications—Edited *College Echoes*, 1922-3; edited *Scottish University Verses* 1918-23 (1923) and various booklets and pamphlets.

DOWNFIELD

HENRY DODD, his wife, Elizabeth
1919 Scott, died at Edinburgh 26th Feb. 1932; dem. 2nd Feb. 1941; died 4th June 1942.

ST DAVID'S

GEORGE LEWIS, his daugh., Florence
1839 Mary (marr. Harold B. Milne of Ridgwood, London), died 13th July 1929.

GEORGE MURDOCH MACLEAN,
1909 died at Monifieth 14th May 1948; his daugh., Mairi (marr. 27th Sept. 1934 Lewis Drummond Carmichael, Mill of Bendochy).

(*United with St Paul's 28th May* 1947.)

ST JOHN'S

PETER GRANT, his son, John Guillan,
1851 died at Tayport 28th July 1930.

JOHN ANTHONY MACRAE, trans.
1919 to Partick 10th Jan. 1928.

McINTOSH MOWAT, trans. from
1928 Ruthrieston (*q.v.*) 11th July 1928; trans. to Campsie, High Church, 23rd April 1941; died 22nd May 1948; his daugh., Marjory (marr. 16th Sept. 1939 James Wilson Anderson, min. of Bonhill North). Publication—*Straight from the Shoulder*.

ST PAUL'S

1662 WILLIAM RAIT, Regent of King's College, Aberdeen, 1641. Marr. cont. 21st July 1642 Elizabeth Gordon, sister to Alexander Gordon, the Gudeman of Birsemore, and had issue—James, bapt. 2nd Sept. 1654; Robert, bapt. 21st Nov. 1655; William, bapt. 14th Feb. 1657; Catherine, bapt. 4th Oct. 1658; David, bapt. 8th Feb. 1660; Laurence, bapt. 6th July 1661; Alexander, bapt. 11th Aug. 1663; Agnes, bapt. 30th March 1665.

1682 ROBERT RAIT, had issue—William, born 24th Aug. 1685; Janet, born 24th Aug. 1686; Alexander, born 26th March 1688.

1691 WILLIAM MITCHELL. Addl. issue—Alexander, bapt. 24th March 1669; a child buried Aberdeen 4th Oct. 1669.—[*Aberdeen Reg.*]

1883 WILLIAM SMITH, his widow, Jessie Bayne, died 10th Nov. 1941.

1897 JAMES BOATH WOOD, his wife, Elizabeth Hair, Doctor of Osteopathy, died 6th July 1925.

FAIRMUIR

1903 DONALD DEWAR MACDONALD, son of Donald M., Parish Schoolmaster, Kilmacolm; died at Dundee 14th June 1926.

1926 WILLIAM ANGUS WALLACE, born 27th March 1883; educ. at St John's College, Manitoba Univ.; ord. deacon by Archbishop of Rupert's Land; *locum tenens* St Mark's, Minnedosa; ord. priest 18th June 1916; rector of St Thomas, Winnipeg, 1916–19; dem. on appointment as Western Canadian Provincial Organising Secretary for the World Brotherhood Movement; rector of Elgin, Manitoba, 1921; dem. June 1922; returned to Scotland; assistant Ferry Port on Craig; adm. on probation by General Assembly 24th May 1923; adm. by Presb. of Hamilton 1924; adm. to Law 11th Feb. 1925; trans. and adm. 15th Dec. 1926; trans to Guthrie 21st Nov. 1935. Marr. 25th Sept. 1916 Elizabeth Haslam Bethune and has issue—William Bethune, born 9th May 1922; Elizabeth Naomi, born 20th May 1925; Eleanor May, born 25th Sept. 1932.

HILLTOWN

1838 JOHN BAXTER, died 12th Aug. 1893; his wife, Janet Soutar, died 11th Jan. 1879, aged 69; had issue—John born 10th Aug. 1841, died 3rd April 1908; George Chalmers, born 16th July 1843, min. U.F. Church, Cargill, died 2nd April 1918; Jane, died 10th June 1849; Richard, died 9th July 1849.

LOCHEE

The church was dedicated by Bishop de Bernham 11th Sept. 1243.

1871 WILLIAM WRIGHT, his widow, Margaret Asher Bell, died 22nd Dec. 1935.

1920 RICHARD GIBB, trans. to Lochmaben 17th Feb. 1925.

1925 HUGH SHIRLAW, born Loanhead 15th April 1881, son of William S. and Agnes Merry Thomson; educ. at Univ. of Edinburgh, M.A. (1907), B.D. (1911); licen. by Presb. of Edinburgh 1910; served in Argyll and Sutherland Highlanders and in Royal Scots, Lieut., in Great War; assistant at Robertson Memorial, Edinburgh; ord. to Fogo 11th Sept. 1919; trans. and adm. 1st Oct. 1925. Marr. 4th Feb. 1918 Florence, daugh. of William Dunnett, min. of Kilmarnock.

LOCHEE, ST LUKE'S

1879 WILLIAM MAY, died 7th Jan. 1925; his widow, Anna McDougall, died 7th Nov. 1946.

1917 EVELYN GALL, trans. to Kirkcaldy 27th April 1927.

1927 MATTHEW McPHAIL, trans. from Castle Douglas 12th Oct. 1927; trans. to Arbirlot 16th May 1929.

LOGIE

The church was granted to Scone Abbey by William, Bishop of St Andrews 1202–12, being confirmed by William the Lion. The church was dedicated by Bishop de Bernham 25th Aug. 1243.—[*Book of Scone*, 28.]

JOHN CHRISTISON, M.A., had issue also, Mr John.—[*Dunfermline Sas.*, ii, 201.]
1576

JAMES WILSON MUGGOCH, trans. to Martyr's, Paisley, 18th Jan. 1928.
1922

HENRY MATTHEW BARTLETT, born Insch 31st Oct. 1902; son of Henry B., master baker, merchant and farmer, and Isabella Dunbar Matthew; educ. at Univ. of Aberdeen, M.A. (1923), B.D. (1926); licen. by Presb. of Garioch 1926; assistant Galashiels; ord. 6th July 1928. Marr. 27th June 1940 Elizabeth Auld Nicholson, elder daugh. of William J. Wallace, 11 Strawberry Bank, Dundee, and had issue—Anne Susan, born 17th June 1941, died 20th Nov. 1942; Peter Henry, born 19th June 1944.
1928

MARYFIELD

JAMES DOWIE, died at Cupar 17th May 1932.
1887

JOHN McILWRAITH, trans. to St Ninian's, Aberdeen, 20th Feb. 1929.
1922

WILLIAM CECIL BIGWOOD, born Burnside, Forfar, 9th Dec. 1903, son of William John B. and Annabella Valentine; educ. at Forfar Academy and Univ. of St Andrews, M.A. (1924), and Edinburgh B.D. (1929); licen. by Presb. of ——— 1929; ord. 19th June 1929; trans. to Keith, St Rufus, 2nd Oct. 1935; trans. to Fetteresso 5th April 1944. Marr. 12th Nov. 1930 Isabella Hunter, daugh. of Joseph Farquhar, Dundee, and Christian Hunter, and has issue—Anne Margaret, born 9th Feb. 1932, died 15th Feb. 1932; William Francis Nathan, born 1st Feb. 1933; Winifred Katherine, born 14th Dec. 1935; Joan Mary, born 28th Jan. 1937.
1929

ROSEBANK

ALEXANDER FORBES BLACK, trans. to Advie 4th May 1928.
1920

JOHN HOWAT, born 23rd Jan. 1903, son of Adam H., M.A., schoolmaster, Pittenweem, and Henrietta Taylor; educ. at Madras College and Univ. of St Andrews, M.A. (1924), B.D. (1927); licen. by Presb. of St Andrews 5th May 1927; assistant at West Church, Aberdeen; ord. 27th Sept. 1928; trans. to Ballater South 29th June 1933; trans. to St Rule's Monifeith, 24th Feb. 1943; app. Assembly Secretary for Department and Director of Religious Education, 1948. Marr. 29th Dec. 1938 May, eldest daugh. of James Owen Angus, Aberdeen, and has issue—Angus John, born 5th Aug. 1944.
1928

ST ANDREW'S

JAMES EWING, his son, Sir James Alfred, died 7th Jan. 1935.
1837

HARCOURT MORTON DAVIDSON, died 5th June 1926.
1886

ROBERT FORRESTER VICTOR SCOTT, trans. from Strathmiglo (*q.v.*) 26th Jan. 1926; trans. to Barony, Glasgow, 3rd Oct. 1935; trans. to St Columba's, Pont Street, London, 7th Oct. 1938; D.D. (Edinburgh, 23rd June 1944); has issue—Frances, born 23rd Jan. 1925; Agnes Henrietta, born 16th Nov. 1926; Thomas Harry, born 11th May 1932. Father-in-law's name, for "F. J." read "Frank Scott."
1926

ST ENOCH'S

HUGH GEORGE WATT, his widow, Amy Stanley Allan, died at Milngavie 1st Sept. 1928.
1877

WILLIAM YOUNG COLQUHOUN, died 11th March 1928.
1923

JOHN HENDERSON SEAFORTH BURLEIGH, trans. from Fyvie (*q.v.*) 3rd Oct. 1928; dem. 30th Sept. 1931 on app. to Chair of Ecclesiastical History, Univ. of Edinburgh; D.D. (Aberdeen, 30th March 1938). Marr. 25th Aug.
1928

ST MARK'S

CHARLES MARTIN GRANT, line 32,
1877 for "1915" read "1918."

JOSEPH ROBERT PRENTER, dem.
1913 2nd June 1925; adm. to St Ninian's, Linlithgow, 9th April 1930; dem. June 1937; died 8th July 1946; his daughs.—Kathleen Louisa (marr. 3rd April 1937 Kenneth Anderson, leader of Reid Orchestra); Lucie Blanche Woods (marr. 17th April 1937 Dr Philip Murphy, Colonial Medical Service).

DAVID BRUCE NICOL, formerly of
1925 Skelmorlie (*q.v.*); trans. from St Margaret's, Edinburgh, 18th Dec. 1925; trans. to Govan 5th Sept. 1929.

ST MATTHEW'S

MATTHEW WELSH NEILSON, trans.
1920 to New Deer 16th May 1924.

HUGH CLARKE McCOLL, trans.
1924 from Kilbirnie (*q.v.*) 9th Oct. 1924; dem. 31st May 1928; assistant St Mungo's, Alloa; adm. to Milton, Glasgow, 28th March 1933; died 7th Jan. 1944.

COLIN ROSS MUNRO, born Kilmuir,
1928 Ross-shire, 25th Jan. 1886, son of John M., forester; educ. at Univ. of Aberdeen, M.A. (1910); ord. to Mure Church, Irvine, 1916; trans. to West U.F. Church, Hamilton, 1922; trans. and adm. 14th Nov. 1928; dem. 12th March 1931; trans. to Old Church, Alexandria, 14th Sept. 1932. Marr. 4th April 1917 Isabella Margaret, daugh. of David Hamilton, teacher, Bellevue, Meikleriggs, Paisley, and has issue—Iain Ross, born 10th April 1918; David Hamilton, born 31st Oct. 1921.

WALLACETOWN

STANLEY BUCHANAN CAREY,
1919 dem. 23rd Feb. 1926 and went to St Andrews, Guelph, Canada, 1927; 1926 Mary, daugh. of Charles Giles, min. of Forglen, and has issue—Elizabeth Anne, born 1st Nov. 1927; John Karl, born 14th Jan. 1931. Publication—*Christianity in the New Testament Epistles*.

adm. to St Andrews Presb. Church, Pictou, Nova Scotia.

JOHN ALEXANDER MACKAY,
1926 trans. from Cluny, Kincardine o'Neill (*q.v.*) 8th Sept. 1926; dem. 7th Oct. 1930; adm. to Chapelton 23rd Dec. 1930; trans. to St James, Clydebank, 30th Jan. 1936.

INCHTURE

The church was dedicated by Bishop de Bernham 11th Aug. 1243. In 1165–72 King William the Lion granted the church, with its lands and the Chapel of Kinnaird, to the Priory of St Andrews, the grant being confirmed by Richard, Bishop of St Andrews, 1170–2. In 1372 Pope Gregory XI confirmed a charter of William Landel, Bishop of St Andrews, granting the Mensal Church of Inchture with the Chapel of Kinnaird for the fabric of the Cathedral, on the ground that the action of the sea had destroyed a large part of the rock on which the Cathedral was situated and threatened the greatest danger to the foundation and fabric of the same, and that the fruits, annual rents, and revenues devoted to the work of the fabric, through wars and the mischievousness of men, had become so small and so alienated that they did not suffice for the repair of the rock and the upkeep of the Cathedral. In the church there was an altar dedicated to St Katharine.—[*Reg. Priory of St Andrews*, xxxvi, xlv, 59, 138–9, 218–19.]

NICOL SPITTAL, M.A., min. at
1563 Foulis, also in charge here 1563–72.—[*Comps. Sub Coll. of Thirds, Fife*, etc.]

JOHN SMYTH, exhorter 1565–6.—
1565 [*Cal. of Charters*, ix, 2105.]

JAMES WICHTAND, pres. to vicarage
1574 15th Aug. 1573 on death of Arthur Taillyour.—[*Reg. Pres. Bene.*, i, (4), 10.]

ALEXANDER SCRYMGEOUR, pres.
1599 to vicarage 17th Dec. 1606 on dem. or transportation of John Ogilvy, min. at Kingoldrum.—[*Reg. Sec. Sig.*, lxxv, 211.]

1710	THOMAS CARSTAIRS, episcopal min., intruded here Oct. 1715 to Jan. 1716 and lured men for the Pretender.—[*Justiciary Records.*]
1884	JOHN ADAMSON HONEY, his widow, Jessie Syme, died 9th Dec. 1935.
1920	THOMAS DOWNIE MEREDITH, trans. to St Luke's, Edinburgh, 30th Sept. 1927.
1928	PETER JOHN McIVER, trans. from Craigneuk 17th Feb. 1928.

(*United to Kinnaird 12th Jan. 1941.*)

ROSSIE

The Church of Rossinclerach (Rossie) was dedicated to St Laurence and St Coman by Bishop de Bernham of St Andrews 13th Aug. 1243. The church along with its pertinents was granted to the Priory of St Andrews by Matthew, Archdeacon of St Andrews—confirmation by Malcolm IV, 1153–65. The "Abbey" of Rossie indicates that there was an early Christian settlement here, with dependent churches or chapels.—[*Reg. Priory of St Andrews*, 64, 126, 200–1, etc.; *Church of Scot. in 13th Century*, 56.]

1565	DAVID ROBERTSON, pres. in 1570 on death of David Henderson.—[*Reg. Pres. Bene.*, i, (2), 5.]
1607	GEORGE HAITLIE, pres. to vicarage 11th Aug. 1607 on death of Robert Gray, last vicar, who was brother of Patrick, Lord Gray.—[*Reg. Sec. Sig.*, lxxvi, 147.]
1628	JAMES BLAIR.—[*G. R. Sas.*, lx, 437.]

INVERGOWRIE

The church was founded by St Boniface (Curitan) about 715. At Invergowrie there was a church site called *Kil-curdy* (Church of Curitan), called in 17th century Kincurdy, Kincuddy. The church, along with the lands called Dargoch on the west side of the church, was granted to Scone Abbey by Malcolm IV, 1153–65.—[Scott's *Pictish Nation*, 375; Simpson's *Celtic Church in Scot.*, 111; *Book of Scone*, 12.]

1561	WILLIAM CAVELL, vicar 1561.—[*Comps. Gen. Coll. of Thirds.*]
1563	JOHN BUCHAN, min. in 1563, also at Liff.—[*Comps. Sub Coll. of Thirds, Forfar*, etc.]
1563	DAVID DENMUIR, reader.—[*Comps. Sub Coll. of Thirds, Forfar*, etc.]
1568	NINIAN HALL, min. 1568–9.—[*Comps. Sub Coll. of Thirds, Forfar*, etc.]
1579	JOHN CHRISTISON, M.A., pres. to vicarage 14th Jan. 1579–80 on death of William Hepburn, Chalmoner of Scone.—[*Reg. Pres. Bene.*, ii, 28.]
1901	DONALD DAVIDSON, died 16th Feb. 1929; his widow, Lily Munro, died Bournemouth 26th June 1946.

(*Charges united 2nd Sept. 1945.*)

KINNAIRD IN GOWRIE

Kinnaird was a dependent chapel of Inchture and as such was given by William the Lion, 1165–1214, and Richard, Bishop of St Andrews 1163–77, to the Priory of St Andrews.

1579	JAMES WICHTAND, reader 16th Feb. 1567–8.—[*Edin. Tests.*, ix, 248.]
1649	THOMAS KINNARES.—[*G. R. Sas.*, 2 Ser., x, 149.]
1678	JOHN SHAW, his first wife, Anna Bennet, died 15th March 1671. Addl. issue—Elizabeth, born 6th Feb. 1668; his son, John, was by first marriage; marr. (2) Isobel Strachan and had issue—Janet, born 8th Feb. 1673; Isabel, born 14th July 1674, died 31st July 1675; Catherine, died 18th Dec. 1676.—[*Carnock Register, Memo.*, Rev. J. M. Webster.]
1899	JOHN MILNE ANDERSON, dem. 12th Jan. 1941.

LIFF and BENVIE

The church was confirmed to Scone Abbey by William, Bishop of St Andrews 1202-12, being one of a group of churches described as granted to the Abbey by Alexander I, Malcolm IV, William the Lion.—[*Book of Scone*, 31.]

1563 JOHN BUCHAN, min. in 1563. (See Invergowrie.)

1566 NICHOLAS SPITTALL, min. of Foulis Easter and Longforgan, in charge here.

1601 JOHN CHRISTISON, called min. of Liff 2nd Oct. 1605.—[*Dunfermline Sas.*, ii, 201.]

1919 WILLIAM SUTHERLAND BUCHAN, trans. to St James, Portobello, 8th Oct. 1924.

1925 JOHN MACLEAN, trans. from Renton (*q.v.*) 25th March 1925. Addl. issue—Kenneth F., born 25th Feb. 1921, died 25th Jan. 1922; Alisdair Edmund, born 14th Sept. 1922, killed falling from a tree 22nd Feb. 1930; Iain Gordon Cameron, born 10th Jan. 1924; his wife, Ann O'Brien, died 3rd Aug. 1934; his daugh., Moira (marr. 16th July 1946 James, elder son of J. D. McGibbon, Gray Cottage, Liff.)

BENVIE

The church was dedicated by Bishop de Bernham 9th Sept. 1243. About 1350-60 there are mentioned at Benvie, the land of St Martin and the Vennel of St Mary, the latter no doubt being the parish church.—[*Misc. Scot. Hist. Soc.*, v, 17.]

1599 JOHN OGILVIE, min. 14th March 1601, when Alexander Scrymgeour claimed possession as successor to Thomas Ramsay.—[*Acts and Dec.*, clxvi, 55.]

1665 ALEXANDER SCRIMGEOUR, his wife had a son, Patrick Chalmers.—[*Deeds Dal.*, 1705, No. 142.]

1731 THOMAS LAWRIE, line 11, for "Begs" read "Bogs."

LONGFORGAN

1565 JOHN SMYTH, exhorter 18th Jan. 1565-6.—[*Cal. of Charters*, ix, 2102.]

1566 NICOLAS SPITTAL, exhorter 18th Jan. 1565-6, may be identical with N.S., son of Henry S. of Blairlogie; had a sister Christina.—[*Cal. of Charters*, ix, 2105; Stephen's *Inverkeithing and Rosyth*, 480-1; *Edin. Tests.*, v, 142.]

1661 JAMES MIDDLETON, had issue—David, bapt. 15th Feb. 1656; Jean, bapt. 9th Dec. 1658; Grizel, bapt. 30th March 1660; Catherine, bapt. 14th April 1661.—[*Montrose Reg.*]

1702 THOMAS MITCHELL, had issue—Marjorie, bapt. 11th May 1698.—[*St Martin's Reg.*]

1709 JAMES HODGE, his daugh., Jean (marr. cont. 12th Aug. 1732).

1715 WILLIAM ELPHINSTONE, intruded here 1715 to Jan. 1716 and waited upon the Pretender at Glamis.—[*Justiciary Records*, 12th Feb. 1717.]

1843 WILLIAM RITCHIE, his sons—Edward Thomas, died 3rd March 1928; William Marshall, died at Broughty Ferry 25th Sept. 1932.

1885 NEIL KENNEDY MACKENZIE, died 5th Aug. 1924; his daugh., Cecilia Emily Grant (marr. 6th Aug. 1924 Capt. David Heron Watson, Cameron Highlanders); his widow, Edith Henrietta Frances Grant, died 2nd Dec. 1941.

1925 WILLIAM MACNICOL, trans. from Chapel of Garioch (*q.v.*) 16th Jan. 1925.

LUNDIE and FOULIS EASTER

1566 ALEXANDER CRICHTON, parson.—[*Acts and Dec.*, xxxi, 173, xlix, 107.]

1577 JOHN KNOX, M.A., min. 1st Dec. 1577.—[*Edin. Tests.*, vi, 168.]

1595 ANDREW MORTON, his son, Andrew, min. of Carmunnock.

1701 WALTER AINSLIE, marr. (3) Beatrix Chalmers, whose father was a merchant and not a writer; his son, Walter, adm. merchant burgess of Edinburgh 14th Sept. 1737.

1711 GEORGE FLEMING, marr. Agnes, daugh. of Alexander Hamilton of Kinkell and widow of Robert Hamilton; his son, William, apprenticed to Robert Boyd, merchant, Edinburgh, 17th May 1732.

1919 JOHN SINCLAIR, trans. to Mains and Strathmartine 14th April 1926.

1926 ROBERT LAMOND MACNIE, trans. from Loth 1st Dec. 1926; died at Dundee 14th Feb. 1929.

1929 JOHN ROGAN, trans. from Burntisland (*q.v.*) 14th June 1929, died 22nd Dec. 1929; his daugh., Elizabeth Agnes (marr. 27th Dec. 1929 William Stevenson, min. of Kinghorn).

FOULIS EASTER

The church was dedicated by Bishop de Bernham 31st Aug. 1242.

1574 PATRICK MORTIMER, reader, pres. to vicarage 7th March 1574-5 on dem. of John Row and death of Andrew Row.—[*Reg. Pres. Bene.*, i, (2) 31.]

MAINS and STRATHMARTINE

Strathdighty. In 1201-7 the church was granted to Arbroath Abbey by Gillechrist, Earl of Anegus. In the church there was an altar dedicated to the Virgin Mary. A dispute between Robert Graham of Fintry, heir of late Robert G. of Fintry, and Matilda Scrymgeour, widow of the said late Robert G., as to the altar was settled on 20th May 1490, when the arbiters in the dispute received the goods and ornaments of the altar in a chest before the altar from Sir Andrew Bachlane, chaplain, and the arbiters and said Matilda gave them to Robert Graham, who in turn gave them to the altar in honour of God, the Blessed Virgin, and St Joseph, vowing at the same time to found a perpetual chantry in their honour. The foundation took place on 7th June 1490.—[*Reports Hist. MSS. Commis.*, ii, *Graham of Fintry*, 199; *Reg. Great Seal*, ii, 2130.]

1563 NINIAN HALL, exhorter 1563.—[*Comps. Sub Coll. of Thirds, Forfar*, etc.]

1568 WILLIAM AUCHMOUTIE, M.A., min. in 1568.—[*Comps. Sub Coll. of Thirds, Forfar*, etc.]

1575 ALEXANDER GRAHAM, vicar.—[*Acts and Dec.*, liv, 33.]

1585 WILLIAM BRUCE, pres. to vicarage 21st Feb. 1588-9 on death of Alexander Graham.—[*Reg.Sec.Sig.*, 35.]

1590 WILLIAM RAIT.—[*G. R. Sas.*, lix, 151.]

1673 PATRICK STRACHAN, had issue—John, bapt. 13th April 1676; George, bapt. 26th May 1677.

1795 ALEXANDER STRACHAN, his daugh., Jean (marr. 3rd April 1795).

1820 DAVID CANNON, marr. Margaret, sister of James Lewes, Trinidad, and had issue—James, died young; Joseph, died young; Helen (marr. James Forgan, writer, Dundee); John, surveyor, factor and agent, South Australia and Van Dieman's Land, died at Edinburgh 27th Aug. 1852; Alexander, Captain, H.E.I.C.S.

1918 ALEXANDER ANDERSON, dem. 25th Nov. 1925; adm. to Robertson Memorial, Glasgow, 12th Jan. 1928.

1926 JOHN SINCLAIR, trans. from Lundie (*q.v.*) 14th April 1926; app. clerk of Presbytery 1925; dem. 1st Oct. 1945; app. assistant clerk of Presb. of Glasgow 1945. Marr. (1) 16th June 1927 Hannah Winks (died 21st Sept. 1935), daugh. of Robert Black Hunter and Anne Steele Morris; (2) 5th June 1940 Margaret MacGillivray McMurtrie and has issue—Marie Williamson, born 4th Feb. 1944.

STRATHMARTINE

The church was dedicated by Bishop of Bernham 18th May 1249.

1562 THOMAS CUMMING, vicar 1562–6.—[*Comps. Sub Coll. of Thirds, Forfar*, etc.]

1563 JAMES WEICHT, exhorter 1563, min. 1567.—[*Comps. Sub Coll. of Thirds, Forfar*, etc.]

1568 THOMAS MORRISON, pres. to vicarage 14th May 1568 on death of James Tyrie.—[*Reg. Sec. Sig.*, xxxvii, 64.]

1572 WILLIAM AUCHMOUTIE, min. pres. to prebend of quarter of parsonage 20th March 1572 on death of Sir James Weicht.—[*Reg. Sec. Sig.*, xli, 58.]

1718 WILLIAM THOMSON, marr. Helen, daugh. of William Ged, merchant, Edinburgh.

1744 HUGH MAXWELL, his sons—Robert of Halkerton; George of Balmyles, provost of Dundee.

1751 DAVID MAXWELL, his daughs.—Janet, died 1833; Ann (marr. Capt. Bell), died 1826; Helen (marr. George Blair of Adamstone), died 1831.

MONIFIETH

The church was granted to Arbroath Abbey by Gillechrist, Earl of Angus (Leneges), *cir.* 1201–7. About 1230 Malcolm, Earl of Angus, granted to Nicolas, son of Bryce, priest of Kirriemuir, the whole land of the Abthan of Monifieth. Abthan denotes that there was here a Celtic community of clerics governed by an Ab or Head. At Eglismonichty there was a chapel dedicated to St Andrew. If the name contains that of St Nechtan (Mo-Nechtan), St Andrew may be a later dedication.—[Skene's *Celtic Scotland*, ii, 395; Watson's *Celtic Place Names*, 311; *Cal. of Charters*, i, 31; *Reg. of Arbroath, vetus*.]

1563 JAMES LOVELL, reader.—[*Comps. Sub Coll. of Thirds, Forfar*, etc.]

1565 GILBERT GARDEN, on his complaint that Henry Wood of Ballumby and others had deprived him of the fruits of the glebe since 1565 by ejecting his tenants of the same, the Privy Council on 21st July 1569 ordained the said Henry to desist from the occupation of the glebe and put Gilbert in possession.—[*Reg. Privy Council*, i, 686–7.]

1616 PATRICK DURHAM, had issue—Andrew, bapt. 17th April 1615, died 13th Oct. 1659; Charles, bapt. 9th July 1616; Jean, bapt. 7th Aug. 1617; Agnes, bapt. 13th June 1619; Alexander, bapt. 21st May 1624.

1626 JOHN RUTHERFORD, called "King James the Fifth and Sixth man."—[*Reports Hist. MSS. Commis.* vi, 736.]

1649 JOHN BARCLAY, marr. 14th Nov. 1648 Helen, daugh. of John Fotheringham, and had issue—George, bapt. 5th Jan. 1650; John, bapt. 1st July 1651; John, bapt. 27th Nov. 1652; David, bapt. 25th Feb. 1654; Jean, bapt. 20th May 1655, died 31st July 1687; Alexander, bapt. 22nd Sept. 1656; William, bapt. 15th April 1658; Marion, bapt. 17th June 1659; Margaret, bapt. 30th July 1660; Elizabeth, bapt. 16th Feb. 1662; Jean, bapt. 27th June 1663; George, bapt. Nov. 1666; Thomas, bapt. 18th June 1668; Henry, bapt. 4th April 1670.

1676 JOHN DEMPSTER, had issue—Mary, bapt. 8th Dec. 1676; George, bapt. 24th Jan. 1678; John, bapt. 29th April 1679; Charles, bapt. 15th Nov. 1680; James, bapt. 24th April 1682, died 18th June 1684; Henry, bapt. 20th Aug. 1683; Jean, bapt. and died 1st Nov. 1685.

1900 DAVID DUTHIE McLAREN, died at Culter, Aberdeenshire, 8th April 1939.

1921 GORDON QUIG, died at Edinburgh 18th March 1946; his only daugh., Pauline Margaret Janet (marr. 12th May 1947 Flying Officer David Falconer Robertson).

MONIKIE

1561 MATTHEW GRIEVE, vicar pensioner, reader and exhorter 1561-8; pres. 1567-8 on death of Thomas Scrymgeour.—[*Reg. Pres. Bene.*, i, 3; *Comps. Sub Coll. of Thirds, Forfar*, etc.; *Reg. Privy Council*, 1, 684.]

1563 GILBERT GARDEN, min. 1563-8.— [*Comps. Sub Coll. of Thirds, Forfar*, etc.] (See Monifieth.)

1574 HENRY GRIEVE, pres. to vicarage 10th July 1571 on death of Matthew Grieve.—[*Reg. Pres. Bene.*, i, (4), 23.]

1585 JOHN DURHAM, his daugh., Barbara (marr. cont. 1st, 2nd and 10th March 1638 Andrew, son of Patrick Durham, min. of Monifieth).—[*Forfar Deeds*, 28th Jan. 1642.]

1680 WILLIAM RAIT, marr. cont. 12th April 1673, and had issue—George, M.D., bapt. 8th July 1674; Marat, bapt. 20th May 1676; Isabel, bapt. 9th Jan. 1678 (marr. 15th June 1704 John Robertson of Balharrie); Elizabeth, bapt. 19th Feb. 1679 (marr. James Smyton, merchant, Dundee); Marie, bapt. 6th Dec. 1683; Rachel, bapt. 3rd June 1686; Janet, bapt. 8th Jan. 1688; James, bapt. 29th Jan. 1689; Catherine, bapt. 25th Dec. 1689; Agnes, bapt. 18th May 1691.

1827 JAMES MILLER, born 20th June 1777; his son, David, died 22nd Aug. 1839; his daughs.—Elizabeth, died 10th Dec. 1873; Mary Ann, died 31st July 1862 (marr. 26th Dec. 1849 Malcolm McIntyre, min. of Free Church, Monikie); Janet, died 3rd Aug. 1840; Jane Martin (marr. 26th Dec. 1848 Alexander Comrie, min. of Free Church, Carnoustie); his son, John, died 27th Jan. 1879.

1896 ANDREW ARMIT, died 5th Aug. 1938; his widow, Elizabeth Wilson, died 28th Aug. 1942; his daugh., Elizabeth, died 24th June 1925.

MURROES

In 1201-7 the church was granted to Arbroath Abbey by Gillechrist, Earl of Angus (Leneges).—[*Reg. of Arbroath, vetus* 31.]

1563 WILLIAM OLIVER, reader, pres. to vicarage 20th Nov. 1579 on death of Ninian Cook.—[*Reg. Pres. Bene.*, ii, 251.]

1563 ANDREW AUCHINLECK, min. in 1563 and 1574.—[*Comps. Sub Coll. of Thirds, Forfar*, etc.] (See Barry.)

1648 ROBERT EDWARD, line 15, delete "Elizabeth Adamson, who survived him and had issue."

1715 JAMES DUNDAS, episcopal min. intruded here, Nov. 1715 to Jan. 1716. —[*Justiciary Records*.]

1873 JAMES NICOLL, died 3rd Sept. 1935; his widow, Cecilia Clark Baird, died 26th Jan. 1938.

1919 WILLIAM AUGUSTUS FORBES, died 16th Aug. 1942. Marr. 2nd Sept. 1926 Margaret Janet Ann, daugh. of John Tulloch and Janet Muir, and has issue—William Surrene, born 1st June 1929; John Augustus, born 16th Aug. 1931; Alexander Tulloch, born 24th Aug. 1934.

BALLUMBIE

1564 JOHN WIGTOUN, alleged vicar pensioner.—[*Acts and Dec.*, xxx, 48.]

ST MARGARET'S, BARNHILL

1884 THOMAS NEWBIGGING ADAMSON, his widow, Christina Fraser, died 15th Feb. 1929.

1921 GEORGE BREMNER, dem. 10th Nov. 1946; died 27th Nov. 1946; his wife, Jeannie Mackay, died 18th Nov. 1943.

TEALING

The church was granted to the Priory of St Andrews by Hugh Gifford and his son,

Willliam, 1178–80, and 1189–98 confirmed by William the Lion.—[*Reg. Priory of St Andrews*, xxxiii, 72, 325.]

1561 ADAM FOWLIE, vicar 1561, also parson 1563 and min. 1568.—[*Comps. Gen. Coll. and Sub Coll. of Thirds, Forfar*, etc.]

1567 ANDREW GIBB, pres. to vicarage 2nd June 1573 on death of Adam Fowlie.—[*Reg. Pres. Bene.*, i, (4), 6.]

1590 JOHN RAMSAY, pres. to parsonage 30th April 1591; the charge "has much pepull and requiring an able person to travel in the function of thir ministrie."—[*Reg. Sec. Sig.*, lxii, 42.]

1623 ALEXANDER BRUCE, his daugh., Catherine (marr. 6th Dec. 1649 John, son of James Scrimgeour of Fordell).

1665 PATRICK MAKGILL, marr. Marjory Durham, who marr. (2) Thomas Herring of Callie.—[*Deeds Dal.*, 1706, No. 1839.]

1835 DAVID BARCLAY MELLIS, his daugh., Mary Campbell, died from motor accident, Edinburgh, 17th April 1933.

1889 SAMUEL MACAULAY, his father min. at Annaclone, Bannbridge; died 5th June 1925; his widow, Helen Scott Shiell, died 16th April 1941; his daughs.—Helen Scott (marr. 20th Sept. 1941 Charles Kendal Hamlyn Rae); Mary Margaret (marr. 10th Oct. 1946 Rev. Cassells Cordner, M.A., Cooke Centenary Church, Belfast).

1925 IAN FORBES McCULLOCH, born 29th May 1898, son of John Hutton McC., min. of North Leith; educ. at Edinburgh Institution, Univ. of Edinburgh, M.A. (1924); licen. by Presb. of Edinburgh 19th Dec. 1923; assistant St Stephen's, Edinburgh, 1924; ord. 19th Nov. 1925; trans. to Greenock East 27th Nov. 1928; trans. to Grahamston East 2nd April 1937. Marr. 17th March 1926 Jane McWaters, daugh. of Robert Semple, Kilmarnock, and has issue—Alexander Forbes, born 16th July 1927; George Morison, born 18th March 1930; Elizabeth Ann Scott, born 24th June 1934.

1929 JAMES ALEXANDER SUTHERLAND WILSON, trans. from Bridge of Allan (*q.v.*) 15th June 1929; dem. 31st May 1941; died 12th Nov. 1944; his son, Leslie Rose, died 15th April 1917.

PRESBYTERY OF BRECHIN

BRECHIN, KILMORE and BUTTERGILL

Kilmoir and Buttergill were included in the charge of Brechin not later than 1574.

The Church of Kilmoir was situated on the north side of the South Esk, a short distance from the Cathedral and in the garden of Brechin Castle. Andrew Lauche (Leitch ?) was rector of Kilmoir *cir.* 1566–7.

The Church of Buttergill or Buthergill was a prebend of Brechin Cathedral. The church stood upon a knoll on the south side of the South Esk about 200 yards west of Brechin Bridge. The ruins of the church and the gravestones were removed about the close of the 18th century. At the site there was a spring which bore the name of "Inscen Well." Sir Robert Abercromby was parson of Buttergill, apparently at and certainly soon after the Reformation, and *cir.* 1566–7 John Leslie, son of John L. in Brechin, was granted "the benefice called the parsonage and vicarage of Buttergill," vacant or when vacant by the decease or demission of the said Sir Robert.

In the Cathedral there were also altars as follows: St Andrew, in the parish church; the Virgin Mary, at which on 18th Nov. 1360 Robert Erskine of Dun founded two chaplains; St John the Baptist; St James, at which there was a chaplainry of St Ann; All Saints, at which on 6th June 1541 Sir David Brown, vicar pensioner of Edzell, founded a chaplainry of the Name of Jesus. The bishopric was founded prior to 1153, and most probably in 1150. The abbot of the Celtic monastery appears to have become the Bishop; and the Culdees, at first conjoined with the Chapter, were ultimately, in 1248, superseded by it. The Vicarage of Brechin was a prebend of the Cathedral, the vicar, no doubt, having the parochial cure and serving at the parochial altar. On 31st Oct. 1429, Walter Palatine of Stratherne, Earl of Athole and Caithness, lord of Brechin, son of Robert II, founded a college of four priests and six boys to celebrate in the Cathedral, apparently as choristers, providing them with land and with houses which he built thereon. Ten upper chambers were built after his death, and completed by the Bishop; and three lower chambers were built by two chaplains. The round tower attached to the south-west angle of the Cathedral was built probably in the reign of Kenneth IV Macmael-Cholium 971–95. Apparently in 1267, William de Brechin, son of Sir Henry de Brechin, son (natural) of David, Earl of Huntingdon, founded the *Maison Dieu* with chapel dedicated to the Virgin Mary, the endowment being, in addition to the site, the Mill of Brechin, with three-tenths of the multures of Brechin, and the multures of other lands. Between the Bishop's Palace and the Castle of Brechin there was a House of the Trinity Friars founded in 1260, and at Woodside, near Brechin, there was a chapel dedicated to the Virgin Mary. On 7th Nov. 1454, the "Provost of St Anscharies's of Brechin" is a mandatory of Pope Nicholas V; but there is no known religious foundation corresponding to that designation.

The chapel at Errot or Arrat was dedicated to St Mary Magdalene. By Bull of Pope Eugene in 1435 it was united to the Holy Rood Altar in Brechin Cathedral.— [*Reg. Great Seal*, ii, 494, 1358, iii, 757, 1345; *Excheq. Rolls*, xv, 146; *Reg. Sec. Seal*, i, 1761, ii, 1487; *Reg. of Brechin*, i, 11, 13, 20, 52, 68–9, 181–4, 230–4, ii, 42, 44, 175–80, 304, 332, 361; *Cal. Papal Regs.*, *Letters*, vii, 242, viii, 343, ix, 83, x, 689, xi, 273; *Book of Assumptions*, i, 356; Skene's *Celtic*

Scot., 396–402; Simpson's *Celtic Ch. in Scot.*, 115; Jervise's *Memorials of Angus and Mearns*, 469–71.]

SIR ROBERT ABERCROMBY, vicar of Buttergill 9th Oct. 1561.—[*Cal. of Deeds, Decreets*, xxviii.]
1561

JOHN HEPBURN, on 15th Jan. 1587-8, as min. of Brechin, Kilmoir, Cuikstone and Buttergill, he received a gift of the Chaplaincy of St Leonard in Finavon to be paid to him yearly for his services at said kirks.—[*Reg. of Brechin*, ii, 361.]
1562

JOHN HAY, reader 1563.—[*Comps. Sub Coll. of Thirds, Forfar*, etc.]
1563

JOHN SHARP, reader 1563.—[*Comps. Sub Coll. of Thirds, Forfar*, etc.]
1563

DAVID WATT, vicar 1566.—[*Comps. Gen. Coll. of Thirds*.]
1566

RICHARD FINLAYSON, reader 3rd June 1576.—[*Edin. Tests.*, vi, 159.]
1576

JOHN ERSKINE, pres. to vicarage 27th Feb. 1578-9 on death of David Watt.—[*Reg. Pres. Bene.*, ii, 13.]
1578

ROBERT KINNEIR, vicar 31st July 1576; on 26th Nov. 1579, in succession to the late John Erskine, he was pres. by James VI to the vicarage with manse and glebe, having been "found qualified by the Superintendent of Angus to exercise the office of reader within the Kirk of God"; died after 15th May 1608; had a son, John.—[*Reg. of Brechin*, ii, 230, 286, 296, 340.]
1576

ALEXANDER BISSET, M.A.; to him and his wife, Jean Ogilvy, belonged the Office of the Mayor (Mair) of Fee of the Sheriffdom of Aberdeen, with the lands of Pitmukstoun (Pitmuxton) belonging to the said office, lying near the Dee in the parish of St Machar; the office and lands passed to the Crown as ultimate heir.—[*Reg. Great Seal*, xi, 70.]
1608

JAMES WATT, reader 29th April 1623. —[*Reg. Great Seal*, viii, 644.]
1623

ROBERT NORRIE, M.A., son of Alexander N., min. of Dunipace; in succession to his father, he was pres. by Hon. Patrick Maule of Panmure on 29th Aug. 1636 to the office of Preceptor of the *Maison Dieu* of Brechin, "to fulfil the duties of the office, serving the cure of an ordinary minister in the Chapel of the said Preceptory and exercising the charge of a Master of the Grammar School in the City of Brechin."—[*Reg. of Panmure*, ii, 321–2.] (See Dunipace.)
1639

ROBERT GRAY, his son, Robert, apprenticed to James Seton, merchant, Edinburgh, 21st Nov. 1739.
1717

JAMES MACKAY, his daugh., Elizabeth Herd, died Ray Basses, Pyrenees, 19th Oct. 1945.
1875

JOHN ALEXANDER CLARK, his daugh., Elspeth Eadie, died 3rd June 1927; his widow, Margaret Eliza Ann McIntyre, died 11th July 1937; his daughs.—Dorothy Campbell, died at Loughborough 8th May 1941; Barbara MacMillan, died 10th June 1942.
1892

WALTER WILLIAM COATS, his wife, Margaret Janet Hamilton, died 3rd Jan. 1926; he died 21st June 1941.
1901

SECOND CHARGE

ADAM DUNCAN TAIT HUTCHISON, dem. 10th Feb. 1942; died 8th Jan 1949; his wife, Margaret Menzies, died 7th Nov. 1936.
1893

(*First and Second Charges united* 10*th Feb.* 1942.)

BRECHIN EAST

REGINALD FREDERICK WHITELEY, trans. to Thornliebank 7th June 1927.
1921

JOHN MEIKLE GRAY, formerly of Georgetown, British Guiana (*q.v.*), and Elderslie; adm. 5th Oct. 1927; dem. 10th Jan. 1937; adm. to Fetlar 4th May 1938; trans. to Bressay 4th Sept. 1942;
1927

dem. 21st Oct. 1946; adm. to Lauder West 11th Dec. 1947; his son, Neil Alexander, died 12th April 1944; Gwendoline Mary Lloyd, born 6th May 1934.

GARDNER MEMORIAL

1899 ALEXANDER MIDDLETON, dem. 1937, died 9th Nov. 1942.

CARESTON

The church was built by Sir Alexander Carnegie of Balnamoon (Bonnymoon) in 1636, and on 17th Nov. 1641 his lands of Careston and Pitforkie were disjoined by Parliament from Brechin and erected into the parish of Careston, Sir Alexander being patron. The church was considerably altered in 1808, and its story is further unfolded by a tablet over the entrance bearing this inscription: "In loving memory of Mrs Campbell of Stracathro this Church was restored in 1905 A.D."—[*Acts Scott. Parl.*, v, 478; *Trans. Scott. Eccles. Soc.*, 1906–7, 131, 133, 141.]

1666 GILBERT SKENE. Addl. issue—Agnes, bapt. 3rd Jan. 1664; Jean, bapt. 14th April 1665; Elizabeth, bapt. 3rd Feb. 1666.—[*Montrose Reg.*]

1710 ALEXANDER LINDSAY, M.A., intruded here again Sept. 1715 to Feb. 1716 and gave support to the rebels.—[*Justiciary Records.*]

1905 ROBERT PAISLEY, dem. 17th Nov. 1925, died at Brechin 5th June 1926; his widow, Amy Taylor, died 22nd Dec. 1948.

1926 ROBERT MATTHEW WATSON, trans. from Clova (*q.v.*) 17th March 1926; died 8th Jan. 1939 unmarr.

(*United to Fern 4th July* 1937.)

CRAIG INCHBRIOCH or INCHBRAYOCK and DUNNINALD

Craig. The church was dedicated by Bishop de Bernham 23rd Aug. 1243. By Bull of Pope Sixtus IV, 26th Feb. 1473, Inchbrioch was made a Mensal Church of St Andrews.

Dunninald. Dedicated to St Skioch or St Struy, thought by Reeves to be a corrupt form of St Echad, one of St Columba's disciples from Ireland. The church or chapel, no longer in existence, stood on a burying-ground which, called St Kae's, is romantically situated on the margin of the sea-cliffs, the rock being known locally also as Elephant Rock. On 17th Nov. 1470 Pope Paul II decreed that the Chapel of St Seaffron (St Skiach) be served by the Priory of Restennet and the sacraments dispensed to the inhabitants, the chapel with the lands of Donmacht (Dunninald) belonging to the Priory. The parish of Skeochy is mentioned 26th Jan. 1539–40, and called also parish of St Skeoch and Senetskay. The parish of Craig was formed by the union of St Skeoch parish and the parish of Inchbrayoch, i.e. the island of Brioc, in the South Esk near Montrose, where the old church was situated. The lands of Dunninald, which seem chiefly to have made up the parish of Skeoch, belonged with their harbour and fisheries to the Priory of Restennet.—[*Reg. Great Seal*, iii, 26th Jan. 1539–40; *Retours*, iv, 153, F. 50; *Archaeologica Scotica*, v, 312; *Cal. Papal Regs., Letters*, xii, 361; *The Apostolic Camera of Scottish Benefices*, 173.]

1562 RICHARD MELVILLE, vicar in 1562–3.—[*Comps. Sub Coll. of Thirds, Forfar*, etc.]

1562 JOHN MELVILLE, brother of preceding, min. here 1562. In 1576 it is recorded that "Sanct Skae or Dunnynand neides na reidare," and this may point to the discontinuance of the chapel.—[Article in *Dundee Advertiser*, 26th June 1928; *Acts and Dec.*, liii, 471.]

1587 JAMES MELVILLE, reader 10th Dec. 1587, also reader at Maryton.—[*Reg. of Brechin*, ii, 361.]

1908 PETER SMITH BISSET, dem. 17th May 1943; his wife, Maria Greasham Elrick Milne, died 24th Sept. 1938.

DUN and ECCLESJOHN

Dun and Ecclesjohn were united 2nd May 1583, when it is narrated "yair is within the said parochine of Dun and boundis thereof a small benefice callit the benefice of Ecclesjohn being of auld ane chapel erectit for pilgrimage and having only the teind of a pleuch of land or thairby, wanting ane kirk these many yeiris bygane." There was in the church an altar dedicated to the Virgin Mary.—[*Retours*, iii, 45.]

1563 WILLIAM GRAY, M.A., min. in 1563 and at Logie Montrose.—[*Comps. Sub Coll. of Thirds, Forfar*, etc.]

1563 JOHN BATY, reader 1563.—[*Comps. Sub Coll. of Thirds, Forfar*, etc.]

1563 ROBERT ARBUTHNOT, M.A., vicar.—[*Comps. Sub Coll. of Thirds, Forfar*, etc.]

1567 JAMES ERSKINE, M.A., may be identical with James, son of Sir John E. of Dun and his second wife, Barbara (? Agnes) de Bearle. He studied under Melanchthon; pres. in 1570 on death of Euphame, prioress and last possessor.—[*Reports Hist. MSS. Com.*, v, 632; *Reg. Pres. Bene.*, i, (2), 3.]

1574 THOMAS ERSKINE, min. here, pres. to parsonage and vicarage 24th March 1574 on death of James Erskine.—[*Reg. Pres. Bene.*, i, (4), 31; *Reg. Sec. Sig.*, xlii, 124.]

1575 SIR JOHN ERSKINE of DUN, he appears on 20th Dec. 1560 among those "whilk are thoght apt and able the ministers and commissionars forsaids to minister"; and it is recorded of him in the Presentation to Dun 11th Aug. 1575 that he has had "lang travellis in yr ministrie within ye kirk of God"; to Andrew Mylne and other mins. commission was given by John Winram, Superintendent of Fife, to enter him in office "be placing of hym in ye pulpit and delyvering of ye buke of God in his handis," which was done 20th Aug. 1575.—[*Reg. Epis. of Brechin*, ii, 307-8; *Booke of the Univ. Kirk*, 4.]

1583 ANDREW STRACHAN, grandson of John S. of Thornton, pres. on resignation of John Erskine of Dun 1583; had issue—John.—[*Brechin Com. Decreets*, 25th July 1598; *Reg. Pres. Bene.*, ii, 88; *Memorials of the Family of Strachan*, 30; *Reg. Mag. Sig.*, ii, 274.]

1622 JAMES LEIGHTON, brother to Robert L. of Ulysseshaven; had addl. issue James, bapt. 19th Nov. 1621; Elspet, bapt. 18th Sept. 1622.—[*Reg. of Deeds, Scott.*, 11th Jan. 1619; *Montrose Baptisms*.]

1646 WILLIAM LEIGHTON, died before 23rd June 1703; had issue—Elizabeth, bapt. 17th Aug. 1656; James, bapt. 15th June 1658.

1685 JOHN DOUGALD, marr. cont. 29th May 1697 Isabel Erskine.

1701 JAMES KER, M.A. William Simpson, episcopal min., intruded here Sept. 1715 to Feb. 1716.—[*Justiciary Records*, 12th Feb. 1717.]

1873 ALEXANDER ANDERSON, his wife, Amelia Emily Rodger, died 11th Oct. 1929.

1914 WILLIAM PATERSON BLACK, died 5th Dec. 1935.

ECCLESJOHN

1566 SIR JOHN FORAIT (Forrat), parson in 1566 and 1577, when he is described as a "poor blynd man."—[*Comps. Gen. Coll. and Sub Coll. of Thirds, Forfar*, etc.]

EDZELL

1563 THOMAS RAMSAY, reader 1563 and 1567.—[*Comps. Sub Coll. of Thirds, Forfar*, etc.]

1573 JOHN FULLARTON, M.A., pres. to parsonage and vicarage on dem. of John Duncanson 9th July 1573.—[*Reg. Pres. Bene.*, i, (4), 10.]

1644 DAVID FULLARTON, marr. 29th July 1647 Anna Lichton, buried 3rd March 1674.

1841 ROBERT INGLIS, his sons—Henry, died 15th April 1931; George Brown, died Sept. 1936.

1905 DAVID WILLIAMSON, trans. to Plean 12th Oct. 1927.

1928 JOHN COPELAND, M.A., Ph.D., born Co. Down 1st Aug. 1865; ord. 1894; adm. to St Andrews Presb. Church, Hebburn, Newcastle-on-Tyne, 1915; trans. to Livingstone 7th April 1920; trans. 23rd Feb. 1928; died at Brechin 14th Dec. 1931; unmarr.

NEWDOSK

1563 PATRICK BONKILL, min. in 1563; also at Fordoun and Fettercairn.—[*Comps. Sub Coll. of Thirds, Forfar*, etc.]

1565 WILLIAM CHALMERS, M.A., parson 3rd April 1565.—[*Collegiate Churches of Midlothian*.]

FARNELL

There was in the church an altar dedicated to St Michael. Apparently not long before his death on 19th April 1598 Mr David Carnegie of Kinnaird obtained the consent of the Presbytery of Brechin and the General Assembly to a scheme whereby the lands of Kinnaird, Balnamone, Pentoskell, Over Dalgetie, Middle Drumms and Greendene, lying in the parish of Brechin, and the parish of Cuikston were united to constitute a distinct parish to be designated Kinnaird, with a church built by the said Mr David near Kinnaird Castle. Mr Carnegie's son and successor, Sir David, acting on his father's testament, carried the project to completion, and in 1604–6 secured the resignation of the following parties of their rights in favour of the Church of Kinnaird—Alexander, Bishop of Brechin, to the teind sheaves of Kinnaird, Balnamone, Pentoskell and Over Dalgetie; Robert Kinneir, vicar of Brechin, to the small teinds of the foregoing lands and the teinds of Middle Drummis and Greendene; and Mr John Wemyss, min. at the Church of Kinnaird, to the revenues of the prebend of the Sub-Dean of Brechin, and the rectory and vicarage of Cuikston; and by Charter of 16th April 1606 James VI mortified the foregoing to the Church of Kinnaird, along with the manse and glebe, the patronage passing to Sir David C. Ratification was made by Act of Parliament on 11th July of the same year; and the parish of Cuikston thus became part of the new parish of Kinnaird. The reasons for the project were that the people of the lands concerned in Brechin Parish were far distant from Brechin Church, that the Church of Cuikston was completely demolished, and in any case was not sufficient to accommodate the people, and that the revenues of the rectory and vicarage of Cuikston were an insufficient provision for a minister. In 1787 the parish of Kinnaird was suppressed, the larger part being attached to Farnell Parish, and the remainder, the north-west portion, being annexed to Brechin. The Church of Cuikston was situated about a mile north of the present Church of Farnell, near a mound called Rume's Cross, probably the site of a vanished cross, and by its name indicating, it has been conjectured, the patron saint of the parish. Of Kinnaird Church only the foundations remain. Near by is Pader or Pater Well.—[*Acts Scott. Parl.*, vi, 358; *Reg. Great Seal*, vi, 1730.]

1573 THOMAS SHEWAN, reader here, still in office 1588, pres. to vicarage in 1573 on death of John Meldrum.—[*Reg. Pres. Bene.*, i, (4), 10; *Comps. Sub Coll. of Thirds, Forfar*, etc.]

1577 JAMES THORNTON, M.A., parson and vicar, died before 24th Nov. 1577.—[*Reg. of Brechin*, ii, 334.]

1577 JAMES NICOLSON, pres. to the parson and vicarage 24th Nov. 1577.—[*Reg. of Brechin*, ii, 334.]

1581 DUGALD CAMPBELL, M.A., pres. to the Deanery of Brechin, and the parsonage and vicarage of Farnell 30th Nov. 1581, "being found qualified to be a minister of the Church of God" by the Superintendent of Angus.—[*Reg. of Brechin*, ii, 340.]

JOHN LAMMIE. Addl. issue—James.
1673 —[*G. R. Sas.*, lii, 296.]

ANDREW GEDDIE, son of Patrick G.,
1703 min. of Balmaclellan.

IVO MACNAUGHTON CLARK,
1912 Ph.D. (Aberdeen, 1926); assistant clerk of Presb. 9th March 1937. Marr. 19th July 1930 Margaret Donaldson, only daugh. of James Hanton, Brechin.

KINNAIRD

JOHN OGILVIE, M.A., min. of Cuikston and Kinnaird 6th Jan. 1601–2
1601 in succession to Archibald Sibbald dep. 3rd March 1601.—[*Acts and Dec.*, clixvi, 375.]

DAVID RAIT, had issue—Jean, bapt.
1664 19th June 1646; Helen, bapt. 4th July 1648; Henry, bapt. 6th June 1651; William, bapt. 4th Aug. 1653; John, bapt. 1st June 1655.

FERN

WALTER FAIRWODDER (Fairweather), reader in 1563.—[*Comps.*
1563 *Sub Coll. of Thirds, Forfar*, etc.]

JAMES MELVILLE, min. in 1563.—
1563 [*Comps. Sub Coll. of Thirds, Forfar*, etc.]

PATRICK MURE, parson 30th May
1584 1584.

ALEXANDER NORIE, had issue—Alexander; Robert, min. of Stracathro.—[*Reg. Bishop. of Brechin*,
1586 347.]

JAMES WATSON, episcopal min. intruded in the church Sept. 1715 to
1715 Feb. 1716.—[*Justiciary Records.*]

ROBERT CONSTABLE MITCHELL, was assistant at St Paul's, Perth, and
1907 afterwards at Wormit; dem. 16th Feb. 1937; died 26th June 1945.

HILLSIDE

MICHAEL CUNNINGHAM WILSON, dem. 27th July 1926.
1907

ROBERT WILSON MERRY, trans. from Canisbay (*q.v.*) 24th Feb. 1927;
1927 his wife, Dr Jean M. Crawford, died 16th Nov. 1937.

LETHNOT and NAVAR

JOHN LINDSAY, trans. to Lochlee
1591 after 1595.

ROBERT NORIE, had issue—Robert, Bishop of Brechin, min. of South
1639 Church, Dundee.

ROBERT THOMSON, intruded at Montrose Sept. 1715 to Feb. 1716.—
1685 [*Justiciary Records.*]

JOHN TAYLOR, his daugh., Margaret,
1775 died at Bridge of Allan 29th May 1858.

JAMES GOODLET ROBERTSON,
1905 dem. 31st July 1938; died 17th Feb. 1943.

NAVAR

GEORGE SWINTON, vicar 1563.—
1563 [*Comps. Sub Coll. of Thirds, Forfar*, etc.]

JAMES FULLARTON, reader 1563.—
1563 [*Comps. Sub Coll. of Thirds, Forfar*, etc.]

LOCHLEE

JOHN LINDSAY, M.A., formerly of Lethnot; described as "sometime
1607 minister of Lochlee" on 25th June 1607, when he was denounced as a rebel by the Privy Council for his part in the assault on Lord Spynie at the "Stair fit" of the latter's lodging in High Street, Edinburgh; on 3rd July following he was put to the horn at the Market Cross.—[*Reg. Privy Council*, xiv, 477–8, 480.]

JOHN STEWART, his daugh., Janet
1885 May (marr. 12th July 1939 Peter Dow, C.A., Rangoon).

JOHN McRORIE KAY, dem. 15th May 1932; his wife, Christina Mc-
1922 Martin, died at Killin 1st Dec. 1927. Marr. (2) 18th Dec. 1934 Janet Ferguson Macfarlane, who died 20th Dec. 1944.

LOGIE PERT or LOGIE MONTROSE

The union of the parishes of Logie Montrose and Logie-Pert was ratified by Parliament 12th March 1647, the heritors agreeing to build a new church near the middle of the parish. The renewal of the Act of Union was ratified by Parliament in 1661.—[*Acts Scott. Parl.*, vi, (1), 740; vii, 291.]

1554 ALEXANDER FORREST, parson and vicar; was in office as parson 12th June 1554 and 2nd April 1565; died before 6th Feb. 1573.—[*Reg. Great Seal*, iv, 2825; *Laing Charters*, 623; *Reg. Pres. Bene.*, i, (4), 16; *Wemyss Book*, ii, 289.]

1563 WILLIAM GRAY, M.A., min. in 1563. (See Dun.)

1563 JOHN WILSON, reader 1563, vicar 1574.—[*Comps. Sub Coll. of Thirds, Forfar*, etc.]

1563 ALEXANDER RAE, vicar.—[*Acts and Dec.*, lvi, 115.]

1566 ALEXANDER FEROUS (Forrest), parson of Logy Montrose, charged to produce Registers of the Bishopric of St Andrews 8th July 1566.—[*Acts and Dec.*, xxxviii, 21; *Cal. of Charters*, x, 2109.]

1573 WILLIAM GRAY, M.A., pres. in 1563 on death of Alexander Ferous.—[*Reg. Pres. Bene.*, i, (4), 16.]

1603 JOSHUA DURIE, pres. in 1603 on death of William Gray.—[*P. S. Reg.*, lxxiii, 227.]

1717 JAMES BELL, his son, John, apprenticed to Hugh Hamilton, merchant, Edinburgh, 13th July 1748.

1864 ARCHIBALD BUCHANAN, his daughs. — Elizabeth Sutherland, D.C.S., died 26th March 1936; Grace Marshall, died 18th Dec. 1932; Margaret Mill, died 8th Jan. 1936.

1884 JAMES LANDRETH, died 22nd Feb. 1934; his widow, Janet Patton Gerrie, died 14th Dec. 1946.

MARYTON

In 1211–14 King William the Lion granted to Arbroath Abbey the Church of Old Montrose (Maryton) along with the lands of the same church, which in Gaelic is called Abthen; that designation indicates that there was here an old Celtic settlement abbey or monastery.—[*Reg. of Arbroath, vetus*, 4.]

1561 DAVID MELDRUM, vicar and reader 1561–3, died before 11th April 1580.—[*Comps. Sub Coll. of Thirds, Forfar*, etc.]

1567 JOHN MELVILLE, reader, was in office 28th May 1575 and pres. to the vicarage by James VI, 11th April 1580 in succession to David Meldrum.—[*Reg. of Brechin*, ii, 340; *Edin. Test.*, v. 140.]

1587 JAMES MELVILLE, reader 10th Dec. 1587; also reader at Inchbrioch.—[*Reg. of Brechin*, ii, 361.]

1594 JOHN GRAHAM, M.A., servitor to John, Earl of Morton, pres. to vicarage 9th July 1594 on death of John Melville.—[*Reg. Sec. Sig.*, lxvi, 168.]

1738 JAMES BAILLIE, his widow, Margaret Farquharson, died at Lawton, Perthshire, 16th April 1780; his daugh., Maria (marr. 1769 George Wright of Lawton.)

1905 JOHN DAWSON MACLEAN, trans. to Barthol Chapel 12th Jan. 1928.

1929 WALTER GEORGE MACKEAN, formerly of Sikhim (vii, 700); adm. 5th April 1929; died at Aberdeen 2nd Nov. 1932.

MENMUIR

Menmuir Church was a prebend of Dunkeld, and as such was held in 1419 by Alan Stewart, natural son of Walter, Earl of Atholl and Caithness, natural son of Robert II. The present church was built in 1842, taking the place of a building erected in 1767. In the Forest of Kilgerrie there were a hermitage and chapel dedicated to the Virgin Mary. The site was in a field near the farmhouse of Chapelton of Dunlappie; and the ruins existed till about the middle of the 19th century. In the vicinity was the Lady's Well; and there was also a graveyard. Hugh Cumynth (Cumming), the hermit in 1445, held the hermitage and chapel on a hereditary title; and on 18th May of that year James II, on the resignation of the said Hugh, granted a charter of the hermitage and chapel, with croft and the green and 3 acres of arable land pertaining to the same, to John Smyth, citizen of Brechin, the reddendo being the benefit of the prayers of the hermit and other rights and services rendered to the Crown according to use and wont before the said resignation. Hugh Cumming seems to have retained some interest, for on 29th Nov. 1454 he granted a Procuratory of Resignation in favour of David Creichton, who in accordance therewith made resignation in the hands of King James on 16th Feb. 1454–5, and the King granted to Alexander de Fowlertone, his special esquire, the whole right and claim of the said Hugh in the hermitage and chapel, croft and green. About six years later, on 8th Aug. 1461, John Smyth, who had received the Crown Charter of 1445, granted to William Sumyre of Balrowdy a feu-charter of "my" hermitage of St Mary of Kingerrie and all and whole the croft of arable land annexed and pertaining to it of old, in exchange for 1 merk annual rent from the tenement of Walter de Crage of Swanstoun in the town of Brechin, to be held off the said John and his heirs.—[*Cal. of Supplications Rel. to Scot.*, 118, S.H.S.; *Reg. of Brechin*, ii, 382–3; *Hist. of the Carnegies*, i, Pref. xvii, ii, 72, 518–20, 541–2; Jervise's *Land of the Lindsays*, 248 and *n.*]

1561 JAMES HAMILTON, parson.—[*Acts and Dec.*, xxiii, 84, xxv, 15, xxvii, 218.]

1563 JAMES MELVILLE, M.A., min. at Fern, in charge here also 1563–8.

1566 ROBERT AUCHENLECK, vicar in 1566; chaplain of Drumlithie.—[*Comps. Sub Coll. of Thirds, Forfar*, etc.]

1567 JOHN AUCHENLECK, pres. to vicarage 21st Jan. 1567–8 on death of Robert Auchenleck.—[*Reg. Pres. Bene.*, i, 4.]

1568 ANDREW ELDER, pres. to vicarage 30th Aug. 1568 on death of Robert Auchenleck.—[*Reg. Pres. Bene.*, i, 15.]

1584 JOHN LINDSAY, M.A., held also the parsonages of Lethnot and Lochlee as well as the parsonage of Menmuir conferred on him 1st July 1566 on resignation of James Hamilton, but probably lay appointments; son of David, ninth Earl of Crawford; app. Lord of Session as Lord Menmuir 5th July 1581; became Lord Privy Seal March 1595–6; ambassador to France 1596–7 but did not go; died 3rd Sept. 1598.—[*Scots Peerage*, i, 516; Grote's *Prot. Book*, 276.]

1636 THOMAS COUPAR, trans. from Saline; adm. before 29th Aug. 1636.—[*Reg. of Brechin*, 321–2.]

1644 DAVID CAMPBELL, his son, Mr George.—[*Forfar Sas.*, 6th May 1696.]

1715 JAMES WATSON, episcopal min., intruded here Sept. 1715 to Feb. 1716.—[*Justiciary Records.*]

1908 DAVID AVENEL VIPONT, his widow, Flora Macdonald, died at Brechin 12th Aug. 1931; his sons—Francis, min. of Saughtree, 1925; Roland, min. of Scots Church, Belize, 1934.

1923 WILLIAM BUCHANAN, trans. to St Mary's, Dalziel, 23rd Feb. 1927.

1927 JAMES GEGG, ord. 12th May 1927; trans. to Sorn 19th Sept. 1928.

1929 LEWIS McGLASHAN, pres. by Presb. *jure devoluto* and trans. from Dalbeattie (*q.v.*) 12th July 1929; dem. 19th Oct. 1943; died 3rd Dec. 1944.

(*Charges united 26th June* 1942.)

MONTROSE

The church was rebuilt in 1791, the old steeple being left till *cir.* 1842, when it was replaced by the present steeple designed by Gillespie Graham. There was in the church an altar dedicated to the Holy Trinity, founded by Elecso and Thomas Falconer, burgesses of Montrose on 12th July 1434. There was also an Altar of the Holy Rood founded by Thomas Bull, Canon of Aberdeen and Brechin and perpetual vicar of Montrose, on 18th Aug. 1432, and on 10th March 1432–3 its endowments were augmented by the annexation of the Chapel of St John. At the Altar of St Sebastian in the church Mr Walter Stratoun, parson of Dunnottar, founded a chaplainry on 19th Oct. 1502. There was also in the church an altar dedicated to the Saviour and His Precious Body and Blood, founded by David Stirling of Easter Brekky, and Sir John Gilbert, vicar of the Hospital of Montrose, son and heir of John Gilbert, burgess of Montrose. On 20th Jan. 1531–2 the said David Stirling granted for the support of a perpetual chantry-chaplain at the altar, who should be skilled in art, music, and grammar, and act as song-master of the burgh, an annual rent of 10 merks of the 10 pound lands of Easter Brekky. The said 10 merks had formerly been mortified by the said David Stirling's late father, Mr George Stirling of Easter Brekky, and his uncle, Patrick Stirling, to a perpetual chaplain at the Altar of the Virgin Mary in the Church of Kinnell. The Hospital of Montrose, dedicated to the Virgin Mary, was a house for lepers, and was situated apparently on a part of the Common Links, which bears or bore the name of St Mary, a short distance east of the Victoria Bridge. A Crown Charter of 1516 states that it was founded by the progenitors of James IV, and was endowed with the lands of Spittalchelis, Denside, etc. Long prior to the early part of the 16th century the house had passed out of use, the buildings had become ruinous, and the lands had been alienated and set to members of the nobility at a small feu, all because of the negligence of the masters. Before 18th Aug. 1512 Patrick Paniter, Abbot of Cambuskenneth and Master of the Hospital, had embarked upon the project of applying the house to another purpose. He redeemed the hospital from the hands of secular persons, recovered the alienated lands, and at his own charges built a new settlement, church, manse, and other buildings, with lands for the place and gardens on each side of the Market Place of Montrose. Thereafter by Crown Charter of 14th Nov. 1516 and Act of Parliament he received power to change the constitution of the hospital and erect it *de novo* into a House of Blackfriars and also confirmation of his grant of the place to Friar John Adamson, the Blackfriars' Provincial. Among the conditions which Paniter attached to the grant were masses at the Altar of St Lawrence in the church of the place, a burial-place for himself, etc., on the north side of the choir of the church near the high altar, and the life rent of the front house built by him adjacent to the church. The original Settlement of the Blackfriars at Montrose was founded by Sir Alan Durward in 1230, and was situated adjacent to the hospital on the Common Links. A letter of James V *cir.* 1516 narrates that it "was destroyed by fire by the enemies of the Kingdom 200 years ago," and describes it as "to-day untended and neglected." Apparently therefore the transference of the Blackfriars to the new settlement was for them advantageous. But after a time it emerged that the friars found the variety of noises of the Market Place, and the crowds that there assembled, uncongenial to their divine celebrations and their private devotions; and on their petition they were transferred to the old abode by Crown Charter of 1524 and Act of Parliament of 1525. In accordance with a letter of Queen Mary and Darnley of 22nd Feb. 1559, which described the Blackfriars as "sturdy beggaris" who "under colour of almess and moyoin of courte for the tyme spulzet the poor" by intruding themselves and "takand the haill place and rentis thairof," the Lords of Secret Council appointed the Blackfriars' place with all lands, etc., to be distributed to the poor of Montrose, and ordered a hospital to be erected thereon for the entertainment of the poor as time and money permitted. By charter of 1st June 1570 James VI granted to the burgh the chapel, houses, revenues, etc., of the place for behoof of the poor, and included the same under the Royal Foundation of the hospital of the burgh of Montrose.—[*Reg. Great Seal*, ii, 3765, iii, 113, 138, 1725, iv, 1146, 1953; *Acts Scott. Parl.*, ii, App., 389, 396; *Epistles of Kings of Scotland*, i, 290; *Reports Hist. MSS. Commis.*, ii, 39–40; Keith's *Cat. of Scott. Bishops*, 443; *Reg. of Brechin*, i, 34, 37–8.]

FIRST CHARGE

1565 THOMAS ANDERSON, min. in 1560.—[*Comps. Gen. Coll. of Thirds.*]

1571 JOHN BEATTIE, reader March 1571-2 and 26th Oct. 1579.—[*Edin. Tests.*, iv, 281; vii, 251.]

1615 JOHN OGILVY, reader 31st May 1615.—[*Montrose Reg.*]

1629 JOHN CROLL, reader 8th March 1629, and Master of the Music School; held office apparently till about close of 1669. Marr., with issue—Marie, bapt. 8th March 1629; James, bapt. 22nd March 1644; David (1), bapt. 20th June 1645; David (2), bapt. 12th Aug. 1646.—[*Montrose Reg.*]

1631 ARCHIBALD SYMMER, his daugh., Grizel, bapt. 28th Oct. 1631, and his son, Archibald, 23rd June 1633.—[*Montrose Reg.*]

1633 JAMES DUNCAN, his son, James, bapt. 9th Jan. 1638, and his daughs.—Jean, 23rd Oct. 1639, Mary 9th July 1641.—[*Montrose Reg.*]

1642 THOMAS COUPER, his son, James, bapt. 13th Feb. 1644, his daugh., Eliza (Elizabeth), 3rd Feb. 1651.—[*Montrose Reg.*]

1673 DAVID LYELL, had children buried 1st Jan. 1661 and 19th May 1671.—[*Aberdeen Reg.*]

1870 WILLIAM EWAN BULL GUNN, his widow, Sophia McChater, died 4th Feb. 1926.

1918 JOHN STEWART ROBERTSON, adm. to united charge 23rd May 1936; dem. 28th April 1948.

SECOND CHARGE

1563 JOHN BATY or BEATTIE, reader 1563, pres. to vicarage of Hospital of Montrose 20th July 1571 on death of Sir John Gilbert.—[*Reg. Pres. Bene.*, i, (2), 18.]

1899 HUGH CALLAN, died 13th Aug. 1924.

1925 NEIL ALEXANDER MACLEAN, ord. 3rd Feb. 1925; trans. to St Andrews, Edinburgh, 7th June 1927.

1927 WILLIAM CARRIE CLARK, born 15th Feb. 1886, fourth son of Andrew Shearer C., Kingscroft, Stanley Road, Trinity, and Rose Harper Carrie; served as Captain in R.G.A. in Mesopotamia during Great War; licen. by Presb. of Edinburgh 1920; assistant Kirknewton and Morningside; ord. to Newton 3rd April 1924; trans. and adm. 7th Dec. 1927; trans. to St Mary's, Partick, 12th Oct. 1930; trans. to Stobhill 5th Nov. 1941. Marr. 9th July 1924 Effie, only daugh. of William Wallace Dunlop, headmaster, Daniel Stewart's College, Edinburgh.

(*First and Second Charges united 23rd May* 1931.)

MONTROSE, MELVILLE

1867 WILLIAM JOHN STEVEN, his widow, Jessie Spence, died 27th Nov. 1937; his son, William, died Kingston Hill, Surrey, 8th Dec. 1934.

1891 WILLIAM TAYLOR, his daugh., Kathleen (marr. 1929 William Francis Smith, Nigerian Government Service).

1917 JULIUS McCALLUM, died 15th May 1935; his son, Julius, ord. to Killernan 28th Dec. 1933. Marr. 15th Aug. 1934 Margaret Ferguson, youngest daugh. of John W. Fairweather, Montrose.

STRACATHRO

The church pertained to the Precentor of Brechin. By letters of 20th March 1583–4 James VI united the vicarage, hitherto a "distinct benefice," to the parsonage, making them one benefice for the future. The church was rebuilt in 1799, and thoroughly repaired in 1844–5. In the churchyard on 7th July 1296, three days prior to his surrender of his kingdom and his Royal Seal "enclosed in a little purse," etc., to the Bishop of Durham on behalf of Edward I, at Brechin Castle, John Baliol, King of Scotland, at the hour of vespers, "renounced his league with France and confessed his sins against his liege lord the king (Edward I), desiring to be reconciled with him."—[*Reg. of Brechin*, i, xvi*n*, ii, 345–6; *Cal. of Docs. Rel. to Scotland*, ii, 188–9, 194.]

1561 JOHN GUTHRIE, M.A., vicar 1561–3.—[*Comps. Coll. Gen. and Sub Coll. of Thirds, Forfar*.]

1563 ANDREW MYLNE, min. in office 1563.—[*Comps. Sub Coll. of Thirds, Forfar*, etc.]

1567 PAUL FRASER, M.A., pres. to vicarage 27th Sept. 1583 and again 20th March 1583–4 on death of John Sym.—[*Reg. Pres. Bene.*, ii, 91, 100.]

1571 JOHN SYM, reader in 1563, pres. to vicarage 18th Oct. 1571 on death of David Guthrie.—[*Reg. Pres. Bene.*, i, (2), 7; *Comps. Sub Coll. of Thirds, Forfar*, etc.]

1610 ROBERT NORIE, second son of Alexander N., min. of Fern.

1909 WILLIAM NEWLANDS, died 11th May 1941; his son, Arthur, died 29th May 1933.

DUNLAPPIE

1561 JAMES LYCHTOUN, parson, son of Helen Stirling, Lady Ullishaven; pursued her murderers, who protested he should lose his benefice.—[Pitcairn's *Crim. Trials*, i, 411.]

PRESBYTERY OF ARBROATH

ARBIRLOT

About 1208 the Abbot of Arbroath granted permission to Sir Philip de Moubray to have an oratory in his place of Kelly, on condition that the mother church was not deprived of her dues and other festivities, and that Sir Philip and his heirs and families attend the mother church on all principal solemnities, if not prevented by reasonable indisposition.—[*Reg. of Arbroath, vetus*, 86.]

1563 WALTER LINDSAY, reader 1563.— [*Comps. Sub Coll. of Thirds, Forfar*, etc.]

1591 JAMES AUCHTERLONIE, pres. to vicarage 18th Dec. 1591 on death of Charles Michaelson.—[*Reg. Sec. Sig.*, lxiii, 62.]

1591 PATRICK LINDSAY, M.A., pres. to vicarage 2nd Feb. 1591-2 on death of Charles Michaelson.—[*Reg. Sec. Sig.*, lxii, 163.]

1592 GEORGE GLEDSTANES, pres. to vicarage 17th May 1592 on death of Charles Michaelson.—[*Reg. Sec. Sig.*, lxiii, 264.]

1603 DAVID LINDSAY, min. St Andrews; pres. to vicarage 14th Jan. 1603 on death of David Black.—[*Reg. Sec. Sig.*, lxxiii, 166.]

1617 JAMES IRVING, died Aug. 1625.— [*Reg. Sec. Sig.*, lxix, 45.]

1687 GEORGE MAKGILL, his son, Alexander, apprenticed to Alexander Nisbett, mason in Edinburgh, 16th June 1697.

1832 JOHN CHRISTIE, his daughs.—Margaret Finlayson, died 10th Jan. 1938; Mary Cathcart, died 27th Sept. 1934.

1923 ARCHIBALD COWAN KENNEDY, trans. to St Enoch's, Glasgow, 8th May 1928 and to Chair of Hebrew, Aberdeen, 16th May 1932; D.D. (Edinburgh, 1944).

1929 MATTHEW McPHAIL, born 1st Oct. 1893; assistant New Monkland and Govan; ord. to Castle Douglas 7th Nov. 1923; trans. to St Luke's, Lochee, 12th Oct. 1927; trans. and adm. 16th May 1929. Marr. 28th Oct. 1921 Elizabeth H.

(*Charges united* 1929.)

ARBROATH

The altars in the abbey, St Catherine, St Peter, St Laurence, St Nicolas, were dedicated on 26th Aug. 1485 by Bishop George Bran of Dromerie. The Altar of the Virgin Mary in the abbey was situated near the door of the vestry. In the abbey there was also an altar dedicated to St Mary Magdalene. In the Chapel of the Virgin Mary, which was at the west end of the Bridge of Arbroath, there was also an Altar of St Nicholas. The Chapel of St Michael was in the street of the Almory of Arbroath, and at Seton of Arbroath there was a chapel dedicated to St Ninian.—[*Reg. of Arbroath, Niger*, 56, 226, 227, 356, 357, 432, 438–42; *Reg. Great Seal*, iii, 2702; v, 559, 2150.]

1563 NINIAN CLEMENT, min. in 1563.— [*Comps. Sub Coll. of Thirds, Forfar*, etc.]

1563 THOMAS LINDSAY, reader and exhorter.—[*Comps. Sub Coll. of Thirds, Forfar*, etc.]

ARBROATH—CARMYLIE

1579 JOHN GRANGER, pres. to vicarage 1st March 1577 on dem. of Robert Auchmowtie; still in office 1597.—[*Reg. Pres. Bene.*, i, (4), 66; *Comps. Sub Coll. of Thirds, Forfar*, etc.]

1788 GEORGE GLEIG, his daugh., Ann Forbes (marr. 23rd Nov. 1822).

1844 WALTER FORBES IRVINE, his daugh., Leonora Jane, died 6th May 1946; his son, Louis Godfrey, M.D., died Johannesburg 15th March 1946.

1905 JAMES SPENCE CUTHILL, dem. 31st July 1946; died 24th Aug. 1946.

ARBROATH ABBEY

1909 ANDREW DOUGLAS, his widow, Alice Sinclair, died 20th June 1933.

1919 PETER HILL NICOLL, dem. 30th Jan. 1923 on app. to British Guiana; adm. to Dalmarnock 27th Sept. 1927.

1923 ALEXANDER CLARK, trans. to Cortachy 25th June 1931; died 17th Jan. 1942; his wife, Mary Maclaren Hamilton, died 14th July 1936. Marr. (2) 5th Aug. 1941 Helen Stewart, third daugh. of George Gordon, Glenallan, Dalkeith.

INVERBROTHOCK

1876 GEORGE LOGAN, his widow died 19th Nov. 1929; his daugh., Christina Kirkhope Craig, died at Glasgow 5th April 1930.

1904 THOMAS DOW STEWART, his widow, Agnes Duncan, died 23rd June 1937.

1909 GEORGE HITCHCOCK, dem. 30th Dec. 1945; his daugh., Annie Morrison Gray (marr. 18th July 1934 Robert Knox Lorimer, son of John Burr, min. of Bowden); his wife, Margaret Anne Spence, died at Corstorphine 4th March 1948.

LADYLOAN

1901 JOHN McWILLIAM, licen. 1st May 1895; dem. 20th July 1941.

(*Charges united 20th July 1941.*)

ST MARGARET'S

1923 WILLIAM EWART GLADSTONE MILLAR, had addl. issue—Carol Mary Gladstone, born 13th April 1930; Hazel Lynne Gladstone, born 16th Dec. 1931.

AUCHMITHIE

1886 JAMES CHRISTIE, his widow, Eliza Matilda Hill, died 9th July 1925.

BARRY

The church was dedicated by Bishop de Bernham 18th Aug. 1243.

1591 JOHN GARDYNE, pres. to parsonage and vicarage 4th March 1590 on dem. of Harry Kinnear.—[*Reg. Sec. Sig.*, lxii, 8.]

1636 PATRICK LYON, his widow marr. (2) John Gray in Forfar; his daugh., Agnes.—[*Forfar Com.*, 16th June 1664; *Forfar Sas.*, i, 286, 28th July 1663.]

1724 WILLIAM DALL, his wife, Rachel Russell, was sister to David R., surgeon in Kennaway.—[*Session Papers*, 133, 21st Jan. 1745.]

1895 JOHN HEGGIE, died 29th April 1945.

(*Charges united 26th Aug. 1945.*)

CARMYLIE

On 5th March 1500-1 David Strathauchine of Carmylie founded a chapel dedicated to the Virgin Mary, the endowment being 5 merks annual rent from the Manor and Mill of Carmylie, 40 sh. annual rent from the husband-lands of Carmylie, etc. Mass was to be celebrated for King James, etc., and the donor himself, and Janet Drummond, his wife; and there was also provision that the chaplain shall be bound continually to keep a school at the chapel for the instruction of youth. Sir Malcolm Struble was chaplain 1511–12. On the site of this chapel there was erected the church built as the parish church in 1609.—[*Reg. Great Seal*, ii, 3684; *Reg. of Brechin*, i, 223–4; *Acts Scott. Parl.*, iv, 442.]

WILLIAM WILSON, his daugh., Eliza Jane, died at Broughty Ferry 10th March 1937.
1837

PATRICK BELL, his son, John, solicitor, died in Aberdeen.
1843

JAMES GORDON LYON, died 23rd Feb. 1926.
1900

ROBERT BARR McVICAR, trans. from Carnoch (*q.v.*) 22nd Sept. 1926 died 13th March 1943; his son, Robert Barr, min. of Cairneyhill, ord. 3rd Nov. 1943.
1926

(*Charges united 25th July* 1943.)

CARNOUSTIE, Q.S.

ALEXANDER ROBERTSON GIBSON, died 23rd Aug. 1928; his widow, Catherine Jane Bowie, died 16th Jan. 1939.
1880

JAMES BAILLIE, born Larkhall 19th July 1893, son of Archibald B. and Ann Henderson Stewart; educ. at Univ. of Glasgow, M.A. (1914); commanded 304 Howitzer Battery, 76 (H) Field Brigade, Royal Artillery, Dundee, retired as Major 1936; licen. by Presb. of Hamilton 1921; assistant Elgin 1921, St Michael's, Edinburgh; ord. 5th June 1924; dem. 25th Oct. 1941; app. to Nassau, Bahamas, 1941; dem. 1942; C.F. Halifax Naval Station; adm. to Knox Church, Belmont, Ontario 1946. Marr. 23rd March 1932 Isabel Rose, daugh. of Robert Campbell, Adelaide, South Australia, and Helena Honora Rose, and has issue—Isabel Rose, born 22nd Dec. 1932. Publication—*The Old Parish Church of Carnoustie: The First Hundred Years Centenary 1937* (Carnoustie, 1937).
1924

COLLISTON

ALEXANDER MILLS, died at Arbroath 17th Dec. 1929; his wife, Georgina Anderson, died 5th April 1929; his son, David William, died at Victoria, British Columbia, 16th April 1940.
1883

FRIOCKHEIM

ALEXANDER SETON, his widow, Lilla Eglese, died 5th Sept. 1931.
1877

PATRICK ARTHUR ANDREW, dem. 16th Dec. 1924; died 13th April 1927.
1888

NORMAN DOUGALL KENNEDY, born 21st Nov. 1895, son of William Black K., B.D., min. of Eyemouth; educ. at George Watson's College and Univ. of Edinburgh, M.A. (1919); served in Great War as Lieut. K.O.S.B., M.C.; licen. by Presb. of Edinburgh 26th April 1922; assistant St Stephen's, Edinburgh; St Mungo's, Glasgow, 1924; Markinch, 1924; ord. 23rd April 1925; dem. 19th June 1928 and became min. of First Presbyterian Church, New Glasgow, Nova Scotia; trans. to First Presbyterian Church, Regina, Sept. 1942. Marr. 7th June 1930 Marion Kennedy.
1925

STEWART BAILLIE, born Larkhall 24th April 1903, son of Archibald B. and Annie Henderson Stewart; educ. at Univ. of Glasgow, M.A. (1926); licen. by Presb. of Glasgow May 1929; assistant Maxwell, Glasgow; ord. to united charge 1st Aug. 1929. Marr. 18th June 1929 Margaret Hinshelwood Thomson.
1929

GUTHRIE

In 1189–99 the church was granted to Arbroath Abbey by William the Lion. It was erected into a collegiate church for a provost and three prebendaries by Sir David Guthrie of Guthrie, who had acquired the church from Arbroath Abbey—a Bull of Confirmation being granted by Pope Sixtus IV on 14th June 1479. By charter of 18th Sept. 1505 Sir Alexander Guthrie of Guthrie, Kt., with consent of his son and heir David, granted to the provost, Sir David Guthrie, and the prebendaries, Mr David Fotheringham, Sir David Lundy and Sir David Kyd, four manses erected at the charges of the collegiate church on pieces of land which the said late Sir David Guthrie had assigned to them and had intended to convey to them if it had pleased God to spare him; and by another charter of 30th Sept. 1505 the said Sir Alexander Guthrie, for the souls of the said David Guthrie and Janet, his wife, granted an annual rent of 10 lib. from the lands of Lowr in the barony of Kincardine, Forfar, to a canon to celebrate in the said collegiate church. Prebends of the church were Guthrie, Hilton and Langlands, and Lowr. The present church was erected in 1826. The Church of Crebyauch (Carbuddo, Kirkbuddo) is included in the Taxation of 1275. By charter of 2nd Sept. 1472 James III confirmed a charter of David, Earl of Crawford and Lord Lindsay, granting to his kinsman, Mr David Guthrie of Guthrie, 6 acres of land beside the Church of Kirkbuddo, the pasture of six cows, and the patronage of the said church, which later was attached as a rectory to the Collegiate Church of Guthrie. At and subsequent to the Reformation continued attached and united to Guthrie, and constituted the southern and detached part of the parish. Till about 1682 the people of Carbuddo had a chapel of their own in which the min. of Guthrie officiated each third or fourth Sunday. The churchyard is situated on a knoll, on the south side of which is the chapel well.

On 3rd April 1576 Alexander Guthrie disponed the provostry of the church to his son, Gabrielle, student, St Leonard's College, and the prebendary called Hilton and Longland to his son, Andrew.—[*Reg. Pres. Bene.*, i, (4), 52; *Reg. of Arbroath, vetus,* 5, 67, 241; *Reg. Mag. Sig.,* ii, 1078, 2910; *Reg. Privy Council,* ii, 565.]

1563 JAMES BALFOUR, M.A., min. in 1563.—[*Comps. Sub Coll. of Thirds, Forfar,* etc.]

1574 GEORGE HAWICK, reader at Kirkbuddo.—[Jervise's *Epitaphs,* ii, 151.]

1660 WALTER KEITH, M.A.; he represented to the Privy Council that "the Kirk being vacant, he was called by the elders and deacons by Act of 7th Oct. 1660, to serve as minister; he accepted the call and served the Cure by preaching, yet on account of the troubleness of the times and the unsettledness of Church Government he had not got a formal presentation and collation, but seeing he hath discharged the ministry by preaching all the time, he craves for the stipend for 1661, 1662," which the Council granted; afterwards min. at Channelkirk.—[*Reg. Privy Council,* 3 Ser., iii, 333.]

1663 GEORGE STRACHAN, his daugh., Elizabeth (marr. cont. 15th Jan. 1697 David Ochterlony, merchant, Montrose).

1692 JAMES GUTHRIE, son of David G. of Pitforthie and Margaret Livingston.—[*Forfar Sas.,* ix, 473, 20th Sept. 1697.]

1850 PETER MILLIGAN, his daughs—Agnes Leighton, died at Elie 24th Dec. 1927; Janet, D.C.S., died 16th Sept. 1928; Helen Wood, died 30th July 1945; his son, Patrick Fraser, bank agent, Elie, died at Perth 30th June 1930.

1907 WILLIAM GUTHRIE LAW, died 3rd April 1929.

1929 PETER MILNE, trans. from Gilmerton 7th Aug. 1929 (vii, 701); dem. 15th May 1935; died at Edinburgh 18th Sept. 1939.

INVERKEILLOUR

The patron saint is said to be Mo Chonoc or Mo Chonog of Cell Mucroisse, whose day is 19th Dec. In 1178 the church was granted to Arbroath Abbey by Walter de Berkeley, chamberlain of the King. The church was dedicated by Bishop de Bernham 17th Aug. 1242. At Kinblethmont there was a chapel dedicated to St Laurence, which in the early part of the reign of Alexander II was given by Richard de Melville to Arbroath Abbey. The chapel at Whitefield was dedicated to the Virgin Mary. The Temple lands of Kinblethmont belonged to St Germain's Hospital, Tranent.—[*Reg. of Arbroath, vetus,* 37, 99–100, *niger,* 165; Lockhart's *Church of Scotland in the* 13*th Century,* 50–1; *Retours,* vii, 312; Watson's *Celtic Place Names,* 282.]

ALEXANDER FORRESTER, vicar 1561–3.—[*Comps. Sub Coll. of Thirds, Forfar*, etc.]
1561

CHARLES MICHAELSON, min. in 1563.—[*Comps. Sub Coll. of Thirds, Forfar*, etc.]
1563

CHARLES ROSSIE, reader in 1563.—[*Comps. Sub Coll. of Thirds, Forfar*, etc.]
1563

JOHN PITCAIRN, reader, pres. to vicarage 9th July 1574 on death of Alexander Forrester.—[*Reg. Pres. Bene.*, i, (4), 23; *Edin. Tests.*, iii, 461.]
1573

JOHN FULLERTON, min.; may be identical with John F. of Kinnaber, thought apt by the Assembly on 20th Dec. 1560 to be a min. and commissioner.—[*Book of Univ. Kirk*, 4.]
1576

ARTHUR FITHIE, pres. in 1604 on dem. of John Pitcairn of Kirkton Mill, Inverkeiler.—[*Reg. Sec. Sig.*, lxxiv, 139.]
1598

JOSHUA DURIE, his marr. cont. 5th Dec. 1593 calls him John Durie and his wife Euphame, daugh. of James Mackein.—[*Yester Writs*, 920].
1613

JOHN RAIT, his second wife, Euphame Mudie, daugh. of Janet Ramsay; had issue, James, bapt. 3rd March 1649, died young.—[*Montrose Reg.*]
1650

JAMES RAIT, his daugh., Margaret (marr. cont. 30th July 1700). He intruded at Kirriemuir Sept. 1715 to Jan. 1716 and was in attendance on the Pretender at the house of Kinnaird.—[*Justiciary Records*, 23rd Jan. 1717.]
1672

ANDREW BRUCE, had issue—David Elizabeth, Magdalen, George, Ann, Christian.—[*Forfar Burgh Reg. of Deeds*, Bundle 1730.]
1705

ANDREW HALDEN, died at Montrose 25th May 1928.
1887

ANGUS MACASKILL, born 14th Nov. 1901, son of Alexander Jack M., postman, Stornoway, and Johan Macleod; educ. at Nicolson Institute and Univ. of Aberdeen, M.A. (1923); licen. by Presb. of Arbroath 1926; assistant Arbroath 1926; ord. assistant and successor 18th April 1928; trans. to London Road, Edinburgh, 12th Nov. 1947. Marr. 23rd Nov. 1932 Maureen Reith, daugh. of Norman Baxter Anderson and Ruth Lilian Matthewson, and has issue—Alistair Angus, born 17th Dec. 1933; Norman Roy, born 1st May 1936.
1928

(*Charges united 7th March* 1948.)

ETHIE

DAVID MYLNE, reader, vicar in 1586. —[*Comps. Gen. Coll. of Thirds.*]
1586

KINNELL

By Bull of Pope Sextus IV, 26th Feb. 1473, Kinnell was made a mensal church of St Andrews.—[*The Apostolic Camera and Scottish Benefices*, 173.]

JOHN JOHNSTONE, vicar and reader reader 1561.—[*Comps. Gen. Coll. of Thirds.*]
1561

PATRICK LIDDELL, parson and vicar (Prebend of St Salvator's) 1563, which he dem. before 19th March 1566–7, died before 1st April 1588.—[*Comps. Sub Coll. of Thirds, Forfar*, etc.; *Reg. Sec. Sig.*, xxxvi, 26; lvii, 81.]
1563

DAVID FYFE, reader 1563.—[*Comps. Sub Coll. of Thirds, Forfar*, etc.]
1563

JAMES GRAY, app. to the Prebend (parsonage of Kinnell) of St Salvator's, St Andrews, by John, Archbishop of St Andrews; confirmation by Crown Charter 19th March 1566–7; died before 28th Jan. 1587–8.—[*Reg. Sec. Sig.*, xxxvi, 26; lvii, 86.]
1563

JOHN JOHNSTONE of Barnecleuch, vicar 1578–82.—[*Reg. Abbrev. Feu Charters of Church Lands*, ii, 173, 315.]
1578

ARTHUR FITHIE, M.A., pres. 28th June 1587 to parsonage "callit of old Chalmaines Chaplaincy of St Salvator's College, St Andrews" on death
1587

of James Gray; and as min. here to parsonage 1st April 1588 on death of Patrick Liddell.—[*Reg. Sec. Sig.*, lvii, 81.]

1599 JOHN GUTHRIE, pres. in 1599 on dem. of Arthur Fithie.—[*Reg. Sec. Sig.*, lxxi, 47.]

1603 WILLIAM KINNEAR, pres. to parsonage and vicarage 1603 on dem. of John Guthrie.—[*Reg. Sec. Sig.*, lxxiv, 24.]

1883 DUNCAN MACARTHUR, died 26th May 1925; his widow, Isabella Fleming, died 2nd Jan. 1926.

1925 WILLIAM MARTIN, trans. from Braes of Rannoch (*q.v.*) 15th Oct. 1925; trans. to Dallas 11th May 1932; dem. 12th April 1947; died at Garmouth 14th April 1948.

KIRKDEN

In 1388 the church was situated beside a ford upon the Vauny Water, near "the foot of the rock called Craignacre." In the vicinity was a well called "Sinruie," a corruption of St Malrubh. The present church was built in 1825.—[*Reg. Priory of St Andrews*, 409–10.]

The church was dedicated by Bishop de Bernham 1st Sept. 1243.

1594 JAMES HEPBURN, M.A., pres. to parsonage and vicarage 18th July 1594 on dem. of Harry Duncan.—[*Reg. Sec. Sig.*, lxvi, 179.]

1594 JOHN LINDSAY, M.A., pres. to parsonage and vicarage 10th Sept. 1594 on death of Robert Ramsay.—[*Reg. Sec. Sig.*, lxvi, 203.]

1594 GILBERT GRAHAM, M.A., pres. to parsonage and vicarage 9th Dec. 1594 on dem. of Harry Duncan.—[*Reg. Sec. Sig.*, lxvii, 92.]

1617 THOMAS RAMSAY, had issue—John, Robert, Thomas, Patrick, Helen, Barbara.—[*St Andrews Tests.*, 30th April 1635.]

1646 JOHN RUTHERFORD, was Dean of St Andrews Univ.—[*Rep. Hist. MSS. Com.*, vi, 736.]

1685 WILLIAM BALVAIRD, min. at Airlie 1678. Marr. Elizabeth Spalding and had issue—Elizabeth, Catherine, Grizel.—[*Forfar Sas.*, vi, 450, 25th Sept. 1678.]

1893 JOHN BOYLE, dem. 31st Jan. 1931; died 11th Dec. 1934; his daugh., Margaret Edward (marr. 2nd April 1931 David Gardyne Dorward, B.Sc.).

(*United to Dunnichen 6th Sept. 1931.*)

IDVIE

1571 WILLIAM HAY, parson 27th June 1571.—[*Cal. of Charters*, x, 2225.]

LUNAN

In the Accounts of the General Collector of Thirds for 1573 there appears this entry: "To the relict of the late Walter Mylne according to the allowance of the old compts £6 8 4." If the reference is to Walter Myln or Mill, priest of Lunan, who suffered martyrdom at St Andrews on 28th Aug. 1558, it would throw further light upon the extent to which he had parted company with the Roman Catholic Church.

1567 JOHN BATY, vicar 24th Oct. 1570.—[*Acts and Dec.*, xlvi, 267.]

1867 ALEXANDER FRIDGE, his widow, Elizabeth Catherine Macdonald, daugh. of a shipmaster, Arbroath, died 22nd Feb. 1936, aged 80.

1907 WALTER PERCY COX, dem. 11th Feb. 1939; his wife, Wilhelmina Agnes Brown, died 3rd Oct. 1940. Marr. (2) 6th Oct. 1941 Jane Leck.

PANBRIDE

There was at Panmure a chapel dedicated to the Virgin Mary. By Bull of 27th Jan. 1484–5 Pope Julian granted permission to Sir Thomas Maule of Panmure to celebrate mass and other divine offices within the chapel, though as yet unconsecrated, and to have a portable altar, and that either by his own chaplains or other suitable priests secular or regular. There was also a chapel at Boath, to which Christian de Valoniis, Lady of Panmure, who succeeded her father, William de V., and died after 1254, granted the lands of Botmernoch or Bothmernoch, and also 2 merks annual rent from the lands of Brechys. By Christian de Valoniis' great-grandson, Walter de Maule of Panmure, who died in 1348, the chapel with its lands, annual rents, and all rights, was given to Brechin Cathedral. Included also in the gift were the lands of Cairncorty, and on 24th Aug. 1348 Adam, Bishop of Brechin, gave the chaplainry and its foresaid endowments for the sustenance of two perpetual chaplains founded by him anew in the cathedral. In augmentation of the chaplainry the Bishop also united thereto an annual rent of 20 sh. which the Abbot and Convent of Arbroath were held to pay to Brechin Cathedral at Pentecost in virtue of a composition lately made between the Bishop and Chapter and the said Abbot and Convent. The chaplains were to celebrate mass, one at the Altar of the Virgin Mary, and the other at the Altar of the Holy Rood in the cathedral, for the souls of the said Adam, his predecessors and successors as bishops, the canons, and Hugh, the Chancellor. It was further stipulated that the vicar of Panbride should say a Mass of the Virgin Mary each Saturday, and the vicar of Monikie a Mass of St Marnoc for all time. The latter part of the stipulation and the name of the lands, Bothmernoch, granted originally to the chapel, suggest that the chapel may have been dedicated to St Marnoch. There was another chapel at Boath, dedicated to St Laurence. It belonged to Arbroath Abbey. To William de Monteath, son of son of Sir Michael de M., William, Abbot of Arbroath 1276-88, became bound to support a chaplain at the said William's Chapel of St Laurence at Boath, the said William to bestow upon the abbey the lands of Konan-Mor-Capil. In the 17th century both the chaplainry and the chapel appear among the possessions of the Earls of Panmure.—[*Reg. of Panmure*, ii, 141–2, 171–2, 173, 253–4; *Reg. of Brechin*, i, 10–12, 13, 14, ii, 363; *Reg. of Arbroath, vetus*, Pref., xiv, 189; *Retours*, xxvi, 168, xxx, 186, xxxviii, 340.]

1562 WILLIAM LAING, vicar 2nd Dec. 1562.—[*Reg. of Deeds*, v, 376.]

1588 JOHN LAING, M.A., vicar 1588; also at Forteviot; chancellor of Brechin 1590.—[*Comps. Gen. Coll. of Thirds.*]

1680 PATRICK MAULE, marr. Maria, daugh. of John Maule; his son, James, bapt. 7th Dec. 1694, fought at Sheriffmuir and escaped to France; wrote a journal of his travels 1716–20 (in possession of George Burn-Murdoch of Gartincaber); factor to Earl of Moray, Donibristle; buried 25th Nov. 1753.

1717 ROBERT TRAIL, his son, John, apprenticed to Hugh Penman, goldsmith, Edinburgh, 12th May 1736.

1851 JAMES CAESAR, his daugh., Agnes Cowan, died 10th July 1935.

1895 JOHN CAESAR, D.D. (St Andrews, 26th June 1931), died 13th Feb. 1938.

ST VIGEANS

The church was dedicated by Bishop de Bernham 19th Aug. 1242 and by the Bishop of Dromore on 25th Aug. 1485. The Altar of St Sebastian was founded by John Brown in Letham in 1506. On 17th Feb. 1543-4 Alexander Ouchterlony, brother of Alexander O. of Kelle, was escheited "through being fugitive fra the law at the horne for non-finding of souirte to underlie the law for breiking and spulyeing Sanct Vegeanis kirk of Arbrotht and oure Lady Chapell of the same, and for other crimes." In the Den of Seaton there was a chapel dedicated to St Ninian, founded by the Abbot and Convent of Arbroath, and consecrated on 24th Aug. 1485 by George de Brane, Bishop of Dromore. St Ninian's Croft marks its site; and near are St Ninian's Well and a cliff called St Ninian's Heuch. To the chaplainry of the chapel Sir John Tod, son and heir of Simon T., burgess of Arbroath, was presented by David, Abbot of Arbroath, on 22nd July 1492, the presentation to become effective on the death of the chaplain, Sir William Gybsoune.—[*Reg. of Arbroath, niger*, 174, 271; *Reg. Sec. Seal*, iii, 636; David Miller's *Arbroath and its Abbey*, 129–30, 146; Lockhart's *Ch. in Scot. in 13th Century*, 51.]

1563 NINIAN CLEMENT, min. in 1563.—[*Comps. Sub Coll. of Thirds, Forfar*, etc.] (See Arbroath.)

1602 ROBERT BRUCE, M.A., min. 4th Nov. 1602.

1602 JOHN YOUNG, reader.—[*Acts and Dec.*, clxv, 457.]

1665 PATRICK STRACHAN, his daughs.—Anna, bapt. 20th June 1672; Margaret (marr. cont. 3rd Jan 1695 David Ramsay, younger of Cairnton.)—[*Forfar Sas.*, ix, 30th April 1695.]

1696 GEORGE STRACHAN, died before 20th Sept. 1700; his son, John, going abroad 1729.—[*Arbroath Burgh Court*, 20th Sept. 1700.]

1734 JOHN HENDERSON, his son, Robert, apprenticed to Edward Lothian, goldsmith, Edinburgh, 16th May 1733.

1754 JOHN AIKEN, died Father of the Church.

PRESBYTERY OF FORDOUN

ARBUTHNOTT

By charter of 30th May 1505 Sir Robert Arbuthnott of that ilk for the soul of Maud Scrymgeour, his wife, etc., granted to a chaplain at the Altar of the Blessed Virgin Mary, situated at the south side of the choir of the church, certain annual rents with a manse, garden, and croft near the Chapel of St Ternan, as a residence for the chaplain. This refers to the Lady Chapel previously founded by Sir Robert. At Peattie there was a chapel dedicated to St Mary.—[*Reg. Mag. Sig.*, 5th Aug. 1505; *Trans. Aberdeen Eccl. Soc.*, 1897.]

1563 ANDREW PATRICK, reader in 1563.—[*Comps. Sub Coll. of Thirds, Forfar*, etc.]

1567 PATRICK RAMSAY, min. at Conveth, also in charge here.

1569 ALEXANDER ARBUTHNOTT, his pres. in 1569 to parsonage and vicarage on res. of Robert Hallet.—[*Reg. Pres. Bene.*, i, 27.]

1665 ALEXANDER ARBUTHNOTT, in addition to *John Bull*, his son, Dr John, wrote *The Art of Political Lying* and *The Memoirs of Martinus Scriblerus*.

1715 ALEXANDER ROBERTSON, son of Alexander R., min. at Longside, intruded here Oct. 1715.—[*Justiciary Records.*]

1850 ROBERT MOIR SPENCE, his daughs.—Margaret Anne, died 15th April 1933; Anne Gerard, died 30th May 1934.

1921 JOHN SIMPSON MUTCH, trans. to Newport 18th May 1925.

1925 ALFRED SAUNDERS BARRON, born New Blyth 10th April 1890, son of George B., schoolmaster, and Robina Eliza Gray Collier; educ. at Univ. of Aberdeen, M.A. (1912), B.D. (1915); served in Great War with Gordon Highlanders; licen. by Presb. of ——— 1915; *locum tenens* at Kintore; teacher, Nicolson Institute, Stornoway; schoolmaster, Strathdon, 1922; ord. 16th Sept. 1925; trans. to Longside 19th Oct. 1933. Marr. 6th Sept. 1922 Alice Ann Mary, daugh. of Alexander Mitchell, store manager, Kintore.

BENHOLME

1563 WILLIAM ELDER, reader 1563; designated vicar 16th April 1568 and reader 1573.—[*Comps. Sub Coll. of Thirds, Forfar*, etc.; *Edin. Tests.*, iv, 333; v, 83.]

1563 JOHN GUDEFALLO, min. in 1563, also at Ecclesgreig.—[*Comps. Sub Coll. of Thirds, Forfar*, etc.]

1566 JAMES THORNTON, parson 1566.—[*Comps. Sub Coll. of Thirds, Forfar*, etc.]

1577 WILLIAM DOUGLAS of Glenbervie, pres. to parsonage and vicarage 27th Dec. 1577 on death of John Thornton.—[*Reg. Pres. Bene.*, i, (4), 68.]

1577 WILLIAM MORRISON, M.A.; his pres. in Feb. 1577-8 on death of John Thornton.—[*Reg. Pres. Bene.*, i, (4), 65.]

1587 JOHN ERSKINE, M.A., in Bingfurde, pres. to vicarage 20th Nov. 1587 on death of William Morrison.—[*Reg. Sec. Sig.*, lv, 103.]

1648 JAMES MELVILL, marr. (2) Isabel, daugh. of Alexander Straton of that ilk.—[*P. R. Sas.*, *Kincardine*, v, 146.]

1715 ANDREW SKENE, intruded here and conducted episcopal services in a meeting-house at Brotherston and gave support to the rebels.—[*Justiciary Records.*]

1843 ALEXANDER SMART MYERS, his daughs.—Helen Forrest, died at Edinburgh 5th Feb. 1929; Diana Cooper, died 30th May 1938; Eliza, died 14th Feb. 1940; Jane, died Edinburgh 17th Oct. 1945.

1923 JOHN BARCLAY DAVIE, father a merchant; trans. to Kerse 18th May 1927.

1927 GEORGE ARTHUR EVERETT WALKER, trans. from Corgarff (*q.v.*) 7th Sept. 1927; dem. 6th July 1947; his wife, Edith Donaldson, died 27th May 1936. Marr. (2) 14th Oct. 1942 Annie Webster Japp Henderson or Wylie.

(*United with Johnshaven 6th July* 1947.)

BERVIE

At Inverbervie there was a friary of the Carmelites, situated at the place designated "Friars' Dubb." The friary held the Churches of Kingussie and Dunnottar. By Crown Charters of 15th Oct. 1570 and 1st Aug. 1587 Mr David Lindsay acquired the endowments of the friary—lands, salmon fishings and white fishings in the water of Bervie, fresh and salt, tofts, crofts, annual rents, mills, multures, money and victual fermes, customs, canis, and other profits, and the patronage of churches, benefices, chaplainries in the county of Kincardine or in any other part of the Kingdom. In the latter year, 1587, the grant was ratified by Parliament, which at the same time conveyed to the Burgh of Montrose for the hospital there the sum of 45 merks 5 sh. 4d., being the sum for which the endowments had previously been given to Mr David Lindsay.—[*Reg. Great Seal*, iv, 1932, v, 1332; *Acts Scott. Parl.*, iii, 489, 504*b*; Walcott's *Anc. Ch. of Scot.*, 337, 408; *Retours*, xxiv, 94.]

1563 JAMES SYMSON, reader in 1563.— [*Comps. Sub Coll. of Thirds, Forfar*, etc.]

1591 JAMES RAIT, had Kinneff also in charge till his death.

1674 PETER RAIT, his daugh., Mary (marr. cont. 22nd July 1712 James Carnegie, surgeon apothercary, Brechin.

1924 GRAHAM NICOLL WARNER, trans. to Elgin Second Charge 16th Dec. 1926.

1927 NEIL McGILL, formerly of Duntocher (*q.v.*); trans from Tomintoul 27th April 1927; died 3rd Oct. 1944; Provost of Inverbervie.

COOKNEY

In 1840 the Sabbath service was conducted by a preacher who was also second parochial schoolmaster at Fetteresso. The sacraments were dispensed by the parish min. (See Fetteresso and Portlethen.)

1919 ANDREW ELVIN HART, trans. to Coylton 1st Sept. 1932; his wife, Ethel Burns, died 13th June 1939. Marr. (2) 4th Feb. 1942 Wilhelmina Thom, and has issue—Archibald James, born 12th March 1943.

DUNNOTTAR

On the Crag of Dunnottar, it is said, a chapel was founded early in the 5th century by St Ninian. To this view some support comes from the fact that on the top of an isolated neighbouring rock, called Dinnacair, there were found in 1832 several stones incised with early Christian symbols, believed to have been in use prior to the 8th century, one of the stones having the fish, the symbol of Christ, and the triangle which signifies the Trinity. Dinnacair may have been a "retreat" connected with the chapel on the crag. The church was dedicated by Bishop de Bernham 15th May 1276. In any case certain it is that at a later period there was upon the rock St Ninian's Parish Church of Dunnottar, dedicated by William Wishart, Bishop of St Andrews, on 15th May 1276. Twenty years later, on 28th Aug. 1296, Wautier de Kerringtoune, parson of Dunnottar, swore fealty to Edward I. In the following year the rock, which was held by the English, was assaulted by Wallace. The attack was successful; and, the garrison having sought sanctuary in the sacred building, Wallace, according to Blind Harry, "Brynt up the kyrk, and all that was theirin." It is said that the church was rebuilt, and in turn was burned by Edward III. That, however, does not seem certain. On 30th March 1346 William, Earl of Sutherland, and his wife, Margaret Bruce, received from David II a charter of the Crag, with power to build a fortalice thereon. Probably the power was not exercised; but Sir William Keith, Great Marishal of Scotland, who acquired Dunnottar on 8th March 1392-3, by excambion with his son-in-law, Sir William Lindsay of Byres, built a "castle and fortalice" upon the rock. For that deed, regarded as an encroachment on sacred ground, Sir William was excommunicated by the Bishop of St Andrews. On appeal to the Holy See, Sir William, in virtue of a Bull of Pope Benedict XIII, on 14th June 1395, secured the withdrawal of the sentence, at the hands of the Bishop, on condition that he paid suitable compensation to the Church of Dunnottar for the use of the rock. In his appeal Sir William, besides justifying the tower as necessary for his own protection and for the security of his dependents and their goods, and as inferring no injury to the "new Church" or its rector, stated that when in time past during the wars that raged in the Kingdom of Scotland the Parish Church of Dunnottar with the churchyaird, situated on a rock overlooking the sea, required to be rebuilt and put in order, the late John, lord of the barony of Dunnottar, with the consent and authority of the Bishop of St Andrews for the time, built and established another church with churchyard on the mainland of the parish church; and the rock was left empty and deserted. It would appear that the foresaid lord of the barony was John, Ninth Earl of Athol, who had right to Dunnottar through his mother, Ada, Countess of Athol, who married John of Strathbogie, Eighth Earl of Athol in right of his wife. The said Countess Ada in turn had right to Dunnottar through her mother, Ferneleith, Countess of Athol, who married David de Hastings, connected with the Mearns and holding the title Seventh Earl of Athol in right of his wife. The said Earl John was executed at London in 1306. Clearly, therefore, if he transferred the parish church from the rock, the church burned by Wallace was left a ruin. In any case, some time prior to the advent of Sir William Keith at Dunnottar, the church, on account of the disabilities of wars that frequently involved Dunnottar Crag because of its fortress value, was removed to the mainland, apparently to the site which the parish church still occupies; and the church on the rock became the chapel of the castle. The existing ruins of the chapel, on the south side of which is the churchyard, show portions of the 13th-century church burned by Wallace; but the work is in the main of the 16th century. For her own soul and the soul of her deceased husband, David de Hastings, Ferneleith, Countess of Athol, granted Dunnottar to Cupar-Angus Abbey. The grant was confirmed by her daughter, Countess Ada, but it does not appear that it actually took effect. In 1504 the annexation of the church to the Trinity Collegiate Church, Edinburgh, was confirmed by Pope Julius. One half of the parsonage and vicarage of the church was given to the Dean of the Collegiate Church, and the other half to the Sub-Dean. The church was rebuilt in 1782 on the site of the old church, of which only one part survives— the Marischal Aisle, the tomb of George, Earl Marischal, built in 1582. On 16th June 1903 the church was reopened for worship after a scheme of restoration had been carried out.—[*Reg. Great Seal*, i, App. i, 122; *Transcripts from the Vatican*, i, 356, MS. Reg. Ho.; *Hist. MSS. Commis. Reports* iii, 405, 408; *Statua Ecclesiae Scoticanae*, i, ccciii; *Cal. of Docs. Rel. to Scot.*, ii, 214; *Scots Peerage*, i, 425-6; Simpson's *Dunnottar Castle*, 6 and n, 52; *Lives of the*

Lindsays, 317; Barron's *Castle of Dunnottar* 21; *Collegiate Churches of Midlothian*, 143; *Reg. Pres. Bene.*, i, 81; *Memo.*, Rev. J. C. Campbell, B.D.]

JOHN CHRISTISON, min. at Fetteresso, in charge also here.—[*Comps. Sub Coll. of Thirds, Forfar,* etc.]
1560

JAMES PAWTON, reader, in charge 1563.—[*Comps. Sub Coll. of Thirds, Forfar,* etc.]
1563

JOHN ELDER, one of the rectors 3rd April 1563, having the fruits of the half of the parsonage and vicarage of the church, which belonged to the deanery of Trinity Collegiate Church; died before 8th April 1578.—[*Colleg. Churches of Midlothian*, 126–7, 131, 139, 226.]
1563

WILLIAM SALMOND, one of the rectors 3rd April 1563, having the fruits of the half of the parsonage and vicarage of the church, which belonged to the sub-deanery of Trinity Collegiate Church; died before 4th Sept. 1576.—[*Colleg. Churches of Midlothian*, 126–7, 131, 137, 226.]
1563

ANDREW MYLNE, M.A., pres. in 1574 and 1578 on death of John Elder. On presentation by James VI he was admitted by the Superintendent of Angus 4th Sept. 1576 to the half of the parsonage and vicarage that had pertained to William Salmond, and on 3rd Nov. 1578 he was presented to the half that had pertained to John Elder.—[*Colleg. Churches of Midlothian*, 137, 139; *Reg. Pres. Bene.*, i, 81, ii, 87.]
1574

ALEXANDER KEITH, pres. in 1579 on dem. of Andrew Mylne.—[*Reg. Pres. Bene.*, ii, 23.]
1579

JAMES RAIT, reverse marriages—marr. (1) pro. 8th April 1660 Jean Edmonston (? Erskine), Montrose.
1654

GILBERT KEITH, son of Gilbert K. of Caldhame and Mary Rait; had addl. issue—Alexander, buried 6th May 1711; Mary, buried 3rd May 1711.
1686

WILLIAM SETON, episcopal preacher, who, ordained by an "enaucterated bishop," had been deposed by the Presbytery of Fordoun for various misdemeanours, intruded in Dunnottar Oct. 1715 to Feb. 1716, and, encouraged by the Earl and Countess Marischal, ejected Mr Mitchell with his wife and family from the manse and occupied the same; from the foregoing it would appear that Mr M. had an earlier marriage than that of 1732.—[*Justiciary Records.*]
1715

DOUGLAS GORDON BARRON, died at Aberfoyle 18th Feb. 1947; his wife, Louise Eliza Brydon, died 4th Feb. 1938. Addl. Publications—*The Castle of Dunnottar and its History* (1925); *Jean Charlier de Gerson, the Author of De Imitatione Christi.*
1885

JOHN GAIRDNER WHITE HENDRIE, line 8, for "R.F.C." read "R.F.A."; licen. by Presb. of Ayr May 1920; trans. to Colombo, Ceylon, 8th July 1933.
1923

FETTERCAIRN, alias TRINITY

The church was made a mensal Church of St Andrews by Bull of Pope Sixtus IV, 26th Feb. 1473. The Chapel of St Martin is mentioned in 1445 and 1493, in connection with a croft "lyand at the bridgend beside St Martin's Chapel betwixt the lands of Dullach and Disclune."—[*Reg. Great Seal*, ii, 767; *Mems. of Angus and Mearns*, 438; *The Apostilic Camera and Scott. Benefices*, 173.]

WILLIAM STRATHAUCHIN, reader in 1563.—[*Comps. Sub Coll. of Thirds, Forfar,* etc.]
1563

PATRICK BONKLE, min. in 1563.—[*Comps. Sub Coll. of Thirds, Forfar,* etc.]
1563

JOHN THOM, reader, succeeded William Strathauchin 1563.—[*Comps. Sub Coll. of Thirds, Forfar,* etc.]
1563

JAMES STRATHAUCHAN, parson, brother of John S. of Claypotts.—[*Acts and Dec.*, lvii, 407.]
1576

1576	JAMES LINDSAY, pres. in 1576 on death of James Strathauchan.—[*Reg. Pres. Bene.*, i, (4), 43.]
1580	JOHN COLLACE, pres. to parsonage and vicarage 15th Aug. 1580 in succession to James Lindsay.—[*Reg. Sec. Sig.*, xlvii, 1.]
1867	WILLIAM ANDERSON, his son, James Edward, C.B.E., died 18th Jan. 1945.
1910	CHARLES LAMB HUNTER, adm. to united charge 1929; dem. 30th Nov. 1948.

FETTERESSO

The church was dedicated by Bishop de Bernham on 25th May 1246. In the churchyard on the south boundary of the parish, about a mile from Stonehaven, stands the roofless church which was in use till 1813, when it gave place to the present church built at Stonehaven. Part of the ruin is an aisle built opposite the pulpit in 1720. In 1621 a petition by Thomas Burnet of Leyis, craving the erection of a new church in the parish "most ewest for the Instructioun of the Parochoneris of Fetteresso quha duell most remote from the present Kirk," was remitted by Parliament to the Commission for the Plantation of Kirks, etc. Nothing appears to have resulted. In 1649 the Presbytery of Aberdeen petitioned Parliament for the erection of a parish kirk with "glaib and manse and other accommodatioun" for the remoter parts of Fetteresso and Netherbanchi. "It is almost impossible to thame Especiallie in the winter tyme to repair to their owne paroche kirk for the worship of God and the educatioune of their souls. The way being deip and almost impossible." The number of communicants within the said bounds was given as "about 8 or 9 hundreth souls." The area in question was the north part of Fetteresso and the south part of Banchory-Devenick. In this case also there was no result. But about 1760 a small place of worship was built at Newhall in the north part of the parish. It was called the "Sod Kirk," doubtless because the roof was covered with turf which at a later period gave way to tiles. Efforts towards securing a better building, which were strongly supported by Mr Silver of Netherley, culminated in the erection of a house at Cookney, capable of accommodation for 400 people. The latter in turn gave place to the present Cookney Church. The Chapel of Cowie was dedicated by Bishop de Bernham on 22nd May 1276, "so that no prejudice may arise to the mother-church of Fetteresso." The chapel was under the joint invocation of St Mary the Virgin and St Nathalom. The Lady Well is in the neighbourhood.—[*Acts Scott. Parl.*, iv, 607*a*, vi, (2), 343; Lockhart's *Ch. in Scot. in 13th Century*, 62, 63; *Trans. Aberdeen Eccl. Society*, 1897, 241.]

The present church was built in 1810–13 and enlarged 1876–8. The Chapel of Cowie, described in 1722 as situated near the ruins of the Castle of Cowie, was consecrated by Bishop Wishart of St Andrews on 22nd May 1276. The dedication was St Mary the Virgin and St Nathalan. In 1496–1504 James IV made various offerings in "Our Ladie Chapell of Cowie." On 28th Dec. 1502 the same monarch confirmed grants as follows: certain crofts, including "le Abbottiscroft" in the town of Cowie by late William Hay of Urie, an annual rent from lands near Cowie by the late Gilbert Hay of Urie, and a croft called the Temple Croft near the town of Cowie by late Alexander Strachan of Dillevard, for the support of a perpetual chaplain in the chapel. Mr Robert Hay was Chaplain of "the chaplainry of St Nathalan in the Chapel of Cowie" on 26th Nov. 1568. It is said that the chapel was demolished soon after the Reformation "by reason of superstitious resorting thereto." St Mary's Well, near the chapel, was also a place of superstitious resort, and in 1722 was "yet held in veneration by the country people." There was at Cowie a Fair of St Nathalan.—[*Reg. Great Seal*, ii, 2681; iii, 2299, iv, 2191; *Statua Ecclesiae Scoticanae*, i, 303; Macfarlane's *Geog. Colls.*, i, 249, 255, iii, 236–7.]

ROBERT RAIT, reader in 1563.—
1563 [*Comps. Sub Coll. of Thirds, Forfar*, etc.]

ANDREW MYLNE, M.A., pres. in
1576 1576 on death of Patrick Brown.—
[*Reg. Pres. Bene.*, ii, 23.]

PETER ROSS, an episcopal min., intruded in Fetteresso, ejected Mr
1715 Burn and his family from the manse, and took the poor-box and money and the session books and papers; he was dep. by the Presb. of Fordoun in 1716 for "scandalous practices"; at the same period William Cruickshank, an episcopal min., conducted services at Muchalls and was dep. by the presb.—[*Justiciary Records*.]

JOHN WATT, his daugh., Elizabeth
1845 (Mrs J. P. Sym), died 20th April 1944.

JAMES BEATTIE BURNETT, D.D.
1905 (Aberdeen, 1st April 1931), died at Aberdeen 1st Oct. 1945; his wife, Helen Mary Christison, died 20th Jan. 1943; his son, James, died 30th Jan. 1942. Publications—*The Kirks of Cowie and Fetteresso*; *Seaside Sermons*.

FORDOUN

At the instance of William, Earl Marischal, the burgh of Kincardine was created anew by Crown Charter of 27th Jan. 1531–2, with a Fair of St Catherine the Virgin, and a Fair of St Catherine of Siena, and by Crown Charter of 3rd March 1540–1 the towns of Kincardine, Cowie, and Durris were erected into free burghs with the following fairs—at Kincardine, a Fair of St Catherine the Virgin in winter, and a Fair of St Catherine of Siena in summer; at Cowie, a fair on the Feast of St Nachtalan; and at Durris, a fair on the day of St Monan. St Catherine's was the church of the now vanished burgh of Kincardine, whose fair and cross were removed to Fettercairn in 1670. The church, too, has disappeared, but its burial-ground still exists on the farm of Castleton.—[*Reg. Great Seal*, iii, 1113, 2299, vii, 737; *Ordnance Gazetteer*, 391; Jervise's *Epitaphs and Inscrips.*, i, 65.]

JOHN SMYTH, reader in 1563.—
1563 [*Comps. Sub Coll. of Thirds, Forfar*, etc.]

PATRICK BONCLE, min. here in 1563;
1563 pres. to vicarage 28th Jan. 1576–7 on death of Walter Callam, when he also held Laurencekirk.—[*Comps. Sub Coll. of Thirds, Forfar*, etc.; *Reg. Pres. Bene.*, i, (4), 52; *Edin. Tests.*, ii, 301, v, 22, 82.] (See Fetteresso and Newdosk.)

GILBERT ANDERSON, his daugh.,
1714 Elizabeth, died at Edinburgh 13th June 1782.

WILLIAM FORBES, marr. Susanna,
1747 daugh. of William Walker, dyster, Aberdeen; his children—Mary Ann (marr. Rev. Austin Johnson), died 1812; Elizabeth (marr. Professor William Duncan, King's College, Aberdeen), died 1931; Middleton, died 1834; Phoebe (marr. –. Scott, purser, R.N.).

CHARLES FORBES BUCHAN, his
1846 father, Peter B., was poet and antiquary.

JOHN MENZIES, his widow, Susan
1875 Gordon Garland, died 20th Jan. 1930.

ROBERT GALBRAITH, dem. 31st
1902 Aug. 1934, died 23rd Oct. 1937; his daugh., Jane (marr. 10th June 1931 Neil Garland, Hong Kong); his widow, Eliza Alison, died 14th May 1947.

GARVOCK

JAMES SYMMER, reader in 1563.—
1563 [*Comps. Sub Coll. of Thirds, Forfar*, etc.]

ALEXANDER KEITH, reader; pres.
1563 to vicarage on death of John Wardlaw, 9th Feb. 1586–7; also at Kinneff.—[*Reg. Sec. Sig.*, lv, 17; *Comps. Sub Coll. of Thirds, Forfar*, etc.]

JOHN WARDLAW, vicar 1564–5.—
1564 [*Acts and Dec.*, xxxiii, 25.]

WALTER MORRISON, M.A., pres. to vicarage 13th May 1588 on dem. of Alexander Keith.—[*Reg. Sec. Sig.*, lvii, 81.]

1588

ROBERT ARBUTHNOTT, M.A., pres. in 1604 on death of Walter Morrison.—[*Reg. Sec. Sig.*, lxxiv, 138.]

1604

JOHN KEITH, had issue—James.—[*Aberdeen Sher. Court Deeds*, 1st Sept. 1694.]

1653

ROBERT OCHTERLONY, marr. Anne, daugh. of Captain William Keith of Reidcloak.—[*Montrose Deeds*, 11th Oct. 1689.]

1685

WILLIAM STEPHEN, died at Barnton 25th March 1934; his widow, Jane Latto Morrison, died 30th March 1936; his son, Charles, F.R.S.E., Keeper of Natural History Department, Royal Scottish Museum.

1877

FRANCIS McHARDY, trans. to Logie, Cupar, 26th July 1928.

1923

MUNRO SOMERVELL, formerly of Drumelzier (*q.v.*), trans. from Ballantrae 13th Dec. 1928; dem. 16th May 1935; died at Peebles 6th May 1936.

1928

GLENBERVIE

By Papal Bull of 4th May 1422 the church, which was dedicated to St Michael, was erected a prebend of Brechin Cathedral in response to a petition by the Earl of Mar. There was at Drumlithie a chapel of which on 2nd June 1536 Sir James Auchleck was chaplain. The Well of St Carran at Drumlithie in all probability indicates the saint to whom the chapel was dedicated. Carran is Ciaran, apparently Ciaran of Cluain mac Nois, whose day was 9th Sept. and who died in 549. The endowment of the chapel was the lands of Drumlithie, which on 18th Dec. 1549 Sir James Reid, Presbyter-Perpetual Chaplain, with consent of Mr Robert Erskine, Dean of Aberdeen, patron of the chaplainry, set in feu to William Douglas, son and heir of the late Archibald Douglas of Glenbervie. William Douglas had granted a piece of land of his Templar Lands of Templehill beside the parish church of Glenbervie, for building a dwelling and a garden for the chaplain. At Dillavaird there was a chapel dedicated to St Mary the Virgin. There is said to have been a Chapel of St Conon at Drumlithie.—[*Transcripts from the Vatican,* 1421–59, 47, *MS., Reg. Ho.*; *Reg. Great Seal*, v, 876; *Sir John Cristison's Prot. Bk.*, 201; *Trans. Aberdeen Eccles. Society*, 1897, 241; Watson's *Celtic Place Names*, 278.]

JOHN CHRISTISON, min., described as parson and min. 1568.—[*Comps. Sub Coll. of Thirds, Forfar*, etc.]

1560

JOHN AUCHENLECK, reader 1563.—[*Comps. Sub Coll. of Thirds, Forfar*, etc.]

1563

JOHN IRVINE, probably natural son of Sir Robert I. of Monboddo.—[*G. R. Sas.*, 3 Ser., ii, 44.]

1636

ALEXANDER ROBERTSON, son of Alexander R., min. at Longside, conducted services in a meeting-house at Drumlithie, and there also William Seton, episcopal min., performed like functions for several years.—[*Justiciary Records.*]

1715

PATRICK LINDSAY GORDON, died 27th Aug. 1948.

1894

KINNEFF

The church was dedicated by Bishop de Bernham on 5th Aug. 1242. St Arnty's Well gives the name of the saint, Adamnan, in another form. Between the church and the castle there is the remnant of a building called St Arnty's Kell, or St Arnold's Cell, denoting a religious building. St John's Chapel was near the Temple-lands, and in the vicinity is St John's Hill with a farm at the foot called Chapel of Barras. The chapel may have been connected with the Knights Templar and Knights of St John. Of the Church of Kingorny there is now no trace; but at the end of the 18th century there were the remains of a small chapel said to occupy the spot where in 1342 David II with his queen landed from

France, and had High Mass performed for his safe return. Near the place is a spring called the Chapel Well.—[*Retours*, xi, 245; *Acts Scott. Parl.*, v, 625; *Mem. of Angus and Mearns*, 438, 442; Lockhart's *Ch. in Scot. in 13th Century*, 48-9.]

1561 SIR WILLIAM OWSTEAN (AUSTIN), vicar pensioner, 1561.—[*Comps. Sub Coll. of Thirds, Forfar*, etc.]

1563 ALEXANDER KEITH, min. in 1563. (See Garvock.)

1563 JOHN PATRICK, min. in 1563. (See Arbuthnott.)

1574 JAMES SIMSON, reader, designated exhorter 1575.—[*Edin. Test.*, iv, 10.]

1613 JAMES RAIT, called vicar 10th July 1602 and had Bervie also in charge. Marr. Margaret Douglas.—[*Kincardine Sas.*, i, 83.]

1640 JAMES GRANGER, had issue—Margaret, bapt. 19th July 1664.

1663 JAMES HONYMAN, had also issue, Margaret.

1701 ANDREW HONYMAN, his widow, Helen Rait, buried 12th March 1743.

1908 WILLIAM CRUICKSHANK, D.D. (Aberdeen, 1926), died 4th July 1932; his daugh., Mary Barbara (marr. 19th Aug. 1937 Donald Campbell, M.A., min. of Church of Scotland, Lausanne); died 29th March 1947.

CATERLINE

1563 ARCHIBALD WATSON, reader 1563. —[*Comps. Sub Coll. of Thirds, Forfar*, etc.]

1682 DUGALD JAMESON, marr. Elizabeth, daugh. of James Allan, bailie of Brechin, and had issue—James; Dougall; Janet; Helen, all under 18 in 1691.—[*Deeds Dal.*, 1706, No. 759.]

LAURENCEKIRK

The present church was built in 1804, superseding a building erected in 1626. At Chapelknap of Scotston there was a chapel dedicated to St Anthony; and Taunton Fair preserved the name of the saint in altered form.—[Fraser's *Hist. of Laurencekirk*, 212-13; *Trans. Aberdeen Eccl. Soc.*, 1897, 244.]

1563 PATRICK RAMSAY, min. in 1563.— [*Comps. Sub Coll. of Thirds, Forfar*, etc.] (See Arbuthnott.)

1563 ALEXANDER WYLIE, reader 1563.— [*Comps. Sub Coll. of Thirds, Forfar*, etc.]

1594 ROBERT MOIR, reader 1594.— [*Comps. Surplus of Thirds of Benefices.*]

1677 WILLIAM DUNBAR, min. at Montrose 1704, had a son, William.— [*Deeds, Durie*, 1705, No. 49.]

1872 CHARLES MORRISON, his widow, Margaret Dickson, died 30th Sept. 1924; his daugh., Anne Latto, died 21st May 1933.

1891 THOMAS SCOTT, dem. 1st June 1931; died at Brechin 4th June 1942; his daugh., Robina (marr. 15th Dec. 1930 Frank A. Brown, Ichang, China).

MARYKIRK

There was an altar dedicated to the Virgin Mary in the aisle of the Virgin built by John Strachan of Thornton and his son and heir, David, on the south side of the church. On 7th Oct. 1490 they granted 11 merks annual rent from the barony and mill of Thornton to Sir Thomas Smyth and his successors, chaplains at the altar. The church was dedicated by Bishop de Bernham on 9th Aug. 1242. The saint was the Virgin Mary. The church belonged to St Germain's hospital, Tranent, and, later, to King's College, Aberdeen University. There was a chapel at Inglismaldi. The name occurs in earlier form as Eglismaldi, Ecclismaldi, Church of Maillie, Maillidh— a saint not mentioned in the calendar.— [Watson's *Place Names*, 295; Lockhart's *Ch. in Scot. in 13th Century*, 50-1; *Reg. Mag. Sig.*, ii, 1987, 2777.]

1563	JOHN PATRICK, min. 1563; also at Kinneff.—[*Comps. Sub Coll. of Thirds, Forfar*, etc.]
1563	**THOMAS RAMSAY**, reader 1563.—[*Comps. Sub Coll. of Thirds, Forfar*, etc.]
1567	THOMAS LINDSAY, reader March 1574.—[*Edin. Tests.*, v, 161.]
1594	JOHN STEWART, reader 1594.—[*Comps. Surplus of Thirds of Benefices.*]
1617	JAMES RAIT, marr. pro. 14th July 1618 Isabella, daugh. of Peter Blackburn, Bishop of Aberdeen.—[*Aberdeen Reg., Kincardine Sas.*, ii, 252.]
1643	WILLIAM RAIT, adm. before 21st July 1642.
1666	ROBERT RAIT, his children—Katherine (marr. cont. 21st April 1688 David Rait of Bryanston); Robert; Margaret (marr. cont. 12th Oct. 1702 Patrick Cruickshank, merchant, Aberdeen); Jean, born 19th June 1666.—[*Forfar Sas.*, viii, 284, 15th May 1688.]
1857	JAMES CAMPBELL McCLURE, his son, George John, died at Edinburgh 26th Jan. 1925; his daughs.—Jane Thomson, died 16th Oct. 1939; Elizabeth Anne, died 10th Jan. 1939.
1908	WILLIAM ALEXANDER MACFARLANE FORBES, died 14th Feb. 1933.

(*United with Muirton* 21*st May* 1933.)

RICKARTON

1872	JOHN REITH, his widow, Isabella Carmichael Blackwood, died 1st May 1924.
1924	JOSEPH McKENZIE McPHERSON, trans. to Dunnichen 27th Feb. 1929.
1929	ALEXANDER CHRISTIAN WILLIAM SAUNDERS, trans. from Braemar (*q.v.*) 3rd Sept. 1929; dem. 28th Feb. 1933; died at Dumfries 8th Sept. 1933.

ST CYRUS

The church was dedicated by Bishop de Bernham on 7th Aug. 1242. To the Priory of St Andrews, 1178–81, it was granted by William the Lion, along with the Chapel of St Regulus and half a ploughgate of land situated at the chapel, and also the land of the Abbey of Ecclesgrig according to its right and ancient measurements. The earlier name appears in various forms, Ecclegrig, Ecclesgrig, Egglisgirg, Egglisgirgh. St Curig is Cyrie, Cyricus, martyr in Antioch, commemorated as Girie by Oengus at 16th July. Ciricius or Girg is mentioned in the Pictish Chronicle, A.D. 776–885. The early church stood in the old churchyard below the Heughs of St Cyrus on the shore not far from the mouth of the North Esk. In 1632 a new church was built on an eminence above the Haughs, about three-quarters of a mile north of the early church; and it in turn gave place to a building erected 1785–7, and repaired and enlarged in 1835. Near St Cyrus Well was a piece of land called St Cyrus Ward. In Dec. 1243 Bishop de Bernham granted licence to Alexander de Strivelyn to have a chantry chapel at Laurenciston on condition that all obventions and oblations of the chapel should belong to the mother church of Ecclesgreig, and that the said Alexander and his heirs should pay annually, in token of subjection, a pound of wax, the value of which was to be fixed with reference to the value at the markets of Montrose. The dedication of the chapel was St Laurence the Archbishop. The Chapel of St Regulus with its attached land, called Eglisreul, was situated at Morphie. Of the "Abbey of Ecclesgrig," already noted along with its land, nothing is known, except that it was "ancient" in 1178–81. Manifestly it was identical with "the Priory of Ecclesgrig," which is mentioned in a mutilated writ of 1135. St Siras Hope, later St Cyrus Bay, preserved the name of the patron saint in a different form, as do also white and salmon fishings "at the arena called Sanct Schirras, Sanct Siras, and Sanct-Seirece Sands," between the *Prestis-rod-fute* on the east, and the Machrie Burn on the west. Other fishings bore the name "Net of St Thomas" and also simply "St Thomas." The church with the lands of the abbey was granted to the Priory of St Andrews 1163-72 by Richard Bishop of St Andrews. Abbey indicates that here was a Celtic abbey or monastery.—[*Reg. Priory of St Andrews*, 27, 56-9, 85, 149-52, 166, 218, 229, 254, 256, 336, 337; *Reg. Great Seal*, ii, 1039, v, 1633; *Retours*, vii, 151, 166, xliv, 327, xlvi, 92; Macfarlane's *Geograph. Colls.*, iii, 236; Watson's *Celtic Place Names*, 324; Lockhart's *Ch. in Scot. in 13th Century*, 50, 51.]

1563 JAMES WILKIE, vicar.—[*Comps. Sub Coll. of Thirds, Forfar*, etc.]

1563 ROBERT NEILSON, reader.—[*Comps. Sub Coll. of Thirds, Forfar*, etc.]

1563 JOHN GOODFELLOW, min. in 1563.—[*Comps. Sub Coll. of Thirds, Forfar*, etc.]

1569 ROBERT BURNETT, reader 6th Sept. 1576.—[*Edin. Tests.*, iv, 370.]

1587 GEORGE GLEDSTANES, M.A., min. here, pres. to vicarage 23rd Sept. 1590 on death of Walter Wilkie.—[*Reg. Sec. Sig.*, lxi, 38.]

1592 JOHN ERSKINE, M.A., pres. 17th May 1592 on death of George Gledstanes.

1614 DAVID MELDRUM, line 7, for "John" read "Joshua," min. of Trinity, Edinburgh.

1848 THOMAS MACKINTOSH, his daugh., Jane Christina, died 20th June 1947.

1884 ROBERT DAVIDSON, died 3rd May 1936; his son, Frederick Churchill, Colonel R.A.M.C., died at Murrie, India, 13th July 1935.

(*Charges united April* 1933.)

SYNOD OF ABERDEEN

PRESBYTERY OF ABERDEEN

ABERDEEN EAST

WILLIAM (WALTER) LESLIE, M.A.,
1585 appears with Peter Blackburne as exhorter and min. 17th Oct. 1588 and as min. in succeeding years up to 19th Oct. 1589 and may have served in East Second Charge. Marr. pro. 8th Jan. 1586–7 Marion Lawson.

JAMES ROSE. Addl. issue—Katherine, bapt. 7th Feb. 1605; Elspeth, bapt.
1602 15th Aug. 1606; Marjorie, bapt. 3rd Aug. 1610; Isobel, bapt. 6th June 1616.

GEORGE GORDON, marr. Anna Crichton (buried in Bishop Scougal's
1683 aisle, Old Machar, 23rd Oct. 1695); had issue—Henry, bapt. 22nd Sept. 1679; Isabel, bapt. 11th Oct. 1680; Anna, bapt. 10th Jan. 1683; George, bapt. 15th Feb. 1684; James, bapt. 29th Sept. 1686.—[*Old Machar Reg.*]

THOMAS RAMSAY, his son, Matthew,
1693 bapt. 22nd Aug. 1697.

JOHN BISSET, had issue—Agnes, bapt. 6th April 1724, died young; Mar-
1728 garet, bapt. 27th Jan. 1726; John, bapt. 17th April 1727; George, bapt. 2nd Aug. 1728; Agnes, bapt. 25th Aug. 1729; Elizabeth, bapt. 18th Dec. 1730; James, bapt. 23rd March 1732.

ROBERT DOIG, born 3rd Sept. 1768, son of Robert D., manufacturer,
1812 Dundee, and Margaret Cook.

GEORGE WALKER, T.D. (1921), dem.
1899 16th May 1934, died 8th Oct. 1937; his sons—Charles William, M.C., M.A., M.D.; Ralph Spence, M.A. (Cantab.), Univ. Lecturer; Ronald Powlett, M.A., M.B., Ch.B. Publication—*The Idealism of Christian Ethics* (Baird Lecture, 1928).

FERRYHILL

CHARLES MONCREIFF ROBERTSON, trans. to St Oswalds, Edin-
1924 burgh, 19th April 1929.

JOHN HARRIS BURRY, trans. from Alves (*q.v.*) 19th Dec. 1929; has
1929 addl. issue—John Neilson, born 15th Dec. 1926; David Roddick, born 20th Jan. 1929; Mary Lorena, born 18th Aug. 1930; Muriel Sheffield, born 9th Feb. 1932; Sheila Isabel, born 31st Jan. 1934, died 31st July 1941; Alastair Thomas, born 10th July 1936.

GILCOLMSTON

JOHN MONTGOMERY McQUITTY,
1925 trans. to Monimail 29th Nov. 1928.

DAVID SIME STEVEN, born Dundee 16th Feb. 1896; son of David
1929 Russell S., consulting engineer, Dundee, and Jane Sime; educ. at Harris Academy, Dundee, Univ. of St Andrews, M.A. (1919), B.D. (1922); served in Egypt and France in Royal Scots in Great War, M.C.; licen. by Presb. of Dundee 4th May 1922; assistant St Cuthbert's; ord. 11th Jan. 1925; adm. to Teviothead 6th Feb. 1925; trans. and adm. 16th May 1929; trans. to Inveresk 18th March 1937. Marr. 18th Dec. 1923 Margaret Peddie, daugh. of James Cattanach McIntosh, fruit farmer, Blairgowrie, and has issue—Jean, born 1st Nov. 1924 (marr. 27th Sept. 1947 William Norman Roy Scotter, Stanwix, Carlisle); David Russell, born 10th Jan. 1926; James

GREYFRIARS

WILLIAM OLIVER, his widow, Anne
1881 Ross Duncan, died 13th May 1929.

GORDON JOHN MURRAY, dem.
1886 31st Dec. 1936; died 21st Dec. 1941.

HOLBURN

JAMES ALEXANDER McCLYMONT, died 19th Sept. 1927; his
1874 widow, Agnes Smith, died 4th Sept. 1939.

HENRY COULTER, trans. to Bella-
1919 houston 8th Feb. 1927.

JAMES THOMAS HALL, O.B.E., formerly of Tillicoultry (*q.v.*), trans.
1927 from West Linton 2nd Sept. 1927; trans. to Townend Street, Belfast, 29th Sept. 1932; trans. to Dalziel South 28th Nov. 1934; trans. to Newlands 22nd March 1945. Addl. issue—Lawrence Graham Murray, Sub-Lieutenant, born 10th Oct. 1922, killed in war Oct. 1944.

JOHN KNOX'S

HERBERT BELL, his daugh., Jane
1877 Harriet, died 10th Nov. 1943.

GEORGE DUNDAS NISBET, born
Dalbeattie 14th March 1887; LL.B.
1914 (Edinburgh, 1920); dem. status 24th Nov. 1920; barrister, Middle Temple (adm. 1927); readm. to status of min. 26th May 1934; *locum tenens* at Kirkmabreck.

DAVID FINDLAY CLARK, his father
1918 of Kerlaw, Girvan.

JOHN JAMES SCOTT THOMSON,
trans. to Larbert 7th Jan. 1932; died
1925 15th Dec. 1943.

MANNOFIELD

JOHN AULAY STEELE, trans. to St
1915 Vincent, Glasgow, 17th June 1926.

JAMES FOREST KELLAS, born 2nd
Aug. 1898, son of John K., min. of
1926 Rathen; educ. at Strichen Secondary School and Univ. of Aberdeen, M.A. (1920), B.D. (1923); Union Theological Seminary, New York, 1923; licen. by Presb. of Deer 1st May 1923; assistant, Rathen, and St Bernard's, Edinburgh, 1925; ord. to Forteviot 18th Sept. 1925; trans. and adm. 15th Dec. 1926. Marr. 27th June 1934 Mary Isabel, daugh. of Captain James Roger and Mary Grant, Aberdeen, and has issue—James Grant, born 16th May 1936.

NORTH

GEORGE CHALMERS, identical with
"Mr George Chalmers," described
1599 27th Oct. 1619 as "Minister at Dumbennan (Huntly), burgess of this burght (Aberdeen), and sumtyme one of the ministers thairof and regent in the said College" (Marischal); the date of his ministry here is uncertain.—[*Marischal College and Univ.*, 32, *New Spalding Club.*]

JOHN BLACKBURNE, adm. before
1st Sept. 1602, when he appears
1602 third in the list of three mins. of Aberdeen.—[*Aberdeen Reg.*]

ALEXANDER ROSS, his daughs.—
Bessie (marr. George Meldrum, min.
1636 of Fintray); Jean (marr. Capt. James Ogilvie); Isobel (marr. cont. 29th July 1665 Adam Innes of Towiebeg).—[*Banff Sas.*, i, 430.]

WILLIAM BLAIR, marr. 12th Nov.
1668 Marie Morrison (died before
1680 1696) and had issue—Agnes, bapt. 5th Sept. 1669; Margaret, bapt. 24th Jan. 1671; Alexander, bapt. 13th Feb. 1673; Elizabeth, bapt. 1st Feb. 1674; Robert, bapt. 15th April 1685.—[*Aberdeen and Forglen Regs.*]

WILLIAM MACKNIGHT WILSON,
dem. Campbeltown, Canada, 1863;
1879 adm. to Chatham 1868.

JAMES RAE, trans. to Midmar 27th
1904 March 1928.

1929 CHRISTIAN VICTOR AENEAS MacECHERN, M.A., formerly min. at Colombo, Ceylon (Vol. vii, 567); adm. 3rd June 1929; trans. to Kirkmabreck 11th March 1938.

(*Charge united with Trinity by General Assembly 21st Nov. 1928.*)

OLD MACHAR

The cathedral was dedicated to St Mary the Virgin and St Machar. The twofold designation was in use up to about the close of the 13th century, and thereafter the name of the Virgin was usually alone employed. In addition to the altars already noted there were the following: Altar of St Columba; Altar of St Anne; Altar of the Wounds of Christ and of St Devenic, founded in 1507 by Alexander Cabell, Prebendary of Banchory-Devenick; Altar of Our Lord; Altar of St Congan, the Abbot, and St Katharine, St Margaret (Antioch), St Martha, and St Barbara (Nicomedia), virgins, founded, apparently on 18th May 1491, by Alexander Vaux, Prebendary of Turriff; Altar of St Sebastian, St Stephen, and St Laurence, founded *cir.* 1500 by Andrew Liell, Treasurer of Aberdeen, as executor of the late Mr Alexander Lindsay, Rector of Belhelvie, son of Alexander L.; Altar of St Sebastian the Martyr, St Katharine of Egypt, and St Barbara, Virgin and Martyr, founded in the south aisle next the choir by Gavin Dunbar, Bishop of Aberdeen, who on 23rd Sept. 1531 granted an annual rent of £20 from certain lands for its endowment; Altar of St Ninian. On 20th July 1473 William de Camera of Balnacrag, as executor of late Mr Walter Ydyle, Canon of Aberdeen and Brechin and Prebendary of Deer, granted an annual rent of 20 sh. from lands at Kintore to the chaplains of the choir to celebrate a stated mass in the Chapel of St Ninian the Confessor; Altar of St Mauricius (Machar), evidently the altar already noted under the name Muireach, which, however, denotes not St Mauricius but St Muireadhach. Like St Machar, the Virgin Mary had also an altar, apart from the High Altar and situated in the choir. On 1st March 1501–2 Mr Duncan Scherar, Prebendary of Clat and Canon of Aberdeen, son of William S., burgess of Aberdeen, granted his newly built tenement lying in the university, to amplify, endow, and augment a chaplainry at the Altar of St Andrew, in honour of the Trinity, the Virgin Mary, St Andrew, St Moloc, and St Fotinus. Among the possessions confirmed to the bishopric by the Bull of Pope Adrian IV, 10th Aug. 1157, was the Church of St Machar, which became the seat of the bishopric. It may have been identical with the church which appears later as the Church of the Kirkton, a prebend of the cathedral and pertaining to the dean. When the new cathedral took the place of the church, the parochial work was carried on in the nave by a chaplain at an altar there. This work was divided when by the Statutes of 19th April 1256 it was decreed that the dean who was the rector of the church of the Kirkton have two parochial chaplains, one with a cleric in the Church of the Kirkton, performing parochial sacred ministrations outside or beyond the choir of the cathedral, and the other, also with a cleric, in the Chapel of Monycabok (St Columba's, New Machar), performing parochial sacred ministrations there. In 1182–99 a hospital dedicated to St Peter was founded by bishop; and on 23rd Feb. 1531–2 Bishop Gavin Dunbar founded a hospital for twelve poor men west of the cathedral outside the churchyard. In the Church of St Mary of the Nativity in King's College there were, besides the High Altar, the following: Altar of the Virgin Mary, situated in the nave; Altar of St Germanus; Altar of the Holy Cross in the rood loft; Altar of St Catherine the Virgin, built by the executors of Hector Boece, Principal of the University 1500–36; Altar of the Blessed Sacrament, founded by Alexander Galloway, Rector of Kinkell 1520–50, and several times Rector of the University. Saints in whose honour endowments were given for masses at altars in the church, by William Cumming of Inverallochy in 1506, and Mr Barnard Carngyll, Perpetual Vicar of Banff and Inverbryndie, in 1542, were the Virgin Mary, St John Baptist, St

ABERDEEN] OLD MACHAR 529

Andrew, St Ninian, St Ternan, St Ethernan, St Columba, St Mary Magdalene, St Brandon the confessor, St Anne, and St Thomas the Martyr. An inventory of the ornaments, vessels, furnishings, etc., of the church is given in *Fasti Aberdonenses*, 560ff. —[*Reg. Epis. of Aberdeen*, i, 5–7, 11, 39, 48, 199, 220, 304, 337, 347, 348, 352, 353, 387, ii, 39, 48, 147, 197–8, 198; *Reg. Great Seal*, ii, 2560, iii, 837, 1145, 2073, 3196; *Reg. Sec. Seal*, ii, 1017; *Fasti Aberdonenses*, 40, 64, 68, 115–16, 116–18, 121, 560, 561, 562, 564, 565, 566, 567, 570, 571.]

1567 JOHN ERSKINE, M.A., exhorter 1567. —[*Reg. of Min.*, 66.]

1621 ALEXANDER SCROGIE, M.A., marr. 17th Nov. 1607 Jean Ross.

1640 WILLIAM STRACHAN, had issue—Alexander, bapt. 7th Nov. 1641; William, bapt. 23rd Jan. 1643; Arthur, bapt. 3rd March 1644, buried 26th Feb. 1645.

1656 JOHN SEATON, marr. Jean Forbes, died after 25th Jan. 1672, had issue—John, died 27th Jan. 1672; William, buried 7th Feb. 1649; Rachel, bapt. 9th Dec. 1656; George, bapt. 10th Jan. 1669.

1659 ALEXANDER SCROGIE, buried in south aisle of cathedral 4th April 1661, had issue—Alexander, bapt. 26th Oct. 1659; George, bapt. 9th Aug. 1661.

1665 ROBERT REYNOLD, buried 20th Nov. 1670; his widow, Janet Douglas, marr. (2) 5th Aug. 1674; his daugh., Mary, bapt. 19th June 1667; his sons—Robert, buried 27th Sept. 1671; Patrick, born 26th Feb. 1670.

1672 GEORGE STRACHAN, buried in right aisle of cathedral 6th Nov. 1678.

1684 JOHN KEITH, buried in Scougal's aisle 12th March 1694; his son, James, graduate of Univ. of Aberdeen.—[*Mystics of the North East*, 25.]

1694 FRANCIS ROSS, min. at Renfrew, of which Charge he had been deprived in 1690; received a call to the Charge in 1694; appeared before the Commission of Assembly in Aberdeen in July of that year, and on being asked whether he was willing to apply to them and conform to the Church Government now established, he gave a negative answer, whereupon the Commission, finding that he was not qualified, declared the call null and void and ordered the church to be declared vacant.— [*Records of Old Aberdeen*, ii, 94, *Spalding Club*.]

1699 THOMAS THOMSON, buried in porch of church 28th Oct. 1704.

1705 DAVID CORSE, his sons, Alexander and David, bapt. 16th March 1706 and 29th March 1707. Addl. issue—John, bapt. 9th June 1708; George, bapt. 9th June 1709; Elizabeth, bapt. 26th June 1710; Margaret, 25th Sept. 1711; Katherine, bapt. 3rd Feb. 1713.—[*Old Machar Reg.*]

1714 ALEXANDER MITCHELL, M.A., was of Colpna; of issue, Thomas was bapt. 29th May 1700; Margaret, born 1701 and marr. John Osborne, Principal of Marischal College; John, bapt. 25th Oct. 1705, and apparently died young; Jean, bapt. 20th April 1708; John, bapt. 7th July 1712; Anna, bapt. 7th Nov. 1714, and was interred two days later. Addl. issue—Marjorie, bapt. 15th Oct. 1704.— [*Belhelvie Reg.*; *Old Machar Reg.*]

1714 JOHN SHARP, D.D., was illegally intruded on a Sunday in April 1714 "in a most tumultous manner," "the mobb having broken open the Church door on Saturday night in order to his entry"; he "set up an English service in the Church," but appears to have kept possession only for two Sundays; on his departure he took with him the "Church Bible, pulpit, and latron green cloathes with there silk fringes, bason and bason cloath, and sand-glass," which were returned in the following October by "William Baverly a soldier."—[*Records of Old Aberdeen*, ii, 125, 126, 127.]

1878 GEORGE JAMIESON, his daugh., Georgina Jane (Mrs Wallace) died 1st Jan. 1937; his son, William, died Feb. 1926.

1923 JOHN MacGILCHRIST, died 18th Aug. 1928; his wife, Hon. Agnes Caroline Burns, died 20th May 1928; his son, Ian Charles, killed in flying accident 1st Oct. 1933; his daugh., Beatrice Betty (marr. 2nd June 1932 Douglas Poole Henshaw, Colinton).

(*First and Second Charges united 21st Nov.* 1928.)

SECOND CHARGE

1704 DAVID HEDERWICK, M.A., unlawfully intruded into the church, apparently on the First Sunday of April 1704; a request for the use of the Communion vessels for a Communion celebration by him was refused by the Kirk Session; is said to have been summoned by the Privy Council to answer for the intrusion, but there is no further record.—[*Records of Old Aberdeen*, ii, 115.]

1715 ALEXANDER BARCLAY, M.A., "sometyme incumbent at Peterhead"; intruded and took possession of the church on 30th Oct. 1715, by order of Patrick Sandilands, Sheriff-Depute of Aberdeen, who refused access to the min., Alexander Mitchell, "unless he would go in on such terms as he proposed"; the min. refused and protested, and adjourned to the manse with the congregation, and there conducted the service.—[*Records of Old Aberdeen*, ii, 127.]

1717 WILLIAM SMITH, M.A., was a probationer in parish of Strichen 4th Feb. 1715; died 29th March 1731. Issue—Alexander, bapt. 30th Oct. 1717; William, bapt. 19th March 1719, and died same year (bur. 23rd Sept.); Margaret, bapt. 22nd Feb. 1721, and died same year (bur. 29th Oct.); Jean, bur. 25th Jan. 1726.—[*Old Machar Reg.*; *Strichen Reg.*]

1925 MELVILLE DINWIDDIE, C.B.E. (1943); dem. 31st Aug. 1933 on appointment as Scottish Regional Director of British Broadcasting Company; has addl. issue—Arna Mary, born 13th Jan. 1927; James Melville, born 10th Nov. 1929.

(*Second Charge abolished by General Assembly 21st Nov.* 1928.)

OUR LADY OF THE SNOW

The church was founded in virtue of a Bull of Pope Alexander VI to Bishop Elphingstone, 1st March 1497, and appears to have been completed in 1499, when the bishop united the church and university to the new university; the vicars of the church to be graduates, or at least, Bachelors of Law. The purpose of the foundation was that the church was to be the parish church of Old Aberdeen, so that the cathedral might be free for its own proper functions. It was dedicated to St Mary of the Snows, suggested, it is thought, by the dedication of the Church of Santa Maria Maggiore in Rome, alternatively known in Latin as Santa Maria ad Nives. Not long after the Reformation the cathedral became the parish church; and on 15th May 1583 King James VI united and annexed to the parish and parish kirk of St Machar, the "kirks of Snaw and Spittal (the latter attached to the Hospital of St Peter founded by Bishop Matthew Kinninmond, 1172–99), parsonage and vicarage of the same." The reasons for the union were that the Snow and Spittal churches "are situat within the midder of the parochin of St Machar, and all three are unit and annexit to the College and University, and the fruits of the said kirks of Snaw and Spittal are not able to sustaine ane minister, nether zit ar yair congregations of great boundis or oyrwyse populous but maist convenuallie may resort to ye ad Cathedral, the parochin kirk of Old Aberdeen." Orme states that one of the first acts of Dr Guild after he became Principal of the University in 1640 was to decree the destruction of the Snow Church, masons to "cast down the walls thereof, and to transport the stones to build the College Yard dykes and to employ the hewn work to the decayed chamber windows within the College." In 1661, however, the roofless walls continued intact, and ten years later portions of them still survived. All traces are now gone; and the site alone remains as a much-reduced burial ground behind the tenements of the main street of Old Aberdeen, and near the Powis Burn.—[Fraser's *Hist. of Aberdeen*, 80–100; *Reg. Sec. Seal*, xlix, 117; Orme's *Description of the Chanonry*, etc., 176.]

1561 JOHN LESLIE, M.A., prebendary and parson 1561; reader 1563; was in office 15th July 1557.—[*Comps. Gen. Coll. of Thirds*; *Reg. Great Seal*, iv, 18th Dec. 1557.] (See Oyne.)

1580 ALEXANDER CHEYNE, M.A., son of Laurence C., commissary of Aberdeen, and Margaret, daugh. of William Troup of that ilk, was prebendary and parson 15th March 1580–1. On 13th Oct. 1581 he conveyed to Mr George Barclay, burgess of Aberdeen, and Marjory Cheyne his wife, the "tenement, place and lugeing of the Snaw now ruinous"; Canon of King's College and Commissary of Aberdeen; died 1587. He marr. Katherine, daugh. of Patrick Bruce of Pitcullo, and had issue—John.—[*Coll. Shires of Aberdeen and Banff*, 304; *Aberdeen Sas.*, ii, 206, 21st May 1620; *Reg. Mag. Sig.*, v, 19th Aug. 1585; *Cal. of Charters*, xi, 2585; *Reg. Abbrev. Feu Charters of Church Lands*, ii, 319; *Officers and Graduates, King's College*, 30.]

POWIS

1924 ALEXANDER MOIR, died 27th March 1940; his wife, Mary Strachan, died 24th Dec. 1938; his son, Robert Scott, died 6th June 1923.

ROSEMOUNT

1914 JAMES KISSOCK WILKEN, dem. 18th Feb. 1938; died 18th Feb. 1946; his wife, Ann, daugh. of John Bremar, builder, Macduff, died 10th Oct. 1934.

RUBISLAW

1883 ROBERT THOMSON, died Father of the Church 31st Jan. 1935; his daugh., Violet (marr. Charles E. Ritchie, St Helier, Jersey), died 27th July 1933.

1923 VINCENT CASSELS ALEXANDER, trans. to St Mark's, Dundee, 30th Jan. 1930; trans. to Kilbarchan West 5th Oct. 1940.

RUTHRIESTON

1920 McINTOSH MOWAT, trans. to St John's, Dundee, 11th July 1928.

1928 ROWELLYAN RAMSAY, born New Elgin 2nd April 1898, son of William R., insurance superintendent, and Agnes Veronica Campbell Inglis; educ. at Robert Gordon's College and Univ. of Aberdeen, B.Comm. (1923); served in 6/8 Batt. Gordon Highlanders 1916–19, in France April 1917 to April 1918; prisoner of war 11th April to 11th Nov. 1918, Rhine Army Sept., 1919; licen. by Presb. of Aberdeen 5th May 1926; assistant John Knox's, Aberdeen, and West Church, Aberdeen; ord. to Wanlockhead 21st Oct. 1926; trans. and adm. 8th Nov. 1928; dem. 30th Sept. 1933 and went to Brisbane, adm. to Ithaca, Queensland, 31st Jan. 1934. Marr. 7th Sept. 1926 Johan Alexandra, daugh. of Archibald Ross, insurance agent, and Helen Duguid, and has issue—Rowena Olivia, born 16th July 1927; Stanley John Archibald, born 29th June 1929; Mervyn Ross, born 22nd Nov. 1934; Rowellyan Ross, born 8th Dec. 1937.

ST CLEMENT'S

1652 ROBERT DOWNIE, his mother was Isabel, eldest daugh. of James Reid, min. of Banchory-Ternan; on 3rd Aug. 1652 he was nominated by the Town Council to the office of Catechist of Fettie, the salary for that duty as well as for the duty of Librarian being 700 merks Scots per annum.—[*Recs. of Marischal Coll. and Univ.*, i, 202*n*, 235*n*; ii, 207*n*.]

1683 ALEXANDER GRAY, marr. Margaret Peacock and had issue—Thomas, bapt. 1st May 1687; Alexander, bapt. 21st Feb. 1690; George, bapt. 8th May 1692; John, bapt. 29th Oct, 1693; Robert, bapt. 18th Nov. 1694; William, bapt. 28th May 1696; Margaret, bapt. 2nd Aug. 1702.—[*Aberdeen Poll Tax Roll*, ii, 624.]

ALEXANDER SPENCE, his daugh., Catherine Easton, marr. James McKissock Shiach, at Castlehill, Aberdeen, 6th July 1871, and died at F.C. Manse, Dunfermline, 19th Aug. 1885; and his daugh., Mary Jane (Mrs Urquhart), died at the English Presbyterian Manse, Walkton, 9th Oct. 1877; by his second wife, Janet Auchie, whom he marr. at Edinburgh 19th Oct. 1852, he had issue—a boy stillborn 15th Sept. 1853; Margaret Lucy, born 7th April 1855 and died at Ardgilzean, Elgin, 14th Dec. 1939; Janet, born 30th Dec. 1856, and died at Ardgilzean, Elgin, 27th April 1942; William Alexander, born 30th Oct. 1858, and died at Aberdeen 7th Dec. 1887; Alexander Easton, born 1st Aug. 1860, min. at the West Church, Dollar, marr. 21st May 1890 Barbara Mill, younger daugh. of Robert Cowan, min. of the Free High Church, Elgin, and died 8th April 1919 on service with the Scottish Church's Hut at Cologne, interred there; James Auchie, born 8th April 1862, and died at Liverpool, New South Wales, 18th Aug. 1929; Robert Stuart, born 6th Aug. 1864, Caroline Anne, born 10th Dec. 1865 (marr. 15th Aug. 1891 Gordon Reid Shiach (L.D.S., Edinburgh), Elgin) and is now of Ardgilzean, Elgin; George Henry, born 9th Dec. 1867, C.A., died at Sydney, Australia, 9th Sept. 1923, and interred in Gorehill cemetery there; his second wife, Janet Auchie, was aged 74 at her death 24th Dec. 1899.—[*Family Bible penes* Mrs Shiach, Ardgilzean, Elgin.]
1837

CHARLES CADELL MACDONALD, his son, Ronald William Cadell, died at Inverness 26th Jan. 1942; his daughs.—Ethel Olivia Maga (Mrs Straith) died 15th Dec. 1926; Minnie Elizabeth Mary, died 4th Dec. 1943.
1879

JOHN STUART CAMERON, trans. to Springburn 17th May 1926.
1920

GERALD KERR JENKINS, born 25th, Nov. 1893, son of William J., M.A., headmaster, James Gillespie's School, Edinburgh, and Margaret Bell Kerr; educ. at Daniel Stewart's College and Univ. of Edinburgh, M.A. (1921); served in France Belgium and Italy, Major R.F.A. 1914–19, M.C.; licen. by Presb. of Edinburgh 29th June 1923; assistant North Leith 1923–6; ord. 16th Sept. 1926; trans. to Shettleston, Glasgow, 13th May 1932; trans. to Cromarty 22nd Dec. 1948. Marr. 29th July 1931 Margaret Winifred, daugh. of Alexander Maitland Ross, Aberdeen, and Margaret Falconer Eddie, and has issue—Margaret Wilson, born 18th Nov. 1933.
1926

ST FITTICK'S

JOHN GORDON, dem. 4th June 1928; died at Edinburgh 14th April 1930.
1911

CHARLES MACARTHUR, formerly of Gardenstown (*q.v.*); became Naval Chaplain; adm. 28th Sept. 1928; trans. to St Leonard's, Kinghorn, 12th July 1934. Marr. 6th Aug. 1925 Kathleen Lovelace, daugh. of Thomas Holman and Elizabeth Lovelace.
1928

ST GEORGE'S IN THE WEST

NEIL MELDRUM, dem. 14th Sept. 1943. Addl. issue—Mary Elizabeth Helen, born 28th Nov. 1927. Publication—*Forteviot—The History of a Strathearn Parish* (1926).
1925

ST NINIAN'S

MAXWELL JAMES WRIGHT, died 1st Nov. 1927; his widow, Edith Graham Campbell, died 5th Dec. 1947. His sons—James Campbell Graham, M.B., Ch.B.; Ninian Blundell, B.D., min. of Dalmellington; Maxwell Campbell, M.C., M.B., Ch.B., died 29th April 1937; his daugh., Effie, M.A., Aberdeen (for Conway read Cowan).
1901

LEWIS LEGERTWOOD LAGG CAMERON, trans. to Mortlach 26th Sept. 1928.
1925

JOHN McILWRAITH, B.A., trans. from Maryfield, Dundee, 20th Feb. 1929; had addl. issue—Margaret Graham, born 18th Sept. 1925; Joyce, born 28th March 1928.
1929

SOUTH

1878 WILLIAM DAVID SCOTT, line 10, delete "*s.p.*" and add: "had issue— David Barclay Houston, C.A., born 5th May 1905; Thomas Wharrie Falconer, merchant, born 1st Jan. 1908; Margaret Stuart, born 5th Nov. 1906 (marr. 3rd Dec. 1933 Rupert Saumarez Carey, merchant younger son of Sir Bertram Carey, K.C.I.E., C.S.I.)."

1912 WILLIAM LINDSAY GORDON, died 29th Feb. 1940.

ST NICHOLAS or WEST

In addition to altars in the church already noted, there were: Altar of St Stephen, founded by Stephen Balrone, burgess, 10th March 1444-5; Altar of St Lawrence and St Ninian, founded in the choir in 1356 by William Leith of Bernys, who to provide the necessary space "augmented" the choir 16 feet to the south; Altar of St Mary the Virgin and St Joseph, founded before 1444; Altar of St Barbara; Altar of the Name of Jesus, described on 14th Aug. 1525 as "newly founded by John Artour, burgess"; Altar of Our Lady of Pity, in the crypt; Altar of St Mary the Virgin, St Barbara, and All Saints, founded by Alexander Gray, burgess, 2nd May 1509; Altar of St Mungo and St Tovine (? The new, mother of St Mungo, or Teunon, St Adamnan), permission for the foundation of which "in the triangle of thar east end of their Choir" was granted by the Town Council to William Leslie, Parson of Menmuir, on 9th Sept. 1502; erection may not actually have taken place. On 31st July 1464 William Scherar, burgess, and his wife, Isabella (Rutherford), in honour of the Trinity, the Virgin Mary, St Duthac, and St Bridget the Virgin, granted various lands and annual rents to amplify, endow, and augment a chaplainry at the Altar of St Duthac, "anciently founded in part by the Alderman, Bailies, and Community of Aberdeen." At the Altar of St Laurence there was a chaplainry of St Fergus. In 1425-38 Lady Elizabeth Gordon granted half of the lands of Cocklarachy in Drumblade for the endowment of the Chaplainry of St Mary of Cocklarachy in the "Yle of Cocklarachie" which she built in the church, and where she and her husband, Sir Alexander Seton, were buried. Altars with dual dedications were: St Helen and St Margaret, St Thomas the Apostle and St George the Martyr, St Crispin and St Crispianus, St Duthac and St Bridget. The Altar of St Mary Magdalene was a prebend of the University Chapel. On 23rd June 1499 the vicarage of St Nicholas was united to the university by Bishop Elphinstone, and on 28th March it was granted by Bishop William Gordon for the provostry of St Nicholas.

On 2nd May 1504 Robert Blinseik, burgess of Aberdeen, endowed with part of his property on the west side of the Shiprow, the Chapel of St Ninian, then newly built on the Castle Hill, for the souls of James III and Margaret his queen and of James IV and Margaret his queen, for his own soul and the souls of Robert B. his father, Elizabeth Rutherford his mother, and Isabella Wood his wife. Mr Thomas Chamer was then master and chaplain of the chapel. But there was a chapel on the Castle Hill in 1264.—[*Chart of St Nicholas*, i, xxxiii, liv-lv, 17-21, 33, 106, 108, 115, 128, 131, 144, 241, ii, 19, 267, 341, 381; *Reg. Great Seal*, iii, 419, iv, 548; *Fasti Aberdonenses*, 29; *Cal. Papal Regs., Letters*, vii, 235; Macdonald's *Place Names West Aberdeenshire*, 13; *Scots Peerage*, iv, 519, 521; *Book of Assumptions*, i, 390; *Trans. Aberdeen Eccles. Soc.*, 1888, 26; *Excheq. Rolls*, i, 12.]

1560 ANDREW CULLEN, vicar, son of Andrew C., Provost of Aberdeen; died 7th July 1560; was also parson of Fetterneir.—[*The Chronicle of Aberdeen*, 34, *Mis.* ii, *Old Spalding Club.*]

1560 SIR JOHN COLLISON, chaplain of the Altar of the Virgin Mary in the church in 1559, and was also subchanter of Aberdeen; he became vicar of the church, probably in succession to Andrew Cullen, in 1560; on 26th June 1577 "be ane ryng" he dem. the vicarage, subject to his life-interest, in the hands of

William Gordon, Roman Catholic Bishop of Aberdeen, who up to his death discharged the temporal and in some cases the spiritual duties of his office; died 25th July 1584.—[*The Chronicle of Aberdeen*, 45, 56, *Mis.*, ii, *Old Spalding Club*; *Extracts from the Council Reg. of Aberdeen*, 1398–1570, 321.]

1567 JOHN LESLIE, reader here and at Nigg in 1567.—[*Reg. of Ministers*, 66, *Maitland Club*.]

1570 WALTER CULLEN, born 2nd Nov. 1526, son of Walter Cullen, bailie of Aberdeen, and his wife, Bessie Pratt, daugh. of Thomas Pratt, bailie, and grandson of Andrew Cullen, Provost of Aberdeen; was burgess of the burgh; was reader in Nov. 1570, and probably was app. in that year; on 26th June 1577, on the demission of his uncle, Sir John Colliston, in his favour, he was coll. to the vicarage by the placing of "ane ryng on his finger" by William Gordon, Roman Catholic Bishop of Aberdeen, and on 3rd March 1577-8 he received royal presentation to the office. On 19th Jan. 1578-9 the Council ord. him as reader and vicar "to be answered and obeyed of the haill teyndis of the vicarage sic as lamb, geyss, lynte, eggs, woll, hempt and other dewties of the vicarage, and for every mylk cow to haff twelft penneis"; as reader he received £20 of stipend with an addition of £10 granted by the Council on 8th Oct. 1574 "for reading the prayers efter nune"; he is on record on 25th Oct. 1576 as performing the sacrament of baptism, and on 5th June 1578 the Kirk Session ord. part of his duties to be "to read ane portioun of the Catechisme and the bairnes answer him." He died after 23rd March 1595-6, and apparently before 13th Oct. 1605, when two readers were in office, as below. On 4th Feb. 1610 the Kirk Session awarded to his daugh., Margaret, £10 for his "Bookes of Baptisme, Mariage, and Buriall," delivered by her to the Bishop for the use of the town. He marr. (1) Janet Tulidefe (died 23rd April 1561), with issue—Duncan, who on 15th Aug. 1574 "departed out of Aberdeen to Dayneskin (Danzig) in ane ship of Monross" (Montrose); (2) Elspet Tulidefe, with issue—John, bapt. 7th July 1571; Margaret, bapt. 20th Oct. 1572; Janet, bapt. 28th March 1577. Author of *The Chronicle of Aberdeen*, printed in Miscellany ii, Old Spalding Club.—[*The Chronicle of Aberdeen*, xxiii–xxvi, 32, 34–5, 37, 39–41, 45, 51, 52, 55–7, 64, 66–7; *Extracts from Council Records of Aberdeen*, 1570–1625, 20, 31, 45; *Genealogy of an Aberdeen Family*, 3; *Reg. Pres. Bene.*, i, 151.]

1573 JOHN CRAIG, min.; on 14th Sept. 1579 "Mr John Craig, sometime minister Aberdeen, departhit with his wife and barnis and haill hoissell owit of the said burght, and left his flock onprowyditt of ane minister to be preschour to the kingis grace as he allegit." "Master John Craig, Minister, coyme to Abden, who was apoynttit be the Gennaral Kyrk (the united Kirk Sessions of the burgh) minister of the said burgth," 6th Aug. 1573; died Father of the Church; his son, William, was bapt. 9th Oct. 1575.—[*Aberdeen Reg.*; the *Chronicle of Aberdeen*, 51, *Mis.* ii, *Old Spalding Club*.]

1585 WILLIAM LESK, M.A., exhorter, 17th Oct. 1585.—[*The Chronicle of Aberdeen*, 57, *Mis.* ii, *Old Spalding Club*.]

1601 ARCHIBALD BLACKBURNE, if he was a son of the Bishop of Aberdeen, he was the child of an earlier marriage; he marr. proc. 30th Sept. 1617 Anne Blak, with issue—Issobell, bapt. 19th Sept. 1618; Archibald, bapt. 30th Nov. 1620.—[*Aberdeen Reg.*]

1605 WALTER ANDERSON, M.A., reader 13th Oct. 1605; afterwards min. of Kinellar (*q.v.*).—[*Extracts from Council Recs. of Aberdeen*, 1570–1625, 48.]

1605 GILBERT LESLY, reader 13th Oct. 1650.—[*Extracts from Council Recs. of Aberdeen*, 1570–1625, 48.]

1623 RICHARD ROSS, M.A., reader, died 9th June 1623.—[*Extracts from Council Recs. of Aberdeen*, 1570–1625, 386.]

ST NICHOLAS or WEST—BANCHORY DEVENICK

1623 ALEXANDER GRAY, son of –. Gray, burgess of Aberdeen; app. reader by the Council 25th July 1623; had issue—William, buried 25th Dec. 1616.—[*Extracts from Council Recs. of Aberdeen, 1570–1625*, 386.]

1625 JAMES SIBBALD of Kair; his wife, Elizabeth Nicolson, died in (buried 12th Nov.) 1671; issue—Thomas (1), bapt. 1st Dec. 1628, and died young; James, bapt. 29th Dec. 1630; Marjorie, bapt. 31st Dec. 1631 (marr. Robert Forbes, M.A., Regent of Marischal College, and Regent and Canonist of King's College); Thomas (2), bapt. 27th May 1635.—[*Aberdeen Reg.; Marischal Coll. and Univ.*, 35–6; *King's Coll. and Univ.*, 30, 57.]

1684 ANDREW BURNETT. Addl. issue—Thomas, bapt. Oct. 1693; William, bapt. 9th Oct. 1694; Andrew, bapt. 15 Sept. 1703.—[*Aberdeen Reg.*]

1688 JOHN FORBES, reader 11th May 1688, his son has an illuminated title page in Baptismal Register on that date; was in office till 12th Dec. 1704.

1702 COLIN CAMPBELL, M.A., marr. proc. cont. 16th Aug. 1703, marr. 17th June 1704 Margaret Walker, daugh. of Alexander W., late Provost of Aberdeen; his sons—Colin, bapt. 28th Jan. 1711; George, 27th Sept. 1719. Addl. issue—Ann, bapt. 5th Oct. 1704; Jean, bapt. 20th Jan. 1706; Marjorie, bapt. 11th March 1707; John, bapt. 22nd June 1708; Alexander, bapt. 10th Oct. 1709; Helen, bapt. 24th April 1712; Anna, bapt. 19th Jan. 1718.—[*Aberdeen Reg.*]

1729 JAMES OGILVIE, marr. Elizabeth, daugh. of Thomas Strachan, bailie, Aberdeen, and had issue—Helen, bapt. 20th Nov. 1729; Isobel, bapt. 15th July 1731.

1919 AUGUSTINE WENTWORTH SCUDAMORE FORBES, D.D. (Glasgow, 18th June 1930); trans. to Park, Glasgow, 7th Oct. 1932, died 6th Feb. 1945; his widow, Mary Elizabeth Burns, died at Bearsden 14th Aug. 1948.

TRINITY

1880 ROBERT SLESSOR, his son, Dr Francis Stewart, died 30th July 1940.

1907 WILLIAM BRUCE MUIR, died at Charlottetown, Prince Edward Island, Sept. 1930.

1923 ROBERT LOGAN, dem. 4th June 1928, died 3rd Oct. 1930. His son, John Black, B.D., min. of St Stephen's, Edinburgh; his daugh., Anne, M.A., lecturer in English, on staff of Scottish Churches College, Calcutta (marr. 30th Sept. 1937 Rev. Martin Andrew Simpson, Professor of History, Calcutta); his son, James Cameron Purse, medical student; his son, Robert Frederick Russell, M.A., min. of Ferguslie.

WOODSIDE

1836 ROBERT FORBES. Addl. issue—James, Mount Grace, Potters Bar, Middlesex, whose son, Admiral Sir Charles Moston Forbes, Commander-in-Chief of Home Fleet.

1924 ROBERT LAIRD SNEDDON, trans. to St James, Portobello, 4th April 1930; died 7th May 1947. Addl. issue—Daphne Vyvian, born 28th Feb. 1932.

BANCHORY DEVENICK

There was a chapel of St Ternan with a churchyard on a rock at Findon, now in the parish of Portlethen. Near it was St Ternan's Well, to which medicinal qualities were ascribed.—[*Coll. of Shires of Aberdeen and Banff*, 264–6.]

1563 THOMAS BELTY, reader 1563.—[*Comps. Sub Coll. of Thirds, Forfar*, etc.]

1567 ROBERT MERCER, M.A., was in office in 1566.—[*Comps. Sub Coll. of Thirds, Forfar*, etc.]

1578 ROBERT MERCER, M.A., Canon of Aberdeen, on 14th June 1580 he conveyed to Henry Mercer, son of Laurence Mercer of Meikleour, "the manse

Place and Bigging of Banchory Devenick in the Aldtoun of Aberdeen."—[*Reg. of Abbrev. of Feu Charters of Church Lands*, ii, 103.]

ANDREW MELVILL, delete from line 7 "and" to line 10 "1644."
1622

WILLIAM ROBERTSON, had issue—Katherine, bapt. 4th Dec. 1638; Isabel, bapt. 20th June 1640; William, bapt. 23rd Dec. 1642; Margaret, bapt. 27th Jan. 1648; his wife, Isabell Gordon, buried 6th March 1673.
1652

JAMES GORDON, his sons—James, rector of Hawnby, Yorks; Peter, episcopal min., London and New York, died 1703; John.
1673

WILLIAM PAUL, his daugh., Catherine, Lloyd, died at Newark, New Jersey, 18th Dec. 1928 (marr. Fitz Hagemann, who died before Great War, when his widow assumed her mother's maiden name of Stewart); his son, Sir George Morrison, died 4th May 1926.
1834

WILLIAM FYFE LAWRENCE, his widow, Elizabeth Milne Duncan, died 29th Dec. 1939.
1882

ALEXANDER MACKENZIE, died 14th July 1931.
1919

BELHELVIE

In 1304–5 the Bishop of Aberdeen showed that one of his prebend churches, Belhelvie, possessed in King Alexander's time a piece of land called "St Ternan's Land," between St Ternan's Chapel and the sea on the north, which was leased to the Thane of Belhelvie by the parson of Lony, and after his death wrongfully attached to the thanage by the King's servants, and taken by force from the church in time of war. The Lieutenant and Chamberlain of Exchequer were ordered to make enquiries and certify the King by next Parliament.—[*Cal. of Docs. Rel. to Scotland*, ii, 1727, 468.]

GILBERT KELLO, reader in 1563.—[*Comps. Sub Coll. of Thirds, Aberdeen*, etc.]
1563

JAMES STRACHAN, M.A., parson 1567, died before 29th May 1576, and had issue—William, evidently of Chapel of Garioch (Logie Durno) (*q.v.*).—[*Reg. Pres. Bene.*, i, (4), 43; *Reg. Epis. Mora*, 405, 407.]
1567

JAMES LINDSAY, M.A., pres. to parsonage and vicarage 5th June 1576 on death of James Strachan.—[*Reg. Pres. Bene.*, i, 28; i, (4), 43.]
1574

GEORGE INNES, marr. 30th May 1661 Elizabeth, daugh. of Thomas Gordon in Keithoksmiln.
1668

WILLIAM DYCE, marr. 13th Feb. 1719 Katherine Anderson.
1716

ALEXANDER JOHN FORSYTH, certain relics of his inventive industry are now in the Tower of London, to which they were pres. by Emeritus Professor Reid of Aberdeen; a grand-nephew of Forsyth was the late Major-General Sir Alexander John Forsyth Reid, K.C.B., M.A., LL.D., Colonel of the 29th Punjabees, who wrote the brochure on his grand-uncle as stated. At Cromwell Tower, King's College, Aberdeen, a memorial was placed about ten years ago, a replica of that at the Tower of London to his memory.
1791

MALCOLM TOWER SORLEY, died 3rd May 1933.
1888

CRAIGIEBUCKLER

JAMES NIMMO CUTHBERT, retired 8th June 1938; his wife, Maud Mary Couper, died 28th Oct. 1931.
1893

CULTS

CHARLES SINCLAIR CHRISTIE, dem. 10th Dec. 1928, died 5th May 1936. Line 9, delete "2" and read "27."
1888

LOUIS HERBERT WATSON, born Portobello 28th Aug. 1899, son of John W. of Church of Scotland Social Scheme, and Margaret Robertson; educ. at George Heriot's School and Univ.
1929

of Edinburgh, M.A. (1923); served as 2nd Lieut. in Tank Corps in Great War 1918; licen. by Presb. of Edinburgh 26th Dec. 1924; assistant St Michael's, Edinburgh; ord. to Kirkcowan 1st June 1927; trans. and adm. 11th April 1929; trans. to Dalserf 27th Oct. 1937; trans. to St Luke's, Edinburgh, 19th April 1945. Marr. 1st June 1927 Elizabeth Mitchell, younger daugh. of Robert Stewart, min. of Crosshill, and has issue—Jean Stewart, born 23rd July 1928; Linda Margaret, born 17th Oct. 1936.

DRUMOAK

Mayota or Mazota is said to have been the chief of the nine maidens who came to Scotland with St Brigit and who was the daugh. of a St Dovenald who lived in the Den of Ogilvie in Angus. The saint, however, seems to be M'Aedoc or M'Aodhog, probably identical with M'Aedoc of Lismore. The present church was opened for worship 13th Nov. 1806.—[Watson's *Celtic Place Names*, 328.]

1566 CUTHBERT REID, pres. to parsonage and vicarage 25th May 1566 in place of Andrew Leslie and Alexander Wright.—[*Reg. Sec. Sig.*, xxxiv, 84.]

1621 JOHN GREGORIE, his son, James, "invented an engine of destruction so terrible that Sir Isaac Newton implored him to destroy the plans of it"; John, bapt. 7th March 1656.—[*Aberdeen Weekly Journal*, 24th Dec. 1942.]

1883 CHARLES MACKIE, died 12th Aug. 1926; his son, William Soutar, M.A. (Hons.) (Aberdeen, 1906), B.A. (Oxon) 1st Cl. Hons. Eng. Lang. and Lit., 2nd Class Hons. Mod. Hist., 1909; Lecturer in English Languages and Literature, Univ. College, Southampton, before going to Cape Town; his daugh., Helen, M.A. (Aberdeen, 1913); his daugh., Elsie (marr. (1) 15th Nov. 1923 Harry Vincent Sherlock Horne, Army Pensioner, and (2) 1941, John West, Fishcurer, Lossiemouth).

1922 JOHN LESLIE ROBERTSON, trans. to Charlotte Street, Aberdeen, 3rd Sept. 1930; trans. to Kinellar and Blackburn 26th Nov. 1936; died 17th Dec. 1946. Addl. issue—Margaret Leslie, born 30th March 1924; Isabel, M.A. (marr. 3rd Feb. 1944 Captain John Gray, R.A.M.C.).

(*Congregations united 16th Sept.* 1934.)

DURRIS

1563 ALEXANDER GERRIT, reader in 1563.—[*Comps. Sub Coll. of Thirds, Aberdeen.*]

1595 ALEXANDER YOUNGSON, M.A., pres. to parsonage and vicarage 1st Dec. 1595 on death of Archibald Hogg.—[*Reg. Sec. Sig.*, lxviii, 21.]

1717 ROBERT MELVILLE, marr. 23rd July 1717 Isabella Fordyce, who died 5th Sept. 1719.

1883 ROBERT REITH SPARK, dem. 6th Dec. 1932; died at Aberdeen 30th June 1947; his daugh., Gladys, M.B., Ch.B. (marr. 19th Sept. 1929 Gordon Lang Collie, Banrawela, Ceylon), died at Durban, South Africa, 13th Dec. 1942.

(*Congregations united 12th March* 1933.)

DYCE

The church pertained to the parsonage of Kinkell.

1563 THOMAS MILL, reader in 1563.— [*Comps. Sub Coll. of Thirds, Aberdeen, etc.*]

1594 ARTHUR FORBES, was in office in 1594.—[*Comps. Surplus of Thirds.*]

1717 JOHN REID, his daugh., Isobel, bapt. 8th March 1719.

1888 JAMES TAYLOR COX, dem. Charge 12th Jan. 1936; app. Depute Clerk of General Assembly 24th May 1927; D.D. (Aberdeen) 28th March 1928; app. Principal Clerk of General Assembly 22nd May 1928; app. Joint Senior Clerk of General Assembly of the reunited Church of Scotland 2nd Oct. 1929; nominated unanimously, 16th Sept. 1936, for the office of Moderator of the General Assembly of 1937, but declined; app. sole Principal

Clerk of General Assembly 25th May 1939, and dem. 23rd May 1946 (on dem. was pres. with portrait in oils, now in Gallery of Assembly Hall). Clerk of Presb. of Aberdeen 1903–47; Synod Clerk 1913–48, thus holding office, it is believed, for a longer period than any clerk, since the Reformation, of any of the five largest Presbs. in the Church of Scotland; died at Aberdeen 5th Nov. 1948. Publication—Editor of *Practice and Procedure in the Church of Scotland* (Edinburgh, May 1934; 1939; 1945; 1948). His daugh., Lilian Oswald, assistant nurse, Stobhill Hospital, Glasgow.

FINTRAY

1563 STEPHEN MANNERS, M.A., designed vicar in 1563 and formerly Master and Provost of the Hospital of Old Aberdeen.—[*Comps. Sub Coll. of Thirds, Aberdeen.*]

1571 ANDREW KEMP, M.A., pres. to vicarage 29th Aug. 1571 on death of Stephen Manners; his widow, Isobel Adamson, received a pension 1571.—[*Reg. Pres. Bene.*, i, (2), 19; *Comps. Sub Coll. of Thirds, Linlithgow.*]

1572 THOMAS FLEMING, M.A., pres. to vicarage 9th March 1572–3 on death of Andrew Kemp.—[*Reg. Pres. Bene.*, i, (4), 57.]

1574 ROBERT WOOD, pres. to vicarage 12th Aug. 1574 on death of Thomas Fleming.—[*Reg. Pres. Bene.*, i, (4), 27.]

1573 GEORGE WATSON, reader 1573.—[*Comps. Gen. Coll. of Thirds.*]

1594 WILLIAM NEILSON, M.A., pres. to vicarage 13th Feb. 1594–5 on depriv. of Robert Wood.—[*Reg. Sec. Sig.*, lxvii, 60.]

1662 GEORGE MELDRUM, marr. Bessie (buried 9th March 1684), eldest daugh. of Alexander Rose, min. of Aberdeen North, and had issue—Elspeth, executor of her brother.

1699 ROBERT BURNETT, had addl. issue—Thomas, bapt. 6th June 1683; George, bapt. Jan. 1687.

1702 JAMES HUTCHISON, his wife, Margaret Keir, buried in Greyfriars, Edinburgh, 15th Oct. 1699; a child buried 3rd Dec. 1688; Hugh.—[*Deeds Dal.*, 1705, No. 724.]

1856 WILLIAM OGILVIE, his son, Charles Green, Union Bank of Australia, died at Taurango, New Zealand, 27th April 1933; his daugh., Helen (marr. Thomas Rennie, M.B., C.M., M.D., Formosa and Foochow, China (died at Aberdeen 11th April 1912), with issue, including Major-General Thomas Gordon Rennie, Commander of 51st Division, killed at Rhine crossing March 1945).—[*Aberdeen Roll of Grad.*, 1860–1900, 446; *Memo.*, Mrs Rennie, Fairview, Kintore.]

1885 JOHN CATTO, his widow, Eliza Watt, died 19th March 1936; his sons—John, M.B., Ch.B., 1900 (Aberdeen), died at Assam 7th May 1908; Gavin James, manager, Union Bank, Aberdeen; William Robert, M.B., Ch.B., 1904 (Aberdeen), Medical Officer, Rand Mines, Transvaal, 1906–11, District Surgeon, Rhodes, Cape Province, 1912–14, Cape Town, Resident Medical Officer, East Griqualand, 1925, died at King William's Town 13th Jan. 1940; Alexander Godsman, now min. at Duffus; Patrick Thomas, M.B., Ch.B., 1915 (Aberdeen), Lieut. R.A.M.C. June 1915, served at home 1915–16, and in Egypt, Palestine, April 1916, final rank, Captain, now at Coventry; Forbes Shepherd, M.B., Ch.B., 1923 (Aberdeen), Private, 4th Gordon Highlanders, 27th March 1914, served with 5th Gordons at home 1914–17, and with B.E.F. June–Aug. 1917, final rank, Corporal, now of Hulme, Manchester; his daugh., Lizzie Jane (marr. 18th Sept. 1912 James Robertson, M.B., Ch.B., M.D., Ch.M. (Aberdeen), who was killed in action near Bapaume 21st March 1918, when as Lieut.-Col. he was in command of the 2/Gt. Highland Field Ambulance, R.A.M.C.).—[*Memo.*, Rev. A. G. Catto, Duffus.]

JAMES ANDREW CRAWFORD, line 3, delete "15th Jan. 1864" and read "22nd Feb. 1863"; died 9th June 1947.
1909

KINELLAR

The church pertained to the parsonage of Kinkell. Cairntradlin in the parish is Triduana's Cairn. St Triduana is "the lady of the three days fast." It may not be the real name of the saint, but may have been given to her because of the rigour of her fasting.—[Watson's *Celtic Place Names*, 334–5.]

JOHN WYLIE, M.A., exhorter 1563, and at Skene.—[*Comps. Sub Coll. of Thirds, Aberdeen*, etc.]
1563

JAMES HENDERSON, reader in 1563. —[*Comps. Sub Coll. of Thirds, Aberdeen*, etc.]
1563

WALTER ANDERSON, marr. Margaret Skene, who was buried 19th Oct. 1671.
1606

JOHN MERCER, marr. 1652 Lilias Row and had issue—Agnes, bapt. 20th Feb. 1656.
1607

JOHN ANGUS, marr. (1) cont. 6th May 1700; (2) 21st May 1707, Anna, daugh. of James Cheyne in Auchencreve and had issue—John, bapt. 1st Sept. 1710.—[*Methlick Reg.*]
1697

JAMES JOHNSTON TINDAL, died 4th April 1927.
1881

ROBERT LITTLEJOHN BARR, died Aberdeen 14th April 1932; his widow, Isabella Garland Gray, died 23rd Feb. 1942.
1899

(*Charges united 31st July* 1932.)

MARYCULTER

Included in a charter of King William the Lion to Kelso Abbey, confirming grants to the Abbey by his father, King David, and his brother, King Malcolm, is the Church of Culter. Later, between 1221 and 1236, there was established at Culter, on the south side of the Dee, a preceptory of the Knights Templar with a chapel dedicated to the Virgin Mary. Subsequently a dispute arose between the Abbot of Kelso and the Knights Templar as to the right of the latter to have a chapel within the parish of Culter. The matter was brought before Pope Urban IV, who remitted it to delegates, the Abbot of Jedburgh and the Abbot of Holyrood. The finding was in favour of the Knights Templar; and as an ultimate outcome of the subsequent settlement between them and the Abbot, the parish of Culter was divided into two parishes. The portion on the north side of the Dee, where the church was dedicated to St Peter, was designated Peterculter; and the portion on the south side, in which was situated the Templars' Chapel of the Virgin, was called Maryculter.—[*Reg. of Kelso*, i, 15, 23, 181–5; *Reg. Epis. Aberdeen*, ii, 288–93.]

JOHN BROWN, his mother was Ann Touch.
1812

ANDREW TWEEDIE, dem. 3rd Nov. 1936, died 4th Oct. 1938.
1917

NEWHILLS

THOMAS CREVEY, min. of a chapel in Elgin, charged by Isobel, daugh. of John Leslie, min. of Rothes, of being the father of her child.—[*Records of Elgin*, ii, 378.]
1679

ROBERT BURNETT, his son, Thomas, bapt. 16th July 1715.
1702

CHARLES NAIRN BARKER MELVILLE, his son, Charles James, died in London 13th May 1935.
1867

ANDREW CURRIE, dem. 16th Jan. 1943.
1918

NEW MACHAR

There was a chapel or cell and oratory on a small island on Loch Gowl, Bishop's Loch, where the bishops of Aberdeen had a residence, and where Bishop de Bernham died in 1282.—[Macfarlane's *Geogph. Coll.*, i, 85.]

1570 ALEXANDER GARIOCH, reader, son of Alexander G.; died 7th July 1578.—[*Chron. of Aberdeen*, 50.]

1576 BEROALD INNES, line 4, delete "became min. of Alves."

1626 JAMES HERVIE of Mains of Elrick, which he acquired in 1642 from Gilbert Hervie, burgess of Aberdeen; dem. before 13th Aug. 1650, but was alive at that date; issue—an only son, Robert, fiar of Mains of Elrick.—[*Aberdeen Sas.*, xii, 293, (1642), xiv, 246, 420 (1650).]

1650 JAMES CHALMERS, Regent in Marischal College in 1648.—[*Marischal Coll. and Univ.*, 35, *New Spalding Club*.]

1669 JAMES GARDEN, recommended for ordination 19th May 1669.

1687 GEORGE SEATON, he was catechist and preacher of the Gospel in St Machar's Church, Old Aberdeen, apparently when acting as Librarian at King's College; had issue—Anna, bapt. 21st May 1688; Alexander, bapt. 15th Jan. 1691; George, bapt. 4th May 1692; James, bapt. 8th Dec. 1696; Archibald, buried 18th Nov. 1729.

1706 WILLIAM MITCHELL, on 29th Oct. 1708 the Synod of Moray recommended that contributions be made on his behalf, he having "a numerous family and reduced to straits."

1723 JAMES KEITH, a dep. episcopal min. intruded here 1723-4.

1866 WILLIAM ROBERTSON BRUCE, his widow, Elizabeth Gilzean Cruickshank, died 5th Jan. 1928; his daugh. Jane (marr. James Snavie Cooper, M.B., C.M., D.P.H., M.D., Leeds).

1904 ALEXANDER HOOD SMITH, died Aberdeen 16th June 1927.

1927 ANDREW MILNE MITCHELL GILES, born 7th March 1902, son of Charles G., min. of Forglen; educ. at Robert Gordon's College, Aberdeen, and Univ. of Aberdeen, M.A. (1927); licen. by Presb. of Turriff 14th May 1926; assistant Holburn, Aberdeen, 1926; ord. 24th Nov. 1927; trans. to St Aidans, Broughty Ferry, 27th Aug. 1941. Marr. 30th April 1929 Isabel Ogston, daugh. of James Gauld and Jane Ogston, Aberdeen, and has issue—Isabel Audrey, born 18th Feb. 1930; Andrew Charles Hamish, born 22nd Dec. 1932; Peter, born 19th Aug. 1936; Sheena Elizabeth, born 21st July 1941.

(*Charges united 7th Aug.* 1932.)

NIGG

The church was granted to Arbroath Abbey by King William the Lion *cir.* 1189–99, and in 1202–4 the church with its chapels was confirmed to the abbey by William Malvoisin, Bishop of St Andrews. It was dedicated by Bishop de Bernham of St Andrews 30th July 1242. Before 1829 the church was in a ruinous condition, and in that year the present church was built on the hill at Kincorth. The ruins of the church stand on the east side of the Bay of Nigg. The belfry is remarkable as being on the east end of the church, and on the die are the date 1704 and the initials of the min. of that time, Richard Maitland. There is a pennon vane of date 1763, and there is also a fleur-de-lis north point. St Fiachra's Well, named after the patron saint, which was near the church, disappeared through the action of sea erosion. In the vicinity were the kirklands and the manse. Nigg Bay also bore variations of the Saint's name—St Ficker's, Sandy Fittick's, San Fittich's, Sanct Moffatis-bay, Sanct Mussets-bay, Sanct Moffot's-bay. On 3rd July 1233 the whole land of Nigg was granted to Arbroath Abbey by Alexander III; and on 11th Dec. 1495 James IV, "for the singular devotion which he had for St Thomas and for St Fotinus, patron of the 'town' of Torry,'' erected the "town" into a free burgh of barony under the Abbot of Arbroath, with power to elect bailies, etc., have a market cross, a weekly market on Friday, and an annual fair on St Fotinus' Day (23rd Dec.) and four subsequent days. One purpose of the erection was the provision of entertainment and sustenance for foreigners and lieges requiring hospitality in the said "town," who, coming from beyond the mouth to the burgh of Aberdeen and other northern regions of the Kingdom, were unable to cross on account of the tempestuous river of Dee. The Abbot of Arbroath had at Torry a residence called Abbotshall, depicted on the map of Old Angus and Mearns from drawings by Pont and Gordon, *cir.* 1640, as situated near the south bank of the Dee opposite the inches, that is, west of the site of the Victoria Bridge. The gardens of the manor *lie Abbotshall* occur in a charter of 13th Nov. 1564; the house itself is apparently the "ruined building" described in 1581 as near the river Dee, and on the south side of the same, with garden between *lie Raik* and *lie Midchingill*, extending along the bank of the said river, and doubtless it was "the ruins of an edifice belonging to the Abbot which were dug up on the upper part of the Harbour" just prior to 1793, and at that time were still designated "Abbot's Walls." Near by was a burial ground, almost certainly the burial ground attached to the chapel designated on 28th Aug. 1475 as "the Chapel of the said Lord Abbot" (George, Abbot of Arbroath), the abbot's private chapel. The chapel was dedicated to St Fotinus. There was also at Torry a piece of land, described on 30th Sept. 1535 as "the Lordis Croftis," belonging to the grain barn of Torry, and situated a short distance above the Dee; and farther west, near the Dee below Kincorth, is situated Abbotswell, called earlier Abbots Walls. The proximity of the Spittal Burn suggests that here there was an hospitium for travellers, belonging to the abbot. On the shore of the parish was *lie Coif*, commonly called *Hailymanis Coif*, a name due to a cave in this vicinity reputed as the abode of a hermit. Hence the modern designation of the district, Cove. To the abbey also belonged two ferry boats on the Dee, *lie Netherferry-boit* at Nether Torry opposite Fittie, and *lie Uverferry-boit* at Over Torry west of the bridge.—[*Reg. of Arbroath, Nigrum,* 173, 182, 292–5, 524–5, *vetus,* 3–8, 17, 74–5, 111; *Reg. Great Seal,* ii, 2292, v, 252, 1214, 2119; *Retours,* xxv, 23, xi, 215; *Church of Scot. in* 13*th Century,* 48.] (See Gordon of Rothiemay's *Map of Aberdeen,* 1661, and *Map of Old Angus and Mearns in Reg. of Arbroath, Nigrum.*)

JOHN ROCHE, grandson of Alexander R., dyer, Aberdeen; his pres. in 1597 was on death of John Davidson.—[*Reg. Sec. Sig.,* lxix, 129; *Aberdeen City Sas.,* 7th June 1621.]
1588

JAMES DOUGLAS, M.A., had issue— Ann, buried 25th Aug. 1681.—[*Old Machar Reg.*]
1657

RICHARD MAITLAND, his son, Charles, apprenticed to Walter Paterson, peutherer, 30th May 1718.
1674

JAMES FARQUHAR, marr. Ann Maitland. Addl. issue—John, bapt. 1st Sept. 1700; Elizabeth, bapt. 2nd Oct. 1702.
1717

HUGH MACONNACH SMITH, his widow, Jane Beattie, died 2nd June 1945.
1888

JOHN EDMUND MITCHELL, died 2nd June 1928; had issue—Joseph John Edmund Downie, born 9th Feb. 1927.
1923

WALTER SIMPSON, trans. from Rattray (*q.v.*) 12th Dec. 1928. Publication—*The International Labour Organisation* (Booklet).
1928

PETERCULTER

There was a Well of St Mark, and a piece of land was called St Cuthbert's Croft. For the parish of Culter and its ultimate division, see Maryculter.—[*Place Names of West Aberdeenshire,* 306.]

WILLIAM MELDRUM was vicar in 1554.—[*Collegiate Churches of Midlothian,* 221.]
1554

ALEXANDER ROBERTSON, reader, was in office in 1563.—[*Comps. Sub Coll. of Thirds, Aberdeen,* etc.]
1563

WILLIAM WALLACE, as reader here pres. to vicarage 30th Jan. 1577-8 on death of Sir William Meldrum.—[*Reg. Pres. Bene.*, i, (4), 64.]

1578

FRANCIS THOMSON. Addl. issue—Margaret, bapt. 19th June 1646.—[*Peterculter Reg.*]

1636

JOHN KENNEDY, his son, John, bapt. 23rd May 1710; Anne, bapt. 22nd Oct. 1719; Mary, bapt. 20th July 1722. Addl. issue—Alexander, bapt. 17th March 1713; James, bapt. 17th March 1715; Elizabeth, bapt. 10th Dec. 1716.

1704

JOHN STIRLING, born 21st Dec. 1785, son of Patrick S., writer, Dunblane, and Ann White; his son, John, born 1828, not 1829.—[*Scot. Notes and Queries*, March 1934, 47.]

1812

JAMES AIRD, his widow, Margaret Clark, died 31st May 1938.

1888

JAMES LAING THOMSON, dem. 30th April 1948; his sons—James Laing Stephen, M.B., Ch.B. (Aberdeen, 1932), London; William Eddie Spalding, M.A., Assistant to Radon Centre, Univ. of Aberdeen; his wife, Mary Spalding, died 18th May 1939.

1905

PORTLETHEN

About 1635 Mr Robert Buchan, proprietor of the local estate, built here a Roman Catholic church or chapel. After a time it fell into disuse; and gradually it came to be used for Presbyterian worship. In 1725 it is narrated that "the present Minister (at Banchory-Devenick) preaches once in 15 days in the afternoon in summer, and once in 20 days in winter." About 1744 a licentiate named Wilkie was appointed to preach on alternate Sundays here and in the "Sod Kirk" at Newhall in Fetteresso parish. After his death both churches were closed; and at Portlethen "any strolling preacher officiated." But in 1785 the parish min. secured the appointment of a licentiate to conduct the services.

At the end of the 18th century a Mr Scorgie officiated. He was followed by Mr Pirie, who died in 1827; and the latter's successor was Mr William Law.—[*New Stat. Acc.*, xi, *Kincardine*, 185-6 and *n*; Macfarlane's *Geog. Colls.*, i, 108, S.H.S.; Henderson's *Hist. of Banchory-Devenick*, 153-5.] (See Fetteresso.)

ALEXANDER ROBERTSON GRANT dem. 31st Dec. 1938, died 24th April 1942; his sons—Alister, Medical Superintendent, County Mental Hospital, Whittingham, Preston, M.B., Ch.B. (1913), M.D. (Aberdeen) 1924, Lieut. R.A.M.C. 4th Jan. 1914, served in France and Belgium Feb. 1915 to April 1919, Captain; Ronald Kirkham, M.B., C.M., Georgetown, British Guiana; his widow, Annie Elizabeth Robertson, died 4th May 1943.

1883

SKENE

The church pertained to the parsonage of Kinkell. "Jesus Fair," mentioned in 1720 as held at the Park of Slioch, may be a dedication to Our Lord.—[Mackinley's *Ancient Church Dedications*, 54.]

JOHN WYLIE, M.A., exhorter 1563. (See Kinellar.)

1563

JOHN PHILP, M.A., min. 1563; in charge also at Alford and Forbes.—[*Comps. Sub Coll. of Thirds, Aberdeen*, etc.]

1563

THEOPHILUS STEWART, M.A., Master of Aberdeen Grammar School, held the vicarage 1573.—[*Comps. Gen. Coll. of Thirds.*]

1573

DAVID STEWART, parson, died before 1578-9. Marr. Grissel Bruce of the Auchinballive family; she marr. (2) Robert Skene of Woolary.—[*Acts. and Dec.*, lxxiii, 403.]

1578

GILBERT KEITH, marr. Marie Hay.—[*Reg. of Deeds*, cccxxxvi, *Durie*, 29th May 1623.]

1610

ABERDEEN] **SKENE** 543

1664 LUDOVIC DUNLOP, his son, Alexander, rector of Nunnington, Yorks, died 23rd Jan. 1722; his son, Andrew, watchmaker, London. Delete "min. of Whitern."—[*Deeds. Durie*, 1706, No. 492.]

1870 WILLIAM MARSHALL PHILIP, his widow, Mary Hardy, died 28th Dec. 1930, aged 97.

1911 JOHN McMURTRIE. Addl. issue—Beatrice Somerville Brodie, born 13th March 1926; Isobel Jean, born 25th Sept. 1929; Elspeth Anne, born 5th March 1932; John, born 21st May 1937.

(*Skene and Lochside united 20th April* 1941.)

PRESBYTERY OF KINCARDINE O'NEIL

ABOYNE

The present church seems to have been erected in 1842. It has a stone with the date 1761, which probably was the year of the erection of a central church on this site to take the place of the Church of Aboyne, which was situated at the Kirktown east of the village, and the Church of Glentanar, the ruins of which may still be seen farther west, and which, thatched with heather, was called "The Black Chapel on the Muir." "Muchrieha's Well" is about 1½ miles north-west of Aboyne Church. Near it is a stone with a cross cut on it; and near to the cross there was a stone cut in hollow shape and called "Muchrieha's Chair." It was broken up about the beginning of the 19th century. The saint seems to be not Malrubh but *Mo-cridhe, Mo-chridoc*, but it is impossible to identify which of the saints who bore that name is here concerned.—[Watson's *Celtic Place Names*, 331.]

1563 JOHN CUSHNIE, reader in 1563 and 1567.—[*Comps. Sub Coll. of Thirds, Aberdeen*, etc.]

1574 ROBERT BOYD, pres. to vicarage 5th April 1574 on death of Arthur Taylor.—[*Reg. Pres. Bene.*, i, (4), 4.]

1679 LUDOVIC GORDON, marr. cont. 18th Oct. 1676, Catherine Burnett.—[*Aberdeen Sher. Court Books*, 14th Nov. 1684.]

1784 THOMAS GORDON, his mother, Isabel Shepherd, was daugh. of John Shepherd, min. of Logie-Coldstone.

1902 JAMES DUNCAN MACKENZIE, dem. 27th Nov. 1935, died at Kirkcaldy 6th Jan. 1939.

(*Charges united 9th Feb.* 1936.)

GLENTANAR

1563 JOHN ROSS, reader in 1563.—[*Comps. Sub Coll. of Thirds, Aberdeen*, etc.]

BANCHORY TERNAN

Torannan (Ternan), one of the seven sons of Aengus, son of Aed of the 6th century, was a disciple of Palladius, and was called *Abb Bencair*, Abbot of Bennchar, being, it is said, the head of a Columban monastery here; and here he is reputed to have been buried. His bell, called the Ronnecht, was preserved here till the Reformation; and here too, tradition states his head was preserved. The "dewar"—hereditary keeper—of the bell, held in virtue of his office a piece of land called the "Deray Croft of Banquhori-terne." It has been suggested that a small square iron bell, discovered when the Deeside railway was under construction at this point, and subsequently lost sight of, may have been the Ronnecht. Kilduthie, situated in the parish, may suggest a dedication to St Duthac.—[Watson's *Celtic Place Names*, 280, 298, 300; Skene's *Celtic Scot.*, ii, 30; MacKinlay's *Anc. Ch. Dedications* (non-script.), 107.]

1529 THOMAS CURROR was app. perpetual vicar 1st Feb. 1529 in succession to Alexander Spittal, who became prebend of Auchindoir.—[*Reg. of Arbroath, niger*, 497.]

1562 THOMAS MYRTON, M.A., vicar 1562.—[*Comps. Sub Coll. of Thirds, Forfar*, etc.]

1563 JAMES RYND, reader 1563.—[*Comps. Sub Coll. of Thirds, Forfar*, etc.]

BANCHORY TERNAN—BRAEMAR

1567 JAMES REID, pres. in 1582 on deaths of Sir Thomas Curror and Burnett; his son, John, min. of Logie Buchan, servitor to Mr George Buchanan; Isabel, his eldest daugh. (marr. William Downie in Banchory, with issue, including Robert, min. of St Clement's, Aberdeen); his son, Thomas, by his will of 19th May 1624, bequeathed to the town of Aberdeen his "whole Library of Books" for a library at Marischal College, and the sum of six thousand merks for the support of a librarian; his son, Alexander, on 4th Oct. 1633, mortified to the Provost and Bailies of Aberdeen the sum of £110 Stg. for bursaries for two or three poor scholars at Marischal College, and by his will of 1st Feb. 1639–40 bequeathed to the said Provost and Bailies £100 Stg. to augment the salaries of the regents of the college.—[*Reg. Pres. Bene.*, ii, 86; *Recs. of Marischal College and Univ.*, i, 194, 195, 197, 226–8, 234–5n; ii, 207n.]

1646 ALEXANDER CANT, marr. (cont. 8th Sept. 1648) Isobel (not Margaret); had issue—Andrew, bapt. 1649; William, bapt. 16th Feb. 1665.

1699 MARTIN SCHANK, had issue—Alexander, bapt. 14th Aug. 1703; Margaret, bapt. 9th Dec. 1705.

1894 JAMES HALL, his widow, Christian Jamieson, died 30th Oct. 1942.

BIRSE

1563 ANDREW HOG, reader.—[*Comps. Sub Coll. of Thirds. Aberdeen*, etc.]

1593 ALEXANDER IRVING, pres. to Chancellary in 1593 in succession to Alexander Seton.—[*Reg. Sec. Sig.*, lxxii, 171.]

1618 JOHN ROSE, marr. (2) Elizabeth, daugh. of James Wood of Over Tippertie; his daugh., Margaret (marr. William Ross of Drumachie).—[*Aberdeen Sas.*, xii, 557, 570, 7th and 14th Dec. 1643.]

1663 ALEXANDER STRACHAN, buried at Old Machar; his sons—John, bapt. 19th June 1664; Alexander.

1864 CHARLES DUNN, his wife, widow of W. L. Thomson, wine merchant, Aberdeen, died 6th May 1930.

1923 JOHN PATON MURRAY, dem. 17th May 1926 and became Army Chaplain 1st June 1926; adm. to Dun 2nd April 1936; dem. 30th Sept. 1943.

1927 ARNOLD LOW KEMP, trans. from Millbrex (*q.v.*) 8th Oct. 1926; dem. 13th June 1948; his son, Robert, on staff of *Manchester Guardian;* died Edinburgh 22nd March 1949.

BRAEMAR or KINDROCHET

In the *Liber Cartarum Prioratus Sancti Andre* there is a copy of a charter, cir. 1237–40, by which Duncan, Earl of Mar, gifts the Church of Kindrochet to the Priory of Monymusk, which was confirmed by Bull of Pope Innocent in 1200. The church is named *Ecclesiam Sancti Andrae de Kindrouch*. The river Cluny is called by its ancient name "Alvan." The date is 1214–34. Later in 1228–39 there is confirmation of the gift "de ecclesia de Kindraich by Gilbert, Bishop of Aberdeen," and on 28th May 1245 the same church of St Andrew of Kindrochet was confirmed to the prior and convent of Monymusk by Pope Innocent IV.

According to the legend the church of Kindrochet was founded in the eighth century by King Angus and dedicated to St Andrew before that of St Andrew in Fife.

1563 JAMES HANYE (Hannie), reader in 1563.—[*Comps. Sub Coll. of Thirds, Aberdeen,* etc.]

1608 JOHN ROSS, marr. Elizabeth Wood.

1907 ALEXANDER CHRISTIAN WILLIAM SAUNDERS, trans. to Rikarton 3rd Sept. 1929.

CLUNY

JOHN WEBSTER, his widow, Alexandrina Hay, died 28th March 1932.
1866

GEORGE FERRIES, his wife, Mary Lumsden, died 14th Nov. 1934; he died 27th Aug. 1938.
1883

JOHN ALEXANDER MACKAY, trans. to Wallacetown, Dundee, 8th Sept. 1926.
1923

WILLIAM MURDOCH, adm. from Culsalmond 22nd Feb. 1927; died 8th Sept. 1941; had issue—Elizabeth Helen, born 14th Aug. 1924; Ian Martin Calder, born 9th Oct. 1926.
1927

(*Charges united* 18*th June* 1933.)

COULL

GEORGE LAWSON, reader in 1563.—[*Comps. Sub Coll. of Thirds, Aberdeen*, etc.]
1563

WILLIAM BRUCE, pres. to vicarage 2nd Sept. 1571 on death of Andrew Leslie.—[*Reg. Pres. Bene.*, i, (2), 32.]
1574

ROBERT LINDSAY, pres. to vicarage 30th April 1591 on dep. of Thomas Mallison.—[*Reg. Sec. Sig.*, lxii, 41.]
1585

ANDREW GRAY, marr. Marjory Robertson.—[*Aberdeen Sas.*, viii, 212.]
1624

JAMES PATERSON, line 12, for "Gollan" read "Gellan."
1734

ALEXANDER MACKENZIE, dem. 13th Dec. 1927, died at Aboyne 4th July 1929.
1882

ROBERT HILL RICHMOND, formerly of Shapinsay (*q.v.*); trans. from Kirkmaiden 4th July 1928.
1928

CRATHIE

In the 6th century St Colin, a British saint, settled in Crathie. He is commemorated by a pool in the Dee called Polhallock (Pol-Colin-oc) and by a fair which was formerly held at Clachantuin. At each of the places named he founded churches, but his name was afterwards confused with that of St Columba, the great apostle of the Scots. Some time later a follower of St Kentigern came to Crathie, called St Monire. There was a fair in Crathie on the day of his commemoration, 18th Dec., and a pool in the river Dee opposite the grounds of Balmoral Castle is still called Polmanaire, as he is said to have baptised his converts to Christianity in its waters.

In the time of Thomas, the last Earl of Mar of the Celtic line, the Abbey of Cambuskenneth possessed the church and teinds of Crathie. In the Cartulary of Cambuskenneth there is a confirmation dated 11th Jan. 1347 at Fetternear, granting in consideration of the poverty of the abbey, permission to the abbot to appropriate the fruits of the Church of Crathie to his own use and that of the convent and to serve the parish by a qualified chaplain, removable at their pleasure, reserving to the bishop and his successors the episcopal rights in the said church, which they had in the neighbouring churches.

SIR LAURENCE COUTTS, reader 1563.—[*Comps. Sub Coll. of Thirds, Aberdeen*, etc.]
1563

ALEXANDER FERRIES, his daugh., Katherine (marr. –. Farquharson); wife alive 1675.
1626

ARCHIBALD ALEXANDER CAMPBELL, his daugh., Alice, born 21st died 23rd Feb. 1877.
1874

JOHN STIRTON, app. Chaplain to the King 26th Sept. 1936; C.V.O. 26th Sept. 1936; app. Chaplain in Ordinary to King George VI 1939; present at coronation of King George VI and Queen Elizabeth and led the Procession of Clergy in Westminster Abbey 12th May 1937; dem. 3rd Sept. 1941; died at Edinburgh 9th Oct. 1944. Column 2, lines 20 and 21, insert brackets before "Proceedings" and after "1910." Addl. publications—*The Red House* and other papers (1926). *Notes on the Chapel Royal of Scotland and the Order of the Thistle* (1927); *My Manuscript*
1919

Portfolio (1929); *Links with Lady Nairne and the Oliphants of Gask* (1930); *Three Periods of English Poetry, 1670–1824,* (1930); *St Fergus the Saint of Glamis* (1930); *Erasmus, a Character Study* (1930); *Incident in the Life of H.M. Queen Elizabeth* (1931); *The Very Rev. James Cameron Lees, K.C.V.O., an Appreciation* (1931); *A Royal Letter* (1931); *Crathie Parish Church, an Historical Survey* (seventh edition) (1938); *The Spanish Match* (1933); *Funeral Expenses of King William III* (1934); *Notes on some Manuscripts and Early Printed Works* (1934); *The Chantry Chapel at Glamis* (1936); *The Innes of Balnacraig and Ballogie —a Family History* (1938); *Glamis Castle, its Origin and History* (1938).

(*Charges united* 1st Jan. 1930.)

DINNET

1903 WILLIAM SAWERS, his wife, Isabella Alexander Giffen, died 16th April 1929.

ECHT

In the reign of Alexander II, 1214–49, the church was granted to the Abbey of Scone by Thomas, son of Malcolm of Lunden, confirmed by Bull of Pope Honorius III 15th Dec. 1225.—[*Book of Scone*, 58, 67.]

1563 JAMES GRAY, M.A., vicar 1563.— [*Acts and Dec.*, xli, 5; *Comps. Sub Coll. of Thirds, Aberdeen*, etc.]

1599 ROBERT FORBES, pres. in 1602 on dem. of James Gray.—[*Reg. Sec. Sig.*, lxxii, 218.]

1658 WILLIAM ALEXANDER, M.A., buried 27th Dec. 1686.—[*Aberdeen Reg.*]

1695 THOMAS KINNEAR, marr. Ann, daugh. of Andrew Straton, apothecary, Montrose; his son, Arthur, apprenticed to William McVey, wright, 25th Aug. 1729.

1873 ANDREW SOUTTER, his daugh., Emilie Leith, died 17th July 1930; his widow, Florence Augusta Baker, died at Joppa 21st May 1948.

1915 THOMAS ARNOTT MUNRO, marr. 19th Sept. 1934 Margaret Anderson, eldest daugh. of Donald Butter, Glenlyon, Inverness.

FINZEAN

1921 JAMES ROSS, trans. to Slains 22nd Sept. 1927.

1928 CHRISTOPHER CHARLES BARNETT, born 27th March 1903, son of Christopher Charles B., insurance agent, Aberdeen, and Mary Ann Davidson; educ. at Grammar School and Univ. of Aberdeen, M.A. (1925), B.D. (1927); licen. by Presb. of Aberdeen 4th May 1927; assistant John Knox's Church, Aberdeen; ord. 26th Oct. 1927; adm. 6th March 1928; trans. to Bellie 24th Sept. 1934; trans. to Hilltown, Dundee, 15th May 1947. Marr. 19th Sept. 1928 Sarah Jane Ogg, daugh. of Henry Russell Davie, evangelist, and Margaret White, and has issue—Charles Henry, born 29th July 1929; Jean Margaret Mary, born 3rd May 1932.

GLENGAIRN

It appears that St Mungo was a later dedication. Professor Watson states that *Cill Mo-Thatha* was the old name of the church, and that there was held a fair called *Feill Mo-Thatha.* "Mo-Thatha is the form assumed in Scottish Gaelic of the Irish name *Tua,* 'the silent one,' for an earlier *Toe.*" The old church was used for worship for the last time on 7th Dec. 1800. But already, and prior to 1794, there was "another place of worship at the upper bridge of Gairn," that is the old military bridge across the Gairn at Gairnshiel, about five miles up the Glen, constructed 1750–3; and in it and the church up to 1800, by appointment of the Royal Bounty Committee, through the aid of whose grant the work was carried on, a service was conducted each alternate Sunday. After 1800 the services appear to have taken place in the other "place of worship" which probably occupied the site of the present church opened early in 1804. Up to 1800 or thereby the missionary assisted the min. in the work of Glenmuick and Tullich, but thereafter his duty seems to have applied only to Glengairn.

The church originally belonged to the Augustinian Hospital of St Germain of the Order of Cross-Bearers with the Star of Bethlehem; and by charter of James IV, 22nd May 1497, it was granted to King's College, Aberdeen. There was a chapel with burying-ground at Dalfad, and a burying-ground at Rineatan (Renatton).—[*Glenmuick Kirk Session Records—Memo.*, Rev. I. Howat, B.D.; Fraser's *Old Deeside Road*, 192 and *n*; *Petition for Erection of Parish*, 1862–3; Watson's *Celtic Place Names*, 297–8; *Fasti Aberdonenses*, 11–14; *Spalding Club*; Jervice's *Epitaphs and Inscriptions*, ii, 147.] (See Tranent.)

CHARLES BOG, missionary at Braemar, and also at Glenmuick, Glengairn and Tullich, and from 1739 only at Glengairn and Tullich; on 19th June 1748 it is stated that he "is now removed to aneyr corner."—[*Glenmuick Kirk Sas. Recs.*; *Memo.*, Rev. I. Howat, B.D.] (See Braemar.)
1728

WILLIAM FORSYTHE, entered upon duty as missionary on 19th June 1748; pres. to Aboyne and ord. 19th June 1754.
1748

THOMAS JACKSON, app. apparently in 1754; preached on the last occasion on 12th Aug. 1759; went to New York.
1754

LUDOVIC GRANT, M.A., ord. as missionary in or about 1781; preached on last occasion 28th Feb. 1799; adm. to Methlick 3rd April 1799.
1781

ANDREW WATSON, app. missionary 29th Nov. 1798; ord. to Tarland (*q.v.*) 29th Aug. 1799.
1798

ROBERT MacGREGOR, ord. as missionary 2nd July 1799; adm. to Kilmuir-in-Trotternish (*q.v*) 27th Sept. 1822.
1799

JAMES SMITH, described in 1823 as "preacher of the Gospel in this parish," appears to have succeeded Mr MacGregor; he marr. Charlotte Farquharson, Old Meldrum; proc. of banns 2nd Nov. 1823.
1823

DONALD CAMERON, ord. as missionary 21st March 1824; adm. to Laggan (*q.v.*) 1st Aug. 1832.
1824

DONALD STEWART, born in Contin Parish in 1797, son of John S., catechist of Contin parish, and Catherine, daugh. of Thomas Stewart, catechist of Contin parish; acted as teacher in various schools both before and after his university course; educ. Aberdeen Univ., M.A. (March 1824); app. parish schoolmaster at Crathie 1824; licen. in 1830, probably by Presb. of Kincardine O'Neil; ord. as missionary 1833; "came out" in 1843, and the congregation took the name of Cromar; retired in 1877 on account of ill health, and died in Aberdeen, July 1879, and interred at Old Machar. Marr. in 1839 Marie Louisa, only daugh. of Andrew Wilson, sea-captain, Aberdeen; she died in Spring of 1883, without issue.—[*Memo.*, Miss A. A. Stewart, 28 South Street, Halifax, Nova Scotia; *King's College—Officers and Graduates*, 281, *Spalding Club*.]
1833

ROBERT NEIL, his widow, Mary Reid, died 11th Feb. 1899; his daughs.— Barbara, died 24th Feb. 1873; Mary Erskine, died at Ballater 18th Nov. 1939.— [*Tombst.* at Glengairn.]
1846

JAMES ROBB ALLAN, died 28th Oct. 1943.
1918

THOMAS DAVID WATT, died suddenly at Ballater 10th Feb. 1927; his widow, Catherine Erskine Ferguson, died 8th April 1939.
1924

(*Parish united to Glenmuick May* 1927.)

GLENMUICK

The church originally belonged to the Augustinian Hospital of St Germain of the Order of Cross-Bearers with the Star of Bethlehem; and by charter of James IV, 22nd May 1497, it was granted to King's College, Aberdeen. Near Monaltrie House there was a chapel dedicated to St Nathalan, the garden of the house occupying the ancient burying-ground of the chapel. The foundation stone of the first church at Ballater was laid in 1798; and the building, a plain structure with wooden spire, was opened for worship on 10th Dec. 1800. The last services in the three old churches all took place towards the close of that year, as follows: Glenmuick on 23rd Nov., Tullich on 30th Nov., and Glengairn on 7th Dec. Soon after, Glenmuick Church was destroyed by a fire which originated in the thatch of the roof. The foundation stone of the present church at Ballater was laid by Lord Huntly in 1873; and the first service in the church was held on Thursday, 25th June, 1874—the Fast Day preparatory to Communion.—[*Fasti Aberdonenses*, 11–14, *Spalding Club*; *Deeside Guide Books;* Fraser's *The Old Deeside Road*, 183, 190.] (See Tranent.)

JOHN FERRIES or FERGUSON, 1651 marr. Agnes, daugh. of John Auchterlony, provost of Brechin.

JAMES ROBERT MIDDLETON, dem. 1884 6th June 1928, died 29th Oct. 1934; his widow, Elizabeth Davidson Grant Wilson, died at Montrose 1st Oct. 1948.

JAMES WAUGH, born at Eskdalemuir 1928 19th Feb. 1894, son of Walter W. and Annie Carmichael; educ. at Langholm and Dumfries Academies and Univ. of Glasgow, M.A. (1919), B.D. (1921); licen. by Presb. of Glasgow 4th May 1921; assistant St Mungo's, Glasgow, 1921–3; ord. to Hurlford 10th May 1923; trans. and adm. 26th Oct. 1928; trans. to John Knox's, Aberdeen, 2nd Sept. 1932; trans. to Stow 2nd Feb. 1939. Marr. 26th June 1923 Mary, daugh. of David and Annie Crocket.

TULLOCH

The church was a canonry and prebend of Aberdeen, Hugh Kennedy being canon and prebendary in 1438.—[*The Apostolic Camera and Scottish Benefices*, 246.]

KINCARDINE O'NEIL

Kincardine O'Neil formed part of the patrimony of the Columban monastery at Banchory Ternan. On 31st Oct. 1330, Duncan, Earl of Fife, ratified the erection of the church into a Prebend of Aberdeen by Alexander, Bishop of Aberdeen. In 1733 the roof of the old church, which was of heath, was burned by a young man who was engaged shooting pigeons. It was renewed with slates, and re-slated in 1799. There was a chapel at Boganchapel, *Bog an t'seipeil*, Chapel at the Bog. At "Drumcassie," evidently Drumlasie in the north part of the old parish, there was a famous village well to which, as narrated in the first half of the 18th century, crowds from Kincardine O'Neil resorted on the morning of the first Sunday of May. Lasie may denote Laisren, a saint who died in 639 and whose name, with the prefix Mo, elsewhere appears as Mo-Lasse and Mo-Laise; and it may be that the spring was attached to a chapel of that name. On 3rd March 1233–4, Alan Durward, justiciary of Scotland, gave to God and the Virgin Mary, and the Hospital of Kincardynonel "at the bridge which my father caused to be built across the Dee," apparently to the south of the old church towards the ferryboat station on the Dee, a davach of land called Suthcluthy and the Church of Kincardin in Mar. Alan Durward granted a second charter in 1250, which contained two davachs of land, one called Sudluyth, and the other called Kincardynonel, with two lands lying within the davach of Kincardynonel, to wit at Pathhellok and Garslogie, also the Church of Kyncardynonel with pertinents, and two acres in which is situated the Church of Lumphannan, with the right of patronage of the same church, with its Chapel of Forthery pertaining to the same church. Confirmation by Bull of Pope Innocent followed in 1359. At Kincardine O'Neil there was a Barthol-Fair (St Bartholomew), which is recorded in 1725 as beginning on the last Tuesday of August and extending for three days.— [*Reg. Epis. of Aberdeen*, i, 83, ii, 268, 273; *Place Names of West Aberdeenshire*, 61, 67,

Spalding Club; Watson's *Celtic Place Names*, 305-6, 518-19; Macfarlane's *Geog. Colls.*, i, 102, 103.]

1559 ROBERT HAMILTON, M.A., called parson 18th Sept. 1559.

1559 ROBERT WITHERSPOON, M.A., stated to be his successor; was parson 17th Sept. 1575, when he held the parsonage and vicarage, i.e. Lumphanan, Midmar, Cluny and Glentanar.—[*Cal. of Charters*, viii, 1796; *Reg. Sec. Sig.*, xliii, 39.]

1563 ALEXANDER EUSTACE, reader in 1563.—[*Comps. Sub Coll. of Thirds, Aberdeen*, etc.]

1563 ALEXANDER LIVINGSTONE, min. in 1563.—[*Comps. Sub Coll. of Thirds, Aberdeen*, etc.]

1582 JOHN STRACHAN, son of John S. of Thornton and Margaret Livingston, and brother of William S. of Kirkton of Kincardine O'Neil and Tilliefroskie; pres. in 1582 on death of Robert Witherspoon; canon and prebendary of Aberdeen; rector of King's College, Aberdeen, 1600, 1602, 1605, 1608-10, 1612-14; died after 6th Aug. 1621. Marr. before 19th Nov. 1604 Isabel Symmer and had issue—Robert; Thomas; Isabel (marr. James Forbes of Cloak). Marr. (3) Agnes Troup and had issue—Jean; his son, John, M.A., served in Muirton as heir of his father Oct. 1628.—[*Reg. Mag. Sig.*, iii, 2893; v, 1142, 1786, vi, 726, 1256, 2186, viii, 222; *Retours*, iv, 130; *Aberdeen Sas.*, ii, 265, 267, iii, 421, xvi, 207; *Reg. Pres. Bene.*, ii, 136; *Aberdeen Inhib.*, 11th Oct. 1636; *Books of Adjournal*, viii, Old Series, 798, 5th April 1650; *Kincardine Sas.*, iii, 107.]

1625 ALEXANDER STRACHAN, should be JOHN STRACHAN, formerly of Lumphanan; adm. before 12th Sept. 1625, held the parsonage of which Glentanar, Lumphanan, Cluny, Midmar were pendicles, and appears to have continued Lumphanan in the charge; died after 6th Nov. 1635 and before 26th Feb. 1636. Marr. before 23rd May 1615 Agnes Troup, probably daugh. of William T. of Balnacraig, with issue—John, eldest son (marr. soon after 28th July 1634 Nicholas Burnett, daugh. of Thomas B. of Camphill by his wife, Margaret Keith); Jean; his wife, Agnes Troup, died after 5th April 1650.—[*Book of Adjournals*, Old Ser., viii, 5th April 1650; *Aberdeen Sas.*, v, 154, 314 (1625), ix, 378, 485, 502 (1635), xi, 109 (1638), etc.; *Kincardine Sas.*, iii, 370 (1634); *Reg. Pres. Bene.*, vii, 63.]

1658 GEORGE BURNETT, marr. (2) Jean Reid.—[*Kincardine Sas.*, vi, 48.]

1710 WILLIAM MAIN, had issue—William. Marr. (2) 15th June 1714.—[*Scot. Notes and Queries*, Feb. 1930, 40.]

1772 WILLIAM MORICE. Addl. issue given parish register—Rachel, born 22nd April 1776; Ann, born 5th Oct. 1779.

1928 GAVIN ELMSLIE ARGO, dem. 15th May 1931; died 21st Aug. 1931; his daugh., Ruth Elmslie (marr. 8th Dec. 1931 Alexander M. Hay, Shotley, Umkomaas, Africa); his son, Gavin Alexander Elmslie, M.C., O.B.E. (Military) 1923, Major, R.A.M.C., served in France and Afghanistan 1914-18; died at Durban, Natal, 15th March 1945.

LOGIE-MAR and COLSTONE

The parish of Logie-Mar was termed, in the 12th and 13th centuries, Logyruthuen, Logy Ruthuen, Logyruthman, Logyrothuen, and the name survives now in Rothuen or Riven. Before 1200 the church, under the designation Ruchaven, was bestowed upon the Priory of Monymusk by Gilchrist, Earl of Mar (1182-1211). Whether the gift actually took effect is not clear. At all events, in 1239-41, Duncan, Earl of Mar, granted the church for the support of a chaplain to celebrate for the souls of his wife, etc., in the Cathedral of Aberdeen, where he desired to be buried.

The Church of Colstone is variously designated in the 13th, 14th, 15th and 16th centuries, Colessen, Kilchodiscam, Kilchodistan, Codlessen, Codlessery, Coddylstane, Codlystanys, Codilstane, Colquholdstane. By charter at Kildrummy on 8th

Nov. 1402, Isabella de Douglas, Lady of Mar and Garioch, in her widowhood, granted the patronage and advowson of the church to Lindores Abbey, to be converted to the proper use of the abbey on the death or resignation of Simon, then rector, "if confirmation of the grant could be obtained." Evidently the Bishop of Aberdeen did not confirm the grant, and in 1424 the church was made a canonry and prebend of Aberdeen Cathedral, under lay patronage, by Henry de Lichton, Bishop of Aberdeen.

When the parishes were united in 1618, a new church was built in a central position. The church was rebuilt in 1780, and almost entirely rebuilt in 1876.—[*Reg. Priory of St Andrews*, 372; *Reg. of Aberdeen*, i, 16, ii, 52, 55, 85–6, 253, 255; *Chart of Lindores*, 294 and *n; Cal. Papal Regs., Letters*, iii, 75, 81, 200, 202; iv, 200, viii, 159, 549; *Petitions*, i, 104; *Reg. Pres. Bene.*, i, 94; Jervise's *Epitaphs*, i, 281; *Ord. Gazeteer*, v, 548.]

1563 ARTHUR SKENE, reader 1563, probably identical with A.S., vicar of Glenbuchat.—[*Comps. Sub Coll. of Thirds, Aberdeen*, etc.]

1563 HENRY SPARK, reader at Colstone 1563.—[*Comps. Sub Coll. of Thirds, Aberdeen*, etc.]

1563 WILLIAM CRICHTON, M.A., parson 14th June 1563, died before 9th May 1565.—[*Acts and Dec.*, xxvii, 356, xxviii, 256, 388, 423, xxx, 4, 43; *Reg. of Deeds*, vi, 468; *Reg. Sec. Sig.*, xxxiii, 34.]

1565 ALEXANDER CRICHTON, pres. to parsonage and vicarage 9th May 1565.—[*Reg. Sec. Sig.*, xxxiii, 34.]

1570 DAVID STEWART, reader at Colstone, holding the parsonage with the glebe and manse and £16 yearly; in 1574 he was successful in an action against James Reid, adm. parson in 1573, who had refused Stewart the fruits of 1573 as being annat and threatened to eject him from the manse and glebe. Reid was ordered to make payment, or to be put to the horn.—[*Privy Council, Reg.* ii, 393, 25th Aug. 1574.]

1572 GEORGE LIVINGSTONE, pres. to parsonage 18th Feb. 1572.—[*Reg. Pres. Bene.*, i, (4), 4.] (See Glenbuchat.)

1573 JAMES REID, pres. in 1573 on death of Alexander (? William) Crichton. —[*Reg. Pres. Bene.*, i, (4), 8.]

1580 ROBERT SKENE, vicar, died before 22nd Sept. 1580.—[*Reg. Pres. Bene.*, i, 41.]

1580 WILLIAM MORRISON, pres. to vicarage 22nd Sept. 1580.—[*Reg. Pres. Bene.*, i, 41.]

1585 JAMES DUFF, parson and vicar, dem. before 26th April 1585; also parson of Kinnoir (*q.v.*).—[*Reg. Sec. Seal*, lii, 181.]

1585 DAVID STRATON, his presentation to the parsonage and vicarage on 26th April 1585 was in succession to James Duff.—[*Reg. Sec. Seal*, 411, 181.]

1597 GEORGE GORDON, reader 10th and 17th April 1597.—Michie's *Hist. of Logie Coldstone*, 39, 40.]

1608 JAMES STRACHAN, marr. Marjorie Symmer and had issue—John.—[*Aberdeen Inhib.*, 18th Nov. 1633.]

1748 JOHN McINNES, marr. (1) 30th April 1717 Mary Strachan.—[*Old Machar Reg.*]

1857 GEORGE DAVIDSON, his son died in South Africa 15th Nov. 1934; his daugh., Elizabeth Georgina, died at Aboyne 23rd Jan. 1942.

1910 ROBERT ROBERTSON, died 25th April 1933.

(*Charges united* 27th *Aug.* 1933.)

LUMPHANAN

The pre-Reformation font which had been absent from the church for more than a century, first at Pitmurchie and then at Stranduff, Kincardine O'Neil, and used as a watering trough, was restored to the church in Oct. 1933. The font, of roughly dressed stone, is more or less circular in form and measures approximately 36 inches across the outside, 24 inches inside, and is 18 inches deep. Underneath there is a cylindrical socket cut into the centre of the bottom with a raised ridge round, about three inches back from the outside edge of this socket. This was evidently for the purpose of securing the font on a pedestal, of which, however, no trace can be found. In 1250 the patronage of the church, with the Chapel of Forthary, was given by Alan Durward to the Hospital of St Mary founded by him at Kincardine O'Neil (*q.v.*). For a time after the Reformation, Lumphanan was a dependent of Kincardine O'Neil.—[*Aberdeen Weekly Journal*, 13th Oct. 1933.]

1563　JOHN MICHAEL, reader in 1563.—[*Comps. Sub Coll. of Thirds, Aberdeen*, etc.]

1583　JOHN STRACHAN, min.; apparently identical with John Strachan, min. at Kincardine O'Neil (*q.v.*).

1615　ALEXANDER STRACHAN, Alexander is a mistake for John; he was John S., eldest son of William S. of Kirkton of Kincardine O'Neil, and of Tulliefroskie, by his wife, Christian, daugh. of Archibald Irvine of Whitestane, and nephew of Mr John Strachan, rector of Kincardine O'Neil; trans. to Kincardine O'Neil before 16th Sept. 1625 but appears to have continued in charge here.—[*Reg. Great Seal*, vi, 726, 1533, vii, 686, 1236, 1717.]

1668　ALEXANDER MITCHELL, M.A.; resident with his wife and daugh., Margaret, in Aberdeen in 1696; his wife, Marjory, was daugh. of Gilbert Menzies, burgess of Aberdeen.—[*Aberdeen Poll Tax Roll*, ii, 623.] (See John Menzies, vii, 362.)

1683　PATRICK LEITH, son of George L., min. of Meldrum, and Anne Forbes. Marr. Margaret, daugh. of Patrick Forbes of Gardenstown.—[*Reg. of Deeds, Mack.*, 177, 178, 1683.]

1882　MATTHEW CHARTERIS THORBURN, his daugh., Jean Charteris (marr. 23rd Dec. 1933 Bernard, son of Cornan J. Casson, Croft, Leicester).

1913　FRANCIS CANTLIE DONALD, app. Clerk of Presb. Jan. 1927; his wife, Mary Reid, died 27th June 1945; had issue—Craig Reid Cantlie, born 7th Sept. 1914, scholar at Emmanuel College, Cambridge; Betty Mary, born 11th Sept. 1915, died 29th Nov. 1934; Gwendolen Beatrice Annette, born 27th Jan. 1917; Heather Margaret, born 23rd June 1922.

MIDMAR

In a writ of 29th May 1536, the name of the Saint is given as Monidusnidus with the preface Mo (my). For a time after the Reformation Midmar was a dependent church of Kincardine o'Neil.—(Sir John Cristisone's *Prot. Book*, 198-9.]

1563　WILLIAM ROBERTSON, reader 1563.—[*Comps. Sub Coll. of Thirds, Aberdeen*, etc.]

1651　WILLIAM DOUGLAS, was alive 7th April 1684, when he had a child interred at Aberdeen.

1859　EDWARD LUMSDEN, his daugh., Mary (Mrs Ferries), died 14th Nov. 1934.

1917　DAVID CRAWFORD, trans. to Cortachy 24th Aug. 1927.

1928　JAMES RAE, trans. from Aberdeen, North (*q.v.*), 27th March 1928, died 15th Aug. 1935. Marr. 1st March 1927 Ada Isobel Fernando, widow of William Ludovic Grant, solicitor, Edinburgh.

(*Charges united 5th Jan.* 1935.)

KINAIRNEY

There was a chapel at Corsindave mentioned on 2nd June 1535.—[*Prot. Bk. of Sir John Cristisone*, 155, *Scott. Rec. Soc.*]

1563　JAMES LESLIE, reader 1563.—[*Comps. Sub Coll. of Thirds, Aberdeen*, etc.]

1565 ROBERT MAITLAND, M.A., vicar 12th April 1565.—[*Yester Writs*, 727, *Scott. Rec. Soc.*]

1579 WILLIAM SKENE, pres. to vicarage 2nd Feb. 1579–80, vacant by the death of Mr Robert Maitland.—[*Reg. Sec. Seal*, xlvi, 105.]

1607 WILLIAM BURNETT, his daugh., Helen (marr. cont. 7th March 1657 Thomas, son of Patrick Forbes, burgess of Aberdeen).—[*Aberdeen Sas.*, xix, 143, 14th March 1657.]

STRACHAN

The church was dedicated to the Virgin Mary. The present church was built in 1866. The old bell probably belongs to the beginning of the 16th or end of the 15th century, or even somewhat earlier. In 1866 it was removed from the belfry in the old church and hung in a beech-tree in the churchyard, whence it was taken down in 1895, and in the following year placed in the Session House for preservation.—[*Trans. Aberdeen Eccles. Soc.*, 1897, 220, 248.]

1599 THOMAS BURNETT of Slowie; was Archdeacon of St Andrews. Marr. (1) –. Lauder, daugh. of John Lauder, one of His Majesty's Domestics.—[*Reg. Mag. Sig.*, vii, 1803; *Reg. of Deeds*, cclxxii, 160.]

1659 JOHN STRACHAN, his daugh., Jean, bapt. 23rd Oct. 1657. Addl. issue—Elizabeth, bapt. 3rd July 1659.—[*Montrose Reg.*]

1861 ALEXANDER McLEAN, line 12, for "26th Feb. 1913" read "22nd July 1931"; his son, William James, died Quebec 30th Sept. 1943.

1920 JAMES ALEXANDER WADDELL MULLIGAN, his sons — John Henry, M.B., Ch.B., Carnegie Teaching Fellow in Anatomy, Aberdeen, 1923–6; demonstrator in anatomy St Thomas Hospital, Medical School, London, 1926; Lecturer in regional anatomy, Univ. of St Andrews; James Anderson, M.B., Ch.B., Inverbervie; Hugh Waddell, M.B., Ch.B., M.D. (Hons)., D.Sc., Captain, Indian Medical Service.

TARLAND and MIGVIE

The Church of Tarland was granted by Morgrund, Earl of Mar, *cir.* 1165–71, to the Priory of St Andrews, with the stipulation that he and Agnes, his countess, wherever they may die in Scotland, be buried in St Andrews. The patron saint is Mo-Luoc of Lismore, who died in 592, and whose day is 25th June. The name is an affectionate form of Lugiad.

Before 1178 the Church of Migvie was granted to the Priory of St Andrews, by Morgrund, Earl of Mar, and Agnes, his countess, and *cir.* 1153–78 the said Countess Agnes made the same grant on her own account. The patron saint is St Finan "the Infirm," whose day is 16th March.—[*Reg. Priory of St Andrews*, xxxix, 246–7, 248–50; Watson's *Celtic Place Names*, 283, 290.]

1563 ALEXANDER SCOTT, M.A., vicar 1563.—[*Comps. Sub Coll. of Thirds, Aberdeen*, etc.]

1563 ROBERT SKENE, M.A., exhorter in 1563 and 1576, probably vicar of Logie Mar; also at Tough.—[*Comps. Sub Coll. of Thirds, Aberdeen*, etc.; *Reg. of Ministers*, 66.]

1563 JOHN IRVINE, reader in 1563 and 1567.—[*Comps. Sub Coll. of Thirds, Aberdeen*, etc.]

1582 WILLIAM SCOTT, min. 8th July 1582. —[*Cal. of Charters*, xiv, 3178.]

1591 ALEXANDER YOUNGSON, M.A., pres. to vicarage of Migvie 25th Dec. 1591 on death of John Chalmers.—[*Reg. Sec. Sig.*, lxiii, 82.]

1668 JAMES ROSS, his daugh., Janet (marr. cont. 17th Jan. 1704).

1906 JOHN DICKIE, D.D. (Aberdeen, 1918), Principal, Theological College, Presbyterian Church of New Zealand, 1929; Moderator of General Assembly, New Zealand, 1934–5; died at Dunedin 24th June 1942; his widow, Barbara Trotter, died at Dunedin July 1946. Addl. Publications—*Fifty Years of British Theology, a Personal Retrospect* (Gunning Lecture), Edinburgh 1937; *The Organism of Christian Truth* (1930).

1915 WILLIAM MARSHALL LOW, died 14th Dec. 1942.

(*United with Migvie* 18*th Feb.* 1940.)

TORPHINS

1884 DUNCAN McGREGOR, his widow Mary Ann Reid, died 12th Dec. 1934; his son, Duncan Gerald, W.S., Captain, R.A.F.

(*Charges united* 4*th Jan.* 1942.)

PRESBYTERY OF ALFORD

ALFORD

The church was granted to the Priory of Monymusk by Gilchrist, Earl of Mar, before 1207.—[*Reg. Priory of St Andrews*, 372.]

1563 JOHN PHILP, min. in 1563. (See Skene and Forbes.)

1573 JOHN COULSON, vicar.—[*Acts and Dec.*, 1, 459.]

1591 JOHN STRACHAN, min. here, pres. to vicarage 31st March 1591 on depr. of James Smyth.—[*Reg. Sec. Sig.*, lxii, 35.]

1585 JAMES SMITH, pres. to vicarage 17th Jan. 1584-5 on death of Sir John Colleson; confirmed 24th May 1585. —[*Reg. Sec. Sig.*, 1, 179; lii, 134.]

1737 WILLIAM BADENOCH, marr. Ann, daugh. of John Cuming Farquharson of Kellas and Haughton.

1812 JAMES FARQUHARSON, his mother was Annie Littlejohn.

1896 PETER ADAM, dem. 22nd Dec. 1926, died 5th Oct. 1927.

1927 ROBERT CRAWFORD, born Glasgow 1st April 1878, son of John C. and Louisa Waters; educ. at Denniston School, Glasgow, and Univ. of Glasgow; licen. by Presb. of Hamilton, Dec. 1924; ord. to Plean 23rd April 1925; trans. and adm. 17th June 1927. Marr. 5th Oct. 1906 Agnes, daugh. of Alexander Aitchison, and has issue—Jean Mearns, born 22nd Aug. 1907 (marr. 10th March 1935 James Watt Smith); John Branwill, Glasgow Police Force, born 9th Sept. 1909; Robert Alexander Nelson, Banton, born 21st Oct. 1914.

AUCHINDOIR

A question between Andrew, Bishop of Moray, and Gilbert, Bishop of Aberdeen, regarding the diocesan rights over the church was temporarily settled in 1236 by each party agreeing to waive the matter in their lifetime. On the gift and at the request of Thomas, Earl of Mar, Bishop Alexander de Kynninmonth II, on 28th May 1361, united the Church of Dauchyndore (Auchindoir) to the prebendial Church of Invernochtie. On 25th March 1513 Bishop Elphinston, at the instance of Thomas Myrton, Archdeacon of Aberdeen and Rector of Auchindoir, and with consent of James V, erected the church into a prebend of Aberdeen Cathedral, the rector to provide a vicar for the cure of Auchindoir; and on 14th June 1531 Bishop Dunbar, with the consent of the said Thomas Myrton, incorporated the Prebend of Auchindoir with the Univ. of Aberdeen, making it a prebend and canonry of the college church, with Thomas Myrton as prebendary and canon. There was a Nine Maidens' Well.—[*Reg. of Moray*, 101; *Reg. Epis. of Aberdeen*, i, 89-90, 382; *Fasti Aberdonensis*, 74, 94; *Place Names of West Aberdeenshire*, 266.]

1589 WILLIAM THOMSON, min. here, pres. to parsonage and vicarage 26th Dec. 1591 on dem. of George Lauder of Bass.—[*Reg. Sec. Sig.*, lxiii, 86.]

1834 WILLIAM REID, his daugh., Isabella Elizabeth, M.B.E., died 15th Oct. 1938.

1882 ALEXANDER JOHN ANDERSON, died 13th March 1929.

1922 JOHN HARKNESS, trans. to Morebattle 19th May 1927.

WILLIAM LAWYS DAVIES, born Llansadwrn, Carmarthenshire, 22nd Dec. 1871, son of David D. and Anne Davies; educ. at Carmarthen and Trevecca Colleges; associated with Univ. of Wales, M.A., B.D. (1922); licen. by London Welsh Presb. 31st July 1899; ord. to Prestatyn 13th Dec. 1900; min. of Young Bland Presb. Church, New South Wales, 1906; adm. to United Free Church 27th May 1914; adm. to Saline and Steeland U.F. Church 6th Dec. 1917; dem. 6th Jan. 1920; adm. to St John's, Cawnpore, India, 22nd Dec. 1920; returned to Scotland, assistant St Cuthbert's, Edinburgh, and South Leith; adm. to Sorn 12th March 1925; trans. and adm. 16th May 1928; died 30th Nov. 1941. Marr. 24th Oct. 1899 Ada, daugh. of John and Anne Richards Lougharne, who died 30th May 1935, and has issue—John Alan, Chaplain to Forces, born 9th Dec. 1902. [1928]

(*Charges united 15th Jan.* 1930.)

KEARN

JAMES COUTTS, reader in 1563.—[*Comps. Sub Coll. of Thirds, Aberdeen*, etc.] [1563]

ALEXANDER LAW, he was deprived by the Synod of Aberdeen 4th April 1716 for adherence to the Rebellion, but he continued to possess the manse, and, under pretence of orders from Bishop Falconer at Glamis, preached and exercised the office of the ministry at the Manse of Kearn and elsewhere within the bounds of the Presb. of Alford and the Sheriffdom of Aberdeen, Oct. 1718 to Feb. 1721.— [*Justiciary Records.*] [1713]

CABRACH

A chapel with churchyard was situated near Lesmurdie.—[*Coll. of Shires of Aberdeen and Banff*, 615.]

THOMAS CHRISTISON, reader in 1563.—[*Comps. Sub Coll. of Thirds, Aberdeen*, etc.] [1563]

JOHN IRVING, apparently identical with John I., resident in Aberdeen with his wife, Margaret Thomson, and had issue—George, bapt. 16th Oct. 1681; Patrick, bapt. 29th July 1683; Christian, bapt. 21st Dec. 1686; and three children buried at Aberdeen 8th Jan. 1681, 15th Aug. 1683 and 10th March 1687. [1648]

ANDREW BURT, trans. to Insch 17th Feb. 1927. [1920]

HUGH MACKENZIE, born Glenorchy 27th Jan. 1893, son of Duncan M. and Isabel Mackenzie; educ. at Kingussie School and Univ. of Edinburgh; licen. by Presb. of Lorn 12th Aug. 1919; missionary at Brae Lochaber; ord. to Hylipol 16th Sept. 1925; trans. and adm. 9th Sept. 1927; trans. to Glass 17th Dec. 1942; died 9th May 1946. [1927]

(*Charges united 5th June* 1932.)

CLATT

JOHN HENDERSON, reader in 1563. [*Comps. Sub Coll. of Thirds, Aberdeen*, etc.] [1563]

JOHN GORDON, M.A., son of Alexander G. of Lesmoir, pres. to parsonage and vicarage 19th Oct. 1594 on excommunication of James Gordon; trans. to Crimond before 1st June 1597.— [*Reg. Sec. Sig.*, lxvi, 231, lxxii, 66–7.] [1594]

ROBERT YOUNGSON, pres. to parsonage and vicarage 1st June 1601 on trans. of John Gordon.—[*Reg. Sec. Sig.*, lxxii, 67.] [1601]

THOMAS GAIRDYNE, inst. 12th Jan. 1670. [1669]

JAMES WALKER, his daughs.—Helen Grant, died at Edinburgh 4th Dec. 1929; Emma Katherine Gordon, died 15th Oct. 1926. [1844]

GEORGE ALEXANDER SELBIE, dem. 5th Oct. 1908; adm. to Coll. 14th Dec. 1927. [1864]

1867 ROBERT McKERRON was schoolmaster at Drainie while studying Divinity; his daugh., Isabella, died 21st May 1933; his son, Robert, died at Edinburgh 21st March 1937, was to have received LL.D., Aberdeen, 31st March 1937.

1909 ANDREW GRAY, his widow, Annie Amelia, daugh. of Peter Sanderson, The Birks, Galashiels, died at Edinburgh 8th April 1930.

1922 ALEXANDER WILLIAM WATT, dem. 31st Dec. 1942; his son, Adrian Gray, min. of Baillieston Old 30th April 1941.

CORGARFF

At Corriehoul there was near the Chapel of St Machar a well still known as Tobar Machar, or St Machar's Well. It was a place of pilgrimage. On 13th June 1613 the Kirk Session of Elgin decreed "that all merchants and others leave of to gang to the Well at Strathdon callit Michell (Machar ?) under pain of 10 merks each time."—[*Records of Elgin*, ii, 134.]

1923 GEORGE ARTHUR EVERETT WALKER, trans. to Benholme 7th Sept. 1927.

1928 HARRY LEGGATT, formerly of Wormit (*q.v.*); assistant Galston; adm. 16th Feb. 1928; dem. 12th Nov. 1930; died 13th May 1946. Marr. 23rd Feb. 1928 Isabel, daugh. of James Webster Morris and Sybilla Corrigall.

GLENBUCKET

Glenbucket was a chapel in Logie-Mar, but on 22nd April 1473 it was erected into a parish by Bishop Thomas Spens of Aberdeen, with consent of the Dean and Chapter of the Cathedral and of Sir Edward Makdowel, vicar of Logie-Mar. The deed of erection narrates the perils of storms and floods of waters that beset the inhabitants in travelling to and fro between Glenbucket and Logie through an uninhabitable tract of country and desert mountains, amid which in one day five or six people had perished when going to keep Easter at Logie Church. The Church of Glenbucket was to be served by a resident parochial chaplain, who was to have the church land of Chapeltone along with the great tithe both of Chapeltone and of the town of Balnaboth in Glenbucket and others, which belonged to Logie. He was also to have the altarages and other small emoluments, which also of old belonged to the vicar of Logie; with 20 sh. Scots yearly from the vicar of Logie in respect of his release from the cure of Glenbucket.—[*Reg. Epis. of Aberdeen*, i, 308–9.]

1567 WILLIAM COWPER, reader; in office 1563.—[*Comps. Sub Coll. of Thirds, Aberdeen*, etc.]

1572 GEORGE LIVINGSTONE, pres. to the parsonage and vicarage of Logiemar, "with the pendicle called Glenbucket, one of the common kirks of the Chanonry of Aberdeen," 18th Feb. 1572–3. —[*Reg. Pres. Bene.*, i, (4), 4.]

1582 ARTHUR SKENE, designated vicar 8th Dec. 1582, probably identical with A.S., reader at Logie-Mar 1567.—[*Reg. Mag. Sig.*, v, 859.]

1843 JOHN BREMNER, his daugh., Helen, died at Archieston 15th May 1945.

1886 WILLIAM ARTHUR SPARK, dem. 18th Dec. 1931; died 17th May 1932; his son, John, at Woodhead, Keithhall; a daugh. (marr. George Clerihew, Tilliefourie, Alford); his widow, Isabella Ogg, died 4th May 1948.

(*Charges united 4th July* 1932.)

KEIG

The Church of St Dianconianus (Diaconanus) of Keig was confirmed to the Priory of Monymusk by Bull of Pope Innocent III in 1200. It was also confirmed to the priory by William, Bishop of St Andrews, 1202–38.—[*Reg. Priory of St Andrews*, 366, 372.]

1576 JOHN STRACHAN, died before 13th Nov. 1603.—[*Aberdeen Sas.*, iii, 91.]

1683 ANDREW LIVINGSTONE, M.A., had issue by 2 marr.—Isabel, bapt. 4th Aug. 1722; a child, buried 4th Nov. 1729.

1876 THOMAS BELL, his widow, Eliza Foster Johnston, died 8th March 1926.

1906 JAMES STEWART, born 23rd Oct. 1864, dem. 16th May 1939; died 9th July 1942; his daugh., Isobel Rankin, M.A., LL.B.(Edin.), marr. 23rd Nov. 1932 Edgar Ralph Wide, M.B., Ch.B., D.T.M. & H., Medical Missionary at Baringa, Congo, and Govt. (Belgian) M.O.H. for District; his widow, Janet Turnbull, died 20th Feb. 1946.

(*Charges united 16th May*, 1937.)

KENNETHMONT

1587 WILLIAM BARCLAY, M.A., pres. to vicarage of "Kynathmont Christis Kirk" 27th May 1587 on death of James Spittal.—[*Reg. Pres. Bene.*, ii, 176.]

1607 GEORGE SPENS, vicar, son of James S., vicar of Insch.—[Macfarlane's *Gen. Coll.*, ii, 43.]

1687 WILLIAM GARIOCH, marr. 5th Feb. 1712 Helen, daugh. of George Leith of Treefield.—[*Rayne Reg.*]

1870 THOMAS BURNETT, died at Aberdeen 27th May 1926.

1924 ANDREW WELSH FARMS, trans. to Glenlivet 9th Nov. 1926.

1927 DAVID DUTHIE MACLAREN, trans. from Bressay 10th March 1927; dem. 30th Dec. 1931; died 8th April 1939.

(*Charges united 21st Feb.* 1932.)

RATHMUREAL or CHRIST'S KIRK

1563 WILLIAM THOMSON, reader in 1563; also at Leslie.—[*Comps. Sub Coll. of Thirds, Aberdeen*, etc.]

1587 WILLIAM BARCLAY, M.A., pres. to vicarage 27th May 1587 on death of James Spittal.—[*Reg. Pres. Bene.*, ii, 176.]

KILDRUMMY

Owing to the fact that at one time the church was surrounded by a marsh, it was called "the Chapel of the Loch." Of the old church there remain only parts of the north and east walls and the Elphinstone burial-place which was the south aisle. After the Elphinstones left Kildrummy the tomb fell into a state of disrepair, but, as its inscription tells, it was "Restored by William, 15th Lord Elphinstone, 1862." There was also a chapel dedicated to St Moluag, now called Sammiluah's Chapel, near Battlehillock.

At Clova there was a Columban monastery. The church and monastery stood on rising ground on the left bank of the Burn of Littlemill, a tributary of the Mossat Burn. Foundations indicate a church 31 feet long and 15 feet wide. The monastery was annexed to the Monastery of Mortlach, and later to the See of Aberdeen. In 1266 Robert, Bishop of Aberdeen, gave the church, along with the Church of Dalmeath, for the maintenance of the lights and ornaments of the High Altar in the cathedral. On 18th Jan. 1362-3 Alexander Kinninmonth, Bishop of Aberdeen, united the Churches of Clova and Kildrummy, on account of the weakness of the fruits of the two benefices, and presented a fit vicar.—[*Reg. Epis. of Aberdeen*, i, 102, 103, ii, 29; McConnachie's *Donside*, 84; *Place Names of West Aberdeenshire*, 295.]

1560 SIR JOHN GREIG, vicar 29th April 1560, and designated vicar-pensioner 18th Nov. 1577; died before 24th Jan. 1587-8.—[*Reg. Great Seal*, iv, 1638, 1647; *Acts and Dec.*, lxviii, 369; *Reg. Sec. Seal*, lvi, 151.]

1587 ALEXANDER CHEYNE, M.A., pres. to vicarage 21st Jan. 1587-8 on death of Sir John Greig.—[*Reg. Sec. Sig.*, lvi, 161.]

DONALD STEWART MACKENZIE,
1910 dem. 24th Feb. 1926; app. min. of Gartcosh, Glasgow, 3rd April 1926.

JOHN HEGGIE, trans. from Crieff West (*q.v.*) 9th Sept. 1926; dem. 1st Dec. 1931; died 13th Feb. 1932; his widow, Jessie Baird Hislop, died 5th April 1946.
1926

LEOCHEL

The church was granted to the Priory of Monymusk by Gilchrist, Earl of Mar *cir.* 1182–1211; he also granted ½ davach of land comprising the site of the church, which was confirmed by Colin, Hostiarius of the King, for the souls of himself and Ada, his wife, and by Philip de Monte, and Anna, his wife, daugh. and heiress of Colin. Apparently about 1220 a dispute about the church between Duncan, son of Morgrund, Earl of Mar, and David (Donald ?), son of the Earl (i.e. of Morgrund), was settled, at the request of Alexander, by each surrendering his rights in the church in the King's hands in favour of the priory.

There was a chapel at Lenturk. Chapel Croft, a short distance south-east of Craigievar, and Chapel Yard on the farm of Corbanchory, suggest ancient places of worship; and on the farm of Newton Corse is the site of Terry Croft.—[*Coll. of the Shires of Aberdeen and Banff*, 597; *Reg. Priory of St Andrews*, 63–4, 373.]

GEORGE FORBES, brother of John Forbes of Newe; his mother, Christian, daugh. of John Shepherd, min. of Leochil.
1768

WILLIAM MALCOLM, son of William M. Line 3, delete "M.A. (1812)"—[*Scot. Notes and Queries*, May 1935, 79.]
1821

ALEXANDER TAYLOR, his daugh., Isabella, died 3rd Dec. 1930.
1839

GEORGE HENDERSON GRASSICK, dem. 8th June 1927, died 18th Feb. 1934; his widow, Anne Reid, died 30th Aug. 1940.
1879

JAMES MONTGOMERIE BINNIE, trans. from Unst (*q.v.*) 9th Nov. 1927; dem. 1st Oct. 1937; his wife, Jenny Pollok, died at Glasgow 21st March 1939.
1927

CUSHNIE

WILLIAM FORBES, was chaplain here 31st Aug. 1574; had a natural son, James, burgess of Aberdeen, who received letters of legitimation 1st Sept. 1574.—[*Reg. Mag. Sig.*, iv, 181, 2299.]
1574

PATRICK COPLAND, his daugh., Agnes (marr. 22nd Oct. 1702 William Forbes, Buchaam, Strathdon).
1672

STRATHDON or INNERNOCHTIE

There was a chapel at Corriehoul, on the east bank of Allt Coire Tholl, at Corgarff, dedicated to St Machar. There was also a graveyard used for interments as late at least as the 18th century. A well near by still bears the saint's name. Another chapel in the Corgarff district was situated at Ord. Tomanchapil in the parish is "Chapel Knoll," Tom an t-seipeil. A church that dated from 1757 was demolished in 1851, and the present edifice erected on the site.—[McConnochie's *Donside*, 115, 120; *Coll. of the Shires of Aberdeen and Banff*, 616; *Place Names of West Aberdeenshire*, 328.]

Innernochtie. The church was granted to the Priory of Monymusk by Gilchrist, Earl of Mar, before 1200. On the gift of Thomas, Earl of Mar, Bishop Alexander de Kinninmond II, on 12th July 1356, erected the church into a prebend of Aberdeen Cathedral. From 1361 to 1513 the prebend was augmented by the Church of Auchindoir. —[*Reg. Priory of St Andrews*, 370–2, 374; *Reg. Epis. of Aberdeen*, i, 82.] (See Auchindoir.)

ALEXANDER ROSS, reader, in office 1563.—[*Comps. Sub Coll. of Thirds, Aberdeen*, etc.]
1567

JAMES ELPHINGSTONE; this is a mistake; should be John Elphingstone, M.A., second son of Alexander, Lord Elphingstone, born 4th June
1581

1536; pres. to the parsonage when an infant; on 29th Oct. 1537 purports as parson to have witnessed an instrument, and again on 19th Aug. 1538; appears in 1542 as Canon of Aberdeen and Prebendary of Invernochtie; on 26th Sept. and 8th Oct. 1581 he conveyed to Mr George Barclay, burgess of Aberdeen, and Marjorie Cheyne, his wife, "the land of Iugeing pertaining to the parsonage, within the Chanonry of Old Aberdeen, on the west side, between the tenement and lodging of the rectory of Turriff on the north, the common way to the Cathedral on the east, the common vennel to the loch of Aberdeen on the south and the said loch on the west"; died in Aug. 1616. Marr. Agnes, daugh. of Sir David Bruce of Clackmannan, with issue—Michael; George; Mary.—[*The Lords of Elphingstone*, i, 86-8; *Sir John Cristisone's Prot. Bk.*, 248, 269; *Officers and Graduates of King's College*, 7, Spalding Club; *Reg, Abbrev. Feu-Charters of Ch. Lands*, ii, 320; *Stirling Test.*, 19th Oct. 1616.]

1651 WILLIAM WEDDERBURN, marr. before 27th May 1635 Marjorie Seaton, daugh. of Marjorie Lawsoune.—[*Aberdeen Sas.*, ix, 316.]

1881 WILLIAM WATT, his widow, Catherine Taylor, died 30th Jan. 1940.

1926 WILLIAM ARCHIBALD DOUGLAS COWIE, born at Maud 4th Oct. 1900, son of William C., min. of Maud; educ. at Peterhead Academy and Univ. of Aberdeen, M.A. (1922); licen. by Presb. of Fordoun June 1924; assistant Morningside, Edinburgh; ord. 28th July 1926; dem. 16th May 1932; adm. to Cummertrees 25th July 1935. Marr. 27th Nov. 1926 Janet, daugh. of James Ross Campbell, M.A., schoolmaster, Daviot, Aberdeenshire, and Annie Garden, and has issue—William Campbell, born 3rd July 1928; Ian Douglas, born 8th Aug. 1931; Constance Margaret, born 5th Aug. 1933.

TOUGH

1563 GILBERT BROWN, reader 1563.—[*Comps. Sub Coll. of Thirds, Aberdeen*, etc.]

1563 ROBERT SKENE, exhorter 1563, also at Tarland.—[*Comps. Sub Coll. of Thirds, Aberdeen*, etc.]

1563 JOHN STRACHAN, min. in 1563.—[*Comps. Sub Coll. of Thirds, Aberdeen*, etc.]

1663 JOHN MAIR, his eldest son, George.—[*Deeds, Durie*, 1706, 20, 574.]

1706 PATRICK COPLAND, son of Patrick C., min. of Cushnie; had issue—Agnes; William, min. of Forbes.

1897 THOMAS DAVIDSON, dem. 30th Sept. 1939; died 13th Jan. 1947. Marr. 24th June 1925 Elsie Marie, daugh. of James Christie.

TOWIE or KINBATTOCH

Kinbattoch appears also as Kynbethot, Kynbethoc, Kilbethok, Bethoc, now Beathay, is a woman's name; and here it may be the name of an otherwise unknown saint.—[Watson's *Celtic Place Names*, 312.]

1561 SIR THOMAS STEVENSON, chaplain of Towie.—[*Comps. Sub Coll. of Thirds, Aberdeen*, etc.]

1562 DAVID GUTHRIE, parson 1562.—Orme's *Description of the Chanonry*, etc., 159.]

1563 DAVID ARROT, reader in 1563.—[*Comps. Sub Coll. of Thirds, Aberdeen*, etc.]

1888 ALEXANDER JACK, his widow, Jane Ann Loch, died at Helensburgh 23rd Nov. 1926.

1921 GEORGE PORTEOUS McWILLIAM, trans. to Beath 16th Oct. 1929. Addl. issue—a daugh., born 5th Feb. 1933.

(*Charges united 3rd Feb.* 1930.)

TULLYNESSLE and FORBES

The church was confirmed to Aberdeen Cathedral by Bull of Pope Adrian IV in 1157; and on 22nd April 1376 it was erected into a prebend of the cathedral by

Bishop Alexander de Kinninmond II. At Whitehaugh there are fields called respectively Temple Close and St John's Close.—[*Reg. Epis. of Aberdeen*, i, 5-7, 119; *Place Names of West Aberdeenshire*, 344.]

1562 SIR WILLIAM CABELL, parson 1562-3.—[*Comps. Sub Coll. of Thirds, Aberdeen*, etc.]

1564 JOHN KENNEDY, M.A., clerk to the Diocese of Aberdeen, received from William Gordon, Bishop of Aberdeen, on 8th Jan. 1564-5, the parsonage then possessed by William Cabell, canon of Aberdeen, or any other rectory or benefice to be vacant; confirmed by Crown Charter 23rd Jan. 1565-6; he entered on the parsonage soon after; was also vicar of Inverurie and Gamrie.—[*Cal. of Charters*, ix, 1975; *Reg. Sec. Sig.*, xxxiv, 38.]

1573 JAMES FORBES, M.A., pres. to vicarage of Tullynessle 21st Nov. 1573, vacant by non-compearance of Alexander Anderson.—[*Reg. Pres. Bene.*, i, (4), 13.]

1589 ALEXANDER GUTHRIE, M.A., pres. to parsonage and vicarage 7th Aug. 1590 on death of John Kennedy.—*Reg. Sec. Sig.*, lxi, 23.]

1858 WILLIAM PAULL, his widow, Mary Charlotte Stephen, died at Banchory 22nd Oct. 1930; his daugh., Eliza Erskine, died at Banchory 2nd April 1939; his son, James George, O.B.E., Advocate, Aberdeen, died 11th Feb. 1947.

1924 WILLIAM GREIG STRACHAN, trans. to Aberfoyle 23rd Nov. 1927.

1928 JAMES CHRYSTAL MUIR, formerly of Fowlis Wester (*q.v.*); adm. 18th May 1928; dem. 1st Nov. 1940.

(*The parishes were united in* 1808.)

FORBES

1563 JOHN PHILIP, min. in 1563.—[*Comps. Sub Coll. of Thirds, Aberdeen*, etc.] (See Alford and Skene.)

1574 PATRICK MORTIMER, as reader here pres. to vicarage 7th March 1574 on dem. of John Row and Andrew Row.—[*Reg. Pres. Bene.*, i, (4), 31.]

1574 JAMES WALKER, reader Nov. 1570.—[*Reg. of Ministers*, 66.]

1763 WILLIAM COPLAND, son of Patrick C., min. of Tough.

PRESBYTERY OF GARIOCH

BLAIRDAFF

1887 GEORGE KEITH, brother of Sir Arthur K., dem. 1926, died at Cheltenham, New South Wales, 7th May 1930.

1890 RICHARD ROBB, dem. 31st Aug. 1934; died 23rd Sept. 1938; his wife, Jane Tinning, died 17th Oct. 1927.

(*Charges united 2nd Sept. 1934.*)

BOURTIE

1566 ALEXANDER HARVIE, M.A., "ane chaplain of the chaplainry Cullane, founded at the High Altar thereof"; pres. to vicarage 12th April 1566 on dem. of Sir David Harvie.—[*Reg. Sec. Sig.*, xxxiv, 37.]

1567 ANDREW DUMBRECK, reader 1563; pres. to vicarage 4th Oct. 1575 on death of Sir David Harvie.—[*Reg. Pres. Bene.*, i, 222; i, (4), 36, ii, 117; *Comps. Sub Coll. of Thirds, Aberdeen*, etc.]

1611 GILBERT KEITH, marr. Katherine Burnett and had issue—Gilbert; John; George, bapt. 25th Dec. 1650. —[*Aberdeen Sas.*, xii, 416, 29th May 1643.]

1644 ROBERT BROWNE, had issue—Isabel, bapt. 13th July 1654; William, bapt. 1st April 1657; Mary, bapt. 9th June 1659; Anne, bapt. 10th Nov. 1661; Robert, bapt. 25th March 1664.

1878 WILLIAM LESLIE DAVIDSON, died at Elgin 4th Sept. 1929.

1896 MICHAEL JAMES MACPHERSON, died 5th June 1932; his wife, Anne Grant, died 9th Aug. 1929; his daugh., Margaret (marr. 7th Nov. 1930 Alastair G. M. Macpherson, son of John G. M., schoolmaster, Cruden).

(*Charge united with Meldrum 3rd Nov. 1940.*)

CHAPEL OF GARIOCH and LOGIE DURNO

In the concluding part of the 12th century the Church of Durnach (Logiedurno) was granted to Lindores Abbey by David, Earl of Huntingdon, brother of William the Lion, who had founded the abbey on his return from the Holy Land in 1178. In 1599 a new church was built at the site of the Chapel of Garioch, from which the united parish subsequently took its name. In the charter of the Lordship of Lindores to Patrick Leslie, Lord Lindores, on 31st March 1600, the said Patrick is held bound to pay 100 merks stipend to "the minister of Logiedurno, now translated to Chapel of Garioch." Apparently some time elapsed before the new name was in general use, but on 3rd July 1637 there occurs "the parish of Logiedurno called Chapel of Garioch." The church of 1599 was repaired about 1744; and in 1813 it was replaced by the present church. The Church of Fetternear is said to have granted to the See of Aberdeen by Malcolm IV on 21st Aug. 1164; and it was confirmed on 26th Nov. 1359 by Pope Adrian. The Chapel of Garioch, dedicated to the Virgin, was in existence in the first half of the 14th century. In the Exchequer Rolls of 1364 there appears the sum of £5 Scots expended for boards to repair the chapel. James IV visited the chapel on 23rd Oct. 1497, and in Sept. 1562 Queen Mary, on a visit to the district, was present in it at a celebration of Mass. In a charter of 1519 it was designated the Royal Chapel, which may indicate that it was founded by a Scottish

CHAPEL OF GARIOCH and LOGIE DURNO

sovereign. In the chapel there were six chaplainries, to each of which there were attached a manse and croft for the chaplain. They were Colliehill, Conglas (Knokinglass), Pitcaple, Pitgavny, Wardis (Wardhouse) and Wartle. Of the foundations of the chaplainries there are the following records: Between 1328 and 1342 Christian Bruce, lady of the Garioch, sister of Robert I and widow of Sir Andrew de Moray, founded a chaplainry in the chapel for the souls of Robert I, herself, her late husband, Sir Andrew de Moray, the endowment being a toft and a croft of 1 acre in the tenement of Drumdarnach, and an annual rent of 100 sh. sterling from the lands of Meikle Wartle. In 1384 Christian Bruce's granddaugh., Margaret Countess of Douglas, lady of Mar, daugh. of Donald, third Lord of the Isles, granted for the souls of herself, William, Earl of Douglas, her late husband, the late Thomas, Earl of Mar, and James, Earl of Douglas, her son, ten pounds from two parts of Pitgavny, and the whole town of Collishill with pertinents (except Westfield in Bourtie). Alexander Stewart, Earl of Mar, is said to have founded a chaplainry, possibly Conglas, for the souls of those slain at the Battle of Harlaw in 1411. In 1420 Isabel Mortimer, daugh. of Bernard M. of Craigievar, and widow of Sir Andrew Leslie of Balquhain, founded a chaplainry for the souls of her six sons slain at Harlaw, and of her husband killed at Braco by the Sheriff of Angus. On 28th Nov. 1474 James III confirmed a mortification of 12 merks annual rent from Balcomy, Fife, in the first instance, and Wardis and Quyltpat, Aberdeenshire, made by Alexander Leslie of Wardis, for the souls of himself and his wife Isabella. The Chaplainry of Pitcaple was founded before 24th Aug. 1511. On 14th April 1426 James I confirmed a grant by Sir Patrick de Ogilvie Kt. of Grandown, with consent of his father, Alexander de Ogilvie, Sheriff of Forfar, to a perpetual chaplain to celebrate for the soul of late Andrew de Leslie, Kt., of an annual rent of 10 merks from his lands of Strathalva, Banffshire, which failing, from the lands of Auchterhouse and Essy, Forfarshire. Sir Alexander Galloway, Chaplain of the Chaplainry of Colliehill, granted to the chaplainry 2 acres in the barony of Balquhain sold to him by William Leslie of B., for a manse for the chaplain of said chaplainry, who was to pay 5 sh. to the other five chaplains in the chapel, 12 pence each. This was confirmed by James IV on 24th Jan. 1505-6. The General Assembly on 29th Aug. 1639 and Parliament on 17th Nov. 1641 ratified the erection of the Hospital of Balhaggardy by Thomas Erskine of Pittoddrie, who gave as endowment the Chaplainries of Wartle, Colliehill, Pitgavny and Knokinglass, of which he was patron. "He had built a house of tua houses heighte at the Chapel of Garioch, with the intention to put some old poore and decrepit men therein for ther bettir accomodatione of ther service to God."— [*Reg. Mag. Sig.*, i, App. i, 61, 70, App. ii, 30, 133; ii, 41, 1188, 2914, 3124, vi, 1032, vii, 1778, 1873, viii, 1466, ix, 734, 1501; *Reg. Sec. Seal*, i, 1268, 3037, ii, 4803, iii, 842; *Acts Scott. Parl.*, v, 513, 605a; *Excheq. Rolls*, ii, 166, xiii, 478, 548; *Lord High Treasurer's Accs.*, i, 364; *Reg. Epis. of Aberdeen*, i, 57, 66-7, 84-6, 167-9, 222; *Chart. of Lindores*, 8, 9; Davidson's *Inverurie and Earldom of Garioch*, 80, 146-7.]

1561 SIR JOHN PHILP, vicar 1561 and 1563.—[*Comps. Gen. Coll. and Comps. Sub Coll. of Thirds, Aberdeen*, etc.]

1563 STEPHEN MASON, M.A., min. 1563.—[*Comps. Sub Coll. of Thirds, Aberdeen*, etc.]

1563 ANDREW SPEARS, reader 1563.—[*Comps. Sub Coll. of Thirds, Aberdeen*, etc.]

1567 JOHN LESLIE, reader in office 1563.—[*Comps. Sub Coll. of Thirds, Aberdeen*, etc.]

1588 WILLIAM STRACHAN, M.A., evidently son of James S., parson of Belhelvie; pres. to vicarage 11th Feb. 1588-9 on death of John Philp and on 14th Aug. 1589 and 19th July 1591 in succession to John Leslie.—[*Reg. Sec. Sig.*, lix, 22, 44, lxiv, 140.]

1592 ALEXANDER PATERSON, pres. 21st Oct. 1592 on death of William Strachan.—[*Reg. Sec. Sig.*, lxiv, 160.]

1635 ALEXANDER STRACHAN, the name of his wife, Katherine Strachan, indicates his identity with Alexander Strachan, son of Andrew S., min. of Duns, who marr. Katherine, daugh. of John Strachan, min. of Kincardine O'Neil, cont. 7th Oct. 1625; by mandate of the Bishop of Aberdeen, 8th June 1631, the Presb. cognosed designed, and by sasine of 5th July 1638 gave him possession of a glebe from church lands nearest the church, including four rigs called the Priest's Croft, with foggage, pasture, feall and divot, and a manse with toft and orchard. His daugh., Elizabeth (marr. William Strachan of Luesk, min. of Daviot); his sons—George; John, regent of King's College, Aberdeen, in 1651, 1655, and described as "the best scholar that ever was in the College," dem. the office of regent "because he could not live with the Covenanters," went abroad and "studied physick," and became a Doctor of Medicine, and after a visit to his native land, again went abroad, and "turned popish," became Rector of the Scots College at Rome, and died in that office.—[Oram's *Description of the Chanonry*, etc., *Old Aberdeen*, 160, 176–8; *Officers and Graduates of Univ. and King's College*, 191, 193; *Aberdeen Sas.*, xi, 104, 13th Feb. 1652, 214; *Gardenston Papers*; *Reg. of Deeds*, ccccviii, 356.]

1870 ALEXANDER YOUNG, his daugh., Helen Maitland (marr. Joseph Lawrence Hogan, Johannesburg), died at Aberdeen 21st March 1930; his sons—Andrew, died 7th Feb. 1928; Charles Maitland Cook, died at Aberdeen 16th May 1945.

1912 WILLIAM McNICOL, B.D., his daugh., Winifred Isobel, M.B., Ch.B., Medical Officer R.A.F. (marr. 22nd June 1942 Surgeon Lieut. Harold Preston Watson, son of Flight Lieut. Preston, R.N.A.S., Dundee).

(*Charges united* 31st Aug. 1941.)

FETTERNEIR

1560 ANDREW CULLEN, M.A., parson, died 7th July 1560, also vicar of St Nicholas, Aberdeen.—[*The Chronicle of Aberdeen*, 34.]

1569 ANDREW LESLIE, in office before 19th April 1568.—[*Cal. of Charters*, x, 2118.]

1571 JAMES CURRIE, pres. to parsonage and vicarage 20th May 1571 in succession to Andrew Leslie.—[*Reg. Sec. Sig.*, xxxix, 120.]

CULSALMOND

1563 STEPHEN MASON, M.A., min. in 1563. (See Logie Durno.)

1563 WILLIAM STRAITH, reader in 1563. —[*Comps. Sub Coll. of Thirds*, Aberdeen, etc.]

1574 ANDREW SPENS, had charge here as well as at Drumblade and Forgue 1574–6.

1607 THOMAS SPENS, son of Thomas S., tailor burgess of Aberdeen.

1916 WILLIAM MURDOCH, trans. to Cluny 22nd Feb. 1927; delete lines 5 and 6 "in 1913" and read "5th May 1914."

1927 ROBERT CHALMERS ANDERSON, trans. from Dulnain Bridge (*q.v.*) 15th July 1927; died 25th Feb. 1931; his widow, Jeanie Marshall Smith, died 14th April 1939.

DAVIOT

The Well of Our Lady was connected with the chapel and graveyard at Fingask, dedicated to the Virgin Mary. At the site about the beginning of last century, workmen digging to secure a foundation for a mausoleum discovered a silver crucifix.

1563 ANDREW THOMSON, exhorter 1563. —[*Comps. Sub Coll. of Thirds*, Aberdeen, etc.]

JOHN LESLIE, reader in 1563.—
1563 [*Comps. Sub Coll. of Thirds, Aberdeen*, etc.]

GEORGE PATERSON, pres. 13th July
1573 1573 to Treasurership of Aberdeen, which is the parsonage and vicarage of Daviot, vacant through Patrick Myrtoun failing to give consent to Articles of Religion, to take oath acknowledging Our Sovereign Lord and to give ordered prayers in Daviot Church.—[*Reg. Sec. Sig.*, xlii, 94.]

WILLIAM STRACHAN, along with
1613 his first wife, Grizel Smith, he acquired Leweck, Bayne, from John Leith of Harthill, 8th June 1631. Marr. (2) before 12th Feb. 1652 Elizabeth, daugh. of Alexander Strachan, min. of Chapel-of-Garioch; died after 26th July 1654; his son, William, M.A., marr. (1) 26th Nov. to 22nd Dec. 1637 Mabel, daugh. of George Garioch of Little Endownie, and (2) before 4th July 1654 Elizabeth Abercrombie.—[*Aberdeen Sas.*, vii, 359, (1631), xi, 559, (1637), xv, 214, (1652), xvii, 252, (1654).]

ALEXANDER LUNAN, line 10, for
1672 "daughter" read "sister." Marr. Janet, daugh. of William Elphinstone of Ross.

WILLIAM ANDERSON, marr. (1) 4th
1717 March 1720 Jean, daugh. of William Keith, min. of Keithhall.

ROBERT SHEPHERD, his son,
1788 Thomas, became laird of Kirkvilde, Skene.—[Michie's *Logie Colstone*, 192.]

ALEXANDER SMART, Ph.D., trans.
1923 to Broughty Ferry 24th March 1926; trans. to St Cuthbert's, Saltcoats, 11th Dec. 1940.

JAMES FYFE RENNIE, born Tarves
1926 13th Jan. 1897, son of William R., farmer, and Janet Fyfe; educ. at Kemnay School and Univ. of Aberdeen, M.A. (1922), B.D. (1925); licen. by Presb. of Garioch 27th March 1925; assistant at Riccarton, Kilmarnock; ord. 17th June 1926. Marr. 19th April 1939 Kathleen Mary Lauder and has issue—Helen Kathleen, born 21st March 1941; Winifred Helen Orton, born 23rd May 1943.

INSCH

Inchmabany, the former name of the parish, denotes my Bean's Haugh—St Bean. About the beginning of the second quarter of the 13th century, Sir Bartholomew Fleming was granted permission by the Abbot and Convent of Lindores to erect a chapel at Weredos (Wardhouse), he giving to the Church of St Drostan of Inchmabanin (Insch) and its rectors, that is Lindores Abbey, a toft and 2 acres of arable land adjoining the toft in his town of Ravengille between the great road and the moor towards Gillandreston, with the common easement of the same town, with common pasture for six "animals," one horse, and forty sheep, and also pledging himself that the said Church of Inchmabanin would suffer no injury nor lose any of its rights by the existence of the said chapel.—[*Chart of Lindores*, 65.]

WILLIAM BALLINGALL, reader in
1563 office 1563.—[*Comps. Sub Coll. of Thirds, Aberdeen*, etc.]

JAMES SPENS, pres. to vicarage 17th
1578 Sept. 1578 on dem. of William Ballingall; had issue—George, vicar of Kinnethmont; William; Alexander; a daugh.—[*Reg. Pres. Bene.*, ii, 4; Macfarlane's *Gen. Coll.*, ii, 43.]

WALTER LESLIE, pres. to vicarage
1578 8th Nov. 1578 on death of William Ballingall.—[*Reg. Pres. Bene.*, ii, 8.]

WILLIAM BARCLAY, pres. to
1596 vicarage 4th March 1598 on dep. of James Spens.—[*Reg. Sec. Sig.*, lxxxi, 49.]

ALEXANDER ROSS, probably adm.
1631 1631. Marr. Bessie Logie and had issue—Patrick.—[*Aberdeen Sas.*, xiv, 314, 9th June 1693; *Reg. of Deeds*, ccccxli, 10th June 1631.]

WILLIAM BURNETT, his daugh., Margaret (marr. Alexander Barclay, min. of Peterhead), who with her son-in-law and daugh. was living in Peterhead 1696.—[*Aberdeen Poll Tax Roll*, i, 572.]
1661

ALEXANDER MEARNS, line 5, delete "Father of the Church."
1729

JOHN MACK, died 12th Dec. 1932.
1899

ANDREW BURT, trans. from Cabrach (*q.v.*); adm. 17th Feb. 1927; trans. to Monikie 12th July 1939. Addl. issue—Robina, born 2nd Jan. 1925; Amelia Kirkwood, born 6th April 1927. Publication—*Our Village* (1933).
1927

INVERURIE

The Church of Inverurie with the Chapel of Monkegie appears in the charter granted to Lindores Abbey by the abbey's founder, David, Earl of Huntingdon, brother of William the Lion. In Pope Celestine III's Bull of Lindores, 8th March 1195, the grant takes the form—the Church of Rothkel with its chapels of Inverurie and Munkegie, and the same occurs three years later in the Bull of Pope Innocent III. Rothkel and Munkeggie appear in combination in the Register of the Episcopate of Aberdeen in a charter of King William the Lion, of date 1175-99. But Rothkel as applied to a parish passed out of use at an early stage. Apparently about the beginning of the second quarter of the 13th century Sir Simon of Garentuly (Gartly) received permission from the Abbot and Convent of Lindores to erect a private chapel at his manor of Crimond, within the enclosure of his court, where he and his family may hear Divine Service. The conditions were that he and his tenants holding of him should come, on the principal festivals, in the accustomed manner, to the mother Church of Inverurie; that Sir Simon and his heirs do fealty to said church, as likewise should the chaplains serving in the chapel; and that Sir Simon and his heirs should give annually to the said church 2 lb. of wax at the Feast of the Assumption of St Mary—15th Aug.—[*Chart of Lindores*, 2-3, 64, 102, 107; *Reg. Epis. of Aberdeen*, i, 9.]

SIR WILLIAM CABELL, vicar 1562-3.—[*Comps. Sub Coll. of Thirds, Aberdeen*, etc.]
1562

JAMES RYND, reader 1563.—[*Comps. Sub Coll. of Thirds, Aberdeen*, etc.]
1563

JOHN KENNEDY, M.A., his gift of and collation to the vicarage of Inverurie and Montkeggie by William Gordon, Bishop of Aberdeen, confirmed by Crown Charter 22nd Jan. 1565-6.—[*Reg. Sec. Sig.*, xxxiv, 35.] (See Tullynessle.)
1565

ALEXANDER MACKIE, as min. pres. to vicarage 13th Sept. 1589 on death of John Kennedy.—[*Reg. Sec. Sig.*, lix, 57.]
1574

JOHN MILL or MILNE, his first wife, Margaret Leslie, was daugh. of William L. of New Leslie, by his second wife, Elizabeth Forbes; issue—his son, Andrew, died 8th Feb. 1636, and daugh., Jean, 14th Feb. 1637.—[*Inverurie Reg.*]
1600

WILLIAM FORBES, had issue—Margaret, bapt. 26th Nov. 1646; Elizabeth, bapt. 4th Nov. 1648.
1643

WILLIAM MURRAY, his son, William, M.A., died 23rd Jan. 1754, aged 46, apparently identical with William Murray, preacher of the Gospel, Old Aberdeen, who marr. Elizabeth Irvine (died 16th Feb. 1725), with issue—Elizabeth (buried 17th Dec. 1724); John (buried 8th Nov. 1725).—[*Old Machar Reg.*]
1679

JOHN DAVIDSON, his daugh., Isabella, died at Dollar 15th June 1941.
1844

JAMES BLACK, his father was schoolmaster of Cruden; died 10th July 1936.
1890

KEITHHALL

Monkeggie. Monkeggie does not appear as a separate parish in the 12th century.

The "paroch Kyrk of Monkege" occurs in 1481. There was in the church an altar of St Serf.—[*Chart. of Lindores*, xii; *Coll. of the Shires of Aberdeen and Banff*, 569.] (See Inverurie.)

1683 WILLIAM KEITH, marr. cont. 25th July 1695 Elspeth (died before 18th June 1702), daugh. of John Logie of Boddome.—[*Deeds, Dal.*, 1705, No. 1018.]

1821 JOHN KEITH, his daugh., Frances Alexandrina, died at Edinburgh 24th July 1940.

1923 ALEXANDER RAE GRANT, trans. to Cults West 17th March 1938. Marr. 21st Sept. 1926 Elizabeth, M.A., elder daugh. of William Frain, Aberdeen, and Jean Maclean, and has issue—Alexander Frain, born 5th April 1929; Mayra Esme Rae, born 20th July 1933.

KINKELL

The Kirk of Kinkell was "of auld erected in ane benefice and parsonage quhairof" these "kirkis were proper parts and pendicles"—Dyce, Drumblade, Skene, Kintore, Kemnay, Kinellar. By Act of Parliament in 1649 those churches were separated from Kinkell, along with the right of patronage and the title to the teinds in each case, and each became an independent parish, each min. becoming titular and having right to the teinds, fruits, rents, and other emoluments. In 1663, after the establishment of Episcopacy, those churches, described along with Kinkell as the parsonage of the same, were annexed to the Deanery of St Andrews, and that was ratified by Act of Parliament in that year. After the Revolution Settlement each parish resumed its independent status.

Among its notable rectors in pre-Reformation times were Henry de Lichten, who in 1426 became Bishop of Aberdeen and erected the Cathedral of St Machar; Alexander Anderson, who became the last Roman Catholic Principal of King's College; and Alexander Galloway, one of the chapter of the cathedral, who erected the Church of Kinkell, of which the ruin is all that remains.—[*Acts of Parl.*, vi, (2), 183, vii, 453.]

1561 JOHN DAVIDSON, M.A., parson and, in 1563, Principal of Glasgow University.—[*Comps. Gen. Coll. and Sub Coll. of Thirds, Aberdeen*, etc.]

1563 ALEXANDER ANDERSON, M.A., vicar; also at Methlick and Tyrie.—[*Comps. Sub Coll. of Thirds, Aberdeen*, etc.]

1574 JAMES CURRIE, reader here, pres. to vicarage 5th July 1573 vacant by Alexander Anderson, sometime Principal of the College of Aberdeen, not compearing before the Commissioners of Kirks.—[*Reg. Pres. Bene.*, i, (4), 9.]

1583 THOMAS LUMSDEN, M.A., pres. 15th Dec. 1566 to the parsonage of Kinkell "callit a prebendarie of the Cathedral Kirk of Aberdeen, on res. of Harry Lumsden, his father's brother"; his son, William of Ardmurdo, advocate in Aberdeen 1624; his daugh., Katherine (marr. Patrick Gordon 2nd of Nethermuir).—[*Reg. Sec. Sig.*, xxxv, 102; *Comps. Gen. Coll. of Thirds*,] (See Kirkforthar.)

1644 WILLIAM LEITH, min. 15th April 1644.

1650 JOHN GELLIE, M.A., marr. 30th Jan. 1649 Maria Jeffrey.—[*Aberdeen Reg.*]

1683 THOMAS WEMYSS of Fingask. Marr. Janet, daugh. of Patrick Wemyss of Gradney.—[*Signature*, 19th Dec. 1697.]

KEMNAY

The church pertained to the parsonage of Kinkell (*q.v.*). The pre-Reformation building, the High Altar of which was apparent, though built over, was removed to make way for the present church in 1844.—[McConnochie's *Donside*, 61.]

1561 SIR JOHN CRISTISON, vicar 1561-3; chaplain of Kirkinglass.—[*Comps. Gen. and Sub Coll. of Thirds, Aberdeen*, etc.]

1563 THOMAS GRAY, reader 1563.—[*Comps. Sub Coll. of Thirds, Aberdeen*, etc.]

1563 JAMES MURRAY, min. 1563; also at Monymusk.—[*Comps. Sub Coll. of Thirds, Aberdeen*, etc.]

1641 JOHN SEATON, min. here before 5th July 1641; Regent and Professor of Natural Philosophy at Marischal College cir. 1626–41; nominated Professor of Divinity at Marischal College 11th March 1646, but the nomination does not appear to have taken effect.—[*Recs. of Marischal College and Univ.*, i, 130n, 170 and n, 251, ii, 34, 35.]

1650 DAVID LEITCH, had issue—Marie, bapt. 4th Nov. 1643; Andrew, bapt. 9th Dec. 1644; George, bapt. 6th Feb. 1648.—[*Old Machar Reg.*]

1924 ROBERT KELTIE, trans. to Humbie 24th Sept. 1931; died in his garden 14th Sept. 1937. Addl. issue— Janie Thomson, born 5th Dec. 1925.

(*Charges united 3rd Dec.* 1929.)

KINTORE

The church pertained to the parsonage of Kinkell (*q.v.*). The present church was built in 1879. There was a chapel at Halforrest. Lands of the Holy Cross and of the Holy Rood and the "Lammies Rood" at Kintore may indicate altars in the church dedicated to the Holy Cross and to St Peter in Chains.—[*Coll. of the Shires of Aberdeen and Banff*, 249; McConnochie's *Donside*, 37; Sir John Cristison's *Prot. Book*, 266, 284, 422; *Reg. Mag. Sig.*, v. 1836.]

1563 JOHN CHALMERS, reader in 1563.—[*Comps. Sub Coll. of Thirds, Aberdeen*, etc.]

1649 ANDREW STRACHAN, marr. Jean Irving (who marr. (2) James Wilson, Kintore) and had issue—Patrick (eldest), min. of Dramoir, Ireland; Janet.—[*Aberdeen Sas.*, xi, 242, 22nd June 1682.]

1727 GEORGE MOIR, his daugh., Agnes (marr. 27th July 1748).

1833 ROBERT SIMPSON, his sons—William Lawrence, died at Dunedin 10th June 1927; Archibald Foote, died Aberdeen 27th April 1930; David, died Sydney 3rd April 1936.

1843 WILLIAM ROSS, his daugh., Jane Anne, died 29th June 1938.

1920 JOHN FRASER, trans. from Monquhitter (*q.v.*) 10th July 1929; adm. to United Charge 29th Dec. 1929; trans. to Dunfermline North 4th July 1929.

1929 FRANK ROBERTSON, trans. from Monquhitter (*q.v.*).

(*Charges united 3rd Dec.* 1929.)

LESLIE

The Church of Leslie was granted to Lindores Abbey by Norman, Constable of Inverurie Castle, son of Malcolm, confirmation by John, Earl of Huntingdon, in 1219–32. At the Reformation the church was united to the Church of Premnay. The union was dissolved apparently soon after 29th April 1625. The church was rebuilt in 1815. There was a chapel at the place called Chapelton.—[*Chart of Lindores*, lvi, 18, 82, 90, 340; *Reg. Great Seal*, vi, 1032, vii, 1717, viii, 548, 780.]

1561 SIR THOMAS RAITH, vicar in 1561.—[*Reg. Abbrev. Feu Charters of Church Lands*, i, 152.]

1563 ANDREW OGILVY, M.A., min. also at Premnay.—[*Comps. Sub Coll. of Thirds, Aberdeen*, etc.]

1563 WILLIAM THOMSON, reader in 1563, also at Christ's Church.—[*Comps. Sub Coll. of Thirds, Aberdeen*. etc,]

1580 WALTER INNES, pres. to vicarage 23rd Feb. and 25th March 1582–3 on death of Thomas Raith; still in office 1584.—[*Reg. Pres. Bene.*, ii, 86; *Reg. Sec. Sig.*, lii, 15.]

1600 WILLIAM FORBES, M.A., min. here, pres. to Kingoldrum 28th Dec. 1588.—[*Reg. Sec. Sig.*, lxix, 263.]

1720 ROBERT ABERCROMBIE, his son, John, died 1820.

JOHN RUSSELL, his daugh., Isabella
1876 Margaret, died 9th March 1936.

JOHN DALGLEISH CARMICHAEL,
1926 dem. 31st Dec. 1934, died 2nd Sept. 1940. Marr. Isa Watson Cameron Stuart Bayne, died 6th Dec. 1938.

(*Charges united 1st Jan.* 1934.)

MELDRUM or BETHELNIE

The Lady's Well was connected with the chapel at Chapelharsey dedicated to the Virgin Mary.—[Mackinlay's *Ancient Church Dedications*, 109.]

THOMAS MILL, reader 1563.—
1563 [*Comps. Sub Coll. of Thirds, Aberdeen*, etc.]

WILLIAM FORBES, M.A., min. before 28th Dec. 1588, when he was
1588 pres. to vicarage of Kingoldrum.—
[*Reg. Sec. Sig.*, lxix, 261.]

GEORGE LEITH, marr. (2) Anna
1643 Forbes and had issue—Patrick, min. of Lumphanan.

JAMES CRUICKSHANK EASTON,
1852 his son, Harry Montgomery, W.S., died 28th March 1932; his daugh., Mary (marr. –. Roger at Balerno Hall, Balerno).

JOHN CHRISTOPHER NISBET, marr.
1924 15th Sept. 1934 Ella, daugh. of Robert Anderson; line 6, for "1914" read "1915," and line 8, for "1920" read "1921"; dem. 27th Nov. 1943.

MONYMUSK

It is said that about 1080 a Culdee priory was founded here by Malcolm Canmore. Proceeding upon a military expedition against the people of Moray, he halted at Monymusk, and there he made a vow that, should the expedition prove successful, he would devote the village to St Andrew and at it found and endow a priory. He returned successful, having secured a bloodless victory through the intervention of priests; and the priory was duly established. Before 1200 Gilchrist, Earl of Mar *cir*. 1182–1211, took steps to convert the settlement into an Augustinian priory. He built a cell in the Church of St Mary of Monymusk where the Culdees were, and conveyed to the same the Churches of Leochel, Ruchaven (Logy-Ruthven, Logie-Mar) and Invernochtie (Strathdon). He also granted the Church of Alford before 1207. Other churches belonging to the priory were Inverdrochit (Braemar), the gift of Duncan, Earl of Mar 1228–43, and Keig, confirmed by William, Bishop of St Andrews 1202–38. In 1211 the Abbots of Melrose and Dryburgh, and the Archdeacon of Glasgow, acting as Papal Delegates, confirmed an agreement between William, Bishop of St Andrews, and the Culdees of Monymusk, which provided that the Culdees have a prefectory, a dormitory, and an oratory without a cemetery, and the right of burial in the cemetery of the parish church, the rights of the Mother Church being reserved, and further that there be twelve Culdee canons, and the thirteenth, Bricius, be the master or prior, in conformity with the constitution of the Augustinian Priory of St Andrews. It may be that the oratory was situated outside the parish church. In the first part of the 16th century there occurs mention of the "Parish Church of St Mary of Monymusk," of the "Nave of the Church of the Monastery of Monymusk," of the "Cemetery of the Parish Church of Monymusk," and of the "Cemetery of the Monastery of Monymusk." In any case the parish church, in which there was an altar dedicated to St Michael, was made a Prebend of Aberdeen in 1445. Of the 12th-century church there survive in the present church the tower with Norman doorway, vaulted basement and Norman arch entering into the church, and the choir with Norman arch. In 1822 the church was enlarged by the addition of a north aisle. At the same time the roof was repaired, the church was equipped with seats, and the spire of the tower renewed. In 1890 the spire, then in a dangerous condition, was removed, and the existing Norman battlements were erected by Sir Arthur H. Grant. In the parish there were three chapels, one at Balvach near Ton Burn, another west of the site of the toll-house at Tillyfourie, and another, dedicated to St Finan, at Abersnithock, near Braehead.—[*Reg. Priory of St Andrews*, 362–3, 370–1, 372–4; *Reg. Epis. of Aberdeen*, i, 16; Sir John Cristison's *Prot. Bk.*, 28, 61, 81, 136, 138, 144.]

1563 JAMES MURRAY, min. in 1563; pres. in 1573 on death of John Hay, Commendator of Balmerino.—[*Comps. Sub Coll. of Thirds, Aberdeen*, etc.; *Reg. Pres. Bene.*, i, (4), 15.]

1574 JAMES JOHNSTON, pres. in 1574 on death of John Hay; had issue—James, M.A.—[*Reg. Pres. Bene.*, i, (4), 23; *Aberdeen Sas.*, i, 1 Ser. 178.]

1605 ALEXANDER SCROGIE, M.A., pres. to vicarage and parsonage 20th May 1605 on depriv. of James Johnston.—[*Reg. Sec. Sig.*, lxxvi, 310; *Gordonston Papers*.]

1629 JOHN GELLIE, his widow marr. (2) Walter Ogilvie, min. of Deskford.

1678 JOHN BURNET, had issue—Isabel, bapt. 15th March 1680; Jean, bapt. 15th May 1686.

1853 THOMAS HENRY DAWSON, his widow, Mary Milne, died 8th Dec. 1926.

1869 WILLIAM MEARNS MACPHERSON, his daugh., Bessie Beadnell, died at Wells 25th Aug. 1942.

1920 FREDERICK WILLIAM LOVIE, his widow, Alice Gordon Wyness, marr. (2) 27th May 1932.

1924 JAMES GRANT FORBES, trans. to Forteviot 17th May 1927.

1927 ROBERT CAMPBELL MARSHALL, trans. from Ardallie (*q.v.*) 14th Nov. 1927; died 31st May 1937; had issue—Duncan, born 1st, died 2nd April 1912; Hilda Margaret, born 7th April 1916 (marr. 7th Dec. 1940 David Sinclair, 2nd Lieut. R.A., son of G. B. Tonybee, Rosegarth, Dalkeith); Eric, born 7th April 1918, died 10th April 1918.

OYNE

There was a Chapel of St Ninian at Pitmedden.

1559 JOHN LESLIE, D.D.; ind. to parsonage and vicarage 2nd July 1559; born 1526 or 29th Sept. 1527; said to be the son of Gavin L., fourth son of Alexander L. of Balquhane, but Buchanan calls him "priest's geitt" (spurious son of a priest), and Knox calls him "bastard," on the ground that his father, Gavin Leslie, parson of Kingussie and Commissary of Ross, was in priest's orders, and was not married to his reputed wife, Miss Butter, daugh. of the laird of Gormack. On 19th July 1538 a dispensation or legitimation under papal authority was granted by Alexander Sutherland, official of Moray, in favour of John Leslie, scholar in Moray, enabling him, notwithstanding defect of birth, to receive holy orders; Canon of Aberdeen and Ellon; prebendary of Aberdeen, vicar of Dyce; Professor of Canon Law at Univ. and King's College, Aberdeen; Abbot of Lindores 1564; Bishop of Ross in Jan. 1565 in succession to Henry Sinclair; Lord Ordinary of the College of Justice Jan. 1565; sent to France by the Catholic Party to offer Queen Mary their services, and to invite her back; accompanied her on her return, and afterwards rendered her service; died at Brussels 3rd May 1596; said to have had three daughs.—Janet (marr. Andrew Leslie of New Leslie); ——, marr. Richard Irvine; ——, marr. –. Cruickshank of Tillymorgan. In 1578 he published his *De Origine Moribus et Rebus Gestis Scotorum*.—[*Records of the Leslies*, iii, 401–2; Brunton and Haig's *Senators of the College of Justice*, 116; both of which see for full account.]

1570 ALEXANDER LESLIE, M.A., parson before 20th July 1570, died before 21st July 1571.—[*Reg. Sec. Sig.*, lxi, 12; *Reg. Mag. Sig.*, iv, 2222; *Reg. Pres. Bene.*, i, (2), 17.]

1571 JOHN ABERCROMBY, son of Alexander A. of Petmeddan, pres. to parsonage and vicarage 4th July 1571 on death of Andrew Leslie and forfeiture of John Leslie, Bishop of Ross.—[*Reg. Pres. Bene.*, i, (2), 17.]

ROBERT BURNETT, Margaret Leslie
1596 was his widow, not his first wife.

JAMES STRACHAN had licence to
1668 marry Elizabeth, daugh. of John Leith of Newlands.—[*Old Machar Reg.*, 17th Nov. 1683.]

DUNCAN GEORGE MEARNS, his
1874 widow, Mary Margaret Agnes Magdalen Grant, died at St Andrews 30th Aug. 1931; his sons—William, died at Ardrossan, Alberta, 20th Oct. 1936; Duncan George Morrison, died 31st March 1945.

WILLIAM WATSON, D.D. (Aberdeen,
1909 27th March 1929). Addl. Publication—*Morals of Scottish Clergy*.

(*Charges united 12th Aug.* 1940.)

PREMNAY

Before 1198 David, Earl of Huntingdon, founder of Lindores Abbey, gave to that abbey the Church of Premnay. At the Reformation the church was united to the Church of Leslie; and the union continued till apparently soon after 29th April 1625. The church was rebuilt in 1792 and repaired in 1828. There was a Chapel of St James at Auchleven and a Well of St Lawrence.—[*Chart of Lindores*, 3–5; *Place Names of West Aberdeenshire*, 304.] (See Leslie.)

ANDREW OGILVIE, M.A., min. in
1563 1563. (See Leslie.)

JOHN STEWART, his son, Hugh, was
1876 also awarded Croix de Guerre (with Palms); author of the Official History of the New Zealand Expeditionary Force; app. Professor of Latin, Leeds Univ., 1926 and Principal of University College, Nottingham, 1930; died at sea on voyage home from New Zealand 22nd Sept. 1934.

FRANCIS GARDEN, his son, Donald
1912 John, M.A., B.Com., lecturer on Industrial Administration, Manchester, died at Manchester 26th June 1943.

JOHN LEISHMAN NELSON, dem.
1918 10th May 1946; died 15th Jan. 1948.

RAYNE

There was at Rotmais a chapel dedicated to the Virgin Mary.—[*Coll. of Shires of Aberdeen and Banff*, 577.]

ANDREW THOMSON, exhorter 1563.
1563 —[*Comps. Sub Coll. of Thirds, Aberdeen*, etc.]

ANDREW SPENS, pres. to vicarage
1567 17th Jan. 1567 on death of Sir Andrew Thomson.—[*Reg. Pres. Bene.*, i, 2.]

JOHN STRACHAN, pres. to vicarage
1568 2nd July 1568 on death of Sir Andrew Thomson.—[*Reg. Pres. Bene.*, i, 12.]

ROBERT HEPBURN, vicar.—[*Acts*
1569 *and Dec.*, xlvi, 487.]

WALTER ABERNETHIE, M.A., had
1582 also a son, Walter, to whom for his "intertainment at scholis" for seven years, pres. was made 18th July 1590 of the Chaplainry of Meikle Wartle vacant by death of Alexander Leslie, parson of Oyne.—[*Reg. Sec. Sig.*, lxi, 12.]

WILLIAM GREIG, his daugh., Mary
1875 Isabella Harvey, died at Aberdeen 9th June 1945.

JOHN SYMINGTON WEIR, marr.
1909 15th Nov. 1914 Irene Alice Bussell, and had issue—Elizabeth Irene, born 7th March 1916; Evangeline Mary, born 28th Jan. 1918; Stephanie Margaret, born 15th Jan. 1919; Frances Jean, born 17th Aug. 1924.

ALEXANDER REAPER, trans. to
1914 Linwood 16th March 1927.

DONALD ALLAN CAMERON, trans.
1927 from Evie 2nd Sept. 1927; his daughs.—Ena Macnee, died 7th Sept. 1932; Catherine Anne, died 4th Sept. 1943.

PRESBYTERY OF ELLON

BARTHOL CHAPEL

ALEXANDER ROBERTSON SUTTER, 1914, died at Banff 14th July 1939.

WILLIAM GEORGE ROBERTSON, 1925, trans. to Cullen 28th Sept. 1927.

JOHN DAWSON MACLEAN, 1928, trans. from Maryton (*q.v.*) 12th Jan. 1928; trans. to Finzean 21st Feb. 1935.

CRUDEN

ALEXANDER TRAIL, reader 1563, 1563.—[*Comps. Sub Coll. of Thirds, Aberdeen*, etc.]

WILLIAM DUNBAR, M.A.; 1691, after his deposition he lived in Peterhead, where, June 1719 to June 1720 and later, he conducted services in his own house at the time of public worship in the church, and performed other ministerial functions, particularly on 30th Sept. 1720, delivering a seditious discourse at the interment of Sir William Keith of Ludquharn in the choir of the church; later, after he became Bishop of Moray, he took part in the duties of the episcopal church at Peterhead, but not as pastor.—[*Justiciary Recs.*; I. T. Findlay's *Hist. of Peterhead*, 166-7.]

JAMES WARDLAW, 1717, he encountered bitter opposition, led by Mr William Ogilvie, chamberlain to the Countess of Errol, being "inhumanly treated, few or none in the parish durst avowedly and openly converss with him, the usual and necessary service due to the minister, yea, the necessary supports of human life were denied to him in the parish, so that he was obliged to provide himself from neighbouring parishes, and at last necessitated to leave the place."—[*Justiciary Records.*]

JOHN WEBSTER, 1720, also met keen opposition, and in 1721 a crave for the "speedy redress of his insupportable grievances" was presented to the justices.—[*Justiciary Records.*]

ALEXANDER PHILIP, 1838, his son, Alexander, L.LB., solicitor, Brechin, died 21st Jan. 1932.

JOHN MACQUEEN, 1915, his son, John Gordon McGirr, died 6th July 1938.

ELLON

To God, the Virgin Mary, St Machar, and Matthew, Bishop of Aberdeen, the church with pertinents was granted by Malcolm IV on 21st Aug. 1164. Apparently in the early part of his reign Robert I gave the patronage of the church to Kinloss Abbey, the abbot and convent having to pay to a perpetual chaplain in St Mary's Cathedral, Aberdeen, 100 sh. yearly, find him an honest habit for his use in the choir, and have a house built for him. In 1320 Henry, Bishop of Aberdeen, made an appropriation of the church, the fruits of which, it is narrated, were by a former bishop divided into two portions, the rector taking the tithes of corn, and the vicar the tithes of lambs, wool, cheeses, and all oblations, funeral and other parochial dues. Bishop Henry appropriated to the abbot and convent the rectory which had been and continued to be their patronage, together with the said tithes of corn, the appropriation to take effect upon the resignation or death of the rector. Upon the resignation of William Comyn of Buchan, the abbot and convent entered upon possession of the rectory and tithes, and, as stated in the Papal Confirmation of the appropriation, 29th July 1376, "have held them for 56 years." In 1328, consequent upon the resignation of Sir Robert de Peebles, vicar of the church, a concordat was made between Bishop Henry and the abbot and convent, in virtue of which the bishop apportioned the fruits of the vicarage thus—24 merks annually, through the hands of the abbot and convent, for a prebendary and canon created anew by the bishop in the Cathedral Church of Aberdeen, with a stall in the choir and inclusion in the chapter; 4 merks annually, out of the foregoing 24 merks, for a deacon to serve in the stall; 100 sh. salary for a chaplain in said cathedral church; and the cure of Ellon to be served by a vicar who shall continually reside there, and have a manse with garden. In or about 1532 the church was remodelled and embellished by Thomas Crystall, Abbot of Kinloss. He placed in the church an altar piece "which combined statuary with painting as in the Chapel of B.V.M. at Kinloss." and added several vestments. At the same time he built an abbot's palace, probably at the place called Abbotshall, near to which are the Abbot's Haugh and the Abbot's Well in the vicinity of Mains of Waterton. In the first quarter of the 18th century the church was described as being in the form of a cross, having a choir, nave, and transepts, one transept for the Cheynes of Esslemont, and the other for the Bannermans of Elsick, and then for the Forbeses of Waterton. The church passed out of use in 1777, and all that now remains is part of the chancel wall, divided into three compartments. The left compartment commemorates Alexander Annand of Auchterellon, who died 9th July 1601, and his wife, Margaret Fraser (daugh. of Alexander Fraser, 7th of Philorth, and widow of Alexander Cumyn of Inverallochy), who died Aug. 1602, and bears their arms; the centre compartment is now blank, save that it has the Annand arms with motto "Sperabo," the shield being flanked respectively by "DDA" and "obiit 1326"; and the right compartment is to the memory of Alexander Annand of Auchterellon, son of the foresaid Alexander A., and his wife, Margaret Cheyne, daugh. of the laird of Esslemont, the dates of deaths being blank, and likewise bears their arms. Built into the south wall there is a sculptured stone, indicating the site of the Waterton transept, and bearing the inscription, "Built by T. F. of W., son to W. F. of Tolqn., and J. R., daut. to Balmain, in 1637. Rebuilt by T. F. of W., and M. M. (Margaret Montgomery) in 1755." There was in the church an altar of the Holy Rood; and there were also two fairs, Rood Fair and Mary Mass Fair. Attached to the church were four scolocs or scologs, for whose support there was an endowment of land divided into four parts. It would appear that scolocs or scholars—convertible terms—were a lower ecclesiastical order with certain duties in the church assigned to them, and perhaps directly connected with training for the priesthood. Of their lands it is narrated that in 1265 Gamelin, Bishop of St Andrews, let in lease to Alexander, Earl of Buchan, and his two sons, his lands of Ellon, which the Scolocs of Ellon hold, for 2 merks yearly and certain dues with which the lands were burdened, with reversion to the bishop on the deaths of the said Earl and his two sons. Later, at an inquest held by Walter, Bishop of St Andrews, in 1387, it was declared by good men and true that the church lands in Ellon called the Scoloc lands were of the yearly value of £15 13s. 4d. stg., and were worth of old £20 stg., that from these lands there were to be found for the Parish Church of Ellon four clerks with copes and surplices, able to read and sing sufficiently; that a quarter or quarter part of Easter Ellon was bound to find a house for the scholars; that the quarter or ¼ part of Candellon (Candle-Ellon) was bound twice in every year to find 24 wax candles for the perch before the High Altar; and that a quarter or ¼ part of Ferley was bound to find a smithy for Ellon. The inquest further shows that the scolocs were heriditary owners admitted to their heritage by ordinary legal seisin; but they held off the bishop, and the practice was that the heir of a deceased scoloc should be entered in his heritage by the bailef of the lands without a letter of inquest from the overlord. It would appear, therefore, that in 1387 the lands had been diverted from their original purpose, being held by laymen, while the scoloc's office in the church was performed by substitutes for whom the scoloc lands had to make provision. There was a chapel at Chapelton at Esslemont; and the Chapel of Udny was also attached to the church. On 4th Oct. 1547 Francis Cheyne was appointed by the Bishop of Aberdeen to the office of Clerk of the Parish Church in succession to his late brother, Patrick Cheyne. The present church was built in 1777, repaired in 1828, and renovated and decorated in 1876 and again in 1907.—[*Reg. Epis. of Aberdeen*, i, 7–8, 134, 177; *Collections of the Shires of Aberdeen and Banff*, 308–9, 311–12; *Spalding Club*; *Misc. of Spalding Club*, v, 36–62; *Trans. of Aberdeen Eccles. Soc.*, 1889, 23–5, 15–16; Pratt's *Buchan*, 437, 442–7; *Book of Buchan*, 341; Macfarlane's *Geog. Collections*, iii, 226; *Thanage of Fermartyn*, 482–9; *Records of Kinloss*, Pref., xlvi, 121; *Cal. of Papal Registers, Letters*, iv, 225–6.]

1563 ALEXANDER OGILVY, min. 1563, and at Fyvie, Tarves and Methlick. —[*Comps. Sub Coll. of Thirds, Aberdeen*, etc.]

1563 JOHN RAY, reader, 1563.—[*Comps. Sub Coll. of Thirds, Aberdeen*, etc.]

1563 JOHN GREIG, reader 1563.—[*Comps. Sub Coll. of Thirds, Aberdeen*, etc.]

1575 JAMES CHEYNE, servitor to Lord Regent; pres. to Prebendary of Ellon 25th Oct. 1575 on death of John Chalmers.—[*Reg. Pres. Bene.*, i, (4), 38.]

1588 JOHN HERIOT, pres. to vicarage 1st March 1588–9 on death of Walter, Abbot of Kinloss, last vicar.—[*Reg. Sec. Sig.*, lix, 46.]

1678 WALTER STEWART, he marr. Elizabeth Forbes (died 1st April 1750) on 16th Oct. 1681; his daugh., Margaret, died in 1771 and before 12th Sept.; her husband, Charles Gordon, was grandson of Thomas Gordon of Cloves and Monaughty, and great-grandson of Sir William G., 6th of Lesmoir; and was served heir to his father, Alexander G., of Cloves 20th May 1718; he, along with his wife and his son William, acquired Fetterangus from Charles Morrison 20th July 1733.—[*Ellon Reg.*; *House of Gordon*, ii, 74–6.]

1872 THOMAS YOUNG, his daughs.— Dorothy Mary (marr. 16th Dec. 1933 Paymaster Commander Frederick R. Mack, R.N., O.B.E.); Eileen, died at London 2nd Feb. 1935.

1923 HAMILTON DAVID FORRESTER DUNNETT, dem. 28th Dec. 1947; his son, William Fleming, B.A., C.A., Madrid. Publication—*Ivnera'an, a Strathspey Parish*.

(*Charges united* 28th *Dec.* 1947.)

FOVERAN

In 1261 Alexander, Earl of Buchan, gave to six poor prebends at Newburgh ½ acre of land at the manse and precincts which lies between the manse of the chaplain on the east and the port of the said town, to celebrate Mass in the chapel of the said town, for his own soul, and the soul of Isabella, his countess, and the souls of all the faithful.—[*Reg. Epis. of Aberdeen*, i, 276.]

1563 DAVID LORD, reader, 1563.—[*Comps. Sub Coll. of Thirds, Aberdeen*, etc.]

1648 JOHN SEATON had charter of Schethin from George Seaton of Schethin.—[*Reg. Mag. Sig.*, x, 1655; *Aberdeen Sas.*, xvii, 421.]

1667 JOHN ROSS, had issue—John, bapt. 25th Aug. 1671; Margaret (marr. James Lorimer).

1692 JAMES GORDON, became episcopal min. at Montrose 1696–9; rector of Hawnby, Yorks, 1703; had issue— George, bapt. 6th Oct. 1696.—[*Old Machar Reg.*]

1727 JAMES GILCHRIST, marr. Ann, daugh. of William Fraser of Inverallochy, and had issue—John, bapt. 27th Feb. 1730.

1840 WILLIAM STRACHAN WATT, his son, James Peter, died at Aberdeen 22nd March 1933.

1880 JOHN SMEATON LOUTIT, his widow, Susan Abernethy Harvey, died 7th March 1930.

1912 THOMAS McWILLIAM, dem. 18th May 1931, died Aberdeen 14th Dec. 1936; his widow, Helen Porteous Murray, died 24th Nov. 1948.

(*Charges united 6th Dec.* 1931.)

LOGIE BUCHAN

The present church was erected in 1787. Logyn-Talargy, the old name of the parish, contains the name of St Talorgan. In 1275 the church was designated Logyntalargy. The latter part of the name denotes St Talarican or Talorgan, who may have been the saint prior to St Andrew. In the second part of the 14th century the designation is Logie-in-Buchan, in the middle of the 16th century it is Logie, and in the early part of the 17th century it is Logye-upon-Ethensyde.—[Theiner's *Vet. Mon.*, 111; *Reg. Great Seal*, iv, 1422, vi, 1858, vii, 1032, 1927; Watson's *Celtic Place Names*, 298.]

1563 JOHN STRACHAN, exhorter.—[*Comps. Sub Coll. of Thirds, Aberdeen*, etc.]

1583 JOHN CHEYNE, M.A., pres. to parsonage and vicarage 30th Dec. 1583 on death of Alexander Arbuthnott.—[*Reg. Pres. Bene.*, ii, 95.]

1593 THOMAS BISSET, M.A., without a charge, pres. to parsonage and vicarage 9th May 1593, vacant by inability of John Cheyne.—[*Reg. Sec. Sig.*, lxv, 63.]

1594 JOHN REID, son of James R., min. of Banchory Ternan; min. here 5th July 1594; his wife, Isabel Meldrum, buried Auld Kirk, Aberdeen, 20th June 1621.—[*Reg. Sec. Sig.*, lxvi, 166.]

1626 PATRICK GUTHRIE, son of Alexander G. of Kincaldrum; Regent, King's College, 1602, Sub-Principal 1610. Marr. pro. 14th June 1613 Jane Blackburn.

1696 ALEXANDER GORDON, took episcopal ordination and was assistant here 1st Oct. 1695, when he was appointed Humanist at King's College; he continued in that office till his death in Dec. 1738. Marr. Barbara, daugh. of John Colsone of Ardo.—[*Old Machar Reg.*, 16th Dec. 1704.]

1889 WILLIAM FRANK SCOTT, his widow, Henrietta Porteous Hardy, died at London 21st July 1947.

1919 JAMES COUTTS, died 29th Jan. 1933; his daughs.—Emily Isabel, North of Scotland Agricultural College; Patricia Jane, M.A., Medical Missionary, Zamba (marr. 8th Aug. 1933 Thomas Price, M.A., Clydebank).

METHLICK

The Chapel of St Ninian and its churchyard disappeared about the beginning of the nineteenth century.

1560 THOMAS BURNETT, parson 1563.—[*Comps. Sub Coll. of Thirds, Aberdeen*, etc.]

1563 ALEXANDER ANDERSON, parson and vicar; also at Tyrie.—[*Comps. Sub Coll. of Thirds, Aberdeen*, etc.]

1563 ALEXANDER OGILVY, M.A., min. (See Ellon, Tarves, Fyvie.)

1563 NICOL SMYT, reader, 1563 and 1567.—[*Comps. Sub Coll. of Thirds, Aberdeen*, etc.]

1583 WALTER STEWART, M.A., pres. in 1582 and 1583 on death of Thomas Burnett.—[*Reg. Pres. Bene.*, ii, 87.]

1641 ROBERT OGILVIE, M.A.; his wife, Isobel Adie, died (buried 18th April 1667).—[*Aberdeen Reg.*]

1683 ALEXANDER CLARK, M.A.; his widow, Ann Garden (buried 19th Jan. 1729); had issue—Anna, bapt. 15th Oct. 1685; Jean, bapt. 6th Nov. 1686;

Alexander, bapt. 25th Nov. 1687; Isobell, bapt. 30th Dec. 1688; William, bapt. 7th May 1691.—[*Methlick Reg.*]

1704 JOHN MULLIGAN, issue by first marriage—William, bapt. 17th Aug. 1704.—[*Methlick Reg., Old Machar Reg.*]

1839 JAMES WHYTE, his son, George Gordon, died at Aberdeen 21st Dec. 1934; his daughs.—Anne Murray, died at Aberdeen 9th March 1927; Catherine (Mrs Parr), died at Aberdeen 8th July 1934; Mary, died at Aberdeen 18th Aug. 1935; Eleanor (Mrs Smith), died 17th Jan. 1945.

1906 CHARLES GORDON MACKENZIE, dem. 24th June 1924; adm. to West Church, Crieff, 24th Feb. 1928.

1925 ROBERT WILSON FORBES, died 23rd Feb. 1928; his widow, Alice Victoria Dickie, died 29th Jan. 1932.

1928 WILLIAM SUTHERLAND, trans. from Gartly (*q.v.*) 6th Sept. 1928; died 21st July 1945.

(*Charges united 16th July* 1933.)

SLAINS

By charter of 19th Aug. 1498 James IV granted the church to the Univ. of Aberdeen for the advancement of the Sciences, and building and repairing the university; and for the support of two chaplains in the college church. This was confirmed by Bishop Elphinstone on 7th Dec. 1498, and by Alexander, Earl of Buchan, on 12th Nov. 1499; and on 7th Dec. of the latter year the bishop united the church to the university. The Church was rebuilt in 1599; and the present church was built in 1806 and renovated in 1882. In the churchyard stands a portion of the old church—an aisle which formed the burial-place of the Earls of Errol from 1631 to 1758.—[*Reg. Mag. Sig.*, ii, 2442; *Fasti Aberdonenses*, 26, 27, 28.]

1840 JAMES RUST, his daugh., Elizabeth, died at Edinburgh 4th Sept. 1939.

1897 JOHN OGILVIE, his widow, Mary Ann Munro Menzies, died 2nd Feb. 1929; his son, Ian, born 23rd May 1886.

1919 DAVID NORMAN MASSON, trans. to Kilmarnock, High Church, 23rd June 1927.

1927 JAMES ROSS, trans. from Finzean (*q.v.*) 22nd Sept. 1927; trans. to Glenbuchat 24th Oct. 1946.

FORVIE

1561 JOHN STEVENSON, still in office 1564. —[*Comps. Sub Coll. of Thirds, Aberdeen*, etc.]

TARVES

The Church of Tarves with the Chapel of Futhcul appears in the confirmation charter of John, Bishop of Aberdeen 1200-7, to Arbroath Abbey. The Chapel of Futhcul appears to be identical with the chapel that existed in what is now part of the parish of Barthol-Chapel (*q.v.*). The old church was described in 1730 as a choir with two aisles, one aisle of the Gordons of Haddo, and the other of the Forbeses of Tolquhon. The remains of the latter aisle is in the centre of the churchyard. On the tomb are the Forbes and Gordon arms, with the initials W. F. (William Forbes of Tolquhon) and E. G. (his wife, Elizabeth or Elspet Gordon, daugh. of George G. of Lesmoir), and the date 1589. Upon the scroll of the Forbes arms is the Tolquhon motto, "Salus per Christum"; and above the Gordon arms are the words "dochter to Lesmoir."—[*Reg. of Arbroath, vetus*, 136; *Thanage of Fermartyn*, 370-3, 382.]

1563 DONALD REOCH, reader, 1563.— [*Comps. Sub Coll. of Thirds, Aberdeen*, etc.]

1563 ALEXANDER OGILVY, min. 1563.— [*Comps. Sub Coll. of Thirds, Aberdeen*, etc.] (See Methlick, Ellon and Fyvie.)

1593 JAMES ORD, M.A., pres. to vicarage 20th Feb. 1593-4 on death of Alexander Ogilvie.—[*Reg. Sec. Sig.*, lxvi, 70.]

1706 WILLIAM FORBES, line 2, for "Thomas" read "John."

1917 ALEXANDER WOOD McNAIR, trans. to St Boswells 23rd Jan. 1929.

1929 JAMES MURRAY, born Bucksburn, Newhills, 20th March 1905, son of Robert Ririe M. and Jeannie Edwards; educ. at Robert Gordon's College, Aberdeen, and Univs. of Aberdeen and Edinburgh, M.A. (1926); licen. by Presb. of Edinburgh 2nd May 1929; assistant Lady Glenorchy's, Edinburgh; ord. 18th July 1929; trans. to St Mark's, Greenock, 19th May 1947. Marr. (1) 15th Dec. 1931 Lily Knowles, M.A. (died 17th June 1934), daugh. of Alexander Anderson Pirie, M.A., Tarves, and Mary Knowles, and had issue—Elspeth Ann, born 2nd Dec. 1932; Jean Bridget, born 9th May 1934; marr. (2) 20th July 1942 Margaret Barclay Rogers.

UDNY

On 11th Nov. 1406 Ronald de Uldeny (Udny) granted to a chaplain serving in the Chapel of the Holy Trinity of Uldeny, for the soul of Patrick de Uldeny, his father, all his lands with pertinents, on which the old Chapel of Uldeny was situated, his lands between the waters of the Brony and the Couly, the lands which the hermit possessed by leave of his father, the brew-house of Uldeny with the pasture on the common of Uldeny for a mare, a pig, twelve cattle, and forty sheep, and an annual rent of 33s. 4d. from the lands of Auchinloun (Auchlown).—[*Reg. Epis. of Aberdeen*, i, 209.]

1682 ALEXANDER MYLNE, M.A., his daugh., Agnes, buried 17th Feb. 1724.—[*Old Machar Reg.*]

1722 ROBERT INNES, marr. Elizabeth, daugh. of Gordon of Shielagreen.

1850 JOHN LESLIE, his son, Alexander Milne Leslie of Pittruchie, died 9th Sept. 1937.

1876 ALEXANDER SPENCE, his daugh., Johanna, M.A., Cults; his widow, Agnes Morton Barclay, died at Cults 19th March 1940, aged 94.

1923 ROBERT WILSON, trans. to St Andrew's, Perth, 30th Sept. 1927.

1928 WILLIAM McNUTT, trans. from Olrig (*q.v.*) 22nd Feb. 1928; adm. to united charge 10th May 1931. Addl. issue—Donald Campbell, born 6th May 1928; Alistair Bain, born 13th June 1932.

(*Charges united 10th May* 1931.)

PRESBYTERY OF DEER

ABERDOUR

In "ye yle" of the church there was an altar dedicated to Our Lady of Pity. An inscription on the outside of the south wall of the present church, near the village, bears that it was erected in 1818 by John Dingwall Esq., of Brucklay, patron and principal heritor of the parish, and Charles Forbes Esq., of Auchmedden. What remained of the chapel at Chapel Den was removed in 1855, and the site ploughed up. —[Pratt's *Buchan*, 314; *Reg. Sec. Sig.*, xxxv, 80.]

1563 WILLIAM MASON, M.A., min. in 1563.—[*Comps. Sub Coll. of Thirds, Aberdeen*, etc.]

1574 ALEXANDER RAMSAY, schoolmaster and reader 1563, probably identical with Alexander Ramsay who on 24th Sept. 1566 held the chaplainry of Our Lady of Pity in the church.—[*Reg. Sec. Sig.*, xxxv, 80; *Comps. Sub Coll. of Thirds, Aberdeen*.]

1567 DAVID HOWISON, pres. in 1577 on death of Robert Carnegy.—[*Reg. Sec. Sig.*, lxix, 128.]

1614 GEORGE CLARK, marr. (1) Magdalen Forbes, probably of Pitnycalder (died 1629), and had issue—William, doctor; (2) Jean Ogston of the family of Auchmaleddie near Strichen.

1651 WILLIAM RAMSAY, marr. Janet Mowat.—[*Deeds Mack*, 1705, No. 429.]

1884 CHARLES BINNIE, his son, Harry, one of the Brethren of Trinity House, London.

1920 ALEXANDER GODSMAN CATTO, trans. to Duffus 1st Dec. 1926.

1927 WILLIAM POTTER, ord. to Gardenstown 25th Sept. 1912; trans. to Sheuchan (*q.v.*) 17th May 1916; trans. to Ordiquhill 31st May 1918; trans. and adm. 18th March 1927; found drowned near manse 1st July 1936.

(*Charges united 24th June* 1930.)

ARDALLIE

1909 ROBERT CAMPBELL MARSHALL, trans. to Monymusk 14th Nov. 1927.

1928 CHARLES MACDONALD, formerly of Appin (*q.v.*), trans. from Enzie 4th April 1928; died at St Madoes 12th Feb. 1947; his wife, Helen Milne, died 23rd Oct. 1927; his son, Hector Kennedy, min. of St Madoes; his daugh., Mora (marr. 30th Aug. 1936 Robin Ingram Mitchell, min. of Haddington West); Helen Milne (marr. 17th July 1925 William Wilson Dunlop of Beardmores Ltd., Dalmuir); Margaret Jessie (marr. 2nd Dec. 1941 John Young Simpson, min. of Chalmer's Church, Wishaw).

BLACKHILL

1910 ALEXANDER BLACK, his father schoolmaster of Cruden; dem. 17th Nov. 1931; died 28th Nov. 1932; his widow, Jeannie Russell, died 29th Dec. 1940.

BODDAM

1901 WILLIAM McHARDY, dem. 30th June 1938, died 18th May 1941.

CRIMOND

The present church was built in 1812. In the churchyard, the writer of the *New Statistical Account* tells us, part of a wall of the old church, in which was a "font stone," was still standing in 1845. Probably the "font stone" was the piscina. On the wall was the date 1576, possibly denoting that repairs were carried out then. In this parish was situated the Chapel of the Virgin in the now defunct Burgh of Rattray.

ANTHONY TAILZEFAIR, parson, died before 1573.—[*Acts and Dec.*, xxvii, 217, liv, 131.

1563

ARCHIBALD KEITH, pres. in 1573 on death of Arthur Taylor; brother of William K. of Ludquharn and son of Gilbert K. of Ludquharn.—[*Reg. Pres. Bene.*, i, (4), 10.]

1573

SAMUEL KEITH, M.A., pres. to parsonage and vicarage 25th Feb. 1595-6 on death of Archibald Keith. —[*Reg. Sec. Sig.*, lxviii, 118.]

1595

JOHN GORDON, trans. from Clatt before 1st June 1597.—[*Reg. Sec. Sig.*, lxxii, 667.]

1597

WILLIAM HAY, marr. (2) 20th May 1649 Elspet Burnet.

1628

WILLIAM LAW, in 1717-21 he intruded in Ellon, preaching in a meeting-house and performing other functions of the ministry; had issue—Anna, buried 24th April 1727.—[*Justiciary Recs.*, 1717-21, 20th March 1721.]

1701

JOHN GORDON, his daugh., Janet, bapt. 27th Oct. 1718.

1711

WILLIAM BOYD, his sons—Robert, died Soorabaya 1873; George, died in Ceylon 21st Nov. 1838.

1797

JOHN CALDER, his sons—John, Colonial Service, Nigeria; Hew Maclaren Nevill, M.B., Ch.B., Lowestoft; his daughs.—Enid, M.B., Ch.B.; Margaret Winifred, M.B., Ch.B. (marr. 1st Nov. 1922 George William Watson, M.R.C.S., L.R.C.P., Distington, Cumberland).

1880

ROBERT TAYLOR MONTEITH, trans. to Forgue 9th Sept. 1927.

1909

JAMES WALLACE SIMPSON, born at Scarfskerry, Dunnett, 20th Sept. 1891, son of Walter Muir S. and Margaret Wallace; educ. at Bonar Bridge, Tain Academy and Univ. of Edinburgh, M.A. (1922); licen. by Presb. of Edinburgh 19th Dec. 1923; assistant St Bernard's, Edinburgh; ord. to Calderbank 22nd April 1925; trans. and adm. 1928; trans. to St Serf's, Alva, 9th July 1930. Marr. 31st Oct. 1930 Catherine Simpson, daugh. of Andrew Faichney.

1928

DEER, OLD

The Celtic Monastery of Deer may have been situated either where the old parish church now is, or perhaps at St Colm's Hillock, about a mile to the south and almost certainly not on the position of the later abbey, as the Cistercians usually sought out new sites for their foundations. The surviving memorial of the monastery is the *Book of Deer*, whose vernacular entries furnish proof that the monastery maintained its identity until as late as the 12th century. Whether it was suppressed to make way for the Cistercian Abbey of Deer, founded in 1218 by William Cumyn, first Earl of Buchan, or had already decayed, is not clear. About seven years ago the abbey ruins situated on the left bank of the South Ugie, some distance west of the village of Old Deer, were acquired, with the adjacent grounds, by the Roman Catholic Church. The ruins have been put into a condition of preservation; and excavations have revealed many additional features of great interest. Until recently a fair, St Drostan's, was held in the parish in December. Sir William Grantully was vicar of Deer on 14th Dec. 1541, when his natural son, Mr James, received letters of legitimation.

There was a chapel at Knevin. The "Lady's Well" is situated in a hollow between Bruxie and Clachriach; and on the west side of the hill of Dens was "Anna's Well," possibly indicating St Anne, the reputed mother of the Virgin Mary.

The present Church was built in 1788, and in 1880-1 it was reseated and the tower was erected. In 1898 the church was internally remodelled. In or about 1403 Robert III granted to the Abbot and Convent of Deer all the Great Custom of the whole wool of their own sheep and of the teind of the Church of Deer, not exceeding 20 sacks, for perpetual celebrations annually and daily at the Altar of St Michael in the church of the abbey, for his own soul, the souls of Elizabeth Mure and Anabella (Drummond), late queen, and of the Duke of Rothesay, etc.—[*Reg. Sec. Sig.*, xv, 55; Pratt's *Buchan*, 125, 171n; *Coll. for the Shires of Aberdeen and Banff*, 397, Spalding Club; Lawson's *Book of the Parish of Deir*, 11-12; *Reg. Great Seal*, i, App. ii, 1836; *Excheq. Rolls*, iii, 631.]

JOHN WARDLAW, M.A., son of John W., burgess of Edinburgh, was pres. to the Prebendary of Deer 1st Feb. 1576-7 on death of Walter Chalmers; was still in office 29th Dec. 1612.—[*Reg. Pres. Bene.*, i, (4), 55; *Reg. of Deeds*, Hay, 19th Dec. 1612.]
1576

ABRAHAM SIBBALD, prés. by George, Earl Marischal.—[*Acts and Dec.*, cxiii, 227.]
1581

ALEXANDER MARTIN, his son, James, bapt. 29th Oct. 1633; his daugh., Jean (marr. Patrick Strachan tailor in Aberdeen).
1635

ROBERT KEITH, marr. 19th June 1645 Euphemia Kinnear.—[*St Andrews Reg.*]
1649

ALEXANDER GAIRDYNE, marr. July 1666.—[*Clatt Session Record.*]
1665

GEORGE KEITH, M.A.; his son, Alexander, M.A. (Marischall College, 1726), was dep. by the Presb. of Ellon from the office of schoolmaster at Cruden, but "continues to keep a school in the parish (Cruden), outhounds his scholars to injure and molest the legally established minister and his family," beating his horse at pasture, destroying "the fruits of his yard," throwing stones at the door of the manse, and making up "ryms"; though informed of the guilty persons, he refused to chastise them; and under pretence of Orders from "exauctorated Bishops," he and Mr Cook, Chaplain to the Countess of Errol, took up a meeting-house in Cruden, where they preached, and also performed baptisms and marriages, in 1718-19 and Jan.-Feb. 1720. He marr. (cont. 19th Oct. 1726) Elizabeth, daugh. of John Irvine of Kingcausie.—[*Justiciary Records*, 1717-21.]
1683

WILLIAM LIVINGSTONE, late episcopal min., dep. by the Presb. of Deer, intruded here, preached and dispensed communion in a meeting-house near the church and discharged other functions of the ministry Dec. 1719 to Feb. 1721.—[*Justiciary Records.*]
1719

ALEXANDER LAWSON, his widow, Elizabeth Laing Stewart, died 10th July 1936.
1893

(*Charges united 24th June* 1930.)

FETTERANGUS

The confirmation charter of Adam de Crail, Bishop of Aberdeen 1207-28, to Arbroath Abbey includes the Church of Muirhugin (St Fergus) with the Chapel of Fetheranus (Fetterangus); probably, therefore, the chapel was included by implication in the grant of the Church of Inverugin to Arbroath by Radulf le Naym or Neym as confirmed by charter of King William the Lion 1165-1214. Fetterangus became a parish later; and after the Reformation it was under the charge of the min. of St Fergus, who gave supply every third Sabbath until 1618, when Fetterangus was united to Deer. On 6th Oct. 1589 George, Earl Marischal, and his son, William, received a Crown charter of the patronage of the parsonage and vicarage; and the church lands belonged to William Keith of Ludquharn to whom in 1607 his grandson, William, was served heir. The patron saint may have been St Angus, a disciple of St Columba, associated with Balquhidder, the name, on this basis, being Angus' *fetter*, a slope or terraced declivity, as here. The ruins of the church, 33 by 12 feet, stand near the north side of the churchyard, which is situated on a slight eminence in a field about a quarter of a mile south of the village. There was a local belief that before the death of an old inhabitant of the place an unseen bell was heard ringing in the churchyard. By decreet of the Commission of Plat, which was dissolved in July 1618, the parish of Fetterangus was united to Deer; and the decreet was put into execution by the Presb. of Deer on 12th Nov. 1618.—[*Reg. of Arbroath, vetus*, 6, 137; *Reg. Great Seal*, v, 26th Sept. 1592; *Retours*, iv, 123; Watson's *Celtic Place Names*, 510, 272; *Cal. of Papal Reg., Letters*, i, 30; *Reg. Epis. of Aberdeen*, ii, 247; Macfarlane's *Geog. Coll.*, i, 65; Lawson's *Book of the Parish of Deir*, 11–12.]

1580 Served by a reader, but vacant 1580.— [*Comps. Gen. Coll. of Thirds.*]

1599 DAVID ROBERTSON, was a member of Assembly at Aberdeen 1605.— [Spottiswood's *History*, 486.]

NEW DEER

The church was erected in 1839, a short distance north of the site of the old church built in 1622 by the Earl Marischal and other proprietors, close to the site of a pre-existing chapel which belonged to the Abbey of Deer. The old church, to which an aisle was added in 1773, had a pointed, richly moulded west doorway.—[Pratt's *Buchan*, 1755–6.]

1554 GILBERT CLERK, had issue—Margaret.

1682 DAVID SIBBALD, his daughs.—Elizabeth, bapt. 15th March 1685; Catherine, bapt. 12th July 1691, buried 20th Feb. 1692. Addl. issue—a daugh. bapt. 7th April 1688; Patrick, bapt. 28th April 1690, buried 20th Feb. 1692; Sophia, bapt. 7th Dec. 1692; Anna, bapt. 26th Jan. 1696; James, bapt. 9th July 1698; Camilla, buried 29th July 1698.—[*New Deer Reg.*]

1722 GEORGE MAIR, line 3, delete "and brother of Thomas M., min. of Orwell."

1879 GEORGE FORBES INNES PHILIP, his son, James Porter, O.B.E., died at Aboyne 29th Sept. 1939.

1924 MATTHEW WELSH NEILSON, M.A., B.D.; also Ph.D. (Aberdeen, 1928); as Mr Adams died on the day of the voting for the colleagueship, procedure began *de novo*, the same candidates were put forward for the Full Charge, and Mr Neilson, having been selected, was adm. on 16th May 1924.

FRASERBURGH or PHILORTH

At Fingask, south-west of Fraserburgh, there is a place designated "the College," in Gaelic *Achyseipal*, "Field of the Chapel," denoting that here in early Christian times there was a community of clerics whose ab or head directed the supply of daughter churches. Its site, now completely obliterated, is said to have been traceable in the early part of last century. At Chapelton in the same quarter there was a chapel or cell, with a well, belonging to the Abbey of Deer. Portions of the walls of the chapel were still in existence about a century ago, and somewhat later the well was drained and filled up.

The Church of Philorth was situated in the old churchyard at Kirkton, on the links to the south of Fraserburgh. The church, built in Fraserburgh in 1571 by Sir Alexander Fraser of Philorth, the founder of the burgh, was cruciform. It was enlarged in 1628, and further repaired sixty years later. The present church was built in 1802, renovated in 1873–4, and considerably reconstructed in 1898–9. There were of old chapels at Fingask and Chapelton.— [Scott's *Pictish Nation*, 135; Pratt's *Buchan*, 284, Ed. 1901; Pratt's *Buchan*, 278; *Coll. of the Shires of Aberdeen and Banff*, 443.]

1563 ROBERT SMYT, reader in 1563, also at Rathen.—[*Comps. Sub Coll. of Thirds, Aberdeen.*]

1563 DAVID BRODIE, reader in 1563.— [*Comps. Sub Coll. of Thirds, Aberdeen.*]

PETER MACLAREN, his daugh., Agnes Finlayson (Mrs Davidson), died at Beildside 2nd Oct. 1934.
1861

WILLIAM NEIL SUTHERLAND, trans. to Dalmeny 18th June 1926.
1919

DONALD CAMPBELL BRYCE GORDON, trans. from Dunrossness (*q.v.*) 24th Nov. 1926, died 16th Nov. 1928; his only son, John Macilrick Bryce, sergeant, R.A.F., killed 10th Sept. 1945.
1926

JOHN KENNEDY MACKENZIE, trans. from Stornoway (*q.v.*) 12th June 1929, died 10th June 1945. Addl. issue—Ian Murdo, born 3rd Aug. 1931.
1929

INVERALLOCHY

DUNCAN MACGREGOR, his widow, Ann Andrew, died at Dunfermline 1st Feb. 1928; his daugh., Elizabeth (marr. 29th July 1933 James Christian, son of Robert Reith Spark, min. of Durris); his son, Andrew, master, Kirkcudbright Academy.
1881

JAMES COLHOUN, adm. 18th Aug. 1926; trans. to Maud 15th March 1928.
1926

ALEXANDER GILLON, ord. 26th June 1928; trans. to Kilmun 16th Aug. 1929.
1928

(*Charges united* 24th June 1930.)

KININMONTH

There was a chapel, probably dedicated to St John, situated on the south border of the old parish of Lonmay, about a mile from Kininmonth proper. In the first part of the 18th century there existed remains of the chapel and the burial-ground, and the site is still pointed out. The church was built in 1837.—[Pratt's *Hist. of Buchan*, 244, Ed. 1901.]

JAMES SMITH, his sons—John Leslie Sidney, min. of Langton 25th Sept. 1932; James, M.A., Malayan Civil Service 1930, Retrenchment Officer 1932;
1886
his daugh., Katherine Elizabeth Mary, died in Inverness 3rd Jan. 1949.

GEORGE PETRIE, died 25th Sept. 1928.
1918

JOHN RUTHERFORD GREENLAW, born 17th Nov. 1904, eldest son of John G., min. of Buckie; educ. at Buckie Secondary School and Univ. of Aberdeen; licen. by Presb. of Fordyce 30th April 1929; ord. 22nd Aug. 1929; dem. 17th March 1940. Marr. 19th Dec. 1929 May Helen Ross (died 7th April 1940) and has issue—Catherine, born 27th June 1932.
1929

(*Kininmonth and New Leeds united* 17th *March* 1940.)

LONGSIDE

The church was built about 1620 by William, Earl Marischal, and rebuilt 1799.—[*Acts Scot. Parl.*, v, 608*n*; Pratt's *Buchan*, 207.]

ALEXANDER IRVING, marr. Margaret Guthrie, buried 4th May 1670; his son, Andrew, apprenticed to Alexander Anderson, merchant, Edinburgh, 2nd Jan. 1678.
1634

THOMAS ROBERTSON, M.A. Addl. issue—Grizel, bapt. 19th Jan. 1669; Elizabeth, bapt. 11th Dec. 1669; William, bapt. 16th May 1675.
1662

ALEXANDER ROBERTSON, M.A.; by sentence of the Justices of 2nd Jan. 1718 he was ordered to remove from the church and manse and glebe in favour of the lawful min., and to give up the utensils of the church, and was also forbidden to exercise the functions of the ministry in the parish; yet he retained the registers of the church, the mortcloth, and the bonds and other documents of the poor-money, troubled and molested the min., and conducted services in his own house at Nether Kinmundy, and also bapt., 1718 to 20th Jan. 1721. His son, Alexander, became an episcopal min., having been licensed by "an exauctorate Bishop," and conducted services at a meeting-house at Drumlithie for more than a year prior to
1687

Feb. 1717, and intruded in the Church of Arbuthnott in Oct. 1715. Addl. issue—Alexander, bapt. 8th Oct. 1690; Lilias, bapt. 29th Oct. 1691; Arthur, bapt. 13th May 1694; Christian, bapt. 17th June 1695; George, bapt. 16th Nov. 1696; James, bapt. 14th March 1698.—[*Longside Reg.*; *Justiciary Records*, 1712 to 20th March 1721.]

1717 JOHN LUMSDEN, M.A., marr. 3rd Aug. 1725 Frances, daugh. of Robert Fullarton, Craighall, Ellon, with issue—Eupham and Barbara (twins), bapt. 13th Aug. 1726; Robert, bapt. 18th Sept. 1727; Mary, bapt. 25th Sept. 1728; John, bapt. 2nd Oct. 1729; Agnes, bapt. 2nd Nov. 1731.—[*Longside Reg.*; *Ellon Reg.*]

1877 ROBERT CUSHNEY, his widow, Mary Williamson, died at Sunbury-on-Thames 24th March 1937.

1904 RICHARD HENDERSON, died 6th Dec. 1932; his daugh., Elizabeth Mary (marr. 29th July 1929 Thomas Westmoreland Forrest of the Anglo-Ecuadorian Oil Company, South America); Aileen, M.A. (marr. at Rangoon 4th Feb. 1932 Alexander Grosert Rae, Chank); Dorothy, M.A. (marr. 22nd April 1930 Alistair Chisholm Mackenzie, M.A., son of Duncan M., Inverness); daugh. (marr. James Slater, Braeside, Banffshire); his sons —Richard Bruce, M.B., Ch.B., Sierra Leone, born 20th May 1901; George Andrew Falconer, born 19th March 1895; his widow, Margaret Falconer, died 26th Dec. 1946.

LONMAY

The present church was built in 1787.

1552 JAMES GORDON, M.A., parson 14th July 1552, died before 16th June 1574.—[*Reg. Pres. Bene.*, i, (4), 226; *Spalding Club Mis.*, iv, 54.]

1574 GILBERT CHISHOLM, min. here, pres. to parsonage and vicarage 6th June 1574 on death of James Gordon.—[*Reg. Pres. Bene.*, i, (4), 21.]

1878 JAMES FORREST, his widow, Katherine Gray, died 24th July 1939.

1914 JAMES MACDONALD FINLAYSON, died 17th Aug. 1945.

MAUD

The church was built and opened in 1876.

1883 WILLIAM COWIE, app. 15th June 1883; his widow, Christian Ewen Simpson, died 6th Oct. 1944; his son, Alexander Ross Murison, rector of Marr College, Troon; his daugh., Mabel Margaret, M.A. ("Lesley Storm"), the novelist (marr. 21st July 1921 James Thomson Doran Clark, M.B., Ch.B., London); his son, William, min. of Strathdon.

1919 WILLIAM SIMPSON, trans. to St Mary's, Hawick, 23rd Nov. 1927.

1928 JAMES COLHOUN, born Londonderry 7th July 1867, son of Robert C. and Annie Walker; educ. at Londonderry Academical Institution and Univ. of Magee College; licen. by Presb. of Derry April 1893; ord. to Benvarden 20th Dec. 1893; trans. to Glassville, New Brunswick, Canada, 26th Nov. 1912; trans. to Castle Bellingham, Co. Louth, Ireland, 14th March 1917; adm. to Inverallochy 18th Aug. 1926; trans. and adm. 15th March 1928; trans. to Greenbank, Co. Derry, 25th Sept. 1932; died 2nd Nov. 1941. Marr. 3rd June 1903 Ellen, daugh. of David Camac, min. of Boyle Presbyterian Church, Connaught, and has issue—Robert Eric Camac, born 16th July 1908.

(*Charges united 26th Oct.* 1932.)

PETERHEAD

The ruins of the old church are situated in the churchyard on the links. They consist of the side walls of the chancel, the entire chancel arch, and a square tower in the centre of the west wall of the nave. The chancel is Norman; the remainder of later style. The old church was replaced by a building erected in the town in 1770; and the latter in turn was succeeded by the present church, which has this inscription:

"Founded, 25th May 1804: Opened, 14th August 1806." At what is now known as Windmill Brae there was a settlement called Monksholm which may have been a chapel or cell connected with the Abbey of Deer. Excavations have revealed fragments of a wall or pavement and sculptured stones and many slates. Near this is the Abbot's Well.—[Pratt's *Hist. of Buchan*, 4 Ed., 82*n*.]

1562 SIR PATRICK OGSTON, vicar 1562-3. —[*Comps. Sub Coll. of Thirds, Aberdeen*, etc.]

1563 ARCHIBALD REID, reader in 1563.— [*Comps. Sub Coll. of Thirds, Aberdeen*, etc.]

1585 THOMAS BISSET, pres. 8th Oct. 1594 on death of Patrick Ogilvie.—[*Reg. Sec. Sig.*, lxvii, 23.]

1664 JOHN CHALMERS, his son, George, bapt. 7th June 1669.

1682 ALEXANDER BARCLAY, M.A.; he is said to have been a cadet of the Barclays of Gartly. In 1695 he was discharged by Parliament on his renunciation of his protest against the Commission of the General Assembly in Aberdeen in 1694; described as "tenant in Prora" in 1695, and he was designated as "formerly" min. at Peterhead in 1696, when he was resident in the town with his wife, family, and mother-in-law; in Oct. 1704 he intruded in Auchterless. With the help of Rev. John Barclay, formerly min. at Edrom, and Rev. Alexander Hepburn, formerly min. at St Fergus, he opened an episcopal meeting-house in Peterhead 21st Sept. 1706, at what is now No. 3 Port Henry Lane (off the Longate); for said intrusion he was ordered by the Synod on 12th May 1708 to compear before the Presb., and as he appeared only by procuration and not personally at the Presb. on 2nd Jan. 1709 he was declared contumacious by the Presb. and also discharged from exercising any part of the ministerial office either in Peterhead or in the bounds of the Presb.—said sentence to be intimated to him. Along with Rev. Alexander Hepburne he served the Church of Peterhead after the Pretender landed there on 2nd Dec. 1714, and kept possession several months, conducted episcopal services, prayed for King James, and read the Proclamation levying men for his service—for which he was dep. in 1716. He died apparently before Aug. 1721, when Mr Alexander Cumming was episcopal incumbent at Peterhead. Marr. Margaret, daugh. of William Burnet, min. at Insch, and had issue—Marie, bapt. 8th Feb. 1683; George, bapt. 14th Nov. 1685; William, bapt. 17th Oct. 1687; Alexander, bapt. 23rd July 1689; Alexander, bapt. 22nd March 1693; Marie, bapt. 30th Sept. 1695; his daugh., Jean, had no second marriage.— [*Recs. of Presb. of Deer*, 1708-9; *Memo.*, Rev. Dr M. Welsh Neilson, Presb. Cl.; *Acts Scott. Parl.*, ix, 423a; *Aberdeen Poll Tax Roll*, i, 572; *Reg. of Deeds Mack.*, 6th Oct. 1720; *Memo.*, Rev. E. F. Esson, M.A., B.Sc., Rector, Episcopal Church, Peterhead; Burke's *Landed Gentry*, 1939, 909; *Justiciary Records*, 1717-21, 20th March 1721; Findlay's *Hist. of Peterhead*, 166-7.]

1915 HUGH DOUGLAS SWAN, his daughs. —Dorothy Fortune (marr. 11th May 1948 George D. Miln, Warrington, Lancashire); Norah Kathleen (marr. William G. Miln).

PETERHEAD EAST

1921 ALBERT ALEXANDER DIACK, trans. to St Bernard's, Edinburgh, 7th July 1926.

1926 JOHN ANDREW INGLIS, born 2nd June 1890, son of John Inglis, tweed designer, and Isabella Turnbull; educ. at Univ. of Edinburgh, M.A. (June 1912); served in France as Captain in Black Watch; licen. by Presb. of Jedburgh 1917; ord. to Rosewell 13th May 1919; trans. and adm. 12th Nov. 1926; trans. to Carnbee 22nd Nov. 1929. Marr. (1) 25th Nov. 1917 Isabella Wear, daugh. of Thomas Douglas and Mary Wear; she died 20th Jan. 1938 and had issue—Muriel Douglas, born 5th Jan. 1919; John Gladstone, born 2nd Jan. 1926; (2) 23rd Dec. 1940 Nancy Miller, daugh. of James Wilson and widow of John Monro Garlick.

PITSLIGO

The church was built about 1603 by Sir Alexander Forbes of Pitsligo, afterwards Lord Pitsligo. In the sands a little south of Pitsligo Castle there was a chapel believed to have been dedicated to the Nine Maidens. Near it was a spring of the same name. The priest's house is said to have stood near by at a spot called the Priest's Knowe. Tradition also tells of a burying-ground there. The walls of the old church, which had mingled features of Gothic and Renaissance work, are still standing. The lower part of the south or "Pitsligo" aisle was the burial-vault of the Pitsligo family, and it has now been enclosed, its oak door having a brass plate with an inscription recording the members of the family, including the founder of the church who died in 1636, interred in the vault. The present church was built in 1890, in Early English style of the 13th century, with a nave, three-sided apse, north transept, and a south aisle or transept, which is an exact reproduction of the Pitsligo aisle of the old church. In this aisle has been fitted the beautifully carved woodwork of the old aisle, regarded as one of the best extant examples of Jacobean Scottish woodwork, and probably executed under the guidance of Dutch woodcarvers. The aisle has also an alcoved roof with panels containing coats of arms carved in oak, and with elaborately carved pendants. These also belonged to the old church, as did also samples of old pew-panelling which, recovered from various quarters, have been fitted into the pulpit and otherwise distributed in the new church.—[Mackinley's *Ancient Church Dedications in Scotland*, i, 17; Pratt's *Hist. of Buchan*, 4 Ed., 288.]

1647 DUNCAN FORBES, had issue—John, died unmarr.; Duncan in Ackenway; George, merchant, Aberdeen; Alexander, min. of Dyke; Margaret in Moy, died unmarr. 1703; Mary (marr. George Stewart, provost of Banff).

1689 WILLIAM SWAN, M.A.; in 1718 to Jan. 1721 he conducted a meeting-house in the parish.—[*Justiciary Records.*]

1720 WILLIAM MERCER, was chaplain to Sir Harry Innes of Innes 30th Oct. 1717, when Synod of Moray recommended a Royal Bursary for his study of theology.

1863 WALTER GREGOR, col. 2, line 5, for "William" read "Wallace."

1910 JAMES WALKER MORRISON WILLIAMSON, trans. to Polmont 12th Aug. 1926.

1927 GEORGE ARTHUR SEFTON, born Aberdeen 3rd March 1900, son of Alfred S., Assistant Superintendent, Post Office, Aberdeen, and Elizabeth Monro; educ. at Robert Gordon's College, Univs. of Aberdeen, M.A. (1921), B.D. (1924), and Strasbourg; licen. by Presb. of Aberdeen 8th May 1924; assistant St Andrew's, Glasgow; ord. 28th Jan. 1927; trans. to Fern 1st Oct. 1937. Marr. 20th June 1928 Mary Chenoweth, daugh. of Thomas O. and Mary Keay, Dundee, and has issue—Henry Keay, born 15th Jan. 1931; Catherine Mary, born 21st Feb. 1933; Arthur Monro, born 21st June 1937.

NEW PITSLIGO

1886 ALEXANDER REID CRAIB, his widow, Annie Hutcheon, died 4th Feb. 1939.

1913 JOHN McWILLIAM, dem. 30th Sept. 1934. Marr. (2) 26th Aug. 1930 Margaret, daugh. of George Mair and Margaret Ferguson, and has issue—Ruth Agnes, born 21st Feb. 1934; Ann Margaret, born 15th Dec. 1935. Publication—*Criticism of Philosophy of Bergson* (Edinburgh, 1929).

(*Charges united 30th Sept.* 1934.)

RATHEN

The patronage of the church was bestowed upon the Bishopric of Aberdeen by Robert I on 21st March 1328–9. It was the Church of Ruthven (Angus), not Rathen, that belonged to the Abbey of Arbroath.

On the east side of Mormond Hill there is a den called "Saint Eddran's Glack," said to have been the Hermitage of St Ethernan. Near the church there are two hillocks, one of which is called St Oyne's. There is also a spring of the same name. In 1723 the hillock and well were both known as St Owen's. That may indicate a dedication to St Owen. There was a Rood Well on the boundary of the parish with Lonmay.—[Pratt's *Buchan*, 246*n*; Macfarlane's *Geog. Colls.*, i, 56; *Reg. of Priory of St Andrews*, 373-4; *Reg. Epis. Aberdeen*, i, 47.]

1563 ROBERT SMYT, reader 1563, also at Philorth.—[*Comps. Sub Coll. of Thirds, Aberdeen*, etc.]

1574 GILBERT CHISHOLM, min. here, pres. to parsonage and vicarage 28th Oct. 1574 on death of Adam Heriot. —[*Reg. Pres. Bene.*, i, (4), 24.]

1574 DUNCAN DAVIDSON, pres. to parsonage and vicarage 20th Feb. 1574-5 on death of Adam Heriot.— [*Reg. Pres. Bene.*, i, (4), 30.]

1703 JAMES ANDERSON, probably identical with James, son of Dr George A., Professor of Divinity, King's College.

1842 JOHN FORBES MITCHELL COOK, his son, Alexander, died 11th Oct. 1928.

1894 JOHN KELLAS, his son, James, min. of Mannofield; John, Principal Scottish Churches College, Calcutta; his daugh., Kate Gray, died at Little Ardo, Methlick, 29th Sept. 1932.

1925 JOHN BELL, trans. to St Margaret, Glasgow, 23rd April 1928.

1928 ALEXANDER MAUCHLINE, formerly of St Matthew's, Dundee (*q.v.*); assistant at St Bride's, Glasgow; adm. to St Mary's, Dalziel, 12th Sept. 1923; trans. to St Thomas, Leith, 22nd Sept. 1926; trans. and adm. 14th Sept. 1928; trans. to Kemback 22nd Dec. 1932; dem. 11th Nov. 1948.

ST FERGUS or LONGLEY

Prior to 1616 the church stood in the old churchyard near the seashore about two miles east of the present building. At the removal in 1616 the parish took the name of St Fergus, its titular saint.

1562 GILBERT KEITH, son of William, Earl of Marischall; vicar 4th May 1566; was in office 30th March 1543-4, died after 28th Feb. 1580.—[*Reg. Abbrev. Feu Charters of Church Lands*, i, 224; *Reg. Sec. Sig.*, xxxv, 23; *Reg. Mag. Sig.*, iii, 2940, iv, 175.]

1590 JAMES KYD, reader in 1570.—[*Reg. of Ministers*, 69.]

1637 JOHN ROBERTSON, marr. 25th Nov. 1641 Elizabeth, daugh. of Alexander Middleton of Berryhillock.—[*Old Machar Reg.*]

1703 ALEXANDER HEPBURN, after his deposition, he assisted Rev. Alexander Barclay at Peterhead in carrying on episcopal ministrations; intruded there 1714-15 and continued after Mr Barclay's death.—[J. T. Findlay's *Hist. of Peterhead*, 166-7.]

1895 ANDREW WATT, his wife, Mary Douglas Mitchell, died 3rd March 1942; he died 14th July 1946.

SAVOCH OF DEER

The church was opened in Dec. 1834.

1887 WILLIAM WALLACE WILSON, his daughs.—Louise, M.A., headmistress of Shannas Public School; Agnes, M.A. (marr. Queenstown, South Africa, 16th Feb. 1927, Leslie George Panton); his sons—Robert, min. of St Andrew's, Perth, 1927; William, M.B., Ch.B., Pembroke Dock, South Wales, 1925, and Hay, Hereford, 1927.

1924 THOMAS NELSON ALLEN, adm. 22nd Feb. 1924; trans. to Orwell 22nd March 1928.

DAVID NESS, trans. from Whiteinch (*q.v.*) 16th Aug. 1928; trans. to Cardross 8th Dec. 1932; died 1st Dec. 1935; his widow, Mary Adam, died 25th Dec. 1945.
1928

(*Charges united 21st March* 1933.)

STRICHEN

The Wardlaw MS. states that Strichen was erected into a parish by Thomas Fraser of Knocky in 1599, and Mr. John Reid planted as min. By Act of 1633 Parliament ratified and approved Acts of the Diocesan Synod of 1st May 1622 and 19th April 1629 for the disjunction of lands from Rathen and Fraserburgh, and the erection of the same into the parish of Strichen, and for the "erection of ane new paroche kirk of Strichen." The present church was built in 1798–9. The existence of a Lady Well may mean that the chapel on the Chapelmuir, evidently the level ground near the railway station and the former site of fairs, was dedicated to the Virgin.—[*Wardlaw MS.*, 191; *Acts Scott. Parl.*, v, 153, x, 109; Pratt's *Buchan*, 197, Ed. 1901.]

JAMES WHYTE, had a Fraserburgh connection, and probably identical with Mr James Whyte, "governor to the laird of Strichen" 20th Sept. 1686; buried in Cheyne's Aisle, Old Machar Cathedral; had issue—Elizabeth, born 6th Nov. 1694; William, born 8th Jan. 1696.—[*Strichen Reg.*]
1694

THOMAS UDNY, had a "helper," Colin Campbell, M.A., 14th Aug. 1743; his daugh., Elizabeth, bapt. 7th Feb. 1706, and his son, Thomas, bapt. 18th Feb. 1714. Addl. issue—Robert, bapt. 23rd Sept. 1708; Nathaniel, bapt. 20th Aug. 1711; James, bapt. 4th Feb. 1715; Isabel, bapt. 9th July 1719.—[*Strichen Reg.*]
1701

CHARLES STEWART, his daugh., Margaret Thomson, died at Aberdeen 15th June 1945.
1862

RICHARD GOODWILLIE was an officer of excise at Dundee; educ. E.U. Theological Hall; died 6th Jan. 1934; his daughs.—Margaret Philip (marr. William Hepburn, Strichen); Elizabeth (marr. William Ingram, Strichen); his widow, Rachel Philip, died 13th Dec. 1936.
1888

CHARLES McGLASHAN, died 29th June 1932.
1925

(*Charges united 1st Jan.* 1933.)

TYRIE

The present church was built in 1800.

ALEXANDER ANDERSON, M.A., parson and vicar. (See Methlick and Kinkell.)
1563

DAVID HOWIESON, pres. to parsonage and vicarage 10th Nov. 1573 on removal of Alexander Anderson (? Ogston) for non-confession of faith.—[*Reg. Pres. Bene.*, i, (4), 15.]
1583

WILLIAM CHEYNE, M.A.; on 27th April 1630 the Synod of Moray lodged a complaint against him with the Bishop of Aberdeen for having unlawfully married "these children" in Elgin; and on 27th Oct. 1640 the Synod excommunicated him "for making some unlawful marriage," the said sentence to be intimated in all the parishes of the Province of Moray.
1615

ALEXANDER MILNE, his daughs.—Mary Louise, died 13th Jan. 1929; Alexina, died 1st Jan 1900; Caroline, died 6th March 1937.
1856

ADAM NELSON, died at Crathie 17th July 1929.
1901

PRESBYTERY OF TURRIFF

ALVAH

The church, with the church lands, was granted to Cupar Abbey by Marjory, Countess of Athol, widow of John, Earl of Athol, with consent of her son and heir, David of Strathbogie, in 1314. Confirmation was given in the same year by Henry le Chen, Bishop of Aberdeen, Cupar Abbey being bound to pay 6 merks stg. annually for a chaplain to celebrate in the Cathedral of Aberdeen.—[*Reg. of Cupar Abbey*, i, 3; *Reg. Epis. of Aberdeen*, i, 41.]

1556 SIR GEORGE SCOTT, pres. by Donald, Abbot of Cupar, to vicarage 3rd Jan. 1556 in succession to Sir Gilbert Bard.—[*Reg. of Cupar Abbey*, ii, 126.]

1563 HENRY MORTIMER, reader in 1563.—[*Comps. Sub Coll. of Thirds, Aberdeen*, etc.]

1636 ROBERT BLAIR, had also a daugh., Isabel.—[*Aberdeen Poll Tax Roll*, ii, 624.]

1917 ROBERT JAMES VICTOR MARTIN, line 14, for "Thornlea" read "Thornilea," and line 15, for "Rendell" read "Randall." Has issue—Victor David Randall, born 19th March 1919; Helen Catherine Halley, born 8th June 1921.

AUCHTERLESS

The former church was built in 1780, and an aisle was added in 1832. The present church was erected in 1879; and subsequently the spire was added by the Blackford family in memory of J. P. Watson of Blackford and his wife and younger daugh. At Seggat were situated the Chapel and Well of the Virgin. Long after 1560 these continued to be objects of superstitious resort and practices; and in April 1649 the Synod of Aberdeen, finding that "the Chapel and the Chapel Well of Segget were not demolished, nor the well filled up according to ane former ordinance," ordained the Presb. of Turriff to visit the Kirk of Auchterless and "demolish the said Chapel, Altar, and well." But the well at least survived ecclesiastical attacks; and it is related in 1840 that within the memory of some of the oldest inhabitants, "money and other articles were deposited on Pash Sunday by those whose superstitious feelings led them to frequent the well in expectation of some benefit to be derived from drinking the water dedicated to the Holy Virgin."—[Pratt's *Buchan*, 389; *The Thanage of Formartyn*, 133.]

1561 ARCHIBALD BELL, M.A., parson 1561–3; chanter of Aberdeen.—[*Comps. Gen. Coll. and Sub Coll. of Thirds, Aberdeen*, etc.]

1563 ROBERT ALLARDYCE, reader in 1563: vicar pensioner 1567.—[*Comps. Sub Coll. of Thirds, Aberdeen*, etc.]

1595 ROBERT MAITLAND, chanter of Aberdeen 1614.

1647 ANDREW MASSIE, adm. to Drumblade before 2nd July 1631; his son, Andrew, Regent, King's College, Aberdeen, 1656, and Principal there 1673–8, afterwards Regent, Edinburgh University.—[*King's Coll.*, 41, 57.]

1682 PATRICK SETON, his sons—James, apprenticed to James Gooden, currier, 6th Nov. 1695; William, bapt. 21st May 1687.

1704 ALEXANDER BARCLAY, he intruded in the church in 1704 with a "Presentation" from Patrick Duff of Hatton, who seems to have ignored the abolition of patronage in 1690 and kept possession of the keys: the "Presentation" was unacceptable to the congregation, and was not recognised by the Presb.—a decision which was upheld by the Synod; he refused to surrender the keys to the Presbytery's representative, but was ultimately outed, and returned to Peterhead before 1708.—[*Recs. of Presbytery of Turriff; Memo.*, Rev. Dr A. A. Duncan, Presby. Clerk.]

1706 ALEXANDER ROSE, marr. (1) 17th April 1707 Christian Harvie in Boddam and had issue—James, bapt. 2nd Sept. 1712; Katherine, bapt. 7th Oct. 1715; Alexander, bapt. 29th Aug. 1717; William, bapt. 24th Aug. 1718.

1898 ALEXANDER ADAM DUNCAN, D.D. (Aberdeen, 29th March 1933); his wife, Janet Black Galloway, died 22nd Feb. 1942; his daughs.—Elizabeth Craven, M.A. (marr. 26th July 1935 George Robert Bruce, M.A., English Master, High School, Dundee); Christina, L.L.B. (Aberdeen, 1935), (marr. 19th July 1941 W. J. Bruce Munro, M.A.). He marr. (2) 3rd July 1943 Bessie Macpherson Fraser.

FORGLEN

The present church was built in 1806. On a stone in the south wall of its immediate predecessor was this inscription—"This Church was re-edified by George Ogilvie, Master of Banff, 1692." To the Abbey of Arbroath William the Lion, 1165–1214, granted the custody of the Brachbennach (the consecrated banner of St Columba) and the lands of Forglen given to the Lord and St Columba for its maintenance, which land of Forglen had of old been granted for that purpose. The pre-Reformation church was situated where the rivulet falls into the Deveron, about half a mile west of the present church. For a time Forglen was conjoined with Alvah, but it became a separate parish early in the 17th century. Later the major part of the lands of Carnousie were detached from Marnoch and joined to Forglen.—[*Reg. of Arbroath, vetus*, 5, 10.]

1582 ALEXANDER IRVINE, described as reader at Drum 1580; held parsonage and vicarage.—[*Comps. Gen. Coll. of Thirds.*]

1676 JOHN DUNBAR, M.A.; his daugh., Jean, bapt. 18th Nov. 1678. Addl. issue—Mary, bapt. 16th Dec. 1679; Helen, bapt. 14th April 1682; Ann. bapt. 18th Nov. 1684; Alexander, bapt. 6th Feb. 1687; George, bapt. 31st Aug. 1689. Marr. (2) 9th March 1707 Susanna Fairfoul.— [*Forglen Reg.; Peterhead Reg.*]

1873 ARCHIBALD BOWMAN, his widow, Helen Maclean, died 30th June 1929.

1915 CHARLES GILES, dem. 18th Oct. 1927 on app. as chaplain to Aberdeen Royal Infirmary; died 27th Nov. 1937; his son, Andrew Milne Mitchell, min. of New Machar; his daughs.—Mary (marr. John H. E. Burleigh, min. of Fyvie); Isabella (marr. William Noble Chisholm, F.R.C.S., son of John C. Gibson, Huntly); his son, Robert, M.B., Ch.B.; his wife, Elizabeth Seton, died 20th Oct. 1932.

1928 JOHN WOOD, formerly of Whalsay (*q.v.*); trans. from Lowick 24th Feb. 1928; dem. 11th Nov. 1930; died 10th Oct. 1947; his wife, Elizabeth Addison Rutherford, died 25th Aug. 1945.

FORGUE

The church, under the designation of the Church of Fornixdraut or Ferendracht (Frendraught), was granted to Arbroath Abbey by Sir William de Frendraught, Kt., without the consent of the bishop, the abbey to supply a perpetual chaplain for the cure of the parish. On 3rd Jan. 1257-8 the grant was confirmed by Bull of Pope Alexander IV, who by another Bull of the same date decreed that the church be applied by the abbot and convent for the purpose of hospitality, subject to a competent reservation for the perpetual chaplain. By still another Bull by the said Pope, on 8th Jan. 1257-8, the chaplaincy was erected into a perpetual vicarage with emoluments of 100 sh. annually, the whole altarage, manse, and teind sheaves of lands then under cultivation, the residue over and above the 100 sh. to pertain to the abbey. By Charter of John, Abbot of Arbroath, on 15th Aug. 1268, after the death of Duncan, last rector, it was set forth that the abbey was to appoint a chaplain to serve the parish, the altarage, church lands and manse to pertain to the chaplain, and the abbey to have the great tithes of the whole lands, and 8 merks annually of the lesser tithes of wool or lambs. After 1257-8 the parish was designated Forgue. By charter of 8th May 1535 James Creichton, Kt., of Frendraught granted to Sir William Cristison, perpetual chaplain, and his successors, at the Altar of the Virgin Mary in the cell or chapel built by the said James in the church, an annual rent of 24 merks from the lands of Bogny in the barony of Frendraught. This was afterwards called the chaplaincy of the "Isle of Forgue." The present church was built in 1819. In the church, apparently in a transeptal aisle, there was an altar dedicated to the Virgin Mary, founded on 8th May 1535 by Sir James Creichton, Kt., of Fyndraucht (Frendraught), the endowment being 24 merks from the lands of Bogny in the barony of "Frendraucht." The first chaplain was Sir William Cristisoun.—[Theiner's *Vet. Mon.*, 73, 74; *Reg. of Arbroath, vetus*, 188, 197–8, *Niger*, 212–13; *Reg. Epis. of Aberdeen*, i, 18–23; *Reg. Great Seal*, iii, 1474, 3297.]

1561 SIR ALEXANDER HOME, vicar 1561–3.—[*Comps. Gen. Coll. and Sub Coll. of Thirds, Aberdeen.*]

1608 JAMES HAY, trans. to Culter about 1623.—[*Banff Sas.*]

1627 WILLIAM DOUGLAS, adm. 1627, not 1628.

1644 ALEXANDER GARDEN, adm. 17th March 1644. Marr. 28th Jan. 1644; his wife, Isobel Middleton, died after 1696; his son, James, born 3rd May 1645; his daugh., Margaret.—[*Scot. Notes and Queries*, Nov. 1933, 164; *Mysteries in the North East*, 33; *Aberdeen Poll Tax Book*, ii, 202.]

1677 GEORGE GARDEN, for "1677" read "1674."

1680 PATRICK HARVIE, his wife, Margaret Scougall, buried 13th Aug. 1722. Line 7, for "daughter" read "Helen." Addl. issue—Christian.—[*Abbrev. of Adjud.*, 30th Aug. 1734.]

1871 JAMES BREBNER, died 23rd Jan. 1927; his daugh., Helen, died at Aberdeen 2nd April 1937; his son, Robert, factor at Dalmeny.

1916 CHARLES WALKER STOBIE, trans. to Ferryport-on-Craig 27th April 1927.

1927 ROBERT TAYLOR MONTEITH, trans. from Crimond (*q.v.*) 9th Sept. 1929; has issue—Robert Dougall, born 23rd Jan. 1916; Margaret Duncan, born 28th March 1918; Eleanor Mary, born 22nd Feb., died 12th June 1922; Lorna Graham, born 12th Jan. 1928.

FYVIE

The Tyronensian priory at Fyvie was founded by Sir Reginald Cheyne in or before 1285 in honour of the Lord Jesus Christ and the Blessed Virgin. In that year he granted a charter of the lands of Ardlogy and Lethendy to Arbroath Abbey and the monks of the abbey inhabiting the priory or cell (at Fyvie); and in the same year Sir Reginald's second son, Henry, Bishop of Aberdeen, united the vicarage of Fyvie to the priory, the cure to be served by a perpetual chaplain, who shall attend to the parish day and night as often as necessary and administer the sacraments to the parishioners.

The priory founded by Reginald de Chene seems to have been a reconstitution of a Celtic ecclesiastical establishment. To the priory, it is said, belonged the group of Pictish sculptured stones built into the east gable of the parish church, a fleur de lis in the manse wall, and several stones built into All Saints Church, Woodhead. On 21st Aug. 1459 Malcolm, Abbot of Arbroath, and the convent of the same, presented to the Pope a petition craving that the priory be united to and appropriated by the abbey. The priory, states the narrative, is not conventual, nor a dignity, nor a *personatus*, but it depends on Arbroath, and has been wont to be assigned to one of the monks, and its value does not exceed £18 stg., and the assignation to the monk is revokable at the abbot's pleasure. But a monk, Alexander Mason, of the said monastery, holds and detains possession by the help of King James (II). The Pope ordered the Abbot of Deer, the Prior of Restonnet, and Walter Yohl, canon of Aberdeen, to summon said Alexander and others concerned, and if the foregoing be found true, to unite and appropriate the priory to the monastery in perpetuity, so that when the said Alexander has for a just and reasonable cause been removed by the said Malcolm or the abbot for the time, and recalled to the convent, and got a monk's portion assigned to him, Malcolm and the convent may take possession. In 1865 a cross was erected on the site of the priory by Colonel and Mrs Gordon of Fyvie. It is said that there was at Follarule a Chapel of St Rule founded in 1376 by Adam Pyngle, burgess of Aberdeen. The first part of the statement may accord with fact; but what Adam Pyngle did found on 20th August 1376 was a chaplain for perpetual celebration at the new altar erected by Alexander Kinninmonth, Bishop of Aberdeen 1356–80, in the south corner of the Cathedral Church of Aberdeen, for the souls of himself, his wife, Marjorie Blackwater, the said Bishop of Kinninmonth, etc., the endowment being the lands of Folethrowle; and with consent of his said wife he gave the mill of Folethrowle with adjacent land and the water rights, and a piece of arable land in the lands of Folethblackwater, as an additional endowment lest at any time in the future the revenues and farmes of the lands of Folethrowle should prove inadequate for the sustenance of the chaplain. This was designated the chaplainry of Follarule; and according to the confirmation charter of Robert II on 11th Aug. 1381, the chaplainry was "to God, the Blessed Virgin Mary, and All Saints." The manse, yard, and glebe of the chaplain were situated at Meikle-Folla; and it may be that it was vestiges of the manse, not of a chapel as stated, that were recorded as existing in 1724–5, and in part at the close of the 18th century in the "town-land" of Meikle-Folla, and that entirely disappeared in 1847 when the whole foundations were dug up in a field about 300–400 yards west of the Church and churchyard of Follarule. By charter of James VI, 10th Sept. 1574, the chaplainry was conveyed to King's College, Aberdeen. Somewhat earlier, on 10th July 1573, Mr Alexander Cheyne, parson of the Snow Church, Old Aberdeen, was presented to the chaplainry which was within the yearly rent of £30, and was vacant through the last chaplain, Mr. John Strathauchin, not having subscribed to the Articles of Religion, as an additional sustenance in "his office of teching the lawis" in King's College. It may be that Mr John Strathauchin was the successor of Sir William Silver, who was chaplain at least from 1528 to 1541, and as such was one of the vicars of the choir of the cathedral. On 19th July 1449 John Henrison, clerk, had been coll. and provided to the chaplainry, vacant by the death of William Liel.—[*Procs. Soc. of Antiqr.*, lxxiii, 1938–9, 32–3; *Thanage of Fermartyn*, 54, 60, 61, 66; *Cal. of Papal Registers, Petitions*, x, 711, xi, 405; Pratt's *Buchan*, 412; *Reg. Epis. Aberdeen*, i, 109–11; Orem's *Description of the Chanonry*, etc., *Old Aberdeen*, 87; *Fasti Aberdonenses*, 129; *Reg. Pres. Bene., Regent Morton*, i, 8–9; Sir John Cristisone's *Prot. Bk.*, Nos. 73, 326, 360; *Reg. of Arbroath* No. 234, 255, pp. 166–8.]

ALEXANDER OGILVY, min. in 1563. 1563 (See Tarves, Methlick and Ellon.)

WILLIAM CHALMERS, reader in 1563.—[*Comps. Sub Coll. of Thirds, Aberdeen*, etc.]
1563

HIEROMYMUS INNES, his daugh.,
1594   Jane (marr. William Bannerman of Asleid).

JOHN MANSON, his daugh., Agnes
1829   Eliza, died 18th Aug. 1932.

JOHN HENDERSON SEAFORTH BURLEIGH, trans. to St Enoch's,
1924   Dundee, 3rd Oct. 1928.

FRANKLIN ROSS TAYLOR LORNIE, born at Allanton, Lanark-
1929   shire, 23rd Oct. 1893, son of Peter L., Allanton, Shotts, and Christina Catherine Taylor; educ. at George Watson's College and Univ. of Edinburgh, M.A. (1914); licen. by Presb. of Edinburgh 5th Sept. 1917; assistant West St Giles; Lieut. in Royal Scots and Capt. 5th K.O.S.B. 1922 and 1940 in Great War; ord. to Anwoth 13th Feb. 1919; trans. to Buccleuch, Glasgow, 26th March 1925; trans. and adm. 20th Feb. 1929; trans. to Newhaven on Forth 22nd Oct. 1937; recalled as combatant officer 1940, dem. 2nd May 1944. Marr. 17th April 1919 Catherine, eldest daugh. of Thomas Douglas Dobson, timber merchant, Leith, and Agnes Mitchell, and has issue—Franklin Neil, born 21st March 1920; Agnes Dobson, born 24th July 1923; Thomas Douglas Dobson, born 21st March 1926.

GAMRIE

The Church of Gamrie, with the Chapel of Trub (Trup, Troup) appears in the confirmation charter granted by John, Bishop of Aberdeen 1200–7, to Arbroath Abbey. The church had been granted to the abbey by King William the Lion between 1189 and 1198. The Chapel of Troup had been situated on the lands of that name. In the north wall of the ruined old church are three holes which contained a corresponding number of skulls, traditionally said to have been those of three Danish chiefs who were slain in a battle in 1004 at the place afterwards called the "Bleedy Pots." The invaders, who were defeated, are said to have polluted the church. Hence the exhibition of the skulls, which were removed bit by bit by visitors to the place about the close of the first quarter of the 19th century. The present church, situated about a mile inland, was built in 1830.—[*Reg. of Arbroath, vetus,* 136; Pratt's *Buchan,* 328–9, 335.]

WILLIAM MASON, M.A., min. in
1563   1563.—[*Comps. Sub Coll. of Thirds, Aberdeen,* etc.]

THOMAS CRISTISON, reader 1563.—
1563   [*Comps. Sub Coll. of Thirds, Aberdeen,* etc.]

GILBERT CHEYNE, M.A., pres. to
1576   vicarage 10th Oct. 1576 on death of John Cockburn.—[*Reg. Pres. Bene.,* i, (4), 48.]

ALEXANDER FRASER, M.A., pres.
1585   to vicarage 24th April 1584 on dem. of John Kennedy, parson of Tullynessle.—[*Reg. Sec. Sig.,* 1, 124.]

JOHN KENNEDY, M.A., vicar 1588.
1588   —[*Comps. Sub Coll. of Thirds, Aberdeen,* etc.]

JOHN MURRAY, pres. to vicarage
1592   12th May 1592, vacant by non-residence of Alexander Fraser.—[*Reg. Sec. Sig.,* lxii, 262.]

JOHN GORDON, marr. 17th June
1717   1712 Janet, daugh. of George Gordon, merchant, Aberdeen.

JAMES WILSON, died Father of the
1732   Church.

JAMES CRUDEN, his daugh., Sophia,
1855   died 11th Feb. 1933.

PATRICK THOMAS CLARK, his
1875   daugh., Margaret Murdoch, died 30th March 1934.

DAVID WALKER MACLEAN, died
1925   18th April 1932.

GARDENSTOWN

JOHN SCOTT THOMSON, dem. 17th
1925   May 1932; died 18th April 1946.

(*Charge united to Gamrie* 17*th May* 1932.)

INVERKEITHNY

On 26th Feb. 1640 the min. produced to the Synod "two gryt silver pieces worth sax scoir libs," gifted to the use of the church by the laird of Frendraught. There was in the parish a Chapel of St Peter.—[*Coll. of the Shires of Aberdeen and Banff*, 65.]

1562 SIR PATRICK OGSTON, vicar 1562–3.—[*Comps. Sub Coll. of Thirds, Aberdeen*, etc.]

1590 WALTER BARCLAY, M.A., min. here, pres. to parsonage and vicarage 7th July 1590 on death of Hew Craigie.—[*Reg. Sec. Sig.*, lxi, 3.]

1661 JOHN MAITLAND, his son, David, M.A. (Aberdeen, 1705), received Orders from an "exauctorate" bishop, in 1717–21, intruded in Inverkeithny, conducting a meeting-house at the manse, and performing other functions of the ministry. Had addl. issue—Alexander, Charles, William.—[*Records of Marischal College*, ii, 281; *Justiciary Records*, May 1721.]

1701 JAMES MAITLAND, M.A.; on 2nd Jan. 1718 the Justices ordered him to find caution not to disturb his successor in the possession of the manse and glebe and the utensils of the church, and further prohibited him from exercising the functions of the ministry; but in 1718 to Jan. 1721 he preached in a meeting-house in Forgue and performed baptism.—*Justiciary Records*, 1717–21, 20th March 1721.]

1721 WILLIAM MILNE, line 12, for "Duff" read "Gordon."

1809 JAMES MILNE, his widow, Isabella Milne, bequeathed £500 for supplementing the stipend of the parish.

1922 DAVID SMITH, father schoolmaster, Glamis; trans. to Ceres 14th May 1926.

1926 EDMOND STEUART RUSSELL, formerly of Poolewe (*q.v.*); trans. from Arisaig 12th Aug. 1926; app. by Presb. of Garioch to Bourtie for three years 6th Sept. 1939; dem. 2nd Nov. 1940.

KINEDWARD

The ruins of the old church are situated on the north bank of the King-Edward burn. A stone with the name and arms of Forbes in the west gable may indicate that the church was built soon after Lord Forbes entered into possession of the Castle in 1509. An addition was made to the east end, probably in 157–, the partly obliterated date which occupies a place at the top of one corner along with the initials R.K.—Robert Keith, Commendator of the Abbey of Deer, to which the Church belonged. The Craigstone aisle on the south side, which contains memorials of the Urquhart family, was built by John Urquhart of Craigfintray; and an archway erected by him for his private use carries the initials of himself and his third wife, Elizabeth Seton and the date 1621. Above the west doorway are the initials of Dr William Guild, min. 1608–13, indicating possibly that repairs were carried out during his incumbency.—[Pratt's *Buchan*, 346–7.]

1570 DAVID HOWESON pres. to the vicarage-pensionary 28th July 1572 on death of Andrew Shand.—[*Reg. Sec. Sig.*, xi, 115.]

1905 WILLIAM ALEXANDER RATTRAY SELKIRK, died Clarkston Glasgow, 21st Nov. 1946; his sons—Alastair Logie, died through enemy action 4th Jan. 1941; William, Wing Commander, R.A.F., killed 4th Feb. 1942.

MACDUFF

1920 WILSON SUMMERS LESLIE trans. to Whiteinch 13th Dec. 1928.

1929 LOUIS EDMOND McVICKER, trans. from Monigaff 4th July 1929; dem. 30th June 1945; died at Port Stewart 24th Oct. 1945; had issue—a daugh. still-born 3rd Nov. 1917; John Louis Armitage, M.B., Ch.B., born 8th Nov. 1919; Joan Hogg Elizabeth, born 23rd May 1923.

MILLBREX

ARNOLD LOW KEMP, trans. to Birse 8th Oct. 1926.
1915

SYDNEY MELROSE McEWAN, trans. from Deerness (*q.v.*) 9th Feb. 1927.
1927

MONQUHITTER

The church was erected in 1764, taking the place of a building that was the gift of William Cumine of Auchy and Pittullie, who died 1707, and to whose memory there is a monument in the present church.—[Pratt's *Buchan*, 375–6.]

ADAM HAY, his son, Adam, apprenticed to Colin Mackenzie, chirurgeon, 16th March 1720.
1678

JOHN SPENCE EWEN, his son, Alister, M.A. (Aberdeen, 1923), B.Sc. Agriculture (Edinburgh, 1930), assistant professor of Animal Husbandry, Univ. of Saskatchewan, Canada, 1931.
1920

FRANK ROBERTSON, trans. to Kintore, 10th July 1929.
1924

GEORGE EDDIE THOMSON, formerly of Murthly (*q.v.*); trans. from Newcastle 22nd Oct. 1929; adm. to united charge 8th April 1931. Marr. (2) 13th Dec. 1941 Mary Anne Barclay.
1929

(*Charges united 8th April* 1931.)

NEW BYTH

The old church gave place to the present building in 1852.

ALEXANDER PATERSON, dem. 30th Nov. 1936; died 19th Jan. 1941.
1918

TURRIFF

The present church was built in 1794, enlarged in 1830, and altered and improved in 1897. The ruins of the old church stand at the west end of Castle Street. The belfry bears the date 1635, the Hay Arms, the initials of William, Earl of Erroll, and the initials of the min. of that time, Thomas Mitchell. In 1861, when a portion of the south wall of the choir was being demolished to furnish material for the repair of the churchyard wall, a fresco painting of a mitred abbot was discovered on a splay of a window that had been built up. On each side of the head were stars painted red, and the words S. NINIAN in black. Unfortunately it was destroyed soon after the discovery; and a similar fresco on the opposite splay suffered destruction in the actual demolition. It is probable that there was a series of frescoes round the choir, the work, maybe, of Andrew Baerkum, who in 1538 was employed by the Abbot of Kinloss to adorn certain portions of that monastery. At the Haugh of the Laithers there was a chapel, said to have been dedicated to St Carnac, apparently identical with the Welsh St Caranog. There was a Celtic monastery, generally regarded as having been dedicated to St Congon, a follower of St Columba, and possibly founded by him. In 1272 Alexander Comyn, Earl of Buchan, founded a hospital for a master, six chaplains, and thirteen poor husbandmen, giving to it in 1273 his lands of Knockhill. In 1329 Robert I added a mass chaplainry for his brother, Sir Nigel Bruce, captured by the English at Kildrummy Castle, and "hanged and drawn" by order of Edward I, the endowment being the lands of Petty at Fyvie. By charter of 10th March 1511–12, James IV, for his special favour towards his domestic clerk, Mr Thomas Diksoun, prebendary of Turriff, within the Cathedral Church of Aberdeen, and for the edification and policy carried on at the Parish Church of Turriff for entertainment of the lieges, with the consent and desire of William, Earl of Erroll, patron of the church and prebend, erected the church lands, town and glebe of the said Church of Turriff into a free burgh of barony, with power to the inhabitants to sell and buy, and have the position of burgesses, and the power to elect bailies, etc., with the advice of the said Mr Thomas and his successors, and to have a market cross, a weekly market each Saturday, and two annual fairs, at the Feast of St Peter-in-Chains, and of St Congon, and power to the said Mr Thomas to lay out the said lands as burgh roods for the good of the inhabitants.

1583 WILLIAM HAY, parson 10th Feb. 1574-5, 1578.—[*Reg. Mag. Sig.*, iv, 2360; *Comps. Gen. Coll. of Thirds.*]

1590 GEORGE HAY, born 1563, son of John H. of Leys.

1664 ANDREW SKENE, had issue—Joanna.

1844 WILLIAM LESLIE, his son, William, shipbuilder, Aberdeen, died 29th Jan. 1927.

1907 DUNCAN MACLAREN, died 21st Nov. 1926; his widow, Joan Hamilton Gillieson, died at Edinburgh 14th May 1927; his daugh., Mairi Ann (marr. 13th Sept. 1939 John, elder son of W. H. Elliott, Edington Mains, Chirnside).

1927 PETER CRAIK MacQUOID, born Carisbrooke, Isle of Wight, 19th July 1895, eldest son of James MacQuoid, customs officer, and Bessie Craik; educ. at Fordoun School, Mackie Academy, Stonehaven, and Univs. of Aberdeen and Edinburgh, M.A. (1919); licen. by Presb. of Edinburgh 29th June 1921; assistant, Hawick; ord. to Bothkennar 22nd April 1924; trans. and adm. 20th April 1927. Marr. 4th Aug. 1924 Margaret Florence Smith, second daugh. of John Weir, Thurso, and Elizabeth Anderson Thom, and has issue—Vera Florence Elizabeth, born 30th Aug. 1926; Peter Craik, born 22nd Jan. 1936.

YTHAN WELLS

1890 ALEXANDER WILSON, his daugh., Charlotte, M.A., M.B., Ch.B., assistant practitioner at Lincoln 1925–8 (marr. 31st July 1928 Percy John, son of Rev. S. B. Brydges, rector of Potter Hanworth, Lincolnshire).

1917 DANIEL ALEXANDER FORREST, dem. 25th Feb. 1948.

PRESBYTERY OF FORDYCE

BANFF

There was a chapel near the Castle dedicated to the Holy Rood, and a chapel dedicated to St Thomas. There was also, near the town, a chapel dedicated to the Virgin Mary. In 1324 it gave place to a house of the Carmelites, King Robert I, in that year, granting it and its ground to God, the Blessed Virgin Mary, and the brothers of Mount Carmel, for building there a church and other buildings of their order, and giving besides to the said brothers and their successors that davoch of land with its pertinents wont hitherto to belong to the said chapel, for supplying bread, wine, and wax for the more devout performance of the worship of God. St Catherine's Green and St Catherine's Street in the town seem to point to a dedication to that saint.—[Mackinlay's *Anc. Ch. Dedications*, script.), 166, 258, 366; (non-script.), 420.]

1590 JOHN GUTHRIE, pres. in 1597 on death of William Carnegie.—[*Reg. Sec. Sig.*, lxix, 115.]

1716 JAMES INNES, line 14, for "Avon" read "Aven."

1873 WILLIAM STRATON BRUCE, died at Edinburgh 30th March 1933; his son, Robert Duncan, Canadian Pacific Railway, died from an accident at Calgary 5th June 1926; his daughs.—Ethel (marr. 6th Sept. 1930 Robert G. Sheriffs, Sheriff clerk, Banff); Alice Straton (Mrs. McIver), died 22nd Jan 1934; his son, Arthur Nicol, Italian Consul at Edinburgh, died 28th June 1943.

1925 DAVID FINDLAY CLARK, awarded the Norwegian Freedom Cross 1947. Marr. 2nd Sept. 1927 Anna Whyte, third daugh. of James Mackenzie, Lochgelly, and Anna Whyte, and has issue—David Findlay, born 30th May 1930; Thomas James Macdonald, born 8th April 1932.

BOYNDIE

The patron saint is Brenaind Moca Alte, son of Findlay, of Clonfort. Designated the "Voyager," he died in 577. His feast was on 16th May, and here his fair was held in Brannan Howe on 26th May, new style. "The Brannan Stanes" are in this parish.—[Watson's *Celtic Place Names*, 274.]

1563 WILLIAM SMYTH, reader in 1563.—[*Comps. Sub Coll. of Thirds, Aberdeen*, etc.]

1863 JAMES LEDINGHAM, his son, Sir John Charles Grant, professor of Bacteriology, Univ. of London, F.R.S., F.R.C.P.E., LL.D. (Aberdeen, 1895), Knight Bachelor 1937.

1896 JAMES GARDINER LEDINGHAM, dem. 30th Sept. 1940 in favour of A. and S.

BUCKIE

The Church was built in 1835.

1908 JOHN GREENLAW, his sons—John Rutherford, min. of Kininmonth; Karl Stewart Guthrie, min. of Kinloss and St David's, Dundee; his wife, Katherine Paterson Stewart, died 7th March 1943.

CULLEN

In a settlement between the Bishop of Moray and the Bishop of Aberdeen in 1236 there appears the Chapel of Inverculan which is petitioning for the status of a church. As a church it occurs in the Taxation of 1275, being valued along with Fordyce and Tulywhill (Ordiquhill) at 60 merks; and in 1498 the designation is the Parish Church of Cullen. In 1327 Robert I founded a chaplainry in the church for the soul of Queen Elizabeth, his second wife, who had died at Cullen in Nov. of that year, the endowment being £5 Scots from the Burgh Roods annually and 33 sh. 4 pence in augmentation, payable at the hands of the bailies and community of that burgh. The payment is mentioned in the Exchequer Rolls in 1327 and subsequent years; and the foundation was ratified by James III under the Great Seal on 6th March 1455, and by Queen Mary under the Privy Seal on 10th July 1543. On 10th Dec. 1536, John Duff of Muldovet founded the Chaplainry or Altar of St Anne. In the first quarter of the 15th century John Hay, lord of the Forest of Boyne and Tullibole, founded an altar, probably the Altar of St Mary Magdalene, for the soul of Alexander Sinclair, lord of Deskford, with an endowment of £5 Scots annual rent from his lands of Ordinhove. And in 1539 the aisle of St Ann on the south side of the church was built by the said John Hay's granddaugh., Elene or Helen, daugh. of David Hay and wife of Archibald Dick of Craighead. For the upkeep of the aisle and its ornaments she mortified a croft and tofts in the burgh. The particular dedication of the collegiate church was St Mary the Virgin; but the erection was for the honour and glory of the Trinity, the Virgin Mary, St Anne, St John the Baptist, St Andrew, St Mary Magdalene, and all the Saints of the Heavenly Host. It was founded by Alexander Ogilvy of that ilk, Mr Alexander Dick, Archdeacon of Glasgow, John Duff of Maldovat, the bailies and community of the burgh, and the parishioners of the Church of St Mary of Cullen, confirmation being given by William Stewart, Bishop of Aberdeen, on 23rd April 1543, and ratification by John Hamilton, Archbishop of St Andrews, as Papal Legate, in Feb. 1552. To the provostry were assigned the fruits of the vicarage of Rathven, with manse and garden and 2 acres of arable land on the south side of the church. Mr William Elphinstone, vicar of Rathven, was the first provost. To each prebend was allotted 20 merks in lands and money, with apartment and garden, the lands being crofts in the town. The prebends were—St Anne, to which pertained tofts and crofts and 35 bolls barley, being the endowment by Helen Hay and her son, Alexander Dick, Archdeacon of Glasgow, both already mentioned; Holy Cross; St Mary the Virgin, whose prebendary had the cure of souls of the parish of Cullen; St John the Baptist; St Andrew, the endowment of which included the revenue of the foundation made by Robert I for the soul of his queen, and given by Queen Mary in 1543 "in help and supplement of our College Kirk in the burgh of Cullen"; and St Mary Madgalene, to which belonged the endowment from the lands of Ordinhove granted by John Hay as already mentioned. There were also two singing boys. At the Reformation the prebendary of St Andrew's prebend was Sir George Hay, who in 1566–7 acted as Master of the Grammar School. On 2nd March 1582–3 and 2nd April 1583 the possessions of the prebends of St Mary Magdalene, Holy Cross, St Andrew, and St John the Baptist, were conveyed to Alexander Hay of Easter Kennet, Clerk Register, by the respective prebendaries, with consents. The Crown charter of Confirmation gives in detail the possessions of each prebend. After the Reformation Cullen was attached to Fordyce, of which on 26th March 1622 it is given as "a pendicle." Apparently soon after it was disjoined from Fordyce. The church, described in 1724 as situated "about the middle of the town" (Old Cullen), stands at Old Cullen about a mile from the new town, in a recess of the walls of the grounds of Cullen House, St Anne's Aisle or Chapel being the south transept of the church. In the north wall, near the site of the High Altar, is the aumbry. The recess at the base is surmounted by the figures of two angels holding a monstrance—the utensil used for presenting the consecrated Host for the adoration of the people.—[*Reg. Great Seal*, v, 301, viii, 302; *Reg. Sec.*

Seal, i, 2436, iii, 356, 1420; *Exchequer Rolls*, i, 61, 458, 477, 549, vi, 172–3, x, 621, xi, Pref., xxxiii, and 65, 126, xii, 106, 384, 608, xiii, 110, 584, xiv, 113, 447, xviii, 107, 344, 351, 391; *Reg. of Moray*, 101; *Reg. of Aberdeen*, ii, 53; *Reports Hist. MSS. Commis.*, iii, 404; Macfarlane's *Geog. Colls.*, i, 72; Cramond's *Ch. of Cullen*, 11–12, 25–6, 46, 56.]

1563 ANDREW HAY, reader in 1563.—[*Comps. Sub Coll. of Thirds, Aberdeen*, etc.]

1573 JAMES ANDERSON, pres. to parsonage on dem. of John, Archbishop of St Andrews.—[*Reg. Pres. Bene.*, i, (4), 10.]

1601 GEORGE DOUGLAS, marr. (1) Catherine Stewart.—[*Banff Sas.*, 22nd June 1601, 22nd May 1607, 13th Feb. 1608 and 4th Nov. 1633.]

1623 JAMES HAY, formerly of Forgue.—[*Banff Sas.*, 31st May 1623.]

1652 JAMES CHALMERS, it is recorded in minutes of Elgin Kirk Session 6th June 1659 that he had been unanimously elected min. at Elgin by the elders and heritors, but the Presb. of Fordyce had refused translation.—[*Recs. of Elgin*, ii, 290.]

1663 WILLIAM BURNETT, had issue—Christian, bapt. 9th March 1677; William, bapt. 13th Nov. 1681.

1717 JAMES LAWTIE, marr. (2) cont. 15th Jan. 1757 Margaret, daugh. of James Innes, min. of Banff (she died 1st July 1763).

1901 WILLIAM GEORGE GREEN McLEAN, dem. 16th May 1927, died at Longniddry 16th March 1939; his daugh., Ella Mary (marr. 30th June 1931 Dr Angus Cameron, M.C.); his son, Douglas Gordon, min. of Innellan.

1927 WILLIAM GEORGE ROBERTSON, trans. from Barthol Chapel 28th Sept. 1927; D.D. (Aberdeen, 3rd April 1935); dem. 30th Sept. 1936; his wife, Elizabeth Ann Iverach, died 22nd April 1932; marr. (2) 21st Nov. 1934 Daphne Drucilla, daugh. of Henry Fripp, M.D., London, and widow of Arthur Wilson Taylor, Newcastle-on-Tyne. Publication—*The Church Annals of Cullen* (1938).

DESKFORD

There was at Skeith a chapel dedicated to Our Lady of Pity, in which her wooden image was preserved.—[Mackinlay's *Ancient Church Dedications in Scotland* (script), 111.]

1578 JOHN PILMAIR, reader 28th April 1578.—[*Edin. Tests*, vi, 102.]

1654 WALTER OGILVIE, marr. Helen Leith, widow of John Gellie, min. of Monymusk.—[*Farquhar Papers.*]

1659 ANDREW HENDERSON, his daugh., Mary (marr. cont. 17th Feb. 1693 Walter Ogilvie of Ardoch). Line 13, for "213" read "215, 433."—[*Banff Sheriff Court Rec.*, 11th Jan. 1705.]

1843 JAMES MACKINTOSH, senior graduate of King's College, Aberdeen, 1900; his son, John Fraser, died 3rd July 1918; James, died 2nd Aug. 1900; William, died 25th Dec. 1928; Alexander Watson Mackenzie, died 25th Nov. 1917; Francis William Innes, M.B., C.M., died at Evie, Orkney, 11th May 1931; his daugh., Ellen Jane (marr. 30th Aug. 1888 Alexander Emslie, stockbroker, London); his son, Sir Ashley Watson, F.R.C.P.E. (1916), LL.D. (1930), K.C.V.O. (1931), Physician to Aberdeen Royal Infirmary 1909–30; Regius Professor of Medicine, Univ. of Aberdeen, 1912–30; Hon. Physician in Scotland to King George V and King Edward VIII; Consulting Physician to Scottish Command; died 14th Oct. 1937; Edith Frances Wheen, died 24th Sept. 1943.

1890 GEORGE MATHIESON PARK, dem. 18th May 1931; his wife, Anne Keith, died 29th June 1938.

(*Charges united 30th Aug.* 1931.)

ENZIE

For the inauguration of mission work at Enzie, the Presb. of Strathbogie on 25th Aug. 1725, under the plea that "all kirks and chappels and places for uses" were "by law in the hands of the present Establishment," made choice of St Ninian's Chapel at Chapelford in the parish of Bellie, a house in good repair and "at a good distance from both Kirks of Bellie and Rathven." Almost at once trouble occurred, and on 27th Oct. 1725 the Synod of Moray concurred "with the Presbytery of Strathbogy for prosecuting the poppish rabblers, violence having been done to Mr Walter Morrison, preacher of the Gospel, and his hearers at St Ninian's Chapel in the Enzie. Information to be laid before the Commission of the General Assembly. The Moderator also to write to such officers of State as he shall think proper anent the said rabble." A year later, on 25th Oct. 1726, the Presb. was appointed by the Synod "to make further enquiry and get what evidence possibly they can for supporting their claim to that Chappel, and transmit the same to the advocate of the Church for his advice, and that application be made to the Duke of Gordon desiring that Chappel for publick worship as to the suppression of popery." Whatever was the immediate result of such action, it was later resolved to build a "meeting-house in the Enzie," and in 1729 the General Assembly appointed a voluntary collection through the nation for the building the same and for providing the preacher in a subsistence and necessary accommodation. The heritors concerned showed reluctance to grant a building site, apparently due to their impression that a "house for public worship would lead to the erection of a third parish with the consequent claim upon the heritors for a Manse, Glebe, and Stipend." Accordingly, on 22nd Oct. 1729, the Synod appointed a committee to wait on the Duke of Gordon and the Duchess, his mother, and assure them that the church had "no design for a new erection in the Enzie to the burthening of the heritors," and to crave ground for a "Meeting-house" and a manse. These buildings appear to have been erected in the following year, or soon after, on a site in the west part of the parish of Rathven. Of the church built in 1785 we are told that the cost was also met from a fund accruing from a collection made throughout the church. It was under the management of the Royal Bounty Committee; and the salary of the missionary was defrayed in part by the Royal Bounty, and in part by an endowment arising from lands left by a Mr Anderson, which were purchased by Alexander, Duke of Gordon, "the price being invested more advantageously in other property." There was a glebe of 8 acres and a "comfortable house" for the missionary. On the Braes of Enzie there was a chapel dedicated to St Ninian. The burying-ground is called St Ninian's and sometimes Chapelford.—[*Presby. Recs.*, 25th Aug. 1725; *Memo.*, Rev. John Will, B.D.; *Recs. of Synod of Moray*, 27th Oct. 1725, 25th Oct. 1726, 22nd Oct. 1729; Mackinlay's *Ancient Church Dedications* (non-script.), 33.]

WALTER MORRISON, on 25th Aug. 1725 he was app. by the Presb. of Strathbogie to repair to the Chapel of St Ninian at Enzie and to begin preaching, catechising, etc., till he was orderly withdrawn therefrom; he was described as "a preacher commissioned to this Presbytery and other places thereto adjacent upon the Royal Fund granted by H.M. King George and the last General Assembly."—[*Presby. Records*, 25th Aug. 1725; *Memo.*, Rev. John Will, B.D.]
1725

WILLIAM SMITH CAIE, his sons— William James, M.B., Ch.B., Mayor of Bury St Edmunds, died at Edinburgh 3rd Feb. 1927; John Morrison, C.B. (1943), Assistant Secretary, Board of Agriculture for Scotland.
1883

ROBERT HOWIE, dem. 17th May 1926, died at London 25th Sept. 1926; his widow, Jeanie Porter, died at Kilmarnock 19th March 1937; his son, Robert, M.A., Principal, Norbury College, London.
1898

1926 CHARLES MACDONALD, trans. from Appin 6th Oct. 1926; trans. to Ardallie 4th April 1928.	**1902** JOHN CHARLES MACGREGOR, his daugh., Mona Rosaleen (marr. 11th Aug. 1934 George, son of John Macdonald, Marden Moor, Galashiels).

(*Charges united 2nd March* 1930.)

FORDYCE

To Sir Alexander Symson and his successors, perpetual chaplains at the Altar of the Virgin Mary in the church, William Ogilvie of Stratherne, Kt., Royal Treasurer, gave two annual rents on 15th July 1516, for the souls of Alison Roull, his wife, etc. In 1275 the Churches of Cullen and Tulywheel (Ordiquhill) were depends of Fordyce; and after the Reformation, and apparently till 1622, these two churches, along with Deskford, continued in the same position. There were fairs of Tallerean and of New Summariffs, the latter suggesting that there was a dedication to St Macbrubha.—[*Reg. Great Seal*, iii, 95, 3157, viii, 302; *Reg. Epis. of Aberdeen*, ii, 53; Mackinlay's *Anc. Ch. Dedications* (nonscript.), 176; Watson's *Celtic Place Names*, 318.]

1563 JOHN ROBERTSON, vicar.—[*Acts and Dec.*, 27, 37; 36, 197.]

1569 GILBERT GARDEN, M.A., pres. to parsonage and vicarage 15th July 1568.—[*Reg. Pres. Bene.*, i, 14.]

1574 THOMAS ROBERTSON, reader, pres. to vicar-pensionary 31st Aug. 1574 on dem. of Sir John Robertson, usufructer, and non-compearance of James Robertson, vicar pensionary.—[*Reg. Pres. Bene.*, i, (4), 27.]

1684 ALEXANDER GILLIES, died 11th May 1715.

1865 JAMES GRANT, his daughs.—Caroline Stuart, died at Edinburgh 3rd Aug. 1930; Jane Watson, died at Banchory 2nd Dec. 1938; Katherine (Mrs. Stewart), died at Edinburgh 16th Nov. 1939; his son, Lachlan Gordon Duff, died at Manchester 6th April 1941.

1914 GEORGE ARTHUR MACDONALD DICKSON. Addl. issue—Dugald Macdonald, born 3rd July 1924.

(*Charges united 28th Oct.* 1934.)

ORD

1864 JAMES DAVIDSON, son of James D., shipmaster, Macduff, and Ann Watt. Line 15, for "Jemima" read "Jamima"; had issue—Isabella, M.A., Glasgow; Alexander Gardner, born 15th June 1872; James Milne, architect, Office of Works, Major, 3 Bat. Queen's Own Cameron Highlanders, born 10th Oct. 1876.

1890 JAMES AIKEN, died Glasgow 18th May 1933.

1898 GEORGE GRANT, dem. 4th Dec. 1928; died 2nd Feb. 1935; his sons—Alexander Ronald, died 3rd June 1926; William, born and died 7th Aug. 1891; his wife, Williamina Calder, died 19th Oct. 1929.

ORDIQUHILL

Ordiquhill was a pendicle of Fordyce till 22nd March 1622.—[*Reg. Great Seal*, viii, 302.]

1574 GILBERT GARDYNE, min. at Cullen, had also charge here till 1589. (See Cullen and Fordyce.)

1599 PATRICK DARG, min. at Cullen, had also charge here. (See Cullen.)

1918 WILLIAM POTTER, trans. to Aberdeen 18th March 1927.

1927 JAMES GEORGE MACDONALD, trans. from Elchies (*q.v.*) 20th Oct. 1927; died 28th Jan. 1941.

(*Ordiquhill, Cornhill and Ord united 28th Dec.* 1941.)

PORTSOY

THOMAS EDMUND HILL JONES, formerly of Durness (*q.v.*); assistant Kirkcaldy; trans. to Wanlockhead 29th March 1929; died 23rd Feb. 1943.
1926

JOHN MATHESON MACLEOD, trans. from Erchless (*q.v.*) 30th Sept. 1929. His daugh., Allina Catherine, in the nursing profession.
1929

RATHVEN

On 12th May 1333 Thomas de Hay of Urchny, for his own soul, and for the soul of his wife, Janet, and the soul of the late Christian Cruickshank, founded a chaplainry at the Altar of our Lord in the church, the endowment being five merks Scots annually from his lands of Urchny in Nairn. At the farm of Farskane there was a chapel dedicated to the Virgin Mary. On 19th June 1226 John Bysett, for the souls of William and Alexander, Kings of Scotland, and for the souls of his ancestors and successors, gave to God and the Church of St Peter of Rothven (Rathven) for the sustenance of seven lepers, the patronage of the Church of Kyltalargy (Kiltarlity). The hospital so founded had a prior who was admitted a canon of the Cathedral of Moray, a chaplain, and a menial.

The church was rebuilt in 1794. The old church was then described as in part "as old as Edinburgh Castle," having "couples of oak that grew in the estate of Rannes," "a roof of different altitudes," and "of venerable appearance." A question between the Bishop of Moray and the Bishop of Aberdeen as to the diocesan rights over the Church of Farskine in this parish was temporarily settled in 1236 by each party agreeing to waive the matter in their lifetime. In 1275 the Churches of Rathven were valued at 22 merks. Situated on the seashore about a mile west of Cullen, the Church or Chapel of Farskane seems always to have been attached to Rathven. It was dedicated to the Virgin Mary.—[*Reg. of Moray*, 27-8, 101; *Reg. of Aberdeen*, i, 39, ii, 53; Jervise's *Epitaphs*, i, 12, 273.]

SIR GEORGE DUFF, Provost of Cullen, vicar in 1565; on 8th Dec. 1545, when designated chaplain, he was presented to the provostry of the college of the B.V., Cullen, lately founded with the fruits of the vicarage of Rathven, resigned by Mr William Elphinston, chaplain, with reservation of his life rent.—[*Reg. of Abbrev. Feu Charters of Church Lands*, i, 138; *Reg. Sec. Sig.*, iii, 1420.]
1565

THOMAS HAY, min., his pres. to vicarage 17th Sept. 1582 on death of Sir George Duff.—[*Reg. Pres. Bene.*, ii, 78.]
1582

NICHOLAS TULLOCH, Sir Nicholas T., vicar 26th Dec. 1574, and burgess of Forres; died 20th Nov. 1582; survived by his wife, Isobel Ross, and had issue—James, Michel, Katherine, Elspeth.—[*Edin. Test.*, vii, 364, xii, 305.]
1585

THOMAS GARDEN M.A. pres. to parsonage 3rd Feb. 1588-9 on death of George Hay.—[*Reg. Sec. Sig.*, lix, 8.]
1588

JAMES LYLE min. of Bellie, pres. to parsonage 2nd Oct. 1589.—[*Reg. Sec. Sig.*, lix, 66.]
1589

JOHN HAY, brother-germane of George Hay, intruder 1713.—[*Justiciary Records*, 1712-17, 15th March 1715.]
1710

GEORGE HAY, in 1713 he intruded in the Church and Manse of Rathven, and continued so for two years, "so that the Presbytery have had no access either to supply or plant the Church by any qualified conform to law"; on 28th Dec. 1714 a petition presented by the congregation to the Presb. for his continuation as min. was refused, and when Mr Alexander Irvine, min. of Cullen, went to supply Rathven by order of the Presb., he was attacked by the people and stoned to the effusion of blood.—[*Justiciary Records*, 1712-17, 15th March 1715.]
1713

ANDREW KER.—*Aberdeen Genealogies*, 38.]
1723

1879 GORDON IRVING DONALD, his sons—Abercrombie of Kepong Rubber Estates Ltd., Malaya; James of Jeluke, Malay; his daugh., Barbara Mary Lizars (marr. 7th Sept. 1939 T. Brian Lisle, Leamington).

1901 JOHN LAWRIE SYMINGTON, dem. 30th Nov. 1938; died at Edinburgh 27th July 1947; his daugh., Nettie Agnes Lawrie (marr. 30th Sept. 1934 William Stuart Taylor, C.A.), died 19th Feb. 1936; his widow, Nettie Scott, died at Edinburgh 18th Dec. 1947.

SEAFIELD

1877 JAMES McINTYRE, dem. 5th Oct. 1926; died at Portknockie 25th Oct. 1928.

1927 JOHN FAULDS, formerly of Milton of Balgonie (*q.v.*); trans. from Clyne 18th May 1927; died 9th Oct. 1942.

(*United with Portknockie North* 31*st Dec.* 1942 *and with Cullen* 22*nd Dec.* 1946.)

SYNOD OF MORAY

PRESBYTERY OF STRATHBOGIE

BELLIE

Situated in the churchyard about two miles from Fochabers, near the junction of the Spey with the Moray Firth, the church belonged to the Priory of Urquhart. It was dedicated to St Peter. In 1720, on a petition by the min., the Presb. took steps for the erection of a new church. Delay ensued; and on 1728, when the church was described as "largely ruinous," and too long and too narrow, the Presb. set aside the idea of a new church, and decreed the repair of the old building, which was to be reduced to 70 feet in length and increased 3 feet in breadth by setting back the rear wall, making the breadth 20 feet within the walls. Two years later the work was incomplete, and even in Nov. 1732 the building was without doors and was otherwise insufficient. Eventually, in 1733, the work was completed. Subsequently the Duke of Gordon agreed to erect a new church in Fochabers. Plans were prepared in 1787; but the church was not finished till 1797. In 1720 it was reported to the Presb. that the manse consisted of two rooms and was built "of a mudwall," was "thecked with divots," and "like to fall." A new manse was secured at a cost of £900 Scots. On the burn of Tynet, about two miles south-east of the old church, there stood the Chapel of St Ninian. For a time after the Reformation it was used for worship alternately with the parish church. Later it became ruinous, and some years prior to the Revolution it was repaired by "priests and papists" and "enlarged to the bulk of many country churches in the Kingdom," and was used as a Roman Catholic place of worship both before and some time after 1688. In 1722-3 it was described as "well sclated and hath a large arch on every side by which they ('priests and papists') designed it in form of a Cross." It has attached to it a churchyard with "ruined dykes," which at that time was used as a "common burial-place." At Bellie there were also Fairs of St Catherine, St Mungo, and Holyrood.—[Macfarlane's *Geog. Colls*, i, 240-1; Jervise's *Epitaphs*, i, 12, 15; Cramond's *Church of Bellie*, 10, 12-14, 17-19.] (See Enzie.)

The chapel at the Bog of Gight, apparently in the vicinity of Gordon Castle, was founded by John Hay, Lord of Tullybethoyle, in or about 1374 and was dedicated to All Saints.—[*Reg. Epis. Moray*, 321.]

ROBERT GRANT, reader, charged before the Privy Council 11th Aug. 1590 with having baptised a child of the Earl of Huntly at Bog of Gight.—[*Privy Council Reg.*, xiv, 375.]
1574

JAMES LYLE, pres. to parsonage of Rathven 2nd Oct. 1589.—[*Reg. Sec. Sig.*, lix, 66.]
1589

WILLIAM SANDERS, he was ordained by the Synod in 1632 "to pay ten merks *ad pios usus* for being altogidder out of anie kirk on Whytsunday last as he was in his jurney betwixt this and Aberdone and to be depryved if he fall again in the lyk will example." Marr. (1) 1627, Margaret (died Oct. 1629), daugh. of Adam Duff of Drummuir and widow of David Henderson, min. of Botriphnie; (2) Christian Gregor, and had issue—John; Robert; Walter; Marjorie (marr. Alexander Shand); (3) Violet Henderson, widow of
1607

Alexander Innes of Petinich.—(*Com. of Moray Decreets*, 24th Jan. and 24th and 27th March 1632.]

1770 JAMES GORDON, his daugh., Jean, died 18th Dec. 1794.

1899 ROBERT VENTERS, dem. 16th May 1934; died Kirton, Dumfries, 28th Sept. 1945; his daugh., Margaret, M.B., Ch.B. (marr. 2nd Dec. 1940 John Rawson Elder, M.B., Ch.B., son of Professor J. R. Elder, Univ. of Otago).

(*United with Fochabers 30th Nov. 1947.*)

BOTRIPHNIE

Called Pettrifnie 6th April 1647.—[*Recs. Synod of Moray*, 6th April 1647.]

1574 JAMES FARQUHARSON, pres. to the vicarage of Pettary (Botarie) and Pettruthny (Botriphnie) 26th Aug. 1574, vacant by the death of Sir Walter Bunsche or the deprivation of John Hepburne.—[*Reg. Sec. Seal*, xlii, 67v.] (See Botarie-Cairney.)

1599 DAVID HENDERSON, died Dec. 1622. Marr. Margaret Duff, who marr. (2) William Sanders, min. of Bellie, and had issue—Margaret; Joan; Bessie (marr. John Wilson, Haugh of Grange).—[*Com. of Moray Decreets*, 27th March 1632.]

1879 ALEXANDER MACKAY, died suddenly 14th April 1930.

(*Charges united 16th Nov. 1930.*)

CAIRNEY
(formerly Botarie and Rivin)

Botarie occurs as Potarie in 1529 and Pottarie in 1611. On a visitation on 22nd May 1650 the Synod of Moray, finding that the people of the united parishes were "disaffected," so that "none of either the parishioners will come to the other parish kirk, but will be served *per vices* at their own respective kirks," much to the hindrance of the work, ordained the Presb. of Strathbogie to approach the Lords of Plantation of Kirks with a view to provision being made for each church being erected a separate charge. Eight years later, on 7th April 1568, the Synod disjoined the parishes, the min., Robert Jamieson, denuding himself of the Kirk of Riven; and on 3rd April 1660 it was intimated to the Synod that the Presb. had disjoined the two churches and declared the Church of Rivin vacant. Apparently nothing further was done, for on 7th Oct. 1686 the min., Alexander Rose, represented to the Synod that he served the two annexed Churches of Botarie and Ruthven, that the fabric of Ruthven Church was so ruinous that there was no conveniency to exercise doctrine or discipline, and that there was little expectation of the church being speedily repaired, and accordingly he craved the Synod to allow discipline at either church; his crave was granted.—[*Recs. of Synod of Moray*, 22nd May, 1650, 7th April 1658, 3rd April 1660, 7th Oct. 1686.]

1567 SIR NICHOL TULLOCH, vicar of Riven, 6th Aug. 1567, and 26th Nov. 1573, when he was put to the horn by the Privy Council for failure to appear to answer for certain crimes; probably still in office 31st Jan. 1576–7; evidently identical with Nicholas Tulloch, vicar of Drumdelgie in 1585.—[*Reg. Great Seal*, iv, 2639; *Reg. Privy Council*, ii, 305–6.]

1567 ALEXANDER LESLIE, pres. in 1569 as the vicarage of Botarie being in the hands of the King through the unlawful provision made to William Strathauchin, son of Mr James S., parson of Belhelvie.—[*Reg. Pres. Bene.*, i, 28.]

1573 JOHN HEPBURN, vicar in 1573 and 1575.—[*Comps. Gen. Coll. of Thirds.*]

1574 JAMES FARQUHARSON, pres. to vicarage of parish Kirk of Pettary and Petenthny 26th Aug. 1574 on death of Sir Walter Bunscht, last vicar, and John Hepburn, pretended vicar, not being lawfully provided thereto.—[*Reg. Sec. Sig.*, xlii, 67.]

SIR JOHN LESLIE, reader, pres. to vicarage of Pettary and Petenthny 10th Sept. 1574, on death of Sir Walter Bunscht.—[*Reg. Pres. Bene.*, i, (4), 28.]
1574

JAMES ANDERSON, min. here pres. to hail vicarage of Pettary and Petenthny 22nd Jan. 1591-2 on death of John Hepburne.—[*Reg. Sec. Sig.*, lxi, 126.]
1591

ALEXANDER ROSE, described as "Episcopal preacher at Ruthven and Botary," he was summoned before the Presb. of Strathbogie "for his having a scandalous access to the late unnatural rebellion," and was suspended and referred to the Synod, who, on 30th Oct. 1716, dep. him from the ministry for having, on his own confession, "read the pretender's proclamation calling up the subjects to his camp at Perth, and also a proclamation for a thanksgiving for the pretender's safe arrival in Scotland."
1680

JOHN ANNAND, his son, William, died at Huntly 27th July 1922.
1858

JAMES JOLLY CALDER, dem. 11th Oct. 1932; died at Stonehaven 21st Jan. 1946.
1900

(*Charges united 5th Oct. 1930.*)

DRUMDELGIE

The old church was burned about the close of the 16th century; hence the name "Burnt Kirk" applied to it.

1585 NICHOLAS TULLOCH, vicar 1585.

RUTHVEN

ANDREW HAY, reader 1563.—[*Comps. Sub Coll. of Thirds, Aberdeen*, etc.]
1563

DAVID CUMMING, pres. to vicarage 30th July 1580 on death of Robert Carmichael.—[*Reg. Pres. Bene.*, ii, 88.]
1580

DAVID RAMSAY, pres. to parsonage and vicarage 19th April 1582 on dem. of David Cumming.—[*Reg. Pres. Bene.*, ii, 37.]
1582

DAVID HENDERSON, M.A., pres. to parsonage and vicarage 17th July 1591 on dem. of Alexander Hay.—[*Reg. Sec. Sig.*, lxix, 281.]
1593

DRUMBLADE

The church pertained to the parsonage of Kinkell (*q.v*). "Jesus Fair," mentioned in 1720 as held at the park of Slioch, may indicate a dedication to Our Lord. At Chapelton in the parish was a chapel called in 1624 the "Nynemaidin chapell" near the old house which had been occupied by the late Sir George Rothrie, chaplain of Sidel chapel.—[*Reg. Mag. Sig.*, 24th June 1624.]

GEORGE ROTHNIE, was reader in 1563 and 1567.—[*Comps. Sub Coll. of Thirds, Aberdeen.*]
1563

ANDREW SPENS, had charge of Drumblade, Forgue and Culsalmond in 1574-6.—[*Book of Univ. Kirk*, 336, 351.]
1574

ALEXANDER BARCLAY, his pres. in 1598 was on the death of David Henderson.—[*Reg. Sec. Sig.*, lxix, 281.]
1598

WILLIAM GARDEN BLAIKIE, his sons—Walter Biggar, died 3rd May 1928; James Andrew, died 21st Dec. 1929; Robert Henry, died 5th Oct. 1933.
1842

WILLIAM GRANT, dem. 14th Oct. 1930; died Edinburgh 14th Feb. 1943; his daugh., Mary Crawford (marr. 2nd April 1938 Lieut. William Reginald Michell, R.N.); his son, Laurence, Inspector of Taxes, Newcastle-on-Tyne.
1891

(*Charges united 9th Nov. 1930.*)

GARTLY

St Finnan's Well was next the Chapel of Tillathrowie, which probably therefore had the same dedication.—[Henderson's *Place Names in West Aberdeenshire.*]

THOMAS GARDEN, M.A., Clerk of the Diocese of St Andrews; on 19th June 1566 he was provided to the perpetual vicarage of Grantuly (Gartly) and Dundelgie (Drumdelgie) by Patrick Hepburne, Bishop of Moray, who placed his ring on the finger of the said Thomas, committing to him the care and administration of the charge, and commanded the Dean of Christianity of Strathbogie, and rectors and vicars, etc., to induct him; uncertain whether he conformed.—[Grote's *Prot. Bk.*, 275.]
1564

JOHN CHALMERS, on 2nd Oct. 1649 he was suspended by the Synod "three lord's days for his unorderlie baptising and marrying and receing delinquents."
1649

JAMES THOMSON, his daughs.—Sarah Elizabeth (marr. William Henry Stewart, M.D., Dep. Inspector-General, R.N.), died 15th Sept. 1935; Catherine Hay, died at Linden Gardens, London, 18th Feb. 1934.
1843

ALEXANDER ANDERSON, his daugh., Jane, died 31st March 1935.
1878

WILLIAM SUTHERLAND, trans. to Methlick 6th Sept. 1928.
1908

WILLIAM KAY WHITE, trans. from Glenrinnes (*q.v.*) 17th Jan. 1929; delete "M.A. (1909)" and insert "M.A. (1908)."
1929

(*Charges united 1st Jan.* 1933.)

GLASS

SIR JAMES GLASS, vicar 1561, also of Kirkmichael.—[*Comps. Gen. Coll. of Thirds.*]
1561

JAMES GRANTULLIE, parson 1562–3, also at Kirkmichael.—[*Acts and Dec.*, xxix, 433; *Comps. Sub Coll. of Thirds, Aberdeen.*]
1564

GEORGE MELDRUM, dem. his charge prior to his deposition 5th Oct. 1664.
1644

PATRICK ROSS, had issue—George.—[*Aberdeen Sas.*, x, 341, 18th Dec. 1679.]
1688

WILLIAM GALLETLY GUTHRIE, died 21st May 1942.
1913

(*Charges united 8th Oct.* 1933.)

DALMEATH

The church belonged to the Monastery of Mortlach, and later to the See of Aberdeen. In 1266 Robert, Bishop of Aberdeen, granted the church, along with the Church of Clova, for the maintenance of the lights and ornaments of the High Altar of the cathedral.—[*Reg. Epis. of Aberdeen*, ii, 29.] (See Mortlach and Clova.)

WILLIAM ABERCROMBIE, min. here, pres. to parsonage and vicarage 11th June 1575.—[*Reg. Pres. Bene.*, i, (4), 35.]
1575

WILLIAM LESLIE, M.A., parson 1586–90.—[*Comps. Gen. Coll. of Thirds.*]
1586

GRANGE

In the barony of Strathisla granted to Kinloss Abbey by William the Lion, the abbey built a chapel dedicated to the Virgin Mary. Abbot Thomas Crystall, who died 20th Dec. 1535, placed in the chapel a beautiful statue of the Virgin, on a pedestal. On the erection of the parish in 1618 the chapel became the parish church. The present church was built in 1795. The parish takes its name from the Grange of Kinloss Abbey, which was situated in Strathisla Barony. Ladyhill and Ladywell in the parish recall the Virgin dedication.—[*Recs. of Kinloss*, 36.]

JOHN RUSSELL, his daughs.—Joanna Maria (marr. –. Brown); Isabella Helen (marr. George Edward Renwick); his son, Alexander, First Puisne Judge of Colony of Trinidad and Tobago, died at Port of Spain 13th Oct. 1934.
1867

JOHN GRAHAM CRANMER, died 9th April 1936; his wife, Catherine Mary Gordon, died 12th Aug. 1928.
1915

HUNTLY, formerly DUNBENNAN and KINNOIR

A chapel dedicated to St Menimus, the Confessor, was founded on the banks of the Deveron by Symon, Thane of Aberchirder 1253-99. On 27th June 1469 the two parishes were designated the "United Parishes of Kynnore and Dunbenane." On 22nd May 1650 the Synod resolved that "Dunebennan will need an able man it alone, it having within it the house of Huntly," and further, on 7th April 1658, it passed an Act disjoining the two parishes, the min., Mr William Jamieson, agreeing to denude himself of Dunbennan—the parishes remained united.—[*Reg. of Moray*, No. 218; *Cal. Papal Regs., Letters*, xii, 336; *Recs. Synod of Moray*, 22nd May 1650, 7th April 1658.]

1561 PATRICK HEPBURNE, rector, Kinnoir; one of the natural sons of Patrick Hepburne, Bishop of Moray, and grandson of Patrick Hepburne of Beynstoun; legitimised 4th Oct. 1545; summoned for treason along with his father and brothers 20th Dec. 1567, when he was still rector.—[*Acts Scott. Parl.*, v, 6; *Reg. Great Seal*, iii, 3169; *Scots Peerage*, ii, 142-3.]

1561 JAMES GORDON, M.A., vicar at Kinnoir and Dunbennan 1561-3; died before 24th June 1574.—[*Comps. Gen. and Sub Coll. of Thirds, Aberdeen*; *Reg. Sec. Sig.*, xiii, 45.]

1563 ROBERT KEITH, reader 1563.—[*Comps. Sub Coll. of Thirds, Aberdeen*, etc.]

1563 ROBERT FRASER, min. at Kinnoir and Dunbennan 1563.—[*Comps. Sub Coll. of Thirds, Aberdeen*, etc.]

1565 JOHN CHRISTISON of Renno.—[*Acts and Dec.*, xxxvi, 147.]

1567 JOHN PHILIP (PHILP), he was one of the monks of Kinloss Abbey and at the Reformation he left the abbey and "entered in the Lordis wyneyard planting the Gospel of truth according to the small talent given unto him, sen quhilk tyme it semyng gude to God to cast his pouer Kirk under the croce of povertie be withdrawing the stipendis appointit for the ministeris fra them in the yeir of God 1565 yeirs, the said Johnne enterit in societie with said abbot (Walter of Kinloss) and techit the Evangell to his people of Strathlay (Strathisla) and Kinloss at his chargeis till sum provisioun was maid for the sustentatoune of the ministrie and thane he was appointit agane be the Kirk to certain kirkis, quhair he now travellis according to his charge"; during all that time he had been without the benefit of his monk's portion of the abbey, and on his complaint the Privy Council on 9th July 1569 decerned that Abbot Walter pay him his annual pension from the abbey for ten years bypast according to the practice of the realm; on 20th July following, the Council suspended the decree till the said John "satisfy the Kirk and report the Superintendent's testimonial thereupon." —[*Reg. Privy Council*, i, 680-1, 684.] (See Alford, Turriff, Kinedward, Forglen, Auchterless, Keith, Forgue, Rothiemay.)

1574 WILLIAM SPENS, reader; pres. to the vicarage of Kinnoir and Dunbennan 24th June 1574.—[*Reg. Sec. Seal*, xlii, 45v.]

1580 JAMES DUFF, min. here, pres. to vicarage and parsonage 31st Dec. 1580 on death of Robert Keith; he held the parsonage of Kinnoir, and on 26th April 1585, when the parsonage and vicarage of Kinnoir were united, he received presentation to the vicarage, which was dem. by Mr Alexander Gordon of Hilside.—[*Reg. Pres. Bene.*, ii, 45; *Reg. Sec. Seal*, lii, 181.]

1604 GEORGE CHALMERS, was for a time one of the mins. at Aberdeen (North).

1692 LUDOVIC GORDON, died Aug. 1734. —[*Scot. Notes and Queries*, June 1934.]

1924 ADAM MACKAY, died at Aberdeen 24th Jan. 1931.

KEITH

1567 ANDREW GUTHRIE, called exhorter 1568.—[*Comps. Sub Coll. of Thirds, Moray*, etc.]

1665 Sir JAMES STRACHAN, had a child bapt. 28th Jan. 1669. His son, Hugh "commonly known under the name of Ramsay," carried on work as R.C. missionary in Crathie, Kindrochit, Glenmuick and Glencarden (Glengairn) in 1713, and was declared fugitive by the Lords Justiciary at Aberdeen.—[*Elgin Reg.*; *Justiciary Records*, 1712-17, 10th March 1715, 1717-21, May 1721.]

1700 JOHN GILCHRIST, died 4th June 1713. Marr. Sarah, daugh. of James Guthrie, merchant, Edinburgh, and had issue—James, bapt. 21st May 1701; Katherine, bapt. 14th Dec. 1702; John, bapt. 29th Dec. 1704; Mary, bapt. 18th June 1706; died 21st Nov. 1714; Margaret, born 1707 (marr. Alexander Tarras, merchant, Banff.)

1898 SYDNEY SMITH, adm. to Roslin 30th March 1927.

1914 MATTHEW STEWART, trans. to Hamilton Second Charge 3rd Sept. 1926.

1927 JOHN FREELAND, trans. from St Andrew's, Perth, 4th March 1927; dem. 26th Feb. 1935; adm. to Woodside, Glasgow, 11th Dec. 1945; his daugh., Margaret, died 6th Nov. 1940.

MARNOCH, of old ABERCHIRDER

The old church is said to have been built in the middle of a Druid circle of standing stones. The Chapel of St Neminius the Confessor, situated near the Deveron, was founded about 1286-7 by Alexander, Thane of Aberchirder, for the soul of Alexander, King of Scotland, the soul of his father, and his own soul, the endowment given to the chaplain, Sir Cristinus, being four silver merks annually from the mill of Carnoussexth (Carnousie), and the whole haugh called Dolbrech, with all the buildings built or to be built in the churchyard at the said chapel. St John's Chapel was situated at Chapelton, were are St John's Well and St John's Ford. On 26th Feb. 1640 the min. reported to the Synod "that the Laird of Frendraucht had given to his Churche two gryt cupps of silver worth nyne scoir libs, and that Sir Alexr. Lesly gave a silver bason, a Church bell, and a hand bell."—[*Reg. of Moray*, 279-80; MacKinlay's *Anc. Ch. Dedications* (script.), 280.]

1563 JOHN WILSON, reader at Aberchirder 1563.—[*Comps. Sub Coll. of Thirds, Aberdeen*, etc.]

1574 GEORGE DOUGLAS, reader, pres. to vicarage 23rd Aug. 1574 on death of John Thom. He was one of those who, as related on 18th Oct. 1577, assailed Alexander Dunbar, Dean of Moray, and killed the Dean's daughter, Elizabeth, aged 13 years.—[*Reg. Pres. Bene.*, i, (4), 27; Young's *Annals of Elgin*, 114.]

1579 JAMES DUNBAR, pres. to vicarage 11th March 1579-80, on death of George Douglas.—[*Reg. Pres. Bene.*, ii, 32.]

1597 ALEXANDER HAY, min. here, pres. to vicarage 18th June 1597, on death of Florence Winchester.—[*Reg. Sec. Sig.*, lxix, 115.]

1631 RICHARD MAITLAND, M.A.; in 1632 he was ord. by the Synod "to keep his kirk and to be resident at his Mans and to keep the presbiterie as he sould in tyme coming and to quyt his deposed reedare": was suspended by the General Assembly at Aberdeen 28th July 1640, for some apparent miscarriages in his life and some in his doctrine, and on 27th Oct. following he was reponed by the Synod, having cleared himself of popery, armenianism, etc.

1648 JOHN REIDFURD, adm. to Forglen before 1624; trans. to Towie 1634.

1707 ALEXANDER CHALMER, his widow, Barbara Burnett, died Tuesday, 26th March 1776.

1842 DAVID HENRY, his daugh., Mary Frances, died at Aberdeen 12th Nov. 1930.

1917 NEIL WILLIAM WILSON, died 5th Dec. 1943.

MORTLACH

To the Monastery of Mortlach belonged the Church and Monastery of Clova with land and the Church of Dalmeath with land. By Bull of Pope Andrew in 1157 the Monastery of Clova and the Monastery of Mortlach, with the five churches pertaining to same, were annexed to the See of Aberdeen.—[*Reg. Epis. Aberdeen*, i, 5-6, 84.]

1559 JOHN LESLIE, parson 27th May 1559 and 1570. (See Oyne.)

1562 ALEXANDER ANDERSON, parson in 1562.—[*Acts. and Dec.*, xxix, 67.]

1573 GEORGE LESLIE, pres. to parsonage and vicarage 18th Aug. 1573, vacant on non-compearance of Alexander Anderson, sometime principal of College of Aberdeen, before Commissioners of Kirks; had also a daugh., Helen.—[*Reg. Pres. Bene.*, i, (4), 10; *Rec. of Elgin*, ii, 10.]

1594 NORMAN DUNCAN, M.A., his pres. on depriv. of George Leslie.—[*Reg. Sec. Sig.*, lxvi, 67.]

1601 ALEXANDER LESLIE, pres. in 1601 on depriv. of Norman Duncan.—[*Reg. Sec. Sig.*, lxxii, 139.]

1661 ALEXANDER INNES, reponed by Synod "on his petition has his mouth opened to preach the Gospel," 4th April 1660, before adm. here. Marr. pro. 18th Aug. 1661, Marjory Scrogie.—[*Old Machar Reg.*]

1669 ARTHUR STRACHAN, on 26th Oct. 1708 the Synod decerned that the Presb. of Strathbogie "be appointed to apply the civil magistrate for stopping the irregular and scandalous practices of Mr Arthur Strachan, schismaticall preacher at Mortleigh (in Cairney) and that they proceed to censure him as they see cause."

1698 HUGH INNES, line 2, for "Feichnet" read "Leichnet"; his son, Alexander, apprenticed to Adam Lindsay, surgeon, 10th Dec. 1729.

1837 JAMES ALEXANDER CRUICKSHANK, his daugh., Jean, died 6th Dec. 1933.

1886 JOHN BARR CUMMING, dem. 5th June 1928; his daughs.—Janet Stalker (marr. 28th June 1933 Arthur Douglas Phillip, son of Sydney Phillip Aitkens, Cranleigh House, Addleston); Margaret Cowie, died 18th Jan. 1948.

1928 LEWIS LEGERTWOOD LEGG CAMERON, served in 4th Gordon Highlanders, wounded 1916; trans. from St Ninian's, Aberdeen (*q.v.*), 26th Sept. 1928; trans. to Bo'ness 19th April 1934; dem. on app. as Secretary of Social and Welfare Committee 1937. Marr. 3rd Sept. 1925 Margaret Ann, daugh. of James Middleton, Aberdeen, and has issue—Margaret Middleton, born 22nd Dec. 1926; Eileen Middleton Petrie, born 7th April 1929; Neil, born and died 14th Nov. 1931.

(*Charges united* 22*nd July* 1934.)

NEWMILL

1924 KENNETH JOHN CAMERON, trans. to Gamrie 2nd Nov. 1932. Addl. issue—Kenneth Sutherland, born 23rd Oct. 1928; John Mowat, born 27th Jan. 1935.

RHYNIE

There are the remains of a chapel near Finglenny called Chapel Cairn. Bell Hillock is beside the cairn.—[*Place Names of West Aberdeenshire*, 100.]

1563 THOMAS DALLACHIE, reader 1563.—[*Comps. Sub Coll. of Thirds, Aberdeen*, etc.]

1609 HENRY ROSS, on 1st July 1640 he was libelled before the Synod of Moray for "sindrie grosse faults and oversights," and on 21st Jan. 1641 the Synod found thirteen counts of the libel proved and suspended him, but reponed him at the same meeting. On 8th June 1641 he was ord. by the Synod to "denude himself of his lairge labouring of fermeland, as it hath bene a gryt distraction to him"—he did so 5th April 1642.—[*Recs. of Synod of Moray*, 8th June 1641, 5th April 1642.]

1643 GEORGE CHALMERS, had a son buried 16th June 1662.

1680 JAMES GORDON, on 29th Oct. 1718 the Synod recalled the sentence of deposition, but continued his suspension till next Synod.

1900 JAMES CAMERON McHARDY, dem. 2nd June 1931. Marr. (2) 30th June 1945 Annie Christina Murray Bremner Esson.

(*Charges united 7th June* 1931.)

ESSIE

1569 HEW CURRIE, parson.—[*Acts and Dec.*, xlvi, 75.]

1573 GEORGE ARNOT, parson.—[*Acts and Dec.*, liv, 206, 255.]

ROTHIEMAY

The first church was built by St Drostan in the haugh below Rothiemay Castle in the sixth century. In 1752 the Earl of Fife, who had acquired Rothiemay, pulled down the church because it interfered with his view from the castle, and utilised the stones in building, at the Midtown, a new church which was the predecessor of the existing church. What was left of the old church was grown over and the exact site became unknown. But recently the site was brought to light through the labours of Colonel Ian Forbes of Rothiemay Castle and one of his men, and the excavations had laid bare the foundations, altar stone and font.—[Dr Douglas Simpson, *Trans. Banffshire Field Club.*]

1567 LAURENCE DONALDSON, pres. to vicarage 10th Dec. 1573 vacant by James Clerk not compearing for admission.—[*Reg. Pres. Bene.*, i, (4), 14.]

1641 JAMES GORDON of Zeochry, at "a visitation of the Kirk holden by James, Lord Bishop," on 24th Oct. 1678, it was reported that "Mr James Gordon has continued in sickness, and Mr William Logie, schoolmaster, has preached and thus his school has been spoiled"; Mr Gordon promised to give 300 merks for a helper with the use of his books; issue by first marriage—Margaret. Marr. (2) 17th Sept. 1663 Katherine, daugh. of Thomas Gordon, sheriff depute of Aberdeen; she died May 1703, and had issue—James; Alexander of Kinminity, died 1722; Ludovic, who with father and mother had a sasine 18th Dec. 1671; Catherine.—[*G. R. Sas.*, 3 Ser., xxviii, 361; *Banff Sas.*, 22nd July 1667, 20th Aug. 1670; *Scot. Notes and Queries*, 3 Ser., xii, 70, May 1934.]

1880 WILLIAM ALLARDYCE, his son, Robert Moir, M.A., LL.B., O.B.E., C.B.E., Director of Education, Glasgow, 1929, and chief official of Education Department, Glasgow Town Council; Alexander, M.A., B.L.; his daugh., Marion Jane, M.A., LL.B. (London, 1932), called to English Bar 1933, in Pensions Branch, Customs and Excise Department, London, 1923.

1913 DAVID ALEXANDER ANDERSON, dem. 26th Oct. 1946. Addl. issue—Beatrice Margaret, born 12th April 1925.

(*Charges united 21st July* 1935.)

PRESBYTERY OF ABERLOUR

ABERLOUR

On 8th Nov. 1451 Aberlour is designated Lochlin or Inncrim, now called Aberlour.—[*Reg. Epis. Moray*, 223.]

1566 LEONARD LESLIE, M.A., parson in 1566 and 1568.—[*Comps. Sub Coll. of Thirds, Moray*, etc.]

1607 WILLIAM DOUGLAS, vicar; natural son of Mr Alexander Douglas, burgess, Commissioner, and Provost of Elgin, and received letters of legitimation 5th Feb. 1554-5, when he was designated Sir William Douglas, Chaplain; was vicar here 27th Sept. 1565, and probably was in office at the Reformation.—[*Reg. Great Seal*, iv, 981, 1681, 1877.]

1669 ROBERT STEPHEN, his daugh., Margaret (marr. cont. 22nd July 1707 William Cuming of Tomore).—[*Reg. of Deeds, Mack.*, cxii, 2nd Jan. 1713.]

1707 ROBERT STEPHEN, on 27th Oct. 1713 the Synod refused consent to his translation to Craig, but gave consent on 14th April 1714, as there was no hope of his grievances being removed.

1709 GEORGE HAY, intruded in Aberlour before 1709, preaching and exercising other functions of the ministry, sentenced by the Lords Justiciary at Aberdeen in that year; intruded later at Rathven.—[*Justiciary Records*, 1712-17, 13th March 1715.] (See Rathven.)

1917 ALFRED DRUMMOND DUFF, trans. to Mearns 22nd Oct. 1929; his wife, Edith Hart, died 11th Feb. 1937. Marr. (2) 21st Aug. 1938 Nellie Shaw, youngest daugh. of James Murray, Strachanshaw, Busby. Prisoner of War in Germany 1940.

BOHARM

The Hospital of St Nicholas, for the sustenance of poor persons resorting thither, was founded in 1222-35 by Muriel de Pollok, daugh. of late Peter de P., the endowment being the lands of Innerorkall, and the mill of the same, with the water rights. She also gave the Church of Rothes. The lands of Aginvay were the gift of Walter de Moravia between 1222 and 1242; and on 7th Oct. 1232 Alexander II granted a charter of 4 merks annually from the farm of Mill of Invernairn for the sustenance of a chaplain and a clerk in the chapel of the hospital. Prior to 1530 the cadets of the house of Rothes took possession of the revenues of the hospital, which soon thereafter became ruinous; and shortly after 1829 its remains were cleared away to facilitate the construction of the approach to the suspension bridge then under erection.—[*Reg. Epis. of Moray*, 120-5.]

1568 WILLIAM PETERKIN pres. to parsonage sometime pertaining in common to Chanonry of Moray Cathedral 26th Jan. 1567-8; pres. to vicarage in 1582 on death of John Robertson.—[*Reg. Pres. Bene.*, i, 5, ii, 80; *Comps. Sub Coll. of Thirds, Moray*.]

1580 JOHN ROBERTSON, M.A., vicar, was dead 1582.—[*Comps. Gen. Coll. of Thirds*.]

DUNDURCAS

1567 WILLIAM PETERKIN, exhorter, designated min. 1569.—[*Edin. Test.*, ii, 108.]

1568 WILLIAM LEITH, reader 1565, also at Dipple.—[*Comps. Sub Coll. of Thirds, Moray*, etc.]

PATRICK BALFOUR, M.A., Elgin, pres. to vicarage 15th Sept. 1572 on death of Sir William Wiseman.—[*Reg. Pres. Bene.*, i, (3), 21.]
1572

JOHN MODERATUS (Mudrach Murdoch), pres. to vicarage 3rd Dec. 1574 on dem. of Patrick Balfour.—[*Reg. Pres. Bene.*, i, (4), 29.]
1574

JAMES DOUGLAS, pres. to vicarage 8th Aug. 1576 on death of John Mudrach.—[*Reg. Pres. Bene.*, i, (4), 47.]
1576

JOHN KNOX, M.A., pres. to vicarage 30th Oct. 1576 on death of John Mudrach.—[*Reg. Pres. Bene.*, i, (4), 48.]
1576

JOHN RAY, M.A.; Regent and Professor of Moral Philosophy at Marischal College *cir.* 1633–48; Editor of Cicero's *Epistdarum libri* iv, Aberdeen, 1630, 1635. "He made an excellent funeral Oration on King Charles the Martyr."—[*Recs. of Marischal College and Univ.*, i, 65n, 213, ii, 34, 35.]
1652

ADAM HARPER, assistant at Duffus 1683–6.
1686

ELCHIES

The old church was situated at Easter Elchies, where the churchyard still exists, and appears to have been ruinous at or soon after the union with Knockando in 1625. Subsequently steps seem to have been taken to secure the rebuilding of Elchies Church, for on 10th Oct. 1671 the Synod recommended the Presb. of Aberlour to meet in Elchies parish and there, along with the heritors, "design a plot of ground most convenient for erecting a new Church which work was intended and concluded upon many years ago." The matter was again before the Synod on 9th April 1672, when that body, on the ground that the people of Elchies were a great distance from Knockando Church "and that few or anie of those people did frequent the ordnances at the said place," and that therefore there was need for a new church at Elchies, ratified and approved of the church being erected on a platt of ground called Cargill. Owing to difficulties in securing that site the Synod on 14th Oct. 1673 ord. the min. at Knockando "to use all legal diligence against the heritors to build a new church in the plat of ground at Easter Elchies where it was of old." That church became ruinous about 1750.

JAMES STRACHAUCHAN, parson.—[*Acts and Dec.*, xxviii, 417, xxix, 433, xxxii, 108, 223.]
1563

ALEXANDER LESLIE, pres. to vicarage of Botarie 13th June 1569.—[*Reg. Pres. Bene.*, i, 28.]
1567

WILLIAM STRACHAUCHIN, parson and prebender.—[*Acts and Dec.*, liii, 413.]
1574

JOHN LESLIE, reader at Botarie.—[*Acts and Dec.*, lv, 557.]
1574

JAMES GEORGE MACDONALD, trans. to Ordiquhill 20th Oct. 1927.
1914

JAMES ALEXANDER SUTHERLAND MACKAY, born Dornoch 3rd Sept. 1901, son of John M. and Christina Sutherland; educ. at Dornoch Academy and Univ. of Edinburgh, M.A. (1923); licen. by Presb. of Edinburgh April 1927; assistant at St Mary's, Dundee; ord. 5th April 1928; trans. to Cardenden 24th June, 1931; died 8th Jan. 1943. Marr. 13th June 1928 Emma Forrest, daugh. of James Myles and Catherine McLellan Myles.
1928

(*Charges united* 7th *Jan.* 1934.)

GLENLIVET

Chapel Chriosd was situated at Nevie. It was called Neuechin Christ, Neuin Crist, "Christ's Sanctuary"; and the lands attached to the chapel were called the lands of Neuchin Christ or Neuchincrist, and belonged to the Bishopric of Moray. Nevi is from *Nemeton*, Nemed, "Holy," and signifies an institution, originally pagan, taken over by the Christian Church. On 28th Oct. 1714, following a representation by the Presb. of Aberlour that the country of Glenlivet was about eight miles distant from its parish church of Inveravon, that it abounded with papists, defections being made by "traffiquing priests," and that the Synod should use its endeavours to have another ord. min. in Inveravon parish, the Synod recommended the Presb. to apply to the Commission for the Plantation of Kirks for the erection of Glenlivet into a separate parish; the matter was not pressed.—[*Reg. of Moray*, 12, 68; Watson's *Celtic Place Names*, 246, 249.]

JAMES STEVENSON, on 13th April 1713 the Synod prohibited the Presb. of Aberlour to ordain him as assistant in the parish of Inveravon, "considering it is ane highland paroch abounding with papists and popish priests traffiquing amongst them whose dependence is mainly upon these having the Irish language which language Mr Stevenson hath not."
1712

ALEXANDER INNES, born Rothes 1738, son of Jonathan I. in Peteraigie, and Margaret Grant; died 14th May 1819. Marr. his cousin, Elizabeth, daugh. of John Innes in Balvenie and Magdalen Grant, and had issue—John Alexander Robert, Lieut. 48th Regiment.
1768

JAMES BAIN, was assistant schoolmaster at Duffus in 1853.—[*Recs. of Elgin Presb.*, 7th Dec. 1853.]
1865

ROBERT HOGG CALDER, dem. 2nd June 1926; died 6th May 1930.
1883

ANDREW WELSH FARMS, trans. from Kennethmont (*q.v.*) 9th Nov. 1926; trans. to Canonbie 21st Nov. 1930. Marr. 15th Sept. 1931 Isabella Jane, daugh. of Charles Watson, Estate Office, Leith Hall, Kennethmont, and has issue—Christian Edith Welsh, born 11th July 1941; Hazel Taylor Ross, born 14th Jan. 1944.
1926

(*Charges united 21st Jan. 1932.*)

GLENRINNES

ALEXANDER FALCONER, born 17th March 1777, son of John F., min. of Sandwick, Orkney.
1809

CHARLES BRUCE, his son, Hon. Robert Randolph, Lieut.-Governor of British Columbia, died 21st Feb. 1942.
1864

WILLIAM KAY WHITE, trans. to Gartly 17th Jan. 1929.
1912

DONALD MACGILLIVRAY BEATON, formerly of Leslie, Garioch (*q.v.*); trans. from Tannadice 31st May 1929; died 10th Sept. 1942; his wife, Janette Simpson, died 2nd April 1928. Marr. (2) 16th July 1935 Helene, daugh. of Robert Clyde and Elizabeth Power.
1929

INVERAVON

JOHN STEWART, his widow, Christian Fordyce, marr. (2) cont. 21st May 1702, Robert Grant, writer, Edinburgh.
1682

WILLIAM ASHER, his daugh., Robina (marr. Captain Robert Skinner, Bengal Army), died 7th Aug. 1876.
1883

EDWIN MAXWELL MURRAY DAVIDSON, trans. to St Drostan's, Markinch, 1st Oct. 1930. Marr. 22nd June 1922 Christina, daugh. of David G. Donaldson, M.B., C.M., Dunning, and had addl. issue—Moyra Donaldson, born 17th Sept. 1926; David Gilbert Donaldson, born 23rd Aug. 1931; Jack Cunningham, born 2nd Dec. 1938.
1924

KNOCKANDO

JOHN CLARK his son, William Esdaile Cattley, died at Bridge of Allan 21st Jan. 1939; his daugh., Caroline, died 17th March 1938.
1855

PATRICK RIDDELL, died 3rd March 1940; his widow, Isabella Logan Williamson, died 16th June 1944.
1901

ROTHES

The church was granted to the Hospital of St Nicholas at the Boat of Brig by Muriel de Pollok, daugh. of Peter de P., and the grant was confirmed by her daugh., Eva, Lady Morthach, lady of Rothes.

There was a chapel in Rothes Castle.—[*Reg. Epis. of Moray*, 124; *Reg. Great Seal*, iii, 148.]

JOHN LESLIE, his son, John, succeeded to Findrassie; his daugh., Isobel, had a child by Thomas Crevey, min. of Newhills.

1663

JAMES ALLAN, on 19th June 1705 he was charged by the Synod for absenting himself from meetings of Presb. and Synod, and for not having subscribed his renouncing the errors of Antonia Bourignon, and for not adhering to the Confession of Faith, and was suspended till next meeting of Synod. On 30th Oct. 1705 the Synod, on learning that the congregation at Rothes had boycotted the service at which his suspension was to be intimated, again suspended him till the next meeting. On 5th March 1706 the Synod cited him to the next ensuing General Assembly, and on the General Assembly referring the process back to the Synod on 9th April 1706 the Synod on 29th May following dep. him "for his absence from the Presb. for his unjust reflections upon the Synod of Moray in reference to the errors of Bourgignonism, in refusing to own the Confession of Faith as the Confession of his Faith," etc. His intimated appeal to the General Assembly produced no result in his favour, and on 25th Oct. 1709, when he craved to be restored to the exercise of the ministry, the Synod referred the case to the Committee for Overtures. On 27th Oct. following, the Synod records that "Mr James Allan gives no satisfaction to the Synod, and desists from prosecuting his address."

1696

WILLIAM FALCONER JENKINS, dem. 26th March 1939; died at Burghead 27th Sept. 1939.

1895

PRESBYTERY OF ABERNETHY

ABERNETHY

PATRICK GRANT, M.A.; apparently identical with Patrick Grant, son of John Grant of Freuchie, whom the said John provided with the "Living of Rothiemurchus" before 1584. In 1624 he offered to demit the Kirk of Kincardine as part provision for a min. at Rothiemurchus. But Kincardine seems to have remained under his charge, for he was held responsible by the Synod for building the church there 1625-7. He had issue, Janet.—[*Recs. Synod of Moray*, 25th Oct. 1625, 25th Oct. 1626 (see Rothiemurchus); *Banff Sas.*, 8th July 1630.]
1585

WILLIAM FORSYTH, his son, William, died while shooting 10th Dec. 1935.
1863

DUNCAN ROBERTSON, formerly min. here (*q.v.*), adm. to Boat of Garten 5th May 1932, dem. 24th Nov. 1933, died 15th July 1941.
1907

ARCHIBALD WATSON ROSS, dem. 2nd Feb. 1932, adm. to Glenlivet and Craggan 4th Sept. 1941. His first wife divorced 7th March 1941. Marr. (2) 16th July 1941, Catherine Stuart.
1922

(*Charges united 3rd March* 1932.)

KINCARDINE ON SPEY

ALEXANDER STEWART, pres. to parsonage on 9th July 1569 when a student at St Andrews Univ., on death of John Gray.—[*Reg. Pres. Bene.*, i, 25.]
1569

ADVIE

The church was probably dedicated to St Bridget. About one and a half miles northeast of Advie station are the ruins of the old church. Over the doorway are the initials W.G., A.G., and the date 1706. The initials are said to be those of the builder and his wife, inserted by the builder himself; and it is further affirmed that the Laird, irritated by the action of the builder, banned further procedure with the work. At Dalvey there are or were the remains of the ecclesiastical establishment of Devek, called the Chapel, and probably identical with the Church of Deveth which about 1213-21 Bricius, Bishop of Moray, at the instance and on the petition of his uncle, Friskyn de Kerdal, patron of the church, granted and confirmed to the Church of the Holy Trinity of Spynie, for the fabric of the same. The grant was confirmed by Andrew, Bishop of Moray, to the Church of the Holy Trinity of Elgin, after it became the cathedral church in place of Spynie Church in 1224.—[Mackinlay's *Anc. Ch. Dedications* (non-script.), 130; Rev. Dr Reid's *Grantown*, 88-9, 1906 Ed.; McConnochie's *Strathspey*, 122; *Reg. Epis. of Moray*, 61-2, 65.]

THOMAS AUSTIN, M.A., pres. 1574 on death of James Thornton.—[*Reg. Pres. Bene.*, i, 24.]
1574

JOHN LIDDELL, dem. 6th Dec. 1927; died 23rd Jan. 1939; his widow, Euphemia Eliza Norah McAlistir, died 14th May 1947.
1888

ALEXANDER FORBES BLACK, trans. from Rosebank, Dundee (*q.v.*), 4th May 1928; Clerk of Presb. dem. 1948.
1928

ALVIE

A chapel of the Blessed Virgin Mary was founded at Kincraig by John Hay of Tulliebethell 3rd May 1374, with £40 annually from the lands of Lochlwy, 2 acres of land and a house at Rate.—[*Reg. of Moray*, No. 320.]

1572 JOHN GLASS, in 1570 had haill common Kirk of Alvy as min., pres. to vicarage 14th March 1572-3.— [*Reg. Pres. Bene.*, i, (4), 5; *Comps. Sub Coll. of Thirds, Moray*, etc.]

1575 ANDREW OSTLER, reader, pres. to vicarage 6th Nov. 1575 on death of Mr John Brown.—[*Reg. Pres. Bene.*, i, (4), 38.]

1580 WILLIAM MacINTOSH, pres. to parsonage and vicarage 24th Sept. 1580 on death of Sir John Glass.—[*Reg. Pres. Bene.*, ii, 40.]

1632 RODERICK MACLEOD, on 3rd Nov. 1642 the Synod suspended him and appointed him to appear before the Presb. of Abernethy for final sentence of deposition, on charges of immorality, absence from his charge without notice, neglect of discipline, failure for four years to administer the Sacrament of the Lord's Supper, and non-catechising, and also of being under suspicion of "medling with the commone guid and penalties."

1880 JAMES ANDERSON, ord. to Wallace, Nova Scotia, June 1865; trans. to Newcastle, New Brunswick, 1873.

1914 DUGALD McLEAN, dem. 27th July 1932, died 29th Nov. 1936.

(*Charges united 27th July* 1932.)

CROMDALE

The present church was built in 1809. At Congash there was a chapel with a burial-ground, probably prehistoric. In it are two remarkable sculptured stones, one of which bears an object of helmet shape. At Achnahannet, "field of the Annat," in the north part of the parish, there is the site of a little chapel in a field, enclosed by a "cashel." Down below near the town is *Tobar an Domhnaich*, "Sunday's Well."— [*New Stat. Acc.*, xiv, 441; Cramond's *Grantown*, 24; Bruce-Lockhart's *My Scottish Youth*, 149; Watson's *Celtic Place Names*, 252.]

1568 WILLIAM SYMSON, reader in 1568. —[*Comps. Sub Coll. of Thirds, Moray.*]

1590 PATRICK GRANT, as min. of Advie, Cromdale and Inverallan, pres. to vicarage of same 20th March 1590-1 on death of Thomas Rattray.—[*Reg. Sec. Sig.*, lxii, 207.]

1640 GILBERT MARSHALL, on 3rd June 1640 he was censured by the Synod "for marrying the Laird of Grant (James Grant) to my Laird of Murray's sister (Mary Stewart, daugh. of James, second Earl of Moray), and for not taking security that she shall adhere to the true religion, she having been bred and brought up in papistrie"; he pleaded that he did it "at the earnest desire and sollicitation of the Laird of Grant, and for saving them from the sin of fornication"; on 8th Oct. 1651 he was suspended by the Synod for two Sabbaths for irregular baptising and marrying; and on 2nd Feb. 1659 he was again suspended by the Synod for two Sabbaths for "his gross omission and neglect of so important a dutie as prayer in and with the Laird of Grant's family when he hapnd to be in the said family"—the said Laird had been accused of neglect of family worship and of having priests in his home, and his wife of practising certain forms of Popish worship, idolatry and superstition.—[*Recs. Synod of Moray*, 3rd June 1640, 8th Oct. 1651, 7th April, 1652, 3rd April 1655, 2nd Feb. 1659.]

1909 THOMAS SHERETT CARGILL, died 4th Nov. 1936; his wife, Nellie Alexander, died at Edinburgh 3rd Nov. 1928. Marr. (2) 9th Oct. 1930 Mary Jean Laurie, who died 4th Nov. 1936.

(*Charges united 15th May* 1930.)

DUTHIL

In 1660 the church, which was fallen to the ground, was rebuilt by the Laird of Grant. The present church was built in

1826. At a meeting of the parishioners in the church on 13th Jan. 1537-8, Mr Andrew Grant was elected Clerk of the Parish in succession to the deceased William Grant. The Grants of Grant, afterwards Earls of Seafield, had a burial aisle here from 1586. The mausoleum adjoining the church was built in 1821 by Francis William, sixth Earl of Seafield, and a new mausoleum, a counterpart of the former, was erected to the east of the churchyard about 46 years later by the Dowager Countess of Seafield. In the churchyard is the grave of Ian Manndoch or Lom, the celebrated Jacobite poet.—[*The Chiefs of Grant*, iii, 268; McConnachie's *Strathspey*, 108; Shaw's *Hist. of Province of Moray*, i, 255; *Reg. of Synod*, 3rd April and 2nd Oct. 1660.]

1566 ALEXANDER OGILVY M.A., parson in 1566 and 1568.—[*Comps. Coll. of Thirds, Moray*, etc.]

1623 WILLIAM WATSON, before the Synod in July 1646 "he confessed that James Grahame (Marquis of Montrose) was a night at his house"; and for compliance with the Marquis he was suspended by the Synod from 6th April to 5th Oct. 1647. On 2nd Oct. 1649 he was referred by the Synod for trial to the Presb. of Aberlour on a charge of contemptuous reception of the General Assembly's order to mins. to "speak boldlie against the Scots in England"; and three years later he was suspended for three months "for giving the communione to the people kneeling."—[*Recs. Synod of Moray*, July 1646, 6th April, 5th Oct. 1647, 2nd Oct. 1649, 7th April, 15th June 1652.]

1652 JAMES WATSON, for various misdemeanours, including service with Montrose at Lesmoir, he had his licence suspended by the Synod in July 1646 till 5th Oct. 1647; and he was rebuked by the Synod on 2nd Oct. 1649 for going "through the country in Highland apparell"; he died before 3rd April 1660.

1667 WILLIAM SMITH, suspended by the Synod for two months on 13th April 1675 for "ministerial failings, neglects, and escapes, and his conversation not becoming the gravity of a minister."

1695 DONALD McINTOSH, ord. to Farr, 15th July 1674. Marr. Janet Mackay.—[*Deeds Mack*, 1704, No. 733.]

1820 WILLIAM GRANT, on 24th April 1844 the Synod recorded its appreciation of his liberality in having built a school in the parish and set aside a considerable sum for its endowment. Lines 21 and 22, for "Stewart" read "Stuart."

1912 PETER MACGREGOR, died 30th Dec. 1935; his daugh., Margaret Una Cameron (marr. 10th July 1931 Reginald John Fry, Radipole, Weymouth).

(*Charges united* 15*th May* 1930.)

INSH

It would appear that Insh had a later dedication of St Mary. On 28th July 1294 William le Franseys was sued by Thomas the Clerk of Elgin, for being found in possession of 476 lamb skins which the plaintiff deposited in the Church of St Mary of Insh for security against robbers and which had been carried off. Franseys stated that he had bought them from some men unknown in Elgin "last Thursday." By leave of court parties compromised. Near the Great North Road, in a field below Dunachton House, there is an ancient burial-ground with ivy-covered remains of a chapel said to have been dedicated to St Drostan.—[*Cal. of Docs. relating to Scotland*, ii, 192; McConachie's *Strathspey*, 35.]

1564 SIR GILBERT DUFF, chaplain of St Katherine's Chapel in Innes.—[*Comps. Sub Coll. of Thirds, Moray*.]

1897 GEORGE MACKAY MUNRO, his widow, Lucy Hyde Turnbull, died 27th Jan. 1940.

1918 JOHN ROBERT DE LINGEN KILBURN, line 20, for "Ide" read "Iole"; M.B., Ch.B.

	ROBERT MONTGOMERY BRIGHT, trans. to Kirkmichael, Dunkeld, 19th July 1928.
1921	

(*United to Alvie 27th July* 1932.)

INVERALLAN

Portions of the walls of the old church in the churchyard near the Spey existed till about forty years ago, when they were removed in connection with churchyard alterations. Futach's (Fiacre's) Stone has an incised cross on each side, the east face of the stone being dressed. Built into the west wall of the churchyard is a symbol stone; the symbols are believed to be of Pictish origin influenced by association with the early Christian crosses, and of the 6th or 7th century. The old baptismal font, circular, rough-dressed, and with circular orifice, is near the entrance to the churchyard. St Futach's Well, in part filled with mud and growth of grass, is situated on the west side of the road along the Spey, a short distance from the churchyard. The first church, built in Grantown, bore the date 1801, the year of its erection. It gave place to the present church, the Seafield Memorial Church, erected on the same site and opened on 1st May 1886. It was the gift of Caroline Stuart, Countess of Seafield, in memory of her husband, John Charles, seventh Earl of Seafield, and of their son, Ian Charles, eighth Earl of Seafield. The pulpit was made from a piece of elaborate old carving brought from Castle Grant. In front of the Seafield gallery is a piece of carved woodwork found in 1874 when an old house was in process of demolition at the farm of Shillochan, Duthil. It consists of three rows of panels. The topmost row of eight panels has the arms of the following families: Cumming of Altyre; Gordon of Huntly; Rose of Kilravock; Calder of that ilk; Grant of Auchernach; Forbes of Auchintie; Leslie of Balquhain; Lumsden of Cushnie. Below is inscribed:

Mark the upright man, and behold the just,
For the end of that man is peace.

The middle row, also of eight panels, displays floral and figure designs, and below is:

The righteous cry, and the Lord heareth them,
And delivereth them out of all their troubles.

The lowest row, of seven panels, carries less ornate designs.—[Crammond's *Grantown*, 7–8; *Inscrips. in Church*; Memo, Mr. Wm. McGregor, Grantown.]

	JOHN THOMSON, his son, Alexander Stuart Duff, died at Glasgow 9th Sept. 1927.
1878	

	WILLIAM GREEN, his widow, Flora MacDonald Manson, died 18th May 1937.
1888	

	IAN ROBERT WILSON GILLAN, dem. 23rd Aug. 1929; adm. to St Columba's, London (Second Charge); dem. on appointment to Fairmilehead Church Extension Charge, 12th April 1938.
1925	

DULNAIN BRIDGE

	ROBERT CHALMERS ANDERSON, trans. to Culsalmond 15th July 1927.
1923	

KINGUSSIE

The church along with the Chapel of Benchory (near Newtonmore) was granted to the Bishopric of Moray by Gilbert de Kathera' (Strathern ?), with confirmation by William the Lion 1203–11. The church was rebuilt in 1624 and 1792. The priory was founded by George, Earl of Huntly, *cir.* 1490. It belonged to the Order of the Carmelites. Croft-maluag, now Chapelpark, at Raitts, indicates that there was a chapel there dedicated to St Mo-Luoc of Lismore, who died 592, Mo-Luoc being an affectionate form of Lugiad, Lughaidh.—[*Reg. of Moray*, 14; *Recs. of Synod of Moray*, 13, 14th April 1624; *Reg. Sec. Seal*, ii, 797; Watson's *Celtic Place Names*, 292–3.]

	ROBERT CARNEGIE, parson 1558.—[*Reg. Abbrev. Feu Charters of Church Lands*, ii, 317.]
1558	

KINGUSSIE—LAGGAN

1571 ARCHIBALD LINDSAY, M.A., parson, 18th April 1566, Jan. 1571-2.—[*Reg. Sec. Sig.*, xl, 47; *Reg. Mag. Sig.*, iv, 2518.]

1649 LACHLAN GRANT, his son, James, min. of Ruthrie.—[*Synod Reg.*, 4th Oct. 1670.]

1810 JOHN ROBERTSON, ord. at Achrenie, Halkirk; trans. to Eriboll 1794.

1857 GREGOR STUART, line 8, for "29" read "24."

1867 KENNETH ALEXANDER MACKENZIE, his widow, Mary Isabella MacDonald, died 7th April 1929; his daugh., Elizabeth Hannah Fairbairn (marr. 17th Jan. 1931, Edward Robertson, M.A., schoolmaster, Kingussie).

1906 DUGALD MACFARLANE, D.D., Moderator of General Assembly 18th May 1937. His wife, Roma Constance Campbell, died 1st Oct. 1947.

KIRKMICHAEL

In 1625 and again in 1671 and 1673 the parish was named Strathavin.—[*Rec. of Synod.*]

1561 SIR JAMES GLASS, vicar 1561. (See Glass.)

1562 SIR JAMES GARNTULLIE, vicar 1562-3. (See Glass.)

1624 JOHN RAY, M.A.; on 4th Feb. 1640 he "professit his willingness to subscryvie the Covenant, but affirmed that he durst not hazard to subscryvie for feare of the Clangregour and other brocken men daylie conversing about him, enemies to the Covenant."—[*Recs. of Synod of Moray*, 4th Feb. 1640.]

1686 COLIN NICOLSON, eldest son and heir of George N., master mason, and Janet Campbell.—[*G. R. Sas.*, 3 Ser., xxxv, 207, 24th May 1675.]

1897 JAMES WILLIAM FRASER, his widow, Catherine Roy Paterson, died 19th Oct. 1942.

1907 JOHN GARROW DUNCAN, D.D. (Aberdeen, 29th March 1933), dem. 31st Dec. 1942; his wife, Katherine Reid, died 12th Dec. 1933. Marr. (2) 3rd July 1940 Robina (died Dundee, 12th Feb. 1944), daugh. of John MacHattie, Woodside, Portknockie; (3) 31st Oct. 1945 Eliza Lily Mathews; his daughs.—Phyllis (marr. 12th Nov. 1934, at Capetown, Murdo Alexander MacRae, Beauly); Mary, M.A., missionary, Calcutta (marr. 12th Oct. 1932 Ralph Wood Smith, Upper Assam, son of Rev. J. J. Smith, Filey, Yorkshire). Addl. Publications—*Ophel Irion Excavation* (with Prof. A. S. Macalister, LL.D.); *The Accuracy of the Old Testament* (S.P.C.K.); *Digging up Bible History* (2 vols., S.P.C.K.); *Corpus of Palestinian Pottery* (1928); *New Light on Hebrew Origins* (1936, S.P.C.K.).

LAGGAN

1560 SIR JOHN NICOLSON, vicar 1560 and 20th June 1566.—[*Old Ross-shire and Scotland*, i, 16.]

1575 JOHN DOW MacCONDOQUHIE, his pres. in 1575 on death of Alexander Clerk.—[*Reg. Pres. Bene.*, i, (4), 38.]

1637 ALEXANDER CLARK, "seiking to be planted at the Kirk of Laggan," he was ord. by the Synod in Oct. 1637 "to go unto the Marquess of Huntlie to seik his favourable consent to his plantation"; and on 3rd April 1638 the Bishop reported to the Synod that he had admitted Mr Alexander Clark to the Kirk of Laggan with the consent and assent "both of the Marquess of Huntlye and the parochiners of Laggan"; on 15th April 1640 he was suspended by the Synod on charges of being non-resident, of keeping not his charge as he ought, and of absence from the Synod that day without excuse; on 3rd June following he was questioned by the Synod about his habit of going to public places "in hieland clothes," particularly being in that garb in Inverness, and also about his residence and keeping his charge, his excuse being the non-payment of his stipend and the want of a manse and glebe; he was rebuked for his former miscarriage and reponed to his Charge, with warning of deposition in the event of further transgression; on 6th July 1646 was sharply rebuked by the Synod and referred to the Presb. of Aberlour for having "drunk much aquavity at the Presbytery Meeting"; and on 15th June 1652 he was ord. by the Synod to give his repentance in sackcloth a day in ilk ane of the Kirkis of Badenoch, viz. Kingussie, Laggan and Alves, for marrying and baptising, after his deposition in 1647 (but before his deposition was publicly intimated).

LACHLAN GRANT is stated to have had a daugh., Christian (marr. Muriach Macpherson).
1649

JOHN MACLEOD, his daugh., Jamesina Balmain, died 6th Sept. 1931.
1851

DUNCAN SHAW MacLENNAN, died at Newtonmore 6th Dec. 1930; had issue—Norman Macpherson, born 24th Sept. 1895, M.B., Ch.B. 1921, D.P.H. 1923, M.D. 1924 (Aberdeen), A.U.O.T.C., N.Z. Forces 1912–14, 2nd Lt. 3rd Cameron Highlanders, Dec. 1915, attached to 6th Cameron Highlanders; served—Home, 9 months, France, 10 months, Hospital, 1 year; Final Rank, Lieutenant; Assistant M.O.H., Woolwich, 1926–7; Sanitation Officer, Colonial Medical Service, Kenya, 1928; Senior Health Officer, Palestine, 1930; Northern Rhodesia, 1931.
1881

NEIL MACLEOD ROSS, D.Litt. (Edinburgh, 1928), D.D. (Glasgow, 17th June 1936), C.B.E. (1933), died at Edinburgh 17th Dec. 1943; his son, Norman Macleod, died 29th Sept. 1930. Publication—Editor, *An Gaidheal*.
1923

(*Charges united 23rd Oct. 1931.*)

ROTHIEMURCHUS

The church was granted to the Cathedral Church of Moray by Andrew, Bishop of Moray, 1221–42, to provide lights for the cathedral. It was dedicated to St Duchaldus, who is said to have come from Iona after one of the Norse raids in the west, and for a time settled in the district. A marsh near the church was termed St Duchald's Pool; and St Duchald's Fair was held in the district up to the close of the 18th century. At Achnahatnich, about a mile from Coylum Bridge, there was a chapel with burying-ground, dedicated to St Eata, who may be Eate, one of the twelve English pupils of St Aidan and afterwards Abbot of Melrose and Lindesfarne, or the Irish Saint Ide.—[Watson's *Celtic Place Names*, 318; Mackinlay's *Ancient Church Dedications* (non-script.), 505; *Reg. Epis. Moray*, 70.]

PATRICK GRANT, in the will of John Grant of Freuchie, 23rd Nov. 1584, it is stated, "I have provided Patrick Grant, my son, to the Living of Rothiemurchus." Apparently he was identical with Patrick Grant, min. at Abernethy and Kincardine, and probably retained his interest in the Living of Rothiemurchus. That at least might serve to explain his consent in 1624 to help in furnishing provision for a min. at Rothiemurchus, and his further consent to the admission of Mr Henderson there.—[*The Chiefs of Grant*, iii, 292.] (See Andrew Henderson, following.)
1584

ANDREW HENDERSON, in April 1624 Mr Patrick Grant, min. at Abernethy and Kincardine, stated that he was "content to demitt the soume of ane hundreth merks money of the benefice of Kincarden with the gleib thiroff yeirly for the mantinance of Mr Andrew Hendersone at the Kirk of Rothiemurchus and consents to the present nominatione and plantatioun of the said Mr Andrew." To the Synod on 13th Oct. of the same year it was intimated that Mr William Watson, min. at Duthil, "is content of his own accord to demitt the Kirk of Rothiemurkis with the whole benefit thairoff, that ane minister may be planted thairoff," and that Mr Patrick Grant "willinglie condiscendit to dimitt the kirk off Kincardin togidter with ane hundreth merks out of the provision thairoff" for the same purpose; and the Synod ord. the Presb. upon those
1625

grounds to consider how the Kirks of Rothiemurchus and Kincardine may be served, "and see out for persons quha may undertake the charge." In Oct. 1625 Mr Grant was ord. by the Synod to put Mr Henderson in possession of the glebe of Kincardine and pay the 100 merks out of the stipend of Kincardine for 1625 and so forth; and on 27th April 1630 the Synod, while agreeing to the transportation of Mr Henderson to Balquhidder, resolved that Mr Grant be "summoned for withdrawing the means of provision" from him. There appears to be no further reference to the matter.

1925 MURDOCH LAMONT, died 13th Aug. 1927; his sons—Ewen, M.A., D.Sc.; Malcolm, C.A.; his widow, Euphemia Ann Hume, died at Glasgow 30th June 1933.

1928 ROBERT WILSON, born Annbank, Ayrshire, 17th Jan. 1870, son of James W., colliery manager, and Janet Wyper; educ. at Irvine Academy and Univs. of Glasgow, M.A., and Edinburgh, B.D.; assistant East Church, Stirling, Lothian Road, Edinburgh, Claremont Church, Glasgow; ord. to Thornliebank U.P. Church 5th Sept. 1899; adm. from United Free Church by General Assembly 1926; adm. 1st Feb. 1928; dem. 30th Sept. 1930; died at Collesdene, Strathaven, 24th July 1934.

(*Charges united 1st March* 1931.)

TOMINTOUL

There was a Chapel of St Bridget at the farm of that name between Tomintoul and the river Avon.—[Mackinlay's *Ancient Ch. Dedications* (non-script.), 130.]

1854 JOHN AULAY MACLENNAN, died at Brechin; his son, John Norman Emslie, died at Darlinghurst 5th Dec. 1914; his daugh. (marr. –. Gerard, chemist, Leicester.)

1886 WILLIAM DUNBAR DEY, died at Forres 15th Jan. 1932; his widow, Isabella Parker, died at Forres, 20th Oct. 1940.

1926 NEIL McGILL, trans. from Duntocher (*q.v.*) 21st April 1926; trans. to Bervie 27th April 1927.

1928 WILFRED SCOTT GOODERE, trans. from Flotta (*q.v.*) 24th Jan. 1928; dem. 31st Jan. 1942. Has issue, Albert Scott, born 29th July 1926.

PRESBYTERY OF ELGIN

ALVES

The church was dedicated to the Virgin Mary.—[Macfarlane's *Geographical Coll.*, i, 236.]

1564 JOHN THORNTOUN, chantor of Moray, parson.—[*Acts and Dec.*, xxxii, 114.]

1567 PATRICK BALFOUR, 1567 and 1586,—[*Comps. Sub Coll. of Thirds, Moray*, etc.]

1625 ROBERT ROSS, his daugh., Christian (marr. John Calder of Little Urchyne).—[*Elgin Sas.*, ii, 10, 19th Jan. 1625.]

1649 WILLIAM CAMPBELL, trans. to Olrig, 2nd Jan. 1661.

1676 BEROALD INNES, line 2, for "said to be" read "natural."

1781 WILLIAM SMITH, his father not min. of, but licentiate at.

1850 JAMES MACKIE, his son, Alexander Grant, went to Ceylon, thence to Malaya, first as road contractor and later in tin industry; became one of the pioneers of that country; died at Port Said, 28th Oct. 1933; his daughs.—Eliza Jane, died London 27th Dec. 1931; Alice, died Edinburgh 10th Aug. 1935.—[Bruce Lockhart's *Return to Malaya*, 33-4.]

1886 WILLIAM FORREST HAMILTON, dem. 9th June 1925; died at Bournemouth 30th May 1938.

1925 JOHN HARRIS BURRY, line 10, for "Algarra" read "Algoma"; lines 18 and 20, for "Lorne" read "Lorena"; trans. to Ferryhill North, Aberdeen, 19th Dec. 1929.

(*Charges united* 12*th April* 1931.)

BIRNIE

The church was the first seat of the Bishopric of Moray. In 1171-84 King William the Lion granted a charter in favour of the Church of the Holy Trinity of the Bishopric of Moray and Simon, Bishop of Moray. If Birnie Church was at that time the seat of the bishopric, then its dedication was the Holy Trinity. But the seat of the bishopric may then have been the Church of Spynie. At Pittendreich there was a hermitage or desertum, of which all trace has disappeared. The fragment of a sculptured stone belonging to it is in Elgin Museum. In 1731 the church was reported to the Presb. as ruinous "in gables, doors, windows," and "the roof like to fall," and steps were taken to have the building thoroughly repaired—the west gable to be rebuilt from the foundation, with a window 2 ft. × 6 ft., and a bell-house erected upon the same; the two side walls of the nave and choir with the two windows repaired from the foundation; the mid-gable and the easter gable also to be repaired, including pointing of "the old work." The date on the belfry, 1734, marks the completion of the work. In 1890 the church was repaired in a manner in keeping with its style.—[*Reg. of Moray*, 4; *Recs. Presb. of Elgin*, 28th Dec. 1731; *Pilgrimages in Moray*, 41.]

1560 JOHN STANIS, described as "vicar and minister" and "reader and exhorter," probably 1560-5.—[*Book of Assumptions*, 413.]

1567 ROBERT PONT, M.A., pres. to vicarage 18th Jan. 1567-8.—[*Reg. Sec. Sig.*, xxxvii, 26.]

JAMES JOHNSTON, pres. to vicarage 26th Feb. 1567-8 on dem. of James Douglas, and to parsonage on dem. of Robert Pont.—[*Reg. Sec. Sig.*, xxxvii, 39; *Reg. Pres. Bene.*, i, (4), 24.]

1567

ALEXANDER INNES, M.A., pres. to parsonage and vicarage 25th July 1593 on death of James Johnston.—[*Reg. Sec. Sig.*, lxv, 200.]

1589

GEORGE DOUGLAS, pres. in 1598 on depriv. of Alexander Innes.—[*Reg. Sec. Sig.*, lxx, 22.]

1598

ALEXANDER SPENS, his son, Jerome, commanded a troop in Colonel Villiers' Regiment of Horse in Ireland 1689.—[*Reg. of Deeds, Mack.*, cxv, 197.]

1627

WILLIAM SANDERS, his eldest daugh., Margaret (marr. cont. 7th June 1684 Thomas Wood, merchant, Elgin).—[*Reg. Ho. Charters.*]

1663

GEORGE GORDON, his daugh., Anna, died Elgin 8th Jan. 1932.

1832

JOHN KENNEDY, died 20th Oct. 1928, his widow, Eliza Bruce Scott, died 30th Aug. 1945.

1890

THOMAS MURRAY INGLIS, formerly of Tewchar (*q.v.*); trans. from Quarter 26th June 1929; dem. 11th Oct. 1932; died at St Andrews 4th Oct. 1933. His daugh., Agnes Hutchison Murray (marr. 3rd Sept. 1943 Thomas Charles, son of Rev. Robert Edwards, Trofarth, Abergele); Margaret Elizabeth Keir (marr. 10th Dec. 1943 David M. Fairbairn, R.N.).

1929

BURGHEAD

The Chapel of St Æthan or Ethan was situated at Chapelyard. The name may be a corruption of Aidan, first Bishop of Lindisfarne, who died in 651, or of Eata, one of Aidan's "twelve boys of the English Nation," who was first abbot of the Monastery at Old Melrose, and successor of Aidan in the See of Lindisfarne, and died 683. On a representation to the effect that "Seceders" were trying to draw off from the church the inhabitants of Burghead, and had secured a granary in which their clergy were to officiate, the Presb. on 7th May 1821 appointed a committee to interview Mr W. Young of Burghead about securing a Church of Scotland man to officiate, and to use endeavours for a place of worship; and on 28th Nov. 1822 it was reported that Mr Young had expressed agreement with the proposal and that by individual subscriptions and collectors in various parishes a place of worship was now erected, a site having been granted by Mr Young. The sphere of the church was Burghead, Cumineston, and Hopeman. The church was enlarged in 1838 and repaired in 1858-9. On 29th Nov. 1899 a proposal for a new church was submitted to the Presb. Strong support was forthcoming; the foundation stone was laid on 31st March 1902, and the church was opened for worship on 30th Nov. of the same year. Since the Union of 1929 the former U.F. church became the place of worship, and the old parish church has served as the church hall. —[*Procs. of Soc. of Antiqs. Scot.*, iv, 321, 368, 1863; *Recs. of Elgin Presby.*, 7th May 1821, 28th Nov. 1822, 20th Aug. 1838, 22nd Feb. 1859, 26th Feb. 1862, 29th Nov. 1899, 6th Feb. 1901, 7th Nov. 1900; *Memo*, Rev. Theo. M. G. Lamb, M.A.]

ROBERT WOODSIDE, his widow, Fanny Helen Clarke, died 9th April 1925.

1885

WILLIAM MURRAY, trans. to Mossgreen, 17th May 1926.

1920

CONSTANTINE SINCLAIR, ord. 4th Nov. 1926; trans. to Buchlyvie 1st Feb. 1929.

1926

WILLIAM GEORGE DUNCAN MACLENNAN, born Inverness 27th Aug. 1899, third son of Donald M., goods inspector, Rockville, Inverness, and Mary J. Cran; educ. at Royal Academy, Inverness, and Univs. of Aberdeen, M.A. (1922), Cambridge, B.A. (1926), and Marburg; tutor at Westminster College, Cambridge, 1927; licen. by Presb. of Inverness

1929

1927; ord. 14th July 1929; trans. to Bearsden North 4th Oct. 1933. Marr. 5th Sept. 1929 Elspeth, daugh. of W. E. Shaw, min., Lossiemouth, and has issue—Alistair Seomas, born 16th Dec. 1930; Elizabeth Mary, born 1st July 1932; Duncan Hugh, born 26th June 1934.

(*Charges united 8th Dec.* 1929.)

DRAINIE

The Church of Kinedar was dedicated to St Gerardine, the name, it is said, being a form of St Gervadius, Bishop of Brechin, and was granted to the Priory of St Andrews by Simon, Bishop of Moray, 1171-84. For a time the church, which consisted of nave, choir, and transepts, served as the Cathedral Church of Moray, particularly in the early part of the 13th century. In 1207 it was described as "situated on a peninsula of the sea, to which none of the parishioners could approach without difficulty." The cave of the patron saint, which has now disappeared, was situated on the shore at Stotfield, west of Lossiemouth.

The Church of Ogston, dedicated to St Peter, was situated in the churchyard near the South Lodge of Gordonstown.

On 5th April 1642 the Synod of Moray recommended to the Commissioners for the Plantation of Kirks that Ogston be disjoined from St Andrews and united to Kinedar; and in the same year it was recorded that Kinedar and Ogston "were united in law by the Presbytery." To the Synod's recommendation effect was given by the Commissioners on 28th July 1647, and ratification was made by Parliament on 10th June 1648, it being decreed that the parishioners of Ogston were to receive the Sacraments and burial at Kinedar. Before 15th Nov. 1649 the Church of Kinedar was a ruin, decayed "by the iniquitie of tyme," and required to be rebuilt; and Sir Robert and Sir Ludovic Gordon petitioned the Presb. for a central church. Objection was made by the parishioners of Ogston, who refused to attend Kinedar Church but were willing to attend their own church, which was "commodious for them," and also by the min., who wished Ogston to be disjoined from Kinedar. Further consideration was given to the proposal for a central church, and though on 29th May 1650 the Presb. disjoined Kinedar and Ogston, later it reversed its policy, passing an Act on 18th Dec. 1650, constituting the union of the two. On 31st Dec. of the same year the heritors of the two parishes agreed to modify a stipend for the united kirks, ". . . whilk offer the Presbytery accept, the Kirks to continue united for the tyme coming." Meantime, on 2nd Sept. 1650, the Synod expressed approval of the policy of a central church, and on 2nd Jan. 1651 it designed a site for the same—"a piece of ground called the Broomfield lying upon the north of the House of Drenny upon the west of the Lummielochs." It was also arranged that there be a churchyard on the south-east part of the said ground. On 3rd April 1653 it was reported to the Synod that no beginning had been made with the new church, and that the Church of Ogston was incapable of accommodating more than a third of the people. On 4th Oct. 1653 it was further reported that Sir Robert Gordon had undertaken the building of the new church; and eventually the work was begun on 2nd May 1654, and before 3rd Oct. of that year the walls were "advanced above the height of the doors." In his will of 11th July 1654 Sir Robert Gordon said, "I do recommend the building of a share of the Church of Drenie to my wyfe; for seeing we have taken down the old Church of Kinnedar, it is reason that we help to build another"; but for many years little or nothing was done. A supplication to the Synod by the parishioners of Kinedar on 21st Oct. 1662 that "the old decayed edifice of the Kirk of Kinedar may be repaired" led to nothing; and on 1st April 1672 the min. laid a complaint before the Synod regarding the lack of a church, the building of the new church being "still delayed by the negligence and unwillingness of the heritors to be at expense in that so necessarie a work." That may indicate that Ogston Church had become unfit for worship. In any case a few years later it had passed out of use, for a Kirk Session minute of 14th Jan. 1677 records that worship in Ogston Church was impossible "by reason it was open and unthacked, and worship was carried on sometimes in the dining-room at Gordonston, sometimes in the barn of Drainie, and sometimes in the Girnal House at Kinedar. Eventually the Church was used for worship for the first time on 2nd April 1677. Even then it was but half-sclaited." Soon afterwards it was completed. The date on the belfry is 1675. Meantime, on 3rd Oct. 1665, the Synod had ratified the Union of Kinedar and Ogston; and on 2nd April 1667 a contract between the Bishop of Moray and others anent the Union was recorded in the Synod minutes. The foundations of Kinedar Church were still to be seen in the churchyard in 1760, but nothing now remains above ground. In the churchyard there is an old cross; and fragments of stones taken from the manse walls and now in Elgin Museum appear to be relics of the old church. A sculptured stone, found in the churchyard, is at the manse. East of the churchyard stood the Castle of Kinedar, which for many years was the residence of the Bishops of Moray. Attached to it was a chapel.

The foundations of the Castle as well as of the enclosure were visible in 1760. On the site of Ogston Church and with stones from the same, Dame Elizabeth Dunbar, widow of Sir Robert Gordon, third of Gordonston, built the Gordonston mausoleum in 1705 in memory of her husband. The churchyard contains an old cross.

On 1st Oct. 1794 the min., Mr Lewis Gordon, presented a petition to the Presb., representing that the church built 1654–77 was both incommodious and insufficient—the floor below the level of the ground outside causing difficulty of access and also water from the roof in bad weather to find its way into the area of the Church; the roof ruinous and decayed; the walls rent in various places; the church neither paved, ceiled, nor plastered, and so cold in winter as to affect the health of the people. Besides, the absence of a wall round the churchyard left the graves exposed to the attacks of dogs, swine and other animals.

Whatever was done produced no lasting effect; and on 4th July 1820 the Presb. adopted a resolution that a new church be built about a mile farther to the east. The site finally chosen on 28th Nov. 1822 was "on rising ground in a new plantation where 4 roads meet upon the north side of the road from Lossiemouth to Westfield"; and the plans ultimately agreed upon were by James Gillespie, after the style of Rafford Church, as abridged by George Alexander. On 26th Jan. 1825 it was reported that the new church was near completion; and on 17th Feb. following it was taken over from the contractors. The roofless walls of the old church still survive. In 1915 steps were taken by the Presb. and the Drainie Kirk Session towards getting the parish church transported to St Gerardine's Mission Church, Lossiemouth. Considerable negotiations followed; and eventually on 14th Dec. 1917 the Court of Session granted decree of transportation. By disposition of 26th and 29th March 1918 the trustees of St Gerardine's Church conveyed it to the heritors as the parish church. By agreement between parties the old church became the property of the valued rent heritors of Drainie; and in 1923 it was demolished.—[*Recs. of Synod of Moray*, 31st Dec. 1650, 3rd Oct. 1665, 1st April 1672; *Recs. of Elgin Presby.*, 15th Nov. 1649, 13th April, 1st May, 29th May, 18th Dec., 31st Dec. 1650, 3rd Oct. 1654, 12th Nov. 1662, 4th June 1672, 17th Feb. 1825; *Reg. of Moray*, 59, 63; *Acts Scot. Parl.*, vi, (2), 111; Pocoke's *Tour in Scot.*, 190; *Recs. of Drainie Heritors; Pilgrimages in Moray*, 73, 74; *Recs. of Elgin*, ii, 97.]

SIR JAMES DOUGLAS, vicar 1570.—
1570 [*Book of Assumptions.*]

DAVID COLLACE, buried with his wife in Drainie Kirk; had issue—
1633 John; Robert, bapt. 19th Dec. 1645.

MICHAEL CUMMING, had issue—
1666 David, bapt. 3rd Jan. 1668; Isaac, bapt. 5th Aug. 1669; Alexander, bapt. 9th May 1672; Anna, bapt. 30th June 1674; Elizabeth, bapt. 9th Feb. 1675; Isabel, bapt. 4th Aug. 1678; Jean (marr.

John Hay, Younger of Echreis).—[*Banff Sas.*, 4th Oct. 1698.]

1846 JAMES WEIR, his daugh., Janetta, died 7th Feb. 1947.

1883 JOHN WELLWOOD, his widow, Isabella Herkless, died Brechin 4th May 1946.

1919 JOHN GEDDES RITCHIE, trans. to Stevenston, 24th Nov. 1927.

1928 MALCOLM MANFORD CORNER, born Inverness 28th July 1901; son of William C. and Hedwig Dorothea Just; educ. at Inverness and Univ. of Aberdeen, M.A. (1925), B.D. (1928); licen. by Presb. of Inverness 5th May 1925; assistant St Giles, Edinburgh, 1926–8; ord. 2nd May 1928. Marr. 2nd July 1947 Agnes Doreen, daugh. of James Mathers, min. of Rosewell, and widow of Arthur C. Gordon, B.D., C.F., min. of Foveran.

LOSSIEMOUTH (DRAINIE)

A chapel was built here in 1847–8, being described on 7th June of the latter year as "lately erected." Toward "finishing it" the Home Mission Committee gave a grant of £112 on 11th Oct. of the same year. The site, on the west side of the town, was conveyed to the Kirk Session of Drainie free of all charge on 22nd June 1849 by Dr Richard Rose, min. of Drainie, and his sister, Elizabeth; and there was provision on the site both for the church and a school and other buildings. In 1877 a request was made that the Home Mission build a new church, but nothing further was done. On 4th Feb. 1885 the min. of Drainie submitted to the Presb. plans for a new church which, he proposed, should become the church of the parish. The matter was delayed, but eventually, on 17th Oct. 1894, the Presb. agreed to a church being built nearer the burgh, the existing church being deemed inadequate. A site was granted by Captain Dunbar of Pitgavenay; and on 16th Aug. 1899 the foundation stone of the building was laid by Sir Charles Dalrymple, Bart., M.P. On 22nd Jan. it was resolved to ask for the church, which was called St Gerardine's, a Chapel-of-Ease Constitution, and this was granted by the General Assembly in May of that year. In 1917 St Gerardine's became the parish church. From the time the chapel was opened in 1848 the min. conducted a service there each Sabbath in addition to the service in Drainie Church. On 18th Feb. 1857 a proposal was made to secure a probationer for the work, but without success. Later suggestions to the same effect led to the Presb. agreeing on 30th March 1870 that a probationer be appointed to undertake all competent work. In Sept. 1877 and March 1882 fruitless proposals were made to secure endowment with a view to Lossiemouth being erected into a parish.

1871 CHARLES HENRY, M.A.; on 29th March 1871 he was received by the Presb. as a preacher in the bounds for work at Lossiemouth; he belonged to the Presb. of Hamilton, but for several years prior to 1871 had been at work in the Presb. of Dundee; on 29th Aug. 1883 he received a certificate from the Presb., having left the bounds; may have been identical with Charles Henry, min. at Banton 1858.—[*Recs. of Presby. of Elgin*, 29th March 1871, 29th Aug. 1883.] (See Banton.)

1886 JAMES EWING CAMERON, recorded on 3rd March 1886 as missionary at Lossiemouth, from the Presb. of Glasgow; received a certificate on 24th April 1889 on return to that Presb.; afterwards assistant at Huntly in 1906; Shiskine, ord. 1910; and at Chapel of Garioch 1911. —[*Recs. of Presby. of Elgin*, 3rd March 1886, 24th April 1889.]

1889 WILLIAM McHARDY, received by the Presb. on 2nd Oct. 1889 from the Presb. of Aberdeen, on appointment to Lossiemouth; became min. at Boddam 1901.

1903 NORMAN McLEOD, assistant Canonbie; ord. 11th March 1903; app. to the chapel-of-ease 6th Sept. 1903, and ind. 11th Oct. following; trans. to Belhaven, 7th Jan. 1914.

DUFFUS

It is said that to St Peter's Church of Duffus there fled for sanctuary the occupants of St Aethan's fane at Torridun (Burghead) when about the end of the 9th century the Norsemen, under Sigrud the Powerful, captured Torridun and desecrated the fane. Evidence of a later church is found in a charter of Richard, Bishop of Moray 1187-1203, conveying to William, son of Freskyn, certain lands, and the full teinds of said lands to God and to the Church of St Peter at Duffus, and to Andrew the parson and our clerk, "his" son (i.e. son of William), as is shown by the charter of "our" predecessor, Symon. That indicates the existence of a church in 1171-84, when Symon de Tonei, monk of Melrose, was Bishop of Moray. In it there was an altar, dedicated to St Catharine, which was in existence in 1214, and beside which were buried Hugh de Freskyn de Moravia, who died before 1226, and his son, Walter de Moravia, who died 1262-3. There was also in it a Chapel of St Laurence founded before 1248 by Walter de Moravia's second son, Freskyn de Moravia, who died in 1296 and was buried in the chapel. For the endowment of the chapel he gave of his lands of Duffus and of Dalvey in Strathspey. In addition to the High Altar of St Peter there may have been another altar in the church dedicated to that Apostle, for on 18th Sept. 1240 Walter de Moravia, son of Hugh de M., granted a croft and toft to the Chaplain of St Peter in the Church of St Peter at Duffus to celebrate for the souls of his father and mother, etc. The church seems to have undergone repairs in 1303, when John de Spalding, Canon of Moray, "hoste" of Edward I in Elgin, successfully petitioned that monarch "that he would give him 20 oaks in his forest of Laund Morgun (Longmorn), to build his Church of Duffus, whereof he is Canon." The fact that, as we shall see, the arms of Alexander Sutherland of Duffus, who died on 12th Oct. 1479, appear on the boss of the extant medieval porch and above the lancet window in the west wall of the burial vault which manifestly belongs to the same period as the porch, and on tablets in the main walls of the building, indicates that at least he carried out extensive work on the church and may have actually rebuilt it. For the next notice of the church we have to pass to 17th May 1672, when it was described as "ill accomodate for the public worship and stands in need of reparatioun and plenishing." At that time the "back" of the church and the roof were repaired; and the Presb. further ord. that "for the better hearing of the word" the kirk be divided between the two heritors according to their rents, Alexander, Lord Duffus, and Sir Ludovic Gordon, "who shall replenish their respective parts with convenient seites, desks, and lofts" for themselves and their tenants. A line was drawn down the middle of the church, and the space available for accommodation was, on the north side 21 ells from gable to gable, and, on the south side, 15 ells, made up of 6 ells from the east gable to the pulpit, and 9 ells from the pulpit to the "great door," plus "a little bounded at the syd of the steeple staire." That these measurements refer to the nave is evident from the fact that at the same time Lord Duffus received permission from the Presb. "to close up the passage betwixt the Kirk and the quire for the better accomodation of the Church and the forsaid reparation." In the autumn of 1717 the north wall of the church was "mended" with the addition of a buttress. A few years later, in or about 1720-1, there occurs a brief description of the building as then existing,—"a very pretty Church, well lighted; it has at the west end of it a stately steeple of four storie high, built be the Lord Duffus predecessors which is their burial place. It hes on the east end of the quire a very handsome monument built be Mr Archibald Dunbar of Tundertoune." Further information about the tower may be gleaned from a Kirk Session Minute of 7th March 1641, recording a payment "to Alexander Anderson, mason, for ye upplifting of four stones that fell off ye platform of ye stipel and for ye biging of twa windows in ye stipel." It can hardly be doubted that the church of 1720-1 was substantially the church of medieval times, consisting of a nave, choir, and west tower, with a south porch and a stair to the tower inside the church at the south-west corner. That the church was subsequently rebuilt is, as we shall see, certain; and probably the work was carried out in 1730–2. The question of repairs to the church was raised before the Presb. on 17th Jan. 1724; and on 5th July 1726 that body adopted a report which required the renewal of the roof and the provision of three buttresses for the "back wall" which was "insufficient and coming out over," and in danger of collapse. Delay ensued; and though the Synod as well as the Presb. took action, on 22nd Oct. 1730 it was reported that, while Thunderton (Archibald Dunbar), the heritor concerned, had promised in April 1729 that "he was to order the reparation of the Church," nothing had been done. To the matter no further reference is made; but on 13th June 1732 when the Presb. carried out a visitation of Duffus, it placed on record that the church was "in good repair"—a clear indication that some effective work had been done. On 24th Oct. 1780 it was reported to the Presb. that the church was "in a ruinous condition." Of what was done there is no record; but the writer of the *New Statistical Account* (1845) states that the church was "thoroughly repaired" in 1782. He also refers to it as being "like most old Churches in Scotland constructed without the least regard to appearance, comfort, or commodious arrangement." He would hardly thus have written of a church rebuilt in 1782, only 63 years previous to the publication of the Account. In any case what was actually done subsequent to 1720–1, and probably *cir.* 1729–30, may be learned from an examination of the church as it now exists in the old churchyard at Kirkton about 300 yards east of Duffus village. With the exception of the south porch and the adjacent part of the inner wall, and the lower part of the west gable, the nave was taken down and rebuilt, with the north and south walls upon the old foundations, and the east gable apparently upon the line of the old choir arch. Except the basement, which constituted the Sutherland burial-vault with entrance from the church, the tower was also taken down, and the west gable was carried up to terminate in a belfry, access to the bell rope being got by means of a ladder to the roof of the burial-vault. There were lofts on the north side and east end of the church, each with an outside stair, and a loft on the west end with access by the old stair of the tower, a small portion of which may still be seen. The east loft was also furnished with a fireplace. The medieval porch was left "covered with turf flat on the roof." It has a vaulted roof, and two doorways, an outer and an inner. On the right side of the latter, inside the church, there is a piscina. On the floor of the church there are many tombstones and also fragments of heraldic stones, and also in the interior there is a recess in the east gable in which is the bust of a stone effigy. On the floor level near the east end of the north wall there are built into the wall what appear to be fragments of a medieval tomb. The existence of the arms of Alexander Sutherland of Duffus on the boss of the south porch, on the west wall of the burial-vault and on shields on the north and the south walls of the church, has already been noted. Near the east end of the north wall there are a stone with an incised sceptre and sword, and another stone bearing a figure seated on a sphere and blowing a trumpet, evidently a representation of Gabriel and the last trump. It may be presumed that the choir was taken down when the church was rebuilt. The foundations of the side walls, showing that the choir was of the same width as the nave, may be clearly traced, and the lower part of the east wall survives as the west wall of the Dunbar burial enclosure, built soon after 1711. Inside the choir space on the west side of the Dunbar enclosure there is another burial enclosure constructed presumably when the choir was removed. It contains various tombstones, including the marble slab of Alexander Sutherland of Duffus, who died in 1479, and Morilla Chisholm, his wife, both of whom presumably had been interred near the High Altar. Towards the close of 1867 complaints as to the condition and suitability of the 18th-century building led to negotiations between the Presb. and the heritors, which ended in the present church at the west end of the village being built in 1868-9, being completed in June of the latter year. The pulpit windows were filled in stained glass at the expense of parties respectively in Hopeman and in the Landward Part of the parish; and the cost of the rose window, also in stained glass, was defrayed by Lady Dunbar Brander. At a cost of £405 the spire was built by the min., Rev. Dr Brander, to be associated, at his express desire, with the names of Sir Archibald Dunbar, Bt. of Westfield, and Mary Lady Dunbar Brander of Northfield and Pitgaveny. In the early part of 1870 the materials of the old church were sold, and the building was left roofless. But under the care of the Office of Works its walls have been made secure against any deterioration. Probably also in 1870 a stable that was built on the north side of the west gable adjacent to "Lord Duffus Tomb," and is mentioned in 1867, was removed. In the churchyard a short distance south of the porch there is a cross, probably of the 14th century. Among the vessels of the church there is a solid silver plate, shaped almost like a basin, which is $17\frac{5}{8}$ in. in diameter and weighs 4 lb. avoirdupois. On the under rim is the inscription, "Deo et ecclesiae M. Joannes Guthrie Rector Duffus consec.," and on the upper rim, "The Bread that I will give is my flesh which I will give for ye life of the word IOH* 6* 51." Probably it may have been the gift of Mr Guthrie, min. 1631–41. It is said to have disappeared about the time of the termination of Mr Guthrie's ministry. On the other hand, it has to be noted that a "silver bason," sometimes designated a "large dish" of silver, occurs at regular intervals in inventories of Duffus church vessels in the Presb. minutes from 14th Nov. 1649 to at least 11th Sept. 1756. In any case the plate did disappear, and ultimately came into the possession of a London silversmith about 1860. From him it was acquired by a gentleman who presented it to St Patrick's Church, Hove, for use as an alms-dish. There it came under the notice of Sir Edward Dunbar and Mr Chalmers, min., who identified it as the property of Duffus Church. The result of a conference between Sir Edward and Mr Chalmers on the one hand, and the vicar and chief vestryman of St Patrick's on the other, was that the plate was acquired for £250, and restored to Duffus Church in 1925. An inscription on the under rim tells of its removal in 1641, its reappearance in London in or about 1860, its transference to St Patrick's, and its ultimate recovery in 1925. In 1871, at the expense of Rev. Dr Brander, two old silver salvers were converted into two filigreed patens somewhat resembling cake-baskets. At the east end of the village near the road is the Well of St Peter, which is kept in excellent condition. It provided water for the village prior to the introduction of the gravitation supply. In the field in front of Duffus House there is a well bearing the name of St Lawrence. In addition to the Chapel at Burghead (*q.v.*) there were in the parish at least two chapels. One was at the "College" of Roseisle, the designation "College" no doubt denoting an early community of clerics whose Ab or Head directed the supply of daughter churches. The other, dedicated to the Virgin Mary, was founded by permission of Bricius, Bishop of Moray 1203-21, on the north side of Duffus Castle, by Hugh de Moravia, Lord of Duffus and Strathbrock, whose son, Andrew, was then parson of Duffus. To it were assigned the teinds of Aldetoun; and there was a manse, also on the north side of the Castle. On 13th Sept. 1542 Patrick Hepburne, Bishop of Moray, with consent of William Sutherland of Duffus, patron of the chapel, created it a Prebend and Canonry of Elgin Cathedral, called the Prebend of Unthank, with the manse at the Castle, a garden and croft, and a manse at the cathedral. By this erection Unthank became a parsonage. Hence, in all probability, arose the mistaken view that Unthank was originally a parish. About 1720-1 the Chapel of Unthank was described as "a very bonnie Chappell, the remnant of it is yet extant."—[*Reg. of Moray*, Pref., xxxv-vi, 273, 401, 429, 481; *Cal. of Docs. Rel. to Scot.*, ii, 434; *Reg.*

Great Seal, vi, 1714; *Recs. of Presby. of Elgin*, 14th Nov. 1649, 16th Oct. 1660, 23rd March 1664, 17th May and 12th July 1672, 15th Oct. 1717, 28th Oct. 1728, 17th Jan. and 16th April 1729, 14th April 1730, 13th June 1732, 14th Oct. 1736, 11th Sept. 1756, 24th Oct. 1780; *Kirk Sess. Recs.*, 7th March 1641; Macfarlane's *Geog. Colls.*, i, 233–4; Duffus *Heritors' Recs.; Memo*, Rev. A. G. Catto, B.D.]

1561 WILLIAM HEPBURNE, parson 17th and 21st Nov. 1561.—[*Papal Bulls and Eccles. Docs.*, 74, *MS. Reg. Ho.*]

1567 PATRICK HEPBURNE, parson, deceased in 1567.—[*Acts and Decreets*, xxv, 304, xxvi, 398.]

1567 JOHN KEITH, owned one-third of Duffus and therefore was probably identical with John, third son of William, Earl Marischal, who had lands in Duffus; his son, Mr Alexander, was of Unthank, and his tombstone with date 1616 is built into the outside of the east gable of the old Church of Duffus; his daugh., Margaret—the arms of her husband, Alexander Gordon of Sidra, and herself are on the tombstone of their son, Alexander, who died 1st Sept. 1597, within the enclosure of the choir space of old Church of Duffus.—[*Reg. Great Seal*, vi, 1442, 1653, 1655; *Recs. of Elgin*, i, 225; *Scots Peerage*, vi, 50.]

1567 WILLIAM CLARK, reader; described on 24th May 1574 as Sir William Clark, vicar of Duffus; in 1546–7 he was chaplain of St Duthac's Altar in Elgin Cathedral, and was also chaplain of "the Chaplaincy of St James of Flens," also in the cathedral.—[*Recs. of Elgin*, i, 89, 145; *Reg. Pres. Bene.*, i, 135–6.]

1570 JOHN KER, M.A., parson 1570.—[*Comps. Sub Coll. of Thirds, Moray*, etc.]

1570 SIR JOHN GIBSON, parson of Unthank, so designated 8th May 1580, held the Prebend of Unthank in Elgin Cathedral, but does not seem to have discharged any duties in Duffus; had a son, William, cousin of Gavin Dunbar, Dean of Moray.—[*Recs. of Elgin*, 145, 155, 245.] (See Llhanbryd and Alves.)

1576 JAMES DOUGLAS, reader, pres. to vicarage 16th Sept. 1576, vacant by the death of Sir William Clerk.—[*Reg. Pres. Bene.*, i, (4), 84.]

1603 ROBERT SUTHERLAND, reader 13th May 1603.—[*Recs. of Elgin*, i, 225.]

1608 PATRICK DUNBAR, M.A., son of Patrick D. of Blervie; his tombstone with his arms within the enclosure in the choir space of the old Church of Duffus bears that he died 28th Aug. 1629, aged 53 years; his daugh., Agnes, bapt. 14th July 1612.

1631 JOHN GUTHRIE, by warrant of the General Assembly at Aberdeen July 1640, the Sub-Synod of Moray deposed him and declared Duffus Church vacant on 21st Jan. 1641; to the Sub-Synod it was reported on 8th June 1641 that he had showed signs of repentance and that it was remitted to the Sub-Synod that he might subscribe the Covenant and preach with a view to being restored to the ministry where the Lord shall call him; he sincerely subscribed the Covenant, and the Sub-Synod appointed him to preach a penitential sermon at Elgin, Spynie and Duffus; he petitioned the Sub-Synod to be restored to Duffus; the Sub-Synod resolved to refer the matter to the General Assembly, and the Assembly refused it a hearing; on 10th Nov. 1642 it was represented to the Presb. that for a long time the parish had "been destitute of preaching upon everie Lord's Day." Addl. issue—Lucretia (marr. David Collace, min. of Drainie); a daugh. (marr. Thomas Guthrie of Logie).—[*Recs. Synod of Moray*, 21st Jan. and 8th June 1641, 6th June 1642; *Recs. Presby. of Elgin*, 10th Nov. 1642.]

1643 ALEXANDER SYMMER, he had, as assistant, Adam Harper, afterwards of Boharm, at least from 1683 to 1686; his son, George, educ. at King's College, Aberdeen Univ., M.A. (19th July 1666), died 11th March 1683; his daugh.,

Jean, died at Kirkhill 20th Jan. 1695.—[*Univ. and King's Coll.*, 200, *New Spalding Club*; *Duffus Reg.*]

1687 ADAM SUTHERLAND, adm. 17th Feb. 1687 by order of the Archbishop; his son, James, was bapt. 9th July 1682. Addl. issue—Janet, bapt. 14th Oct. 1683; Patrick, bapt. 20th Nov. 1684 (buried in Light Aisle, Old Machar Cathedral, 6th April 1699); Hugh, buried in Light Aisle, Old Machar, 26th Dec. 1728; Anna, bapt. 15th Jan. 1686; Adam, bapt. 6th May 1688; Robert, bapt. 2nd Feb. 1691.—[*New Machar Reg.*; *Old Machar Reg.*; *Duffus Reg.*]

1724 JAMES DUNBAR, brother of John D., merchant, Inverness.

1778 JOHN REID, was assistant at Drainie prior to admission here.—[*Recs. Presby. of Elgin*, 25th Aug. 1778.]

1907 HENRY REID CHALMERS, trans. to Abernyte 16th June 1926.

1926 ALEXANDER GODSMAN CATTO, trans. from Aberdour, Deer (*q.v.*), 1st Dec. 1926. Marr. 12th Aug. 1920 Elizabeth Kate, daugh. of John Macleod and Johanna Campbell. Addl. issue—Gordon Duffus, born 26th Oct. 1929; William Leslie, born 30th Sept. 1931.

ELGIN

The church, a prebend of Elgin Cathedral, was sometimes called the Prebend of 100 shillings, because included in the prebend there was 100 shillings of the altarage of the church. In or soon after 1187 King William the Lion, for the augmentation of the Bishopric of Moray, gave the church, along with the Chapel of St Andrew and the Chapel of Monbeen, to Bishop Richard and his successors, the gift to take effect after the decease of Richard de Prebend, his cleric, and of Walter, Cleric of Richard. The church was burned by the Wolf of Badenoch in 1390. In it there were the following altars—the Virgin Mary, at which chaplainries were founded, on 20th Oct. 1363 by William de Soreys, burgess of Elgin, on 12th Nov. 1343 by William Pope, son of William Pope, burgess of Elgin, and in 1365 by Richard, son of John, burgess of Elgin; the Holy Rood, at which in 1286 a chaplainry was founded by Hugh Herok, burgess of Elgin; and St Duthac the Bishop, at which a chaplainry was founded on 9th May 1528 by Alexander Gaderer (Gatherer), Elgin, his son, Mr Thomas, being then the chaplain. In 1596 a new loft was built in the west end of the church; and in 1598 the choir, the upkeep of which had previously devolved upon the Bishops of Moray, was thoroughly repaired in "theck, ruff, wallis, windois glais, and pleneeshing," the cost, 800 merks, being met by a stent imposed on the fruits of the Bishopric of Moray. About 1621 the choir, under the name of the Little Kirk, was constituted a separate place of worship by the closing of the chancel arch. Probably it was then that the Rood Loft, access to which was by a stair in the choir, was removed. Subsequently there occur in the Kirk Session minutes notices of services conducted by the mins. in the two churches, sometimes termed the old and the new. On 10th Nov. 1653, when the Presb. assembled for their meeting at the church, "the meeting was interrupted by ye Inglis Troupers also had a number of yr horsis in the Church which was the place of meeting." The Presb. accordingly adjourned. On 2nd April 1661 there was submitted to the Synod of Moray a reference from the Presb. of Elgin "anent the building an edifice of a new Kirk at Elgin." In respect of the absence of some heritors, the matter was delayed; and nothing more appears to have been done. On Sunday, 22nd June 1679, the roof of the church collapsed, but the pillars and central arched tower remained. In the following year rebuilding was inaugurated; and the work was completed in 1682. The church was demolished in 1826, and was replaced by the present church, which was opened for worship in Oct. 1828. About 1605 the churchyard was removed, recourse being had to the churchyard at the cathedral.

The auxiliary Church of St Columba, built on a site between Moss Street and

Duff Avenue, was opened for worship on 17th June 1906. It is a mixture of Norman and Gothic architecture, and consists of a nave with south aisle of four bays, a choir with transeptal chapel on the south side and an organ chamber on the north, and a chancel. The pulpit, of carved oak in the Renaissance style, was the pulpit placed in the parish church when it was rebuilt in 1684. When the present parish church was built, the pulpit was removed to Pluscarden Priory. When the priory was acquired from the Duke of Fife by the Marquis of Bute, the pulpit was reserved by the Duke, who subsequently returned it to the Church of Scotland. It differs in style from St Columba's Church, but was used by the architect, Dr MacGregor Chalmers, as the model for all the church's oak furnishings.

To the Chapel of St Andrew and the Chapel of Monbeen reference has already been made. It is not clear whether the former was the Chapel of St Andrew situated above Pluscarden Glen, or the chapel which afterwards became St Andrew's Parish Church. The chapel on the Castlehill, dedicated to the Virgin Mary, was repaired and rebuilt in 1459–69. In it there was an altar dedicated to St John the Baptist, at which on 10th July 1351, Isabel Countess of Moray, founded a chaplainry for celebrations at stated times for the soul of Thomas Randolph, Earl of Moray; and in the second quarter of the 15th century James Dunbar, Earl of Moray, granted certain annual rents and also provision for bread, wine, and wax to "the Chaplain of the King in the Chapel." Near the ordeal pot, a testing-place for women delinquents, the site of which, situated at the east end of Chanonry Road, is marked by a stone at the foot of the railway enbankment, there was another chapel dedicated to the Virgin Mary, called the Chapel of Grene or Lady of Grene. There were also a Chapel of the Holy Trinity and a Chapel of St John.

In or about 1226 Andrew de Moravia, Bishop of Moray, founded on land "between the King's Way and the river Task" a maison-dieu with chapel, dedicated to St Mary and St John the Evangelist, for the reception of the poor, both "brothers and sisters," and the sustenance of the same. To the endowments given by the Bishop there were added by Alexander II on 27th Feb. 1234–5 the lands of Monbeen and Kellas. In 1390 the house was "destroyed and burned" by the Wolf of Badenoch. By Charters of 22nd March 1594–5, 10th Dec. 1599, and 29th Feb. 1620, James VI granted to the burgh of Elgin, for the support of the poor and of a music school with a music master, the hospital, the preceptory and the right of patronage of the same, the lands of Over and Nether Monbeen and the Haughs of Monbeen, the lands of Nether Cardellis, and Over and Nether Pettinseiris, which pertained to the hospital of old. The maison-dieu was replaced by the Bede Houses in 1626; and the latter were rebuilt in 1864. In 1770 the walls of the maison-dieu were blown down, but a remnant seems to have been in existence in 1860. The site was on the west side of Maison Dieu Road, and is in fact occupied by Anderson's Institution.

The friary of the Blackfriars was dedicated to St Andrew and was situated near the Lossie, north-west of the Castlehill. On 29th March 1285 Alexander III gave mandate to the Sheriff and Bailies of Elgin to pay from the fermes of the burgh certain quantities of victual to the friars; and on 21st Oct. 1313 Robert I granted to them 10 merks annually from the Thanage of Aberchirder. Of the Settlement, the name of which is perpetuated in Blackfriars' Haugh and Blackfriars' Road, some slight foundations were in existence in 1740.

Apparently in the third quarter of the 13th century William, Earl of Ross, who died in May 1274, gave to God, the Holy Trinity, and the Bishops of Moray, the lands of Cadboll in Ross, and a quarter of the lands of Pethkenny, for the life and sustenance of the Minorite (Grey) Friars, who for the time were dwelling in the house belonging to them near the Cathedral of Elgin, or shall dwell in it for the future, and, failing that, for the sustenance of chaplains in the cathedral church. Clearly, therefore, about the middle of the 13th century an unknown donor provided a house in Elgin for the Greyfriars; and it would also appear that in it they took up their abode. But the fact that Cadboll and Pithendie (Pethkenny) subsequently constituted a chaplainry in the cathedral shows that the Greyfriars did not fulfil the condition of permanent residence; and, therefore, nothing more was done towards the establishment of the house. Dunfermline House at the east end of the town is said to occupy the site of the Greyfriars' original abode. The second and complete foundation was made by John Innes, Sheriff of Moray, apparently some years prior to 1479. That year is the date of the Bull of Pope Sixtus IV confirming the foundation; and the Bull describes the monastery as "now founded and built." Associated with the founding of the house is the following story. Described as "a man seldom given to pious deeds," Sheriff Innes was also known by repute as a "raider of church possessions, an oppressor of the lieges, and a disturber of the peace." A band of Caterans raided Moray, and carried off much booty of cattle and corn. With a force of Moray men the Sheriff followed the reavers to the Pass of Abernethy, where a fight took place. The men of Moray were defeated; and they fled, leaving their leader, as they thought, dead on the field. Badly wounded, he turned to Heaven for help and vowed to amend his ways, restore his ill-gotten gains, and found a monastery for Franciscans if he were rescued from his plight. At that time his uterine brother, Francis, one of the friars of the Franciscan Monastery at Aberdeen, and noted for his piety and learning, was at Abernethy in the course of one of the periodical missions in the north which he and other Franciscan friars from Aberdeen carried out for the conversion of "the rude and barbarous people of the neighbourhood." Forewarned of the fight in his sleep, he set out for the pass, and found and rescued his wounded brother. Restored to health, the latter implemented his vow, including the founding of the monastery at Elgin. Subsequently, when he was free from business claims, he sometimes spent weeks at the monastery, observing its rules, rising even for the nocturnal vigils, and sharing the meagre diet of the cloisters. The first friars at Elgins, who came from Aberdeen, were twelve in number, with Francis Innes, the founder's brother, and Doctor of Both Laws of France, as the first guardian of the monastery. Among the twelve there were at least three of special note—Bernard Chisholm, whose work in converting cattle thieves earned for him the nickname of "associate of caterans"; Anthony Fraser, and Robert Stuart. In 1480 Alexander Sutherland of Quarrelwood granted the Friars the right to cut down in his woods what trees they required for repairs, etc., of their buildings. After the Reformation, the place was put to various uses; and ultimately, in 1891, it was acquired by the Sisters of the Convent of Sainte Marie of Mercy; and, thereafter, the church which had become ruinous, and the conventual buildings, of which the west wing survived, were restored through the generosity of the Marquis of Bute.

Annual rents pertaining "of old" to the "white Friars of Elgin" occur in a charter of 1581, but of such friars nothing further seems to be known, and the description may be a copyist's error. To the east of the maison-dieu there was a leper house, with about six acres of land attached, in the angle of the Tyock Burn and the Fochabers road. Near the cathedral there was a place or land belonging to the "Brethren of St Lazarus beside the Wall of Jerusalem." In 1360 Bishop John Pilmou granted and confirmed the land (or part thereof) extending to $3\frac{1}{2}$ roods, described as lying on the west side of the stone wall of the canonry between the two common ways, to four perpetual chaplains of the cathedral, to be divided proportionally for the building of manses for themselves and their successors. St Lazarus' Wynd indicates the site.

The Bishopric of Moray was in existence in the time of Alexander I (1107-24), Bishop Gregory (1115) being the first bishop mentioned. That for nearly a century the see had no fixed cathedral seat appears both from the narrative of Bishop Bricius (1203-21), contained in his petition to Pope Innocent III craving that the Church of Spynie be declared the cathedral, and also from the narrative in his writ of foundation of the canonry. He states that his predecessors, having no fixed place as cathedral, had from the point of view of convenience adapted the seat in one or the other of three churches—Birnie, Spynie and Kineddar, that most of them had held Spynie Church as the cathedral, and that in it they had been installed. It would appear, therefore, that Birnie Church had at first been regarded as the cathedral, and that it had given place to Spynie, which seemed to be much in favour. When the petition was addressed to the Pope, Kineddar Church was the seat. But, as the Bishop further narrates, Kineddar was held by consensus of opinion, clerical and lay, to be most unsuitable, situated as it was "on a peninsula of the sea to which none of the parishioners could approach without difficulty." And there were other considerations which induced the "Chapter and other prudent men" to favour Spynie, "the difficulty of places," "the roughness of ways," and "the change of times," and chiefly greater security against the works of evildoers, and better facilities for the bishop in the ministrations of his office alike in spiritual and temporal things. It was craved, therefore, that the Pope decern the Holy Trinity Church of Spynie to be the seat of the Bishop of Moray for the future. On 26th March 1207 the Pope acceded to the petition, and remitted to the Bishops of St Andrews and Brechin, and the Abbot of Lindores, to make inquiry and give effect to the crave, which was done. About sixteen years later steps were taken to secure the transference of the seat from Spynie. On 13th April 1224 Pope Honorius III narrates that "coming into our presence, our venerable brother, the Bishop of Moray, has often expounded to us and repeatedly poured into our ears" that the cathedral was in a position by no means safe from guerilla raids and was so solitary that provisions were difficult to obtain and the clerics had to go a long way to buy what was necessary, and consequently were hindered in no small degree in the performance of their devotions. For those reasons the Bishop "with much insistence of entreaties has craved that the seat be transferred to a place more suitable," the Holy Trinity Church beside Elgin. The personal character of the approach to the Pope has led to the inference that it was made by Bishop Bricius when he attended the Lateran Council at Rome in 1215. But, apart from the fact that Honorius did not become Pope till 1216, it will be observed that the Papal narrative speaks, not of the late bishop, but of the bishop alive at the time, and that in recording the consent of the King and the chapter to the change, it adds "as the said Bishop (i.e. the Bishop craving the change) asserts." Evidently, therefore, the bishop was Andrew de Moravia, who was app. in 1222 and consecrated in the following year, and must have visited Rome at the outset of his episcopate. On 13th April 1224 Pope Honorius made remit to the Bishop of Caithness, the Abbot of Kinloss, and the Dean of Ross, empowering them to make the change, if on the grounds of necessity and utility they saw fit; on 5th July of the same year Alexander II addressed a letter to these Papal mandatories, expressing his great desire that "there be effected the translation of the Episcopal Seat to that Place beside Elgin which we have given to the Bishop and Clergy of Moray for the building of that Church," and his further wish that it be done "in our time," and giving them mandate for, and asking them to take into consideration, the carrying out of the Papal remit; and on the 19th of the same month the Bishop of Caithness and the Dean of Ross met at Elgin, and on the grounds already stated, app. the said Church of the Holy Trinity beside Elgin to be the Cathedral of Moray and at the same time granted confirmation of the transfer in the church, with the Bishop of Moray presiding. Of the origin of the Holy Trinity Church then existing, nothing is really known. It may be inferred that Alexander II gave the site for the church with a view to the ultimate transference of the episcopal seat; and possibly the "church" at the time of the transference may have been the first portion of the cathedral. In any case the foundation stone of the cathedral was laid also on 19th July 1224, and the building was carried on by Bishop Andrew, and probably completed before his death in 1242. The cathedral was burned and mainly destroyed by the Wolf of Badenoch in 1390, and was rebuilt. On 14th Feb. 1567-8 the Priory Council ord. that the lead of the roof which "is for ane greit part be diverse personis thiftuously stowin and being taken away," "be taken down and desponed upon for interteneing and sustentatioun men of weir and uther needful charges." Of an opposite nature was the policy of the Privy Council on 8th July 1569, when beneficed men in the Diocese of Moray were charged to contribute for the repairing of the cathedral, "for mending the theking and reparating" the Church, "to the effect that the same may be a convenient place to conven the people for hering of the Word of God." The proposal was not carried into effect. In the cathedral there were altars dedicated as follows—the Virgin Mary in the south aisle of the chancel; St Laurence; St Peter in the south aisle; St Paul in the south aisle; Holy Rood; St Katharine; St John; St James, called St James Chaplainry of Flens; St Columba; St Thomas the Martyr in the north aisle; St Martin; St Giles; St Anne; St Nicholas; St Andrew; St Ninian, called St Ninian's Chaplainry of Flens; St Mary Magdalene; St Michael; St Duthac. On 16th May 1328 Thomas Randolph, Earl of Moray, granted an annual rent of £23 6s. 8d. from the fermes of the Sheriffdom of Elgin to five Chaplains to celebrate for the souls of Robert I, his uncle, etc., in the "magnificent chapel" dedicated to St Thomas the Bishop and Martyr, which he had built in the churchyard on the south side of the cathedral. Described in 1456 as "in the cathedral," and in 1502 as "within the same, the chapel" may have been incorporated in the main building some time after its foundation.—[*Reg. Great Seal*, i, 245, ii, 245, 1334, 2625, iii, 781, 835, iv, 638, v, 93, 393, 1101, 1590, 1697, 1742, 1893, 2030, vi, 249, 267, 652, 953, 1709, vii, 853, 2136, 2141, 2169, viii, 1612, 1634, 1651, 2169; *Reg. Sec. Seal*, ii, 81, iii, 1811; *Acts Scott. Parl.*, v, 595; *Excheq. Rolls*, iii, 77, vi, 219, 220, 270, 464, 466, 483-4, 517, vii, 17, 20, 238, 355, xii, 52; *Cal. Papal Regs., Letters*, i, 94, 96, ix, 103, 105, 447, 480, x, 315-16, xii, 363; *Petitions*, i, 580; *Cal. of Docs. Rel. to Scot.*, ii, 434; *Retours*, iii, 155, iv, 273; Theiner's *Vet. Mon.*, 22; *Reg. Pres. Bene.*, i, 133-4, ii, 23; *Extracts from Recs. of Kirk Sess. of Elgin*, 344; *Recs. of Elgin*, i, 70, 89, 149, 324, 444, ii, 69, 483, 489, 501; *Brockie MSS., St Mary's College, Blairs; Memo.*, Rev. John McKee, B.A. (Cantab); *Recs. of Synod of Moray*, 6th April 1658, 2nd April 1661; *Recs. Presby. of Moray*, 10th Nov. 1653; *Family of Innes*, 111, 116; *Scots Mag.*, xxxv, 106; Pocoke's *Tours Thro' Scotland*, 190. For details, see Rhind's *Sketches of Moray*, Shaw's *Province of Moray*, Young's *Annals of Elgin*, Macintosh's *Elgin Past and Present*; and for Canonries, etc., of the Cathedral, see *Preface of Reg. of Moray*.]

ALEXANDER WINCHESTER, had charge also of Pluscarden 1568.—[*Comps. Sub Coll. of Thirds, Moray*, etc.]

1566

WILLIAM DOUGLAS was chaplain of the Altar of St Laurence in the cathedral, and one of the prebendaries. On 10th Sept. 1566 he was Clerk of Consistory, and on 12th Jan. 1578-9 he was app. clerk of the burgh for one year; in 1576 he was reader at Elgin and St Andrews, part of his duties being "to warne the parishioners to their examinationes agane the Communion"; was still reader in 1607; he had a natural son, James, of whom a Kirk Session minute of 17th July 1594 records that he "has actit himself to be baneist gif evir he beis found at pastyme the tym of preaching or nit found ane common player."—[*Exts. from Recs. Kirk Sess. of Elgin*, 8, 23, 344-7; *Recs. of Elgin*, i, 121-2, ii, 21, 47, 64,.]

1569

ROBERT LESLIE, reader in 1591, when it is narrated that "the minister and eldaris inhibits Robert Leslie, reader, that he nether marie nor bapteis without he haif the express commandment of the minister and eldaris"; on 15th July 1598 his attitude to baptism was again under review, when the Kirk Session commanded

1591

him to baptise the infant of John Innes, elder, notwithstanding the fact that said John was under sentence of excommunication for being "artt and part" in an act of murder; it would seem, therefore, that he was qualified to perform marriages and baptisms; still in office 11th March 1604, when there was brought against him the vague charge of having "raissit himself under the pulpit."—[*Exts. from Recs. of Kirk Sess. of Elgin*, 12; *Recs. of Elgin*, ii, 66, 122.]

GEORGE DOUGLAS, reader 24th Sept. 1616; evidently identical with George D., son of Archibald D., mason, Old Aberdeen, who was app. Master of the Song School and the Grammar School 9th Nov. 1600; had issue—Robert, bapt. 28th Feb. 1611; James, bapt. 22nd March 1612; Margaret, bapt. 15th Aug. 1613.—[*Recs. of Elgin*, ii, 398, 401.]
1616

JOHN GUTHRIE, after his deposition, the Senior Charge remained vacant; later a supplication was pres. to Parliament by "the Minister and towne of Elgin, craving ane mantenance for two ministers and ane reider, they being now altogidder destitute"; and on 9th Sept. 1639 Parliament resolved that the supplication be recommended to His Majesty as proceeding from the General Assembly, but that there be no Act of Parliament regarding it.—[*Acts Scott. Parl.*, v, 595.]
1623

DAVID MURRAY, reader 22nd May 1628, when he ratified his promise of marriage to Janet Grant in the parish of Spynie, daugh. of the late Gregor G. in Gartinmore; also Master of the Music School.—[*Recs. of Elgin*, ii, 205.]
1628

GILBERT ROSS, probably son of Oliver R., notar in Maybole, and Janet Graham. Marr. (2) Elizabeth, daugh. of Francis Napier, burgess of Edinburgh.—[*Gen. Reg. Sas.*, liii, 64; *Reg. of Inhibitions*, i, 457, 9th March 1630; *Edinburgh Burgess Roll*, 4th July 1636.]
1640

WILLIAM MURRAY, reader 12th Sept. 1641, held the vicarage and the vicar's lands; was also Master of the Music School; dem. office 2nd Aug. 1668.—[*Recs. of Elgin*, ii, 240, 405, 408.]
1641

THOMAS INNES, reader 1667. Marr. Nicolas, probably daugh. of Thomas Craig, min. of Spynie, and had issue—Robert, bapt. 26th Nov. 1667.
1667

ROBERT LANGLANDS, his son, George, apprenticed to Robert Elliot, surgeon, Edinburgh 13th July 1709.
1696

ALEXANDER TOPP, his daugh., Margaret (marr. Thomas Blackie Park, Haddington); died 14th May 1934.
1841

WILLIAM MOFFAT, died 17th Jan. 1943; his widow, Frances Low, died 15th Oct. 1947.
1894

JAMES MILLAR MOORHEAD MADILL, his wife, Margaret Helen Scott, died 14th Sept. 1928. Marr. (2) 4th Feb. 1931 Isabella Gordon, daugh. of Robert Stuart Christie, Manitoba.
1916

SECOND CHARGE

ALEXANDER WINCHESTER, min., pres. to vicarage 26th Feb. 1567–8 on dem. of George Hepburn.—[*Reg. Pres. Bene.*, i, 6.]
1566

WILLIAM DOUGLAS, pres. to vicarage 24th March 1567–8 on assignation of George Hepburn, treasurer of Moray, and to vicarage 27th Nov. and 8th Dec. 1569, on resignation of Alexander Winchester.—[*Reg. Pres. Bene.*, i, 7, 32.]
1569

DAVID PHILP, on 14th Oct. 1622 the Kirk Session ord. that Mr David Philp "quhen he teitches that he turn the glass quhen he goes to the pulpit, that the prayers, psalme, and preitching be all endit within the hour, under pain of 6/8."—[*Recs. of Elgin*, ii, 167.]
1609

JOHN GORDON, he was dep. for (1) neglect of weekly sermon; (2) lack of discipline in Kirk Session; (3) often deserting his charge, particularly when "maid doctor at Aberdene," and, "as a man unsatled in his judgments,"
1633

taking to the hills "in a gray playd and trewes," remaining there on one occasion for about eighteen days; (4) being scandalous, profane, and irreligious; (5) careless wandering in the country on the Sabbath days; (6) fighting in the High Street and open churchyard in Elgin with an Irish phisitiane, both of them wrestling "in dubbs and myres" until separated; (7) scandalous and unsound in doctrine; (8) cursing all that entered into the Covenant. On 4th April 1648 it was reported to the Synod that he encouraged malignants; and at the same meeting he confessed that he had exercised part of the ministerial function since his deposition. He was referred to the Commission, and on 3rd May of the same year the Synod recorded that the General Assembly had appointed the Presb. of Elgin to excommunicate him. It was further reported to the Synod on 2nd Sept. 1650 that he was frequenting the bounds of the Presb. of Aberlour and the "prime families theirin, abusing ministers with his tongue when he say them," and at "gentlemen's tables" blessing and giving thanks.—[*Recs. of Synod of Moray*, 30th April 1639.]

JOHN GORDON, fourth son of John G. of Craig; went to Portyone in Wales. Marr. Elizabeth, daugh. of Hon. Alexander Gordon of Strathaven; his second son, Alexander, died before 15th Dec. 1657; his daugh., Elizabeth (marr. George Gordon of Tewchines).
1633

THOMAS LAW, had issue—Robert; Thomas.—[*Banff Sas.*, 6th May 1659; 7th Dec. 1666.]
1645

JAMES HORNE, his daugh., Agnes, bapt. 16th Dec. 1668.
1659

JAMES HAY, born 1736, son of Hugh H. of Park family; his daugh., Ann, died at Aberdeen 21st March 1793.
1779

LEWIS GORDON, his mother, Isabel Rae.
1815

JAMES CHARLES CONN, trans. to St Stephen's, Broughty Ferry, 4th Aug. 1926.
1922

GRAHAM NICOLL WARNER, trans. from Bervie (*q.v.*) 16th Dec. 1926; trans. to St James, Clydebank, 25th June 1931; trans. to St John's, Lochwinnoch, 2nd May 1935; app. Assistant Secretary and Deputy, Church and Ministry Department, 24th May 1946. Marr. 23rd July 1924 Sheila L. G. Macaulay, and has issue—Sheila Elizabeth Macaulay, born 11th Feb. 1926; Patricia Helen Gordon, born 4th Dec. 1930, died 24th Aug. 1946; Robert Graham, born 29th Dec. 1932, died 31st Jan. 1933; Ian Graham, born 4th April 1934; Kenneth Boath, born 10th Dec. 1938.
1926

PLUSCARDINE

The Old Store which was situated a short distance east of the Lodge became on the erection of a Mission in the Glen, the place of worship known as the "Old Ha'." In 1821 Lord Fife fitted up the old parlour of the priory as a church and in 1843 he gave the use of it to the Free Church. Services continued to be held till about 1898, when the Marquess of Bute entered into possession.

In the Glen of Pluscarden there was a chapel dedicated to St Andrew and prior to 1230, the glen was called the Vale of St Andrew.

ALEXANDER WINCHESTER, min. in 1568. (See Elgin.)
1568

ST ANDREWS and LHANBRYDE

JOHN WALKER, M.A.; his son, Henry William, was in Tuticorin, India; his son, Robert Duff, was in Sydney, Australia; and his son, John, was in Springfield, Tasmania; his daugh., Elisa Catherine (marr. Hugh Alexander Duff of Kenern, New Zealand), died 25th Sept. 1925.— [*Inscrip.*, St Andrew's Churchyard.]
1839

CHARLES ALEXANDER DAVIDSON, his widow, Phoebe Cruickshank, died at Hawick 1st Feb. 1930, aged 93.
1863

JOHN ROBERTSON DUNCAN, trans. to Inveraven 25th Sept. 1931; died 1st Sept. 1933 as result of motor accident at Elgin; his widow, Margaret
1897

ST ANDREWS

Smart, died 2nd Sept. 1935; his daugh., Elspet Margaret (marr. William Strathdee, distiller, Glenfarlass, Banffshire).

ST ANDREWS

1569 ALEXANDER LESLIE, M.A., pres. to vicarage 4th June 1569 on death of Sir John Chalmers; dep. before 13th Oct. 1573.—[*Reg. Pres. Bene.* i, 28, 97.]

1576 PATRICK BALFOUR, pres. to vicarage 15th Oct. 1576 on death of Sir John Chalmers.—[*Reg. Pres. Bene.*, i, (2), 87.]

1576 GEORGE DOUGLAS, reader here, pres. to vicarage 3rd Oct. 1573, John Chalmers having failed to compear to make confession of faith on succession to Alexander Leslie.—[*Reg. Pres. Bene.*, i, 97; i, (4), 11.]

1586 JAMES LAUDER, min. 29th April 1586, had issue—Andrew.—[*Acts and Dec.*, lv, 303.]

1640 ROBERT TERRAS, had issue—Robert, min. of Olrig.

1663 THOMAS CRAIG, line 8, for "11" read "6"; was son of Thomas C., min. of Spynie; had issue—Isobel.—[*Elgin Sas.*, iv, 168.]

LHANBRYDE

1710 WALTER STEWART, marr. pro. 23rd Feb. 1710 Barbara, probably daugh. of Andrew Munro, Sheriff of Moray. Addl. issue—Robert, bapt. 13th Sept. 1723; Hugh, called only son; John, his successor, probably a near relative, but not a son.—[*Inverkeithney Sas.*, 2nd Feb. 1738.]

1727 JOHN STEWART, line 1, delete "son of preceding."

1735 PATRICK DUNCAN, his daugh., Jean (marr. William Tulloch, merchant, Forres).

SPEYMOUTH, formerly DIPPLE

The church, commonly called the "Red Kirk," was founded on 10th July 1732, near St Leonard's Well at Stynie which mysteriously dried up many years ago. On 18th March 1746 Lord John Drummond of the Jacobite army came to the manse, which for a time became the rebels' headquarters. The rebels retired on the approach of the Duke of Cumberland's army and the Duke slept at the manse on the night of 12th April 1746.—[*Session Record.*]

A small house, called "The House of the Holy Ghost," stood at the churchyard gate. Round it in the direction of the sun's course the people carried the corpse at burial—a superstitious practice that was not abolished till the walls were razed to the ground.

By decreet of 14th July 1731 the Commissioners for Plantation of Kirks decreed that the parishes of Dipple and Essil and the barony of Garmouth be united into one parish under the name of Speymouth. This was in accordance with a suggestion of the Synod of Moray on 22nd April 1730, the min. of Urquhart and the min. of Essil each having refused any relation to the people of Garmouth.—[*Recs. Presby. of Elgin*, 1st Feb. 1732; *Recs. Synod of Moray*, 22nd April 1730; Shaw's *Province of Moray*, iii, 385.]

1565 ADAM HEPBURNE of Bonhard, Dean of Caithness, was parson of Dipple 25th May 1565.—[*Reg. of Deeds*, iv, 193, viii, 200.]

1567 WILLIAM PETERKIN, vicar and exhorter, 1567–90.—[*Comps. Sub Coll. of Thirds*, Moray, etc.] (See Arndilly.)

1568 WILLIAM KEITH, reader 1568. (See Dundurcas.)

1588 WILLIAM MCQUEEN, vicar 1588.—[*Comps. Sub Coll. of Thirds, Moray*, etc.]

1731 ROBERT MILN, bapt. 20th Aug. 1697; his wife, daugh. of Alexander McIntosh, not William.

1785 JAMES GILLAN, line 12, for "Allangarth" read "Allanpark."

GEORGE BIRNIE, D.D. (Aberdeen, 4th April 1940), dem. 11th March 1940; died 22nd Jan. 1941; his wife, Margaret Lobban, died 24th Oct. 1937; his daughs.—Jeanie Morrison, M.B., Ch.B. (marr. 2nd June 1934 Lieut. Harold Vitler Clarke, R.N.R.S., son of George Clarke, Cheam, Surrey); Margaret Helen Kemp (marr. 2nd Sept. 1947 Rev. James Smith, Moray House, Edinburgh). Publications—Various Treatises on Botany.

1890

(*United with Garmouth 21st July* 1940.)

ESSIL

SIR ALEXANDER DOUGLAS, died before 18th Aug. 1587.—[*Reg. Sec. Sig.*, lvi, 18.]

1574

ALEXANDER HAY, M.A., pres. to vicarage from Rhynie 18th Aug. 1587 on death of Sir Alexander Douglas.—[*Reg. Sec. Sig.*, lv, 19.]

1587

SPYNIE

The Church of the Holy Trinity of Spynie was decerned the Cathedral of the Bishopric in 1207, and continued so till 1224. Whether that was the church that existed at and after the Reformation has not been determined. Upon the latter church repairs were carried out in 1708, especially in the case of the south wall and the west half of the roof; and attention was again given to the faulty state of the building in 1724, when it was estimated that the cost of necessary repairs would be £488 12s. Little appears to have been done; and on 4th Nov. 1731 it was reported to the Presb. that the church was ruinous, the east gable being rent and falling from the side walls, and the larger part of the roof insufficient. From this emerged the question as to whether the building should be repaired; and after full consideration the Presb. on 11th July 1732 agreed to the transportation of both church and manse "which are at present very inconveniently situate, the said Church lying in a distant corner of the parish very far from the body of the people and the best inhabited places of the parish"; transportation "would tend much to the good of souls in the parish." Eventually agreement was made between the heritors and the min. for the building of a new church upon "a piece of barren moor at the Mains of Quarrywood," which was also to be the site of the new manse. The min. was also "to get a piece of ground from Braco sufficient to be a yard." It was further agreed that the new church was to be of the same dimensions as the old church, with the addition of an aisle 20 ft. square. Later it was found that to that stipulation there was close approximation. Whereas the old church, on measurement taken prior to its removal, was 66 ft. long, 21½ ft. broad, with walls 12 ft. high, the new church was 67 ft. long, 22 ft. broad, with walls 12 ft. high, besides the aisle on the north side 20 ft. square. The new church was founded on 10th March 1735, and on 13th April 1736 it was reported to the Presb. that it was "nearly finished." The division of the church among the heritors was made on 4th May 1736, when it was further decreed that "for the accommodation of servants and strangers a Common Loft be built in the west end of the Church." The east end was occupied by the Westfield Loft. On 28th Aug. 1739 the church was declared sufficient by the Presb. The belfry, built in 1723, and two windows, one of them arched, were removed from the old church and incorporated with the new; and on the south wall there is a dial with the date 1740 and the inscription, Ion Dugal fecit, the said John being a son of the contemporary min. It was in 1740 that the church was actually completed, though apparently it was used for worship prior to that date. Extensive repairs were begun in 1803 and completed on 3rd Dec. 1805—two windows, one on each side of the pulpit, were enlarged; a door in the aisle was built up, and a door in the east gable was opened up, with a window above the same; outside the latter door there was built a semicircular portico with north and south doors; the church was completely paved and reseated; there was provided a new pulpit, a precentor's desk, and a baptistry "as in St Andrew's Church"; the Westfield loft was repaired, and the common loft was renewed, a stair being furnished in the south-west corner. To a petition of the Presb. 10th Oct. 1734 that the church and manse be called New Spynie, effect was given by the Commissioners before 11th March 1735. The Palace or Castle of Spynie, the residence of the Bishops, was built by John Innes, Bishop 1407-14. Situated a few hundred yards south of Inchbroom House there was a chapel dedicated to the Virgin Mary, called the Chapel of the Island of Spynie, Our Lady Chapel of the Inch. Apparently it is this chapel to which reference occurs on 28th July 1296, when William le Franseys was sued by Thomas the Clerk of Elgin for being found in possession of 476 lamb-skins which the plaintiff had deposited in the "Church of St Mary of Inch for security against robbers."

At Kintrae farms there was situated the Church of Kintrae, called in a Charter of Bricuis de Douglas, Bishop of Moray 1203-22, "the old Church of Kyntra." For the purpose of augmenting the prebend of Spynie, founded by Bishop Bricuis, his predecessor, Andrew de Moravia, Bishop of Moray 1222-42, joined the Church of Kintrae to the Church of Spynie. All vestiges of the church and churchyard have disappeared, but the site may still be traced. In at least part of the period 1187-1203, Lambert, Chaplain of King William the Lion, was parson of Kintrae. There was a chapel at Inchbrock between Wester Kintrae and Westfield House.—[*Reg. Epis. Moraviende*, 39, 94, 273, 359; Mackintosh's *Pilgrimages in Moray*; *Recs. of Presb. of Elgin*, 29th July 1708, 10th Sept. 1724, 4th Nov. 1731, 11th July 1732, 1st Oct. 1734, 11th March 1735, 13th April 1736, 4th May 1736, 28th Aug. 1739, 21st April 1803, 8th Jan., 3rd Dec. 1805; *Cal. of Docs. Rel. to Scotland*, ii, 192; *Family of Innes*, 111.] (See Elgin.)

SIR ALEXANDER SUTHERLAND, vicar 15th Feb., 15th March 1567.—[*Reg. Great Seal*, v, 1215.]
1567

ROBERT INNES, M.A., pres. to parsonage 24th June 1574 on Thomas, Commendator of Glenluce, being declared a rebel.—[*Reg. Sec. Sig.*, xlii, 119.]
1574

ALEXANDER DOUGLAS, pres. to vicarage 27th Oct. 1574 on death of Sir John Dowall.—[*Reg. Pres. Bene.*, i, (4), 24.]
1574

ALEXANDER WINCHESTER, min. here, pres. to parsonage 19th Feb. 1574-5 on Thomas, Commandator of Glenluce, being declared a rebel.—[*Reg. Pres. Bene.*, i, (4), 29.]
1576

ALEXANDER RAWSON, pres. to parsonage and vicarage 15th Feb. 1580-1 on death of Thomas Hay.—[*Reg. Pres. Bene.*, ii, 44.]
1581

THOMAS CRAIG, apparently Nicolas Craig, wife of Thomas Innes, reader, Elgin, was a daugh.—[*Elgin Bapt. Reg.*, 26th Nov. 1667.]
1624

WILLIAM CLOGIE, his daugh., Margaret, bapt. 23rd June 1612, and Alexander 25th June 1614.—[*Elgin Reg.*]
1647

ROBERT BATES, cont. of proc. of second marriage with Margaret Dunbar, 3rd Oct. 1714.—[*Forglen Reg.*]
1707

ALEXANDER SIMPSON, in or about 1839 he became incapacitated for duty by "an afflictive visitation of Divine Providence"; in Jan. 1846 a "new" assistant was app., Mr P. J. Gilruth, from St Andrews Presb., and afterwards min. of South Ronaldsay and Burray; Mr Gilruth left before 2nd Dec. 1846, on which date Mr Simpson craved the Presb. that the patron be asked to appoint an assistant and successor; the patron refused, and on 3rd Feb. 1847 the Presb. agreed to the appointment of an ordained assistant, and Mr James Bain was ord. on 10th March following; he was licen. by the Presb. of Strathbogie in 1837, became assistant schoolmaster at Urquhart 29th June, and schoolmaster 4th Dec. 1839 in succession to the late Mr James Cooper.
1826

JOHN MAIR, dem. 19th Feb. 1946.
1907

URQUHART

The old church stood in the churchyard at the east end of the village. A hollow to the north-east of the churchyard is held to have been the site of the priory. Near at hand is the Abbey Well. In the parish there was a chapel dedicated to the Holy Rood.—[*Reg. Mag. Sig.*, iii, 2153; *Pilgrimages in Moray*, 86–7.]

1567 JOHN BLINDSHIELD, reader, also at Lhanbryd.—[*Comps. Sub Coll. of Thirds, Moray*, etc.]

1574 PATRICK BALFOUR, probably identical with Mr Patrick Balfour, son of Patrick B. of Oldmill, adm. by Elgin Town Council as Master of the Grammar School 10th Sept. 1566; his daugh., Agnes, was betrothed to John Robb, merchant, Elgin, but it is not certain that the marriage took place.—[*Recs. of Elgin*, ii, 25, 396.]

1682 JAMES GORDON, had a son, Frederick.—[*Deeds, Durie*, 1704, No. 573, 599.]

1695 JAMES URQUHART, his son, Joseph, apprenticed to William Henderson, merchant, 14th Nov. 1677; his daugh., Jean (marr. cont. 5th March 1713 Bailie Robert Logan, litster in Forres).

1695 JOHN URQUHART, marr. Anne Innes, and had issue, Jean (marr. Lawrence Sutherland of Greenhall).

1734 JOHN McGILCHRIST, marr. cont. dated 28th July 1730, Elizabeth, daugh. of William Fraser of Broadlands, and had issue, Anne (bapt. July 1738).

1847 HARRY WALKER, line 10, for "J" read "Alexander."

1859 GORDON INGRAM, his son, James Kyd Duncan, M.D., died at Puerto Orotava, 21st April 1933; William, K.C., died 13th July 1943.

1894 PATRICK CAMPBELL SINCLAIR, dem. 31st Aug. 1937.

(*Churches united 12th Nov. 1937.*)

PRESBYTERY OF FORRES

ALTYRE

ANDREW SIMSON, M.A., pres. to the "Common Kirk of Altair" 16th Jan. 1567-8.—[*Reg. Pres. Bene.*, i, 3.]
1567

ALEXANDER URQUHART, min. at Rafford, in charge here.—[*Comps. Sub Coll. of Thirds, Moray*, etc.]
1568

JOHN CLERK, reader; also at Dallas.—[*Comps. Sub Coll. of Thirds, Moray*, etc.]
1568

DALLAS

SIR JAMES SPENS, pres. to vicarage 1st July 1560, probably identical with Sir J. S., vicar of Alves.—[*Reg. Mag. Sig.*, iv, 1963, 2639.]
1560

JOHN CLERK, reader 1568. (See Altyre.)
1568

ANDREW BROWN, pres. to vicarage 25th Oct. 1574 on death of Sir James Spens.—[*Reg. Sec. Sig.*, xlii, 83.]
1574

PATRICK CUMMING, M.A., pres. 11th July 1576 to Sub-Deanery of Moray, which is the parish of Dallas and the vicarage of Auldearn. "Before the change of religion" it had been held by Mr William Pattison, on whose resignation Sir Michael Willet had received presentation 6th July 1576.—[*Reg. Pres. Bene.*, i, (4), 43.]
1576

GEORGE DOUGLAS, pres. to parsonage and vicarage 6th Aug. 1588, the Sub-Deanery being vacant by depriv. of Patrick Cumming.—[*Reg. Sec. Sig.*, lviii, 3.]
1588

ALEXANDER RICHARDSON, marr. Agnes Chapman (she marr. (2) George Cumming, his successor)
1601
and had issue, William of "Riniver," not "Rininel."

GEORGE CUMMING, marr. Agnes Chapman, widow of Alexander Richardson, min. of this parish. Suspended by Synod 6th Oct. 1646 for "complyance he had with the enemie" (Montrose) and referred to the Commission of Assembly at Edinburgh, but he was reponed by the Synod 6th April 1647, having given full satisfaction.
1624

JOHN CROCKAT, had a son, Thomas.
1708

WILLIAM ROBERTSON, served in France 1917–20 (wounded), Chaplain to the Forces 1920; trans. to Kirkton 8th May 1931; dem. 16th May 1940. His wife's father was of Keills, Islay. His daugh., Flora Douglas (marr. 16th Sept. 1939 Donald Alexander MacCalman, Leamington, son of Alexander M., Bearsden).
1925

DYKE and MOY

There was in the parish a Chapel of St Ninian, with manse and garden.—[*Reg. Mag. Sig.*, viii, 434.]

ANDREW SIMSON, min. in 1568. (See Forres.)
1568

WILLIAM DUNBAR, vicar before 16th Nov. 1583, pres. in 1585 on death of Andrew Simson.—[*Reg. Sec. Sig.*, liii, 29.]
1585

WILLIAM FALCONER, marr. 19th April 1625 Margaret, daugh. of Thomas Tulloch of Tannachie and Isabel Dunbar. Line 27, delete "Jean (marr. George Chalmers of Linkwood)." His second wife was daugh. of John Sutherland of Kinstearie and Lilias Hay.
1625

DYKE and MOY—EDINKILLIE

1674 WILLIAM FALCONER, his daugh., Jean, bapt. 17th Aug. 1677 (marr. (1) George Chalmers of Linkwood, and (2) before 1707, William Cumyng of Craigmill); evidently identical with Bishop Falconer, resident at Slains cir. 1716–20, and exercised at least some of the functions of a bishop, assuming "a prelatical authority derived from the exauctorated prelates."—[G. R. Horn, 8th Feb. 1707; *Justiciary Records*, 1717–21, May 1721.] (See Kearn, Alexander Law.)

1692 ALEXANDER FORBES, was twice marr. and had issue by first marriage, Alexander and James, and by second, Robert, Jean, Lillias and Agnes. In Oct. 1706 he intimated his demission to the Synod, "he being habituallie valetudinarie, being much brokn with gravel, gout, and several other distempers"; but on a letter from the parishioners objecting to the acceptance of the demission because of "the serious effects that would follow to the parish," the Synod resolved to give him all help and encouragement, and, delaying consideration of the case till next Synod, app. supplies for Dyke for half a year. Later, steps seem to have been taken to secure full assistance for Mr Forbes, for on 2nd May 1707 Mr John Cumming, "now under a call to Dyke," was rebuked by the Synod, who at the same time directed a letter to be sent to the Presb. of Fordoun, for having given "great offence by travelling upon the Lord's Day from Breichen to Fettercairn before sermon and having come in about the end of the lectur and heard both sermons, by crossing the Kairn immediately after sermon," and because "both ministers and people in the Presbytery of Fordoun were offended by this his practice when he did come north."

1727 ROBERT DUNBAR, line 3, for "Kincorth" read "Kirkhill."

1876 JOHN MACEWAN, his son, Hugh Henry Lyall, Staff Sergeant R.A., killed in Burma March 1944.

1914 THOMAS ALEXANDER WARNOCK, died 1st Nov. 1940. Addl. issue—Grizel, born 20th Aug. 1917; Doris, born 13th Nov. 1927.

(*United with Moy West 2nd March 1941.*)

MOY

1564 WILLIAM SUTHERLAND, parson 1567–8.—[*Comps. Sub Coll. of Thirds, Moray*, etc.]

1566 PATRICK LIDDELL, M.A., parson in 1566, also at Croy.—[*Comps. Sub Coll. of Thirds, Moray*, etc.]

1570 JAMES VAUS, exhorter 1570, also at Croy.—[*Comps. Sub Coll. of Thirds, Moray*, etc.]

1589 THOMAS ANNAND, pres. to parsonage 10th March 1590–1 on death of William Sutherland.—[*Reg. Sec. Sig.*, lxii, 11.]

EDINKILLIE

In March 1287 Archibald, Bishop of Moray, gave to John, Archdeacon of Moray, the whole land of the Church of St John the Baptist of Logyfythenach, the said John to provide a chaplain for the church and to give for the sustenance of the chaplain a merk from the vicarage of Dyke.—[*Reg. of Moray*, 284.]

1582 JOHN FORRESTER, M.A., pres. to vicarage 10th Dec. 1582 on death of Sir Alexander Sinclair.—[*Reg. Sec. Sig.*, xlix, 52.]

1586 THOMAS DUFF, reader 8th Nov. 1582.—[*Edin. Tests.*, xii, 305.]

1599 JOHN STRATON, pres. to vicarage 20th Feb. 1607 on death of Sir Alexander Sinclair.—[*Reg. Sec. Sig.*, lxxvi, 7.]

1614 ROBERT DUNBAR, probably son of Thomas Dunbar of West Grange near Forres, min. of Auldearn.

1649 PATRICK GLASS, marr. Marie, daugh. of Patrick Dunbar of Blervie (she marr. (2) Patrick Tulloch of the Tannochy family). He had issue—Patrick, merchant in Forres.

1672 DAVID CUMMING, his mother was Margaret Dunbar of the Boath family. Delete "as son James of Pressley who was his grandson and son of Patrick or Peter, doctor in Inverness." He had a daugh., Jean. Line 22, for "Slug" read "Sluie."

1909 JOHN MORRISON, adm. to united charge 26th June 1930; dem. June 1940; his wife, Gertrude Johnstone, died 26th Sept. 1936; he died at Aberdeen 17th Nov. 1944.

(*Charges united 26th June* 1930.)

FORRES

The foundation stone of the present church was laid by Lady Strathcona on 17th Aug. 1904, and the church was opened for worship on 4th March 1906.

In 1305 Adam le Chapelayn of Moraf (Moray) asked 6 merks for serving "a Chapel built in honour of St Laurence in the county of Forros (Forres), of the alms of King Alexander, for the soul of Margaret, late Queen of Scotland." He was to receive his "stipend" on exhibition of his charter.—[*Cal. of Docs. Rel. to Scotland*, iv, 375.]

Forres was the seat of the Archdeacon of Moray Cathedral. The church, along with the Archdeacon's manse, many other houses, and the burgh records and charters, were burned by the Wolf of Badenoch in May 1390. The present church, built in 1905, took the place of a church erected in 1777. The Chapel of St Leonard was situated at Chapelton, between Rafford and Forres; and the chapel at Logie was dedicated to St John. There was in the parish a chapel dedicated to St Duthac.—[Mackintosh's *Pilgrimages in Moray*, 52–3; *Acts of Lords of Council in Public Affairs*, 490, 19th July 1540; *Reg. Mag. Sig.*, vii, 519.]

1567 ANDREW SIMSON. min. (See Dyke.)

1567 JOHN PATERSON, reader, and in 1568; died after 8th Nov. 1582.— [*Comps. Sub Coll. of Thirds, Moray*, etc.]

1582 JOHN FORRESTER, was schoolmaster and min. in 1582.

1599 JOHN STRATON, son of Arthur S. of Snawdoun, and Margaret Keith. Marr. cont. 12th and 21st May 1602 Janet, daugh. of David Murray of Little Ardath and his wife Margaret Kirkcaldie. —[*Kincardine Sas.*, i, 84.]

1792 JOHN MACDONNELL, his daugh., Robina, born 1803 (marr. 25th Aug. 1828 Captain John Douglas, R.N.), died 1874.

1912 GORDON BEATTIE WATT, died at Edinburgh 23rd Nov. 1928; his widow, Agnes Milne Dobie, died at Edinburgh 6th Feb. 1939.

1918 WILLIAM PHILIP WISHART, had issue—William Alexander, born 25th Dec. 1923; John Laurence, born 28th April 1932.

KINLOSS

It appears that for some time prior to the middle of the 17th century worship of the Church of Scotland was conducted in the chapter house of the abbey. At that period various parts of the abbey fabric were removed to Inverness to provide material for the construction of a fort there by Cromwell; and it was then proposed that the stones of the chapter house should be utilised for the same purpose. Protest was made by the Presb. of Elgin with a view to saving the chapter house, especially in view of the fact that "it is agreed that there shall be a Church and a special Parish for Kinloss and the people thereabouts who are now almost without the means of the Gospel." In reply Alexander Brodie of Lethens, who had acquired Kinloss, stated that the abbey stones had been removed against his will, and also offered to build a church and manse with the money that he had received for the stones, and also to provide a sufficient glebe from the lands of Kinloss. Negotiations followed in 1650-3, and eventually on 20th July 1653 agreement was reached on the basis of the offer of Alexander Brodie, with this reservation by him, that the church should not be built in the precincts of the abbey. The place chosen for the church was "William Kere's house, the kill yard, and remanent ground yrabout from the high gate to ye burne, and that the walls of the old Kill (Skene's Kiln) be repaired and enlarged and made wider, and the middle wall removed to ye effect the kirk may be built yrupon." A churchyard was provided on "the commontie north of the Abbey precincts"; and the glebe was designed in part from the lands called George Yard. The church was ready for worship before 1657; and on 6th May of that year the parish was erected by the Presb. of Elgin, confirmation by Parliament being forthcoming on 15th March 1661. The present church was built in 1765. At Laurenston, Burgie, there was a Fair of St Lawrence which was ultimately removed to Forres.

The Abbey was founded on 20th June 1151 (the *Chronicle of Melrose*, p. 74, gives the date 21st May 1150). To it belonged the Churches of Avoch and Ellon, and the Hospital of St John the Baptist, of Hebuisden, in the parish of Loth. Abbot Thomas Crystall, who died 30th Dec. 1535, repaired the Chapel of St Jerome, and erected in it Altars of St Jerome, St Anne, and of the dead.—[*Recs. of Presby. of Elgin*, 27th Dec. 1649, 17th, 31st Jan. 1650, 3rd, 10th, 17th Feb., 2nd March, 8th, 20th July 1653; *Acts Scott. Parl.*, vii, 74-5; *Recs. of Kinloss*, xxv, xxxix-xl, 30, 120, 134.]

JAMES RAWSON, reader in 1568; also at Rafford.—[*Comps. Sub Coll. of Thirds, Moray*, etc.]
1568

JAMES URQUHART, marr. Agnes or Anna Brodie.
1659

JAMES GORDON, son of Thomas G. of Cloves and Monaghty and his wife Helen Seton, and grandson of Sir William G. of Lesmoir.
1699

WILLIAM HENRY EDIE, his son, Henry Scott Ker, killed in motor accident, Southampton, 23rd Dec. 1934.
1877

GEORGE ALEXANDER McKEGGIE, trans. to Craigie 11th Nov. 1929; has issue, Marjorie E.
1925

(*Charges united* 19*th May* 1930.)

RAFFORD

Among the eight canonries erected by Bishop Bricius when he founded Elgin Cathedral (1208-15) was that of Cantor with a davoch of land and the Church of Alves and the Church of Rafford. On 12th May 1226 twelve new canonries were added, including a prebend from the Church of A—— for a succentor, the first being Lembertas. In addition to Rafford, the succentor had the Church of Ardclach.

In note on vi, 427, delete lines 5, 6 and 7.

When the parish of Kinloss was erected in 1657 from portions of Rafford, Alves and Forres, Rafford received the small parish of Altyre in compensation.

At the Reformation Alexander Dunbar the succentor had just been appointed Dean as well, both of which offices he retained for some thirty years when he pres. his second son Robert to the former, but his elder son Thomas to the latter. Then followed some crooked transactions in the teinds to the financial benefit of the family.

JAMES RAWSON, reader in 1568. (See Urquhart.)
1586

ROBERT DUNBAR, son of Alexander D., dean of Moray, pres. to the parsonage and vicarage which is the "sub-chantre of Moray" 3rd July 1591, on res. of his father.—[*Reg. Sec. Sig.*, lxii, 103.]
1590

THOMAS DUNBAR, son of Alexander D. of Inchbrok and Janet (marr. cont. 30th Dec. 1583), daugh. of Thomas Cumyng of Altyre.—[*Duffus Papers.*]
1620

ALEXANDER FORDYCE, his son,
1668 Thomas, died 5th May 1755.

WILLIAM PORTEOUS, marr. Helen, daugh. of Alexander McIntosh of Blervie and Isobel, daugh. of William Duff of Dipple, and had issue, James.
1727

ROBERT LOGAN, his mother was Ann, daugh. of James Urquhart, barber in Forres. He had issue—Margaret, born 23rd Feb. 1744; Robert, born 28th Aug. 1745; Elizabeth, born 3rd July 1747. Four of his children died between June and Aug. 1752.
1738

WILLIAM STEPHEN, had issue—John,
1784 farmer, Covesea, near Hopeman.

GEORGE MACKAY, his wife was daugh. of John Johnstone and Elizabeth Norris; his sons—David, born 15th Sept. 1817, died 26th Jan. 1875; Lewis, born 25th Oct. 1822; his daugh., Helen, died 19th Jan. 1886.—[*Tombst.*, Rafford.]
1816

ARCHIBALD SCOTT BALLANTYNE, dem. 22nd June 1942; his daugh., Jean Sinclair Paton, L.D.S., R.C.S. (Edinburgh) (marr. 17th Oct. 1934 Robert George Smith, Mayfield, Forres); his wife, Elizabeth Jane Brownlee, died 27th Oct. 1938. He marr. (2) 29th Nov. 1939 Charlotte Christina Murchison.
1904

PRESBYTERY OF NAIRN

ARDCLACH

The church was rebuilt in 1626.—[*Reg. Synod of Moray*, 24th Oct. 1626.]

1580 WILLIAM SIMSON, pres. to vicarage 23rd Dec. 1579 on death of Sir Robert Brown.—[*Reg. Pres. Bene.*, ii, 287.]

1883 DAVID MILLER, his son, James Webster, Medical Superintendent, Mental Hospital, Salisbury.

1916 ROBERT KERR, trans. to St Matthew's, Dundee, 16th May 1933; trans. to Kinnell, 17th May 1946.

(*Charges united 27th Sept. 1933.*)

ARDERSIER

1569 THOMAS FERGUSSON, exhorter in 1569.—[*Comps. Sub Coll. of Thirds, Inverness*, etc.]

1599 THOMAS URQUHART, third son of Thomas U. of Davidston and Christian Murray, and not as stated; had issue by first marriage—Christina, only daugh. (marr. cont. 19th March 1619 William Campbell of Galcantray).—[*Inverness Sas.*; *Elgin Sas.*, 31st May 1619; *Reg. of Deeds, Hay*, ccclxxxvi, 277.]

1695 LACHLAN McBEAN, marr. Mary, sister to John Stewart, younger, of Killemickly. On 16th Feb. 1698 there was submitted to the Presb. of Tain a letter from Sir Hugh Campbell of Cawdor, requesting that Mr Lachlan McBean be allowed to continue at Ardersier, and that he might do so with the sanction of the Presb. The Presb. replied that while not satisfied with his conduct in entering Ardersier Church without their permission, yet upon hearing that he enveighs bitterly against himself for his former ways, and testifies publicly against the evils of the late defection in the land, they were willing to tolerate him till they be better informed about him, or know him better.—[Macnaughton's *Ch. Life in Ross and Sutherland*, 15–16; *Sas.*, lxxvi, 10, 28th June 1699.]

AULDEARN

Eren, Erin or Eyrn seems to have been the old name of Auldearn. To Richard, Bishop of Moray 1187–1203, King William the Lion granted a confirmation charter of the Church of Eren with the Chapel of Rath and the Chapel of Moythus, and also of the Church of Eren with the Chapel of Innernarn (Nairn), the Chapel of Rathe and the Chapel of Morchus. The charter of Bricius, Bishop of Moray 1203–21, founding the canonry of Spynie, included the Church of Eryn with the Chapel of Innernarren. At Auldearn there was land called St Columba's acre.—[*Reg. Epis. Moray*, 37, 40–1, 67; Watson's *Celtic Place Names*, 229; *Reg. Mag. Sig.*, ix, 774.]

1571 PATRICK CUMMING, M.A., min. of Dallas, pres. to parsonage and vicarage 11th July 1576, Sub-Deanery of Moray.

1591 THOMAS DUNBAR of Grange, had two sons—Robert, probably min. of Edinkillie in 1614; Thomas, tutor of Westgrange, died 1674.

1622 JOHN BRODIE.—[*G. R. Sas.*, 3 Ser., xxxvii, 331.]

1874 JAMES BONALLO, his widow, Nina Helen Dunbar, died 6th Sept. 1945.

GEORGE McWILLIAM, trans. from Clepington 15th April 1926; adm. to united charge 8th Jan. 1930; has addl. issue—Eileen Vanora, born 18th May 1923 (marr. 18th Sept. 1945 James Howie Haldane, Captain R.A.M.C., son of James Howie H., min. of U.F. Church, Sauchie); Sheila Maureen Lorimer, M.B., Ch.B. (marr. 30th Oct. 1940 Surgeon Lieut. Richard Howell Roberts, R.N.V.R.).
1926

CAWDOR

The old church was situated at Barevan, for *Barr Eibhinn*, now contracted into *B'reibhinn* in Gaelic, as in "the Church of Breven," which occurs in 1665. In 1275 the name is "the Church of Ewen." The patron saint is Aibind, daugh. of Mane, of Cluain Draignech, and one of the holy maidens subject to Brigit. Her name means "delightful," and would now be *Eibhinn* or *Aoibhinn*. About 1619 the church gave place to a church erected in a more central position by Sir John Campbell of Cawdor. Attached to the residence of the Thanes of Cawdor was a chapel dedicated to the Virgin Mary; and when the castle was built, there was included a chapel to which Sir Walter de Tarbett was inducted chaplain in 1467. An old bell, a relic of the chapel, is at Cawdor Castle. By Bull of 15th Dec. 1225 Pope Honorius III confirmed to Scone Abbey the Church of Evein (Cawdor), with its chapels. There is no further reference to the grant.—[Watson's *Celtic Place Names*, 271; Shaw's *Moray*, ii, 274, 277; *Book of Scone*, 67.]

GEORGE STRANG, M.A.; on 8th Feb. 1564 was vicar of Ewan, apparently Braeven (Cawdor).—[*Reg. of Deeds*, vii, 123.]
1564

ALLAN McINTOSH, pres. to parsonage 19th June 1569.—[*Reg. Pres. Bene.*, i, 25.]
1569

HUTCHEON ROSS, pres. to the vicarage 3rd April 1577.—[*Reg. Sec. Sig.*, xliv, 55.]
1577

JOHN CAMPBELL, parson of Dunlochie, pres. to vicarage 13th Oct. 1589 on death of William Hepburn.—[*Reg. Sec. Sig.*, lx, 683.]
1586

DONALD MACPHERSON, his daugh., Jean (marr. Andrew Macpherson of Nuide Beg).
1642

ALEXANDER HAY FORBES, trans. to Methil 8th Sept. 1927.
1909

WILLIAM METCALFE, formerly Army Chaplain (*q.v.*), adm. 8th Feb. 1928.
1928

(*Charges united 9th Dec.* 1945.)

CROY and DALCROSS

PATRICK LIDDELL, M.A.; rector 11th June 1561, res. 1566–7; parson 1566, min. 1578.—[*Wardlaw MS.*, 157; *Reg. Mag. Sig.*, v, 562; *Reg. Pres. Bene.*, i, 130.] (See Moy.)
1566

JAMES WAUS, exhorter 1576; pres. to vicarage of Dalcross 5th Dec. 1576, vacant by death of Robert Melville.—[*Reg. Sec. Sig.*, xlii, 96.] (See Moy.)
1570

DONALD RUTHVEN, son of William R. of Corriburgh; pres. to parsonage and vicarage vacant by death of Patrick Liddell 26th May 1589.—[*Reg. Sec. Sig.*, lix, 14.]
1589

THOMAS FRASER, born 1822; his son, William Garden, senior wrangler, H.M. Inspector of Schools, died at Aberdeen 25th Feb. 1935; his daugh., Helen Mary, died at Aberdeen 1st Nov. 1933.
1853

CHARLES FRASER, line 1, for "Gaudrigg" read "Gaulrigg"; dem. 1st Oct. 1933; died 29th Aug. 1944; his sons—Francis Stewart Gordon, min. of Nairn; John Annand, min. of Second Charge, Hamilton.
1890

(*Charges united 4th Feb.* 1934.)

NAIRN

The Chapel of the Virgin Mary at Easter Geddes was founded in 1473 by Hugh Rose of Kilravock, for his own soul and the souls of his ancestors and successors, the endowment being five pounds Scots of stipend and a croft for a glebe and site of a manse. At Feynesfield there was a chapel dedicated to St Finan, Seiepil Fhinan.—[Watson's *Celtic Place Names*, 286.]

1585 SIR JAMES TARRAS, vicar 1585.—[*Comps. Gen. Coll. of Thirds.*]

1687 GEORGE DUNBAR, marr. Elizabeth Leslie.—[*Elgin Sas.*, 2 Ser., vii, 237.]

1884 JAMES BURNS, his widow, Jane Isabella McDougall, died 13th Nov. 1939.

1898 WILLIAM ROBINSON PIRIE, dem. 28th July 1931; died at Newhaven 20th Dec. 1934; his son, George, M.B., Ch.B.; his widow, Mary Jane Stewart, died 25th Feb. 1943; his son, David Yoolow Stewart, died at Barnard Castle 25th Nov. 1946.

PRESBYTERY OF INVERNESS

BOLESKINE and ABERTARFF

1563 JAMES DUFF. (See Dores.)

1579 PATRICK DUNBAR, pres. to vicarage 12th Dec. 1579 on death of –. Brown.—[*Reg. Pres. Bene.*, ii, 27.]

1625 ANDREW DOW FRASER, on 4th Oct. 1636 the Synod granted to him liberty to intromit with the "buriall silver of Abertarff" to erect "ane stone house, as some evill disposed persones had alreadie burned his present dwelling hows"; had issue, Donald, recommended to charity by the Commission of the Kirk in 1647 because of the death of his father, "killed by the cruell Irishes."—[*Recs. of Synod of Moray*, 4th Oct. 1636, 24th Nov. 1647.]

1648 THOMAS HOUSTON, born 1618. Marr. Mary (died 13th March 1681), daugh. of Alexander Fraser of Erchit.

1859 MALCOLM MacINTYRE, his widow, Annie, daugh. of James Clark, Port Askaig, Islay, died at Corpach 28th Feb. 1927.

1893 JOHN BROWN MACARTHUR, dem. 3rd Oct. 1934; died at Glasgow 17th March 1948; his sons—Angus Alexander; Ian Edward; Archibald Norman and Duncan (died 1948), all M.B., Ch.B.

DAVIOT

1623 ALEXANDER THOMSON, on 13th April 1624 he was ord. by the Synod to reside at his kirk under pain of deprivation; a similar order was given on 25th Oct. 1625, and at the same time he was ord. "to urge the building of his kirks"; was in residence soon after, but considerable delay took place in regard to church building, and nothing was done at 30th Oct. 1627; on 26th April 1634 the Synod ord. the "Kirk of David this year to be perfyted and compleetlie builded"; and in Oct. 1637 he reported that "his kirks were both compleatly theked"; in April 1637 the Synod intimated to him "that heirafter he be not sene in Innerness at all on Saturday nor at no tyme so frequentlie as he hes been befor."

1664 ALEXANDER FRASER, son of Thomas F. and Katherine, daugh. of Sir Robert Gordon of Anbolls (Embo).—[*Wardlaw MS.*, 117.]

1859 JAMES MACDONALD, his son, Donald George Gordon, M.D., died in London 21st April 1928.

1922 ALISTAIR MACLEAN, died 12th Dec. 1936. Addl. issue—Gilleasbuig, born 22nd June 1926; line 7, for "Ian" read "Ian Macfarlane Lamont"; delete line 8 and read "Alistair Stuart, born 21st April 1922," Publications—*Volume of Sermons*; *High Country*; *Gaelic Phono Grammar*.

(*Charges united 3rd Oct. 1934.*)

DORES

In 1233 Andrew, Bishop of Moray, at the instance and petition of Alexander II, patron of the Church, granted the church to the Priory of Pluscarden.—[*The Religious House of Pluscarden*, 201–2.]

1889 THOMAS SINTON, his widow, Catherine Macfarlane, died at Bridge of Tilt 21st Dec. 1941; his son, Thomas Christopher John, min. of Tower Church, Stanley, 1st March 1933; Chaplain to the Forces, died on active service Oct. 1943.

1924 JOHN MacCALLUM, dem. 7th March 1943.

BONA

1565 ALEXANDER STEWART, brother of James of Fincastle, pres. to vicarage 7th Dec. 1565 on death of Sir Robert MacNair.—[*Reg. Sec. Sig.*, xxxiv, 15.]

1584 THOMAS INNES, parson 4th Aug. 1591.—[*Reg. Sec. Sig.*, lxii, 132.]

ERCHLESS

1884 JAMES FRASER, his widow, Margaret Jane Caskey, died 22nd Feb. 1935.

1915 NEIL MACLEOD, died at Connel 17th July 1934.

1929 JOHN MATHESON MACLEOD, trans. to Portsoy 30th Sept. 1929.

(*Charges united 9th Jan. 1930.*)

GLENMORISTON

1891 ARCHIBALD MacNEILL, dem. 8th Oct. 1929; died at Lewiston 6th Dec. 1929.

INVERNESS

The church, along with ½ caracute of land and chapels, was granted to Arbroath Abbey *cir.* 1189-99 by King William the Lion in honour of the Virgin Mary. There were in the church altars dedicated respectively to the Virgin Mary, apparently in addition to the High Altar, and to the Holy Rood, St John the Baptist, St Michael and St Catherine. In the Chapel of the Virgin Mary in Inverness David II on 26th Oct. 1359 founded a chaplain, the endowment being a piece of land *de la Cras*—11 acres beside the lands of the Virgin Mary Parish Church; and the same monarch confirmed to the chapel a donation by John Scott, burgess of Inverness. On 16th April 1435-6 Pope Eugenius IV granted relaxation of penance to penitents who on the Feast of St Ann visited and gave alms for the repair, etc., of the Church of Blackfriars, Inverness, "in which the body of Alexander, Earl of Mar and Garioch, was buried on said Feast, and which has been greatly deformed, especially on account of wars, and is going to ruin."—[*Reg. of Arbroath*, 3-8, 24; *Reg. Great Seal*, i, App. ii, 1327, iv, 2518, 2760, v, 999; *Reg. of Moray*, 309-10; *Cal. Papal Regs., Letters*, viii, 681.]

1565 THOMAS HOWIESON, his daugh. marr. Rannald Bain Sirduncanson, burgess of Dingwall, and had issue, Alexander.—[*Foulis Writs*, 145, 10th Jan. 1607.]

1574 GEORGE ROSS, chaplain.—[*Acts and Dec.*, liii, 230.]

1674 ALEXANDER CLERK, marr. (1) 1653 Esther, probably daugh. of Robert Elliot of Reidheugh and Lady Jean Stewart; and (2) Jean, sister of Robert Fraser, advocate.—[*G. R. Sas.*, 2 Ser., v, 7.]

1688 HECTOR MACKENZIE, marr. Margaret, daugh. of Sir James Strachan of Thornton; his daugh., Barbara (marr. (1) John Mackinnon of Torrin, Strath, and (2) Alexander Maclennan).

1727 ALEXANDER MACBEAN, marr. (1) 25th Sept. 1712 Marjorie Macbain, Inverness, and had issue—William, died in infancy 2nd Dec. 1713; Archibald; Alexander, died 22nd Nov. 1739; William, attorney, London; Aeneas, bapt. 15th May 1721, died 22nd Aug. 1722; Forbes, General, bapt. 28th June 1725, died 1800; Elizabeth; line 29, delete "sheriff clerk."

1801 ALEXANDER FRASER, marr. (1) 17th Oct. 1785 Isobel, daugh. of George Munro of Culcairn.

1852 DONALD MACDONALD, his daughs. —Ann Marjory, died 14th Aug. 1925; Grace Shaw, died 23rd June 1934.

1907 DONALD MACLEOD. Addl. issue— Ursula Mary Eva, born 5th Jan. 1930; his daugh., Lorna Helen Janet (marr. 28th Aug. 1948 Rev. Sir George Frederick Macleod, Bart., D.D., min. of Govan).

SECOND CHARGE or WEST

WILLIAM FRASER, his widow, Alison Fraser, died 9th Nov. 1687.
1648

ALEXANDER FRASER, son of Alexander F. Yr. of Balnain.
1727

GAVIN LANG, his daughs.—Anna Graham, died 14th July 1931; Jean Stewart Corbet, died at Invergordon, 16th Aug. 1933; his son, Alexander Matheson, died at Barbados, 11th April 1948.
1882

NEIL MacLELLAN, died 8th Nov. 1935.
1917

ST MARY'S or THIRD CHARGE

ANDREW MACPHAIL, still called Andrew Brebner in 1568, when he was exhorter at Petty and the Yrirche Kirk at Inverness.—[*Comps. Sub Coll. of Thirds, Moray*, etc.]
1566

THOMAS INNES, reader, son of James I. of Drainy; pres. to vicarage 25th July 1574 on death of Sir George Hepburn, Treasurer of Moray.—[*Reg. Pres. Bene.*, i, 26.]
1574

ROBERT MACPHERSON, his sons—John, barrister; Robert Alexander, died 1877.
1834

CHARLES MACECHERN, his widow, Christina Cameron, died 25th Aug. 1936; his son, Charles, died Nevada, U.S.A., 2nd Aug. 1945.
1879

ST STEPHEN'S

ARTHUR ALEXANDER HAMILTON, marr. 26th April 1928 Anne Christian, eldest daugh. of William Sutherland, Slaggan, and has issue—Catherine Thomson, M.A., teacher, Bridge of Earn, Perthshire; Euphemia Jean, teacher of Domestic Science; Alexandrina, in nursing profession.
1922

NORTH CHURCH

ARCHIBALD COOK, his daughs.—Barbara (marr. –. Mackintosh, rector of Inverness Academy); Christine (marr. John Ross, min. of Free Church, Stoer).
1837

KILTARLITY

In 1224–6 John Bisset gave to the Church of St Peter of Rathven for the support of the lepers there serving God, the patronage of the Church of Kiltarlity and whatever right he had in the gift, provision also being made for a chaplain to minister at the leper house.—[*Reg. of Moray*, 77.]

GEORGE HAY, parson 18th March 1561 and 2nd May 1573; son of William Hay of Talla, and brother of William Hay of Talla and Wyndene; also parson of Eddleston, Renfrew, and Rathven (*q.v.*).—[*Reg. of Deeds*, vi, 398, xii, 148.]
1561

ROBERT MAKRUDDER, reader, pres. to vicarage 5th Dec. 1574.—[*Reg. Pres. Bene.*, i, (4), 29.]
1574

JOHN WRIGHT, called "John Wrycht or Bann" in his presentation, min. here, pres. to vicarage 3rd April 1577.—[*Reg. Pres. Bene.*, i, (4), 54; *Reg. Sec. Sig.*, xliv, 71.]
1576

DONALD DOW FRASER, priest of Kidhill, descended from Clan Chrigger; son of Sir Andrew F., priest of Urray; had letters of legitimation 12th Jan. 1567; had issue—John, min. of Rosskeen; William, min. of Kiltarlity.—[*Reg. Sec. Sig.*, xxxvii, 30; *Ardentoul MS.*]
1592

WILLIAM FRASER, died Oct. 1665; his daugh., Janet (marr. Thomas, son of James Fraser of Phopacy).—[*Wardlaw Reg.*; *Wardlaw MS.*, 115.]
1618

PATRICK NICOLSON, marr. a daugh. of Hugh Fraser of Craigscorrie.
1716

MALCOLM NICOLSON, marr. Barbara, daugh. of Lieut. William Fraser and Barbara Robertson.
1761

ARCHIBALD MACDONALD, D.D., dem. 11th Nov. 1929; died Father of the Church 29th Jan. 1948; his wife, Margaret Hope Tolmie, died at Glenormiston 7th April 1931; his daughs.—Christina, born 9th March 1895, died 22nd
1892

Dec. 1897; Flora Amy Macruari, delete (twin). Addl. Publications—*Memorials of the '45* (1930); *The Old Lords of Lovat* (1934).

KIRKHILL

The old name of the parish was Dulbachlach, Dulbatelach, Dulbachlack, *cir.* 1203. In 1210-12 an agreement was made between John Bisset of Lovat and Bricuis, Bishop of Moray, whereby the church at Dunbachlach was to be transported to Fingasch, to the place which is called Wardlaw, in the Gaelic, Balabrach, and after transportation to become a mensal church of Moray. The church at Dunbachlach is also said to have been dedicated to St Mauritius, in whose honour a fair was held annually at Dunbachlach on 11th November. This would point to St Mauritius being St Machar, whose day was 12th Nov. By Hugh, Lord Lovat, the fair was removed in Nov. 1641 to Beauly, where under the name of *Fail Mhauri* it was also held annually on 11th Nov. The church at Wardlaw was abandoned in 1790, when the present church was built on a site "removed 2 gunshots from Mary Hill." On the site of the former church in the churchyard is the mausoleum of the Lord Lovats, which is itself supposed to be the chancel of the medieval church. When the Priory of Beauly was demolished, Lord Simon Fraser of Lovat transferred the large bell, Clag M'Mannachi, to Kirkhill, where it was erected on a wooden frame on a hill south-east of the church, called Tome Chluig, Bell Hill. As it was too big for an ordinary steeple, it was sent by Lord Hugh Fraser of Lovat to Holland, where it was recast by Michael Burgerhouse in 1634, and made in a dimension for the kirk steeple, in which it was hung in the following year. At the same time a large hand-bell was also made from the material.—[*Reg. of Moray*, 15-16; *Wardlaw MS.*, Pref., xv, xvi, 61, 159, 265-6n, 275; Pollock's *Beauly and District*, 25; Watson's *Celtic Place Names*, 267.]

1588 SIR DAVID CUTHBERT, vicar, 19th June 1566-7, 1588-9.—[*Cal. of Charters*, xviii, 2990; *Reg. Mag. Sig.*, iv, 276.]

1611 JOHN HOUSTON, line 21, for "Anna" read "Elspeth"; his daugh., Katherine (marr. cont. 11th May 1677 Robert Dunbar of Drakies); his son, James, min. of Resolis.—[*Tain Sher. Court Deeds*, 31st Dec. 1692.]

1661 JAMES FRASER, his sons—William, physician to the Emperor of Russia; Hugh; his daugh., Helen, schoolmistress of Tain 1715 (marr. William Leidge).

1848 EWEN MACKENZIE, his daugh., Cecilia Margaret, died at London 12th April 1929.

1917 KENNETH MACLEAN, dem. 30th Sept. 1942; his wife, Jane Steen, died Greenock 8th Jan. 1947.

(*Charges united* 18*th Jan.* 1934.)

FARNUA

1569 ANDREW BRABONER, pres. to parsonage 18th June 1569, died before 1575; had issue, Andrew, who succeeded him in the charge.—[*Wardlaw MS.*, 183; *Acts and Dec.*, lv, 132; *Reg. Pres. Bene.*, i, 25.]

1575 ANDREW McPHAIL, min. here, pres. to parsonage 6th Nov. 1575 on death of Andrew Braboner; trans. to Kingussie 1581.—[*Reg. Pres. Bene.*, ii, (4), 38; *Wardlaw MS.*, 183.]

MOY and DALAROSSIE

The Church of Dalarossie was granted to the Cathedral Church of Moray by Andrew, Bishop of Moray, 1221-42, to provide lights for the cathedral.—[*Reg. Epis. Moray*, 7.]

1624 ANDREW DOW FRASER, after being provided to Abertarff and Boleskine, continued to hold Moy and Dalarossie, and apparently in 1626 the Synod granted him a "month to resolve qlk he sall demit."—[*Rec. Synod of Moray*, 1626.]

THOMAS McLAUGHLAN, his sons—John David, died 11th April 1943; Simon Lachlan Fraser, died Rio de Janeiro 7th Feb. 1943. **1838**

NORMAN MACKENZIE, died 8th May 1931. Marr. 20th June 1929 Gladys Winifred, M.A. (Cantab), youngest daugh. of Daniel McDougall, Struan, Bearsden. **1925**

PETTY

JAMES DUNBAR, M.A., pres. to parsonage 26th Nov. 1595.—[*Reg. Sec. Sig.*, lxviii, 37.] **1580**

DONALD MacQUEEN, pres. in 1596 on death of James Chisholm.—[*Reg. Sec. Sig.*, lxviii, 169.] **1595**

JOHN DUNCANSON, had issue—Thomas; Alexander, apprenticed to James Gordon, saddler, Edinburgh, 25th June 1740; Robert; John; Finsella; James.—[*Abbrev. of Adjud.*, 3rd Jan. 1751.] **1728**

JOHN FRASER, his daughs.—Christiana Beatton, died Dundee 26th Dec. 1942; Margaret, died 9th March 1943. **1852**

DONALD MACGILLIVRAY, died Edinburgh 3rd Aug. 1941; his daugh., Lorna Margaret (marr. 20th June 1947 John, only son of Allan Steven, Under Bolton, Haddington). **1902**

(*Charges united 29th April* 1934.)

URQUHART and GLENMORISTON

On 21st Aug. 1536 Queen Mary confirmed the presentation made by her father of Sir John Donaldson to the Chapel of St Ninian with the 40 sh. lands called Pitkerrell and a croft pertaining to said chapel, and with the croft reliquary and the iron crucifix of St Drostan, in succession to Sir Duncan McOlrig.—[*Chiefs of Grant*, iii, 121–4; *Reg. Sec. Sig.*, ii, 2070.]

ALEXANDER GRANT, in Oct. 1625 he was heavily rebuked for failure to attend the two previous meetings of the Synod, also rebuked for celebrating a marriage after being discharged by his brethren from so doing, and ord. to make public repentance in the Kirk of Glenmoriston and pay the sum of forty pounds "ad pios usus."—[*Reg. Synod of Moray*, 24, 25th Oct. 1625.] **1624**

ANGUS BOYD, Chaplain to Forces in Great War for two years; died at Aberdeen 3rd Jan. 1946, unmarr. **1921**

(*Charges united 1st May* 1946.)

SYNOD OF ROSS

PRESBYTERY OF CHANONRY

AVOCH

The church was beautified and repaired by Abbot Thomas Crystall of Kinloss, who died 30th Dec. 1535.—[*Recs. of Kinloss*, 32.]

1560 ALEXANDER PEDDER, son of James P., Chamberlain to Bishop of Ross and Vicar of Urray.—[*Comps. Sub Coll. of Thirds, Inverness*, etc.]

1569 ANDREW MYLNE, pres. to vicarage 7th Nov. 1569.—[*Reg. Pres. Bene.*, i, 29.]

1607 JAMES LAUDER, son of John L., one of H.M. domestics.—[*Reg. of Deeds*, cclxx, 161.]

1714 ALEXANDER McLENNAN, intruded in the church 4th June 1714, also set up a meeting-house in the parish, performed irregular marriages 1714-16, and in Dec. 1715 to Jan. 1716 accompanied the rebels under Donald Murchison, Chamberlain to William, Earl of Seaforth, to attack Col. Robert Munro of Foulis.—[*Justiciary Records.*]

1756 THOMAS SIMPSON, his grandson was Sir George S., Governor of Hudson Bay.

1914 EDWIN JAMES BRECHIN, son of James Brodie B., bookbinder, Dundee; dem. 14th Oct. 1941; died at Monifieth 2nd June 1942.

CROMARTY

The Chapel of St Duthac was situated at Navitie, which was Church land high on the ridge of the South Souter. This is of interest when it is remembered that Nativity denotes an institution, originally pagan, taken over by the Christian Church. There was an old local belief that the final judgment is destined to take place on the Moor of Navitie. St Michael's Chapel was at the same place. The Chapel of St Regulus was founded and endowed by the inhabitants of the burgh. All three chapels were within the liberties of the burgh; and they were granted to the burgh by Crown Charter of 4th July 1593, ratified by Act of Parliament in 1641. There were two fairs, St Norman's Fair on 8th March, and St Regulus' Fair on 14th March.—[*Acts Scott. Parl.*, v, 538*b*; *Reg. Great Seal*, v, 2350; Watson's *Celtic Place Names*, 249.]

1876 WALTER SCOTT, his widow, Mary Ann Brydon, died 11th May 1932. She was in Lucknow with her parents during the siege during the Indian Mutiny.

1917 GORDON MOORE, trans. to Old Church, Wick, 28th Sept. 1932; trans. to Gask 12th May 1948. Addl. issue—Mary Elsie, born 4th May 1926.

FORTROSE

On 15th June 1572 James VI made to William, Lord Ruthven, a gift of the lead of the roof of the cathedral which, by the forfeiture of the bishop, was in the King's hands "throw being the said Cathedral kirk na paroch kirk bot ane monasterie to sustaine ydill bellies."—[*Reg. Sec. Seal*, xl, 106.]

1569 WILLIAM HAY, reader 1575; was son of Robert Hay; was one of the vicars of the cathedral 2nd April 1559, and designated also chaplain of the cathedral;

KILLEARNAN

In 1275 the parish is designated Edorador or Ederdover. The patron saint, Jurnan, seems to be Itarnan or Itharnan, who died among the Picts in 669, and is said to have been buried at Cairn Jurnein, the stone circles on the summit of Mull-Buie, in the parish, which are regarded as bearing his name. The church, which was "in the form of a cross," seems to have been partly rebuilt about 1690–5. It was thatched with heather, but about 1750 it was "raised in the walls, slated, and seated; but in opposition to the then minister's wishes, the Heritors continued its former Popish form."—[Theiner's *Vet. Mon.*, 69; Watson's *Celtic Place Names*, 32.]

1559 SIR JOHN SAIDSARF, perpetual vicar, 2nd April 1559; died probably after 6th May 1583.—[*Reg. Great Seal*, vi, 563.]

1700 JOHN MACKENZIE, described in 1717 as "late Meeting-House keeper at Killearnan"; helped the rebels at Urray Muir, Dec. 1715.—[*Justiciary Recs.*]

1814 JOHN KENNEDY, his daugh., Margaret Jess (marr. Hugh Mackay, min. of Milton, Glasgow).

1890 ANGUS JOHN NORMAN MACDONALD, D.D. (Glasgow, 18th June 1930); died 28th Nov. 1932; his widow, Elizabeth Hector, died 8th Dec. 1937; his sons—James William, died New York 17th Aug. 1932; Ranald Aeneas Hector, died Los Angeles 29th Dec. 1935; his daugh., Marion (marr. 1934 Flying Officer William E. Galting, Maldon, Essex).

(*United to Redcastle* 11*th June* 1933.)

KNOCKBAIN

Near Allangrange House there exist the east gable and a small portion of the south wall of a chapel which was dedicated to St John and belonged to the Knights Templar. —[*Book of Ross*, 14.]

1567 WILLIAM SOMERVELL, vicar.— [*Acts and Dec.*, xxxvii, 448; li, 422.]

1568 SIR DAVID BRACHANE, vicar in 1568, also vicar of Suddie (*q.v.*).

1568 JOHN REID, pres. to vicarage 10th March 1568–9 on death of Sir David Brachane.—[*Reg. Pres. Bene.*, i, 18.]

1586 ANDREW CROMBIE, pres. to vicarage 28th May 1592 on death of John Reid.—[*Reg. Sec. Sig.*, lxiii, 270.]

1695 JOHN MACKENZIE, M.A.; it was reported to the Presb. on 25th Sept. 1695 that he had intruded on the parish, and had been summoned to the diet on that day; he failed to appear, and accordingly the Presb. discharged him from preaching here, and appointed Mr William Stewart to preach in the church and intimate the sentence. On 8th April 1696 Mr Stewart reported that he went to Kilmuir Wester, finding no access to the kirk, preached in a barn, where but few came to hear him, as the intruder had obstructed the people; he intimated the Presbytery's prohibition, but the intruder still continued to preach; the Presb. resolved to apply to the Laird of Balnagowan as Sheriff-Principal of the Province to put the law against intruders into execution against the said John Mackenzie.—[Macnaughton's *Church Life in Ross and Sutherland*, p. 10.]

1721 HUGH CAMPBELL, eldest son of Alexander C. of Torrich.—[*Elgin Sas.*, viii, 441, 4th March 1776.]

1791 RODERICK MACKENZIE, his daughs.—Catherine, died unmarr. 1878; Anne, died in childhood; Margaret (marr. Rev. William Fraser, Balnain); Jean, died 1868; his son, Alexander, judge in India.

1892 JOHN DOW, D.D. (St Andrews, 29th June 1934); died 4th July 1938; his daughs.—Beatrice Anna Mackenzie (marr. 4th May 1936 Norman Leslie Auchterlonie, M.B., Ch.B.); Leila Annie (marr. 2nd June 1936 Murdoch Duncan Gray); Margaret Isobel (marr. 26th March 1940 Donald, son of D. Macfarlane, Kirklena, Ardrishaig).

---

still in office as reader 2nd Oct. 1594.— [*Reg. Great Seal*, vi, 168, 563, 716, 738, 1992.] (See Killearnan.)

SUDDIE

1568 SIR DAVID BRACHANE, vicar 26th Oct. 1568 to 10th March 1568-9; also vicar of Kilmuir Wester.—[*Edin. Tests.*, i, 341; *Reg. Pres. Bene.*, i, 18.]

1568 SIR DUNCAN LOGAN, vicar in 1568. —[*Edin. Tests.*, i, 341.]

1569 ANDREW MYLNE, min. of Avoch, also in charge here.—[*Comps. Sub Coll. of Thirds, Inverness*, etc.]

1569 DAVID THOMSON, pres. to vicarage 7th Nov. 1569 on death of Sir David Brachane.—[*Reg. Pres. Bene.*, i, 29.]

1570 JAMES BUSCHART, reader on death of David Thomson.—[*Comps. Sub Coll. of Thirds, Inverness*, etc.]

1669 THOMAS FRASER, his daugh., Isabel (marr. Alexander Fraser 14th Sept. 1715).—[*Justiciary Records*, 1717-21, 12th Feb. 1717.]

RESOLIS, or KIRKMICHAEL

The Church of Kirkmichael was situated at the east end of the parish near the seashore. St Martin's farmhouse, on the road from Conon Bridge to Cromarty, marks the site of the old Church and Churchyard of Cullicudden, dedicated to St Martin of Tours. Locally the parish was called Sgire Mhartiunn, "the parish of Martin." The Church of Culycudin of "Cultudyn" occurs in a reckoning of teinds 24th May 1275. Before 10th March 1641 the church gave place to the church near the seashore, now a ruin, for on that date Parliament transferred to Inverness "the Fair callit Martimes fair qlke was holdine of old at St Mairtaines kirk in Ardnannoch now Lyand waist."—[*Acts Scott. Parl.*, v, 540b, vii, 122a; Theiner's *Vet. Mon.*, 112.]

1567 SIR JAMES GRAY, vicar in 1567 and 1571.—[*Comps. Sub Coll. of Thirds, Inverness*, etc.]

1569 THOMAS DENOUNE, parson, was dead 1569.—[*Comps. Sub Coll. of Thirds, Inverness*, etc.]

1571 ALEXANDER CLUNES, reader 1571-2.—[*Comps. Sub Coll. of Thirds, Inverness*, etc.]

1586 ALEXANDER REID, pres. to vicarage 14th March 1586-7 on death of Sir James Gray.—[*Reg. Sec. Sig.*, lv, 36.]

1662 JAMES HOUSTON, son of John H., min. of Wardlaw.

1921 RODERICK MACKENZIE, his wife, Annie Jane Macdonald, died 4th Nov. 1945.

CULLIECUDDEN

1569 ROBERT MUNRO, exhorter 1569.— (See Logie Easter.)

ROSEMARKIE

Rosemarkie Church was dedicated to St Moluag and by Cuiritan the dedication was changed to St Peter. The site of Rosemarkie Church is still called *Kilcurdy* "Curitan's Church." On 15th June 1572 James VI made to William, Lord Ruthven, a gift of the lead of the roof of the Cathedral of Ross, in the King's hands, "throw being the said cathedral kirk na paroch kirk bot ane monasterie to sustene ydill bellies," and through forfeiture of the bishop.—[*Reg. Sec. Seal*, xl, 106; Scott's *Pictish Nation*, 376, 377.]

1560 GEORGE DUNBAR, vicar in 1560 and 1570.—[*Comps. Sub Coll. of Thirds, Inverness*, etc.]

1633 PATRICK DURHAM, Dean of Ross, marr. Janet Sinclair.

1908 ROBERT SHAW MASTERTON, dem. 3rd July 1945; died 27th Sept. 1947.

PRESBYTERY OF DINGWALL

ALNESS

The church was built in 1780. Near the head of Loch Moire, Mary's Loch, on its north-west side, there was a chapel with burying-ground, dedicated to the Virgin Mary. At the place there is a spring, *Tobar Mhoire*, "Mary's Well," with which healing virtues were formerly associated. At Culcraggie there was a chapel, mentioned in 1435–6. North of the farmhouse of Assynt, Novar, there is a small rectangular burying-ground called *Cladh Churadain*, "the graveyard of Cuiritan" (Boniface), indicating that at that place there may have been a chapel dedicated to that saint.—[*Cal. Papal Regs., Letters*, viii, 532–3; *Book of Ross*, 50–1; Watson's *Celtic Place Names*, 315; Macfarlane's *Geog. Colls.*, i, 212–13.]

1560 THOMAS ROSS, M.A., parson 1560–1; had a brother, John.—[*Reg. Abbrev. Feu Charters of Church Lands*, i, 236.]

1562 ALEXANDER MORRISON, exhorter, parson and vicar 1562.—[*Comps. Gen. Coll. of Thirds.*]

1570 SIR THOMAS BUCHAN, rector 20th May 1570.—[*Laing Charters*, 154.]

1574 ALEXANDER DOUGLAS, reader, pres. to vicarage 4th Sept. 1574 on death of Sir James Spens.—[*Reg. Pres. Bene.*, i, (4), 27.]

1588 ROBERT ROSS, M.A., pres. to Chaplaincy of Alness pertaining to John Robertson, one of the Ministers of the New College of St Andrews.—[*Reg. Sec. Sig.*, lxiii, 182.]

1635 THOMAS ROSS, marr. (cont. 19th Dec. 1639) Margaret, daugh. of Murdoch Mackenzie of Tollie.—[*Reg. of Deeds, Mack.*, 22nd July 1642.]

1771 ANGUS BETHUNE, his daugh., Janet (marr. 18th July 1791 Dr Alexander Strath, Tain).

1918 JOHN MARTIN, died 29th June 1946.

CARNOCH and STRATHCONON

The churches united 1928.

1928 JOHN MURRAY, min. of Free Church, Lybster, 1922; trans. and adm. 8th Nov. 1928; trans. to Old Church, Oban, 16th Dec. 1932; died 20th Dec. 1936.

CONTIN

Apparently about 1477 a force of the Macdonalds, led by Gillespick, brother-natural of John of Illa, invaded Ross, laid waste Kintail and Strathconon, burned Contin Church and the women and children and priest who had fled to the church for sanctuary. At the west end of Loch Garve is the farm of Killin, *Cill Fhinn*, "the Church of St Fion," the site, no doubt, of the old Church of Strathgarve, dedicated to St Fion. Loch Garve is still called *Loch Maol-Fhinn*, "Fionn's servant's loch." There is a Gaelic saying that this church was one of the oldest in Scotland—"Cill-Phinn's, Cill-Duinn's, Cill Donain, na tri cilltean is sine an Albainn," Killin, Kildun, Kildonan, the three oldest cells (chapels) in Scotland.—[Fraser's *Earls of Cromarty*, ii, 478; Watson's *Celtic Place Names*, 320; *The Book of Ross*, 68.]

1575 ROBERT BURNETT, M.A., parson; his natural sons—Alexander and Robert, legitimated 30th June 1575.—[*Reg. Mag. Sig.*, iv, 2433.]

1592 THOMAS BURNETT, M.A., pres. to vicarage and parsonage 17th March 1592–3 on death of Robert Burnett.—[*Reg. Sec. Sig.*, lxv, 36.]

1689 AENEAS MORRISON, pres. from Kilmorie, Arran, 5th Sept. 1687; intruded in the Church 18th July 1716, undertook commission from Earl of Seaforth to raise Lewis men for the rebel army Sept.-Oct. 1715, and preached in the camp at Urray Muir Dec. 1715.—[*Justiciary Records*; *Deeds Dal.* 1706, No. 1702.]

1826 CHARLES DOWNIE, his son Kenneth, Lieut.-Colonel, I.M.S., died at Cannes 17th Feb. 1912.

1884 JAMES DUNCAN MACRAE, his widow, Christian Robertson, died 7th Nov. 1933.

1906 ANDREW COLQUHOUN MACLEAN, died 18th Sept. 1937; his daugh., Cairine Ross (marr. 7th Sept. 1940 James Beattie Petrie, Lieut., R.A.M.C., Aberdeen).

DINGWALL

The church was united to the Priory of Urquhart before 1455. In the churchyard to the north of the church there is an enclosure called St Clement's Aisle, which in part is the remains of the old Church of St Clement. The former parish church was burned in 1733; and the present church was erected in 1801. In Dingwall there were chapel lands designated respectively St Catherine and St Mary; and there were also a Chaplainry of the Trinity and Chaplainry of St Michael "founded in the burgh." The Chapel of St Laurence was in the Castle. On 2nd Nov. 1547 Sir Andrew Dow was presented to the chaplainry in succession to the late Sir Alexander Roresoun.—[*Cal. Papal Regs., Letters*, xi, 288; *Reg. Great Seal*, v, 1959; *Book of Ross*, 30; *Acts Parl.*, xi, App., 143; *Reg. Sec. Sig.*, iii, 2521.]

1579 ROBERT PHILIP, pres. to parsonage and vicarage 26th Nov. 1579 on dem. of Donald Adamson.—[*Reg. Pres. Bene.*, iii, 24.]

1591 JOHN MACKENZIE, pres. 27th Jan. 1591–2 to parsonage and vicarage of Dingwall and Lemlair with the Trinity and St Michael's Chaplainries in the Kirk of Dingwall and to the parsonage and vicarage 21st March 1594–5 on death of Thomas Ker.—[*Reg. Sec. Sig.*, lxvii, 81, lxiii, 144.]

1640 JOHN MACRAE. Addl. issue—William; Murdoch.—[*Inverness Sas.*, 1673.]

1674 JOHN MACRAE, line 24, for "Agnes" read "Anne"; line 25, for "John" read "George."—[*Reg. of Deeds, Mack.*, cxxxiv, 12.]

1708 DONALD BAYNE, son of Alexander B., bailie of Dingwall and not as stated; was schoolmaster of Kiltearn from 1701.

1716 JOHN BAYNE, his son, Lieut. Duncan, app. delegate for election of M.P. 9th June 1754.—[*Scottish Notes and Queries*, Jan. 1929, p. 18.]

1743 ADAM ROSE, had issue—Margaret, bapt. 3rd May 1749; Donald, born 1751; Alexander, bapt. 4th May 1756.

1899 JAMES ROSE MACPHERSON, his daughs.—Audrey Primrose (marr. 28th March 1930 William Scott Taylor, min. of Inverallan); Ann (marr. John Marshall, min. of Tingwall).

1921 DAVID YOUNG ROBERTSON, trans. to Erskine 6th March 1929.

1929 RODERICK FRASER, served in Great War 1914; formerly of Rousay (*q.v.*); trans. from Lintrathen 26th Sept. 1929; has issue—Chrystabel Jean, born 10th Feb. 1926 (marr. 1st March 1946 Hakon, younger son of Anton Lie, Lervik, Onsay, Norway); James Alasdair Angus, born 24th Dec. 1928.

FODDERTY

The churchyard of Fodderty, containing the site of the old church, lies on the south side of the road to Dingwall. In 1807 the church was rebuilt on a site west of the churchyard, and it was enlarged in 1842. About 1901 steps were taken to secure the transportation of the parish church to the church which had been built at the west end of Strathpeffer, and on 7th March 1902 the Court granted authority to the trustees of Strathpeffer Church, if decree of transportation were granted, to convey the church to the heritors as the parish church; and on 4th July of the same year decree of transportation was obtained. By the heritors the old church was conveyed to the foresaid trustees in 1904 for use as a church. Later, that idea was abandoned, and the church was sold and was converted into a dwelling-house—a purpose which it still fulfils. The Chapel of Innis Ruaraidh (Inchrory), dedicated to the Virgin Mary, was situated on the north side of the road opposite Fodderty churchyard. On 13th Feb. 1348-9 Adam de Urquhart granted to a chaplain in the chapel certain lands and annual rents with manse, etc. Adjacent to the site of the chapel is *Croitan Teampuill*, "Temple Croft," probably a pagan dedication, where in 1830 stone coffins, urns, and relics of the Bronze Age were discovered. At the foot of the east shoulder of Knockfarrel lies the Well of St John the Baptist, indicating possibly that there had existed at that spot a chapel dedicated to that saint. The well was a place of pilgrimage for the sick and insane in search of cure. In the Strath of Peffery is *Dabhach Mo-Luag*, Dochmaluag, "My Luag's davoch," indicating St Moluag. The Church of Kinettas was situated in the churchyard of that name west of Strathpeffer.—[*Recs. of Fodderty Heritors*; *Book of Ross*, 37-8, 43; Scott's *Pictish Nation*, 237; Watson's *Celtic Place Names*, 293; *The Earls of Cromarty*, ii, 319-20].

1572 WILLIAM HAY, pres. to vicarage 15th Jan. 1571; called "sometime vicar" 1576.—[*Reg. Pres. Bene.*, i, (2), 5; *Comps. Gen. Coll. of Thirds.*]

1573 WILLIAM CHALMERS, vicar 27th May 1573.—[*Reg. Abbrev. Feu Charters of Church Lands*, ii, 30.]

1574 RORIE BAYNE, reader here, pres. to vicarage 19th May 1574 on death of Sir John Smith.—[*Reg. Pres. Bene.*, i, (4), 20.]

1574 ALEXANDER ANTON, pres. to vicarage 25th Nov. 1574 on death of Rorie Bayne; died before 1582.—[*Reg. Pres. Bene.*, i, (4), 48.]

1586 IVER McIVER, pres. to parsonage 17th Nov. 1591.—[*Reg. Sec. Sig.*, lxiii, 18.]

1662 JOHN MACKENZIE, died Oct. 1666. Marr. Christian Weym and had issue—Roderick; John.—[*Tain Sher. Court Deeds; Reg. of Deeds, Mack.*, 30th Oct. 1699.]

1900 JOHN GUNN NICOLSON, dem. 1st Oct. 1947; his daugh., Margaret (marr. 3rd Oct. 1935 Ian Menzies, son of John Menzies, Maryburgh).

(*Charge united with Strathpeffer 2nd Oct.* 1947.)

KINETTAS

1572 GEORGE MUNRO, M.A., min. 1572; Chancellor of Ross.—[*Comps. Sub Coll. of Thirds, Inverness*, etc.] (See Suddie.)

KILMORACK

1560 SIR JOHN NICOLSON, vicar 1560 and 1570.—[*Comps. Sub Coll. of Thirds, Inverness*, etc.]

1576 DONALD FRASER (DOW), called "unplaced minister" in 1576.—[*Comps. Gen. Coll. of Thirds.*]

1674 WILLIAM FRASER, had issue—William, M.D., bapt. 18th Jan. 1683; Alexander, bapt. 29th April 1684; Mary, bapt. 5th July 1685; John, bapt. 19th Jan. 1688; Margaret, bapt. 14th March 1689; Hugh, bapt. 27th Aug. 1691; Jean, bapt. 16th May 1693; Anne, bapt. 15th Aug. 1697.

1846 SIMON FRASER, his daugh., Catherine, died 6th March 1929.

1891 EWEN ARCHIBALD RANKEN, line 10, for "Sept." read "April"; dem. 4th Oct. 1932; his wife, Elizabeth Jackson, died at Trinity 3rd March 1936; he died at Trinity 21st July 1948.

KILTEARN and LEMLAIR

The Church of Kiltearn may have been dedicated to St Tighernach, who died in 506. The Church of Lemlair was situated in the old churchyard by the seaside near Waterloo, east of Dingwall. The churchyard is designated *Cladh Mo-Bhrigh*, the graveyard of Brigit, and that renders it doubtful whether St Mary superseded St Brigit as patron saint. In Lemlair Church, it is said, the Presbyterian doctrines during the Reformation were first taught in the north. The present parish church, on the right bank of the Skiach close to the shore, was built in 1790–1. A short distance from the old Churchyard of Lemlair in the direction of Dingwall, the railway passes through a deep cutting called Mountrich, which was the site of the Chapel of Kilchoan, *Cill Chomhghain*, the saint being Comgan, said to have been the brother of Kentigerna, of the 8th century, daugh. of Cellach Cualann of Leinster. The Chapel at Balconie was dedicated to St Monan, probably Moinenn, who was Bishop of Brendan's Monastery at Clonfert and died in 572.—[*Reg. Pres. Bene.*, i, 143; Watson's *Celtic Place Names*, 312, 328–9; *The Book of Ross*, 46.]

1572 FARQUHAR MUNRO, reader 1572.—[*Comps. Sub Coll. of Thirds, Inverness.*]

1576 JOHN SANDILANDS, parson on 11th Aug. 1576.—[*Munro of Foulis Writs*, 90.]

1585 ARCHIBALD MONCRIEFF, M.A., pres. to parsonage and vicarage 30th Nov. 1585 on death of John Sandilands.—[*Reg. Pres. Bene.*, 30th Nov. 1585.]

1587 ROBERT MONTGOMERIE, M.A., pres. to vicarage 24th Jan. 1587–8 on death of John Sandilands.—[*Reg. Sec. Sig.*, lv, 161.]

1589 ROBERT MUNRO, pres. to parsonage and vicarage 6th May 1605 on death of John Sandilands.—[*Reg. Sec. Sig.*, lxxiv, 302.]

1594 JOHN MUNRO, M.A., son of Hugh M. of Assynt; pres. to parsonage and vicarage 13th Feb. 1594–5 on death of John Sandilands.—[*Reg. Sec. Sig.*, lxvii, 52.]

1620 DAVID MONRO, was min. 5th July 1620.—[*Reg. of Deeds*, cccli, 132.]

1698 WILLIAM STUART. Publication—*A Letter concerning the Oath of Abjuration* (Inverness, 1712).

1849 ALEXANDER MACLEAN, his daugh., Susan, died at Edinburgh 25th July 1931 (marr. William Martindale Galbraith).

1875 WILLIAM WATSON, his widow, Isabella Allan, died 29th Sept. 1934; his daugh., Margaret Janet, died at Bowden, Cheshire, 1st Feb. 1937.

1920 ARCHIBALD CAMPBELL, his daugh., Helen Mairi Iseabel (marr. 5th June 1942 William Hugh Galloway, M.B., Ch.B.).

LEMLAIR

The earlier saint is St Brig, Brigh. There were several saints of this name. Brig, daugh. of Amalgad, of Achad Aeda, and Brig, daugh. of Fergus, of Cell Brigi, were among the holy maidens who were subject to Brigit. The name of the old churchyard of the church, by the seaside near Waterloo, is called *Cladh Mo-Brigh*.—[Watson's *Celtic Place Names*, 312.]

KINLOCHLUICHART

1914 GEORGE BRUCE, died 19th March 1929; his daugh., Theodora Janet Middleton (marr. 24th May 1939 John Mackenzie, Strathpeffer); his widow, Margaret Learmonth, died 4th July 1942.

URQUHART

The old name of the parish of Urquhart, or Ferintosh, was Logiebride, a designation arising from a chapel at Conon, which was dedicated to St Bride. The church was rebuilt in 1795. At what is now called Logie-side on the banks of the Conon, about 300 yards north-west of Conon House, there is an old graveyard called St Bride or St Brigit, in which there was a chapel dedicated to that saint. Hence arises "Logiebride," associated of old with the designation of the parish. The teinds of "Urquhart and Logiebride" are mentioned in a letter of Pope Alexander IV to the Bishop of Ross on 9th Feb. 1256–7, and "the Church of Logiebride" occurs in a reckoning of teinds of 24th May 1575. *Allt Brighde*. "St Bride's Burn," is near Conon House.—[Theiner's *Vet. Mon.*, 69, 112; Watson's *Celtic Place Names*, 275; *The Book of Ross*, 4.]

1571 ROBERT KEITH, min. 1571.—[*Comps. Sub Coll. of Thirds, Inverness*, etc.]

1574 ROBERT MONRO, his son, Hector.—[*Foulis Charters*, 176, 2nd Dec. 1624.]

1609 JOHN MACKENZIE. (See Dingwall.)

1665 DONALD FRASER, had issue—Thomas; Alexander of Powis, regent and Sub-Principal, King's College, Aberdeen, died 15th Jan. 1742.—[*Powis Papers; Primitive Beliefs in North East of Scotland*, 202.]

1685 ANDREW ROSS, marr. Anna, daugh. of George Cuming, min. of Urray, and had issue—Andrew; James; William; Katherine (marr. cont. 29th Nov. 1714 Thomas Lindsay, writer, Inverness); Janet; Margaret.—[*Elgin Sas.*, iii, 380, 8th April 1692; *Reg. of Deeds, Mack.*, cxxix, 31st Jan. 1721, cxxvii, 22nd April 1720.]

1729 ALEXANDER FALCONER, his daugh., Elizabeth (marr. Thomas Fyers, overseer of works, Edinburgh).

1918 JOHN SELLAR, his son, Andrew, B.Sc., killed in Wales Sept. 1945.

URRAY

There was a chapel with graveyard at Conon House. The name of the church and parish was Inneraferyn, occurring also as Inverferan, Inveraferan, Inverasfran, Euraferayne, Euraferane, between 1256 and 1440. On 9th Feb. 1256 and 11th June 1257 the designation is the Succentory Church of Bron; and in 1257 it appears as Inverasfran and Lochbren Church. The designation Urray was in use not later than 3rd Feb. 1545–6. The Church was dedicated to St Madidus. The present church was built about 1780–1.—[*Cal. Papal Regs., Letters*, ix, 426, 445; *Reg. Sec. Seal*, ii, 1526, 2656; Theiner's *Vet. Mon.*, 69, 112; Fraser's *Earls of Cromarty*, ii, 316, iii, 315–17; Macfarlane's *Geogr. Colls.*, ii, 357.]

1560 ALEXANDER PEDDER, vicar, died between 26th Oct. 1568 and 7th Nov. 1569; had a son, James.—[*Pres. of Elgin*, i, 147; *Reg. Pres. Bene.*, i, 39, 341.]

1567 SIR ANDREW DOW FRASER, vicar 2nd Feb. 1547–8, died before 12th Jan. 1567–8, when his natural son, Donald Dow Fraser, received letters of legitimation.—[*Reg. Sec. Sig.*, xxxvii, 30.] (See Kirkhill.)

1569 ALEXANDER GRIERSON, pres. to vicarage 7th Nov. 1569 on death of Sir Alexander Pedder.—[*Reg. Pres. Bene.*, i, 39.]

1569 DONALD ADAMSON, exhorter here and at Dingwell and Chaplain of St Laurence in Arisdaill, pres. to vicarage 8th Dec. 1569 on death of Sir Alexander Pedder.—[*Reg. Pres. Bene.*, i, 33; *Comps. Sub Coll. of Thirds, Inverness*, etc.]

1573 DAVID HALIBURTON, pres. to parsonage before 18th Sept. 1573 on failure of Donald Adamson to accept Articles of Religion.—[*Reg. Pres. Bene.*, i, (4), 11.]

1574 DONALD WILLIAMSON.—[*Acts and Dec.*, l, 307.]

1579 WILLIAM RITCHIE, pres. on 26th Nov. 1579 on dem. of Donald Adams.—[*Reg. Pres. Bene.*, ii, 23.]

1593 JOHN MACKENZIE, M.A., when a student at St Andrews was pres. to parsonage and vicarage 28th Jan. 1591-2 on death of Donald Adamson.—[*Reg. Sec. Sig.*, lxiii, 148.]

1605 JOHN MALCOLM, marr. Isabel Mackenzie, and had issue—Andrew; still min. April 1638.—[*Munro of Foulis Writs*, 199, April 1638.]

1658 GEORGE CUMMING, his daugh., Annie (marr. Andrew Ross, min. of Urquhart).

1715 DUNCAN MURCHISON, chaplain to Sir John Mackenzie of Coull; intruded in Urray 1715-16, kept a meeting-house, performed other functions of the ministry, and preached at the rebel camp of William, Earl of Seaforth, at Urray Muir and Brahan.—[*Justiciary Records.*]

1861 JOHN ADAM MACFARLANE, his daugh., Helen Muriel, died Yarrow Manse 29th March 1932.

1916 SAMUEL KNOX JOHNSTON, died 25th Sept. 1935.

(*Congregations united 8th June* 1937.)

PRESBYTERY OF TAIN

CROICK

ROBERT WILLIAMSON, in sustaining his presentation on 19th June 1828, the Presb. declared "that the Presbytery cannot, by so doing, be considered as in the least approving of the Act on which the presentation is founded"; and on 25th Sept. 1828 he was ord. and adm. to be min. of the Government Church of Croick, in the parish of Kincardine, as assistant to the parish min.—[Macnaughton's *Church Life in Ross and Sutherland*, 343.]
1828

JOHN COUTTS, died 7th Aug. 1933.
1919

(*Charge united with Kincardine 8th June 1947.*)

EDDERTON

On 17th March 1841 the Presb. declared the church totally unsuitable for worship and incapable of repair, and ord. a new church to be built, the site selected being on the moor of Corrieblair, south-west of the manse. The church was completed in Oct. 1842.

SIR FARQUHAR REID, exhorter and min.; also at Kincardine.—[*Comps. Sub Coll. of Thirds, Inverness*, etc.]
1567

WILLIAM ROSS, his son, David, apprenticed to William Bishop, apothecary, Edinburgh, 19th Dec. 1694.
1665

ALEXANDER MUNRO, son of John M., tenant in Barrowen, and Mary Mackenzie, bapt. 11th Jan. 1757; was schoolmaster of Edderton.
1785

DONALD MACRAE, his son, Kenneth, died 10th May 1929.
1902

FINLAY McNICOL McKINNON, his daugh., Elizabeth Helen (marr. 23rd April 1938 Dermot Michael Fitzgerald Lombard, R.N.R.).
1924

FEARN

At Hilton of Cadboll there was a chapel dedicated to the Virgin Mary. Beside it was a sculptured cross-slab that some time ago was removed to Invergordon Castle. After the collapse of the roof of the church on 10th Oct. 1742, the Presb. after giving full consideration to the condition of the buildings resolved on 23rd March 1743 not to repair the roofless church but to build in the cloister-yard a new church 75 ft. long and 20 ft. broad (inside measurements), with a slated roof. Delay ensued; but ultimately building proceeded in 1746, and on 12th Nov. of that year the Presb. met at Fearn, took over the new church, and declared it to be the church of the parish. The church had a short period of existence, for at a meeting on 12th Oct. 1771 the heritors, on the ground that the church was in a "ruinous condition," deliberated as to rebuilding it or repairing the old abbey, and ultimately approved of a plan by Captain Ross of Balnagown, one of the heritors, by which he undertook, if the heritors paid him £200 stg., to repair the abbey church, and have it sufficiently finished by 1st Nov. 1773. Again there was delay, but on 12th Oct. 1775 the church was ready for occupation. The total cost was £386 14s. 9¾d.; and in addition Captain Ross met the cost of repairing the part of the fabric called the "Ross Aisle" at an outlay of £38 15s. The abbey church again became the parish church, and the "new church" was completely demolished. — [Macnaughton's *Church Life in Ross and Sutherland*, 165–73, 262–3, 276.]

1584 PATRICK MUIR, M.A., min. 30th Nov. 1584.—[*Cal. of Charters*, xii, 2764.]

1644 WILLIAM ROSS, marr. (3) cont. 30th June 1660 Isabel, daugh. of Andrew McCulloch, provost of Tain.

1663 JAMES McCULLOCH, M.A., given in Wardlaw MS. as min. of Fearn, may have been in office in the period 1663–70.—[*Wardlaw MS.*, 117, S.H.S.] (See Kilmuir Easter.)

1670 ALEXANDER ROSS, died Oct. 1676.

1677 DONALD MACLENNAN, marr. Janet Ross.—[*Inverness Sas.*, cclxxxix, 1684.]

1689 KENNETH MACKENZIE, on 9th June 1697 he craved the Presb. that in regard his persuasion was now Presbyterian, the Presb. would be pleased to revise his processes, or refer him to the Superior Judicatories, or allow him themselves the exercise of his ministry. The Presb., while satisfied that he was reformed in principles and practices, recorded their inability to act as craved, because the Presb. which deposed him was an associate Presb. of brethren from Moray, Ross and Sutherland, of which there were none among them except Mr Denune, and besides, Mr Mackenzie in his process had appealed to the first lawful General Assembly. A further petition to be reponed was rejected by the Presb. 25th May 1698. —[Macnaughton's *Church Life in Ross and Sutherland*, 11–12, 18.]

1869 HUGH FRASER, his daughs.—Ursula Gilman, died at Harrow 14th April 1933; Janet, died at Edinburgh 2nd May 1929; his son, Hugh, M.D., died at Harpendean, Herts, 17th Jan. 1941.

1895 CHARLES ROBERTSON, his widow, Agnes Shaw Cameron Munro, died 16th March 1948.

1925 JACKSON LOUDON McFADDEN, M.A. (1917). Line 2, for "Nov." read "Oct."; his mother was Mary Wallace Loudon. Marr. 8th Jan. 1936 Mary Elizabeth, younger daugh. of John Robertson Forbes, min. of Logie Easter, and has issue—John James Forbes, born 6th April 1937.

KILMUIR EASTER

At the east end of the church is the burial-vault of the Cromarty family, apparently a part of the earlier church. Attached to the vault is a round-tower with the inscription "Biggit 1616," but the lower part of the tower may be as early as the first part of the 11th century. The chapel at Balnagowan was dedicated to the Virgin Mary.—[*Book of Ross*, 55; *Reg. Great Seal*, iii, 372, 2661.]

1560 GEORGE DUNBAR, parson in 1537, reader in 1571.—[*Reg. Abbrev. Feu Charters of Church Lands*, ii, 278.]

1569 WILLIAM ROSS THOMASSOUN, exhorter 1568; pres. to vicarage 20th June 1569–70 on death of Alexander Arbuthnott; also at Logie Easter.—[*Comps. Sub Coll. of Thirds, Inverness*, etc.]

1569 ROBERT MUNRO, exhorter 1569–71. (See Culicudden.)

1575 NEIL MUNRO, pres. to vicarage 7th Nov. 1574–5 on dem. of William Ross, parson of Rosskeen (*q.v.*).—[*Reg. Pres. Bene.*, i, (4), 24.]

1618 ALEXANDER HOSSACK, his son, William, portioner of Nigg.

1655 JAMES McCULLOCH, marr. Elspet, daugh. of James Fraser and Janet, daugh. of John Denune of Pittogarty and granddaugh. of James Fraser, provost of Nairn, and had issue—John in Glastullich of Knockbreck.—[*Tain Town Sas.*, 5th May 1682. (See Fearn.)

1687 DONALD FORBES, M.A.; on 2nd Sept. 1700 it was reported to the Presb. that upon the 29th Aug. last, being a day app. for a National Fast, he did most unwarrantably intrude himself upon and contumaciously preach in the Kirk of Kilmuir-Easter, and that upon the following Sunday he came to the churchyard and behaved in a tumultuous manner towards Mr Fraser of Alness, who had been app. by the Presb. to supply the vacancy that day; he was summoned to a meeting of Presb. on 29th Oct., but did not appear; in deference to a letter from Viscount Seafield, the Presb. delayed further procedure, and of the matter nothing more is heard.—[Macnaughton's *Church Life in Ross and Sutherland*, 27-30.]

1851 WILLIAM MACPHERSON, his sons —Charles Edward Walker, died 6th Dec. 1931; Sir Duncan James died 18th Jan. 1936; his daugh., Katherine Penuel, died 13th Sept. 1947.

1886 DONALD STUART, his son, William Laing, died London 29th June 1939.

1914 JOHN CAMPBELL MACNAUGHT, dem. 12th Nov. 1939, died 15th June 1940.

KINCARDINE

That there existed in the parish a chapel dedicated to St Colman, probably Colman whose day is 18th Feb., is denoted by Kilmachalmaig, "Church of Colman."—[Watson's *Celtic Place Names*, 279; *The Book of Ross*, 65.]

1567 FARQUHAR REID, exhorter 1569. (See Edderton).

1569 THOMAS DENUNE, parson, was dead 1569.—[*Comps. Sub Coll. of Thirds, Inverness*, etc.]

1573 ALEXANDER LESLIE, designated parson 29th June 1582.—[*Hist. MSS. Commiss.*, vi, 717.]

1574 ANDREW MARTYN, M.A., parson, was dead before 30th April 1574.—[*Cals. of Charters*, x, 2313.]

1620 JOHN (? JAMES) ROSS, marr. Helen Rose and had issue—Samuel in Culess (eldest son).—[*Reg. of Deeds, Mack.*, 2nd May, 1663.]

1655 THOMAS ROSS, his son, Andrew, min. of Tarbat.

1671 GEORGE ROSS, marr. cont. 8th Feb. 1673 Katherine, daugh. of Malcolm Ross of Kindeas; she marr. (2) cont. 22nd Jan. 1684 Alexander Sutherland of Inchfurie.—[*Reg. of Deeds*, Dal., 4th Jan. 1710; *Ross Sas.*, 26th June 1684.]

1711 ROBERT MUNRO, line 3, delete "and brother of Hugh Munro, min. of Tain."

1919 HUGH FRASER MacNEILL, dem. 8th June 1947; died 22nd Jan. 1948.

(*Charges united with Croick 8th June 1947.*)

LOGIE-EASTER

In 1763 the min. reported to the Presb. that the church "has for many years been in a most ruinous condition; that the timber of the roof was rotten, and the heather thatch did not hold out a drop of rain; the walls were out of plumb, and there was not a pane of glass in any of the windows." The Presb. resolved to take immediate steps to deal with the matter; and on 4th June 1764 John Ross of Balnagowan, one of the heritors, sent a letter to the Presb. containing an offer to provide a site for a new church on an eminence to the east of the manse on his lands of Logie, as the situation of the existing church was difficult of access. The matter was delayed in the hands of the heritors, some of whom, two years later, proposed that Logie-Easter be annexed to Fearn and Kilmuir-Easter. The proposal was rejected by the Presb. on 2nd April 1766; and early in the following year, on representation by the heritors, the Presb. approved of a site for the new church on an eminence east of the manse. In 1778, in connection with an excambion by which Captain John Ross of Balnagowan acquired the manse and glebe in return for an equivalent glebe at the place of Pitmaditty and a new manse built by him at the Chapel-Hill there, "an acre of ground in the Chapel-Hill was proposed to be set apart for a Church and Churchyard in case the Church shall be brought thither." On 13th April 1815 the Presb. acceded to a crave of the min. that a new church should be built at Chapel-Hill, and on 11th Feb. 1818 it agreed to a plan for a new church there at an estimated cost of £1076 stg., which the heritors, "after much deliberation and mature consideration," had resolved to build. The ruins of the first of the three churches just enumerated are situated in the old graveyard called *Lagaidh*, hence Logie, near Marybank farmhouse on the Balnagowan river; and the ruins of the second are also marked farther east on the O.S. Map.—[Macnaughton's *Church Life in Ross and Sutherland*, 247, 248, 254, 278–80, 330, 332; *Book of Ross*, 56.]

1574 SIR THOMAS HAY, parson 1560.—[*Reg. Abbrev. Feu Charters of Church Lands*, ii, 228.]

1574 ROBERT MUNRO, exhorter 1569. (See Culicudden.)

1581 JOHN ROSS, M.A., pres. as min. on death of Sir Thomas Hay.—[*Reg. Pres. Bene.*, ii, 57.]

1624 DAVID ROSS, his sons—Hugh of Auchnacloich; George.—[*Tain Sher. Court Records*, 1721.]

1665 KENNETH MACKENZIE, marr. cont. 10th April 1671 Mary, daugh. of James Fraser of Pitkinty.—[*Tain Sher. Court Deeds*, 19th June 1677.]

1730 JOHN McARTHUR, was schoolmaster of Kilmuir Easter.

1843 ALEXANDER MACKENZIE, was parish schoolmaster of Kiltarlity previous to appointment as min. here; his daugh., Mary, died 2nd Oct. 1944.

1916 DUGALD MACDONALD, his daugh., Isabel Eunson (marr. 23rd May 1942 Charles John Radcliffe, son of Lieut.-Colonel J. C. R. Husband).

1924 JOHN ROBERTSON FORBES, dem. 16th May 1934, died 19th Sept. 1936; his daugh., May Elizabeth (marr. Jackson Loudon McFadden, min. of Fearn); his only son, John Seivwright, Squadron Leader, R.A.F., killed March 1942.

NIGG

At the church there is an early Christian Pictish sculptured stone and a somewhat similar stone at Shandwick.—[*Book of Ross*, 57–8.]

1577 ALEXANDER CLUNES, M.A., pres. to vicarage 19th Feb. 1577-8 on dem. of Finlay Mason.—[*Reg. Sec. Sig.*, xlv, 53.]

1578 FINLAY MASON, M.A., pres. to vicarage 27th March 1594 on depriv. of John Leslie, Bishop of Ross, and vicar here "an obstinat papist," and again on 30th May 1594.—[*Reg. Sec. Sig.*, lxvi, 120, 128.]

1603 ALEXANDER CLUNES, reader 1603. —[*Comps. Surplus of Thirds.*]

1653 JAMES MACKENZIE, his daugh., Margaret (marr. cont. 15th Oct. 1697 Hugh Rose, min. of Creich). He died before 9th April 1701 when the heritors and parishioners, on the plea that their kirk was now vacant by the death of Mr Mackenzie, "who also of a long time had not preached to them by reason of weakness, and in regard of the desolate condition of the parish," craved supply from the Presb.—[Macnaughton's *Church Life in Ross and Sutherland*, 32.]

1706 GEORGE MUNRO, marr. (2) cont. 21st Nov. 1717.

1729 JOHN BALFOUR, his son, Andrew, apprenticed to William Tod, merchant, 10th June 1741.

1756 PATRICK GRANT, his son, Lewis, died in Jamaica 4th April 1822.

1865 JOHN FRASER, his daugh., Simona, died 6th March 1944.

1901 NORMAN DONALD MACKAY, born 1872, not 1871; licen. 29th June 1899; died 26th Oct. 1948; his daughs.—Mary Flora, Hospital Nurse, Cambridge; Catherine Yvonne, M.A. (Aberdeen) (marr. 9th Feb. 1946 Walter Edward, son of W. Darby, Leyton, London).

ROSSKEEN and NONEKILL

Originally there were two parishes; and in a reckoning of teinds of 24th May 1275 the Church of Nevoth (Newnakle, Nonakiln) and the Church of Rosskevene appear separately. At or soon after the Reformation the parish is called Rosskeen and Newnakle. At Newnakle, Nonakiln, *Nao'na Cille* for *Neimhead na Cille*, "the nemed of the Church," nemed being an old sacred place taken over by the church, there is a burying-ground with the ruins of the parish Church of Newnakle, which fell in 1714. Attached to the church there appears to have been a large area of land which constituted at one time a sacred pagan sanctuary, including Dalnavie, *Dail Neimhidh*, "the Dale of the Church land," Inchnavie, *Innis Neimhidh*, "the Haugh of the Church land," Cnoc Navie, *Cnoc Neimhidh*, "the Hill of the Church Land," and the estate of Newmore, *Neo'Mhor* "the big or large *Nemed*." Near Dal Neich, west of Cnoc Navie, there was a small chapel. At a Presb. visitation on 15th July 1719 the min. reported that he had two churches, Rosskeen and Nonekill, the latter ruinous, the former in fairly good condition, only the thatch stood in need of repair. In 1832 the present church at Rosskeen was built "on a piece of ground contiguous to and closely connected with the Churchyard," and occupied early in 1833. On 30th Sept. 1824 it was arranged that the glebe and churchyard grass at Nonekill be given in excambion for land contiguous to the glebe at Rosskeen. The Presb. agreed to the excambion on 1st Feb. 1859, and the matter was finally settled in March 1869. The church at Nonekill was dedicated to St Ninian, and near the churchyard are St Ninian's Well and St Ninian's Field.—[Theiner's *Vet. Mon.*, 112; *Reg. Pres. Bene.*, i, 88, 91; Watson's *Celtic Place Names*, 249, 287; *Book of Ross*, 51–2; Macnaughton's *Church Life in Ross and Sutherland*, 315–16, 350, 341–2, 416–17, 423; Simpson's *Celtic Church in Scot.*, 56.]

1568 GAVIN DUNBAR, parson 19th April 1568; died 1570.—[*Cal. of Charters*, x, 2118.]

1569 SIR HOMER FRASER, vicar 1569.—[*Comps. Sub Coll. of Thirds, Inverness*, etc.]

1572 JAMES HERING, pres. to parsonage and vicarage of Rosskeen and Newynkill 5th Jan. 1572-3 on death of Gavin Dunbar.—[*Reg. Pres. Bene.*, i, (4), 2.]

1572 WILLIAM ROSS, pres. 1572 on death of Gavin Dunbar.—[*Reg. Pres. Bene.*, i, (4), 5.]

1607 DAVID MUNRO, student of divinity when pres. to parsonage and vicarage 7th Feb. 1607 on death of John Dow Fraser.—[*Reg. Sec. Sig.*, lxxv, 267.]

1784 THOMAS URQUHART, had issue—Thomas (second of name); Colin; youngest and second of name.—[*Test.* of mother.]

1870 GEORGE MACDONALD his widow, Catherine Rae died 11th April 1938; his son, William Rae, died Edinburgh 30th March 1946.

1918 DUGALD McCALLUM, born 15th March 1875; M.A. 1903, not 1904; died 7th June 1942; daugh. Aenea, born 1919, not 1918; his widow, Mary Baxter, died 19th June 1943.

TAIN

In addition to the Church of St Duthac, built in 1471, and made collegiate ten years later, there were the Chapel of St Duthac in the churchyard, and the Chapel of St Duthac. The latter chapel, reputed as marking the birthplace of St Duthac, stood on the sandy beach north of the town, where, it is said, the town itself was at first situated. This chapel appears to have been the original Church of St Duthac. It was a famous place of sanctuary. Thither in 1307 the Queen of Robert the Bruce and their daugh. fled for safety from Kildrummy Castle, only to be seized by the Earl of Ross, who cared nought for religious scruples, and delivered by him to the English. Thither also, about 120 years later, came for security Mowat of Freswick and his followers, who had suffered defeat at the hands of his foe, McNiel of Creich, and his band. The latter were in close pursuit, and at the sanctuary slew Mowat and his men, and gave the chapel to the flames. It is uncertain when the chapel was restored; but, at any rate, James IV made various offerings to the church and each of the two chapels, including in Nov. 1501, 5s. "to the hermit of the Chapel of St Duthos." By command of the same monarch a silver relique of St Duthac was made in 1503-4 and sent from Edinburgh to Dunfermline and thence to Tain; on the same order on 3rd Aug. 1506 there was given "xxxii unce and iii quarters to be ane relique of Sanct Dutho"; and again on the king's command in 1511 there was delivered to "John Aitkin, goldsmith, to be ane relique to Sanct Dutho, ane of the auld silvir platis brokin, contenand xxxiii unce and quartair unce." In 1535 it is recorded that there was delivered to James V "ane relict of Sanct Dutho set in Silver weyand xxxvi unce iii grote wecht." Cosmo Innes described the Church of St Duthac as consisting of a chancel and nave, a ruinous chapel at the east send of the chancel, a south porch, a detached tower in the middle of the town, and a detached chapel a little south of the former chapel. The detached chapel was probably the chapel of St Duthac in the churchyard. The church ceased to be used for worship in 1815, when a new parish church was built. About 1790 the remains of a small chapel were still to be seen near Lochslin three miles from Tain. In modern times at least St Mary's Well was covered at high water.

On a petition from the min., the Presb. on 28th Nov. 1813 gave consideration to the question of a new church as distinct from enlarging the old church, which was "highly uncomfortable and by far too small to accommodate the parishioners." The old church had been repaired in 1788. There followed considerable negotiations with the heritors and magistrates, and eventually agreement was reached on the basis of a new church on a site at the east end of the town at a cost of £2849 9s. 6d. inclusive of ground and enclosing the same. On 3rd Aug. 1814 the completed church was accepted by the Presb. At a meeting of Presb. on 31st Oct. 1838 the min. "spoke of getting the old Church repaired, with a view to having it erected into a preaching station in the first instance, and then in the hope of having it erected into a parish"; he further stated that "the heritors have all agreed to make said old Church over to the Kirk Session for said purpose, and that a draft of the Deed of Conveyance was being made out." The Presb. gave approval and made remit to the min. to carry out further procedure. The church was acquired by the Guildry Trust formed by a number of local gentlemen, and was restored in 1871 to constitute St Duthus (Duthac) Memorial Church. In the collegiate church there was a Chapel of the Dead.—[*Lord High Treasurer's Accs.*, ii, 125, 265-8, iii, 81, 280, iv, 40, 533, vi, 248; *Origines Parochiales Scotiae*, 426 (*q.v.*), 416, for full account of the provostry; Macnaughton's *Church Life in Ross and Sutherland*, 317-23, 326-7, 371-2; *Reg. Sec. Sig.*, ii, 259.]

1586 JAMES ROBERTSON, pres. to vicarage 1st Dec. 1591 on dem. of Thomas Ross.—[*Reg. Sec. Sig.*, lxiii, 29.]

1665 ROBERT ROSS of Ballon, his sentence of deposition was confirmed by the General Assembly in 1701; on 11th June of the same year he appeared personally before the Presb. and protested against anyone accepting a call to Tain till his appeal to the Lords of Privy Council had been disposed of. For various reasons the Presb. declined to entertain the protest. —[Macnaughton's *Church Life in Ross and Sutherland*, 32-3.]

1701 HUGH MUNRO of Kiltearn. Marr. cont. 26th Aug. 1707 Katherine Barnett; issue—Alexander of Kiltearn, Jean (marr. 14th April 1702 William Munro of Teanaird); Andrew, merchant, Cambridge; Mary, bapt. 15th April 1720; John, bapt. 11th April 1721; John, bapt. 28th Sept. 1722.—[*Reg. of Deeds, Dal.*, cxxxiii, 19th Feb. 1733; *Foulis Writs*, 365, 368.]

1770 HUGH ROSE, probably son of Hugh R., Barrivan, Cawdor, and Jean Macarthur; preacher and schoolmaster at New Bridge of Balnagowan.

1844 LEWIS ROSE, grandson of David R. of Leanach, descended of Holme Rose.

1883 COLIN MACNAUGHTON, his son, Colin, assistant art master, George Watson's College, drowned at St Abb's 4th Aug. 1936.

1920 GEORGE THOMAS THOMSON, app. Professor of Systematic Theology, Aberdeen, 1928.

1924 JOHN MACECHRAN, dem. 1942; his wife, Margaret Black, died at Crieff 13th April 1942.

TARBAT

The Chapel of St Finn Barr, Chapel Barr, was built, 1486–1516, by Thomas McCulloch, Abbot of Fearn. Until 1707 or later there was a vault, 30 feet long, said to have been built as a church by St Columba (Colman ?). On the coast near the old Castle of Tarbat or Ballone there was a chapel known as *Teampul Eraich*, and near it was Tobair Mhuir Well (Mary's Well). The old church seems to have been rebuilt about 1628. A new church was erected in 1756.—[*Origines Parochiales Scotiae*, ii, (2), 439.]

1593 JOHN MUNRO, marr. (2) Christian Urquhart, who survived him.—[*Tombs*.]

1652 ANDREW ROSS,, son of Thomas R., min. of Kincardine. Marr. cont. 18th Nov. 1656.

1885 DONALD MACLEOD, died 27th April 1930; his daugh., Isabella (marr. 22nd Oct. 1929 Harold Graham Grieve, Johore, son of James G., min. of Logiealmond); his widow, Kate Isles Wise Rodger, died 3rd April 1935.

1927 MURDO MACLEOD, trans. from Uig (*q.v.*) 20th July 1927. Addl. issue—Isobel Joan Macphail, born 5th Oct. 1927; Anna Matheson, born 4th Dec. 1929; Roderick Montgomery, born 16th Oct. 1931; Murdo, R.A.F., killed 30th June 1944.

SYNOD OF SUTHERLAND AND CAITHNESS

PRESBYTERY OF DORNOCH

ASSYNT

1565 ALEXANDER STEWART, son of James S. in Fincastle and brother of John S. of Tulipowrie, vicar 3rd Dec. 1565, also Prebendary of Inchemarannoche.—[*Reg. of Deeds*, viii, 186.]

1575 WILLIAM MACQUEEN, parson.— [*Acts and Dec.*, lx, 77.]

1576 WILLIAM McANDREW, parson 1576-7.—[*Comps. Gen. Coll. of Thirds.*]

1728 WILLIAM SCOBIE, his son, John, apprenticed to Archibald Gibson, cordiner, 11th July 1750.

1919 DONALD MACKINNON, trans. to Cumlodden 19th Aug. 1927.

1928 ALLAN MACLEOD ARMSTRONG, born Inverness 19th May 1903, son of Adam A., Telegraph Superintendent, G.P.O., and Isabella Ann Macleod; educ. at Univ. of Aberdeen, M.A. (1925); licen. by Presb. of Aberdeen 10th May 1928; assistant West Aberdeen; ord. 26th July 1928; trans. to Blackhill, Deer, 18th May 1932; trans. to Duthil 4th June 1936; dem. 27th June 1944; went to Aberdeen and engaged in teaching. Marr. 22nd Dec. 1928 Catherine Frances, eldest daugh. of Duncan Graham, Marybank, Stornoway, and Emily Craggs, and has issue—Frederick Adam, born 8th Dec. 1929; Frances Isabella, born 9th Dec. 1931; Alexander Graham, born 30th April 1933; Duncan, born 14th Aug. 1936.

(*Charges united 30th Aug. 1932.*)

CLYNE

1621 JOHN GRAY, marr. (2) 1631.

1697 EYE MACKAY, his son, Hugh, died in Flanders 1745; his daugh., Barbara (marr. John Sutherland, tacksman, Balvaird).

1889 JOHN SPARK, his widow, Christina Fyfe, died 7th April 1937.

1926 JOHN FAULDS, trans. from Milton of Balgonie 15th Dec. 1926.

1927 HECTOR WILLIAM MACKAY, trans. from Snizort (*q.v.*) 23rd Nov. 1927; dem 12th June 1938.

(*Charge united with Brora 12th June 1938.*)

CREICH

1569 WILLIAM GRAY, younger son of William G., min. of Lairg, exhorter here and at Dornoch 1569.— [*Comps. Sub Coll. of Thirds, Inverness*, etc.]

1660 GEORGE McCULLOCH, min.—[*Reg. of Deeds, Mack.*, ii, 311.]

1682 HUGH ROSE, son of Alexander R. of Mereton, Nairnshire. Marr. (2) 15th Oct. 1697 Marie, daugh. of James Mackenzie, min. of Nigg. On 12th Aug. 1696 it was reported to the Presb. that Mr Hugh Rose, dep. some years previously for gross scandals, had intruded upon the church here, exercising ministerial acts, and that in a mercenary way to the scandal of religion. The Presb. app. one of their number to apply in their name to the Sheriff of Sutherland, requesting him to put

CREICH—KILDONAN

the Act of Parliament anent intruders into execution against Mr Rose.—[Macnaughton's *Church Life in Ross and Sutherland*, 10; *Reg. of Deeds, Mack.*, lxxxiv, 22nd June 1699.]

1855 NEIL MACKINNON, born 10th Aug. 1815; his son, Farquhar, died in Australia; his daugh., Jane, died at Edinburgh 22nd Aug. 1939.

1887 ROBERT LAMONT RITCHIE, missionary at Guisachan before admission; died 8th June 1933.

(*Charges united 9th Aug.* 1931.)

DORNOCH

1569 WILLIAM GRAY, younger, exhorter 1569. (See Creich.)

1575 WILLIAM HAY, reader 5th Dec. 1575.—[*Cal. of Charters*, xi, 2528.]

1578 JOHN ROSS, trans. from Latheron before 1578. Marr. Hester, daugh. of James Sutherland of Forse.—[*Forse Writs*, 66.]

1878 DONALD GRANT, his widow, Henrietta Philipina Hall, died at Dornoch 13th March 1945.

1907 CHARLES DONALD BENTINCK, dem. 11th Nov. 1934; died at Edinburgh 27th Jan. 1940; his wife, Helen Green Fraser, died 22nd Feb. 1932. Marr. (2) 26th Nov. 1936 Ann Henderson (died 21st April 1941), daugh. of Donald Mackenzie and widow of George Robert Maclennan, min. of Thurso; his daughs.— Evelyn Helen (marr. 6th Oct. 1931 Dr George Marcus Greig, son of Sir Robert Greig); Elizabeth Hoyes (marr. 21st March 1936 Eric Leslie McIntosh, son of L. McIntosh, Ealing, London).

GOLSPIE

The church was vacant 1649-50.—[*Acts of Parl.*, vii, 390.]

1569 SIR RICHARD MADDER, chaplain of Golspie 1569.—[*Comps. Sub Coll. of Thirds, Inverness*, etc.]

1682 HUGH ROSE, schoolmaster of Petty 1670-4, Dornoch 1674-82.

1690 WALTER DENUNE, marr. Anne, daugh. of Mr William Alexander.— [*Reg. of Deeds, Dal.*, cxxvi, 1st Aug. 1729.]

1817 ALEXANDER MACPHERSON, his wife, Harriet Matheson, died 29th May 1816.

1926 DAVID HEDLEY GILLAN, line 5, for "1893" read "1892"; line 11, for "1906" read "1904"; served in Tirah Expeditionary Force with 1st Gordons 1897-8; in Great War with Calcutta Scottish and Madras Guards 1915-17; Presidency Senior Chaplain, Madras, 1918; dem. 5th Feb. 1936; his son, Wing Commander John Woodburn, D.F.C., A.F.C., a distinguished flying officer, killed 29th Aug. 1941; his daugh., Squadron Leader Agnes Christian, M.B., Ch.B., awarded C.B.E. Jan. 1946 (marr. 26th Sept. 1947 William Proctor Wilson, C.B.E., Group Captain, R.A.F.). Publications—Contributions to various Indian newspapers.

KILDONAN

By Bull of Pope Honorius III, 15th Dec. 1225, the Church of Kildonan with its chapels and lands was confirmed to the Abbey of Scone. In 1332 the church was set in feu by the abbey to David Lytil and his brother, Robert, of Sutherland, who were held bound to build the church with stones and lime through 4 merks allocated, and to meet the ordinary burdens falling upon the church. When the church was made a prebend of Dornoch Cathedral, the Abbot of Scone was instituted a canon and ministered through a vicar-priest in the cathedral. At Naviedale there was a chapel with churchyard, dedicated to St Ninian. Naviedale is *Neimhe dail, nemed*, an old sacred place taken over by the church. There was here a sanctuary—a place that had the right of sanctuary or "girth." The formation is Norse, the second part being Norse, *dalr*, a dale. The Norsemen found the place important, and named the dale after it. Near the churchyard are St Ninian's Well and St Ninian's Field. The Church of Helmsdale was restored and extended in 1896. St Donnan's Church, Kildonan, was restored 1918.—[*Book of Scone*, 67, 162; *The Book of Sutherland*, i, 35, iii, 3–5; Watson's *Celtic Place Names*, 250; Simpson's *Celtic Church in Scotland*, 56.]

1574 ANDREW ANDERSON, exhorter 1574 and at Loth.—[*Comps. Sub Coll. of Thirds, Inverness*, etc.]

1740 HUGH SUTHERLAND, brother to Andrew S. of Braegrudie.

1894 ARCHIBALD BLACK SCOTT, D.D. (Glasgow, 20th June 1928); died 28th Dec. 1947. Addl. Publications—*Rise and Relation of the Church of Scotland* (Edinburgh, 1932); *The Historical Sequence of Peoples and Culture in Scotland 400 B.C. to 950 A.D.* (Peterhead, 1936).

(*Charges united with Loth 4th Jan. 1948.*)

LAIRG

1569 WILLIAM GRAY, elder, exhorter 1569–74; Treasurer of Caithness; had addl. issue—William, exhorter at Creich and Rogart.—[*Comps. Sub Coll. of Thirds, Inverness*, etc.; *Reg. Sec. Sig.*, lxxv, 114.]

1607 JAMES GRAY, treasurer of Caithness in succession to his father.—[*Reg. Sec. Sig.*, lxxv, 114.]

1888 JOHN MACNAUGHTON, died at Montreal 5th Feb. 1943.

1919 JOHN CUNNINGHAM MOORE, dem. 6th July 1931; adm. to Yarrow 28th Nov. 1935; dem. 6th July 1937; died at Vancouver 5th July 1945; his widow, Marguerite Maxwell Lowry Patterson, died 1st June 1946.

LOTH

The Hospital of St John the Baptist of Hebruisden of Helmsdale was granted to Kinloss Abbey on 21st May 1362 by William, Earl of Sutherland.—[*Reg. of Kinloss*, xxxix-xi.]

1567 ANDREW ANDERSON, exhorter 1569, pres. to vicarage 25th Dec. 1595 on dem. of James Maxwell.—[*Reg. Sec. Sig.*, lxviii, 46.] (See Kildonan.)

1569 JAMES MAXWELL, M.A., vicar 1569–72.—[*Comps. Sub Coll. of Thirds, Inverness*, etc.]

1656 JOHN ROSE, adm. 28th Aug. 1655.—[*Orkney Sas.*, viii, 78.]

1739 WILLIAM ROSE, marr. Jean, daugh. of David Anderson, Professor of Divinity, King's College, Aberdeen.

1803 GEORGE GORDON, his daugh., Isabella, died 4th June 1828.

1908 JAMES SINCLAIR McIVOR MOWAT, his sons—Alistair McIvor, min. of Fochabers, trans. to Martyrs, Glasgow, 28th Jan. 1936; James Philip, died 18th Sept. 1939.

(*Charge united with Kildonan 4th Jan. 1948.*)

ROGART

1569 WILLIAM GRAY, elder, exhorter in 1571. (See Lairg.)

1753 HUGH SUTHERLAND, brother of Andrew S. of Braegrudie.

1926 WILLIAM CAIRD TAYLOR, his father, solicitor, Cupar; died at Carnoustie 2nd Oct. 1935. Addl. issue—daugh., stillborn 15th April 1928; John Caird, born 23rd Feb. 1930; Kathleen Bruce Georgeson, born 27th Jan. 1932; Lucy Leighton Logan, born 11th Nov. 1933.

(*Charges united 4th Jan. 1948.*)

STOER

1877 ALEXANDER GRANT, died at Harthill Manse 13th April 1932; his wife, Barbara Grant, died at Greenock 23rd Feb. 1929; his son, Alexander George Macpherson, M.D., Medical Superintendent, Manchester Sanatorium, Abergele, Wales, 20th Oct. 1930.

1919 WILLIAM JOHN MACKENZIE, trans. to Knoydart 24th April 1929; his wife, Margaret Smith, died 2nd June 1933.

PRESBYTERY OF TONGUE

DURNESS

In the churchyard of Balnacille there is said to have been a monastery founded by some of Columba's missionaries; and there was a church assigned by Gilbert, Bishop of Caithness 1222–45, for providing light and incense for Dornoch Cathedral.—[*The Book of Ross*, 124.]

1576 GEORGE MERNIS, pres. in 1576 on dem. of James Makson.—[*Reg. Pres. Bene.*, i, (4), 48.]

1580 WILLIAM MERNIS, pres. in 1580 on dem. of George Mernis.—[*Reg. Pres. Bene.*, ii, 51.]

1663 HEW MUNRO, marr. Ann, daugh. of Donald, first Lord Reay and widow of Alexander Macdonald, son of Sir Donald M., first Bart. of Sleat.

1726 MURDOCH MACDONALD, his son, Joseph, author of *Compleat Theory of the Bagpipe*, died in India.

1856 WILLIAM CHARLES MIDDELTON GRANT, son of John G. in Toraslan and Penuel, daugh. of Samuel Middleton, Mains of Inveraurie, Kirkmichael; his son, Alexander Donald Mackenzie, M.A., died at Grootvlei, Transvaal, 6th May 1936; his daugh., Catherine Jane, died 25th Jan. 1936.

1918 JAMES WALLACE MACDONALD, died 10th April 1931; his widow, Helen Polson, died 30th Nov. 1941.

EDDRACHILLES

1744 JOHN MUNRO, line 14, for "Obe" read "Ore."

1901 GEORGE HENDERSON, his widow, Agnes D. Niebuhr, died 19th Sept. 1937.

1913 WILLIAM JOHN LUNDIE, trans. to Tongue 14th Aug. 1928.

FARR

1572 ARCHIBALD DAVIDSON, parson and vicar 1572.—[*Comps. Sub Coll. of Thirds, Inverness*, etc.]

1584 WILLIAM DAVIDSON, pres. 10th May 1584 on res. of Archibald Davidson.—[*Reg. Sec. Sig.*, iv, 129.]

1697 JOHN MACPHERSON, described as "a curate from Caithness" he appeared before the Presb. of Tain on 25th Sept. 1695, and gave in a petition in writing, acknowledging the evil of Prelacy and the Divine right of Presb. and therefore desiring to be received into the Presbyterian Communion, with liberty to exercise his licence to preach the Gospel which he had received some time previously under Prelacy. The Presb. after full consideration refused the prayer of the petition.—[Macnaughton's *Church Life in Ross and Sutherland*, 8–9.]

1920 JOHN DEAS LOGIE, died at Perth 10th Aug. 1932.

1927 NORMAN MORRISON, trans. to Uig, Balnacille, 15th April 1931; his wife, Annabella Macdonald, died 26th Sept. 1934. Addl. issue—Mary Bella, born 8th Jan. 1926; Donald John, born 1st died 8th Aug. 1928; Ewan Morrison, born 20th April 1930.

KINLOCHBERVIE

1899 ALEXANDER CRERAR, died 12th Feb. 1929.

(*Charges united* 1929.)

STRATHY

1899 ALEXANDER YOUNGSON, died 16th July 1933.

(*Charges united 21st Nov. 1931.*)

TONGUE

1767 WILLIAM MACKENZIE, died Father of the Church.

1889 DAVID LUNDIE, dem. 2nd June 1928, died 26th March 1934; his wife, Elspet Fleming Butter, died 9th July 1929.

1928 WILLIAM JOHN LUNDIE, licen. 9th Oct. 1912; trans. from Eddrachilles 14th Aug. 1928; dem. 31st March 1937; died at Bettyhill 16th Jan. 1946.

PRESBYTERY OF CAITHNESS

BOWER

1569 THOMAS BRYDIE, min. at Watten, also in charge here; held the chaplaincy of Helmsdale.—[*Comps. Sub Coll. of Thirds, Inverness*, etc.]

1908 DUGALD MACECHERN, died 31st Oct. 1946.

CANISBAY

The Church of Canisbay, cruciform in shape, was repaired about 1790, and again thoroughly repaired in 1832-3. There was a chapel called the Kirk of Strubster, described in the early part of the 18th century as "rather an hermitage, being a small spot of green in the midst of a remote wide desert"; and reputed as the "place where Protestants assembled to worship before the Reformation, when they could not do it safely in places more public and accessible." St Irchard's Chapel was identical with "St Ardach's Chappell," a place of pilgrimage in post-Reformation times. The saint is Erchard, Yrchard, the saint of Kincardine O'Neil. On the island of Stroma there were two chapels, the Kirk of Stava or Stara, and the Kirk of Old Skoil.—[Macfarlane's *Geog. Colls.*, i, 156; Mackinlay's *Church Dedications* (non-script.), 506; Watson's *Celtic Place Names*, 320.]

1567 ALEXANDER PATRICK GRAHAMESON, exhorter 1569.—[*Comps. Sub Coll. of Thirds, Inverness*, etc.]

1569 HERCULES BARCLAY, vicar, died before 1569.—[*Acts and Dec.*, xxxii, 97; *Comps. Sub Coll. of Thirds, Inverness*, etc.]

1572 DAVID CARMICHAEL, M.A., pres. to parsonage and vicarage 8th April 1572 on death of Hercules Barclay.—[*Reg. Pres. Bene.*, i, (3), 16.]

1572 JOHN WATSON, pres. on death of Hercules Barclay.—[*Reg. Pres. Bene.*, i, (2), 19.]

1581 HERCULES BARCLAY, parson, 31st July 1581.—[*Cal. of Charters*, xi, 2595.]

1924 ROBERT WILSON MERRY, his wife, Dr Jean McMurray Crawford, died 6th Nov. 1937.

1928 WILLIAM FULTON, born 26th Nov. 1882; son of John F. and Sarah Paterson; licen. by Presb. of Glasgow 16th Dec. 1921; ord. to Gorbals 5th Dec. 1922; trans. and adm. 18th July 1928. Marr. 1st Jan. 1909 Mary, daugh. of David Cumming and Margaret Stewart, and has issue—John, born 4th Oct. 1909; Sarah Paterson, born 13th Oct. 1910.

DUNNETT

1574 THOMAS DUNNET, reader in 1594.—[*Comps. Surplus of Thirds.*]

1697 GEORGE OSWALD, described as "a curate from Caithness," he appeared before the Presb. of Tain on 25th Sept. 1695, and gave in a petition in writing acknowledging the evil of Prelacy and the Divine right of Presb., and therefore desiring to be received into the Presbyterian Communion, with liberty to exercise his licence to preach the Gospel which he had received some time previously under Prelacy. The Presb. after full consideration refused the prayer of the petition. He appears to have been a preaching deacon under Episcopacy; and the Presb. of Edinburgh in licensing him in 1697 no doubt acted under reference from the General Assembly.—[Macnaughton's *Church Life in Ross and Sutherland*, 8-9.]

1876 ARCHIBALD JOLLY, his widow Agnes Dunlop Paxton, died at Musselburgh 13th April 1939.

1889 WILLIAM JAMES STUART FALCONER, his widow, Matilda Rose Elmslie, died 16th Sept. 1935.

1901 JOHN GORDON STEVENSON, his wife, Elizabeth Stroyan, died 6th Jan. 1927.

1916 DAVID SCOTT, died 4th Dec. 1928.

1929 ALEXANDER FRASER, trans. from Glenshiel (*q.v.*) 30th Sept. 1929; dem. 15th May 1932; died at Invergordon 5th April 1941.

HALKIRK and SPITTAL

1566 WILLIAM GORDON, parson, died before 20th May 1566.—[*Reg. Sec. Seal*, xxxv, 25.]

1566 JOHN GORDON, pres. to the parsonage 20th May 1566.—[*Reg. Sec. Seal*, xxxv, 25.]

1567 JAMES SCOTT, reader in 1567 and 1569.—[*Comps. Sub Coll. of Thirds, Inverness*, etc.]

1579 JOHN MOSMAN, reader, pres. to vicarage 17th Sept. 1579 on death of Sir Thomas Anderson.—[*Reg. Pres. Bene.*, ii, 21.]

1706 JOHN MUNRO, his son, Robert, apprenticed to John Smith, cordiner, 27th July 1739.

1902 JOHN RITCHIE, his widow, Jean Singer Bisset, died at Insch 1st Nov. 1940, aged 82.

1924 JOHN LAMB, son of John Cameron L., Portree, died 18th Oct. 1932; his son John Kevan MacGregor, died 8th May 1934.

KEISS

1920 GEORGE WALSH, dem. 28th July 1946; died 31st March 1947; his only daugh., Elizabeth (marr. 5th Aug. 1946 Bernhard Citron, Ph.D., min. of Pleasance, Edinburgh).

(*Charges united 28th July* 1942.)

LATHERON

1570 SIR WILLIAM SINCLAIR, vicar, died in 1570.—[*Comps. Sub Coll. of Thirds, Inverness*, etc.]

1572 WILLIAM SINCLAIR, pres. to vicarage 12th Jan. 1572-3 on death of Sir William Sinclair.—[*Reg. Pres. Bene.*, i, (4), 2.]

1578 JOHN ROSS, trans to Dornoch, before 1578.—[*Forss Writs*, 66.]

1599 GILBERT ANDERSON, marr. Janet Davidson.—[*Forss Writs*, 24.]

1634 DAVID MUNRO, raised an action with regard to the teinds against the heritors 7th Dec. 1649.—[*Forss Writs*, 36.]

1880 JAMES McHARDY, his widow, Elizabeth Jane Sim, died at London 15th March 1933; his daugh., Elizabeth, M.B., Ch.B. (Aberdeen), 1909.

1919 ALEXANDER GILFILLAN, died 26th March 1938; his widow, Margaret Smeaton MacNeilage, died 8th Oct. 1939; his daughs.—Kathleen (marr. 12th Jan. 1939 Joseph Smith Easton, min. of Milnathort); Eileen Margaret Mitchell (marr. 11th Oct. 1939 James Millar Manson, Royal Artillery).

LYBSTER

1857 JAMES RODDICK, his son, Robert Murray McCheyne, died 9th Aug. 1945.

1897 CHARLES DUNN, his widow, Tina Ann Duncan, died 26th Sept. 1946.

1919 ROBERT WILSON, died 18th March 1938.

OLRIG

1563 WILLIAM SINCLAIR, parson, canon of Caithness, was dead before 23rd July 1563.—[*Reg. Abbrev. Feu Charters of Church Lands*, ii, 100.]

1564 WILLIAM SINCLAIR, M.A., parson and vicar 1st May 1564.—[*Reg. Abbrev. Feu Charters of Church Lands*, i, 158; *Cal. of Charters*, ix, 1948; *Acts and Dec.*, xxxv, 212; xl, 364; xli, 454; l, 214, 268.]

1564 Y———— MACKINTOSH.—[*Antiq. Notes.*]

1572 ALEXANDER URQUHART, pres. in 1572 on death of William Sinclair.—[*Reg. Pres. Bene.*, i, (4), 2.]

1574 ANDREW MYLNE, min. pres. to parsonage and vicarage 26th July 1576 on dem. of Alexander Urquhart.

1587 JOHN HUTCHISON, M.A., pres. to vicarage on death of Thomas Keir.—[*Reg. Sec. Sig.*, lvi, 4; *Acts and Dec.*, lv, 315; *Reg. Mag. Sig.*, v, 247.]

1591 JOHN MANSON, pres. to vicarage on depriv. of John Hutchison.—[*Reg. Sec. Sig.*, liii, 62.]

1874 ARCHIBALD HAMILTON GILLIESON, his widow, Jane Murray, died at Moffat 20th Nov. 1933.

1925 WILLIAM McNUTT, trans. to Udny 22nd Feb. 1928. Line 15, delete "a son born 6th May 1927."

1929 JOHN KENNETH MACLEAN, trans. from Morven (*q.v.*) 17th Jan. 1929; died at Spean Bridge 27th Oct. 1941; his daugh., Jean Robertson (marr. 14th Aug. 1929 Dr George Douglas Roche, Scalloway); his wife, Alison Mary Macaulay, died at Spean Bridge 16th Nov. 1940; his sons—Kenneth, 2nd Lieut., Argyll and Sutherland Highlanders, died of wounds 25th Dec. 1941; John Kenneth, M.B.E., Major, Tank Corps, prisoner of war 1942.

PULTENEYTOWN

1878 WILLIAM HARLEY ANDERSON, his widow, Mary Benvie, died 12th Feb. 1922.

1894 ALEXANDER ROSS, died 5th May 1936.

REAY

1569 SIR MALCOLM REID, vicar, was dead in 1569, survived by his wife, Agnes Keith.—[*Comps. Sub Coll. of Thirds, Inverness*, etc.] (See Thurso.)

1878 DONALD MACAULAY, line 2, for "Zachary" read "Donald"; his daugh., Alice Hall, died 20th Oct. 1942.

1909 DUGALD CARMICHAEL, died 4th Sept. 1944; his son, Hugh, educ. at Thurso Academy and Univs. of Edinburgh and Cambridge, Ph.D. (May 1936); Research Fellowship, St. John's College, at Cavendish laboratory, Cambridge, in 1936, conducted research in the cosmic rays under supervision of Lord Rutherford with new and very sensitive apparatus of his own design.

SHURRERY

1920 EDMUND EDWARD WILLIAMSON, died 14th July 1932.

THURSO

The Churches of Thurso, Reay, Wick and Latheron are described on 31st July 1581 as ruinous and roofless.

1561 WALTER INNES, vicar, reader and min. 1561-2.—[*Comps. Gen. Coll. of Thirds.*]

1785 PATRICK NICOLSON, his daughs.—Janet Dunbar (marr. Dr Featherstone); Mary (marr. Major Jackson); Isabella (marr. Dr Simon Nicolson); Margaret (marr. Lieut.-Colonel Western).

1831 WALTER ROSS TAYLOR, his widow, Isabella Macdonald, died 5th April 1928; his daugh., Christina Barbara Ross, died 26th June 1928.

GEORGE ROBERT MACLENNAN,
1910 died 12th Sept. 1935; his widow, Annie Henderson Mackenzie, marr. (2) 26th Nov. 1936 Charles Donald Bentinck, min. of Dornoch.

WATTEN

1569 **THOMAS BRYDIE,** M.A., min. and exhorter 1569. (See Bower and Thurso.)

1649 **WILLIAM SMITH,** burgess of Edinburgh 1st Aug. 1649; marr. Sara, daugh. of John Davidson, surgeon, Edinburgh.

1875 **WILLIAM LAING REID,** his widow, Annie Sutherland, died 14th April 1936; his daugh., Anne Henderson (marr. 15th July 1944 Simon, son of Robert Linton, Leadclune, Inverness).

1892 **DAVID LILLIE,** died at Lybster 21st Feb. 1940; his wife, Frances Margaret Brown, died 10th Dec. 1931.

WICK

The pre-Reformation church was situated at Mount-Hallie or Halie near the east end of the town. Its successor was built in the present churchyard before 1576, and was repaired in 1728 and 1752. A new church was erected in 1830. The Chapel of St Tears seems to have been dedicated to St Drostan; and later it was under the invocation of the Holy Innocents. In 1834 it is narrated that within the memory of persons living it was customary for people to visit the "Chapel of St Tears on Innocent's Day, and leave in it bread and cheese as an offering to the souls of the children slain by Herod." In the first half of the 18th century, and maybe later, people frequenting the chapel had their recreation and pastimes on the third day of Christmas.—[Macfarlane's *Geog. Colls.*, i, 151.]

1567 **ANDREW PHILP,** pres. to vicarage 25th Nov. 1574 on dem. of Andrew Graham.—[*Reg. Pres. Bene.*, i, (4), 28.]

1569 **SIR ALEXANDER MENZIES,** vicar pensioner 1569–72.—[*Comps. Sub Coll. of Thirds, Inverness,* etc.]

1876 **ALEXANDER CLARK,** his daugh., Eliza Gertrude, died at Edinburgh 23rd April 1943.

1916 **JOHN MacDOUGALL,** trans. to St Michael's, Edinburgh, 30th Sept. 1929.

SYNOD OF GLENELG

PRESBYTERY OF LOCHCARRON

APPLECROSS

1568 SIR MURDOCH JOHNSTONE, described in 1568 as one of the chaplains of Applecross of St Morenss (Movrie, Maolrubha).—[*Comps. Sub Coll. of Thirds, Inverness*, etc.]

1569 SIR WILLIAM STEWART, chaplain of Applecross of St Morenss, was dead in 1569.—[*Comps. Sub Coll. of Thirds, Inverness*, etc.]

1588 THOMAS GORDON, M.A., pres. to parsonage and vicarage 3rd Feb. 1588-9 on death of George Hay.—[*Reg. Sec. Sig.*, lix, 8.]

1777 JOHN MACKENZIE, had issue—Farquhar, H.E.I.C.S.

GAIRLOCH

West of the hollow known as *Leabdiah na babaine*, "the bed of the white cow," scooped out by Finn to enable his white cow to calve, and used by large congregations at Communion seasons, is the site of a chapel with burying-ground, dedicated to St Maolrubha. On the seashore near Laide, in the old parish, is the ruined chapel of Sand of Udrigle, reputed locally to be one of the earliest Christian churches on the West Coast.—[*The Book of Ross*, 79, 85.]

1583 ALEXANDER MACKENZIE, pres. to parsonage and vicarage on death of Sir –. Stewart 11th Jan. 1582-3.—[*Reg. Pres. Bene.*, ii, 82.]

1649 RODERICK MACKENZIE, died Father of the Church.

1914 DONALD MACLEOD, dem. 31st May 1939, died 24th May 1945; his widow, Amelia Gunn, died 20th Dec. 1946.

GLENELG

1694 SWEYN McSWEYN, M.A., min. of Kilcalmonell and Kilberry; intruded here and was dep. by the Synod 15th Oct. 1694 for contumacy. (See Kilcalmonell and Kilberry.)

1890 ALEXANDER MacTAGGART, dem. 11th Nov. 1931, died 15th Nov. 1946.

(*Charges united 2nd July* 1931.)

GLENSHIEL

The church was erected in 1758. The Chapel of St Kentigerna was situated near the church and manse, in the old burying-ground called *Cill Chaointeoirn* or *Cill Chaointeord*, "Church of Kentigerna." A disused burying-ground opposite Shiel School, called *Cill Fhearchair*, "Church of Ferchar," may commemorate a saint of that name who does not appear in the Calendar.—[Watson's *Celtic Place Names*, 301–2, 304; *The Book of Ross*, 73.]

1730 JOHN BEATON, his daugh., Flora (marr. Roderick Macleod of Borline, Bracadale).

1917 ALEXANDER FRASER, trans. to Dunnett 30th Sept. 1929.

KINTAIL

The Chapel of St Fillan, said to be the burial place of that saint, was situated near the head of Loch Long, at Killalan, *Cill*

Fhaolain, "Fillan's Church." *Eilean Donnain*, "Donan's Isle," at the head of Lochalsh, may commemorate St Donnan of Eigg, whose day was 17th April. Loch Duich, *Loch Dubhthaich*, is named after St Duthac.—[Watson's *Celtic Place Names*, 155, 284–5; *The Book of Ross*, 72.]

1574 JOHN MURCHISON, pres. in 1574.—[*Reg. Pres. Bene.*, i, (4), 28.]

1582 DONALD MURCHISON, pres. in 1582 on dem. of John Murchison.—[*Reg. Pres. Bene.*, ii, 86.]

1618 FARQUHAR MACRAE, his eldest son, Thomas.—[*Reg. of Deeds, Gibson*, 508, 1st June 1634.]

1920 DUNCAN MacRAE MacLENNAN, died at Kingussie 1st Oct. 1941; his sons—Roderick, app. May 1933 Professor of Philosophy, McGill Univ., Montreal; Norman Macpherson, Director of Medical Services, British Guiana.

KNOYDART

The patron saint of the old parish was *Chomhghain*, Comgan, hence Kilchoan.—[Watson's *Celtic Place Names*, 281.]

1890 JOHN FORBES MENZIES, his widow, Charlotte Kerr Macphail, died 19th Nov. 1931.

1916 JOHN MACKAY, died at Corstorphine 6th Nov. 1935.

1929 WILLIAM JOHN MACKENZIE, trans. from Stoer (*q.v.*) 24th April 1929; dem. 31st Oct. 1943. Marr. (2) 9th Oct. 1934 Susan Amelia, youngest daugh. of Duncan McGilp, Craignish.

LOCHALSH

The patron saint is *Chomhghain*, Comgan, said to have come from Ireland with Kentigerna and Fillan.—[Watson's *Celtic Place Names*, 281.]

1577 ALISTAIR MOIR, min. in 1577.—[*Acts and Dec.*, lv, 149.]

1695 FINLAY MACRAE, dep. after 12th Feb. 1717.—[*Justiciary Records.*]

1910 JOHN MACLEAN, dem. 17th April 1946; died 26th Oct. 1946.

LOCHBROOM

On Isle Martin there are the ruins of a chapel dedicated to St Martin, and near the ruins a curious gravestone with double arms, said to have been a memorial of the saint.

1569 SIR JOHN MUNRO ALEXANDERSON.—[*Reg. Pres. Bene.*, i, 29.]

1683 JOHN MACKENZIE, adm. 7th June 1683.

1808 THOMAS ROSS, born 10th Dec. 1768, educ. at Marischall College, Aberdeen, M.A. (1796), and divinity at Edinburgh; tutor to Sir James Matheson of the Lewis. His children—Abigail (marr. James Noble, min. of St Oran's Gaelic Chapel, Edinburgh); Alexander, private secretary to President Polk of United States, American Consul at Rio de Janeiro, died at sea 1851; Donald, studied for Church but became merchant in New York; Georgina (marr. John Thomson, D.D., min. of Fourth Presbyterian Church, New York); Lillian, unmarr.; Kenneth, master of *Martin Luther*, died in London 24th Oct. 1855; Thomas; George, manager of Bank of Hindustan at Yokohama; Jane (marr. Angus Polson, merchant, Galt, Canada), died 19th July 1866; Catherine, unmarr.; Anna, unmarr.; Elizabeth (marr. 12th Oct. 1853 William Sinclair, min., Free Church, Plockton), died 31st March 1858; Patrick Campbell, partner in a Commission House, New York.

1895 WILLIAM SUTHERLAND, his widow, Catherine Margaret Clark, died at Edinburgh 30th April 1935.

LOCHCARRON

1582 MURDOCH MURCHISON, pres. 1582.—[*Acts and Dec.*, lv, 253.] (See Lochalsh.)

1587 MURDOCH MACKENZIE, M.A., min., pres. to parsonage 18th July 1582 on death of Alexander the Grudie.—[*Reg. Sec. Sig.*, xlix, 24.]

LOCHCARRON—ULLAPOOL

1923 DONALD MACPHAIL, trans. to Kennethmont 23rd June 1932; trans. to Kilmany 27th June 1935; died 19th April 1942.

PLOCKTON

1918 SAMUEL NICOLSON, died 18th April 1944.

POOLEWE

1889 WILLIAM CAMERON, his widow, Elizabeth Florence Ogilvy, died June 1927.

SHIELDAIG

1861 ALEXANDER AENEAS RANALDSON MACDONELL MACINTYRE, marr. 31st March 1878.

1919 JOHN CURRIE, trans. to Acharacle 6th Nov. 1930; died 29th March 1940.

ULLAPOOL

1920 WILLIAM URQUHART MACNAB, trans. to Kilcalmonell 17th May 1929.

PRESBYTERY OF SKYE

BRACADALE

LAUCHLAN FRASER, ord. by Synod 10th Oct. 1642 to serve at Snizort *per vices* during the vacancy. Line 4, for "1641" read "1643"; dep. 1645. The parish had been vacant for four years in Oct. 1649.—[*Synod of Argyll*.]
1642

JOHN BETHUNE, was min. before 6th July 1667.—[*Rothesay Parish Records*.]
1667

DANIEL MACAULAY, his daugh., Alice (marr. John Macqueen, min. of Snizort).
1708

HUGH BLACK, dem. 12th May 1938.
1920

(*Charges united 17th May* 1938.)

DUIRINISH

FINLAY CORMOCSOUN, held the parsonage and vicarage apparently at and before 1560; died before 1st May 1564.—[*Reg. Sec. Seal*, xxxvi, 8.]
1560

MALCOLM MACPHERSON, pres. to parsonage and vicarage of Duirinish and St Breda, Harris, in succession to Finlay Cormocsoun by the Earl of Argyle 1st May 1564; coll. 18th Dec. 1566; ratification by the Crown 13th Feb. 1566-7.—[*Reg. Sec. Seal*, xxxvi, 8.]
1566

ALAN O'COLGAN, adm. about 1600; trans. to Kilchoan in this parish about 1614.
1600

EWEN MACQUEEN, adm. in 1614; designated Mr Hew MacQueen, min. at Kilvorich (Duirinish); he was charged by the elders at a meeting of the Commission of Synod at Kilvorich on 8th July 1642 with neglect of his elders—"they were in the matter as cyphers," with negligence in preaching, with failure to have any celebration of the Lord's Supper, with the non-appointment of a beadle, and with absence of censure of adulterers and fornicators.—[*Recs. of Synod of Argyle*, 45, S.H.S.; Earls of Cromartie, 37.]
1614

MARTIN MACPHERSON, adm. here about 1644, not 1661.
1644

DUGALD MACPHERSON, adm. before 1667, not 1684.
1667

NORMAN MACLEOD, son of —— M. of Oze.
1717

JOHN MACLEOD, brother of preceding; his son, Roderick, a sea-captain, tacksman of Ballamore, Bracadale in 1760.
1741

DONALD MACLEOD, marr. Anne, daugh. of John Maclean, min. of North Uist. Line 29, for "Alexander" read "Andrew"; for "Balranald" read "Griminish"; line 31, for "Alexandrina" read "Margaret"; line 22, add Alexandrina (marr. (1) Walter Bethune, (2) —— Watson); Catherine (marr. Angus Macdonald of Griminish, N. Uist).—[*Hist. of the Macleods*, 268.]
1754

WILLIAM BETHUNE (or Beaton), marr. Janet, daugh. of John Mackinnon of Glas-na-Kill, Strath (nephew of Lachlan M., the Skye Bard).
1767

JOHN MACGREGOR SOUTER, lines 20-22 read:
"Cuid dhith na Laiduin
Na-h-cabhra 's na Greugais
'S cheud nach tuig each."
1814

DUNCAN McCALLUM, his daugh., Margaret Isabella Anne, died at Edinburgh 8th Jan. 1936.
1844

DONALD MACLEAN, his daugh., Harriet (marr. 1st Oct. 1932 Roderick Matheson Maclean, min. of Grange, Grangemouth); Jane (marr. 20th Jan. 1934 Archibald Macdonald, B.L.); his widow, Harriet Hopkins, died Strathaven 28th Sept. 1948.
1889

LACHLAN MACLEOD, born Bernera, Harris, 10th Nov. 1892; son of Malcolm M., missionary, and Mary Munro; educ. at Univ. of Aberdeen, M.A. (July 1921); served in Great War as Lieut. 7th Cameron Highlanders and was a prisoner of war in West Prussia March to Dec. 1918; Headmaster, Stockinish School, Harris, 1921; ord. to U.F. Church May 1927; adm. to united charge 1928; trans. to Knock 21st Feb. 1930; trans. to St Columba's, Stornoway, 25th Sept. 1935; trans. to Kilmichael, Glenurquhart, 22nd Feb. 1945; adm. to united charge 1st May 1946. Marr. 29th Dec. 1921 Jessie Mary, daugh. of Murdoch Morrison, min. of U.F. Church, Bernera, Harris, and has issue—John Morrison, born 19th Nov. 1922; Mairi Margaret, born 7th Aug. 1924; Muriel Rhoda, born 10th Nov. 1926; Calum Alexander, born 25th July 1935.
1927

HALLIN in WATERNISH

JOHN LAMONT, his daugh., Joanna Elizabeth, died at Inverness 26th Nov. 1933.
1845

RODERICK McINNES, trans. to Uig 26th March 1928.
1924

KILMUIR in TROTTERNISH

ARCHIBALD MACQUEEN, said to have been trans. from Snizort (*q.v.*), but the Synod, May 1643, ordains Presb. to admit him here.—[*Synod Reg.*]
1644

DONALD NICOLSON, marr. (3) Margaret, daugh. of Donald Morrison, min. of Barvas. He had issue— Margaret (marr. her cousin, William Nicolson, in England); Malcolm, M.A., licentiate, but never officiated, was tacksman of Scorrabreck, Portree; Donald, tacksman of Stenscholl, Portree; John, tacksman of Scuddiburgh, Kilmuir; Alexander, min., intruded at Kilmuir 1715; Patrick, min. of Kiltarlity; George, ancestor of James, Dean of Brechin; James; Jane (marr. Lauchlan Mackinnon of Corry); Rachel (marr. 1716 John Macdonald of Culnancnoc); Mary (marr. Alexander Macqueen of Brunistet, son of Archibald M., min. of Snizort); Neil; Margaret (marr. Norman Macdonald of Tetscor); Donald of Stenscholl; Margaret (marr. Donald Macdonald of Scuddiburgh); Janet (marr. Alexander Macdonald of Balranald); John, died young; Jane; William; John; and five others.—[*Clan Donald*, iii, 474; *McLaglan MSS., Glasgow Univ.*; *Scot. Notes and Queries*, 3 Ser., vi, 212; *The Clan Nicolson*, 71.]
1663

DUGALD MACPHERSON, min. in 1667.—[*Rothesay Burgh Register*, i, 303.]
1667

ALEXANDER NICOLSON, son of Donald N., min. of this parish, and Margaret Morrison. Marr. (1) Marion, daugh. of John Macdonald of Castleton, and had issue—Donald, tacksman of Aird, Sleat; John, surgeon in Sleat.
1715

DONALD MACQUEEN, his daugh., Isabel (marr. (1) James Macdonald of Cuidreach, who died of fever in North Carolina in 1780; (2) James Macdonald of Skeabost, merchant, Portree). Line 37, for "Jane" read "Janet"; his son, Donald, tacksman of Ullinish, Bracadale, died 17th April 1786.
1740

ROBERT MACGREGOR, bapt. 10th Oct. 1767; son of Alexander M. in Garth, Fortingall and Margaret Menzies. Marr. 16th Dec. 1804 Janet Menzies, and had issue—Alexander, born 26th May 1806; Margaret, born 31st July 1808; Isabella, born 16th Aug. 1811; Ann Brown, born 1818. He was a Gaelic poet. —[*Trans. of Gaelic Society of Inverness*, xxxiii, 3.]
1822

JOHN MacIVER, his daugh., Alexa, died 28th Sept. 1944.
1851

1926 DONALD ALEXANDER MAC-DONALD, born Iona 21st Sept. 1845, son of John M. and Margaret MacCormack; educ. at Univ. and Free Church College, Glasgow; ord. to Free Church, Fort Augustus, 19th Sept. 1878; trans. to Free Church, Kilmuir, Feb. 1888; became min. of united charge 1926; dem. 15th May 1932; died at Edinburgh 26th Feb. 1934. Marr. 20th Dec. 1898 Frances Charlotte Jean, daugh. of John Ingram, min. of Unst, and had issue—Margaret Augusta, born 9th Dec. 1899, died 15th Feb. 1912; Frances Mabel, born 31st May 1902; Ian Rainy Ingram, M.D., born 9th Oct. 1905; Anne Matilda Macphail Croan, born 15th June 1907, died 11th June 1909.

PORTREE

1727 HUGH MACDONALD, suspended from the exercise of any part of the ministerial function for four full weeks from 27th July 1755 for drunkenness.

1756 JOHN NICOLSON, son of John N. of Scuddiburgh and Una, daugh. of Alexander Macdonald of Flodigarry.

1799 ALEXANDER CAMPBELL, line 2, for "Carelaroch" read "Corlaroch."

1854 HUGH MACARTHUR, his widow, Mary Macgregor, died 29th Oct. 1919.

1894 ALEXANDER BLACK, died 30th Aug. 1936; his wife, Margaret MacDougall, died 6th March 1933.

SLEAT

The first church is said to have been built by a priest called Crotach MacGhillie Gorm—the Hunch-backed son of the Blue Servitor—and a Canon of Beauly. In a battle in a neighbouring field in the 17th century between the Macleods and the MacIntyres the latter were defeated, and they sought refuge in the church. The victors locked the door and, setting fire to the church, burned both it and the MacIntyres. A second church was built by Macdonald of Sleat in 1691, and it now stands a ruin beside the church which replaced it in 1876.—[Barnett's *Autumns in Skye*, 64–5.]

1633 NEIL MACKINNON, translated the Shorter Catechism into Gaelic in conjunction with Angus Macqueen, min. of North Uist, for which he received thanks of Synod of Argyle in 1652. Marr. Janet, daugh. of Donald Macleod of Drynoch. A curious case between him and Kenneth Mackenzie, parson of Sleat, recorded *Reg. of Deeds*, Hay, cccxcvii, 450.

1646 ALEXANDER FRASER, called min. 26th June 1640.—[*Argyll Synod Rec.*]

1669 ANGUS MACQUEEN, dep. by the visitors from the Synod of Argyll in 1695 for "neglecting the catechising for 18 years, being a habitual drunkard and swearer, quitting the singing of Psalms in public worship." His daughs.—Margaret (marr. Roderick Macleod of Gesto); Mary (marr. (1) 15th July 1705 William Macleod of Ferinlea, (2) 7th July 1715, Donald Shaw of Bernisdale, (3) Alexander Macleod of Greshornish); his son, James, writer in Sleat 1723; his daugh., Marion (marr. John Maclean of Muck).—[*Clan Gillean*, 409.]

1726 EDMUND MACQUEEN, delete issue.

1915 KENNETH ROSS, his wife, Margaret Macfarlane, died 18th June 1931. He died 21st June 1939.

SMALL ISLES

1757 MALCOLM MACASKILL, son of John M. of Rhu-an-dunan.—[*Morrison MSS., Stornoway Library.*]

1848 PETER GRANT, his daugh., Isabella (Mrs. Robertson) died at Ringwood, Hants, 26th Dec. 1939, aged 93.

1864 JOHN SINCLAIR, his daugh., Sarah, died Inverness 1st April 1934.

ANGUS MACDONALD, his daugh., Selma, nursing sister, died Glasgow 13th May 1944.
1913

JOHN STEWART, dem. 16th May 1929, died 29th May 1933; his daugh., Agnes, died 7th Feb. 1927.
1926

SNIZORT

ARCHIBALD MACQUEEN, line 4, for "12" read "26"; adm. after 10th Oct. 1642, when the charge was vacant and Synod ord. Lachlan Fraser, min. of Bracadale, to serve *per vices* during the vacancy. Adm. to Kilmuir 1644, but continued to serve here till 1649, receiving half of the stipend.—[*Records of Synod of Argyll*, 47; *Synod Reg.*, May 1650.]
1642

GEORGE MUNRO, settled about 1650.
1650

DONALD MACQUEEN, adm. before 6th July 1667; he marr. (1) a lady, name unknown, and had issue as stated.
1667

ARCHIBALD MACQUEEN, his sons —Murdoch, tacksman of Skirinish, Snizort; Archibald, tacksman of Glentallin; Kenneth, died at Dublin 6th Feb. 1750.
1706

WILLIAM MACQUEEN, delete "born 1718"; died 21st (not 17th) Sept. 1787. Marr. Alice, daugh. of Daniel Macaulay, min. of Bracadale.
1753

MALCOLM MACLEOD, his daugh., Christian (marr. Donald Murchison, Bernisdale, and emigrated to Prince Edward Island).
1786

RODERICK MACLEOD, had issue— Mary, born 1824, died 1851; Donald, born 1826, died 1828; Margaret, born 1829, died 1849; Ann Robertson, born 1831, died 1852; Malcolm, born 1832; Susan MacAllister, born 1833, died 1855; Christina, born 1837, died 1858; Jessie, died at Oban; Isabella, died at Oban; J. W. Lillingston; John, died at Pau 1842; Dr Roderick, died April 1922; Colonel James, C.I.E., V.D., died at Oban April 1919.
1838

ANGUS MARTIN, his son, Nicol of Glendale, died 15th March 1935; his daugh., Mary Isabel, died 17th June 1935.
1844

JOHN MacRURY, line 4, for "as" read "at"; his daughs.—Mairi (marr. 5th Dec. 1929 John Herbert Maclaren, officer of China Navigation Co., Hong Kong); Johanna (marr. 12th April 1935 Magnus Ross Mackay, M.C., M.B., Ch.B.); his widow, Flora Elizabeth Brown, died at Edinburgh 10th Dec. 1945.
1886

DUNCAN MACKENZIE, born Jura 10th Aug. 1873, son of George M. and Catherine MacPhail; educ. Luing school and Rothesay; licen. by Presb. of Lochaber 1927; ord. 6th June 1928; died 5th March 1940. Marr. 6th June 1891 Margaret (died 23rd Nov. 1941), daugh. of Neil Campbell and has issue—John George Campbell, born 27th Aug. 1903; Catherine, born 2nd, died 23rd April 1905; Ian Samuel, born 7th May 1907; Nigel A., min. of Holywood 28th Sept. 1939, born 21st Nov. 1909; Susan Ann, born 9th Dec. 1911.
1928

STENSCHOLL

JOHN NICOLSON, son of Alexander N., innkeeper, Kylerhea, and Abigail Nicolson. He was uncle of Sheriff Alexander Nicolson.
1829

CAMERON MACKAY, died Inverness 13th April 1937; his widow, Caroline D. Macfarlane, died 4th Feb. 1946.
1913

NORMAN LAING, died 27th Sept. 1939.
1924

STRATH

NEIL MACKINNON, see case between him and Kenneth Mackenzie, parson of Sleat.—[*Reg. of Deeds, Hay*, 379, 450.]
1627

DONALD NICOLSON, son of Neil N. and Kate Macdonald, and grandson of Donald N., min. of Kilmuir.
1750

1779 DONALD MACKINNON, born Tarscavaig, Skye. Marr. Catherine, daugh. of Neil Maclean of Kilphedair and granddaugh. of John Maclean of Borerey; his daughs.—Marion (marr. Donald Calder, schoolmaster, Kilmuir); Mary, died 1860.

1856 DONALD MACKINNON, his sons—Lauchlan Kenneth, died at Kilbride, South Yarra, Australia, 24th Aug. 1935; Charles John, resident magistrate, Basutouland, died 27th March 1935; Archibald Donald, died at Hove 5th Sept. 1937.

1914 HECTOR MACLEAN, D.D. (Glasgow, 22nd June 1938); killed in motor accident near Dalwhinnie 30th Nov. 1943; his daughs.—Elizabeth Ramsay (marr. 26th Oct. 1937 Duncan Harold Macneil, M.A., LL.B., solicitor, Inverness); his sons—William, M.B., Ch.B.; Alastair Donald, M.B., Ch.B., Kingussie; his daugh., Mairi Ishbel (marr. 16th July 1942 Robert S. Allison, B.Sc.).

PRESBYTERY OF UIST

BARRA

1813 ALEXANDER NICOLSON, had addl. issue—Jessie (marr. Donald Fraser, son of min. of Kiltarlity); Malcolm, died young; Caroline; Malcolm; Grace Hay.—[*Clan Nicolson*, 78.]

1847 HENRY BEATSON, a daugh. marr. William Donald, purser, *Dunira Castle*, Glasgow.

1871 ARCHIBALD MACDONALD, line 2, for "1843" read "1832"; dem. 15th May 1929; died 1st April 1931.

BENBECULA

1781 DUNCAN FERGUSON, 1781–92.

1792 DUNCAN ROBERTSON, 1792.

1832 WILLIAM BETHUNE, born 20th Dec. 1804, son of Alexander B., min. of Harris.

1869 JOHN MACPHERSON.

1874–5 D. J. MACLEAN.

1878 DUNCAN MacINTYRE.

1881–2 NEIL MACKINNON.

1882 ANGUS J. MACDONALD, adm. to Ullapool 18th June 1884, afterwards of Killearnan.

1896 MURDO MACPHAIL, his daughs.—Ann (marr. 3rd July 1931 John Inwood Forrest, Uphall); Norma (marr. 16th Aug. 1934 Gilbert Sidney Ferliky, London).

BERNERA

1917 NORMAN MORRISON, trans. to Farr 15th Sept. 1927.

1928 MURDO SMITH, born 24th May 1877; ord. U.F. missionary at Strath 1921; trans. and adm. 1928; adm. to united charge of Bernera and Benbecula 5th May 1932; dem. 19th June 1935; died 19th March 1936. Marr. 17th July 1919 Margaret Matheson, and had issue—Peggy Main, born 23rd Nov. 1921; Dora Isabel, born 25th June 1923; Kenneth Donald, born 19th Feb. 1925; Morag Sybil (twin) born 19th Feb. 1925.

HARRIS

1560 FINLAY CORMOCSOUN, held the parsonage and vicarage, apparently at and before 1560; died before 1st May 1564.—[*Reg. Sec. Seal*, xxxvi, 8.]

1566 MALCOLM MACPHERSON, pres. to Duirinish and St Bride's, Harris, in succession to Finlay Cormocsoun by the Earl of Argyle 1st May 1564; coll. 18th Dec. 1566; ratification by the Crown 13th Feb. 1564–7.—[*Reg. Sec. Seal*, xxxvi, 8.]

1625 JOHN MACPHERSON, held Barra in conjunction.

1667 JOHN CAMPBELL, son of Malcolm C. of Strone, factor to Macleod; adm. before 10th July 1667; had issue—Donald, student of Theology under the Synod of Glenelg 1674.

1713 AULAY MACAULAY, had a son, Alexander, student in 1757.

1806 ALEXANDER BETHUNE, his son, William, min. of Benbecula.

1910 JOHN KERR, died 10th July 1930.

NORTH UIST

In the parish there is *Cladh Chomhghani*, "Comgan's Cemetery," indicating that there was a chapel dedicated to that saint.

In 1455 the church was designated St Mary's, Alwasca. The chapel, dedicated to the Holy Trinity, Teampul-ne-Trianaid, with the lands of Karynch (Carinish) and others, was granted to the Abbey of Inchaffray by Christina, daugh. and heiress of Alan and lady of Uist, with confirmation by Reginald, called M'Roary (son of Roderick), lord of Uist, Godfrith of the Isles, lord of Uist, on 7th July 1389, and Donald, lord of the Isles, brother of Reginald, on 6th Dec. 1410.—[*Charters of Inchaffray Abbey*, xlvii, 136, 137; *Cal. Papal Reg.*, Letters, xi, 286; Watson's *Celtic Place Names*, 281.]

JOHN MACLEAN, marr. Ann, daugh. of Donald Macleod, min. of Duirinish.
1708

DONALD MACQUEEN, his son, John, student 1776; his daugh., Margaret (marr. John Maclean, third of Hosta, North Uist).
1755

ALLAN MACQUEEN, line 10, for "Codrum" read "MacOdrum."
1770

JAMES MACQUEEN, line 14, for "officer" read "Captain."
1802

FINLAY MACRAE, line 18, delete "and Balranald."
1818

DONALD MACDONALD, dem. 30th June 1837; died 24th March 1940, unmarr.
1887

ST KILDA

ALEXANDER BUCHAN, he began his work at St Kilda in Aug. 1704, that, according to his own statement, being the date "when I first went to the island"; previous to his advent, the people there did not have "any to instruct them in the principles of the Christian Reformed Protestant Religion, nor any to teach them to read." He returned to this country in Aug. 1709, the reason being "for want of subsistence, there being no settled maintenance for one in his station in that place"; indeed, "he was not in a capacity to go back and continue there except some assurance be given that he will be taken care of." Here it was strongly felt that it would be a serious loss to St Kilda if his services were no longer available for the island; and accordingly efforts were made to induce him to return and resume the work. At the appointment of the Commission of the General Assembly he was ord. by the Presb. of Edinburgh on 15th March 1710. On the following day he pres. to the S.P.C.K. a petition which reveals something of the spirit that animated him. He points out that "the island is much upon my heart, and I have denied myself the ease and other worldly accommodations I might have had elsewhere, to serve the interests of the Gospel in that place"; now that he had been ord. a min. of the Gospel for the use of that island, "in obedience to the call of Providence, the orders of the Reverend Judicatories of the Church, and the Desire of the Honourable Societie, I resolve to return to Hirta and give myself up to His Service in the Gospel of His Sone, being persuaded the Societie will find themselves in dutie and honour obliged to take care that I and my family have a competent subsistence." He then gives expression to his concern about successors to himself in the work, for "my tyme cannot be long in the world, the fatigue and bareness of my diet has brought me low"; realising the difficulty of prevailing upon strangers to go to St Kilda, and anxious to have "some persons bred to succeed me in that place," he "had been at some pains to instruct Finlay McDonald and Murdo Campbell, two natives of that island whom I have been entertaining and learning since August 1704." He had brought them to this country and was keeping them at school for reading, writing and music at his own charges, and as he was about to return to St Kilda, he was anxious to secure the sum of 100 merks to maintain them for a year at the grammar school in Skye. "I thought it my duty for my exoneration to use all proper means to have the Gospel continued in that place after I am dead and gone, and it will ease my mind that I have left this before you." One further matter was set forth in a postscript—"I have procured some books, and charitable persons are giving me more, and I am resolved to leave a catalogue of them with your Secretar and preserve them in the island for the use of my successors." (The catalogue is recorded in the minutes of the Society.) On 30th March 1710 the S.P.C.K. app. him schoolmaster on the island, authorising and empowering him to "erect and keep up a school in the said island, and to teach the inhabitants thereof to read, especially the Holy Scriptures and other good and pious books, as also to teach writing, arithmetick, and such lyke Degrees of Knowledge, and to use such means for instructing the people in the Christian Reformed Protestant Religion as may be proper"; he was further instructed "to be careful of Finlay McDonald and Murdo Campbell and of their education in order to their being useful in the said island." Several promises of financial help were forthcoming, especially from members of the S.P.C.K., who engaged themselves to assist till the Society was in possession of funds for a regular grant. If not then, certainly later, an annual grant was made by the Committee for the Reformation of the Highlands. On 13th April 1710 he settled in the island for the second time. Success attended his labours; but his closing days were darkened by the ravages of smallpox some time between 15th Aug. 1727 and 13th May 1728. According to the report of Mr Daniel Macaulay, min. of Bracadale, who visited St Kilda in 1728, of the 21 families on the island 17 succumbed to the disease, leaving 26 orphans to be supported by the surviving four families. Of those whom Alexander Buchan had taught to read, only two were left. Among the survivors were three men and eight boys, who during the prevalence of the malady were marooned on a rock whence they had gone in Aug. 1727 to catch a loading of young solan geese, the chief food of the island. With his work outwardly ruined, it is small wonder that Alexander Buchan's apparently fragile health gave way. He died in Feb. 1729. His wife, Katherine Campbell, "a poor widow with diverse children," was resident in Edinburgh on 2nd April 1730 when the S.P.C.K. agreed to petition the Barons of Exchequer to have her put on His Majesty's Charity Roll. Two of his sons, George and Dougal, were boarded on 6th Aug. 1728 with Mr Dewar, Schoolmaster, Edinburgh, who recommended to the S.P.C.K. that Dougal be apprenticed to a wright in town. The Society were of the opinion that Dougal be bred to succeed his father in St Kilda.—[*Recs. of S.P.C.K.*, ii, 38, 76, 408; iii, 52, 57–8, 59, 71, 186, 625.]

RODERICK McLENNAN, M.A., was a student of Divinity when app.; ord. apparently in June 1730, and immediately thereafter went to St Kilda.—[*Recs. of S.P.C.K.*, iii, 384, 396, 410.]

ALEXANDER MACLEOD, delete 1755 entry, "same as preceding."

ANGUS MACLEOD, line 16, for 1780 "Royal Navy" read "Army."

LAUCHLAN MACLEOD, line 10, delete "Admiral R.N."; line 12, 1788 after 1877 add "father of Angus, Admiral, R.N."

SOUTH UIST

MARTIN MACPHERSON, trans. to 1642 Duirinish about 1644.

JOHN MACAULAY, nephew of Aulay 1772 M., min. of Harris.

RODERICK MACLEAN, his mother was a daugh. of James Macdonald, 1816 son of the Kingsburgh who befriended Prince Charles; he was at Corrie in Skye when Dr Johnson and Boswell knocked at Mackinnon's hospitable door there.—[See Boswell's *Journal of the Tour to the Hebrides.*]

MALCOLM LAING, trans. to Alness 20th Feb. 1947. Marr. 17th Aug. 1926 1928 Mary Catherine MacRury, Grogary, South Uist, and has issue—Anne Margaret, born 23rd Aug. 1929; Eoghann

MacRuaraidh, born 2nd Feb. 1931; Mairi Catriona, born 15th Nov. 1932; Ranald, born 23rd Dec. 1934; Calum, born 8th Nov. 1936; Christina Kathleen Morag, born 11th Oct. 1938; Mary Normana Agnes, born 9th Nov. 1942.

(*Charge united with Howmore 17th June 1947.*)

TRUMISGARRY

1824 WILLIAM MACQUEEN, marr. Christian Ann, daugh. of William Macleod, tacksman of Fintray, Skye, who survived him.

1873 WILLIAM MACKINTOSH, son of Robert M., teacher, Dunvegan.

PRESBYTERY OF LEWIS

BARVAS

1643 DONALD MORRISON, his daugh., Margaret (marr. Donald Nicolson, min. of Kilmuir.)

1858 JAMES STRACHAN, his daugh., Helen Ross (marr. Dugald Campbell McQuarrie, New Zealand); his son, Peter Donald, M.A., M.D., O.B.E., died at Fort Hare, Alice, South Africa, 7th May 1941.

CROSS

1840 JOHN FINLAYSON, line 1, for "Mugare" read "Mugary."

1905 JOHN MACPHAIL, died 9th Nov. 1934.

KNOCK

1878 DONALD MACKAY, his daughs.—Catherine Hughina, died 23rd Jan. 1937; Jessie (marr. John Newall).

LOCHS

1889 DONALD MACALLUM, died 23rd April 1929.

1921 DUNCAN MATHESON, dem. 31st Aug. 1943; died 25th Dec. 1944. Marr. (2) 12th Dec. 1933 Margaret, daugh. of Donald Macdonald and Annie Macleod.

STORNOWAY

In the Eye peninsula is Eye burying-ground with a Norman chapel dedicated to St Columba.—[*Book of Ross*, 88.]

1689 DANIEL MORRISON, line 2, for "Donald" read "Roderick."

1789 COLIN MACKENZIE, line 18, for "11" read "16."

1924 JOHN KENNEDY MACKENZIE, served in Great War as 2nd Lieut. in 3rd Cameron Highlanders; trans. to Fraserburgh 12th June 1929.

UIG

The church was dedicated to St Coman.—[*Cal. Papal Reg., Letters*, xi, 284.]

1777 HUGH MUNRO, marr. Janet, daugh. of John Macaskill.

1928 RODERICK McINNES, trans. from Hallin-in-Waternish 28th March 1928; suspended by Presb. of Lewis Dec. 1930, having joined Free Presbyterian Church; min. in Lewis 1931–6; re-adm. by General Assembly 24th May 1941. Marr. 30th April 1925 Marion Macaskill, who died Durness 28th May 1944, and had issue—Christina, born 6th March 1926; John, born 3rd April 1930.

SYNOD OF ORKNEY

PRESBYTERY OF KIRKWALL

ST ANDREW'S

1562 GAVIN WATT, reader in 1562 and 1568.—[*Comps. Gen. and Sub Coll. of Thirds, Orkney*, etc.]

1568 ARCHIBALD REID, reader in 1568. (See Holm.)

1582 CUTHBERT HENDERSON, M.A., min. on 5th Dec. 1582.—[*Acts and Dec.*, lv, 289.]

1928 DAVID WILSON BAIRD, trans. from Cross and Burness 19th Dec. 1928; dem. 31st Oct. 1947; his wife, Minnie Anna McKnight Knox, died 21st July 1939. Marr. (2) 1st April 1941 Isabel Macleod Muir; his daughs.—Anne Frances (marr. 1940 William Fern); Agnes Alexandra (marr. Frank Hardy).

BURRAY

1922 ROBERT FORSYTH McGARRITY, trans. to Saughtree 15th Feb. 1929; died at Edinburgh 8th May 1933; his wife, Jeannie Gloag, died 13th May 1935.

(*Charges united 12th Aug.* 1930.)

DEERNESS

1929 HARALD LAMB MOONEY, born 1st Sept. 1906, son of John M., company secretary, and Isabella Jane Barron; educ. at Grammar School, Kirkwall, and Univ. of Edinburgh, M.A. (1926); licen. by Presb. of Kirkwall 1st July 1929; ord. 23rd July 1929; adm. to united charge 8th Sept. 1931.

EVIE and RENDALL

The Church of Evie was dedicated to St Nicholas. Described as "a poor affair, annually thatched with straw," it was deserted in 1788. Chapels in the parish were St Peter's Kirk at Costa, and the Kirk of Norrisdale in Woodwick, the latter apparently being identical with the Virgin Chapel of Woodwick. The Church of Rendall was dedicated to the Virgin Mary; but St Laurence has also been suggested. It was last occupied in 1794, and its ruins are situated in the old churchyard near the shore. North-east of the Hall of Rendall there was a chapel dedicated to St Thomas; and there was also a chapel at Langskail.—[*Procs. Orkney Antiq. Soc.*, iv, 35, vi, 71, vii, 43–4; Neile's *Ecclesiological Notes*, 27.]

1561 DAVID ANDERSON, vicar-pensionary 1564.—[*Comps. Gen. Coll. of Thirds.*]

1566 JOHN STEWART, reader 1566.—[*Comps. Sub Coll. of Thirds, Orkney,* etc.]

1580 ROBERT BLACK, pres. on dem. of Sir John Anderson.—[*Reg. Pres. Bene.*, i, 407.]

1620 HARRY SMYTH, min. in 1620, afterwards of Hoy in 1628.

1621 JAMES MORISON with his wife, Elizabeth Ogilvy, had sasine 22nd May 1676.—[*G. R. Sas.*, 3 Ser., xxxiii, 403.]

1925 DONALD ALLAN CAMERON, his daugh., Ena Macnee, died at Fort Augustus 7th Sept. 1932; his wife, Isabella Jane Macnee, died 25th March 1945.

(*Charges united 10th Feb.* 1931.)

HAM or HOLM

1562 NICOL CRAIGIE, vicar and exhorter 1562.—[*Comps. Gen. Coll. of Thirds.*]

1568 ARCHIBALD REID, reader 1568; also at Deerness.—[*Comps. Sub Coll. of Thirds, Orkney,* etc.]

1570 JOHN STEWART, pres. to vicarage on death of Nicol Craigie.—[*Reg. Sec. Sig.,* xlvii, 31.]

1614 ROBERT STEWART, marr. Anna Paplay and had issue—James; Isabel (marr. 1631 Edward Pottinger, indweller, in Kirkwall).

1688 JAMES GRAHAM, his daugh., Marjory (marr. Andrew Sinclair, shipmaster, Shetland).

1724 WILLIAM MOIR, marr. (1) proc. 7th May 1748.

1895 ANDREW LANG, his widow, Elizabeth Key Balsillie, died at Edinburgh 22nd Feb. 1946.

1915 ALBERT JAMES LAING, died 6th June 1934. Marr. Elizabeth Lawson Low.

(*Charges united 15th March 1945.*)

KIRKWALL

There were in the cathedral other altars with dedications as follows: Our Lady of Pity; the Holy Trinity; St Olaf; St Mary the Virgin in the aisle of St Magnus; St John the Evangelist; St Lawrence; St Catherine; St Duthac; the Holy Cross; St Ninian; St James; St Andrew; St Peter; St Salvator; and St Salvator and St Peter is also given as the dedication of one altar. In the parish church of St Ola there was an altar of Our Lady of Pity, founded in the early part of the 16th century by John Leith, burgess of Kirkwall. At Pickequoy near Kirkwall there was a chapel dedicated to St Duthac, which appears to have been erected by William, third Earl of Orkney.—[*Reg. Great Seal,* iii, 3102, iv, 1758, 2815, v, 1047, 1287, 2265, vi, 44, 1038; *Procs. Orkney Antiq. Soc.,* iv, 30, 32; *Procs. Soc. Antiq. of Scot.,* xvi, 195; *Cal. Scott. Supplications,* 81, S.H.S.]

1561 ROBERT FOWLIE, vicar also at Birsay and Harray 1567.—[*Comps. Sub Coll. of Thirds, Orkney,* etc.]

1567 JOHN STEWART, reader, Kirkwall, pres. to vicarage of St Ola 4th Oct. 1580 on death of Sir John Saidler.

1568 SIR JOHN SAIDLER, pres. to vicarage on death of Sir Magnus Muir.—[*Reg. Pres. Bene.,* i, 21.]

1620 WILLIAM BRUCE, vicar of St Ola and reader.—[*Orkney Sas.,* 124.]

1919 WILLIAM BARCLAY, trans. to Shawlands, Glasgow, 3rd June 1936; his son, Ian Robert Garden, born 1st Nov. 1927; his daugh., Fiona Margaret, born 24th, died 26th April 1932.

SECOND CHARGE

1723 WILLIAM SCOTT, marr. 30th April 1724.

1859 JAMES WALKER, his daugh., Wilhelmina, died 26th Feb. 1949.

RENDALL

1920 JOHN LIVINGSTON MACPHEE, died 12th Sept. 1935; his widow, Katherine Macdonald, died 26th July 1945.

(*Charge united with former U.F. station 8th Dec.* 1936.)

SOUTH RONALDSHAY and BURRAY

1561 THOMAS RATTRAY, vicar and reader 1561–2; also at Shapinshay.—[*Comps. Sub Coll. of Thirds, Orkney,* etc.]

1574 JAMES JOHNSTON, min. of Burray 28th April 1574.—[*Acts and Dec.,* lv, 22.]

1590 WILLIAM HALCRO, line 14, for "Henry" read "Ralph."

PATRICK GORTHY GILRUTH,
1851 assistant at Spynie 1846.

JAMES CAMERON STEEN, marr. (2) 17th June 1926 Catherine McIntosh Sanderson, daugh. of Charles O. R. Omand, and has issue—James Cameron, born 28th June 1927; Letitia Blanche Cameron, born 27th Oct. 1934.
1927

ST MARY'S, SOUTH RONALDSHAY

According to tradition the church was built by one Gallus, who, being expelled from the country, went on board a ship to find asylum elsewhere. In a storm the ship was wrecked, and Gallus jumped upon the back of a sea-monster. In that perilous position he prayed to God and vowed to God that if he reached safety he would build a church in honour of the Virgin Mary. Carried to land by the monster, he fulfilled his vow; and the monster being changed into a stone of its own colour, he placed the stone in the church. Early in the 16th century there was in the church a stone of grey whin 6 × 4 feet, which bore the impress of two naked feet.—[Macfarlane's *Geog. Colls.*, iii, 310.]

ROBERT WALLACE, his widow, Margaret Marr, died 1st Dec. 1933.
1875

JAMES FORBES, his widow, Mary Tough, died 1st Oct. 1932.
1880

THOMAS DONALDSON, trans. to Airth 14th Nov. 1928. Marr. 5th Aug. 1927 Katherine Mary, daugh. of Donald MacLennan, and has issue—Katherine Mary, born 27th Feb. 1929; Elizabeth Alexandrine, born 31st Aug. 1931.
1925

(*Charges united 7th June* 1932.)

PRESBYTERY OF CAIRSTON

BIRSAY

The Church of Birsay, dedicated to Christ, was erected by Earl Thorfinn, *cir.* 1050. It was the church of the bishopric prior to the erection of Kirkwall Cathedral. Earl (St) Magnus, murdered in 1115, was interred in the church, as was also Earl Thorfinn. Subsequently the relics of St Magnus were transferred to St Olaf's Church, Kirkwall, where they were kept till they found a resting-place in the cathedral. On the Brough of Birsay there was a church dedicated to St Peter erected in the 11th century. An earlier church there was dedicated to St Colme.—[*The Orkneyniga Saga*, Pref., xcv–vi, xcviii, 44, 67; *Proc. Orkney Antiq. Soc.*, iii, 24–5.]

ROBERT MAITLAND SOUTER, dem.
1908   13th Jan. 1942, died 21st April 1943.

FIRTH and STENNIS

The Church of Firth was dedicated to the Virgin Mary, as was also the chapel on the island of Damsay. The Church of Stennis was dedicated to the Holy Cross.—[Macfarlane's *Geog. Coll.*, iii, 307; *Proc. Orkney Antiq. Soc.*, iv, 22, 31, v, 51.]

WILLIAM MUREHEAD, pres. to
1560   vicarage 1st Dec. 1579 on death of Sir James Layng.—[*Reg. Pres. Bene.*, i, 25.]

HENRY COLVILLE, brother to
1580   Robert C. of Cleish, pres. to vicarage of Orphir and Stennis 6th June 1580 on death of Magnus Halcro, and to parsonage and vicarage 30th July 1580.—[*Reg. Pres. Bene.*, i, (4), 35, 38.]

ANDREW GRAHAM, marr. Christian,
1782   daugh. of John Scott in Kirkwall, and had issue—Janet, born 24th Feb. 1727; Elspeth, born 8th Feb. 1728; James, born 9th July 1729; John, born 17th April 1731.

PETER BARR REID, dem. 9th Nov.
1918   1927; died at Ayr 23rd May 1941; his widow, Letitia Caskey, died 15th April 1947.

ALEXANDER BURNETT, born 18th
1929   Feb. 1873; son of Andrew B., Kiltarlity, and Mary Macdonald; educ. at Raining School, Inverness; on Blantyre Mission Staff, Nyasaland, 1900–25; on home service with Foreign Mission Committee 1925–9; licen. by Presb. of Cairston 12th June 1929; ord. 22nd June 1929. Marr. 25th Aug. 1905 Jessie Barclay (died 27th May 1938), daugh. of James Dewar, and had issue—Andrew Ian, born 24th Oct. 1906, min. of Newhaven 1931; trans. to Springburnhill 31st March 1937; James Alexander, born 12th Feb. 1909; Robert Dewar, born 31st July 1913. Marr. (2) 11th April 1940 Sarah Kate Clappen, Cropstown, Leicester.

(*Charges united 1st Aug.* 1945.)

HARRAY and BIRSAY

ROBERT FOWLIE, min. in 1562;
1562   archdeacon of Orkney.—[*Comps. Sub Coll. of Thirds, Orkney*, etc.]
(See Kirkwall.)

WILLIAM DAVIDSON, had been
1666   blind fourteen years 1687.—[*P. C. Reg.*, 3 Ser., 13, xx, xliii, xlviii.]

JOHN GARSON, his son, John George,
1841   M.D., Ewell, Surrey, died 31st May 1932.

WILLIAM JOHN STEELE DICKEY,
1895   his widow, Elizabeth Rachel Ferguson, died Kella, Co. Londonderry, 9th July 1936; his daugh., Mabel Elizabeth

Anne (Mrs Allison), died Belfast 9th Sept. 1946.

1922 GEORGE FREDERICK COX, app. Clerk to Presb. of Orkney March 1930.

(*Charges united 1st Feb.* 1946.)

HOY

In the parish there was a chapel dedicated to St Columba.—[*Reg. Mag. Sig.*, iv, 2472.]

1562 JOHN MOLYSON, vicar pensioner and reader 1562-8.—[*Comps. Gen. and Sub Coll. of Thirds, Orkney*, etc.]

1688 JAMES STRACHAN, marr. Beatrix Gordon.—[*Orkney Sas.*, vi, 31, 1697.]

1698 ALEXANDER MAIR, marr. 23rd May 1695.

1895 JAMES DUNCAN ANDERSON, died 9th Dec. 1937.

ORPHIR

1560 MAGNUS HALCRO of Brugh, natural son of Andrew H.; he died before 1580; his natural daugh., Jonet, on 31st March 1587 received Royal Letters of Legitimation which willed that her sons Henry and Robert Elphingstone be the heirs of said Jonet and her father, Magnus.—[*Reg. Great Seal*, v, 1045, 1177, vii, 159.]

1580 HENRY COLVILLE, pres. 1580 on death of Magnus Halcro.—[*Reg. Pres. Bene.*, i, (4), 35.]

1610 PATRICK WATERSTON, his mother, Margaret Fairlie.

1698 EDWARD IRVINE, son of Patrick I. of Lee in Quholm, Orkney.—[*Orkney Sas.*, 16th July 1712, 13th Dec. 1715.]

1927 JAMES SABISTON, born Flotta 26th Jan. 1882; son of Gavin S. and Janet Sutherland; educ. at Flotta Public School and Church of Scotland Normal College, Aberdeen; schoolmaster, Tain; missionary, Blantyre Staff, Nyasaland; served in R.N.V.R. in German East Africa in Great War; schoolmaster, Tankerness; licen. by Presb. of Cairston 27th July 1927; ord. 30th Aug. 1927; trans. to Bourtie 3rd Feb. 1933; died 9th Nov. 1938. Marr. 11th Nov. 1909 Jean Ann, daugh. of Joseph Simpson, farmer, and had issue—Kenneth, born 15th Nov. 1910; Mary, born 17th Sept. 1912; James, born 11th Sept. 1915; Louis, born 8th Jan. 1921; Ernest Bowman, born 17th April 1925.

SANDWICK

1904 JAMES RAE MURDOCH, dem. 11th Nov. 1935; died 22nd Feb. 1938; his son, James Rae, assistant St Mark's, Dundee, drowned 4th March 1937.

(*Charges united 14th Jan.* 1936.)

STENNIS

The Church of Stennes was dedicated to the Holy Rood. The Church of Firth was dedicated to the Virgin, and the same dedication pertained to the chapel on the isle of Damsay. The present church was erected in 1813. In the village of Finstown there was a chapel called the "Black Chapel."—[*Procs. of the Orkney Antiq. Soc.*, iv, 22, 31, v, 51, 53, 54; Macfarlane's *Geograph. Colls.*, iii, 307.]

1889 GEORGE RAYMOND MURISON, died 12th Feb. 1931; his daugh., Isabel Heriot Gordon (marr. 14th Aug. 1930 Victor Stewart Clouston, bank accountant); his widow, Jeanie Moir Irvine, died at Aberdeen 21st Jan. 1946.

(*Charge united with former U.F. Mission Station 12th Feb.* 1935.)

SANDWICK and STROMNESS

The chapel in the township of Yesnaby was situated about 100 yards from the shore at the Noust of Bigging, where there are traces of a churchyard. It appears to have been identical with the Chapel of St Bride near Forsewell.—[*Procs. Orkney Antiq. Soc.*, iii, 27.]

1561 ANDREW WHYTE, reader.

JOHN DUNCANSON, M.A.—[*Comps.*
1561 *Sub Coll. of Thirds, Orkney*, etc.]

JOHN GARDYNE, min. before 6th
1619 March 1619.

THOMAS DANIEL WINGATE, his
daugh., Helen Murray, died at Lyn-
1865 stone, Exmouth, 29th Dec. 1940; his
son, John Bruce of Sumburgh, died 8th
Sept. 1939.

JOHN MAIR HUTCHEON, had issue
—William Douglas, born 23rd Nov.
1925 1916; Isabella Nora, born 27th June
1918 (marr. 4th July 1942 Alexander
Thomson Smith, M.A., B.Com.); Laura
Ella, born 4th Nov. 1922; Raymond, born
27th Sept. 1925; Robert Mackinnon, born
27th Sept. 1925.

WALLS and FLOTTA

JOHN MOLYSON, vicar pensioner and
1562 reader.—[*Comps. Gen. and Sub Coll.
of Thirds, Orkney*, etc.]

ADAM MOODIE, min. here when
1577 pres. in 1577.—[*Reg. Pres. Bene.*,
i, (4), 58.]

JOHN KEITH, had issue—Ann, bapt.
8th June 1708; Archibald, bapt. 12th
1707 June 1709; Jean, bapt. 8th March
1711; Edward, bapt. 12th Feb. 1712;
Charles, bapt. 21st Oct. 1713; Isabella,
bapt. 7th March 1715.

**LOUIS CLARENCE DUNCAN
DOUGLAS**, dem. 15th Nov. 1926;
1918 adm. to Murthly 16th Feb. 1928.

PRESBYTERY OF THE NORTH ISLES

CROSS and BURNESS

There was in the parish a chapel dedicated to St Augustine.—[*Proc. Orkney Antiq. Soc.*, iv, 34.]

1560 WILLIAM PIERSON, designated reader April 1577.—[*Reg. Mag. Sig.*, v, 1047.]

1657 WILLIAM COCHRANE, assistant, Aberdour, Fife, 1656–7.—[*Ross's Aberdour and Inchcolm*, 231–4.]

1704 MURDOCH MACKENZIE, marr. Janet Thomson.—[*Orkney Sas.*, vii, 217.]

1866 MATTHEW FISHER, his son, Harold, died Aug. 1937.

1925 DAVID WILSON BAIRD, trans. to St Andrew's 19th Dec. 1928.

EDAY and FARAY

1920 DAVID SUTHERLAND, died 28th Oct. 1935.

(*Charges united 9th June* 1931.)

LADY

1568 JOHN GRAHAM, parson 18th Sept. 1568; rector 9th April 1586 and 12th May 1587.—[*Cal. of Charters*, x, 2129; *Reg. Mag. Sig.*, v, 1220.]

1585 ALEXANDER CLUNE, pres. 23rd April 1585.—[*Reg. Pres. Bene.*, ii, 133.]

1585 JAMES COCK, marr. Jean Sinclair.—[*Reg. House Charters*, x, 8th May 1596.]

1635 THOMAS COCK, marr. Janet Scollay.—[*Charter and Sas.*, 1628, *Orkney and Shetland Documents.*]

1647 PATRICK WEMYSS, described as having "for many years been put from his charge for his loyalty and affection to His King's Majestie," "with his wife and children forced to live on charity of good people," he received from Parliament on 6th June 1662 a grant of the vacant stipend of Lasswade for crop and year 1659.—[*Acts Scott. Parl.*, vii, 375.]

1675 THOMAS LYALL, had issue—Mr Thomas; Robert.—[*Deeds Dal.*, 1706, No. 849.]

1900 JOHN HARDIE PEARSON, his widow, Mary McCririck, died 26th Nov. 1931.

1919 HENRY SMITH, died 11th May 1932; his daughs.—Jane Mary Cruickshank, died 23rd Nov. 1929; Cecilia, died 2nd July 1919.

(*Charges united 14th March* 1933.)

NORTH RONALDSHAY

1585 CUTHBERT HENDERSON, M.A., was min. here in 1585, when James Cock, M.A., was alleged to be min. of the same.—[*Acts and Dec.*, 135, 281, 15th and 16th June 1592.]

1908 WILLIAM RICHMOND SCOTT, dem. 26th June 1929; died at Tarbrax, West Calder, 30th Nov. 1944.

(*Charges united 12th May* 1931.)

PAPA WESTRAY

1911 MATTHEW RICHMOND, died 19th Jan. 1944.

ROUSAY and EGILSAY

The Church of Rousay was probably dedicated to the Virgin Mary. The Chapel of St Peter, called "Cobbie Rows Chapel," on the Island of Weira, probably of 12th and 13th century, may have been built by Bishop Bear in 1188–1223, son of Kolbein Hruga.

The Church of Egilsay was probably built after the conversion of the Norsemen in 998. The upper chamber of the chancel was doubtless the priest's room, but traditionally it is said to have been used as a prison. That is said to account for its title, "the Grief House." But that designation may have been bestowed upon it because the body of Earl Magnus had been laid there after his assassination by the followers of his cousin Hakon at a conference called by the Bishop on the Isle of Egilsay for the purpose of composing the difference between the cousins. A proposal has been made to restore the church.—[*Procs. Orkney Antiq. Soc.*, ii, 19; *Orkneyinga Saga*, xcvi, xcvii.]

THOMAS BENSTOUN, vicar and min. 1561—[*Comps. Gen. Coll. of Thirds.*]

LAURENCE YOUNG, parson and reader 1561.—[*Comps. Gen. Coll. of Thirds.*]
1561

JOHN BALFOUR, vicar 1568. (See Westray.)
1568

DAVID WATSON, marr. cont. 21st and 22nd June 1630 Janet, daugh. of James Stewart of Graemsay and Helen Monteith of Egilshay.—[*Perth Sas.*, 2 Ser., iv, Aug. 1636.]
1626

ALEXANDER SPARK, his widow, Jane Hannah Reid, died 14th Jan. 1940.
1885

RODERICK FRASER, trans. to Lintrathen 30th Sept. 1925.
1923

(*Charges united 15th Nov.* 1932.)

SHAPINSAY

THOMAS RATTRAY, vicar and reader 1561-2. (See South Ronaldsay.)
1561

DUNCAN COLQUHOUN KERR, his widow, Penelope Charlotte Campbell Grandison, died 7th Oct. 1932.
1898

ROBERT HILL RICHMOND, trans. to Coull 4th July 1928.
1920

(*Charges united 9th May* 1933.)

STRONSAY

There was a chapel dedicated to St Salvator, the patronage of which was held by the family of Halcro of that ilk. The endowment included "the nine-penny land of Grobustar, with three towmales of Grobustar."—[*Cal. Laing Charters*, 1836, 2502.]

JAMES MAXWELL, M.A., pres. 11th March 1540-1 to the Altar of St Catharine in Kirkwall Cathedral in succession to Sir John Maxwell.—[*Reg. Sec. Seal*, ii, 3893; *Reg. Great Seal*, v, 1287.]
1569

ALEXANDER SOMERVILLE, eldest son of William S., merchant, Edinburgh; adm. burgess of Edinburgh 28th June 1643.
1635

WILLIAM ELMSLIE WILKIE BROWN DEMPSTER, died at Slamannan 1st March 1933.
1901

ROBERTSON MILLER, formerly of Tewchar (*q.v.*), adm. 6th Feb. 1929; dem. 14th July 1931; adm. to charge in Presb. Church of Canada.
1929

(*Charges united 10th Nov.* 1931.)

WESTRAY

In 1585 it is narrated there is no such kirk as the Cross Kirk of Westray, but the Cross parsonage is assigned to the min. there.—[*Comps. Gen. Coll. of Thirds.*]

WILLIAM ANNAND, M.A., pres. to parsonage of Cross Kirk of Westray 5th Dec. 1566, ratified 26th April 1569 on death of Alexander Scott.—[*Reg. Pres. Bene.*, i, 21.]
1566

1568	JOHN BALFOUR, vicar in 1568, also at Rousay.—[*Comps. Sub Coll. of Thirds, Orkney*, etc.]
1626	DAVID WATSON, marr. cont. 21st and 22nd June 1630 Janet, daugh. of James Stewart of Graemsay and Helen Monteith.—[*Perth Sas.*, v, 59, 90.]
1699	WILLIAM BLAW, had issue—James; Janet (marr. James Spence, N.P.); Sarah (marr. Thomas Loutit of Lyking); Elizabeth (marr. Thomas Mackenzie of Noup); Jean (marr. Andrew Cowan, min. of this parish); Marion (marr. William Manson, Notary); Barbara, unmarr.; Ann, unmarr.; Thomas; William; Marjory (marr. Thomas Traill of Tirlot).

SYNOD OF SHETLAND

PRESBYTERY OF LERWICK

BRESSAY, BURRA and QUARFF

1560 ALEXANDER KINCAID, was vicar some time of Burra subsequent to 1560. (See Walls.)

1567 JOHN MacQUHAILL, reader in 1567 and 1568.—[*Comps. Sub Coll. of Thirds, Orkney*, etc.]

1715 JOHN DUNCAN, his son, John, apprenticed to James Hunter, wright, Edinburgh, 26th June 1734.

(*Charge united with St Olaf's, Lerwick, 21st Oct. 1945.*)

DUNROSSNESS

In Pitcairn's Report of the Revenues of the Parochial Benefices of Shetland early in the 17th century there are enumerated under Dunrossness four churches, St Matthew, St Magnus, St Colme, and St Paul, corresponding to Dunrossness, Sandwick, Cunningsburgh, and Fair Isle. Each of the churches of Dunrossness and Fair Isle was designated the Cross Kirk. That might indicate that they were dedicated to the Holy Rood. It may be, however, that the designation arose from the cruciform shape of the buildings, and that, as indicated, the respective dedications were St Matthew and St Paul. Dunrossness Church was situated near the sea at Quendale till 1790, when a new church was built some distance away. Within the church there was a chaplainry called the Prebend or Chaplainry of the Cross Stouk, of which in 1578 David Sinclair was perpetual prebendary. "St Peter's Stowke" on the Fair Isle may indicate some ecclesiastical revenue or, more probably, a small building attached to the church with an altar dedicated to St Peter. From 1593 Sandwick was attached to Dunrossness.—[*Procs. Soc. of Antiq. of Scot.*, xvi, 197, xviii, 295, 297, 298, 302; Mill's *Diary of Shetland*, 195; *Reg. Great Seal*, v, 1723.]

1561 GEORGE BELLENDEN, vicar 1561.—[*Comps. Gen. Coll. of Thirds.*]

1569 WALTER ECHLINE, M.A., pres. to vicarage 14th Jan. 1569 on death of George Bellenden.—[*Reg. Sec. Sig.*, 14th Jan. 1569.]

1570 ALEXANDER THOMSON, M.A., pres. to vicarage 24th Nov. 1570 on death of Henry Echline.—[*Reg. Pres. Bene.*, i, (2), 11.]

1574 JOHN DRYNNANE (Drennan), M.A., pres. to vicarage 4th April 1574 on death of Alexander Thomson.—[*Reg. Pres. Bene.*, i, (4), 18.]

1575 MALCOLM SINCLAIR, pres. on death of John Kingson.—[*Reg. Pres. Bene.*]

1869 WILLIAM BRAND, his daugh., Mary, died at Corstorphine 12th March 1930.

1927 MILLAR OGILVIE, trans. to Rattray 16th May 1929.

FAIR ISLE

1731 JAMES WILLIAMSON, line 4, for "1744" read "11th Sept. 1739."

LERWICK

1740 THOMAS MILLER, his son, William, died in Jamaica 24th Oct. 1791.

WILLIAM MARSHALL TAIT, died 1st March 1931. Marr. (2) 13th June 1928 Constance Margaret Woods; his daugh., Isabel Mary, secretary, St Marylebone Hospital; his son, Herbert, in Indian Civil Service. — 1910

ARCHIBALD MACINTYRE, dem. 16th May 1933; his daugh., Ruby (marr. 17th Dec. 1937 David Darby Palmer, Colonial Service, Malaya). — 1918

QUARFF

DAVID JOHNSTONE, his daugh., Gertrude, died 24th Sept. 1936; his son, David, bank accountant, Union Bank, died at Whitehills Manse, Grange, 23rd Jan. 1942. — 1882

JOHN LOVE, died at Edinburgh 28th Jan. 1932. — 1910

CHARLES DAVIDSON, died 12th Aug. 1930; his widow, Sarah Lindsay Neill, died 4th Nov. 1930. — 1917

SANDWICK

CHARLES NAIRNE BALDIE, his widow, Elizabeth Powrie, died at Glasgow 3rd Dec. 1930. — 1885

TINGWALL, ETC.

The Church of Whiteness was dedicated to St Ola, and was known as St Ola's Chair. The Church of Weisdale was dedicated to the Virgin Mary. Of old it was much frequented by people who held the belief that by making an offering at the shrine of Our Lady they would be delivered from any trouble under which they were labouring. Tradition tells that the inception of the church was due to two wealthy ladies, who, overtaken by a storm at sea, made a vow to Our Lady that if deliverance was vouchsafed to them they would in honour of her erect a church at the spot when they landed. Weisdale was the place of their deliverance; and at once they proceeded to fulfil their vow. Each morning, it is further stated, the masons engaged on the construction of the building found at the site as many stones as they required during the day. In Tingwall parish there was a chapel dedicated to St Giles with an endowment of lands in the town of Ousta extending to 24 merks of the land, with *le skattis*, Hoiswick, Cunnisburg, Quarfe, and Uterbuster, and also the island of *lie Holm* of Ousta.—[*Reg. Great Seal*, v, 1045.]

JEROME CHEYNE, vicar, archdeacon of Zetland.—[*Comps. Gen. Coll. of Thirds.*] — 1561

JOHN MITCHELL, died before 6th Aug. 1659.—[*Shetland Sas.*, iii, 363.] — 1629

DAVID ALBERT MURDOCH, trans. to Newton on Ayr 14th Nov. 1928. — 1924

JOHN MARSHALL, born 1st Dec. 1897, son of Henry M. and Mary Elizabeth Grace Margaret Rogers; educ. at Whitehaven School and Univ. of Edinburgh, M.A. (1928); teacher in Egypt 1920–4 and Edinburgh; licen. by Presb. of Lerwick 10th May 1929; assistant Inveresk 1927; ord. 10th May 1929; trans. to Crieff West 14th Oct. 1931; dem. 26th March 1936; adm. to Hanley Presbyterian Church, Staffordshire, 1937. Marr. 11th July 1921 Jane Ann, daugh. of James Rose Macpherson, min. of Dingwall. — 1929

WHITENESS

WILLIAM GORDON, his son, William Andrew, schoolmaster, Crathes, died 28th Oct. 1933, aged 31. — 1882

CHARLES LEYS, dem. 12th Nov. 1935; adm. to Rothes High 29th Jan. 1936; died 7th Dec. 1943. — 1926

PRESBYTERY OF BURRAVOE

FETLAR

JOHN REID, vicar 1560, died 1562.
1560

WILLIAM LAUDER, M.A., notary public at Kirkwall 1560, pres. by Bishop Adam Bothwell to prebendary of Woodwick, in Orkney and Fetlar, 1563; had also charge of Unst 1567-74 and Yell in 1567; was chamberlain of the Bishop and was imprisoned at Edinburgh in 1569 for non-production of his accounts; res. vicarage of Yell in 1592 and probably died shortly thereafter. Marr. Elspeth Kennedy, who survived him and was alive in 1604, and had issue—James, min. of Yell; Thomas; and possibly Abraham.
1562

MATTHEW LITSTER, pres. 14th Oct. 1574 to vicarage, reader here and in Yell.
1574

JAMES LAUDER, vicar in 1593 here and in Yell.
1593

JOHN BONAR, his son, William, apprenticed to Andrew Bruce, merchant, Edinburgh, 28th Nov. 1744.
1729

JAMES ARCHIBALD CAMPBELL, his widow, Eliza Wallace Hunter, died at Lerwick 1st Dec. 1938; his son, James, M.B., Ch.B., Aberdeen, Lieut. R.A.M.C., served in Macedonia 1918-19.
1881

WILLIAM GRAHAM CARSON, born Auldearn 1891, son of James C., schoolmaster, and Jessie Grant; became schoolmaster at Olnafirth School, Voe, 1911; assistant Lerwick Central School 1913-15; educ. at Univ. of Glasgow, M.A.; missionary and assistant in St Paul's, Glasgow; ord. 25th Sept. 1922; died on board *Earl of Zetland* steamer 11th Sept. 1937. Marr. 30th June 1923 Janet Houston, daugh. of Alexander Hill, writer, Glasgow, and Annie Park, and had issue—Annie Park, born 1924; Janet Grant, born 6th May 1928; James Grant, born 19th Dec. 1935.
1924

UNST

The Lady Kirk of Aluastel occurs on 13th Nov. 1455.—[*Transcripts from Vatican*, iii, *MS., Gen. Reg. House.*]

SIR ANDREW HILL, vicar in 1528, held office at Reformation but doubtful if he conformed; was vicar 15th June 1560; died after 27th July 1567.—[*Cal. of Charters*, ix, 1844.]
1560

WILLIAM LAUDER, min. of Fetlar (*q.v.*), had also charge here.
1567

FRANCIS BOTHWELL, designated perpetual vicar 12th Nov. 1572; nephew of bishop.—[*Reg. Mag. Sig.*, v, 2389.]
1568

JAMES HAY, pres. 1574 on death of Francis Bothwell; dep. for non-residence 1592.—[*Reg. Pres. Bene.*, i, (4), 28.]
1574

PETER MAXWELL, min. in 1585, afterwards min. of Fetlar.
1585

ALEXANDER CRAIG, intruded at Fraserburgh, where, on 11th June 1706, he was deprived by Privy Council.—[*P. C. Acta*, 11th June 1706.]
1683

JOHN HAY, his sons—William, apprenticed to William Mein, merchant, Edinburgh, 25th April 1744; Thomas, apprenticed to Patrick Henderson, merchant, Edinburgh, 22nd Aug. 1744.
1720

JOHN INGRAM, his daugh., Caroline Augusta, died 20th Jan. 1944.
1838

1869 WILLIAM SMITH, his son, Laurence Dundas, LL.B., died at Winnipeg 17th Nov. 1925.

(*Charges united* 1*st Jan.* 1931.)

MID YELL

1562 JAMES FALLOWSDAILL, son or brother of David F., prebendary of Kirkwall, was vicar of Yell in 1542 and joined the reformed church in 1560, but was only app. reader; died before 14th Oct. 1574; had issue—David of Lumbister and probably Janet in Windhouse in 1600.

1574 MATTHEW LITSTER, reader here and in Fetlar, 1574-9.

1593 PETER MAXWELL, min. here and in Fetlar.

1592 JAMES LAUDER, M.A., son of William L., min. of Fetlar, pres. to vicarage 1st Feb. 1592-3 on resignation of his father.—[*Reg. Sec. Sig.*, lxv, 12.]

1844 JAMES BARCLAY, his daugh., Mary Isabella Buist, died 29th May 1937.

1918 GEORGE ALBYN DOUGLAS LAURIE, died unmarr. 11th July 1928.

SOUTH YELL

1876 JOHN WATSON, his widow, Grace Reid, died 3rd May 1936.

1920 ANDREW NOBLE SCOTT, his widow, Jessie A. N. Macmanus, died 21st Nov. 1942.

PRESBYTERY OF OLNAFIRTH

DELTING

1573 JOHN DENOON, pres. in 1573 on death of Donald ——.—[*Reg. Pres. Bene.*, i, (4), 17.]

1589 ROBERT WOOD, M.A., pres. to vicarage 20th June 1589 on death of John Denoon.—[*Reg. Sec. Sig.*, lx, 21.]

1846 JOHN DUNCAN McINTYRE, his daughs.—Elizabeth Harrison, died 6th Aug. 1932; Andrienne Alexandra, died Levenhall 25th Jan. 1940.

1920 KENNETH ALEXANDER MACLEAY, died 26th Dec. 1931; his second wife divorced. Marr. (3) 22nd Nov. 1928 Christian MacIntyre.

1926 JOHN McLAREN WILSON, dem. 11th June 1929.

NESTING

1567 ALEXANDER SPITTAL, his pres. printed in *Proc. Soc. Antiquaries* (N.S.), iv, 198, 20th April 1882, and in *Antiquities of Shetland*, 147.

1847 ALEXANDER WATSON SHAND, his son, James, died at Broughty Ferry 8th Nov. 1929.

1924 JOHN HENDERSON MACKENZIE, adm. to Carfin 30th July 1929.

LUNNA

1900 WILLIAM STABLES SMITH, died at Edinburgh 30th March 1939.

NORTHMAVINE

There was in the parish "ane small Stowk called 'St Michael's Stowk.'"—[*Proc. Soc. of Antiq.*, xviii, 297.]

1577 ALEXANDER LAWSON, reader, pres. to vicarage 11th July 1577 and 1st March and 22nd Sept. 1578 on death of Sir John Gifford.—[*Reg. Pres. Bene.*, i, (4), 587.]

1579 JAMES PITCAIRN, pres. in 1579 on death of Sir John Gifford and also 19th Nov. 1578 on dem. of Alexander Lawson.—[*Reg. Pres. Bene.*, ii, 9.]

1889 JOHN MACDONALD, his widow, Mary Armstrong Peck, died 9th Jan. 1933.

SANDSTING and ARTHSTING

It is said that men saved from the wreck of the Spanish Armada in 1588, in gratitude for their preservation and for the kindness shown them here, built a church at Sand about a mile and a half from the holm, and dedicated it to the Virgin Mary. When the Reformation reached Sandsting about 1600, the church was used by the Protestants, and in 1760–70 it was allowed to become a ruin. In addition to the church at Sand in Sandsting there was a church at Twatt in Aithsting, and their place was taken by a central church in 1780.

1864 WILLIAM ROSE, his sons—Alfred Ernest, died at Park Vale, Carterton, New Zealand, 10th Nov. 1928; James, W.S., Depute Town Clerk, Rothesay, died 7th March 1941; William John, died Edinburgh 21st Oct. 1942; Thomas Montford Adie, died Edinburgh 31st Jan. 1943; his daugh., Wilhelmina Adie, died 2nd Nov. 1943.

1909 JOHN MACLEAN, dem. 30th June 1931, died at Edinburgh 2nd Jan. 1936; his son, Hugo Baillie, D.D., min. of Queen Street, Broughty Ferry, 11th

April 1938; his widow, Jessie Lindsay Armstrong, died 24th Nov. 1939; his son, Herbert Stewart, min. of Coldstream West and Galston.

WALLS and SANDNESS

1564 MAGNUS MURRAY, vicar; this may refer to Walls in Orkney.

1567 ALEXANDER KINCAID, sometime servitor to the Bishop 1580 and to the Earl of Orkney, vicar here before 23rd March 1567–8 and also of Bressay and Burra, died after 2nd April 1587.—[*Reg. Mag. Sig.*, v, 80, 1181; *Proc. Soc. of Antiq. of Scotland*, xviii, 296.]

1885 ROBERT ANDREW, died at Edinburgh 3rd May 1944; his daugh., Vaila (marr. 31st July 1935 Alexander Sutherland Mowat, M.A., Professor, Dalhousie College, Halifax, Nova Scotia). Addl. issue—Theodore Philip Simpson Stewart, born 6th Nov. 1930; Allan Urquhart, born 14th June 1933.

1926 THEODORE ANDREW, trans. to Chapelshade, Dundee, 20th March 1930; trans. to Kineff 21st Sept. 1933; trans. to Torthorwald 10th Oct. 1946.

WHALSAY

1876 CHARLES STOBIE, died at Ferryport-on-Craig Manse 9th Dec. 1935.

1917 MATTHEW DON, died 15th June 1930. His estate of £4,000 fell to the Crown *ultima haeres*.

1927 ANGUS MACKAY, line 4, for "Luxmore" read "Luxmoore"; M.A., St Andrews (1923); dem. 26th Nov. 1935; died at Cambridge 13th May 1943. Marr. (1) 5th July 1928 Emily Brown, M.A., daugh. of Alexander, architect, Aberdeen, and Marjory Brown; she died 7th Aug. 1929; (2) 9th Oct. 1930 Edith Gerard, daugh. of George Storry and Edith Gerard.

ARCHBISHOPS

GLASGOW

JAMES BOYD, had a daugh., Janet.
1578

WALTER STEWART, delete from "Having done so," etc., to "Vol. iii, 352." Afterwards Lord Treasurer, created Lord Blantyre 1606; died 8th March 1617.
1587

PATRICK LINDSAY, his wife, Helen Whitelaw, buried at Deane, Lancashire, 14th March 1642.—[*Scot. Notes and Queries*, 3 Ser., viii, 118.]
1635

JOHN PATERSON, was a prisoner in Edinburgh Castle 21st Jan. 1692; his son, Alexander, writer, adm. burgess of Edinburgh 10th Sept. 1708; his daugh., Alice, marr. Oct. 1688.—[*Laing Charters*, 2894.]
1687

ST ANDREWS

GEORGE GLEDSTANES, had issue, George.
1604

BISHOPS

ABERDEEN

1600 PETER BLACKBURN, held the lands and barony of Dyce, and also part of the lands of Endowie, Alford; proclamation of marriage with Isabel Johnston 13th Oct. 1586; his son, Peter, served heir to his father 17th July 1616, in lands and barony of Dyce and in Meikle Endowie and died in (buried in the "auld kirk," Aberdeen, 9th Oct.) 1619; his son, William, M.A., burgess of Aberdeen, was served heir to his brother Peter, in part of Endowie, 30th Nov. 1619; his daugh., Isabel, apparently identical with Isabel Blackburn, wife of James Rait, min. of Aberlethnot; if Archibald Blackburn, min. of St Nicolas', Aberdeen, was a son, he was born of an earlier marriage.—[*Aberdeen Reg.*; *Retours*, vi, 115, 140, vii, 183; *Aberdeen Sas.*, i, 164 (1601), ii, 168 (1620), v, 231 (1626), ix, 180 (1635); *Kincardine Sas.*, i, 133 (1603).]

1618 PATRICK FORBES OF CORSE, line 9, delete "and Oxford"; 2 col., line 7, delete "of Corse"; line 14, add "A later translation was made by his son, John, 1646"; delete lines 16 and 17 and "(Middleburg 1614)"; line 24, for "Calderwood's Hist., iv" read "(Middleburg, 1614)." He had also a son, William, M.A. —[*Aberdeen Sas.*, v, 231, 232.]

1664 PATRICK SCOUGALL, his son, John, buried Old Machar 30th March 1681.

ARGYLL

1666 WILLIAM SCROGGIE, had also issue —Patrick, born 26 Sept. 1666.— [*Old Machar Register*; *G. R. Sas.*, 3 Ser., xxxiii, 426, 27th May 1674.]

BRECHIN

1635 WILLIAM WHITEFORD, his son, Adam, adm. burgess of Edinburgh 31st March 1637.

1682 GEORGE HALIBURTON, born 1635, M.A., St Andrews (17th June 1652); Archdeacon of Dunkeld and min. of Cupar Angus about 14th June 1659.

CAITHNESS

1681 ANDREW WOOD, his daugh., Elizabeth (marr. James Wood, burgess of Edinburgh).

DUNKELD

1607 JAMES NICOLSON, line 13, for "George" read "Gilbert."

1686 JOHN HAMILTON, marr. (1) Magdalene Halyburton, and had issue— Margaret, bapt. 13th Jan. 1667; (2) Elizabeth Urry, and had issue, John, born 27th March 1677.—[*S. Leith Reg.*]

EDINBURGH

1624 DAVID LINDSAY, his daugh., Agnes (marr. Laurence, son of John Lindsay of Dowhill).—[*Gen. of Lindsays of Dowhill*; *Gask Papers*, xxviii, 60.]

1688 ALEXANDER ROSE, educ. at Marischal College, not King's.

GALLOWAY

1610 GAVIN HAMILTON, marr. cont. 16th Oct. 1590 Alison, daugh. of James Hamilton of Bothwellhaugh and Alison Sinclair, and had issue, Anne.— [*Hamilton Com. Dec.*, 6th Jan. 1574-5.]

1680 JAMES AITKEN, described as a "suffering minister for Royalty" received from Parliament on 15th May 1661 a grant of £100 stg. from vacant stipends of Orkney.—[*Acts of Parl.*, vii, 202.]

THE ISLES

NEIL CAMPBELL, line 19, delete "but probably not admitted."
1634

MORAY

JOHN GUTHRIE, line 3, for "Hart" read "Rait"; 2 col., line 30, for "Gaigie" read "Craigie."
1623

COLIN FALCONER, line 17, for "Andrew" read "Bartholomew."
1680

WILLIAM HAY, his daugh., Jean, bapt. 26th April 1683.
1688

ORKNEY

THOMAS SYDSERFF, line 2, for "James" read "Thomas."
1662

ANDREW HONYMAN, his daugh., Eupham (1), bapt. 8th Feb. 1652, died young; Eupham (2), bapt. 30th May 1654; Margaret, bapt. 26th Feb. 1656; Ann, bapt. 13th April 1658 (probably marr. Sheriff Murray of Orkney).—[Craven's *Church Life in South Ronaldshay*, 50.]
1664

ANDREW BRUCE, his son, James, bapt. 7th March 1676.
1688

ROSS

JOHN MAXWELL, marr. Elizabeth, sister of Alexander Innes, min. of Mortlach.
1633

JOHN PATERSON.—[*Aberdeen Sas.*, xiv, 61.]
1662

JOHN LESLIE. (See under Oyne.)
1665

ALEXANDER YOUNG, marr. (2) 3rd Oct. 1676.
1679

JAMES RAMSAY, his son, George, born 1666.
1684

UNIVERSITY OF ABERDEEN

MARISCHAL COLLEGE PRINCIPALS

GILBERT GRAY. Addl. issue—Jean, bapt. 13th April 1609; Isobell, bapt. 3rd Aug. 1610; Gilbert, bapt. 20th June 1613; Alexander, bapt. 28th July 1614.—[*Aberdeen Reg.*]
1598

ANDREW ADIE, issue—Christian, bapt. 26th Feb. 1618; a daugh., buried 28th Nov. 1619.—[*Aberdeen Reg.*]
1616

WILLIAM FORBES, his son, Patrick, bapt. 6th Dec. 1618. Addl. issue—Issobell, bapt. 7th July 1617; Paul, bapt. 6th June 1629.
1634

WILLIAM MOIR of Scotstoun, add. Maidment.—[*Catalogue of Scottish Writers*; G. R. Henderson's *Religious Life in 17th Century Scotland*, 108.]
1649

PATRICK GORDON, buried in Gordon's Aisle, Old Machar Cathedral, 15th Aug. 1703; had a child, died June 1668; his son, Thomas, was Regent (Philosophy) at Glasgow Univ. 1682-9, was tried before the Court of Justiciary for opposition to the Revolution, and confined by them a prisoner to his father's house. The sentence was afterwards enlarged to the country and later altogether removed.—[*Old Machar Reg.*; *Univ. and King's College*, 47-8.]
1673

ROBERT PATERSON, his daugh., Agnes, bapt. 9th Jan. 1683; Isobell, bapt. 11th June 1685; Robert, bapt. 20th Sept. 1686. Addl. issue—Helen, bapt. 18th Sept. 1682; William, bapt. 16th March 1689.—[*Aberdeen Reg.*]
1678

THOMAS BLACKWELL, his son, Thomas, bapt. 12th Aug. 1701; Alexander, bapt. 10th Oct. 1709, executed 9th Aug. 1746; Christian (2), bapt. 5th Jan. 1721. Addl. issue—Helen, bapt. 21st Feb. 1703; John, bapt. 10th Feb. 1704; Elizabeth, bapt. 19th May 1706; David, bapt. 24th May 1707; Christian (1), bapt. 23rd Oct. 1711; Katherine, bapt. 27th Sept. 1713; Charles, bapt. 1st April 1716.—[*Aberdeen Reg.*]
1717

JOHN OSBORNE, marr. 28th Aug. 1718 Margaret Mitchell, daugh. of Alexander M., min. Old Machar; his daugh., Jean, bapt. 28th Aug. 1721; his son, Alexander, bapt. 15th Nov. 1724. Addl. issue—James, bapt. 21st Feb. 1720; John, bapt. 13th June 1727; Margaret, bapt. 16th Oct. 1728; Helen, bapt. 29th Oct. 1732.—[*Aberdeen Reg.*; *Old Machar Reg.*]
1728

KING'S COLLEGE, PRINCIPALS

DAVID RAIT, son of John R. of Sillieflat and Elizabeth Straton. Addl. issue—William; Robert; John.—[*Kincardine Sas.*, i, 141-2, iii, 43-8, 320, iv, 16; *Aberdeen Sas.*, 1 Ser., v, 231.]
1592

WILLIAM LESLIE, line 19, for "Gardner" read "Garden"; lines 20-21 read "Johannis Forbesii."
1632

WILLIAM GUILD, line 44, for "Church" read "Churchyard"; 2nd last line, for "Shirefs" read "Shirrefs."
1640

JOHN ROW, line 17, for "1646" read "1645." Marr. Elspet Gillespie and had issue—John, bapt. 13th Jan. 1642; Grisel (marr. Hugh Anderson, min. of Cromarty). Addl. issue—Patrick, bapt. 2nd Nov. 1643; Anna (marr. proc. 16th June 1657 Alexander Gordon, M.A., son of Sir William G., sixth of Lesmoir, who went to the Continent "merely as a spy on places of Catholic Education" and had a varied career.—[*Aberdeen Reg.*; *Old*
1652

Machar Reg.; *House of Gordon*, ii, 74; *Scottish Notes and Queries*, 1893–4; Henderson's *Religious Life in 17th Century Scotland*, 108.]

1662 ALEXANDER MIDDLETON, had issue—George, his successor; John, vicar of Burnhouse and rector of Crickside, bapt. 9th Aug. 1646, died 1704–5; William, bapt. 16th Nov. 1647; Alexander, bapt. 1st April 1649, died young; Thomas, writer of Spottiswoode's *Appendix*, bapt. 31st Aug. 1651; Alexander, bapt. 3rd April 1653, rector of St Alphagi, Canterbury; Catherine, bapt. 18th Aug. 1654; Elizabeth, bapt. 2nd June 1661; Jean, bapt. 12th Oct. 1662; Charles, bapt. 31st Jan. 1664; Mary, bapt. 3rd June 1666. Line 15, for "1686" read "1666."

1748 THOMAS BLACKWELL, marr. Barbara, daugh. of James Stark, dean of Guild, Aberdeen, and Agnes Fordyce.

1757 ROBERT POLLOCK.—[Ramsay of Ochtertyre's *Scotland and Scotsmen*, i, 469.]

DIVINITY

1625 ROBERT BARRON, marr. Jean Gibson and had issue—John, bapt. 1st Aug. 1629; William, bapt. 19th April 1631; James, bapt. 31st Oct. 1632; Marie, bapt. 16th Nov. 1633.

1649 JOHN MENZIES, line 4, for "1649" read "1647"; line 18, for "18" read "10"; line 19, for "1681" read "1680"; line 28, delete from "Positiones" to "(1674)." Marr. (1) 30th Oct. 1649 Elizabeth Forbes, and (2) Margaret Forbes, and had issue—Bethia, bapt. 21st Nov. 1658, died young; Margaret, bapt. 20th Nov. 1659 (marr. 7th June 1679 John Buchan, son of James B. of Auchmacoy, regent in King's College, Advocate); Jean, bapt. 1st June 1662; Ann, bapt. 26th Aug. 1666 (marr. 21st April 1683 George Fraser, Sub-Principal of King's College), died before 19th April 1707; Bethia, bapt. 10th Dec. 1668; Elizabeth, bapt. 2nd Feb. 1671; Barbara, bapt. 4th July 1672; and two children, buried 1st March and 19th May 1671.

1684 PATRICK SIBBALD, marr. 14th June 1669 Joanna or Jean Scougal, who was buried 2nd March 1680.

1684 GEORGE MIDDLETON, ejected as a Jacobite 1716; had addl. issue—Patrick, bapt. 22nd Nov. 1670; James, bapt. 31st Jan. 1674; Margaret, bapt. 3rd June 1675; Thomas, bapt. 21st June 1677; Helen; George, buried 6th May 1661, and George, buried 28th July 1685; Elizabeth, bapt. 20th Sept. 1685; Janet, bapt. 31st Jan. 1690 (marr. William Walker, litster, Aberdeen); Thomas, bapt. 26th Nov. 1695; Charles, apprenticed to Colin Mackenzie, goldsmith, 10th July 1695; Alexander, captain, 1725; John.—[Orem's *Description of Old Aberdeen*.]

1697 JAMES OSBURNE, his son, Alexander, apprenticed to George Mossman, bookseller, 25th Sept. 1702; had children, buried 16th Nov. 1647, 8th July 1649, 8th Oct. 1650, 14th Nov. 1654, 12th July 1661, a son 19th Oct. and a daugh. 27th Oct. 1664.—[*Old Machar Reg.*]

HEBREW (KING'S COLLEGE)

1673 PATRICK GORDON, his son, Patrick, buried 29th Oct. 1711.

1693 GEORGE GORDON, died 30th Aug. 1730. Marr. 12th Sept. 1705 Margaret (bapt. 17th Feb. 1685), eldest daugh. of George Fraser, Sub-Principal, King's College, and had issue—George, born 23rd Dec. 1711; Thomas, bapt. 18th Aug. 1714. Addl. issue—Ann, bapt. 11th July 1707 (marr. Theodore Gordon, min. of Kennethmont); Isobel, bapt. 24th June 1708; Patrick, bapt. 14th March 1710, buried 29th Oct. 1711; Margaret, bapt. 26th Feb. 1713; Frances, bapt. 6th May 1716, buried 12th March 1717; Alexander, bapt. 8th Dec. 1717; James, bapt. 6th July 1719, buried 17th March 1720; Barbara, bapt. 15th Jan. 1720, buried 10th Oct. 1729.—[*Old Machar Reg.*]

JAMES BENTLEY, born 24th Nov. 1771; his mother, Ruth Powell; his daughs.—Janet, born 26th Jan. 1811; Ruth, marr. 29th Oct. 1839.

1798

JAMES GILROY, died 29th Oct. 1931. Line 9, for "Aberdeen" read "St Andrews."

1895

DIVINITY

ANDREW STRACHAN, eldest son of Andrew S., min. of Dun; Regent, King's College, Aberdeen, 1626 and 1628–32. Marr. proc. 8th Oct. 1632 Margaret, daugh. of James Mowat of Ardo, with issue—Margaret, to whom his brother, Alexander, min. of Chapel of Garioch, was tutor; another daugh., Christian, wife of Thomas Burnett, min. of Strachan, had been born of an earlier marriage; his wife, Margaret Mowat, survived him, and marr. (2) cont. 12th Feb. 1637 Alexander, son of John Hay of Crimondmogate. Publications—D.D. Inaugural Thesis, *De Natura et Objects Religiosi*, Aberdeen, 1634.— [*Aberdeen Reg.*; *Univ. and King's Coll.*, 40, 55, 68, 98; *Reg. of Deeds*, ccclxxxvii, 499; *Inquis. Ret. de Tutela*, xvii, 29; *Aberdeen Sas.*, vii, 447, 1636, x, 331, 1637; *Aberdeen Univ. Review*, Nov. 1934.]

1634

JOHN FORBES of Corse, his son, George, succeeded him in Corse. Line 10, for "Heidelburg" read "Middleburgh"; line 15, delete from "in 1639" to "conjunction"; p. 370, line 12, for "by" read "of"; line 19, "after returned to" read "Scotland and in September to"; line 33, "after charity" shut quotation; line 41, for "before" read "23rd July"; 2nd column, line 1, for "*Theologia*" read "*Theologiae*"; line 13, delete "Aberdeen 1646"; line 15, delete "from His Diary to Aberdeenshire," Latin translation of his Diary appears in *Opera Omnia*. Transcripts of diary at King's College, Aberdeen, and Scottish Episcopal College, Edinburgh. Line 20, delete "Professor Gurtler of Deventa and". Addl. publications—Latin translation of *An Exquisite Commentarie*, by his father (1613); *Commentaries on Apocalypsii* (Amsterdam, 1616); *Scottish Notes and Queries*, Sept. and Dec. 1928; G. D. Henderson's *Religious Life in 17th Century Scotland*.

1635

WILLIAM DOUGLAS, son of Alexander D., M.D., provost of Banff; adm. to Forgue 1627; line 7, delete from "He was" to "His Majesty"; selected Oct. 1643; adm. Jan. 1644; buried in Cathedral 31st Jan. 1666. Marr. proc. 3rd Jan. 1628 Elizabeth Ross, and had issue—James, min. of Nigg; Maria, bapt. 3rd March 1635; Helen, bapt. 23rd Sept. 1641.—[*Scottish Notes and Queries*, April 1929, Jan. and Aug. 1633, May 1634; Gordon's *Scots Affairs*; Spalding's *Troubles*.

1644

HENRY SCOUGAL, line 6, delete from "and" to "1669–72"; line 11, for "11" read "12"; line 13, delete "Univ."; line 33, delete from "He is" to "disappeared," and read "Students transcripts of his lectures in Logic and in Ethics are preserved at King's College Aberdeen." An edition of his works appeared London 1726. Line 43, for "Hist. of" read "Description of Old."

1674

JOHN MENZIES, line 2, for "10th Oct. 1678" read "2nd Jan. 1679"; line 3, for "1681" read "1680."

1678

JAMES GARDEN, born 3rd May 1645, recommended for ord. to New Machar 19th May 1669; pres. to Balmerino 22nd March 1676; pres. to Carnbee by Archbishop Sharp 6th Sept. 1678; adm. to chair 2nd Feb. 1681. Marr. Margaret Irvine (buried 3rd July 1704) and had issue—Patrick, bapt. 5th April 1682, died 1759; Elizabeth, bapt. 27th April 1684; Elizabeth, bapt. 20th Sept. 1685; Patrick, bapt. 8th Sept. 1686, buried 2nd Nov. 1699; George, bapt. 25th June 1688; Isabel, bapt. 19th Aug. 1689; Margaret, bapt. 31st March 1692 (marr. David Gordon, episcopal min. Pittenweem); Robert in London, bapt. 16th Feb. 1693; Charles, bapt. 2nd June 1694; James, rector of Slingsby, Yorks., died 1772; Thomas, M.D. (Aberdeen, 1728). Publications—*Theologia Comparativa* (1699), English translations (London, 1700), (Glasgow, 1752), (Bristol,

1680

1756); other Latin editions (Amsterdam, 1702 and 1708).—[G. D. Henderson's *Mystics of the North East*.]

1704 GEORGE ANDERSON, line 11, delete "D.D. that day"; died 4th April 1709. He marr. probably a sister of aforesaid James Garden, and had issue— Alexander, buried 27th June 1671; Anne, bapt. 31st May 1672, buried 26th Feb. 1673; Anne, bapt. 24th Nov. 1673; Alexander, bapt. 11th Feb. 1675, buried 28th Dec. 1675; James, probably min. of Rathen, bapt. 19th Sept. 1676; Isabel, bapt. 15th Nov. 1677; Patrick, bapt. 14th Jan. 1679; William, bapt. 29th June 1680; Susan, bapt. 8th Jan. 1682, buried 6th May 1683; Robert; Gilbert; Margaret and Elspeth.— [*Scot. Notes and Queries*, May 1933, 65.]

1711 DAVID ANDERSON, line 3, for "Cushney" read "Campbell"; line 6, delete "D.D. that day"; his wife, Katherine Mitchell, died 14th May 1728; his daugh., Jean (marr. 6th June 1727 William Rose, min. of Loth). He had issue —Katherine, bapt. 30th Jan. 1701 (marr. William Dyce, min. of Belhelvie); Jean, bapt. 12th May 1702; Janet, bapt. 1st Oct. 1704; Elizabeth, bapt. 18th Oct. 1705; James, born 25th May 1708, graduated at King's College 1725; Rachel, bapt. 8th July 1709; Margaret, bapt. 18th May 1712.

1735 JOHN LUMSDEN, line 4, delete "and Kinkell"; adm. to chair "14," not "10"; his daugh., Jean (marr. John Maxwell, min. of New Machar), died 31st July 1758; his sons—Alexander, M.D., King's College, died 1778; Charles, died 1738, aged 3.—[Ramsay of Ochtertyre, *Scotland and Scotsmen*, i, 300; Morren, *Annals of the General Assembly*, ii, 267; *University Commission Reports*, 1826-30 (*Aberdeen*), 52; *Miscellany of Spalding Club*, i, 433.]

1771 ALEXANDER GERARD, licen. "1749" not "1748"; adm. to chair 18th June. Addl. issue—William, born 3rd Feb. 1762, died 18th Jan. 1763. Col. ii, line 11, for "Corruption" read "Corruptions."—[John Wesley's *Journal*; *Autobiography of Alexander Carlyle*; Boswell, *Journal of a Tour to the Hebrides*.]

1795 GILBERT GERARD, licen. at Aberdeen 1st Aug. 1781; ord. 28th April 1782.

SYSTEMATIC THEOLOGY (KING'S COLLEGE)

1915 WILLIAM FULTON, line 15, for "1927" read "1st Jan. 1928"; his son, David, died 23rd May 1936.

1928 GEORGE THOMAS THOMSON, D.D. (Edinburgh, 28th June 1935), min. of Tain (*q.v.*); trans. to chair of Christian Dogmatics, Edinburgh, 1st Oct. 1936; his wife, Charlotte Isabel Martin, died 7th Jan. 1937. Marr. (2) 19th March 1938 Alice, youngest daugh. of Alexander Davidson, Perth. Publication— Translation of Karl Barth's *The Doctrine of the Word of God* (Prolegomena to Church Dogmatics, being Vol. I, Part 1).

CHURCH HISTORY

1877 JOHN CHRISTIE, his daughs.—Margaret, D.C.S., died 30th Jan. 1935; Isabel (marr. Thomas Everard, Durban), died in South Africa, 10th July 1934; Florence, died 23rd May 1945; Jean, died 13th Dec. 1945.

1889 HENRY COWAN, died 2nd July 1932; his son, Francis Ogston, died 31st May 1899.

1924 GEORGE DAVID HENDERSON, D.Litt. (Glasgow, 1931), D.D. (Glasgow, 15th June 1935); Master of Christ's College, May 1947. Line 5, delete "1st Oct." and read "19th Sept."; has issue—Robert Thomas Smith, born 17th Dec. 1927; George David Smith, born 7th May 1931. Publications—*Mystics of the North East* (Third Spalding Club, 1934); *The Scottish Ruling Elder* (James Clark and Co., 1935); *Religious Life in the 17th Century Scotland* (Cambridge Univ. Press, 1937); *Memorandum Book of John Grant* (Miscellany, Third Spalding Club, 1935); *The Kirk through the Centuries* (1938); *The Scots*

Confession 1560 (1938); *Scottish National Covenant* (1938); numerous articles and reviews in theological and historical journals and newspapers.

BIBLICAL CRITICISM

1860 WILLIAM MILLIGAN, his son, Sir William, died 19th Dec. 1929; his daugh., Elizabeth, died 2nd Jan. 1944.

1899 THOMAS NICOL, his widow, Ann Underwood, died 12th April 1934; his son, John Underwood, died 18th March 1946; his daughs.—Christian Dorothy, Senior Superintendent of Nurses, Edinburgh Royal Infirmary, died 22nd Jan. 1937; Margaret Melville, M.A. (Aberdeen, 1904).

1919 ANDREW CUMMING BAIRD, dem. 1st June 1938; LL.D. (Aberdeen, 1939); died 12th Jan. 1940.

PRINCIPALS, UNIVERSITY OF ABERDEEN

1855 PETER COLIN CAMPBELL, his daugh., Grace Alexina, died at Aberdeen 10th March 1937.

1877 WILLIAM ROBERTSON PIRIE, his daugh., Penelope Elizabeth, died 23rd July 1932.

1900 JOHN MARSHALL LANG, his son, John Douglas Hamilton, died in South Africa 31st Aug. 1945; his son, Cosmo Gordon, Archbishop of Canterbury and Baron Lang of Lambeth, died 5th Dec. 1945.

1909 SIR GEORGE ADAM SMITH, app. Chaplain to the King 3rd Oct. 1933; D.D. (Cambridge, 7th June 1934); dem. 31st Oct. 1935, died 3rd March 1942.

EDINBURGH UNIVERSITY

PRINCIPALS

1685 ALEXANDER MONRO, marr. Marion Collace, and had issue—Elizabeth, born 24th May 1677; Christian, bapt. 28th Feb. 1684.

1916 SIR JAMES ALFRED EWING, dem. 30th Sept. 1929, died 7th Jan. 1935.

1929 SIR THOMAS HENRY HOLLAND, K.C.I.E., K.C.S.I., app. 1st Oct. 1929, dem. 1944; died 17th May 1947.

DIVINITY

1860 THOMAS JACKSON CRAWFORD, his daughs.—Mary Ranken, died 27th May, 1932; Helen Sarah Pemberton, died Hindhead 7th Aug. 1934.

1903 WILLIAM PATERSON PATERSON, dem. 30th Sept. 1934; LL.D. (Edinburgh, 2nd July 1937); D.D. (St Andrews, 28th Sept. 1937); died 10th Jan. 1939; his daugh., Violet Reid (marr. 16th April 1932 George Laurence Ormerod, M.B., Westbury on Trym, Bristol). Publication—*Conversion* (1940).

HEBREW

1732 WILLIAM DAWSON, adm. burgess of Edinburgh 30th April 1735. Marr. 29th Sept. 1723 Jean, daugh. of William Blackwood, merchant, Edinburgh.

1880 DAVID LAIRD ADAMS, his son, Charles William, died at Closeburn 28th March 1932; his daugh.,Louise Emma (Lady Browne), died 14th Oct. 1931; his son, Herbert Frederick Wilfred, died 2nd Jan. 1940.

1894 ARCHIBALD ROBERT STIRLING KENNEDY, LL.D. (Aberdeen, 29th March 1933); dem. 30th Sept. 1937; died 24th Oct. 1938; his daugh., May, M.A. (marr. Noel Alexander Williamson, son of John Linton Dinwiddie, min. of Ruthwell).

BIBLICAL CRITICISM

1898 JOHN PATRICK, died at Edinburgh 17th Jan. 1933.

1915 WILLIAM ALEXANDER CURTIS, LL.D. (Edinburgh, June 1946); app. Dean of Faculty and Principal of New College 1935; dem. 30th Sept. 1946; his wife, Florence Malseed, died 17th Jan. 1933.

CHURCH HISTORY

1878 MALCOLM CAMPBELL TAYLOR, his daugh., Margaret Gordon MacIan, died 17th March 1943.

1908 JAMES MACKINNON, his wife, Pauline Klein, died 20th Oct. 1930; dem. 31st Dec. 1930, died at Forfar 12th July 1945. Publications—*The Historic Jesus* (1931); *The Gospel in the Early Church* (1933); *From Christ to Constantine* (1936); *Calvin and the Reformation* (1936); *Origins of the Reformation* (London, 1939).

GLASGOW UNIVERSITY

PRINCIPALS

1651 ROBERT RAMSAY, marr. (2) before 17th Jan. 1629.

1660 ROBERT BAILLIE, his son, Robert, M.A. (Glasgow, 1653).

1898 ROBERT HERBERT STORY, his daughs.—Elizabeth Maria Margaret Arnott, died 29th May 1941; Helen, died Glasgow 21st Aug. 1942.

1907 SIR DONALD MACALISTER, Bart., dem. 16th Oct. 1929, died 15th Jan. 1934.

DIVINITY

1674 DAVID LIDDELL, marr. Mary Muirhead (who marr. (2) Joseph Cleland, min. of Dalserf), and had issue— Mr John; Elizabeth.

1740 MICHAEL POTTER, marr. 25th April 1706 Elizabeth, daugh. of James Hamilton of Parkhead and Jean Morton.

1778 WILLIAM WIGHT, line 4, for "Glasgow" read "Edinburgh."—[*Scots Mag.*, April 1786, 105.]

1927 WILLIAM FULTON, app. Principal, Trinity College, Glasgow, 1st June 1938; LL.D.(Edinburgh, June 1946); LL.D. (Glasgow, 1948); his daugh., Elizabeth Hope Sutherland (marr. 19th Feb. 1944 Harold Noel Waller, Wellington, Surrey).

BIBLICAL CRITICISM

1910 GEORGE MILLIGAN, D.D. (Aberdeen, 1904), dem. 30th Sept. 1932, died 25th Nov. 1934; his widow, Margaret Catherine Gloag, died at St Andrews 24th Jan. 1940.

HEBREW

1687 JAMES WEMYSS, had issue— James.

1757 JAMES BUCHANAN, son of William B., gardener, Calton, M.A. (1744), app. Oct. 1757.

1850 DUNCAN HARKNESS WEIR, his son, Charles Spence, C.B.E., died at Dulnain Bridge 22nd Dec. 1932; his daugh., Janet Currie, died 27th Feb. 1948.

1877 JAMES ROBERTSON, his daughs.— Lilias (Mrs Alexander Glen), died 7th May 1939; Margaret (marr. (2) Captain Thomas W. Stewart), died 8th Sept. 1940.

1907 WILLIAM BARRON STEVENSON, dem. 30th Sept. 1937; LL.D. (Glasgow, 22nd June 1928).

ECCLESIASTICAL HISTORY

1874 WILLIAM LEE, his son, William John, died at Jedburgh 13th Nov. 1932.

1877 JAMES ROBERTSON, his wife, Catherine Martin, born 30th Sept. 1844, died 8th Sept. 1918.

1898 JAMES COOPER, his widow, Margaret Williamson, died at Elgin 17th May 1947.

1922 ARCHIBALD MAIN, LL.D. (Glasgow, 23rd June 1943); Chaplain to the King 1925; Moderator of General Assembly 1939; dem. 1942; adm. to Kirkbean 30th April 1942; dem. 13th Feb. 1946; died at Glasgow 14th March 1947; his daugh., Maisie (marr. 11th Dec. 1940 Robert Henderson Budge, min. of Selkirk West).

UNIVERSITY OF ST ANDREWS

ST LEONARD'S, PRINCIPALS

JOSEPH DREW, son of John D., elder, merchant burgess of Glasgow.
1708

ST LEONARD'S and ST SALVATOR'S COLLEGE PRINCIPALS

ALEXANDER SKENE, marr. Christian Forbes, and had issue—Margaret and Helen (twins), bapt. 20th April 1672.—[*St Andrews Reg.*]
1680

ROBERT RAMSAY, marr. (1) Christian Russell and had issue—Moses, bapt. 26th June 1702; Lillias, bapt. 26th Oct. 1705; (2) Jean Young, and had issue, Alexander, bapt. 25th Oct. 1711.—[*St Andrews Reg.*]
1698

ROBERT WATSON, marr. Margaret, daugh. of Andrew Shaw, Professor of Divinity, St Andrews; his daughs.—Margaret, died 11th Feb. 1786; Katherine, died at Greenhill 3rd Sept. 1796.
1778

SIR JOHN HERKLESS, his widow, Harriet Sedley Caie, died 2nd Feb. 1934; his son, William, born and died 19th March 1884.
1915

ST MARY'S COLLEGE

SAMUEL RUTHERFORD, by his second marriage with Jean McMath had issue—Catherine, bapt. 25th Feb. 1641; John, bapt. 27th June 1642; Agnes, bapt. 20th May 1649; Samuel, bapt. 2nd March 1651.
1647

JAMES LORIMER, marr. Margaret, daugh. of Alexander Rose, min. of Monymusk.
1687

WILLIAM VILANT, marr. (1) pro. 19th Jan. 1660 Jean Oglivie, Rescobie.
1691

THOMAS FORRESTER, spent some time in Holland, whence he returned in the company of the Earl of Argyll, landing at Campbeltown on 20th May 1685. At a meeting-house there four days later he preached, Exodus xxxiii. 14-15.—[Erskine of Carnock's *Journal*, 119.]
1698

JAMES HADOW, line 11, delete "15th Feb. 1758." Marr. (2) Margaret Forrester (died 18th Feb. 1758). Addl. issue—John, bapt. 18th Sept. 1703; James, bapt. 7th Nov. 1704; William, bapt. 12th April 1706; James, born 1st June 1708, buried in St Mary's Church, Warwick, 1793; David, bapt. 16th Aug. 1709; Archibald, 22nd Feb. 1711; George, bapt. 11th July 1712; Professor of Hebrew; Thomas.
1707

JAMES GILLESPIE, his daugh., Anna (marr. Harry Davidson, W.S.), died 3rd April 1814.
1779

JOHN TULLOCH, his son, Francis Grant, died at Guildford 27th Dec. 1930; his daughs.—Edith Rose, died 15th Jan. 1930; Isobel, died at Malvern 4th Aug. 1932.
1854

ALEXANDER STEWART, his son, Major Alexander Marshall, died in Ontario, Canada, 17th Aug. 1945.
1894

GEORGE GALLOWAY, died at Exmouth 1st March 1933.
1915

HEBREW

GEORGE HADOW, born 1712, marr. Susan Scott of Rossie.
1712

JOHN BIRRELL, his widow, Elizabeth Wallace, died 13th April 1943.
1871

DAVID MILLER KAY, died at St Andrews 5th April 1930; his widow, Hilda Helen Halliday Gillies, remarr. 6th Sept. 1940.
1902

DIVINITY and BIBLICAL CRITICISM

1675 DAVID FALCONAR, had issue, John, born 26th June 1670, advocate 27th June 1699, died June 1710.

1713 ALEXANDER SCRYMGEOUR, D.D., marr. Janet Falconer and had issue—John, bapt. 16th March 1699; Margaret, bapt. 21st May 1700; Janet, bapt. 12th Oct. 1702; Joan, bapt. 3rd Nov. 1703; Magdalene, bapt. 4th July 1705; David, bapt. 29th April 1708.—[*St Andrews Reg.*]

1799 ANDREW SHAW, his daugh., Margaret (marr. 29th June 1757 Robert Watson, principal of St Leonard's and St Salvator's Colleges, St Andrews).

1919 GEORGE SIMPSON DUNCAN, D.Theo. (Paris, 1938), D.D. (Edinburgh, 1930), LL.D. (Edinburgh, June 1948); app. Principal of St Mary's College 12th March 1940; awarded the Norwegian Freedom Cross 1947. Marr. (2) 27th June 1929 Muriel, elder daugh. of Dr James Smith, 4 Merchiston Gardens, Edinburgh, and has issue, Douglas James McKerrow, born 14th June 1931. Publications—*St Paul's Ephesian Ministry* (1929); *The Epistle of Paul to the Galatians* (Moffat's New Testament Commentary, 1934); *Jesus Son of Man* (1948).

CHURCH HISTORY

1730 ARCHIBALD CAMPBELL, his sons—George, merchant, Kingston, Jamaica, died 15th Oct. 1781; Major John, died Island, near Cape Gracias a Dies, 21st Aug. 1787.

1793 CHARLES WILSON, his daugh., Catherine (marr. 1st Nov. 1801 Francis Jeffrey, Lord of Session), died 8th Aug. 1805.

1868 ALEXANDER FERRIER MITCHELL his daugh., Christian, died at Brechin 26th Jan. 1940.

1922 JAMES HOUSTON BAXTER, D.Litt. (St Andrews, 1930), D.D. (Glasgow, 15th June 1932). Secretary of British Academy Committee on New Dictionary of Medieval Latin; Trustee of Scottish National Library; engaged in excavating Byzantine Imperial Palace, Istambul, since 1935. Addl. Publications—Contributor to *Dict. et Hist. et cla. Geogr. ecclésiastiques* (Louvain); co-editor of the *Annuaire de bibliogr. historique* and of *Corpus Philosorum Medii Aevi*; editor of a *Dictionary of Later Latin, A.D. 125–750*; co-editor of the *Bulletin du Conge*; *History of the Church, 312–800* (in History of Christianity) (1928); *Copiale Prioratus S. Andrée* (1930); co-editor of *Books printed abroad by Scotsmen to 1700* (1932); Index to *Scottish Historical Review*, vols. 13–25 (1932); *Select Letters of St Augustine* (1930); *A St Andrews Music Manuscript* (1932) (edited R. F. Murray); *The Scarlet Gown* (1932); co-editor of *Index of British and Irish Latin Writers* (1933) and of *A Word List of Medieval Latin* (1934).

MODERATORS OF GENERAL ASSEMBLY

1928 JAMES MONTGOMERY CAMPBELL, D.D., min. of Dumfries.

1929 JOSEPH MITCHELL, D.D., min. of Mauchline.

MODERATORS SINCE UNION

1929 JOHN WHITE, C.H., D.D., LL.D., min. of Barony.

1930 ANDREW NISBET BOGLE, D.D.

1931 JOHN ANDERSON GRAHAM, C.I.E., D.D., Kalimpong.

1932 HUGH ROSS MACKINTOSH, D.D., Professor of Dogmatics, Edinburgh.

1933 LAUCHLAN MacLEAN WATT, D.D., LL.D., Glasgow.

1934 PETER DONALD THOMSON, D.D., Glasgow.

1935 MARSHALL BUCHANAN LANG, D.D., Whittinghame.

1936 DANIEL LAMONT, D.D., Professor of Practical Theology, Edinburgh.

1937 DUGALD MACFARLANE, D.D., Kingussie.

1938 JAMES BLACK, D.D., Edinburgh.

1939 ARCHIBALD MAIN, D.D., D.Litt., Glasgow.

1940 JAMES RAE FORGAN, D.D., Ayr.

1941 JAMES HUTCHISON COCKBURN, D.D., Dunblane.

1942 CHARLES WALLACE GRAY TAYLOR, D.D., Edinburgh.

1943 JOHN BAILLIE, D.D., D.Litt., Professor of Divinity, Edinburgh.

1944 EDWARD JAMES HAGAN, D.D., Edinburgh.

1945 ANDREW JAMES CAMPBELL, D.D., Evie.

1946 JOHN MACKENZIE, D.D., Bombay.

1947 MATTHEW STEWART, D.D., Hamilton.

1948 ALEXANDER MACDONALD, D.D., Glasgow.

ARMY AND NAVY CHAPLAINS

FRANCIS PIRIE WILSON ALEXANDER, O.B.E. (1940); born 15th May 1898; son of W. W. A., commercial traveller; educ. at Univ. of Aberdeen; assistant Aberdeen and Glasgow; served in France and Belgium, Dec. 1917 to 11th Nov. 1918; app. 1st Jan. 1928 Hong Kong; chaplain to Forces (3rd class) 15th Oct. 1934; Palestine 1936–9 (M. & C.); mentioned in despatches 21st July 1940; assistant D.C.G., Air Force; a son, born 29th June 1930.

JOHN TURNBULL BIRD, died at Belford 21st July 1930; his daugh., May, died at Edinburgh 3rd June 1936.

JOHN CAMPBELL, died at Dollar 3rd March 1939.

THOMAS HENDERSON CHAPMAN, marr. Jessie Macgregor Martin, who died at London 15th Aug. 1931, and had issue—Jessie; Katherine.

ALAN MUNRO DAVIDSON, A.C.G. Scottish Command 1944; D.D. (Edinburgh, 22nd June 1945); C.B.E. 1st Jan. 1949.

HUGH DRENNAN, born 23rd Dec. 1828, son of William D., Tarbolton, and Agnes Wallace, ord. 25th Oct. 1854. Marr. 5th Sept. 1882 Mary (died 5th July 1930), daugh. of William Walker, King's Lynn, and had issue—Hugh Sutherland, born 4th July 1883; Keith Wallace, born 13th Sept. 1887.

WILLIAM STEVENSON JAFFRAY, C.M.G., C.B.E., D.D., K.H.C.; app. Second Chaplain Commandant Feb. 1932; dem. March 1937; died at Torphins, Aberdeenshire, 7th Nov. 1941.

GEORGE KIRKWOOD, his widow, Elizabeth Brown, died at Bournemouth 19th Nov. 1932; his daugh., Beatrice Elizabeth, died 9th Jan. 1948.

ARCHIBALD McHARDY, app. Hon. Chaplain to the King Nov. 1942; D.D. (Edinburgh) 23rd June 1944.

JOHN PATON MURRAY, served with Cameron Highlanders 1917, Argyll and Sutherland Highlanders, 13th and 14th Yorkshire Reg., 2nd Lieut.; adm. to Dun 2nd April 1936; dem. 30th Sept. 1943.

GEORGE DOUGLAS SEMPILL, adm. to Drumelzier 23rd Nov. 1933.

FRANK WHITE STEWART, died 30th March 1933.

ALEXANDER ROSS YEOMAN, Deputy Chaplain General 1933–4; app. Chaplain to the King Jan. 1933; D.D. (Edinburgh, 28th June 1934.)

JAMES ALEXANDER WILLIAMSON, M.A., born 21st March 1904; licen. 1929; app. Temporary Chaplain (4th class) 11th Sept. 1929; Chaplain (4th class) 13th Sept. 1932; served in Palestine 1936–9 (M. & C.); Chaplain (3rd class) 9th July 1940. Marr. Heather Margaret, and has issue—a son, born 24th Aug. 1943.

CHAPLAINS TO INFIRMARIES AND OTHERS

WILLIAM CRAWFORD FRASER, died Crawford 29th May 1942.

JOHN KNOX, his wife, Eleanor Johnson, died 18th Feb. 1938; Secretary for Scotland for United Society for Christian Literature, Edinburgh; died at Edinburgh 24th Oct. 1947.

ROBERT LIPPE, his daugh., Margaret Elizabeth, died 8th July 1928.

GEORGE WAUGH, died 28th Apr. 1929.

SYNOD OF SCOTTISH CHURCH IN ENGLAND

PRESBYTERY OF NORTH OF ENGLAND

BERWICK, ST ANDREWS

1874 JAMES KEAN, his widow, Jessie Alston, died at Edinburgh 3rd Dec. 1943.

1927 JOHN HENDERSON MACKENZIE, trans. to Carfin 30th July 1930.

TWEEDMOUTH

1700 WILLIAM METHVEN, min. 13th Nov. 1700; had issue, James.—[*Deeds, Durie*, 1705, No. 437.]

1879 WILLIAM FOTHERINGHAM CAMERON, his son, John Young Scott, died Manchester 3rd Oct. 1930.

1920 JAMES DUNN BOWMAN, son of Thomas B., Hamilton, and Margaret Garden Dunn; dem. 1929; died 21st June 1933.

1929 VICTOR WILLIAM WANDS, formerly of Nyasaland (*q.v.*); trans. from Garvald 19th June 1929; trans. to Mid Yell 20th Nov. 1930; Chaplain to the Forces; dem. 31st July 1944; adm. to Fortingall 16th Oct. 1945. Addl. issue, Graham Carson, born 11th Nov. 1933.

LOWICK

1911 GEORGE TAIT, marr. 1931, Lucia Jamesina, daugh. of Thomas Wilson Candlish.

1925 JOHN WOOD, trans. to Forglen 24th Dec. 1928.

1929 WILLIAM MURDOCH GILLESPIE, formerly of Argentina (*q.v.*); adm. 1929; trans. to Tweedmouth 1931; dem. 1st July 1941; died 11th Dec. 1941.

NEWCASTLE upon TYNE

1925 GEORGE EDDIE THOMSON, trans. to Monquhitter 30th Oct. 1929.

SILVER STREET

1744 GEORGE OGILVIE, marr. Anne (died 19th March 1800), daugh. of Gabriel Wilson, min. of Maxton.

PRESBYTERY OF WEST OF ENGLAND

CARLISLE

ROBERT TROUP SIVEWRIGHT,
1920 dem. 31st Dec. 1948.

LIVERPOOL

JAMES HAMILTON, died 24th Feb.
1889 1935; his widow, Barbara Robertson, died 11th Oct. 1936.

PRESBYTERY OF LONDON

CALEDONIAN ROAD, HOLLOWAY

WILLIAM THOMSON, died 6th Nov.
1918 1935.

CROWN COURT

JOHN CUMMING, marr. 6th Aug.
1832 1833.

JOSEPH MOFFETT, D.D. (St Andrews, 25th June 1948); his daugh.,
1917 Jean Elizabeth (marr. 22nd Feb. 1941 Lieut. Ian Benson Stewart, Cameron Highlanders); his son, Patrick Johnston, min. of Gilmerton, 29th Sept. 1948.

ST COLUMBA'S, PONT STREET

DONALD MACLEOD, his son, Kenneth, born 1890, not 1900.
1884

ARCHIBALD FLEMING, died at Windsor 2nd July 1941; his daughs.
1902 —Christian Isobel, died Jan. 1931; Roberta Cecilia Helen (marr. 1st July 1936 Thomas Buston Robson, London).

IAN ROBERT GILLAN (colleague); trans. from Inverallan (*q.v.*) 23rd
1929 Aug. 1929; app. and adm. to Fairmilehead 12th April 1938.

(*The church was destroyed by air raid in* 1941.)

CHARGES IN ENGLAND NOW EXTINCT

LONDON FOUNDERS HALL

1827 HUGH BAILLIE MACLEAN, marr. 20th March 1833 Ruth, daugh. of Alexander Handerson of Warriston, banker, Edinburgh.

CALEDONIAN CROSS STREET and NATIONAL SCOTS CHURCH, REGENT SQUARE

1822 EDWARD IRVING, his daugh., Margaret, died 22nd Nov. 1853; his sons —Samuel, born 26th June 1828; Martin Harvey, died 23rd Jan. 1912; Ebenezer, born 12th Sept. 1832; his daugh., Isabella, born 23rd March 1834 (marr. 7th Jan. 1856), died 17th Nov. 1878.

WARK

1880 ADAM THOMSON LANDRETH, died at Aberdeen 8th March 1946.

WOOLER

1734 ALEXANDER WILSON, son of Andrew Wilson of Hightoun, Roxburghshire; ord. 20th Nov. 1734, died 1st June 1777. Marr. Alice ——, and had issue—Richard, bapt. 9th Dec. 1751; Robert, bapt. 15th July 1754; William, his successor; Sir Alexander, bapt. 15th May 1759, knighted 10th May 1813; physician to the Duke of Kent; Ord, bapt. 21st Nov. 1765, lost at sea.

1776 WILLIAM WILSON, son of preceding; educ. at Univ. of Glasgow, M.A. (1775); ord. 5th Jan. 1776; dem. Dec. 1783; went to Clermont, New York, and practised medicine; app. First Judge of the County of Columbia, died 20th Dec. 1828. Marr. Mary Hervey (born 11th June 1753, died 15th Sept. 1801), and had issue —William Henry, physician and surgeon, born 3rd Feb. 1791, died 9th March 1884; Stephen Bayard, Captain, U.S. Navy, born 18th Aug. 1795, died 16th March 183–.

CHARGES IN IRELAND

JAMES KILPATRICK. (See Vol. i, 305.)

JOHN SINCLAIR, min. of Strabane, marr. Elspeth Innes.—[*Wadset G. R. Sas.*, 3 Ser., xxxiii, 20, 17th Nov. 1673.]

DAVID YOUNG, formerly of Monzievaird, now in Strabane, Ireland, 4th Sept. 1705. Marr. sister of Duncan Tosheock of Monzievaird.—[*Deeds. Durie*, 1705, No. 911.]

CHURCH OF SCOTLAND OVERSEAS

CONTINENT OF EUROPE

In times described in 1441 as "long gone by," traders of Scotland founded in the Church of the Carmelite Friars at Bruges an altar or chapel, to the honour of God, the Virgin Mary, and St Ninian, whose chaplain was to minister to traders and other Scottish people living in that town the Divine Offices and Church Sacraments. It may be that the foundation took place when Scottish trade with the Low Countries was very prosperous, in the period prior to the Wars of the Scottish Succession that followed the death of Alexander III. On a petition "of certain faithful of the realm of Scotland" the work was confirmed by Papal Bull of 26th March 1446–7, which decerned that the chaplain not only minister to Scots at Bruges but also "pass to other places distant not more than two or three days from the said town, there to minister to Scots." In March 1441 the General Council of Scotland at Perth ord. that for the support of the chaplain and the decoration of the chapel there be paid the passage freight of a bundle or package of whatsoever ship or goods loaded for parts of Flanders, Holland, and Zealand; and on 29th Aug. 1450, as the result of a complaint by the chaplain, Sir John Hyndeloch, that payment was either deficient or was withheld, the decree was confirmed by charter of James II. In 1470 the magistrates of Bruges, in granting privileges to Scottish merchants, agreed to give a sum of money for the repair of the chapel; and in 1489, when Andrew Russell was chaplain, the magistrates of Edinburgh expressed concern at the poverty of the chapel and the theft of its cups and other ornaments. But Edinburgh's concern also showed itself in a more practical way. On 22nd Jan. 1437–8 the Town Council ord. that "quhat persouns frauchtis a schip outward sall give a sek ($\frac{1}{6}$) fraucht to Sanct Rynenes Ile in Bruges"; and on 18th July 1494 the Council further ord. that "frauchts of ships within the burgh take clerk or depute to make their charter party, and cause to be insert therein specially the sek fraucht of the schip above fyve lastis of guids, and under that birth, of a half sek fraucht to thair Chaplaine of St Ninian's Altar in Bruges," the same to be paid to the present chaplain, Mr James Wawne. A somewhat similar levy was decreed by the Town Council on 18th July 1494, the chaplain being James Wawne. On 24th Sept. 1538 Sir William Thomson in Antwerp was pres. to the chaplainry by James V in succession to the late Mr Alexander Fotheringhame. Apparently the work was discontinued at the Reformation. At Roscoff in Brittany there was a chapel, variously called the Chapel of Marie Stewart and the Chapel of St Ninian, which is said to have been erected by Mary Queen of Scots to commemorate her safe landing there on 15th Aug. 1548 after her voyage from Scotland. The chapel was destroyed at the Reformation. In the parish church at Roscoff there are, or were, a silver statue of the Virgin and an amber rosary reputed to have been gifts from the Scottish Queen to the chapel. At Elsinore there was a chapel dedicated to St Ninian, which may have been used by the Scots at that place. It is said that to the chapel belonged an altar-piece, now in the museum at Copenhagen.—[*Reg. Great Seal*, i, 392, 3787; *Reg. Sec. Seal*, ii, 2722; *Acts Scott. Parl.*, ii, 57; *Cal. Papal Regs., Letters*, ix, 578; *The Scott Staple at Vere*, 270n; *Extracts from Recs. of Burgh of Edinburgh*, i, 5, 66–7; *Procs. Soc. of Antiq. of Scot.*, xlii, 15, **17.**]

BELGIUM—BRUSSELS

ROCHE, GEORGE RALPH MALVERN, sometime Army Chaplain in India, died at Penzance 15th July 1948.

MACFARLANE, JOHN, trans. from Pollokshaws and app. 30th Sept. 1927; dem. 30th June 1936; adm. to Martyrs West, Glasgow, 24th Aug. 1937; his daugh., Margaret, born 12th Sept. 1928.

FRANCE—PARIS

ROBERTSON, WILLIAM COWPER, trans. to Barthol Chapel 27th June 1935; his daugh., Katherine Macgregor (marr. 20th Sept. 1947 Andrew Maxwell, elder son of John A. Struthers, Muirend, Renfrewshire).

GERMANY—DRESDEN

BOWDEN, JOHN DAVIS, his son, William Douglas, C.B.E., died 24th April 1944.

HOLLAND—AMSTERDAM

WILLIAM MACFARLANE, line 2, for "1839" read "1838."

WILLIAM THOMSON, Officer of the Order of Orange Nassau 1935; O.B.E. June 1936; dem. July 1935.

CAMPVERE

In the contract of 1541 between Scottish merchants and the town of Campvere, by which that town became the Scottish Staple Port, the privileges granted by Maximilian of Burgundy, Lord Beven of Campvere, etc., included the proviso that the said merchants shall have the choice and option of a suitable place in the Collegiate Church of Campvere, with a chaplain so as it shall please the Scottish nation, who shall be provided with a prebendary of canons upon the first vacancy in the said church. Right of burial in the said place or chapel was also granted to Scots dying at Campvere, without the usual payment exacted for burial in the church. The privilege was utilised up to the Reformation, when the chaplain was John Dawson, who had been in office in 1552 and received from the town of Campvere an annual payment of £3 Flemish. Probably at the Reformation the work lapsed. Subsequently steps for renewal were taken. By contract of 1578 the magistrates of Campvere, in order that Scottish people resident at Campvere "be not frustrated of the Word of God and exercitation of the religion as it is for the present used in Scotland," granted them "the quire of the Great Kirk" and a dwelling-house for the minister, with free excise of bear and wine for his household and family. At that time nothing further was done. On 3rd May 1586 the Convention of Burghs, on account of the great abuses by merchants and other Scotsmen in Campvere, "uncomely behaviour in civil life and outward manners" and "no regard for conscience and religion," condescended upon the erection of a church at Campvere without delay; and on 4th July and 3rd Nov. 1587 an agreement was made whereby Campvere undertook to erect a church, make provision for the min. as when the Staple was first established there, including a house. The choir of the Great Church was again granted for worship. Repeated efforts were made by the Convention to carry the project to completion; and eventually a min. was app in 1612. At that time the contract was renewed; and a further renewal took place in 1676. On 25th May 1686 the church was burned, and the Scottish congregation worshipped in the Scottish Poor-house in Winegaert Street till rebuilding was completed in 1699. In 1795 the staple was broken up and the church privilege was withdrawn. The Communion cups seem to have been committed to an elder of the church for the purpose of being given to Middelburgh Church. He died before giving effect to the plan; and his widow is said to have sold them. It may be noted that on 9th Aug. 1641 the General Assembly approved of a motion that "for the weal of this kirk," the Scots Kirk at Campvere should be joined to the Kirk of Scotland as a member thereof, and ord. that a letter be sent to Mr William Spang, min. at Campvere, and the Kirk Session thereof, willing them to send their min. and a ruling elder, instructed with a commission to the next General Assembly at St Andrews in July 1642, when they will be enrolled as commissioners from Campvere Church.—[*Recs. of Convention of Burghs*, i, 211–12, etc., ii, 79–80, etc.; Yair's *Acc. of Scotch Trade in Netherlands*, 111–17, 162; *Scott. Staple at Vere*, 418, 423, 430; *Scott. Church at Vere*, 304–5; *Proc. Soc. of Antiqs. of Scotland*, xxv, 169–70; Peterkin's *Recs. of Kirk of Scot.*, 297.]

ALEXANDER MACDUFF, M.A.; on remit from the Convention of Burghs to certain burghs 15th July 1613, he was app. min. 20th Jan. 1614 with the consent of the King and the Archbishop of St Andrews, and entered on his ministry 1st March 1614; on 4th July 1616, in response to his petition to the effect that the collection of his stipend was unsatisfactory, the Convention of Burghs agreed that in lieu of the collection he be paid 800 gulden annually; his name appears on the four Communion cups presented to the church by the factor in 1620.—[*Recs. of Convention of Burghs*, ii, 426, 439, iii, 8–9, 22–3.]

THOMAS EWING, son of Alexander Ewing, factor in Campvere. On 8th July 1614 the Convention of Burghs resolved to appoint a reader at Campvere, and on 13th July following issued injunctions to him as reader and officer; on 4th July 1616 he was still in office, and on 10th July he was adm. as factor for the nation at Campvere; on 8th July 1619 he continued as Collector of Stipend, one of his duties when he was app. reader.—[*Recs. of Convention of Burghs*, ii, 464, 467, iii, 22, 30, 67, 83.]

GEORGE SYDSERFF, app. by the Convention of Burghs on 3rd Nov. 1625, John, Archbishop of St Andrews, agreeing to admit and receive him to the Kirk, and his appointment being ratified on 7th July 1626; he resigned 4th July 1628 on the ground that Campvere was prejudicial to his health.—[*Recs. of Convention of Burghs*, iii, 209, 228, 252.]

JOHN FORRET, M.A.; app. 10th July 1628 by the Convention of Burghs with the consent of the Archbishop of St Andrews, to take up duty before 1st Nov. following; on 10th July 1629 he laid before the Convention of Burghs a complaint as to the estate of the church, and that Mr Patrick Drummond, conservator of the privileges of the nation in the Low Countries, encroached upon the government of the church contrary to the order of the Church of Scotland, and no conclusion by the Minister and Session did the said Mr Patrick put or suffer to be put into execution; the Convention agreed that the ministers and elders govern the Kirk and the discipline thereof conform to the daily order in the Kirk of Scotland, and debarred interference by the conservator, whose position, however, as ruling elder and civil magistrate was to be recognised in the Session. Forret died in office in Sept. 1629; the statement as to his demission in Oct. 1628 refers to his pastorate at Newburg.—[*Recs. of Convention of Burghs*, iii, 272–4, 287–8, 295, 305–6.]

WILLIAM SPANG, M.A.; on 27th Jan. 1630 there was laid before the Convention of Burghs a letter from the Scottish people of Campvere, regretting the want of a pastor, and deploring their hard estate through the lack of the comfort of God's Word whereof they had been deprived ever since the death of Mr Forret, and the Convention app. William Spang, student of Divinity, who was taken bound to assume office not later than 1st July of the same year, and it was remitted to certain burghs to deal with the Archbishop of St Andrews to receive and admit him; on 1st Dec. 1652 it is recorded that the church was vacant by the desertion of Mr William Spang.—[*Recs. of Convention of Burghs*, iii, 305, 307, 367.]

ROBERT BROWNE, or BROUN, was min. of Kirkbean; on 7th July 1654, when he was exercising the place of min. at Campvere, he was "entreated" by the

Convention of Burghs "to remain until the Burghs' further order."—[*Recs. of Convention of Burghs*, iii, 378.] (See Kirkbean.)

ROBERT FLEMING, in July 1691 he was invited by the Conservator and the church here to be min., but did not assume office; afterwards min. at Rotterdam and Founder's Hall (*q.v.*).—[*Recs. of Convention of Burghs*, iv, 142.]

ALEXANDER WILSON, his widow, Sarah French, died 15th March 1793; his daugh., Sara Christina (marr. John Bower, min. of Maryculter).

MIDDELBURG

WILLIAM SPANG (Secundus), born Nov. 1659, died 6th May 1683.

ROTTERDAM

Portfolio of papers in General Register House.

JOHN DAVID PALM, born 1816, son of –. P., min. at Wolfundahl, Dutch Reformed Church, Colombo, Ceylon, whom he succeeded. Marr. –. Wells, and had issue, –. Lloyd, in Chinese Customs; Theobald, M.D., medical missionary in Japan; a son, died young; William Stuart, doctor, Largo, died 1908; Hilary; Alice; Emma (marr. –. Burnet).

JOHN IRWIN BROWN, O.B.E., Officer of the Order of Orange Nassau; died 2nd Feb. 1937.

ITALY—VENICE

ROBERTSON, ALEXANDER, died 20th March 1933.

SWITZERLAND—GENEVA

WATT, THOMAS MEIKLE, D.D. (Aberdeen, 6th July 1932); trans. to Ballater North, 13th June 1935; died 22nd April 1938.

CONTINENT OF AFRICA

EGYPT—ALEXANDRIA

MITCHELL, DAVID RUSSELL, Chaplain to Ulster Division in France and Egypt 1914–19; adm. to Aberfeldy, 27th Aug. 1926.

MACKIE, GEORGE MUNRO, his widow, Louisa Ross, died at Beyrout 10th March 1934.

ROBERTSON, CHRISTIAN ARTHUR, dem. 1929; adm. to Wellpark West, Greenock, 14th May 1930, and Avondale, 22nd Feb. 1939.

KENYA—NAIROBI

ORR, JAMES FLEMING GORDON, died Nairobi, 4th May 1935; his widow, Grace Ellen Mann, died 29th Oct. 1947.

YOUNGSON, JAMES, adm. to St John's, Kirkcaldy, 19th Sept. 1928; trans. to Nelson, British Columbia, Aug. 1931; adm. to St Andrew's South, Dunfermline, 20th May 1935; trans. to Tullynessle, Forbes, 30th May 1941.

MAURITIUS

JOHN ROBERT DE LINGEN KILBURN, app. first chaplain to the *Queen Elizabeth*, Mediterranean Fleet, 10th Oct. 1920; Senior English Master, Royal College of Mauritius, 1921; Principal of Training College, 1926–31; Senior English Master, Royal College, 1931; Deputy Commissioner A.R.P. for Colony, 1942; dem. 1944 and returned to Scotland.

CONTINENT OF ASIA

BURMA—RANGOON

MUDGE, JAMES, trans. to Sauchie 5th Sept. 1929.

CEYLON

MACARA, JOHN, adm. to Kiltarlity East, 20th Sept. 1932; dem. 26th June 1943.

MACECHERN, CHRISTIAN VICTOR AENEAS, trans. to North and Trinity, Aberdeen, 3rd June 1929.

MACMICHAEL, DAVID COLVILLE, his widow, Jean Grace Marian Govan, died 15th April 1939.

FORD, JAMES ALBERT MUNRO, born 1883; educ. at Scottish College, Adelaide, 1909, Ormond College, Melbourne, B.A. (Adelaide, 27th Dec. 1919); B.D. (Melbourne, 14th May 1922); licen. by Presb. of Melbourne Nov. 1913; ord. to Murray Bridge, South Australia, by Presb. of Onhaparinga 13th Aug. 1915; trans. to Mount Pleasant 1st April 1917; dem. 1st Feb. 1923 on app. as Chaplain and Classical Master, Scots College, Sydney, 1923; adm. to Hinton, Morpeth, New South Wales, 10th March 1925; dem. 15th July 1927; came to Scotland, assistant at North Leith 1927; adm. by General Assembly 24th May 1928; app. to Colombo 1929; dem. 1933, and returned to Australia.

INDIA

ALLAN, JOHN BLACK, licen. by Presb. of Aberdeen; ord. to Indian Chaplaincy 10th Sept. 1929; adm. to Evie 25th July 1933; trans. to Greenhill, Rutherglen, 12th July 1936; trans. to St Brandon's, Boyndlie, 26th March 1941; dem. 26th March 1942. Marr. 12th July 1933.

BLACK, JAMES, O.B.E., formerly of Balfron (*q.v.*), dem. 1928 on app. as Chaplain, Royal Air Force; died at Windsor 5th Jan. 1941.

CAMERON, JOHN, his daugh., Catherine Agnes (marr. 10th Feb. 1934 Alexander, son of Sir John Hope); his son, Alastair R.

CAMERON, SAMUEL WOOD, served as Gunner, R.G.A., March 1917, 2nd Lieut. 4th Feb. 1918; served at Home 1917–18, France April 1918 to May 1919; Lieut., attached Black Watch 1926; died 23rd Dec. 1933; his wife, daugh. of Rev. John Findlater, Indian Chaplain (Wesleyan) died at Chakrata, United Provinces, 20th April 1929, and had issue—a son, born 25th March 1929.

CRAIK, DAVID, born St Cyrus 27th Dec. 1884, son of George C.; educ. at Univ. of Aberdeen, M.A. (1907), St Andrews, B.D. (1912); joined Air Force 1915, D.F.C.

DODD, GEORGE EDWARD, adm. to Monigaff, 12th June 1935; his daugh., Elizabeth Sheila Mary (marr. 3rd July 1942 Captain Gareth Kirkham Du Pre, R.A.).

FERRIER, ALEXANDER, Chaplain to 72nd Highlanders at Kabul and took part in Lord Roberts' famous march to Kandahar; three times mentioned in despatches; died 29th Aug. 1934; his wife, Beatrice Hallowes, died 18th July 1931; his daugh., Lilian Kathleen (marr. 20th April 1938 James Clairmont Fleming, Auchencairn).

HAMILTON, ROBERT KERR, adm. to Bayswater 1859.

HERON, JOHN, died 23rd Feb. 1950.

INGRAM, JAMES WILLIAM, adm. to Tundergarth 18th Dec. 1942.

LEE, ROBERT EWING, M.C., app. to Nice 1937; dem. 1938.

McCAUL, MATTHEW WILSON, adm. to Ruthwell 2nd July 1936.

MACKAY, JAMES HUTTON, died at Fochabers 7th Aug. 1933; his sons—John, in Burma; Joseph, in Nigeria; daugh., Caroline, domestic science teacher, Malay States.

MACKENZIE, DONALD FRANCIS, M.A., dem. 1939; adm. to Clunie 15th Jan. 1941. Marr. 3rd June 1937 Anny Damute.

MACKINTOSH, KENNETH, born Glen Urquhart 10th Jan. 1903, son of Kenneth M., Lewiston, and Lillias Fraser; educ. at Glen Urquhart School and Univ. of ———; licen. by Presb. of Inverness 4th May 1927; app. Indian Chaplain and ord. 2nd March 1928. Marr. 5th April 1929 Annie Stewart, M.A., daugh. of Rev. Peter Brown, B.Sc., Cullen.

McLEAN, LAUCHLAN, dem. 1937, died Nov. 1942.

McLELLAN, DUNCAN TAIT HUTCHISON, adm. to Hounam 29th Aug. 1944; trans. to Boarhills 31st July 1946.

MACPHERSON, GEORGE COOK, dem. 3rd Aug. 1933; adm. to Tarbet West 15th Dec. 1933; died 11th Feb. 1939.

MITCHELL, JAMES DONALD, adm. to Aberfeldy 14th May 1930; his wife, Constance Maria Edward, died 16th Feb. 1938.

PHILIP, JAMES GIBSON, adm. Fellow of the Royal Society of Arts, London, 1934.

REID, JAMES POTTER, M.A., adm. to Trinity, Saltcoats, 2nd April 1941; trans. to Lowick 4th Oct. 1945.

RENNIE, JOHN YULE, app. Superintendent, St Andrew's Colonial Homes, Kalimpong, April 1942, in succession to Dr J. A. Graham; dem. 1943; adm. to Fowlis Wester 2nd Feb. 1945.

RUTLEDGE, JAMES WILLIAM RENWICK, adm. to Longbridge and Breich 21st April 1948; his wife, Elizabeth Brown Hovell, died 5th April 1930. Marr. (2) 3rd Sept. 1935 Christian Mary, youngest daugh. of James Campbell, Tullich, Killin.

SCOTT, THOMAS, died 12th March 1936.

SHORT, GEORGE MURRAY DAVIDSON, adm. to Newburn 22nd Sept. 1943; his son, George M., M.B., Ch.B., missionary, Calabar. Addl. issue—John Thomson, born 5th June 1927.

PALESTINE

HILL, NINIAN, born at Greenock 27th Nov. 1861, only son of James Fleming H. and Mary Jane Ramsay, daugh. of James Johnston Grieve, M.P. for Greenock; educ. at Hawtreys School, Slough, preparatory for Eton, but his education was interrupted by an accident and serious illness, which necessitated it being continued by private tutors. When his health was restored, he attended the Univ. of St Andrews and studied at Oxford, and in later life Divinity at Edinburgh. He became a shipowner in Greenock and took a prominent part in public affairs, being Dean of Guild and Treasurer of the Burgh and Director and Chairman of the Greenock Provident Bank. In 1901 he removed to Edinburgh and was General Secretary for the Society for the Prevention of Cruelty to Children, during which time he reorganised its whole administration. He also took an active interest in Church affairs and became an elder in Murrayfield Church. At a meeting of the Presb. of Edinburgh on 12th Dec. 1917, the day that Allenby entered Jerusalem, he proposed that to celebrate the delivery of that city from seven centuries of Moslem rule, a church and hospice should be erected there to commemorate this, and he was app. by the General Assembly Hon. Secretary of the committee by whom this was carried out. He was licen. by the Presb. of Edinburgh 28th June 1922 and was ord. by them first chaplain of the Church of Jerusalem, and was also Honorary Min. of St. Cuthbert's, Edinburgh, for twenty-three years. He also became in 1919 Secretary to the Committee on Chaplains to H.M. Forces. D.D. (Edinburgh, 1st July 1935); died at Edinburgh 10th April 1946. His ashes were interred in St Andrew's Church, Jerusalem, on 30th Nov. 1947, where a plaque to his memory was dedicated 4th Jan. 1948. He marr. 4th April 1935 Marguerite, youngest daugh. of Henry Richer and Marie Thérese de Portemer. Addl. Publications—Edited first two *Annuals of the Church Service Society*.

AUSTRALIA AND NEW ZEALAND

AUSTRALIA

HUNTER, CHARLES HAY, was fourth son, died 11th July 1928.

SMYTHE, KIRKPATRICK DICKSON, died at Don Bank, Aberdeen, 9th March 1864.

NEW ZEALAND

Contributed by Dr Alexander Cumming, 193 Dominion Road, Auckland.

Instead of "Commonwealth of Australia" write "Australasia." (New Zealand and Fiji are not part of the Commonwealth.)

COMRIE, WILLIAM, eldest son of William Comrie, Foulis Wester, Perthshire. Univ. of St Andrews. Arrived in New Zealand in 1841. Marr. 23rd Jan. 1849 Jessie Miller (who died in Auckland 10th Nov. 1875); held no Charge in N.Z.; died 27th Sept. 1884 at Pukekohe, near Auckland, aged 84.

DICKIE, JOHN, D.D., died in Dunedin, N.Z., 24th June 1942.

GELLIE, JOHN CAITHNESS, born 1834.

JACKSON, ROBERT WINCHESTER, died 29th Aug. 1933.

KILLEN, JAMES MILLAR, born 1847, died 1928.

MACKELLAR, JAMES, born Dec. 1859, died 30th March 1895. For "Waikara" read "Waikari."

MILNE, JAMES, M.A. (Abd.); born 14th Dec. 1865 at Bucksburn, Aberdeen, died 5th June 1943 in Auckland, N.Z.

MORICE, GEORGE. For "Morris" read "Morice"; for "Taurango" read "Tauranga."

PATTULLO, JAMES LEBURN, ord. to Waihi (not Waiki) 1904; to Whangarei 1907; res. 1911; to Kaurihohore 1914; res. 1917.

RANKIN, WILLIAM PILLANS, add —adm. min. New Lynn, Auckland, 1926; Huntly, 1939; died 4th April 1943.

RITCHIE, WILLIAM, trans. to Kaiapoi 1901; died 1945 in Palmerston North.

SOUTAR, ALEXANDER CHALMERS, on page 501 "Pictou" should be "Picton."

THOMPSON, WILLIAM, M.A., B.D.; adm. Waipu (delete "North") June 1898; Coromandel 1905; Waipu (again); died 19th March 1912, aged 56.

WALLIS, JAMES, born 1825. Marr. 1862 Elizabeth, daugh. of Richard Poole, M.D., F.R.C.P.E.; she died in 1904. Arrived in Auckland 1865 as surgeon on the *Rangitoto*. First min. of St David's, Auckland, Oct. 1865; dem. 1st July 1868; Member, House of Representatives for Auckland City West 1877–81; from 1881 to 1896 farmed at Riverhead, Auckland; in 1896 settled in Richmond, Auckland, and died there 25th May 1912.

WALLS, THOMAS, ind. into Woodville 1893; res. 1894; Ngaruawahia 1896; Te Aroha 1898; res. 1905.

CANADA

CAPE BRETON

MURDOCH STEWART, born at Contin 18th May 1810, son of John Stewart and Catherine Stewart, daugh. of Thomas Stewart, Catechist of Contin Parish; educ. at Contin School and at Crathie, and Aberdeen Univ. (King's and Marischal) 1830–4, M.A.; teacher at Calcot's School for Boys, near Elgin, 1837; licen. by Presb. of Elgin 5th Dec. 1838; joined Free Church 1843; ord. to West Bay in latter part of 1843; retired in 1882 and died 30th July 1884 at Pictou; on visit to Scotland marr. 29th June 1847 Catherine (died at Halifax 19th Sept. 1906), daugh. of James MacGregor and Mary Davidson, Achcallater, Braemar, with issue, all born at Black River, West Bay—John, born 3rd July 1848, farmed for a time in Scotland, arts student, Edinburgh Univ. 1871–2, medical student at Halifax, Nova Scotia, 1872–4, and Edinburgh Univ. 1874–7, where he graduated, one of four chosen by Lister to accompany him to London on his appointment to King's College Hospital; returned to Canada 1878, and after engaging in general practice in Pictou, took up surgical work at Halifax and became distinguished as Lecturer in Surgery at Halifax Medical School, afterwards re-attached to Dalhouse Univ.; from the close of 1915 he was head of the Dalhouse Hospital, No. 7 Stationary, at Thorncliff, and in France, and later was Consultant to the Canadian Hospital in England; received C.B.E., and after returning to Canada in 1919 he acted as Consultant in Halifax to the Camp Hill Hospital for returned soldiers till his death 22nd Dec. 1933; was awarded LL.D. by Edinburgh Univ. in 1913, and also by McGill and Dalhouse Univs., Canada; he visited this country in 1927 when he spoke at the Lister Centenary Meeting of the British Medical Association, and received the Honorary Fellowship of the Edinburgh Royal College of Surgeons; Margaret Mary, born 20th Jan. 1850 (marr. J. Farquharson) and died at Calgary 2nd Nov. 1937; Donald Alexander, born 2nd Nov. 1851, Civil Engineer, Railways, died at Halifax 20th Oct. 1897; James MacGregor, born 29th June 1853, lawyer, died at Pictou 18th June 1897; Thomas, born 16th Dec. 1855, clergyman, died at Halifax 8th Jan. 1923; Katherine Isabel, born 9th July 1857 and died at Halifax 12th April 1938; Anne Amelia, born 19th March 1859; Elizabeth Helen, born 5th Sept. 1860; Maria Louisa Jessie, born 2nd Sept. 1862; Alexander Forrester, born 8th Jan. 1864, Civil Engineer, Railways, and died at Halifax 30th Oct. 1937.—[*Memo.*, Miss Anne Amelia Stewart, 28 South Street, Halifax, Nova Scotia.]

MATTHEW WILSON, marr. Christian Scouller, who died 28th March 1852.

NOVA SCOTIA

JOHN STEWART, his wife, Alicia Murray Drysdale, was a sister of Anne Scott Drysdale, wife of Dr Alexander Duff of India; had issue—at least—John, a sea-captain; William, painter, died at New Glasgow, Nova Scotia, in 1929; and two daughs., one of whom died young, and the other marr. a min. in the Province of Quebec.—[*Memo.*, Miss Anne Amelia Stewart, 28 South Street, Halifax, Nova Scotia; *Memo.*, Rev. Dr Hugh Munroe, Westminster Church, New Glasgow.]

PRINCE EDWARD ISLAND

LAMONT, DONALD McDONALD, min. in 1921; adm. to Kilninian and Kilmore 9th Jan. 1935; dem. 11th Nov. 1941; died 31st May 1942.

ONTARIO and QUEBEC

LEATHEM, WILLIAM HARVEY, D.D. (Ottawa, 1930); died 23rd Feb. 1937.

SNODGRASS, JOHN ALLAN, died at Maxwelltown, 8th July 1929.

NEWFOUNDLAND

St Andrew's Church, St John's, celebrated its centenary in 1942, when a history of the congregation was published. In the course of looking over some old papers a record was found that in 1622 an expedition fitted out by Sir William Alexander for Nova Scotia came to Newfoundland through distress. The settlers had with them a min., who died there during the winter of 1622–3. The name of the min. is unfortunately not given.—[*Information from R. A. Templeton, Session Clerk.*]

UNITED STATES OF AMERICA

DUNLOP, WILLIAM, left South Carolina when the Colony was destroyed by Spaniards.—[*Scot. Hist. Review*, 1928.]

STOBO, ARCHIBALD, marr. 9th July 1699 Elizabeth, daugh. of James Park, writer, Edinburgh.—[*Deeds Dal.*, 1706, No. 1819.]

BRITISH WEST INDIES

GRENADA

GIVEN, HUGH O., marr. Margaret (died at Clevedon, Somerset, 11th June 1923, aged 70).

MACFARLANE, DUNCAN, became missionary at Kinlochewe 1933; at Kirkipol and Cornaig, Tiree, Oct. 1933; adm. by General Assembly as ord. min. May 1934; adm. to Tiree 11th July 1934; trans. to Kilchrenen 15th Dec. 1940; has issue—Flora Marion, born 28th Sept. 1927; Annie Laurie, born 17th Nov. 1929.

JAMAICA

MAXWELL, JOHN, son of John M. of Kirkhill, Dalton, died 25th Feb. 1930.

ST VINCENT

McPHAIL, DOUGALD NEIL, dem. 1936.

BRITISH HONDURAS

ADAMSON, ALFRED ERNEST, trans. to St Anne's, Trinidad, 1932.

ANDERSON, JAMES STORIE, his widow, Helen Duff Farquhar Clarke, died 9th Feb. 1943.

BRITISH GUIANA

All Saints

CAMERON, CHARLES McK., dem. **1928** 1934.

St Andrew's

LESLIE, GEORGE NEAVE, trans. from Kincardine in Monteith (*q.v.*); **1928** died 8th Aug. 1937.

St Clement's

CASSOU, MORTIMER ALOYSIUS, afterwards of St Luke's.

St Luke's

MENZIES, ROBERT, died 18th Aug. **1840** 1844.

WALLACE, JAMES BELL; his widow, Eliza, daugh. of Andrew Chrystal **1893** Hamilton, died from effects of accident at Demerara 13th Jan. 1939.

St Saviour's

HUSKIE, JAMES, his sons—Dr David, died at Moffat 7th June 1944; **1879** James, M.B., Ch.B., died 15th March 1945.

DYETT, ALFRED E., died 1946.

SOUTH AMERICA

ARGENTINE—BUENOS AIRES

BRUCE, DOUGLAS WILLIAM, C.B.E., D.D. (Edinburgh, 30th June 1939); his wife, Cecily Mary Kirby, died 5th April 1942.

FLEMING, JAMES WILLIAM, his widow, Elizabeth Ann McDiarmid, died 7th Aug. 1929.

GILLESPIE, WILLIAM MURDOCH, app. to Lowick 1929.

KELLY, GRAEME ISMAY DAVIDSON, son of John Davidson K., M.A., Headmaster, Stanley House, Bridge of Allan, and Anne Baines; educ. at Univ. of Glasgow, M.A. (1926); ord. 1929; adm. to Dunscore 28th Oct. 1930; dem. on app. to Santiago, Chile, July 1939; locum Hopemount, Arbroath, 1942–4; app. to St Ninian's, Paisley, 14th Sept. 1944. Marr. 15th Dec. 1930 Beryl Marjorie, only child of Walter and Jemima Wooley, Junin, Argentina, and has issue—Walter John Davidson, born 6th May 1932; Norman Ismay Davidson, born 13th Sept. 1937.

MACDONALD, HECTOR KENNEDY, adm. to St Madoes 23rd April 1930. Marr. 15th March 1932 Kristeen, daugh. of William Baird Laing, M.I.C.E., and has issue—William Hilton Charles, born 19th Oct. 1935; Kristeen Ann, born 26th Oct. 1936.

MACINNES, ALASDAIR ROBERT ELLIS, dem. 1928; assistant, Mauchline; ord. to Cadder (*q.v.*) 5th June 1929.

McRURY, DONALD ARCHIBALD, adm. to Duncansburgh 20th July 1932; adm. Indian Chaplain 10th Sept. 1935; served in war 1939–45.

TAYLOR, JAMES SHEPHERD, born 3rd Dec. 1900; son of Peter Chalmers T., printer, and Helen Chalmers Shepherd; educ. at Univ. of Glasgow, M.A. (1922); licen. by Presb. of Perth 10th June 1925; assistant, New Kilpatrick; ord. assistant Buenos Aires 9th Feb. 1926; app. min. in charge Northern Suburbs Nov. 1927; adm. to Stevenson Memorial, Glasgow, 17th May 1933; Chaplain to Forces, H.L.I., 1940; killed in action 30th June 1944. Marr. 10th June 1931 Evelyn Ramsay, daugh. of Gilbert Ramsay Darbyshire, railway official, Buenos Aires, and Margaret Macdonald Grant, and has issue—Flora Ramsay, born 16th June 1932; Kenneth Iain, born 29th Dec. 1934; Gilbert Ramsay Darbyshire, born 31st May 1938.

CHILE—VALPARAISO

LAING, WILLIAM MACKIE, dem. Oct. 1933; adm. to Colinton 4th Oct. 1934. Addl. issue—Charles Walbaun, born 31st July 1935.

FOREIGN MISSIONARIES

Introduction, page 686, line 19, for "Choriza" read "Chogorie."

ALEXANDER, JAMES FREDERICK, trans. to Blantyre 1933; Member of Legislative Council, Nyasaland; served until 1938. Line 3, for "Archibald John" read "John Archibald," died 6th June 1941.

ALEXANDER, JOHN ARCHIBALD, adm. to St John's, Symington, 14th April 1938; dem. 10th Feb. 1946.

ANDERSON, ANDREW MELVILLE, served until re-transfer of Iringa Mission to the Berlin Missionary Society 1929; died at Sadani, Tanganyika, 16th Sept. 1939.

ANDERSON, JOHN, his widow, Mary Johnston Veitch, died 4th April 1944.

ARTHUR, JOHN WILLIAM, D.D. (St Andrews, 28th June 1946); adm. to Dunbog 26th July 1938; dem. 22nd July 1948. Addl. issue—Caroline, born 6th Feb. 1926; David, born 23rd Feb. 1930.

BAILEY, THOMAS GRAHAME, served until 1920; died 5th April 1942; his son, Wellesley Grahame, ord. missionary to the Punjab 10th Dec. 1939.

BAIN, JAMES, died at Stirling 10th Nov. 1928.

BORROWMAN, PATRICK HAMILTON, B.D., formerly of Tighnabruach (*q.v.*); app. to Blantyre Mission 30th Sept. 1929; died at Zomba, Nyasaland, 30th Jan. 1948; had issue—a son and a daughter.

BOWMAN, ERNEST DREWITT, retired 1928; app. 1928 Principal of the Jeanes School, Zomba, under Nyasaland Government.

CALDERWOOD, ROBERT GEORGE MATHESON, app. to St Andrew's, Jerusalem, 1936; Secretary, Missionary Council, Kenya, April 1937. Addl. issue—Anne, born 1st Nov. 1925; son, born 2nd Nov. 1928; his wife, Isobel Shaw Cowan, died 6th May 1943.

CAMERON, ALLAN, Principal of Scottish Churches College, Calcutta, 30th June 1937; adm. to Forgandenny 17th May 1945; his daugh., Jean (marr. 17th Aug. 1940 Ian Fraser Mackenzie, M.B., D.P.H., assistant medical officer, Blyth); Mildred (marr. 9th Aug. 1941 Lieut. Robert Burdon Stoker, Normans Hall, Prestbury, Cheshire); his son, Donald Lyon Scott, killed in war 1944.

COCKBURN, GEORGE, his widow, Johnann Garden Thomson, died at Aberdeen 14th March 1936; his daugh., Alice, died at Longniddry 7th June 1935.

DALGETTY, WILLIAM, dem. 1930; died 4th Aug. 1935; his widow, Elizabeth Reid Simpson, died Winnipeg 31st May 1944; his son, William, M.B., Ch.B.

DEANS, WILLIAM, formerly of Tewchar (*q.v.*) and Vol. vii, 690; died at Alexandria, Egypt, 11th Nov. 1934. Marr. (2) Agnes Daffe, who died at Herne Bay 6th June 1935.

DUNCAN, HENRY CECIL, his son, James Edwards, min. of Provanmill, Glasgow, 1940.

DUNCAN, JOHN MENZIES BAILLIE, adm. to Moonzie 19th July 1939; dem. 31st Dec. 1946; his daugh., Clara, died 6th Sept. 1934.

EDWARDS, JAMES, his son, James Sutherland, M.D., died at Perth 8th Feb. 1930.

FERRIE, WILLIAM WINKS, licen. 6th June 1923; adm. for work in India by General Assembly May 1934, and by Presb. of Edinburgh 5th June 1934.

GARRETT, JOHN, Punjab, dem. 1947; assistant Springburnhill, Glasgow, 1947; elected to Duntocher West, 1947, but died on way to church 10th Jan. 1948.

GRAHAM, JOHN ANDERSON, Moderator of the General Assembly May 1931; dem. 1932; D.D. (Aberdeen); died at Kalimpong 15th May 1942. His daughs.— Betty Hughes (marr. 3rd Nov. 1942 Major George Sherriff); Isobel Anderson (marr. Thomas M. Coffey, C.I.E.), died 24th March 1947.

HETHERWICK, ALEXANDER, O.B.E., D.D., dem. 1929, died at Aberdeen 3rd April 1939; his widow, Elizabeth Barclay Pithie, died at Aberdeen 13th Feb. 1945. Addl. Publications—*The Romance of Blantyre*, and enlarged edition of *Dictionary of Nyanja Language*.

KELLAS, JOHN, app. Professor of Economics, Scottish Churches College, Calcutta, 1923; ord. 9th June 1935. Marr. 22nd Aug. 1922 Evelyn Margaret, daugh. of David Ritchie, Peterhead, and has issue —Marshall, born 23rd Aug. 1925, died June 1926; Jean Campbell, born 29th April 1929; Evelyn Lindsay, born 25th Jan. 1931; a child, born 16th Aug. 1939.

KILGOUR, ROBERT, Chaplain to Scots Guards and other Presbyterian troops in London District; died at London 28th Jan. 1942.

KNOX, ROBERT BRODIE, M.A., B.Sc.; born Colac, Victoria, Australia, 25th March 1897; son of Edward K.; app. to Young Men's Guild Mission, Kalimpong, 16th Nov. 1926. Marr. 14th Jan. 1928 Gladys Ivy, daugh. of Richard Lewis Reed, and has issue—Dorothy Margaret, born 23rd Oct. 1928; Gladys Catherine, born 27th Nov. 1929; Elizabeth Mary, born 15th Jan. 1932; Kenneth William, born 12th July 1933; Jean, born 13th Aug. 1937.

LILLIE, WILLIAM, ord. 29th March 1931; adm. to Dulnain Bridge 1948; D.D. (Aberdeen, 1948). Marr. 17th Sept. 1929 Florence Jean Crawford, daugh. of David Watson, D.D., min. of St Clement's Church, Glasgow, and had issue—Adziel, born 3rd July 1931, died 31st Oct. 1935.

LORNIE, JAMES TAYLOR, his widow, Marjory Agnes Jackson, died 7th May 1945.

MacINTOSH, JAMES ARCHIBALD, born Minden, Ontario, Canada, 24th Aug. 1870; son of Alexander M., hardware merchant; educ. Univ. of Aberdeen, B.D. (1904).

MACKEAN, WALTER GEORGE, adm. to Maryton, Montrose, 5th April 1929; died at Aberdeen 2nd Nov. 1932.

MACKENZIE, EVAN, adm. to Glenmorriston 30th July 1930; died 8th Jan. 1934. His daugh., Christina Elizabeth, died at Georgetown, Demerara, 28th Nov. 1940.

McLEAN, LAUCHLAN, died Nov. 1942.

McLEAN, RODERICK MATHIESON, born Conon Bridge, Ross-shire, 13th Feb. 1887, son of Donald M., Glengynach, Kingussie; educ. at Kingussie School and Univs. of Edinburgh and Glasgow; went to Canada 1906; served in Great War in 90th Winnipeg Rifles and Gordon Highlanders 1914; 1st Lieutenant, 25th Sept. 1915; Captain, March 1916; Major, 1918 (despatches); assistant, St George's in the Fields, Glasgow, as student, and St Cuthbert's, Edinburgh; ord. missionary to Nyasaland 29th Sept. 1929; adm. to Grange, Grangemouth, 5th Oct. 1932; trans. to Erchless 11th Oct. 1934; trans. to Lawson Memorial, Forfar, 18th April 1940; trans. to Grenada 14th July 1942. Marr. 1st Oct. 1931 Harriet, second daugh. of Donald Maclean, min. of Duirinish, and has issue—Rona Matheson, born 24th July 1933; Roderick John, born 13th Feb. 1935.

MILL, GEORGE SCOTT, India, dem. 1947; adm. to Garvald 16th Feb. 1948;

his daughs.—Elizabeth Wilson, born Gordon 30th Aug. 1920, M.A. (1940) (marr. 4th July 1942 James Aitken Whyte, min. of Dunollie Road, Oban); Catherine Carlyle, born Calcutta 22nd Sept. 1922 (marr. 6th June 1946 Edward Beaumont Packham).

MORRISON, JOHN, died at Edinburgh 14th Feb. 1932.

NICOLSON, ANGUS, dem. 1941, and returned to Scotland; assistant at West St. George's Church, Edinburgh; adm. to Lawers 18th July 1947; had issue—son, born 20th Feb. 1925; daugh., born 28th Aug. 1928.

OGG, GEORGE, dem. and became locum tenens Tighnabruaich 1928; adm. to Anstruther Easter 27th Feb. 1929.

OGILVIE, JAMES, his daughs.—Mary, died at Portobello 16th March 1935; Maria Frances, died 15th March 1949.

PATERSON, KEITH NORMAN, born Gujerat 23rd Feb. 1902, son of Robert McCheyne P., foreign missionary, Punjab; educ. at George Watson's College and Univ. of Edinburgh; licen. by Presb. of Edinburgh 2nd May 1929; ord. to Punjab Mission, Sialkot, 26th May 1929; dem. 1938. Marr. 9th April 1934 J. C. D., M.A., daugh. of William G. Jeffrey, min. of Millburn, Renton, and has issue—Robert Crozier, born 25th July 1935.

PATERSON, ROBERT McCHEYNE, O.B.E. Line 17, for "J.S." read "Thomas Stanley"; licen. 1941; died Kashmir 5th June 1942.

PHILIP, HORACE ROBERT ANDREW, adm. to Newcastle upon Tyne 1930; his son, Robert Andrew, missionary, Kenya.

REID, JAMES, born 27th March 1869; son of Andrew Reid, engineer; app. general agent to Nyasaland Mission 1891; ord. by Presb. of Blantyre, Nyasaland, 1907; adm. by General Assembly 1934; served several periods as unofficial member of Nyasaland Legislative; Central Africa Medal 1894–8; served till 1933. Marr. 11th Sept. 1901 Maria Jean, M.B.E. (died 12th April 1943), daugh. of John Sanderson, Leith, and has issue—Irene Margaret Isobel, born 30th Nov. 1902; May Dorothy, born 6th May 1906.

RICE, HENRY, his widow, Louisa Hill Cumine, died at Liberton 16th Nov. 1941, aged 91.

SCOTT, HENRY EDWARD, his widow, Isabella Govan, died at Edinburgh 19th June 1939.

SCOTT, WILLIAM, died at Edinburgh 24th Aug. 1936; his son, David Leslie, missionary, Punjab; his daugh., Elizabeth May, teacher, Punjab Mission.

SCOTT, WILLIAM MACKENZIE, had issue—Helen, born 16th May 1927; Shena, born 13th June 1929; Margaret, born 29th June 1933.

STIRLING, JAMES CLARK PAUL, born Edinburgh 30th April 1903; son of Rev. James S. and Isabella Davidson Paul; educ. at Westfield House School, Manchester Grammar School, Victoria Univ., Manchester, Univ. of Edinburgh, M.A., B.D. (1928); distinguished athlete; licen. by Presb. of Edinburgh 1928; assistant, St Cuthbert's, Edinburgh; ord. to Mills and Steamers Chaplaincy, Calcutta, 23rd Oct. 1928; chaplain at Rawalpindi, Burree, Secunderabad and Madras 1938; was chaplain attached to Queen's Own Cameron Highlanders, Argyll and Sutherland Highlanders and Cameronians (Scottish Rifles); Presidency Senior Chaplain, Madras; was chaplain in various campaigns on Indian Frontier; served as combatant officer 1940–4 as Company Commander 1st Batt. Baluch Regiment Frontier Campaign 1940; Intelligence Officer, 27th Indian Infantry Brigade, Iraq and Persia; Military Secretary's Branch 10th Army at General Headquarters, India; dem. 1943; adm. to Trinity, Coatbridge, 16th Feb. 1946; dem. 3rd Feb. 1948. Marr. Ruth Evelyn, daugh. of William Alexander Chisholm, K.C., and has issue—Robin Alasdair Chisholm, born 23rd April 1933.

STOTT, IAN FERGUSSON GORDON, app. Government Supervisor of Education, Nyasaland.

TOCHER, FORBES SCOTT, D.D., Aberdeen (1934); adm. to Botriphnie 21st April 1948; his daugh., Agnes Forbes, 3rd Officer W.R.N.S. (marr. 22nd March 1945 Captain Gilbert George Michael, Intelligence Corps).

TURNBULL, ARCHIBALD, his daugh., Christina Brooks Macdiarmid, died 18th July 1933.

WATSON, HARRY STEEL, adm. to Lochcraig 22nd Sept. 1937; trans. to Neilston South 24th April 1946; has issue—Alexander Cameron, born 23rd Feb. 1927; Harry Milne, born 5th Dec. 1929; Helen Elizabeth, born 29th June 1936.

WATT, JOHN ALEXANDER ROBSON, son of Archie Crawford W., min. of Comrie U.F. Church; ord. 23rd June 1929 to Gold Coast; trans. to Kenya; adm. to Ordiquhill and Cornhill 5th Feb. 1947. Marr. 11th Aug. 1931 Jessie Mary, daugh. of Colonel Imrie, I.M.S., Edinburgh, and has issue—a son, born 31st Oct. 1933; a son, born and died 13th Feb. 1938; a daugh., born 6th Feb. 1939; Dorcas, born July 1942, died 7th April 1945.

WAUGH, GEORGE, died 28th April 1929; his widow, Jane Braid, died 25th Jan. 1938.

YOUNGSON, JOHN FORBES WHITE, his daugh., Margaret (marr. 15th Sept. 1908 Dr John Clark Wilson), died 7th Feb. 1925; his son, Alexander, died 19th Feb. 1943.

GREEN, STEPHEN, missionary, Nyasaland, 1928–37; returned home; assistant St Nicholas West, Aberdeen; adm. to Pulteneytown 29th Aug. 1940; dem. on re-app. to Nyasaland April 1946. Marr. 16th March 1932 Marion Cowan. youngest daugh. of John Henderson, Uddingston.

JEWISH MISSIONARIES

The first Jewish Missions of the Church were those opened at Jassy, Rumania, in June 1841, and at Budapest, Hungary, in Aug. 1841.

SPENCE, DAVID BROWN, his son, John W. L., M.D., died 15th March 1930; his daugh., Elizabeth J. W., died 17th March 1944.

APPENDIX

CHURCH OF SCOTLAND

List of Principal Clerks; Sub- or Depute Clerks; Procurators; Agents

PRINCIPAL CLERKS OF THE GENERAL ASSEMBLY

Cir. 1572	JOHN GRAY, succeeded by
Cir. 1589	JAMES RITCHIE, succeeded by
	THOMAS NICOLSON, succeeded by
	–. SANDILANDS.
1638	ARCHIBALD JOHNSTON of Warriston. (Also Advocate for the Church.)
1690–1694	JOHN SPALDING.
1694–1695	ROBERT PARK, advocate.
1695–1701	JOHN BANNATYNE, min. at Lanark.
1701–1703	DAVID DUNDAS, advocate.
1703–1731	JOHN DUNDAS of Philipstoun, advocate. (Also Procurator from 1706.)
1731–1746	WM. GRANT, advocate—afterwards Lord Prestongrange. (Also Procurator.)
1746–1778	Dr GEORGE WISHART, min. at Tron, Edinburgh.
1778–1785	Dr GEORGE WISHART and Dr JOHN DRYSDALE (assistant and successor), min. at Tron, Edinburgh.
1785–1788	Dr JOHN DRYSDALE.
1789–1807	ANDREW DALZELL, Professor of Greek, Univ. of Edinburgh.
1807–1827	Dr ANDREW DUNCAN, min. at Ratho.
1828–1859	Dr JOHN LEE, Principal of Univ. of Edinburgh.
1859–1861	Dr ALEX. LOCKHART SIMPSON, min. at Kirknewton.
1862–1874	Dr JOHN COOK, min. of Haddington (First Charge).
1875–1886	Dr JOHN TULLOCH, Principal of St Mary's College, St Andrews.
1886–1893	Dr WM. MILLIGAN, Professor of Biblical Criticism, Univ. of Aberdeen.
1894–1907	Dr ROBERT HERBERT STORY, Principal of Univ. of Glasgow.
1907–1911	Dr NORMAN MACLEOD, min. at Inverness (First Charge).
1912–1926	Dr DAVID PAUL, min. at Grange, Edinburgh.
1926–1927	Dr JAMES ALEXANDER McCLYMONT.
1928–1929	Dr JAMES TAYLOR COX, min. at Dyce.

After Union of the Churches

SENIOR CLERKS

1929–1939   Dr JAMES TAYLOR COX and Dr. JAMES HARVEY, Joint Clerks.

PRINCIPAL CLERKS

1939–1946   Dr JAMES TAYLOR COX.
1946–1948   LOUIS CARRICK PHILIPS, min. at Logie, Fife; died 5th Nov. 1948.
1949   Dr THOMAS CALDWELL.

SUB- OR DEPUTE CLERKS OF THE GENERAL ASSEMBLY

After 1589 ROBERT WINRAME.
1638   ALEX. BLAIR.
1701–1738   NICOL SPENCE.
1738–1743   NICOL SPENCE and ROBERT McINTOSH.
1743–1753   ROBERT McINTOSH and JOHN BAILLIE.
1753–1754   JOHN BAILLIE and JAS. EDMONSTON.
1754–1781   JAS. EDMONSTON.
1781–1802   Dr WM. GLOAG, min. at West St Giles, Edinburgh.
1802–1808   Dr DAVID RITCHIE, min. at St Andrew's (Second Charge), Edinburgh; afterwards Professor of Logic in the Univ. of Edinburgh.
1808–1826   Dr THOS. McKNIGHT, min. at Old Kirk, Edinburgh.
1826–1828   Dr THOS. McKNIGHT and Dr JOHN LEE, Principal of Univ. of Edinburgh.
1828–1836   Dr THOS. McKNIGHT and Dr ALEX. LOCKHART SIMPSON, min. at Kirknewton.
1836–1859   Dr ALEX. LOCKHART SIMPSON.
1859–1862   Dr JOHN COOK, min. at Haddington.
1862–1875   Dr JOHN TULLOCH, Principal of St Mary's College, St Andrews.
1875–1886   Dr WILLIAM MILLIGAN, Professor of Divinity and Biblical Criticism, Univ. of Aberdeen.
1886–1894   Dr ROBERT HERBERT STORY, Principal of Univ. of Glasgow.
1894–1907   Dr NORMAN MACLEOD, min. at Inverness (First Charge).
1907–1912   Dr JOHN GILLESPIE, min. at Mouswald.
1912–1913   Dr WM. SIMPSON, min. at Bonhill.
1914–1926   Dr JAMES ALEXANDER McCLYMONT.
1926   Dr JAMES NICOLL OGILVIE.
1927–1928   Dr JAMES TAYLOR COX, min. at Dyce.
1928–1929   DUNCAN CAMERON, min. at Kilsyth.

APPENDIX

After Union of the Churches

JUNIOR CLERK

1929–1938 Dr JAMES GORDON SUTHERLAND.

DEPUTE CLERKS

1939–1946 Dr LOUIS CARRICK PHILIPS.

1946 Dr THOMAS CALDWELL, min. at Aberlady. (Principal Clerk May 1949.)

ADVOCATES AND PROCURATORS OF THE CHURCH

1638 ARCHIBALD JOHNSTON of Warriston. (Also Clerk.) Executed 22nd July 1663.

1706–1731 JOHN DUNDAS. (Also Clerk.)

1731–1745 WILLIAM GRANT (afterwards Lord Prestongrange). (Also Clerk.) Died 23rd May 1764.

1746–1778 DAVID DALRYMPLE, died 26th April 1784.

1778–1806 WILLIAM ROBERTSON (afterwards Lord Robertson), died 20th Nov. 1835.

1806–1831 SIR JOHN CONNELL, died April 1831.

1831–1856 ROBERT BELL, died 27th April 1861.

1856–1869 ALEXANDER SHANK COOK, died 16th Jan. 1869.

1869–1880 ROBERT LEE (afterwards Lord Lee), died 11th Oct. 1890.

1880–1886 WILLIAM MACKINTOSH (afterwards Lord Kyllachy), died 19th Dec. 1918.

1886–1891 SIR CHARLES PEARSON (afterwards Lord Pearson), died 15th Aug. 1910.

1891–1906 SIR JOHN CHEYNE, died 15th Jan. 1907.

1907–1918 Sir CHRISTOPHER NICOLSON JOHNSTON (afterwards Lord Sands), died 26th Feb. 1934.

1918–1922 Hon. WILLIAM WATSON (afterwards Lord Thankerton), died 11th June 1948.

1923–1929 Sir WILLIAM CHREE.

PROCURATORS

1929–1936 Sir WILLIAM CHREE, died 9th Jan. 1936.

1936–1937 Sir ARCHIBALD CAMPBELL BLACK.

1938–1948 JAMES FREDERICK STRACHAN.

AGENTS FOR THE CHURCH

1690–1706	JOHN BLAIR.
1706–1722	JOHN BLAIR and NICOL SPENCE (died Feb. 1743), Joint Agents.
1722–1738	NICOL SPENCE.
1738–1743	NICOL SPENCE and ROBERT McINTOSH, Joint Agents.
1743–1753	ROBERT McINTOSH (died 4th Jan. 1753) and JOHN BAILLIE, W.S., Joint Agents.
1753–1754	JOHN BAILLIE (died 9th Jan. 1754) and JAMES EDMONSTON, Joint Agents.
1754–1781	JAMES EDMONSTON.
1781–1795	GEORGE CAIRNCROSS.
1795–1809	WILLIAM MURRAY.
1809–1831	WILLIAM MURRAY and JOHN MURRAY, W.S. (died 13th April 1836).
1831–1855	WILLIAM YOUNG, W.S., died 22nd April 1855.
1855–1868	JOHN BEATSON BELL, W.S., died 18th May 1869.
1868–1905	Sir WILLIAM J. MENZIES, W.S., died 14th Oct. 1905.
1906–1925	ALAN LOCKHART MENZIES, W.S., died 12th Nov. 1926.
1926–1929	JOHN ALEXANDER STEVENSON MILLAR, W.S.

After Union of the Churches

AGENTS

1929–1938	JOHN ALEXANDER STEVENSON MILLAR, W.S. (died 5th Nov. 1938); ARTHUR HENRY McLEAN, W.S.; and EDWARD JOHN McCANDLISH, W.S., Joint Agents.

Note. It may be noted: (1) that Mr Archibald Johnston of Warriston, Mr John Dundas, and Mr William Grant held the offices both of Clerk of Assembly and Procurator for the Church; (2) that the office of Principal Clerk was held by a layman up to 1746, and again from 1789 to 1807, and similarly that of Sub-Clerk up to 1781; and (3) that all the ministerial Principal Clerks had filled the office of Moderator of the General Assembly with the exception of Dr Cox, who declined nomination.

FATHERS OF THE CHURCH OF SCOTLAND

	Name	Parish	Year of Birth	Ordination	Death
1.	David Ferguson	Dunfermline	1533?	1560	1598
2.	John Craig	Aberdeen		1560	1601
3.	John Duncanson	Stirling		1560	1601
4.	David Lindsay	South Leith		1560	1613
5.	David Wemyss	St Mungo's, Glasgow		1565	1615
6.	Thomas Duncan(son)	Bowden		1568	1621
7.	George Johnston	Ancrum		1572	1631
8.	John Durham	Monikie		1576	1639
9.	Andrew Bennet	Monimail		1583	1639
10.	Thomas Baxter	Dunbog		1585	1644
11.	James Stirling	Strathblane		1586	1650
12.	Luke Stirling	Kilmarnock		1591	1655
13.	John Wemyss	Kinnaird		1597	1659
14.	David Mayne	Dalziel	1572?	1607	1676
15.	James Scott	Ancrum		1616	1679
16.	John Cunison	Dull		1624	1681
17.	James Ker	Abbotrule	1601	1624	1694
18.	John Gemmell	Symington (Ayr)		1642	1705
19.	Roderick Mackenzie	Gairloch		1649	1710
20.	Alexander Gordon	Inveraray		1650	1713
21.	Patrick Simson	Renfrew	1628	1653	1715
22.	Alexander Warner or Verner	Balmaclellan		1657	1716
23.	Alexander McLachlan	Arrochar		1658	1731
24.	William Garioch	Kennethmont	1649?	1677	1738
25.	John Anderson	Drymen		1682	1740
26.	David Meldrum	Tibbermore		1684	1741
27.	John Mackenzie	Laggan		1686	1745
28.	John Cranstoun	Ancrum		1696	1747
29.	James Ramsay	Kelso	1672	1693	1749
30.	Robert Bell	Crailing	1670	1694	1755
31.	James Guthrie	Kirkpatrick Irongray		1694	1756
32.	David Pitcairn	Dysart	1672	1695	1757
33.	Archibald Lundie	Saltoun	1674	1696	1759
34.	Alexander Robeson	Tinwald	1676	1697	1761
35.	Andrew Cumin	Largs	1680	1701	1762
36.	James Nairne	Anstruther Easter	1680	1703	1771
37.	James Nasmyth	Dalmeny	1683?	1711	1774
38.	John McInnes	Logie-Coldstone	1690	1715	1777
39.	Alexander Simson	Monymusk	1698	1720	1781
40.	David Turner	Greenock West	1695	1721	1785
41.	George Reid	Ochiltree	1696	1725	1786
42.	Robert Farquhar	Chapel of Garioch	1699	1726	1787

FATHERS OF THE CHURCH OF SCOTLAND

	Name	Parish	Year of Birth	Ordination	Death
43.	Alexander Johnson	Lyne and Megget	1686	1728	1788
44.	James Thomson	Dunfermline	1699	1728	1790
45.	Sir Robert Preston, Bart.	Cupar	1706	1731	1791
46.	David Hunter	Saline	1698	1732	1792
47.	James Wilson	Gamrie	1694	1732	1792
48.	Malcolm Brown	Kilbirnie	1695	1734	1794
49.	John Baird	Stobo	1710?	1734	1795
50.	John Steele	Stair		1735	1804
51.	David Bannerman	St Martin's	1713	1742	1810
52.	John Aitken	St Vigeans	1726	1754	1816
53.	James Innes	Yester	1733	1760	1821
54.	Patrick Macdonald	Kilmore and Kilbride	1729	1756	1824
55.	Paul Fraser	Inveraray	1731	1761	1827
56.	Thomas Somerville	Jedburgh	1746	1767	1830
57.	William Mackenzie	Tongue	1731	1767	1834
58.	Robert Home	Polwarth	1744	1769	1838
59.	John Burns	Barony, Glasgow	1744	1774	1839
60.	William Leslie	St Andrew's, Lhanbryd	1747	1775	1839
61.	John Kellock or Cuninghame	Crichton	1744	1776	1839
62.	Peter Barclay	Kettle	1749	1778	1841
63.	John Monteath	Houston	1752	1781	1843
64.	James McDonald	Kemback	1752	1781	1843
65.	Andrew Murray	Auchterderran	1749	1783	1844
66.	George Morison	Banchory-Devenick	1758	1783	1845
67.	Joseph Crichton	Ceres	1754	1786	1849
68.	Duncan Macfarlan	St Mungo's, Glasgow	1771	1792	1857
69.	Peter Young	Wigtown	1772	1799	1864
70.	Matthew Gardner	Bothwell	1776	1802	1865
71.	David Harris	Fern	1772	1803	1867
72.	David Duff	Kenmore	1780	1806	1872
73.	Robert Buchanan	Peebles	1786	1813	1873
74.	Alexander Lawson	Creich, Fife	1788	1815	1875
75.	Robert Stirling	Galston	1790	1816	1878
76.	John Stewart	Liberton	1793	1823	1879
77.	Walter Home	Polwarth	1798	1823	1886
78.	James Grant	St Mary's, Edinburgh	1800	1824	1890
79.	James Smith	Cathcart	1803	1825	1897
80.	James Chrystal	Auchinleck	1807	1833	1901
81.	John Duncan	Abdie	1814	1839	1902
82.	John David Palm		1816	1839	1909
83.	John Anderson	Culter, Biggar	1821	1846	1922
84.	James Curdie Russell	Campbeltown	1830	1854	1925
85.	George Thomas Jamieson	Portobello	1838	1863	1926
86.	Thomas Peter Johnston	Carnbee	1836	1864	1932
87.	Robert Thomson	Rubislaw, Aberdeen	1843	1866	1935
88.	William Lang Baxter	Cameron	1841	1867	1937
89.	James Lindsay	Balfron	1846	1871	1938
90.	William Innes	Skene, Lochside U.F.	1843	1873	1940
91.	James Murray	Kilmacolm	1849	1875	1939
92.	Archibald Macdonald	Kiltarlity	1853	1877	1948

INDEX OF PARISHES AND CHAPELS

SCOTLAND

ABBEY, Edinburgh, 6
Abbey St Bathans, 115
Abbotrule, 138
Abbotsford, Glasgow, 188
Abbotshall, 429
Abdie, 437
Aberchirder, 608
Abercorn, 36
Abercrombie, St Monans, 453
Aberdalgie, 360
Aberdeen
  East St Nicholas, 526
  Ferryhill, 526
  Gilcolmston, 526
  Greyfriars, 527
  Holburn, 527
  John Knox, 527
  Mannofield, 527
  North, 527
  Old Machar First, 528
    Second, 530
  Our Lady of the Snow, 530
  Powis, 531
  Rosemount, 531
  Rubislaw, 531
  Ruthrieston, 531
  St Clements, 531
  St Fittick's, 532
  St George's in the West, 532
  St Ninian's, 532
  South, 533
  Trinity, 535
  West St Nicholas, 533
  Woodside, 535
Aberdour, Fife, 404
Aberdour, Deer, 578
Aberfeldy, 354
Aberfoyle, 395
Aberlady, 85
Aberlemno, 479
Aberlour, 611
Abernethy, Perth, 360
Abernethy, Strathspey, 615
Abernyte, 485

Aberuthven, 372
Abertarff, 343
Aboyne, 544
Acharacle, 337
Addiewell, 1
Advie, 615
Airdrie, East, 250
  West, 250
Airlie, 471
Airth, 36, 386
Aithsting, 706
Aldbar, 479
Aldcambus, 105
Aldhame, 113
Alexandria, 273
Alford, 555
Alloa and Tullibody, 386
  St Andrew's, 387
Alloway, 211
Alness, 658
Altyre, 642
Alva, 387
Alvah, 588
Alves, 622
Alvie, 615
Alyth, 471
Amulree, 354
Ancrum, 135
Anderston, 288
Annan, 165
Annbank, 211
Anstruther Easter, 453
  Wester, 454
Anwoth, 199
Appin, 331
Applecross, 680
Applegarth and Sibbaldie, 155
Arbirlot, 508
Arbroath, Abbey, 509
  Inverbrothock, 509
  Ladyloan, 509
  St Margaret, 509
Arbuthnott, 516
Ardallie, 578

INDEX OF PARISHES AND CHAPELS

Ardchattan, 331
Ardclach, 647
Ardentinny, 316
Ardersier, 647
Ardgour, 343
Ardler, 472
Ardnamurchan, 337
Ardoch, 376
Ardrishaig, 312
Ardrossan, 228
   New, 228
Ardwell, 187
Arisaig, 343
Armadale, 36
Arngask, 416
Arnsheen, 187
Arrochar, 273
Ashkirk, 148
Assynt, 671
Athelstaneford, 86
Auchencairn, 199
Auchengray, 266
Auchindoir, 555
Auchinleck, 211
Auchmithie, 509
Auchterarder, 376
Auchterderran, 422
Auchtergaven, 346
Auchterhouse, 485
Auchterless, 588
Auchtermuchty, 437
Auchtertool, 422
Augustine, Greenock, 247
Auldearn, 647
Avondale, 251
Avoch, 655
Ayr, 212
   St James, Newton, 213
   St Leonard, 213
   Wallacetown, 213
Ayton, 122

BAILLESTON, 257
Baldernock, 273
Balfron, 273
Balgay, Dundee, 487
Ballachulish, 343
Ballantrae, 187
Ballingry, 416
Ballumbie, 405
Balmaclellan, 200
Balmaghie, 200
Balmerino, 438
Balquhidder, 396
Balshagray, 289
Banchory Devenick, 535
Banchory Ternan, 544

Banff, 596
Bannockburn, 387
Banton, 285
Bargeddie, 251
Bargrennan, 193
Barnhill, St Margaret, 495
Barnwell, 226
Barony, Glasgow, 289
Barr, 214
Barra, 688
Barrhead, 237
Barrowfield, Glasgow, 290
Barry, 509
Barthol Chapel, 572
Barvas, 692
Bathgate, 36
Battlefield, Glasgow, 290
Beach, Broughty Ferry, 485
Beath, 406
Bedrule, 135
Beith, 229
Belhaven, 105
Belhelvie, 536
Bellahouston, 290
Bellie, 603
Bellshill, 252
Belmont, Glasgow, 290
Benbecula, 688
Bendochy, 472
Benholme, 516
Benvie, 492
Bernera, Uist, 688
Bervie, 517
Bethelnie, 569
Biggar, 51
Birnie, 622
Birsay, 696
Birse, 545
Blackbraes, 37
Blackford and Strageith, 377
Blackfriars, Glasgow, 290
Blackhall, St Columba, 5
Blackhill, 578
Blair Atholl, 346
Blairdaff, 562
Blairgowrie, 472
   St Mary, 473
Blairingone, 417
Blantyre, 252
Bluevale, Glasgow, 291
Boarhills, 454
Boddam, 578
Boharm, 611
Boleskine and Abertarff, 650
Bolton, 87
Bona, 651
Boness, 37
Bonhill, 274

INDEX OF PARISHES AND CHAPELS

Bonnington, Edinburgh, 20
Bonnybridge, 387
Boquhanran, 274
Borgue, 201
Borthwick, 67
Bothkennar, 388
Bothwell, 252
Botriphnie, 604
Bourtree, 562
Bowden, 148
Bower, 676
Boyndie, 596
Bracadale, 683
Braemar, 545
Braes of Rannoch, 354
Brechin, Cathedral, 497, 498
   East, 498
   Gardner Memorial, 499
Bressay, 702
Bridge of Allan, 396
Bridge of Weir, 237
Bridgegate, Glasgow, 291
Bridgeton, Glasgow, 291
Brodick, 322
Broughton, 52
Broughty Ferry, 485
   Beach, 485
   St James, 96
Broxburn, 38
Brydekirk, 166
Buccleuch, Edinburgh, 7
   Glasgow, 291
Buchanan, 274
Buchlyvie, 396
Buckhaven, 423
Buckie, 596
Buittle and Kirkennan, 202
Bunkle and Preston, 115
Burghead, 623
Burnbank, 254
Burntisland, 423
Burra, Shetland, 702
Burray, Orkney, 693

CABRACH, 556
Cadder, 285
Caddonfoot, 149
Cadzow, 254
Caerlaverock, 170
Cairney Botarie and Rivin, 604
Calderbank, 254
Caldercruix, 254
Calderhead, 254
Caldwell, 237
Callander, 396
Calton, Glasgow, 291
Cambus Kenneth, 394
Cambuslang, 254

Cambuslang, West, 255
Cambusmichael, 373
Cambusnethan, 255
Camelon, 38
Cameron, 454
Campbeltown, 322
   Lochend, 323
Campsie, 285
Canisbay, 676
Canonbie, 162
Canongate, 7, 8
Caputh and Logie Mached, 347
Cardonald, 237
Cardross, 275
Careston, 499
Carfin, 261
Cargill, 347
Carluke, 265
Carmichael, 265
Carmunnock, 286
Carmylie, 509
Carnbee, 455
Carnoch, 658
Carnock, 407
Carnoustie, 510
Carntyne, St Michaels, 292
Carnwath, 265
Carriden, 39
Carrington, 68
Carsphairn, 202
Carstairs, 266
Cartsburn, 247
Castle Douglas, 203
Castle, Edinburgh, 37
Castleton, 168
Cathcart, 286
Catrine, 214
Catterline, 523
Cavers, 135
Cawdor, 648
Cellardyke, 455
Ceres, 439
Chalmers, Glasgow, 292
Channelkirk, 143
Chapel of Garioch, 562
Chapelshade, Dundee, 487
Chapelton, 255
Charteris Memorial, Edinburgh, 20
Chirnside, 122
Chryston, 287
Clackmannan, 388
Clarkston, 255
Clatt, 556
Cleish, 417
Cleland, 255
Clepington, Dundee, 487
Closeburn, 182
Clova, 479

Clunie, 348
Cluny, 545
Clydebank, 275
Clyne, 671
Coatdyke, 255
Coats, 255
Cockburnspath, 105
Cockenzie, 88
Cockpen, 68
Coldingham, 122
Coldstream, 124
Colinton, 1
Coll, 338
Collace, 361
Collessie, 439
Colliston, 510
Colmonell, 187
Colonsay, 328
Colston-Wellpark, Glasgow, 292
Coltness, 256
Colvend, 170
Comrie and Tullichetle, 377
Condorrat, 287
Connell, 332
Contin, 658
Cookney, 517
Corgarff, 557
Corrie, 322
Corsock, 203
Corstorphine, 1
  St Anne, 4
Cortachy, 479
Coull, 545
Coulter, 53
Coupar Angus, 471
Covington, 54
Cowdenbeath, 407
Cowlairs, 292
Coylton, 214
Craig and Dunninald, 499
Craigie, 214
Craigiebuckler, 536
Criaglockhart, 4
Craigmillar, 33
Craigmore, 316
Craigneuk, 256
Craignish, 312
Craigrownie, 275
Crail, 455
Crailing, 136
Cramond, 4
Cranshaws, 116
Cranstoun, 68
Crathie, 545
Crawford, 266
Crawfordjohn, 267
Creich, Fife, 440
Creich, Ross, 671

Crichton, 69
Crieff, 378
  West, 379
Crimond, 578
Croick, 664
Cromarty, 655
Cromdale, 616
Cross, Lewis, 692
Cross and Burness, 699
Crosshill, 215
Crosshouse, 229
Crossmichael, 203
Croy and Dalcross, 648
Cruden, 572
Crugilton, 196
Cullen, 596
Culliecudden, 657
Culross, 407, 408
Culsalmond, 564
Cults, Aberdeen, 536
Cults, Fife, 441
Cumbernauld, 287
  East, 288
Cumbrae, 246
Cumlodden, 312
Cummertrees, 166
Cumnock, Old, 215
  New, 216
Cupar, Fife, 441, 443
Currie, 5
Cushnie, 559

Dailly, 215
Dairsie, 443
Dalbeattie, 171
Dalgarno, 182
Dalgety, 404
Dalkeith, 71
  West, 73
Dallas, 642
Dalmarnock, 292
Dalmeath, 606
Dalmellington, 216
Dalmeny, 40
Dalmuir, 275
Dalreoch, 275
Dalry, Ayr, 229
  Kirkcudbright, 209
  West, 230
Dalrymple, 217
Dalserf, 256
Dalton, 155
  Little, 156
Dalziel, 256
  St Andrew, 257
  St Mary, 257
  South, 257
Darvel, 230

INDEX OF PARISHES AND CHAPELS

Daviot, Garioch, 514
Daviot, Inverness, 650
Dawyck, 65
Dean, Edinburgh, 8
Dean Park, Glasgow, 292
Deer, New, 581
   Old, 579
Deerness, 693
Delting, 706
Dennistoun, 307
Denny, 389
Deskford, 598
Dingwall, 659
Dinnet, 347
Dipple, 638
Dirleton, 88
Dollar, 389
Dolphinton, 54
Dores, 650
Dornoch, 672
Dornock, 166
Douglas, 267
Douglas Water, 268
Dowally, 349
Downfield, Dundee, 487
Drainie, 624
Dreghorn, 230
Dron, 261
Drumblade, 605
Drumchapel, 280
Drumdelgie, 605
Drumelzier, 58
Drumoak, 537
Dryfesdale, 156
Drymen, 275
Duddingston, 6
Duffus, 627
Duirinish, 683
Dull, 354
Dulnain Bridge, 618
Dumfries, Greyfriars, 172
   St Mary, 172
   St Michael, 171
Dun and Ecclesjohn, 500
Dunbar, 106
Dunbarney, 362
Dunbarton, 276, 277
Dunblane, 397
Dunbog, 444
Duncansburgh, 343
Dundee, Balgay, 487
   Chapelshade, 487
   Clepington, 487
   Fairmuir, 488
   Hilltown, 488
   Lochee, 488
   Logie, 489
   Maryfield, 489

Dundee (*continued*)
   Rosebank, 489
   St Andrew, 489
   St Clement, 486
   St David, 487
   St Enoch, 489
   St John, 487
   St Luke, 488
   St Mark, 490
   St Mary, 486
   St Matthew, 490
   St Paul, 488
   Second or South, 486
   Wallacetown, 490
Dundonald, 217
Dundurn, 379
Dundurcas, 611
Dundyvan, 252
Dunfermline, 409, 410
   North, 410
   St Andrew, 410
   St Leonard, 410
   Townhill, 410
Dunino, 456
Dunipace, 391
Dunkeld, 348
Dunkeld, Little, 350
Dunlappie, 507
Dunlop, 230
Dunnet, 676
Dunnichen, 480
Dunning, 379
Dunnottar, 517
Dunoon, 316
Dunrod, 207
Dunrossness, 702
Duns, 116
   Boston, 117
Dunscore, 173
Dunsyre, 54
Duntocher, 277
Durness, 674
Duror, 333
Durris, 537
Durrisdeer, 182
Duthil, 616
Dyce, 537
Dyke and Moy, 642
Dysart, 424, 425

EAGLESHAM, 288
Earlston, 143
Eassie and Nevay, 474
East Calder, 33
Eastwood, 237
Eccles, 117
Ecclesjohn, 500
Ecclesmachan, 40

3 B

Ecclesmoghridain, 562
Echt, 547
Eckford, 136
Eday and Faray, 699
Edderton, 664
Eddleston, 58
Eddrachilles, 674
Edgerston, 137
Edinburgh, Abbey, 6
  Bonnington, 20
  Buccleuch, 7
  Canongate, 7, 8
  Castle, 35
  Charteris Memorial, 20
  Dean, 8
  Gaelic, 8
  Greenside, 8
  Greyfriars, New, 9
    Old, 9
  High (St Giles), 10, 11
  Lady Glenorchy, 12
  Lady Yester, 13
  Lockhart Memorial (St Mungo), 31
  Mayfield, 13
  Morningside, 13
  Murrayfield, 13
  Newington, 14
  New Street, 35
  Old Kirk, 12
  Prestonfield, 14
  Restalrig, 14
  Robertson Memorial (Grange), 14
  Robertson Memorial (Grassmarket), 9
  Roxburgh Place, 35
  St Aidan, 14
  St Andrew, 15
  St Anne, 4
  St Bernard, 15
  St Bride, 26
  St Cuthbert, 15, 19
  St David, 20
  St George, 20
  St Giles, 10, 11
  St James, 21
  St John, 21
  St Leonard, 21
  St Luke, 21
  St Margaret, 22
  St Mary, 22
  St Matthew, 22
  St Michael, 22
  St Mungo, 31
  St Oran, 8
  St Oswald, 23
  St Serf, 23
  St Stephen, 23
  Tolbooth, 24
  Trinity, 24, 25

Edinburgh (*continued*)
  Tron, 25, 26
  Tynecastle, 26
  West Coates, 26
  West St Giles, 26
Edinkillie, 643
Ednam, 130
Edrom, 124
Edzell, 500
Elchies, 612
Elder Park, Glasgow, 293
Elderslie, 238
Elgin, 631
Elie, 456
Ellom, 128
Ellon, 572
Enzie, 599
Erchless, 651
Errol, 363
Erskine, 246
Eskdalemuir, 162
Essie, 610
Essil, 639
Ethie, 512
Ettrick, 149
Evie and Rendall, 693
Ewes, 162
Eyemouth, 125

FAIR ISLE, 702
Fairlie, 247
Fairmuir, Dundee, 488
Fala and Soutra, 73
Falkirk, 41
Falkland, 444
Farnell, 501
Farnua, 653
Fauldhouse, 42
Fearn, Ross, 664
Fenwick, 231
Fergushill, 231
Fern, Brechin, 502
Ferryhill, 526
Ferryport-on-Craig, 456
Fetlar, 704
Fetterangus, 580
Fettercairn or Trinity, 519
Fetteresso, 520
Fetterneir, 564
Fintray, 538
Fintry, 277
Finzean, 547
Firth and Stennis, 696
Fisherton, 217
Flisk, 446
Flotta, 698
Flowerhill, 258
Fodderty, 659

INDEX OF PARISHES AND CHAPELS

Fogo, 118
Forbes, 560
Fordoun, 521
Fordyce, 600
Forfar, 480
   Lowson, 481
   St James, 481
Forgan, 457
Forgandenny, 363
Forglen, 589
Forgue, 589
Forres, 644
Fort Augustus, 344
Forteviot, 364
Forth, 268
Fortingall, 355
Fortrose, 655
Forvie, 576
Foss, 355
Fossoway, 418
Foulden, 126
Foulis Easter, 492
Foulis Wester, 380
Foveran, 574
Fraserburgh or Philorth, 581
Freuchie, 447
Friockheim, 510
Fullarton, 218
Fyvie, 590

GAIRLOCH, 680
Galashiels, 149
   West, 150
Galston, 218
Galtway, 206
Gamrie, 592
Gardenstown, 592
Garelochhead, 277
Gargunnock, 390
Gartcosh, 293
Gartly, 605
Gartmore, 398
Gartsherrie, 258
Garturk, 258
Garvald, 89
Garvock, 521
Gask or Findo-Gask, 380
Gelston, 205
Giffnock, 238
Gigha, 323
Gilcolmston, 526
Gilmerton, 27
Girthon, 204
Girvan, 218
   South, 218
Gladsmuir, 90
Glamis, 480
Glasford, 258

Glasgow, Abbotsford, 288
   Anderston, 288
   Balshagray, 289
   Barony, 289
   Barrowfield, 290
   Battlefield, 290
   Bellahouston, 290
   Belmont, 290
   Blackfriars, 290
   Bluevale, 291
   Blythswood, 291
   Bridgegate, 291
   Bridgeton, 291
   Buccleuch, 291
   Calton, 291
   Carntyne, St Michaels, 293
   Chalmers, 292
   Colston-Wellpark, 292
   Cowlairs, 292
   Dalmarnock, 292
   Dean Park, 292
   Dennistoun, 307
   Elder Park, 293
   Gorbals, 293
   Govan, 293
   Govanhill, 294
   Greenhead, 295
   Hillhead, 295
   Hogganfield, 308
   Hutchesontown, 295
   Hyndland, 295
   Kelvinhaugh, 295
   Kelvinside, 296
   Kingston, 296
   Kinning Park, 296
   Langside, 296
   Laurieston, 297
   Macleod, 297
   Martyrs, 297
   Maryhill, 297
   Maxwell, 297
   Merrylea, 298
   Milton, 298
   Newhall, 298
   Newlands, 298
   North Albion Street, 298
   Oatlands, 298
   Parkhead, 298
   Partick, 298
   Plantation, 299
   Pollokshields, 299
   Possil Park, 299
   Queen's Park, 299
   Renfield, 300
   Robertson Memorial, 300
   St Andrew, 300
   St Bernard, 300
   St Bride, 300

INDEX OF PARISHES AND CHAPELS

Glasgow (*continued*)
  St Clement, 300
  St Columba, 300
  St Cuthbert, 301
  St David, 301
  St Enoch-Hogganfield, 301
  St George, 301
  St George's in the Fields, 302
  St Gilbert, 302
  St James, 302
  St John, 302
  St Kenneth, 303
  St Kiaran, 303
  St Luke, 303
  St Margaret, 303
    Tollcross, 304
  St Mark, 305
  St Mary, Partick, 299
  St Matthew, Blythswood, 304
  St Mungo Cathedral, 304
  St Ninian, 306
  St Paul, 306
  St Peter, 306
  St Stephen, 306
  St Thomas, 306, 307
  St Vincent, 307
  Sandyford, 307
  Shettleston, 311
  Springburn, 307
  Steven Memorial, 290
  Strathbungo, 307
  The Park, 307
  Titwood, 308
  Tollcross, St Margaret, 304
  Townhead, 308
  Tron or St Mary, 308
  Whiteinch, 308
  Wilton, 308
  Woodside St Oswald, 308
Glass, 606
Glassary, 312
Glasserton, 193
Glenapp, 188
Glenaray, 313
Glenbervie, 522
Glenbuck, 218
Glenbuckat, 557
Glencairn, 183
Glencoe, 333
Glencorse, 73
Glendevon, 381
Glenelg, 680
Glengairn, 547
Glengarry, 344
Glenholm, 52
Glenisla, 474
Glenlivet, 612
Glenluce, 190

Glenlyon, 355
Glenmoriston, 651
Glenmuick, 548
Glenorchy, 333
Glenprosen, 482
Glenrinnes, 613
Glenshee, 350
Glenshiel, 680
Glentanar, 544
Gogar, 4
Golspie, 672
Gorbals, 293
Gordon, 144
Gourock, 247
Govan, 293
Govanhill, 294
Grahamston, 43
Grange, Edinburgh, 14
Grange, Strathbogie, 606
Grangemouth, 43
Granton, 27
Grantully, 356
Greenbank, 239
Greengairs, 259
Greenhead, Glasgow, 295
Greenknowe, 167
Greenlaw, Duns, 119
Greenlaw, Paisley, 244
Greenock, Augustine, 247
  Cartsburn, 247
  East, 247
  Gaelic, 247
  Ladyburn, 248
  Middle, 248
  North, 248
  South, 248
  St Paul, 248
  Wellpark, 248
  West, 248
Greenside, 8
Gretna, Kinpatrick or Redkirk, 167
Greyfriars, New, 9
  Old, 9
  Aberdeen, 527
Gullane, 90
Guthrie, 510

HADDINGTON, 92, 95
  St Martin, 95
Haggs, 390
Half Morton, 163
Halkirk and Spittal, 677
Hallin in Waternish, 684
Hallside, 259
Ham, 694
Hamilton, 259, 260
Harray and Birsay, 696
Harris, 688

INDEX OF PARISHES AND CHAPELS

Harthill, 260
Hassendean, 140
Hawick, 137
   St John, 137
   St Margaret, 137
   St Mary, 137
Haywood, 269
Heatherlie, 150
Helensburgh, 278
   West, 278
Heriot, 75
High or St Giles, Edinburgh, 10
Hillhead, Glasgow, 295
Hillside, Montrose, 502
Hilton, 129
Hobkirk, 138
Hoddam, 168
Hogganfield, Glasgow, 308
Holburne, 527
Holm or Ham, 694
Holytown, 261
Holywood, 173
Hope Kailzie, 59
Horndean, 127
Houndwood, 126
Houston, 239
Hownam, 138
Howwood, 239
Hoy, 697
Humbie, 95
Hume, 133
Huntly, Dunbennan and Kinnoir, 607
Hurlford, 231
Hutchesontown, 295
Hutton and Corrie, 156
Hutton and Fishwick, 727
Hylipol, 338
Hyndland, Glasgow, 295

Idvie, 513
Inch, 188
Inchbrayock, 499
Inchinnan, 239
Inchture, 490
Inishail, 333
Innellan, 317
Innerleithen, 59
Innernochtie, 559
Innerwick, 108
Insch, 565
Insh, Abernethy, 617
Inverallan, 618
Inverallochy, 582
Inveraray, 313
Inverarity, 482
Inveravon, 613
Inverbrothock, 509
Inverchaolain, 317

Inveresk, 75
Invergowrie, 491
Inverkeillor, 511
Inverkeithny, 593
Inverkip, 248
Inverness, 651
   Gaelic, St Mary, 652
   North, 652
   St Stephen, 652
   West, 652
Invertiel, 429
Inverurie, 566
Iona, 338
Irvine, 232

Jamestown, 278
Jedburgh, 138
John Knox, Aberdeen, 527
Johnstone, Dumfries, 157
Johnstone, Paisley, 239
   St Andrew, 240
Juniper Green, 27
Jura, 328

Kearn, 556
Keig, 557
Keir, 183
Keiss, 677
Keith, 608
Keithhall, 566
Keith Marischal, 95
Kells, 204
Kelso, 130
   North, 130
Kelton, 205
Kelty, 406
Kelvinhaugh, Glasgow, 295
Kelvinside, Glasgow, 296
Kemback, 458
Kemnay, 567
Kenmore, 556
Kenmuir, 261
Kennethmont, 558
Kennoway, 425
Kerse, 43
Kettins, 475
Kettle, 447
Kilarrow, 328
Kilbarchan, 240
Kilberry, 324
Kilbirnie, 231
Kilbowie, 279
Kilbrandon, 333
Kilbride, Oban, 334
Kilbride, Arran, 323
Kilbride, Dunblane, 398
Kilbride, East, 261
Kilbride, West, 235

3 B*

INDEX OF PARISHES AND CHAPELS

Kilbucho, 52
Kilcalmonell, 324
Kilchievan, 323
Kilcholumkill, 326
Kilchoman, 329
Kilchrenan, 333
Kilconquhar, 458
Kildalton, 329
Kildonan, 672
Kildrummy, 558
Kilfinan, 317
Kilfinichen, 339
Killean and Kilchenzie, 324
Killearn, 278
Killearnan, 656
Killillan, 239
Killin, 357
Kilmacolm, 249
Kilmadock, 398
Kilmahog, 397
Kilmallie, 344
Kilmany, 448
Kilmarnock, Laigh, 233
   High, 233
   St Andrew, 233
   St Marnoch, 233
Kilmaronock, 279
Kilmartin, 314
Kilmaurs, 234
Kilmeny, 329
Kilmodan, 318
Kilmonivaig, 344
Kilmorack, 660
Kilmore, 334
Kilmorie, 325
Kilmuir, Skye, 684
Kilmuir Easter, 665
Kilmun, 318
Kilninian and Kilmore, 339
Kilninver, 334
Kilpatrick, New, 280
  Old, 279
Kilrenny, 459
Kilspindie and Rait, 365
Kilsyth, 308
Kiltarlity, 652
Kiltearn and Lemlair, 661
Kilwinning, 234
Kinairney, 552
Kincardine, Abernethy, 615
Kincardine in Menteith, 399
Kincardine O'Neil, 549
Kincardine, Tain, 666
Kinclaven, 350
Kindrochet, 545
Kinellar, 539
Kinettas, 660
Kinfauns, 366

Kingarth, 319
Kinedward, 593
Kinghorn, 426
Kinglassie, 428
Kingoldrum, 476
Kingsbarns, 460
Kingscavil, 46
Kingston, Glasgow, 296
Kingussie, 618
Kininmonth, 582
Kinkell, 385
Kinkell, Garioch, 567
Kinloch and Lethendy, 351
Kinlochbervie, 674
Kinlochluichart, 661
Kinloch Rannoch, 358
Kinlochspelvie, 339
Kinloss, 644
Kinnaird in Gowrie, 491
Kinnaird, Brechin, 502
Kinneff, 522
Kinnell or Boness, 37, 43
Kinnell, Arbroath, 512
Kinnettles, 482
Kinning Park, Glasgow, 296
Kinnoull, 366
Kinross, 418
Kintail, 680
Kintore, 568
Kippen, 399
Kirkandrews, 201
Kirkbean, 174
Kirkbride, 186
Kirkcaldy, Abbotshall, 429
  Invertiel, 429
  Pathhead, 430
  Raith, 430
  St Bryce, 430
  St James, 431
  St John, 431
Kirkchrist, 210
Kirkcolm, 189
Kirkconnell, Annan, 168
  Penpont, 183
Kirkcormack, 206
Kirkcowan, 194
Kirkcudbright, Galtway and Dunrod, 206
Kirkden, 513
Kirkennan, 202
Kirkfieldbank, 269
Kirkforthar, 433
Kirkgunzeon, 174
Kirkhill, 653
Kirkhope, 150
Kirkinner, 194
Kirkintilloch, 309
  St David, 310
Kirkliston, 43

INDEX OF PARISHES AND CHAPELS

Kirkmabreck and Kirkdale, 195
Kirkmadryne, 196
Kirkmahoe, 175
Kirkmaiden, 189
Kirkmichael, Abernethy, 619
Kirkmichael, Ayr, 219
Kirkmichael, Chanonry, 657
Kirkmichael, Dunkeld, 351
Kirkmichael, Lochmaben, 157
Kirknewton, 28
Kirkoswald, 219
Kirkpatrick Durham, 176
Kirkpatrick Fleming, 168
Kirkpatrick Irongray, 176
Kirkpatrick Juxta, 157
Kirkton, 140
Kirkurd, 60
Kirkwall and St Ola, 694
Kirn, 319
Kirriemuir, 481
    South, 481
Kirtle, 169
Knapdale, North, 314
Knapdale, South, 315
Knightswood, 279
Knock, 692
Knockando, 613
Knockbain, 656
Knoxland, 280
Knoydart, 681

LADHOPE, 150
Lady, 699
Ladybank, 448
Ladyburn, 248
Lady Glenorchy, Edinburgh, 12
Ladykirk, 127
Ladyloan, Arbroath, 509
Lady Yester, Edinburgh, 13
Lagganallachie, 350
Laggan, 619
Laing, 673
Lamington, 57
Lamberton, 128
Lanark, 269
    St Leonard, 270
    New, 270
Langbank, 249
Langholm, 163
Langside, Glasgow, 296
Langton, 120
Larbert and Dunipace, 390
Largo, 460
Largoward, 464
Largs, 250
Larkhall, 262
Lasswade, 77
Latheron, 677

Lauder, 144
Laurencekirk, 523
Laurieston, Glasgow, 297
    Falkirk, 42
Law, 271
Leadhills, 271
Lecroft, 400
Legerwood, 144
Leith, North, 28
    St John, 29
    St Paul, 29
    St Thomas, 30
    South, 30
Lemlair, 661
Leny, 397
Lenzie, 310
Leochel-Cushnie, 559
Lerwick, 702
Leslie, Kirkcaldy, 431
Leslie, Garioch, 568
Lesmahagow, 271
Leswalt, 189
Lethendy and Kinloch, 351
Lethnot and Navar, 502
Leuchars, 461
Levern, 241
Llanbryde, 638
Libberton and Quothquan, 55
Liberton, 31
Liff and Benvie, 492
Lilliesleaf, 151
Linlithgow, 44
Linton, Kelso, 131
Lintrathen, 476
Linwood, 241
Lismore, 335
Little Dalton, 156
Little Dunkeld, 350
Livingston, 46
Loanhead, 78
Lochalsh, 681
Lochbroom, 681
Lochcarron, 681
Lochee, 488
    St Luke, 488
Lochgelly, 432
Lochgilphead, 315
Lochgoilhead, 319
Lochlee, 502
Lochmaben, 158
Lochranza, 325
Lochrutton, 177
Lochryan, 190
Lochs, 692
Lochwinnoch, 241
Lockhart Memorial, Edinburgh, 31
Logie Murdoch, Cupar, 449
Logie, Dunblane, 400

INDEX OF PARISHES AND CHAPELS

Logie, Dundee, 489
Logiealmond, 367
Logiebride, 346
Logie Buchan, 575
Logie Colstone, 550
Logie Durno, 562
Logie Easter, 666
Logie Pert, 503
Logierait, 358
Logie Wester (see Knockbain)
Longcastle, 194
Longforgan, 492
Longformacus, 120
Longnewton, 135
Longside, 582
Lonmay, 583
Lossiemouth, 626
Loth, 673
Loudoun, 234
Lowson Memorial, Forfar, 481
Luce, New, 190
Luce, Old, 190
Lugar, 220
Lumphanan, 551
Lunan, 513
Luncarty, 370
Lundeiff, 352
Lundie and Foulis, 492
Lunna, 706
Luss, 280
Lybster, 677
Lyne and Meggat, 60

Macduff, 593
Macleod, Glasgow, 297
Madderty, 381
Mains and Strathmartin, 493
Mailer, 365
Makerstoun, 131
Mallaig, 343
Mannofield, Aberdeen, 527
Manor, 60
Markinch, 432
Marnoch or Aberchirder, 608
Martyrs, Glasgow, 297
Maryculter, 539
Maryfield, Dundee, 489
Maryhill, Glasgow, 297
Marykirk, Stirling, 394
Marykirk, Fordoun, 523
Maryton, 503
Mauchline, 220
  New, 220
Maud, 583
Maxton, 151
Maxwell, Glasgow, 297
Maxwelltown, 177
Maybole, 221

Maybole West, 222
Mayfield, Edinburgh, 13
Meadowfield, 262
Mearns, 242
Meathie, 482
Meigle, 477
Meldrum or Bethelnie, 569
Melrose, 151
Melville, Montrose, 506
Menmuir, 503
Menstrie, 401
Merrylea, Glasgow, 298
Mertoun, 145
Methil, 433
Methlick, 575
Methven, 567
Mid Calder, 33
Middlebie, 169
Midmar, 552
Migvie, 553
Millbrex, 594
Milngavie, 282
Milton, Glasgow, 298
Milton of Balgonie, 433
Minto, 140
Mochrum, 195
Moffat, 159
Moneydie, 368
Monifieth, 494
Monigaff, 195
Monikie, 495
Monimail, 449
Monkland, New, 262
Monkland, Old, 262
Monkton and Prestwick, 222
Monquhitter, 594
Montrose, 505, 506
Montrose, Melville, 506
Monymusk, 569
Monzie, 382
Monzievaird and Strowan, 383
Moonzie, 450
Mordington and Lamberton, 128
Morebattle, 131
Morham, 95
Morningside, Edinburgh, 13
Mortlach, 609
Morton, 184
Morvern, 340
Mossgreen, 415
Mosspark, Paisley, 244
Moulin, 352
Mouswald, 159
Moy, 645
Moy and Dalarossie, 653
Muckairn, 335
Muckersie, 365
Muckhart, 419

INDEX OF PARISHES AND CHAPELS

Muiravonside, 46
Muirkirk, 223
Murrayfield, 13
Murroes, 495
Murthly, 353
Muthil, 384

NAIRN, 649
Navar, 502
Neilston, 242
Nenthorn, 131
Nesting, 706
Nevay, 474
New Abbey, 177
Newark, 250
Newbattle, 79
Newburgh, 450
Newburn, 462
New Byth, 594
Newcraighall, 79
New Deer, 581
Newdosk, 501
Newhall, Glasgow, 298
Newhaven, 28
Newhills, 539
Newington, 14
Newlands, Glasgow, 298
    Peebles, 61
New Machar, 539
Newmill, 609
New Pitsligo, 585
Newport, 462
New Street, Edinburgh, 35
Newton, Dalkeith, 80
Newton on Ayr, 213
Newtyle, 477
Nigg, Aberdeen, 540
    Tain, 667
Norrieston, 401
North Albion Street, Glasgow, 298
North Berwick, 96
North Bute, 320
Northesk, 80
Northmavine, 706

OA, 329
Oathlaw or Finhaven, 483
Oatlands, Glasgow, 298
Oban, 336
    St Columba, 336
Ochiltree, 223
Oldhamstocks, 108
Old Kirk, Edinburgh, 12
Old Machar, 528
Olrig, 678
Ord, 600
Ordiquhill, 600
Ormiston, 81

Orphir, 697
Orwell, 420
Overtown, 262
Oxnam, 141
Oyne, 570

PAISLEY ABBEY, 242, 243
    Greenlaw, 244
    High, 244
    Low or St George's, 244
    Martyrs, 244
    Middle, 244
    North, 244
    St Columba, 244
    South, 244
Panbride, 513
Papa Westray, 699
Park, Glasgow, 307
Parkhead, Glasgow, 298
Partick, 298
Parton, 208
Pathhead, Kirkcaldy, 430
Patna, 223
Peebles, 61
Pencaitland, 99
Penicuik, 81
Penningham, 196
Penpont, 184
Pentland, 82
Persie, 477
Perth, East, 369
    Middle, 369
    St Andrew, 369
    St John, 368
    St Leonard, 370
    St Mark, 369
    St Paul, 370
    West, 369
Peterculter, 541
Peterhead, 583
    East, 584
Pettinain, 271
Petty, 654
Pierston, 230
Pitsligo, 585
    New, 585
Pittenweem, 463
Plantation, Glasgow, 299
Plean, 391
Plockton, 682
Pluscardine, 637
Pollokshaws, 244
Pollokshields, 299
Polmont, 47
Polwarth, 121
Poolewe, 682
Port of Monteith, 402
Port Glasgow, 250

Portlethen, 542
Portmoak, 420
Portnahaven, 329
Portobello, 34
  St James, 6
Port Patrick, 191
Portree, 685
Portsoy, 601
Possil Park, Glasgow, 299
Powis, Aberdeen, 531
Premnay, 571
Prestonfield, Edinburgh, 14
Prestonkirk, 110
Prestonpans, 99
Prestwick, 223
Prinlaws, 433
Pulteneytown, 678

QUARFF, 703
Quarter, 262
Queensferry, 47
Quothquan, 55
Queens Park, Glasgow, 299

RAFFORD, 645
Rait, 365
Raith, 430
Rathen, 585
Rathmoral, 558
Ratho, 34
Rathven, 601
Rattray, 353
Rayne, 571
Reay, 678
Redgorton, 370
Rendall, 693, 694
Renfield, Glasgow, 300
Renfrew, 245
Renton, 282
Rerrick, 208
Rescobie, 484
Resolis, 657
Restalrig, 14
Restennet, 480
Rhu or Row, 283
Rhynd, 370
Rhynie, 609
Riccarton, Kilmarnock, 224
Rickarton, 524
Roberton, Lanark, 272
Roberton, Selkirk, 152
Robertson Memorial, Edinburgh, 9, 14
  Glasgow, 300
Rogart, 673
Ronaldshay, North, 699
  South, 694
Rosebank, Dundee, 489
Rosemarkie, 657

Rosemount, Aberdeen, 531
Rosewell, 82
Rossie, 491
Rosskeen and Nonekill, 668
Rosyth, 412
Rothes, 613
Rothesay, 320
  New, 320
  Gaelic, 320
Rothiemay, 610
Rothiemurchus, 620
Rousay and Egilsay, 700
Roxburgh, 132
Roxburgh Place, Edinburgh, 35
Rubislaw, 531
Rutherglen, 310
  West, 310
Ruthrieston, 531
Ruthven, Meigle, 478
  Strathbogie, 605
Ruthwell, 169

SADDELL, 325
St Aidan, Edinburgh, 14
St Andrews, Fife, 464, 469, 470
  Edinburgh, 15
  Glasgow, 300
  Dundee, 489
  Orkney, 693
  Llanbryde, 637
St Anne, Edinburgh, 4
St Bernards, Edinburgh, 15
  Glasgow, 300
St Bride, Edinburgh, 26
  Glasgow, 300
St Clements, Aberdeen, 531
  Dundee, 486
  Glasgow, 300
St Columba, Glasgow, 300
St Cuthbert, Edinburgh, 15, 19
  Glasgow, 301
St Cyrus or Ecclesgreig, 524
St David, Edinburgh, 20
  Glasgow, 301
  Dundee, 487
St Duthus, 668
St Enoch, Dundee, 489
  Glasgow, 301
St Fergus, 586
St Fittick, Aberdeen, 532
St George, Edinburgh, 20
  Glasgow, 301
St George's in the Fields, Glasgow, 302
St George's in the West, Aberdeen, 532
St Gilbert, Glasgow, 302
St Giles, Edinburgh, 10
St James, Edinburgh, 21
  Glasgow, 302

INDEX OF PARISHES AND CHAPELS

St John, Edinburgh, 21
  Glasgow, 302
  Dundee, 487
St Kenneth, Glasgow, 303
St Kiaran, Glasgow, 303
St Kilda, 689
St Leonard, Edinburgh, 21
  St Andrews, 470
St Luke, Edinburgh, 21
  Glasgow, 303
  Lochee, 488
St Madoes, 372
St Margaret, Edinburgh, 22
  Glasgow, 303
St Mark, Glasgow, 305
  Dundee, 490
St Marnoch, 233
St Martin, 372
St Mary, Edinburgh, 22
  Partick, 299
  Dundee, 486
  Orkney, 695
St Mary's Isle, 208
St Matthew, Edinburgh, 22
  Blythswood, 304
  Dundee, 490
St Michael, Edinburgh, 22
St Modans, Falkirk, 42
St Monans, 453
St Mungo, Edinburgh, 31
  Glasgow, 304
  Annandale, 160
St Nicholas, Aberdeen, 526, 527
St Ninian, Glasgow, 305
  Aberdeen, 532
  Stirling, 371
St Ola, Kirkwall, 694
St Oran, Edinburgh, 8
St Oswald, Edinburgh, 23
St Paul, Edinburgh, 29
  Glasgow, 306
  Dundee, 488
St Peters, Glasgow, 306
St Quivox, 224
St Serf, Edinburgh, 23
St Stephen, Edinburgh, 23
  Glasgow, 306
St Thomas, Leith, 30
  Glasgow, 506, 507
St Vigeans, 514
St Vincent, Glasgow, 307
Salen, 340
Saline, 413
Saltcoats, North, 228
Saltoun, 100
Sandbank, 321
Sandness, 707
Sandsting, 706

Sandwick, Cairston, 697
Sandwick, Lerwick, 703
Sandyford, Glasgow, 307
Sanquhar, 185
Sauchie, 392
Saughtree, 163
Saulseat, 188
Savoch of Deer, 586
Scone, 373
Scoonie, 434
Seafield, 602
Selkirk, 153
Sennick, 201
Shapinsay, 700
Shawlands, 245
Shettleston, 311
Sheuchan, 191
Shieldaig, 682
Shotts, 262
Shurrery, 678
Simprim, 128
Sinclairtown, 431
Skelmorlie, 250
Skene, 542
Skipness, 326
Skirling, 55
Slains, 576
Slamannan, 48
Sleat, 685
Smailholm, 146
Small Isles, 685
Snizort, 686
Sorbie, Kirkmadryne and Crugilton, 196
Sorbie, 338
Sorn, 224
Soutra, 73
Southdean, 141
Southend, 326
Southwick, 178
Speymouth or Dipple, 638
Spott, 112
Springburn, Glasgow, 307
Springfield, 451
Sprouston, 132
Spynie, 639
Stair, 224
Stanley, 374
Stenhouse, 392
Stennis, 697
Stenscholl, 686
Stenton, 112
Stepps, 311
Steven Memorial, Glasgow, 296
Stevenston, 235
Stewarton, 235
Stichell and Hume, 133
Stirling, East, 393
  North, 394

Stirling (*continued*)
  West, 393
    Marykirk, 394
    Chapel Royal, 394
Stobhill, 83
Stobo, 64
Stoer, 673
Stonefield, 263
Stonehouse, 263
Stoneykirk or Stephenkirk, 191
Stornaway, 692
Stow, 146
Stracathro, 507
Strachan, 553
Strachur and Strathlachlan, 321
Strageith, 377
Straiton, 225
Stranraer, 192
Strath, 686
Strathaven East, 251
Strathblane, 283
Strathbungo, 307
Strathdon or Innernochtie, 559
Strathfillan, 283
Strathkinness, 470
Strathmartine, 494
Strathmiglo, 451
Strathy, 675
Strichen, 587
Stromness, 697
Strone, 321
Stronsay, 700
Strontian, 345
Strowan (Auchterarder), 384
Suddie, 657
Swinton, 128
Symington, Ayr, 225
Symington, Biggar, 56

TAIN, 668
Tannadice, 484
Tarbat, Ross, 670
Tarbert, Argyll, 315
Tarbolton, 225
Tarland and Migvie, 553
Tarves, 576
Tealing, 495
Temple, Dalkeith, 83
Temple, Dunbarton, 284
Tenandry, 353
Terregles, 178
Teviothead, 141
Thankerton, 54
Thornliebank, 245
Thornton, 434
Thurso, 678
Tibbermore, 374

Tighnabruaich, 321
Tillicoultry, 402
Tingwall, 703
Tinwald, 179
Tiree, 340
Titwood, Glasgow, 308
Tobermory, 341
Tolbooth, Edinburgh, 24
Tomintoul, 621
Tongland, 209
Tongue, 675
Torosay, 341
Torphichen, 49
Torphins, 554
Torryburn and Crombie, 414
Torthorwald, 180
Tostertoun, 192
Tough, 560
Toward, 317
Towie, 560
Townhead, Glasgow, 308
Townhill, Dunfermline, 410
Trailflat and Dungrie, 180
Trailtrow, 166
Tranent, 101
Traquair, 65
Trinity, Aberdeen, 535
Trinity, Edinburgh, 24, 25
Trinity-Gask, 385
Tron, Edinburgh, 25
Tron or St Mary, Glasgow, 308
Troon, 227
Troqueer, 180
Trossachs, 402
Trumisgarry, 691
Tulliallan, 403
Tullibole, 418
Tullichetle, 378
Tulloch, 549
Tullynessle and Forbes, 560
Tundergarth, 161
Turriff, 594
Tewchar, 310
Tweedsmuir, 65
Twynholm, 209
Tynecastle, Edinburgh, 26
Tynninghame, 114
Tynron, 186
Tyrie, 587

UDDINGSTON, 264
Udny, 577
Uig, Lewis, 692
Uist, North, 689
Uist, South, 690
Ullapool, 682
Ulva, 342

INDEX OF PARISHES AND CHAPELS

Unst, 704
Upsettlington, 127
Uphall, 49
Urquhart, Elgin, 641
Urquhart and Logie Wester, 661
Urquhart and Glenmoriston, 654
Urr, 180
Urray and Kirkchrist, 662

WALKERBURN, 65
Wallacetown, Ayr, 213
Wallacetown, Dundee, 490
Walls, Orkney, 698
Walls and Sandness, 707
Walston, 56
Wamphray, 161
Wandel, 56
Wanlockhead, 186
Wardlawhill, 311
Waterside, 216
Watten, 679
Wauchope, 164
Weem, 359
Wellpark, Glasgow, 292
Wemyss, 434
   West, 435
West Calder, 33
West Coates, Edinburgh, 26
West Kilbride, 235
West Linton, 66
West St Giles, Edinburgh, 26

Westerkirk, 164
Westray and Papa Westray, 700
Weststruther, 147
Whalsay and Skerries, 707
Whitburn, 50
Whiteinch, 308
Whitekirk and Tynninghame, 113
Whiteness and Weisdale, 763
Whithorn or Whitern, 197
Whiting Bay, 327
Whitsome, 128
Whittingehame, 114
Wick, 679
Wigtown, 198
Wilton, Hawick, 142
Wilton, Glasgow, 308
Winchburgh, 50
Wishaw, 264
Wiston and Roberton, 272
Woodside, Glasgow, 308
Woodside, Aberdeen, 535
Wormit, 470

YARROW, 154
Yell, Mid, 705
Yell, South, 705
Yester, 103
Yetholm, 133
Yoker, 284
Ythan Wells, 595

ENGLAND

Berwick, 723
Caledonian, Cross Street, Regent Square, Carlisle, 724 [724
Liverpool, 724
London Crown Court, 724
Holloway, 724

St Columba, Pont Street, London, 724
Lowick, 723
Newcastle upon Tyne, 723
Tweedmouth, 723
Wark, 725
Wooler, 725

INDEX OF MINISTERS

ABERCROMBIE, Robert, 568
Abercrombie, William, 606
Abercromby, Andrew, 353, 375
Abercromby, Henry, 358, 374
Abercromby, John, 570
Abercromby, Sir Robert, 498
Abernethie, Thomas, 137
Abernethie, Walter, 571
Abernethy, Andrew, 365
Abernethy, John, 100, 139, 141
Abernethy, John Adamson, 241
Acheson, John, 441
Achesoune, Robert, 212
Adair, Archibald, 192
Adair, Cuthbert, 188, 204
Adam, David Laird, Professor, 716
Adam, James, 480
Adam, John, 248
Adam, Peter, 555
Adam, William, 176, 374, 421
Adam, William Henderson, 254
Adams, Alexander McClymont, 306, 392
Adams, John, 27, 42
Adams, Kennedy, 261
Adamson, Alfred Ernest, 737
Adamson, Donald, 662
Adamson, George, 85
Adamson, Henry, 369
Adamson, James, 128, 198, 200, 423
Adamson, John, 32
Adamson, Patrick, 202
Adamson, Robert, 435
Adamson, Thomas Newbigging, 495
Addinstoun, David, 30, 31
Addis, Thomas, 13
Addison, William, 149, 483
Adie, Andrew, Principal, 711
Adie, Charles Smith, 375
Affleck, Sir John, 119
Agnew, John Simpson, 284
Agnew, Robert, 38
Agnew, Robert Andrew, 389
Aiken, James, 600
Aiken, James John Marshall, 122
Aiken, John, 515
Aikman, David (John), 202
Aikman, John, 201, 210
Ainslie, Sir James, 141

Ainslie, James Lyon, 269
Ainslie, John, 141
Ainslie, Walter, 493
Ainslie, William, 141
Ainslie, Sir William, 151
Aird, Francis, 256
Aitchison, John, 42
Aitken, Alexander, 429
Aitken, Andrew, 197
Aitken, James, Bishop, 709
Aitken, James, 481
Aitken, James Richmond, 12
Aitken, Thomas, 139
Aitkenhead, Henry, 98
Aiton, John, 54
Aiton, Thomas, 46
Alason, Adam, 218
Alexander, Francis Pirie Wilson, 721
Alexander, George, 55, 68, 245, 393
Alexander, James Frederick, 739
Alexander, John, 56, 166, 168, 182, 317, 430
Alexander, John Auchinleck, 739
Alexander, Robert, 443
Alexander, Vincent Cassels, 283, 531
Alexander, William, 250, 547
Alexanderson, Sir John Munro, 681
Alison, John, 14
Allan, Alexander Smith, 408
Allan, Andrew, 461
Allan, Archibald, 143
Allan, Arthur, 247
Allan, Charles Orford, 28
Allan, George, 298
Allan, James, 614
Allan, James Robb, 548
Allan, John, 60, 135
Allan, John Black, 731
Allan, Robert, 66, 239, 272
Allan, Thomas, 279
Allan, William, 195
Allanson, John, 304
Allardyce, Alexander, 207, 363
Allardyce, Robert, 210, 588
Allardyce, William, 610
Allen, Thomas Nelson, 316, 420, 586
Allison, Alexander, 437
Allison, Thomas Reid, 213
Alpine, George, 277

INDEX OF MINISTERS

Ambrose, Thomas, 48, 79
Anderson, Adam Ernest, 333
Anderson, Alexander, 300, 493, 500, 567, 575, 587, 606, 609
Anderson, Alexander James, 555
Anderson, Alfred William, 4
Anderson, Andrew, 673 bis
Anderson, Andrew Melville, 739
Anderson, Archibald, 318, 324
Anderson, Charles, 182
Anderson, David, Professor, 714
Anderson, David, 60, 132, 417, 693
Anderson, David Alexander, 610
Anderson, George, Professor, 714
Anderson, George Strang, 460
Anderson, Gilbert, 521, 677
Anderson, Sir Herbert, 205
Anderson, James, 42, 296, 300, 361, 478, 586, 598, 605, 616
Anderson, James Alexander, 34
Anderson, James Duncan, 697
Anderson, James Storie, 737
Anderson, Sir John, 251
Anderson, John, 53, 204, 286, 296, 303, 308, 366, 417, 425, 468, 739
Anderson, John Milne, 491
Anderson, Patrick, 56
Anderson, Robert, 277, 283
Anderson, Robert Chalmers, 290, 504, 618
Anderson, Robert Nicolson Tulloch, 27
Anderson, Thomas, 122, 207, 208, 441, 506
Anderson, Walter, 534, 539
Anderson, Weild, 271
Anderson, William, 61, 282, 293, 389, 520, 565
Anderson, William Henry, 678
Anderson, William White, 280, 290
Andison, John Ferguson, 308
Andrew, Alexander, 251, 356
Andrew, John, 419
Andrew, Muir, 213
Andrew, Patrick Arthur, 510
Andrew, Robert, 707
Andrew, Theodore, 707
Andrew, Thomas, 232
Andrew, William, 232
Andrew, William George, 26
Angill, Sir Adam, 412
Angus, Andrew, 429, 431, 432
Angus, John, 412, 539
Angus, Sir William, 379
Annand, John, 605
Annand, Thomas, 643
Anstruther, John, 460
Anton, Alexander, 660
Anton, Peter, 309
Arbuthnott, Alexander, 516 bis
Arbuthnott, Andrew, 128
Arbuthnott, Robert, 500, 522

Archibald, Charles, 174
Archibald, Hugh, 251
Archibald, Sir James, 476
Archibald, Robert, 262, 275
Archibald, Thomas, 294
Argo, Gavin Elmslie, 550
Armit, Andrew, 495
Armitage, Lewis Frederick, 21
Armstrong, Allan Macleod, 671
Armstrong, James, 355
Armstrong, John Brown, 56
Armstrong, Thomas, 379
Arnot, David, 11
Arnot, George, 177, 610, 474
Arnot, Hugh, 50
Arnot, Hugh Young, 451
Arnot, John Thomas, 438
Arnot, Robert, 450
Arrot, David, 560
Arthur, John, 36, 285, 456
Arthur, John William, 739
Arthur, Robert, 147, 461
Asher, William, 613
Ashon, Thomas, 437
Auchenleck, Alexander, 171
Auchenleck, Andrew, 486, 495
Auchenleck, George of Balmanno, 53
Auchenleck (Affleck) John, 86, 461, 504, 522
Auchenleck, Robert, 504
Auchenleck, Thomas, 454
Auchmouty, Robert, 392, 393
Auchmouty, William, 493, 494
Auchterlonie, James, 508
Auld, William, 220, 407
Austin, John Mein, 160
Austin, Thomas, 615
Auty, David Eastham, 203, 486
Ayre, Joseph Logan, 100
Ayton, Thomas,

Babington, Matthew, 482
Badenoch, William, 555
Baikie, Thomas, 54
Bailey, Thomas Grahame, 739
Baillie, Cuthbert, 272
Baillie, James, 503, 510
Baillie, Robert, Principal, 717
Baillie, Stewart, 510
Bain, James, 613, 739
Bain, Thomas, 157
Bain, William, 49, 433
Bainbridge, Philip, 131
Baird, Andrew, 52
Baird, Andrew Cumming, Professor, 715
Baird, David Wilson, 247, 676, 699
Baird, James, 272
Baird, James William, 410, 469
Baird, John, 243, 278

INDEX OF MINISTERS

Baird, John Wilson, 175
Baird, Robert, 231
Baker, James Archibald Argyll, 326
Balcanquhal, James, 452
Balcanquhal, Walter, 24, 94
Baldie, Charles Nairne, 703
Balfour, Donald, 118
Balfour, George, 434
Balfour, Sir Henry, 389
Balfour, James, 11, 434, 446, 511
Balfour, John, 134, 441, 447, 452, 667, 701
Balfour, Patrick, 612, 622, 638, 641
Balfour, Richard, 210
Balfour, Robert, 46
Balfour, Walter, 66, 420
Balfour, William, 419, 420, 458
Ballantyne, Archibald Scott, 646
Ballenden, Patrick, 132
Ballingall, James, 372
Ballingall, William, 565
Balnaves, Alexander, 369, 375
Balneaves, William, 352(3)
Balsillie, David, 3
Balvaird, Alexander, 401
Balvaird, David, 372
Balvaird, William 513
Bane, Sir William, 238
Banks, Alexander, 40
Bannatyne, Charles, 232
Bannatyne, John, 270
Bannatyne, Thomas, 34, 268
Bannerman, James, 81, 347, 358
Bannerman, James Patrick, 347
Bannerman, Robert, 80
Bannerman, William, 380
Barbour, John, 80, 82, 84, 429
Barbour, William, 78, 189
Barclay, Adam, 369
Barclay, Alexander, 584
Barclay, Andrew, 45, 256, 530, 589, 605
Barclay, David of Easter Touch, 444
Barclay, David, 216, 222, 452
Barclay, George, 49, 132
Barclay, Hercules, 676
Barclay, James, 19, 172, 397, 705
Barclay, John, 25, 125, 132, 494
Barclay, Matthew, 277
Barclay, Robert Stephen, 369
Barclay, Walter, 593
Barclay, William, 207, 230, 445, 558, 565, 694
Barnett, Christopher Charles, 547
Barnie, William, 141
Barr, Andrew Muirhead, 187
Barr, Robert Littlejohn, 539
Barrack, John, 446
Barrie, Alexander, 260
Barron, Alfred Saunders, 516
Barron, Douglas Gordon, 519

Barron, Robert, Professor, 712
Barron, William 161
Barrowman, James Storry, 215, 292
Bartane, Thomas, 348
Bartlett, Henry Matthew, 489
Barton, Adam, 165
Bartone, John, 99
Barty, James Strachan, 472
Barty, Thomas, 189, 383
Bates, Robert, 640
Baty, John, 506, 513
Bawne, Sir Alexander, 363
Baxter, Andrew James Burt, 374
Baxter, David, 151, 462
Baxter, David Brook, 231, 250
Baxter, James Houston, Professor, 187, 719
Baxter, John, 477, 488
Baxter, Mungo, 253
Baxter, Thomas, 440, 444
Baxter, William Lang, 454
Bayne, David, 47
Bayne, Donald, 659
Bayne, John, 231, 306, 659
Bayne, Rorie, 660
Beale, George, 49
Beaton, Donald Macgillivray, 484, 613
Beaton, John, 680
Beaton, Lewis, 266
Beaton, Stephen, 294
Beattie, Irving, 37
Beattie, John, 506
Beattie, John Donald Macfarlane Benny, 160
Bell, Thomas Blizzard, 190
Bell, William, 160, 167
Bell, William Napier, 163
Bell, William Wilson, 115, 256, 384
Bellenden, George, 702
Bellenden, William William, 459
Bennet, Alexander Lyon, 251, 291
Bennet, Andrew, 47, 440, 449, 458
Bennet, John, 146
Bennet, William, 6, 25, 135, 173
Bennie, William, 37
Benson, James Muirhead, 486
Bentinck, Charles Donald, 672
Bentley, James, Professor, 713
Benvie, Andrew, 14, 374
Berrie, Alexander Scott, 115
Berry, James Garrow, 171
Bethune, Alexander, 688
Bethune, Angus, 658
Bethune, Duncan, 339
Bethune, John, 122, 683
Bethune, Joseph, 126
Bethune, William, 683, 688
Betoun Alexander, 5
Betoun, Archibald, 231
Betoun, James, 173

3 C

INDEX OF MINISTERS

Beveridge, John Gardiner, 76
Bickerton, Thomas Alexander, 67
Biggar, Thomas, 428
Biggert, Robert, 184
Bigwood, William Cecil, 489
Binnie, Charles, 578
Binnie, James Montgomerie, 559
Binning, Sir Andrew, 1
Binning, Hugh, 294
Bird, John Turnbull, 721
Birnie, Robert, 270
Birnie, William, 270
Birrell, John, Professor, 718
Bishop, James, 34
Bishop, John, 68
Bisset, Alexander, 498
Bisset, Archibald, 35
Bisset, Douglas George, 460
Bisset, John, 526
Bisset, Peter Smith, 499
Bisset, Robert, 347
Bisset, Thomas, 58, 575, 584
Black, Alexander, 578, 685
Black, Alexander Forbes, 489, 616
Black, David, 476, 483
Black, Duncan, 325
Black, George, 468
Black, Hugh, 683
Black, James, 566, 731
Black, John, 115
Black, John Easton, 280
Black, Peter Cameron, 262
Black, Robert, 271, 693
Black, Thomas, 369
Black, William, 249
Black, William Kilgour, 482, 483
Black, William Macmillan, 199
Black, William Paterson, 500
Black, William Ritchie, 20
Blackadder, Patrick, 403
Blackadder, William, 183, 433
Blackburn, Archibald, 229, 534
Blackburn, John, 275, 527
Blackburn, Peter, Bishop, 709
Blackhall, Andrew, 76, 86
Blackwell, George, 37
Blackwell, Thomas, Principal, 711, 712
Blackwood, Adam, 435
Blackwood, James, 185, 376, 414 bis, 434
Blackwood, Peter, 405, 413
Blackwood, William, 6, 376
Blaikie, William Garden, 605
Blair, Alexander, 218
Blair, Charles Patrick, 186
Blair, David Logan, 374
Blair, George, 262, 383
Blair, Hew, 308, 311
Blair, James, 69, 491

Blair, John, 225, 365, 366
Blair, Peter, 139
Blair, Robert, 87, 212, 468, 588
Blair, Thomas, 124
Blair, William, 225, 279, 527
Blake, James William, 84
Blaney, Thomas, 56
Blaw, Edward, 400
Blaw, William, 701
Blindschall, James, 482, 641
Blindshiell, Robert, 198
Blinschell, Robert, 196
Blinshiell, David, 57
Blyth, David, 205, 207, 210
Blyth, Henry, 118
Boag, James Aitken, 291
Boag, William Goldie, 355
Bodin, Alexander Hastie, 277
Bodin, William, 215, 228
Boe, James, 397
Bog, Charles, 548
Bogie, David Kinnear, 406
Bollo, William, 64
Bonallo, James, 647
Bonaly, Robert, 80
Bonar, Andrew Redman, 7, 119
Bonar, Horatius, 130
Bonar, James, 222
Bonar, John, 704
Bonar, Thomas, 106
Bonkill, Patrick, 501
Bonkle, Michael, 105, 108
Bonkle, Robert, 94
Booth, John Livingston, 65
Booth, Patrick, 59
Borland, Robert, 154
Borland, William, 107
Borrowman, Patrick Hamilton, 321, 739
Borthwick, Archibald, 121
Borthwick, Ninian, 28, 143
Borthwick, William, 462
Boston, Thomas, 149
Boswell, George, 422
Boswell, William, 412
Bothwell, Francis, 704
Bowden, John Davies, 727
Bower, Alexander, 251
Bowie, Archibald, 383
Bowie (Bowes) Robert, 192
Bowman, Archibald, 589
Bowman, Ernest Drewett, 739
Bowman, James Dunn, 723
Boyd, Alexander, 216, 218, 333
Boyd, Andrew, 288, 318
Boyd, Andrew Kennedy Hutchison, 469
Boyd, Angus, 654
Boyd, Archibald, 72
Boyd, Arnold, 413

INDEX OF MINISTERS

Boyd, George, 14, 183, 228, 229
Boyd, James, Archbishop, 708
Boyd, James, 59
Boyd, John, 483
Boyd, John Gage, 225
Boyd, John McGavin, 262
Boyd, Robert, 253, 272, 304, 447, 544
Boyd, Walter, 196
Boyd, William, 204, 214, 279, 579
Boyd, Zachary, 289
Boyle, John, 136, 139, 401, 513
Boyle, Patrick, 94
Boyle, William Wilson, 418
Braboner, Andrew, 653
Brachane, Sir David, 656, 657
Bradfute, James, 55
Bradfute, John, 55, 272
Bradfute, William, 417, 447, 452
Brand, John, 7, 38
Brand, William, 702
Brander, James, 255
Brebner, James, 590
Brechin, Edwin James, 655
Bremner, George, 495
Bremner, John, 157, 557
Brewster, Patrick, 243
Bright, Robert Montgomery, 150, 351, 618
Brisbane, Matthew, 246
Brisbane, William, 246
Brisby, Henry Shannon, 150
Brock, William Peterson, 268
Brodie, David, 581
Brodie, Duncan Hunter, 298
Brodie, John, 647
Brodie, Robert Geddes, 256
Brodie, William, 158
Broun, Francis David, 303
Brown, Adam, 176
Brown, Alexander, 209
Brown, Alexander Douglas, 413
Brown, Alfred, 297
Brown, Andrew, 13, 229, 445, 642
Brown, Andrew Watson, 15
Brown, Archibald, 145
Brown, David, 27, 136, 154, 173, 482
Brown, Ebenezer, 82
Brown, George, 156, 234
Brown, Gilbert, 560
Brown, James, 28, 176, 183, 204, 322, 383
Brown, James Rossie, 13
Brown, John, 33, 53, 84, 120, 121, 164, 181, 183, 208, 290, 428, 433, 539
Brown, John Dunlop, 316, 327
Brown, John Francis, 75
Brown, John Irwin, 729
Brown, John Knox, 250
Brown, John McWilliamson, 316
Brown, Laurence, 477

Brown, Lyon, 182
Brown, Patrick, 177
Brown, Richard, 407
Brown, Robert, 55, 60, 174, 238, 403, 562, 728
Brown, Robert Hope, 309
Brown, Thomas, 89, 157, 361, 414
Brown, Sir William, 184
Brown, William, 108, 124, 183
Brown, William Graham, 317
Brown, William Morris, 22
Brown, William Robertson, 42, 43
Brown, William Rossie, 228
Brown, William Stevenson, 275
Brownhill, John, 408
Brownlie, James Paterson, 363
Brownlie, William, 310
Bruce, Alexander, 496
Bruce, Andrew, Bishop, 477, 710
Bruce, Andrew, 468, 515
Bruce, Archibald, 394
Bruce, Charles, 613
Bruce, Douglas William, 486, 738
Bruce, Edward, 415
Bruce, George, 661
Bruce, John, 15, 47
Bruce, Robert, 155
Bruce, William, 493, 546, 694
Bruce, William Robertson, 540
Bruce, William Straton, 596
Brugh, James, 385
Bryce, Alexander, 28
Bryce, Donald Campbell, 159
Bryce, Sir James, 176
Bryce, James, 306
Bryce, James Clow, 156
Bryce, James Cornwall, 235
Bryce, Sir John, 156, 171
Bryce, John Campbell, 228
Bryce, Morrison, 273
Bryden, James Henderson, 453
Brydie, Thomas, 676, 679
Brydon, Robert, 173
Bryson, Alexander, 172, 386
Bryson, Andrew, 307
Bryson, James, 182
Bryson (Bryce) Sir John, 171
Buchan, Alexander, 689
Buchan, Archibald, 112
Buchan, Charles Forbes, 521
Buchan, Henry Ritchie, 233
Buchan, James, 59
Buchan, John, 491, 492
Buchan, Sir Thomas, 658
Buchan, William Sutherland, 150, 492
Buchanan, Archibald, 503
Buchanan, George, 159, 207
Buchanan, Hamilton, 283
Buchanan, James, Professor, 717

INDEX OF MINISTERS

Buchanan, James, 12, 163, 288
Buchanan, John, 54, 319
Buchanan, Peter, 133
Buchanan, Robert, 63, 308, 439, 458
Buchanan, Thomas, 348, 439,
Buchanan, Walter, 8
Buchanan, William, 257, 504
Buchanan, William Buchanan Cullen, 27
Bullo, John, 59
Buncle, Edward, 176
Bunting, Thomas James, 302
Burdon, Charles Scott, 292
Burdon, James Alexander, 98, 267
Burdoun, John, 396
Burgess, James, 485
Burleigh, John, 130
Burleigh, John Henderson Seaforth, 489, 592
Burne, John, 76, 408, 409, 412 *bis*
Burness, David, 272
Burnett, Alexander, 8, 696
Burnett, Andrew, 215, 297, 535
Burnett, David, 393
Burnett, George, 550
Burnett, James, 139
Burnett, John, 100, 570
Burnett, John Beattie, 521
Burnett, Robert, 33, 525, 538, 539, 571, 658
Burnett, Thomas of Slowie, 553
Burnett, Thomas, 558, 575, 659
Burnett, William, 14, 42, 553, 566, 598
Burns, Alexander Fyfe, 12, 244
Burns, Andrew, 231
Burns, George, 65
Burns, George Stewart, 305
Burns, James, 449
Burns, Stewart, 138
Burns, Thomas, 13, 245, 271
Burr, John, 149
Burry, John Barrie, 526, 622
Burt, Andrew, 556
Burt, James Robert, 99
Burt, Sir Robert, 389
Buschart, James, 657
Butler, Dugald, 150

CABELL, Sir William, 561, 566
Cadell, James, 190
Cadenhead, John, 216
Caesar, James, 92, 514
Caesar, John, 514
Caesar, William, 103
Caie, George Johnstone, 480
Caie, Norman Macleod, 260
Caie, William Smith, 599
Cairns, John Edgar, 420
Calder, George, 284
Calder, James Jolly, 605
Calder, Robert Hogg, 613

Calderwood, John Alexander, 83, 251
Calderwood, Robert George Matheson 739
Calderwood, Robert Sibbald, 255
Calderwood, William, 72
Caldwell, George, 56
Caldwell, John, 191
Caldwell, Thomas, 86
Callan, Hugh, 389
Callan, Richard, 120
Callander, Alexander, 389
Callander, John, 195, 208
Callander, William Corson, 150
Callum, George, 383
Cameron, Alexander, 282, 329
Cameron, Allan, 739
Cameron, Archibald, 274
Cameron, Charles McK, 737
Cameron, Daniel, 75
Cameron, David, 396, 493
Cameron, Donald, 345, 548
Cameron, Donald Allan, 315, 571, 693
Cameron, Donald Mackillop, 29
Cameron, Duncan, 30, 235, 309
Cameron, Ewen of Dunloskin, 316
Cameron, Hector, 314, 315, 336
Cameron, Hugh, 14
Cameron, James Ewing, 626
Cameron, John, 151, 313, 316 (3), 318, 322, 399, 731
Cameron, John Alexander, 145
Cameron, John Arthur, 205
Cameron, John Fawns, 417
Cameron, John Kirkland, 485
Cameron, John Stuart, 307, 532
Cameron, Kenneth John, 609
Cameron, Lewis Legertwood Lagg, 532, 609
Cameron, Peter, 258
Cameron, Samuel, 358, 387
Cameron, Samuel Wood, 205, 731
Cameron, William, 682
Cameron, William Fotheringham, 723
Campbell, Alastair, 335
Campbell, Alexander of Auchnacloich, 334
Campbell, Alexander, 223, 282, 335, 685
Campbell, Alexander Duncan, 207
Campbell, Andrew, 379
Campbell, Andrew James, 302
Campbell, Archibald, Professor, 719
Campbell, Archibald, 313, 329, 333, 335, 409, 661
Campbell, Archibald Alexander, 546
Campbell, Colin, 312, 332, 486, 535
Campbell, Daniel, 334
Campbell, David, 326, 504
Campbell, Donald, 48, 313, 314 *bis*, 336, 342
Campbell, Dugald, 314, 317, 501
Campbell, Duncan, 315
Campbell, George of Kinnochtree, 12

INDEX OF MINISTERS

Campbell, George, 20, 116, 215, 238
Campbell, Gillespie Macgregor, 244, 336
Campbell, Hew, 73
Campbell, Hugh, 320, 656
Campbell, James, 183, 296, 335, 372, 416, 438
Campbell, James Alexander, 180
Campbell, James Archibald, 704
Campbell, James Cameron, 375
Campbell, James Montgomery, 172, 180
Campbell, James Robertson, 324
Campbell, James Stuart, 284
Campbell, John, 7, 24, 116, 234, 281, 315, 318, 329, 332, 333, 339, 383, 480 648, 688, 721
Campbell, John Alexander, 330
Campbell, John James, 192
Campbell, John Macleod, 283
Campbell, John Robert, 376, 384
Campbell, Joseph, 193
Campbell, Laughlan, 322
Campbell, Mungo, 340
Campbell, Neil, Bishop, 710
Campbell, Neil, 312, 314, 322
Campbell, Neil Lewis Arthur, 344
Campbell, Ninian, 282
Campbell, Patrick, 356
Campbell, Peter Colin, Professor, 715
Campbell, Robert, 191, 192, 283, 347
Campbell, Thomas, 52, 195, 249
Campbell, William, 194, 215, 355, 396, 622
Campbell, William Albert, 347
Campbell, William Ballantine, 354
Campbell, William Mackean, 176, 276
Candlish, Robert Smith, 20
Cant, Alan, 441
Cant, Alexander, 545
Cant, Andrew, 11, 24, 79
Cant, John, 204
Carey, Stanley Buchanan, 490
Cargill, Donald of Kirklands of Rattray, 383
Cargill, Thomas Sheratt, 616
Carie, James, 444
Carkettill, Patrick, 113
Carlyle, John, 166
Carment, James, 378
Carmichael, Alexander, 272
Carmichael, David, 676
Carmichael, Dugald, 678
Carmichael, Frederick, 432
Carmichael, Ian, 339
Carmichael, James, 86, 94
Carmichael, John Dalgleish, 569
Carmichael, Patrick, 405
Carmichael, Samuel Gilfillan, 186
Carmichael, William George Hayward, 369
Carnegie, Robert, 618
Carnegy, Robert, 366
Carness, John, 237
Carrick, John Charles, 79

Carrick, Robert, 239
Carrick, William, 261
Carrington, Robert, 478
Carruthers, George, 42
Carruthers, James, 200, 238
Carruthers, John, 156
Carruthers, Sir Mark, 160
Carson, William Graham, 704
Carstairs, Thomas, 491
Carswell, Donald, 333
Carter, Walter Gordon, 137, 265
Cassou, Mortimer Aloysius, 737
Castlelaw, James, 154
Castlelaw, William, 235
Cathels, David, 137
Cattanach, David Lynedoch, 138
Cattanach, Joseph Hardie, 60
Catto, Alexander Godsman, 578, 631
Catto, John, 538
Cavell, William, 491
Chalmer, Alexander, 608
Chalmers, Alexander, 32, 55, 89
Chalmers, Daniel, 148
Chalmers, George, 527, 607, 610
Chalmers, Henry Reid, 485, 631
Chalmers, James, 168, 242, 456, 540, 598
Chalmers, John, 148, 170, 244, 422, 568, 584, 606
Chalmers, Thomas, 302
Chalmers, William, 216, 346, 382, 482, 501, 591, 660
Champare, Robert, 194
Chapman, Alexander, 173
Chapman, Henry, 94
Chapman, Robert, 200
Chapman, Thomas Henderson, 721
Charles, John, 68, 143
Charleson, Charles Forbes, 184
Charleson, John, 245
Charlton, Harcourt Peter, 192
Charteris, Andrew, 219
Charteris, Archibald Hamilton, 178
Charteris, Henry, 29
Charteris, James, 61
Charteris, Laurence, 88
Charteris, Thomas, 95
Chalto, John, Dean, 99
Cheyne, Alexander, 530, 558
Cheyne, Gilbert, 592
Cheyne, James, 574
Cheyne, Jerome, 703
Cheyne, John, 575
Cheyne, Robert, 204
Cheyne, William, 587
Chieslie, John, 3, 55
Chirnsyde, William, 281 *bis*
Chisholm, Alexander, 378, 384
Chisholm, Edward, 484

INDEX OF MINISTERS

Chisholm, Gilbert, 583, 586
Chisholm, James, 226
Chisholm, John, 151
Chree, Charles, 477
Chree, George Johnston, 483
Christie, Charles, 247
Christie, Charles Sinclair, 536
Christie, George, 15
Christie, Henry, 419
Christie, James, 27, 509
Christie, John, Professor, 714
Christie, John, 508
Christie, John George Crocket, 278
Christie, Peter, 115
Christison, Alexander, 126
Christison, David, 249, 254
Christison, Sir John, 567
Christison, John, 52, 409, 489, 491, 492, 519, 522
Christison, John of Benno, 607
Christison, Sir Thomas, 134
Christison, Thomas, 556, 592
Christison, William, 486
Chrystal, James Robert, 256
Clanny, Hugh, 174
Clapperton, John, 130, 154
Clark, Alexander, 509, 575, 619, 679
Clark, Archibald, 344
Clark, David Findlay, 527, 596
Clark, Dugald, 307
Clark, George, 578
Clark, Gilbert, 269
Clark, Ivo Macnaughton, 502
Clark, James Smith, 387
Clark, John, 229, 316, 413, 613
Clark, John Alexander, 498
Clark, John Ashfield, 138
Clark, John Sinclair, 262
Clark, John Young, 188, 297
Clark, Patrick Thomas, 592
Clark, Richard Mackie, 161
Clark, Thomas, 15
Clark, William, 142, 264, 459, 460, 463, 630
Clark, William Carrie, 80, 506
Clark, William Weir, 33
Clarke, Thomas Elliot Simpson, 100
Claxton, Arthur Eugene, 287
Clayhills, Andrew, 136
Cleghorn, George, 167
Cleghorn, John, 435
Cleghorn, Matthew, 156
Cleland, George, 263
Cleland, James, 146
Cleland, Joseph, 256
Clelland, John Skeoch, 220
Clement, Ninian, 508, 518
Clepan, George, 483
Clerk, Adam, 130, 146, 161

Clerk, Alexander, 651
Clerk, Gilbert, 581
Clerk, John, 136, 382, 642 *bis*
Clerk, William, 136
Clerk, William Bruce, 163
Climie, Hugh, 477
Clogie, William, 640
Clune, Alexander, 699
Clunes, Alexander, 657, 667 *bis*
Clunie, David, 105
Clunie, John, 113
Coats, Walter William, 498
Cochrane, James, 480
Cochrane, John, 22, 283, 288
Cochrane, John Douglas, 174
Cock, James, 699
Cock, Thomas, 699
Cockburn, George, 739
Cockburn, Harold Andrew, 162
Cockburn, James, 99, 212
Cockburn, James Hutchison, 397
Cockburn, John of Newholme, 55
Cockburn, John, 81, 334
Cockburn, Patrick, 113, 120
Colden, John, 61
Colden, Thomas, 203
Cole, Alexander, 210
Colherd, William, 268
Colhoun, James, 582, 583
Collace, David, 625
Collace, John, 520
Collier, James, 292
Collier, John, 68
Collison, Sir John, 533
Collow, John, 184
Colquhoun, Adam, 66
Colquhoun, Archibald, 64
Colquhoun, James, 196, 281
Colquhoun, John, 64, 157
Colquhoun, Robert, 107
Colquhoun, William Young, 489
Colt, Adam, 76, 126
Colt, Alexander, 370
Colt, James, 135
Colt, John, 152
Colville, Henry, 419, 696, 697
Colville, John, 33, 287, 325
Colville, Patrick, 229
Colville, Robert, 134, 191
Colville, William, 115
Colvin, James Charles Gillies, 168
Colvin, John, 195, 297
Colvin, Walter Laidlaw, 5
Colwyer, John, 261
Colwyn, John, 234
Compton, Samuel James Moore, 21
Comrie, Alexander, 357
Comrie, Duncan, 378

INDEX OF MINISTERS

Comrie, William, 734
Conacher, Duncan, 254, 325
Condie, George, 311, 385
Condie, John Charles, 237, 486, 637
Condie, Joseph, 402
Condie, William Cochran, 184
Connell, Duncan Macnair, 303
Connelly, Thomas, 9, 130, 258
Constane, Patrick, 450
Conway, William, 259, 431
Cook, Archibald, 652
Cook, George, 120, 146, 201, 379, 449
Cook, John, 94, 275
Cook, John Forbes Mitchell, 586
Cook, Robert, 239
Cook, Thomas, 241, 319
Cooper, Alexander, 154
Cooper, Charles Guthrie, 142, 307
Cooper, James, Professor, 717
Cooper, John, 299, 343
Copeland, John, 501
Copland, John, 46
Copland, Patrick, 559, 560
Copland, William, 561
Cormocsoun, Finlay, 683, 688
Corner, Malcolm Manford, 626
Cornwall, Walter, 45
Cornwall, William, 4
Core, William Granville, 68
Cormack (Gormack), Thomas, 484
Corrie, Robert Clayton, 112
Corsair, John, 409
Corse, David, 529
Corson, William, 218
Corswall, Sir John, 178
Cosens, Alexander Thomson, 52
Coskery, Alexander, 376
Costrane, John, 124
Coull, Patrick, 177
Coullie, James, 99
Coulson, John, 555
Coulter, Henry, 290, 527
Coulthard, William, 423
Coupar, David, 186, 428
Coupar, Robert, 45
Couper, Thomas, 414, 504, 506
Couper, Walter, 3
Couper, William, 369
Courtney, David, 133
Courtney, John of Trolingshaw, 87
Courtney, Thomas, 145, 148
Cousin, William, 117
Coustane, Patrick, 431, 439
Coutts, James, 556, 575
Coutts, John, 664
Coutts, Sir Laurence, 546
Coutts, William, 127
Cowan, Charles James, 131

Cowan, Francis, 90
Cowan, Henry, Professor, 714
Cowan, James, 267
Cowan, Peter, 297
Cowan, William, 20
Cowie, William, 583
Cowie, William Archibald Douglas, 560
Cowley, James Arthur, 239
Cowper, William, 557
Cox, George Frederick, 697
Cox, James Taylor, 537
Cox, William Percy, 513
Craib, Alexander Reid, 585
Craig, Aeneas Nelson, 431
Craig, Alexander, 704
Craig, James, 6, 256, 379
Craig, John, 394, 534
Craig, Robert, 316
Craig, Robert James, 195
Craig, Thomas, 638, 640
Craig, William Pitcairn, 415
Craighead, Robert, 305
Craigie, John, 453
Craigie, Nicol, 694
Craigie, William, 356, 358
Craik, David, 731
Craik, James, 301
Cranmer, John Graham, 606
Cranston, Hector, 61, 382
Cranstoun, James, 30
Cranstoun, John, 135
Cranstoun, Michael, 4, 32
Cranston, Thomas, 148, 165
Cranston, William, 145
Crarer, William, 352
Crawford, Archibald, 229, 235, 249, 279, 338
Crawford, David, 480, 552
Crawford, Gavin, 42
Crawford, Hugh, 215
Crawford, James Andrew, 539
Crawford, James Montgomery, 223
Crawford, John, 71
Crawford, Nicol 56
Crawford, Patrick, 216
Crawford, Robert, 232, 240, 249, 391, 555
Crawford, Robert Brown, 344
Crawford, Thomas, 351
Crawford, Thomas Jackson, Professor, 716
Crawford, Thomas James Campbell, 278, 310
Crawford, William, 214
Creech, Patrick, 98
Creichton, Alexander, 108
Crerar, Alexander, 674
Crevey, Thomas, 539
Crichton, Abraham, 483
Crichton, Alexander, 346, 352, 491, 551
Crichton, George, 200
Crichton, James, 261

Crichton, John, 262
Crichton, Patrick, 368
Crichton, Robert, 185, 363
Crichton, Steven, 168
Crichton, William, 37, 551
Cristison, Alexander, 377, 379, 380
Crockat, John, 642
Crockett, William Shillinglaw, 65
Croll, John, 506
Crombie, Andrew, 656
Crombie, John, 374
Crombie, Thomas, 237
Crombie, William, 112
Crooks, John, 187
Crookes, William, 234
Crosbie, John, 89
Crosbie, John Geddes, 231
Crosby, Thomas, 177
Cross, Alexander, 335
Cruden, James, 592
Cruickshanks, James, 54
Cruickshanks, James Alexander, 609
Cruickshanks, John Rodger, 65
Cruickshanks, Thomas, 347 bis, 352 bis, 473
Cruickshanks, William, 523
Cullen, Andrew, 533, 564
Cullen, James, 198
Cullen, Walter, 534
Cumming, Alexander, 362
Cumming, David, 605
Cumming, George, 642, 663
Cumming, James Elder, 307
Cumming, John, 104, 724
Cumming, John Barr, 609
Cumming, Michael, 625
Cumming, Patrick, 12, 642, 647
Cumming, Thomas, 494
Cumyng, David, 478, 664
Cunningham, Adam, 136
Cunningham, Alexander, 149, 222, 230, 240
Cunningham, David, 251, 270, 274, 439
Cunningham, Gabriel, 309
Cunningham, Hugh, 103
Cunningham, James, 274, 275 bis
Cunningham, John, 187, 219, 225, 230, 265, 400
Cunningham, Patrick, 140
Cunningham, Umphra, 249
Cunningham, William, 25
Cunnison, John, 355
Curle, David, 226
Currie, Adam, 248
Currie, Sir Andrew, 147
Currie, Andrew, 539
Currie, Hew, 474, 610
Currie, Sir Hugh, 379
Currie, James, 263, 564, 567
Currie, John, 94, 652

Curror, Thomas, 544
Currour, John, 177, 352, 353
Curtis, William Alexander, Professor, 716
Cushnie, John, 544
Cushney, Robert, 583
Cussane, Robert, 184
Cuthbert, Alexander, 41
Cuthbert, Sir David, 653
Cuthbert, James Nimmo, 536
Cuthill, William, 200
Cuthill, James Spence, 509

DABB, John Henry Michell, 424
Daes, James, 143
Daill, Thomas, 113 bis
Dalgety, James, 482
Dalgety, James Boath, 243
Dalgetty, William, 739
Dalgleish, Alexander, 45
Dalgleish, David, 56
Dalgleish, John, 48
Dalgleish, Nicol, 463
Dalgleish, Robert, 45
Dalgleish, Walter, 164
Dalgleish, William, 4, 457
Dall, John, 320
Dall, William, 509
Dallachie, Thomas, 609
Dalmahoy, James, 394
Dalrymple, James, 48, 212
Daly, Robert, 258, 302
Dalziel, Ninian, 170 bis, 177, 179, 180
Dalziel, William, 200
Danielston, Peter, 116
Danielston, Robert, 212, 424
Darg, Patrick, 600
Darroch, John, 323, 326, 328
Darroch, Maurice, 324
Darroch, Robert, 261
Daun, Robert, 148
Davidson, Adam, 134
Davidson, Alan Munro, 721
Davidson, Alexander, 29, 48
Davidson, Andrew, 72, 202, 482
Davidson, Archibald, 674
Davidson, Charles, 703
Davidson, Charles Alexander, 637
Davidson, David, 485
Davidson, Donald, 31, 299, 323, 491, 586
Davidson, Edwin Maxwell Murray, 380, 613
Davidson, George, 551
Davidson, George Ramsay, 12
Davidson, George Smyttan, 366
Davidson, Harcourt Morton, 489
Davidson, James, 193, 242, 482, 566, 567, 600
Davidson, John, 99, 115, 187, 260, 385
Davidson, John Edgar, 126
Davidson, Patrick, 420

INDEX OF MINISTERS

Davidson, Ranken, 216, 218, 234
Davidson, Reginald Ian, 355, 476
Davidson, Robert, 34, 525
Davidson, Thomas, 115, 560
Davidson, Walter, 144, 291
Davidson, William, 287, 674, 690
Davidson, William Leslie, 562
Davie, John Barclay, 43, 511
Davies, William Lowys, 224, 556
Davis, John, 202
Dawson, John, 131
Dawson, John Finlay, 314
Dawson, Patrick, 351
Dawson, Thomas Henry, 570
Dawson, William, Professor, 716
Dawson, William, 310, 739
Dempster, John, 372, 494
Denholme, Robert, 54, 122
Denison, Patrick, 333
Denmuir, David, 491
Dennistoun, Archibald, 286
Dennistoun, Robert, 212
Denoon, Benjamin, 194
Denoon, John, 706
Denoon, Thomas, 657, 666
Denune, Walter, 672
Denune, William, 99
Dewar, Alexander, 354
Dewar, Archibald Edmiston, 186
Dewar, Duncan, 355
Dewar, James, 273, 392
Dewar, Peter, 320
Dewar, Thomas, 432
Dey, John, 340
Dey, William Dunbar, 621
Diack, Albert Alexander, 15, 584
Dick, David, 487
Dick, Henry Littledale, 272
Dick, Horace James, 61
Dick, James, 279
Dick, John, 65
Dick, John Crawford, 162
Dick, Robert, 25
Dickey, John Henry, 280
Dickey, Robert James Steele, 255, 406
Dickey, William John Steele, 696
Dickie, David, 303
Dickie, John, 734
Dickie, John McAusland, 320
Dickie, Matthew, 231
Dickson, Adam, 59, 63
Dickson, David of Busby, 11
Dickson, David, 27, 61, 160
Dickson, George, 135, 460
Dickson, George Arthur Macdonald, 600
Dickson, John, 63, 204, 311, 554
Dickson, John Gavin, 21
Dickson, Matthew Scott, 262

Dickson, Richard, 43
Dickson, Robert, 30, 301
Dickson, Robert Marcus, 270
Dickson, Sir Thomas, 49
Dickson, William, 150
Dill, Samuel Marcus, 211
Dill, William, 188
Dimma, Thomas, 48
Dinwiddie, Archibald Hutton, 141
Dinwiddie, John Linton, 169
Dinwiddie, Melville, 530
Dobbie, James, 45, 266
Dobie, Alexander, 288
Dobie, William, 127
Dobie, William Jardine, 428
Dodd, George Edward, 731
Dodd, Henry, 487
Dodds, James, 3, 204, 207
Dods, George, 89, 214
Dods, George Nisbet, 244
Dods, John, 381
Dods, Selby Ord, 89
Doig, Robert, 526
Doig, Thomas, 415
Don, Matthew, 707
Donald, Andrew Thomson, 145
Donald, Sir Donald, 433
Donald, Duncan Macalister, 352
Donald, Francis Cantlie, 552
Donald, George Henry, 150
Donald, Gordon Irving, 602
Donald, Maunsel Grant Mackintosh, 483
Donaldson, Andrew, 409
Donaldson, Charles James, 224, 290
Donaldson, Gavin, 389
Donaldson, James of Murroch, 277
Donaldson, James, 207
Donaldson, Laurence, 610
Donaldson, Robert, 156
Donaldson, Thomas, 386, 695
Donaldson, William Galloway, 480
Donn, Andrew, 70
Donnan, Andrew, 198
Dougald, John, 500
Dougall, James, 192
Dougalson, Donald, 337
Dougalson, George, 352
Dougharty, John Torrens, 268, 296
Douglas, Adam, 134
Douglas, Sir Alexander, 639
Douglas, Alexander, 124, 154, 640, 658
Douglas, Andrew, 509
Douglas, Archibald, 54, 60 *bis*, 61, 66, 100 *bis*, 109, 184, 286, 304
Douglas, George, 140, 265, 598, 608, 623, 636, 638, 642
Douglas, Hector, 135
Douglas, Henry, 309

INDEX OF MINISTERS

Douglas, Sir James, 218, 625
Douglas, James, 127, 541, 612, 630
Douglas, Sir John, 135
Douglas, John, 122, 128, 138, 139, 162, 186, 218, 222
Douglas, John Leonard, 118
Douglas, Louis Clarence Duncan, 353, 698
Douglas, Sir Ninian, 64
Douglas, Robert, 64, 99, 120, 128, 149, 177, 260
Douglas, Thomas, 74, 438, 449
Douglas, Thomas Logan, 267, 293
Douglas, Walter, 131
Douglas, William of Glenbervie, 516
Douglas, William, 112, 134, 582, 590, 611, 635, 636, 713
Dow, David, 177, 287
Dow, John, 656
Dow, William, 209
Dowie, James, 489
Downie, Charles, 659
Downie, John, 324
Downie, Robert, 531
Drennan, Hugh, 721
Drew, John Alexander Caldwell, 36
Drew, Joseph, Principal, 718
Drew, Ninian, 309
Dron, John Archibald, 285
Drummond, David, 356, 368, 379
Drummond, George, 356, 372
Drummond, James Johnstone, 139
Drummond, John, 254, 379, 380
Drummond, Ninian, 366
Drummond, Thomas, 88, 379
Drummond, Sir William, 347
Drummond, William, 377, 378, 379, 382, 383, 385
Drynnane, John, 702
Drysdale, Alexander, 309
Drysdale, James, 430
Drysdale, John, 26
Drysdale, Matthew Robert, 190
Drysdale, Robert, 472
Dudgeon, Thomas, 89
Duff, Alexander, 336
Duff, Alfred Drummond, 611
Duff, Sir George, 601
Duff, George Neilson, 282
Duff, Sir Gilbert, 617
Duff, Henry, 31
Duff, James, 343, 552, 607, 650
Duff, Thomas, 643
Duffus, Robert, 366
Duguid, William, 54
Duke, Ernest Hamilton, 169
Dumbreck, Andrew, 562
Dunbar, Gavin, 246, 668
Dunbar, George, 33, 212, 649, 657, 665
Dunbar, James, 608, 636, 654
Dunbar, John, 215, 589
Dunbar, Kenneth, 31
Dunbar, Patrick, 343, 630, 650
Dunbar, Robert, 643 *bis*, 645
Dunbar, Robert Grant, 359
Dunbar, Thomas of Grange, 647
Dunbar, Thomas, 645
Dunbar, William, 155, 523, 572, 642
Duncan, Alexander Adam, 589
Duncan, Andrew, 34
Duncan, Andrew Bethune, 408
Duncan, David, 81
Duncan, David Alexander, 216, 398
Duncan, George, 177
Duncan, George Gordon Dundas Stewart, 178, 294
Duncan, George Simpson, Principal, 719
Duncan, Henry, 71, 169
Duncan, Henry Cecil, 739
Duncan, Hugh, 258
Duncan, James, 506
Duncan, James Robertson, 637
Duncan, John, 172, 209, 298, 393, 394, 437, 439, 702
Duncan, John Garrow, 619
Duncan, John Gibb, 292
Duncan, John Henry, 235, 372
Duncan, John Menzies, 26 *bis*
Duncan, John Murray Baillie, 739
Duncan, Laurence, 239, 474
Duncan, Leslie, 105, 302
Duncan, Norman, 609
Duncan, Patrick, 638
Duncan, Thomas Ogilvy, 87
Duncan, William, 383
Duncan, William Cairns, 213
Duncan, William Grant, 52
Duncan, William Ogilvy, 255
Duncanson, Andrew, 151
Duncanson, James, 386
Duncanson, Sir John, 359
Duncanson, John, 654, 698
Duncanson, Thomas, 148, 390
Dundas, James, 495
Dundas, William, 39
Dungalson, Michael or Nicol, 194, 195
Dunlop, Alexander, 198, 242
Dunlop, Alexander Slater, 282, 469 *bis*
Dunlop, John, 34
Dunlop, Ludovic, 543
Dunlop, Robert Hamilton, 456
Dunlop, Samuel, 10, 117
Dunlop, William, 230, 354, 423, 737
Dunn, Charles, 50, 545, 677
Dunn, George Macleod, 223, 296, 435
Dunn, Michael, 205, 207
Dunn, Peter, 40

INDEX OF MINISTERS

Dunn, Peter Alexander, 8
Dunnett, Arthur Henry, 137, 141
Dunnett, George Victor, 14, 105
Dunnett, Hamilton David Forrester, 574
Dunnett, Thomas, 676
Dunnett, William, 233
Dunning, Alexander, 361
Dunning, Thomas, 377
Dunmure, Alexander, 365
Durham, James, 305
Durham, John, 495
Durham, Patrick, 494, 657
Durie, John, 14, 31, 40
Durie, Joshua, 503, 512
Durie, Robert, 454
Durie, Simeon, 457
Durward, Charles, 434
Dury, George, 412
Dury, John, 208
Dyce, Thomas, 141
Dyce, William, 536
Dyett, Alfred E., 737
Dykes, John Dalziel, 261
Dykes, Thomas, 213
Dysart, Alexander, 362
Dysart, Sir Michael, 178

EADIE, James, 56
Eadie, William, 312
Eason, Patrick, 272
Easson, David Edward, 68
Easton, James Cruickshank, 569
Easton, John, 37
Eccles, Hew, 225
Echline, Walter, 702
Edgar, Alexander, 65
Edgar, Andrew, 209, 176, 220
Edgar, John, 127, 282
Edgar, Nicol, 175
Edgar, Robert, 451
Edie, William, 77, 296
Edie, William Henry, 645
Edmondston, Biot, 399
Edmondston, John, 148, 391
Edmonston, John of Warroxhill, 275
Edmonstone, Robert, 408
Edmonstone, William, 347, 366, 372
Edward, Alexander, 456
Edward, Robert, 195, 495
Edwards, James, 739
Edwards, George John, 434
Eglinton, Archibald, 192
Eglinton, Hugh, 231
Elder, Andrew, 504
Elder, John, 519
Elder, Thomas, 190, 198
Elder, William, 516
Elisoune, Sir Alexander, 110

Elliot, Henry, 135
Elliot, James, 25
Elliot, Martin, 162
Elliot, Ninian, 49, 270
Elliot, Thomas, 140
Ellis, George, 39
Ellis, William, 213
Elmslie, John Watson, 407
Elphinston, James, 72, 377, 559
Elphinston, John, 426, 437
Elphinston, William, 492
Erroll, Duncan, 281
Erskine, Ebenezer, 394
Erskine, Henry, 122
Erskine, James, 41 *bis*
Erskine, Sir John of Dun, 500
Erskine, John, 498, 500, 516, 525, 529
Erskine, Sir William, 285
Erskine, William, 286
Esdaile, David, 484
Eustace, Alexander, 550
Eveatt, William, 351
Ewan, Gordon Milne, 363
Ewen, John Spence, 7, 33, 594
Ewing, James, 489
Ewing, Thomas, 728

FAIRBAIRN, James, 143
Fairbairn, John, 133
Fairbairn, Patrick, 100
Fairfoul, John, 200
Fairley, John, 390
Fairlie, Henry Alexander, 219
Fairlie, John, 306
Fairlie, Robert Paul, 173, 228
Fairney, Alexander, 445
Fairwodder, Walter, 502
Falconer, Alexander, 389, 613, 662
Falconer, Colin, Bishop, 710
Falconer, David, Professor, 719
Falconer, David, 5
Falconer, James, 198
Falconer, William, 205, 642, 643
Falconer, William James Stuart, 677
Fallowsdaill, James, 705
Fargie, Alexander, 398
Fargy, Alexander, 387, 388
Farish, Charles William, 378, 388
Farms, Andrew Welsh, 558, 613
Farquhar, Henry, 73
Farquhar, James, 541
Farquhar, John Laurie, 159, 296
Farquharson, James, 154, 555, 604 *bis*
Faulds, James, 433
Faulds, John, 602, 671
Fenwick, David Pitkaithly, 449
Fergus, Alexander, 503
Fergushill, John, 213

Ferguson, Adam, 358
Ferguson, Adam Wightman, 486
Ferguson, Alexander, 340, 342
Ferguson, Allan, 275
Ferguson, Daniel John, 283
Ferguson, Donald Fergus, 247
Ferguson, Duncan, 688
Ferguson, Hamilton Russell, 256
Ferguson, James, 205
Ferguson, John, 45, 49, 152, 549
Ferguson, Robert, 202
Ferguson, William, 418
Fergusson, James, 3
Fergusson, John, 137
Fergusson, Peter, 188
Fergusson, Robert Menzies, 401
Fergusson, Thomas, 191, 647
Ferrie, William Winks, 740
Ferrier, Alexander, 731
Ferries, Alexander, 546
Ferries, George, 546
Ferries, John, 549
Fethie, Arthur, 512 *bis*
Fiddes, Alexander, 15
Finch, Charles Sydney, 485
Findlater, Alexander, 268
Findlater, Thomas, 66
Findlay, Peter Charles, 203
Findlay, Robert, 389
Findlay, Thomas, 112, 236
Findlay, William, 394
Finlay, John Agnew, 183
Finlayson, Alexander Wilson, 119, 286
Finlayson, Francis, 233
Finlayson, James Macdonald, 583
Finlayson, John, 692
Finlayson, Joseph Sage, 424
Finlayson, Richard, 498
Finlayson, William Logie, 158
Fisher, James, 154
Fisher, James Annett, 204
Fisher, Matthew, 699
Fisher, Robert, 152, 222, 271, 473
Fisher, Robert Findlay, 447
Fisher, Robert Howie, 13, 19
Fleming, Adam, Dean, 197, 198
Fleming, Alexander, 182
Fleming, Archibald, 370, 724
Fleming, Donald, 39
Fleming, Gideon, 493
Fleming, James, 227, 261, 478
Fleming, James Alexander, 30
Fleming, James William, 738
Fleming, John, 248
Fleming, Lee McKinstery, 160
Fleming, Richard, 48
Fleming, Robert of Balloch, 310
Fleming, Robert, 254, 729

Fleming, Thomas, 13, 277, 538
Fleming, Sir Thomas, 185
Flemington, Hugh, 128
Flescher, Robert, 441
Fletcher, George, 483
Fletcher, James, 131
Flint, Patrick, 184
Flint, William Craig, 344
Flocker, Andrew, 454
Fogo, George Laurie, 180
Fogo, John Laurie, 283
Foirhouse, Alexander, 40
Foord, Robert, 89
Forbes, Alexander, 450, 643
Forbes, Alexander Hay, 433, 648
Forbes, Arthur, 537
Forbes, Augustine Wentworth Scudamore, 297,
Forbes, Donald, 665   [386, 535
Forbes, Duncan, 585
Forbes, George, 559
Forbes, James, 441, 564, 695
Forbes, James Grant, 364, 570
Forbes, John of Corse, Professor, 713
Forbes, John, 51, 535
Forbes, John Mackenzie, 176
Forbes, John Robertson, 667
Forbes, Patrick of Corse, Bishop, 709
Forbes, Robert, 387, 535, 547
Forbes, Robert Wilson, 157, 576
Forbes, William, 476, 477, 521, 559, 566, 568, 569, 577
Forbes, William, Principal, 711
Forbes, William Alexander Macfarlane, 524
Forbes, William Augustus, 495
Forbes, William John, 95
Ford, James Albert Munro, 731
Fordyce, Alexander, 646
Fordyce, George, 3
Fordyce, James, 386
Forest, John, 112
Forfar, James, 297
Forman, Adam, 108
Forman, James, 94
Forman, John, 454, 459
Forrat, Sir John, 500
Forrest, Alexander, 503
Forrest, Daniel Alexander, 595
Forrest, James, 583
Forrest, Robert Gibb, 26
Forrester, Alexander, 103, 139, 197, 512
Forrester, Alexander McCaul, 66
Forrester, Andrew, 3, 400, 425
Forrester, David, 144, 265
Forrester, James, 53
Forrester, John, 394, 643, 644
Forrester, Robert, 205, 210
Forrester, Thomas, Principal, 718
Forrester, Thomas, 152

INDEX OF MINISTERS

Forret, David, 459
Forret, John, 449, 728
Forret, Thomas, 449
Forsyth, Alexander, 453
Forsyth, Alexander John, 536
Forsyth, David, 87, 121, 146
Forsyth, Henry, 421
Forsyth, James, 392, 448
Forsyth, John, 309
Forsyth, William, 190, 568, 675
Fortescue, John Faithful Irvine, 237
Fotheringham, James, 53, 266, 482 *bis*
Fotheringham, John, 149
Foulis, Adam, 197, 254, 476
Foulis, Alexander, 108
Fowler, David, 479
Fowlie, Adam, 496
Fowlie, Robert, 494, 696
Frame, Hugh Fulton, 458
Francis, David Lawrence, 430
Francis, James, 247
Frank, William, 95
Franklin, Foster, 249
Fraser, Alexander, 592, 650, 651, 652, 677, 680, 685
Fraser, Alexander Douglas, 296
Fraser, Sir Andrew Dow, 650, 653, 662
Fraser, Archibald, 432
Fraser, Arthur, 137
Fraser, Charles, 447, 648
Fraser, David Denholm, 103
Fraser, Donald, 662
Fraser, Donald Dow, 652, 660
Fraser, Farquhar, 341
Fraser, Sir Homer, 246, 668
Fraser, Hugh, 332, 665
Fraser, James, 170, 172, 239, 339, 347, 651, 653
Fraser, James Annand, 95
Fraser, James William, 619
Fraser, John, 338, 341, 410, 429, 568, 654, 657
Fraser, Lachlan, 338
Fraser, Lauchlan, 683
Fraser, Lewis, 195
Fraser, Paul, 507
Fraser, Robert, 607
Fraser, Robert George, 30
Fraser, Robert William, 21
Fraser, Roderick, 477, 659
Fraser, Simon, 660
Fraser, Thomas, 648, 657
Fraser, William, 652, 660
Fraser, William Crawford, 722
Frazer, Joseph McNeill, 296
Freebairn, Thomas, 262
Freeland, John, 369, 608
French, James, 165, 166, 270
French, Patrick, 45
French, Robert, 118, 119, 145

Frew, David, 181
Fridge, Alexander, 513
Frizelle, Robert, 443
Frood, Bryce, 191
Fry, Samuel Campbell, 218
Fullar, William, 230
Fullarton, David, 500
Fullarton, Henry McIntosh Robertson, 38
Fullarton, James, 392, 502
Fullarton, John, 180, 184, 243, 500, 512
Fulton, William, 293, 676
Fulton, William, Professor, 714, 717
Furlong, James, 311
Fyfe, Andrew, 173
Fyfe, David, 512
Fyfe, William, 272
Fyfe, William Day, 485
Fyfe, William Wilson, 168

GADERER, Alexander, 218
Gairdyne, Alexander, 580
Gaitles, Patrick, 116
Galbraith, Humphrey, 389
Galbraith, John, 388
Galbraith, Patrick, 89
Galbraith, Robert, 521
Galbraith, William, 33, 98, 139
Gall, Alexander, 384, 385
Gall, Evelyn, 430, 488
Galloway, Alexander, 140
Galloway, David, 191
Galloway, George, Principal, 718
Galloway, George, 193
Galt, Patrick, 121, 361, 437
Garden, Alexander, 437, 438, 440, 590
Garden, Francis, 571
Garden, George, 590
Garden, Gilbert, 494, 495, 600
Garden, James, Professor, 713
Garden, Thomas, 601, 606
Gardiner, George, 28
Gardiner, John, 368
Gardiner, William Wallace Dunlop, 9
Gardner, George, 167
Gardner, James, 65
Gardner, Matthew, 295
Gardner, Robert, 38, 377
Gardyne, Gilbert, 600
Gardyne, John, 509, 698
Gardyne, Thomas, 556
Gardyne, William, 24, 479
Garioch, Alexander, 540
Garntullie, Sir James, 619
Garrett, John, 740
Garrioch, William, 558
Garson, John, 696
Gartshore, George, 207
Garvine, Thomas, 12

Gaw, Alexander, 381
Geddes, Charles, 179, 208
Geddes, Francis Gilbert, 297
Geddes, John, 300, 408
Geddie, Andrew, 502
Geddie, Patrick, 200
Geddie, Robert, 416
Geekie, George, 462
Gegg, James, 224, 504
Gellatly, James, 257
Gellie, John, 567, 570
Gellie, John Caithness, 734
Gellie, Paul, 386
Gemmell, John, 225
Gentles, Thomas, 243
Gerard, Alexander, Professor, 714
Gerard, Gilbert, Professor, 714
Gerrit, Alexander, 537
Getherall, Sir Thomas, 146
Gib, Martin, 196
Gibb, Andrew, 496
Gibb, George, 474
Gibb, Richard, 159, 488
Gibb, William, 49
Gibson, Alexander Robertson, 510
Gibson, Archibald, 13
Gibson, Arthur John Howieson, 300
Gibson, David, 60, 212
Gibson, James, 100, 294, 296
Gibson, James Duncan Walker, 265
Gibson, Sir John, 630
Gibson, John, 19, 191, 192, 238
Gibson, John Sharpe, 150
Gilchrist, John, 135, 388, 608
Giles, Charles, 589
Gilfillan, Alexander, 677
Gilfillan, Brodie Smith, 188, 214, 242
Gillan, Alexander, 319
Gillan, David Hedley, 672
Gillan, George Green, 286
Gillan, Ian Robert Wilson, 618, 724
Gillan, James, 20, 22, 638
Gillespie, Edward, 298
Gillespie, George, 10
Gillespie, James, Principal, 718
Gillespie, James Ewer, 175
Gillespie, James Hogg, 217
Gillespie, John, 160, 273
Gillespie, William Murdoch, 723, 738
Gillies, Alexander, 600
Gillies, Francis Cowan, 353
Gillies, James, 271
Gillies, John, 164
Gillies, John Macdonald, 315, 353
Gillies, Robert, 170
Gillies, Thomas Roger, 350
Gillies, William, 321
Gillies, William Alexander, 357

Gillieson, Archibald Hamilton, 678
Gillieson, Thomas, 26, 116
Gillieson, William Phin, 213
Gilliland, James, 119
Gillon, Alexander, 582
Gilmour, John, 438
Gilroy, James, Professor, 713
Gilruth, Andrew Hutton, 268
Gilruth, James Ruth, 54
Gilruth, Patrick Gorthy, 695
Gilston, William, 407
Given, Hugh O., 737
Glasgow, James, 35, 214
Glasgow, John, 232
Glass, Adam, 86
Glass, Sir James, 606, 619
Glass, John, 616
Glass, John Watt, 307
Glass, Patrick, 644
Glass, Thomas, 358, 368, 383
Glasse, John, 16
Glattisberrie, Robert, 276
Gledstanes, George, Archbishop, 708
Gledstanes, George, 181, 508, 625
Gledstanes, Herbert, 170, 178
Gleig, George, 509
Glen, Alexander, 88
Glen, Archibald, 286
Glen, James, 88
Glen, John, 133, 304
Glen, John Paul, 312, 321
Glen, Robert, 286
Glen, Thomas Stobo, 294, 390
Glen, William, 447
Glendinning, James, 180
Glendinning, Robert, 207
Glennie, John Douglas, 394, 448
Gloag, Andrew, 34
Gloag, Patrick James, 149
Glover, John, 180
Goderrall, Sir Thomas, 64
Gold, John, 53
Goldie, George, 87
Goldie, James, 84
Goldie, Thomas Smith, 27, 124
Goldie, William, 267
Goldie, William McLauchlan, 279
Goodall, Charles, 23, 214, 216, 362
Goodall, James Graham, 464
Goodere, William Scott, 621
Goodfellow, John, 516, 525
Goodman, Christopher, 468
Goodwillie, Richard, 587
Gordon, Adam, 304
Gordon, Aeneas Gunn, 448
Gordon, Alexander, 314, 578
Gordon, Hon. Arthur, 384
Gordon, Arthur Currie, 205

INDEX OF MINISTERS

Gordon, Charles, 148
Gordon, Donald Campbell Bryce, 582
Gordon, George, Professor, 712
Gordon, George, 526, 551, 623, 673
Gordon, Hugh, 275
Gordon, James of Zeochry, 610
Gordon, James, 283 bis, 536, 540, 754, 583, 606, 607, 610, 645, 646
Gordon, James Bryce, 110
Gordon, James Drummond, 135
Gordon, John, 138, 143, 199, 532, 556, 579 bis, 592, 637, 677
Gordon, Lewis, 637
Gordon, Ludovic, 544, 607
Gordon, Patrick, Principal, 711
Gordon, Patrick, Professor, 712
Gordon, Patrick Lindsay, 522
Gordon, Robert, 11, 347, 348
Gordon, Thomas, 79, 137, 546, 680
Gordon, William, 187, 361, 677, 703
Gordon, William Ireland, 209
Gordon, William Lindsay, 134, 533
Goudie, John, 133
Gould, John, 154
Gourlay, Adam, 151
Gourlay, James, 284
Gow, John Miller, 408
Govan, James, 377
Gowan, Peter, 197
Gowanlock, James, 168
Graham, Alexander, 112, 493
Graham, Andrew, 378, 696
Graham, Archibald, 309
Graham, David, 176, 370, 378, 471
Graham, David Cunningham, 81
Graham, George, 185, 356, 368
Graham, Gilbert, 513
Graham, Henry Greig, 132, 295
Graham, James, 184, 188, 471, 694
Graham, James Francis, 190
Graham, James Thomas, 292
Graham, John, 166, 279, 503, 699
Graham, John Anderson, 740
Graham, John Fraser, 290
Graham, Malise, 395
Graham, Manners Hamilton Nisbet, 132, 151
Graham, Robert, 231, 240, 275, 363, 471
Graham, Robert Balfour, 98
Graham, Thomas, 297
Graham, Thomas Forest Harkness, 254
Graham, Thomas Harkness, 250
Graham, William, 266, 278
Graham, William Vilant, 177
Grahamson, Alexander Patrick, 676
Granger, James, 523
Granger, John, 509
Granger, William, 213
Grant, Alexander, 338, 654, 673

Grant, Alexander Brown, 10, 283
Grant, Alexander Rae, 567
Grant, Alexander Robertson, 542
Grant, Andrew, 15
Grant, Charles Martin, 490
Grant, Charles Peter, 248
Grant, Donald, 315, 671
Grant, Donald Macgregor, 65, 283, 462
Grant, George, 600
Grant, George Henry, 141
Grant, James, 22, 30, 32, 600
Grant, James Bell, 306
Grant, James Chalmers, 302
Grant, John, 211
Grant, John Forbes Watson, 23
Grant, Lachlan, 619, 620
Grant, Ludovic, 548
Grant, Patrick, 195, 615, 616, 620, 667
Grant, Peter, 487, 685
Grant, Robert, 603
Grant, Samuel, 376
Grant, William, 136, 345, 605, 617
Grant, William Charles Middleton, 674
Grant, William Kenneth, 136, 469
Grantullie, James, 606
Grassick, George Henderson, 559
Gray, Alexander, 369, 373, 531, 535
Gray, Andrew, 73, 172, 277, 546, 557
Gray, Sir Duncan, 485
Gray, Sir George, 200
Gray, Gilbert, Principal, 711
Gray, Hew, 59
Gray, Sir James, 657
Gray, James, 283, 512, 647, 673
Gray, John, 36, 86, 380, 671
Gray, John Meikle, 238, 498
Gray, Lothian, 112
Gray, Robert, 198, 498
Gray, Thomas, 52, 60, 568
Gray, William, 89, 500, 503 bis, 671, 672, 673 bis
Green, Stephen, 247, 742
Green, William, 618
Greenfield, William, 11
Greenhill, Charles Kinnear, 152
Greenlaw, John, 596
Greenlaw, John Rutherford, 582
Gregor, Walter, 585
Gregorie, Alexander, 213
Gregorie, John, 537
Greig, George, 176
Greig, James, 188, 443
Greig, Sir John, 558
Greig, John, 574
Greig, Michael, 350
Greig, William, 571
Grier, George, 95
Grierson, Alexander, 662

Grierson, Archibald, 246
Grierson, John, 48
Grierson, John Callander, 483
Grieve, Henry, 495
Grieve, James, 367
Grieve, Matthew, 495
Grimwood, William Edward, 68, 121
Grinton, Patrick, 60
Grub, John, 482, 484
Gudefallo, John, 516
Guild, William, Principal, 711
Gullan, Gabriel, 156
Gullan, William, 127
Gunn, George, 133
Gunn, George Gibson, 125, 302
Gunn, Peter Bryce, 141
Gunn, William Ewan Bull, 506
Gunson, John, 296
Gusthart, William, 24
Guthrie, Alexander, 561
Guthrie, Andrew, 608
Guthrie, David, 354, 560
Guthrie, Henry, 361
Guthrie, James, 177, 393 bis
Guthrie, John, Bishop, 710
Guthrie, John, 34, 507, 513, 596, 630, 636
Guthrie, Patrick, 575
Guthrie, Thomas, 21
Guthrie, William Darling, 294, 434
Guthrie, William Galletly, 606

HADDEN, Archibald, 197
Haddow, James Murray, 202
Hadow, George, Professor, 718
Hadow, James, Principal, 718
Haig, William, 52
Haitlie, George, 491
Haitlie, John, 161
Halcro, Magnus of Brugh, 697
Halcro, William, 494
Haldane, Andrew, 512
Haldane, Robert, 477
Haldane, Walter, 266
Haliburton, David, 476, 662
Haliburton, Sir George, 88, 92
Haliburton, George, Bishop, 709
Haliburton, George, 471 bis
Haliburton, John, 132
Hall, George, 131
Hall, Gilbert, 43
Hall, James, 115, 545
Hall, James Thomas, 527
Hall, John, 12
Hall, John Thomas, 66
Hall, Mercer, 152
Hall, Ninian, 491, 493
Hall, Robert, 484
Hall, William, 487

Halliday, Archibald, 240
Halliday, Christopher, 457
Halliday, John, 180
Hamilton, Alexander, 11, 39, 40, 195, 285, 393
Hamilton, Andrew, 193, 286
Hamilton, Archibald, 3, 18, 198, 232, 242, 286
Hamilton, Arthur Alexander, 652
Hamilton, Blaise, 167
Hamilton, David, 262
Hamilton, David Gordon, 23, 130
Hamilton, Gavin, Bishop, 109
Hamilton, Gavin, 240
Hamilton, George, 11, 90, 112, 207
Hamilton, George Wilson, 166, 279
Hamilton, Gilbert, 5
Hamilton, Gilbert of Braehead of Raploch, 236
Hamilton, Hans, 230
Hamilton, Henry, 5
Hamilton, James, 12, 32, 35, 55 bis, 95, 182, 251, 258, 260, 288, 304, 486, 504, 724
Hamilton, James, Bishop, 285, 262
Hamilton, James Buchanan, 233
Hamilton, John of Gilkerscleuch, 267
Hamilton, John, Bishop, 709
Hamilton, John, 10, 36, 57, 87, 148, 157, 230, 242, 253, 258, 279, 459, 486
Hamilton, John Arnott, 79, 269
Hamilton, John Cowan, 53
Hamilton, John Edmund, 22
Hamilton, John Macfarlane, 211
Hamilton, Malcolm, 232
Hamilton, Matthew, 229
Hamilton, Ninian, 6
Hamilton, Patrick, 108, 224
Hamilton, Peter, 38, 46
Hamilton, Robert, 10, 250, 287, 468, 479, 550
Hamilton, Robert Kerr, 731
Hamilton, Samuel John, 253
Hamilton, Thomas, 235, 263
Hamilton, Sir William, 253
Hamilton, William, 5, 27, 87, 113, 156, 160, 215, 254, 258, 259, 279
Hamilton, William Forrest, 622
Hamilton, William Murray Smyth, 373
Hammill, Sir John, 400
Hammyl, John, 376, 379
Hampton, David McHardy, 408
Hanye (Hannie), James, 545
Hardie, Robert Montgomerie, 68
Hardie, William, 469
Hardy, Thomas, 27
Hargreaves, Sir Thomas, 59
Harkness, John, 131, 555
Harlaw, Nathaniel, 81
Harlaw, William, 18
Harper, Adam, 612
Harper, Alexander, 264
Harper, Alexander Bain, 319, 384

INDEX OF MINISTERS

Harper, John, 236
Harper, Thomas, 183, 272
Hart, Andrew Elvin, 517
Hart, Archibald, 379
Hart, James, 10
Harvie, Alexander, 352, 562
Harvie, Patrick, 390
Harvie, Thomas, 138
Hastie, Alexander, 306
Hastie, John, 125
Hastie, Patrick, 201
Hauxwell, Francis Marmaduke, 265
Hawthorn, Sir Michael, 201
Hay, Adam, 594
Hay, Alexander, 608, 639
Hay, Sir Andrew, 104
Hay, Andrew, 245, 598, 605
Hay, George, 59, 478, 595, 601, 611, 652
Hay, Gilbert, 60
Hay, James, 152, 309, 590, 598, 637, 704
Hay, John, 104, 198, 245 bis, 252, 445, 498, 601, 704
Hay, Theodore, 63
Hay, Sir Thomas, 667
Hay, Thomas, 63, 601
Hay, William, Bishop, 710
Hay, William, 116, 513, 519, 595, 655, 660, 672
Headrick, Robert, 38
Hederwick, David, 530
Heggie, David, 384
Heggie, John, 379, 509, 559
Hegy, Sir Andrew, 41, 145
Henderson, Abraham, 198
Henderson, Alexander, 10, 186
Henderson, Andrew, 598, 620
Henderson, Cuthbert, 320, 693, 699
Henderson, David, 234, 604, 605
Henderson, David Ramsay, 400
Henderson, Duncan Smith, 257, 431
Henderson, Frank, 244
Henderson, George, 674
Henderson, George David, Professor, 247, 714
Henderson, Hugh, 172
Henderson, James, 176, 301
Henderson, James Bell, 307
Henderson, John, 103, 213, 223, 417, 440, 539, 556, 575
Henderson, John William, 366
Henderson, Joseph, 272
Henderson, Malcolm, 398
Henderson, Patrick, 76
Henderson, Richard, 205, 252, 583
Henderson, Robert, 258
Henderson, Thomas of Broomfield, 184
Henderson, Thomas, 167, 402
Henderson, Walter Robertson, 199
Henderson, William, 409
Hendrie, George Smith, 216

Hendrie, John Gairdner White, 519
Hendry, Frederic, 36, 386
Henry, Archibald, 348
Henry, Charles, 626
Henry, David, 609
Henry, Donald MacIntyre, 198, 205
Henry, George, 3
Henry, John, 458
Henry, Patrick, 12
Henry, Robert, 9
Henryson, Abraham, 201
Henryson, David, 412
Henryson, John, 447
Hepburn, Adam of Bonhard, 638
Hepburn, Adam, 64
Hepburn, Alexander, 586
Hepburn, Charles Michael, 73, 353
Hepburn, Sir George, 112
Hepburn, George, 229
Hepburn, James, 513
Hepburn, John, 10, 53, 116, 143, 145, 498, 604
Hepburn, Patrick, 607, 630
Hepburn, Robert, 112, 476, 571
Hepburn, Thomas, 86, 109, 110 bis
Hepburn, William, 630
Herald, William David, 117
Herbertson, Archibald, 222
Herbertson, Robert, 212, 245, 377
Hering, James, 668
Heriot, Adam, 467
Heriot, Alexander, 72
Heriot, George, 173, 175
Heriot, John, 232, 574
Herkless, Sir John, 718
Heron, John, 731
Herries, John, 79
Herries, Robert, 156
Hervie, James of Mains of Elrick, 540
Hervy, John, 234
Hetherwick, Alexander, 740
Heughan, Charles, 79, 268, 287, 292, 295
Hewat, Andrew Middlemas, 103
Hewison, James King, 320
Higgins, James, 354
Higgins, James Craig, 226
Higgins, William, 65
Hill, Alexander, 309
Hill, Sir Andrew, 704
Hill, Colin Cecil Pitcairn, 233
Hill, Henry David, 98
Hill, James, 176, 211, 246, 287, 344
Hill, James Niven, 433
Hill, Lawrence, 289
Hill, Ninian, 732
Hill, Thomas, 251
Hilton, John, 200
Himmell, John, 421, 428
Hislop, Thomas, 291

INDEX OF MINISTERS

Hitchcock, George, 509
Hodge, James, 492
Hodge, Robert, 36, 46, 49
Hog, Sir Andrew, 41
Hog, Andrew, 545
Hog, James, 407
Hog, Thomas, 390
Hogg, George, 88
Hogg, James, 174
Hogg, James Allan, 218
Hogg, Robert, 40
Hogg, William, 122
Hoggan, James, 54
Hoggart, Robert, 223
Holburne, Patrick, 418
Home, Abraham, 114, 119
Home, Sir Alexander, 590
Home, Alexander of Houndwood, 107
Home, Alexander, 112
Home, Andrew, 144
Home, Archibald, 116, 120, 128, 129
Home, Charles, 133
Home, David, 105, 116, 126, 127, 128
Home, Francis, 204
Home, George, 115 bis, 122, 129, 133, 146
Home, Henry, 143
Home, John, 82, 122, 128
Home, John of Blackadder, 146
Home, John of Kello, 119
Home, Ninian, 133
Home, Patrick, 121, 127
Home, Robert, 119, 128, 183
Home, William, 122, 415
Honey, John Adamson, 189, 491
Honyman, Andrew, Bishop, 710
Honyman, Andrew, 523
Honyman, James, 523
Honyman, Robert, 469
Honyman, Thomas, 450
Hood, William, 133
Hope, Charles, 57
Hope, James, 173
Hopkirk, Dudley Stuart, 9, 250
Hopkirk, Sir James, 68
Hoppringle, John, 13
Hoppringle, Robert, 124
Horn, Alexander, 149
Horne, James, 637
Horne, Robert Keith Dick, 3
Horne, Robert Stevenson, 48
Horsburgh, Robert, 100
Hossack, Alexander, 665
Houlston, Charles Edward, 23, 410
Houston, Archibald McNeil, 422
Houston, James, 657
Houston, James Edward, 245
Houston, John, 230, 288, 309, 653
Houston, Robert, 279

Houston, Sir Robert, 183
Houston, Thomas, 650
Houston, William, 160
Howat, John, 489
Howat, John Lennox, 239, 300
Howell, Alexander Rutherford, 243
Howie, David Porter, 233
Howie, Robert, 599
Howie, William, 316
Howieson, David, 578, 587, 593
Howieson, John, 254
Howieson, Richard, 76
Howieson, Thomas, 651
Howitt, Stephen John, 157
Hume, Adam, 121
Hume, Alexander, 121
Hume, Charles, 174
Hume, James, 176
Hume, John, 382
Hunter, Adam, 79
Hunter, Alexander, 75, 194
Hunter, Andrew, 25
Hunter, Archibald, 234
Hunter, Charles, 272
Hunter, Charles Hay, 734
Hunter, Charles Lamb, 520
Hunter, David, 150, 407
Hunter, George, 140
Hunter, Henry, 31
Hunter, James, 73, 146, 167, 398
Hunter, John, 82, 192, 213, 219
Hunter, John Crabbe Templeton, 119
Hunter, John Mercer, 429
Hunter, John Sutherland, 20
Hunter, Joseph, 105
Hunter, Peter Hay, 15
Hunter, Robert, 3, 38, 46, 185
Hunter, Robert Condie, 271
Hunter, Robert Love, 175, 308
Hunter, William, 273
Huskie, James, 737
Hutcheon, John Mair, 299, 698
Hutchison, Adam Duncan Tait, 498
Hutchison, Charles Whitehead, 308, 354
Hutchison, George, 24, 383
Hutchison, Gilbert, 59
Hutchison, Hew, 129
Hutchison, James, 247, 286, 538
Hutchison, John, 222, 415, 678
Hutchison, Maxwell, 176
Hutchison, William, 255
Hutchison, William Andrew, 410
Hutsoun, Sir Thomas, 381
Hutton, George Dickson, 388
Hutton, James, 208
Hutton, Robert Shaw, 255
Hutton, William, 110
Hyndschaw, Robert, 448

INDEX OF MINISTERS

INCH, Thomas, 310
Inglis, Alexander, 234
Inglis, David, 462
Inglis, Hew, 419
Inglis, James, 423
Inglis, John, 10, 186, 260
Inglis, John Andrew, 82, 584
Inglis, John Macdonald, 196
Inglis, Robert, 214, 501
Inglis, Thomas, 132
Inglis, Thomas Murray, 262, 310, 623
Ingram, Gordon, 641
Ingram, James, 397
Ingram, James William, 732
Ingram, John, 704
Innes, Alexander, 609, 613, 623
Innes, Beroald, 540, 622
Innes, George, 536
Innes, Hieromymus, 592
Innes, Hugh, 609
Innes, James, 104, 145, 596
Innes, John, 191
Innes, Robert, 577, 640
Innes, Thomas, 636, 651, 652
Innes, Walter, 568, 678
Inverarity, William, 347
Ireland, Alexander, 350, 351, 418
Ireland, George, 128
Ireland, John, 169
Ireland, John Alexander, 258
Ireland, Thomas, 210, 359
Ireland, Walter Foggo, 29
Irvine, Sir Alexander, 477
Irvine, Alexander, 589
Irvine, Alexander Robertson, 347
Irvine, Edward, 697
Irvine, James, 508
Irvine, James Stewart Watt, 423
Irvine, John, 522, 553
Irvine, Walter Forbes, 509
Irving, Alexander, 545, 582
Irving, Edward, 725
Irving, Francis, 176
Irving, James, 208
Irving, John, 556
Irving, Walter, 459
Irwin, James Alexander Hamilton, 30

JACK, Alexander, 560
Jack, David, 311
Jack, George, 31
Jack, Hugh Morton, 204
Jack, James Craig, 476
Jack, John, 291
Jack, John Watson, 230
Jack, Robert, 265, 292
Jack, Thomas, 238,
Jack, William, 261

Jackson, Donald, 312, 315
Jackson, John, 390
Jackson, Robert Winchester, 734
Jackson, Thomas, 548
Jackson, William, 239, 245
Jaffray, John, 222
Jaffray, William Stevenson, 721
James, Wallace Newton, 311
Jameson, Andrew, 160
Jameson, Dugald, 523
Jameson, John, 173, 183 bis
Jameson, William, 139
Jamie, David, 417
Jamie, George Hope, 248, 275
Jamie, William Low, 1
Jamieson, Archibald, 377
Jamieson, George, 530
Jamieson, George Thomas, 34
Jamieson, Hugh Mitchell, 377
Jamieson, James, 476
Jamieson, James Bryce, 172, 257
Jamieson, John, 53, 118
Jamieson, Sir Mark, 365
Jamieson, Robert, 306
Jamieson, Robert George, 20, 349
Jamieson, William, 209
Jamieson, William Cruickshank Eddie, 25
Jamieson, William James, 230
Jardine, Andrew, 53
Jardine, David Bayne, 185
Jardine, David Little, 183
Jardine, Fergus, 428
Jardine, John, 26
Jardine, Matthew, 198
Jardine, Thomas, 187
Jenkins, Gerald Kerr, 532
Jenkins, William Falconer, 614
Jenkinson, John, 86
John, William, 214
Johnson, Donald, 292
Johnson, James Stewart, 254
Johnston, Adam, 70
Johnston, Alan, 266
Johnston, Alexander, 116
Johnston, Andrew, 100, 161
Johnston, David, 244
Johnston, David Silver, 28
Johnston, Frederick John Douteville, 190
Johnston, George, 135, 143
Johnston, George Andrew, 211
Johnston, Gilbert, 311
Johnston, James, 230, 363, 570, 623, 694
Johnston, James Christie, 378
Johnston, John, 35, 38, 43, 52, 118, 161, 197, 512 bis
Johnston, John Archibald, 156
Johnston, Joseph, 59
Johnston, Laurence, 117

Johnston, Michael Shaw Stewart, 196
Johnston, Patrick, 204
Johnston, Quintin, 308
Johnston, Robert of Carristan, 158
Johnston, Robert, 53, 168, 240
Johnston, Robert John, 401
Johnston, Samuel Knox, 663
Johnston, Simon, 165
Johnston, Symon, 189
Johnston, Thomas, 1
Johnston, Thomas Kennedy, 200
Johnston, Thomas Peter, 455
Johnston, William, 49, 81, 124, 135, 158, 161
Johnston, William George, 244, 319
Johnstone, David, 703
Johnstone, George, 447
Johnstone, John McKerlie, 49
Johnstone, Sir Murdoch, 680
Johnstone, Robert, 13, 406
Johnstone, Thomas, 199
Johnstone, Thomas Francis, 248
Johnstone, William, 166
Jolly, Archibald, 677
Jones, Edward Rowland, 392
Jones, Thomas Edmund Hill, 186, 392
Jones, Thomas Snell, 12
Junkene, Robert, 361
Justice, Alexander, 362

KAE, Adam, 201
Kay, Charles, 31
Kay, David Miller, Professor, 718
Kay, George, 10
Kay, John, 193, 197
Kay, John McRorie, 312, 502
Kay, Robert, 147, 197
Kean, James, 723
Kearney, Thomas Ramsay, 20, 259
Keir, John, 441
Keir, Robert, 286
Keith, Alexander, 49, 519, 521, 523
Keith, Archibald, 476, 579
Keith, Edward, 323
Keith, George, 47, 562, 580
Keith, Gilbert, 519, 542, 562, 586
Keith, James, 540
Keith, John, 522, 529, 567, 630, 698
Keith, Norman Coutts, 89
Keith, Robert, 510, 607, 662
Keith, Samuel, 579
Keith, Walter, 143, 511, 567
Keith, William of Aquhortis, 19
Keith, William, 638
Kellas, James Forrest, 364, 527
Kellas, John, 586, 740
Kellie, James, 113
Kellie, John, 54

Kellie, Robert, 166, 368
Kellie, Simon, 51
Kello, Gilbert, 536
Kelly, Graeme Ismay Davidson, 738
Kelly, James, 292
Kelly, William, 61
Kemp, Andrew, 277, 438, 459, 538
Kemp, Arnold Low, 545, 594
Kemp, Sir John, 400
Kemp, William, 85
Kennedy, Alexander, 25, 340
Kennedy, Archibald Robert Stirling, Professor, 716
Kennedy, Charles William, 292
Kennedy, Gilbert Alexander, 255
Kennedy, Hew, 212, 219
Kennedy, Hugh, 25, 136
Kennedy, James, 395
Kennedy, James Russell, 191
Kennedy, John, 280, 435, 481, 542, 561, 566, 592, 628, 656
Kennedy, Norman Douglas, 510
Kennedy, Thomas, 372
Kennedy, Walter, 268
Kennedy, William Black, 126
Kent, John, 122
Ker, Alexander, 65, 435
Ker, Andrew, 601
Ker, Hew, 60
Ker, James, 131, 138, 500
Ker, Sir John, 132
Ker, John, 85, 94, 99, 630
Ker, Mark, 131
Ker, Robert, 148
Ker, Sir Thomas, 132
Ker, William, 135, 149
Ker, William Lee, 234
Kerr, Colin Mackay, 302
Kerr, George Scott, 180
Kerr, John, 89, 286, 688
Kerr, John Alexander, 161, 163
Kerr, John Mitchell, 308
Kerr, Robert, 149, 448, 647
Kerr, Robert Cranston, 120, 131
Kerr, Robert Hogg, 162
Kerr, William, 190
Kesting, August John, 344, 413
Kesting, Norman Gottfried, 58, 280
Kid, James, 48
Kid, William, 107
Kidd, William, 273
Kidston, Andrew Snadden, 273
Kilburn, John Robert de Lingen, 617, 730
Kilgour, Robert, 740
Kilgour, Robert Laurie, 261
Killen, James Millar, 252, 734
Kilpatrick, James, 725
Kincaid, Alexander, 702, 707

INDEX OF MINISTERS

King, James Waters, 280
King, Robert Alexander, 172
King, Thomas, 265
Kinloch, James, 484
Kinloch, John, 379
Kinloch, Robert, 11
Kinnaird, John, 33, 266
Kinnares, Thomas, 491
Kinnear, Alexander, 129, 137
Kinnear, Edward, 33
Kinnear, John, 242
Kinnear, Robert, 498
Kinnear, Thomas, 455, 547
Kinnear, William, 513
Kinninmonth, Thomas, 422
Kinross, William, 223
Kintore, George, 69
Kirk, Adam, 381
Kirk, Andrew, 381, 392, 405
Kirk, James, 107, 201, 320, 395
Kirk, Robert, 395
Kirkcaldie, Andrew, 428
Kirkcaldy, Thomas, 256
Kirke, Robert, 127
Kirkland, Robert, 155
Kirkpatrick, James, 68
Kirkpatrick, James Mackenzie, 149, 300
Kirkpatrick, John, 157
Kirkpatrick, Roger Sandilands, 154
Kirkpatrick, William, 234
Kirkton, Andrew, 141
Kirkwood, George, 721
Kirkwood, James, 140, 186
Kirkwood, Thomas Duncanson, 362
Knight, Thomas Fulton, 128
Knowes, Christopher, 124
Knowes, William, 116
Knowles, Willliam Andrew, 26, 156
Knox, James, 194
Knox, John, 10, 29, 144, 323, 492, 612, 722
Knox, Robert, 130
Knox, Robert Brodie, 740
Knox, Simon, 204
Knox, Thomas, 238
Knox, William, 444
Kyd, David Russell, 356
Kyd, James, 586
Kyd, Robert Joseph, 235
Kyde, William, 486
Kynninmonth, Alexander, 483

LACEY, William Roland, 275, 295
Laidlaw, Andrew, 176, 302
Laidlaw, James, 186
Laing, Albert James, 694
Laing, James, 193
Laing, John, 36, 280, 514
Laing, Malcolm, 690

Laing, Norman, 686
Laing, William, 177, 514
Laing, William Mackie, 127, 738
Laird, Alexander Oswald, 429
Laird, David, 451
Lamb, Andrew, 194
Lamb, James, 87, 105, 106
Lamb, Sir John, 371
Lamb, John, 295, 353, 677
Lamb, William, 103, 135
Lammie, John, 502
Lamond, Hugh, 329
Lamond, John, 8
Lamont, Alan, 425, 426
Lamont, Andrew, 432
Lamont, Donald, 347
Lamont, Donald McDonald, 315, 735
Lamont, Henry Maclaurin, 124
Lamont, James, 263
Lamont, John, 354, 684
Lamont, Murdoch, 303, 621
Lamont, Robert, 348
Lamont, Walter, 318
Landale, David, 155, 346
Landale, William Maxwell, 82, 255
Landell, James, 124
Landells, Adam, 127
Landells, John, 273
Landells, Robert, 266
Landeth, James, 503
Landeths, Adam, 223
Landreth, Adam Thomson, 725
Landreth, Peter Robert, 369
Lang, Andrew, 168, 694
Lang, Gavin, 258, 652
Lang, James, 113
Lang, James Paisley, 393
Lang, John Marshall, Professor, 289, 715
Lang, Marshall Buchanan, 111
Lang, Walter, 3
Langlands, Frederick David, 150, 238
Langlands, John, 137, 142
Langlands, Robert, 636
Langwell, James, 6
Lapsie, James, 286
Lauder, Alexander, 304, 305
Lauder, Andrew, 198
Lauder, James, 113, 346, 638, 655, 704, 705
Lauder, John, 33, 105
Lauder, Robert, 98, 113
Lauder, William, 704 *bis*
Laurence, Andrew Taylor, 22
Laurie, George Albyn Douglas, 705
Laurie, James, 219
Laurie, John, 169
Laurie, Thomas, 272
Laurie, Walter, 192
Law, Alexander, 556

Law, Sir Gilbert, 308
Law, James, 43, 192
Law, John, 56, 242
Law, Mungo, 10
Law, Robert, 3
Law, Thomas, 239, 637
Law, William, 579
Law, William Guthrie, 511
Lawis, Thomas, 59
Lawrence, William Fyfe, 536
Lawrie, Archibald, 234
Lawrie, John, 55, 186
Lawrie, Thomas, 492
Lawrie, William, 272
Lawrie, William James, 192
Lawson, —, 365
Lawson, Alexander, 440, 580, 706
Lawson, Archibald, 176
Lawson, Gavin, 198
Lawson, George, 154, 546
Lawson, James, 10
Lawson, John, 471
Lawson, Lewis of Leuchold, 204
Lawson, Roger, 169
Lawson, Thomas, 450
Lawtie, James, 598
Layng, James, 281 bis
Layng, John, 364
Layng, Patrick, 348, 365, 368
Layos, Edward, 76
Leggatt, Harry, 470, 557
Leighton, James, 500
Leighton, William, 500
Leiper, James, 272
Leishman, James Fleming, 131
Leishman, Thomas, 131, 361
Leitch, David, 568
Leitch, Henry, 438, 449
Leitch, Robert Mackay, 485
Leith, George, 569
Leith, Patrick, 562
Leith, William, 567, 611
Lennox, John, 362
Lesk, William, 534
Leslie, Alexander, 570, 604, 609, 612, 638
Leslie, Andrew, 564
Leslie, David Smith, 127
Leslie, George, 7, 438, 452, 459, 609
Leslie, George Neave, 399, 737
Leslie, Gilbert, 534
Leslie, James, 552
Leslie, Sir John, 605
Leslie, John, Bishop, 710
Leslie, John, 39, 531, 534, 563, 565, 570, 577, 609, 611, 612, 614
Leslie, Norman, 384
Leslie, Robert, 635
Leslie, Walter, 526, 568

Leslie, William, Principal, 711
Leslie, William, 526, 595, 606
Leslie, Wilson Summers, 308, 593
Levack, John Grant, 326
Levack, William Larnoch Tennyson, 290, 462
Leverance, John, 36, 224
Lewis, George, 487
Lewis, Wilfred Joseph, 475
Leys, Charles, 703
Lichton, Matthew, 5
Lichton, Thomas, 105
Liddell, David, Professor, 717
Liddell, John, 615
Liddell, Matthew, 114, 115, 116, 121
Liddell, Patrick, 512, 643, 648
Liddell, Robert Herbert Ramsay, 372
Liddell, Thomas, 158
Liddle, David Francis, 291
Liddle, William, 21
Lillie, David, 679
Lillie, William, 740
Limond, William Gilbert, 147, 270
Lindsay, Sir Alexander, 477
Lindsay, Alexander of Evelick, 372
Lindsay, Alexander, 266, 308, 480, 482, 499
Lindsay, Archibald, 619
Lindsay, David, Bishop, 709
Lindsay, David, 30, 68, 474, 480, 481, 508
Lindsay, George of Blackscolme, 282
Lindsay, George, 29
Lindsay, Henry, 369, 480
Lindsay, Hercules, 214
Lindsay, Sir Hew, 482
Lindsay, Hew, 54
Lindsay, James, 182, 233, 254, 273, 419, 520 536
Lindsay, John of Dowhill, 365
Lindsay, John, 222, 225 bis, 266, 502, 504, 518
Lindsay, Patrick, Archbishop, 708
Lindsay, Patrick, 508
Lindsay, Robert, 3, 56, 270, 546
Lindsay, Robert Robertson, 271
Lindsay, Thomas, 56 bis, 272, 508, 524
Lindsay, Walter, 478, 508
Lindsay, William, 79, 163, 230
Linn, Patrick, 172
Linning, Thomas, 56, 271
Lippe, Robert, 722
Liston, William Alexander, 237
Lithgow, Robert, 148
Litster, Matthew, 704, 705
Little, James, 280
Little, John, 177
Little, Thomas, 192, 270
Little, William, 164
Liver, Robert, 145
Liverance, John, 53, 268
Livingstone, Alexander, 550
Livingstone, Andrew, 558

INDEX OF MINISTERS

Livingstone, Archibald, 53
Livingstone, George, 551, 557
Livingstone, Henry, 400
Livingstone, Hugh, 329, 342
Livingstone, John, 135, 155, 192, 193, 303, 308
Livingstone, Robert, 52, 55
Livingstone, Thomas, 265
Livingstone, William, 580
Loch, Sir Patrick, 168
Loch, Patrick, 179
Lochhead, John, 211
Lockhart, Laurence, 239
Lockhart, Robert, 55
Lockhart, Samuel, 223
Lockhart, William, 1
Logan, Allan, 408, 415
Logan, Duncan, 657
Logan, Donald MacIntosh, 315, 343
Logan, George, 25, 509
Logan, John, 170, 178, 280
Logan, Robert, 535, 646
Logan, Thomas, 123
Logan, William, 170
Logie, John, 371, 481
Logie, John Deas, 374, 475, 674
Logie, Robert Scarth Valentine, 360
Logie, William, 88, 434
Lord, David, 574
Lorimer, James, Principal, 718
Lorimer, John Gordon, 301
Lornie, Franklin Ross Taylor, 199, 299, 594
Lornie, James Taylor, 175, 740
Lorraine, James Joseph, 410
Lorraine, Joseph Currie, 170
Lothian, John, 262
Lothian, William, 7
Loudon, Alexander, 42
Loudon, Joseph, 83
Loutit, John Smeaton, 575
Love, John, 288, 703
Love, Thomas, 479
Lovell, James, 494
Lovie, Frederick William, 570
Low, James Anderson, 178
Low, Thomas, 89, 250
Low, William Marshall, 554
Lownie, Sir Archibald, 347
Lugton, Thomas, 46
Lumsden, Charles, 6
Lumsden, Edward, 552
Lumsden, Henry, 433
Lumsden, James, 35
Lumsden, John, Professor, 714
Lumsden, John, 583
Lumsden, Thomas, 60, 385, 433, 567
Lumsden, William, 409, 417
Lunan, Alexander, 565
Lundie, Archibald, 100

Lundie, David, 675
Lundie, George, 40, 82
Lundie, James, 29, 127
Lundie, John, 110
Lundie, Robert, 462
Lundie, Thomas, 353, 471
Lundie, William John, 674, 675
Lundy, Thomas, 54
Lyall, George, 402
Lyall, Thomas, 699
Lychtoun, James, 507
Lyell, David, 506
Lyell, Hugh Arbuthnott, 485
Lyle, James, 601, 603
Lyle, Thomas, 114
Lyne, Edward, 76
Lyon, Gilbert, 428
Lyon, James Gordon, 510
Lyon, John, 181
Lyon, Patrick, 428, 482, 484, 509
Lyon, Ritchie Doughty, 99, 410
Lyon, Silvester, 483
Lyon, Thomas, 484
Lythgow, Sir John, 36
Lythton, Thomas, 128

MABON, Thomas, 144
MacAlexander, Thomas, 189
MacAlister, Archibald, 329
MacAlister, Hector, 324, 325
MacAllan, Donald, 201
MacAlpine, John, 323
MacAlpine, Walter, 408
MacAlpine, William, 231
Macallum, Donald, 692
MacAndrew, Thomas Watt, 42, 265
MacAndrew, William, 671
Macara, Alexander, 232, 389
Macara, John, 414, 731
Macarthur, Alexander, 321
Macarthur, Archibald, 339
Macarthur, Charles, 311, 532
Macarthur, Duncan, 247, 513
Macarthur, Hugh, 685
Macarthur, John, 667
Macarthur, John Brown, 650
Macaskill, Angus, 512
Macaskill, Malcolm, 685
Macaulay, Aulay, 688
Macaulay, Daniel, 683
Macaulay, Donald, 678
Macaulay, Duncan, 347, 354, 355, 356, 357
Macaulay, John, 490
Macaulay, Robert, 394
Macaulay, Samuel, 496
MacBain, James, 275
Macbean, Alexander, 329, 338
Macbean, Donald, 353

INDEX OF MINISTERS

Macbean, Lachlan, 647
Macbeth, John, 80
MacBlane, Nicol, 197
MacBride, Daniel, 350
MacCaig, Donald, 336
MacCaig, Neil 166
MacCall, John Drennan, 228
MacCallum, Archibald, 312
MacCallum, Dugald, 668
MacCallum, Duncan, 683
MacCallum, John, 303, 333, 334, 338, 397, 650
MacCallum, John Donaldson, 262
MacCallum, John Foster, 225, 480
MacCallum, John Stewart, 247
MacCallum, Julius, 506
MacCallum, Malcolm, 336
MacCallum, Neil, 340
MacCallum, William, 131
MacCalman, Alexander, 335
MacCalman, Archibald, 336
MacCalman, Duncan, 335 *bis*, 337
MacCalman, John, 188
MacCalman, Nicol, 334
MacCardel, James, 231, 311
MacCaughan, Thomas, 264, 268
MacCaughey, Charles Francis, 166
MacCaul, Matthew Wilson, 732
MacClellan, John, 152, 201, 202, 207
MacClellan, Nicol, 189
MacClellan, Robert, 189, 205
MacClellan, Robert Scott, 389
MacClennochan, Ninian, 208
MacClenochan, Ninian, 190
MacCloy, Donald, 318
MacCluggage, Albert, 238
MacClure, James Campbell, 524
MacClymont, James Alexander, 526
MacClymont, John Douglas, 215
MacColl, Archibald, 341
MacColl, Hugh Clarke, 233, 490
MacColl, John, 159, 258
MacCombie, John, 174
MacCondoquhie, John Dow, 619
MacConnachie, William, 144
MacConzie, John, 160
MacCorcadill, John, 257
MacCorkindale, Duncan, 282, 387
MacCorkindale, William Andrew, 127
MacCormick, John Archibald, 332
MacCorquodale, Donald, 299
MacCrathane, John, 420
MacCreath, John Fergusson, 130, 146
MacCuaig, Angus, 328, 329
MacCuard, Robert, 306
MacCulloch, Charles, 204
MacCulloch, Colin, 389
MacCulloch, Donald, 192
MacCulloch, Elias, 199, 200

MacCulloch, Finlay, 301
MacCulloch, George, 671
MacCulloch, Hugh, 29, 119
MacCulloch, Ian, 247
MacCulloch, Ian Forbes, 496
MacCulloch, James, 192, 665
MacCulloch, James Hutton, 29
MacCulloch, Patrick, 198
MacCulloch, William, 254
MacCullough, William Cupples, 137
Maccultrie, Thomas, 210
MacCurrach, James Lawson, 248
Macdermett, John, 213
Macdiarmid, Hugh, 337, 397
Macdiarmid, William Hutchison, 263, 481
Macdonald, Alexander, 285, 301, 303, 313, 332, 386, 456
Macdonald, Angus, 315, 321, 486
Macdonald, Angus John Norman, 656, 688
Macdonald, Archibald, 652, 688
Macdonald, Charles, 331, 578, 600
Macdonald, Charles Cadell, 532
Macdonald, Coll Archibald, 358
Macdonald, Donald, 256, 324, 329, 345, 651, 689
Macdonald, Donald Alexander, 685
Macdonald, Donald Dewar, 488
Macdonald, Donald Henry, 330
Macdonald, Donald John, 324
Macdonald, Duff, 257
Macdonald, Dugald, 667
Macdonald, Duncan David Farquharson, 128
Macdonald, Finlay Robert, 474
Macdonald, George, 608
Macdonald, Hector Kennedy, 738
Macdonald, Hugh, 685
Macdonald, James, 454, 650
Macdonald, James Alexander Donald John, 343
Macdonald, James Duff, 8
Macdonald, James George, 600, 612
Macdonald, James Ronald, 161
Macdonald, James Wallace, 674
Macdonald, John, 378, 706
Macdonald, John Nelson, 298
Macdonald, Malcolm, 338
Macdonald, Murdoch, 674
Macdonald, Neil Gillies, 330, 338, 341
Macdonald, Roderick John Fraser, 458
Macdonald, William Thomson Ponton, 391
Macdonnell, John, 644
Macdougall, George, 361
Macdougall, James, 242, 332
Macdougall, John, 22, 34, 343, 396, 679
Macdougall, Neil, 320
Macdougall, Robert, 317
MacDowall, Hew, 192
MacDowall, Sir Neill, 191

INDEX OF MINISTERS

MacDowall, Sir William, 40, 188, 189
Macduff, Alexander, 728
Macduff, John Ross, 307
Macduff, Robert Charles Henry, 35
MacEachran, John, 274
MacEachran, Robert, 395
Macechern, Charles, 652
Macechern, Christian Victor Aeneas, 323, 528, 731
Macechern, Dugald, 676
Macechern, John, 670
Macewan, John, 643
Macewan, Sydney Melrose, 594
MacFadden, Jackson Loudon, 189, 665
MacFadden, Oliver Kenneth Wallace, 134
MacFadyen, Donald, 337
MacFadyen, James, 188, 329, 345
Macfadzean, Angus, 328
Macfarlane, Alfred, 148
Macfarlane, Bryce, 209
Macfarlane, Donald, 323, 324, 336
Macfarlane, Dugald, 619
Macfarlane, Duncan, 358, 737
Macfarlane, James, 6, 47
Macfarlane, John, 245, 315, 715
Macfarlane, John Adam, 663
Macfarlane, John Warden, 8
Macfarlane, Thomas Malloch, 27
Macfarlane, William, 727
Macfarlane, William Alexander, 355
Macfarlane (Macfarland), William John, 67, 130, 438
Macfarlane, William Leekie, 209
MacFie, David, 329
MacGarrity, Robert Forsyth, 30, 164, 693
MacGeorge, William, 75, 170
MacGhie, Andrew, 88
MacGhie, John, 88
MacGhie, Mungo, 173
MacGibbon, James, 305
MacGibbon, Thomas, 346, 351, 359, 382
MacGilchrist, Daniel, 282
MacGilchrist, John, 294, 315, 329, 530, 641
MacGill, Francis, 390
MacGill (Makgill), George, 508
MacGill, Henry Moncreiff, 80
MacGill, James, 189
MacGill, John Whyte, 164, 171
MacGill, Neil, 277, 517, 621
MacGill, Patrick, 496
MacGilliechallum, Gregor, 357
MacGillivray, Donald, 654
MacGillivray, Duncan, 295
MacGillivray, James, 254
MacGinn, Thomas, 160
MacGlashan, Charles, 587
MacGlashan, Lewis, 171, 504
MacGlass, George, 279

MacGowan, Alexander, 140, 160, 204
MacGregor, Alexander, 338, 354, 396
MacGregor, Alexander Murray, 190
MacGregor, Charles, 13, 316
MacGregor, Duncan, 554, 582
MacGregor, Ewen Macdonald, 188
MacGregor, James, 19
MacGregor, John Campbell, 8
MacGregor, John Charles, 600
MacGregor, John Macnab, 334
MacGregor, John Robertson, 432
MacGregor, Malcolm, 80
MacGregor, Malcolm Blair, 278
MacGregor, Patrick, 367
MacGregor, Peter, 617
MacGregor, Robert, 548, 684
MacGregor, William Covington, 54
MacGude, Sir Thomas, 219
MacGuffie, John, 190
Machamwell, William, 104
MacHardy, Archibald, 721
MacHardy, Francis, 449, 522
MacHardy, James, 677
MacHardy, James Cameron, 610
MacHardy, William, 578, 626
MacIlwraith, John, 246
MacIlvean, Thomas Dale, 170
MacIlvorich, Donald, 313
MacIlvorie, John, 332
MacIlvra, Martin, 339, 341
MacIlwraith, Alexander Hannay, 428
MacIlwraith, John, 489, 532
MacInnes, Aeneas Ede, 152
MacInnes, Alastair Robert Ellis, 285, 738
MacInnes, George, 209
MacInnes, John, 332, 531
MacInnes, Roderick, 684, 692
MacIntosh, Allan, 648
MacIntosh, Charles Douglas, 332
MacIntosh, Donald, 617
MacIntosh, Duncan, 354
MacIntosh, James Archibald, 740
MacIntosh, Lauchlan, 363
MacIntosh, William, 616
MacIntyre, Alexander Aeneas Ranaldson Macdonell, 682
MacIntyre, Archibald, 703
MacIntyre, Archibald Ewing, 245, 317
MacIntyre, Duncan, 344, 688
MacIntyre, James, 602
MacIntyre, John, 340, 345
MacIntyre, John Duncan, 706
MacIntyre, John Walker, 345, 358
MacIntyre, Malcolm, 341, 680
MacIntyre, Walter, 173, 401
MacIver, Iver, 660
MacIver, John, 684
MacIver, Peter John, 256, 491

Mack, John, 566
Mack, John Charles, 157
MacKail, Hew, 24
Mackay, Adam, 299, 607
Mackay, Alexander, 316, 604
Mackay, Angus, 707
Mackay, Cameron, 686
Mackay, Donald, 244, 692
Mackay, Donald William, 116
Mackay, Eye, 671
Mackay, Gavin Kerrill, 183, 239, 257
Mackay, George, 646
Mackay, George William, 358
Mackay, Hector William, 671
Mackay, James, 290, 498
Mackay, James Alexander Sutherland, 612
Mackay, James Cunningham, 351
Mackay, James Hutton, 732
Mackay, John, 315, 681
Mackay, John Alexander, 490, 546
Mackay, Kenneth, 341
Mackay, Niel, 223
Mackay, Norman Donald, 667
Mackay, Robert Henry, 454
Mackean, Walter George, 503, 740
Mackechnie, John, 125, 303
Mackechnie, William, 274
MacKeggie, George Alexander, 645
MacKell, John, 182
MacKell, Matthew, 253
Mackellar, Alexander, 343
Mackellar, Angus, 99
Mackellar, James, 734
Mackellar, John, 336
Mackellar, John Alexander Coull, 287
Mackellar, John Bayne, 333
MacKendrick, Thomas Miller, 262, 297
Mackenzie, Alexander, 303, 314, 315, 320, 536, 546, 667, 680
Mackenzie, Alfred James, 25
Mackenzie, Allan, 341
Mackenzie, Andrew Law McGregor, 177
Mackenzie, Archibald, 213, 274
Mackenzie, Callum, 327
Mackenzie, Charles Gordon, 379, 576
Mackenzie, Colin, 692
Mackenzie, Colin Archibald, 218
Mackenzie, Donald Francis, 732
Mackenzie, Donald Stewart, 292, 559
Mackenzie, Donald William, 342
Mackenzie, Duncan, 686
Mackenzie, Evan, 740
Mackenzie, Ewen, 653
Mackenzie, George, 247, 256, 329, 334
Mackenzie, George Edward, 156
Mackenzie, George Omond, 140, 433
Mackenzie, Hector, 651
Mackenzie, Hugh, 338, 556
Mackenzie, Hugh Skinner, 113
Mackenzie, James, 82, 151, 370, 667
Mackenzie, James Buchanan, 47
Mackenzie, James Duncan, 544
Mackenzie, John, 656, 659, 660, 662, 663, 680, 681
Mackenzie, John Henderson, 9, 261, 706, 723
Mackenzie, John Kennedy, 116, 582, 692
Mackenzie, John Skinner, 350
Mackenzie, Kenneth, 665, 667
Mackenzie, Kenneth Alexander, 619
Mackenzie, Lachlan, 336
Mackenzie, Murdoch, 681, 699
Mackenzie, Neil, 332, 334
Mackenzie, Neil Kennedy, 492
Mackenzie, Norman, 322, 654
Mackenzie, Robert Dunbar, 240
Mackenzie, Roderick, 656
Mackenzie, William, 675
Mackenzie, William John, 673, 681
MacKeracher, Malcolm, 336
MacKerchar, John, 355
MacKerron, David Denholm, 151
MacKerron, Peter, 130
MacKerron, Robert, 557
MacKichan, Peter Neil, 313, 315
Mackie, Alexander, 566
Mackie, Charles, 537
Mackie, George Munro, 730
Mackie, James, 19, 149, 622
Mackie, John, 171
Mackie, Thomas, 246
Mackie, William, 209
MacKillop, Neil, 338
MacKinlay, Alexander Wallace, 318
MacKinley, Henry, 20, 143, 431
MacKinnon, Alexander, 284, 300, 345
MacKinnon, Charles, 257, 306
MacKinnon, Donald, 312, 671, 687 bis
MacKinnon, Finlay, 359
MacKinnon, Finlay McNicol, 664
MacKinnon, James, 329
MacKinnon, James, Professor, 716
MacKinnon, John Campbell, 380
MacKinnon, Lachlan, 335
MacKinnon, Malcolm, 322
MacKinnon, Neil, 337, 372, 385, 386, 388
MacKinnon, Neil Donald Campbell, 334
MacKinnon, Neil Duncan, 284
MacKinnon, Robert Bruce, 50
Mackintosh, James, 329, 598
Mackintosh, John, 216, 264, 291
Mackintosh, Kenneth, 732
Mackintosh, Robert Smith, 211, 218
Mackintosh, Thomas, 525
Mackintosh, William, 342, 691
Mackintosh, Y., 678
MacKirdie, James, 325

Macknight, James, 12
Macknight, Thomas, 12
Macknight, William, 232
MacKune, Christopher, 267
Maclachlan, Alexander, 273
Maclachlan, Archibald, 329
Maclachlan, Donald, 315
Maclachlan, Hugh, 332
Maclachlan, John, 312, 313, 326, 335
Maclachlan, Neil, 333, 334
Maclachlan, Patrick, 335
Maclachlan, William, 314
Maclagan, James, 366
Maclagan, John, 298
Maclagan, Duncan, 352, 355, 356
Maclaine, Aeneas, 318, 339
Maclaine, Angus, 338, 340
Maclaine, Hector, 316
Maclaren, Archibald, 306
Maclaren, Charles Lucius, 137
Maclaren, Daniel, 265
Maclaren, David Duthie, 494, 558
Maclaren, David John, 385
Maclaren, Duncan, 595
Maclaren, John, 390, 403
Maclaren, John Reid, 471
Maclaren, Kenneth Daniel, 363
Maclaren, Peter, 582
Maclaren, William Peter, 1
Maclauchlan, Archibald, 320(3)
Maclauchlan, Colin, 320, 357
Maclaughlan, Thomas, 654
MacLaurin, John, 301
Maclean, Alexander, 243, 311, 553
Maclean, Alexander Duncan, 343
Maclean, Alistair, 650
Maclean, Andrew Colquhoun, 659
Maclean, D. J., 688
Maclean, David Walker, 592
Maclean, Donald, 684
Maclean, Donald F., 329
Maclean, Donald Matheson, 320
Maclean, Douglas Gordon, 317
Maclean, Dugald, 616
Maclean, Duncan, 303, 318
Maclean, Duncan Finlay, 237
Maclean, George Murdoch, 487
Maclean, Hector, 687
Maclean, Hew, 338
Maclean, Hugh Baillie, 725
Maclean, James, 293
Maclean, John, 282, 329, 331, 345, 492, 681, 689, 706
Maclean, John Dawson, 503, 572
Maclean, John Kenneth, 340, 678
Maclean, Kenneth, 653
Maclean, Lachlan, 315, 366
Maclean, Lauchlan, 732, 740

Maclean, Malcolm, 322
Maclean, Neil Alexander, 14, 506
Maclean, Norman, 19 bis
Maclean, Peter Hector, 340
Maclean, Robert Allan, 44
Maclean, Roderick, 690
Maclean, Roderick Matheson, 740
Maclean, Walter George, 740
Maclean, William George Green, 598
Maclean, William Gordon, 273
Macleay, Kenneth Alexander, 247, 275, 708
MacLees, David Patrick, 394
Maclellan, Alexander, 292
Maclellan, Duncan, 350
Maclellan, Duncan Tait Hutchison, 732
Maclellan, Ian, 359
Maclellan, John Campbell, 358
Maclellan, Malcolm, 306
Maclellan, Neil, 652
Maclellan, Sir William, 193
Maclellan, William, 207
Maclennan, Alexander, 655
Maclennan, Donald, 665
Maclennan, Duncan Macrae, 681
Maclennan, Duncan Shaw, 620
Maclennan, George Robert, 679
Maclennan, John Aulay, 621
Maclennan, John Norman, 343
Maclennan, Roderick, 690
Maclennan, William George Duncan, 623
Macleod, Alexander, 690
Macleod, Angus, 223, 324, 340, 690
Macleod, Donald, 139, 172, 307, 651, 670, 680, 683, 724
Macleod, Sir George Fielden, 19
Macleod, Hector Maclennan, 262
Macleod, John, 217, 294, 298, 340, 343, 620, 683
Macleod, John Ford, 26, 273
Macleod, John Matheson, 340, 601, 651
Macleod, Kenneth, 323, 328
Macleod, Kenneth Olans, 347
Macleod, Lachlan, 684
Macleod, Lauchlan, 690
Macleod, Malcolm, 686
Macleod, Murdo, 670
Macleod, Neil, 339, 651
Macleod, Norman, 105, 289, 300, 626, 683
Macleod, Roderick, 616, 686
Macleod, Walter, 470
Macleod, William, 322
Macleod, William Houldsworth, 274
MacLintock, Samuel, 66
MacLuckie, James Morrison, 13, 162
Macmaster, James, 214
Macmath, David Fyfe, 224, 310
Macmeikan, James, 272
Macmichael, David Colville, 344, 731

INDEX OF MINISTERS

Macmichael, Duncan, 461
Macmichael, Neil, 312
Macmillan, Alexander, 338
Macmillan, Angus, 324
Macmillan, Donald, 14, 295
Macmillan, Fingon, 338
Macmillan, Hugh, 150
Macmillan, John, 207
Macmillan, William, 410
Macmorine, Robert, 176, 307
Macmorland, James, 189, 407
Macmorland, John Peter, 140
MacMurray, Andrew Douglas, 214
MacMurray, Charles Robb, 447
MacMurrie, Malcolm, 325
MacMurtrie, John, 15, 543
Macnab, Alexander, 329
Macnab, David Evan, 328
Macnab, Duncan, 355
Macnab, James Simpson, 246
Macnab, James Strathearn, 258, 387
Macnab, John, 326
Macnab, John Rolland, 274
Macnab, Stevenson, 71
Macnab, William Urquhart, 324, 682
Macnair, Alexander Wood, 153, 577
Macnair, Duncan, 350
Macnair, James, 7, 48
McNaught, James, 288
McNaught, John Campbell, 666
Macnaughton, Colin, 670
Macnaughton, Duncan, 337
Macnaughton, George Donald, 376
Macnaughton, George Ferrier Anderson, 203
Macnaughton, John, 673
Macnaughton, John Scott, 370
Macneill, Archibald, 651
Macneill, Hector, 323
Macneill, Hugh Fraser, 666
Macneill, John, 317
Macneill, John Henry Horton, 390
Macneill, Neil, 341, 387
Macneill, Robert, 192
Macnicol, William, 492, 564, 678
Macnie, Robert Lamond, 493
Macniven, John, 244
MacNutt, William, 577
Maconachie, James Hamill, 376
MacOsonage, Malcolm, 322, 324
MacPaul, Sir John, 334
Macphail, Andrew, 652, 653
Macphail, Donald, 682
Macphail, Dougall Neil, 737
Macphail, Duncan, 314
Macphail, John, 196, 692
Macphail, Matthew, 203, 488, 508
Macphail, Murdo, 688
Macphail, Neil, 339

Macphail, William, 312, 333
Macphee, Angus, 318
Macphee, John Livingston, 694
Macpherson, Alexander, 43, 672
Macpherson, Colin, 240, 333
Macpherson, Donald, 287, 341, 648
Macpherson, Dugald, 683, 684
Macpherson, George Cook, 732
Macpherson, George William Kinnaird, 139, 266
Macpherson, James Rose, 659
Macpherson, James Roderick, 301
Macpherson, John, 336, 378, 674, 688
Macpherson, John Forbes, 248
Macpherson, John Gordon, 478
Macpherson, John Roderick, 167
Macpherson, Joseph Mackenzie, 480, 524
Macpherson, Lauchlan, 348, 376
Macpherson, Malcolm, 683, 688
Macpherson, Malcolm Munro, 248, 278
Macpherson, Martin, 681, 690
Macpherson, Michael James, 562
Macpherson, Neil, 313
Macpherson, Ranald, 21
Macpherson, Robert, 36, 83, 652
Macpherson, Thomas Smith, 307, 323
Macpherson, William, 666
Macpherson, William Mearns, 570
Macqueen, Allan, 689
Macqueen, Angus, 685
Macqueen, Archibald, 684, 686
Macqueen, Daniel, 12
Macqueen, David James, 402
Macqueen, Donald, 654, 684, 689
Macqueen, Edmund, 685
Macqueen, Ewen, 683
Macqueen, James, 689
Macqueen, John, 240, 572
Macqueen, Patrick, 314, 320
Macqueen, William, 638, 671, 686, 691
Macquerne. David, 195
Macquhae, Stair Park, 224
Macquhaill, John, 702
Macquirrtie, James, 319
Macquisten, Alexander, 249
Macquitty, John Montgomery, 450, 526
Macquitty, Luke, 203, 223
Macquoid, Peter Craik, 388, 595
Macquorne, John, 216, 225
Macrae, Donald, 664
Macrae, Dugald Cowan, 332
Macrae, Duncan, 356
Macrae, Farquhar, 333, 681
Macrae, Finlay, 681, 689
Macrae, James Duncan, 659
Macrae, John, 659 *bis*
Macrae, John Anthony, 20, 299, 487
Macrae, Martin, 339, 402

INDEX OF MINISTERS

Macrudder, Robert, 652
Macrury, Donald Archibald, 738
Macrury, John, 686
Macsweyne, Sweyn, 324, 680
Mactaggart, Alexander, 680
Mactavish, Alexander, 314
Mactavish, Archibald, 342
MacVean, Colin Archibald, 358
MacVean, Colin Archibald Arthur, 166
MacVean, Donald, 338
MacVean, Duncan Cameron, 345
MacVeritie, Sir James, 319
Macvicar, Angus John, 326
Macvicar, Colin, 357
Macvicar, Donald, 317, 318
Macvicar, John Gibson, 159
Macvicar, Neil, 19
Macvicar, Robert Barr, 510
Macvicker, Louis Edmond, 196, 593
Macwhirrie, Murdoch, 324, 325
Macwilliam, Charles Keith, 30, 130, 254, 271
Macwilliam, George, 267, 487, 648
Macwilliam, George Porteous, 406, 560
Macwilliam, John, 509, 585
Macwilliam, John Morel, 292
Macwilliam, Thomas, 375
Madder, John, 140
Madder, Sir Richard, 672
Madill, James Millar Moorhead, 636
Main, Archibald, Professor, 717
Main, John, 65
Main, William, 25, 243, 550
Mair, Alexander, 697
Mair, George, 403, 560, 581
Mair, John, 180, 640
Mair, Ludovic, 185
Mair, William, 143, 376
Maitland, James, 87, 197, 205, 593
Maitland, John, 593
Maitland, John Carlies, 196
Maitland, Richard, 541, 608
Maitland, Robert, 553, 588
Malcolm, Alexander, 25
Malcolm, John, 174, 333 bis, 334, 663
Malcolm, Neil, 333, 334, 356
Malcolm, Robert, 163
Malcolm, William, 559
Malloch, John, 383
Malseed, Robert William, 169
Manderston, John, 78, 87
Manners, Stephen, 538
Manson, John, 592, 678
Manuel, David Gilmour, 145
Marche, William, 458
Marjoribanks, George, 113
Marjoribanks, Thomas, 1, 3, 113, 214
Marjoribanks, Thomas Stirling, 112
Marr, George Simpson, 13

Marr, Peter Carmichael, 269
Marshall, Adam, 381
Marshall, Alexander, 406
Marshall, Alexander James, 450
Marshall, Gilbert, 616
Marshall, James, 406
Marshall, John, 358, 703
Marshall, John Forsyth, 251, 278
Marshall, Robert Campbell, 570, 578
Marshall, Robert Thomson, 448
Marshall, Theodore, 347
Marshall, Thomas, 407
Marshall, William, 61, 414
Martin, Alexander, 580
Martin, Andrew, 239
Martin, Angus, 686
Martin, Frank Hale, 22
Martin, George, 287, 486
Martin, James, 364, 386
Martin, John, 194, 205, 214, 218, 275, 400, 658
Martin, Robert James Victor, 588
Martin, Samuel, 37, 450
Martin, Thomas, 63
Martin, William, 4, 9, 346, 354, 513
Martyn, Andrew, 666
Mason, Finlay, 667
Mason, John, 452
Mason, Stephen, 563, 564
Mason, William, 578, 592
Massie, Andrew, 588
Masson, Alexander, 44
Masson, David Norman, 233, 576
Masson, Donald Tolmie, 8
Masterton, Alexander, 173
Masterton, Robert Shaw, 657
Mathams, Walter John, 343
Mathers, Henry Alexander, 132
Mathers, James, 33, 82
Matheson, Duncan, 692
Matheson, Robert, 381
Mathieson, Finlay, 7
Mathieson, John, 11
Mauchline, Alexander, 30, 257, 586
Mauchline, John, 257
Maule, Patrick, 514
Maxwell, David, 455, 494
Maxwell, Edward, 170
Maxwell, Gabriel, 217, 239
Maxwell, Gavin, 201
Maxwell, Hugh, 494
Maxwell, James, 200, 673
Maxwell, John, Bishop, 710
Maxwell, John, 174 bis, 175, 377, 737
Maxwell, Peter, 704, 705
Maxwell, Robert, 239, 249
Maxwell, Thomas, 167, 171, 265
Maxwell, William, 275
May, William, 488

INDEX OF MINISTERS

Mayne, David, 159, 257
Mearns, Alexander, 566
Mearns, Duncan George, 571
Meik, James, 254
Meikle, Alexander, 163
Meikle, James, 472
Meikle, John, 60
Meiklejohn, Hugh, 36
Mein, John, 164, 199
Meldrum, Alexander, 173
Meldrum, Andrew, 145
Meldrum, David, 503, 525
Meldrum, George, 25, 538, 606
Meldrum, Neil, 364, 532
Meldrum, Robert, 104, 458
Meldrum, William, 24, 541
Mellis, David Barclay, 496
Melrose, William, 381, 385 bis
Melrose, William Rutherford, 216
Melvill, Andrew, 449, 536
Melville, Charles Nairn Barker, 539
Melville, Ephraim, 45, 463
Melville, James, 453, 463, 484, 485, 499, 502, 503, 504, 517
Melville, John, 112, 499, 503
Melville, Richard, 499
Melville, Sir Robert, 444
Melville, Robert, 537
Melville, Thomas, 179, 285
Melvin, Andrew, 96
Mentieth, Robert, 400, 402
Menzies, Sir Alexander, 679
Menzies, Alexander, 359
Menzies, Andrew, 195
Menzies, Archibald, 166, 167, 170, 184
Menzies, Hugh, 425
Menzies, James, 145, 151, 397
Menzies, John, Professor, 712
Menzies, John, 358, 359 bis, 521
Menzies, John Forbes, 681
Menzies, John Menzies, 341
Menzies, Peter Sinclair, 302
Menzies, Robert, 737
Menzies, Walter, 246
Menzies, William, 90, 183, 222, 356, 357
Mercer, John, 539
Mercer, Laurence, 60
Mercer, Robert, 535 bis
Mercer, William, 585
Merchiston, Robert, 158
Meredith, Thomas Downie, 22, 491
Meritoun, William, 154
Mernis, George, 674
Mernis, William, 674
Merrow, David Scribner, 392
Merry, John Reevie Johnston, 244, 254
Merry, Robert William, 676
Metcalfe, William, 648

Metcalfe, William Musham, 244
Methven, David, 447, 458
Methven, James, 119
Methven, John, 240
Methven, Thomas, 429
Methven, William, 119 bis, 449, 723
Michael, John, 552
Michaelson, Charles, 512
Michaelson, John, 423
Michell, Andrew, 220
Michie, George Bennet Thomson, 247
Middlemas, Savile, 435
Middleton, Alexander, 499
Middleton, Alexander, Principal, 712
Middleton, Arthur Stanley, 8, 255
Middleton, Charles James More, 136
Middleton, George, Professor, 712
Middleton, George, 450
Mill, George Scott, 740
Mill, John, 566
Mill, Thomas, 127, 537, 569
Millar, Andrew, 79, 216, 291
Millar, Archibald, James, 394
Millar, Arthur, 76
Millar, Daniel Jack, 278
Millar, David, 160, 165
Millar, Francis Duncan, 60
Millar, Gavin, 367
Millar, George, 348
Millar, James, 430
Millar, Peter Carmichael, 289, 438
Millar, Robert Gordon, 173
Millar, Thomas, 30, 242
Millar, Thomas Boyd, 272
Millar, Walter, 403
Millar, William, 52, 53
Millard, David Bruce, 431
Miller, David, 48, 647
Miller, David Alexander, 304
Miller, James, 20, 215, 297, 482, 495
Miller, John, 242
Miller, John Russell, 323
Miller, Robert, 223
Miller, Robertson McCallum, 248, 310
Miller, Thomas, 702
Miller, William Ewart Gladstone, 297, 509
Miller, William James Somerville, 26
Milligan, George, Professor, 717
Milligan, George, 159
Milligan, Oswald Bell, 3, 139
Milligan, Peter, 511
Milligan, William, Professor, 715
Mills, Alexander, 510
Milne, Adam of Bewlie, 152
Milne, Alexander, 247, 587
Milne, David Grant, 217, 431
Milne, David Munro, 21
Milne, Gordon Ewan, 310

Milne, James, 593, 734
Milne, James Alexander, 5
Milne, John, 61, 149, 566
Milne, Joseph, 37
Milne, Peter, 27, 377, 511
Milne, Robert, 369, 638
Milne, Thomas, 357
Milne, William, 58, 593
Milne, William Murray, 456
Milroy, John, 187
Milroy, William Liston, 485
Mitchell, Alexander, 529, 552
Mitchell, Alexander Ferrier, Professor, 719
Mitchell, Alexander Gordon, 279
Mitchell, Alexander William, 316
Mitchell, Andrew Fallas, 194
Mitchell, Andrew Milne, 540
Mitchell, Archibald Henderson, 483, 487
Mitchell, David Russell, 354, 730
Mitchell, Frederick Ritchie, 80
Mitchell, George, 387
Mitchell, Gordon, 398
Mitchell, James of Auchinraith, 477
Mitchell, James, 30, 146, 376, 462
Mitchell, James Donald, 732
Mitchell, James Gordon, 402
Mitchell, John, 703
Mitchell, John Edmund, 541
Mitchell, Joseph, 220
Mitchell, Patrick, 56
Mitchell, Robert Constable, 502
Mitchell, Thomas, 110, 492
Mitchell, William, 11, 488, 540
Mitchell, William Carrick, 134
Mitchell, William Gemmell, 7, 447
Moderatus, John, 612
Moffat, Alexander, 288
Moffat, James, 61, 167
Moffat, John, 190, 192, 194, 195, 210
Moffat, Sir Stephen, 103
Moffat, Thomas, 80
Moffett, Joseph, 27, 724
Moir, Alexander, 160, 536
Moir, Alistair, 681
Moir, George, 568
Moir, Henry, 423
Moir, Robert, 523
Moir, Thomas, 131
Moir, William, Principal, 711
Moir, William, 694
Mollison, Patrick, 56
Molyson, John, 697, 698
Moncrieff, Sir Alexander, 477
Moncrieff, Alexander, 377, 434
Moncrieff, Andrew, 461
Moncrieff, Archibald, 361, 661
Moncrieff, Edmond, 375
Moncrieff, Edward, 367

Moncrieff, George, 362, 416
Moncrieff, Sir Henry Wellwood, 19, 261
Moncrieff, John of Tippermalloch, 372
Moncrieff, John, 349, 362
Moncrieff, Robert Kirkwood, 416
Moncrieff, William, 368, 450
Moncrieff, William Hardie, 165
Moncrieff, William Scott, 82
Moncur, Alexander, 370
Moncur, Andrew, 473
Moncur, Matthew, 474 *bis*
Moncur, Thomas, 474
Monilaws, Alexander, 168
Monipenny, Patrick, 46
Monro, Alexander, Principal, 716
Monro, David, 661
Monro, George Ross, 344
Monro, Robert, 662
Monro, Thomas, 286
Monteath, John, 239
Monteath, William Paul, 223, 240
Monteith, James Taylor, 276
Monteith, John, 378
Monteith, Robert, 68, 201, 387
Monteith, Robert Taylor, 579, 590
Montgomery, Archibald, 280, 287, 296
Montgomery, Hugh, 217
Montgomery, James, 23, 235
Montgomery, Robert, 212, 223, 224, 235, 320, 443, 661
Montgomery, William, 212
Moodie, Adam, 698
Moodie, Leslie, 76
Moodie, William Steven, 127
Mooney, Harald Lamb, 693
Moore, Charles, 394
Moore, Gordon, 655
Moore, Hamilton, 235
Moore, John Cunningham, 673
Moore, Thomas, 246
Moore, William, 468
Moray, David, 377
Morgan, Emmanuel, 224
Morgan, George Grandison, 99
Morice, George, 734
Morice, William, 550
Morison, James, 693
Morrell, William Wilson, 238, 240
Morris, Reginald Innes, 412
Morris, Robert, 470
Morris, William Drummond, 138
Morrison, Aeneas, 659
Morrison, Alexander, 658
Morrison, Andrew Mitchell, 20
Morrison, Angus, 325
Morrison, Archibald, 6
Morrison, Charles, 523
Morrison, Daniel, 692

INDEX OF MINISTERS

Morrison, David, 25, 397
Morrison, David Alexander, 425
Morrison, David Anton, 472
Morrison, Donald, 321, 692
Morrison, George, 365
Morrison, Hugh Thomas Sutherland, 161, 194,
Morrison, James, 430 [431
Morrison, John, 644, 741
Morrison, John Scott, 126
Morrison, Norman, 674, 688
Morrison, Thomas, 373 *bis*, 494
Morrison, Thomas Angus, 310
Morrison, Walter, 522, 599
Morrison, William, 341, 516, 551
Morrison, William Pollok, 238
Mortimer, Cyrus Maxwell, 487
Mortimer, Henry, 588
Mortimer, Patrick, 493, 566
Mortimer, Robert, 26
Morton, Alexander Aitken, 36, 449
Morton, Andrew, 286, 492
Morton, Sir John, 166, 184
Morton, Patrick, 455
Moscrop, William 199, 201 *bis*, 204, 208
Mosman, George, 266
Mossman, John, 79, 677
Mothersill, John Elmore, 207
Moubray, James, 36
Moubray, John, 40, 43, 363
Moultray, James, 430
Mowat, James Sinclair McIvor, 673
Mowat, McIntosh, 487, 531
Mowat, Robert, 84
Mowat, William Alexander, 201
Moyes, William Begbie, 283
Mudge, James, 257, 392, 731
Muggoch, James Wilson, 231, 244, 489
Muir, George, 193, 239
Muir, James, 219
Muir, James Chrystal, 380, 561
Muir, John, 42, 104, 244, 294
Muir, John Alexander Russell Brown, 126
Muir, Patrick, 665
Muir, Pearson McAdam, 305
Muir, Robert, 204, 407
Muir, Robert Hugh, 40
Muir, Robert Walker, 307
Muir, Thomas, 56
Muir, William, 23, 72
Muir, William Bruce, 535
Muir, William Muircroft, 287, 425
Muirhead, Allan, 358
Muirhead, George, 5
Muirhead, James, 181
Muirhead, John, 222, 251, 310
Muirhead, Thomas, 255
Muirhead, William, 55
Mulligan, James Alexander Waddell, 553

Mulligan, John, 576
Mungall, William, 214
Munn, Thomas, 458
Munro, Alexander, 435, 664
Munro, Colin Ross, 490
Munro, David, 124, 668, 677
Munro, Farquhar, 661
Munro, George, 660, 667
Munro, George Mackay, 617
Munro, Hew, 674
Munro, Hugh of Kiltearn, 669
Munro, Hugh, 692
Munro, John, 661, 670, 674, 677
Munro, John Dempster, 126
Munro, John McLaine, 307, 457
Munro, John Malcolm, 27, 306, 314
Munro, Neil, 665
Munro, Robert, 661, 665, 666, 667
Munro, Thomas Smith, 547
Munro, William, 388
Murchison, Donald, 681
Murchison, Duncan, 663
Murchison, John, 681
Murchison, Murdoch, 681
Murdo, Andrew, 249
Murdoch, Alexander, 197
Murdoch, David Albert, 213, 703
Murdoch, James Rae, 697
Murdoch, John, 126, 168
Murdoch, William, 217, 546, 566
Mure, Alexander, 445, 447
Mure, Patrick, 502
Mure, Thomas, 246
Murehead, William, 696
Murison, George Reynard, 697
Murray, Adam, 48, 180
Murray, Alexander, 385
Murray, Alexander John, 59
Murray, Anthony, 53, 174
Murray, David, 170, 199, 346, 376, 380
Murray, George, 98 *bis*, 200 *bis*, 374
Murray, Gordon John, 527
Murray, Hotchkis Haynes, 383
Murray, James, 69, 160, 184, 201, 249, 389, 568, 570, 577
Murray, James Alan Cameron, 307
Murray, Sir John, 408
Murray, John, 56, 296, 367, 380, 385, 444, 592,
Murray, John Paton, 545 [658
Murray, John William, 61
Murray, Magnus, 707
Murray, Matthew, 98
Murray, Robert, 200
Murray, Robert Wilson, 502
Murray, Thomas, 351, 454
Murray, Walter, 599
Murray, William, 61, 413, 414, 425, 455, 474, 566, 623, 636

INDEX OF MINISTERS

Muschet, Alexander, 42
Mushet, Gilbert, 287
Mutch, Andrew, 385
Mutch, John Simpson, 463, 516
Myers, Alexander Smart, 517
Mylne, Alexander, 577
Mylne, Andrew, 507, 519, 521, 655, 657, 678
Mylne, David, 512
Myrton, David, 432
Myrton, Thomas, 544

NAIRN, Charles, 458
Nairn, James, 454, 464
Nairne, Thomas, 429
Nairne, William, 425
Napier, John Gordon Smith, 130
Napier, Peter, 290
Nasmyth, Gavin, 48, 230
Nasmyth, James, 40, 189
Neil, Alexander, 13
Neil, David, 250
Neill, Gilmour, 58, 159
Neill, Robert, 548
Neill, William, 462
Neill, William Notman, 261
Neilson, Alexander, 370
Neilson, Matthew Welsh, 490, 581
Neilson, Thomas, 44
Neilson, William, 538
Nelson, Adam, 587
Nelson, Allan Manson, 161
Nelson, David, 479
Nelson, John Leishman, 571
Nelson, Robert, 288, 525
Ness, David, 587
Ness, Donald, 308
Nevay, John of that Ilk, 476, 477, 482
Nevay, John, 476 *bis*
Newbie, Thomas, 140
Newbigging, William, 52
Newlands, William, 507
Nichol, Harvey, 208
Nicholls, John Ashplant, 81, 255
Nicholson, Christopher, 198
Nicholson, Maxwell, 23
Nicol, Alexander Sinclair, 166
Nicol, David Bruce, 22, 256, 294, 490
Nicol, David Durie, 22, 250, 294
Nicol, James, 432, 495
Nicol, John, 477
Nicol, Peter Hill, 509
Nicol, Thomas, Professor, 715
Nicoll, James Bell, 26
Nicoll, Peter Hill, 292
Nicolson, Alexander, 684, 688
Nicolson, Angus, 741
Nicolson, Colin, 619
Nicolson, Donald, 684, 686

Nicolson, James, Bishop, 709
Nicolson, James, 479, 501
Nicolson, James Graham Goodall, 66, 101
Nicolson, Sir John, 619, 660
Nicolson, John, 685, 686
Nicolson, John Gunn, 660
Nicolson, Malcolm, 652
Nicolson, Patrick, 652, 698
Nicolson, Samuel, 682
Nimmo, Samuel, 1
Nisbet, Archibald, 124
Nisbet, George Dundas, 527
Nisbet, James, 2
Nisbet, John Christopher, 569
Nisbet, Robert, 27
Niven, Mungo, 157
Niven, Thomas Brown William, 299
Nivison, Abraham, 169
Nivison, Alexander, 152
Noble, James, 8, 64, 137
Norie, Alexander, 390, 502
Norie, Robert, 498, 502, 507
Norvell, Archibald, 197
Nymbill, John, 69

OCHTERLONY, Robert, 522
O'Colgan, Alan, 683
Ogg, George, 454, 741
Ogil, David, 89 *bis*, 108
Ogill, Richard, 76
Ogilvie, David, 477
Ogilvie, George, 723
Ogilvie, James Nicoll, 9
Ogilvie, John of Queich, 484
Ogilvie, Millar, 353, 702
Ogilvie, Robert, 575
Ogilvie, Walter, 598
Ogilvie, William, 108, 538
Ogilvie, William Falconer, 235
Ogilvy, Sir Robert, 461
Ogilvy or Ogilvie, Alexander, 574, 575, 576, 591, 617
Ogilvy or Ogilvie, Andrew, 131, 568, 571
Ogilvy or Ogilvie, James, 479 *bis*, 535, 741
Ogilvy or Ogilvie, John, 288, 440, 476, 492, 502, 506, 576
Ogilvy or Ogilvie, Thomas, 120, 473, 477
Ogston, Sir Patrick, 584, 593
Ogstoun, George, 54
Oislar, Sir Gilbert, 196
Oliphant, John, 263, 266
Oliphant, Andrew, 458
Oliphant, Johnston, 37
Oliver, George, 178
Oliver, James, 6
Oliver, John, 297
Oliver, William, 495, 527
Omey, Alexander, 363

INDEX OF MINISTERS

Omey, Donald, 319, 322, 337
Omey, Duncan, 326
Omey, John, 372
Omond, John Reid, 383
Ord, James, 577
Orme, David, 449
Orme, William, 449
Orr, Alexander, 168
Orr, Andrew Clark, 67
Orr, David, 293
Orr, George, 225
Orr, James Fleming Gordon, 730
Orr, John, 12, 270
Orr, Norman Farquhar, 186, 374
Orr, Robert Alexander, 275
Osburne, Henry, 226
Osburne, James, Professor, 712
Osburne, James, Principal, 711
Osburne, John, 219
Osburne, Thomas, 88
Ostlair, Sir Robert, 363
Ostler, Andrew, 616
Oswald, Archibald, 134
Oswald, George, 676
Oswald, James, 368
Oswald, James Honeyman, 184
Oswald, John, 100
Oswald, Robert, 250
Oswald, William, 385
Ouke, George, 369
Oustane, Samuel, 184
Owstean (Austin), Sir William, 523

PAGAN, Gavin Lang, 21
Pagan, John, 253, 363
Paine, Sir James, 205
Paisley, John, 242, 277
Paisley, Robert, 392, 499
Paisley, Robert Ninian, 88, 127, 178
Palm, John David, 729
Paplay, William, 372
Park, George, 244
Park, George Mathieson, 598
Park, Hugh, 287
Park, James, 29
Park, John, 192, 373
Parker, Andrew Borland, 271
Parker, James, 202
Parker, Sir John, 202
Parker, John, 302
Parker, Stuart Crawford, 156, 290
Paterson, Alexander, 564, 594
Paterson, Andrew, 129
Paterson, Archibald Morton, 49, 226
Paterson, Charles Edward, 156
Paterson, David Howat, 251
Paterson, George, 565

Paterson, Isaac, 199
Paterson, James, 546
Paterson, James Alexander, 454
Paterson, John, Archbishop, 707
Paterson, John, Bishop, 710
Paterson, John, 28, 110, 161, 170, 218, 405 bis, 440, 644
Paterson, Keith Norman, 741
Paterson, Patrick, 278
Paterson, Peter, 286
Paterson, Robert, Principal, 711
Paterson, Robert, 258, 440, 444, 446
Paterson, Robert McCheyne, 741
Paterson, Thomas, 61, 67 bis
Paterson, Walter, 87
Paterson, William Berry Shaw, 279
Paterson, William Paterson, Professor, 716
Paton, Andrew, 184
Paton, David, 476
Paton, James, 68
Paton, James Aikman, 188
Paton, John, 172
Paton, John Allan Hunter, 6
Paton, Joseph Thomson, 218
Paton, Robert, 172, 179, 194
Paton, Robert Nicol, 432
Paton, Stephen, 61
Paton, William, 216
Patoun, William, 406, 409, 414
Patrick, Andrew, 516
Patrick, John, Professor, 716
Patrick, John, 523, 524
Patterson, James, 316
Patterson, John, 277
Patterson, John Thomas, 178
Patterson, Thomas Maver, 78
Pattoun, John, 414
Pattullo, Henry Alexander, 208
Pattullo, James Leburn, 734
Pattullo, James Mitchell, 96
Patullo, George, 347, 460
Paul, David, 14
Paul, John, 19
Paul, Robert John, 215
Paulin, George, 420
Paull, William, 536, 561
Pawton, James, 519
Pearson, Andrew Forret Scott, 236
Pearson, John Hardie, 699
Pearson, Robert, 127
Pearson, Rodolph, 193
Pearson, Thomas, 28
Peat, John Chalmers, 398
Peat, Patrick, 441
Peattie, John, 120
Pedder, Alexander, 655, 662
Peden, Alexander, 190
Peden, George, 233

INDEX OF MINISTERS

Peebles, Andrew, 424
Peebles, Sir Bernard, 239
Peebles, Guy Steel, 264
Peebles, Robert, 219
Penman, Gideon, 70
Pennell, James, 417
Pennell, William Joseph, 201
Pennycuick, William, 181
Penycuke, William, 81
Peter, Thomas Burnett, 397
Peterkin, William, 611 bis, 638
Peters, David Smith, 248
Peters, William, 419
Petrie, Alexander, 371
Petrie, George, 582
Pettie, Robert Douglas, 164
Pettigrew, John, 294
Philip, Alexander, 572
Philip, George Forbes Innes, 581
Philip, Horace Robert Andrew, 741
Philip, James Gibson, 732
Philip, John of Ormiston, 48
Philip, John, 561, 607
Philip, Pirie, 204
Philip, Robert, 659
Philip, William Marshall, 543
Philp, Andrew, 679
Philp, David, 636
Philp, Sir John, 563
Philp, John, 542, 555
Phin, George, 48
Phin, Kenneth Macleay, 149
Picken, John, 55
Pierson, William, 393, 699
Pinkerton, Robert Lang, 41, 270
Pirie, William Robertson, Professor, 715
Pirie, William Robinson, 649
Pitcairn, Alexander, 362
Pitcairn, David, 425
Pitcairn, James, 374, 445, 706
Pitcairn, John, 512
Pitcairn, Robert, 49
Pitcairn, Thomas, 18
Playfair, David, 36
Playfair, Patrick, 360
Playfair, Patrick Macdonald, 469
Plenderleith, David, 24
Pollock, Henry, 11
Pollock, James Ferrier, 43, 421
Pollock, Robert, Principal, 712
Pollok, John, 273
Pollok, Thomas, 130
Pont, Robert, 18, 468, 622
Ponton, Robert, 426
Porteous, Archibald, 141
Porteous, David John Moir, 250
Porteous, James, 74, 78
Porteous, Thomas, 21

Porteous, William, 53, 646
Porter, George, 222
Porter, William, 191
Porter, William Henry, 441
Porterfield, John, 212, 228
Potter, John, 300
Potter, Michael, Professor, 717
Potter, Michael, 397
Potter, Robert Douglas, 417
Potter, William, 578, 600
Potts, Robert, 149
Pow, John, 124
Power, Gilbert, 192
Powrie, William, 36, 38, 363
Prenter, Joseph Robert, 490
Prentice, Archibald, 79
Preston, David, 163
Preston, Berry, 64, 224
Preston, David, 308
Preston, Symon, 229
Primmer, Jacob, 410
Primrose, Charles, 70
Primrose, James, 48
Pringle, John, 119
Prophet, James, 160
Proudfoot, Robert Forrester, 119
Proudfoot, William, 95
Provand, William Seath, 306
Pryde, James Johnstone, 131, 133, 184
Pryde, John Marshall, 42, 460
Pryde, Robert, 308
Pryde, Robert Hamilton, 79
Pryde, Thomas, 263
Purves, George, 75
Purves, Thomas, 60
Pyle, William, 126
Pyott, Alexander, 107
Pyper, David, 99

Quig, Gordon, 306, 494

Rae, Alexander, 503
Rae, David Neill, 158
Rae, David Smith, 352
Rae, James, 433, 527, 552
Rae, Peter, 184
Rae, Robert Reid, 252
Raff, Eric Maitland Kirk, 138, 412
Rainie, William, 213
Rait, David, 502
Rait, David Phin, 711
Rait, James, 479, 483 bis, 512, 517, 519, 523, 524
Rait, John, 512
Rait, Peter, 517
Rait, Robert, 488, 521, 524
Rait, William, 476, 488, 493, 495, 524
Raith, Sir Thomas, 568

INDEX OF MINISTERS

Raldson, Robert, 450
Ramage, John, 215, 256
Ramsay, Alexander, 12, 126, 578
Ramsay, Andrew, 12, 382
Ramsay, Charles Rolland, 182
Ramsay, David, 477, 478, 480, 605
Ramsay, David Ogilvy, 182
Ramsay, Sir George, 68
Ramsay, George, 78, 429
Ramsay, James, Bishop, 710
Ramsay, James, 130, 180, 382
Ramsay, Sir John, 116
Ramsay, John, 90, 219, 496
Ramsay, John McNicoll, 263
Ramsay, Matthew, 242
Ramsay, Ninian, 32
Ramsay, Patrick 516, 523
Ramsay, Robert, Principal, 717, 718
Ramsay, Robert, 100, 186, 217, 482
Ramsay, Rowellyan, 186, 531
Ramsay, Thomas, 126, 172, 500, 513, 524, 526
Ramsay, William, 355, 356, 359, 448, 578
Randall, Thomas, 393
Ranken, Edward Blackmore, 113
Ranken, Ewan Archibald, 661
Ranken, Henry, 232
Ranken, James, 385, 452
Ranken, Oliver Shaw, 197
Ranken, Robert, 57
Ranken, William, 186
Ranken, William Eric Kilmorack, 104
Ranken, William Pillans, 734
Rankine, John, 224
Rankine, William Henry, 219
Rattray, John, 287, 353, 412, 471
Rattray, Silvester, 353
Rattray, Thomas, 694
Rattray, William, 308, 473
Rawson, Alexander, 640
Rawson, James, 645
Ray, Alexander, 479
Ray, James, 6, 455
Ray, John, 612, 619
Rayes, John, 260, 574
Rayning, Robert, 157
Reaper, Alexander, 241, 571
Reddick or Roddick, George, 180
Redpath, George, 103, 121
Reed, John, 126
Reekie, Henry Kilgour, 351
Reekie, James, 8, 148
Rees, David Daniel 228
Reid, Alexander, 657
Reid, Allan, 49
Reid, Andrew, 151, 423
Reid, Archibald, 335, 584, 693, 694
Reid, Cuthbert, 537
Reid, David Allan, 222

Reid, Duncan Alexander Cameron, 302
Reid, Sir Farquhar, 664
Reid, Farquhar, 666
Reid, Sir George, 94
Reid, Hugh Park, 129
Reid, James, 18, 89, 545, 551, 741
Reid, James Potter, 732
Reid, John, 250, 396, 456, 537, 575, 631, 656, 704
Reid, Malcolm, 678
Reid, Matthew, 100
Reid, Mungo, 242
Reid, Sir Nigel, 335
Reid, Patrick, 274
Reid, Peter Barr, 696
Reid, William, 201, 448, 555
Reid, William Alexander, 222
Reid, William Arnold, 198
Reid, William Lang, 679
Reid, William Walker, 277
Reidfurd, John, 608
Reith, John, 524
Rennie, James Fyfe, 565
Rennie, James Yule, 732
Rennie, Robert, 309
Renton, Sir Andrew, 165
Renton, John, 421, 432
Reoch, Donald, 576
Reynold, Robert, 529
Riach, William Lyon, 14
Rich, Henry, 741
Richardson, Alexander, 642
Richardson, James, 141
Richardson, Robert, 136
Richardson, William, 214
Richers, Joseph Edward, 473
Richmond, John, 199
Richmond, Matthew, 699
Richmond, Robert Hill, 189, 546
Riddell, Archibald, 25
Riddell, Henry Scott, 141
Riddell, Patrick, 613
Riddoch, Alexander, 357
Rigg, John, 452, 480
Rigg, Walter, 37
Rind, Robert, 380
Ritchie, Adam Inch, 113
Ritchie, Alexander, 397, 484
Ritchie, Alexander John Cairns, 105, 420
Ritchie, Charles, John, 57
Ritchie, David, 221
Ritchie, George, 139
Ritchie, James, 186
Ritchie, John, 440, 677
Ritchie, John Geddes, 150, 626
Ritchie, Robert Lamont, 672
Ritchie, William, 87, 492, 663, 734
Ritchie, William Blackley, 387

INDEX OF MINISTERS

Robb, Alexander Barrie, 42
Robb, Richard, 562
Robertson, Alexander, 59, 318, 355, 390, 403, 516, 522, 541, 572, 582, 729
Robertson, Alexander Cameron, 315
Robertson, Alexander Irvine, 388
Robertson, Andrew, 14, 195, 257, 412
Robertson, Archibald, 329
Robertson, Archibald Aeneas, 354
Robertson, Charles, 665
Robertson, Charles Moncrieff, 23, 350, 526
Robertson, Christian Arthur, 277, 730
Robertson, David, 121, 491, 581
Robertson, David Rae, 485
Robertson, David Young, 247, 659
Robertson, Donald John, 328
Robertson, Douglas Dickson, 73, 223
Robertson, Duncan, 615, 688
Robertson, Edward, 375
Robertson, Frank, 310, 568, 594
Robertson, Frederick Lockhart, 300
Robertson, George, 33, 60, 323
Robertson, George Home, 127
Robertson, Harry, 110
Robertson, James, Professor, 717
Robertson, James, 31, 59, 114, 131, 282, 283, 305, 386, 462, 669
Robertson, James Goodlet, 502
Robertson, James Home, 124
Robertson, John, 254, 263, 345, 350, 586, 611, 619
Robertson, John Alexander, 129, 167
Robertson, John Anderson, 4
Robertson, John Balfour, 190
Robertson, John Leslie, 539
Robertson, John Spence, 215
Robertson, John Stewart, 506
Robertson, Joseph MacGregor, 8
Robertson, Robert, 413, 551
Robertson, Thomas, 40, 298, 346 *bis*, 351, 359, 368, 382, 582, 600
Robertson, Sir Walter, 358, 405
Robertson, William, 9, 10 *bis*, 252, 260, 383, 536, 552, 642
Robertson, William Cowper, 417, 727
Robertson, William George, 572, 598
Robeson, John, 257
Robin, Henry, 423
Robin, John, 426
Robinson, James Woodside, 285
Roche, George Ralph Malvern, 727
Roche, John, 541
Roche, Robert, 412
Rock, William, 177, 431
Roddick, James, 167, 677
Rodger, Ernest Ormrod, 239
Rodger, Matthew, 311
Rogan, John, 424, 493

Rogers, David, 170
Rolland, James, 396, 482
Rollo, David Andrew, 307
Rollock, Henry, 25
Ronaldson, John, 337
Rose, Adam, 659
Rose, Alexander, Bishop, 709
Rose, Alexander, 589, 605
Rose, David, 457
Rose, Donald Stewart, 409
Rose, James, 526
Rose, John, 545, 673
Rose, Lewis, 670
Rose, William, 673, 706
Rose, William Charles, 347
Ross, Alexander, 527, 559, 565, 665, 678
Ross, Andrew, 188, 662, 670
Ross, Archibald Watson, 615
Ross, Charles, 417
Ross, David, 341, 667
Ross, Francis, 245, 529
Ross, George, 168, 658, 661
Ross, Gilbert, 636
Ross, Henry, 609
Ross, Hugh, 670, 671, 672
Ross, Hutcheon, 648
Ross, J., 188
Ross, James, 46, 127, 450, 547, 553, 576, 666, 667
Ross, John, 266, 544, 545, 574, 666, 667, 672, 677
Ross, Kenneth, 685
Ross, Lachlan, 265
Ross, Neil, 329
Ross, Neil Macleod, 7, 620
Ross, Patrick, 606
Ross, Peter, 521
Ross, Richard, 534
Ross, Robert of Ballon, 669
Ross, Robert, 622, 658
Ross, Thomas, 658, 666, 681
Ross, William, 94, 299, 568, 664, 665, 668
Rossie, Charles, 512
Rothnie, George, 605
Routledge, James William Renwick, 351
Row, Andrew, 400
Row, Archibald, 64
Row, John, Principal, 711
Row, John, 200, 363, 365, 407, 426
Row, Robert, 36
Row, Samuel, 132
Row, William, 363 *bis*
Rowatt, Alexander, 255
Rowatt, James, 139
Roxburgh, John, 234
Roy, John, 275
Roy, William, 274
Rule, George, 120

INDEX OF MINISTERS

Rule, Gilbert, 9, 128
Rule, Robert, 393
Runciman, David William, 432
Russell, Alexander, 397
Russell, Andrew, 432
Russell, Edmund Stewart, 343, 593
Russell, George, 271
Russell, James, 154, 259, 458
Russell, James Curdie, 322
Russell, James Keddie, 446
Russell, John, 569, 606
Russell, Robert, 154
Russell, Thomas, 266, 426
Russell, William, 64 *bis*
Rust, James, 576
Rutherford, Andrew, 118
Rutherford, Charles Neilson, 476
Rutherford, David Sinclair, 52, 223
Rutherford, George, 209
Rutherford, James, 138
Rutherford, John, 154, 441, 456, 468, 494, 513
Rutherford, Robert William, 258
Rutherford, Samuel, Principal, 718
Rutherford, Thomas Ranken, 349
Ruthven, Donald, 648
Rutledge, James William, 732
Rynd, James, 544, 566
Rynd, John, 429, 432
Rynd, Patrick, 362
Rynd, Robert, 449
Rynd, William, 366
Ryne, Alexander, 197

SABISTON, James, 697
Sabiston, James Robertson, 6
Saidler, Sir John, 694
Saidsarf, Sir John, 656
Salmon, Sir John, 351
Salmon, William, 348
Salmond, William, 519
Sanders, William, 603, 623
Sandeman, James, 471
Sanderson, James, 128
Sanderson, John, 190
Sanderson, Patrick, 59
Sanderson, Samuel Somerville, 450
Sanderson, William, 89, 112, 114
Sandilands, James, 186
Sandilands, John, 54 *bis*, 137, 661
Sandilands, John Macrae, 181
Sandilands, Robert, 27, 128
Sangster, Alexander, 176, 246
Sauchie, Alexander, 426, 433, 434
Saunders, Alexander Christian William, 524, 545
Saunders, Frank William, 199
Saunders, John, 319
Savile, David, 35

Sawers, David Hay, 266
Sawers, William, 547
Scanlan, George, 417, 452
Schank, Martin, 545
Schillingis, Steven, 131
Scobie, William, 671
Scott, Adam Wylie Hempseed, 379
Scott, Alexander, 553
Scott, Alexander Inglis, 373
Scott, Andrew Noble, 705
Scott, Andrew Smith Dingwall, 254
Scott, Archibald, 26
Scott, Archibald Black, 673
Scott, Archibald John Darling, 479
Scott, David, 242, 257, 677
Scott, Francis of Langton, 147
Scott, George, 244, 425, 446
Scott, Sir George, 588
Scott, George Gordon, 5
Scott, George John Chalmers, 213
Scott, Henry Edward, 741
Scott, Hugh, 149
Scott, James, 3, 88, 135, 140, 148, 209, 232, 249, 385, 482, 677
Scott, James MacGlashan, 369
Scott, John, 38, 73, 141, 148, 163, 199, 266, 306, 482
Scott, Patrick, 265, 425
Scott, Richard, 148, 163
Scott, Robert, 59, 95, 148, 260, 304, 305, 412, 452 *bis*
Scott, Robert Baldock, 95, 283
Scott, Robert Forrester Victor, 452, 489
Scott, Symon, 140, 147
Scott, Sir Thomas, 385
Scott, Thomas, 4, 80, 381, 523, 732
Scott, Walter, 147, 655
Scott, Sir William of Balweary, 438
Scott, William, 130, 382, 437, 455, 458, 553, 694, 741
Scott, William David, 533
Scott, William Frank, 575
Scott, William Mackenzie, 741
Scott, William Richmond, 266, 699
Scougal, Henry, Professor, 713
Scougal, Patrick, Bishop, 709
Scougal, Patrick, 100
Scoular, Andrew, 367
Scoular, John Greenshields, 194
Seath, George Allan, 217
Seaton, George, 540
Seaton, John, 568, 574
Sefton, George Arthur, 585
Selbie, George Alexander, 338, 556
Selkirk, Matthew, 70
Selkirk, William Alexander, 593
Sellar, John, 662
Semple, James, 104

INDEX OF MINISTERS

Semple, John of Beltrees, 414
Sempill, George Douglas, 721
Sempill, John, 419
Sempill, Robert, 246, 271
Seright, William, 231, 298
Serle, William, 6
Service, John, 188, 295
Service, John Barr, 88
Service, William Jack Nichol, 248
Seton, Alexander, 510
Seton, James, 129, 440
Seton, John, 529
Seton, Patrick, 588
Seton, William, 519
Seytoun, Alexander of Northrig, 395
Seytoun, Henry, 395
Seytoun, John, 440
Seytoun, Robert, 401
Shand, Alexander Mason, 237
Shand, Alexander Watson, 706
Shanks, William Speirs, 297
Shannon, William Henry, 224
Sharp, James, 77
Sharp, John, 360, 498, 529
Sharp, Patrick, 291
Sharp, Thomas Wylie, 306
Sharp, William, 209, 270
Sharpe, David, 261
Sharpe, James, 30
Sharpe, Robert Meredith, 266
Shaw, Andrew, Professor, 719
Shaw, David, 376
Shaw, George, 401
Shaw, Henry, 401
Shaw, James, 199
Shaw, John of Newmains, 154
Shaw, John, 491
Shaw, Patrick, 154, 248
Shaw, Robert, 163
Shaw, Walter, 9, 290
Shaw, William, 119, 213, 386
Shedden, John, 216, 390, 486
Shennan, Malcolm, 311
Shepherd, Alexander, 41, 156
Shepherd, George, 79
Shepherd, Robert, 565
Shepherd, William Alexander, 362
Sherriff, Thomas Chalmers, 380
Shewan, Thomas, 501
Shields, Alexander, 469
Shields, Patrick, 33
Shiels, Thomas, 186
Shirlaw, Hugh, 119, 488
Short, Charles Maurice, 27
Short, George Murray Davidson, 237, 732
Short, James, 156
Sibbald, Abraham, 580
Sibbald, Adam, 385

Sibbald, David, 581
Sibbald, James of Keir, 535
Sibbald, James Hope, 116
Sibbald, Patrick, Professor, 712
Sibbald, Samuel James Ramsay, 299
Sibbald, William, 95
Sievwright, John Smith, 254, 417
Sievwright, Wilfred Robert, 203, 436
Silver, David, 147
Sim, Frederick Robert, 65
Sim, Robert, 450
Sime, William Lamb, 146
Simpson, Alexander, 640
Simpson, Archibald, 72
Simpson, Donald Murray, 337
Simpson, Frederick Angus, 447
Simpson, George, 291
Simpson, Ian Grindlay, 439
Simpson, James, 36, 58
Simpson, James Smith, 426
Simpson, James Wallace, 254, 579
Simpson, Macduff, 125
Simpson, Robert, 173, 360, 568
Simpson, Thomas, 655
Simpson, Walter, 352, 541
Simpson, William, 26, 138, 274, 583
Simpson, William Mungall, 192
Simson, Andrew, 81, 87, 95 bis, 107, 268, 642 bis, 644
Simson, Archibald, 151
Simson, Arthur, 100
Simson, David, 326, 329
Simson, George, 460
Simson, James, 523
Simson, John, 86
Simson, Matthew, 99
Simson, Patrick, 4
Simson, William, 272, 647
Sinclair, Archibald, 178, 319
Sinclair, Barty Daniel, 388
Sinclair, Constantine, 396, 623
Sinclair, Daniel, 120
Sinclair, Duncan Macrae, 343
Sinclair, Edward Arthur Neil, 293
Sinclair, Henry, 288, 304
Sinclair, Sir John, 180
Sinclair, John, 40, 81, 87 bis, 171, 173, 175, 336, 493, 685, 725
Sinclair, Malcolm, 702
Sinclair, Patrick Campbell, 641
Sinclair, Robert, 85, 375
Sinclair, Thomas, 42
Sinclair, Thomas Gourlay, 218
Sinclair, Sir William, 677
Sinclair, William, 115, 677, 678 bis
Sinton, Thomas, 650
Sivewright, Robert Troup, 724
Skene, Alexander, Principal, 718

INDEX OF MINISTERS

Skene, Alexander, 367
Skene, Andrew, 517, 595
Skene, Arthur, 551, 557
Skene, Gilbert, 499
Skene, Robert, 55, 551, 553, 560
Skene, William, 553
Skeoch, Thomas, 394
Skinner, John, 388
Skinner, Thomas, 216
Skirling, Thomas, 455
Slater, Thomas, 302
Slessor, Duncan Morrison, 177
Slessor, Robert, 535
Sloan, John, 245
Small, James, 103
Smart, Alexander, 485, 565
Smart, Alexander Forteath, 123
Smart, John, 266, 286
Smart, William Robertson, 426, 484
Smeaton, James, 429
Smeaton, John, 403
Smellie, William Thomas, 320, 411
Smith, Alexander, 122
Smith, Alexander Hood, 540
Smith, Alexander Salmond, 268
Smith, Andrew Gray, 433
Smith, David, 163, 184, 399, 439, 593
Smith, George, 24
Smith, Sir George Adam, 715
Smith, George Charles, 219
Smith, George Munro, 394
Smith, George Stuart, 100
Smith, Harry, 75, 279, 406
Smith, Henry, 193, 699
Smith, Henry Wallis, 28
Smith, Hugh, 238
Smith, Hugh Maconnach, 541
Smith, James, 59, 232, 243, 273, 284, 369, 542, 555, 582
Smith, James Cromarty, 255
Smith, James Farquhar, 191
Smith, John, 56, 280, 298, 338
Smith, Kenneth, 329, 332
Smith, Peter George, 400
Smith, Robert, 61, 227
Smith, John Gauld, 228
Smith, Murdo, 688
Smith, Robert Bridges, 116
Smith, Robert Harvie, 245
Smith, Robert Nimmo, 94, 347
Smith, Sydney, 83, 608
Smith, Theophilus, 83
Smith, Thomas, 300, 454, 478
Smith, William, 37, 55, 69, 257, 268, 488, 530, 617, 622, 679, 705
Smith, William Chalmers, 291
Smith, William Grierson, 148
Smith, William Henry Gray, 119

Smith, William James, 38, 233
Smith, William Stables, 706
Smyth, Andrew, 380
Smyth, George, 65
Smyth, Harry, 693
Smyth, James, 363
Smyth, John, 458, 474, 490, 492, 521
Smyth, Kirkpatrick Dickson, 134
Smyth, Patrick, 389
Smyth, Robert, 456, 575, 581, 586
Smyth, Walter, 35
Smyth, William, 410
Snadden, Andrew Mitchell, 5
Sneddon, Robert Laird, 535
Snoddy, Thomas Gillespie, 430
Snodgrass, John Allan, 736
Snodgrass, William, 162
Somers, Robert, 159
Somervell, Mungo, 522
Somervell, William, 190, 656
Somerville, Alexander, 54
Somerville, Alexander Neil, 288
Somerville, Hew, 265
Somerville, James, Lord, 32
Somerville, James, 58, 393
Somerville, John, 5, 152
Somerville, Ludovic, 262
Somerville, Munro, 28, 58, 187
Somerville, Robert, 55
Somerville, Samuel, 28
Somerville, Sir Thomas, 55
Somerville, Thomas, 55, 290
Somerville, William, 174
Sorley, Malcolm Tower, 536
Sorley, William, 105
Sousie, Lucas, 68
Soutar, Alexander Chalmers, 734
Souter, John Macgregor, 683
Souter, Robert Maitland, 696
Soutter, Andrew, 547
Soutter, James Tindal, 113
Spalding, Samuel, 205
Spang, William, 728, 729
Spankie, Thomas, 445, 473
Spark, Alexander, 304
Spark, Henry, 551
Spark, John, 6, 671
Spark, Robert Reith, 537
Spark, William Arthur, 557
Spears, Andrew, 563
Spears, Robert, 424
Spiers, Alexander, 309
Spiers, Ebenezer Brown, 13
Spiers, William, 356
Spence, Alexander, 532, 517
Spence, David Brown, 742
Spence, John, 42, 430
Spence, John Aitken, 217, 402

Spence, John Ryrie, 141
Spence, John W., 20, 56, 423
Spence, Robert Moir, 516
Spencer, Andrew, 105
Spens, Alexander, 411, 450, 460, 623
Spens, Andrew, 564, 565, 571, 605
Spens, David, 446, 455
Spens, George, 43, 558
Spens, Sir James, 642
Spens, James, 565
Spens, Thomas, 569
Spens, William, 607
Spittal, Alexander, 55, 706
Spittal, Nicol, 490
Spittal, Nicholas, 492 *bis*
Spittal, Thomas, 41
Spottiswood, John, 33, 385
Spottiswood, John Robert, 229
Spottiswood, Robert, 138
Sprott, George Washington, 99
Stafford, John Owen, 167
Stalker, George Alexander, 261
Stanis, Sir James, 417
Stanis, John, 622
Stark, David, 133, 428
Stark, John, 390, 449
Stark, Robert, 113, 419
Stark, William Adam, 176
Stedman, Alexander, 406
Stedman, Edward, 95
Steedman, John, 26
Steedman, Robert, 39
Steel, Adam, 75
Steel, James, 387
Steel, William, 158
Steele, John of Palmone, 224
Steele, John, 421
Steele, John Aulay, 307, 527
Steen, James Cameron, 695
Steen, John Charlton, 156
Steill, James, 476
Stenhouse, John, 410
Stephen, James Alexander, 73
Stephen, Robert, 245, 611 *bis*
Stephen, William, 410, 522, 646
Steuart, Frederick Alexander, 239
Steuart, John, 320
Steven, Alexander, 408
Steven, David Sime, 141, 526
Steven, John, 195
Steven, Robert, 217
Steven, William, 25
Steven, William McCulloch, 299
Stevenson, Alexander Wright, 188, 289
Stevenson, Andrew, 107
Stevenson, Donald, 400
Stevenson, George, 193, 194
Stevenson, James, 10, 48, 613

Stevenson, John, 48, 127 135, 261, 453, 481, 576
Stevenson, Sir John, 149
Stevenson, John Gordon, 677
Stevenson, Malcolm, 274, 281, 282
Stevenson, Robert, 390, 410, 480
Stevenson, Robert Home, 20
Stevenson, Sir Thomas, 560
Stevenson, William, 30, 423, 428
Stevenson, William Black, 5
Stevenson, William Ferrie, 311
Stevenson, William John, 506
Stevenson, William Sinclair, 242
Stewart, Alexander, Principal, 718
Stewart, Alexander, 78, 328, 343, 615, 651, 671
Stewart, Allan, 351
Stewart, Andrew, 365
Stewart, Anthony, 190, 195, 196
Stewart, Archibald, 193
Stewart, Archibald Francis, 395
Stewart, Charles, 356, 474, 587
Stewart, Charles Edward, 167
Stewart, Daniel 319
Stewart, David, 237, 246 *bis*, 426, 542, 551
Stewart, David Melville, 246
Stewart, Donald, 341, 548
Stewart, Duncan, 347
Stewart, Francis, 312
Stewart, Frank White, 721
Stewart, Gavin, 216
Stewart, George Lindsay, 30, 211
Stewart, George Wauchope, 94
Stewart, Hercules, 173
Stewart, James, 40, 52, 179, 230, 352, 414, 558
Stewart, John, 33, 195, 204, 249, 274, 291, 341, 471, 502, 524, 571, 613, 638, 686, 693, 694 *bis*, 735
Stewart, John of Traquair, 135
Stewart, John Douglas, 203
Stewart, Matthew, 260, 608
Stewart, Murdoch, 735
Stewart, Patrick, 319, 320
Stewart, Robert of Skerrels, 320
Stewart, Robert, 9, 65, 103, 193, 215, 320, 337, 344, 345, 473, 476, 691
Stewart, Theophilus, 542
Stewart, Thomas Dow, 509
Stewart, Walter, Archbishop, 708
Stewart, Walter, 148, 175, 242, 279, 350, 574, 575, 638
Stewart, Sir William, 680
Stewart, William, 114, 174, 414
Stibbles, Robert, 486
Stirling, David, 126, 215
Stirling, Henry, 479
Stirling, James, 243, 266, 289
Stirling, James Clark Paul, 741
Stirling, John, 214, 232, 542

INDEX OF MINISTERS

Stirling, Luke, 279
Stirling, Patrick, 192
Stirling, Robert, 235, 240
Stirling, William, 395
Stirton, John, 546
Stobie, Charles, 707
Stobie, Charles Walker, 457, 590
Stobo, Archibald, 737
Stoddart, Alexander, 445
Stoddart, John, 285
Stoddart, William, 382
Storie, Thomas, 126, 147
Story, Robert Herbert, Professor, 717
Stott, Ian Fergusson Gordon, 742
Strachan, Alexander, 440, 493, 545, 550, 552, 564
Strachan, Andrew, Professor, 713
Strachan, Andrew, 500, 568
Strachan, Arthur, 609
Strachan, George, 143, 425, 511, 518, 529
Strachan, James, 136, 359, 536, 551, 571, 692, 697
Strachan, James McTurk, 366
Strachan, John, 26, 352, 480, 550 *bis*, 552, 553, 555, 557, 560, 571, 575
Strachan, John Robert, 477
Strachan, Patrick, 373, 493, 515
Strachan, Robert, 170
Strachan, William, 529, 563, 565
Strachan, William Buchanan, 254
Strachan, William Greig, 396, 561
Straith, William, 564
Straiton, James, 144
Strang, Alexander, 182
Strang, George, 648
Strang, George Walter, 323
Strang, William, 232
Strathannan, John, 352
Strathauchan, James, 519, 608, 612
Strathauchan, William, 519, 612
Straton, David, 551
Straton, John, 643, 644
Strong, David, 216, 295
Strong, William Baillie, 75
Strudgeon, John, 201
Strudgeon, William, 201
Stuart, Adam Moody, 21
Stuart, Alexander, 18
Stuart, Archibald Graham, 293
Stuart, Donald, 666
Stuart, Gregor, 619
Stuart, James, 55
Stuart, John, 15, 140
Stuart, Thomas, 451
Stuart, William, 661
Stuart, William Stevenson, 307, 393
Summers, George Drummond, 439
Sutherland, Adam, 631

Sutherland, Sir Alexander, 640
Sutherland, Andrew, 410
Sutherland, David, 699
Sutherland, Hugh, 673 *bis*
Sutherland, Hugh Thomas, 425
Sutherland, Robert, 630
Sutherland, Rollo Russell Graham, 187, 233, 250
Sutherland, Thomas William Grant, 108
Sutherland, William, 178, 238, 576, 606, 643, 681
Sutherland, William Neil, 40, 582
Swan, David, 222
Swan, Hugh Douglas, 584
Swan, John Arbuckle, 301
Swan, Ninian, 265
Swan, William, 30, 555
Swan, William Dalgleish, 457
Swinton, Alexander, 116
Swinton, David, 116
Swinton, George, 474, 502
Swinton, Thomas, 419
Swyne, Robert, 433
Syde, John, 61
Sydserff, George, 728
Sydserff, Thomas, Bishop, 710
Sym, Arthur Pollok, 151
Sym, John, 10
Sym, William John, 13
Symington, James, 271
Symington, John, 225
Symington, John Lawrie, 602
Symmer, Alexander, 630
Symmer, Archibald, 506
Symmer, James, 521
Symmer, John, 437
Symon, James, 231
Symonton, John, 265
Symson, Andrew, 99
Symson, James, 517
Symson, John, 462, 434, 507
Symson, Mathias, 393
Symson, Robert, 218

TAGGART, Moses, 60
Tailzefair, Anthony, 579
Tait, Adam Duncan, 44
Tait, Alexander, 65
Tait, Andrew, 286
Tait, George, 82, 723
Tait, John, 53
Tait, Walter, 25, 372
Tait, William, 53
Tait, William Marshall, 703
Tant, Alexander James Wishart, 329
Tarbett, Albert, 189
Tarras, Sir James, 649
Taylor, Alexander, 559

INDEX OF MINISTERS

Taylor, Andrew Ross, 43
Taylor, Charles William Gray, 21
Taylor, David, 454
Taylor, Gilbert, 36
Taylor, Henry, 147
Taylor, James, 58, 242, 383
Taylor, James Shepherd, 738
Taylor, Sir John, 166
Taylor, John, 24, 161, 170, 184, 205, 218, 440, 502
Taylor, Malcolm Campbell, 172, Professor 716
Taylor, Robert, 6
Taylor, Walter Ross, 678
Taylor, William, 170, 186, 305, 506
Taylor, William Caird, 673
Taylor, William Moncrieff, 395
Telfer, Samuel, 310
Telfer, William, 196
Tennant, Joseph, 138
Terras, Robert, 638
Thaft, James, 361
Thalland, Thomas, 422
Thalland, William, 422
Thom, Patrick Baeda, 418
Thomassoun, William Ross, 665
Thompson, Richard, 34
Thompson, Robert James, 152
Thompson, William, 734
Thomson, —., 191
Thomson, Adam, 189
Thomson, Alexander, 7, 11, 179, 650, 702
Thomson, Alexander McInroy, 137
Thomson, Andrew, 222, 564, 571
Thomson, Andrew Bald, 230
Thomson, David, 61, 657
Thomson, David Livingston, 262
Thomson, Edward, 454
Thomson, Edward Litton, 260
Thomson, Francis, 542
Thomson, George, 448
Thomson, George Eddie, 353, 594, 723
Thomson, George Miles, 43
Thomson, George Speed, 455
Thomson, George Thomas, Professor, 153, 670, 714
Thomson, James, 63, 188, 195, 200, 244, 300, 410, 420, 606
Thomson, James Laing, 542
Thomson, James Ramsay, 251
Thomson, Sir John, 61
Thomson, John, 9, 151, 181, 233, 351, 365, 438, 471, 618
Thomson, John Archibald Glover, 25, 137
Thomson, John Colquhoun, 167
Thomson, John Fernie, 73
Thomson, John Gardner Macleod, 235
Thomson, John James Scott, 147, 527
Thomson, John Knox, 239

Thomson, John Macalister, 424
Thomson, John Scott, 592
Thomson, John Scoular, 317
Thomson, John Youngson, 248, 271
Thomson, Maitland, 360
Thomson, Neil Livingstone, 262
Thomson, Peter, 341, 380
Thomson, Robert, 82, 204, 502
Thomson, Robert Burns, 112
Thomson, Robert John, 124, 253, 386
Thomson, Robert Nicholson, 300
Thomson, Thomas, 141, 155, 403, 438, 529
Thomson, Thomas Bentley Stewart, 23, 257
Thomson, Thomas Reid, 119
Thomson, William, 65, 179, 196, 255, 388, 406, 444, 447, 494, 555, 558, 568, 724, 727
Thorburn, David, 31
Thorburn, John, 28
Thorburn, Matthew Charteris, 552
Thornton, Alexander, 130
Thornton, Cecil Taylor, 5, 22
Thornton, James, 135, 501, 516
Thorntoun, John, 622
Tindal, James Johnston, 539
Tocher, Forbes Scott, 742
Tocher, William Middleton, 446
Tod, George, 52
Tod, James, 53
Tod, Sir John, 28
Tod, John, 39
Tod, Sir William, 135
Tod, William, 202
Todd, Alexander, 460
Todd, George, 126
Todd, John, 119
Tolmie, John William, 345
Topp, Alexander, 636
Torrence, Alexander, 75
Torrie, William, 335
Tough, George, 122
Trail, Alexander, 572
Trail, Robert, 514
Train, Alexander, 177
Trent, Patrick, 45
Trent, William, 95
Trotter, Alexander, 89
Trotter, Ninian, 133
Troughton, John, 189
Tullidelph, John, 362
Tullidelph, Patrick, 457
Tullis, James, 423
Tulloch, Arthur Penryn Stanley, 41
Tulloch, John, Principal, 718
Tulloch, John Lancelot Constantine, 133, 260
Tulloch, Sir Nichol, 604
Tulloch, Nicholas, 601, 605
Tulloch, William Weir, 297
Tullos, James, 435

INDEX OF MINISTERS

Turcan, Alexander, 380
Turnbull, Archibald, 742
Turnbull, Charles Scrimgeour, 252
Turnbull, George, 40, 216
Turnbull, James, 389
Turnbull, John, 152, 458
Turnbull, Robert, 290
Turnbull, Robert Wilson, 55, 157
Turnbull, Thomas, 199
Turnbull, Thomas Hardie, 271
Turnbull, William, 137
Turnbull, William Bell, 90
Turner, Alexander, 402
Turner, Archibald, 67
Turner, Patrick, 67
Turner, William, 176
Tweedie, Andrew, 539
Tweedie, David Jackson, 133
Tweedie, Walter, 52 bis, 53, 56
Tweedie, William, 64
Tweedie, William King, 24
Tyrie, Alexander, 474 bis, 485

UDNY, Thomas, 587
Underwood, John, 207
Underwood, Thomas, 177
Ure, Robert, 386
Urie, Andrew, 47
Urquhart, Alexander, 642, 678
Urquhart, Andrew, 191
Urquhart, James, 149, 641, 645
Urquhart, Patrick, 136, 149
Urquhart, Thomas, 647, 668

VALLANCE, James, 179
Vallance, Sir Matthew, 428
Vallance, Thomas Barr, 231, 441
Vallance, William, 311
Vassie, Thomas, 49
Vassie, William, 162
Vaus, James, 643
Vaus, William, 194
Vauss, Richard, 190
Veitch, Andrew, 311
Veitch, George, 361
Veitch, James, 19
Veitch, John, 129, 147
Veitch, William, 22, 172
Venters, Robert, 604
Vernor, Alexander, 99
Viland, William, 457
Vilant, William, Principal, 718
Vipont, David Avenel, 504

WADDELL, Alexander, 474
Waddell, David, 147
Waddell, Peter Hately, 113
Waddell, Richard, 107, 118

Waddell, Walter, 67
Walker, Alexander, 60, 484
Walker, Archibald, 84
Walker, Duncan, 67, 131
Walker, George, 203, 526
Walker, George William, 290, 439
Walker, George William Everett, 517, 557
Walker, Harry, 641
Walker, Hugh, 400
Walker, James, 7, 143, 202, 235, 274, 556, 561, 694
Walker, John, 8, 65, 168, 277, 637
Walker, John Cunningham, 194
Walker, John Hunter, 119
Walker, John Yuill, 59, 450
Walker, Robert, 7
Walker, Robert William, 8
Walker, Russell, 192
Walker, Samuel Stephen, 69
Walker, Thomas, 217
Walker, William, 213, 355
Walker, William Montgomery, 223
Walkingshaw, William, 60
Wallace, Alexander, 218
Wallace, Andrew Ewing, 117
Wallace, Charles Stuart, 195
Wallace, Henry Owens, 89, 151
Wallace, James, 299
Wallace, James Bell, 737
Wallace, James Mawer, 220
Wallace, Jardine, 65
Wallace, John, 25, 63, 145, 176, 218, 243
Wallace, Michael, 233
Wallace, Sir Patrick, 171
Wallace, Patrick, 250
Wallace, Robert, 27, 103, 190, 696
Wallace, Robert Wilfred, 470
Wallace, William, 227, 238, 542
Wallace, William Angus, 271, 488
Wallis, James, 734
Walls, Thomas, 734
Walls, William, 284
Walters, Edward, 297
Walsh, George, 677
Walwode, Charles, 426, 434
Wands, Victor William, 89, 723
Wann, Andrew Blair, 378
Warden, John, 8
Wardlaw, Alexander, 419
Wardlaw, James, 572
Wardlaw, John, 159, 526, 580
Wardlaw, Samuel, 33
Wardlaw, Thomas, 430
Wardrope, Alexander, 50
Wark, David, 199
Warner, Graham Nicoll, 517, 637
Warner, Thomas, 200
Warnes, Sydney Herbert Rutt, 299

INDEX OF MINISTERS

Warnock, Gavin, 252
Warnock, Thomas Alexander, 643
Warr, Alfred, 283
Warr, Alfred Ernest, 124, 295
Warr, Charles Laing, 11, 248
Warren, Andrew, 455
Warren, Robert Sharp, 192
Waterston, Patrick, 697
Waterston, William, 213
Watson, Adam, 240
Watson, Alexander Cameron, 153
Watson, Alexander Robertson, 244
Watson, Andrew, 548
Watson, Archibald, 486, 523
Watson, Charles, 43
Watson, David, 300, 308, 701
Watson, David Crawford, 310
Watson, George, 138, 277, 538
Watson, George Bruce Scoular, 136
Watson, Harry Steel, 742
Watson, James, 7, 69, 502, 504, 617
Watson, James Patrick, 275, 307, 386
Watson, John, 170, 188, 193, 389, 676, 705
Watson, John Rutherford, 118
Watson, Laurence, 80
Watson, Louis Herbert, 194, 536
Watson, Mungo, 90
Watson, Peter, 429, 432
Watson, Sir Robert, 191
Watson, Robert, Principal, 718
Watson, Robert Matthew, 479, 499
Watson, William, 52, 423, 571, 617, 661
Watt, Alexander, 260, 409
Watt, Alexander Kidd, 478
Watt, Alexander Watt, 557
Watt, Andrew, 586
Watt, Charles James, 121
Watt, David, 498
Watt, Gavin, 693
Watt, Gordon Beattie, 644
Watt, Hugh George, 489
Watt, James, 498
Watt, John, 174, 396, 521
Watt, John Alexander Robson, 742
Watt, John Buchan Adam, 285
Watt, Lauchlan Maclean, 23, 305
Watt, Thomas David, 548
Watt, Thomas Meikle, 42, 729
Watt, William, 560
Watt, William Martin, 263
Watt, William Strachan, 575
Waugh, George, 194, 722, 742
Waugh, James, 30, 231, 549
Waugh, John, 203
Waus, James, 648
Webster, Alexander, 24
Webster, James, 24
Webster, James Moir, 407

Webster, John, 5, 440, 449, 546, 572
Webster, John McKesser, 283
Webster, William Laurie, 37
Wedderburn, William, 560
Wedderspoon, James, 134
Weicht, James, 494
Weir, Duncan Harkness, Professor, 717
Weir, George, 95
Weir, Harold George Mullo, 204
Weir, Hugh, 262
Weir, James, 626
Weir, John, 67, 270, 272, 481
Weir, John Symington, 571
Weir, Richard, 60
Weir, Robert Walter, 172
Weir, Thomas, 160, 186
Weir, William, 45
Wellwood, John, 626
Welsh, Sir John, 173
Welsh, John, 177
Welsh, Sir Robert, 184
Welsh, Robert, 186
Welsh, William, 58
Wemyss, David, 304, 374
Wemyss, James, Professor, 717
Wemyss, John, 117, 361, 362, 437
Wemyss, Matthew, 7
Wemyss, Patrick, 276, 429, 499
Wemyss, Robert, 456
Wemyss, Thomas of Fingask, 567
Wemyss, William, 132, 400
Westwater, John, 39
White, David, 472
White, George, 461
White, John, 95, 187, 189, 289, 378, 406
White, Robert, 457
White, Sir Thomas, 112
White, Thomas, 7
White, William, 229
White, William Kay, 606, 613
Whiteford, William, Bishop, 709
Whiteford, William, 233
Whitehead, William, 211
Whitehead, William Young, 81
Whitehill, Sir Maktor, 357
Whitelaw, Donald Chisholm, 264
Whitelaw, John Morrison, 87
Whiteley, Reginald Frederick, 245, 498
Whitson, John, 203
Whyte, Andrew, 697
Whyte, James, 576, 587
Whyte, John, 48, 321
Wichtand, James, 490, 491
Wight, George, 161
Wight, James, 141
Wight, Robert, 172
Wight, William, Professor, 717
Wight, William Ferguson, 346

INDEX OF MINISTERS

Wightman, Michael, 176
Wightman, William McCaig, 301
Wigtoun, John, 495
Wilkie, Adam, 157
Wilkie, Charles, 40
Wilkie, David, 9
Wilkie, James, 525
Wilkie, James Keith, 312
Wilkie, Patrick, 94
Wilkie, Robert, 233, 234
Wilkie, Thomas, 7, 13, 29, 136, 149, 151, 154
Wilkie, William, 151
Wilkie, Zachary, 121
Wilken, James Kissock, 531
Williamson, Alexander, 27, 222, 403
Williamson, Andrew, 346
Williamson, Andrew Wallace, 11
Williamson, David, 18, 363, 365, 391, 501
Williamson, David Ritchie, 189
Williamson, Donald, 662
Williamson, Edmund Edward, 678
Williamson, Frederick Hunter, 419
Williamson, James, 8, 113, 134, 182, 702
Williamson, James Alexander, 387, 721
Williamson, James Walker Morrison, 47, 588
Williamson, John, 76, 179, 240, 269, 431, 444
Williamson, John Conacher, 163
Williamson, Robert, 425, 440, 444, 447, 664
Willis, George, 432
Willis, Michael, 300
Willison, Alexander, 217
Willison, Alexander Stewart, 414
Wilson, Alexander, 595, 725, 729
Wilson, Charles, Professor, 719
Wilson, David, 218
Wilson, David Wilkie, 83
Wilson, Duncan Macfarlane, 434
Wilson, Gabriel, 151
Wilson, George, 22
Wilson, Hugh, 252
Wilson, James, 29, 125, 150, 177, 224, 370, 429, 432, 592
Wilson, James Alexander Sutherland, 396, 496
Wilson, James Peter, 224
Wilson, James Robertson Sweet, 29
Wilson, James Wyper, 264
Wilson, John, 75, 180, 271, 363, 380, 427, 503, 608
Wilson, John McLaren, 706
Wilson, John Rudge, 142
Wilson, John Stewart, 178
Wilson, Matthew, 272, 735
Wilson, Michael Cunningham, 502
Wilson, Neil Wilson, 609
Wilson, Rhoderick James, 268
Wilson, Robert, 79, 370, 577, 621, 677
Wilson, Roger, 100
Wilson, Stephen, 159

Wilson, Sir Steven, 262
Wilson, Steven, 381, 428, 430
Wilson, Thomas, 127, 271
Wilson, Thomas Clark, 349
Wilson, Thomas Wilkie, 147
Wilson, William, 124, 188, 247, 248, 402, 442, 471, 475, 510, 527
Wilson, William Bower, 48
Wilson, William Lyall, 18
Wilson, William Wallace, 586
Winchester, Alexander, 635, 636, 637, 640
Winchester, Hugh Sinclair, 273
Winchester, James, 139
Wingate, John of Chartershall, 389
Wingate, Thomas Daniel, 698
Winram, Robert, 443
Winter, David, 346
Wiseman, Robert Brown, 54, 431
Wiseman, William Reid, 90
Wishart, William, 25, 26, 43
Wishart, William Philip, 644
Wistoun, Thomas, 142
Witherspoon, James, 104
Witherspoon, Robert, 550
Woddrow, Patrick, 276
Woddrow, Robert, 238
Wood, Alexander, 68, 98, 461
Wood, Andrew, Bishop, 107, 709
Wood, Anson Robertson Craik, 192, 443
Wood, David, 167
Wood, James, 469, 456, 462
Wood, James Boath, 488
Wood, James Gray, 245
Wood, James Richmond, 186
Wood, John, 403, 559, 723
Wood, John Julius, 9
Wood, Mungo, 3
Wood, Robert, 463, 477, 480, 538, 706
Wood, Thomas, 107, 455, 468
Wood, Walter, 147
Woodburn, John Murray, 178
Woodside, Robert, 623
Wordie, James, 443
Workman, William, 147
Wotherspoon, Arthur Wellesley, 298
Wotherspoon, Henry Johnstone, 23
Wotherspoon, John Morrison, 298
Wotherpsoon, William Lang, 366
Wright, George Tod, 23, 156
Wright, James, 222
Wright, John, 205, 374, 397, 652
Wright, Leo, 210
Wright, Maxwell James, 532
Wright, Norman Macleod, 303, 325
Wright, Richard, 394
Wright, Robert, 408, 444
Wright, Robert Hill, 156
Wright, Stewart, 252

INDEX OF MINISTERS

Wright, Thomas Henry, 484
Wright, William, 311, 488
Wyhtman, John, 60
Wyld, Symon, 164
Wylie, Alexander, 520
Wylie, Alexander Matthew, 346
Wylie, James, 199
Wylie, John, 539, 542
Wylie, Matthew, 214
Wylie, Peter, 143

YAIR, Joseph, 137
Yalilee, Alexander, 397
Yeoman, Alexander Ross, 721
Young, Alexander, Bishop, 710
Young, Alexander, 199, 307, 564
Young, Alexander Aytoun, 348
Young, Andrew, 371
Young, David, 245, 725
Young, David Gowans, 368
Young, George, 157
Young, George Hislop, 132
Young, James, 244, 413
Young, James Morough, 220
Young, John, 229, 155, 185, 195, 425, 428, 476, 483, 515
Young, Ninian, 222
Young, Peter, 182
Young, Robert, 310, 376, 432
Young, Thomas, 249, 453, 574
Young, William, 370
Youngson, Alexander, 537, 553, 675
Youngson, James, 431, 730
Youngson, John Forbes White, 742
Youngson, Robert, 556
Younie, John Milne, 400
Yuille, George Simpson, 311
Yule, Robert, 470

www.ingramcontent.com/pod-product-compliance
Ingram Content Group UK Ltd.
Pitfield, Milton Keynes, MK11 3LW, UK
UKHW050937280426
12129UKWH00014B/909